# The Town House
# in Medieval and Early
# Modern Bristol

# The Town House in Medieval and Early Modern Bristol

Roger H Leech

ENGLISH HERITAGE

Published by English Heritage, The Engine House, Fire Fly Avenue, Swindon SN2 2EH
www.english-heritage.org.uk
English Heritage is the Government's lead body for the historic environment.

© English Heritage 2014

Images (except as otherwise shown) © English Heritage,
© Crown Copyright. EH, or Reproduced by permission of English Heritage

First published 2014

ISBN 978-1-84802-053-5 (book) + 978-1-84802-054-2 (CD)

Product code 51533

*British Library Cataloguing in Publication data*
*A CIP catalogue record for this book is available from the British Library.*

**All rights reserved**
No part of this publication may be reproduced or transmitted in any form or by any means, electronic or mechanical, including photocopying, recording, or any information storage or retrieval system, without permission in writing from the publisher.

Application for the reproduction of images should be made to English Heritage. Every effort has been made to trace the copyright holders and we apologise in advance for any unintentional omissions, which we would be pleased to correct in any subsequent edition of this book.

For more information about images from the English Heritage Archive, contact Archives Services Team, The Engine House, Fire Fly Avenue, Swindon SN2 2EH; telephone (01793) 414600.

Brought to publication by Robin Taylor, Publishing, English Heritage.

Typeset in Charter regular 9.5pt

Edited by Catherine Bradley
Indexed by Alan Rutter
Page layout by Francis & Partners
Printed in Belgium by DeckersSnoeck.

# CONTENTS

Preface and Acknowledgements ..... vii
Author's Note ..... xi

1 Introduction ..... 1
2 The Saxon and Medieval Town ..... 13
3 Developers – the Early Modern City ..... 33
4 The Urban Tenement Plot in the Medieval City ..... 59
5 The Hallhouse ..... 69
6 The Shophouse ..... 117
7 The Complexities of Commerce ..... 143
8 The Residential House ..... 179
9 The Garden House ..... 229
10 Spaces and Changes ..... 281
11 'The Company of the town' ..... 329
12 Bristol and the Atlantic World ..... 357
13 Merchant Capitalism and the Streets of Bristol ..... 369

Appendix 1 Documents Relating to the Building of Bristol Houses (ordered by date) ..... 377
Appendix 2 Inventories ..... 381
Notes ..... 405
Bibliography ..... 415
Index ..... 425
A selective inventory of recorded houses ..... on CD, *inside back cover*

*TO PAMELA, THOMAS AND ELEANOR*

# PREFACE AND ACKNOWLEDGEMENTS

This book has its origins in a research project commenced in the late 1970s, inspired by work undertaken for the predecessors of English Heritage (the Ancient Monuments Inspectorate within the Department of the Environment) in evaluating the urban archaeological resource in the counties of Avon, Gloucestershire and Somerset.[1] One particular outcome of this work was a study of 17th-century housing in the town of Frome, Somerset. The research for the study revealed that, in looking for comparative material, almost nothing was available in print to understand the form and character of housing of the same period in Bristol, a city of major importance in the 17th century and only a short distance from Frome.[2] In looking at this vacuum of knowledge it rapidly became evident that a considerable number of houses of the 17th century or earlier survived within Bristol, alongside a potentially vast quantity of relevant documentary material, plans, photographs, paintings and drawings.[3]

In putting together the first stage of a research project to look at this material, the author was especially grateful to the British Academy and the Society for Medieval Archaeology for grants towards the research, and to Professors Peter Fowler, the late Mick Aston and Warwick Rodwell for their help and advice. Colleagues looking at other towns also offered much help and encouragement. Here I must thank especially Helen Bonney, the late Alan Carter, Stanley Jones, Michael Laithwaite, Julian Munby and John Schofield, as well as Frances Neale, whose guided walk around the inner town wall first sparked my interest in Bristol's history, archaeology and buildings.

The precise catalyst to the initiation of the project came one evening in January 1979, while on a trip with my wife Pamela to the Rummer Inn behind High Street. Passing no.43 Broad Street and a skip outside full of medieval timbers, it was evident that building work was taking place within a house already known to be one of Bristol's few surviving medieval dwellings (it is mentioned, like the Rummer, in the ensuing chapters, and is now thought to have been built c 1411). The next day I was able to embark on the recording of this house in collaboration with John Bryant of the Bristol City Museum and Art Gallery's staff. That the project actually commenced in such a way is especially appropriate, as without Pamela's support, encouragement and involvement over the following 30 years this work would never have been completed.

Work on the preparation of reports on individual buildings then commenced. In research at the Bristol City Museum and Art Gallery the encouragement of Francis Greenacre, then Curator of Fine Art, was especially important, as was the guidance on photography received from Gordon Kelsey, Head of the Photographic Unit in the University of Bristol. In surveying individual buildings I was particularly grateful to the late Eric Mercer, Head of Threatened Buildings Recording in the Royal Commission on the Historical Monuments of England (RCHME), for inspirational advice; to Terry Pearson, colleague on the staff of the Committee for Rescue Archaeology in Avon, Gloucestershire and Somerset (CRAAGS); and to Alan Elkan, prominent in the work of the Kingsdown Conservation Group and the Bristol Civic Society. In the RCHME I was also indebted to Stephen Croad and John Hampton for their assistance in looking at building records and air photographs, and to John (J T) Smith for his advice on North American contacts.

Moving soon after the project commenced to direct a new archaeological unit for Cumbria and Lancashire, I owed an especial debt of thanks to the University of Lancaster and the Leverhulme Trust for facilitating and awarding a Leverhulme Fellowship. This allowed the further preparation of reports – on buildings surveyed and particularly those now demolished, but recorded in various documentary sources. In pursuing further the documentary research

I owed a debt of gratitude to the late Dr Kathleen Hughes of Newnham College, Cambridge, who first introduced me to medieval archaeology and the whole process of following up historical research and discovery with that of publication. In the Bristol Record Office I was very appreciative of the help given by the late Professor Patrick McGrath and the late Miss Elizabeth Ralph to members of their extra-mural university documentary research class.

Moving to the Southampton office of the RCHME in 1984, this uncompleted research project continued to move forward. It received a particular boost from the encouragement of Desmond Bonney and Professor Gwyn Merion-Jones to my devoting time to its completion, and from the willingness of RCHME's secretary or chief executive, Tom Hassall, to include completion of the project in my work programme. In 1998 Tom and the Commissioners then agreed to my completing the research and book in a short period preceding my taking early retirement from the staff of the RCHME.

In the initial planning of the book I was most grateful for the comments received from John Bold and Sarah Pearson. At the same time the project itself was lengthened by taking up the suggestion that its scope be widened through changing its terminal date from *c* 1700 to *c* 1800. The first few chapters of the book were then completed, with Professor Derek Keene making a valuable contribution through commenting upon these as they were written. Surveys of houses of importance not yet examined were meanwhile being undertaken by staff of RCHME, including John Cattell, Nigel Fradgley and Barry Jones, but mostly by the author – at times with an insightful, unforgettable and often witty input from Professor Bernie Herman, for whom the work contributed also to his own book *Town House*, published in 2005. Other RCHME staff who made a major contribution at this stage were Veronica Smith with administrative matters, Brian Hopper and Suzanne Ferguson in the supply and digitisation of maps and Ian Leith in advising on some of the byways of the National Monuments Record. RCHME Commissioners were also most supportive.

Time, alas, did not permit the project to be completed at that stage, with the research and book being completed only following retirement from the RCHME. This also might never have happened but for the skilled treatment I was privileged to receive from the staff of the Wessex Neurological Centre in Southampton General Hospital following a brain haemorrhage in August 2005. It was while recovering in the hospital's neurological rehabilitation unit that I received a letter from David Miles, Chief Archaeologist to English Heritage, asking if I would be willing to complete the project through to publication. I am most grateful to David for encouraging the recommencement of work on the chapters, and to Peter Guillery of English Heritage for then reading and commenting upon all the chapters in turn. Having just completed his book on smaller London houses (*The Small House in Eighteenth-Century London: a Social and Architectural History*), he was especially well-placed to offer informed and well-judged comments.

This then led to the final stage of the project, planned to complete the editing of the text and the bringing together of all the illustrations. It was funded by the Historic Environment Enabling Programme of English Heritage (HEEP), and overseen for quality control by Francis Kelly and Rob Iles of the Bristol regional office. In this final stage thanks are due to a number of persons: Tim Cromack, Barney Sloane and Charlie Winter of the HEEP team; Robin Taylor as publications manager; Nigel Clubb, Anna Eavis, Alyson Rogers, Clare Broomfield and Nigel Wilkins of the National Monuments Record; Penny Copeland and James Miles of the University of Southampton for the preparation of most of the line drawings and the maps for the Inventory; Jill Atherton for the townscape reconstructions and cutaway drawings of houses; Allan Adams for his comments on the final drawings; Edward Besly for numismatic advice; Kathleen Thompson for historical advice and assistance with fieldwork; and Pamela my wife, who deserves a second mention at this point for her contribution to the copy editing. In this final stage of the project I have been especially grateful to Colum Giles for his editing of the chapters. He has made many valuable suggestions and has contributed greatly to the final form of the publication. In the final stages of the project I have also been most appreciative of the help and advice received from Catherine Bradley, appointed by English Heritage to see the work through to final publication.

The contribution of a number of photographers to the project is so great that it deserves special mention. Especial thanks must be given to Steve Cole, Head of Photography for English Heritage. It is most pleasing to be able to acknowledge the individual and often stunning contributions of the English Heritage and RCHME photographers involved in the latter stages of the project, notably James Davies, Pat Payne and Peter Williams.

Many photographs originate from work some time ago, including those by Ruding Bryan, Victor Turl and Reginald Frank Wills, and notably those taken by Philip E W Street (PEWS in the Figure captions), all now in the National Monuments Record, and those from the collections of the late Reece Winstone, whom the author met at an early stage in this research. The assistance of his son John Winstone, who took a close interest in the recording and preservation of several important buildings discussed in the publication, is also gratefully acknowledged. Of great assistance too was a meeting with Paul Pritchard, grandson of J E Pritchard.

The contribution of colleagues in the Bristol Record Society has also been particularly important. It was Joe Bettey who, after hearing of my research into the history of houses, suggested that I met with him and the late Elizabeth Ralph to produce the first of what is intended as a series of volumes under the imprint of the Bristol Record Society on the topography of medieval and early modern Bristol. Joe Bettey, Martin Crossley-Evans, Madge Dresser, Peter Fleming and Evan Jones have all engaged in correspondence that has contributed to the study in various ways, as have other historians with particular and overlapping interests. These include Nat Alcock in his researches on the Hearth Tax and Warwickshire towns; the late Dorothy Brown in pressing for the conservation of a number of important buildings; Annie Burnside in her research on the history of Clifton Hill House; the late Edwin and Stella George in their studies of Bristol probate inventories; Mark Girouard in his research into Elizabethan and Jacobean art; Stephen Hague in looking at gentry houses of the 18th century; Sister Kathleen Ireson for researching the history of Emmaus House; Donald Jones for his knowledge of the history of Clifton; Alyson and Michael Marsden for their researches into pewter; David and Penny Mellor for looking at Kingsdown (to whom I am most grateful for the loan of the drawn reconstructions of each side of Kingsdown Parade); Peggy Stembridge in her researches into the Goldney family; James Russell in his study of the suburbs of Bristol; and John Ward of the University of Edinburgh for his researches in building and business in late 18th-century Bristol.

The project has also afforded opportunities for collaboration with other research projects. Some are mentioned below, but they also include the work of the Cotswold Archaeological Trust, Oxford Archaeology and the Avon Archaeological Unit. Several architects have also greatly assisted through making available surveys of particular houses. Here I would like to thank especially Tom Burrough and David Morris of Burrough and Hannam; Eric Franklin of Oatley and Bentnall; the Alec French Partnership; Richard Pedlar; Gordon Priest; the late Alan Rome; Kit Routledge of Beardsworth, Gallannaugh and Partners; the Percy Thomas Partnership and John Warren.

In its completion this publication has been a joint project with Bristol City Council, with various of its departments – an arrangement facilitated by Bob Bewley for English Heritage and Stephen Wray for the City Council. The staff of Bristol City Council have contributed to the research from its very start. Along with the historian the late Bryan Little, the Conservation Officer the late Chris Curtis was one of the many visitors who appeared in our recording of no.43 Broad Street. The role of archaeology in the planning process in Bristol has been transformed by both PPG16 (the planning guidance for sites of archaeological significance issued by the Department of the Environment) and by the appointment of Bob Jones as the City Archaeologist. He and his assistants, both the late Jon Brett and Peter Insole, have made a very great contribution to the project. Photographs by Jon and some historic drawings identified by him have been an important input to the work.

Of equal importance has been the contribution of the Bristol Record Office, of successive City Archivists Mary Williams, John Williams and Richard Burley, and of all the archival, reprographic and storeroom staff who have dealt so patiently, and with such an abundance of knowledge, to help the research on its way. A major input to the project was also made by the staff of the Bristol City Museum and Art Gallery's Departments of Fine and Applied Art in providing access to the collections of illustrations of Bristol houses – notably in the Braikenridge Collection – and in arranging access to the Red Lodge and Georgian House Museum, no.7 Great George Street. Here I must thank especially Andy King for access to the photographic collections of the former Industrial Museum. Thanks are also due to the staff of the City Valuer's Office for access to historic plans and much useful advice.

In looking at historic records advice on palaeography has been gratefully received from Bridget Jones, Alison Brown and Peter Fleming.

Archaeological staff of the Bristol City Museum and Art Gallery and its archaeological unit, Bristol and Region Archaeological Services (BaRAS), have also offered much help. Here I would like to thank especially Bruce Williams, John Bryant, Reg Jackson, Andrew Townsend, Andy King, Tim Longman and Simon Roper, with whom it has been a pleasure to collaborate in the interpretation of particular sites. The assistance of other record offices and collections, including the archives of the Society of Merchant Venturers, the Bodleian Library, the British Library, the National Archives and the County Record Offices for Devon, Gloucestershire, Somerset, Suffolk and Wiltshire, in addition to the Bristol Municipal Charities, is also gratefully acknowledged.

The collections of the Bristol City Reference Library have also been an important source for the research. Here thanks must be given to the local history librarians Geoffrey Langley, Jane Bradley and Dawn Dyer, all of whom were especially helpful in sharing their knowledge of the collections – the core of which is also part of the city's mercantile heritage. A further locally held archive of importance is that in the Special Collections of the University of Bristol and here I must thank especially Michael Richardson for his assistance.

Further afield I must thank those whose support of research in the West Indies has made a significant input to chapter 12 – notably organisations including the University of Southampton, the British Academy, the Joint Information Systems Committee (JISC) and the historical societies for the islands of Barbados, Nevis and St Kitts. I would also like to thank Elaine Morris, Vince Hubbard and Guy Norton for their valued contribution.

The contribution of the University of Southampton has indeed been critical to the completion of the work. Without the library, email and other computing facilities offered to me as Visiting Professor to the Department of Archaeology, the preparation and checking of the final text, illustrations and inventory maps would not have been possible.

At home in Romsey in Hampshire I must also record my thanks to our children Thomas and Eleanor who, as well as tolerating this disruption to the whole of their lives to date, have both contributed in various ways to the research. I would also like to thank Tyrone Freeman for reprographics assistance, my friend the Very Revd. Wesley Carr for theological insights into themes on chimneypieces (along with Dr Anthony Wells-Cole) and my friends Bruce Eagles, David Johnson, Ted Mason, Steve Worner-Gibbs and many others for their encouragement.

Finally I must thank all the householders and occupiers whose warm welcome has enabled the project to take place. Those who provided access to several or more houses are owed an especial thanks, and here I must thank the University of Bristol, its successive Bursars David Adamson and Mike Phipps, and particularly its Estates Officer Jenny Crew; also Bob Lee, Surveyor for the Bristol Municipal Charities, and Petros Birakos and his son Jason for access to Clifton Wood and Mortimer Houses.

# AUTHOR'S NOTE

Abbreviations: those used throughout the book are listed at the beginning of the Bibliography.

Access: inclusion in this book in no way implies any public right of access.

Builders: except where another meaning is obvious, the word 'builder' is used throughout this book to denote the man or woman who caused a house to be built or altered, rather than the artisan or architect who actually did the work or who was employed to supervise it.

Floors: floors and storeys are named throughout in accordance with British usage ie 'ground floor' corresponds to the American 'first floor'; 'first floor' to the American 'second floor' and so forth.

Measurements: imperial measurements are given where the context is one of historic significance; please see the conversion table below for details of metric equivalents:
1ft = 304.8mm
1 yard = 0.914m
1 mile = 1.6km
1 acre = 0.4 hectares

Names: old county names (ie pre-1974) are given where a house was formerly in a different county. The spelling of the names of street names still extant in the 1880s follows that of the Ordnance Survey maps of the same date.

Sources: where not stated, the reader should consult the Selective Inventory provided on the CD-ROM enclosed with the book. Two dates frequently cited are 1775, which will unless otherwise stated be a reference to Sketchley's Directory of that year (see Little (ed) 1971), and 1662, which will unless otherwise stated be a reference to the Hearth Tax returns of that year (for which see BRO F/Tax/1/A: an edition of the Bristol Hearth Tax to be published by the Bristol Record Society and the British Record Society is in preparation).

Drawing conventions used in the plans of houses:

| | |
|---|---|
| ——— | Structural wall |
| ——— | Detail |
| ············ | Overhead/roof line |
| ——— | Hypothetical/demolis |
| - - - - - | Modern cut line |
| – – – – | Modern wall |
| ——— | External doorway |

# 1

# Introduction

## Town Houses

The literature on town houses in England is at first sight extensive. There are studies carried out over long periods of time, focusing on individual cities and towns,[1] but more general studies of urban housing are few. The work of William Pantin, published in the 1960s, initiated the serious analysis of housing in towns and has been particularly influential on subsequent research.[2] He looked at larger town houses of the medieval period, houses with open or large halls, and set out a typology of plans which centred on the positioning of the hall in relation to the house and street. The town house was seen as 'a study in adaptation', the adaptation of rural house plans to the crowded and constrained urban environment. Many subsequent students of town housing have taken Pantin's work as the starting point for their analyses.

More recently, six studies have been of especial importance. Jane Grenville has looked at town houses as part of a wider study of medieval housing, utilising the typology proposed by Pantin alongside that evolved by John Schofield for medieval London houses.[3] Schofield's analysis was based essentially on the number of rooms in the house, an indicator of the social and economic status of the occupier. Grenville's study has focused more on the context of urban housing, on shops and on how commerce and the separateness of towns from the countryside might be seen 'in the social use of space and style'.[4] A significant study has been Roland Harris's review of medieval town houses used commercially on two storeys, much more concerned with origins and development rather than social context.[5]

Fourthly, John Smith's general survey of town houses in England in the period 1450–1560 must be considered here.[6] Smith studied 'the role of towns in generating and diffusing architectural innovation' and the extent to which carpenters devised 'their own solutions to urban problems'. This led him in turn to the identification and discussion of the smallest and often unheated urban dwellings, characteristically tall narrow tenements, numerous but 'none … studied in detail'.

A fifth, far more general study has been Anthony Quiney's broad survey of town houses in medieval Britain, which aimed to provide an overview of the subject rather than to advance a particular argument or set of ideas. Quiney did not discuss why and how town houses had been studied, nor did he consider the directions that such studies might take in the future.[7] A review of Quiney's study concluded that 'the extreme polarisations of wealth implicit in the range of urban housing in cities such as London, Bristol and York, from the largest town houses to the single-room unheated house, invite further research and discussion'.[8] The social context of dwellings such as these in relation to medieval and later urban housing will form an important part of this study.

A sixth study deserving consideration is Bernard Herman's *Town House*,[9] an in-depth review of urban housing close to or on the Atlantic coast of the United States, seen also in the context of urban housing in contemporary England. Herman's approach might be termed 'experiential', looking at urban housing in a range of towns through the eyes and thoughts of those who lived in them: a merchant in Norfolk, Virginia, a widow in Portsmouth, New Hampshire and many others. Coincidentally this experiential perspective has been adopted in much of the design for the displays in the new museum of Bristol, M Shed, and has also influenced this study, where the perceptions of contemporaries, often visible through documentary sources such as rentals or probate inventories, will have an important role.

Impinging on these considerations are the concerns of contemporary urban historians. Medieval towns could be seen as 'little islands of capitalism' within an otherwise almost entirely feudal society. Status in towns, and more especially the larger ones, was in the medieval period and later based principally on commercial success and wealth. The ways in which housing may have enforced or reflected divisions between the extremes of rich and poor in urban society have not been considered by students of medieval towns, but, perhaps because surviving evidence is more abundant, such social divisions have received attention in studies of the early modern period. Elizabeth McKellar has underlined how the development of London's West End and the swallowing up of open spaces 'marked the beginning of that spatial segregation and privatisation of the city which characterised London in the 18th and 19th centuries'.[10] She agrees with John Summerson in seeing the westward expansion of London from the mid-17th century as driven by an increased demand for upper-class housing, but has little or nothing to say of the reasons for London's eastward expansion.[11] Peter Guillery's study of small houses in London provides both a geographical and social complement to McKellar's work, gathering evidence of the housing of poorer levels of society to demonstrate 'the interdependence of high and low cultures, of the vernacular and the polite'.[12]

Bristol too expanded greatly from the mid-17th century onwards and, as in London, upper-class housing formed only a part of what was being built. The social and global contexts of the increase in housing provision from the mid-17th century in cities such as London and Bristol require further exploration, particularly in the context of the still much debated thesis, first advanced by Eric Williams, that the Industrial Revolution in Britain was founded on the wealth produced by the Atlantic trade and African slaves in the West Indies.[13] This thesis, of course, is especially relevant to interpretation of Bristol's expansion for, as is well known, the city was deeply engaged in the triangular trade between Britain, West Africa and the New World.

Historians have recognised the variability of wealth in medieval and later towns. Looking at the commercialisation of English society between 1000 and 1500, Richard Britnell has concluded that in towns there were 'vast differences in prosperity between well-established merchants and propertyless immigrants from the countryside', that by 1500 many distinctions of rank and status had become more pronounced and that 'current research also requires us to accept the Marxist principle that inequalities of wealth and power shaped the way in which economic and social change was to occur'.[14] In an analysis of urban society in the 15th century, David Palliser concluded that there were 'real divisions among townspeople, based on wide inequalities. By and large one can generalise about a twofold or threefold division into powerful, middling and lesser townsfolk … distinctions of wealth and status rather than of occupation'.[15]

Drawing on Charles Phythian-Adams' study of Coventry and Anthony Fletcher and Deborah Stevenson on *Order and Disorder in Early Modern England,* Palliser concluded that 'the traditional concept of order in the late medieval towns, based on ceremonial, myth and ritual, was suited to a localised society in which hierarchy, together with an obligation to those below and deference to those above, made sense of people's lives'.[16]

To illustrate how housing might reflect distinctions in society Palliser drew on the evidence from the Coventry census of 1523 to show how townspeople there 'drew a clear distinction between householders and cottagers … Cottages were often one-roomed, whereas houses included at least a hall and a solar, and often a workshop fronting the street'.[17] Palliser was aware of research by archaeologists and architectural historians and concluded that 'the considerable research on medieval urban housing over the past thirty years has refined but not changed … Pantin's pioneer analysis of late medieval town-house plans'. Using Pantin's evidence, he drew attention to the importance of commercial space in the form of urban houses, showing 'the way in which many houses were built at right angles to the street to economize on valuable frontages, while even the more spacious plots with halls parallel to the street often incorporated commercial premises to let along the street frontage'.[18] This present study will explore whether distinctions of wealth, status and occupation can be drawn as much from the architectural and archaeological evidence as from the documentary sources.

## Bristol Town Houses

The purpose of this study is not simply to add to the literature of single town studies, but to seek whether it is possible to address some of the questions already posed and to transform our understanding of urban housing in medieval and early modern England – especially through looking at the architectural and archaeological data in the context of surviving documentary sources.

Bristol was chosen for this study firstly because of its importance in medieval and early modern England. For much of this period it was England's second city – and yet, unlike London, its medieval housing stock had not been destroyed by a Great Fire. Secondly, preliminary investigation indicated that over 100 houses dating from before *c* 1700 possibly still survived, to varying degrees. Thirdly, no such study of Bristol's town houses had hitherto been undertaken. One recent writer has stated that 'virtually nothing covers the architecture of c.1530 to c.1700, odd since so much survives'.[19] Fourthly, many more houses of this or earlier date were apparently well recorded in topographical illustrations and accounts. Finally, preliminary investigation indicated that surviving and published documentary sources would enable the ownership and tenurial histories of many individual properties to be identified.

A study of the town house in medieval and early modern Bristol therefore provides an opportunity to take a new look at the social and economic context of urban housing in England – in a city that was in the Middle Ages and to the closing decades of the 18th century the most important in the western part of England. By the reign of Stephen (1135–54), then within 150 years of the probable date of its foundation, it had become 'nearly the richest of all the cities of the country … by the very situation of the place the best defended of all the cities of England'.[20] Its location on a low spur, set at the confluence of the Avon and the Frome, overlooking the marshes of the tidal estuary of the Avon and Bristol Channel, favoured not only its defence, but also trade with Ireland and further afield. In 1373 it became a county in its own right, a status not then enjoyed by any other provincial town and justified for Bristol by its straddling two counties and its pre-eminent position in the cloth and wine trades.[21] The near-cessation of the trade in wine, following the capture of Bordeaux by the French in 1453, was a temporary setback in Bristol's fortunes, but recovery was quick, and henceforth trade was based increasingly on exports of manufactured goods and the import of specialist, high-value items. In the late 15th and 16th centuries Bristol mariners became more present in the western seas, with John Cabot, who sailed from the town in 1497 in search of the North West Passage, being the most famous.[22] The way was thereby prepared, from the later 16th century onwards, for the rapid growth in the trade with North America and the Caribbean.[23] Such was Bristol's growth and appearance by the later 17th century that it seemed to Pepys 'in every respect another London'. To Defoe in the early 18th century, it was 'the greatest, the richest and the best port of trade in Great Britain, London only excepted'.[24] Throughout the later 17th and 18th centuries it was one of the most important cities of the Atlantic world, a position it retained until surpassed in the later part of the 18th century by the growth of Liverpool and Philadelphia.

The history of Bristol has been well studied, with a number of scholars making particularly important, wide-ranging contributions in recent decades. The economic development of the city has been studied by Eleanor Carus-Wilson for the medieval period, by David Sacks for the period 1450–1700 and by Kenneth Morgan for the 18th century.[25] Patrick McGrath has revealed much of the life of the merchant community, particularly of the 17th century, while Jonathan Barry has more recently examined popular culture in the 17th and 18th centuries.[26]

A concern central to Barry's analysis of popular culture in 17th-century Bristol was Wrightson's suggestion that in the 17th century social divisions were reinforced by cultural forces, creating a widening gulf between elite and popular cultures. This argument was developed in the context of evidence principally from the countryside. Elements of popular culture discussed by Barry included literacy and education, communication, religious life, civic traditions, guilds and concern for the reformation of manners. How people lived in their tenements and houses was discussed only tangentially. Barry noted that at the end of the century a 'Tudor' vernacular style of architecture was abandoned in favour of the neoclassical style, and that by 1700 'the rich began to own houses on the outskirts of town as well as in the centre … The surge of building after 1660 filled up the green areas of the city; and the wealthy were thereafter increasingly catered for by squares and other areas with gardens, whilst the poor were gradually confined to the poorer suburbs'. Barry concluded that, despite this geographical rift, 'the socio-economic conditions of Bristol, together with the strong sense of communal and civic identity, militated against a clear division between popular and elite culture'.[27]

There is considerable potential for extending Barry's inquiry to look more closely at the domestic and working lives of the townspeople of 17th-century Bristol. The material record may well provide new insights into changing living patterns. If, from the later 17th century, rich and poor were increasingly living in different parts of the city, then more detailed examination of how citizens lived in their homes might well provide a clearer picture of cultural change at the 'popular' level. Such an inquiry would touch also on the arguments developed in a more general context by John H Plumb and Peter Borsay for the increasing differentiation between work and leisure for the better-off by the later 17th century.[28]

In an important contribution to understanding the early development of urban capitalism, Sacks has argued that 'Bristol's history between 1450 and 1700 created a center of early modern capitalism out of a medieval commercial town'. To a citizen of the 15th century, 'Bristol had appeared as a replica of the cosmos, an ordered and harmonious arrangement of parts that made a unified whole'. By the 1670s the social and religious geography of the city had been transformed, these changes reflecting the emergence of a capitalism born of the growth of the Atlantic economy and the new political conditions of Restoration England.[29] This argument was underpinned in part by an analysis of the housing developments thought to have taken place between 1568 and 1673, the dates of the maps of the city by William Smith and James Millerd. A more detailed critique of Sacks's arguments will be reserved for chapters 3 and 11.

Central to Sacks's vision of the capitalist ethic was that man could by his actions transform the world while always remaining open to its shaping influences. The concept that the world is moulded by human agency while being at the same time a powerful and often unpredictable influence on human action is also fundamental to the value of studying material culture as part of the process of writing history. The cultural meanings embedded in the copiously recorded houses and tenements of medieval and early modern Bristol, not thus far much utilised by historians, can play a critical part in deepening understanding of the emergence of the early capitalist city.

Many other studies, drawing both on documentary and archaeological sources, have looked at more specific areas of historical interest, most recently Bristol's involvement in the slave trade.[30] Yet, though much is now known about many aspects of the city's history, there have remained significant gaps. One of these has been the understanding of past social and economic change to be gained through looking at how the inhabitants of the city interacted with their domestic, working and everyday built environment. Walking through the surviving historic streets of the city, perusing the pages of *Bristol Past and Present*[31] or the many thousands of photographs published by Reece Winstone,[32] particularly those of houses pre-dating the 18th century, the historian might ask a number of questions. By whom were these houses built? How and by whom were they used and inhabited? How might the changing patterns of domestic and working life, and of the use of space, embedded in these structures and recorded in the documents relating to these buildings, enhance historical understanding of the development of Bristol and the early modern city? Reece Winstone was especially fascinated by the Dutch House (Fig 1.4; *see* Figs 6.32 and 7.16), which subsequent research has shown was built in 1676 as a shophouse by one Robert Winstone, a glover and prominent citizen. The documentary sources for Robert Winstone's commercial activities are especially pertinent to the concerns of this study. As will be seen, he was involved in the Atlantic trade and used his profits from this not only to build the Dutch House, but also to acquire and probably rebuild Oldbury Court, his second residence or garden house to the north of the city (p250 and Fig 9.44).

For the 18th century, questions of by whom and for whom certain houses were built might be answered through the works of architectural historians. Charles Dening, Walter Ison and Timothy Mowl have in succession written on the Georgian architecture of Bristol, but with an interest primarily in the aesthetics, attribution or execution of the design, most often that of the exterior; Ison especially has much to say on the builders of the Georgian houses of Bristol. How successive generations lived in these houses has not, however, been a concern of the above. The interest in the aesthetics of architectural design has also caused these studies to focus almost entirely on the larger houses.[33]

A similar emphasis on the study of the exterior architecture with a strong leaning to aesthetic qualities was central to Bryan Little's study of the medieval, 16th- and 17th-century architecture of the city.[34] The existing architectural histories of Bristol will not meet the needs of those wishing to know how the city's houses were used and changed in use during the 18th or earlier centuries.

It was initially intended that this study would be of the houses of Bristol before *c* 1700. Subsequently it was decided to extend its scope to *c* 1800. A select number of houses of the 18th century has therefore been included in the

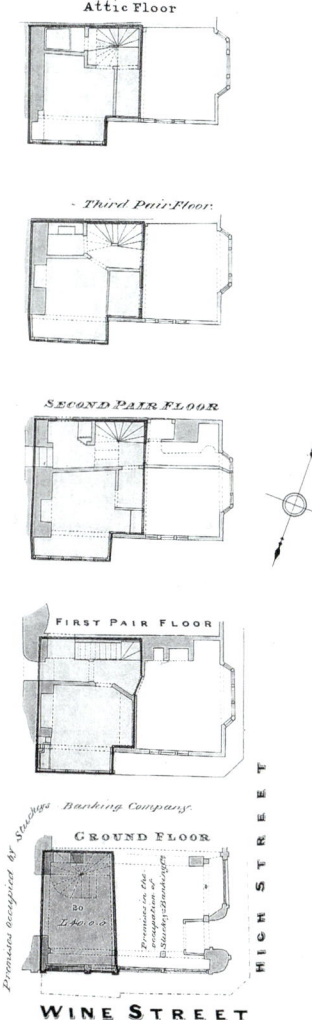

*Fig 1.1*
*The Dutch House, no.1 High Street, photograph of the later 19th century (BRO 17563/1).*

*Fig 1.2*
*The Dutch House, no.1 High Street, plans of ground and upper floors of the mid-19th century, when Stuckeys Bank was in occupation (BRO 33041/BMC/12/PL8 fol 57).*

survey and documentary research, extending the *corpus* of houses considered by authors such as Dening, Ison and Mowl, to address such questions as how and why houses were used, and changed in use.

Fig 1.3
The Dutch House, no.1 High Street, bracket with date '1676' (on shield), photograph of earlier 20th century (BCRL L.38.3).

Fig 1.4
The Dutch House, no.1 High Street, photograph of springing of late medieval fan vault, c 1944, probably identified by Brian St John O'Neil
(English Heritage BB80/2568).

## The Visual Record

The inventory accompanying this study shows that topographical illustrations combined with archaeological data and documentary sources provide a very complete record of a now largely vanished medieval and early modern city. James Millerd, a mercer living on Bristol Bridge, produced in 1673 the first detailed map of the city, complete with vignettes providing close-up views of some of the largest houses.[35] His are the earliest illustrations of individual buildings. From the 18th century an increasing number of illustrations exist, the earliest being a view of the city from Brandon Hill by Bernard Lens of 1714.[36] The panoramas of 1734 by Samuel and Nathaniel Buck, one from the same viewpoint as Lens's drawing, are far more useful to this study, showing in detail a number of the nearest houses.[37] The Bucks were also the inspiration for the work of James Stewart, a schoolmaster who, having encountered the brothers Buck at work on Brandon Hill, proceeded to prepare his own illustrated history of the city, a work which remains in manuscript form only.[38] Stewart's illustrations make a vital contribution to this study. Later 18th-century illustrations come from a variety of sources and notably include two anonymous views of Bristol Quay and a series of drawings by Samuel Hieronymous Grimm.[39]

The record of early Bristol was greatly extended through the work of George Weare Braikenridge, a retired merchant, a collector and an antiquarian. In the 1820s Braikenridge commissioned or purchased over 1,400 drawings and watercolours of the city, mainly of pre-18th century buildings and street scenes.[40] Many of these were separately described in a series of notebooks, now in the City Museum and Art Gallery's collections. Some of these illustrations were published by Joseph Skelton in his *Etchings*, published in 1831, and many more by James Nicholls and John Taylor in their three-volume *Bristol Past and Present*, published in 1881.[41] The latter were able to draw also on the illustrations, plans and accounts of other 19th-century researchers, notably John Bindon, George Pryce and Thomas Shackleton Pope. Bindon's account of the desecrated and destroyed churches of the city was prepared for the meeting of the Royal Archaeological Institute in 1851; unwittingly he included several medieval domestic buildings.[42] Pryce's history of Bristol, published in 1861, includes descriptions of medieval houses and associated structures; his manuscripts include several illustrations.⁴³ The illustrations in Pope's paper on old houses in Bristol very much complement Pryce's account.⁴⁴

From the 1890s the record of Bristol's material past was greatly enhanced by the work of Samuel Loxton and John Pritchard. Loxton's illustrations for the *Bristol Observer*, published between 1890 and 1922, provide a record of many houses, particularly those built behind the main street frontages, often not recorded elsewhere.⁴⁵ Pritchard's work was the first in Bristol to show an awareness of the importance of below-ground archaeology; his observations, published between 1893 and 1929, form in effect a series of watching briefs of buildings and sites about to be redeveloped.⁴⁶ The photographic record and notes of Philip W Street, who met Pritchard in his old age,⁴⁷ form a link between the work of Pritchard and the publications of photographer and collector of photographs Reece Winstone. The grandson of George Edmund Street, the architect responsible for the completion of Bristol Cathedral, Street's records span the 1930s to early 1960s. Street in turn passed some of his notes and photographs to Winstone, responsible for the research and publication of over 30 volumes containing more than 30,000 photographs of Bristol and covering the years 1840–1962.⁴⁸

From the 1940s onwards archaeological excavations have also contributed much to the record of material culture. Over 200 have been undertaken in this period, augmented mainly in the last decade by more than 300 evaluations and some 641 watching briefs. These have produced much information on individual tenements and houses, sometimes of several adjacent tenements.

Archaeological recording has also been extended to standing buildings. The first structure possibly recorded in this way was no.24 Christmas Street⁴⁹ (*see* Fig 5.7), and since 1968, when the Shot Tower on Redcliff Hill was recorded, some 361 buildings have been similarly documented through archaeological work.⁵⁰ For this study specifically some 100 buildings have been separately recorded.

## The Documentary Record

A concept familiar to the antiquaries and historians of the first half of the 19th century was that the material culture of the past could contribute to understanding the history of this city. The Reverend Samuel Seyer utilised his observations made in Baldwin Street during 1813 and 1819 for his history of Bristol, published in 1821–3 in two volumes:

> In this street on the side next to St Nicholas Street about four doors from the Back in September 1813 we examined a house which the inhabitants told us was Fitzharding's, erroneously as I suppose. In the back part of this house was a room, called the Chapel, and which had evidently been such. At the east end was a gallery raised about 8 ft. from the ground, where probably the master of the house had his seat; the gallery communicated with the house on both sides by pointed arched doors. Under this gallery was certainly the altar, the piscina still being perfect in its usual place, with the proper aperture. The floor of the gallery is at present continued over the whole area, which floor divides the chapel into two rooms;.... In the corners we found two or three little figures, rudely carved in freestone; the only one discernible was a priest about a foot high pouring out liquor from a cup into a chalice. The chapel was 25 feet long by 18 feet wide, its greatest length being East and West. Over the gallery was the east window, pointed, having two lights and one mullion ... this house ... was taken down in 1819. Six blocks, which were probably used as corbels, were taken out; one was the crowned head of a king another of a Bishop or mitred abbot.⁵¹

These are possibly the earliest surviving detailed field observations relating to a medieval building in Bristol and at the same time made specifically for the purposes of historical inquiry. Seyer has been rightly described as an historian of outstanding ability, one of 'the best local historians of his own or any generation' and one who could 'undoubtedly have made a notable contribution to the history of England'.⁵² His account of the 'chapel' will serve to introduce and illustrate a number of fundamental concerns.

The establishing of context is vital to understanding material evidence. Seyer identified the Baldwin Street house as a chapel through the presence of a lofty Gothic east window, a *piscina* and by the absence of a medieval fireplace. Other antiquaries and historians of the first part of the 19th century came to similar conclusions. John Evans, in his history published in 1816, conjectured the largest medieval cellar in the city, part of Haddon's Tavern at the junction of High Street and Wine Street (p163; *see* Fig 7.26), to have been a previously unrecorded city centre church. From information, the source of which he could 'not at present recollect', this was thought to have been St Andrew's; the 'crypt of the church' was 'nearly entire, constructed of massive walls and arches'.[53] In his notebooks, written in the 1820s, Braikenridge interpreted a number of buildings with lofty and visible medieval roofs as chapels.[54] A medieval domestic hall, the 'Cyder House' behind nos.51–2 Broad Street (p81), was interpreted by Skelton as 'part of an old monastery'.[55] Bindon interpreted medieval cellars below houses in Corn Street (p157) as having been parts of St Leonard's church.[56] To the early 19th-century historian it was perfectly reasonable to interpret a lofty, unheated, Gothic space, or a decorated vaulted undercroft, as a church or chapel.

Today the Baldwin Street 'chapel' is readily interpreted as a medieval house with an open hall, with its 13th-century origin and its later occupiers identified. This context comes partly from the many studies of town houses now undertaken[57] and also through the more detailed documentation now being provided for property holdings in medieval and early modern Bristol. The former enable the identification of Seyer's chapel as the open hall of a medieval house, with a gallery forming the dais at the upper end of the hall and with a laver or domestic *piscina* for the washing of hands before the meal. The latter is modelled in its methodology on that devised by Keene for Winchester, a 'painstaking and elaborate exercise'.[58] Identifying the past owners and/or occupiers of a house has rarely been possible at the level of a complete English town or city, for no generally applied system of registration existed until the 20th century. For some cities a vast amount of documentary evidence is available, but the amount of work involved in examining it has probably inhibited systematic research.[59] Where this sort of analysis is possible, however, the rewards are great, for it can provide tenement histories which can then be linked, echoing Keene's comments in another context, 'to plots of land and buildings whose size, character, and position within the town are known'.[60] Seyer's 'chapel', 25ft in length, can thereby be identified as occupying the width of a tenement plot bounded by separately owned properties probably by 1273, and certainly by 1548, a rent charge payable to St Ewen's church from then until the 1920s providing the names and other details of successive occupiers or owners.[61] The owner of this hallhouse in *c* 1272 was John Welyschote, a citizen of sufficient wealth to make several grants to the church of St Ewen.[62] By the later 16th century the owner was one William Bird, a wealthy draper and the owner and builder in 1589 of the White Lodge, a second residence on the hillside to the west of the city (p243, pp334–5; *see* Figs 9.2, 9.9 and 11.6).[63]

Such research can often be linked to the results of archaeological investigations. Seyer's chapel was the subject of archaeological excavation (Figs 1.7 and 1.8) in 1974 without it being realised that this was a site well documented in the archives of the Bristol Record Office (Fig 1.6), in the Braikenridge collection in the Bristol City Museum and Art Gallery (Fig 1.5) and in the Seyer manuscripts in the Bristol Central Reference Library. These sources can be used to produce a plan of this long since demolished open hall (Fig 1.9).

For Bristol, the systematic research into tenement histories has in turn enabled a number of wills and in excess of 100 inventories to be related to identified properties. These span the

*Fig 1.5*
*No.59 Baldwin Street, Seyer's 'chapel of St John', copy made in 1821 of original drawing or painting of June 1812 (BRSMG M.2249).*

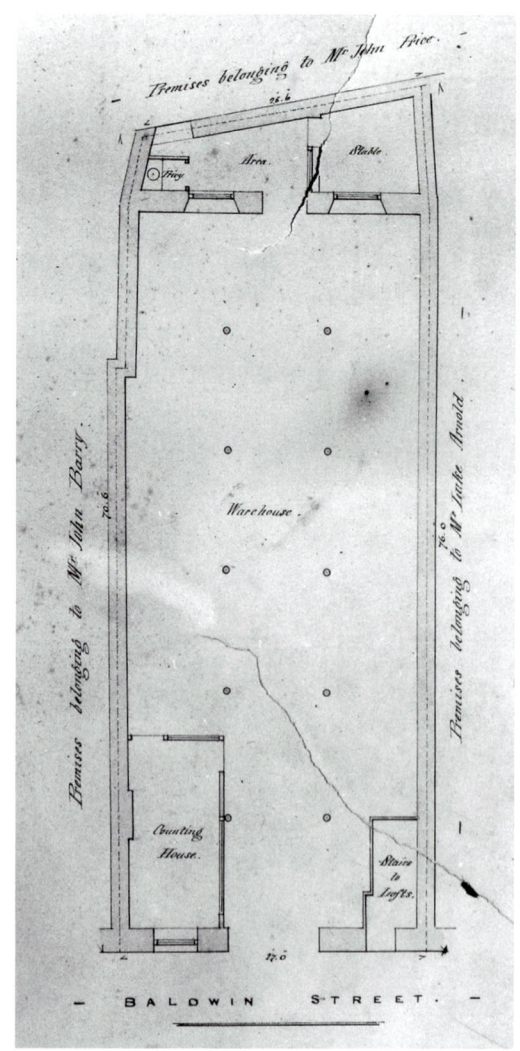

*Fig 1.6*
*No.59 Baldwin Street, Seyer's 'chapel of St John', plan of 1836 (BRO P/St W/ChW/12).*

# INTRODUCTION

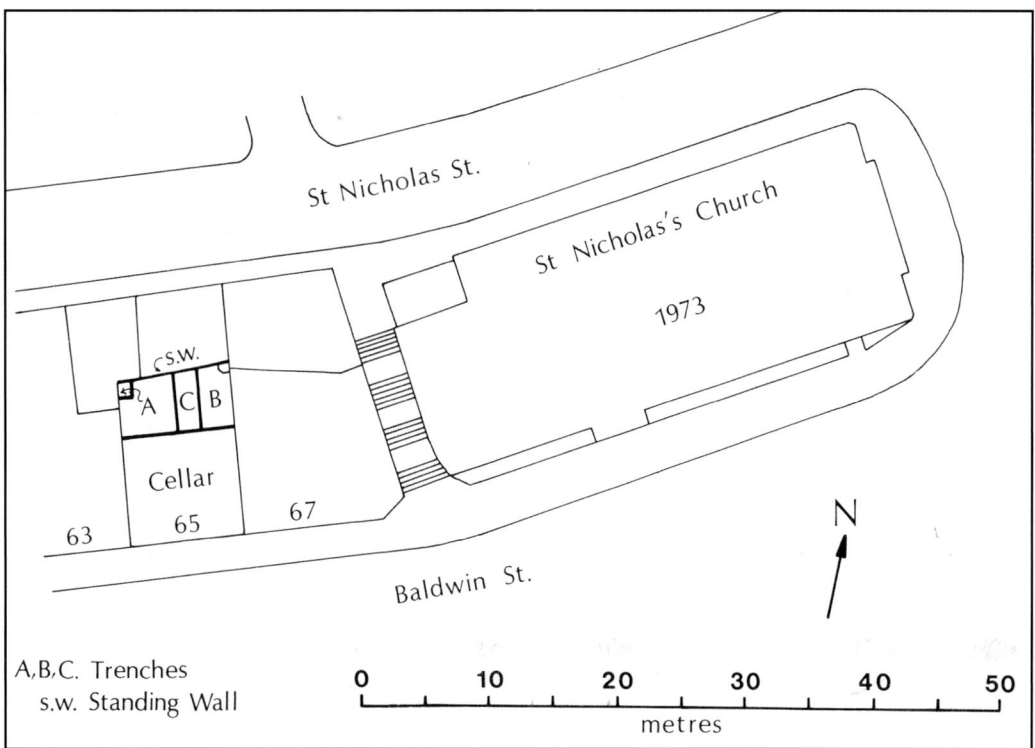

Fig 1.7
No.59 Baldwin Street, Seyer's 'chapel of St John', general plan of archaeological excavations of 1974 (Price 1979, Fig 6).

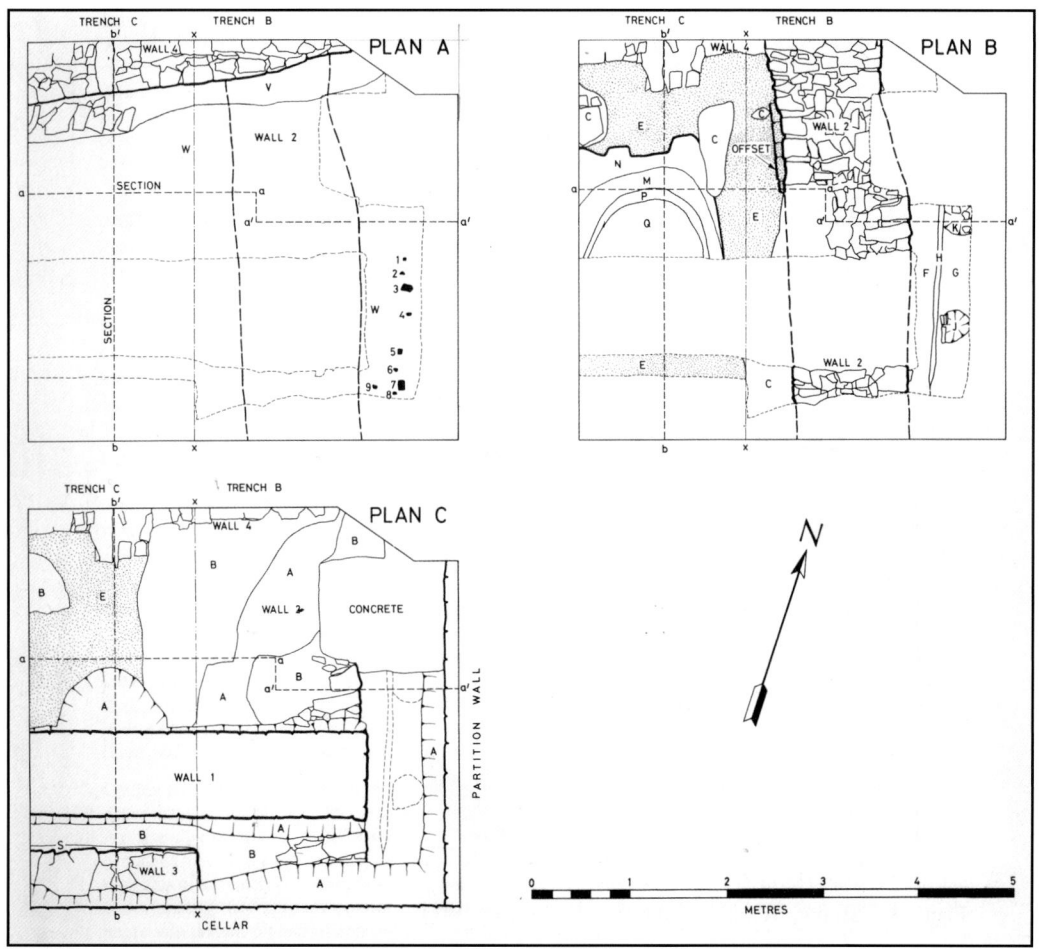

Fig 1.8
No.59 Baldwin Street, Seyer's 'chapel of St John', detailed plans of areas A, B and C of archaeological excavations of 1974 (Price 1979, Fig 7).

*Fig 1.9*
*No.59 Baldwin Street, Seyer's 'chapel of St John', reconstructed plan (RHL, PEC).*

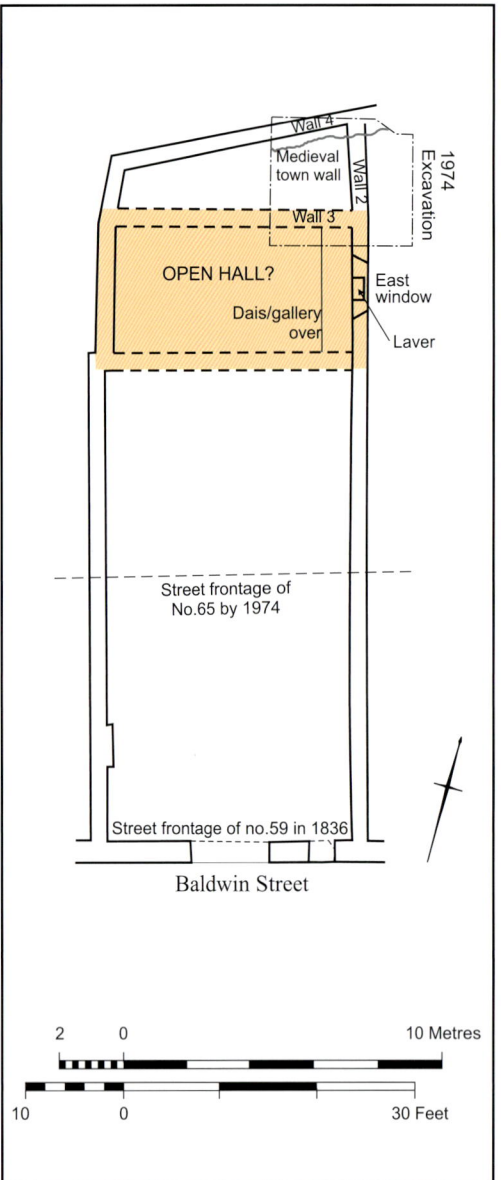

## A Note on the Sources

The reader should be aware of the bias present in the archaeological and documentary sources. The data relating to the physical form of tenement plots and houses has been brought together in an inventory, and in its compilation all available sources have been examined, as widely as possible. The surviving buildings of the later 17th and the 18th centuries have been sampled, rather than surveyed in their entirety. Considered within the text, however, are some buildings, for example those on Bristol Bridge, demolished either anciently or more recently, which were central to the life of the city until that date. The use of earlier illustrations, plans and descriptions, including the information from architectural and archaeological recording and that from institutional records of property holdings and alterations, has ensured that some 900 buildings, often long demolished, could be considered alongside the *c* 100 buildings or parts of buildings surveyed by the author and others in recent times.

Together, these offer a broad sample of buildings of widely varying character across the city for the 17th and 18th centuries. For earlier periods, some areas are less well represented. In the suburbs beyond the walls, in Old Market, Broadmead, Frog Lane and other streets known from documentary sources to have been built up by the end of the 13th century, there were few survivals of buildings of the 16th or earlier centuries even in Braikenridge's time; coincidentally there has been almost no archaeological investigation in these streets.

The survival of early buildings, either to Braikenridge's time or closer to our own, deserves more careful consideration. Christopher Currie has explored the reasons for the rebuilding of earlier housing stock and has shown how models of attrition can be provided for house survival in different regions: 'Apparent waves of rebuilding may be illusory. The richest areas may have the fewest old houses. The earliest surviving houses in an area may not have differed significantly in construction and quality from their lost contemporaries and predecessors'.[64] These comments seem very valid when applied to Bristol in the 1820s, as seen by Braikenridge. Even by then few medieval or even 17th-century houses were visible from the street frontages of High Street, Old Market and Castle Street, the last the most surprising since it was largely built or rebuilt in the 1650s–60s. Conversely the greatest

15th to 18th centuries, linking the lives of individual townspeople to the study of tenement and house during the emergence of the early modern city. They facilitate the search for the overt and more hidden meanings of the nature of personal possessions, their disposition, the names given to rooms by appraisers and, through these, the ways in which those who lived and worked in these houses interacted with the material world. The documentary sources therefore provide important contextual information for our understanding of Bristol's houses. The Inventory accompanying this study draws heavily on the correlations made between such sources for the desk-based reconstruction of buildings long demolished.

concentrations of 16th- and early 17th-century houses were to be found in Lewins Mead – the principal by-pass to the Castle while it stood, of lesser importance once Castle Street had become a through route to the east. The survival or absence of earlier buildings will be noted in subsequent discussion. Here it is sufficient to suggest that survival, either through record or through remaining fabric evidence, inevitably provides only a partial view of the city's housing over the course of the medieval and early modern centuries – a view conferred by forces which acted inconsistently and which are not fully understood. Of particular note is the apparent absence of evidence for the housing of the urban poor: this remains a subject for further investigation.

A further bias in the compilation of this work stems from the documentary sources studied. The survey of property holdings as completed to date and as published covers the early walled city north of the Avon, together with the suburb enclosed by the Marsh wall, also the hillside to the south and west of St Michael's Hill. Research for other areas, as yet incomplete and unpublished, provides a more fragmentary picture.

## The Structure of this Book

In the last few decades architectural historians and historical archaeologists have become increasingly aware, as L P Hartley observed, that 'The past is a foreign country; they do things differently there'.[65] A volume of essays on archaeologies of later historical Britain, published in 1999, was entitled *The Familiar Past*, to reinforce the idea that the recent past is deceptively familiar.[66] A quest for new directions and ways of thinking in vernacular architecture studies has 'argued that if we want to understand houses, we must look at the ideas of the people who inhabited them'.[67]

It is this approach that has determined the structure of the principal chapters of this study of Bristol town houses. Instead of a rigidly chronological analysis, taking in turn medieval, early post-medieval and 'Georgian' periods for successive treatment, the main chapters are focused on contemporary perceptions of the types of houses in which people lived, perceptions which can be related to the economic and social life of the city. In 1473 a clerk of Canynges' chantry in St Mary Redcliff in Bristol compiled an unusually detailed rental of the chantry's endowments. Individual properties were described in detail and within these descriptions a distinction was made between 'hallhouses' and 'shophouses'.[68] It can be argued that this distinction differentiated houses characterised by a hall of impressive appearance, which in the 15th century was open to the roof, and houses that consisted simply of one or more rooms over a shop. Houses with open halls might or might not have one or more shops on the street frontage; such houses could provide significantly more floor space than a house with all its living accommodation over the shop. In 15th-century Bristol the open hall was to be found principally in larger houses; as will be explored further in chapter 5, there is no evidence from Bristol for rows of smaller open-hall houses such as those found in Tewkesbury, Coventry, Battle or Sandwich. Embedded in the contents and arrangement of the open hall in Bristol, and in the juxtaposition of hallhouse and shophouse, was the material evidence for the social relations of urban capitalism – hence in part the reference to 'capitalism' in the title of chapter 13.

Sarah Pearson has recently challenged the validity of this distinction, but to this two rejoinders may be made.[69] Firstly, there is a problem of language and meaning. To people in 15th-century Bristol 'hallhouse' and 'shophouse' conveyed particular concepts not immediately obvious to us. It is the responsibility of the architectural historian to seek out the meanings of these terms. Secondly, Pearson might, in looking at the evidence from Bristol for the use of the term 'shophouse', have given more consideration to Smith's paper on the unheated multi-storeyed town house – critical, it will be argued in chapter 6, to any consideration of what might constitute a 'shophouse'. Both hallhouses and shophouses will be discussed in more detail in chapters 5 and 6.

One of Pantin's two seminal papers was entitled 'Some medieval English town houses. A Study in adaptation'.[70] Pantin was concerned to show how the plan of the house with an open hall was adapted to urban use. An alternative approach would be to show how this plan was *appropriated* for urban use, to meet the needs of elite townspeople who wished to assert their status and position in the urban hierarchy, borrowing a symbol of status in a feudal context to assert social distinction in an urban capitalist context. One might also highlight an omission in Pantin's studies of town houses; neither the smaller shops that often lined the streets in front of a hallhouse complex nor the division of urban society between rich and poor received consideration in his reviews. Furthermore, his focus was very much on elite housing, not on the artisan housing studied in Smith's review, and he was not therefore over-concerned to illustrate the polarisation of urban society between rich and poor. In his typology based on the relationship of the hall to the street, Pantin in all likelihood set out classifications that would have meant little to medieval townspeople. Chapters 5 to 7 touch on the complex relationships that surround these classifications.

Two further descriptors for medieval and early post-medieval urban houses can be found in the rental of 1473. One property was described as a 'corteplace', a term that, like 'hallhouse', can be found in other late medieval documents. A 'corteplace' was a larger property ranged around a courtyard, sometimes including a hallhouse and shophouses on the street frontage. Both Pantin and Schofield identified courtyard houses as belonging to the urban elite.[71] Chapter 11 of this study will look more closely at the courtyard houses of medieval and early modern Bristol.

A second further term used to describe a particular form of house is to be found in a later rental of the properties of the church of St Mary Redcliff. In 1569 another property formerly of the Canynges' chantries was noted as a 'loge'. A 'loge', or 'lodge', was the second residence of a citizen sufficiently wealthy to own two or more properties, a means of investing surplus capital, but also serving other purposes. Chapter 9 will look more closely at the purpose and significance of the lodge or 'garden house' (a 17th-century term for the 'lodge'), an area not previously much considered in studies of the town house in England.

It is intended that the framework for analysis provided by these contemporary perceptions of house types will permit (in chapters 10 and 11) the further exploration of the social meanings of the use of space in an emerging capitalist city. To what extent were the 'inequalities of wealth and power', the 'real divisions among townspeople, based on wide inequalities' and the 'distinctions of wealth and status rather than of occupation' hypothesised by historians studying medieval England or Bristol in particular (above) evident in the planning, construction and use of urban housing?

A further section (chapter 12) will consider the extent to which urban expansion and new building was fuelled by the profits of the Atlantic trade, notably that related to the slavery and sugar-based economy of the West Indies. Such questions will be explored further in this chapter. Trade also carried influences from England and Bristol across the Atlantic, and will permit a consideration of the extent to which the various forms of housing evident in late medieval and early modern Bristol were apparent in the New World, contributing to and forming part of the modes of elite behaviour and discourse that formed part of a wider Atlantic world forged by trade and merchant capitalism. As the philosopher and anthropologist Pierre Bourdieu has written, 'the dialectic of conditions and habitus [most easily understood in this context as lifestyle and expectations: judgements of taste related to social position being themselves acts of social positioning] is the basis of an alchemy which transforms the distribution of capital, the balance-sheet of a power relation, into a system of perceived differences [and] distinctive properties'.[72] Chapter 13 will bring together the various strands of this study, many of which focus on past lifestyles and modes of distinction.

# 2

# The Saxon and Medieval Town

## The Founding of the Saxon *Burh*

Silver pennies minted in the reign of Æthelræd II (979–1016) possibly provide the first evidence for the existence of Bristol – 'possibly' because the letters 'BRIC' could stand for either Bristol or Bridgnorth (Fig 2.1). These coins were struck by his moneyer Elfweard and probably date from 1009–17. The Bristol mint was certainly firmly established by fairly early in the reign of Cnut (1016–35). To have been the site of a mint, Bristol must by this time have been a defended *burh*, with a market and trading connections.[1] From this evidence, and allowing for the absence of any earlier coinage from Bristol, the *burh* is likely to have been founded in the reign of Cnut, Æthelræd II or one of their predecessors. The documentary sources provide no further evidence. Who took the momentous decision to found Bristol remains unknown.

Why Bristol was founded, at this date or before, should be examined at greater length. The position of Bristol was similar to those of a number of *burhs* shown or claimed to have been founded in the reign of Edward the Elder (899–925), at places suited to control estuarine or river navigation, on slightly elevated but accessible spur sites, always associated with bridges over major rivers. It has been argued that the failure of the Viking raids of 914 in the Severn estuary was a direct result of the effectiveness of Edward's defence strategy, with the south coast, and in particular the south side of the Severn estuary, now being protected by fortresses. Bristol may have been part of this strategy, perhaps founded by Edward the Elder before 914 as a *burh* and bridge to control the movement up or down the Avon of the mobile Viking warships.[2] The position of Bristol on the Avon could be compared to that of Chester on the Dee, regained by Edward the Elder from the Norse in 907, or to London, where the bridge across the Thames proved a temporary obstacle to Cnut's attack in 1016.[3]

The majority of the *burhs* founded in the reign of Æthelræd were established as places of defence and refuge, to be utilised in the face of the continuing Danish onslaught. Typical of these foundations were South Cadbury in Somerset and Cissbury in Sussex. The site chosen for Bristol was adequately placed for defence, on a low spur set at the confluence of the Avon and the Frome overlooking the marshes of the tidal estuary. Surrounded on three sides by a low but steep slope, it was connected to the higher ground on the east only by a narrow ridge. However, the low cliff and river banks surrounding the site of Bristol, readily accessible from the sea, could not, for defensive purposes, be compared with the precipitous slopes below the inland hilltops of South Cadbury and Cissbury.

If Bristol's location was adequate for defence, it was superbly situated for trade and commerce, and this is likely to be the principal reason for the establishment of a settlement. The Avon, and most especially its tributary, the Frome, provided an extensive inland port, sheltered from storms and adjacent to land that was to prove eminently suitable for urban development. The tidal Avon provided a link both with the Bristol Channel and the open sea to the west and with the Severn estuary and its tributaries to the north. Although the site was not directly on the open sea, the passage of ships was facilitated through the great tidal range of the Avon, the same river providing access inland to the east. It has been suggested that 'contacts with western England and Norse trading centres in Ireland, especially Dublin, were probably responsible for … the emergence of Bristol as a port in the early eleventh [century], with the slave trade (noted at this date by William of Malmesbury, writing on the life of St Wulfstan) as one of its main concerns'.[4]

*Fig 2.1*
*Silver penny minted at 'BRIC', of Æthelræd II (979–1016), one of two coins from Bristol in a hoard of 1,219 coins found in 1849 when digging for marl at Enner, Denmark (Royal Collection of Coins and Medals, National Museum, Copenhagen; reproduced from Galster (ed) 1966, pl 2, by permission of the British Academy); further information from Helle W Horsnæs, Curator of Ancient Coins, the National Museum of Denmark.*

## The *Burh* Defences and Street Layout

The documents are utterly silent, but the material evidence provides some insights into the considerations of defence and commerce uppermost in the minds of those who founded Bristol. Remarkably, the line that they chose for the defences of the *burh* can still be followed on foot in the modern city (Fig 2.2). The Saxon town defences, built on the crest of the steep slope, were probably superseded in the 13th century, when new walls were built to enclose a much larger area; the form and sequence of these early defences have not been adequately investigated.

The earlier wall appears in documentary references of the 13th century onwards, but is poorly recorded archaeologically. The clearest archaeological evidence is from excavations undertaken in 1990 at nos.3–9 Small Street, which revealed 'the rear of a bank which may have been the precursor of the adjacent early town wall'.[5] Immediately inside the line of the Saxon town defences was a series of intramural lanes, extending from St Nicholas's gate to the Pithay. These survive today as St Nicholas Street, Leonard Lane, Bell Lane and Tower Lane, with each providing an occasional glimpse of the steep slope below. Dolphin Street, known earlier as Defence Street, and Worshipful Street, its course obliterated in the 1760s by the building of Bridge Street, possibly originated as intramural lanes to the defences delimiting the *burh* on the east and alongside the Avon,

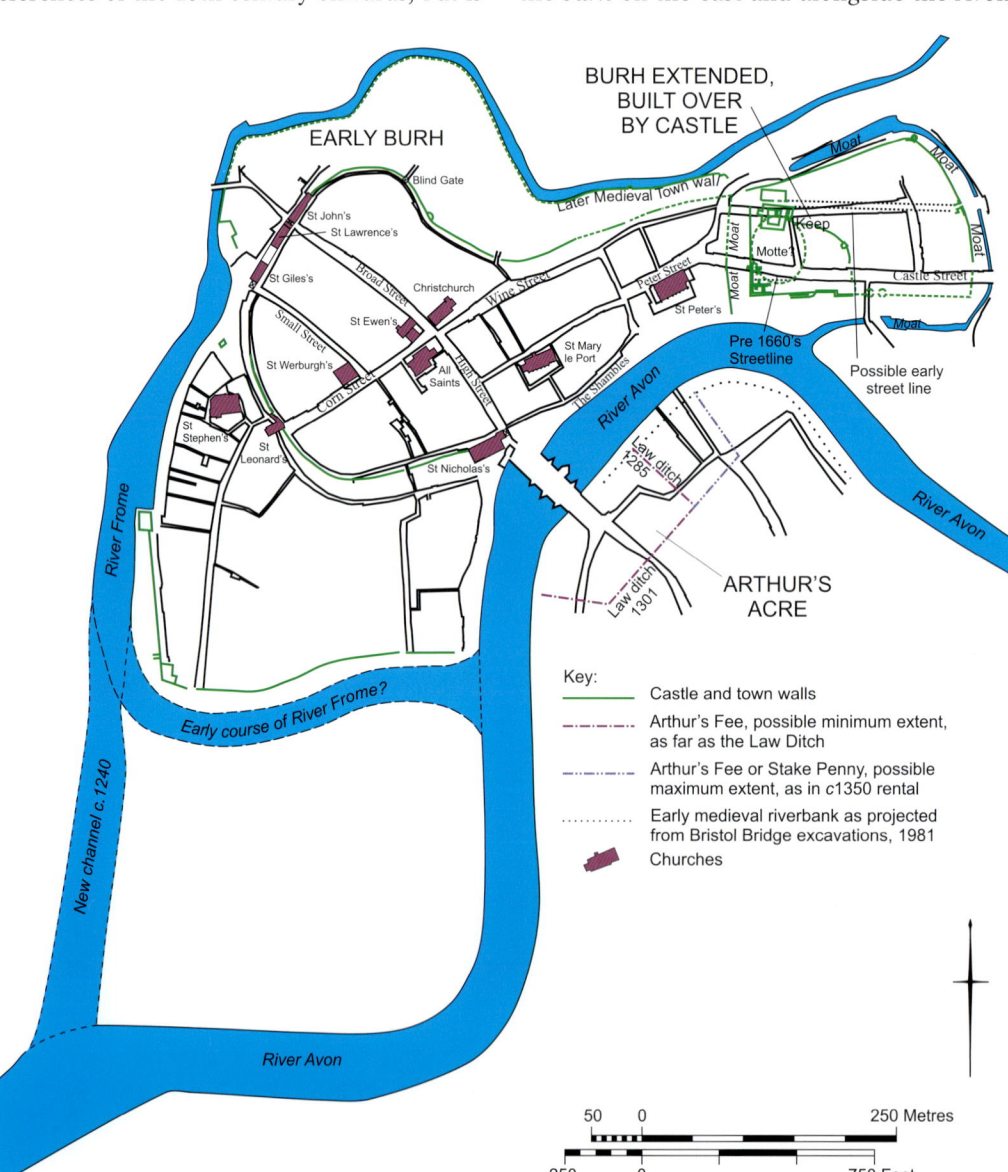

Fig 2.2
Saxon and early medieval Bristol, showing the core of the Saxon burh (the town walls in green), the churches, the Marsh suburb, the location of the medieval quay, the possible course of the Frome before c 1240, the bridge and the probable defended bridgehead of Arthur's Acre (RHL, PEC).

upstream from St Nicholas's gate and the bridge. The bridge certainly existed by the later 12th century and most probably gave its name to the *burh*: 'Bricgstow', the place of the bridge.[6]

With the position of the defences decided, attention would have turned to the apportionment for permanent settlement of the land inside the line of the intramural lanes. It must have been decided to define the principal blocks of land for development through setting out a system of streets, all of which survive today (Fig 2.2). The two principal thoroughfares met at the centre of the *burh*, this carfax to become the site of the high cross. Crossing the ridge from south to north were High Street and Broad Street, while running along the ridge, from west to east, were Corn Street and Wine Street. Each of these streets, and also Small Street, led directly to one of the city gates. A sixth street, Mary le Port Street, could only have led to a gate in the less well understood line of defences on the east. The resulting street system was rectilinear in form, echoing those of other Late Saxon *burhs* founded earlier in the 10th century.[7]

While the intramural lanes must have fulfilled a partly defensive need, facilitating access to the walls in time of attack, some of these and the principal streets were designed for the purpose of trade. East from the Bridge, the butchers' shambles were sited in Worshipful Street by the 13th century. To the west, St Nicholas Street as laid out broadened from 10ft, at the east end of St Nicholas's church, to 20ft in the centre of the street,[8] before this space was infilled with housing backing on to the town wall. The plan of Worshipful Street indicates that it also may have been designed in this way, widening towards the east end to form a market space.

The planning of streets as markets is most evident in the design of the four principal thoroughfares. Broad Street was set out as *c* 24ft wide at each end, the east side broadening out to provide a street nearly twice that width at its mid-point. High Street was set out in an almost identical manner, the east side widening from *c* 30ft at each end to over 40ft at its junction with Mary le Port Street. Wine Street was set out slightly differently, widening from *c* 20ft at the carfax to 50ft at its junction with Tower Lane. In this wide open space was the pillory or 'wynch' which possibly gave the street its name. The west end of Corn Street was also planned to a greater width, 40ft in comparison to the 30ft-wide street closer to the carfax.

This characteristic element in the setting out of a number of streets, so as to accommodate markets in the widened centre parts, set the rectilinear street plan of Bristol apart from those of most other towns in Wessex founded in the late 9th to early 11th centuries. Southampton, another port, was also an exception, with its High Street broadening to accommodate a market.[9] From the very foundation of such towns, their commercial purpose was thus overtly stated.

## Burgages

With the lines of the defences and streets determined, the areas within were subdivided to form 'burgages' or tenements (chapter 4). As this activity commenced, the site must still have appeared largely rural. The extent to which these rural surroundings were familiar to the commercially minded founders of the town can be seen through examining, in more detail, the plans of known property holdings within the medieval city.[10] The principles behind any such examination are well known and can be briefly stated. The physical appearance of a town today or in the past will often in large measure be the result of earlier property development.[11] In the urban landscape, successive earlier properties will often be visible as distinctive 'plan units', identifiable as blocks of tenements with shared characteristic features.[12]

In at least two areas the founders of the *burh* may have utilised elements in an existing landscape of plough-land. On the east side of Broad Street, the sinuous outlines of the properties running back to Tower Lane, as well as the boundaries and lanes in Corn Street running back to St Nicholas Street, possibly derive from the use of furlong alignments during the setting out of the tenement plots. In St Nicholas Street, one of these properties was still known as 'halfurlonge' in the late 15th century; the length of this plot, if extended to Corn Street, would have been *c* 220ft – or one furlong.

Elsewhere, though, a new pattern of boundaries was set out, characterised by its rectilinear form – as between Broad Street and Small Street or between Mary le Port Street and Wine Street. Within these areas development probably proceeded in stages, with smaller blocks of tenements being developed successively; this accounts for the variations visible in the lengths of plots and the alignments of rear boundaries. In each of the principal streets, a number of tenement plots were set out so as to be c 40–50ft wide. In Broad Street and Wine Street, these wide tenements corresponded to those which in 1295 paid a landgable rent (a rent payable to the Crown and charged on each property) of 15d.[13] The 1295 survey records many tenements paying an exact half or quarter of this amount. It is not possible to say whether these plots, consisting of a half or a quarter of the full width, were let as such in the first 50 or so years of the existence of the *burh*.

These perceptions of the ways in which different parts of the *burh* were planned, if accepted as likely, reveal a tension between, on the one hand, the adoption of boundaries that were embedded in rural life as it had been and, on the other hand, the acceptance of a new environment that was wholly urban, owing nothing to what had been here before. The use of earlier furlong boundaries to delimit new burgages might be seen as a matter of convenience, but it might equally have been deeply symbolic to contemporary mentalities. This tension, between the rural past, a town and commercial imperatives, was a long-lived aspect of urban life.

## The *Burh* in the 11th and 12th Centuries

There is further evidence that by the mid-11th century the new *burh* was a place of some importance. In 1051 it was first the destination and then the point of departure for ships of Harold and Leofwine, the sons of Earl Godwin. In 1063 it was the base for Harold's fleet, and in 1068 Harold's sons sailed to Bristol from Ireland. They hoped to take the town by storm, but failed when faced with the stout resistance of its citizens.[14]

Most of the medieval churches of Bristol are first recorded in the 12th century. The density of churches is characteristic of pre-Conquest towns and the greater majority may have come into existence then, rather than after the Conquest.[15] Within the possibly defended area west of Dolphin Street (the area outside that which it is suggested was built over by the Castle) at least ten medieval churches were known to have been in existence in the 12th century (Fig 2.2). Five were located over or between the gates (St Nicholas, St Leonard, St Giles, St Lawrence and St John) and a further five were within the walled town area (All Saints, Christchurch or Holy Trinity, St Ewen, St Mary le Port and St Werburgh). Within the possibly defended area east of Dolphin Street, built over by the Norman Castle, there may have been a further two churches, recorded as chapels by William Worcestre.[16] Beyond the defended area of the *burh*, the churches of St Michael, St Peter and St Stephen were all possibly founded before the Conquest (Fig 2.2).[17] Collectively, these might attest to the rapid success and growth of the town.

Inside the defences, evidence for Late Saxon occupation has come from a number of excavations, but later construction of cellars has made rare indeed the opportunity ever to look closely at the material culture of the early inhabitants. Future archaeological work might, however, show more clearly the growth of the town in the first half of the 11th century. The walled area was possibly extended eastwards before the 1060s. East of the early *burh* the castle built by Geoffrey of Coutances after the Norman Conquest cut across the ridge, separating the city from direct access to its hinterland to the east. In other larger towns and cities in England the Norman castle was almost without exception placed within a corner of the built-up area, partly using the earlier town defences. Whether this was the sequence of events in Bristol has been debated.

Michael Ponsford has argued from the evidence of his archaeological excavations that the earliest Norman castle at Bristol took the form of a newly constructed ringwork. However, this author has argued that the outer defences of the Norman castle possibly utilised the walls of the *burh* as extended eastwards from its original circuit, a recently new east gate of the town then becoming the castle's east gate.[18] As part of the Bristol Castle works, it was then necessary to build another gate, 'Newgate', to provide access to the town from the east, albeit by a tortuous route alongside the castle ditch and mill weir. The extension eastwards of the Saxon *burh* would also provide an explanation for the disjuncture between the street systems to the west and east of Dolphin or Defence Street. The easterly continuation of Wine Street, only 10ft wide, later became known as Narrow Wine Street.[19]

By the 1120s the former *burh* could be described as 'the most populous town of Bristol, where there is a harbour able to receive ships from Ireland, Norway and other lands overseas'.[20] Of particular importance was the trade in slaves, against which Wulfstan, Bishop of Worcester, had preached in Bristol in the later 11th century.[21] The links with Ireland are increasingly attested in the archaeological record, with research now increasing our understanding of the chronology and sources of the trade in pottery and other goods between Bristol, Dublin and other Irish towns.[22] The growth of Bristol from the 11th to the early 12th century was already extraordinary to the chronicler of Stephen's reign.[23] A town founded or almost unknown at the beginning of the 11th century, a mere century and a half later it now ranked in wealth only after London and York. In the next century Bristol would double in area.

## The Earliest Town Houses

Knowledge of the houses built in the town of the 11th and 12th centuries is meagre. The evidence comes solely from excavations and has been much restricted by the extent to which cellars were constructed in the later medieval town (chapter 7). The evidence for earthfast or post in the ground buildings typical of the Anglo-Saxon period has come from two sites.[24] In Mary le Port Street was a building at least 6m long and at least 4m wide, set parallel to the street. Internal features included a hearth near the north-west corner and a drain, possibly taking water from the gable end of the building into a passage alongside.[25] In plan this structure could be interpreted as a hallhouse, the hearth being close to the centre of the room serving as the hall. A second building of similar date and construction was recorded in the excavations at Site D on the site of Bristol Castle, sealed by the castle's defences. The evidence for a structure here came from postholes, stakeholes and beam slots, but the overall plan of the building could not be established.[26]

## The Expansion of Bristol in the Later 12th to Early 14th Centuries

Between the later 12th and early 14th centuries the town of Bristol was much extended through the addition of new suburbs promoted by two feudal lords, the Earls of Gloucester and the FitzHardings of Berkeley, together with the religious houses founded by these families (notably St Augustine's Abbey and the preceptory of the Templars).

Robert, Earl of Gloucester, the illegitimate son of Henry I, acquired the Castle, town and barton (manorial lands) of Bristol as part of the Honour of Gloucester through his marriage to Mabel FitzHamon in 1107. He or his son William was responsible for the development of two new suburbs, beyond the walled city. The *'feria'*, later known as Old Market, was at least part developed for housing by *c* 1165. Broadmead was being developed at a date between *c* 1150 and 1183, when Hawisia, Countess of Gloucester granted to St James's Priory a burgage at the lower and east end of the 'novo burgo prati'.[27]

In determining to develop a new suburb, the Earl of Gloucester was free to place it anywhere on his substantial landholdings to the east and north of the Castle. The choice of precise location presumably depended on where he believed profit might be maximised. In this respect the siting of the Old Market was based on sound judgement. On the main road leading eastwards from the Castle towards Bath, it was well placed as a market for trade with the countryside to the east.[28] Here the street was set out so as to accommodate the market, widening from *c* 30ft at each end to *c* 60ft in the centre. On each side long tenements extended to back lanes, which in turn connected at each end to the main street (Fig 2.3).

The new suburb of Broadmead was similarly well placed, alongside and on the route to Gloucester. Located to the north of the Castle, it was between the Frome on the south and west, the churchyard and fairground in front of St James's Priory on the north, and land, destined to be granted in the 1240s to the Dominican friars, on the east (Fig 2.3).[29] The situation required a different development strategy from that pursued for Old Market. The majority of the tenements in the new suburb faced the street now known as Broadmead, *c* 55ft wide; a smaller number of short tenements faced east on to Old King Street and Merchant Street, leading north to Gloucester. Both these streets were possibly built on a causeway, with Merchant Street widening towards the centre so as to provide a further market area.

Other feudal landlords were active in promoting urban developments to the north and west of the walled town, all identifiable as distinct plan units or blocks of properties (Fig 2.3). St Augustine's Abbey had been founded or re-founded *c* 1140–8, within part of the manor of Billeswick granted to the Abbey by Robert Fitzharding (later Frogmore Street).

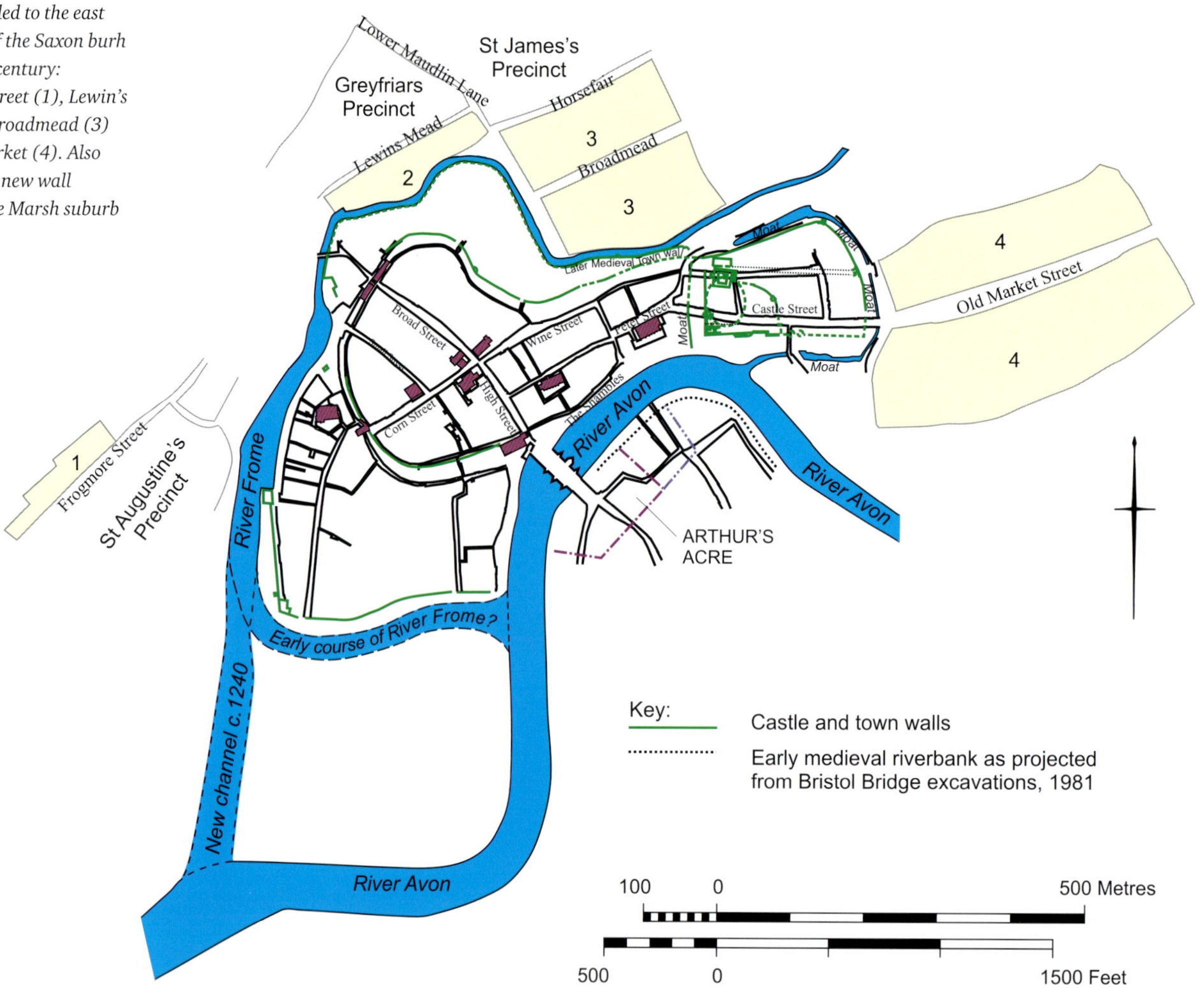

*Fig 2.3*
*Suburbs added to the east and north of the Saxon burh by the 13th century: Frogmore Street (1), Lewin's Mead (2), Broadmead (3) and Old Market (4). Also visible is the new wall enclosing the Marsh suburb (RHL, PEC).*

The north side of part of Frog Lane was probably developed by the Abbot of St Augustine in the later 12th century, being of similar basic plan to the Old Market and Broadmead developments. A single unidentified landowner was responsible for the development of Lewin's Mead (Fig 2.3). In 1285 the 15 listed tenement plots in this street were all held by John de Kerdif.

These developments, along both sides of the Frome and towards St Augustine's Abbey, were individually much smaller projects than those undertaken by the Earl of Gloucester. However, they for the most part exploited to maximum advantage the proximity to the town of what may previously have been small land parcels alongside the Frome. Here, as with the larger developments, the straight and regular boundaries of the new tenements indicate that these were set out anew. In contrast St Augustine's Abbey followed a different strategy in the development of St Augustine's Back. This block of properties appears to have been developed within an existing framework of sinuous narrow plots.

The Marsh suburb to the south of the town wall was probably developed in a similar way. The boundaries to the tenements on the south side of Baldwin Street lacked the regularity of those in streets such as Old Market and Broadmead (Figs 2.2 and 2.3). It has been argued elsewhere that in the 12th century the course of the Frome was to the south of this suburb, and that it was to the burgesses living here, not over the Bridge, that Henry II granted a charter in the later 12th century.[30]

South of the Avon, linked by a bridge to the north bank, feudal lords acting together created an entirely new suburb during the 12th century.[31] The east part was granted by Robert, Earl of Gloucester to the Knights Templar between 1128

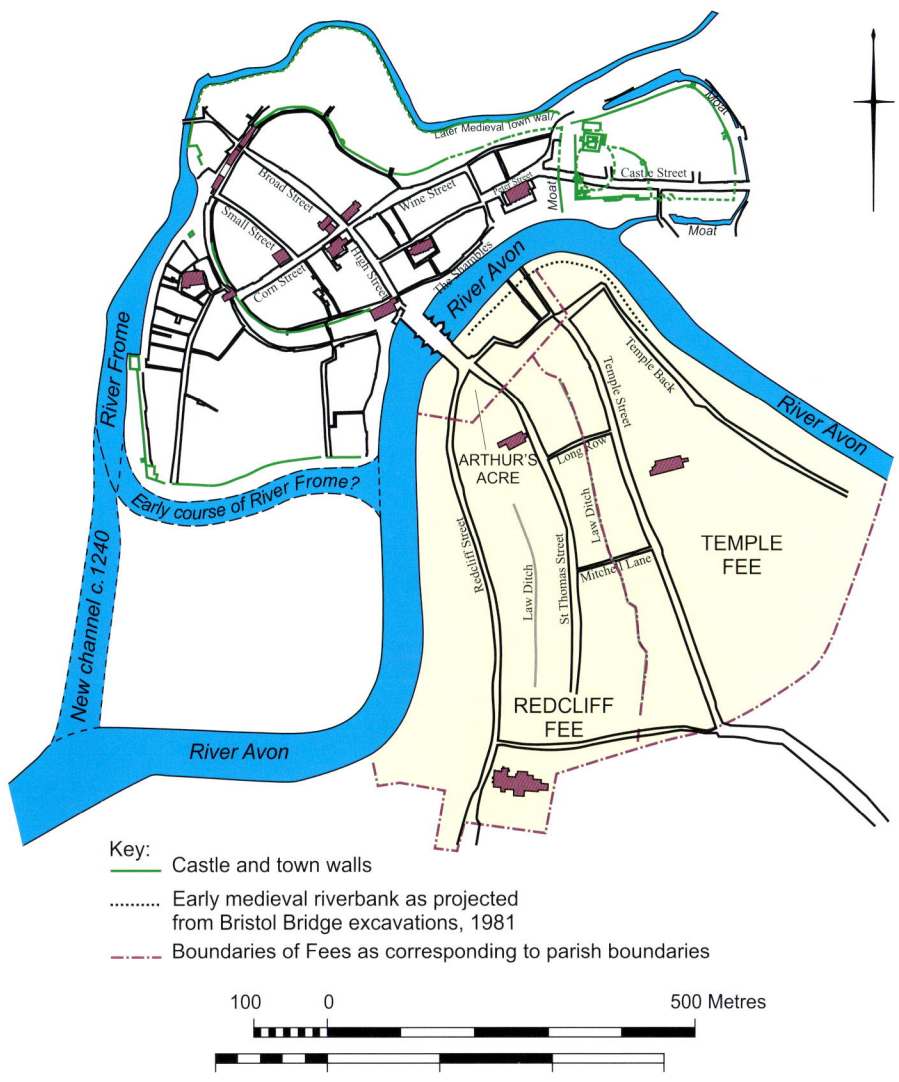

Fig 2.4
Suburbs south of the river in the Saxon and early medieval periods: Arthur's Acre, Temple and Redcliff Fees (RHL, PEC).

and 1148.[32] The building of Temple church and a preceptory followed, together with the setting out of Temple Street and the subdivision of the land either side into burgage plots. The west part of the suburb, Redcliff Fee, was developed by Robert Fitzharding, being part of his manor of Bedminster.[33] Two main streets were laid out, Redcliff Street and St Thomas Street. Both had tenement plots extending back on either side, with those on the west of Redcliff Street stretching to the Avon. Dendrochronological dating has shown that the west side of Redcliff Street was being developed from c 1123–33, and that quays were being built by 1147–8.[34]

Co-operation between the Templars and Fitzharding is evident in the form of the two developments seen together (Fig 2.4). The boundary between the two developments was a 'Law Ditch', which served as a drain for the tenements on both sides. Three streets, Long Row, Mitchell Lane and Pile Street, connected the Templars' suburb to Fitzharding's St Thomas Street. Except for this access from FitzHarding's suburb, the Templars' suburb seems to have been intended as largely self-contained, its contacts as much with the hinterland to the south-east as with the city to the north. In contrast Fitzharding's development was planned with the Bridge to the town on the north side of the river as its focus, Redcliff Street and Temple Street converging just south of the bridgehead. Fitzharding also had the better site. Downstream from the Bridge his development had the advantage of a river frontage accessible to seagoing ships.

A third landowner, not involved in this close collaboration, developed an area close to the Bridge. This was a strip of land that extended from the Law Ditch, which marked the boundary of the Templars' suburb on the east, as far as the 12th tenement in Redcliff Street on the west.[35] Known as 'Arthur's Acre' by *c* 1285, and as 'Arthur's Fee' and also 'Stakepenny' by *c* 1350, the entirely separate development of this area, possibly first by the Crown and then by the Arthur family, can be inferred from a rental of *c* 1350 and from the tortuous route followed by Tucker Street, linking Temple Street to St Thomas Street. Possibly this separate development originated as a settlement created to defend the bridgehead when the bridge leading to the *burh* on the north side of the river was first constructed – most probably when Bristol, 'the place of the bridge', was first founded as a *burh*.[36] In the space of about a century, the initiatives of the Earl of Gloucester, Robert Fitzharding, the Templars and an unknown number of other developers must have more than doubled the area of the city. The pace of building development in mid- and later 12th-century Bristol must have been frenetic, with many persons involved.[37]

## Smaller Developments

Among the more prosperous of the burgesses of mid 12th-century Bristol was Robert, son of Swein. The grant to Robert, by William, Earl of Gloucester, of all four properties and rents from a fifth, all in Old Market, provides one of the first available insights, from a contemporary document, into the property market and the development of property in Bristol.[38] The charter was a confirmation of the grant made to Robert by Adam de Ely, Earl William's chaplain until 1166.

De Ely was part of the Earl's household. His presence is a reminder that a number of persons would have been involved in the promotion and management of William's property developments, which extended across both sides of the Severn estuary and into other parts of southern England. Others had already built upon the four tenements granted to Robert. On three were houses. On the fourth was a longhouse *(longam domum)*, a rural house-type that brought people and animals together under one roof. Among 100 or more deeds relating to property in 13th-century Bristol, there is only this one reference to a longhouse.

In its specific identification in the grant to Robert might be read Adam de Ely's own awareness that this property was sited where town met country. The four properties represented an investment, which strategy or accident might enhance. If the site was sufficiently attractive, an individual burgage might be divided to provide a higher return. It was possibly one of the above tenements that had been so divided when Robert then granted half a burgage to Baldwin the White.[39] A contemporary of Robert was William Fitz Gregory who, at about the same date, granted to his brother Robert another half-burgage in the Market – part of a larger transaction involving six properties.[40] These transactions, not in themselves remarkable, are noteworthy now because Robert and William Fitz Gregory may be regarded as two of the earliest recorded Bristol property investors. The investment of profits in property would be a recurring theme in urban life. Robert and William were also members of a larger urban community, which can be glimpsed as such for the first time in the early 13th century.

## Commercial Imperatives – the Emerging Role of the Townspeople

The principal promoters of the new suburbs of the 12th century were feudal landlords, notably the Earl of Gloucester and Robert Fitzharding, a staunch supporter of Earl Robert, and a burgess of exceptional wealth – to the extent that he and his descendants became Lords of Berkeley. In contrast the transformation of Bristol in the 13th century resulted from the vision and efforts of the urban community, the 'burgesses' mentioned in the royal charters of the 12th and 13th centuries, which were seen most vividly in the works undertaken in the 1240s.

By 1240 the Mayor and Corporation, the names of those involved recorded in contemporary deeds, had prepared plans to excavate a shorter channel for ships coming to the port and the building of new walls to enclose some of the suburbs.[41] The diversion of the Frome (its course shown on Figs 2.2 and 2.3) began in March 1240, facilitated first by an agreement with St Augustine's Abbey and then by the obtaining, at the end of April, of a royal charter exhorting the burgesses of Redcliff to assist in the work. With the new channel completed, the old river course possibly served as the ditch in front of a new wall built to enclose the Marsh suburb. At roughly the same time, new walls extended the defended area of the town on the north, and further new walls were built to enclose the Temple and Redcliff suburbs. On the north various streets now lay within the walled town, notably Christmas Street and Halliers or Grope Lane. On the south the ditch to protect the new walls served also for the diversion of the Avon, as a temporary measure to permit the building of a new bridge to replace the old.[42] The new bridge consisted of four stone arches and was lined with houses by the mid-14th century.[43]

The new walls must have been impressive, particularly those of Redcliff and Temple as seen from the south, or those of the Marsh suburb when approached by river. These were not however for defence, since such long stretches of river frontage were left unprotected for commercial necessity – it being essential to have a quayside on which cargoes could be freely unloaded, and to have river frontages where access was unimpeded for a variety of industries and trades. The royal charter emphasised that the new river channel was 'for the betterment of the port', from which 'no little advantage ought to accrue'. The new defences would act as toll barriers, those on the north and south being known in later times as the Portwall. The walls, and especially the towers marking the principal terminals and corners, can certainly be seen as an expression of civic pride, but the works as a whole were undertaken primarily to fulfill commercial ambitions.[44] The construction of houses, and particularly shops, on high-value sites, tightly constrained but well situated for commercial purposes, is a feature of a successful city.[45]

## New Developments of the 13th Century

The citizens who held houses on the new Bridge occupied one of the prime commercial positions in the city, in one of the most urban situations imaginable. By the mid-l4th century, the widely travelled visitor to Bristol would have seen the Bridge lined with at least 16 or 17 properties, a form of development comparable to the principal bridges of London, Paris and other European cities (Fig 2.5). The new houses and shops built on the Bridge were probably replacements, at least in part, of similar structures on the earlier bridge now demolished. The widely varying rents at which these properties were let by c 1350 indicate that their construction had taken place over lengthy periods, or that the properties were of different sizes.

Fig 2.5
Bristol Bridge shortly before its demolition in 1760; houses on the early medieval bridge would have been lower in height. The arch closest to the church of St Nicholas probably survives below the present street surface. To the left of the arch and shown end-on is the block of five tenements between St Nicholas church and the river (BCRL, Braikenridge collection III.i.389).

It is not known who took the decision to lay out tenement plots in a scarcely less constrained situation, on the narrow steep slope outside the Saxon town defences, now serving neither a defensive nor symbolic purpose. The strips of land between Baldwin Street and St Nicholas Street, between the Quay and Leonard Lane, between Quay Street and Lawrence Lane and between Grope Lane and Tower Lane were all built upon by the early 14th century. Typical were no.7 The Quay, a tenement with a shop and cellar extending back to the town wall, recorded by 1323, and nos.43–4 Baldwin Street, a tenement recorded in *c* 1350 as extending back to St Nicholas Street, with five shops on the frontage to Baldwin Street. Development of these areas must have commenced sooner, however – within a decade or so of the building of the new outer town walls, by *c* 1272–3, when John Welyschote granted to the church of St Ewen a rent of 10s charged upon no.59 Baldwin Street (chapter 1). The development of these tenements is likely to have been by individual landlords.[46]

In the last decade of the 13th century, *c* 1291–3, the parishioners of St Nicholas's church and the Commonalty initiated the development of five tenements at the north-west end of the Bridge. The site was a narrow parcel of vacant land, between the street and the river frontage, and had possibly been part used as a ropewalk between St Nicholas Church and the Avon (Figs 2.3 and 2.5). The rents to be paid thereafter to the Commonalty were evidently determined by the length of street frontage, since the property on the corner with the Bridge counted as two for rental purposes. The parishioners granted this property to Robert Roper in April 1291. By May 1291 the two properties to the south were also held by Roper, together with John Cheddre. In the same month a fifth property, at the south end of the development, was granted by the proctors of St Nicholas's church to the Commonalty, who held it until May 1293 before granting it to Roper and Cheddre. The rents payable to the Commonalty for each unit within this development were identical, contrasting with the varied situation on the Bridge. The same rent was probably paid to St Nicholas's church, but is recorded only for the southernmost property. Roper and Cheddre can therefore be identified as the individuals responsible for the development of this row of five properties. John de Cheddre was one of the most prominent members of the civic community, steward or bailiff in 1288–9, 1294–5 and 1305–6.[47] This new development at the end of the Bridge was safely in the hands of the urban elite.

Certain landlords probably profited by accident rather than design from the altered town plan of the 1240s.[48] Those who held land on the south side of Baldwin Street may have been provided with new investment opportunities. Through the development or realignment of the southern end of Scadepulle or Marsh Street, they may have secured new additional commercial frontages.[49] Conversely, there were also street frontages that were reduced in value. Pile Street below St Mary Redcliff was now separated from the rest of the suburb by the town wall, while St Thomas Street was left without any access to the south.

## Bristol in the Later Middle Ages: Infill and Adaptation

By the end of the 13th century there were few sites within the built-up area, especially ones of high value close to the centre, where new developments could be placed. One exception was possibly the churchyard of Christchurch, where the Broad Street frontage was certainly built up by 1352.[50] Another exception was in Back Street, formerly Baste Street, where Eborard le Frenche was able to build along one side of his garden a row of 11 shops, new in *c* 1350.[51] On the opposite side of the same street, nine shops on the frontage of Spicer's Hall were possibly a development dating from the same time as the mid-14th-century refurbishment of the house and shops on the Welsh Back frontage.[52]

Probably later in date was a development to the south of le Frenche's property, in the same street.[53] By 1567 Edmond Weston's property in the Rackhay consisted of ten tenements and seven gardens.[54] These were probably all rebuilt in the later 16th and early 17th centuries, but could have included four of the tenements on the north side shown in an early 19th-century plan with accompanying watercolour (*see* Figs 8.31, 8.32a and 8.32b). A development similar to the Rackhay (literally a close with racks [for the drying of stained cloths]) was the row of shops (*see* Figs 8.33 and 8.34) at the south end of St Thomas Street. This was the row 'Seynt Mary Reckehey', built by John Haveryng on land leased from the church of St Mary Redcliff before 1416.[55] The developments at the Rackhay and Seynt Mary Reckehey were exceptions, however, with most being notable as developments on sites of lesser value, away from the central streets.

## Working within the Grain of the Town: Adapting Existing Properties to New Needs

From the end of the 13th to the mid-17th centuries Bristol may not have expanded greatly in area, but this is not to say that the city was unchanging. Over the course of these centuries significant developments in property holding took place, many of them designed to exploit the commercial potential of valuable sites – principally by subdivision, but also by laying out development to give plots of different sizes. Close to the carfax, for example, a number of properties had already been broken into smaller units by the end of the 13th century. These were concentrated in High Street, Corn Street and Wine Street. Nos.39–48 High Street, in part of medieval build, still stand on these plots, already subdivided by the 1260s. In plan, this group of tenements can be seen to have been created out of the subdivision of three larger tenements, respectively nos.39–42, 43–6 and 47–8. On the south nos.39–42, separate holdings by the 1260s, were apparently subdivisions of one large tenement that extended back from the street to include also Abyndon's Inn.[56] In the 1295 survey of landgable rents each of the four tenements was assessed at 3¾d, making a total of 15d.

The group of four tenements to the north, now nos.43–6, was similarly assessed, and can be argued to have been a second large tenement later subdivided. The tenements to the north (nos.47–8), grouped around the corner with Corn Street, were by the mid-13th century subdivided into even smaller units. In *c* 1290 the western part of no.48, facing Corn Street, was a parcel of land 9ft 6in wide. This extended back 29ft to abut a tenement used in the early 13th century as a *seld* or bazaar which formed part of the lands of St Augustine's Abbey, shown in much later records to have occupied a plot of similar width, now part of no.47. The indications are that a larger tenement, at the corner of the two streets, had by the early 13th century been subdivided into plots *c* 9ft 6in wide, probably for use as *selds*.[57]

A similar intensity of development had taken place in some of the intramural lanes, their later role as back lanes masking their importance in the earlier history of the town. As in High Street, separately owned properties of varying size fronted these streets at least from the early 13th century. In Tower Lane a tenement, granted to St Augustine's Abbey in the late 12th or early 13th century, formed part of a row of four tenements extending towards the corner with Broad Street. Each was *c* 20ft wide, each assessed at 3¾d for landgable – suggesting an origin as a single large property assessed, like the other larger properties, at 15d per annum.[58] Further south in Tower Lane, a larger house of the 12th century, set at right angles to the street, was excavated from 1979 to 1980.[59] In St Nicholas Street, nos.38–42 were stone houses, certainly dating from the 13th or 14th century if not earlier, occupying plots of a similar size to those of *c* 20ft width in Tower Lane (*see* Inventory).

Some areas beyond the Saxon town defences were also subject to more intensive exploitation of property. In several instances high-status, stone-built dwellings were constructed on sites with comparatively narrow street frontages. On Baldwin Street no.15 was a house with an open hall of the 13th or early 14th century, constructed at right angles to the street. The land attached to the house was, however, considerable, extending nearly 500ft back to the town wall (*see* Inventory). South of the Avon in the Temple suburb, no.5 Temple Street was a stone house of the 13th or early 14th century, situated on a relatively narrow plot (*see* Inventory). It seems likely that, in the new suburbs of the 12th century, these narrow plots did not result from later subdivision, as we have seen in the centre of the city. Instead they were let as such from an early stage in their development, as in Old Market. Dendrochronological dating of the timbers found at Dundas Wharf, nos.128–9 Redcliff Street, has shown that houses with halls at right angles to the street, on relatively narrow plots, were being built from the first half of the 12th century onwards, from the initial development of the suburb.[60] By the 13th century houses of this plan were the norm in Redcliff Street, for instance at nos.80–7, nos.95–7 (Canynges' House) and nos.110–12 (Buchanan's Wharf).

Given the pressure on space revealed by the evidence for subdivision, the retention of large plots in single occupation has a special significance. At nos.51–2 Broad Street (the Cyder House), no.20 Small Street (Colston's House) and at Welsh Back (Spicer's Hall), stone halls of the 13th century or earlier built parallel

*Fig 2.6 (below left)*
*Plan showing suggested subdivision of the Nortons' property at nos.36–9 Baldwin Street and adjacent properties in 1461 (RHL, PEC).*

*Fig 2.7 (below right)*
*Nos.21–5 High Street, indicating suggested subdivision of property by Philip Langley from 1568 onwards (RHL, PEC).*

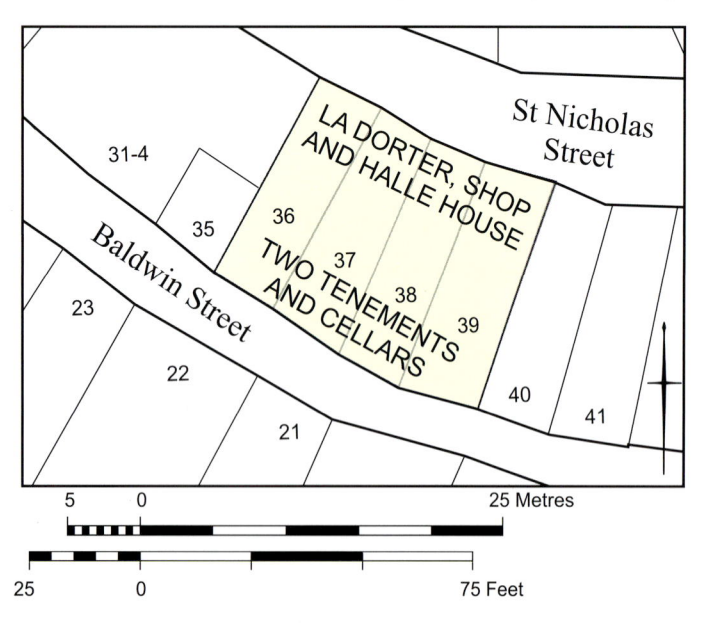

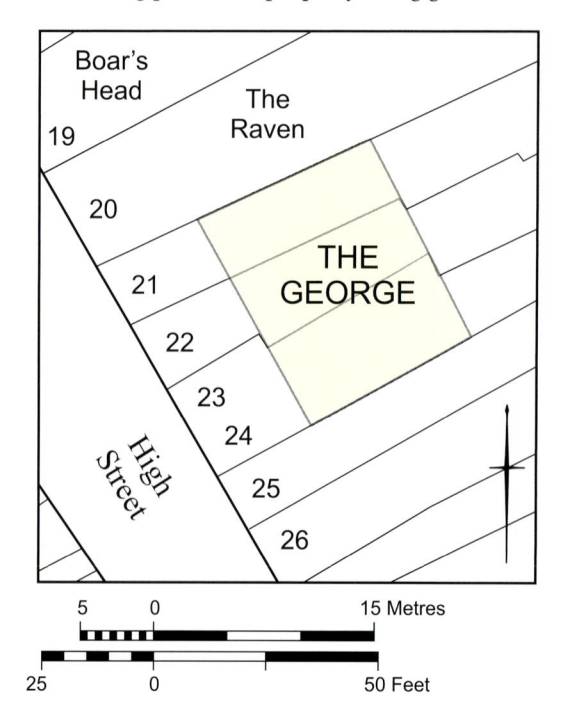

to the street have been recorded. These were the substantial houses of wealthy individuals, for whom it was more important to maintain a spacious tenement in a prestigious location in the midst of the town than to subdivide the plots for commercial development, the opportunity for which almost certainly existed.

For many other landlords, however, subdivision of larger properties into smaller units was a way of exploiting the commercial value of their holdings. The process can be traced from c 1300 through to the mid-17th century, focused mainly on buildings which had outlived their original purpose or on tenements for which continuation of the original use presented a low rate of return. By 1461 a large property between Baldwin Street and St Nicholas Street was owned by Walter and Isabella Norton. They themselves lived in an even larger property close to St Peter's church. Their property at nos.36–9 Baldwin Street was subdivided into three principal parts, each further divided. Fronting Baldwin Street one unit was made up of two tenements and cellars.[61] On St Nicholas Street was a second unit, consisting of houses with solars called 'la Dorter'. The third part fronted that same street and consisted of a shop and a 'hallehouse' (Fig 2.6). In the same street (chapter 5) and elsewhere, other houses with open halls were broken up in a similar way to the 14th and 16th centuries, the commercial return being greater from a subdivided house.

The strategy of the Nortons or their predecessors for redeveloping this property had centred upon utilising its existing division between an upper end, with the chamber or dorter on the first floor, and the open hall. Where an open hall was set back behind shops on the street frontage, an alternative strategy was to utilise the divisions between the shops to extend backwards the boundaries between the tenements. Philip Langley, a grocer with extensive property interests, subdivided nos.21–5 High Street in this way from 1568;[62] the walls of the open hall and its upper end are visible in the plan of the later long narrow tenements (Fig 2.7). In Baldwin Street, the tenement boundaries of nos.31–4, probably of the 17th century or earlier, must have resulted from a similar division of the property, either at the instigation of St Leonard's church or of their tenant.[63] The new boundaries took no note of the earlier hallhouse, which nevertheless remained a visible feature in the structure of the houses (chapter 5). In a third property on the north side of Baldwin Street, to the east of the Nortons' house, nos.40–1 (probably an earlier hallhouse) took the form of two storehouses or warehouses when it was rebuilt in c 1545.[64]

A small number of properties may have been divided through the making of gifts for religious purposes, the giver or his executors then dividing the property. In 1390 the executors of Walter Frampton's will were responsible for the division of no.34 Broad Street, only the rear part passing to the parishioners of St John's to become a priest's house (pp60–1). In the same year Edmund Arthur gave part of his tenement at no.43 Broad Street to the parish of St John, the remaining part of his property being granted in

1402 to the Guild of Merchant Tailors, the Fraternity of St John the Baptist.[65] In 1495 the executors of the will of Richard Erle were responsible for the division of a property in Small Street. Both parts passed to the parish of Christchurch, no.18 becoming part of the endowment of a chantry and no.19 part of the endowment of the lands held by the parish for charitable purposes.[66] By the 16th century, parts of the centre of the city were heavily tenurially subdivided, notably in Cock Lane. Here one tenement, formerly a through-house (these are discussed further in chapter 5), was now subdivided into seven small shops, three cellars and what is enigmatically referred to as a 'stringehouse', probably the same subdivisions shown on a plan of c 1740.[67]

Alongside the frequent subdivisions of property, a contrary trend was evident in the late medieval city, with some tenements being formed by the amalgamation of earlier separate holdings. By c 1500 nos.39–40 High Street were owned by St James's Priory and a chantry of All Saints. They had been combined as one to form the Rose Tavern from at least 1467, an open hall spanning both tenements being approximately of this date. Only in 1565 were they combined in a single ownership.[68] On the other side of the street, nos.9 and 10 High Street were in the same occupation from at least the 1550s, but remained separately owned until the 20th century.[69] Further north, at the corner of High Street with Wine Street, three separate ownerships stood above a single cellar of the 14th or 15th century.[70] By the 1540s the two northernmost parts, the east and west parts of no.1 High Street, were both held by Arthur Edgyn, a tailor. This was probably a single house, replaced by a new house in 1676 (chapters 1 and 6), which was certainly built over the two plots, formerly separately owned.[71]

One of the most long lived amalgamations, or perhaps accumulations, of property holdings was that made in the mid-16th century by John Cutt. By good fortune, possibly because he leased no.39 Corn Street from St Werburgh's parish and was able to keep a close eye on developments in the street, Cutt was able to purchase several adjacent or close properties on the south side of the street (Fig 2.8). In 1549 he

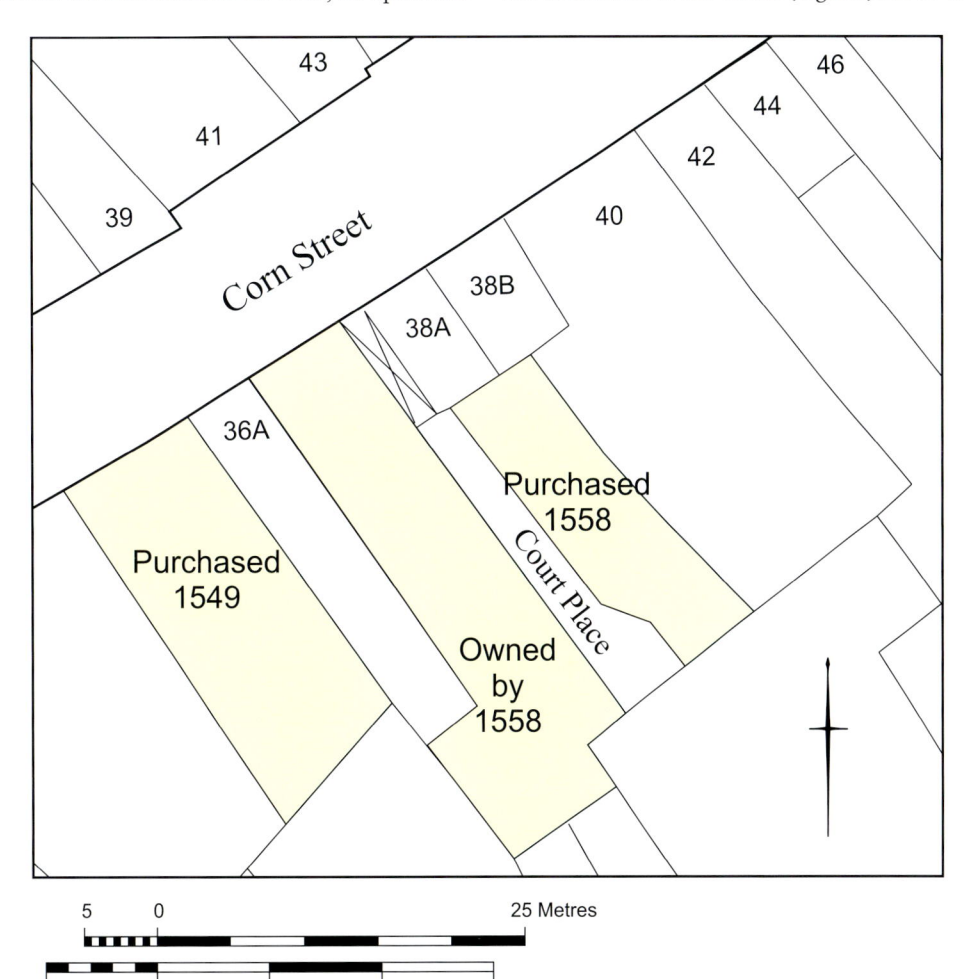

*Fig 2.8*
*John Cutt's properties on the south side of Corn Street in the mid-16th century (RHL, PEC).*

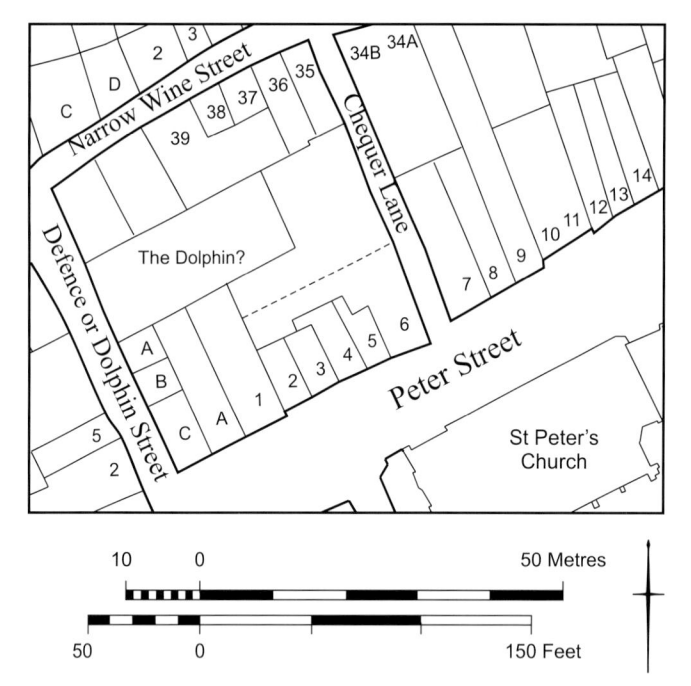

*Fig 2.9*
*Early 15th-century development in Peter Street (RHL, PEC).*

purchased no.34 for 100 marks from John Smythe, a fellow merchant who had possibly purchased it as one of the lands of Bath Abbey. In 1558 Cutt added to this by purchasing for £40 no.36B Corn Street, part ruinous, and no.38C, the Court Place, from the heirs of John Cradocke. A larger but not so well sited property in St Nicholas Street was purchased by 1569.[72] By the time of his death in 1575, when he was mayor, Cutt was possessed of considerable wealth, with extensive property interests in Bristol and Somerset.[73] The Corn Street and St Nicholas Street properties passed first to his son Nicholas and then on his death in c 1580 to his young widow Bridget, thence to her second husband John Whitson. Through Whitson's own charitable bequest this group of properties has remained in single ownership to the present day. There is little evidence, though, that this considerable investment prompted any further injection of capital into house building. Rather Cutt was content to lease several of the substantial buildings on these tenements as company halls, to the Barbers, Tanners and Tilers.[74]

From the end of the 13th century individual landlords undertook little larger scale rebuilding of existing sites.[75] Two exceptions were in the development of Peter Street during the early 15th century, possibly prompted by this area having remained substantially undeveloped since the Burgesses Revolt of 1312. Simon Oliver was seneschal, or steward, to Queen Anne, who held the royal farm, in effect responsible for its management in Bristol. Before 1419 he had built a dwelling house and four shops, now demised to his brother John. These can be identified as nos.4–6 Peter Street and the houses behind in Chequer Lane, described in 1434 as 'the shops of our lady the Queen which Simon Olyver caused to be built anew'.[76] Adjacent were nos.A–C Dolphin Street, demolished in the 1760s, and nos.A, 1–3 Peter Street, probably rebuilt at approximately the same date (Fig 2.9). These had possibly been built by Nicholas Excestre, who in 1434 left to his wife Joan a hall and 14 shops built partly on this site.[77]

Some rebuilding of existing properties was occasioned by fire or the house having becoming ruinous. In 1336 Thomas Thebaud rebuilt a house on the south side of Wine Street, in consideration of which he was absolved from arrears of rent.[78] However, such events as this were rare. Among the properties closely identified there were very few recorded fires, and relatively few houses appear to have become ruinous between the 13th and the early 17th centuries. On the east side of Marsh Street a tenement was ruinous in 1489.[79] In Corn Street, some of the properties purchased by Cutt were ruinous in the 1540s and 1550s.[80] In 1593, 15 Narrow Wine Street was described as 'ruinous'.[81] In 1648 the Starr on the Quay, having burnt down shortly before, was described as 'ruinous and decayed'.[82] The most extensive fire was that on the Bridge in 1647, when 24 houses were destroyed.[83]

## Providing More Housing: Extension and Rebuilding

Investment by landlords in house building between the 13th and 17th centuries was probably for the most part directed at increasing the amount of accommodation on existing sites. This could be achieved through the addition of cellars and extra storeys, and also by extending buildings backwards. Any of these could be achieved by total rebuilding, as well as by excavating within existing structures, or by removing the roof and raising the house upwards.

On the Quay houses were possibly heightened to three storeys by the mid-14th century. In 1323, 1327 and 1331 John de Cobyndone's tenement on the Quay consisted of a shop and a cellar underneath, extending back to the town wall.[84] By 1348 the adjacent house, of John

Hornecastel, extended back to Leonard Lane, which was only possible through its having two storeys (Fig 2.10).

In Broad Street nos.41–2 and 43 formed part of the lands given to the Fraternity of St John the Baptist in 1402. In 1411 the Fraternity undertook a survey of the combined tenement, probably prior to rebuilding no.43.[85] Before this date no.43 had been one of two houses on the site, both being two storeys in height. In the early 15th century, probably *c* 1411, the house was entirely demolished except for the ground-floor rear wall, and replaced by one of three storeys (p120). The Fraternity's rebuilding increased the amount of available accommodation by at least one-third, taking into account the increased space provided by jetties at each floor, and is likely to have also increased its income from the subsequent letting of the property. The rebuilding of no.51, a house of three storeys, built in the 15th century and similar in construction to no.43, may have been prompted by similar considerations. At nos.54–5 William and Joan Prelat rented another such property (p28). It can be concluded that in the 15th century houses on the east side of Broad Street were being raised to three storeys.

In High Street landlords were building houses of four storeys by the 15th century. It is not known who was responsible at some time in that century for rebuilding nos.35–6 to four storeys (Fig 2.11), but clear evidence for the rebuilding

*Fig 2.10*
*Houses fronting the Quay, at first-floor level as seen from Leonard Lane, watercolour of 1823 by H O'Neill (BRSMG M2296).*

*Fig 2.11*
*Nos.35–6 High Street, front elevation, photograph of 1931 (NMR AA78/06659, PEWS).*

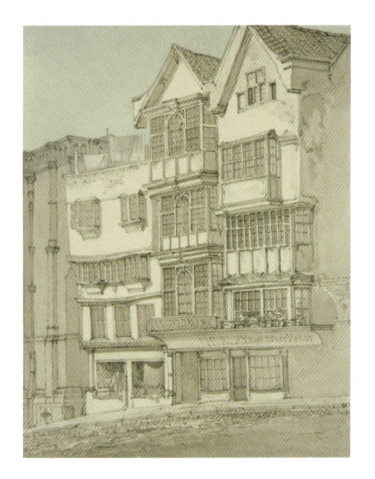

*Fig 2.12*
*Nos.29–31 High Street, watercolour of 1810 by H O'Neill (BRSMG M2246). No.31 was the house built by Stephen Morgan, carpenter for Alison Chestre in 1472 (Appendix 1).*

of no.31 survives. The house that Stephen Morgan contracted to build for Alison Chestre in 1472 was to be of four storeys (Appendix 1).[86] Each of these houses was of one room in depth, and rebuilding is most likely to have been occasioned by the decision to add at least one extra storey.

The distribution of houses of two, three or four storeys in *c* 1500 can be seen as a product of the market in property and an indicator of the value of different areas within the city. By then, landlords had placed the greatest investment in the rebuilding of houses in High Street, where some houses were now of four storeys. In other central streets – Broad Street, Corn Street, Peter Street and Small Street – a number of houses had been raised to three storeys. This concentration of more intensive exploitation of valuable plots continued in the 16th century as landlords invested further in the rebuilding of properties. In Broad Street the Prelats' house was rebuilt and raised to four storeys *c* 1598.[87] In High Street nos.29–30 were rebuilt to be of four storeys and no.31 was raised from four to five storeys (Fig 2.12).

By *c* 1600 houses of four storeys, reflecting the highest land values, were to be found in Broad Street and High Street. Across much of the city, investment had now been made in the building of houses of three storeys. Houses of two storeys were to be found only in areas on the periphery of the Castle precincts, as in Castle Mill Street, Dolphin Street and Lower Castle Street (Fig 2.13a, 2.13b and 2.13c).

## Adapting Older Structures for New Uses

Investment in property could also take the form of adapting older structures for new uses. By *c* 1350 most of the city gates, for example, were now leased to individuals, together with several of the towers between the gates. Also leased were the ditches outside the walls on the south side of the Redcliff and Temple suburbs, and the town ditch outside Lawford's Gate.[88]

Redundant churches were treated in much the same way. By the mid-16th century St Giles's church, extant in 1285, had been acquired by the Corporation and was converted to a house, two cellars and a storehouse. Immediately adjacent was St Lawrence's church, redundant from 1585. It was then immediately leased to the merchant Philip Ellis and was certainly a warehouse by the mid-17th century. A photograph of the 1960s shows the church as

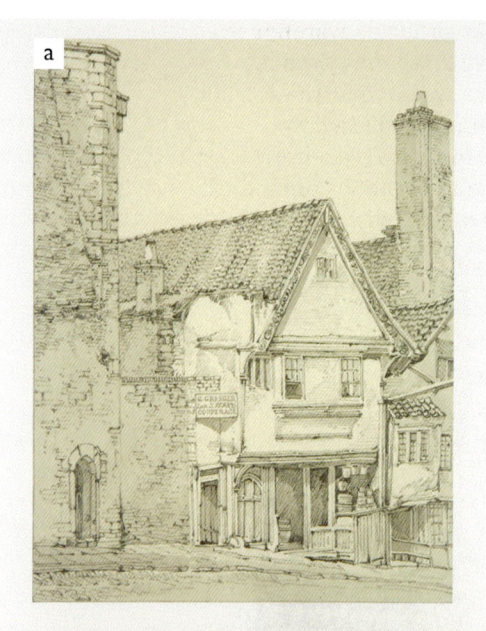

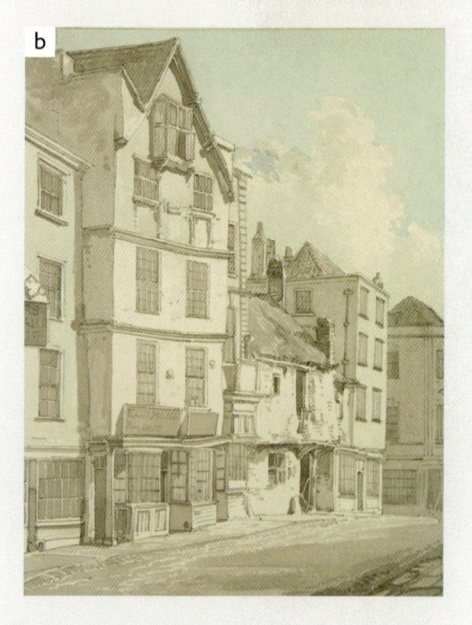

*Fig 2.13*
*Houses of the 16th century and of two storeys: a) in Castle Mill Street, watercolour of 1820 by H O'Neill (BRSMG M2710); b) in Dolphin Street, watercolour of 1821 by H O'Neill (BRSMG M2719); c) in Lower Castle Street, photograph of the later 19th century (BRSMG photographs box 1 fol 1).*

converted to warehouses under demolition (Fig 2.14), only the photographer realising that this was one of the city's medieval churches being demolished.[89]

In Bristol, as elsewhere, the dissolution of the monasteries offered new opportunities to investors wishing to adapt old properties to new uses. The conventual buildings could be converted to houses, used as company halls or demolished and replaced by new buildings, to cite but three possibilities. In several instances the buildings were converted, at least in part, to form new houses. The church of the Greyfriars, purchased by the Corporation and still a church

*Fig 2.14*
*St Lawrence's church, Broad Quay, redundant from 1585, subsequently converted to warehouses. This photograph of 1964 shows the building under demolition (Reece Winstone, Winstone Archive/28471).*

*Fig 2.15*
*Greyfriars, the precinct as redeveloped, plan of the church and claustral ranges, from archaeological excavations by M W Ponsford in 1973 (RHL, PEC, after Ponsford 1975, Fig 1, with further detail added; for the lodges, including that surviving in Blackfriars, see Inventory and Leech 2000c).*

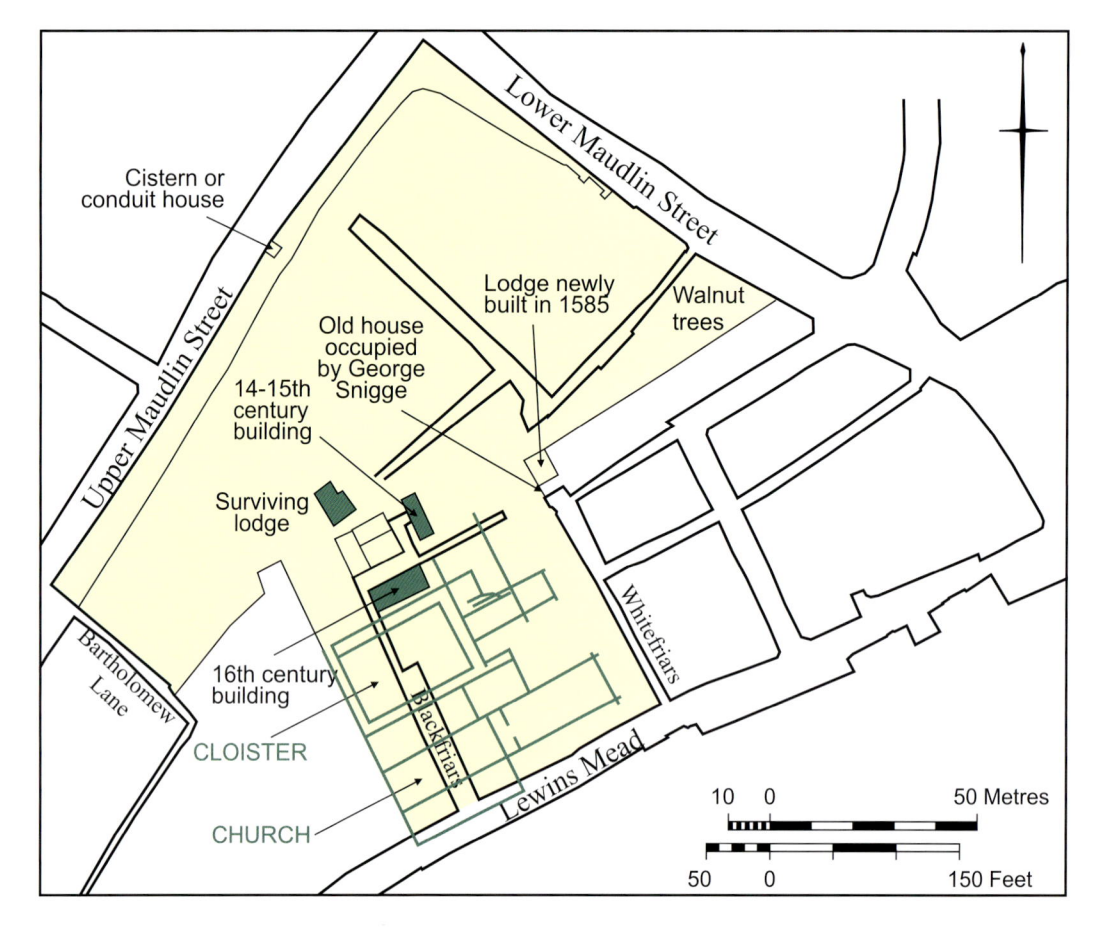

*Fig 2.16*
*Ruins of St James's Priory, in a drawing said to date from 1630*
*(Taylor 1872, author's copy).*

in 1558,⁹⁰ was turned into houses (Fig 2.15), and the north side of the Great Cloister was similarly converted. The remainder of the precinct became an estate of lodges, or garden houses.⁹¹ Henry Brayne, the purchaser of the greatest number of monastic properties in Bristol, adapted St James's Priory, the church excluded, to form a mansion house (Fig 2.16). On St Michael's Hill the former nunnery of St Mary Magdalene was leased by the Crown as a residence.⁹² The Corporation retained the church of the Gaunts' Hospital as the Lord Mayor's Chapel, but most of the hospital buildings were made into residences which were then leased as part of the Corporation's estate.

Other religious houses were converted to non-domestic roles. Alderman William Chester, the purchaser of the Dominican Friary, may have added part of its lands to his own gardens, but the buildings were given other functions (Fig 2.17). The Bakers' Guild utilised the first floor of the south range of the lesser cloister as their hall by the end of the 15th century (Fig 2.18). This use continued, and may have prompted two other guilds to establish their halls in the former friary buildings. The west and south ranges of the great cloister were let, probably by Chester, as the Tanners' and Cutlers' halls. Here, as at Greyfriars, the church probably remained standing – converted, at least in part, to a sugar house or factory during the 17th

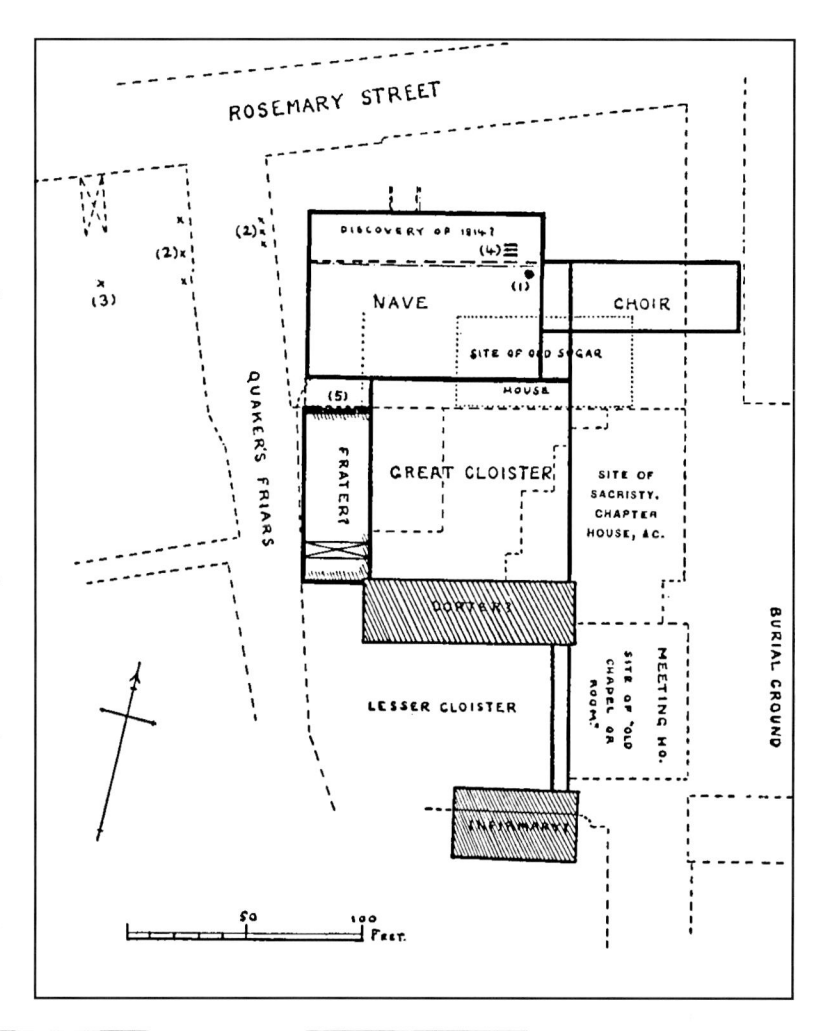

*Fig 2.17*
*Plan of the Dominican Friary, showing parts converted to company halls (Leighton 1933, Fig 21).*

*Fig 2.18*
*The roof structure of the Bakers' Hall, photograph of 2003 (NMR AA 047257, JD).*

# THE TOWN HOUSE IN MEDIEVAL AND EARLY MODERN BRISTOL

*Fig 2.19*
*A hall within the Templars' conventual buildings. Watercolour of 1821 by H O'Neill, who provided three illustrations of an open hall in this location; together these indicate through the portrayal of one end without a stairs and two ends with different stairs that two separate halls are probably shown (BRSMG M2158, M2159 and M2157).*

century. Other buildings were demolished for stone and timber.[93]

The Corporation also acquired Temple Fee, the lands of the Hospitallers. At least one range of the conventual buildings was retained, but its immediate post-Dissolution use is not known. On the north side of the church, an open hall with a 15th-century roof was part of this purchase, remaining largely unaltered until the early 19th century (Fig 2.19). One house was entirely rebuilt. The Carmelite Friary, the third of the Corporation's purchases, was sold in *c* 1558 to William Chester and then demolished 10 years later by a second purchaser, Sir John Young. Its replacement was a large mansion house (Fig 2.20), with the estate being enlarged by various purchases of land made by Young.[94]

## The Absence of Development in mid-16th-Century Bristol

From the mid-16th century landlords in Bristol had at their disposal large tracts of land suitable for redevelopment. John Cutt had assembled a wide swathe of inner city land, extending from Corn Street to St Nicholas Street. For the purchasers of the monastic lands, the precincts of the Blackfriars, Greyfriars, St Bartholomew's Hospital and St James's Priory could have provided substantial areas for new streets and houses, immediately adjacent to the built-up area of the existing city.

Yet no new suburbs were fashioned out of the lands of the dissolved religious houses; the principal new use for the precincts of the Greyfriars and St Bartholomew's Hospital was for them to become estates of garden houses or lodges (chapter 9). The lack of interest shown by the landlords of these newly acquired lands in laying out new streets and building new houses stands in contrast to the investments made in new developments and building projects during the 12th and 13th centuries, and in the Corporation's redevelopment of the Castle and Marsh in the 17th and 18th centuries. The demand for new housing, so evident from the mid-17th century onwards, clearly did not exist in any large measure in mid-16th-century Bristol. The changes that were to take place in the next century were, as subsequent chapters will argue, very much linked to the growth of the Atlantic economy.

*Fig 2.20*
*The Great House in St Augustine's Place on St Augustine's Back, built on the site of the Carmelite Priory, photograph of before 1867 (BRSMG Ma 5745).*

# 3

# Developers – the Early Modern City

The absence of new housing developments which Bristol experienced in the later 16th century was followed by a long period in which the city grew extensively. In the 17th and 18th centuries a mix of greater urban estates and smaller land promotions[1] not only created new streets and neighbourhoods to house an expanding population, but also brought into being a city more in keeping with contemporary aspirations to gentility or refinement. This emphasised distinctions between rich and poor, and brought profits to those involved in the various stages of the development process, much of which was funded by the profits of the Atlantic trade. Through these initiatives the city was reshaped by the urban elite. This chapter will examine Bristol's development in the context of what has been described as the urban renaissance of the late 17th and 18th centuries.

## New Streets and New Neighbourhoods

Barry has outlined how the population of Bristol grew steadily 'from about 12,000 in 1600 (below its medieval peak) up to about 21,000 by 1700, 40,000 or so by 1750 and more than 60,000 by 1800'.[2] Identified new housing developments in this period supplied *c* 3,000 additional dwellings, in which a considerable portion of this increase in population must have been housed.[3] The remainder is likely to have been accommodated in already existing buildings and in unidentified minor developments, especially within courtyards. In Bristol, as in other towns, intensive back-plot development of once substantial properties provided housing for the poorer levels of society: developments such as Broad's Court in Rosemary Street and New Buildings off Broadmead, consisting of houses of one room on each floor, will be discussed further in chapter 8.

The two landlords most active in promoting new housing developments in the 17th century were the Corporation and the Dean and Chapter of the Cathedral, inheritors at the Reformation of the lands of St Augustine's Abbey. From the beginning of the 18th century these were joined by the Society of Merchant Venturers, owner of the manor of Clifton; by the descendants of Henry Dighton, to whom had passed the ownership of the Kingsdown hillside, formerly a possession of St James's Priory; by Nathaniel Wade, the owner of an estate to the east of the Frome on the north side of the city; and by Alderman Day and George Tyndale, the developers of Park Street and the streets adjacent to it.

### The Corporation Estate

The Corporation, so active in the building of town walls and in developments in the 13th century, next embarked on major development projects in the early 17th century. The estates of the Corporation included many individual properties, mostly granted for specific charitable or religious purposes by various benefactors through the preceding centuries, and some larger blocks of land – notably the Castle, the estates formerly of the Greyfriars and the Dominican Friary and the area between the city walls and the great bend of the Avon on the south of the city, known as the Marsh (Fig 3.1).

The largest Corporation development of the 17th century was the redevelopment of the site of Bristol Castle, purchased from the Crown in 1630 and demolished in 1655.[4] By the 1670s over 70 new houses had been built, mostly narrow shophouses in Castle Street with 12 or more larger houses in Castle Green and Tower Street (Fig 3.2). Nearby, the site of the Castle Orchard, comprising six acres to the south of Castle Street, was later laid out as two streets, with Castle Mead, the main thoroughfare,

*Fig 3.1*
*The Marsh, from Millerd's map of 1673 (BRSMG).*

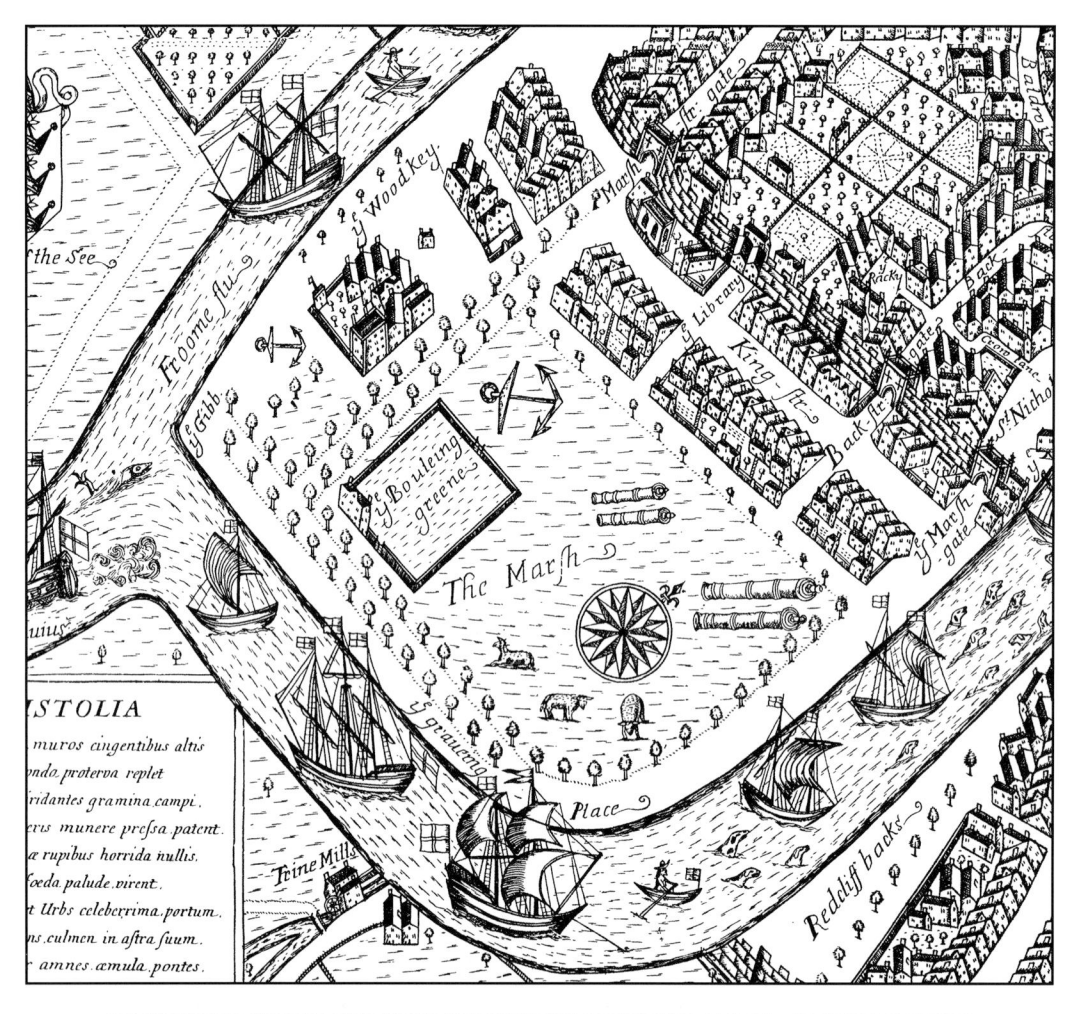

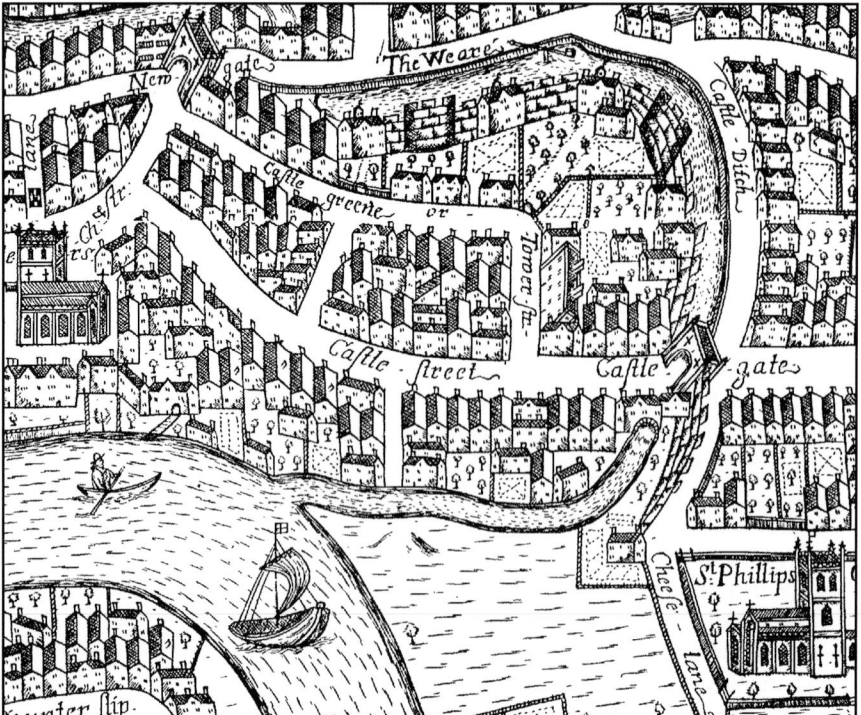

*Fig 3.2*
*The development of the Castle, from Millerd's map of 1673 (BRSMG).*

later being renamed Queen Street (Fig 3.4). Altogether 10 building leases were granted.[5]

The Corporation was the principal developer of the Marsh. This was the first part of the city to receive attention, and was to be the location of the most prestigious of the Corporation's initiatives. Open land on the edge of the built-up area and with water frontages to both the Avon and the Frome, it was ripe for development by the early 17th century. Between 1614 and 1628 many leases of substantial plots, generally with covenants 'to new build', were granted to various individuals between the quayside on the Avon and what was to become Prince Street.[6] By the 1670s the houses built there consisted of a mix of narrow shophouses (chapter 6) and substantial suburban garden houses (chapter 9; Fig 3.1). Meanwhile King Street had been laid out on an east–west alignment at the head of the Marsh. This has been sometimes regarded as a street laid out in the 1660s, but development of the street began *c* 1650 with the lease to Robert Wickham, a carpenter, of a plot 275ft in length on which he was to build six houses within 10 years.[7]

This also was part of the Corporation's estate in the Marsh, to the south of the town wall and adjacent to the area already developed, in what was to become Prince Street (Figs 3.1, 3.3a and 3.3b). The development proceeded in two main phases, the north side from 1650 onwards and then the south side from 1663, all the leases for this side being granted in March of that year.[8] By the 1670s some 44 houses had been built in King Street, 14 on the north side and 30 on the south.

The development of the Marsh was continued by the construction of the imposing Queen Square, a radically new departure in town planning. Laid out by the Corporation on a grand scale in 1699, it took some decades to complete, the last building leases being granted for the houses in the north-west corner in *c* 1725.[9] With the continued development of Prince Street, just to the west of Queen Square, the greater part of the Marsh had been completed through the Corporation's efforts by *c* 1730. Queen Square added 64 new dwellings to the city's housing stock and an additional 52 were built in Prince Street (Fig 3.5).

Contemporary with the completion of Queen Square was the development of the orchard behind St Mark's Hospital church, land held by the Corporation as Governors of the Hospital of Queen Elizabeth. Two new streets were built

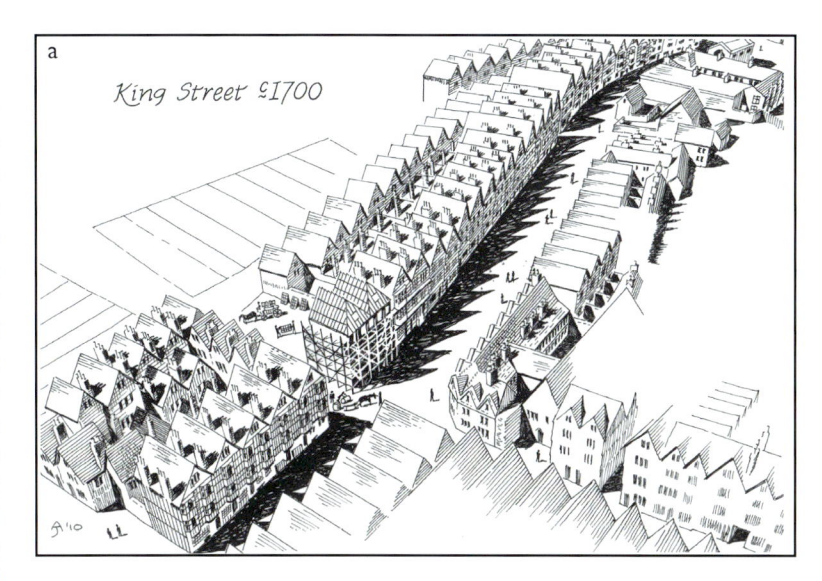

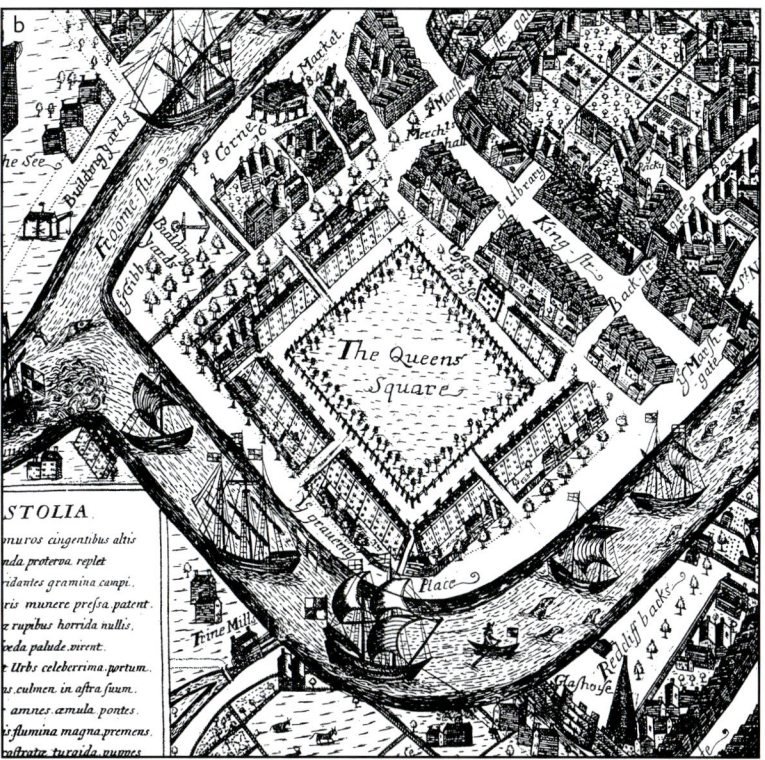

*Fig 3.3 (above)*
*The development of:*
*a) King Street as by c 1700, view as reconstructed from documentary sources (JA);*
*b) the Marsh from Millerd's map, revised in 1710.*

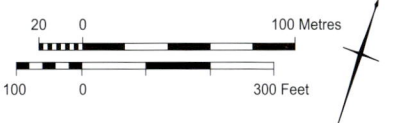

*Fig 3.4 (left)*
*The development of the Castle Orchard (from Ashmead and Plumley's map of 1828).*

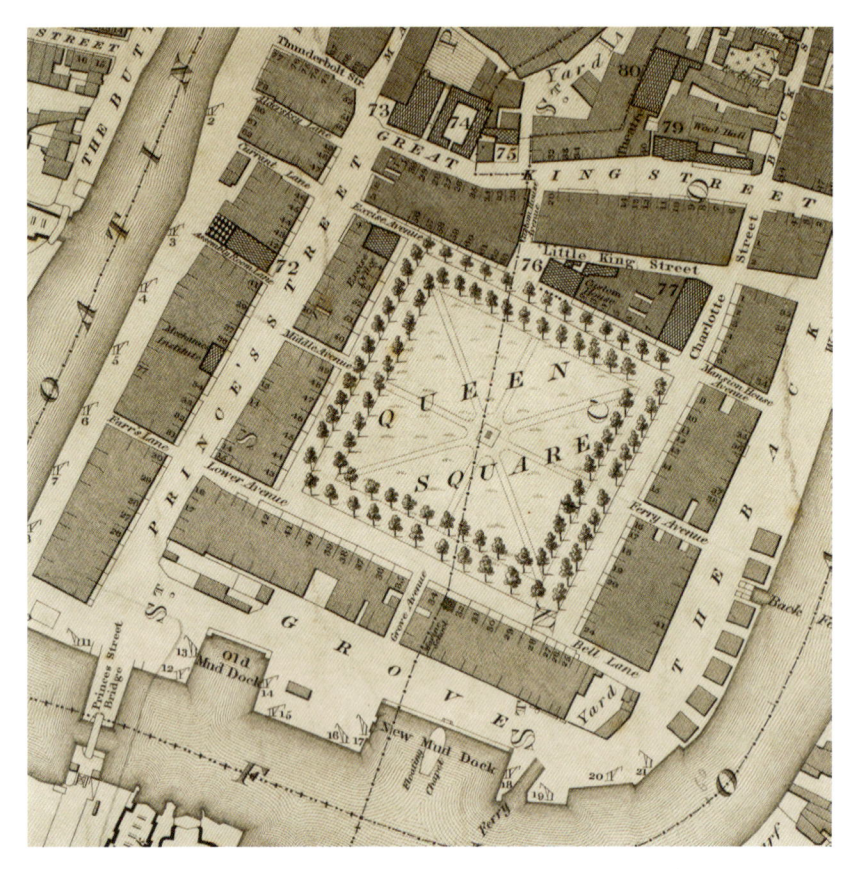

*Fig 3.5*
*Queen Square and Prince Street (from Ashmead and Plumley's map of 1828).*

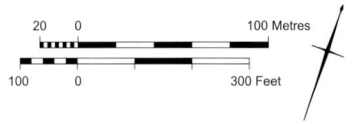

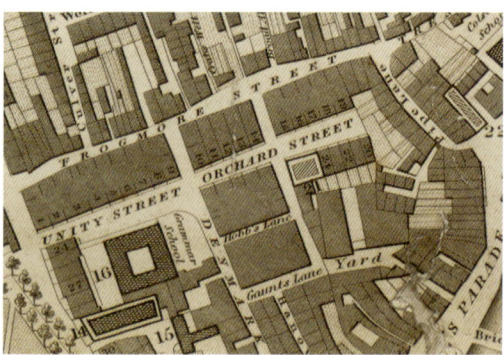

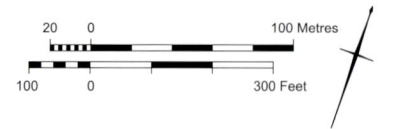

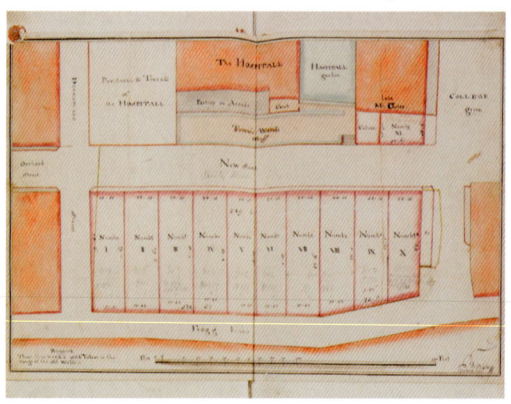

*Fig 3.6 (top right) Orchard Street and Unity Street (from Ashmead and Plumley's map of 1828).*

*Fig 3.7 Unity Street, plan by Jacob de Wilstar, 1742 (BRO 04479(1) fol 14).*

and 3.9b). On the south side of the river no.1 Redcliff Street and five new houses to the south in St Thomas Street were constructed to form a new approach to the Bridge.[10] Subsequently added to these were the 20 new houses of Bath Street, constructed in the 1780s as a new link between the Bridge and Temple Street. On the north side of the river the 42 houses of an entirely new street, Bridge Street, replaced the demolished Worshipful Street or The Shambles in the 1760s.

The building of Bridge Street (Fig 3.10) probably embraced some of the experience gained in the construction of the Exchange some 20 years before, for it involved the demolition of an existing neighbourhood and the displacement of its inhabitants. Its construction – by the standards of the day, a major work of engineering – necessitated the excavation of a deep trench, built up from which were the cellars and superstructures of houses on both sides of the street and the raised roadway. Also on the north bank of the river, as part of the same scheme, one side of Dolphin Street was rebuilt, two new houses were constructed at the entry to Baldwin Street and Union Street was here, Orchard and Unity Streets, providing a further 30 smart residential houses (Figs 3.6 and 3.7).

From the 1740s onwards the Corporation promoted two major building projects, the first being the construction of the Exchange, completed c 1743, and the second being the rebuilding of Bristol Bridge in 1760. The Exchange, as designed by John Wood the Elder of Bath, consisted of a number of separate buildings designed to appear from the exterior as one monumental Classical building. These separate units comprised a tavern, coffee house, market hall and five houses for professional persons (Fig 3.8). The construction work necessitated the demolition of some 44 houses, including a significant part of one entire parish, All Saints, prior to the excavation of a building trench c 150ft by 110ft, in which the cellars of the new Exchange were then built.

The rebuilding of Bristol Bridge in 1760 went hand in hand with the reconfiguration of several of the streets approaching the Bridge (Figs 3.9a

DEVELOPERS – THE EARLY MODERN CITY

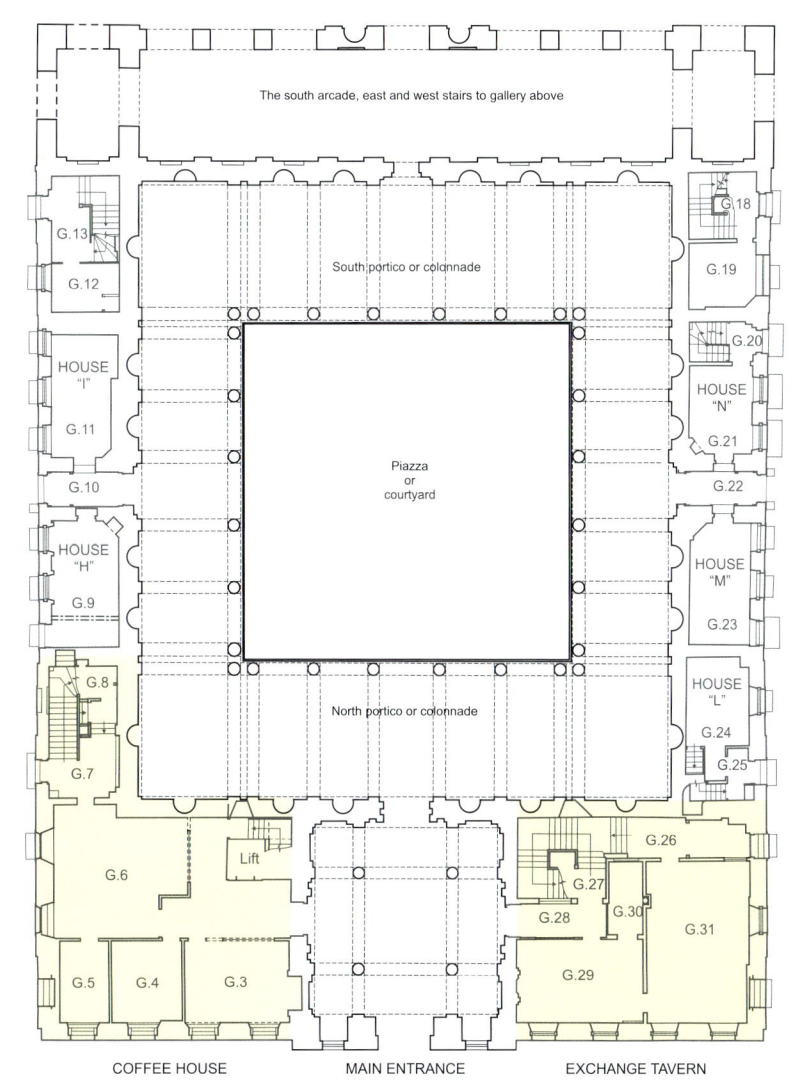

*Fig 3.8*
*The development of the Exchange showing the tavern, coffee house, south arcade market hall and five houses for professional persons (RHL).*

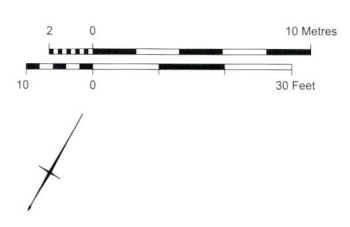

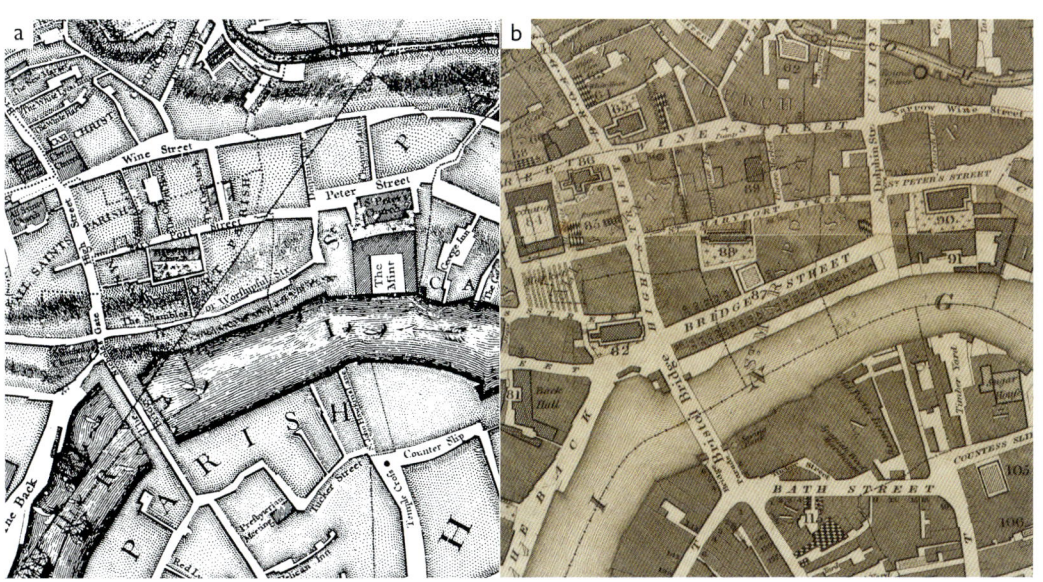

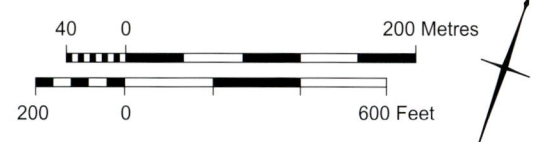

*Fig 3.9*
*The streets approaching Bristol Bridge:*
*a) in 1742, before the building of the new bridge (Roque's map of 1742);*
*b) following its rebuilding in 1760 (from Ashmead and Plumley's map of 1828).*

*Fig 3.10*
*Bridge Street, constructed c 1760, as seen from the air before its destruction from bombing in 1940 (Bristol United Press/Bristol Post archives).*

created, both as a link to Broadmead and to give access to a new market which formed part of the design of the street as a whole (Fig 3.11). The 90 or more new houses constructed in these projects were almost entirely shophouses. So were the 30 new houses of Clare Street (Appendix 1) and the 17 new houses of St Stephen's Street, parts of the scheme to rebuild the area between St Leonard's church, St Stephen's church and the Quay in the 1770s (Figs 3.12a and 3.12b).

The projects of the Corporation in the remaining decades of the 18th century were less ambitious. They included the rebuilding of four houses on both sides of Blind Steps between Baldwin and St Nicholas Streets, the development of some of the Corporation's property on Brandon Hill and the construction of Nelson Street, completed in 1799.[11] The Corporation was not greatly involved in any of the schemes that came to fruition in the building mania of 1786–92 or were aborted following the collapse of 1793 (*see* below).

*Fig 3.11*
*Designs of the later 18th century for the new market in Union Street, following the rebuilding of Bristol Bridge in 1760 (BRO 04479(2) fol 59).*

DEVELOPERS – THE EARLY MODERN CITY

*Fig 3.12*
*The new developments of the 1770s in Clare Street and St Stephen's Street:*
*a) as planned for the City Corporation (BRO 04479(5) fol 95 (b));*
*b) as built, from Ashmead and Plumley's map of 1828.*

## The Dean and Chapter of the Cathedral

The lands of the Dean and Chapter developed for new housing were mainly close to the Cathedral, to the west of the city as built up by the end of the 17th century. Development here probably started in the late 17th century, with the building of new houses at The Butts.[12]

In the last decades of the 18th century the Dean and Chapter were much more involved than the Corporation in new building projects. Close to the Cathedral, the building of 28 houses in Trinity Street was on land leased to Jarrit Smith in 1733 and had commenced by the 1760s (Fig 3.13).[13] More distant from the Cathedral was the development of Culver Close on the hillside above Frog Lane (later Frogmore Street). Some 34 new houses were constructed in two new streets, Culver Street and Wells Street, land leased for building in 1791 (Fig 3.14).[14]

## The Bishop

The lands linked to the Cathedral also included those of the Bishop of Bristol. The Bishop's Park is shown as open ground on maps of 1673 and 1742 and remained largely undeveloped until the 1770s. Then Thomas Gooch, Bishop of Bristol, turned his attention to the lower part of the hill north of the Cathedral, leasing the Park, then pasture, to Samuel Worrall. Covenants stipulated that:

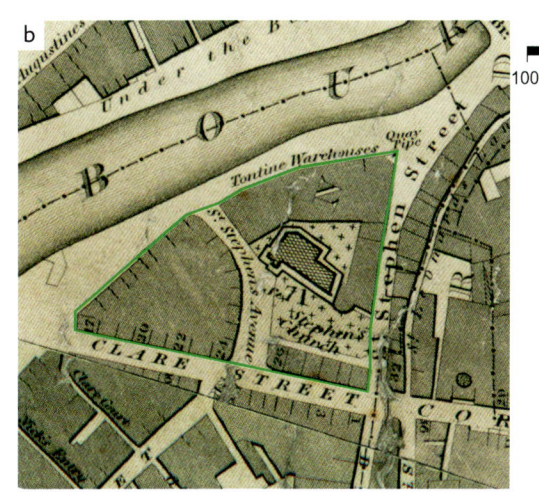

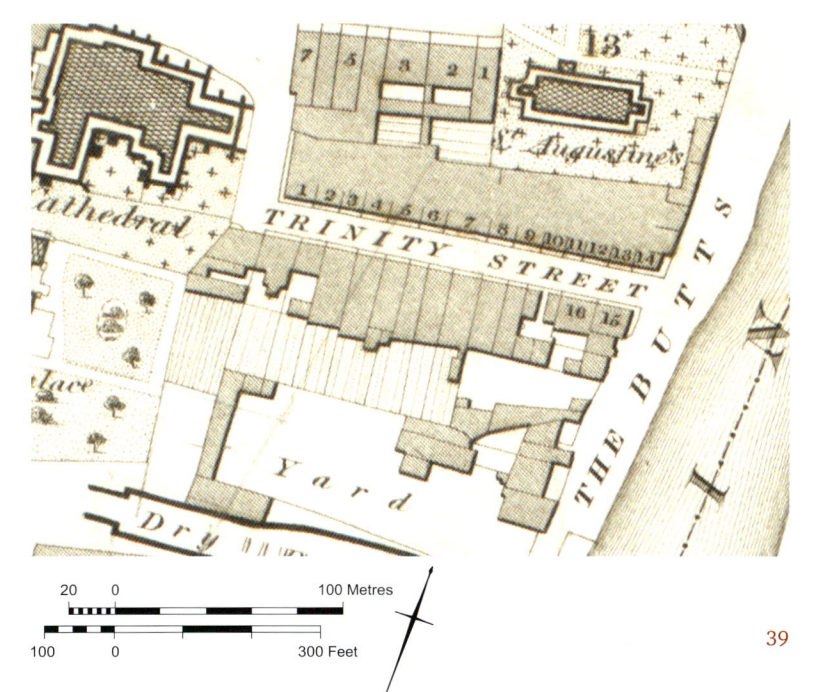

*Fig 3.13 (below)*
*The development of Trinity Street, completed by c 1742 (from Ashmead and Plumley's map of 1828).*

39

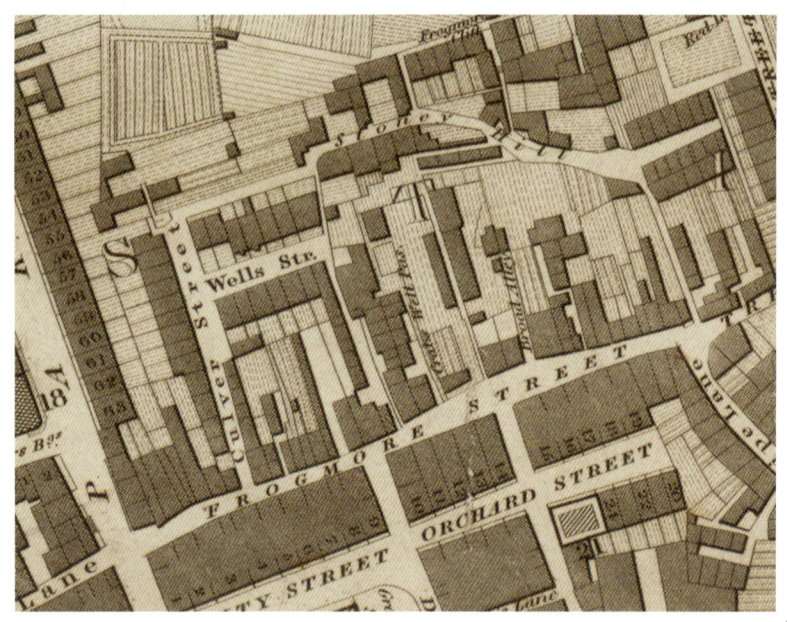

# THE TOWN HOUSE IN MEDIEVAL AND EARLY MODERN BRISTOL

*Fig 3.14*
*The development of Culver Close, in progress by the 1790s (from Ashmead and Plumley's map of 1828).*

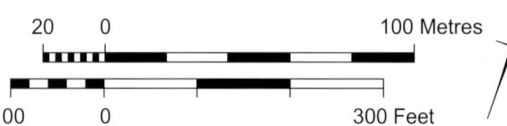

*Fig 3.15*
*The development of the Bishop's Park in progress in the 1770s and 1780s (from Ashmead and Plumley's map of 1828).*

the said close of ground should be improved by buildings to be erected thereon and whereas the said Samuel Worrall hath formed a plan for covering the said close of ground with buildings agreeable to which plan there is a street called College Street of the breadth of forty feet from front to front of the second story of the intended houses out of which is taken three feet for areas or bow windows on the first story or ground floor and five feet for a paved foot-way which leaves twenty four feet carriage which street has hath an entrance at the north east end of the said close of ground near the College Green and opposite to Frog Lane and hath a carriage way on the north west side into Lime Kiln Lane.[15]

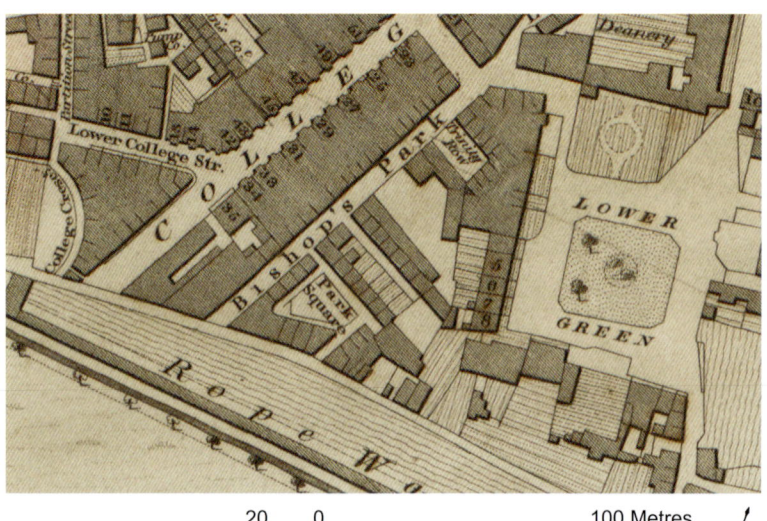

Development had certainly begun by 1775, when eight houses in College Street were recorded as occupied. Building in College Street and its back lane, Lamb Street, was still under way in 1777 and 1778, when the plots for nos.17 and 18, now under Deanery Road, were being let for building;[16] other leases for building were granted as late as 1784, when Thomas Stocking, tiler, was granted a lease for the building of no.54.[17] The development of the Bishop's Park led to the construction of at least 90 houses (Fig 3.15).

## The Growth of the City: Institutional and Individual Developers

If major developments in the central areas of the city and in the Park to the west were undertaken by the Corporation and Bishop, expansion and redevelopment elsewhere provided opportunities for others. As in other English provincial towns, a scatter of small land holdings around the periphery of the city offered scope for many smaller building schemes.[18] Here the landlords active in promoting new housing developments included both institutions, notably the city parishes as owners of lands held so as to generate funds for charitable purposes and also private individuals.

### Developments in the East and North-East

In the early 1700s the building of Queen Square was complemented by that of St James's Square on the east side of the city. This new square, so named because it lay within the parish of St James, was built within what had been the great orchard behind Hobson's Garden, shown as such on Millerd's map of 1673. By the early 1700s this land had passed to Richard Gotley, a Quaker merchant. He must have been the initial promoter of this new square, for at his death in 1705 three plots had been granted for building. Further building leases were then granted by Gotley's widow Rachel, with most of the square being completed by c 1715.[19] This development added some 16 new houses to the city (Fig 3.16).

Richard Gotley's property interests also extended to the north side of the large open space known as St James's Barton. Here he was possibly responsible for the development of a row of 12 large residential houses, nos.9–19 St James's Barton (Fig 3.16).

Not all new developments were on what would today be called 'greenfield' sites. Some took place on sites where existing buildings could be demolished and new ones erected in their place. This was often a strategy for increasing both the rent and the initial payment or fine made at the commencement of a lease, and could be observed in practice in Old Market in the late 17th and early 18th centuries (Fig 3.17). In 1660 no.35 Old Market was the site of two tenements and gardens leased to Edward Fisher and others. This was subsequently assigned to Henry Lloyd, a Quaker merchant, and then in 1705 to Samuel Penry, a baker, and William Barratt, a house carpenter. On 18 September 1705 a new lease was granted to James Penry and William Barratt of the plot, on condition that they demolish the existing two houses and build one new house in their place.

On the adjacent plot was a single house. This too was leased to Penry and Barratt on condition that they build two new houses in its place, now nos.36 and 37 Old Market.[20] Further to the east the four houses nos.38–41 were similarly rebuilt by William Barratt on behalf of the developer Llewellin Evans, a clay tobacco pipe maker.[21]

A little to the north of Old Market, a new suburb developed in the early 18th century. Daniel Defoe passed through it in 1710 and remarked: 'There is one remarkable part of the city where the liberties extend not at all, or but very little without the city gate. Here and no where else, they have an accession of new inhabitants; and abundance of new houses, nay some streets are built, and the like 'tis probably would have been at all the rest of the gates, if liberty had been given'.[22] This was the area now known as St Jude's, an estate with a regular grid of four principal streets, centred on Great George Street, and occupying a large close formerly known as Crotwells. This development lay in Gloucestershire and was outside the city and county of Bristol as defined from 1373 onwards. Defoe's reference to 'liberties' was to the rights of citizens not extending beyond the formal boundaries of the city and county. Building leases for plots in these new streets were being granted in the first three decades of the 18th century, first by Nathaniel Wade and then by his widow and daughter.[23] This development added some 560 new houses to the city (Fig 3.18).

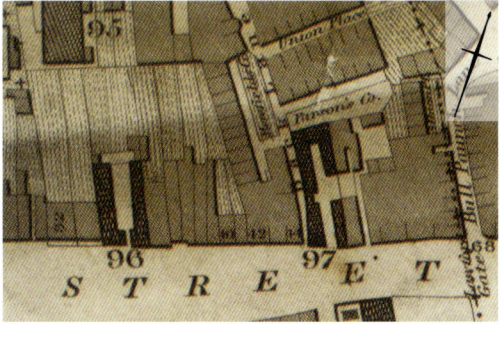

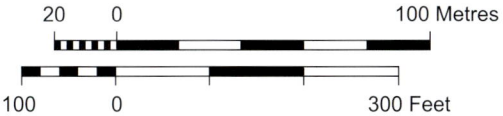

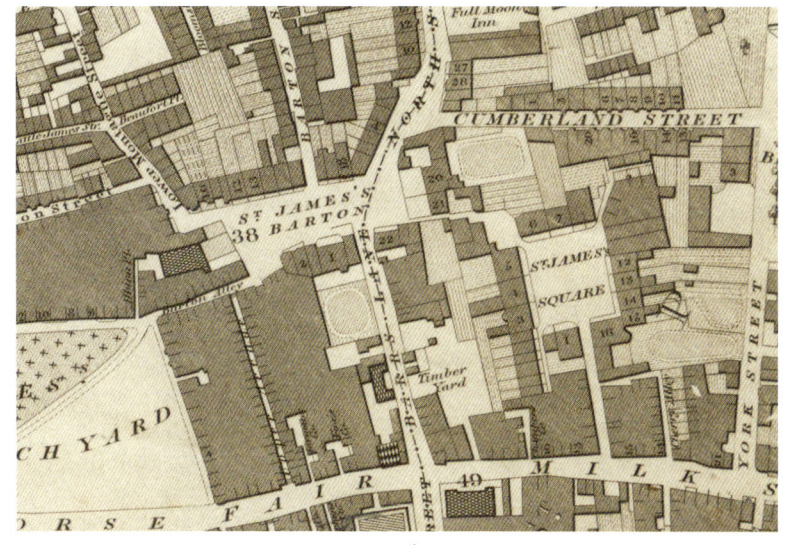

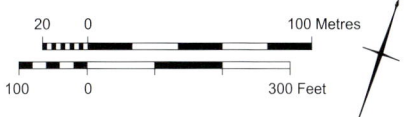

*Fig 3.16 (above) The developments of St James's Square and St James's Barton c 1705–15 (from Ashmead and Plumley's map of 1828).*

*Fig 3.17 (below left) Rebuilding on plots in Old Market, nos.35–41 (from Ashmead and Plumley's map of 1828).*

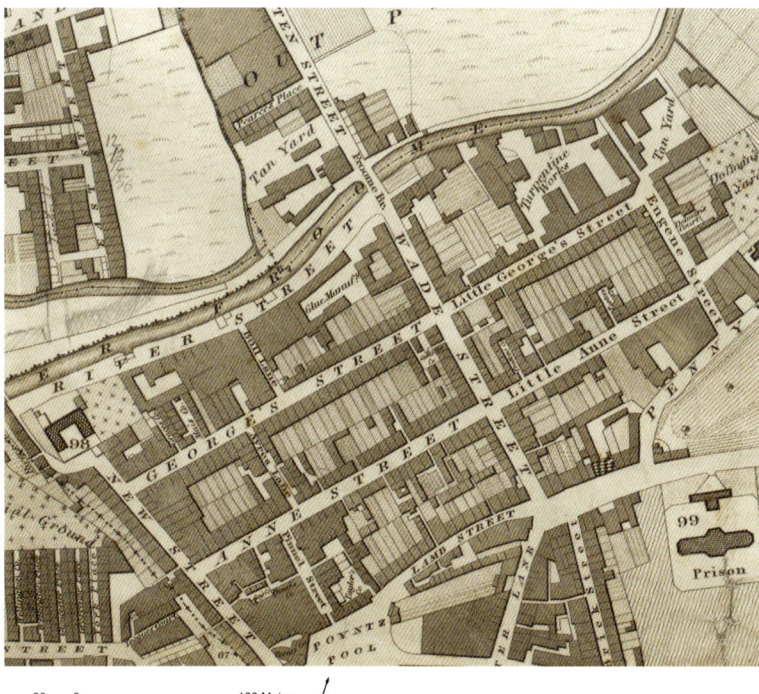

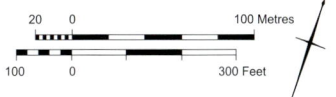

*Fig 3.18 (below) Nathaniel Wade's development of Crotwells (from Ashmead and Plumley's map of 1828).*

*Fig 3.19 (below top)
The Penn family's development of the Brick Leaze (from Ashmead and Plumley's map of 1828).*

*Fig 3.20 (below bottom)
The Penn family's development of the former orchard of the Dominican Friary (from Ashmead and Plumley's map of 1828).*

*Fig 3.21 (below right)
The development of Barrs Leaze, 1784 onwards (from Ashmead and Plumley's map of 1828).*

A second suburb to be developed on the east side of the city was promoted by the Penn family from 1719 onwards.[24] This was within the close formerly known as Barrs Leaze, later known as the Brick Leaze, part of the extensive holdings of the Penn family now living at Ruscombe in Berkshire. The north side of Water Street was developed from 1719 onwards. Callowhill Street, Clarke Street (first named Philadelphia Street), Hanover Street (later Little Hanover Street and Blinkers Steps) and the south side of Milk Street were developed from 1727 onwards. Houses in Callowhill Street were still regarded as 'new built' in 1755 (Fig 3.19).

In a second phase of development the Penn family laid out streets in the former orchard of the Dominican Friary. Penn Street was developed slowly from 1743 onwards, commencing at the north end of the street. Hollister Street was developed from 1749 onwards and Philadelphia Street from 1763. At the south end of the last street an exchange of land was made in 1763, to enable the new street to continue through to Narrow Weir. These two phases of housing development by the Penn family added some 200 new houses to the city (Fig 3.20).

A third phase of the development of this suburb to the east of the city took place from 1784 onwards. Here the remaining part of the close formerly known as Barrs Leaze was subdivided by a grid pattern of new streets, Meadow Street, Stratton Street, Charlotte Street and East Street, adding a further 105 new houses to the city (Fig 3.21).

Land a little to the north of the Penn estate was developed from the mid-18th century, adding a further two squares on this side of the city.[25] Brunswick Square and the adjacent streets (Cumberland, Gloucester, Pembroke, Surrey and York Streets) were developed in the 1760s on land belonging to the merchant Joseph Loscombe. These housing developments added some 65 new houses to the city (Fig 3.22). To the east of Brunswick Square the much larger Portland Square was laid out *c* 1789 on what had been enclosed fields on the east side of the city, shown most clearly on Rocque's map of 1742. Building plots were advertised for sale from March 1790, but the development of the square was halted by the collapse of the building boom in March 1793. In 1801 14 of the 34 houses appear to have been occupied.[26] The construction of the square and the four side streets (Cave, Dean, Paul and Pritchard Streets) was eventually complete by 1814, adding some 107 new houses to the city.[27] The square is shown in detail on the map of 1828 (Fig 3.22).

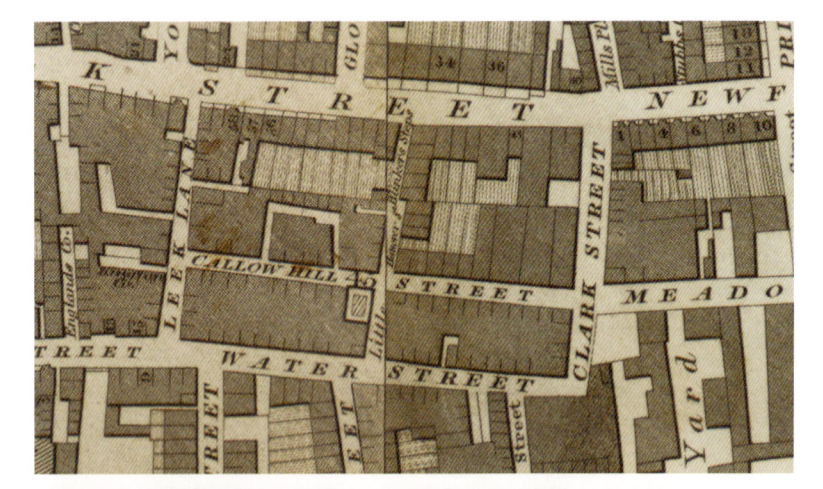

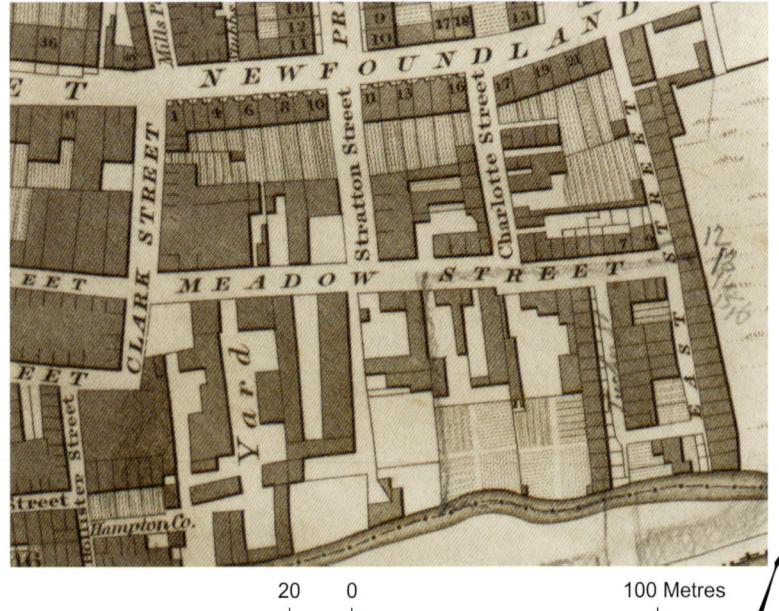

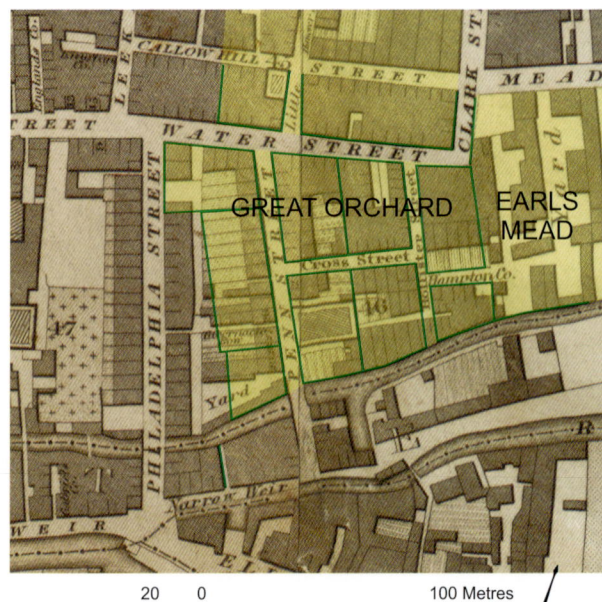

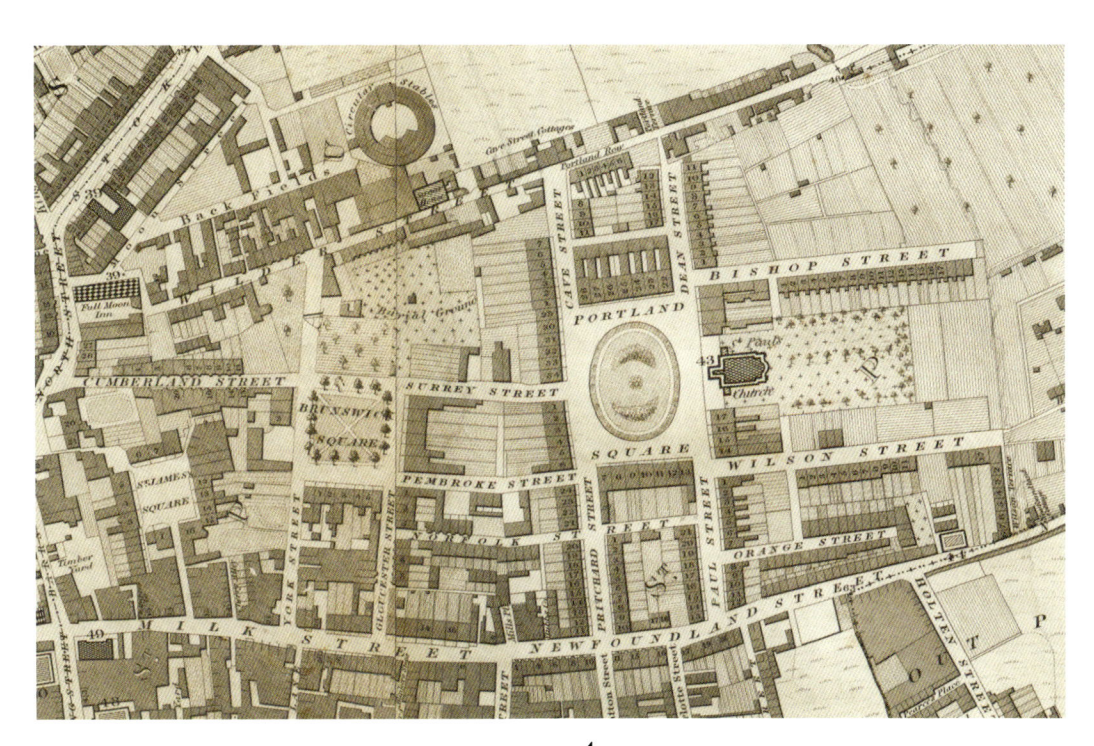

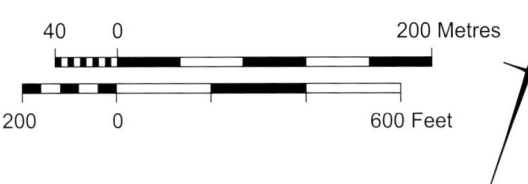

DEVELOPERS – THE EARLY MODERN CITY

*Fig 3.22*
*The development of Brunswick and Portland Squares and of the adjacent streets (from Ashmead and Plumley's map of 1828).*

*Fig 3.23*
*The development of the Little Park, from the 1660s onwards (RHL).*

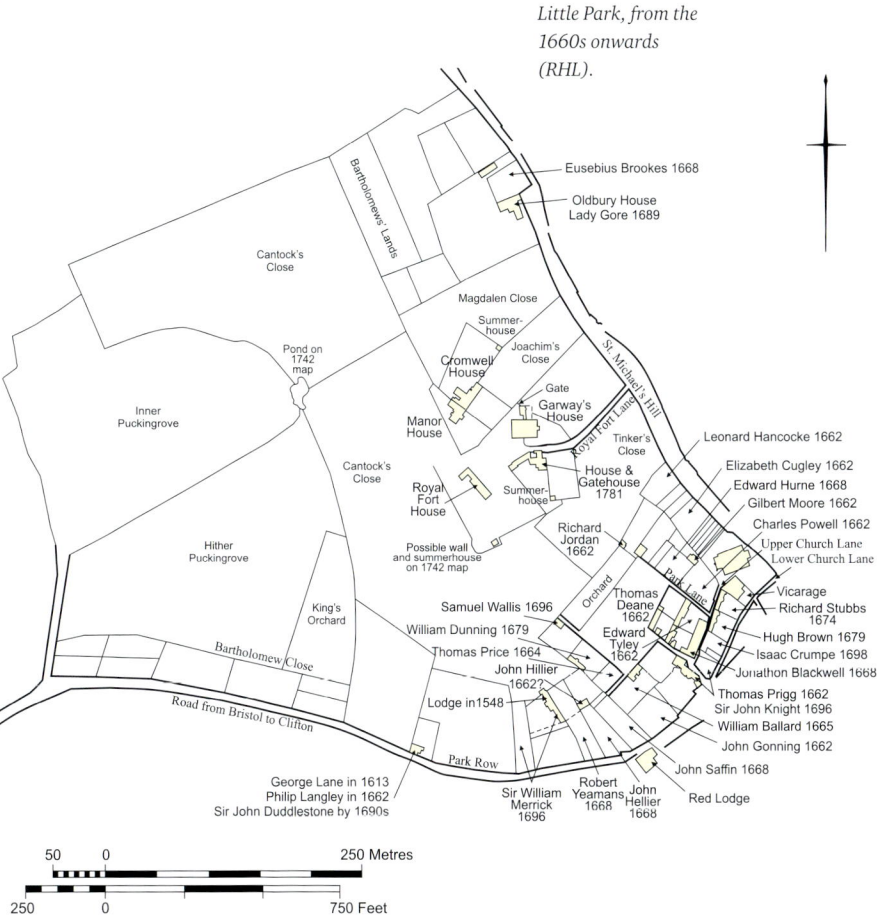

## Developments in the North and West

Leading steeply north-west from the centre of Bristol is St Michael's Hill, the road to the ferry across the Severn at Aust. Here several new developments were planned by individual developers from the mid-17th century onwards. The Little Park was promoted as an estate of some 12 garden houses from *c* 1660 onwards (Fig 3.23; chapter 9).[28] Within the Little Park two rows were developed from 1714 onwards, consisting of 10 houses known as Old Park Hill and 18 known as Vine Row.[29] Higher up the hill, Tinker's Close was developed as an estate of 72 smaller houses between *c* 1735 and 1755. The new development was recorded on a contemporary plan, showing the stage that it had then reached (Fig 3.24).

On the slopes below St Michael's Hill, within the former precinct of the Carmelite Friary, were two separate new developments. The first was a courtyard of workers' houses for the sugar refinery on St Augustine's Back, built at a cost of £1,200 for its proprietor John Knight in 1661[30] (see Fig 8.35). The second was a row of 10 two-storey residential houses on the north side of

43

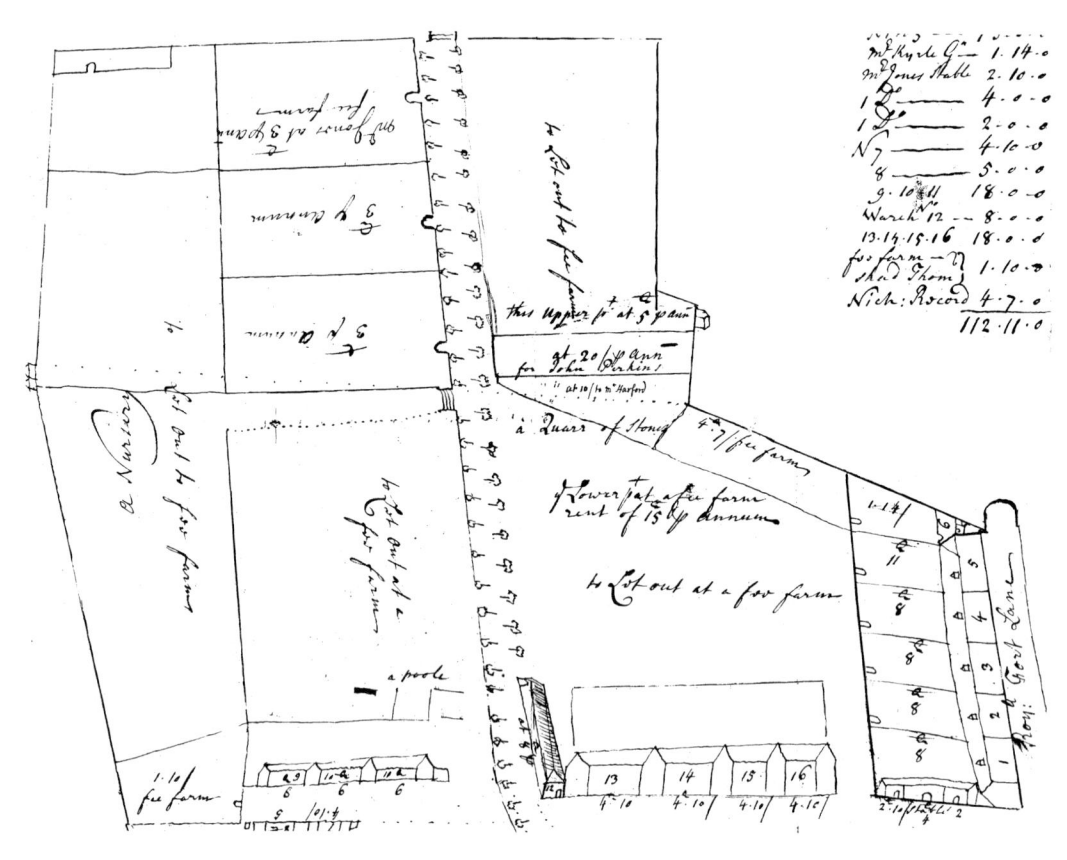

*Fig 3.24*
*Plan of Tinkers' Close*
*c 1735–55*
*(BRO AC/JS 8(61)).*

*Fig 3.25*
*The development of Kingsdown; new streets as developed and planned by 1742 (from Rocque's map).*

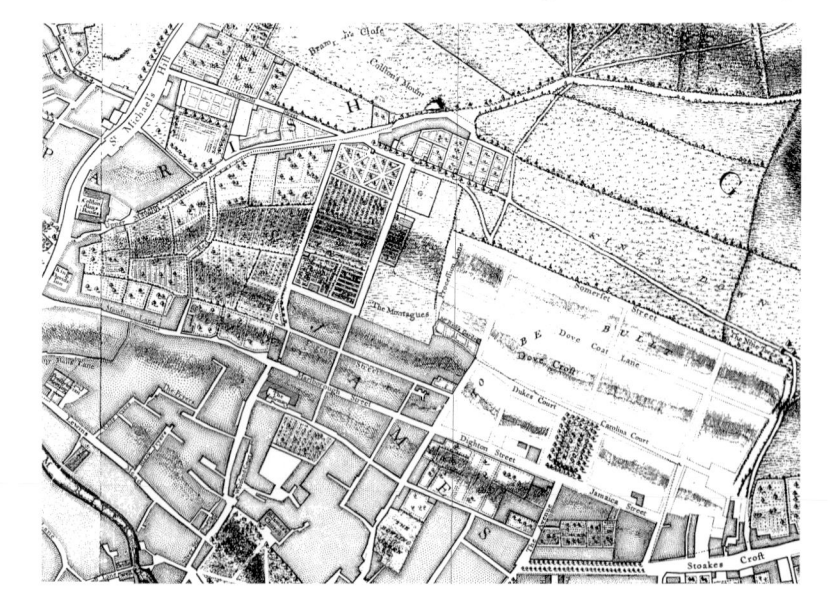

Host Street (*see* Fig 11.21), probably built in the 1690s. Little is known of them in detail, but the developer was apparently the merchant Richard Lane, later owner of the same sugar refinery.[31]

On the steep slopes above the city on the north side, to the east of St Michael's Hill, were the closes known as the Montagues and Kingsdown. Until the dissolution of the monasteries these had belonged to St James's Priory, and the development of this land for housing took place over nearly a century. In the early 18th century the land passed to Henry Dighton, a brewer, and then to his daughters and descendants. By the 1740s, when land was being granted for the building of new houses, they or their agents had laid out at least some of the 10 new streets shown on Rocque's map of 1742 (Fig 3.25). The development of Kingsdown continued until the 1790s when the building of Kingsdown Parade (originally James's Place) began, but it was then brought to a standstill by the collapse of the building boom (see below). Ultimately some 22 new streets added over 560 houses to the city (Fig 3.26).

Contemporary with the development of Kingsdown was the building of Park Street and the streets adjacent to it. This project seems to have been initiated *c* 1740 when Alderman Nathaniel Day was granted the reversion of land near the Boar's Head Inn to enable the building of a new street 40ft wide in the Bullock's Park 'to lead from College Green up into the road towards Jacob's Well'.[32] The plan was perhaps moving forwards in or shortly before 1749, when it was reported that 'we hear a plan of Bullock's Park, situated above the Boar's Head near the College Green, is now under consideration; and that a large way will soon be opened from the College Green thro' Bullock's Park to the road leading from the Red Lodge to Clifton'.³³ Day's plan must have been progressing slowly, for it was not until 1758 that he commenced the development of Park Street, now in partnership with George Tyndale.³⁴ Houses in Park Street were being completed in the early 1760s.³⁵ Great George Street, Charlotte Street and Berkeley Square were evidently constructed as part of the same scheme.³⁶

While all this development was adding to Bristol's built-up area, a new suburb was developing as a separate residential area from the early 18th century. This was Clifton, destined to become one of the most prestigious parts of the city. The larger of the two manors of Clifton was purchased by the Society of Merchant Venturers in 1685.³⁷ The Society, representing the merchant elite of the city, did not immediately involve itself in new housing schemes, and most of the major projects of the earlier 18th century in Clifton were undertaken by individual promoters.

These new schemes of the early 18th century were concentrated close to the hot springs and spa of the Hotwells. Dowry Square and the adjacent Chapel Row were developed alongside the road from Bristol to the Hotwells by the Reverend John Power soon after 1720, providing over 30 new houses. This development proceeded slowly and new houses were still being constructed on the north side of the square in the 1740s.³⁸ Other individual developers were also active in Clifton on the hill above Hotwells. In the centre of the parish was the field known as the Holly Lands, developed for housing from 1736 onwards by Francis Freeman, owner of the second smaller manor. With only three large houses being constructed, this was a very superior development.³⁹

The majority of the terraces and crescents of Clifton were developed in the building boom of 1783–93, some on land leased from the Society of Merchant Venturers: St Vincent's Parade and Prince's Buildings from 1789 onwards; Royal York Crescent and Cornwallis Crescent from 1791; Belle Vue from 1792; the Polygon and Freeland Place from 1826.⁴⁰ Other promoters included John Power, who developed Windsor Terrace in the 1790s; Isaac Cooke, the developer of the Paragon from 1809 onwards; and Samuel Worrall, the developer of Saville Place in the 1790s. Collectively these developments added some 435 new houses to the suburb of Clifton (Fig 3.27).

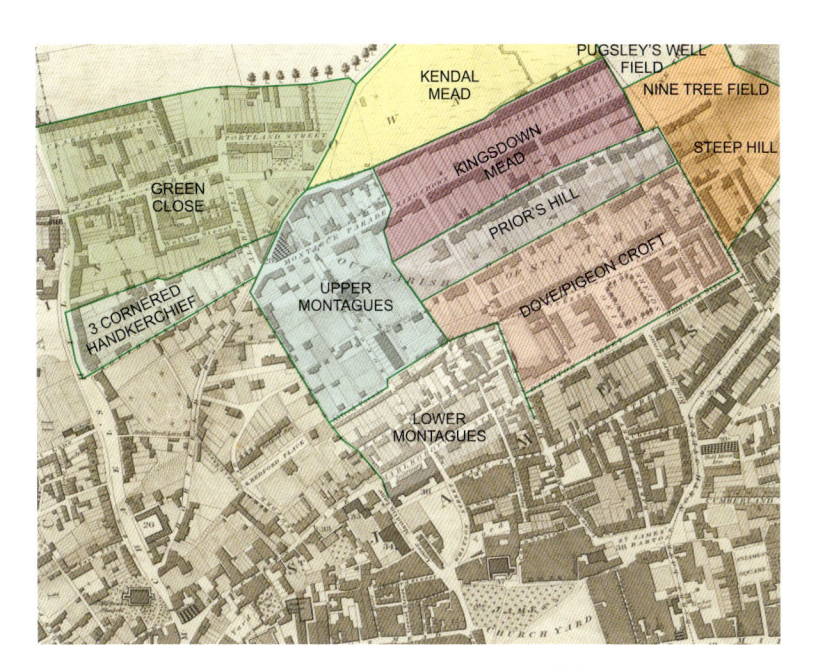

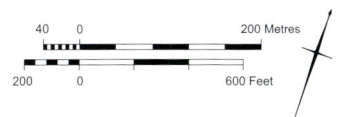

*Fig 3.26*
*The development of Kingsdown, from the 1730s to c 1800 (from Ashmead and Plumley's map of 1828).*

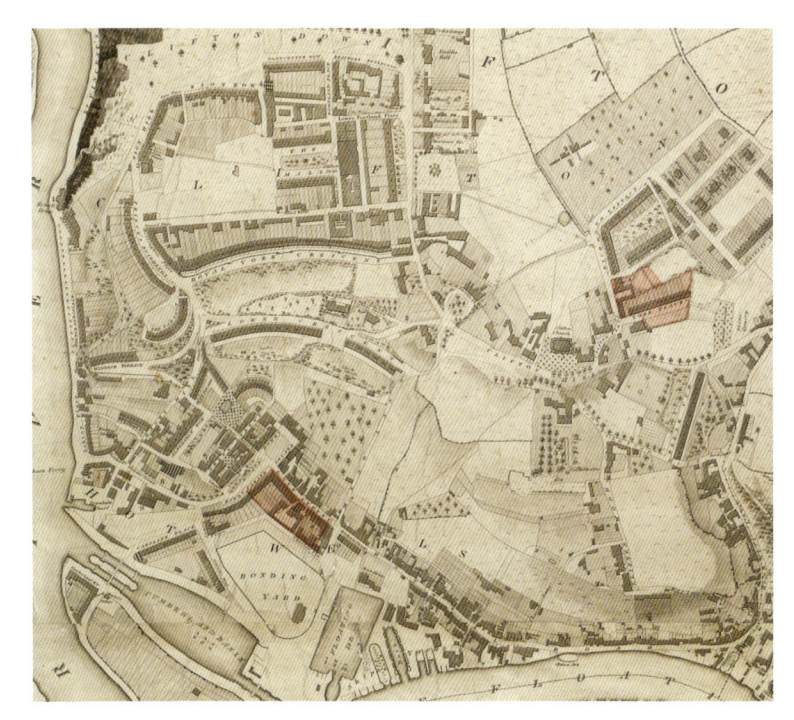

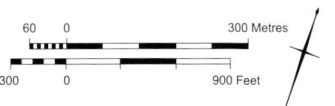

*Fig 3.27*
*The terraces and crescents of Clifton as developed in the building boom of 1783 to 1793 (from Ashmead and Plumley's map of 1828).*

## Developments in the South of the City

On the south side of the city new housing was again provided principally through the promotions of individual developers. One of the largest schemes was the redevelopment by Joseph Haskins, an upholsterer, of the Great Gardens or Spring Garden, a pleasure garden for the paying public at the south end of Temple parish (Fig 3.28). The development of the garden for housing took place from 1725 onwards, with seven new streets being laid out for building, providing some 147 new houses. Development commenced at the south-west end of Avon Street, where nos.11–15 were among the first houses to be built. The north side of Avon Street was being developed four years later, again probably commencing at the south-west end.

By 1731 the leases for all the plots to the corner of Butter Lane had been granted. At the north-east end of the street the entire block in the north-east angle between Tower Street and Avon Street was developed by John Stanton, a wine cooper; his lease was granted by Haskins on 31 May 1728. Development of the remaining parts of the Great Gardens continued slowly, and the last areas to be developed were those on its periphery. A building lease for the north-west side of Church Street, at the corner with Cart Lane, was granted in 1731. The north side of Pipe Lane, as far east as the corner with Rose Street, was granted to John Noades in 1733.

Further to the north-east the entire area between Pipe Lane and the Avon Street houses had been granted to Jonathan Green in 1726, but by 1740 it was still largely undeveloped for housing. Rocque's map of 1742 shows the area still planted with trees, perhaps a surviving part of the Great Gardens (Fig 3.29). In the part of the city to the south and west of St Mary Redcliff church, the development of existing or new streets for housing (Fig 3.30) commenced with Guinea Street, formerly the lane to Trim Mill,

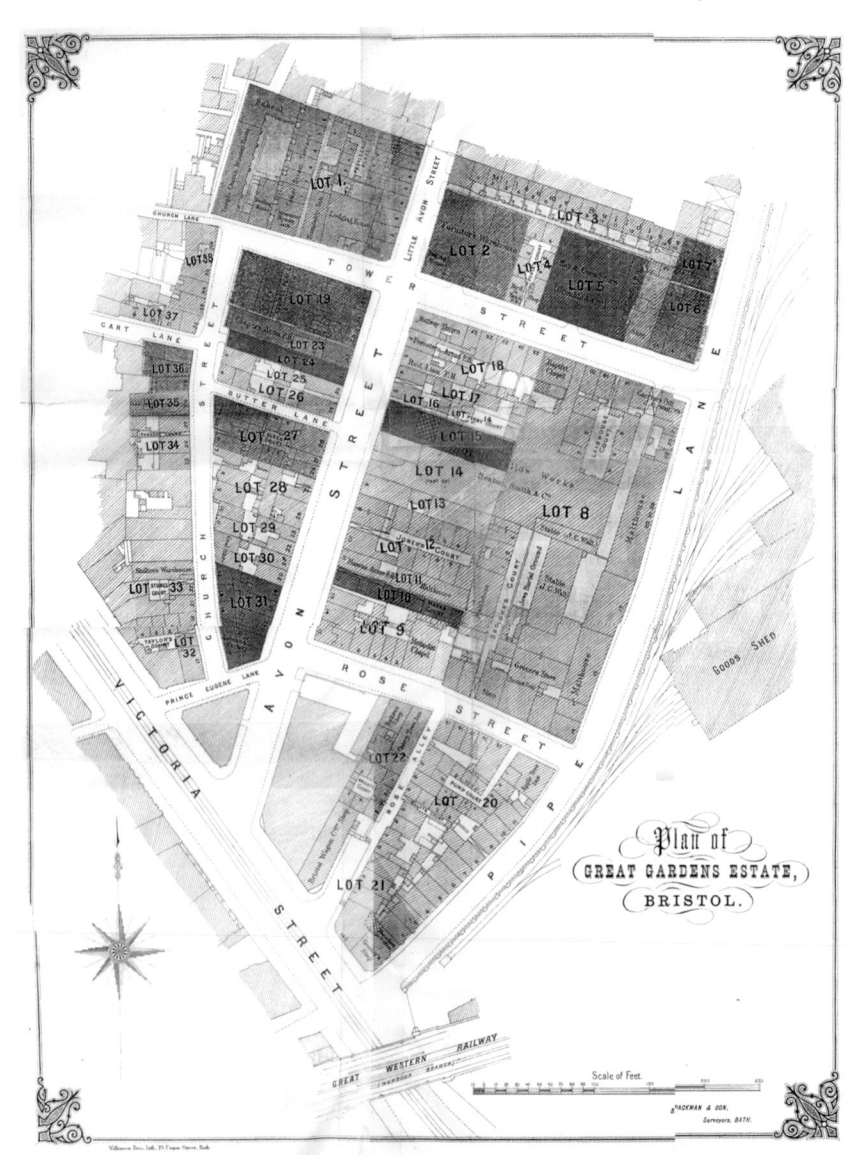

*Fig 3.28*
*The development of the Great Gardens, plan prepared in advance of the sale of ground rents in 1892 (BRO 8484(6) b).*

DEVELOPERS – THE EARLY MODERN CITY

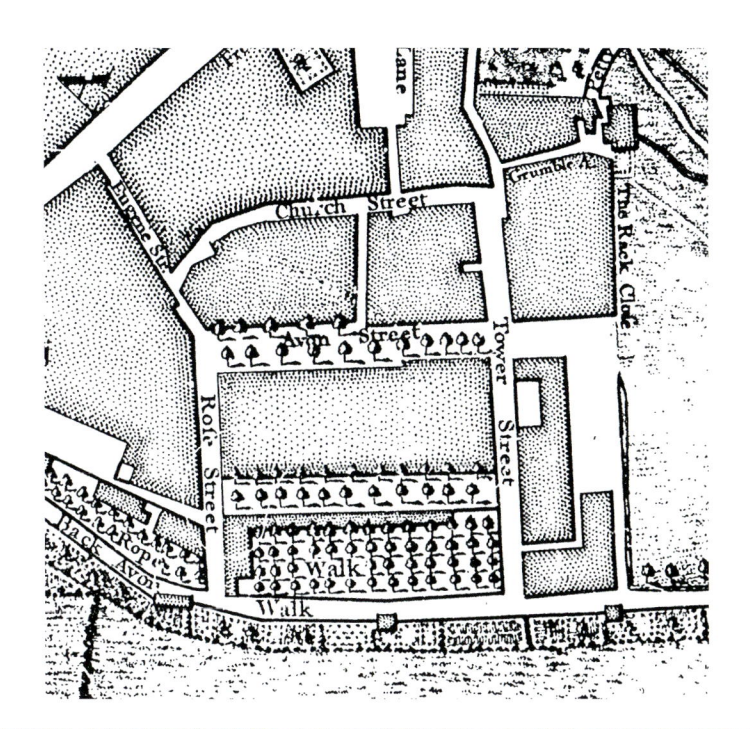

*Fig 3.29*
*The development of the Great Gardens or Spring Garden, from Rocque's map of 1742.*

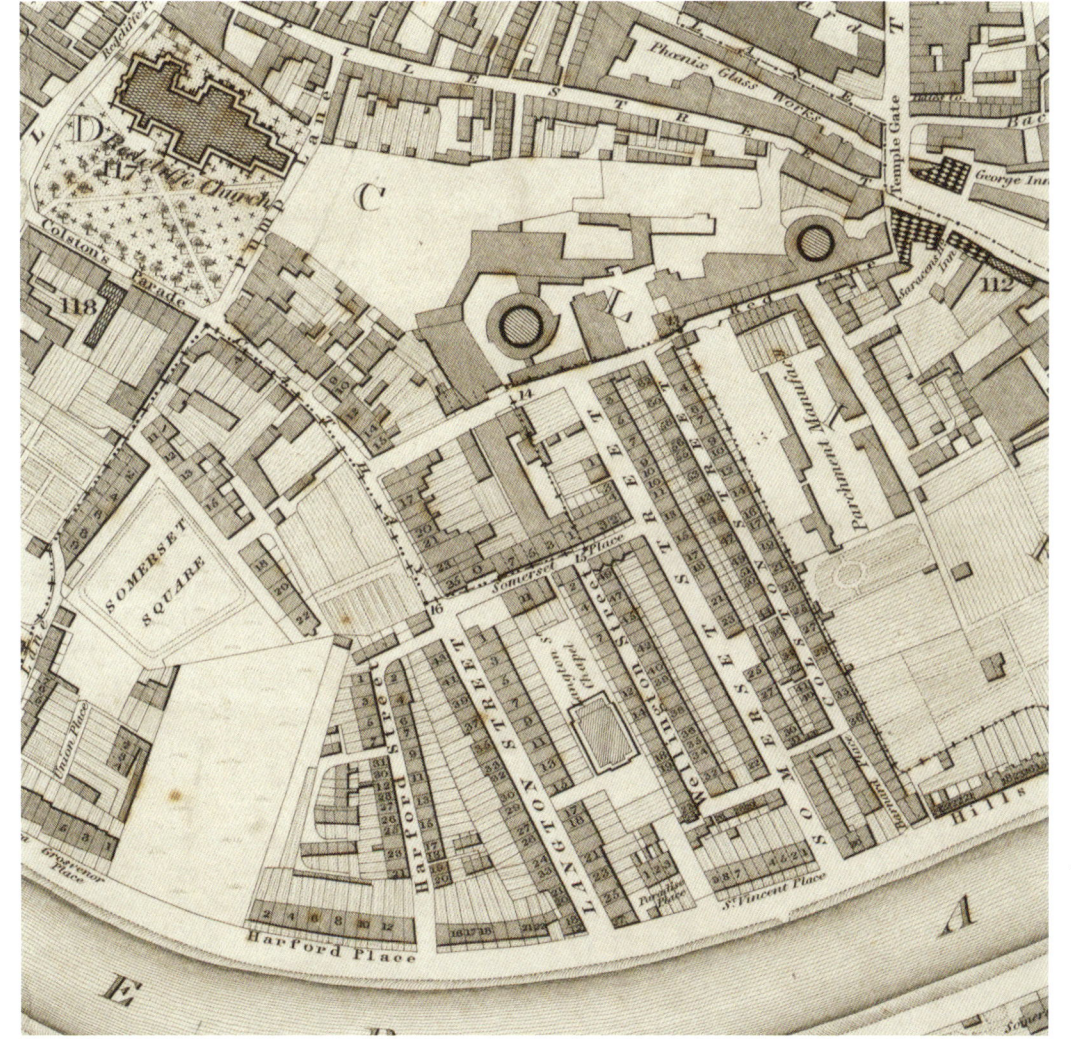

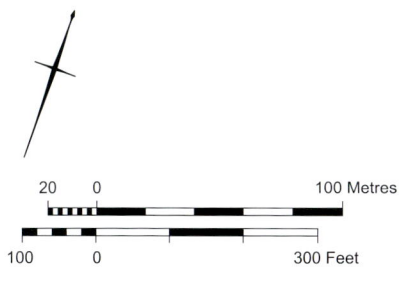

*Fig 3.30*
*New streets to the south and east of St Mary Redcliff church (from Ashmead and Plumley's map of 1828).*

*Fig 3.31*
*Tyndall's Park, the landscape scarred by the new unfinished development (University of Bristol Library, Special Collections).*

*Fig 3.32*
*Tyndall's Park, Repton's view of the park after the proposed landscaping (University of Bristol Library, Special Collections).*

in the 1720s; here 30 new houses were provided. The west part of Redcliff Parade and the north and west sides of Somerset Square were both developed by 1773, and Colston Parade was built from 1776 onwards. These schemes provided some 75 larger terraced houses. By 1826 several streets of smaller houses (216 houses in all) had been built, notably Colston Street, Wellington Street, Somerset Street and Langton Street, together with several separate rows of slightly larger houses (92 in all) fronting on to the New Cut and Clarence Road.[41] Some at least of these new streets originated in the building boom of 1783–93.

## The Building Boom of 1783–93

John Ward has shown how the building boom of the 1780s and 1790s developed after the end of the War of American Independence and the return of peace in 1782. Fifty new streets and squares were laid out within the space of 10 years:

> Portland Square, Berkeley Square, and the principal terraces and crescents of Clifton were all undertaken at this time. About 3,000 houses were completed and many hundreds more were begun,

this for a town of perhaps 45,000 inhabitants and 8,000 houses in 1782. Then early in 1793 came the outbreak of war with revolutionary France and a sweeping financial crisis that ruined many of the builders.[42]

The developments of Portland Square, Berkeley Square, Clifton and Kingsdown have already been discussed. In each of these developments houses remained unfinished until the early 1800s, and for some years the unfinished shells of houses in parts of the city presented a sadly depressing scene. As one visitor commented:

> I do not recollect a more melancholy spectacle, independent of human sufferings, than a walk on a dull day through the silent and falling houses in the western environs of this city; almost all of which are so nearly finished as to represent the deserted streets occasioned by a siege, or the ravages of a plague. Nor can one fail of reflecting on the ruin many families must have suffered, to occasion such a picture of desolation.[43]

One of the most incomplete schemes was that which had been commenced in the parkland close to Royal Fort house. Here, following the bankruptcy of the developers, the uncompleted streets and new houses reverted to the original owner, who then employed the landscape designer Humphry Repton to remodel the grounds and cleverly disguise the damage to the parkland (Figs 3.31 and 3.32). A second unfinished development, its location still unidentified, was that noted by Dr Ward as Mariner's Path, 15 houses each costing £1,000.[44]

## The English Urban Renaissance

It has been argued that in the century after the Restoration, English provincial towns experienced a cultural renaissance. The urban landscape was transformed under the influence of Classical architecture and concepts of urban planning, and through a remarkable expansion in the provision of fashionable public leisure. Prominent public buildings, including town halls, market houses, courts, exchanges, churches, theatres and assembly rooms, all dressed in Classical style, provided a new setting for the formal events in the life of the town, and the town's streets and open spaces were the arena for display and sociability. Domestic architecture also played its part in transforming the image of the town, for increasingly houses were seen not as individual units but instead as contributing to a wider and more formal urban landscape.[45] Bristol shows much evidence for the adoption of new ideas on what a town should be in the early modern period – and indeed in some aspects it provides outstanding illustrations of how the urban landscape changed under the influence of new thinking.

### Urban Design

As has long been recognised, Classical architecture and the building of brick row houses, such as those being constructed in London from the early 17th century, came to Bristol with the building of Queen Square from *c* 1700 onwards.[46] It was as if the City Council had decided that this step, together with the city's first square, was a suitable marker for the beginning of the new century; but it is possible to see some of the concepts of urban design at earlier dates. Symmetry in the design of individual houses can be viewed as part of the same increasing awareness of the Classical world, and it is evident in the 17th century in houses built in Lewin's Mead and King Street (Figs 3.33 and 3.34). The idea of creating Queen Square might also have originated earlier in the 17th century. It is possible that in the building of King Street in the 1660s the Corporation was following a long-term plan for the development of the Marsh, to include ultimately Queen Square. Earlier in the 1610s building leases had established the line of Prince Street, and in the granting of leases for King Street the gap

*Fig 3.33*
*Lewin's Mead, no.69, a symmetrically designed house of the 17th century, probably of c 1642. From left to right: nos.65, 66, 67, 68, 69 (the very tall house to the right of the archway) and 70, watercolour of 1821 by H O'Neill (BRSMG M2855).*

*Fig 3.34*
*Nos.1–5 King Street, symmetrically designed houses of the 1660s, photograph of the later 19th century (NMR Batsford CC60/95).*

between nos.5 and 6 ensured that Queen Charlotte Street could later be built as an avenue leading into one corner of Queen Square.

Also evident from the 17th century onwards was an increasing awareness of urban design, both in the planning of new streets and in ensuring the uniformity of the new houses then built. Some developments, such as those of the Dean and Chapter in Culver Street, Trinity Street and Wells Street, and of the Corporation in King Street, were simply single streets, but most of the more extensive new developments followed what has been termed the gridiron plan. The scheme drawn up for the redevelopment of the Castle, probably in the 1650s, set out two principal streets, Castle Street and Castle Green, parallel to one another and linked by two shorter thoroughfares, Cock and Bottle Lane and Tower Street (Fig 3.2). It is evident from the descriptions of properties in Castle Street that this was a street already in existence, and certainly to that extent the layout of the new suburb was determined by what was already there. But the result of the redevelopment shows the Corporation acting on a large and ambitious scale, informed by some notion of formal planning, to transform a medieval backwater and integrate it into the wider city.

More elaborate concepts of urban planning were evident from the beginning of the 18th century. The standard was set in Queen Square, laid out from *c* 1700. Ison suggested that the inspiration for the building of Queen Square may have come from Lincoln's Inn Fields in London.[47] Certainly the development of squares as a feature of urban planning was first seen in the metropolitan cities of London and Paris. In Bristol, squares and gridiron layouts of streets were prominent in subsequent developments at St James's Square and Crotwells (both in construction by 1710); Orchard Street, commenced in 1718; the Penn family's estate from 1719; and Kingsdown, begun in the 1740s. In the following decades the eastwards expansion of the city included the building of King Square, Brunswick Square and Portland Square (Figs 3.26 and 3.22). The design of the street plan for the development of the parkland below Brandon Hill combined a gridiron pattern for Great George Street and Charlotte Street, with a single main street, Park Street, linking two open spaces, the older College Green and the new Berkeley Square (Fig 3.35).

The most ambitious plans realised were those implemented in the fast developing spa suburb of Clifton. Here, with the example of Bath in mind and in deliberate imitation, large crescents – Royal York Crescent and Cornwallis Crescent, each with its own private esplanade and gardens below for the use of the residents – were begun *c* 1791. To one side of these two crescents were two smaller developments of geometric form, the Paragon completed in the 1810s and below that the Polygon, certainly completed by 1828 (Fig 3.27). But for the collapse of the building boom of the early 1790s these would have been matched by the development planned by the Dean and Chapter for its lands in Tyndall's Park and around Royal Fort house: the Dean and Chapter had in 1792 secured an Act of Parliament to lay out 'a Crescent, Square, Circus, several Streets and other buildings upon a Regular Plan ... the same would form a regular and grand Plan of Building which would very much improve the said City and the lands of the Dean and Chapter'.[48] With the collapse of the building boom, the streets planned by the architect James Wyatt were never built.

Two crescents were built in the crowded suburbs to the south of the Avon. On the south side of the New Cut (of the Avon) 62 houses in York Road formed one long crescent overlooking the tidal river (Fig 3.36). In Temple parish Wilmot Crescent was built by 1828; it was later partly demolished for the building of Victoria Street in 1868, and the remainder was fully demolished by 1885 (Fig 3.37).

## The Uniformity of New Housing

From the 1650s onwards developers also controlled the uniformity and later the form of the new houses in the city's streets. In the development of the Castle, building leases generally stipulated the height of new houses and laid down that they should be uniform with the houses already built. For instance in 1660, at nos.5 and 6 Castle Street, John Evans, mason, was to build 'two faire houses three story in height beside the roofe in uniformity to the castle buildings'; at the adjacent nos.7 and 8 in 1663 Thomas Harding, carpenter, and Robert Drew, carpenter, were each to build one tenement 'in uniformity to the rest of the Castle buildings'; uniformity here was evidently loosely enforced (Fig 3.38).[49]

Thomas Harding would have been well acquainted with what was required, for some four years earlier he had taken a lease for the building of nos.15–16 Castle Street, covenanting

DEVELOPERS – THE EARLY MODERN CITY

*Fig 3.35*
*The development of the hillside below Brandon Hill, Park Street and the adjacent streets linking the older College Green with the new Berkeley Square (from Ashmead and Plumley's map of 1828).*

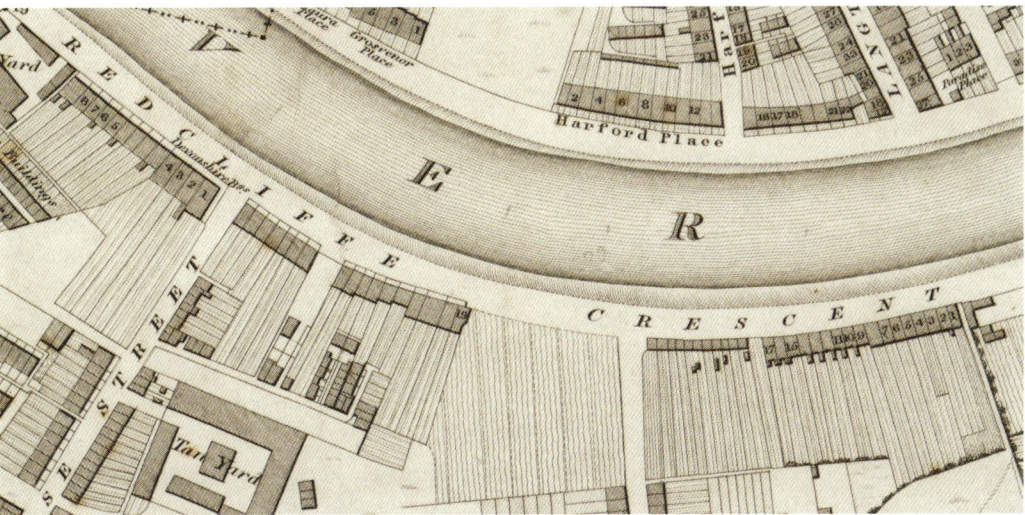

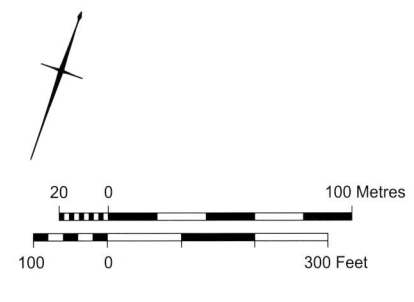

*Fig 3.36*
*Crescent of the 1790s on the south side of the New Cut (from Ashmead and Plumley's map of 1828).*

51

*Fig 3.37*
Wilmot Crescent, Temple parish (from Ashmead and Plumley's map of 1828).

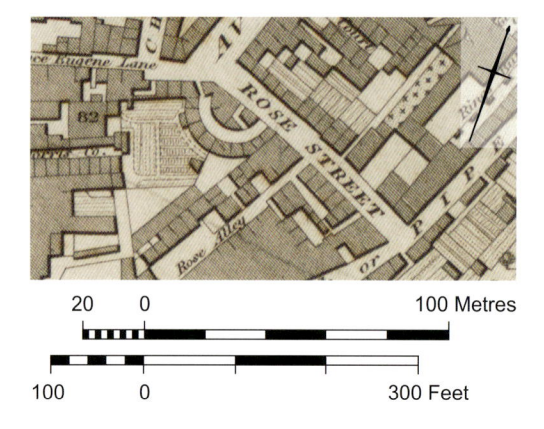

*Fig 3.38*
Nos.7 and 8 Castle Street: Thomas Harding, carpenter, and Robert Drew, carpenter, were each to build one tenement 'in uniformity to the rest of the Castle buildings', watercolour of 1828 by T L Rowbotham (BRSMG M2737).

*Fig 3.39*
Nos.35–7 Old Market, photograph of 1978; part of no.35 (with a hipped roof) on the left, nos.36–7 on the right (extract from NMR BB78/09309).

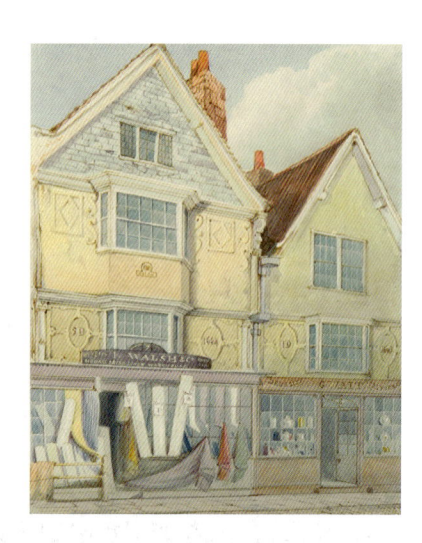

to build 'one or more tenements in height three story and a halfe, bearing uniformity to the rest of the buildings to be erected in the castle according to the platforme that hath been agreed upon'.[50] The 'platforme', or design, would have probably stipulated the maximum extent of any projecting jetties or windows, as was explicit in the building lease for nos.22–3 Castle Street, a plot leased in 1656 to Walter Markes and on which two houses were to be built, 'two tenements three story in height beside the roof uniforme to the rest of the buildings and the juts and windowes not to exceede two foote without the body of the same tenements'.[51]

Similar covenants were applied to the building leases for King Street. In 1663 the land on which nos.6–8 King Street were to be built was leased to Matthew Stephens, merchant, upon condition that he build within three years 'three substantial messuages, three storeys in height besides the roof and in uniformity to the rest of the buildings'.[52] The building lease for nos.2–5 King Street was granted in the same month, the merchant Michael Deyos agreeing to build 'three sufficient messuages fitt & convenient for tenants to live therein, containing in heighth three storyes beside the roof within three yeares next commencing'.[53] Deyos's houses were then built as part of a row of five of symmetrical design so, although there was no requirement for uniformity in this building lease, a row of matching houses was in fact built (Fig 3.34).

With the building of Queen Square far more detailed conditions for the building of new houses were introduced, as for instance for Dr Reade's house in Queen Charlotte Street, the first to be built (Appendix 1). Similarly detailed requirements were set out in later Corporation leases for Queen Square in the 1700s and Prince Street in the 1710s. Even in some of the smaller private developments, the uniformity and appearance of the completed development was of concern to the promoter. In the replacement of two houses with one new one at no.35 Old Market, the Corporation, as trustees for the lands of Trinity Hospital, required that Barratt 'pull down the said two messuages and build one good substantial messuage with an upright front of brick which is to come out into the street three foot beyond Alderman Steevens' Almshouse and is three storys and an halfe in height, the first story eight foot and six inches, the second story eight foot and the third story foure foot and an half in height'. The lease for nos.36–7 set out similar conditions, indicating that it was now the intention of the Corporation that this street should where possible be rebuilt in brick (Fig 3.39).[54]

In the development of the Great Gardens, the lease granted by Haskins and his associates to Peter Whiteing set out some of the conditions attached to the building of the houses. On this plot Whiteing was to build 'three substantial messuages or dwelling houses three story high above the cellar to be in the front forty eight foot and to be built regular and even in the front with the other buildings'. In front of the house Whiteing was to provide 'a sufficient pitching or causeway … before the whole front of the said plot … fifteen foot broad besides six foot out of the said one hundred and thirty foot to be enclosed with palisades and the same from time to time maintain and keep in good repair'. Similar conditions applied in the lease issued a year later to Whiteing for the building of nos.1–3 and 23–7 Tower Street.[55]

By the end of the 18th century private developers were setting out even more detailed requirements. In 1791 the building lease for no.52 Kingsdown Parade, part of Lockier's James's Place development, was accompanied by a separate contract, between Charles Melsom, a sworn measurer or surveyor acting on behalf of the developers, and James Pope, a mason and the builder of the house, setting out the constructional details for the house to be built in some considerable detail (Appendix 1). Further conditions then gave the developers the right to take, complete and sell the house themselves at Pope's expense, if work by Pope had stopped for more than one month.[56]

James's Place is now the north-east part of Kingsdown Parade, and it can be seen that the developer was almost wholly successful in ensuring that uniform terraces were created on either side. No.52 is itself something of an oddity. It was probably one of those houses which remained unfinished after the collapse of the building boom in 1793. The front walls were first constructed so as to be three windows wide, but when completed the house was given a front elevation one sash window wide, rather than the stipulated three.[57] As permitted in the contract (Appendix 1), the rear ground-floor parlour was provided with a bow window (Figs 3.40 and 3.41). The front room on the first floor would have been the Drawing Room, as noted in a later lease for no.58 (Appendix 2).

*Fig 3.40 (left) Nos.54, 52, 50, 48 (and 46) Kingsdown Parade, front elevations, photograph, of 1967 (English Heritage AA67/02829).*

*Fig 3.41 (above) No.52 Kingsdown Parade, rear elevation showing parlour bay window; the lower bay window is a recent addition. Photograph of 2010 (English Heritage DP114084).*

The uniformity of a new row of houses could be ensured partly through written conditions in the lease as in Queen Square, in James's Place or in the Great Gardens development, but was in some instances ensured through covenants in the building lease linked to drawings of the elevation and/or plan of the house to be built. Some of the building leases for the construction of Kingsdown Parade contained such drawings, that for no.79 being a surviving example (Fig 3.42).[58] The construction of Bath Street in the 1780s was enabled through the use of similar drawings in the building leases (Fig 3.43).

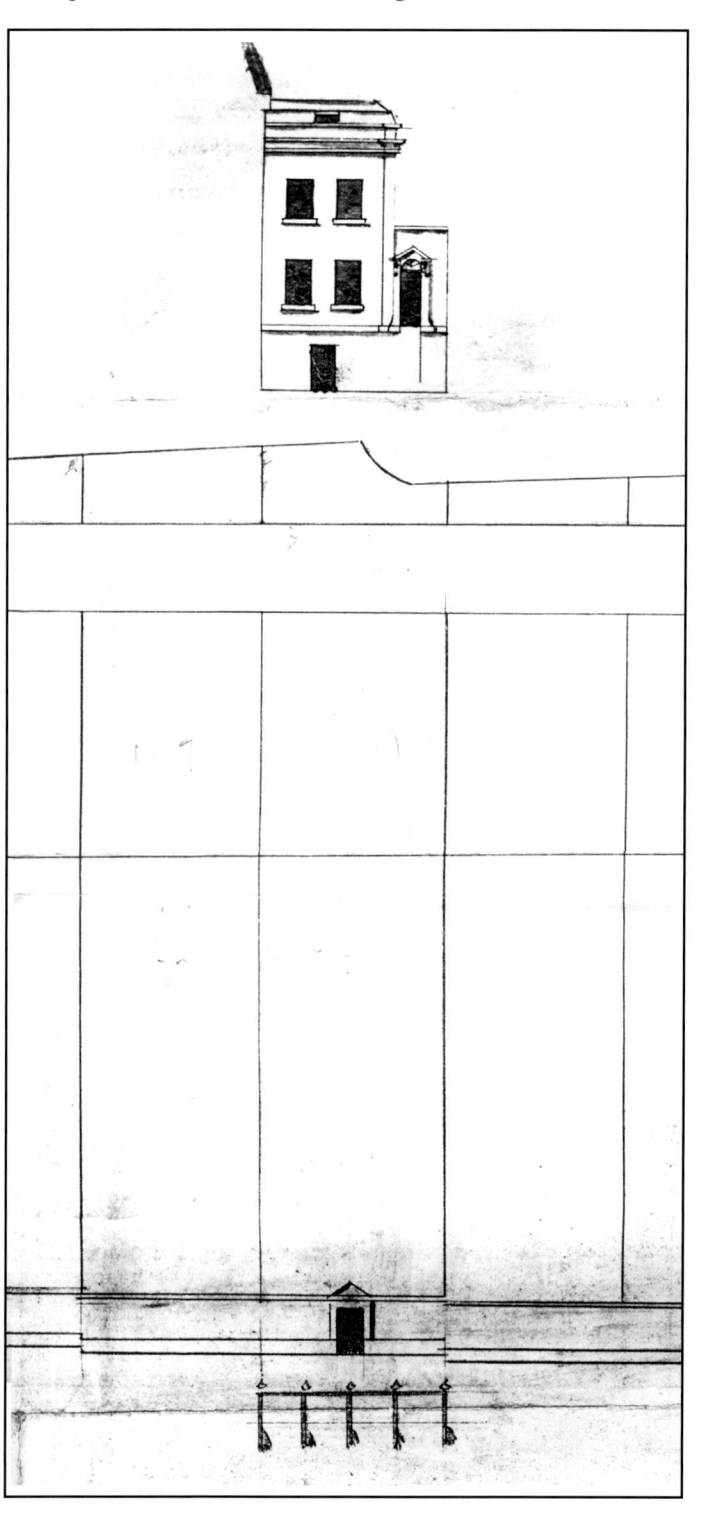

*Fig 3.42*
*No.79 Kingsdown Parade, design of elevation endorsed on lease (BRO 26138(2), conveyance of 13 June 1792).*

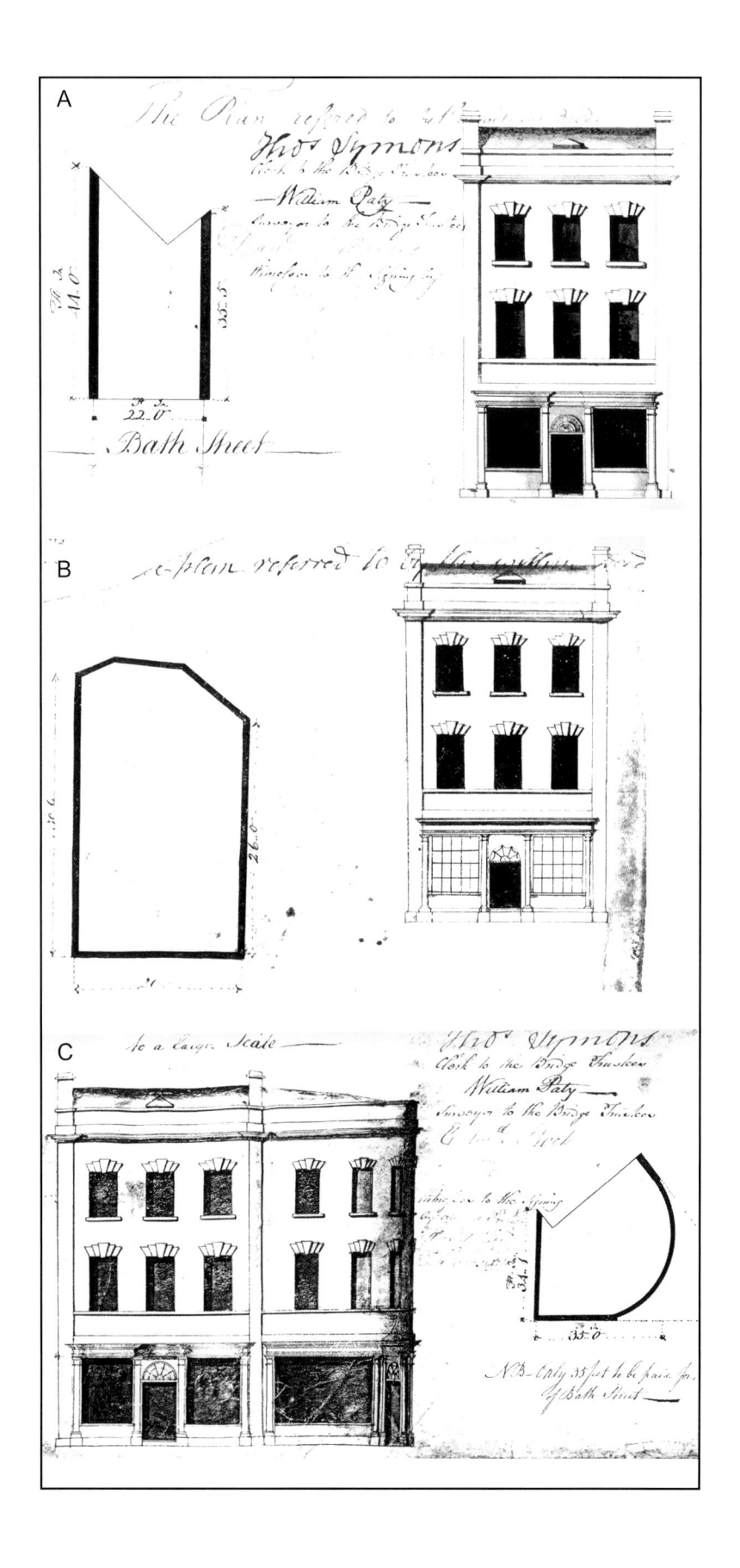

*Fig 3.43
Bath Street, drawings from building leases of the Bath Street houses, 1789 (Courages Archives A.31, Heineken UK).*

## Drainage

Building contracts usually contained no conditions relating to the drainage to be installed, possibly because this was supplied by the developer. This certainly appeared to be the case in the Great Gardens development where it was Joseph Haskins, the promoter of the scheme, who negotiated the consents necessary for the main drain serving the development. In 1771 Temple parish, as the owners of Bastavon and Richard George's Deal Yard, granted a licence to Joseph Haskins and William Barrett, surgeon 'to dig a drain or common sewer of the height of 5 feet & of the breadth of 3 feet thro a piece of ground called the Deal Yard situate at Tower Harratz in Temple Backs ... the said drain to begin & to be carried on in a straight line with the gout then open facing the said Deal Yard down to the River Avon'.[59] This was the sewer that was described in more detail in 1799 in a 'list of the inhabitants names whose gouts communicate with the common sewer to the parish of Temple, beginning at the Back part of the upper end of Avon Street, from there across Tower Street' and thence into the Brick Yard.[60]

## The Naming of Streets

The promoters of new developments must in most instances have been responsible for the naming of the new streets. One individual developer followed the Corporation in allocating names that reflected loyalty to the Crown and Court: the civic naming of King Street, Queen Square and Prince Street was emulated by Nathaniel Wade in his naming of Great Anne Street and Great George Street, plus a modestly named Wade Street (Fig 3.18). Brunswick Square was named for its Hanoverian associations and adjacent streets after the dukedoms held by the King's brothers, Cumberland and York. Portland Square was named in honour of the Duke of Portland, then High Steward of Bristol.[61] Unity Street and Union Street both attested the loyalty of the Corporation to the Act of Union. Loyalty to the Quaker elite was similarly attested in the street names given to the Penn family's developments (Figs 3.19 and 3.20): Callowhill Street, Penn Street and Philadelphia Street all had obvious Quaker associations (William Penn, the founder of Pennsylvania, had married Hannah Callowhill at Bristol in 1695).[62] Loyalty to the Anglican Church might similarly have been part of the attraction of living in Trinity Street, adjacent to the Cathedral.

More streets were allocated names that reflected their historic or topographical associations. The streets fashioned out of the Castle were named Castle Street and Castle Green. The Quaker merchant Richard Gotley named his new St James's Square after the parish in which it was situated. Orchard Street was named after the orchard behind St Mark's Hospital and Culver Street after Culver Close, which in turn probably took its name from a dovecote on the hillside above the hospital. Close to Culver Street was Wells Street, which may have taken its name not from water wells but from the Wells family who would have inherited the garden house or lodge of Thomas Wells built in 1664 (chapter 9).

In the Great Gardens development the naming of Avon Street reflected its proximity to the river, while the naming of Tower Street attested its proximity to the ancient Tower Harratz, part of the extended town defences of the 1240s. In a city where popular culture was taking an increasing interest in history and antiquities, living in streets whose names were taken from the historic landscape may have added to the attraction of these new developments.[63]

One name very significant in promoting the attractiveness of a new development was that of 'Montpelier', accorded to the hillside above and to the north of Ashley Road. This was a name given to a number of new suburbs, for instance in Cheltenham, Gloucestershire and to many new plantations in North America, notably the country house in Virginia of James Madison, fourth President of the United States. The name of Montpellier in France, famous as a resort, seems to have been synonymous with pure, healthy air. Daniel Defoe described Bury St Edmunds as '. . . a handsome town famed for its pleasant situation and wholesome air, the Montpellier of Suffolk and perhaps England.' Edmund Pendleton described the '"Salubrious Air" of the Madison estate as not to be exceeded by any Montpelier in the Universe'.[64]

## Developers and Promoters

The developments initiated by the Corporation were overseen by Council committees appointed specifically for each new project. In c 1650 the redevelopment of the site of the Castle was to be overseen by a committee 'hereby intrusted and impowered to manadge and carry on the whole building of the castle, for the compleat dismantling thereof, making the bridge there, letting and selling the ground and houses and improveing the cittyes revenues by the same, and in all things to have the same power in reference to The castle as other surveirores of the city lands'. The cost of demolishing and refurbishing the existing buildings was considerable, being also augmented by the costs of pitching or cobbling the new streets and of building a new gate into the Castle to facilitate access from Old Market on the east side.[65]

Committees with broadly similar briefs were appointed in 1699 to oversee the issuing of leases for the development of Queen Square, and in 1717 to oversee the planning and construction of Orchard Street. Members of the Council took advantage of their engagement in these schemes by taking leases in the new developments. Of the 10 members of the Committee for the development of the Castle, Alderman Miles Jackson and Councillors Henry Gibbs and Walter Sandy all took out leases for properties; the City Chamberlain, James Powell, leased three separate properties.[66]

Many more leases were taken by speculative builders, sometimes in association with the future tenant or owner of the house to be built. A typical example was no.59 Castle Street, leased in September 1656 to carpenter William Mason. Like most leases in Bristol it was for a specified number of years or for named lives, whichever should prove the longer. In this instance the specified lives were those of Flower Hunt, a tobacco pipe maker, Christian his wife and also those of their two sons, William and Thomas. The Hunt family can be shown from later leases and the Hearth Tax returns to have been the later occupants of no.59. Clearly Flower and Christian Hunt were already identified as the future tenants and owners of the house to be built from the time that Mason took out his lease.[67]

In other examples, the speculator was not a builder and was probably an investor. In King Street, the merchant Matthew Stephens took out the lease for the building of nos.6–8; this was then assigned as two leases, the first to John Peterson the elder, with the lives cited including those of the Peterson family who then lived there.[68] In other instances a speculative builder may have found a purchaser once the house was finished or was under construction.

The building lease for no.7 Castle Street was granted to Thomas Harding, a carpenter, in 1663, but by 1668 he had conveyed this to Christian Dangerfield, a widow, who then leased the property directly from the Corporation.

The speculative builders active in the 17th century and early 18th century came from various trades. In the building of Castle Street in the 1650s they included carpenters, masons, tilers, plasterers and glaziers, all of whom must have subcontracted to other trades as necessary in the management of their individual building projects.[69]

In two developments, Nathaniel Wade's new streets in Crotwells and the streets developed by the Penn family, the promoters were prominent members of the Quaker elite, many of whom were closely linked to various industrial concerns. The houses built in the new streets of these developments were within easy walking distance of a number of Quaker-owned industrial concerns, including Abraham Darby's iron foundry established in 1703, two glassworks – one founded by Abraham Elton *c* 1710 and the other by Edmund Mountjoy and others in 1715 – and the earlier soap works, all in Cheese Lane. Possibly the houses of these new developments accommodated some of the workers in these various industries. If so, they would have been a vehicle for recycling the capital invested in these industries, through workers' wages paying rents, which then became landlords' profits.

The provision of purpose-built housing for industrial workers was on a smaller scale. Purpose-built housing is recorded only in the context of industries where housing was essential to attract workers, sugar-refining in the 17th century and brass-founding in the 18th century. At the sugar house on St Augustine's Back, 13 workmen's houses were built at a cost of £1,200 for its proprietor John Knight in 1661 (*see* Fig 8.35). Disposed around two sides of a courtyard to the west of the Great House, the houses were each of three storeys with one room on each floor and a small yard to the rear.[70] In a similar context, three houses were built in *c* 1666 at the Whitsun Court sugar house at the instigation of its proprietor Thomas Ellis for his works' manager and foreman: it was as important to retain skilled managers as it was to recruit skilled workers. A watercolour of the 19th century shows one of these houses (*see* Fig 7.42); this was probably Ellis's own house, part of which survives. Beyond the city at Baptist Mills, William Champion's brass-works possessed 25 houses for key workers by 1761 (Figs 3.44a and 3.44b). Even with a few additions, this quantity of purpose-built industrial housing would account for a minute proportion of Bristol's expansion from the 1690s onwards.[71]

Those involved in speculative building by the end of the 18th century were broadly the same groups as those involved a century earlier. Dr Ward has identified these as including professional building craftsmen, who 'commonly speculated on their own account in co-operation with financiers from outside the trade'.[72]

In Bristol the developers were, by the end of the 18th century, principally attorneys, such as Harry Elderton, Thomas Morgan and Matthew Mills Coates:

> Conveyancing gave them knowledge of the land market. As trustees and managers of house property, a common middle-class investment, they could keep an eye on the movement of rents. Their supervision of repair work brought them into contact with builders and gave them opportunities to weigh them up. And above all, their employment by clients to place investments gave them access to finance.[73]

One leading developer, James Lockier, was – like Joseph Haskins, the promoter of the Great Gardens estate – an upholsterer or furniture manufacturer. Like Llewllyn Williams in Old Market in the 1690s and members of the Penn family in the mid-18th century, some of these developers were also in the business of investing profits from the Atlantic trade and commerce. Lockier was one of the leading merchants trading with Honduras, importing mahogany for furniture manufacture; the attorney Mills Coates was of an old West Indian family.[74] The links between housing investment and provision in Bristol and the wider Atlantic world will be considered more fully in chapter 12. Similarly, chapters 10, 11 and 13 will explore in greater depth the distinctions of status and wealth embedded in each development through the types of housing provided.

*Fig 3.44*
*Baptist Mills, William Champion's brass-works: a) plan of c 1750, by Jacob de Wilstar (BRO SMV/6/4/14/13); b) reconstruction, as seen from the air (David Martyn).*

# 4

# The Urban Tenement Plot in the Medieval City

## ''Tis So Close Built'

Visitors to Bristol in the later 17th and 18th centuries remarked on the intensity of building in the city. The traveller and writer Celia Fiennes came here from Bath in the 1690s, taking in the 'aire and prospect' of Lansdowne en route. Descending the hill from Kingswood into Bristol, she was very struck by the contrast between the more spacious suburbs on the periphery and then the tightly packed streets towards the centre of the city: 'the buildings of the town are pretty high most of timber work, the streetes are narrow and something darkish, because the roomes on the upper storys are more jutting out, soe contracts the streete and the light; the suburbs are better buildings and more spacious streetes …'[1]

Daniel Defoe's observations, made two or three decades later, were very similar: 'As for the city itself, there is hardly room to set another house in it, 'tis so close built …'[2] Looking at Broad Street *c* 1700 and St Nicholas Street in the 1820s gives an impression of what Defoe must have seen (Figs 4.1 and 4.2).

Fiennes and Defoe walked streets which, in the central part of the city, had been heavily subdivided into many separate tenement plots by the 14th century. A good number of the three- and four-storey houses, especially those which jutted out the most, had been built by *c* 1500. They were looking at a city in which the intensity of its building was in considerable part medieval.

The densely populated medieval city produced a distinct mentality: 'there are some thoughts which will not come to men who are

*Fig 4.1 (left)*
*Broad Street c 1700 view,*
*as reconstructed from*
*documentary sources*
*(JA).*

*Fig 4.2 (above)*
*St Nicholas Street looking*
*west, watercolour by*
*T L Rowbotham, 1825*
*(BRSMG M2262).*

not tightly packed'.³ Some historians have searched for the expressions of these distinct attitudes in faction and disorder. An imperative in these inquiries has been to establish further the relationship and differences between the city and its surrounding countryside.⁴ The mentality of the tightly packed urban population was, however, also expressed in the bonds of secular society, 'the topography of the city and the grouping of its houses may have helped to generate some sense of community between neighbours'.⁵ In looking at the tenement as the context of the urban house, it is inevitable that we look also at the relations between neighbours. The term 'tenement' is used here in its historic sense, to describe the plot of land upon which a house was built, 'land or property held of any other by real tenure',⁶ not in its modern sense of being a building in multiple occupation.

The configuration of the tenement plot, and the rights attached to it, were of fundamental importance to medieval and later townspeople. Through the structures of the tenement can be inferred not only their concerns, but also the co-operation and conflict that occurred between the inhabitants of one plot and the next. For many townspeople, daily lives and work were delimited not by the confines of the house, but by the bounds of the tenement. Of particular concern were matters of ownership, security, lighting, drainage, water supply and sanitation. In all these we see a distinct urban mentality. This chapter is largely concerned with these issues in the medieval period, setting the background and context for the centuries that followed.

## Ownership – Rights and Control

In the tightly packed city, every inch of land was measured and valued. This was very evident in one of the earliest recorded boundary surveys within the town, undertaken by John Wanstre, the civic surveyor, on behalf of the Mayor's Court in 1411. The 'view' or inspection was of the boundaries of a tenement belonging to the Fraternity of St John the Baptist, today known as Tailors' Court and situated on the east side of Broad Street (Fig 4.3). Some of the buildings measured by Wanstre still survive. His measurements were to the nearest half-inch, and were tied in to each of the adjoining properties through carefully recording their respective names.

The immediate need to establish so precisely the bounds of the land owned by the Fraternity can be traced back to another set of measurements, taken nine years previously, when there were two shops and an entry on the street frontage.⁷ In 1411 one of these and the entry were no longer there. Instead, recorded in precise measurements, was a space exactly half of the width of the tenement plot, the part which is today occupied by no.43 Broad Street, the most completely surviving 15th-century house in the city. The main purpose of the 1411 view was thus to confirm the exact boundaries of the building site on the street frontage, on which no.43 was shortly to be constructed. A view in 1479 of the property of St Nicholas's church, opposite the church in St Nicholas Street, was undertaken in similar circumstances to that of the Fraternity's lands. The tenement was described as a void plot, presumably about to be built on.

The concern for exactitude extended also to ownership of the walls surrounding the tenement. John Wanstre and his co-burgesses described the boundary wall on the south side of the tenement behind no.43 Broad Street as 'one half belonging to the said Fraternity and the other half to John Clyve burgess'. The wall was divided down the middle. This was not simply recording an ancient state of affairs. It was current practice to divide responsibility for the boundary wall in this way. In 1415 Wanstre was part responsible for another view, on this occasion of no.34 Broad Street, which had recently been divided (Fig 4.4). In giving

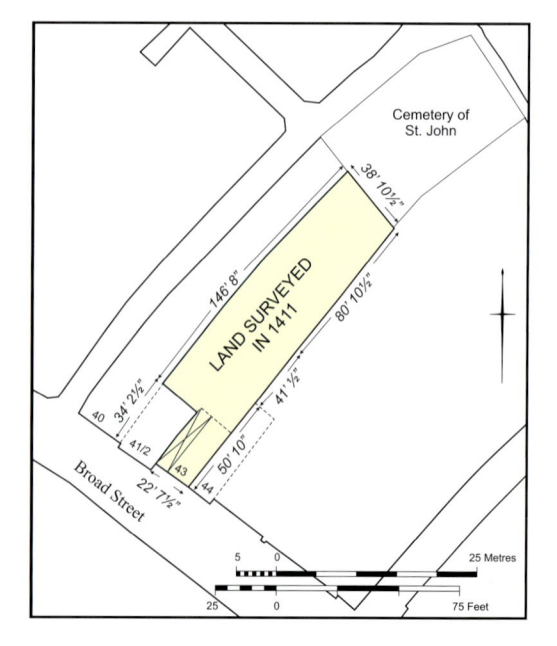

*Fig 4.3*
*Plan of Tailors' Court showing measurements made in 1411 in relation to surviving buildings and boundary walls; see also Fig 7.9 (RHL, PEC).*

*Fig 4.4 (left)*
*Plan of nos.33 and 34 Broad Street showing areas disputed in 1415 (RHL).*

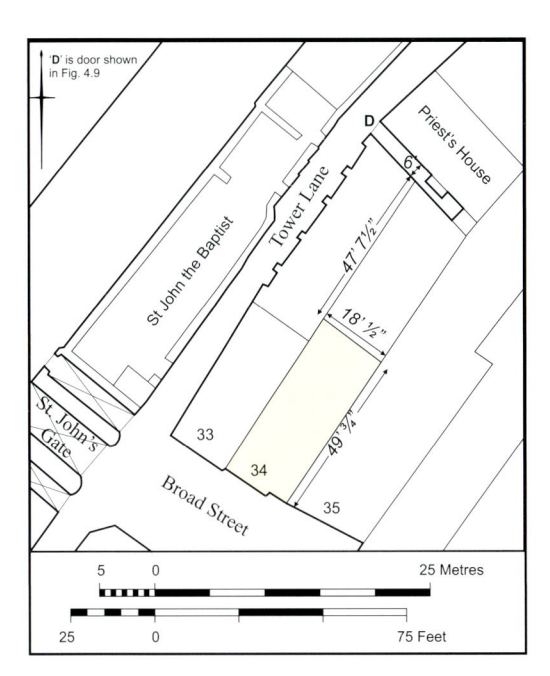

judgement the mayor decreed that 7in of the boundary wall between the two parts would belong to the house fronting Broad Street, 13in to the house behind. On this newly divided tenement, the two neighbours would thereafter be aware of their respective rights. For this purpose, it was of importance that the parish retained this document in the parish chest.[8] Awareness between two owners and their builders of their respective rights is graphically shown in the construction of the wall between the cellars of nos.42 and 43 High Street, both probably of the 15th century. The two sides of the wall were clearly separately constructed, at the same time, using different mortars (Fig 4.5).

Precise rights of ownership assumed an especial importance when it was thought that building works by a neighbour created damage, annoyance or trespass. In 1551 Thomas Welles, at no.27 Christmas Street, secured a view from the Mayor's Court of the damage done by the building works of his neighbour, Phillip Griffiths. These were well advanced by the date of the view. Various timbers had been placed without consent in Welles's walls, 11 along the length of Griffiths' hall and a further six along the length of his pentice (a sloping roof set against a wall), which was probably over a linking first-floor gallery, between his hall and parlour. The court found in Welles's favour. Griffiths was required to make good the damage to the tiles and lead on his neighbour's roof.

In these circumstances, attention often focused on the status of the boundary wall, and whether it was partable, that is a wall with ownership divided down its centre line, the parties on either side therefore each owning and being responsible for one-half of the structure. Over time the ownership of walls could be forgotten and building works were frequently commenced without regard for existing rights. In 1482 the Mayor's arbitrators adjudicated on a disagreement between John Hawkys, merchant, and Thomas Baker, grocer, 'upon a middle pane of a certain wall in High Street between the tenement of Hawkys on north side and the new tenement of [name omitted] Spicer on the south side'. They decreed that the wall was partable.[9] A similar dispute arose in 1472 in the building of Alison Chestre's new house at no.31 High Street, between her and Thomas Vyell, the gentleman owner of the house to the south and west, with regard to the boundary wall at the west end of the tenement plot. A view was obtained and the ruling of the Mayor's Court this time was that the wall was situated on Vyell's ground.[10]

On other occasions a ruling might be sought in advance of building works. In 1422 the parishioners of All Saints, as the owners of the Green Lattice at no.41 High Street, sought a ruling from the Mayor's Court in advance of their neighbour at no.40 rebuilding his house against theirs. The surveyors who undertook the view reported back with the measurements of

*Fig 4.5*
*The partable wall between the cellars of nos.42 and 43 High Street, visible in section during building works in 1979 (RHL).*

the plot and that the boundary 'wall is partable between the tenants'.[11] Some years later in 1439 the parishioners were rebuilding their property and needed a report on the extent to which their neighbours' houses impinged on their property: 'an foresamuch as the said tenement of the priests aforesaid overhangeth the ground of her said mess, for which cause they prayed the said mayor that a view might be had'.[12] The surveyors who reported back to the Mayor, two carpenters and two masons, found that no.42, a house belonging to the Chantry of Walter Frompton, overhung no.41 for a length of 23ft 9in 'abyght 8 inches'. The 'byndyngbeme' (probably the wall plate) of no.42 overhung by 4¼in. Further back no.42 overhung by 3¼in.

The practice of making walls partable continued at least until the end of the 18th century, by which date the ownership of the boundary walls was often explicitly stated in the covenants given in the lease for building. Typical of many was the stipulation in the lease for no.52 Kingsdown Parade of 1791. The walls between the house contracted to be built, and those on each side and between its garden and those adjacent, were to 'be partable'.[13] Disputes regarding boundaries are less easily identified after the mid-18th century, as the latest volume of views by the Mayor's Court is for the years 1653–1736.

### Security

A concern much reflected in the organisation of the tenement was security. The stone walls surrounding the tenement, the locked gates and entries providing access, the shutters and locks to the shops and houses of medieval and later Bristol were all expressions of this concern.

Tenements were provided with substantial stone boundary walls from at least the mid-12th century. At nos.127–9 Redcliff Street, the houses built in c 1150 either side of the common slip had substantial boundary walls extending to the quayside.[14] The provision of such walls was the norm from the 12th to at least the end of the 18th century. Evidence for the construction of boundary walls of the 12th to the 17th centuries has come almost entirely from archaeological excavations, the above instances from documentary sources being important exceptions.[15] Mid-18th-century views of the walled gardens of houses built in the 17th century (see Fig 9.35), the recorded and surviving walls of some streets in Kingsdown and Clifton, provide evidence of the continuing importance attached by townspeople to the effective and secure bounding of the tenement (Figs 4.6 and 4.7). The building leases for the houses in James's Place (now part of Kingsdown Parade), being built in 1791, required that the boundary walls between one

*Fig 4.6 Boundary walls on Marlborough Hill, Kingsdown, photograph of 2012 (English Heritage DP 152575).*

*Fig 4.7*
*Boundary walls below Cornwallis Crescent, Clifton, photograph of 2012 (English Heritage DP 146958).*

*Fig 4.8*
*Doorway in Leonard Lane, dating from the 15th century, now blocked, but formerly providing a rear access to no.10 Small Street; photograph of 2012 (English Heritage DP 146959).*

*Fig 4.9*
*The entrance door to the house or courtyard of Stephen Stepefast, its location shown in Fig 4.4, watercolour by T L Rowbotham, 1827 (BRSMG M2424).*

garden and its neighbours 'be of no greater height in the whole than eight feet nor less than six feet'.[16]

The well-barred door, providing access to an almost hidden property behind, was a characteristic feature of the narrow street in the tightly packed medieval city – an effective and practical symbol of status and power. One such door survives in Leonard Lane, dating from the 15th century, now blocked, but formerly providing a rear access to no.10 Small Street (Fig 4.8). A little further along the intramural lane, across Small Street and Broad Street and into Tower Lane, opposite the vestry door of St John's church, one would have come in the 15th century to a second such door (Fig 4.9). Well hung and set in a most substantial ashlar-faced, four-centred arched entrance, it provided access through a high stone wall to the tenement beyond.

For a stranger to this tenement, and to its occupier, the door very clearly signified the boundary between public and private space. The occupant in 1415 was Stephen Stepefast, one of the chaplains in St John's church on the opposite side of the lane. The doorway provided access to his tenement and also possibly to the back door of that of the Abbot of Malmesbury, at no.35 Broad Street (Figs 4.4 and 4.9). For Stepefast, this was the only access to his tenement and must have provided almost total security for his house.

Stepefast's front door would certainly have provided an effective barrier against drunks or unknown persons wandering the streets at night. That these might be a concern was shown in the 40 proclamations made by the city in the mid-14th century. These provide normative evidence, attempting to curb annoying behaviour documented in legislation. Among the edicts were just two that touched on the security of the tenement. After the nightly curfew had sounded, it was illegal to wander about the town by night without a lighted candle. Drunkenness may well have contributed to such problems, for it was also decreed that no taverner of wine or ale should keep any guests after the hour of curfew, but should immediately close all doors.[17]

Stepefast's solitary front door would, though, have had no place in the principal streets of the town. Here the frontages were lined with shops and houses and had been since at least the 13th century. Nevertheless, there was evidently the same concern with the security of the tenement. In the building of a new church house, at no.1 Broad Street in *c* 1493, the expenses of the proctors of St Ewen's included payments for the 'sprynge locke for the schoppe dore with a keye', together with a variety of locks and 'twystes' for use elsewhere in the house.[18] Maintenance works on houses in the 15th and early 16th century frequently required repairs and replacements. In 1534 a new lock and key was needed for William Wylkyns' 'howse strete dore' in Redcliff Street. In 1509 repairs on another house in Redcliff Street required a new key for the hall door, a further three new locks and keys and eight hasps for the shop windows.[19]

## Ancient Lights

Concern for the availability of natural light must have increased as buildings were constructed to a greater number of storeys and were placed closer together. Problems would have been greatest for the inhabitants of narrower plots. In such situations, light was sometimes taken from an adjacent tenement, with strategies to take light in this way being implemented before the end of the 13th century. The builder of the hall house at no.59 Baldwin Street, Seyer's 'chapel', was able to borrow light from the plot to the east. The occupier of the open hall at no.5 Temple Street benefited in this way from light taken from the tenement to the south (Fig 4.10). At no.24 Christmas Street, the back part of the tenement was occupied by a parlour block of the 13th century, its windows facing on to the rear part of the tenement to the north. Positioned in a similar way by that date was no.44 Broad Street, one of the tenements bounding the area surveyed in 1411. The parlour block, at the rear of the tenement, was lit from Tailors' Court to the north.

One plot to the south, the ground floor of the 12th-century house at nos.51–2 Broad Street, occupying a much wider tenement, was also lit from the plot to the north by a narrow slit window (Fig 4.11). In all these instances no record of the right to take light from the adjoining tenement has been traced, but in each

*Fig 4.10*
*Open hall at no.5 Temple Street, lit from window opening on to property to south; see also p 75 (BCRL Collections for Bristol by G W Braikenridge vol xxii, Temple Parish, fol 291, Mirror Office 1843, 220–1).*

it may have originated in agreements between the owners of adjacent plots.

Light could also be a source of conflict, as in the dispute between Thomas Ryder, a skinner, living in Corn Street in 1574 and John Curtis, a cook, and his neighbour in All Saints Lane. This was the subject of another view. Ryder had been carrying out building works on his boundary with Curtis and had taken some breathtaking liberties in taking these on to Curtis's land. The first of these was a new shed or pentice, said to 'trusse owte and hange over' Curtis's pavement by a full 20in, causing great annoyance and hindrance to Curtis in the 'dymynyshyng' of his light.

## Drains

Another concern that arose from the relationship of the tenement to its neighbours was that of drainage. The engineering of drains was generally facilitated by the natural topography of the oldest part of the city. Drains could flow away from tenements towards the intramural lanes, and thence beyond the walls. The drain from the garderobe of the 12th-century house in Tower Lane, for example, could have operated in this way. In the suburbs set out in the 12th century, the backs of tenements in a number of streets were immediately adjacent to the Frome or the Avon, or to one of the law ditches marking the major boundaries between blocks of properties. To what extent the streets were lined with drains by the 12th century is uncertain.

Co-operation between neighbours was necessary when direct access to the rivers or law ditches was impossible. Such an occurrence was probably most frequent in the heavily subdivided area close to the carfax. In 1310 Henry Pye, the lessee of no.41 High Street, was able to grant an easement to his neighbour Roger Apperlugh at no.40 for a drain to run out of no.40 and through Henry's tenement, provided that it ran freely.[20] Cleaning was to be at their joint expense, indicating that this was part of a collaborative project – possibly another now lost easement taking the drain through into All Saints' churchyard and probably then into All Saints Lane, where there was 'a common gowt'. In 1421 the parish granted a similar easement, this time for a drain from the chaplain's house, across the churchyard and into All Saints Lane.[21]

On other occasions townspeople secured consent for their own individual projects from their neighbours. In 1342 Walter Goby held no.23 Wine Street, extending back to the old town wall. He was able to secure an easement from his neighbour, William Hooke, who held a much larger tenement at no.24, extending back to the new town wall and the Frome. This gave Goby permission to connect into Hooke's drain, provided that his works were made with 'competent' stone walls and that they were maintained at Goby's expense. This drain was still in use in 1423, connected to the latrine of no.23, the easement confirmed by the new owners of no.24.[22]

Drains could also be a source of conflict. Philip Langley purchased no.39 High Street in March 1565, and by December he had secured from the Mayor's Court a view or inspection of the drainage system connecting his property to the 'common gowt' at the back of Gillows Inn – probably that into which the All Saints Lane

Fig 4.11
Ground floor of the 12th-century house at nos.51–2 Broad Street, lit from the plot to the north by a narrow slit window, photograph of probably the late 19th or early 20th century (BRSMG Pl. 712).

drain flowed. Langley's drain passed first into that running through the 'entry' or entrance of his neighbour William Pyll at no.38A, on whom fell the responsibility for resolving the problem. It was certainly much more convenient for Langley to route his drains in this way, since the entire width of his property was occupied by cellars.[23]

The dispute in 1574 between Thomas Ryder and John Curtis also extended to encompass drainage problems. To add insult to injury, further along his boundary with Curtis, Ryder had built his new 'howse of office', or latrine, a 'full three foot four inches' out on to Curtis's land. Over and above using his neighbour's land for his own sanitation, he had also obstructed the drain from Curtis's own 'necessary' r latrine.[24]

It must be remembered that disputes and easements are known about through being carefully recorded in documents. Records of what was normal and accepted do not survive in the same way, at least not from before the 16th or 17th centuries. In this context, the mention in the view of Philip Langley's property of the 'common gowte' at the back of Gillows Inn in 1565 is of importance. Specifically it provides a clue to the former existence of a street or lane continuing the line of All Saints Lane down to St Nicholas Street, emerging through the entrance to Gillows Inn. More generally it hints at the network of common drains that may have existed, and to which most tenements may have had access without dispute or record. One such drain would have been that recorded down the middle of Chequer Lane, recorded in the archaeological excavations of tenements between Narrow Wine Street and Peter Street (Fig 4.12).[25] Responsibility for the construction and maintenance of such drains rested most probably with the Corporation.

The disputes between Langley and Pyll, and Ryder and Curtis, were centred upon tenements in the most intensely subdivided area close to the carfax. Disputes also arose in the less densely settled part of the town, but not with the same

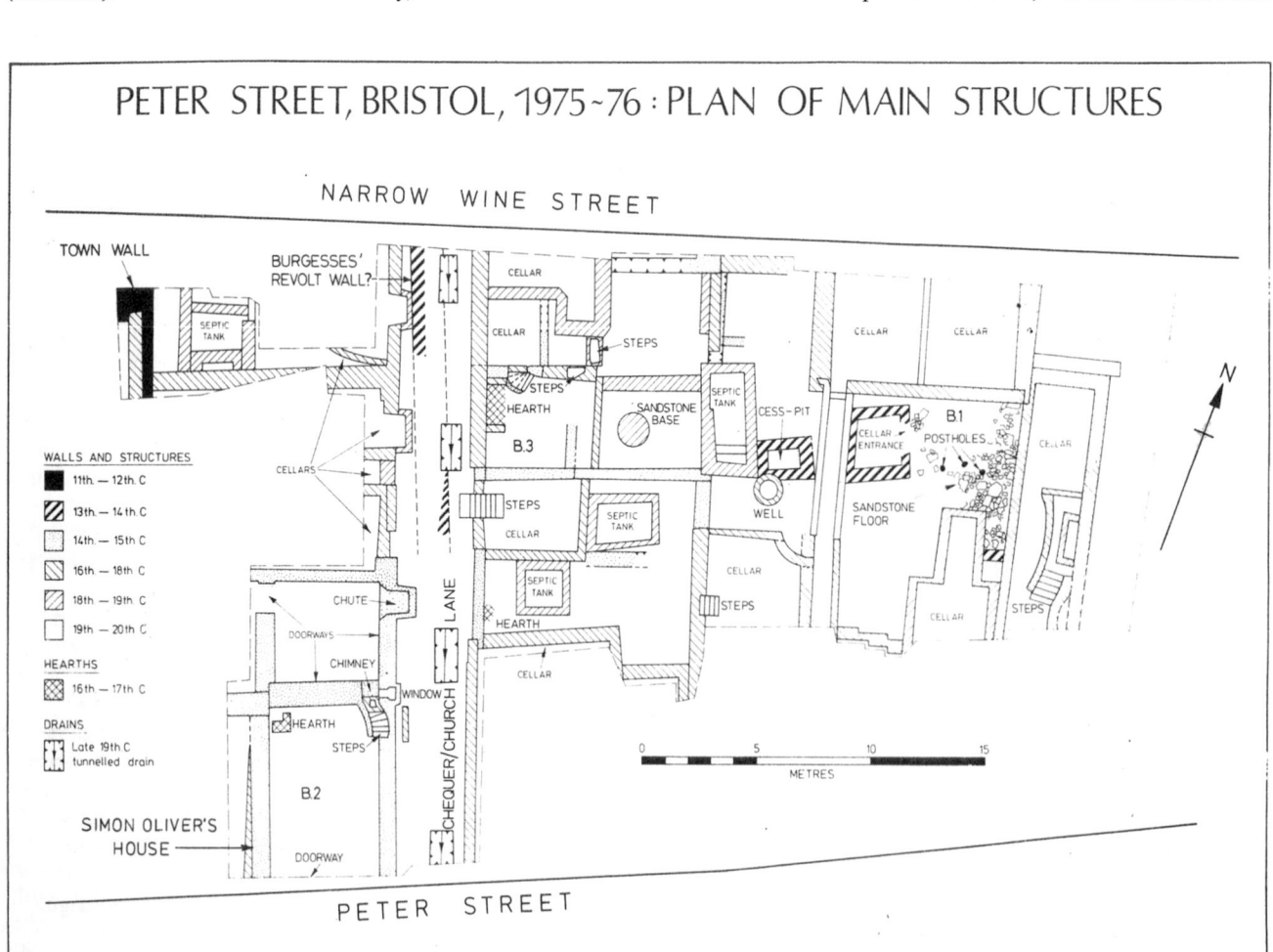

*Fig 4.12*
*Plan of excavations at Chequer Lane, showing medieval drain in centre of street*
*(Boore 1982).*

frequency. It was not surprisingly in the areas where most people lived closest together that the definition of the tenement, and its relation to neighbouring ownerships and rights, assumed the greatest importance.

## The Tenement and the Street

The importance to the owners or occupiers of the medieval tenement of its frontage to the street for commercial purposes is obvious enough. There was also, though, a deeper and more symbolic attachment to the street front. This is evident first in the later 13th and 14th centuries, from the relationship between larger houses and the street.

It has been said that larger houses were frequently set back from the street, the frontage occupied by shops: 'it would be very natural to use the ground floor of the street front for shops, especially in the main streets of a town'.[26] This 'gave the wealthy resident privacy and space, and was an economic use of the land next to the street, which had a high value because of the opportunities it offered for trading'.[27] A closer reading of the evidence for the planning of medieval town houses in Bristol will show that the situation may have been more complex.

In 1307 John Dinnyng took a lease of a shop with a solar above, in Gropecuntelane. This extended back to the tenement of Adam de Temple at the rear and to one side. On the ground floor his shop extended only to the *porticus* or entry of Adam de Temple's house. On the floor above his solar extended as far as Adam's stone house. To one side of the entry, but not to the other, was the front part of Adam's own house. This was described in 1322 as a hall with an entry, but it clearly extended forward to the street, and was prominent there through being built in stone. The adjacent shop, with solar above, let to Dinnyng, was presumably built in timber.[28] The ground floor of Adam's stone house might also have been a shop, but on the floor above would have been his own solar. Adam's house was not therefore set back from the street in its entirety. Rather it retained its own street frontage – marked out, through being built in stone, from the other parts, which were let.

A similar arrangement is evident in the planning of Richard Spicer's house on Welsh Back, as built *c* 1350 (*see* Fig 5.34). The open hall was set back behind two shops on the street frontage, which were separately leased by the mid-15th century and which could not have been structurally connected to Spicer's hall behind. The two shops lay to the north of the entry to the house, which served also as a cross-passage. On the south side of the passage, there was a different arrangement. This part was not leased separately from the house behind until the 17th century. It can be inferred that Spicer's house came forward to the street and that, on the first and second floors, it probably oversailed the entry.

A similar disposition of main house and shops was possibly implemented on several tenements in Baldwin Street, in the narrow strip of land extending back to the old town wall. At nos.33–5 an open hall, with a storeyed chamber at the west end, was set back from the street (Fig 4.13). By 1407 the property was described as a tenement and three shops; the tenement could be interpreted as being the larger property, set back behind the shops. Part of this tenement may, however, have extended forward to the street. The entry leading to the cross-passage was on the street frontage, through a stone two-centred arched doorway, probably of the later 13th century, built after the abandonment of the old town wall.

On one side of the doorway, stone corbelling supported a side wall, jettied at the front to correspond with the superstructure of the shop frontage; from the thickness of the side wall, it must have been of stone. The entrance and front wall of no.17 Temple Street were of similar date and construction (Figs 4.14 and 4.15).[29] The arrangement here was possibly identical to that of the tenement in Gropecuntelane, a stone house coming forward to the street on one side of the entry. The plan was also then possibly the

*Fig 4.13*
*Nos.33–5 Baldwin Street, ground-floor window to storeyed range at west end of medieval house, watercolour by T L Rowbotham, 1827 (BRSMG M2301).*

*Fig 4.14 (below left)*
*Nos.33–5 Baldwin Street, stone entrance doorway, probably to former screens passage, watercolour by H O'Neill, 1823 (BRSMG M2300).*

*Fig 4.15 (below right)*
*No.17 Temple Street, stone entrance doorway, probably to former screens passage, watercolour by H O'Neill, 1821 (BRSMG M2126).*

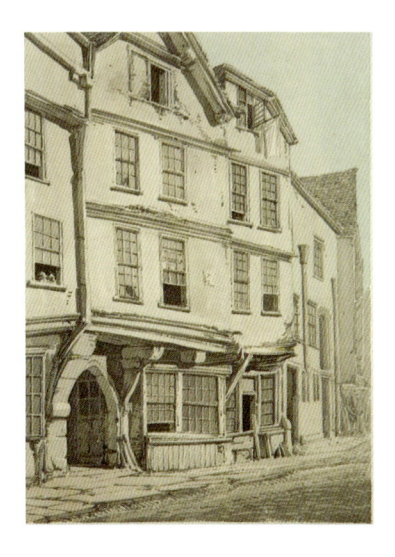

same as for Spicer's house: the open hall of the larger house set back behind shops, the storeyed end to the open hall projecting forwards to the street.[30]

Further instances of this arrangement can be inferred from the plans or descriptions of other tenements in the medieval city. Further to the east in Baldwin Street was a property known by the 15th century as 'le Thoroughouse', owned by William Canynges. An open hall was evidently set back from the street, the property in Canynges' ownership coming forward to the street only at the east end, partly over the line of the cross-passage. It can be inferred that the shops in front of the open hall had been sold as separate freeholds by the 15th century. This property too was in the strip of land below the town wall, developed in the later 13th century.[31] In Wine Street, Haddons Tavern, no.63 and the adjacent properties, were possibly of similar plan. No.63, projecting forward into Wine Street, would have been the storeyed end of the hall, with a range extending to the street. Nos.64–6 Wine Street and nos.1–2 High Street were possibly the shops in front of the property, created as separate freeholds before the grant of the main tenement to St Augustine's Abbey in the early 13th century.[32]

Embedded in these complex plans were the attitudes of some of the more influential citizens towards commerce and the street. In them can be read the balance struck by an original owner, desiring to take a profit from the leases of shops, but wishing also to have a presence on the street front. The richness of the street doorway, often heavily decorated and sometimes emphasised by a porch, hinted at the hidden riches behind and announced the property as one belonging to someone of wealth and power.[33] Furthermore, although the ground floor of the owner's part might often be let as a shop, the owner's chambers above would have given a powerful view of the street and its commerce. Standing at the window of his 'forestreet chamber', Richard Spicer or his successor Robert Sturmy would have looked out over the entry of his house to the waterfront: in one direction to the Bridge, in another to the wharfs and warehouses between Redcliff Street and the river. Rather than being isolated from the bustle and business of the street, the houses of the wealthiest residents might often have offered both quiet and privacy on the one hand and an eye to the town on the other. Chapter 10 will return to the importance of the forestreet chamber.

# 5

# The Hallhouse

## The Hallhouse in the Medieval and Later Town

Chapter 1 has described how in the late medieval town the recording of individual properties' rental values was facilitated by the identification of different types of tenement. A clear distinction was drawn between 'hallhouses', or halls, and 'shophouses', or shops.[1] In 1412 John Droys, collector of rents for the Seymour estate, described most properties as either hall or shop, and occasionally as 'hall and shop'.[2] The halls and shops listed in the Droys rent roll were widely distributed across the early 15th-century city, accounting for over three-quarters of the estate.

Towards the end of the 15th century, in 1473, the clerk of Canynges' charity at St Mary Redcliff used the terms 'hallhouse' and 'shophouse' in his rent roll. No explanation was given in the relevant documents for how the distinction was drawn, nor were any definitions of the terms provided – an omission which suggests that the terms were in common usage and unambiguous, at least for some purposes.

The question arises of how students of medieval urban housing should interpret the terms. What can we infer from these descriptions? To John Droys the distinction between hall and shop was one linked intimately to the rents that might be collected. In 1412 the yearly rents for a property including a hall were generally two to three times the rent for a shop in the same street. In the rental of 1473 for the Canynges' chantry properties, the rents for shophouses were without exception less than those charged for hallhouses. The terms 'shophouse' and 'hallhouse', or 'shop' and 'hall', were possibly shorthand used to distinguish individual house categories. Once identified in such terms, the reference would immediately have a financial context to anyone reading the rental.

The interpretation adopted for this study ties these terms to the types of urban property identified from architectural evidence. The 'hallhouse' is here defined as a property or tenement distinguished by the existence of a hall of impressive appearance, usually the principal element within the late medieval dwelling and open to the roof. In 15th-century London and Bristol the open hall was to be found principally in larger houses. There is no evidence from Bristol for rows of smaller, open-hall houses such as those known from Tewkesbury, Coventry, Battle or Sandwich. The closest parallel in Bristol is the row of 12 or more houses in Averynge's Hayes at nos.69–78 St Thomas Street. Known in the accounts of St Mary Redcliff as Haveryng's, they are probably the 'shops' built for John Haveryng by 1416[3]. Each was $c$ 16ft wide and 20ft in depth, comparable to the houses in Church Street, Tewkesbury which were $c$ 12ft wide and 20ft in depth with a lean-to behind. When excavated in 2006 only the parts of the St Thomas Street houses furthest away from the street could be examined, so the detailed plans remain unknown. A second similar row in Bristol was at nos.69–72 Redcliff Street, where excavations in 1982 revealed at least three houses with open hearths. These houses, 17–18ft in width and of $c$ 40ft or more in depth (Figs 5.1a and 5.1b), were substantially larger than those recorded in Church Street, Tewkesbury, for instance.

The hall was invariably accompanied on the plot by other buildings or rooms to provide what was required for the needs of a household: service rooms, other living rooms and in some cases work rooms. Houses with open halls might or might not have one or more shops on the street frontage: in the same ownership as the buildings behind, these shops might be in separate occupation. Documentary and architectural evidence suggests that 'shophouses' can be defined as separately owned dwellings, generally consisting only of a shop on

# THE TOWN HOUSE IN MEDIEVAL AND EARLY MODERN BRISTOL

*Fig 5.1*
*Houses in rows, examples shown at a common scale for comparative size:*
*a) nos.69-78 Redcliff Street, plan showing 12th- and 13th-century phases of houses with open hearths and therefore open halls (Jones 1983, Fig 2);*
*b) the row of houses of even depth in Averyng's Hayes, nos.69-78 St Thomas Street, built in the 15th century, shown here on a plan of the late 18th century (BRO P/PStMR/E/1);*
*c) the row at Church Street, Tewkesbury (after Platt 1976 and Jones 1968).*

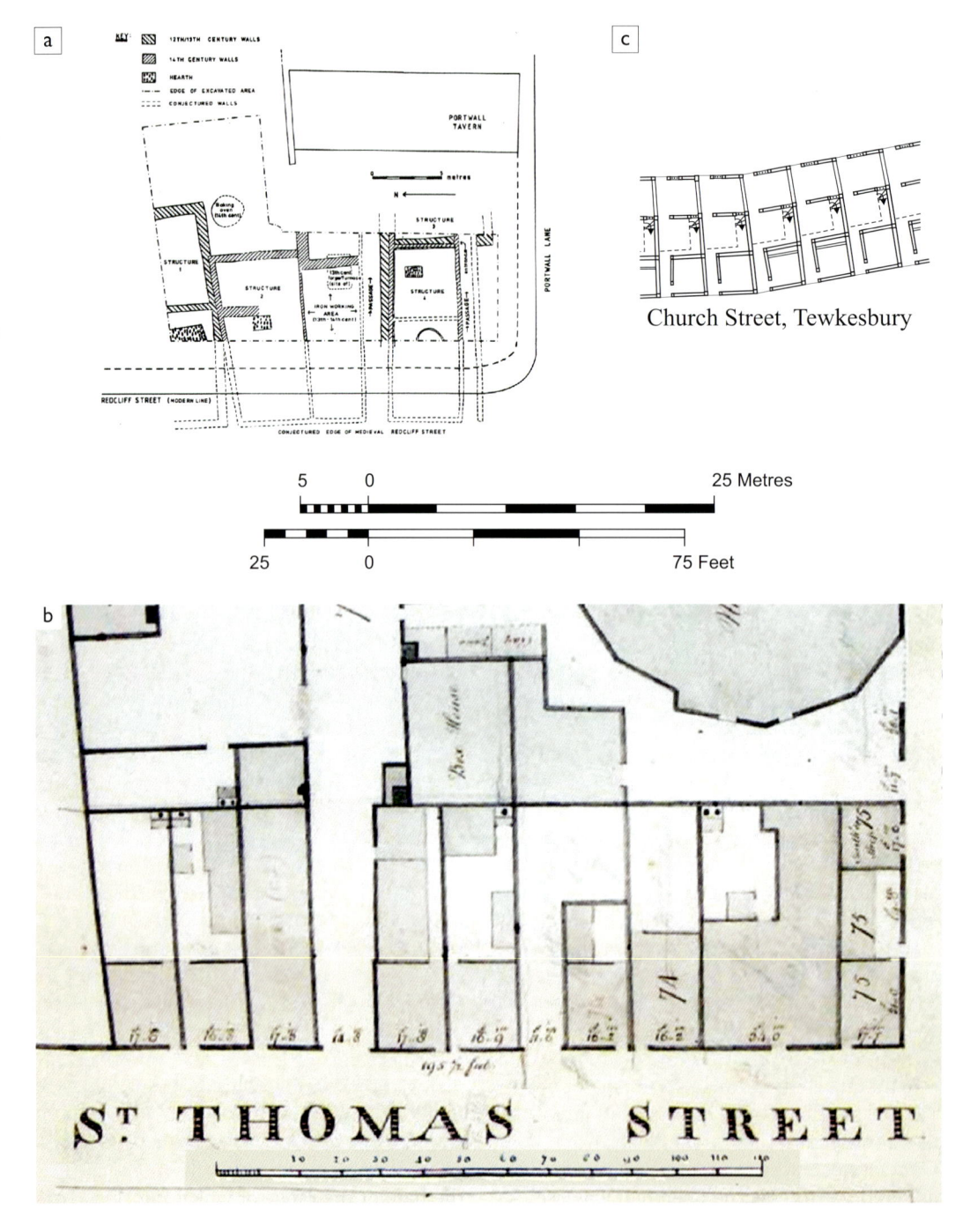

the ground floor and living rooms on the floor or floors above. They were, therefore, usually much smaller than hallhouses, although some multi-storeyed buildings could give more accommodation than suggested by their restricted 'footprint'. Written and material evidence combines, therefore, to suggest social distinctions between those who could afford only a house of one or more rooms built over the shop, sometimes with no heating, and, at the opposite extreme, those who had the means to live in a larger house with a hall open to the roof and comprising a substantial part of the house overall.

This chapter will examine houses which contained an impressive hall and seek to demonstrate how significant changes in customs, social relations and behaviour affected the way in which the house as a whole, and the open hall in particular, were used at different levels of society in Bristol in the medieval and early modern periods. The changes were signalled in the 1370s in Langland's lament that 'now hath each rich man a rule to eaten by himself in a privy parlour … or in a chamber with a chimney, and leave the chief hall, that was made for meals, for men to eaten in'.[4] This complaint has been quoted often enough, but the impact that this social change might have had on the purpose and use of the open hall in the late medieval town has not been much investigated. It is necessary therefore to investigate whether new lifestyles developed as a result of wealthier citizens now using the parlour as the principal social centre of the house, and whether less wealthy citizens aspired to this same lifestyle. In answering these questions we will discover that citizens of the 16th and 17th centuries continued to see the open hall as a significant space within the house.

## The Demise of the Open Hall

Eric Mercer, the author of *English Vernacular Houses*, concluded that in rural England the open hall remained the principal room of the house until the 16th century, though its demise was foreshadowed by the gradual introduction of chimneys and smoke bays to replace open hearths, and by the reduction in size of the hall to provide more storeyed accommodation. By the early 16th century the open hall in the houses of the aristocracy had ceased to be a living room, now serving as an imposing entry to the house. Those of lower rank followed suit in seeing the open hall as obsolete.[5] In the countryside these changes have been seen as part of a wider pattern of emerging individualism: what has been termed closure.[6] There these changes would have affected most of the population.

In the late medieval and early modern city this may not have been so. The work and life of the urban household were very different from those of its rural counterpart. Yet there has been little discussion as to how the open hall was used in large urban centres, or of how such use changed through time – possibly because information on this is not easily found. In the late 14th century some rich citizens may have retreated to the parlour, while other townspeople may have continued to use the open hall as the social centre of the house. For others the open hall was not an essential feature of urban life. As has been seen (and will be investigated further in the next chapter), a substantial number of households may have lived in 'shophouses', without open halls.

Alongside issues concerning the use of the open hall, there are questions concerning its abandonment in an urban context. It must be asked whether townspeople ceased to build and live in houses with open halls for different reasons, and at different times, from their rural counterparts. In seeking to understand social change in the early modern city, the identification of distinctly urban trajectories of changing lifestyles may be of some significance.

## The Construction and Planning of the Urban Hallhouse

The evidence for the construction of hallhouses in Bristol spans the 12th to the 15th or 16th centuries. The extent to which those houses with open halls built and used in these centuries were suited to the needs of townspeople may be looked at from several perspectives. Insights into the strategies of those building or rebuilding such houses may be sought through the analysis of tenement and house plans, looking particularly for the problems inherent in adapting the design of a rural plan and form to an urban situation. Social action within the house, and possibly the ways in which this changed over time, may be considered through the archaeological and documentary evidence for the use of space. In some instances similar evidence may permit the identification of households, providing a context for the hallhouse and its changing use within the social structure of the town.

As in other towns, builders in Bristol adapted the layout and construction of the hallhouse to the constraints of the urban environment. In fitting the hallhouse to a tenement plot, the builder had a choice. If it was set parallel to the street, it was constrained by the width of the plot. If disposed at right angles, however, then the hall, or the range of which it formed part, could be much longer. A further consideration was the storage space and potential rental income that might be obtained from the cellarage that could be placed below the hall.

Such constraints would have been greatest on the narrowest tenement plots. The records of some 15 hallhouses located on narrow plots (the 15 as discussed below) provide a sample from which the strategies devised by builders for the development of the tenement plot can be examined. Where the rear parts of tenements were to be given over to a particular commercial

*Fig 5.2*
*No.87 Redcliff Street (shown here as Building 1 with an open hearth), plan showing 12th-century and later phases (Williams 1981, Fig 4).*

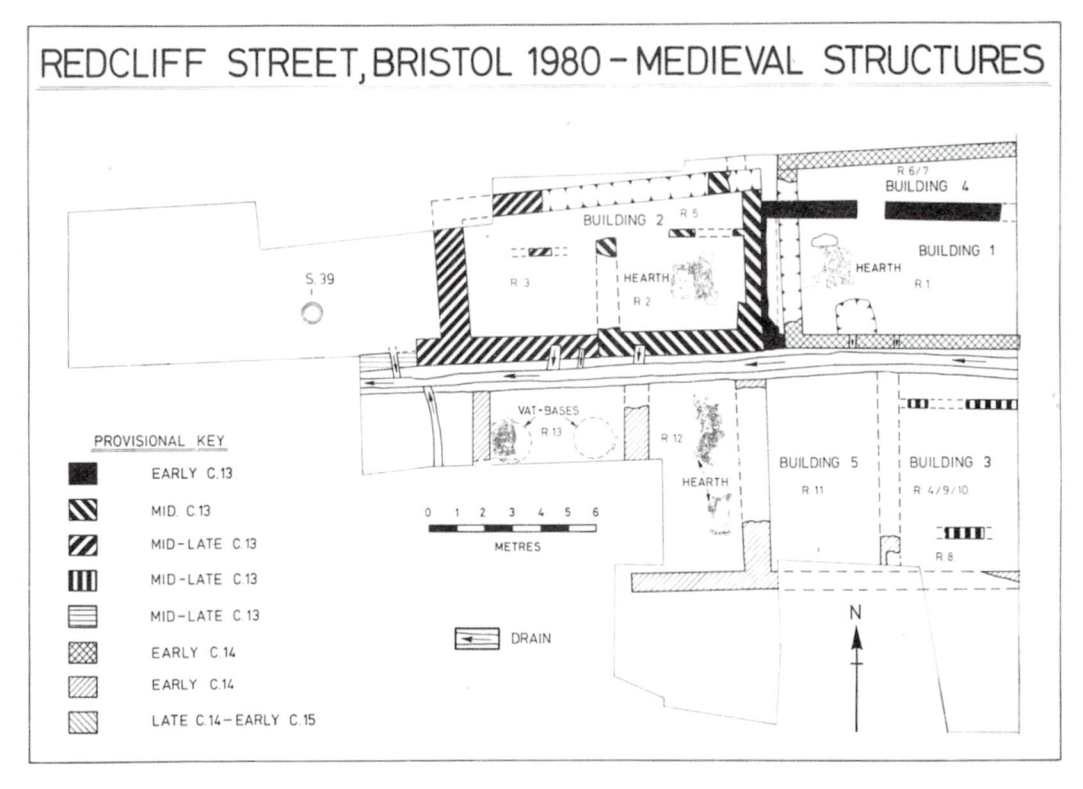

or industrial use, then such strategies would necessarily have embraced the plot as a whole; such information is most likely to come from archaeological excavation.

In Redcliff Street the majority of the houses being built in the 12th and 13th centuries appear from available archaeological evidence to have been set at right angles to the street. Some at least can be argued from the internal siting of open hearths to have been built as hallhouses. At no.87 Redcliff Street the construction of a hallhouse on a plot 20ft wide can now be dated to the early to mid-12th century (Fig 5.2).[7] A side passage provided access to yards, or buildings not identified archaeologically, and the quayside. A little to the north, excavations of the site of Canynges' House have shown that the two phases of 12th-century building at no.95 were of structures set at right angles to the street, but we cannot be certain that these were hallhouses. Across the street, away from the river frontage, nos.70–2 Redcliff Street consisted by the 14th century of three structures at right angles to the street, on plots of 17–18ft in width (Fig 5.1a). Of these no.72 was certainly a hallhouse, a passage on the south side providing access to the rear. At no.144 Redcliff Street a hallhouse extended back at right angles to the street frontage with a passage on the north side (Fig 5.3).

*Fig 5.3*
*No.144 Redcliff Street, side wall of hallhouse at right angles to the street, with window lighting the open hall (RHL).*

# THE HALLHOUSE

A number of other hallhouses of similar plan – a rectangular structure set at right angles to the street, with an open hall occupying the rear part – were placed on similarly constrained sites in other streets. North of the Avon, in the Marsh suburb, nos.15/16 and 17 Baldwin Street may have consisted of single ranges running back from the street, the remnants of the open hall structures shown on early 19th-century watercolours (Figs 5.4 and 5.5). In the walled suburb on the north side, in Christmas Street, nos.1 and 2 on the west side (Fig 5.6) and no.24 on the east side (Fig 5.7), were hallhouses built in the 14th or 15th centuries. In the centre of the town no.41 High Street was built between 1439 and 1442 as a single long range with a lofty open hall set over extensive cellars (Figs 5.8a, 5.8b and 5.8c). Whether the existence on other sites of long cellars of medieval date, running back from the street, can be used as evidence for the former presence of open halls above is not entirely clear; but such cellars existed, for instance, in Broad Street, Corn Street and High Street (chapter 7).

The hallhouses we have discussed thus far appear to have consisted of a single range running back from the street which included an open hall towards the rear. A more complex design, taking more land on a narrow tenement plot, featured the hallhouse as a separate range, contiguous to – but structurally or tenurially distinct from – a range on the street frontage. No.5 Temple Street, with an open hall of the 13th century, was of this plan (Figs 5.9, 5.10a and 5.10b). So was no.124 Temple Street (Figs 5.9, 5.10a, 5.10b and 5.10c), built at least as early as the 15th century; this can be argued from its plan to have included an open hall. Similarly placed was the open hall behind nos.35–6 High Street, the Cock in the Hoop (Figs 5.13a and 5.13b).

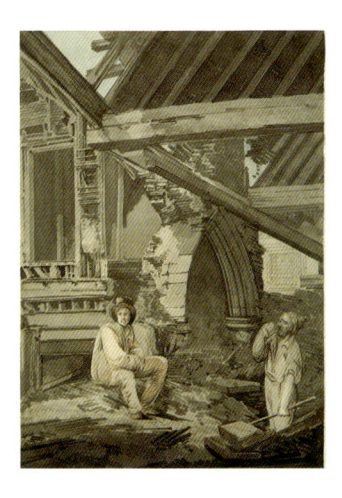

*Fig 5.4*
Nos.15/16 Baldwin Street, arcaded side wall of hallhouse at right angles to the street, watercolour by H O'Neill, 1823 (BRSMG M2223).

*Fig 5.5*
No.17 Baldwin Street, hallhouse at right angles to the street, watercolour by H O'Neill, 1823 (BRSMG M2217).

*Fig 5.6*
No.1 Christmas Street, hallhouse (drawing for Sir George Oatley in private collection).

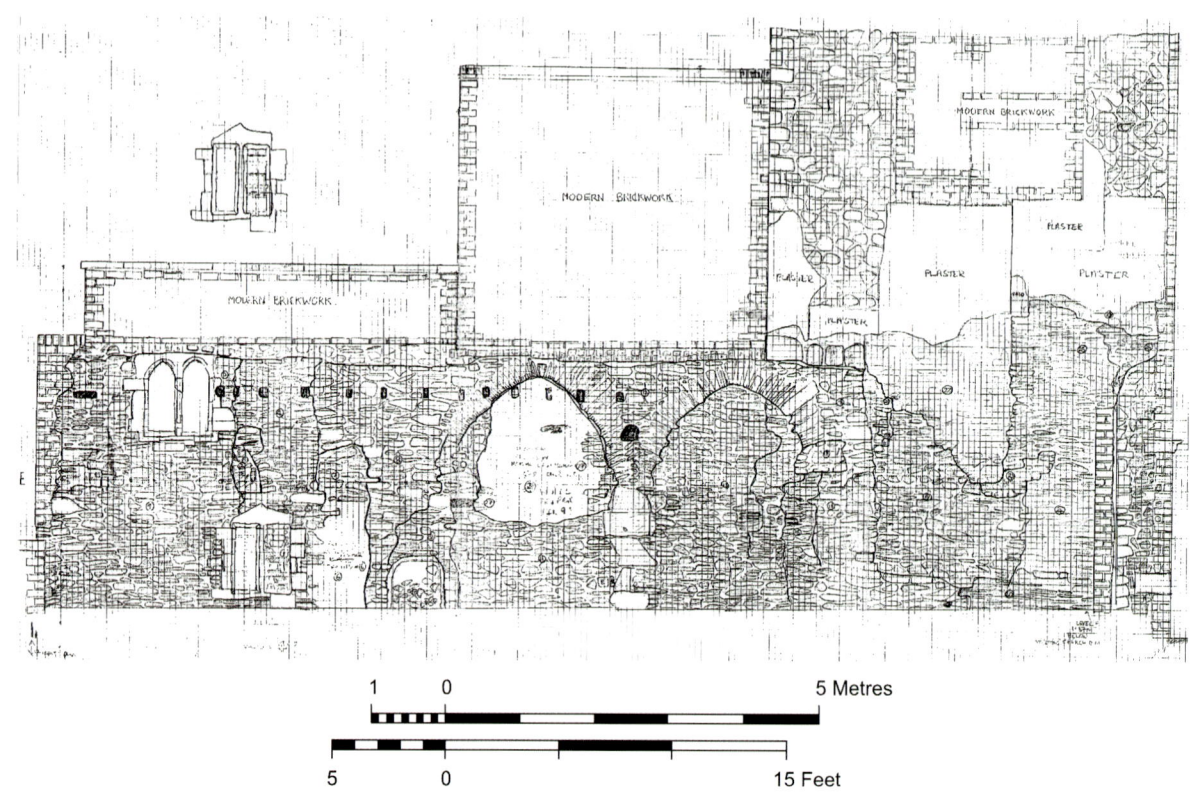

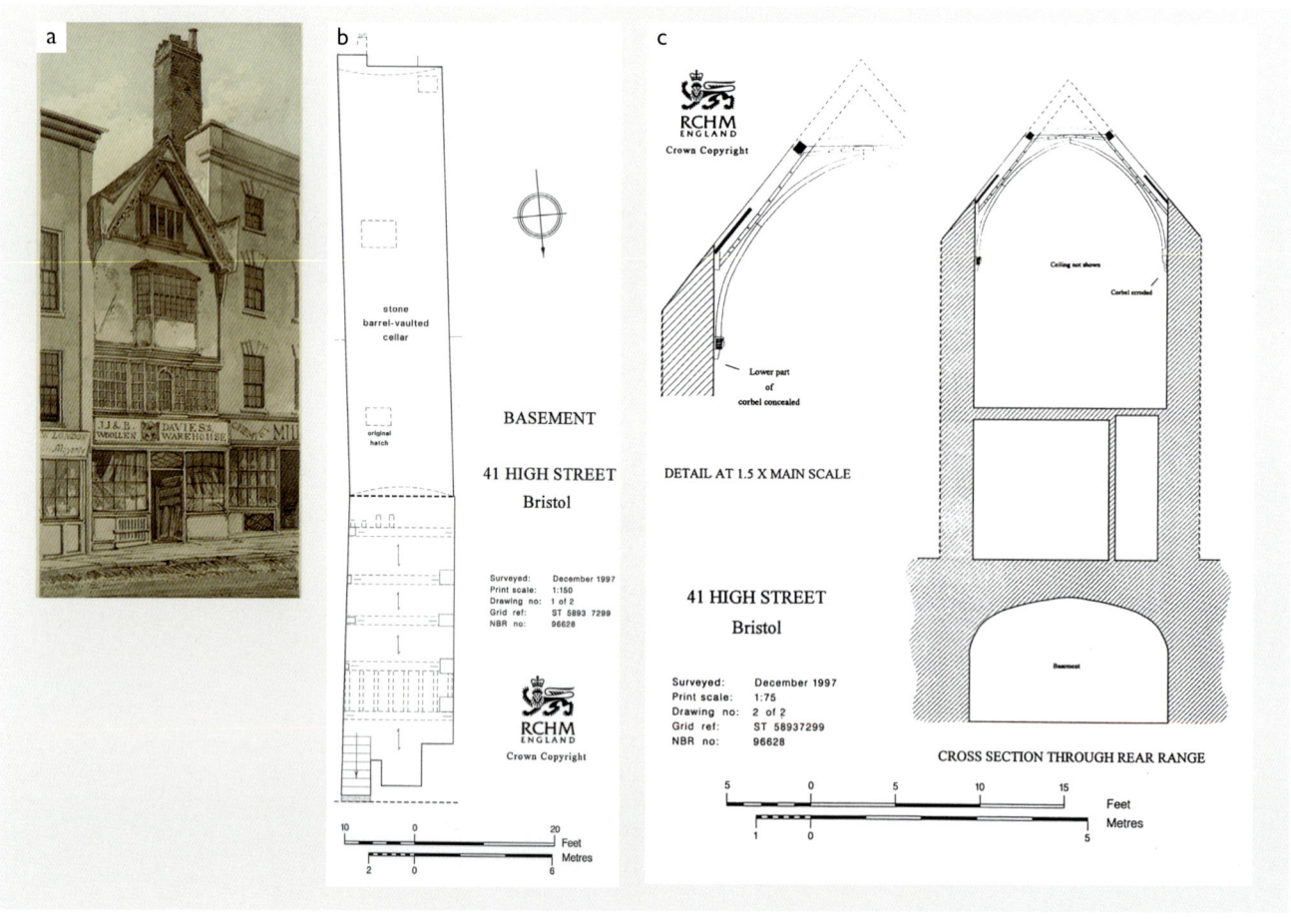

# THE TOWN HOUSE IN MEDIEVAL AND EARLY MODERN BRISTOL

THE HALLHOUSE

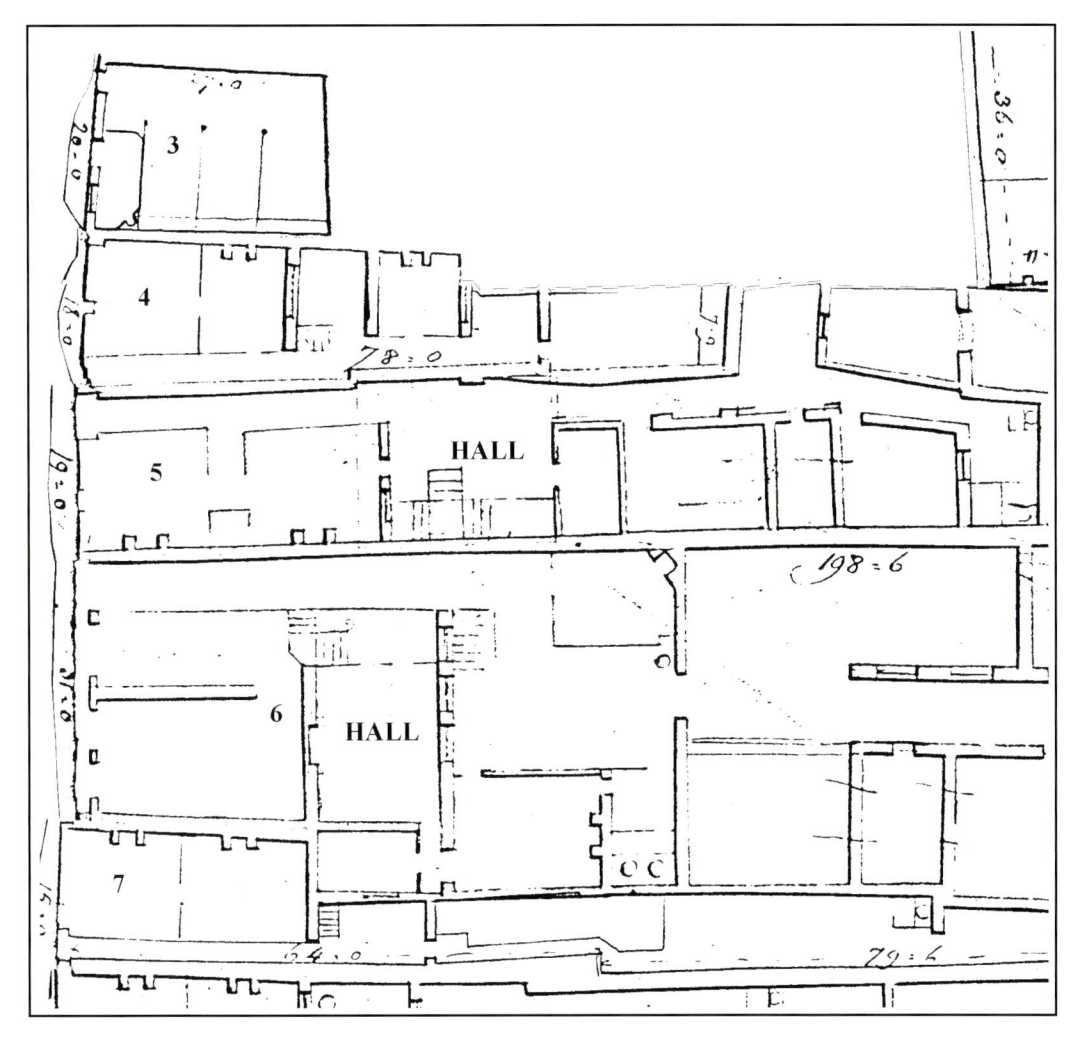

*Fig 5.7 (opposite, above)
No.24 Christmas Street,
hallhouse
(BRSMG drawing located by
Jon Brett, now in the
Bristol City Council Historic
Environment Record).*

*Fig 5.8 (opposite, below)
No.41 High Street:
a) watercolour by H O'Neill
of 1823 (BRSMG M2387);
b) plan of the house;
c): section of the house
(RCHME).*

*Fig 5.9 (left)
Nos.4–7 Temple Street,
plans of c 1804–5 showing
houses with halls
(BRO P.Tem/H/1
fols 29–32).*

*Fig 5.10 (below)'
No.5 Temple Street:
a), b) and c) – blind and
open arcades to open hall
shown in watercolours of
between 1822 and 1825
by H O'Neill. For plan
see Fig 5.9
(BRSMG M 2154–6).*

*Fig 5.11 (above)
No.124 Temple Street, plan and elevation of 1816 (BRO P/StT/Ch/3/31 fol 2).*

*Fig 5.12 (right)
No.124 Temple Street, interpretative plan (RHL).*

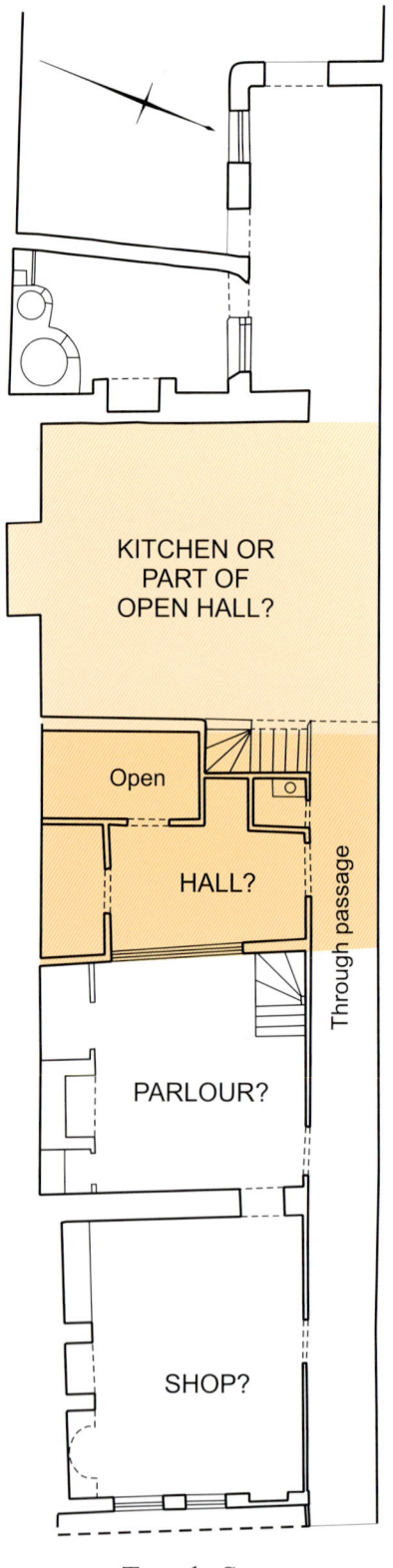

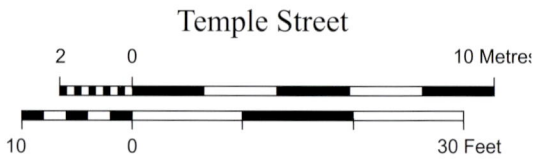

THE HALLHOUSE

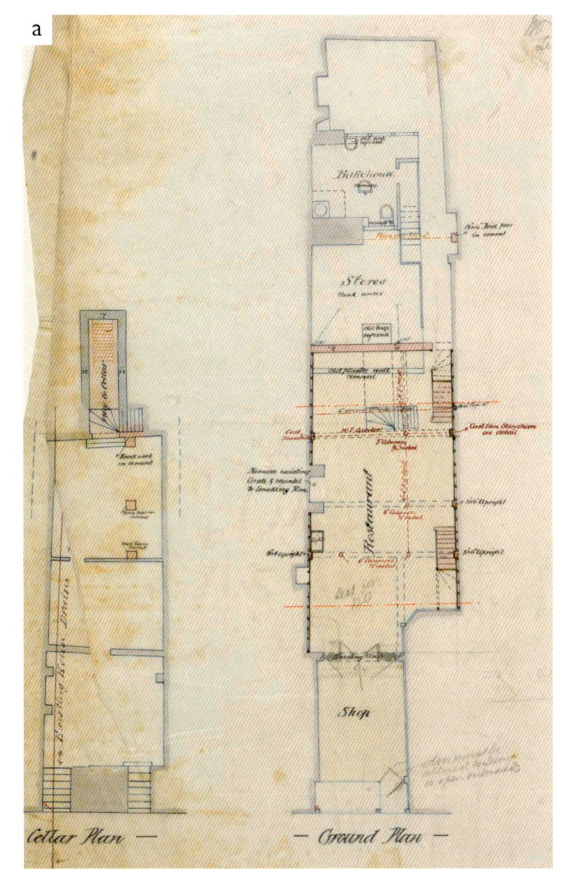

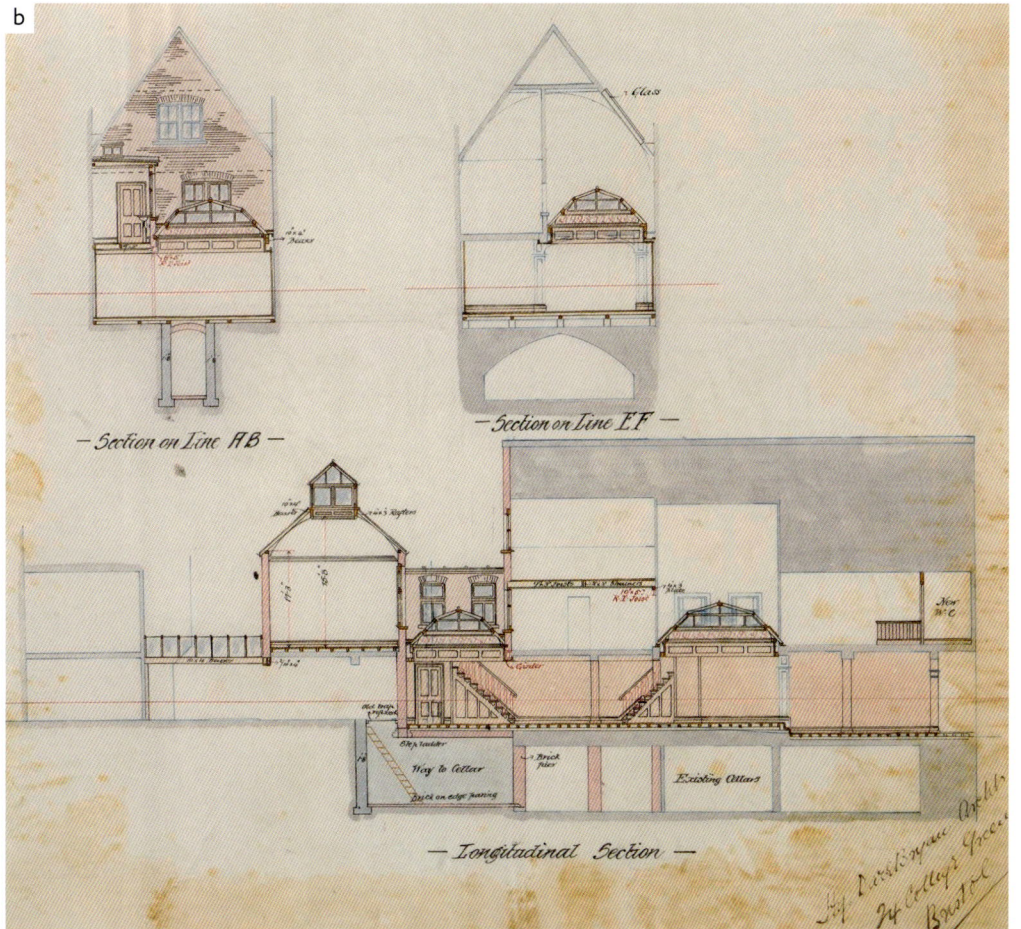

*Fig 5.13*
*Nos.35–6 High Street, the Cock in the Hoop, showing open hall with cellar below, behind street frontage:*
*a) plans of cellar and ground floors;*
*b) longitudinal section (BRO building plans vol 26, fol 26, drawings of 1890, English Heritage DP 146971, 146969).*

On wider plots, builders designed the hallhouse so as to be set parallel to the street. The narrowest of the plots for which we have relevant evidence, and the only one under 30ft wide, was no.59 Baldwin Street (pp7–10). Here a hallhouse *c* 28ft in length, built in the mid-13th century, was placed so as to occupy the whole width of the plot. Unusually it was set right at the rear of the plot, with its front wall 50ft from the street frontage and its rear wall right against the steep slope below the Saxon town wall. Further to the north-west, hallhouses at nos.31–4 and 36–9 Baldwin Street were similarly placed on the slope between the old wall and Baldwin Street – set back from the latter, but on wider plots (p22, 24 and 67).

Even on wider plots, the length of the range containing the open hall usually took full advantage of the total width of the plot. At no.20 Small Street, probably the house belonging to Bath Priory by the 12th century, an open hall of three bays, aisled on the side away from the frontage, was part of a range *c* 55ft in length, extending the full width of the plot (Figs 5.14a and 5.14b). The range was set back 20ft from the street, giving room for a further range on the street frontage, but leaving most of the very substantial plot to the rear free for other purposes. Similarly placed were the ranges set back behind nos.22–5 Broad Street and nos.21–4 High Street (Fig 5.20; *see* Fig 2.7).

A smaller number of larger houses were of different or more complex overall plan, but nevertheless reveal the builders' intention to use the full width of the tenement plot. Norton's House, south of St Peter's church, was probably a 15th-century amalgamation of two houses. One was set 18ft back from, and parallel to, the frontage on to St Peter's churchyard and was by the 15th century possibly a storeyed range. The other was set at right angles on to the street front, and by the 15th century was probably still an open hall. Separately and together these buildings extended the full width of the plots or plot (Fig 5.15).

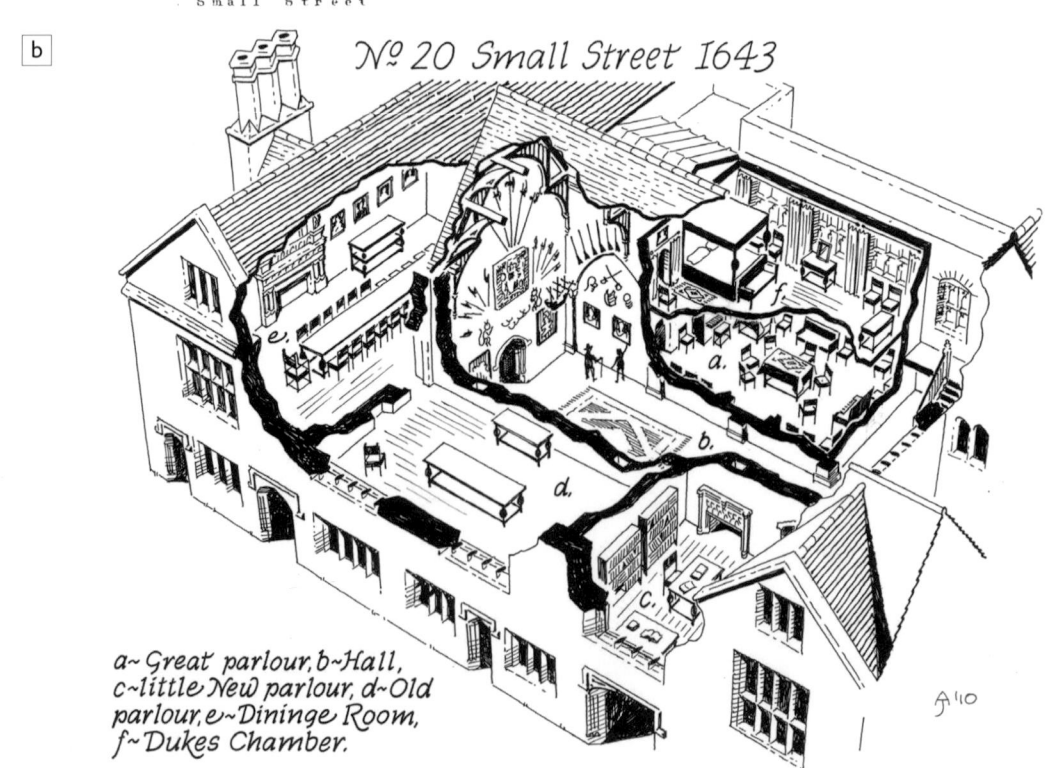

*Fig 5.14*
*No.20 Small Street, the house of John Smythe from c 1540, briefly the residence of Charles I and his sons in 1643 and then of Henry Creswick in 1668:*
*a) plan by Dollman and Jobbins, 1863;*
*b) reconstruction based on documentary sources (JA).*

a~ Great parlour, b~Hall, c~little New parlour, d~Old parlour, e~Dininge Room, f~Dukes Chamber.

THE HALLHOUSE

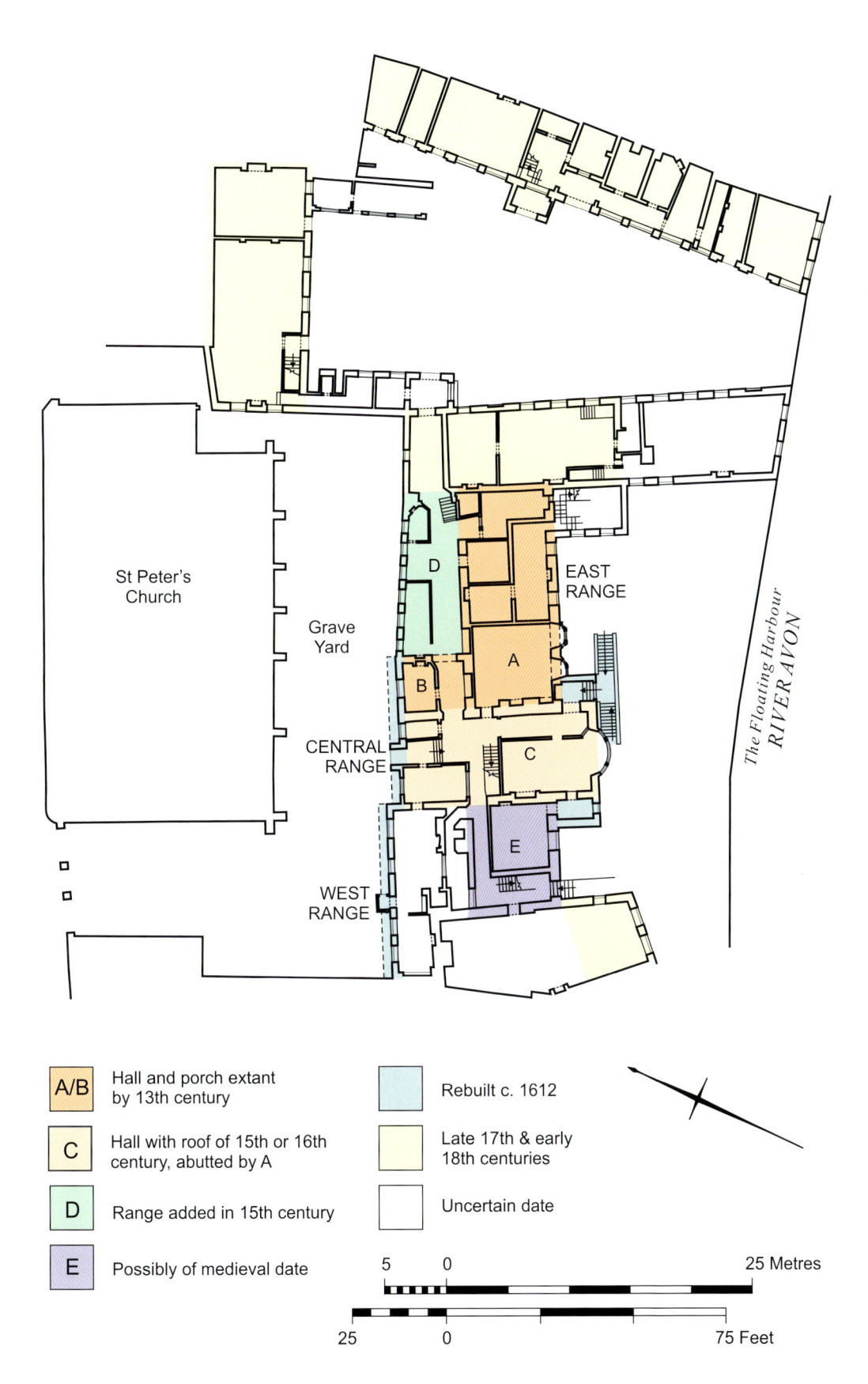

Fig 5.15
Norton's House, later St Peter's Hospital, plan of ground floor, phases deduced from architectural evidence and documentary sources (RHL, PEC, based on plan from an architect's collection, now in University of Bristol Library Special Collections (DM1812/3/9/74, see also Inventory Fig 948).

| A/B | Hall and porch extant by 13th century |
| C | Hall with roof of 15th or 16th century, abutted by A |
| D | Range added in 15th century |
| E | Possibly of medieval date |
| | Rebuilt c. 1612 |
| | Late 17th & early 18th centuries |
| | Uncertain date |

At nos.51–2 Broad Street, the Cyder House was a hallhouse of the 12th century – set parallel to the street, but 140ft back from the Broad Street frontage and *c* 60ft back from Tower Lane. In length *c* 46ft, the Cyder House extended the full width of the tenement plot (Fig 5.16). From its height, and from the arrangements in the 15th or 16th century, it was probably built as a first-floor hall, a further complexity in the design thus being the provision of a passage below the hall to provide access from one end of the property to the other (Figs 5.17a and 5.17b).

At nos.22-8 St Nicholas Street, a plan of different design may indicate the intention of a 12th- or early 13th-century builder to align the various buildings of the property around a courtyard (Fig 5.18). On the north-west was an open hall of the later 12th century, set at right

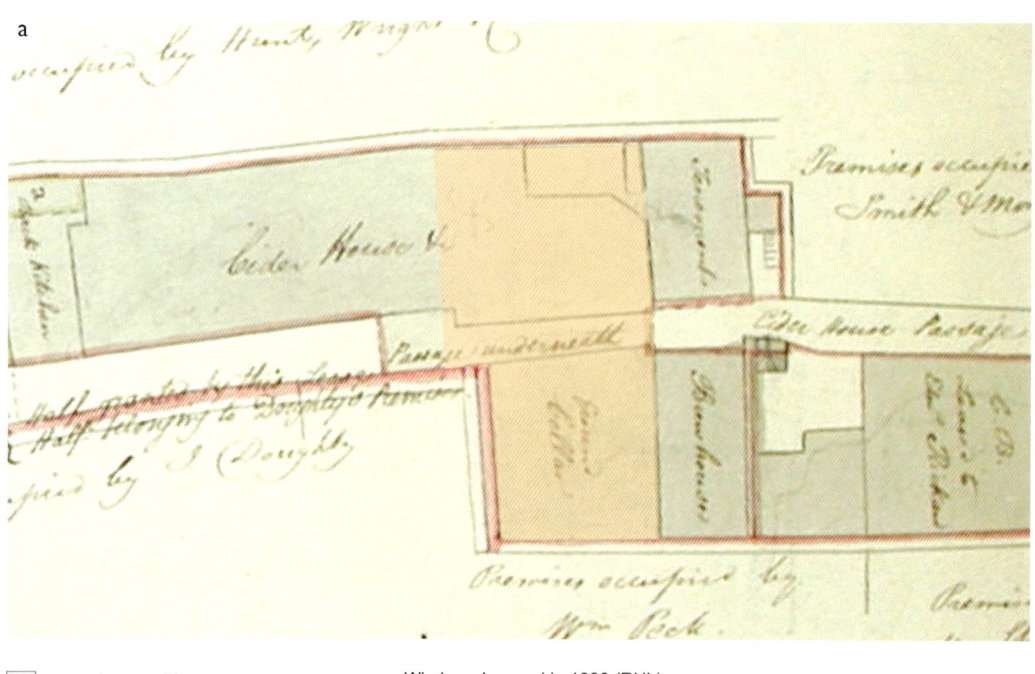

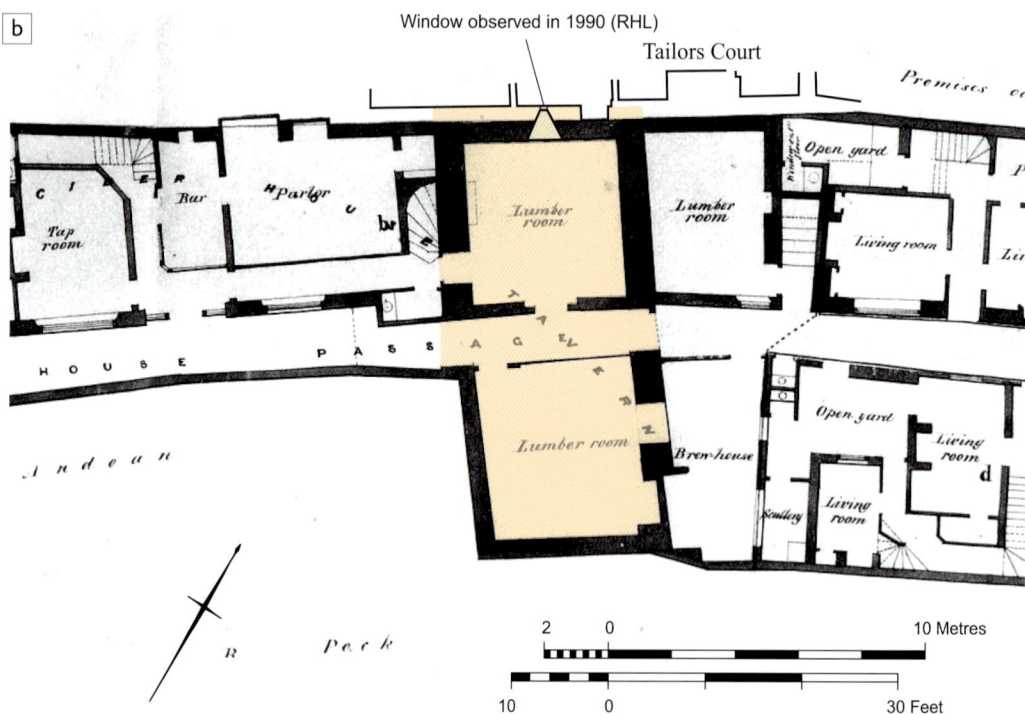

*Fig 5.16*
*Cyder House Passage, Broad Street, surveys of c 1800 (BRO 04479(3) fol 107a) and 1856 (BRO 33041/ BMC/12/PL4 fol 22).*

# THE HALLHOUSE

angles to the street (Fig 5.19). Buildings recorded on the street frontage in the 1820s were of the 16th and 17th centuries, but must have replaced earlier structures. A second and slightly smaller property, also of courtyard plan, was nos.22–5 Broad Street (above), where two ranges with a courtyard between were set back from the street with space for an intervening range on the frontage. A further range forming the north side of a courtyard to the rear was probably rebuilt in the 15th century (Fig 5.20).

A third and far more extensive property, consisting of a number of buildings grouped around a courtyard, was Spicer's Hall, nos.6–9

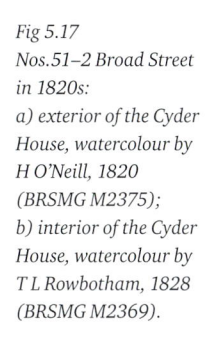

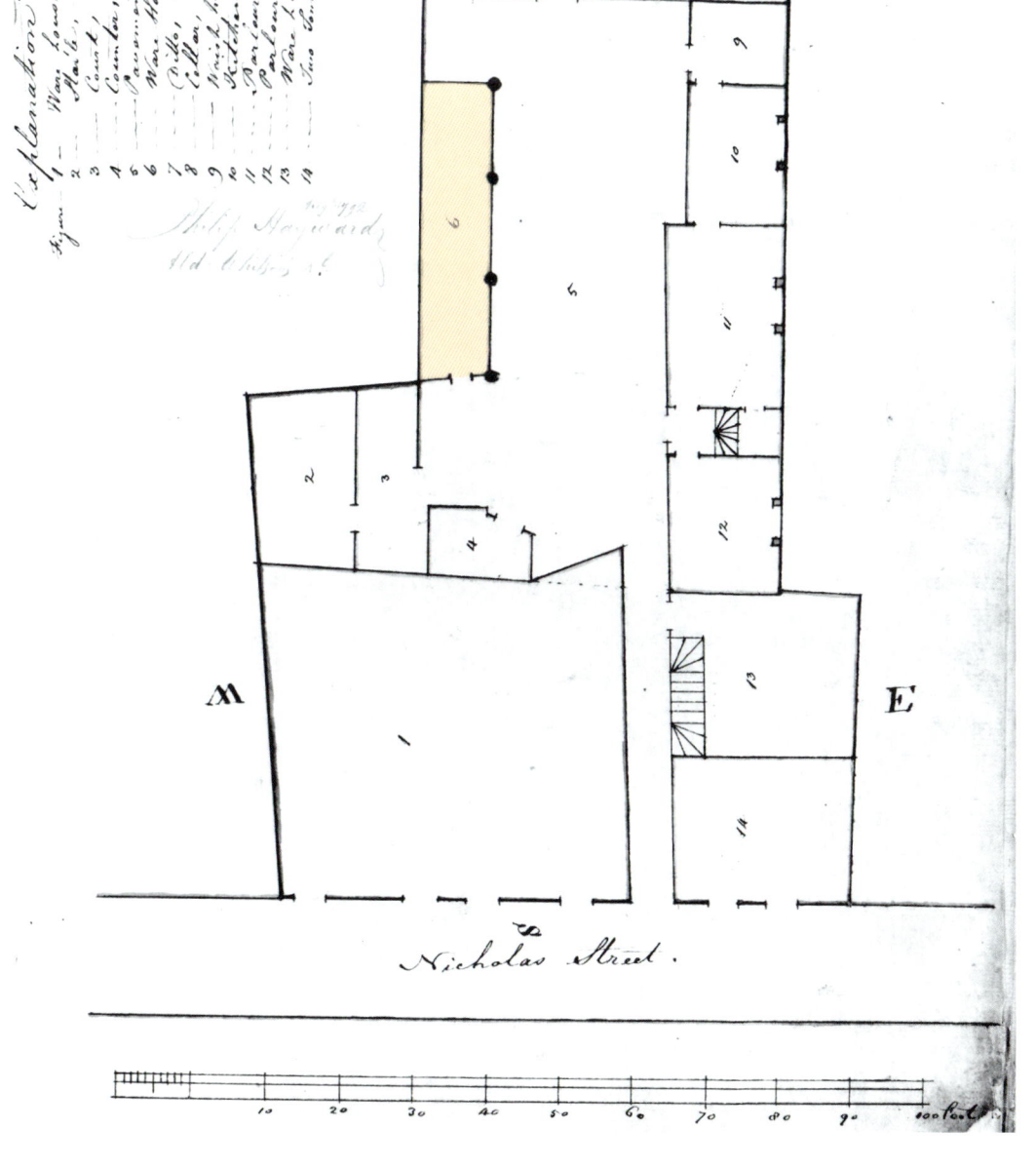

*Fig 5.17*
*Nos.51–2 Broad Street in 1820s:*
*a) exterior of the Cyder House, watercolour by H O'Neill, 1820 (BRSMG M2375);*
*b) interior of the Cyder House, watercolour by T L Rowbotham, 1828 (BRSMG M2369).*

*Fig 5.18*
*Nos.22–8 St Nicholas Street, plan showing location of hallhouse of 12th century (warehouse no.6 on plan), (BRO 04479(1) fol 244).*

*Fig 5.19*
*Nos.22–8 St Nicholas Street, hallhouse of the later 12th century, drawing of mid-19th century (BCRL George Pryce portfolio of drawings).*

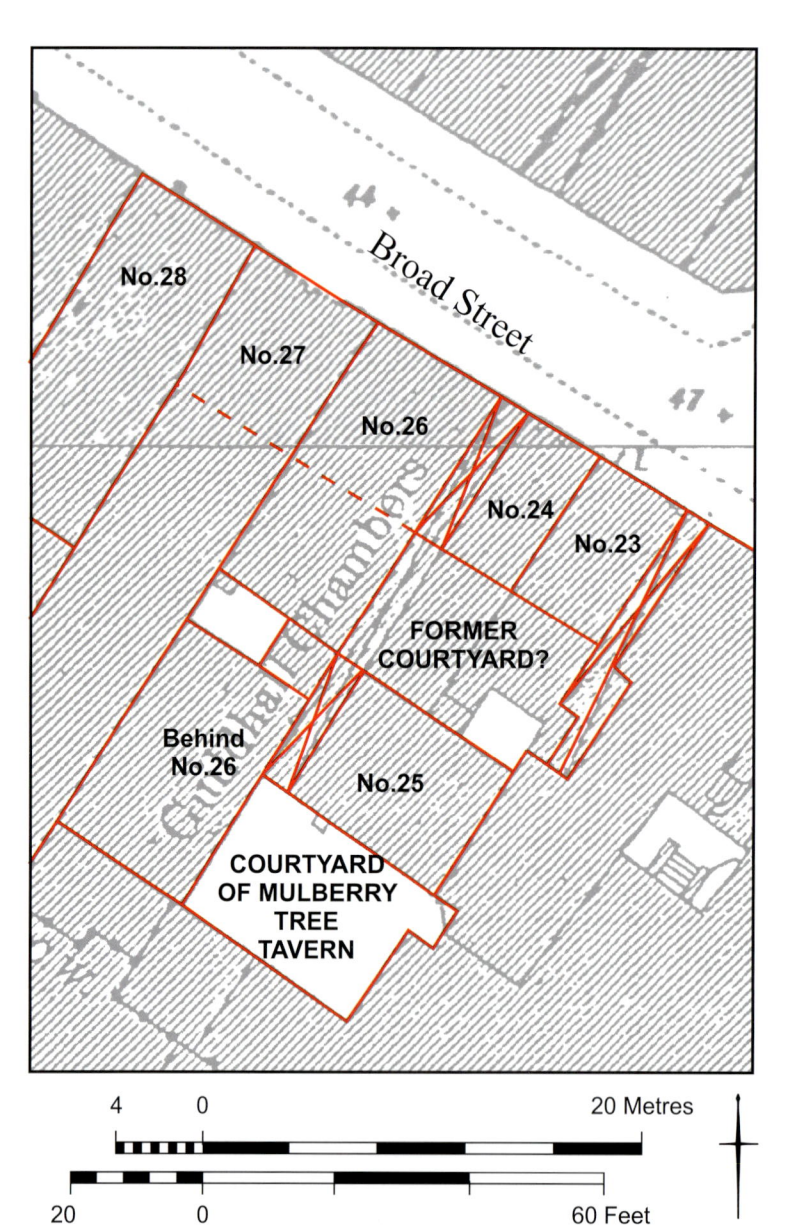

*Fig 5.20*
*Nos.22–5 Broad Street, two surviving ranges possibly of medieval date. The houses are set back from the street and front on to a courtyard, behind two houses with shops built c 1544 and demolished 1819, with possibly a hall to the rear; the cellars below the former shops and the possible hall range still survive (RHL).*

Welsh Back (Fig 5.21). The hall range, featuring a large open hall with storeyed accommodation at one end, extended the full width of the plot – closing the courtyard on the side facing Welsh Back, but in part set back from the street so as to provide space for an intervening range on the frontage. To the rear were separate residential and commercial buildings of the 13th century or earlier.

We can see, therefore, that in a wide range of situations the builders of hallhouses in Bristol were constrained in their choice of site by existing property boundaries. In almost all instances they elected to maximise the use that could be made of the width of the plot, particularly when building close to the street. This constrained siting was very different from that enjoyed by many rural hallhouses. In the countryside, the buildings adjacent to the open hall would generally extend in each direction from its walls. From without, one could walk around the house to pass from one side to another. From within, one could look out in each direction if the house was so designed. In the town these things were not always possible, and we must now look at some of the ways in which the constrained siting of the urban hallhouse impacted on its design.

An immediate problem for most builders was how to enable passage from front to back of the tenement when the hallhouse spanned the width of the plot. For hallhouses built parallel to the street, the solution was to utilise the through-passage, as was done at Spicer's Hall. For those set at right angles to the street, the solution was more complex – demanding in effect that the through-passage become also a side passage, running the length of the hall. Such must have been the plan at no.124 Temple Street (Fig 5.11). Where there was considerable traffic in and out of a particular urban property, and especially where there was also a rear access, the passage through the hall would then be much used by those whose business was essentially elsewhere. Whether this in turn created a peculiarly urban problem is a matter to which we will return later in this chapter.

Another planning problem concerned the need in some hallhouses to link first-floor rooms to the front and rear of the open hall. In a number of instances the provision of a gallery running the length of the hall provided a solution. At Spicer's Hall such a gallery was part of the mid-14th-century plan to provide access between the private accommodation on the street frontage and storeyed rooms at the

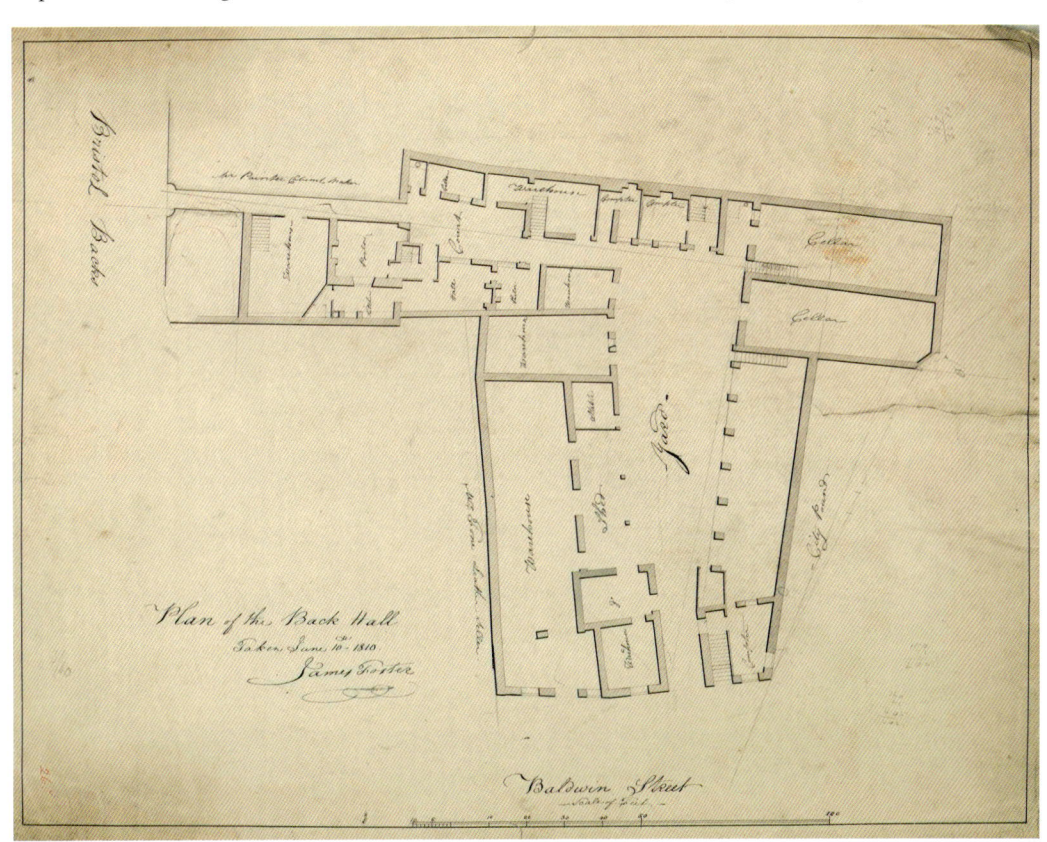

*Fig 5.21*
*Spicer's Hall, nos.6–9 Welsh Back, plan of 1810 (BRO 04479(5) fol 26).*

*Fig 5.22*
*Spicer's Hall, gallery of the mid-14th century, providing access between the private accommodation on the street frontage and storeyed rooms at the south end of the open hall (drawing by Dollman and Jobbins, 1863).*

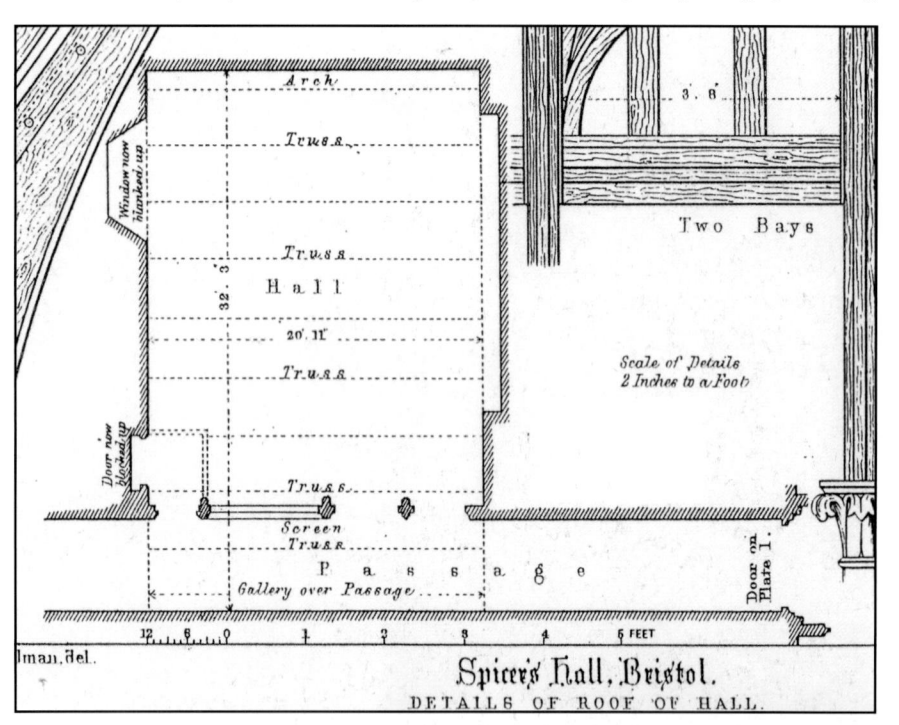

*Fig 5.23*
*Nos.25–26 Small Street Court, Small Street, gallery probably of the 15th century linking the storeyed accommodation on either side of an open hall, photograph of 1908 (Reece Winstone Archive, OB 649).*

*Fig 5.24 (right)*
*Spicer's Hall, Welsh Back, timber-framed entrance porch of the mid-14th century (Seyer 1821).*

south end of the open hall (Fig 5.22). At no.97 Redcliff Street a gallery connected chambers to the front and rear of the open hall.[8] At nos.25–6 Small Street Court, Small Street a gallery, probably of the 15th century, linked the storeyed accommodation at either end of an open hall (Fig 5.23).

Where the hall range was set back wholly or in part from the street, the passage providing access from the street – through the house and thence to the rear of the plot – would need also to pass alongside or through the separate range on the frontage. In a number of instances the entry to this passage from the street was accorded elaborate architectural treatment through the provision of an entrance porch. At nos.nos.33–5 Baldwin Street, a massive, two-centred arched doorway built in ashlar provided access to a hallhouse set back behind the street, built probably in the mid-13th century following the abandonment of the old town wall immediately to the north-east (*see* Fig 4.14). At Spicer's Hall, Welsh Back a timber-framed entrance porch of the mid-14th century provided access both to the owner's accommodation on one side and to the hall and courtyards at the rear beyond (Fig 5.24). At no.124 Temple Street a more simply finished timber-framed porch also supported an oriel window on the first floor, the latter providing further emphasis to the entry to the passage leading to main part of the hallhouse behind (Figs 5.11, 5.25 and 5.26).

It can be argued that these porches were a particularly urban feature, being used to provide emphasis and an imposing principal entry to a house not itself visible from the street. The hall as positioned on the tenement plot in Bristol was generally open only to one or two sides, the others being boundary structures or internal walls separating the open hall from adjacent buildings. This in turn

THE HALLHOUSE

*Fig 5.25*
*No.124 Temple Street, timber-framed porch supporting an oriel widow on the first floor (The British Library Board, Buckler MS, Add MS 36436 fol 516).*

*Fig 5.26*
*No.124 Temple Street, watercolour by H O'Neill, 1821 (BRSMG M2151).*

restricted the number of walls or positions for windows, imposing a constraint on the overall architectural design as seen from the interior. Where possible, windows lighting the hall from the side, often from a side passage, were used. Traces of such windows often survived until the 19th or 20th centuries, encapsulated in later rebuildings of the side wall of the hall, as, for instance, at no.144 Redcliff Street and no.5 Temple Street (Fig 5.3; *see* Fig 4.10). In one case, Spicer's Hall, Welsh Back, a window was set high in the gable wall of the open hall (Fig 5.28). In another, no.20 Small Street, a large Perpendicular window pierced the gable of the hall to match the splendour of the hammer-beam roof (Fig 5.44).

In a number of instances a particular architectural feature, the blind arcade, may have been introduced to provide the rhythm of a bayed structure normally given by windows. Blind arches or arcades were placed in the side or end walls of at least nine halls, generally set in the walls against the boundary of the tenement plot. At nos.22–8 St Nicholas Street a blind arcade of

85

*Fig 5.27*
*Nos.97–8 Redcliff Street, Canynges' House, arcaded side wall of the 15th century, photograph probably of 1931 (NMR BB83/00739 (PEWS)).*

*Fig 5.28*
*Spicer's Hall, Welsh Back, north end wall exposed by wartime bombing, photograph of 1944 (NMR BB80/2562).*

three bays was built into the boundary wall side of a hallhouse of *c* 1200 (Fig 5.19). The side wall of the hall of the Mariners' Guild in Virgin Lane (off Marsh Street), finally demolished in 1880, displayed 'four good arches, which sprang from corbel heads about two feet from the floor'.[9] Similar arcades were built into the boundary side walls of nos.15–16 Baldwin Street (Fig 5.4) and no.24 Christmas Street (Fig 5.7), and into both side walls of no.5 Temple Street later in the 13th century (Figs 5.9 and 5.10; *see* Fig 4.10). At nos. 94, 97–8 and 117–123 Redcliff Street the construction of blind arcaded side walls extended from the 13th to 15th centuries (Fig 5.27).[10]

In Spicer's Hall, Welsh Back, built or substantially rebuilt in the mid-14th century, blind arches were placed both in the end wall of the hall, against the next tenement to the north, and in the east wall, which separated the hall from the range on the street frontage (Figs 5.28 and 5.29). The hall was lit principally from a window on the west side facing on to the courtyard, the south end being closed by a gallery and storeyed range. The gloomy interior is recorded on an early 19th-century watercolour (Fig 5.30). In at least one case, Canynges' House at nos.97–8 Redcliff Street, the rhythm of the blind arcade appears to be related to that of the roof bays, suggesting a strong and

# THE HALLHOUSE

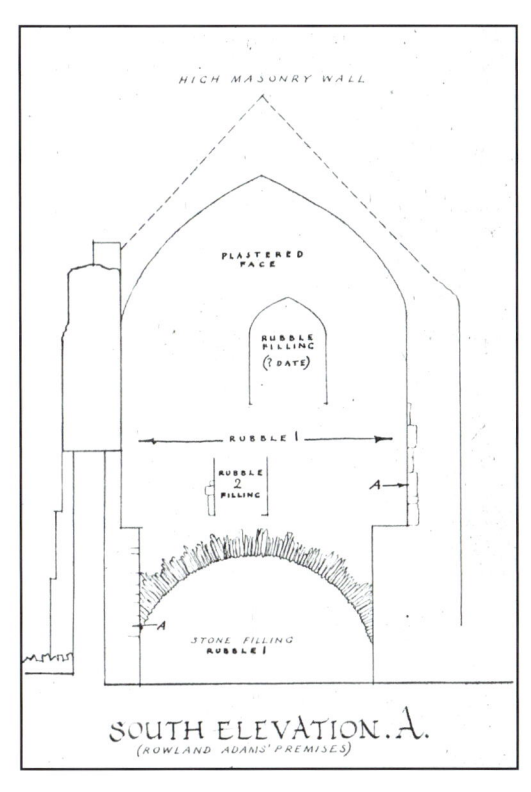

conscious effort to co-ordinate the design of features within the open hall.

Blind arcades or arches of this type are recorded in other urban hallhouses of the 12th and 13th centuries, for instance in London, Kings Lynn and Stamford.[11] In Bristol and in other towns the use of this feature might be interpreted as a reaction to the constraint of the urban tenement plot, an architectural device to fill a blank wall where windows could not be placed. However, it may also have been introduced to lessen the sense of being hemmed in and to give the impression of a curtilage beyond – such as halls of the architectural quality of these examples would indeed have possessed in a rural environment.

In other architectural details the hallhouse as built in Bristol was more similar to its rural equivalents. In their overall design the screens separating the through-passage from the open hall, recorded at Spicer's Hall from the mid-14th century (Fig 5.22) and at nos.21–4 High Street from the 15th century (Fig 5.31), could not be described as distinctively urban. The 14th- and

*Fig 5.29*
*Spicer's Hall, Welsh Back, south end wall exposed by wartime bombing and recorded for the Ministry of Works, by Bryan St John O'Neil in 1944 (BRO Information Box 10/1).*

*Fig 5.30 (above)*
*Spicer's Hall, Welsh Back, watercolour by T L Rowbotham, 1826 (BRSMG M2282); the watercolour omits the blind arcade shown clearly in the wartime photograph (Fig 5.28).*

*Fig 5.31*
*Screen from nos.21–4 High Street, photograph of 1933 (Reece Winstone Archive OB 4620).*

15th-century roofs to the open halls recorded at the Cyder House in Broad Street (Fig 5.17), no.1 Christmas Street (Fig 5.6), Norton's House, no.97 Redcliff Street, no.20 Small Street and Spicer's Hall were all of butt-purlin type (Fig 5.32), conforming to the method of construction used in the surrounding region.

In the sophistication of their finish and detailed design, some of these roofs were altogether exceptional. The significance of this is a point to which we will return later in this chapter when considering the uses to which these houses were put. In terms of heating, the urban halls appear to have been similar to those of rural houses. Archaeology reveals the existence of open hearths set in the centre of the hall. However, the destruction of so many medieval halls makes it impossible today to identify, for example, the presence of smoke blackening in the roof timbers, to see whether the open hearth was the means of heating the hall.

One other architectural element, recorded only in the hall at no.59 Baldwin Street, Seyer's 'chapel of St John' (p7–10), was the provision of

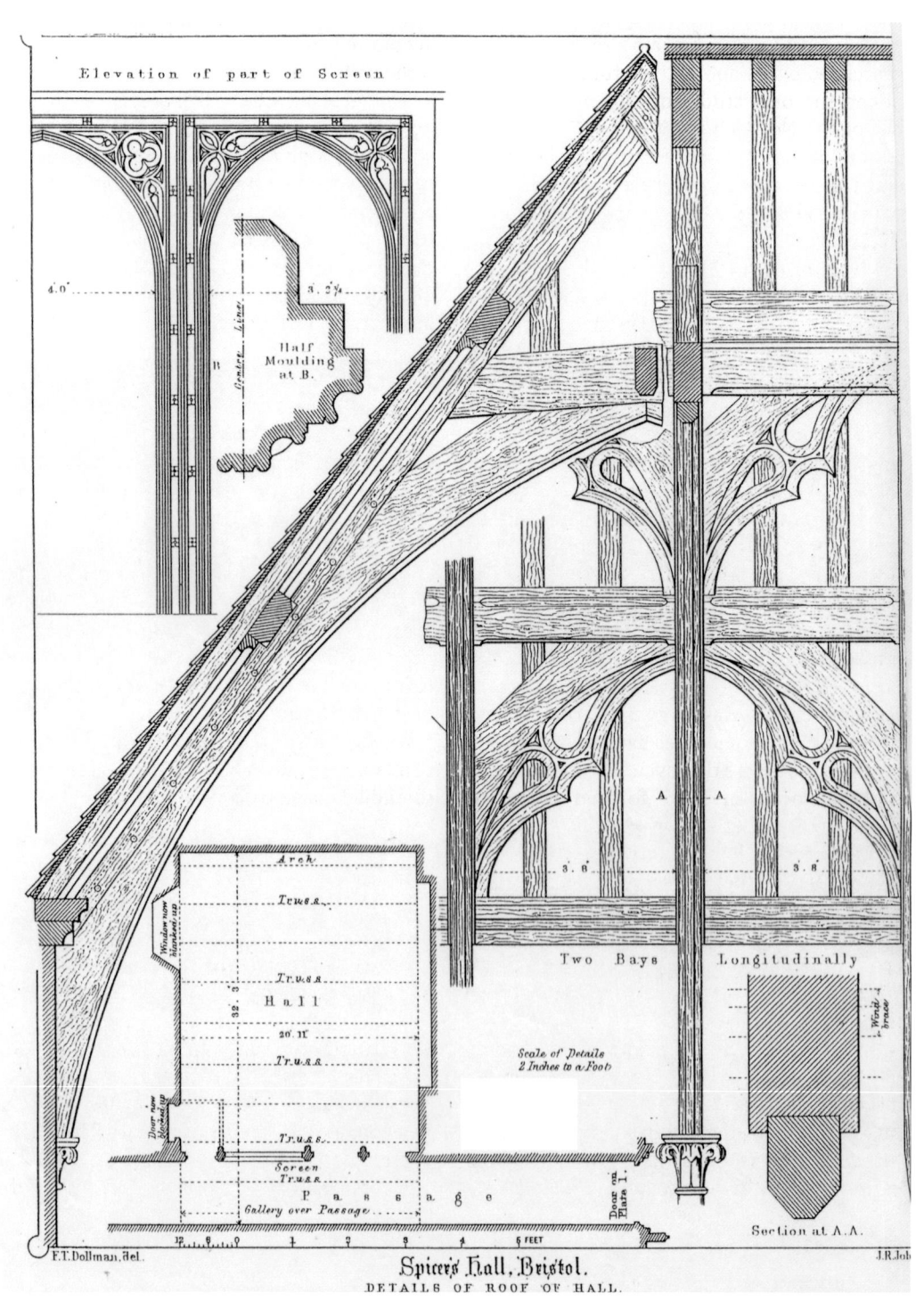

*Fig 5.32*
*Spicer's Hall, Welsh Back, details of roof and floor plan (drawing by Dollman and Jobbins, 1863).*

a laver, for the washing of hands on entering the hall for meals.[12] It would be of interest to know if this had a 17th-century equivalent, providing a link in social behaviour to the provision of washbasins in houses of the 18th century (p318–19).

## Probate Inventories and the Study of Urban Housing

Probate inventories have been little used in the study of urban housing in England. Those for many towns and cities, including those for pre-Great Fire London, remain largely unstudied by archaeologists and architectural historians. Indeed the only study for an English city is that of the Norwich inventories. These were examined exhaustively through statistical methods. Almost no inventories could be linked to identified houses, but the results overall are of considerable interest.[13]

The approach followed for this study of Bristol houses has been to complement the data from Norwich by looking at inventories on a more individual basis, not seeking to establish broad statistically based conclusions, but identifying differences and common threads in the lifestyles of individuals, linked where possible to located, or better still recorded, houses.

Hearths and their furniture have been perceived as presenting particular problems. In Kent the numbers of hearths indicated by the presence of hearth furniture in probate inventories were noted as lower than those listed in the hearth tax returns for Lady Day 1664 or recorded in surviving houses.[14] To explain these discrepancies it was suggested that hearth furniture might sometimes have been removed from a house before the inventory was made, or might on occasion have formed a specific bequest in a will (cited were a jack, plate and furnace recorded in the will for a house in Sevenoaks). In other instances it was suggested that the appraisers may not have thought it worthwhile to itemise the hearth furniture of a parlour or chamber fireplace, or that, when it was summertime, the hearth furniture may have been stored elsewhere.

Specific bequests in a will should be treated with caution; it is evident from a small number of inventories from Bristol, made not for probate but to accompany the leases of houses, that the items regarded as immoveable were those that were affixed to the house, which would have included items such as those cited in the Sevenoaks house.[15] Hearth furniture such as firedogs (both andirons and creepers), tongs and slices did not fall into this category. We need therefore to distinguish between the hearth furniture that could be regarded as immoveable and that which was very definitely moveable. The former was specified in leases and wills because its immoveable status was always at risk – both lease and will were in effect combating what was very often normative behaviour. We might also be cautious with regard to the fireplaces recorded in the hearth tax, but not accounted for in probate inventories for the same house.

One explanation for this absence is that the hearth was visible and open, and therefore also chargeable for the hearth tax, but was not in use. A second possible explanation is that the house was in multiple occupation. Detailed analysis of the hearth tax returns for Bristol has shown that those for 1662–4 list one housekeeper for each dwelling unit, but many houses were in multiple occupation, comprising a number of households and dwelling units. Probate inventories can be shown in a number of instances to relate only to part of a house.[16]

Many of the broader problems identified in using the evidence from inventories remain. For instance, the degree to which all rooms in the house were itemised is sometimes uncertain, making it difficult to be confident that complete houses were being described; and the inherent bias in the criteria for the compilation of inventories means that the documents are generally more representative of the wealthier citizens rather than of society as a whole. But, provided the caveats are kept in mind, there are rewards in looking at inventories in the context of an understanding of known house forms or of identified houses and locations.[17]

## The Hall as the Social Centre of the House

Changes in the way that the hall was used in Bristol's houses, and the relationship of the hall to other rooms within them, are of crucial importance not only to the interpretation of architectural evidence, but also because they reveal significant social and cultural developments in the life of the city. The history is a long one, stretching from the 12th to the 17th centuries, and its principal concern is the

*Fig 5.33*
*Spicer's Hall, nos.6–9 Welsh Back, plan of recorded buildings from documentary sources (RHL, PEC).*

study of where, within the dwelling, the life of the family was focused. The story can be pieced together from a number of sources – archaeology, documents and standing or recorded buildings. In some respects the story is a familiar one: in summary, the decline of the hall as a main living area was complemented by the growing importance of parlours and chambers. But the precise nature of the developments reveals important changes in concepts of privacy, status and household life.

Langland's complaint makes it abundantly clear that, despite alarming trends in the way of life of the rich, the open hall was in the 1370s still widely thought of as the 'chief' room of the house. It was a place for mealtimes, shared by the master and his household, a place which underlined both the communal nature of the household and its hierarchical structure. At the beginning of the 15th century houses of middling men, in cities such as Winchester, Exeter and York, may have contained no more accommodation than a hall and chamber, together with a cellar, buttery, pantry, kitchen and brewhouse.[18] In such situations, the open hall was perforce the principal living room of the house.

In Bristol the use of the open hall as the social centre of the house can be traced from at least the 12th to the 17th centuries. The inhabitants of no.87 Redcliff Street, built in the 12th century, occupied a house two rooms deep. In the rear room of the house was an open hearth; as the only heated room, this can be interpreted as the open hall. From its proximity to the street, the front room can best be interpreted as a shop, possibly with a chamber above. Unless there was a separate kitchen to the rear, beyond the archaeological excavations, the hall must have served also as the kitchen. This arrangement was changed by successive owners or occupants within a century (Fig 5.2).[19]

On the opposite side of Redcliff Street, the inhabitants of no.69 in the 12th and 13th centuries lived in a house of two rooms in depth – possibly with a shop on the street, certainly with an open hall behind and an unheated room to the rear of the hall, probably a parlour. Their later 13th- or early 14th-century successors at no.70 lived in a house of similar plan (Fig 5.1a). The inhabitants of these houses must have regarded the heated open hall as the social centre of their homes.[20]

The evidence relating to the house of Richard Spicer in Welsh Back suggests that the same was still true for one member of the city's ruling elite in the late 14th century. Spicer, mayor three times between 1354 and 1373 and one of the wealthiest Bristol merchants of his age, died in 1377. The estate which he left to the Corporation included various buildings refurbished or rebuilt by him towards Welsh Back, together with a detached chamber block of the 13th century and storehouses of the same date towards Baldwin Street (Fig 5.33).

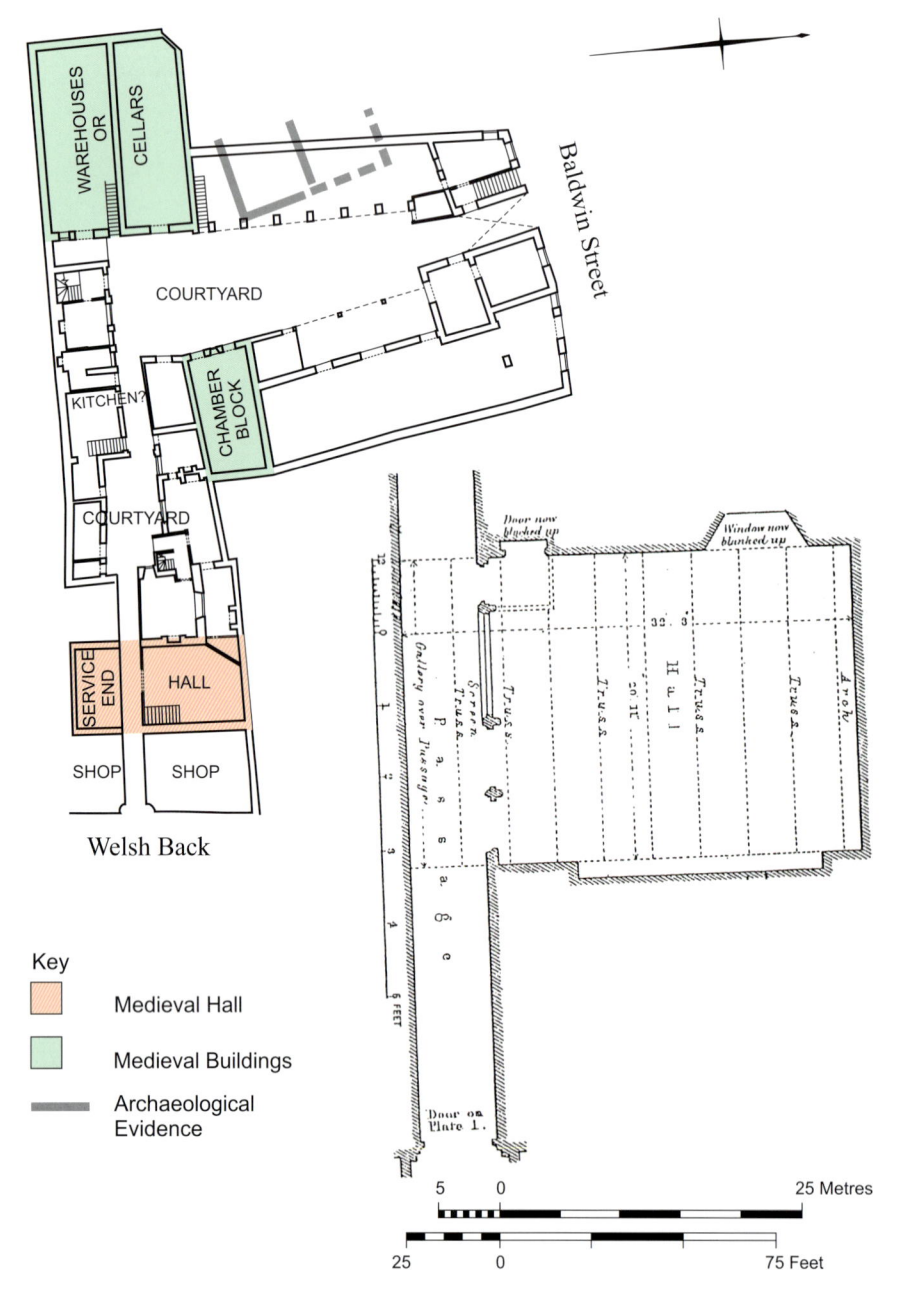

Spicer's residence was organised as two parallel ranges of buildings. Set back from Welsh Back was the range containing the great hall and some storeyed accommodation. The latter lay to the south of the through-passage and consisted of a vaulted room on the ground floor and a room above. The second range, on the street frontage, was divided on the line of an entry and through-passage. To the south of the passage lay a structure of at least three storeys, forming part of Spicer's living accommodation. The greater part of the range fronting the street, lying to the north of the entry, although constructed by Spicer, was not part of his residence, but was built as two shophouses, shown as separately let in the earliest rental for the property, a century later.[21] The through-passage was the route from Welsh Back through the hall to the courtyard and buildings beyond. Visitors would enter via the great door on Welsh Back, its rose-window tracery an instant message that Spicer could afford the best work available. Emerging into the wide through-passage of the great hall they would glimpse the richly decorated roof and gaze closely on the tall, ornately carved but completely solid screen that hid the rest of the hall from sight.

The high table and cloth of estate must have been sited at the north end, lit by a tall oriel window to the courtyard; while in the absence of any chimneystack, a great open hearth must have been placed in the centre of the room. There is no evidence for any direct route from the upper (north) end of the hall to a parlour. Spicer's more private accommodation, a parlour and solar or chambers, can only have been at the lower end of the hall beyond the screen, or in detached structures further back from the street (Fig 5.33). Stairs at the south end of the hall provided access to the chambers and other rooms on the first and second floors – on the west looking on to the courtyard, on the east extending to overlook the Avon, the bustle of the Bridge and waterfront and perhaps some of Spicer's own ships (Fig 5.34). Spicer's new house may have had a parlour and certainly had chambers, but the open hall was at the centre of his dwelling; more expense and lavish decoration was expended here than on any other part of it, except perhaps on the facade to the street. His hall is the best evidence at present available that, in late 14th-century Bristol, the rich man had not yet retreated at mealtimes to his privy parlour.

One hundred years later the lifestyle of widow Giles George, admittedly at a much lower social level, showed a similar focus on the hall. In or close to Broad Street or Small Street, her house comprised two ground-floor rooms, a hall and kitchen. The furnishings of her hall, seen through the inventory of her possessions made in 1496, included the andirons for the hearth, cloth hangings, tables, stools, chairs, a banker (the covering for a bench or chair) and cushions, and a hanging candelabra of five lights. This was the principal living room, the centre of her house (Appendix 2).[22] Probably very similar to George's house was no.44 Broad Street, built in the early 15th century (Fig 5.35). On the street frontage was storeyed accommodation – not included in the inventory made at George's death, but possibly present and in separate occupation. Behind this, however, the dwelling area corresponded closely to the description of George's house; it had an open hall and, at the rear, storeyed accommodation occupying the remaining floor area of the tenement plot.

*Fig 5.34*
*Spicer's Hall, nos.6–9 Welsh Back, view of frontage to Welsh Back (watercolour by Parkman in author's collection).*

# THE TOWN HOUSE IN MEDIEVAL AND EARLY MODERN BRISTOL

*Fig 5.35*
*No.44 Broad Street, plan of first and second floors (RHL, PEC).*

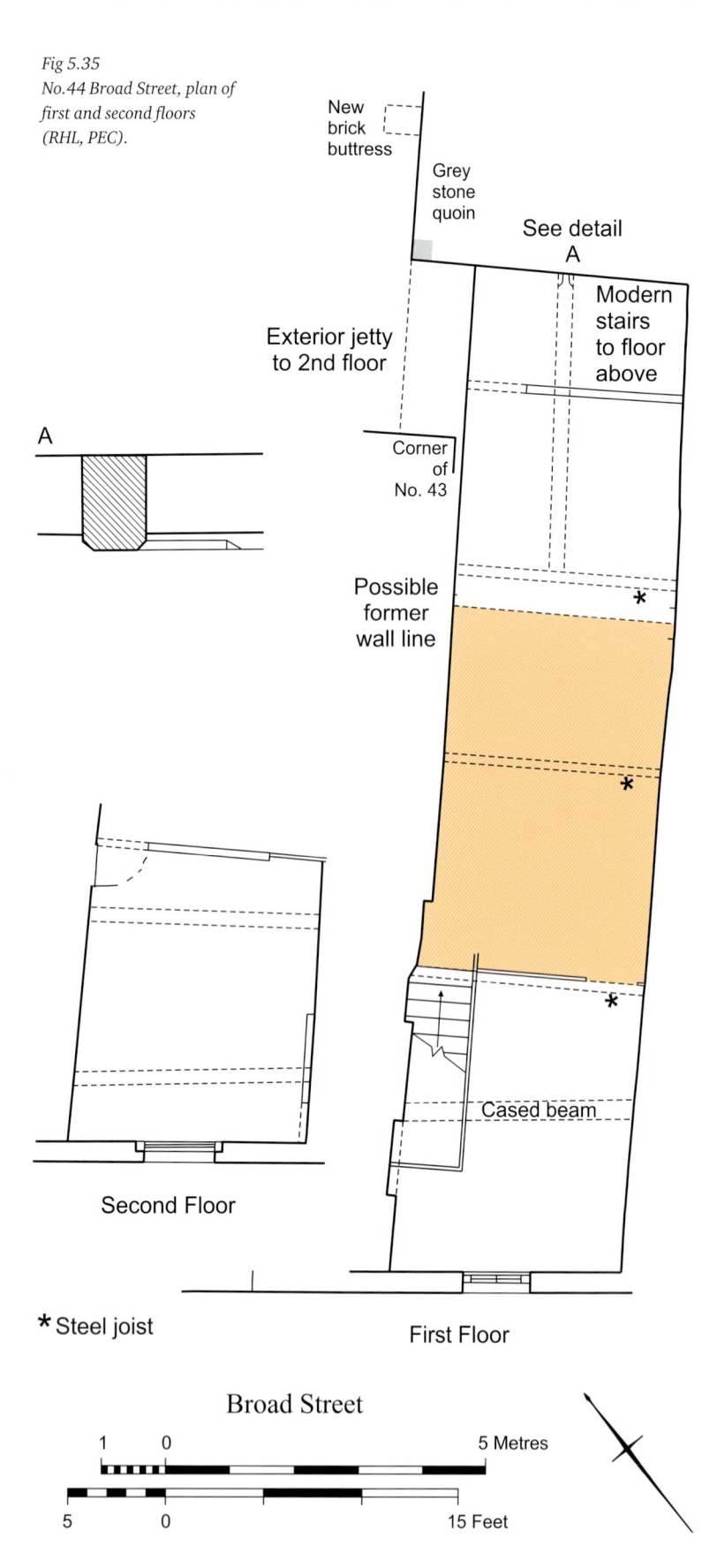

In the early 17th century some citizens still retained the open hall as the principal living room. In 1618 Edward Morris, a merchant, had lived at no.49 Corn Street, a valuable city-centre site at the corner with Small Street. The conjuncture of contemporary probate documents and a detailed plan of the house made in the early 18th century make it possible to follow the route taken by the appraisers in drawing up a list of his possessions (Fig 5.36).[23] Entering the house from the side entrance in Small Street, the first room to be encountered was the kitchen, then an unheated parlour followed by the hall. Upstairs, over the shop fronting on to Corn Street, were two chambers on the first floor and a cockloft (the uppermost attic room rising into the apex of the roof) above.

Morris's living space was distributed between his back parlour and the hall, which was possibly open to the roof, there being no room specified as 'over the hall'. The back parlour was furnished in much the same way as the hall, but only the latter was heated. Perhaps Morris used the hall principally in the winter. The parlour was a much smaller room, but looked south on to a small courtyard which would have caught the sunlight in the summer and would certainly have taken some heat from the kitchen even in winter. Morris's lifestyle was also that of an elderly person, who had left the house much as it was for a considerable period. Many items were broken, among them pewter in the kitchen, two stools in the parlour, even the folding tables in the hall. Many of his possessions were described as old: the leather cushions stuffed with hay in the parlour, the chairs in the hall and his clothes and Bible in his inner chamber or bedroom, to mention but a few.

In 1627 Humphrey Clovill, a goldsmith, had also retained the hall, probably open, as the principal living room of his house, set against the south-east corner of Christchurch in Wine Street. His lifestyle may in this respect have been similar to Morris's, but it was altogether more comfortable in other ways. He lived with rather more possessions, only two of which were described as old. Clovill's hall was moderately well furnished, heated, wainscoted and hung about with pictures and stained cloths. Here there was no parlour.

Some of Morris's contemporaries lived in houses which had been modernised by the insertion of a ceiling within the open hall, providing new rooms on one or more floors above. Despite this important change in the character of the room, some households continued to treat the hall, now ceiled, as the social centre of the house. In St Thomas's parish during the 1640s Barnard Benson, a pewterer, still retained his hall as the main living room of the house.[24] Set between the shop on the street frontage and the kitchen at the rear, the ample furnishings of the hall included chairs and table for dining, carpets and six cushions, together with andirons and a back for the hearth, armour and weapons, together with a looking glass, the Bible and other books. After Benson's death in 1643 the weaponry was removed and, although the contents of the 'stony hall' remained much the same, the lodging chamber overlooking the street began to be used by his widow Mary increasingly for sitting as well as for sleeping, until her death in 1646. Mary, the daughter of Michael Threlkeld, had lived in this way as a child over the shop.

As modernised in the 17th century, the new arrangement of no.44 Broad Street was probably typical of three-room deep houses where the open hall had been ceiled over (Fig 5.35). On the street frontage was a storeyed range, one room in depth, originally of two floors with an attic, now raised an extra storey. Behind was an open hall, with a first and a second floor now inserted. The furthest third of the house had been similarly raised by an extra storey. Benson's household would have fitted comfortably, indeed exactly, into this house as altered. With a shop on the street frontage, separately leased and not mentioned in her probate inventory (Appendix 2), the household of Giles George, an inhabitant of the same parish, would have fitted comfortably into the unaltered house as it was in the 15th century.

In these insights into life in the early 17th-century city can be seen the preferences of individuals and the ways in which these were conditioned by existing structures. Morris was elderly and lived with few comforts, perhaps of his choice, perhaps by necessity. Clovill was certainly able to live with much more comfort. Both he and Morris lived on small, high-value tenement plots in the centre of the city, where the retention of the open hall placed a severe restriction on the expansion of the accommodation; but personal choice must have made their lifestyles seem very different to contemporaries. The Bensons lived in a house where the open hall had been removed, presumably at least in part to increase the available floor area, but it was Mary Benson's preference, as a widow and drawing on her childhood experiences, to live more of the time upstairs, in the forestreet or front chamber.

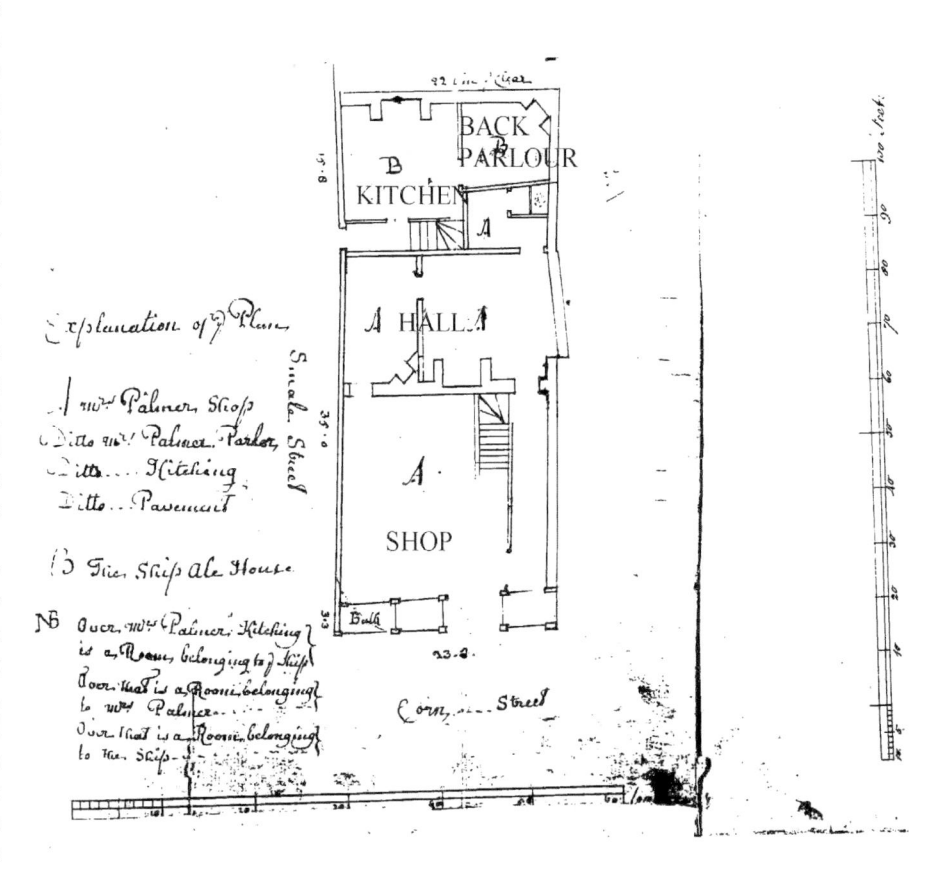

### The Retreat to the Parlour: the Late 15th and Early 16th Centuries

The extent to which the retreat from the hall to the 'privy parlour' lamented by Langland was evident in Bristol by the late 14th century can only be glimpsed. It has been shown that many earlier houses had storeyed accommodation, including probably what would be termed parlours. Richard Spicer's house at nos.7–9 Welsh Back, for example, had extensive accommodation to supplement the hall. Nothing, however, has allowed the certain identification of the transfer of the main living activity, including the important function of dining, from the hall to the parlour before c 1400.

The evidence for this change gathers strength from the late 15th century. The clearest demonstration is the great house of William Canynges, mayor five times and at his death in 1474 a merchant of exceptional wealth. Canynges lived at nos.95–7 Redcliff Street, and a visitor in 1474 would have entered from the street between shops and then passed alongside the great hall

Fig 5.36
No.49 Corn Street, plan of early 18th century, annotated to show the probable location of the rooms mentioned in the inventory of Edward Morris in 1618
(BRO 04479(2) fol 55).

(Figs 5.37 and 5.38). Beyond there was at least one other room followed by a courtyard, with another range of the 15th century traversing the plot from north to south.

Those privileged to cross through the passage in the centre of this range would have entered a second and cobbled courtyard. Eighty feet beyond, the frontage to the river was now completely closed by a newly built structure probably without parallel in late 15th-century Bristol. This structure was described by William Worcestre in *c* 1480 as a 'fair tower built by William Canynges', containing four windows called 'Bay wyndowes ... highly decorated, like the rooms', 60ft long and 48ft wide.[25] Part of the north wall still stands, showing that it was built at least in part of stone, but for direct evidence of its form there is only Worcestre's description.

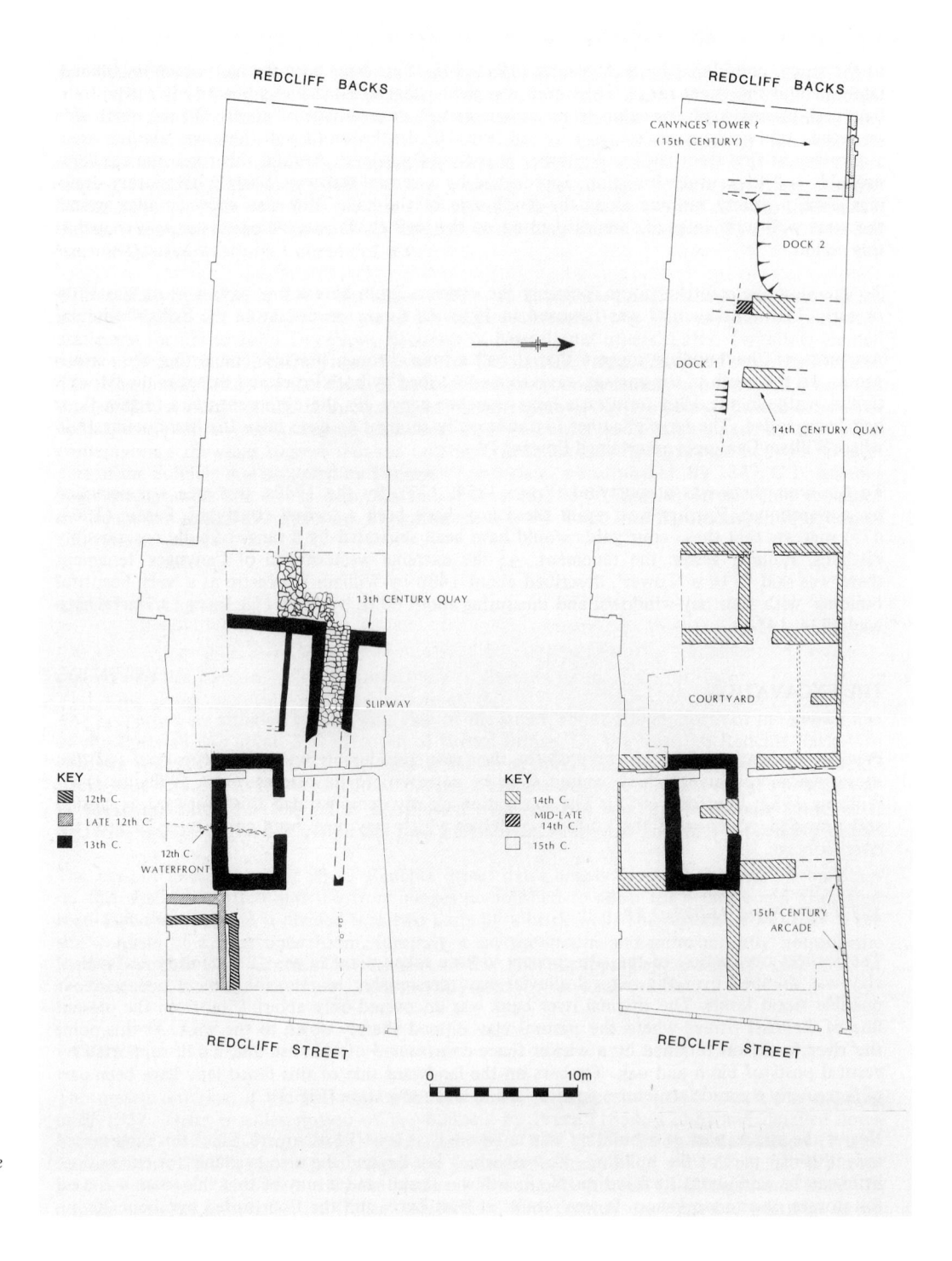

*Fig 5.37*
*Nos. 95–7 Redcliff Street, Canynges' House, plan showing development by the 15th century*
*(Jones 1986, Fig 2).*

# THE HALLHOUSE

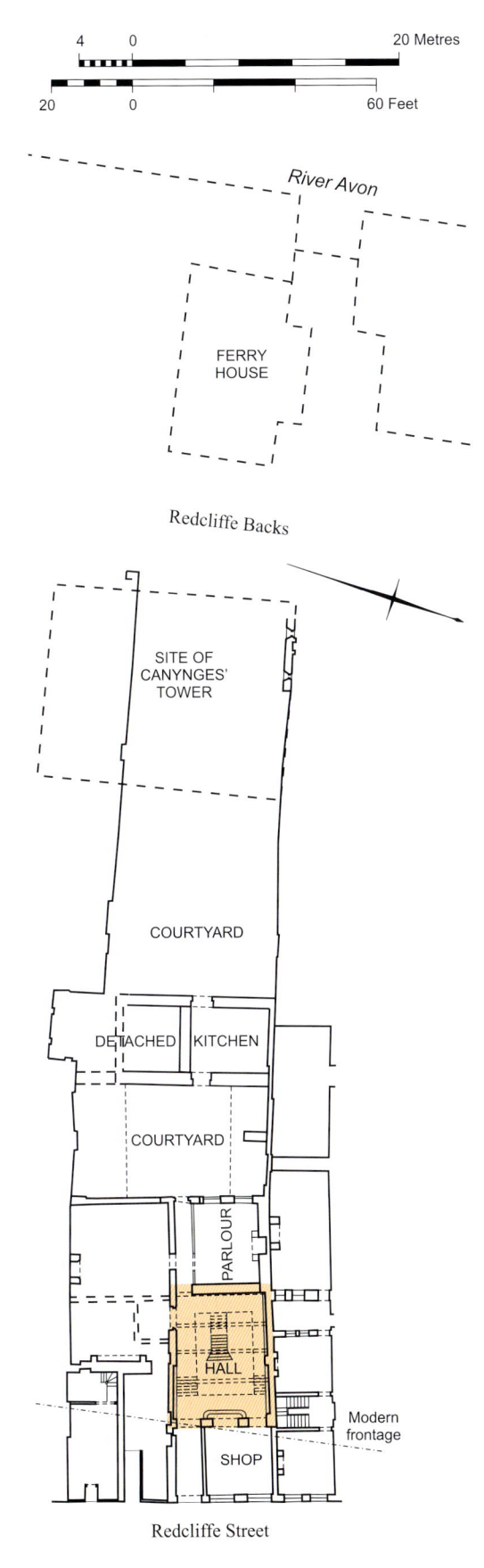

To contemporaries who knew London, Canynges' new tower might have appeared similar to some of the most prestigious dwellings overlooking the Thames waterfront, notably Coldharbour II and Baynard's Castle. Both were refurbished in the later 15th century. The former was an aristocratic residence and one of the settings for a royal marriage in 1501; the rebuilding of the latter was completed by Henry VII in the same year. These Thames-side dwellings or their European counterparts in cities such as Bruges or Venice could certainly have contributed to the inspiration for Canynges' new building works. Worcestre's use of 'tower' would have echoed `la Tour', the name used to describe Coldharbour II in 1401.[26] The view of Canynges' new river frontage, four bay windows in width, might have been very similar to that of Baynard's Castle II, perhaps with similar provision for a water gate (Fig 5.39).

As a Member of Parliament and as a merchant with numerous connections in London, Canynges would have known these and other similarly situated residences.[27] His construction of the new tower on the Avon waterfront was perhaps a deliberate move to assert his status: that of a merchant of exceptional wealth, heavily involved in the political world of the mid-15th century. His house was possibly used (even perhaps extended) to provide hospitality to Edward IV on the king's six-day visit to the city in 1461. As a major addition to his property and from its location overlooking the river, the tower would have provided Canynges with his most splendid rooms for the reception of visitors, and also his most private rooms. It would have certainly much facilitated the retreat to the privy parlour. The shift in the focus of Canynges' investment in his house reveals a great deal about ideas on the relative importance and functions of different elements within the complex.

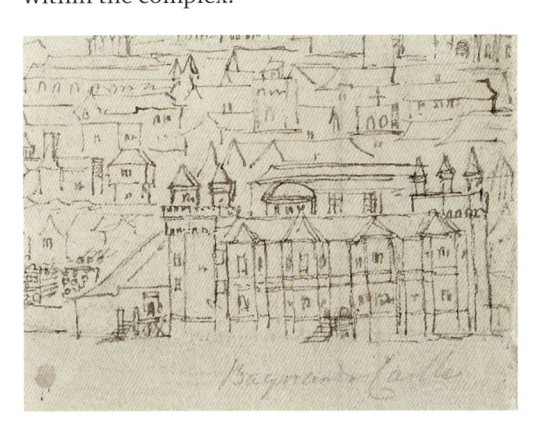

*Fig 5.38*
*Nos. 97–8 Redcliff Street, Canynges' House, plan of recorded buildings from available sources (RHL, PEC, see also entry in Inventory).*

*Fig 5.39*
*Baynards Castle II (Wyngaerde's panorama of c 1540). The illustration shows what Canynges' tower of four bay windows in width may have looked like (Ashmolean Museum, University of Oxford, WA1950.206.3 van der Wyngaerde, Durham House to Baynard's Castle).*

95

When he first purchased the property the hall may well have been the principal room, its use similar to that of Spicer's open hall a century earlier. Canynges, in an early phase of investment in his new property, may have been responsible for the construction of its richly decorated roof. But with the construction of the new range on the river front, its role must have changed. Henceforth the great hall, illustrated by Dolman and Jobbins and demolished in 1937, remained an impressive room with important functions, but it was no longer the social centre of the life of the household (Fig 5.40). This had shifted to the inner part of the complex, to a more private environment.

Across the street, a little closer to the Bridge in St Thomas's parish, was John Gaywode's house. Gaywode's will, made in 1471, offers a further clue to the thinking that had relegated Canynges' great hall to the role of an imposing entry to an increasingly private residence. Gaywode, like Canynges, was a member of the mercantile elite and had twice been sheriff, in one year with Canynges as mayor. His property interests were considerable and extended across the town, but his own residence was, like Canynges', located in Redcliff Street, its precise location not yet identified. Bequeathed to his wife, and then to his son, were the tapestry for the hall and parlour of this house, with bankers and cushions to match, the two best pollaxes [poleaxes], a spear standing in the hall by the entrance to the kitchen, a candlestick of latten hanging in the hall and 'two great andirons for the hall, in use at the feast of Christmas'.[28] Gaywode's hall had become a room for formal occasions only, but it was still at the forefront of his mind, with its furnishings prominent among the items worthy of explicit mention in his will. Here his descendants too would celebrate Christmas, warmed by ancestral tapestry and candlelight.

By the late 15th century, elements of the lifestyle enjoyed by Canynges and Gaywode were evidently shared by a number of their contemporaries. All were wealthier members of the urban community, their domestic lives more visible through inventories of their possessions made for probate in the 1490s and 1500s (Appendix 2).[29] The houses of Thomas Keynes of St James's parish, Thomas Mason of St Stephen's, John Parkyns, a merchant tailor, and Foster, mayor in 1481–2, his house at nos.16-17 Small Street (Figs 5.48 and 5.49), were of remarkably similar form, each including a hall, parlour, buttery, kitchen and at least two or three chambers. Foster's apart, it cannot be proved that these halls were open to the roof, but, with one exception, it is likely that they were, since none of the inventories refers to rooms over the hall. In Keynes' house his 'newe chambre' was possibly over at least part of the hall.

In the houses of the first three, as in the houses of Canynges and Gaywode, the hall was certainly no longer the principal living room; the parlour now fulfilled this function. The halls of Keynes and Mason were not even brought to life at Christmas. Andirons were noticeably absent. In their personal possessions Keynes, Mason, Parkyns and Foster displayed similar taste, with some subtle and a few notable distinctions. Strands of commonality ran through their furnishing of the open hall. All included forms or stools – all, except Mason's, with folding

*Fig 5.40*
*Nos.97–8 Redcliff Street, Canynges' house, open hall of late 14th or early 15th century*
*(NMR BB78/09263 (PEWS)).*

tables. Mason's hall was sparsely filled, the only other item present, by the time the appraisers arrived, being a hanging of green saye or serge; similar hangings adorned the walls of the hall and parlour of Thomas Keynes. With the exception of Mason all had weapons in the hall, probably hanging on the walls, as was certainly the case in Parkyns' house.

Parkyns, Keynes and Foster shared with John Gaywode his preference for furnishing the hall with bankers or cushions, sometimes both. Only Forster's possessions, like those of John Gaywode, included 'a branch of laten tin, with five candlesticks', to hang, it may be surmised, from the open roof above. We can begin to see weapons, a folding table, stools or forms, hangings, bankers and cushions, and less often andirons and hanging branches with candlesticks, as the essential furnishings of a room that held now only a ceremonial and symbolic function – the centre of the household, but not the centre of daily living.

For these citizens this was now the parlour, a heated room which served two or more functions. Tables, spruce for preference, were possibly for dining, and cupboards were to hand for sundry items. Hangings, bankers and cushions, all green for preference, made this a room for sitting in, with candlesticks for dark evenings. This was also a room in which to sleep. Mason's parlour, almost as sparsely furnished as his hall, did not include a bed, but Keynes had one and Parkyns had two – one a double, the other a single. The latter was much the most richly furnished, its tester ceiled with painted cloth and hung with curtains of buckram. Each with coverlets of Norwich cloth, these two beds were a highly prominent feature of Parkyns' parlour. In the furnishing of these rooms a similar lifestyle, the product of a shared taste, was again strongly visible.

The documentary evidence for the retreat by some of Bristol's wealthiest citizens from hall to parlour by the late 15th century is therefore clear. The question arises of whether the form of earlier houses might permit this change to be dated to a period not illuminated by relevant documents. Houses that would have provided accommodation sufficient for this new lifestyle were being built by the 14th century. In Christmas Street, the plan of no.24 allowed for storeyed accommodation two rooms in depth on the street frontage, an open hall of two bays in the centre and a further two-storeyed block one-room deep at the rear (Fig 5.7).

This arrangement would have allowed for a shop on the street frontage, a parlour between it and the hall and a kitchen to the rear, the plain, rectangular, ground-floor window openings to the latter more appropriate to a kitchen.

A similar arrangement could be seen in the outline of no.124 Temple Street, with the open area in the centre of the house, recorded on a plan of 1818, argued to be the ghost of the open hall (Figs 5.11 and 5.12). The plan of this house in the 15th century, certainly the date of the storeyed range on the street frontage (Figs 5.25 and 5.26), would have allowed for a parlour behind the shop, an open hall and a kitchen to the rear. These houses too belonged to wealthy citizens. Standing on an extensive tenement plot, no.24 Christmas Street was the house of Clement Bagot, twice mayor between 1437 and 1443.[30] Nearby, no.2 Christmas Street was in 1423 the house of the burgess and merchant John Stoke and Alice his wife, possibly the merchant and his wife depicted on two of the stone corbels for the arch-braced principal rafters of the roof (Fig 5.41).[31] By 1535 no.124 Temple Street was known as Foster's Place or the Mansion House. The Foster who lived here might have been one of two Richard Fosters, the father or son of John Foster, mayor in 1481–2.[32]

In these houses and others like them the importance of the parlour within the dwelling is apparent in their plans. We cannot be sure in

*Fig 5.41
No.2 Christmas Street, corbels for the arch-braced principal rafters, two of which were carved to represent a merchant and his wife. They possibly portray the burgess and merchant John Stoke and Alice his wife, who held the property in 1423 (Pritchard 1911, 72–3).*

many cases whether it had supplanted the hall as the chief living room, for we know too little about individual houses, but the general trend is clear: documentary and material evidence provides a consistent picture of increasing comfort among the merchant and ruling elite. This development was intimately connected to the increasingly symbolic use of the open hall in the houses of Bristol's wealthiest citizens.

## The Symbolic Hall and the Great Parlour in the 16th and 17th Centuries

In an urban context, the function of the open hall in the larger town house of the 15th to 17th centuries has scarcely been discussed. An aim of this chapter is therefore to examine how and why the large hall remained a feature of large urban houses until towards the end of the 17th century – becoming increasingly a symbolic space, as in Gaywode's house. The use of the hall in this way needs to be seen in the context of the developing use of other parts of the house, especially the parlour and chamber. The changes in the form and use of the house were prompted by the evolving aspirations and lifestyles of the wealthier inhabitants of the early modern city. The central question for the study of the open hall in this later period is this: if no longer the centre of household life, why was it retained with, in some cases, undiminished splendour?

The furnishing and use of the open hall as a largely symbolic space can be discerned in London and other towns between the 15th and 17th centuries. The possessions of Thomas Salle, for example, a draper of London, were appraised in 1468.[33] The hall was simply furnished with tapestry hangings, bankers and cushions, stools, tables and trestles; a 'bordering of iron for the hearth' was presumably for an open hearth, but there is no mention of andirons and fire irons. The remaining contents of the hall consisted entirely of armour and weapons, treated in the inventory as a single group: six spears, two corsletts, 11 bore-spears, one glove, eight battleaxes and 17 parvis [smaller axes(?)] 'great and small'. In contrast the parlour was more richly furnished, with a carpet, stools, turned chairs, fire irons, a birdcage and the *Chronicles of London* in two volumes, supplementing hangings, bankers and cushions similar to those in the hall.

A few years later, in 1476, the appraisal of the possessions of Sir Matthew Phelypp, alderman of London, offers a similar picture. The contents of his hall consisted of hangings, bankers and cushions, tables and trestles, andirons and fire irons, weapons and armour. In Phelypp's house the most sumptuously furnished room was the chamber.[34] In Southampton, the hall of the merchant Richard Thomas in 1447 would have been a familiar setting to merchants of Bristol. Three old cupboards, 20 old stools, 17 lances and four poleaxes would all have served to underline the legitimacy, honour and fighting prowess of Thomas's lineage.[35] More than a century later, in 1573, the halls of the merchants Richard Goddard and Reynold Howse in Southampton were sparsely furnished, but similarly bedecked with arms and armour.[36]

The use of the hall for symbolic and ceremonial purposes in the houses of the Bristol elite of the later Middle Ages has been described above. The continuing use of the hall in these ways through to the 17th century can be studied from the same combination of documentary and architectural evidence, more abundant from the early 16th century. The little-studied inventories of the late 15th century are a rich source of information, but cannot be linked directly to the architectural evidence. The earliest inventory which can be identified with a particular house is that of no.20 Small Street, the home successively of some of the wealthiest citizens of 16th- and 17th-century Bristol (Appendix 2, inventory of John Smythe)[37]

Its owner from *c* 1540 was John Smythe, a merchant whose outstandingly successful career enabled him to purchase a country estate in Long Ashton and a number of the former possessions of Bath Priory. During the years 1545 to 1548 Smythe was living in Corn Street, in St Leonard's parish, but by 1548 he had moved to Small Street, in St Werburgh's parish.[38] By a process of elimination, this house can only have been no.20, purchased by Smythe as part of the Bristol properties formerly belonging to Bath Priory (Figs 5.14, 5.42 and 5.43).[39] Late in 1544 Smythe had paid for the hauling away from his house in Small Street of 364 vats of rubble, at the same time buying in 155 vats of new stone, including 32 of freestone.[40] We can conclude that by 1549 the works were sufficiently complete for Smythe to move in.

His thoughts on the new arrangements for the plan of his house were remarkably similar to those of Keynes, Mason and others some 50 years earlier. A considerable sum must have been spent on re-roofing the open hall, its new roof a cut-down version of the recently

THE HALLHOUSE

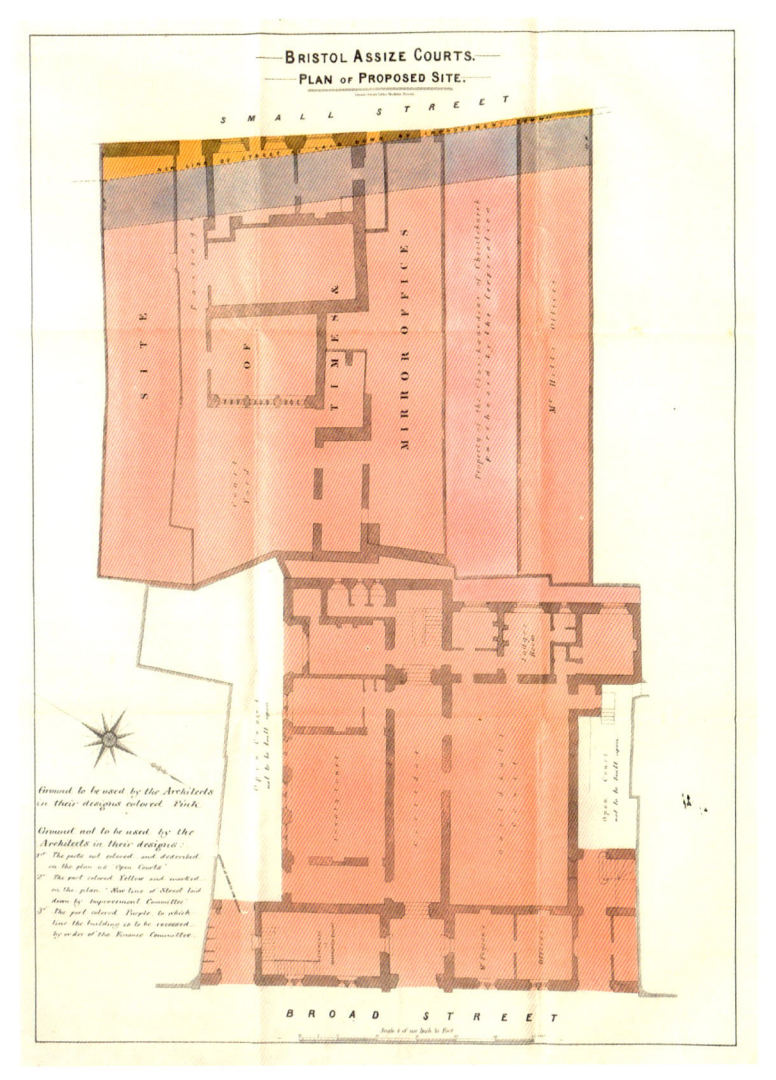

*Fig 5.42*
*No.20 Small Street, plan c 1867 prior to the incorporation of the house in the new Guildhall and courts (BRO 01687(4)).*

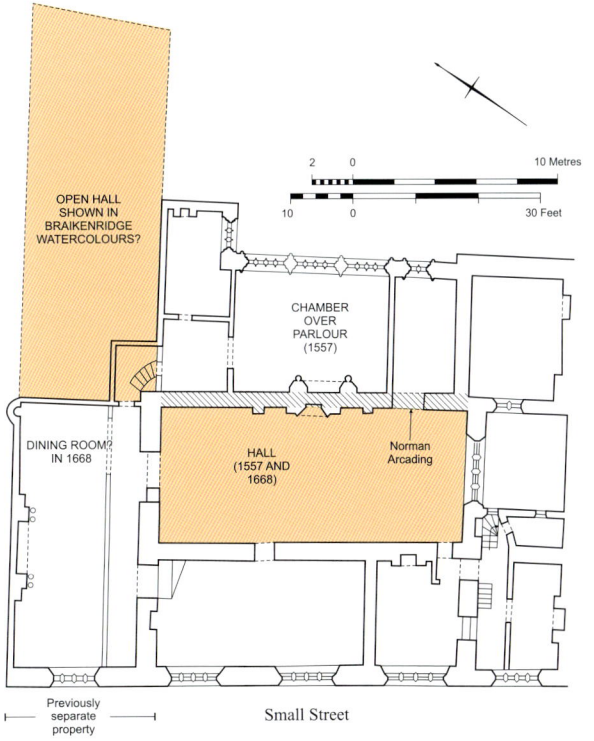

*Fig 5.43*
*No.20 Small Street, recorded buildings (RHL, PEC, see also entry in Inventory).*

99

THE TOWN HOUSE IN MEDIEVAL AND EARLY MODERN BRISTOL

completed hammer-beam roof to Hampton Court (Figs 5.44 and 5.45). In the Small Street hall, as at Hampton Court, the principal roof trusses sprang from columns and capitals characteristic of the Italianate style brought into England from France in these decades. The building alterations probably included the infilling and masking of a late 12th-century open arcade, and possibly the removal of any chimneystack standing in the hall. Certainly it was no part of the new plan to provide one. This was emphatically an unheated room, an entrance hall, albeit nearly 50ft in length. At his death in 1557 this hall was furnished with hangings, wall panels and 18 tapestry cushions, but there was no further seating and no evidence for heating. In this house it appears that the hall had ceased to be used for dining, even at the feast of Christmas.

Contemporary with the rebuilding of the hall was the construction of a new chamber block, together with a stair tower, built against the east side of the hall (Figs 5.14, 5.42, 5.43, 5.46 and 5.47). The ground floor can be interpreted as

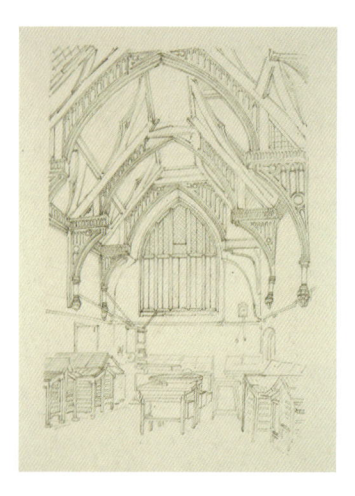

*Fig 5.44*
*The hall of no.20 Small Street, 1820s, with inserted first floor, watercolour by H O'Neill, 1821 (BRSMG M 2466).*

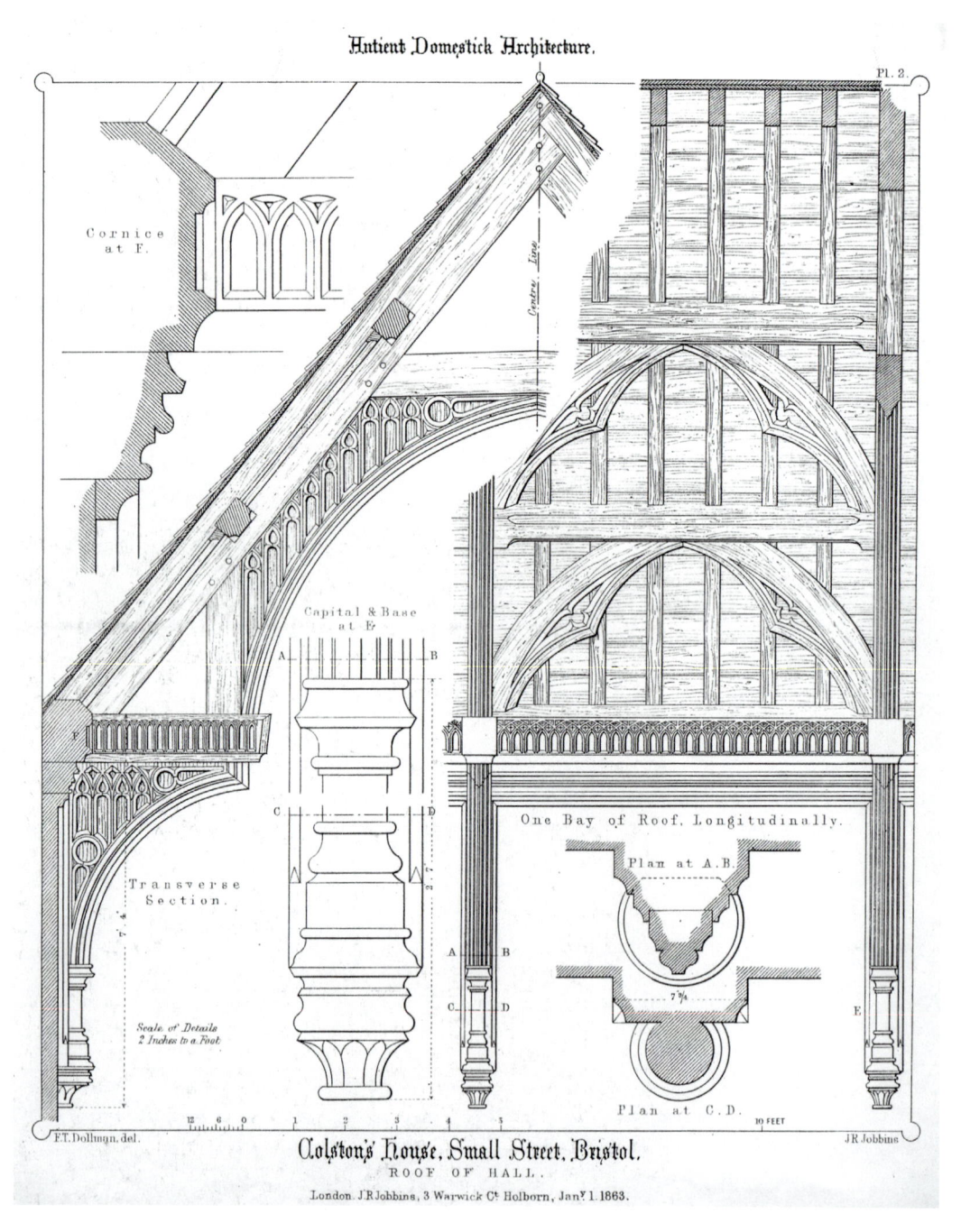

*Fig 5.45*
*No.20 Small Street, detail of roof (drawings by Dollman and Jobbins, 1863).*

THE HALLHOUSE

*Fig 5.46*
*No.20 Small Street, details of parlour wing built in 1540s (drawing by Dollman and Jobbins, 1863).*

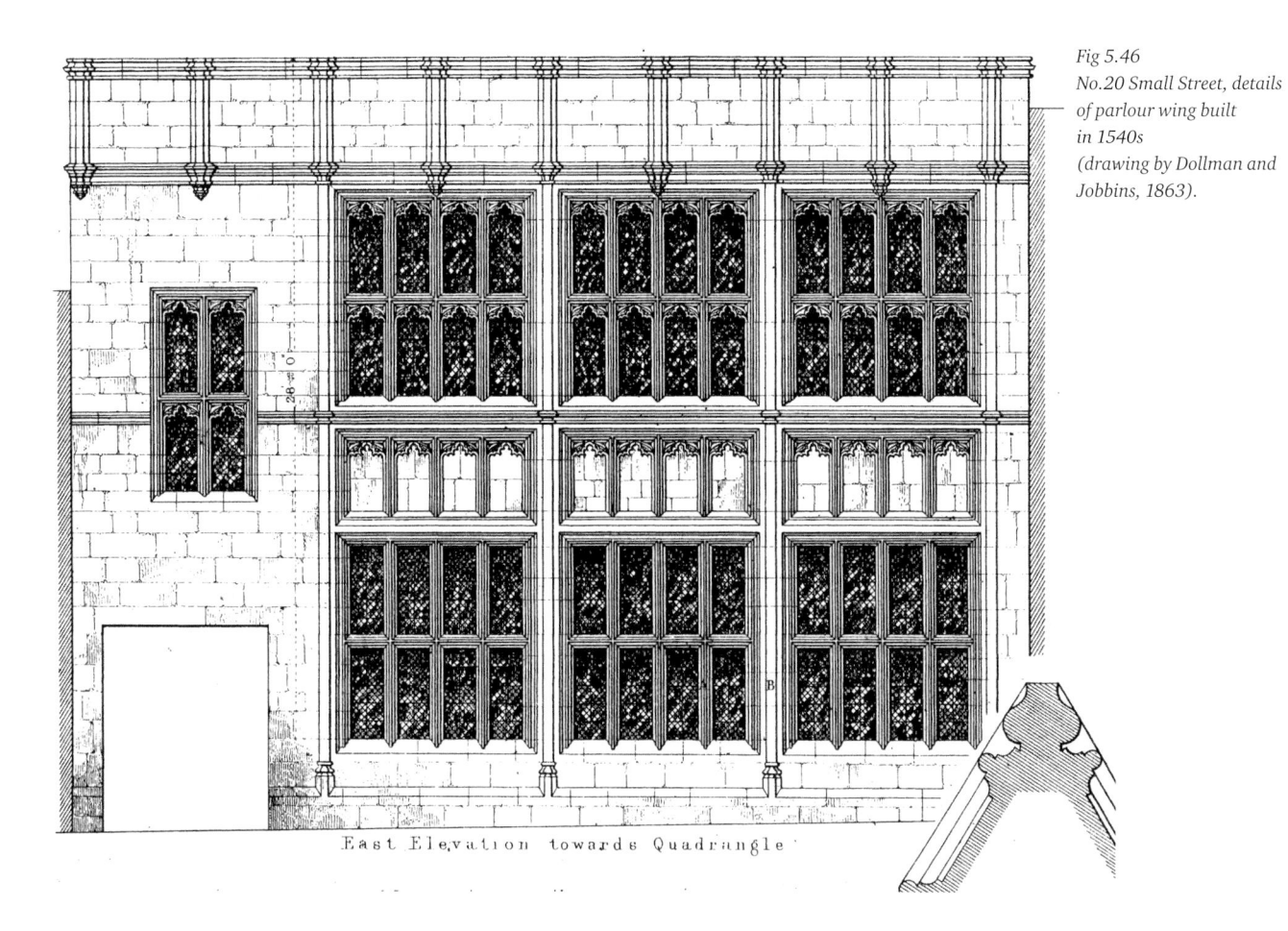

*Fig 5.47*
*No.20 Small Street, drawing of the 19th century of parlour wing built in 1540s (BRSMG Ma6739).*

a parlour, the room above as a new best chamber. In the finish of these new rooms French influences were much more pronounced, most especially in the design of the chimneypieces of identical design on the ground and first floors. The place for formal meals and entertainment was now the parlour, the ground floor of this newly built range faced in freestone. This room offered considerable comfort. Its walls were lined with hangings of red and green saye made especially for the room, and there were small firedogs, an iron fireback and fire irons for use in the winter. A table, two Luxbone chairs and 18 stools denoted that this served as a dining room.

John Butcher, a wealthy draper, alderman and former mayor, also lived in Small Street, at nos.16–17, the house formerly of John Foster (pp96–7). In the 1590s or 1600s the front part of this house was rebuilt, so as to provide five floors of accommodation, comprising cellars, three main storeys and attics, each two rooms wide and one room deep (Fig 5.48). Set back

*Fig 5.48*
*Nos.16–17 Small Street, John Foster's house in 1492, photograph of 1930 by P E W Street (NMR AA78/06658).*

THE HALLHOUSE

behind this front part was a range containing an open hall (Fig 5.49). It could be concluded that in the 1590s it was thought worthwhile to modernise this house at considerable expense, but also important to retain the open hall.

The contents of this house were described in a probate inventory of 1623.[41] Like those of Gaywode and Keynes some 150 years earlier, Butcher's open hall was not a room for everyday living. There was no evidence of any form of heating, and any other domestic comforts were significantly absent. One entered Butcher's hall through a panelled portal. Inside were benches similarly wainscoted; yet one's eyes would have been drawn not to these, but to the various items displayed around the hall. On the walls were four panels containing the *paternoster* and a map of the world, statements of Butcher's faith and horizons. Apart from a hanging candelabrum, everything else in the hall was

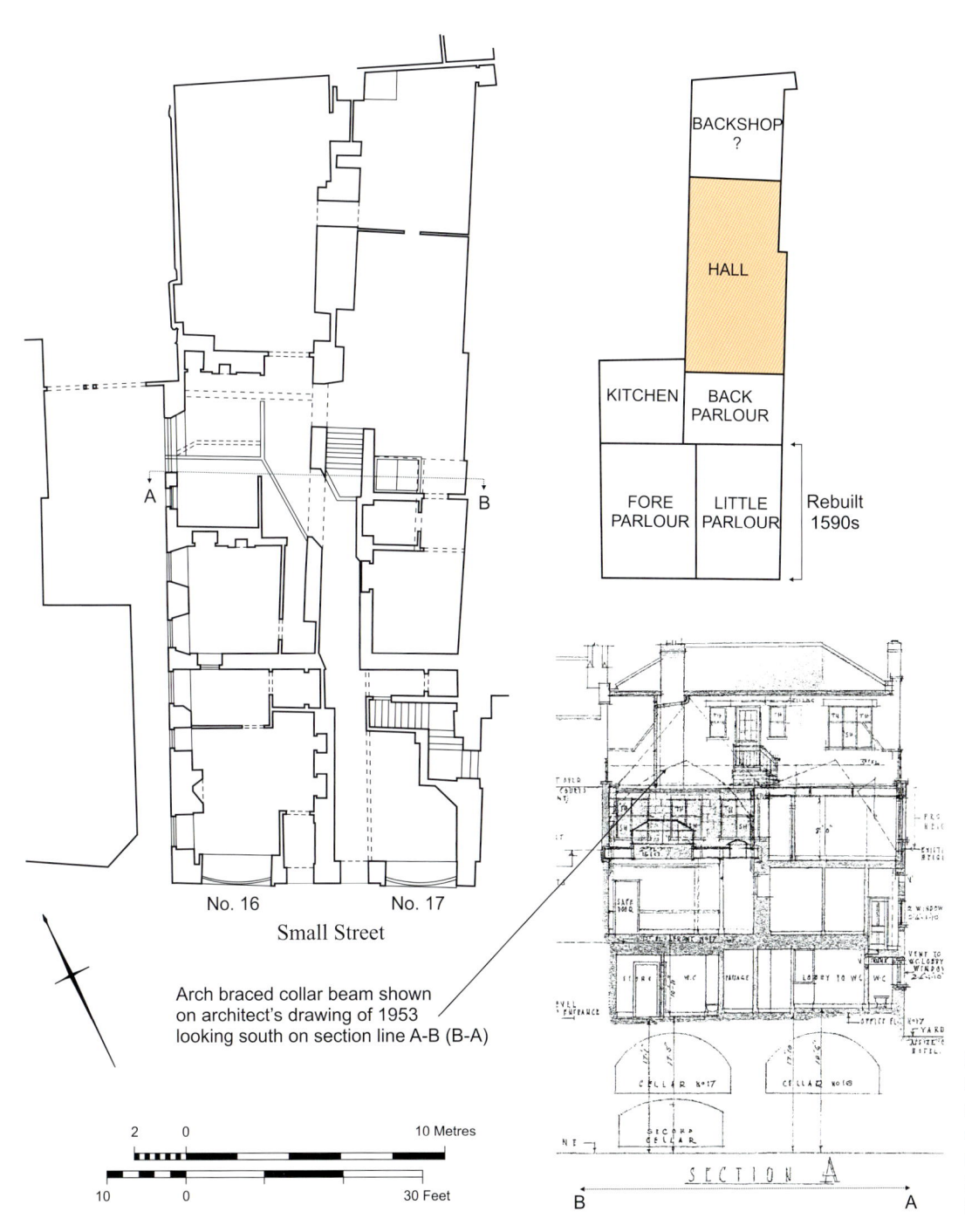

Fig 5.49
Nos.16–17 Small Street, section and plan from author's survey and documentary sources (RHL, PEC, see also entry in Inventory).

weaponry: a complete set of armour, an iron target, spears, a halberd, bill, staff, sword, dagger and four muskets. This display far exceeded that of the 15th-century hall, and could be interpreted as a very overt statement of Butcher's aspirations to gentry status. At his death he held extensive lands in north Somerset. From its position, set back on one side of the courtyard, Butcher's hall could not have served as the everyday entry for visitors. Nevertheless, for those venturing that far, it would certainly have served to underline how John Butcher saw his place in society.

Like his 15th-century predecessors, John Butcher, his family or guests, would have relaxed, sat or read, not in the open hall but in the parlour – of which he had three, all lined with wainscot. In the warmer months the fore-parlour might have been his preferred option, a well-furnished but apparently unheated room, in which a painted ship in a frame was a further reminder of his mercantile interests. This room can be identified as the ground-floor room adjacent to no.18, the flue for the present fireplace contrived within the thickness of the wall and clearly not original to the house. A 'little parlour' comprised the greater part of the more northerly front room, a small stack on the north wall perhaps preserving the location of a former larger chimneystack. In 1623 this room was heated and carpeted, though fairly sparsely furnished. A third 'backer' parlour, unheated, contained only a sideboard with two cupboards, a table, some benches and saye hangings; this was possibly used for dining.

The focus on the parlour as the principal living room of the house would have been equally evident in the newly completed building works of Humphrey Brown, also a merchant, and his next-door neighbour. In the early 1620s Brown was responsible for the construction of the range standing at the back of the tenement plot occupied by no.15 Small Street.[42] When built, this probably consisted of three storeys and an attic, with one principal room on each floor (Fig 5.50). The room on the first floor was ostentatiously finished, having both an elaborately plastered ceiling and a large chimneypiece, the latter now in the Museum of Fine Art in Cincinnati. This was a room for display, centred on the hearth, the sophisticated taste of its owner clearly stated in the portrayal of the five senses on the overmantel above the fireplace (Fig 5.51). Access to this room would have been from a gallery at first-floor level, providing a link across the north side of the courtyard to the hall range extending back from the street, the ghost of this range reflected in the plan of the cellars. Guests might have arrived in Brown's first-floor parlour via an open hall used in much the same way as his neighbour's. Servants would have probably arrived via a stairs within the gallery, affording access to both courtyard and kitchen.[43]

The great parlour in John Whitson's house in St Nicholas Street, completed before 1603, was certainly on the first floor, probably over the formerly open hall. A central feature to the room was the chimneypiece, now firmly of classical form, its heraldry a statement of Whitson's allegiance and social standing (Fig 5.52). Of equal prominence must have been the six great pictures on the wall, one a curtained and full-length portrait of Whitson's second wife, remembered also by Whitson's godson, the

*Fig 5.50*
*No.15 Small Street, section and plan of detached parlour block (RHL).*

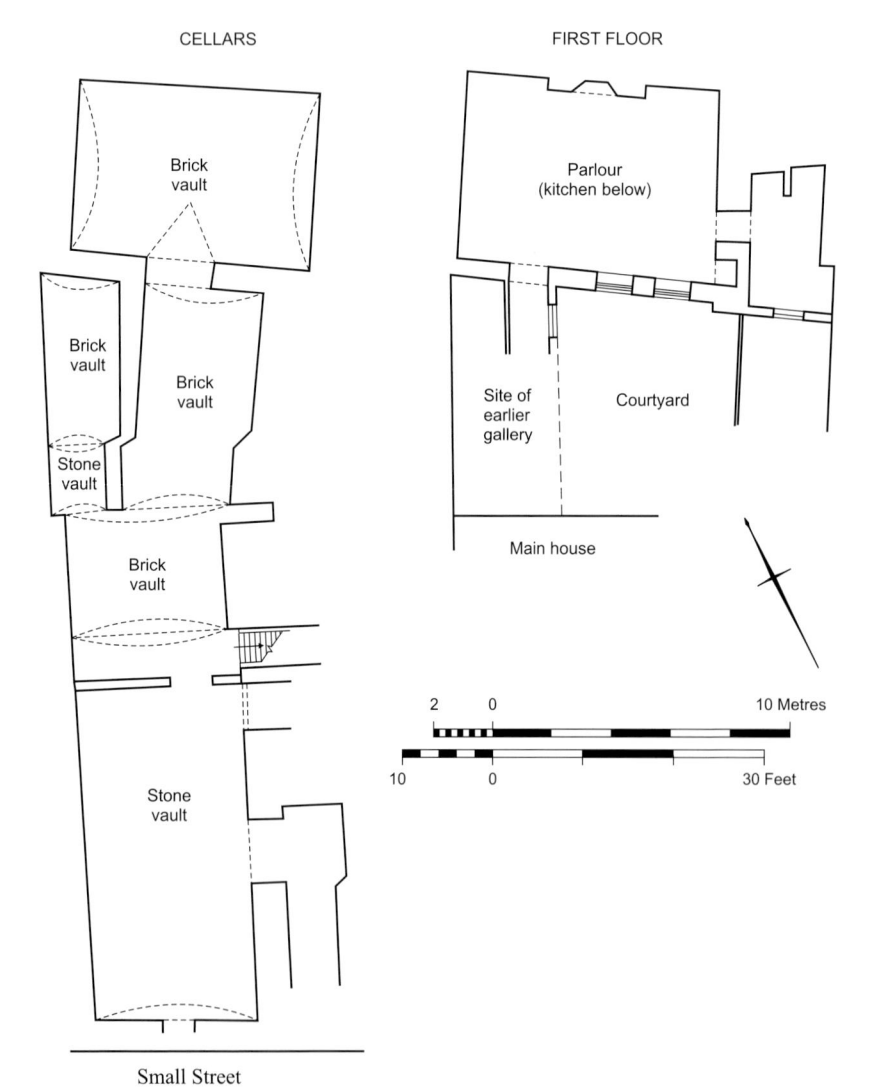

*Fig 5.51*
*No.15 Small Street, detached parlour block, chimneypiece of 1620s depicting the five senses, photograph of 1940 (NMR CC40/00238).*

*Fig 5.52*
*Nos.22–8 St Nicholas Street, Whitson's house, chimneypiece of before 1603, now in the Red Maids' School Hall, photograph of 1927 (Hirst 1927, Pl IV).*

writer and antiquary John Aubrey. From his early childhood visits to this room, Aubrey recollected that Whitson lived 'nobly' and that this was his 'dining room'. He might well have seen the long table with seating for 12 and the eight or more chairs for sitting more comfortably at the fireside.[44]

In several ways Whitson's great parlour had replaced the open hall. Its hearth had no superior in the house; it was the room for important meals and was, with its curtained portrait, of supreme importance to Whitson himself. Years later, it was the one room of which John Aubrey thought to write. Yet Whitson retained also a heated hall, probably the ceiled room below the parlour. Its furnishings included two great pictures, a map and two bucks' horns on the walls. Though weapons and armour were conspicuous by their absence, surprisingly as Whitson was a colonel in the militia, this room would have still been immediately recognisable as the ceiled equivalent of the open hall, the symbolic centre of the house.

In the juxtaposition of the hall and great parlour, the merchant Robert Aldworth followed a different strategy in his rebuilding of Norton's House, the extensive medieval property to the south of St Peter's church (Fig 5.15). As rebuilt c 1612 and as described in a deed of 1648, the hall and parlour were both placed on the first floor, on either side of the stairs.[45] The hall, known in 1619 as the 'upper hall', was fully panelled, but totally unheated. On the opposite side of the stairs was the 'Greate Parlour wainscotted'. This room, far more than the hall, was an area for symbolic display. It was not only panelled, but had an elaborate strapwork ceiling, a richly ornamented entrance doorway and a large decorated chimneypiece emphasising the importance of the hearth (Figs 5.53 and 5.54).

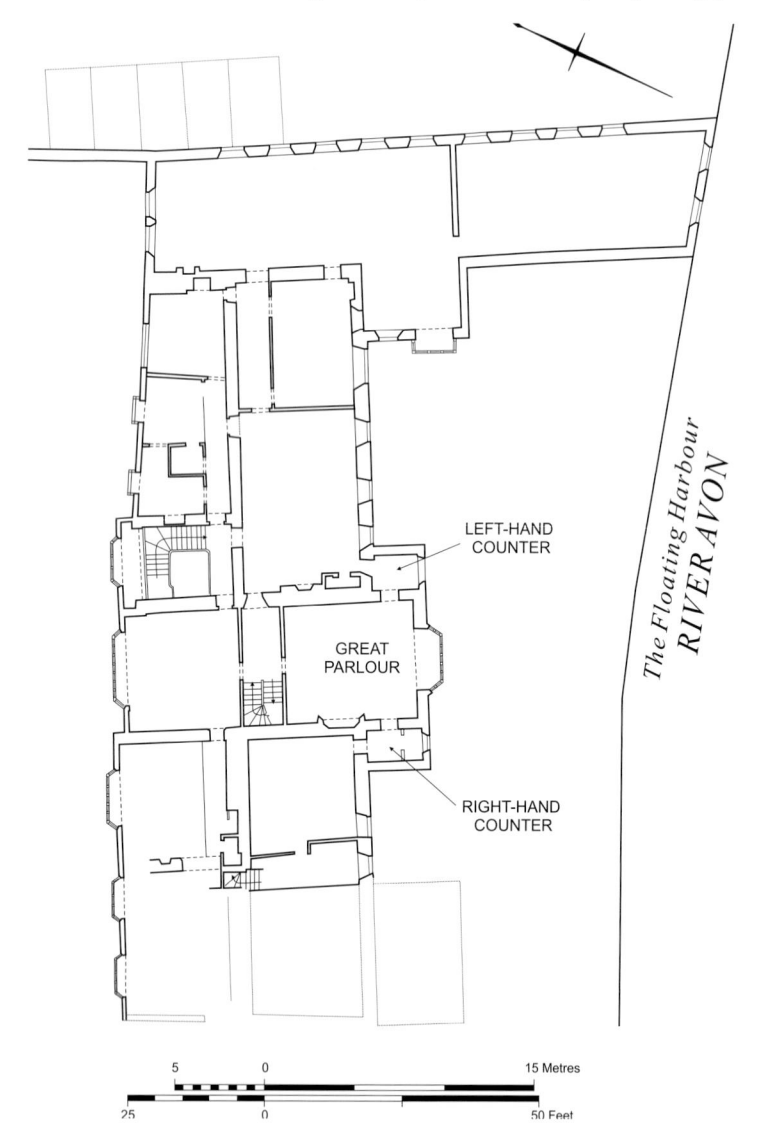

Like a medieval open hall, this great parlour could be seen as graduating from a lower to an upper end. The upper end was marked by a large mullioned bay window, from the outside visibly the largest window in the house and marking out to the exterior world the importance of this room and the organisation of space within it. On the inside, the upper end was marked also by the entrances to two rooms named 'counters', through-closets providing private access to the chambers on each side of the great parlour. More public access to the great parlour was from the elaborate entrance and stairs.

The design of the great chimneypiece contributed to this invoking of medieval values. It was itself of two pieces, the lower part, with the fire arch, dating from the early 16th century. Aldworth had made a conscious decision to retain this earlier feature, but he had also modernised it with the addition of an overmantel bearing the royal arms of James I. The chimneypiece was thus central to the room, not only in a social sense, but also, as with Whitson's room, in subtly noting his own ancestry, and associating that with loyalty to the Crown.

Some households transferred the symbolic role of the open hall to the ceiled-over ground-floor room in the middle of the altered house. The example of John Whitson's house in St Nicholas Street has been noted above. In Small Street Nathaniel Butcher, son of John (pp302–4), had furnished his ceiled hall in 1628 much as his father had done its open predecessor. It had three tables and various

*Fig 5.53*
*Robert Aldworth's house next to St Peter's church, plan of first floor showing great parlour and counters (RHL, PEC).*

THE HALLHOUSE

*Fig 5.54
Aldworth's house, great parlour, photograph of c 1910
(NMR Country Life Collection CTL 01/17031/7033/2).*

stools, two great chests, a pair of virginals, pictures around the walls and an assortment of armour and weapons. This visual display signified that this was the hall, as much the symbolic centre of the house as it had been in his father's time.[46]

As in John Butcher's house, the principal room for extended social interaction, but not for sleeping, was the adjacent parlour. In contrast to the six stools in the unheated hall, the furnishings of the well appointed, heated parlour included a suite of embroidered chairs and stools, together with seating for at least 15 more persons. On the floor above, the newly contrived room over the hall had now become the principal chamber, the status of this room denoted by brass-topped andirons on the hearth, possibly open to what had been the hall roof. Though living in modernised houses, both John Whitson and Nathaniel Butcher chose in the first half of the 17th century to use the hall as the social or symbolic centre of the home. In doing so they were invoking earlier values, ones which would have been familiar to those who lived in houses with open halls in the 15th century. In that sense they were still living with the open hall.

107

The value placed on the symbolic open hall can be demonstrated by a final example, one with very particular and personal meanings related to status and politics. By the 1660s John Smythe's house in Small Street had become the town house of Sir Henry Creswick. Creswick's father, Francis, had been born into a family of Yorkshire gentry and cutlers. He had started his working life in 1598 as apprentice to Henry Hobson, a Bristol hardwareman, and had been admitted as a burgess in 1608. An ardent royalist, he had sheltered the fugitive Charles I and the future Charles II here in 1643, before having his estate sequestered in 1646. The open hall, refashioned in the 16th century, the parlour block built at the same time and the more recently refurbished great chamber overlooking Small Street might all have been utilised for the accommodation of the royal household.[47]

At his death in 1668 an inventory describing the layout and contents of the house was again made.[48] Creswick's open hall was much as it had been a century earlier; it remained unheated and was certainly not a room for daily living. The main purpose of the furnishings of the open hall was to serve as a statement of the family's position. The arms of Elizabeth I, hanging on one wall, would have provided the impression of an ancient lineage, notwithstanding that Creswick's father had been apprenticed in hardware five years before the death of the late queen. A hanging ship symbolised the position of the Creswicks in the merchant community at the centre of the city's fortunes. The size of the room, the three brass candelabra hanging from the hammer-beam roof, the walls adorned with two maps, 13 pictures, two lions carved in wood, a set of deer antlers and an array of muskets, halberds, half-pikes, bandoliers, a shield and three pieces of armour would all have served to impress visitors and guests. Like Smythe, Creswick entertained within the parlour block newly built in the 1540s.

In 1668 Creswick had possessed three parlours. A 'great parlour' was probably the ground-floor room on the east side of the hall mentioned above. It may have served primarily as a room for the reception of visitors. Adjacent to the hall, but heated, its furnishings included a reading desk, an organ, virginals, 12 pictures, tables and stools – as well as 18 chairs, a couch and two carpets, all in the same fabric. The 'old parlour' and 'the little new parlour', both heated, must have been towards the street frontage. The former was barely furnished, but the latter was more a study, with ample shelves, tables and 'books of all sorts'. On the first floor was a further room for living, the 'dining room', again heated. Here the furnishings fulfilled exactly the declared function of the room; they included a table, sideboard, 13 chairs and 12 stools, pictures, glasses and five brass candelabra.

Creswick had made some improvements to the domestic comforts of the house, but he clearly valued the ancient and the antique as settings to promote the legitimacy, honour and lineage of his own dynasty. Six years after the Restoration, the medieval open hall, beatified by the presence of the martyred king, must to Creswick have provided ample legitimacy for a new-founded urban dynasty. To many other citizens it might have seemed an irrelevance, a way of life no longer worth pursuing. In contrast, through the increasing specialisation of function evident in the use of domestic space, the arrangement of his house looked to the future.

In the households of Whitson and Aldworth, the great parlour was the dining room. Forty years later Creswick had both a great parlour and a dining room. The lifestyles of Butcher and Brown were shared by a probably small number of merchants living in the centre of the city. Two further examples can be cited. The merchant John Ware held the lease of the Three Cups, no.63 Corn Street, from 1607 until his death in 1618. On the street frontage, a wide doorway of the 15th century served also as the entry for a processional way through the house into the churchyard of St Ewen's, most probably through Ware's hall.[49] Though moderately well furnished, with a table, three stools and three carpets, the eyes of the occasional procession, including that for his own funeral, would probably been drawn first to the 12 or more pieces of armour and weaponry on the walls. The 'old andirons and doggs', like those of John Gaywode, were probably more for show than for active use. The principal room for entertainment and relaxation was the forestreet parlour, with seating for at least 13 persons – probably the room alongside the entry from the street. This room too was heated, but here the andirons were complete with the other essential hearth furniture, creepers, slice and tongs.[50]

Close to Ware's house was the residence of the merchant Nicholas Meredith, city chamberlain from 1613 to his death in 1639. Visitors to his town house might similarly have been impressed by the visual effect created in his hall. The walls were hung with pictures and a map, together with an assortment of weapons. Two 'high brass andirons' stood in the hearth, but, apart from a chest and sideboard, the room was otherwise sparsely furnished. As in Butcher's house, the principal living room was now the parlour. Two stools and a chair in Meredith's hall provided little seating compared with the 26 chairs and stools kept in the adjoining parlour on the street frontage.[51]

On the same side of Small Street, opposite to Creswick's house, was that of Sir Robert Cann. He died nearly two decades later, and a probate inventory provides a detailed picture of the layout and contents in 1686 (Appendix 2). The hall was unheated and furnished with a variety of old tables and cushions. Its walls were lined with three muskets, 10 swords and 10 bandoleers, and the room must have presented a similar appearance to those of Creswick, Butcher and Meredith. The large, and sometimes still open, symbolic hall in Bristol remained a potent element of merchant housing culture into the 1680s. In an earlier period the hall had already lost its role as the place for formal meals that brought the urban household together on a daily or regular basis. The hall of John Gaywode in the mid-15th century served as the place for formal meals only at such times as Christmas. Two centuries later even this role had probably been abandoned, the place for all formal meals being the dining room.

The principal purpose of the large urban hall was now to symbolise the lineage and honour of wealthy urban families. The room was part of the theatre of the larger house, its medieval ancestry and adornments conveying a powerful statement concerning its owner's status in society.[52] The great andirons in the halls of John Gaywode and other citizens in later periods were symbols as much of the antiquity of the urban family as of the former role of the hall. Old furniture, coats of arms and other ancestral possessions served much the same purpose. Arms and armour too would have served to underline the status of an urban household. The leading citizens of the early modern city had appropriated the form of the medieval open hall for their own new purposes, thereby creating a way of life that could have been easily recognised elsewhere, in London and in other towns and cities.[53] It is clear that by the mid-17th century the lifestyle of the ruling elite of Bristol was part of a much wider commercial culture.

## Merchants and the Gentry: Land, Marriages, Country Houses and the Town House

It has been argued that the 17th century saw a growing consciousness among the Bristol merchants of their place in wider society – reflected, for instance, in requests for grants of arms and the acquisition of country estates.[54] Such requests and acquisitions may have increased in the 17th century, but the awareness of social status was certainly evident by the 15th century. For William Canynges and John Gaywode in the 1460s, John Smythe in the 1540s, John Butcher in the 1620s and Henry Creswick in the 1660s, the open hall would have been seen as an essential component of the lifestyle of the landed classes, an important element of many gentry houses until the early 17th century.[55]

Bristol merchants from the early 15th century onwards would have certainly been familiar with this way of living, featuring as it did increasingly unheated halls, rarely used for mealtimes and often decked with the weaponry for the militia which the gentry themselves would lead. Many illustrations could be given of the close association between merchants and gentry: one Saturday evening in March 1420, the arrival for supper at Berkeley Castle of two merchants of Bristol with their grooms did not seem an unusual event.[56] In the mid-15th century Alice Cokkes, daughter of a wealthy Bristol merchant family, married successively into two important Gloucestershire families, the Berkeleys and the Poyntzs.[57] Canynges' contacts have already been related, and his daughter too married into a gentry family.[58] John Gaywode probably came from Pewsey in rural Wiltshire.[59] In the 1540s and 1550s John Smythe had purchased substantial country estates, notably in Long Ashton, Somerset,[60] while in the 17th century John Butcher and Henry Creswick similarly owned lands outside the city.[61]

The use of the open hall in the 16th and certainly the 17th centuries, in a symbolic sense, might be seen today as an invoking of traditional values, but this was also a lifestyle already evident in Bristol within a century of Langland's complaint. Indeed, for Langland too, the open hall was already a symbol and, with hindsight, we can see that the open hall symbolised values derived from the 14th century or earlier. Among those who lived in what were termed hallhouses in the 15th century, there were already significant differences in lifestyle. Still evident in the early 17th century, these differences reflected the choices of groups distinguished as much by occupational and social status as by wealth. The open hall was retained longest amongst those who were gentry in all but name, much as in parts of rural England.[62]

## The Symbolic Hall, the Status of the Individual and the Militia

Most of the halls which we have examined contained arms or armour. There was a commonality between the hall of John Gaywode in 1473 and that of Sir Robert Cann over 200 years later. The possession of arms was directly linked to the role of the citizenry in the militia, and to the positions held by citizens in the militia. Arms and armour in the hall were not simply, as noted in a study of Norwich inventories, 'prestige items in an imposing entrance to the house'; they were also deeply symbolic of the status of the individual citizen within the militia.[63]

The weapons that each man should keep for the defence of his country, or more strictly speaking his county, were set out according to his wealth, as enacted by the Assize of Arms in 1181, the Statute of Winchester in 1285 and its successive re-issues. These remained binding until repealed by Philip and Mary in 1558. Successive charters confirming the privileges of the city of Bristol, a county in its own right from 1373, set out both the rights and responsibilities of its citizens under the Statute of Winchester. Muster rolls of the period between 1460 and 1480 confirm the increased readiness of especially the urban levies in the mustering of the militia. Maurice Powicke has written that by the end of Edward IV's reign 'a well armed force, somewhat heavily concentrated in the towns, was in being'. In Bristol the militia even possessed artillery,[64] and in London the militia was, from 1537, under the aegis of the Honourable Artillery Company.[65]

By the mid-16th century the special muster had, in Lindsay Boynton's words, become 'an occasion, social as well as military, in the Elizabethan calendar. This was especially true of towns'.[66] In 1572 a general muster of the Bristol militia saw 'all the burgesses fully armed with all sorts of warlike weapons, every craft and science several by themselves with all their drums and colours … a comely show'.[67] In London the muster of some 10,000 men in 1588 was emphatically for the defence of the realm, but events such as the display by 80 'certain gentlemen of the Artillery Garden' of 'moderne armes' triumphing over the Turks, staged in the hall of the Merchant Taylors in 1638, also fulfilled a social function.[68] The organisation of the militia was hierarchical. In London the funeral procession of Sir Phillip Sidney in 1587 gives a good insight into the organisation of the capital's militia. Captains were followed by the lieutenants, sword and target men, musketeers and successive further ranks of fighting men.[69] In Bristol it is evident from the city accounts that the militia were headed by the mayor and aldermen, the latter responsible for their own wards of the city. In London, Bristol and elsewhere, the display of arms within the hall of the individual citizen was thus a display of rank and responsibility within the civic order, matters which were prominent in the annual calendar.

From at least the 15th century, and probably earlier in London, wealthy merchants owned country property, sometimes using a country house as a second residence. In two instances from Bristol, where we can compare the contents of urban and rural residences, it can be shown that the use of the hall to reflect status within the community was confined to the urban setting to which it related. Merchants who possessed a second house in the country may have used one room in the rural house as 'the hall', but its use was very different to that accorded to the hall in an urban context.

Sir Robert Cann's second residence, a weekend retreat, was at Stoke Bishop three miles to the west of Bristol (pp255–8). This was an earlier lodge of one room on each floor, supplemented in 1669 by a larger house with two rooms on each floor. It too was described in the probate inventory of his possessions in 1686.[70] Cann's Stoke Bishop house included a hall, the larger of the two rooms on the ground floor containing also the entry to the house and the stairs to the floor above. The inventory shows that this was the principal living room of the house. Its contents included a table board, six leather chairs, two pairs of brass andirons and the fireplace implements. There were no arms or armour.

The second residence of Andrew Hook, a wealthy brewer, was at Ashley Manor on the other side of the city, a house almost identical in design to Cann's house at Stoke Bishop (chapter 9). In 1689 the absence of arms and armour from a hall which clearly served as the main living room stood in contrast to the weaponry stored in Hook's house in the centre of the city.[71] The display of arms and amour in the halls of the merchant class thus reflected both the status of citizens in the urban militia and a sense of urban identity for families rooted firmly within the city rather than the surrounding countryside. Where wealthy citizens possessed a second house in the countryside beyond, it was the urban hall and not its rural namesake that served to underline the status and honour of its owner and family.

## The Symbolic Hall and the Status of the City

Larger towns and cities of the 16th and early 17th centuries jealously guarded their rights to control the militia within their boundaries, and in this quest they expended considerable sums of money. By Elizabeth's reign and until the Civil War the Corporation of Bristol's annual expenditure invariably included purchases for the equipment and uniforms of the militia. Boynton has highlighted how in local responses to renewed threats in 1613 the 'northern niggardliness' of the Durham gentry, who seem to have resented expenditure on the militia, compared unfavourably with 'Bristol's lavish outlay'.[72] For larger towns and cities such expenditure served to assert civic identity and independence. Thus the halls of leading citizens, where individuals displayed their status in the militia, also expressed this distinctiveness of towns, and especially cities, and the ways in which their wealthier citizens perceived themselves to be set apart from those who lived in the countryside.

Civic expenditure on the militia was at its most excessive when the city was visited by royalty or royal officials. In 1510 Henry VIII's visit to London to see 'the pompous march of the City Watch', the Lord Mayor attended by a giant and two pages on horseback, plus archers, pikemen, bill men and halberdiers, must have occasioned the city considerable expense.[73] On Elizabeth I's first visit to Bristol in 1574 the city mustered 400 of the militia and built two forts above the Avon especially for the occasion, arranging for a mock battle to secure these to take place over three days.[74] Elizabeth and her retinue were provided with hospitality in the large house (Fig 2.20) built by the merchant Sir John Young on the site of the Carmelite Priory; 80 years later the hall within this house still contained 'four wooden racks to hang the armour on'.[75]

In 1587 the city militia, parades and mock skirmishes played a similarly important role in the reception of the Earls of Warwick and Leicester at Bristol. The latter's position as Lord High Steward made him especially well placed to grant favours to the city, and the audits specifically record the visits of the chamberlain to London 'to keep his lordship in mind' of the city's needs. Hospitality for the earls and their retinue was on this occasion provided in the house in Small Street which we have already seen in some detail, earlier in the century the residence of John Smythe. Leicester was so dissatisfied with his subsequent reception in Bath that he wrote back to Bristol asking for a gift of the bed in which he had slept – a request duly granted by an obsequious Corporation anxious not to lose possible favours.[76]

In 1643 this same house, by then belonging to the Creswick family, was briefly the residence of Charles I and his sons following the royalist capture of the city. In 1665 the Lord High Steward and his extensive retinue were again entertained here. The open hall would have served as an entry to the great parlour in which the Duke of Ormond was wined and dined – the arms and armour listed in Creswick's inventory of 1668 perhaps dimly visible through the haze induced by 200 gallons of wine provided to accompany Westphalian hams and tongues especially imported from London (Ormond then prolonged his visit by four days!).[77] Through these events we can see that the open hall of John Smythe's house must have played a role in the affirmation of civic, as well as of individual, identity and obsequiousness – the latter a necessary and often successful element in the city's political relations with the Crown and Court.

## The Imperatives of National Politics

The use of the symbolic hall for public occasions underlined the proximity of leading merchants to the gentry. In Kent, Sarah Pearson noted that 'the gentry required the impressive effect of an open hall for public occasions, and frequently retained such a room – which gradually took on more of the character of an entrance hall – for a long time to come'. In Kent, as in Bristol, the halls of certain houses were 'left open for a very long time'.[78] Halls symbolically furnished were still to be seen in the houses of wealthy merchants in London on the eve of the Great Fire, and in Bristol as late as the 1680s. In the analysis of Norwich inventories it was noted that armour and weapons were often still present in the halls of larger mansions in the second half of the 17th century.[79]

In London and Bristol arms and armour appear to have been totally absent from the halls of prominent citizens by the early 18th century.[80] We might link this to the rapid decline in the importance of the militia that had taken place by the end of the 17th century. In looking at the fortunes of the militia following the Restoration, the years 1660–70 were seen as ones of 'triumph and reverse'; 1670 was seen to mark the beginnings of '80 years of decay'. With the Rye House Plot and Monmouth's Rebellion, the Crown's need for a standing army rather than the militia was reinforced.[81]

We might therefore see the role of the symbolic hall in the early modern city as one linked ultimately to national political considerations and the affirmation of civic identity. From the 15th century or earlier until the 1680s, it remained a potent symbol of the nexus between local and national politics. The walls of the hall lined with arms and armour were signifiers of the Crown's need for the militia, and of the importance attached to this by civic government; they were also a mark of the importance which individual leading citizens accorded to their role and specific status in meeting this requirement. With the passing of the need for the militia, the symbolic and often unheated hall which had been readily identifiable to merchants and citizens from the 15th century or earlier had ceased to have any real significance in the domestic life of the early modern city.

## The Hall in Lesser Houses in the 17th Century: Symbolic Space, Living Room, Work Room, Taverns

If the symbolic hall is seen at its most impressive in the houses of the merchant elite, it may also be glimpsed in diluted form at lower social levels. For some citizens the hall could serve as the symbolic centre of the house without the need to line its walls with weapons. For Teague Jones, a glover living in the parish of St Mary Redcliff in 1612, a table, some stools, two old forms and a solitary javelin were the bare essentials with which to signify the formerly central but now symbolic role of a little used and unheated hall. His main living room was the parlour, heated and lined with wainscot and painted cloths.[82] For William Cradocke, a shoemaker in St Michael's parish, the hall was used more for storage, mainly for the household linen and possibly as a bedchamber; that the Bible and the Communion Book were also kept here might signify it retained a symbolic importance as the centre of the household. In 1612 the principal living room of his three-storey house was the parlour, heated and well furnished with cloth hangings, tables, chairs, stools, a desk and a curtained tester bed complete with an Arras coverlet. His one weapon, a halberd, was also kept here, not in the hall.[83] In George Baldwin's house in Redcliff Street, its contents described in 1613, the principal living room was again the parlour. The hall was unheated, sparsely furnished, but retaining its high table; Baldwin, perhaps because he was a gentleman, felt no need to line his walls with weapons.[84]

It would be interesting to know more of the architecture and design of these houses. As noted earlier in this chapter, rows of small hallhouses or urban Wealden houses such as existed in Kent, Sussex and a number of Midland towns have not been recorded in Bristol – the long row at nos.69–77 St Thomas Street, known as Haveryng's, being a possible exception.

Not all Bristol citizens in the post-medieval city felt the need, or had the means, to use the hall principally as a symbolic or ceremonial room. For some it remained the room for daily living, little changed in function from the hall in many medieval houses. By the early 17th century an increasingly small number of households retained the open hall.[85] Those who used the open hall as their principal living room were not now, for the most part, members of the merchant or ruling elite. The examples of Edward Morris and Humphrey Clovill were noted earlier (pp92–3). Morris was a merchant, but, with goods valued at £18 6s 8d, very impoverished; Clovill was a goldsmith, but was not part of the city's elite.

For many other citizens the open hall seems to have been a relic of an earlier age and had been adapted for new purposes. Close to the Quay was the hall of Henry Marston, the parish clerk to St Stephen's. At the time of his death in 1643 this had become the hall for a school, its contents now including an elm form and five benches for the scholars.[86] Thirty-five years later John Bevill, a painter of arms, had decided to use his now unheated hall, at no.35 Broad Street, in pursuit of his musical interests. At his death in 1678 its contents included his new and old organs, together with a pair of virginals; his seven chairs might have been at least in part for those who came to listen. In making his will Bevill's main concerns, after the bequest of his landed property, were for the disposal of his musical instruments. His principal heated living room was the forestreet chamber, with its curtained tester bed serving also as a bed-chamber; two rapiers provided an echo of what might have once furnished his hall.[87]

By the 17th century open halls had been adapted as workplaces by townspeople involved in other trades. In 1611 John Compton, a butcher in Worshipful Street, used his hall for the storage of calves' pookes, his scales and weights.[88] Once no longer in domestic use, it might still have been known as 'the hall' for many years. In 1668 the hall of John Seager, a tanner in St Peter's parish, was referred to by the appraisers as 'the tan-house called the Hall'. Its principal contents were hides, his furnace, pump and beams.[89]

Neither John Dowles nor Edward Pickrell, a glazier and blacksmith, lived in the open hall, both using the room primarily in the pursuit of their business. The social centre of the house lay elsewhere. In 1617 Edward Pickrell dined and slept in his chamber, storing there a good assortment of his own manufactures.[90] John Dowles lived far more comfortably than Pickrell, but likewise dined and slept in the same room. This was his heated 'forestreet chamber', its many furnishings including a table with seating for eight or more, weapons, a looking glass and two wainscotted tester beds.[91] 'Jonas Seldon in 1618 and John Bisse in 1628, both wiredrawers or metalworkers and living in houses where the hall had been ceiled and turned over to a non-domestic use, similarly used the 'forestreet chamber' both for dining and sleeping.[92]

A small number of contemporaries might have seen this first-floor chamber as synonymous with the parlour. In 1611 Humphrey Ellis, a haberdasher, had as his principal living room the 'parlour over the shop'. This was furnished in a similar way to Dowles' forestreet chamber.[93] Used both for dining and sleeping, this was a room which, as the 17th century progressed, would generally be known as the forestreet chamber, sometimes the lodging chamber, but rarely as the parlour.

Several hallhouses became taverns, the hall of the house becoming the hall or principal room of the tavern. These were concentrated in High Street, extending from St Nicholas's gate to the High Cross at the centre of the town. The first, stretching from High Street to Wine Street, can be argued to have been a hallhouse from the plan of the cellar, the largest of medieval date known of in the town (chapter 7), seen in relation to the overall plan of late medieval shops and at least one cellar, extending around its Wine Street and High Street frontages. This ghost of a hallhouse was by the 15th century Haddon's tavern, the property of St Augustine's Abbey and leased to Richard Haddon, a leading vintner.[94] Further down High Street, at nos.21–5 closer to the Bridge, was a second hallhouse which later became a tavern, known as 'the George' by 1532 (p24). The overall plan of this house can be inferred from the plan of the medieval cellars and from the plan of the ground floor as subdivided from *c* 1568 (*see* Fig 2.7).

Across the street at no.30, the Bull or Angel was also from its name possibly a tavern by 1472. This too was a hallhouse, its open hall adjacent to the St Nicholas Street frontage, with a roof of the 15th century (Fig 5.55). One house away, at nos.33–4, was the Starr, 'le Starretau'ne' in 1467.

*Fig 5.55
No.30 High Street, the Bull or Angel, roof of the 15th century to the open hall adjacent to the St Nicholas Street frontage, watercolour by H O'Neill, 1821 (BRSMG M2248).*

On the other side of the Starr at nos.35–6 was the inn called le Cocke in 1461, known more generally in the later 15th century as the Cock in the Hoop.

Of the Starr we know nothing architecturally, but of the latter we have rather more information (Fig 5.13). In 1462 it was placed behind two shops on the street frontage, all in the same ownership but leased as separate dwellings. The hallhouse at the rear was still seen as separate from the shops on the frontage in 1541 (Figs 2.11 and 5.13) when the property was sold to John Smythe, one of the wealthiest merchants of his age.[95] The property purchased by Smythe was that part of 'the Cocke in the Hope' extending from 'the fore shop' and 'the hawle dore' to 'the farther or ynnar ende'. However, by this date both parts were actually in the same occupation, that of John Pykes, mercer.[96] Of the internal plan of the inn above ground we know nothing except that it had an open hall, the roof probably of the 15th century. Below was a vaulted cellar, extending the length of the range containing the hall.

At least two, if not all, of these 15th-century taverns with halls were earlier the residences of wealthy townsmen. In the early 13th century when first granted to St Augustine's Abbey, what was later Haddon's Tavern had been the land with buildings in the Drapery and in Wine Street. There is at that date no mention of it having been a tavern. The George formed part of the Corporation lands, probably through the gift of Eborard Fraunce (le Frenche), one of the wealthiest merchants of the later 13th century, and by *c* 1350 it was occupied by John Wycombe, mayor in 1346.[97]

## The Through-House

In the most congested and central parts of the town, some open halls ceased to be used either as the social or symbolic centre of the house long before the end of the 15th century. In September 1377 Robert Broun, a merchant, came before the Mayor's Court to defend his right to close the way that passed through his property. 'From time out of mind' this had been 'a common highway leading through the middle of his house in Redyngeslane, by which all men, greatest and least, are used to go from St Nicholas Street to Corn Street between sunrise to sunset whenever they pleased'. The mayor's jury found in favour of Broun, but there is no evidence that the way was closed. Redyngeslane remained open through succeeding centuries under a variety of names: Foster Lane, Hardwellus Lane, St Martins Lane, Symons Lane or the Through-house, the last first recorded in 1446. By 1463 it comprised six tenements, three cellars, a hall, a storehouse and three chambers. It can be argued that it was called the throughhouse because the way passed through it, as described in the law suit and as indeed shown on a much later plan of *c* 1740. Further examination of the property is not possible because any upstanding remains were removed in 1740 for the building of the new Corn Exchange and markets.

The Redyngeslane property was not alone in being termed a 'through-house'. Others existed between Mary le Port Street and Wine Street, and between Baldwin Street and St Nicholas Street. The through-house between Mary le Port Street and Wine Street is first mentioned in 1437 and formed part of a tenement extending between the two streets. William Worcestre described it as 'le through-hows' on the south side of Wine Street, through Haddon's tavern to Mary le Port Street. Further to the east another lane ran between the same two streets through the Swan Inn, a right of way by the later 15th century.[98]

Canynges' through-house in Baldwin Street, first mentioned in William Canynges' will of 1474, can be more precisely placed, a much later plan of 1743 showing the location of part of the property in relation to Blind Steps. By 1474 it was already separated into five parts. Two were said to be within the through-house, one each to the east and west of it, with the fifth in St Nicholas Street. The later plan shows it dissected by what was by the late 15th century 'a hygh grese called a steyr of 32 steppys', later known as Blind Steps.[99] The through-houses in Redyngeslane and on Blind Steps can be seen only in plan. Two further through-houses can be seen more clearly, both also in Baldwin Street.

To the west of Blind Steps, at nos.31–4, was a property owned by the parish of St Leonard and described in 1407 as a house with three shops in Baldwin Street and another three in St Nicholas Street. Although only noted first as a through-house 'still in use' in the early 19th century, records of the 1820s and 1830s reveal a plan appropriate to a through-house dating from the 13th century.[100] On the street frontage was a house of three storeys and an attic, gabled end on to the street. It was mainly of the 17th century, but jettied at the first floor on massive beams, which must have related to an earlier house on the site, and on a stone corbelled bracket, clearly contemporary with the two-centred arched doorway of a house of the 13th century (*see* Fig 4.14). A dark passage led from the arched doorway via a small courtyard and ascended by steps into St Nicholas Street. On the west side of this courtyard the artist Rowbotham painted a window of the 13th or 14th century (*see* Fig 4.13).[101] On the east side of the steps Braikenridge noted that there were 'no dividing floors like the front part of the house, the eye traversing uninterruptedly from the ground to the roof. At the further end from Baldwin Street and about 8 feet from the ground is an enormous beam of oak which serves now as a support to the base of the adjoining house in St Nicholas Street, the basement floor of which projects a few feet into the above mentioned premises'.[102]

Seyer's observation, coupled with the other evidence, confirms that the through-house was none other than the cross-passage of the open hall, here to the east of the passage and steps, set back behind a stone-built range, possibly shops, on the street frontage. A through-house was therefore a house through which passed a right of way. In the case of Redyngeslane it passed through the middle of the house, whatever 'middle' might in this context mean. From the St Leonard's property a clearer picture emerges, the right of way being coincident with the screens passage. Of the other examples cited, Canynges' through-house and the through-house between Mary le Port Street and Wine Street could both have been of similar plan. The 'middle' of John Broun's house may well have been, in effect, the screens passage. The St Leonard's property had evidently been sub-divided into seven separate units by 1407.

Immediately to the south of the St Leonard's property was a third house – not described explicitly as a through-house, but fragmented in a similar way to those described above. This house belonged in 1461 to Walter and Isabella Norton, consisting then of two tenements and cellars in Baldwin Street, lately in the occupation of Robert Goteham and John Coferer. These were the houses with solars called 'la Dorter', and a shop and 'hallehouse' occupied by Thomas Vicarie, both in St Nicholas Street.[103] The juxta-position of dorter and hallhouse could indicate that a larger hallhouse had now been divided, the hall separated from the upper end.

That houses with open halls should have been subdivided in this way, even before the 15th century, need not occasion surprise. In the dense urban environment of the centre of medieval Bristol, men and women would have passed many times through the screens passages of hallhouses to gain access to the courtyards behind. This might have happened much more frequently in the properties between streets, otherwise accessed one from the other with some inconvenience. The circumstances by which such a passage became a right of way vested in law may remain obscure, but might include the frequency with which the right was exercised and the degree to which the owner of the property rights might be absent. Where rights of way had been established, houses with open halls would have become less attractive to live in than others elsewhere. The streets in which through-houses could be found were also, by the 15th century, within the parts of the city where property values were generally highest. In subdividing these houses, owners were possibly influenced both by their reduced value as single residences and their potential value as several separate properties.

The redundancy of these hallhouses is significant from one other perspective. These were houses that had been built in an urban setting in the 12th and 13th centuries, planned according to well established principles that mirrored the hierarchy of the household in the 'upper' and 'lower' ends of the hall. Bristol's elite had appropriated the form of the hall that existed elsewhere in a rural or feudal context, in order to affirm hierarchy in an urban context.

Within such 'through-houses' the through-passage or screens passage ceased to remain just 'lower', but became public rights of way. The barring of entrances behind heavy locked doors to protect property and privacy, as described in chapter 4, was not possible in these situations. In this close-built urban setting some people had little respect for the niceties of status; a notable example was the through-passage of John Broun's house, which had become 'a common highway' (see above). We can here see the through-house as a form of resistance to the imposed values of merchant capitalism.

## Some Conclusions

In Bristol we can see that Langland's complaint about the abandonment of the open hall, and with it a set of traditional values about society and the life of the household, had some substance: it was the rich man who had retreated to his parlour. Within this elite group, and right through to the end of the 17th century, the hall retained symbolic value as affirming status. Up to the mid-16th century considerable sums of money were invested in remodelling the open hall. The roofs of those of Canynges, Smythe and Spicer were of the most intricate and elaborate design, indicating that to their owners these were spaces of the greatest importance. Status was also proclaimed through increasing specialisation in the use of rooms such as the dining room, often richly decorated, and the study. These were markers of refinement and gentility.

Within the wider urban population, the open hall had by the 17th century often ceased to retain value or significance. It became either a short cut from one side of the house to the other or was used for purposes entirely unrelated to its initial construction, such as warehouses or taverns. At no.20 Small Street the open hall, once of the Smythes and later of the Creswicks, suffered this fate by the 19th century, becoming the location of a printing press (Fig 5.44). Canynges' open hall survived to the 19th century through becoming a Roman Catholic chapel.

In the next chapter we will study the second principal type of property recognised by Bristol citizens in the later Middle Ages. The shophouse, seen as distinct from the hallhouse, is a peculiarly urban phenomenon. Its relationship to the hallhouse was complex, but in that complexity is revealed important differences in ways of life. The architecture of the shophouse was to have great significance in the development of Bristol's houses in the 18th century – an era in which the storeyed shophouse form was appropriated for the design of the residential house, and differences in wealth and status were stated through new styles of distinction and gentility.

# 6

# The Shophouse

## Living over the Shop

Making his way across the city of Bristol in 1473, the clerk of Canynges' chantries would have seen a good number of houses that he considered to be 'shophouses' (Fig 6.1).[1] In Redcliff Street stood two belonging to the chantries, each with a vault below and a garden to the rear. As he crossed the Bridge, the clerk would have passed the four-storey house of the widow Alison Chestre in the High Street (later no.31), perhaps completed, perhaps still under construction (*see* Fig 2.12). Following his contract of 1472 with Chestre (Appendix 1), the carpenter Stephen Morgan would have been building 'in the seid house a shop, and a hall above the same with an oryell, a chambre above the hall with an oryell, and another chambre above that'.[2] A little further up High Street were the two similar houses in front of the inn the Cock in the Hoop (*see* Fig 2.11), while at the carfax were shops with solars above, built in front of Christchurch.

In descending Broad Street, the clerk would have passed houses of similar appearance. Below, on the Quay, stood more of the chantries' 'shophouses', one with lofts over (Fig 6.1; *see* Fig 2.10). These houses were characterised by having a shop on the ground floor and further accommodation above, for either living or storage. None of the shophouses possessed an open hall, though this did not preclude the principal room over the shop being called a hall. Such was the case in Alison Chestre's house, and in one of the chantries' shophouses in Redcliff Street, where the expenses in 1509 included the making of a new key for the hall door.[3]

In a late medieval context the word 'house' did not necessarily imply the existence of a dwelling. Workhouse, storehouse, bellhouse and playhouse, for instance, all employed the word 'house' to denote a structure designated for a particular purpose. Nevertheless many shophouses *were* also dwellings, and living over the shop was part of the material culture of the medieval and later town. It can be argued that for contemporaries these houses were distinguished from hallhouses in four ways: firstly through the absence of an open hall; secondly through their more restricted range of accommodation; thirdly, in many instances, by

*Fig 6.1*
*Map showing the locations of shophouses in the 15th to 17th centuries, both Canynges' and others (RHL, PEC).*

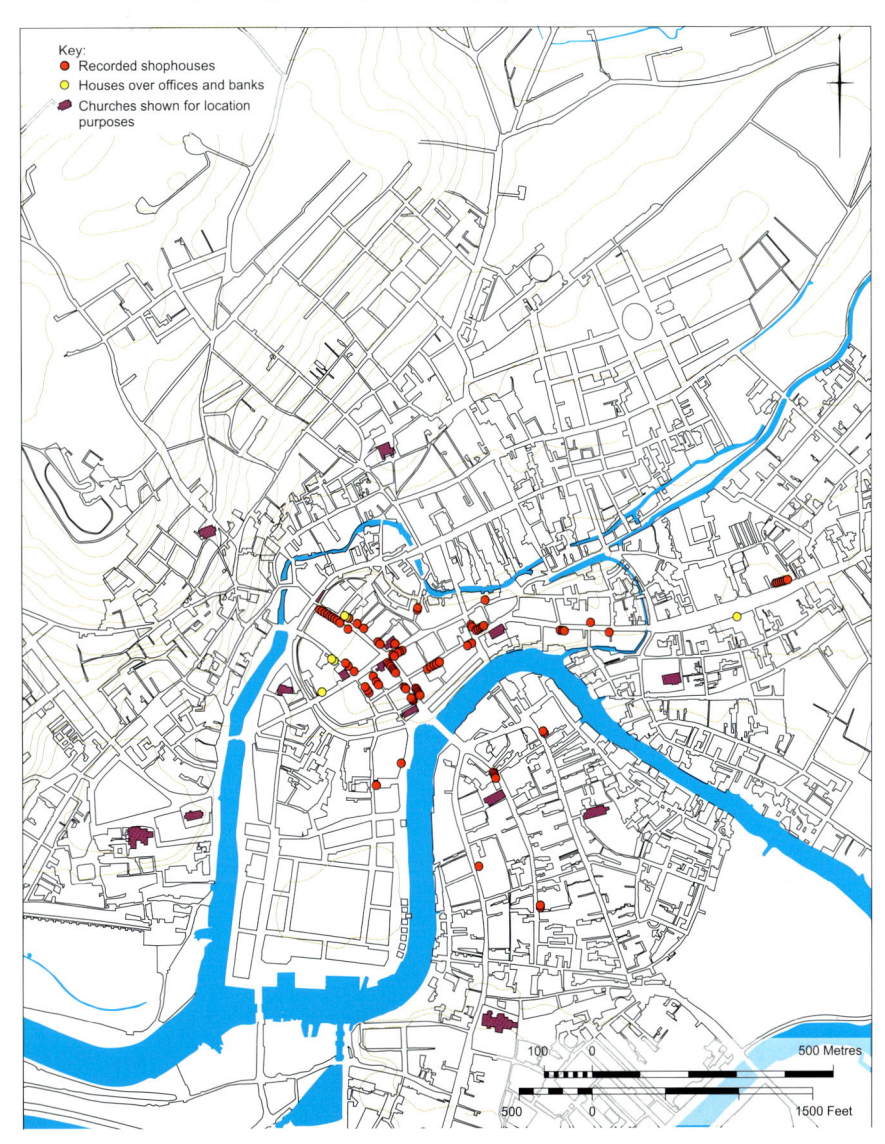

the absence of a hearth for heat; fourthly through the absence of a hearth in the ground-floor room used as the shop. This chapter will explore the chronological and social diversity revealed by shophouses in Bristol. It will show how they were an important type of building in the medieval city, and the manner in which they evolved to accommodate changes in both ways of life and working practice.

## The Shophouse in the English Medieval Town

The shophouse, so named in late 15th-century Bristol, was a characteristic medieval urban building, found in many towns by that date.[4] In 13th- and 14th-century London, for example, the 'row made up of units with a shop on the ground floor and rooms above was a standard feature of the London street scene'.[5] Similar rows have been most readily identified when built as part of a continuous range. Well known examples of the latter include the 14th-century, two-storey rows of York and the Butchers' Row, Shrewsbury, built *c* 1459 by the Abbot of Lilleshall.[6]

Shophouses were also constructed in groups of two or three, or individually, and such smaller developments can be found 'in nearly every old English town'. One of the smallest single houses resulting from one such individual development was at the corner of Frog Street in Exeter; dating from the 15th century, it was 'entirely built upon its tiny shop'.[7] Some of the houses with one room on each floor recorded on early 17th-century plans of London were probably of the 16th century or earlier.[8]

Many shophouses of the 15th century and earlier were evidently constructed without chimneystacks. It has been argued that, in the English climate, the lack of heating would imply that such buildings had no domestic function. Such houses, it has been suggested, must either have had smoke-hoods or chimneystacks which are simply no longer visible, or have been linked to open halls which have disappeared, or have been lock-up shops with storage above.[9] The possibility that some townspeople did live in unheated dwellings should not, however, be dismissed. The extent to which townspeople of the 15th century and earlier lived above the shop, some of them possibly in unheated houses, is of importance in understanding the social structure of the medieval town. It might be inferred that there was a distinction in medieval urban society between those who chose, or were able, to live in houses with open halls and those who lived in rooms over the shop, sometimes without any heating.

'Hallhouse' and 'shophouse' were, it has been argued above (chapters 1 and 5), part of the language of Bristol in the 15th century. Many of the properties forming part of the lands of large urban estates, and recorded simply as 'shop' or 'shops' in rent rolls and other documents of the 15th century and earlier, were probably shop-houses (*see* Fig 7.3). In particular, shops with large gardens behind are likely to have formed part of a dwelling, the plot providing an often considerable area for the growing of fruit and vegetables. In Bristol, the tenements listed in documents as shops in streets away from the central part of the city, such as Old Market, Lewin's Mead and the major streets of the suburbs south of the river, are likely for this reason to have also been dwellings.[10]

The question of whether the lifestyle of townspeople who lived over the shop continued in the post-medieval period to be distinctively different from that of citizens who lived in houses of superficially similar design or appearance, but lacking a shop at the ground floor, remains an open one. The house over the shop could provide essentially the same accommodation as one with family rooms at ground level. It is certainly the case that among the townspeople who lived over the shop, as with those who lived with open halls, there were significant variations in lifestyle, indicative of the complex social structure of an early modern city. Such variations might be evident in the location, size and arrangement of the house.

## The Bristol Shophouse in the Later Middle Ages

In Bristol as in other towns, a number of plots were developed so as to provide shops on the street frontage and a hallhouse behind.[11] In the mid-13th century, after the abandonment of the old inner town wall as a defensive circuit, the strips of land immediately outside the wall were developed in this way, both on the south side of Gropecuntelane and on the north side of Baldwin Street (chapter 4). The phenomenon was found widely across the central part of the city. One of the largest of these developments was that of Richard Spicer's property between

Welsh Back and Baldwin Street. On the north and west, rows of shops fronted on to Baldwin Street and Back Street, probably by the mid-14th century when some of these properties are first recorded. On the east side, facing Welsh Back, the main part of Spicer's own house, built in the mid- to later 14th century, was set back behind two shops on the street frontage (*see* Fig 5.33).

The 11 new shops of the chantry of Eborard le Frenche that stood in Back Street in *c* 1350, with no evidence of a hall behind, and the hall and 14 shops of Nicholas Excestre between Peter Street and Wine Street in 1434 were similarly large developments.[12] Both nos.64–6 Wine Street and nos.1–2 High Street probably had similar origins as shops in front of Haddon's Tavern, a property of St Augustine's Abbey (chapter 5), while nos.21–5 High Street was a row of shops in front of the George, another hallhouse or tavern (chapter 5). In at least some of these developments, the shops were in the same ownership as the hallhouse behind; and it is clear that wealthy citizens and institutions were taking advantage of their location to gain rental income from commercial premises on the busy street frontages. There was, therefore, no sense that the propinquity of commerce detracted from the prestige of the residence, or that privacy was compromised.

In the 16th century such houses, incorporating shops on the street frontage and a hallhouse to the rear, continued to be built or rebuilt. On Broad Street nos.23–30, all probably rebuilt in the 1540s, were properties forming part of the bequest to the City made by Alderman Thomas White of London, a member of a Bristol family who became an important benefactor to his native city. In 1544 nos.23–4 (Fig 6.2) were described as newly built;[13] the barge boards of no.23 bore the initials of Thomas White, indicating that all eight houses were possibly rebuilt by the City following the bequest.

By the middle of the 14th century the shophouses being built in the central part of the city were substantial, multi-storeyed structures. Some were certainly used, at least in the part above the shop, as dwellings. In many cases it can be demonstrated that, where they shared a tenement plot with a hallhouse, the shops were separately occupied and owned, and were therefore shophouses. It is not clear when or how the subdivision of the plots took place. In front of the house of Richard Spicer on the Back, rebuilt in the mid-14th century, stood two properties which by the mid-15th century were held separately from the main house and were described then as shops.[14] As nos.7A and 7B Welsh Back, these remained tenurially distinct until the 19th century (*see* Figs 5.21 and 5.33). Sited to the north of the great entry into and through Spicer's Hall, and contemporary with Spicer's own house, both probably consisted of three storeys.

In the High Street no.31, the house built by Stephen Morgan for Alison Chestre in *c* 1472, was of four storeys and, with its hall and chambers, certainly built as a dwelling house with a shop on the ground floor (*see* Fig 2.12 and Appendix 1).). In the same street, nos.35–6 were one or two houses built in the 15th century, also to four storeys (*see* Fig 2.11). In 1461 this was the property described as two separately leased shops, in the same overall ownership as the Cock in the Hoop to the rear. By 1488 it was apparently one house. Inhabited by John Jay, a tailor and a prominent member of the civic community, it was still separately leased from the house behind.

In Small Street, Broad Street and on the Quay, several shophouses of three storeys were built in the 15th century. Some of these properties appear to have had additional buildings to the rear of the shophouse. During the 14th to 16th centuries nos.25–6 Small Street was a house tenurially distinct from the properties behind, which included at least two halls (Fig 6.3).

*Fig 6.2*
*Nos.23–4 Broad Street, showing one-room deep shophouses built in front of hallhouses set back from the street frontage, rebuilt in c 1544, watercolour by H O'Neill, 1819 (BRSMG M2441, Braikenridge Notebook 2).*

*Fig 6.3*
*Nos.25–6 Small Street, photograph of the 1890s (BRSMG Photographs Box 1, fol B, incorrectly identified as being in Broad Street).*

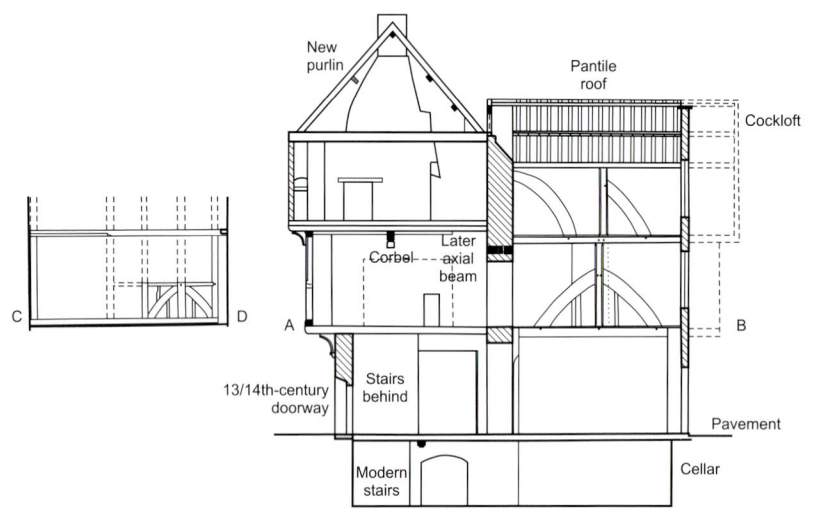

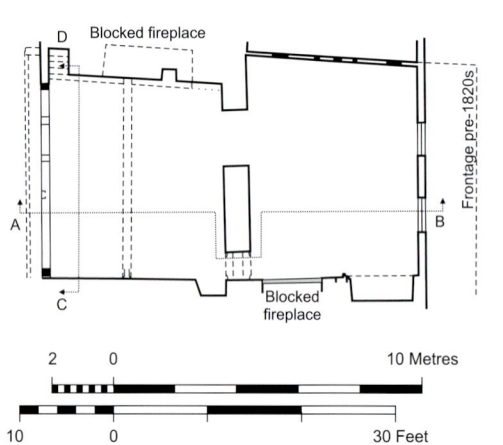

*Fig 6.4*
*No.43 Broad Street, plan and sections, showing chimneystack as added to structure as first built (RHL, PEC).*

*Fig 6.5*
*Broad Street, showing (left to right) no.43 (Guildhall Tavern), no.44 (gabled), nos.49/50 (18th century) and no.51 (two gables), watercolour by H O'Neill, 1821 (BRSMG M2434).*

In Broad Street, no.43 was of three storeys and of two rooms in depth, with a courtyard behind; built *c* 1411, it replaced and partly incorporated the walls of an earlier house of the 12th or 13th century (Figs 6.4 and 6.5). Another, no.51, also consisted of three storeys. A survey of the cellar beneath, and others further to the rear, has shown that this was a house of one or two rooms in depth, extending back to a longer building behind – possibly the Innholders' Hall (Figs 6.5 and 6.6). Fronting the Quay and backing on to Leonard Lane (*see* Fig 2.10), nos.50–1S the Quay. The Quay provided a similar range of accommodation[15]. Before being divided *c* 1500, this property constituted one of the houses of Canynges' chantry listed in the rental of 1473 – Roger Overy's 'Shoppe house to fore the Keye Pype'. If the upper rooms had been solely for storage, these would have been referred to as 'loftys', as entered in the rental for a nearby shophouse by St Stephen's churchyard.

Medieval shophouses in Bristol varied in plan. In the more central parts of the city, one-room deep houses, with shops on the street front, were to be found principally on high-value sites, where the presence of adjacent buildings made it impossible to build a house of two rooms in depth. Many of the shophouses built in front of hallhouses set back from the street frontage were of one-room plan, as at nos.23–4 Broad Street, rebuilt in *c* 1544 (Fig 6.2), as well as in Defence Street (later named Dolphin Street) and Peter Street. Houses of similar plan could also be built on the narrow strips of land between an urban church and the street, as against Christchurch and St Mary le Port. However, such houses do not seem to have been built in the less central streets as a lower-cost form of housing for poorer tradespeople and craftsmen.

Most townspeople in Bristol who lived over the shop possibly did so in houses that were of two rooms in depth, sometimes with further accommodation to the rear. In other large towns and cities such houses were being lived in from at least the 14th century. In London, a row of nine houses in Abchurch Lane was built *c* 1390, the houses initially unheated to judge from the varied manner in which chimneystacks were later distributed across this range of houses.[16] In York, nos.54–60 Stonegate Row were a range of at least seven houses of two rooms in depth, built in the early 14th century.[17]

In Bristol, no.43 Broad Street is the earliest recorded example within the city of a house being built to two rooms in depth. It is also the most complete surviving 15th-century house in Bristol, constructed for the Fraternity of St John the Baptist on the plot of land surveyed in 1411 (Figs 6.4 and 6.5; p60; *see* Fig 4.3). On the ground floor the original arrangements are masked by later alterations, but on the first and second floors the doorways from the front to rear rooms are part of the original plan. Furthermore, the stairs between the first and second floors were sited so as to give direct access to both front and rear rooms. As first built, all six rooms were unheated. The first- and second-floor rooms on the street frontage were lit by a full width window on the first floor and the oriels on the floors above, all possibly original. The adjacent rooms at the rear were lit by further oriel windows, each projecting forward over the entrance way to one side of a window occupying the remaining width of the elevation. All was part of the original design.

This was certainly not a hallhouse. The precise original purpose of the ground floor of

*Fig 6.6*
*No.51 Broad Street, plan of cellars indicating location of storeyed shophouse on street frontage and longer building behind, possibly the Innholders' Hall (RHL, PEC).*

domestic character of the upper floors dates from the 14th century.

In 1307 the tenement of John Dinnyng in Gropecuntelane consisted of a shop on the ground floor and a solar above, extending from the street back to the hall of Adam de Temple.[19] In 1345 Richard Hurrell held a corner shop with a solar on Welsh Back.[20] Shortly before this, in 1343, a more complex set of arrangements may have existed at nos.41–3 Broad Street. The property late of John Hasard, 'Hasardystenement' consisted of 'two shops in the front part … with solar and kitchen adjoining and also in a certain chamber called Godyer behind'; one half of this property was that demolished for the building of no.43 in *c* 1411.[21] In 1395 nos.28–29 High Street were two shops with one cellar and a solar built above, leased to Robert Nemot and Margaret his wife.[22] In 1406 John Dunster held a lease on a shop, with a solar built over it, in Christmas Street.[23] In 1408, no.37 Corn Street was the shop with solar above granted to John Fillyngham and Margaret his wife.[24]

At the south end of Broad Street and in Wine Street, the parish of Christchurch had built two rows of shops backing on to the church. In 1352 no.61 Broad Street comprised a shop with a solar; by 1415 it consisted of two shops with a solar above.[25] In 1402 no.59 Broad Street consisted of a shop with solar, described by 1415 as a solar above.[26] In 1404 a property in Wine Street was described as a shop with solar above, next to another shop described as 'inhabited'.[27] Further to the north in Broad Street, William Prelat and Joan his wife certainly lived over their shops at nos.54–5 in 1448. Their part of the property consisted of two shops at the front facing on to the street, their two solars above and a cellar beneath. The topmost rooms over the Prelats' solars belonged to the tenement behind. From the street this would have appeared as a house of three storeys, perhaps similar to no.51 (Fig 6.5), the complexities of the letting arrangements hidden from the passer-by.[28]

The documentary evidence from these eight houses in Gropecuntelane, Broad Street, High Street, Corn Street and Wine Street shows that rooms generally termed 'solars' were frequently to be found on the upper floors above the shop on the ground floor. Perhaps the clearest evidence for the domestic use of the upper floors is provided by the contract for Alison Chestre's house of *c* 1472 (Appendix 1): with its hall and chambers on the upper floors, the property was certainly built as a dwelling (*see* Fig 2.12).[29]

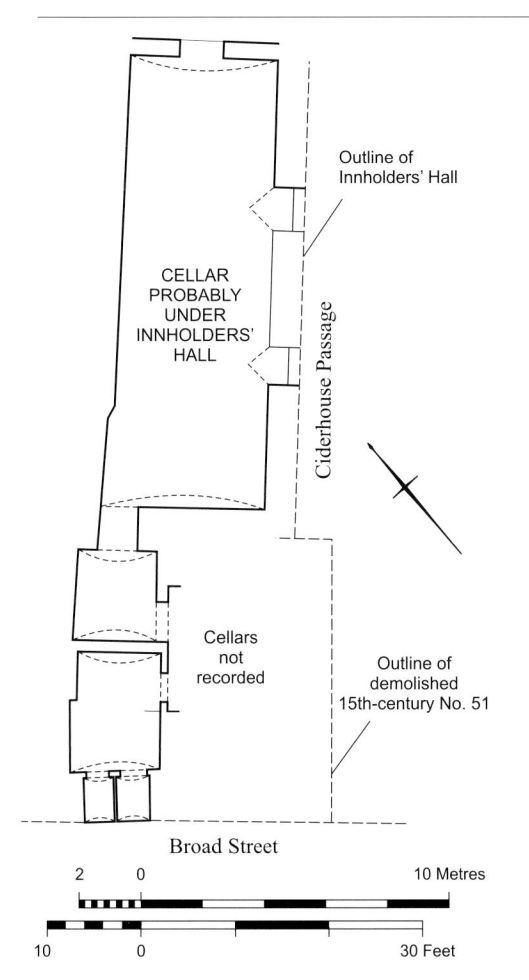

no.43 remains unknown, but, in a street where many shops were recorded in the 15th century, the front room is most likely to have been a shop. Passers-by in the street would have been drawn to this by the elaborate quatrefoiled frieze above the ground-floor entry to Tailors' Court (Fig 6.5). But while the front room was openly accessed from the street, the rear room could only be approached from Tailors' Court, the keys to which were, by the end of the century, held jointly by other parties.[18] From the elaborate fenestration of the first and second floors, both to the street and court, it can be inferred that the upper part of the house was used as living accommodation, though no rooms were heated. This accommodation might have been occupied by one household or shared between two or more. In a 15th-century context, no.43 was probably a shophouse.

The multi-storeyed nature of Bristol's medieval shophouses, and the elaborate fenestration seen at buildings such as no.43 Broad Street, provide the clearest physical evidence for the domestic use of the upper floors: these were more than storage lofts. The earliest documentary evidence for the

## 'A Room still, very Confusingly, called the Hall'

In the shophouse the principal upper room over the shop, generally on the first floor, was frequently referred to as the hall – a term still in use in this context in early 17th-century London, but less so in Bristol. The location and context of the hall within a house of this type is well illustrated in a builder's contract of 1410 for the building of three houses at Friday Street in St Matthew's parish in the City of London. On the ground floor each was to have a shop with a sale-room and office. On the first floor there was to be a hall, larder and kitchen, and on the second floor a principal chamber, privy and retiring room.[30]

In such houses only the hall can have served as the principal living area and social centre of the house, above the shop and below the bedchambers. There were no other rooms for living accommodation, or for sitting, eating and receiving guests. Such a house, we can argue, would have been termed a shophouse – a house over the shop and distinct from one provided with an open hall, which might be termed a hallhouse. In Bristol we have already seen that in 1472 Alison Chestre specified that her house in the High Street should have a hall above the shop (Appendix 1).

It might be asked why this room was called the 'hall'. Like the open hall of the smaller 15th-century hallhouse, it was a heated room and served as the social and domestic centre and seat of power within the household. The use made of this first-floor hall was, however, very different to that made of the open hall in houses such as that of John Gaywode (chapter 5). In Gaywode's house the hall served as an imposing entry to the rooms beyond, asserting the status of the owner, with a fire lit only at the feast of Christmas. In the shophouse, the hall was far more intensively used. In 1531, for example, Kathryn Mason held the lease from the parish of Christchurch for one of the houses built against the south side of its church in Wine Street. It was said in 1558 to extend but five feet beyond the wall of the church. Yet it comprised a shop, a hall and a chamber. These rooms can only have been one above the other, with the hall the room on the first floor.[31] This might have been the context of the room to which Edmond Jones, a clothier, referred in 1573, when he left to his wife Agnes the use of his dwelling house upon the Back, within which was a great spruce table board standing in his 'Haull above'.[32]

It has been said that this room was in the 15th century 'still, very confusingly, called the hall'.[33] To contemporaries the use of the term must, however, have been quite deliberate. The confusion lies more with 21st-century usage of the term, especially by historians of vernacular architecture who have assumed that, in medieval and early post-medieval houses, the hall was almost invariably at ground level and open to the roof. Contemporaries, however, defined the term by the use of the space and the role of the room within the house, rather than by its location or physical form. Even though they defined a type of house – the hallhouse – by the presence of an impressive hall, they did not limit the use of the term itself to the open hall familiar to students of medieval housing.

## The Unheated Shophouse

There is little clear evidence, either in documents or surviving fabric, to demonstrate conclusively whether or not some Bristol shophouses may have lacked any form of heating. Only no.43 Broad Street has been recorded in detail in modern times (Figs 6.4 and 6.5) and no inventories of such houses from before the 17th century have survived. The possibility that, as in other towns, most of these houses were unheated, at least until the late 15th or early 16th centuries, should not, however, be dismissed. There is, at the least, circumstantial evidence to suggest that houses were able to function satisfactorily with neither a means of cooking nor a fire for warmth.

The need for a cooking hearth, clearly essential in an isolated rural dwelling, may not have been felt by some citizens living in the centre of the medieval city. Cooked food could be obtained readily from cookshops, with the greatest concentration of these in Bristol being in High Street. First mentioned in 1306, the area had become known as the 'Cokerewe' by 1370. By 1470 the Cokyn Rewe comprised some seven shops, nos.42–7 High Street.[34] These evidently offered a wide choice of cooked food, including fish, birds and wildfowl large and small, capons, hens, geese and rabbits. Here a well roasted goose could be purchased for 4d, while a baked giblet offered a cheaper alternative. Reheated meat was to be avoided.

None of this should occasion surprise; it was, after all, normal for other victuals to be taken

THE SHOPHOUSE

home ready for consumption. Bread is an obvious example; ale, too, was often sold for domestic consumption. The very concentration of cooks' shops in the centre of the city indicates that the cooks plied a considerable trade – doubtless to those working in the commercial areas, but also perhaps to some who lived without the means of cooking food. The interests of those who sold fresh food to townspeople with cooking hearths were protected by the cooks not being allowed to sell prepared fish or meat before ten in the morning – a further indication that there was a significant trade in cooked food.

It could be a mistaken 21st-century assumption that a domestic hearth for cooking was always necessary in the 15th-century and earlier town.[35] Warmth could be found in the taverns and inns scattered throughout the town, at least until the ringing of the curfew bell of St Nicholas and on Sundays only after mass.[36] Close to the shophouses in Broad Street was the Hart, mentioned as 'the inn called le Hart' in 1442; nos.35–6 High Street were immediately in front of the Cock in the Hoop (*see* Fig.5.13).[37] In a 15th-century context, heating was possibly not considered essential to a room furnished in part for living. The inhabitants of unheated shophouses might for the most part have had the choice of either retreating to bed or enjoying the warmth of a tavern. The concept that a house required a hearth for it to have heating may also be an unwarranted modern assumption, informed also by what was probably normal in a rural context, but was not necessarily so for those who lived over the shop in towns. There were a number of ways of providing a fire for heating without a hearth, including braziers and portable stoves. These would have left no structural evidence to reveal their use.

There are signs, however, that, from the late 15th century, townspeople were no longer content to live in unheated shophouses. Concepts of comfort were changing; chimneystacks were added to existing houses and formed an integral part of new shophouses. In *c* 1500 the owner of no.43 Broad Street inserted a chimneystack in the rear part of the house, providing a kitchen fireplace on the ground floor and large fireplaces to the two rooms above. That on the first floor, with a 4½ft wide fireplace opening set within a four-centred, arched chimneypiece of ashlar, with painted inscription above, certainly heated a room of some importance (Fig 6.4).

## The Shophouse in Post-Medieval Bristol

Many English towns possessed what in Bristol we have termed hallhouses and shophouses.[38] Some, however, also had a type of combined shop and dwelling which does not fit neatly into the categorisation employed in this study of Bristol's medieval houses. The type, best evident at Church Row, Tewkesbury, had a floored shop next to the street and a diminutive open hall to the rear. Is this a hallhouse? Or is it a shophouse? No examples of the type have been recognised with certainty in Bristol; although it is possible that some of the documentary evidence for combined shops and dwellings described such buildings, and that a row of such houses was built as Haveryng's Row in St Thomas Street (chapter 5).

The shophouse remained an important building type in Bristol long after the early 16th century, and better survival of buildings and contemporary documentation allow a fuller picture to emerge of who occupied shophouses, how they were used and how they evolved to meet changing needs.

By the mid-16th century, even those who lived in the smallest shophouses were generally prosperous citizens. In Peter Street the row of houses towards the north-west end, nos.A and 1–4, were among the 14 shops opposite St Peter's Place and extending north into Defence Street mentioned in 1434 and 1474 (Figs 6.7 and 6.8). This was probably a row of one-room deep houses, perhaps with separate kitchens to the

*Fig 6.7*
*Nos.A and 1–4 Peter Street, shophouses of the 15th century, photograph of the later 19th century (BRSMG Photographs Box 1, fol P).*

123

*Fig 6.8*
*(left) no.1 Peter Street in 1856 (BRO 6170(1(a)) located from BRO 04479(1) fol 122);*
*(top right) nos. A and 1–4 Peter Street, shophouses of the 15th century (reconstructed from above)*
*(bottom right) cellar of no.3 Peter Street (BRO Building Plans vol 3 fol 169).*

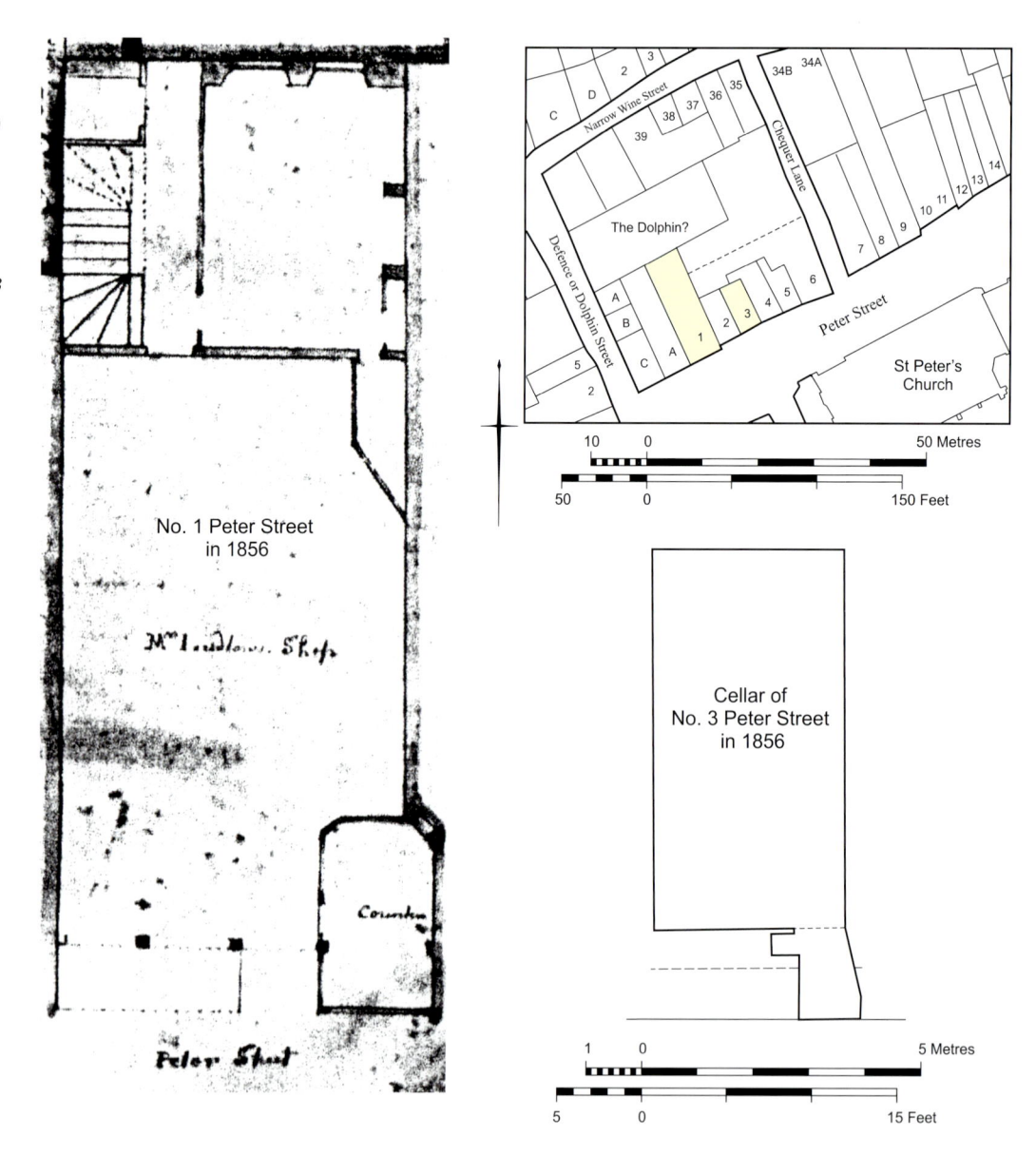

rear, as was certainly the plan of no.1 Peter Street by 1765. By the mid-16th century, the inhabitants of these houses were not poor, but nor were they members of the ruling or merchant elite. In the 1560s and 1570s, for example, no.1 Peter Street was the home of John Frelynge, a goldsmith, then of his widow, and then of her executor Walter Lippett.[39] Part of the same development as the Peter Street houses were nos. A and B Defence Street.[40] One of these two houses was the home of Thomas Clement, a saddler, who died in 1618; his executor and lessee of the other house was John Stibbens, a soap maker.[41]

By the 1530s and throughout the 17th and 18th centuries, townspeople of a similar standing lived in the row of one-room deep houses built against the north side of Christchurch, on the narrow strip of land between the church and the street.[42] Edward Harsell was, like John Frelynge, a goldsmith. He died in 1633, leaving possessions in his house at no.Xch/6 Wine Street valued at £224. For the purposes of preparing an inventory, these seem to have been gathered into two rooms: the 'church chamber' and the kitchen. Gold, gilt and silver were principally stock in trade, but the many items including furniture, linen and books and other goods must have represented the contents of a richly furnished house.[43] Subsequent occupiers of Harsell's house included a succession of goldsmiths, then from the 1730s a hosier, followed by a milliner.

Harsell's neighbour was Anthony Bassett,

a tailor; his house was slightly larger (Fig 6.9). Successive inhabitants of his house in the later 17th and 18th centuries included a pewterer, surgeon, upholsterer and grocer.[44] A similar mix of occupations characterised the inhabitants in 1663 of the four recently built, one-room deep houses set against the north wall of St Mary le Port church (Figs 6.10 and 6.11). These houses had been built between 1648 and 1655 by Thomas Harris, the landlord of the Swan Inn on the opposite side of the street. Nathaniel Cronder and Daniel Harding, both grocers, and John and Samuel Harris, tailor and ironmonger, had all chosen to lead profitable but somewhat cramped lives over their shops in one of the principal shopping streets of the city.[45] Despite consisting of four storeys with attics, nos. 38, 41 and 42 Mary le Port Street offered only half the accommodation of an equivalent house two-rooms deep.

The inventory of the possessions of Thomas Clement, a saddler, in St Peter's parish provides the best available insight into life within one of the 15th-century, one-room deep shophouses on the east side of Defence Street – albeit 200 years after their construction. The rooms described by the appraisers of Clement's goods in 1618 were a shop on the ground floor and a chamber on each of the two floors above. Neither of the chambers was heated, though the forestreet chamber served for sleeping and probably also for dining; its contents included both a curtained bed, a sideboard and four stools. Yet there was no kitchen, and no cooking implements were listed. Like his 15th-century forebears, Thomas Clement may have drawn his sustenance from the cookshop, the baker and the tavern.[46] In contrast, heating was certainly provided in the four houses built in the mid-17th century against St Mary le Port church. Stone chimney-pieces were noted in several rooms.[47]

It might be asked whether poorer townspeople lived in houses of similar plan in the less important streets. From the sample of inventories of houses with a shop on the street front and from the Parliamentary Survey of 1649, such houses were to be found by the mid-17th century only in a small number of

*Fig 6.9*
*Nos.Xch/5 ('D' on plan), Xch/6 (left hand part of 'A') and Xch7 (deeper part of 'A') Wine Street, houses built against Christchurch, plan endorsed on a lease of 1782 (BRO P/Xch/D/65).*

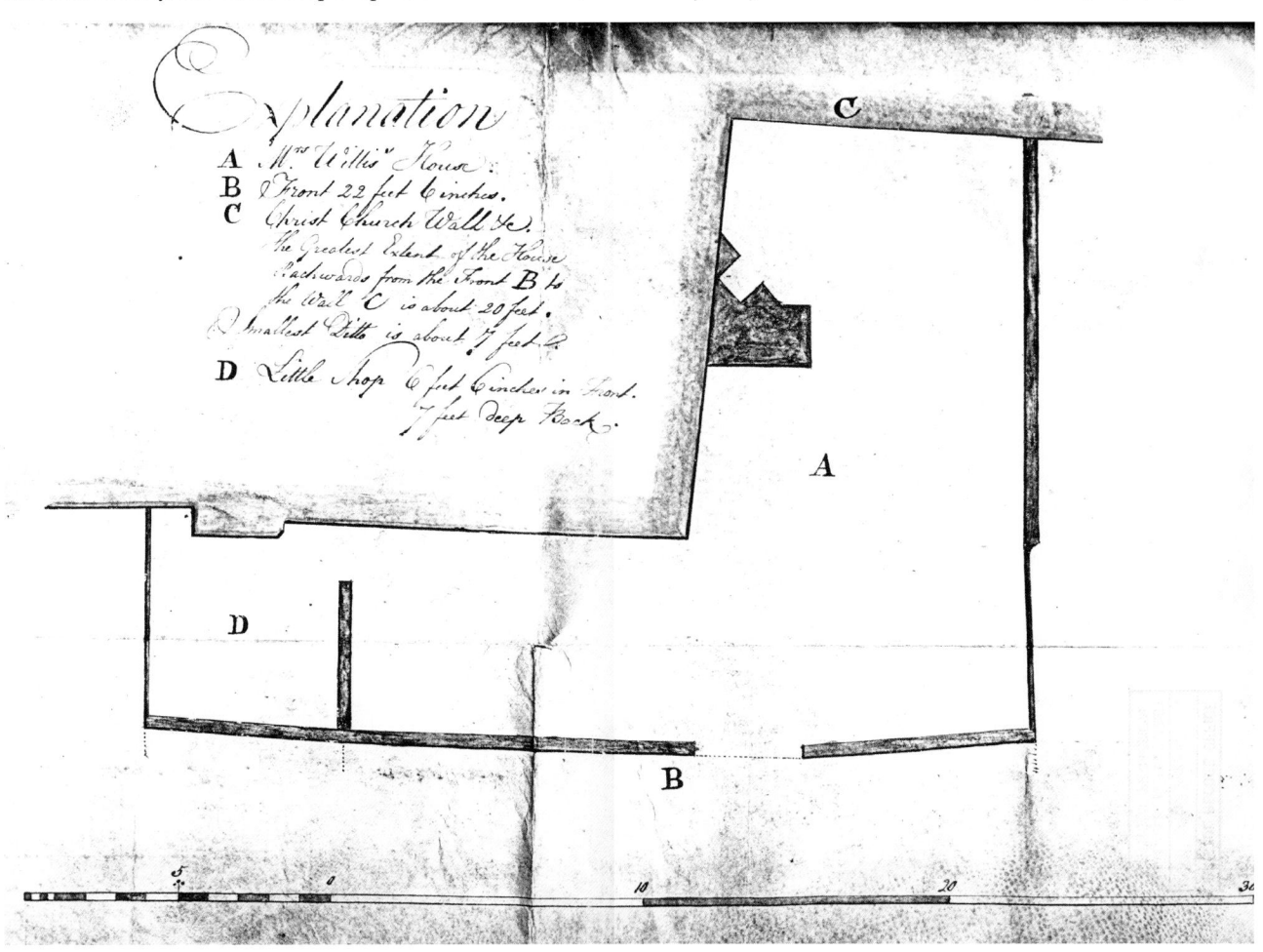

principal streets.⁴⁸ In many streets, notably some of those inhabited by poorer townspeople, such as Frog Lane (later Frogmore Street), there were few or no shops.⁴⁹ Possibly with a few exceptions, the urban poor were not to be found living over the shop.

The occupiers of the shophouses described above were, if not wealthy, then at least of middling status: mainly tradesmen, craftsmen and retailers. By the early 17th century, however, some citizens at the pinnacle of Bristol's mercantile community had begun to eschew the house with the symbolic hall in favour of a luxuriously appointed shophouse of two rooms on each floor. In each case the front part of the house on the ground floor was used for the shop, the room above the shop serving as the principal living room looking out over the street.

Two larger shophouses extant in the 1620s can be identified as the dwellings of wealthy citizens. In 1623 Michael Threkeld, a hosier, had lived at a house in All Saints Lane, described in the probate inventory of his possessions. The shop and kitchen were on the ground floor, with the forestreet chamber and another chamber above. On the second floor were probably the front and back parlours, and above these was the cockloft.⁵⁰

Quite the most sumptuous shophouse was no.12 Welsh Back, the house of the merchant John Langton – a man of wealth sufficient to own a manor in Brislington, just to the east of the city (chapter 9). Langton's house was built *c* 1623 on a plot only 20ft wide (Fig 6.12). The stairs were designed to impress; ornately carved with heraldic figures surmounting the newels, they rose through the full height of the house, and were of sufficient magnificence to be removed in

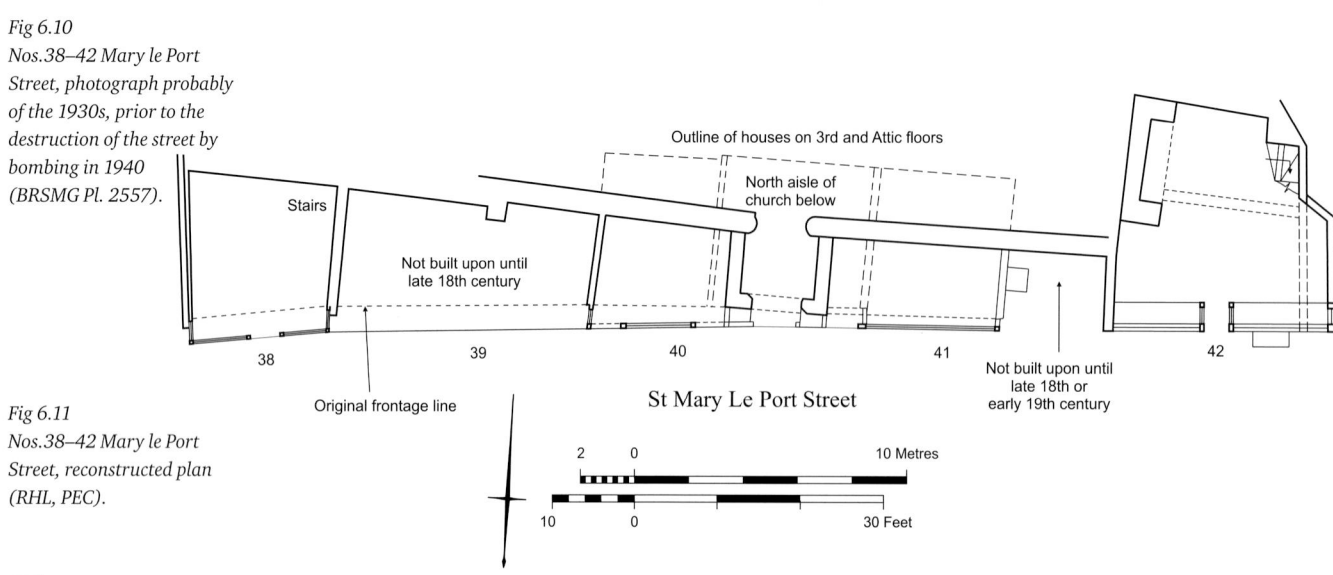

*Fig 6.10*
*Nos.38–42 Mary le Port Street, photograph probably of the 1930s, prior to the destruction of the street by bombing in 1940 (BRSMG Pl. 2557).*

*Fig 6.11*
*Nos.38–42 Mary le Port Street, reconstructed plan (RHL, PEC).*

1906 to a new house in Hampshire, New Place (Fig 6.13).⁵¹ No plan of Langton's house has been traced, but a reconstruction from the surviving fragments at New Place, from illustrations and other sources (Fig 6.14), shows that the stairs must have been visible from the entry and provided access to a belvedere above the roofs – a place from which to see and be seen (Fig 6.12). In a one-room wide house of the 17th century, this placement of the stairs was unusual; the only other certain example recorded was at no.74 Old Market, built in the

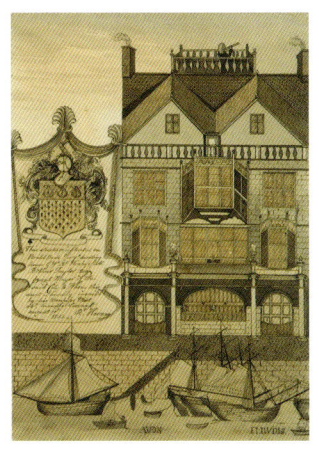

Fig 6.12
John Langton's house at no.12 Welsh Back, watercolour by H O'Neill after R Harman's painting of 1732 (BRSMG M2265).

Fig 6.13
John Langton's house at no.12 Welsh Back, the stairs, photograph of c 1906 (BRO 22885).

*Fig 6.14*
*John Langton's house at no.12 Welsh Back, reconstruction of the plan from notes by PEW Street (given to RHL by Reece Winstone), from Pritchard 1906, photographs of 1931 and later by Street, and measurements of the stairs at New Place, Hampshire (RHL, PEC).*

early 1690s (*see* Fig 8.61). Here, as in Langton's house, an elaborately finished open-well stairs was placed so as to be seen from the entrance to the house. Descriptions from the 19th century say nothing of a shop on the street frontage of Langton's house, but this is clearly shown on the painting of 1732 (Fig 6.12).

Features in the rooms over the shop marked this house out as a dwelling of one of the city's leading citizens. In the forestreet chamber were a chimneypiece dated 1623, bearing the arms of James I (Fig 6.15), a decorated plaster ceiling and a doorway with a door of mahogany (Figs 6.16a and 6.16b). This was elaborately panelled, bearing the date and initials '1628' and 'J L'. It was inlaid with mother of pearl, ivory and silver, and featured caryatides at the sides and a centre panel representing Justice; 1628 was the year when John Langton was mayor.[52] In this house the forestreet chamber amply fulfilled the role of the symbolic hall in indicating the status of the owner, and was possibly known to Langton

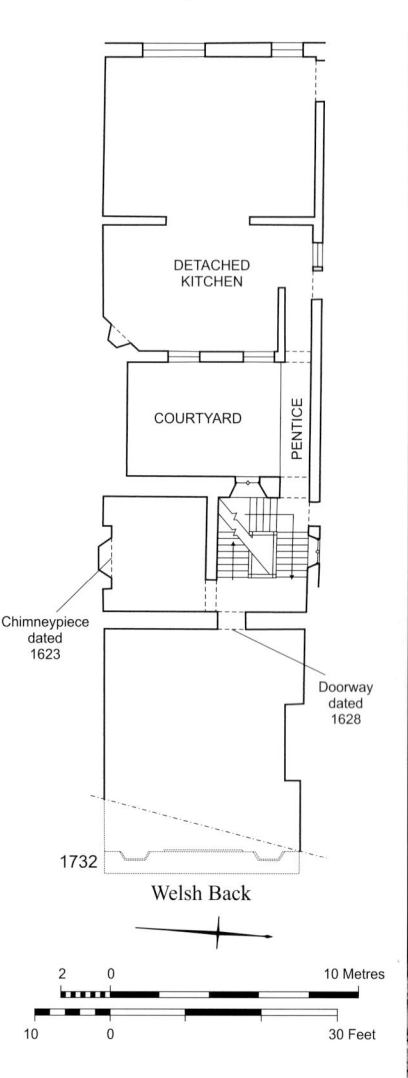

*Fig 6.15*
*John Langton's house at no.12 Welsh Back, first floor, chimneypiece in the forestreet chamber, photograph of c 1906 (NMR Country Life CTL 01/5678/5773/001).*

*Fig 6.16*
*John Langton's house at no.12 Welsh Back, first floor:*
*a) the forestreet chamber, panelled and with a doorway of 1628 to the rear chamber, looking south-west (BRSMG Extra Illustrated Barrett 1789, 2, 494);*
*b) detail of the door of 1628 showing marquetry inlay, looking west (NMR Country Life CTL 01/5678/5773/002). Both photographs of c 1906.*

as 'the hall'. Further along the same street in 1573, the clothier Edmond Jones (above) counted as one of his most prized family possessions 'a great spruce table board standing in my Haull above'.

In the 17th century those living over and next to the shop in two-room deep houses included a few professional men. These included William Nicklus and Gilbert Moore (below: *see* Fig 11.25), barber-surgeons in Castle Street and Broad Street. For the most part, however, the occupiers were involved in manufacturing and retailing. Some were involved in large-scale production and distribution, such as Andrew Gale the soap maker (of no.14A Castle Street); but others were in business in a smaller way, such as John Bisse the wiredrawer and Nicholas Stacy the felt maker (both of Redcliff Street).[53] The lifestyles of this wide range of individuals and their households were necessarily conditioned by a significant part of the ground floors of their dwellings being given over to the uses of the shop.

Details of the internal workings of the post-medieval shophouse can be recovered from documents and the study of recorded or surviving houses. Attention focuses in particular on the extent of heating, particularly on the ground floor. In many instances shops were built without heating. In 1598 nos.54–5 Broad Street were built as a pair of houses, each of two rooms in depth (Figs 6.17a and 6.17b), over and on each side of the entrance to the new market for the flesh shambles (or butchers' stalls). The beam over the passage between the two houses recorded the gift to the city of this land by the wealthy merchant and former alderman and mayor Robert Kitchen. At the entrance to the market, the front ground-floor rooms on the street are likely to have functioned as shops. A 19th-century plan shows only the rear room of no.54 as being heated. The front room can be interpreted as being designed from 1598 specifically as a shop, in which the presence of a fireplace was superfluous.

A similar arrangement must have been intended in a house built at approximately the same date, on the corner of Back Street and Crow Lane. A chimneystack central to a front room, and the 25ft depth to the house, indicated that it was of two-room plan. Two chimneypots on the front stack, for a house of three storeys with an attic, would have indicated to the knowledgeable observer that the front ground-floor room was an unheated shop, only the two principal rooms above being heated (Figs 6.18 and 6.19). A similar vista must have been afforded in the steeply sloping street known as Pithay, where nos.16 and 17 were evidently constructed in the 16th century as a pair of houses, two rooms in depth. The 19th-century plan lacks detail, notably of the stairs, but nevertheless shows clearly that only the rear rooms were heated (Figs 6.20 and 6.21).

Nineteenth-century plans, watercolours of chimneypots and early photographs might seem a tenuous line of argument for the existence of the unheated, street-front shop. This would indeed be so, but for the abundant evidence of this arrangement from later 17th-century houses. This evidence can first be sought in extant houses, notably in two rows, one built in the 1670s and the other between 1684 and c 1705.

The row of four houses built in St Thomas Street (nos.128–131) by Henry Gleson in the 1670s survives as nos.25–31 Victoria Street.[54] Each house was of identical plan, consisting of two rooms on each floor, with the central part of the house being taken up by the stairs and a closet (Figs 6.22 and 6.23). In the rear part of each house a chimneystack rose through all four floors, but in the front ground-floor rooms there was a fireplace only in no.31 – this may well have been an addition, being cut into the side wall rather than contained within a properly

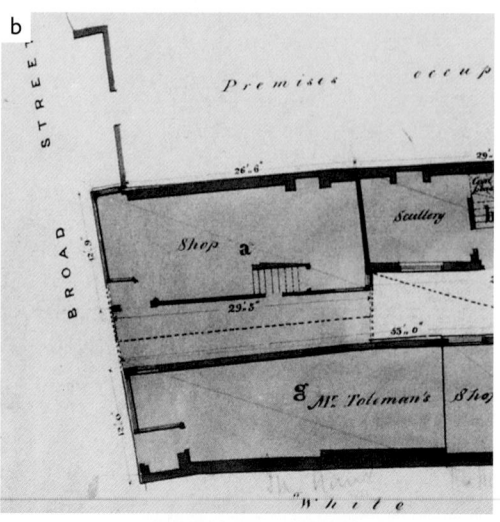

*Fig 6.17*
*Nos.54–5 Broad Street:*
*a) photograph of the late 19th century (extract from BRSMG Ma5651);*
*b) plan of the property, dating from 1855 (extract from BRO 33041/ BMC/PL4/fol 33).*

THE SHOPHOUSE

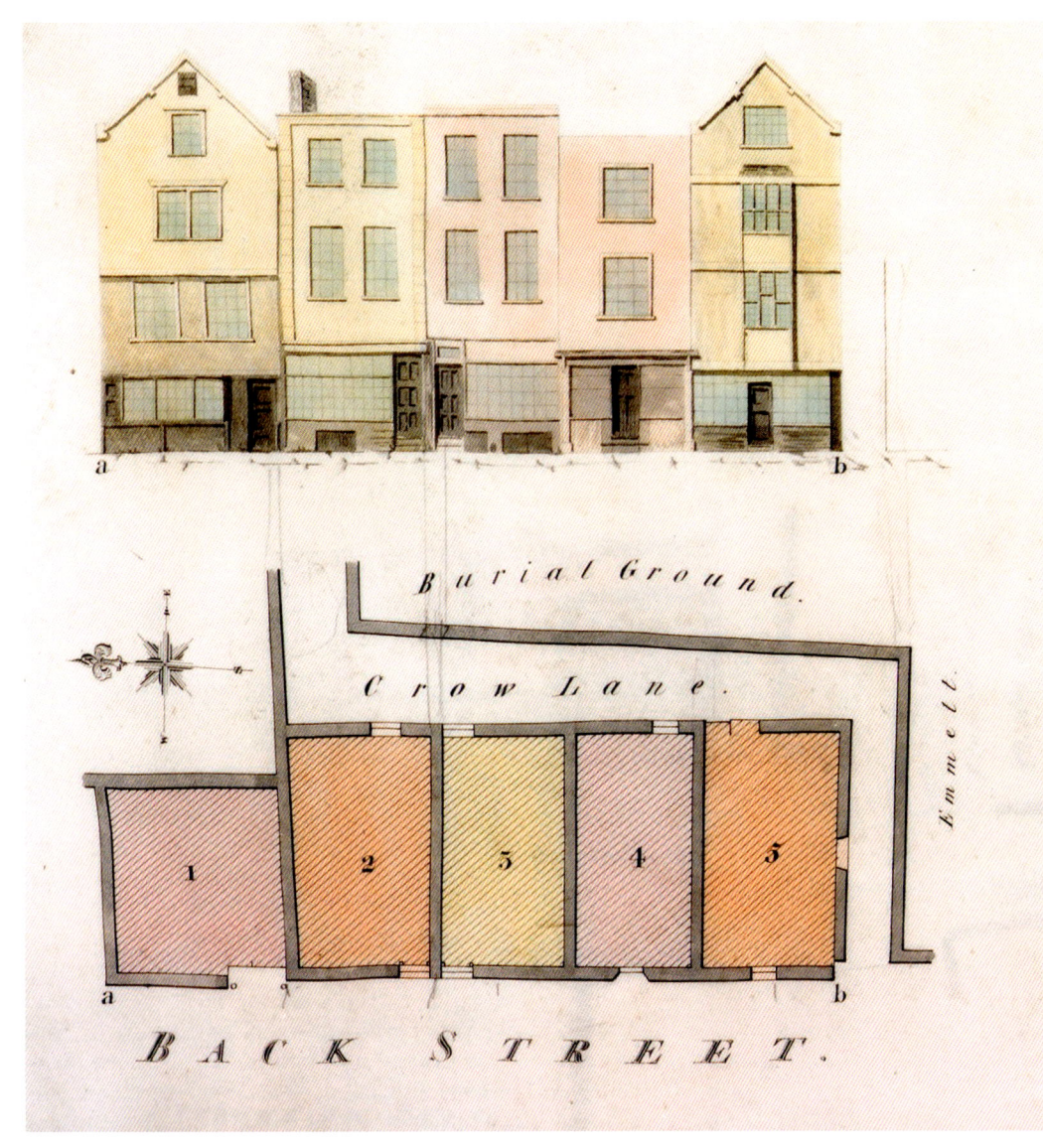

*Fig 6.18 (left)
Corner of Back Street and
Crow Lane, outline plan
of 1828
(BRO 39180 fol 12, part of).*

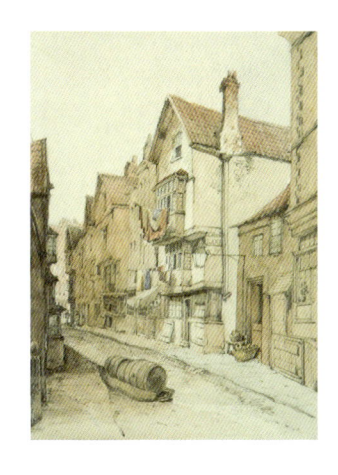

*Fig 6.19 (above)
Corner of Back Street and
Crow Lane, watercolour by
T L Rowbotham, 1825
(BRSMG M2264).*

*Fig 6.20 (below left)
Nos.15 and 16 Pithay,
early 19th-century plan
(BRO P/Xch/plan of Pithay,
house numbers added).*

*Fig 6.21 (below)
Nos.12–13, 14 and 15–17
Pithay
(BCRL Loxton drawings
1649X).*

131

# THE TOWN HOUSE IN MEDIEVAL AND EARLY MODERN BRISTOL

*Fig 6.22*
*Nos.128–31 St Thomas Street (now 25–31 Victoria Street), plan of ground floor (RHL, PEC).*

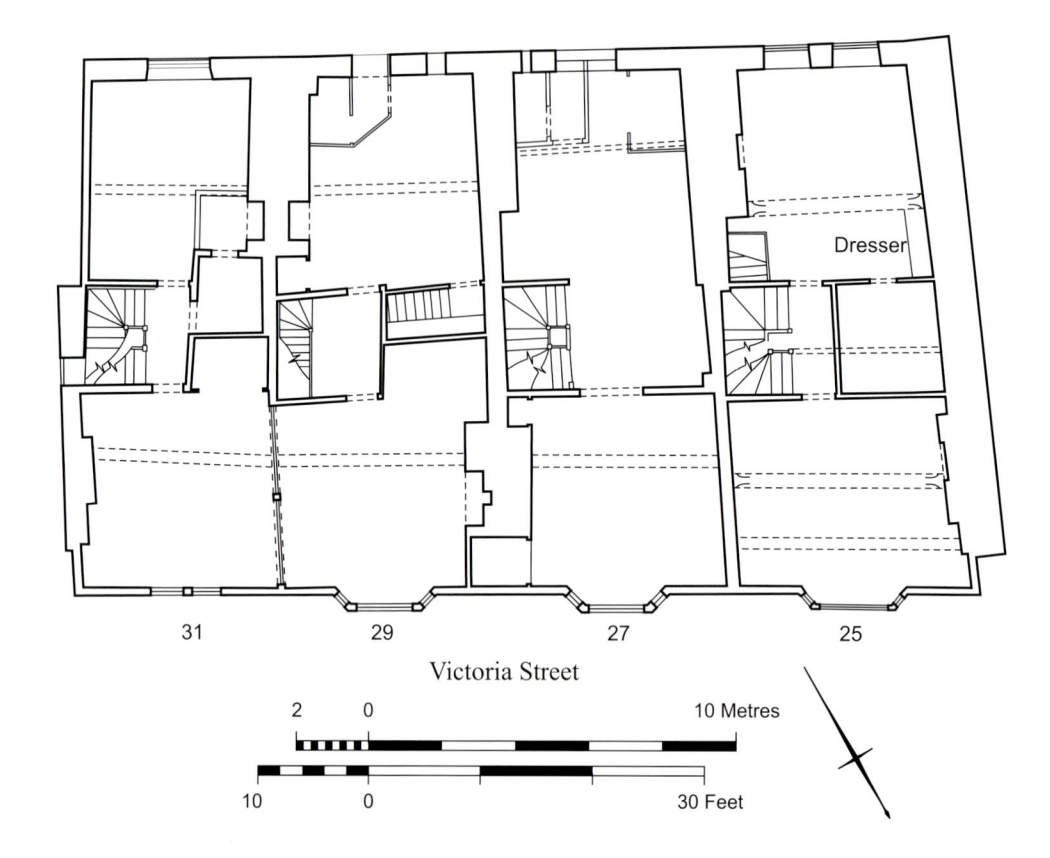

*Fig 6.23*
*Nos.128–31 St Thomas Street (now 25–31 Victoria Street), photograph of 2001 (RHL).*

constructed chimneystack. In contrast, in the first-floor front rooms, chimneystacks existed for all four houses, all supported by the ground-floor ceiling beams. With the exception of no.27, these stacks were positioned on the opposite side of each house to the chimneystacks in the rear rooms. It can be concluded that, in setting out the floor plans of these houses, Gleson intended the front ground-floor rooms to be unheated.

Similar considerations must have influenced Llewellin Evans and William Barrett in the rebuilding of nos.35–41 Old Market (Figs 6.24 and 6.25).[55] Evans, a pipe maker, held the lease on nos.40–1, the first to be rebuilt between 1684 and 1688. The two new houses were built as a pair, each of three and a half storeys, with the front ground-floor room unheated. For economy of building, the chimneystacks were placed along the spine wall separating the two houses. This in turn enabled the stack to the upper front rooms to be balanced and supported centrally on a stone slab, resting on the ground-floor ceiling beam running across the two front rooms.

Barrett, a house carpenter, was probably responsible for the construction of nos.40–1, as he was certainly the builder of the adjacent properties. Between 1692 and 1694 nos.38–9 were built following a plan identical to that of nos.40–1; nos.36–7 and no.35 were built in *c* 1705. In each of these houses, the ground-floor front room was unheated, and the stacks heating the front rooms on the upper storeys were supported on the ceiling beams over the ground floor.

In the redevelopment of the Castle, a demand for houses with unheated front ground-floor rooms was evident from the 1650s. None of the houses then built survive, but a number of inventories, plans and illustrations shed light on the function of the unheated front room.

THE SHOPHOUSE

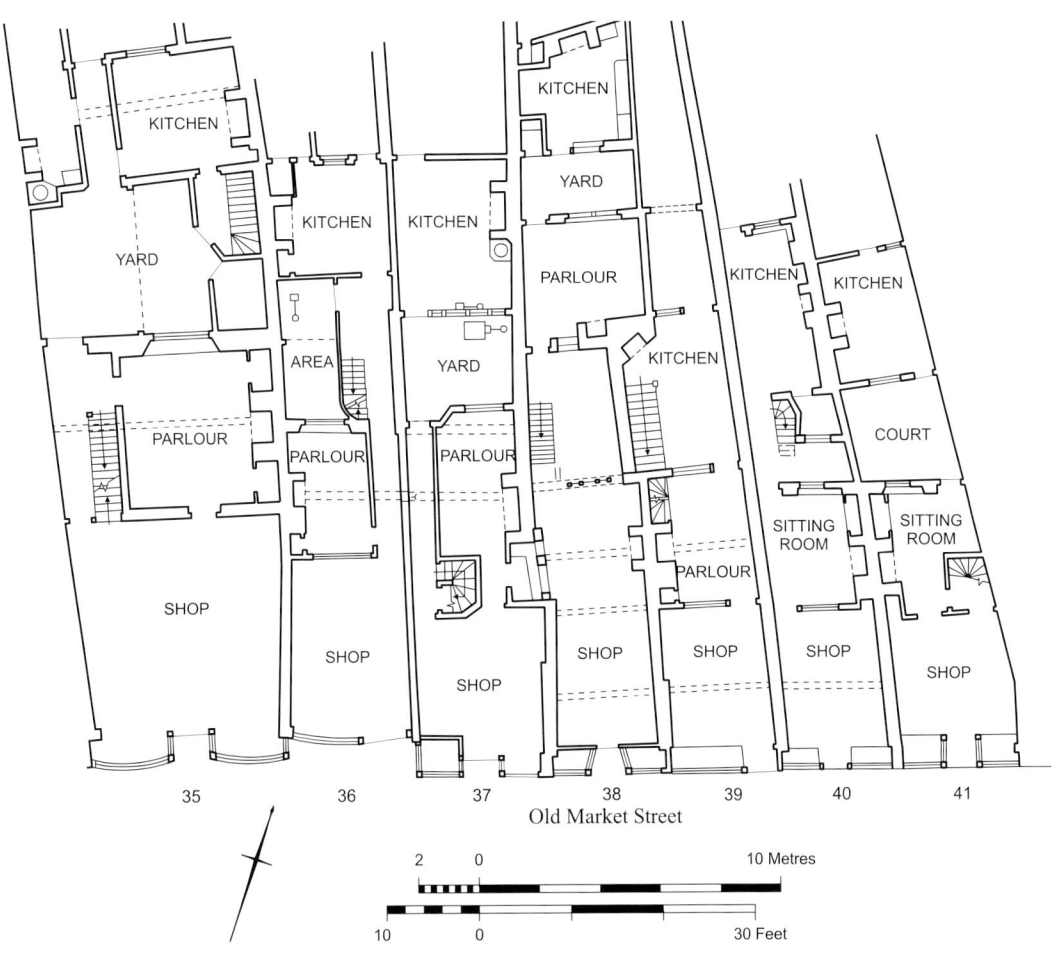

*Fig 6.24*
*Nos.35–41 Old Market, plan of ground floor, names of rooms taken from the plan of 1862*
*(RHL, PEC after BRO 33041/BMC/12/Pl5/fol 6 with additional data from survey).*

*Fig 6.25*
*Nos.35–41 Old Market, photograph of 1978 (NMR BB78/9309).*

133

*Fig 6.26*
*No.26 Castle Street (left), early 18th-century plan (BRO 04479(1) fol 33).*

*Fig 6.27*
*No.56 Castle Street, early 18th-century plan (BRO 04479(1) fol 86).*

No.26 Castle Street was one of two houses of identical layout that were built on a plot leased to Cecily Bush, a widow, in 1661. An early 18th-century plan shows 'bulks' or shop counters projecting into the street under a jettied frontage forward of an unheated shop, with the stairs in the centre and a kitchen in the rear half of the building (Fig 6.26). In 1705 this was the house of William Nicklus, a barber-surgeon. The arrangement of rooms listed in the inventory of his possessions precisely followed that shown on the plan, the front unheated room his shop.[56] On the south side of Castle Street John Harris, a cooper, built no.56 for his own occupation at roughly the same date. The overall plan was a little different from that of Nicklus's house, but the ground-floor front room was again shown on an early 18th-century plan as an unheated shop, bulks projecting forward under the jettied frontage (Fig 6.27).[57]

Further along Castle Street to the west, on a plot leased from the Corporation by Jeremy Holwey, a merchant, three houses of this plan were constructed between 1668 and the early 1670s. John Drew, a house carpenter, was both the builder and the first occupant of no.70 Castle Street, constructed c 1668.[58] The contents of Drew's house were recorded in 1681 for a probate inventory, but do not mention a shop, or the tools and stock of his trade (Appendix 2). Probably the latter had already passed to his wife and son, who were to inherit the property in turn.

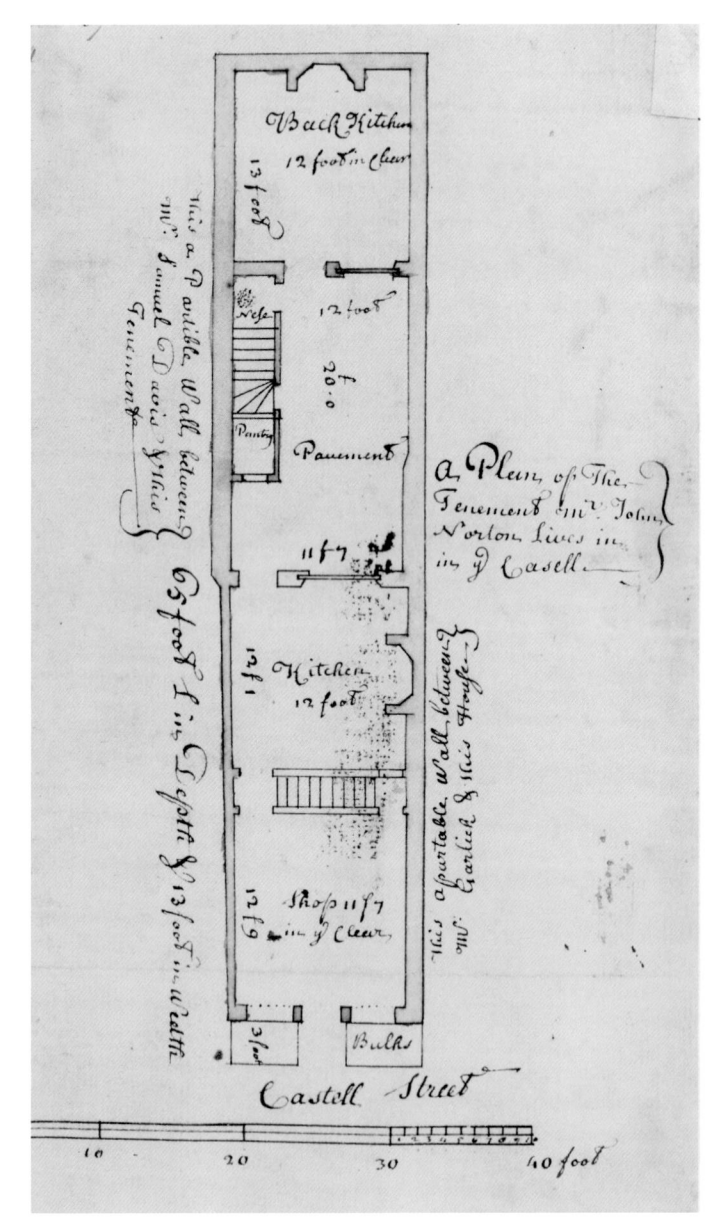

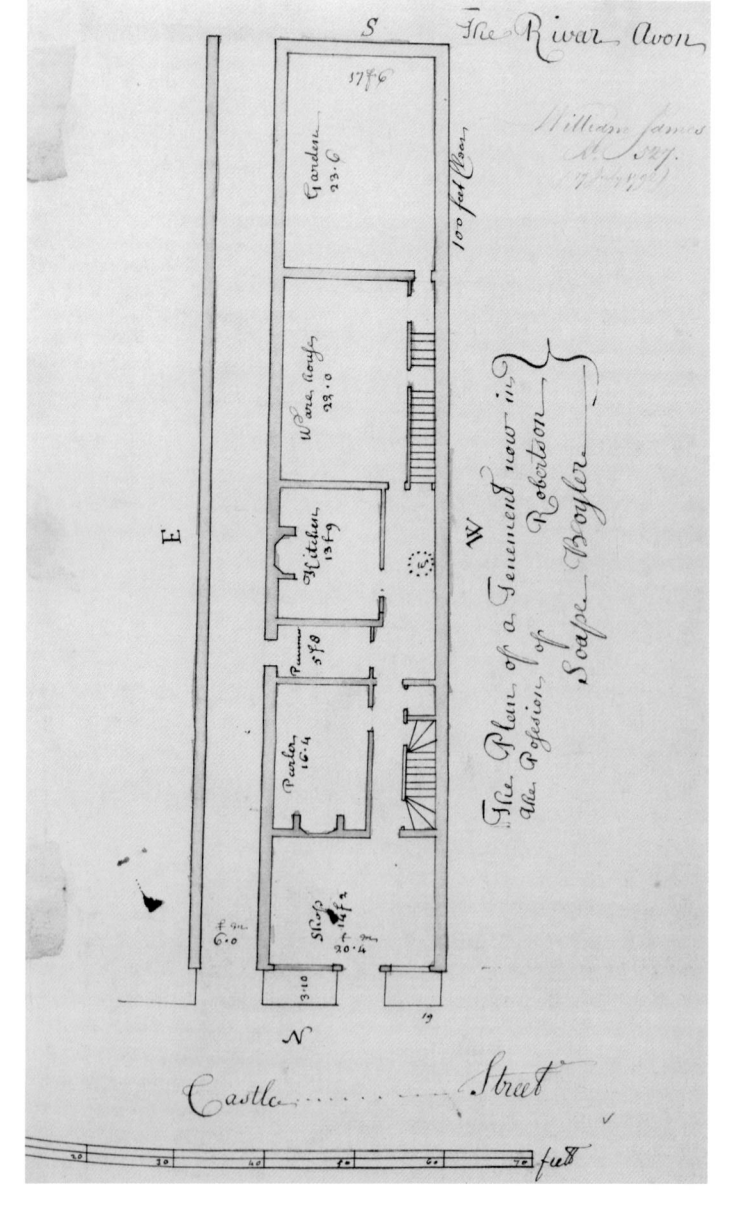

THE SHOPHOUSE

A late 18th-century plan shows the house in detail (Fig 6.28). On the street front was an unheated shop. Behind was a second room, described by then also as a shop; but heated, quite separate from the front room, and probably originally the main kitchen. Echoing the arrangement of no.56, Drew had placed the stairs within the rear half of the house, enabling the shop area to be taken to its maximum possible extent. A similar plan was also adopted for nos.71 and 72, built under leases granted to Thomas Kill, a weaver, and William Taylor, a baker (Fig 6.29).[59] Of the same overall depth as no.70, these two houses were possibly also built by Drew.

Houses with unheated ground-floor front rooms, built in other streets during the 17th and 18th centuries but with no precise historical context known to date, can therefore be interpreted as houses with shops. Rather smaller than the four houses next to St Thomas's churchyard were the two houses at no.61 St Thomas Street, described as 'new built' in 1681 (Fig 6.30).[60] By *c* 1818, one had been converted to first-floor storage space over an entrance way. In the other, a fireplace had been constructed in the front room; its corner position suggests that this was not a feature original to the room. As with no.56 Castle Street, the stairs were placed in the rear half of the house, maximising the area of the shop. In Redcliff Street, no.144 was built to two rooms in depth,

*Fig 6.28*
*No.70 Castle Street, late 18th-century plan (BRO 04479(2) fol 126).*

*Fig 6.29*
*Nos.71 and 72 Castle Street, late 18th-century plan (BRO 04479(5) fol 37).*

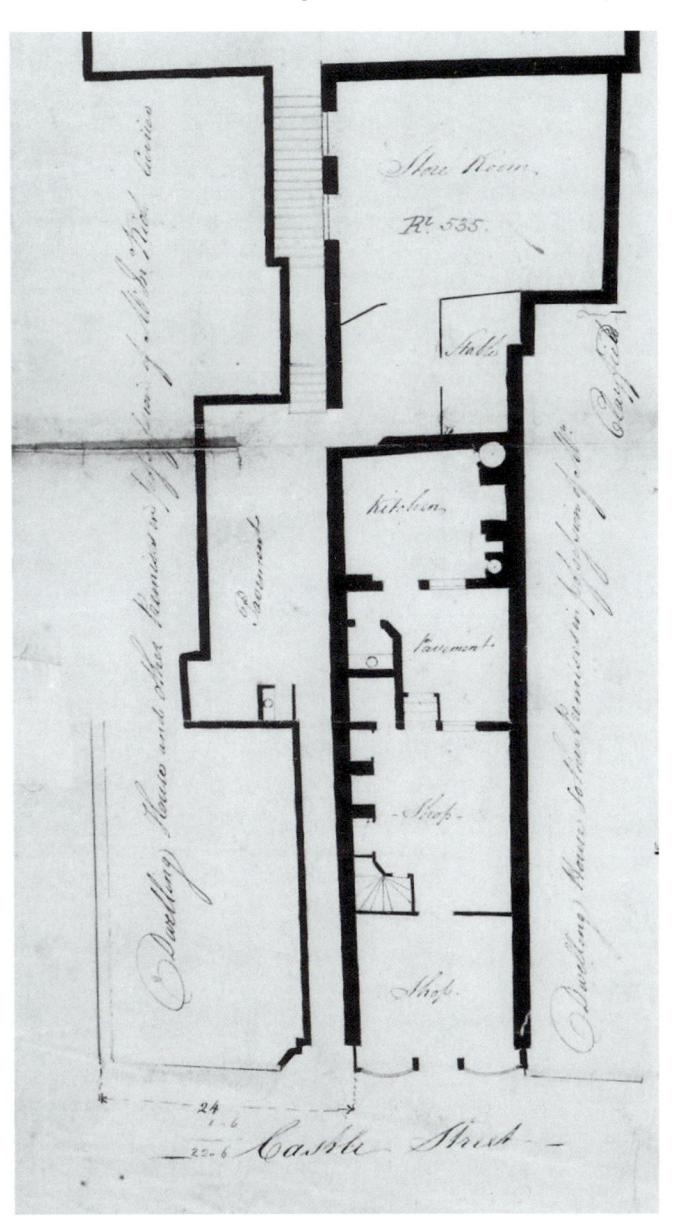

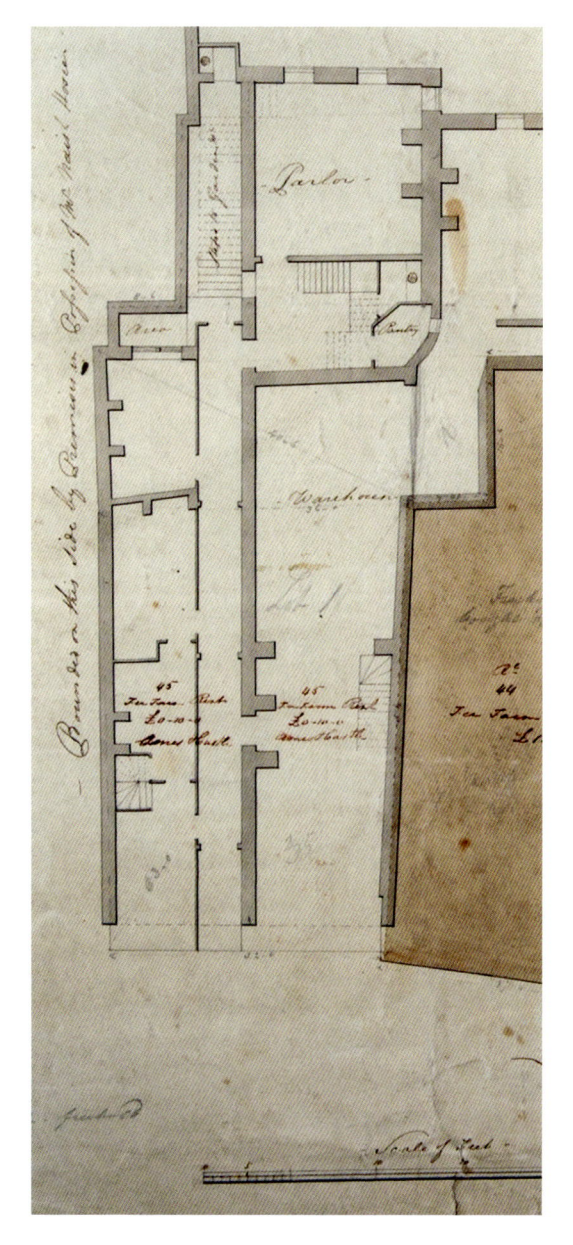

*Fig 6.30
No.61 St Thomas Street,
plan and elevation drawing
of 1818
(BRO P/StT/Ch/3/31
fol 4).*

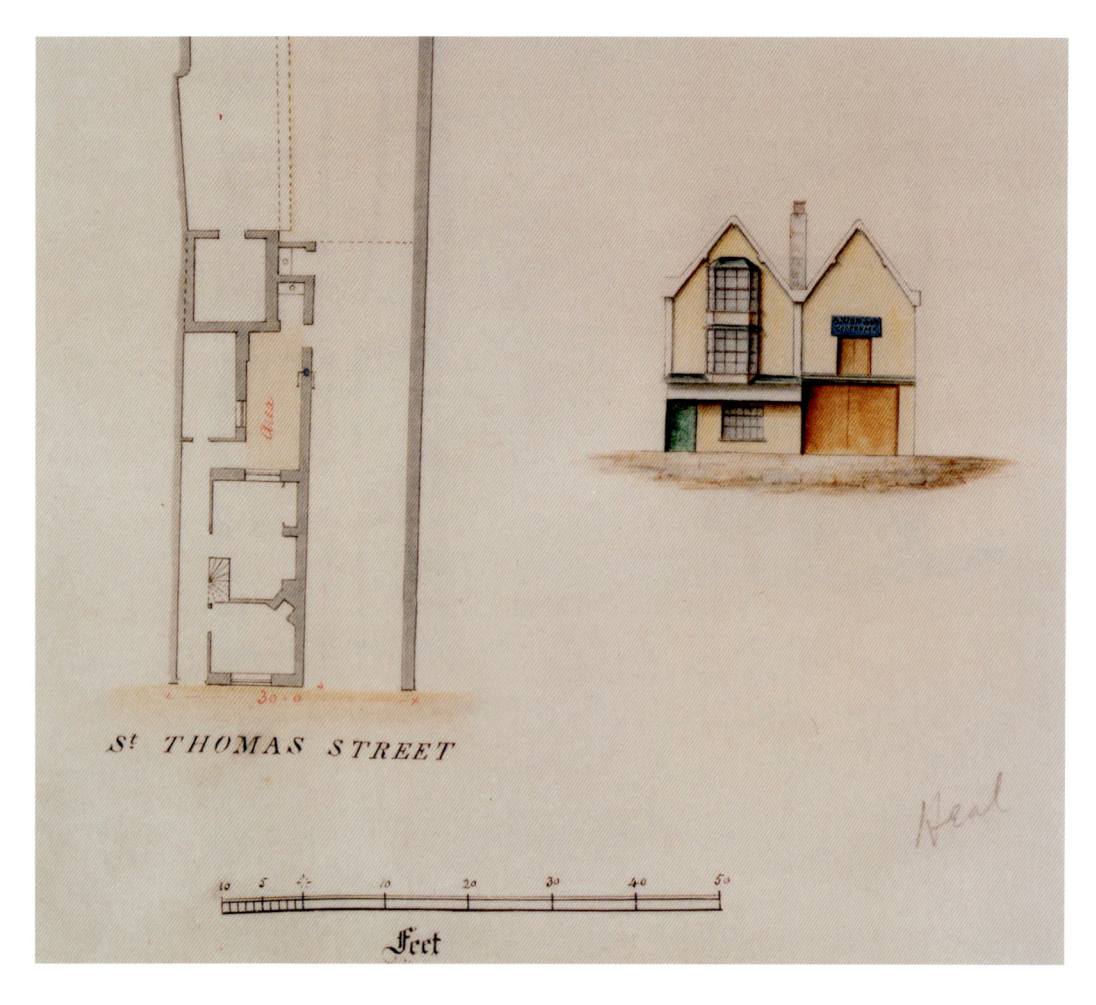

but with an unheated front room (Fig 6.31). In Temple Street, nos.9 and 10 were of similar plan.⁶¹ All these houses are demolished. The best known shophouse was probably that built or rebuilt at no.1 High Street by Robert Winstone in 1676, demolished after bomb damage in the Blitz of November 1940 (chapter 1). A reconstruction of this house from documentary sources reveals that this too had an unheated ground-floor shop (Fig 6.32).

Shophouses with an unheated front room were also to be found in late 17th-century London, for instance at no.45 Greenwich Church Street, constructed *c* 1700, and elsewhere. In London, however, a characteristic lifestyle in the 17th century was to live entirely over the shop. The ground floor was given over wholly to the shop and the house floated, as it were, one floor above.⁶² In Bristol, it appears that this lifestyle was adopted principally by those who lived in houses of one room on each floor. For those living in larger houses, there were often choices to be made in respect of which activities might be located at ground level. Some of the heated rear ground-floor rooms noted above were doubtless kitchens or reception rooms, and therefore an integral part of the dwelling; but others may have been used in connection with the adjacent shop, perhaps as workshops. Tenement plots also varied considerably in size and situation. The amount of land available, and the access to it, influenced the preferences which determined how households might be organised.

## New Houses with Shops – the Developments of the 1740s and Later

Many new shophouses were probably built in the Corporation's developments of the 1740s and subsequent decades. Most of the streets then developed are no longer extant, but there are a few clues to the design of the houses being constructed. A set of drawings relating to the new houses constructed in Union Street in the 1760s includes a design for a house with shop fronts on the ground floor (Fig 6.33). Plans of

THE SHOPHOUSE

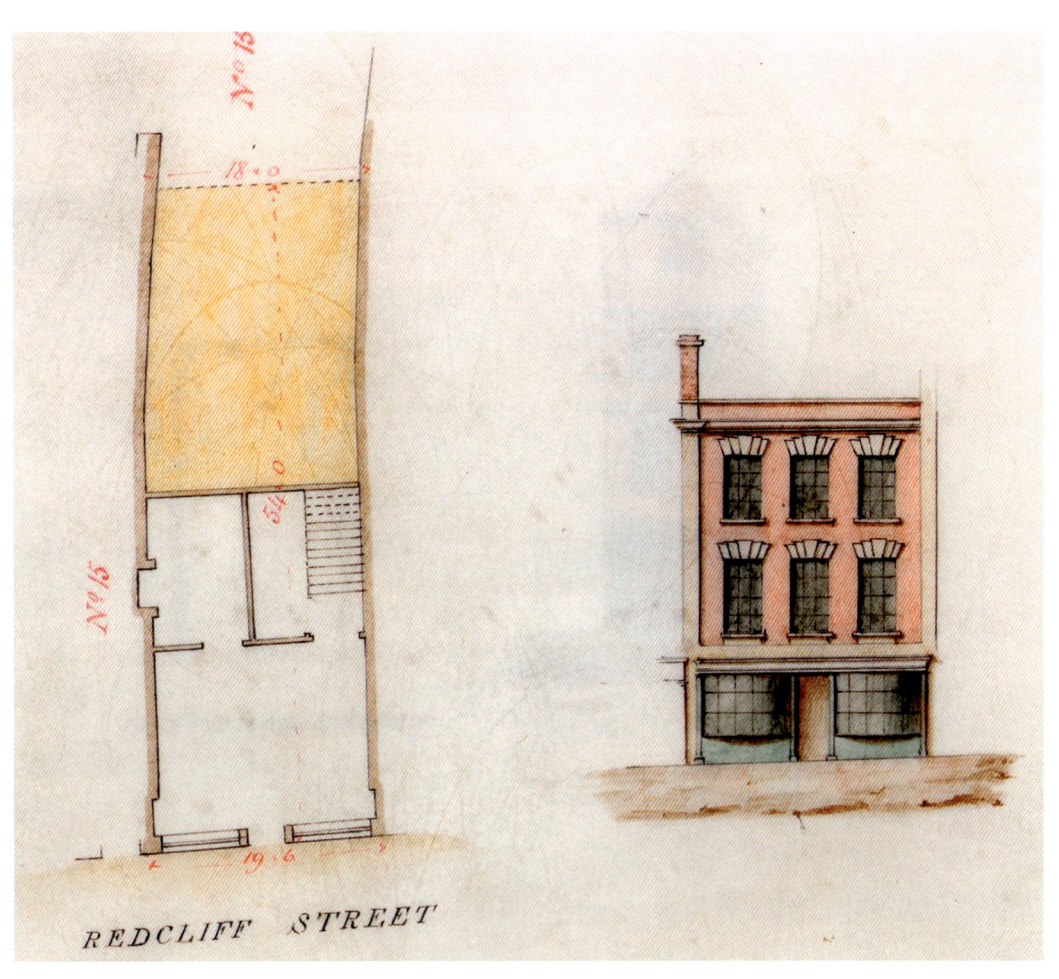

*Fig 6.31*
*No.144 Redcliff Street, plan and elevation drawing of 1818 (BRO P/StT/Ch/3/31 fol 14).*

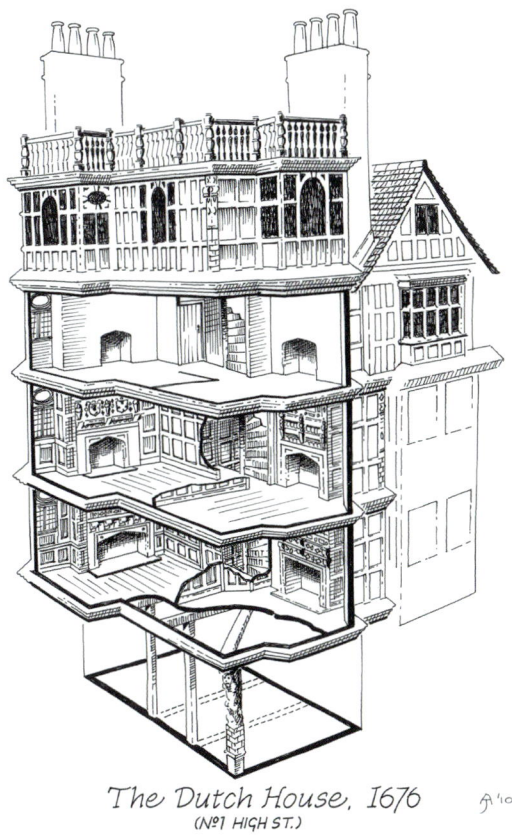

*Fig 6.32 (far left)*
*No.1 High Street, 'the Dutch House', a shophouse built or rebuilt by the glover Robert Winstone in 1676, reconstructed from documentary sources (chapter 1). The unheated ground-floor shop featured a forestreet chamber and other heated chambers above, while the attic floor was possibly the workshop; the reconstruction is of the house from the ground floor upwards (JA).*

*Fig 6.33 (left)*
*Design for a new house to be constructed in Union Street in the 1760s, with shop fronts on the ground floor (BRO 04479(5) fol 22).*

137

*Fig 6.34*
*Three new houses in Dolphin Street, shown on a plan of 1765 for the rebuilding of a property purchased for the widening of the street in connection with improving access to the new bridge (BRO 6170(1)a).*

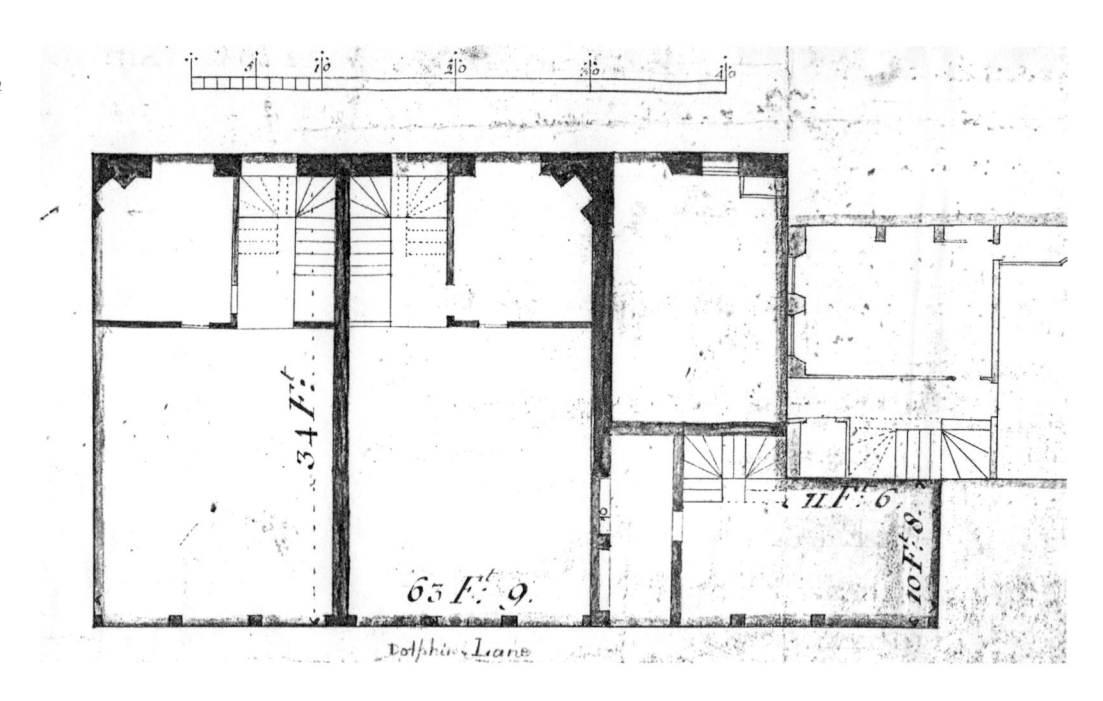

a much later date of nos.23–4 Bridge Street show the chimneystack in the ground-floor front room of no.24 as being of a much smaller size than that in the rear room, and probably added to what had been designed as an initially unheated front shop.[63]

Unheated front-room shops were certainly provided in three new houses in Dolphin Street, shown on a plan of 1765 for the rebuilding of a property purchased for the widening of the street in connection with improving access to the new Bridge (Fig 6.34). As one of the signatories, the craftsman and stone carver Thomas Paty was probably responsible for this design – for a single house next to the house fronting Peter Street and two houses forming a pair, in which the room for the shop was much larger than the rear parlour, a plan that gave primacy to the needs of commerce.[64] Elevation drawings of the late 19th century show most of the houses on both sides of Bridge Street as having ground-floor shop fronts, similar to those known to be of the later 18th century in Bath Street.[65] The building leases for houses in Bath Street, constructed in the 1770s, contained many designs for shop fronts, revealing that this street consisted largely or entirely of shophouses (see Fig 3.43).

The developments of the Corporation also included what appears to have been a new form of commercial dwelling: what John Wood the Elder referred to in his description of the Exchange as 'houses built for Insurance or other Publick Offices; or for trades-people'.[66] Wood's plan showed eight houses on the sides of the Exchange. Survey has shown that three of these were commenced, but not completed. Instead, the spaces were used to accommodate the stairs to the coffee house in the north-east corner, and also to house the two stairs in the south-east and south-west corners to the first floor of the south range (Fig 6.35; see Fig 3.8). These houses were

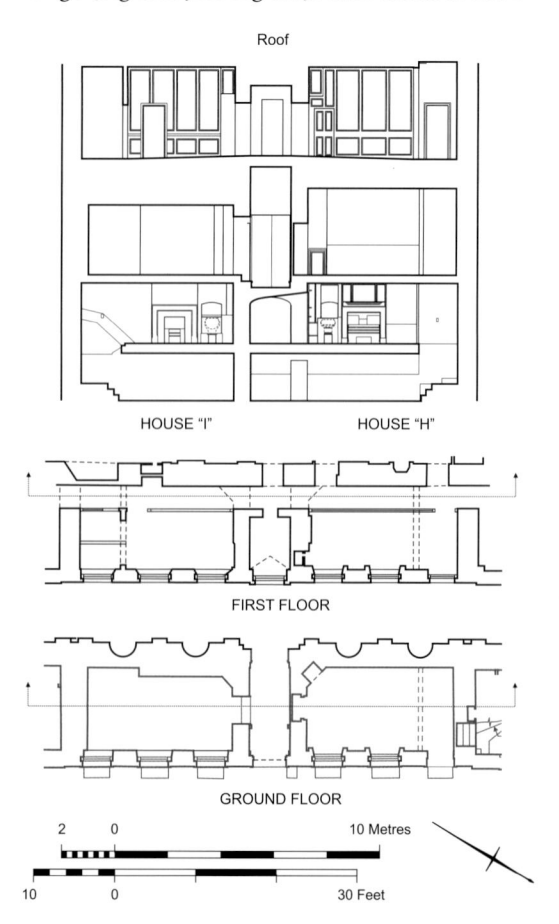

*Fig 6.35*
*Section through two houses on the east side of the Exchange (RHL, PEC).*

THE SHOPHOUSE

of four or five storeys, with a vaulted cellar and kitchen above, plus half- and fully panelled parlours on the ground and first floors. One also possessed a chamber above on a second floor. In 1775 the occupants of these houses included a gunpowder office and insurance, ship and West India brokers, bankers and lawyers, almost all of whom would have had dwellings elsewhere in the city. These were houses primarily for the undertaking of business.

Close by in Small Street, nos.3–4 were rebuilt in the later 18th century to provide similar commercial accommodation. The two houses were, like the Exchange, constructed so as to appear as a single building from the exterior (Fig 6.36). A single entrance with a pedimented doorway provided access to a passage shared by the two houses (Fig 6.37a). By 1775 the two houses were the premises of the attorney Francis Ward and of the bankers Bright and Co.

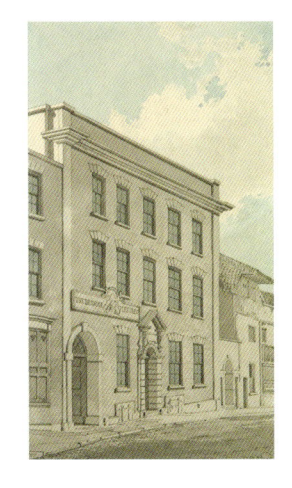

*Fig 6.36 (above) Nos.3–4 Small Street as rebuilt in the later 18th century to provide two houses for business persons; like the Exchange, they were constructed to appear a single building from the exterior. Watercolour by H O'Neill, 1823 (BRSMG M2480).*

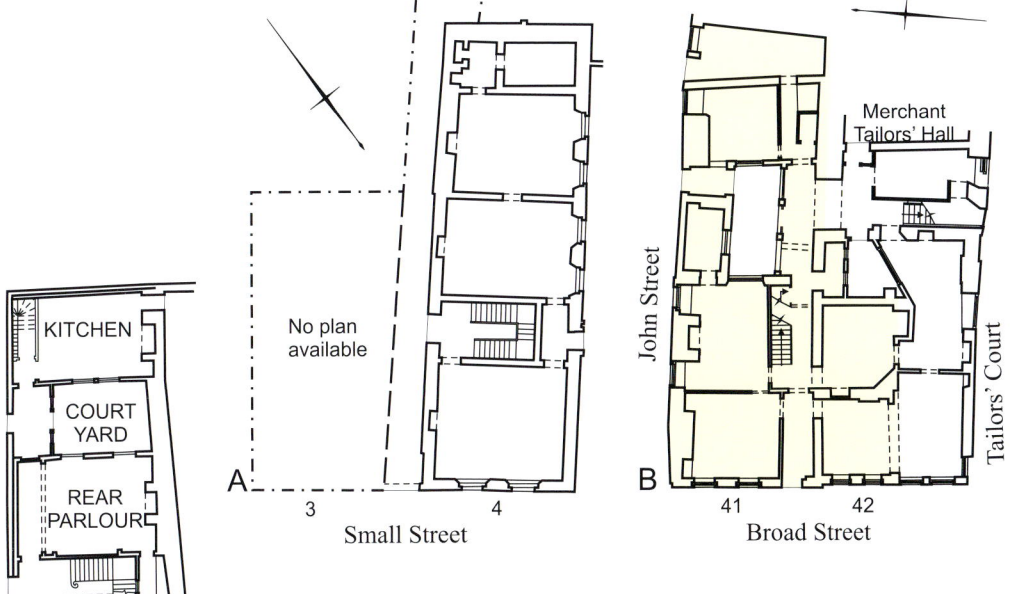

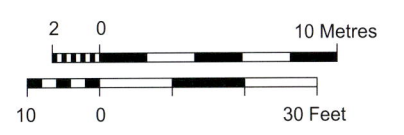

*Fig 6.37 Plans of houses used commercially: a) nos.3–4 Small Street; b) nos.41–2 Broad Street, rebuilt c 1750 as the premises for the bank, plan of ground floor; c) no.35 Corn Street; d) no.69 Old Market (RHL, PEC).*

139

The Corporation was also responsible for rebuilding individual houses as shophouses, for example at no.49 Corn Street, where the Corporation held the property in trust for the Whitson charity. Here the hallhouse once of Edward Morris (chapter 5) was rebuilt c 1800 as a shophouse (Figs 6.38 and 6.39). Comparison of the plans of the house before and after rebuilding show that the hall had now been made part of the shop, and that the former kitchen had become a parlour. On the corner of Small Street, a thoroughfare once dominated by the hallhouses of the urban elite, it was now judged opportune to replace a formerly residential property with a shophouse.

In Broad Street, the house that was once the residence of Andrew Innys, gentleman, was converted c 1750 to become a bank, the premises

*Fig 6.38*
*No.49 Corn Street, mid-19th-century plan of ground floor (BRO 33041/BMC/12/PL1 fol 16).*

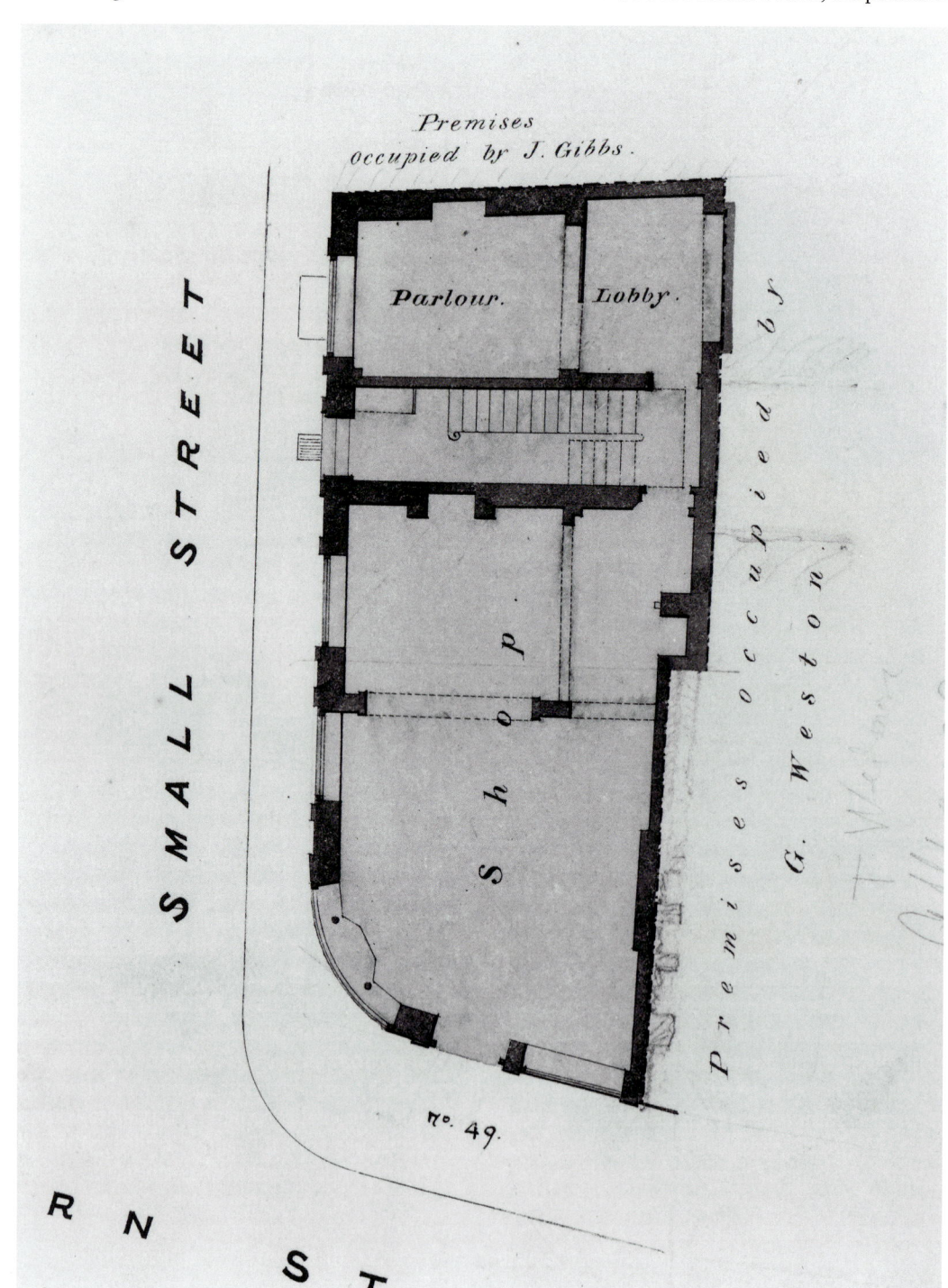

*Fig 6.39*
*No.49 Corn Street, watercolour by G W Delamotte, 1824 (BRSMG M2475).*

THE SHOPHOUSE

of Elton, Lloyd and Co (the first banking company in Bristol). On the street frontage was a brick-fronted house which combined commercial and living accommodation (Figs 6.37b and 6.40). To the rear of the principal rooms on the ground floor were two strongrooms. The floors above were the living accommodation of Robert Langford, clerk to the bank, who was living there in 1775. Behind the courtyard at the rear of the house was a second range, probably dating from the 17th century or earlier, which contained the kitchen and servants' accommodation.

Four decades later another, older property in Corn Street was rebuilt to house this same bank on its relocation from Broad Street. No.35 Corn

*Fig 6.40*
*Nos.41–2 Broad Street, photograph of 2012 (NMR DP 152581).*

*Fig 6.41*
*No.35 Corn Street, arched entrance to front room on first floor, photograph of 2005 (RHL).*

*Fig 6.42 (far right)*
*No.69 Old Market, arched entrance to front room on first floor, photograph of 1998 (NMR BB98/01588).*

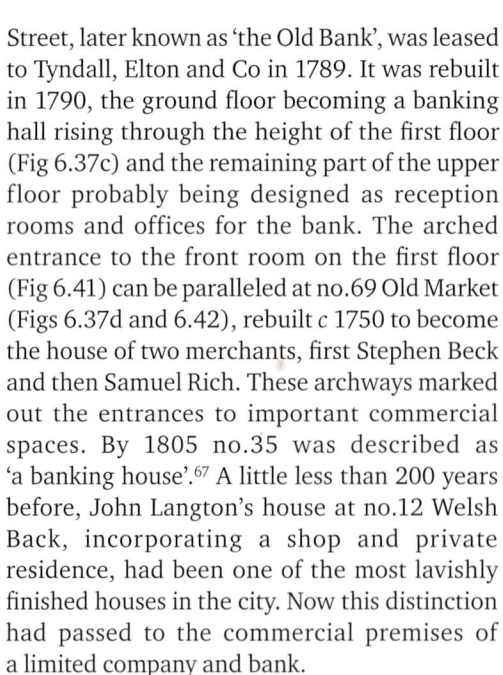

Street, later known as 'the Old Bank', was leased to Tyndall, Elton and Co in 1789. It was rebuilt in 1790, the ground floor becoming a banking hall rising through the height of the first floor (Fig 6.37c) and the remaining part of the upper floor probably being designed as reception rooms and offices for the bank. The arched entrance to the front room on the first floor (Fig 6.41) can be paralleled at no.69 Old Market (Figs 6.37d and 6.42), rebuilt c 1750 to become the house of two merchants, first Stephen Beck and then Samuel Rich. These archways marked out the entrances to important commercial spaces. By 1805 no.35 was described as 'a banking house'.[67] A little less than 200 years before, John Langton's house at no.12 Welsh Back, incorporating a shop and private residence, had been one of the most lavishly finished houses in the city. Now this distinction had passed to the commercial premises of a limited company and bank.

In conclusion, the shophouse was a building with a multiple purpose, both residential and commercial, to be found both in Bristol and in other English cities and towns, including London. In the medieval and early modern periods, it might have been an indicator of social divisions within the urban setting, although, as we have seen, such properties came to house a considerable range of people, from modestly prosperous trading families to some of the wealthiest men of the city. From the 15th century or earlier until the end of the 18th century, the distribution of shophouses across Bristol as a whole might also assist in identifying a central business district, represented in 1837 by 'a central area of parishes where properties were used for predominantly commercial purposes'.[68] The existence of this commercial core went hand in hand with the development of socially segregated suburbs, a process to be examined further in chapter 12.

# 7

# The Complexities of Commerce

In 1795, on the last occasion on which he is known to have visited Bristol, the drawing master John Baptiste Malchair sketched the view across the Avon looking towards St Mary Redcliff church. On that morning, the sun shining wanly through smoke and cloud, he must have been very conscious of the mix of industry and the remains of the medieval city (Fig 7.1).[1] The skyline was still dominated by St Mary Redcliff church, but no longer so exclusively, the truncated base of its spire now half-hidden in the smoke from the cones of the glassworks beyond in Red Lane. Other industrial structures nestled around the church: a pottery kiln or the stump of a glasshouse on the foreshore, the shot tower on Redcliff Hill to the right. Further in the distance, the glasshouse in St Thomas Street was as prominent as the leaning tower of Temple church. Walking through the streets of Bristol on that same day, Malchair would have been conscious of the mix of industry and dwelling houses, characteristic of the early modern city by the later 18th century.

Yet for the most part the study of urban housing in medieval and early modern England has divorced the dwelling house from its integral or adjacent commercial, craft and industrial premises. The reasons are perhaps several. Early houses surviving on street frontages are much more visible than the structures behind. They have frequently been drawn, painted and photographed. Preservation on account of architectural merit has by its very nature protected buildings which can easily be seen; non-domestic buildings behind the frontage are less favoured.

*Fig 7.1*
*View towards St Mary Redcliff, 1795, by John Baptiste Malchair*
*(© private collection).*

In the modern city, working and domestic lives are for the greater number of individuals spatially separated. To what extent was that so in the 18th century or earlier? Can an increasing separation of domestic life from work be seen as a change that took place in the emergence of the early modern city? This chapter is concerned primarily with these questions – with the extent to which the working lives of townspeople were, or were not, intertwined with their domestic lives.

## Retailing, Trade and Industry

Surveying the streets of the town in the 1480s, the traveller and writer William Worcestre would have noted much the same distribution of occupations across the city as could have been observed 200 years earlier. As in other large towns, those engaged in specific trades and crafts tended to congregate in particular parts of the city.[2] In Bristol the locations which they chose related especially to the needs of those concerned with shipping and trade. Worcestre commented on the rope-house alongside the Avon, and the use of the frontage on to the Frome near Marsh Gate for shipbuilding.[3] Nearby, extending back from the quayside, were storehouses and masthouses. In the adjacent streets, notably Marsh Street and Baldwin Street, were carpenters, joiners, turners, cofferers, coopers and hoopers – all making use of timber, some of it doubtless superfluous to the needs of shipwrights. In Baldwin Street and St Nicholas Street could also be found coppersmiths and plumbers. Close to the waterfronts of the Frome and the Avon lived most of the merchants of the city, on hand to supervise the loading and unloading of cargoes and to watch their ships come and go.

Crossing the Bridge, the inhabitants of the Redcliff and Temple Fees were concerned predominantly with various aspects of cloth manufacture. Tuckers (cloth finishers) lived in Tucker Street, weavers in Temple Street and St Thomas Street, and dyers in Redcliff Street. Scattered through these suburbs were inns and taverns. On the Bridge and north of the river, the streets around the central carfax were dominated by retailers, mercers, grocers, drapers, goldsmiths, glovers and other purveyors of high-status luxury items. Here, too, were more inns, taverns and saddlers to serve the needs of visitors on horseback.

Moving east along the ridge were cordwainers (shoemakers and leather workers), predominantly in Mary le Port Street, while butchers and allied trades gathered in the Shambles or Worshipful Street. Tanners, whittawers (leather finishers) and parchment makers were but three more of the trades to be found in streets to the east and north, in Peter and Narrow Wine Streets, and in Broadmead – such as the cordwainers, using the products of butchery. Other trades required water, notably soap makers who were to be found principally in Lewin's Mead and close to the Bridge.[4]

Finally, visitors might note the red light districts. Close to the quays and the mariners were Love Lane and Gropecuntlane, the latter a name found in a number of towns across England.[5] Close to the routes into the town from north and west was the crossroads at the north end of Broadmead, which in c 1480 William Worcestre was sufficently interested in to comment upon at four separate points in his narrative, possibly because of family connections: 'where tenants of my father dwell as wanton women'.[6]

## Shopping in the Street

Not all those engaged in retail trade in the medieval and early modern city plied their wares through shops. The layout of the four main streets radiating from the carfax, broadening in their central areas or at one end to provide greater space, allowed for open-air trading in marketplaces, and specialised markets took place in other parts of the town (chapter 2). By the 14th century meat could be purchased daily from the butchers' stalls in Worshipful Street, fish from stalls in the same street and from the market on the Quay.[7] Beasts could be bought on the vacant space in front of the Dominican Friary in Broadmead, and in no other place.[8] Roughsmiths or their servants were to sell their ironware only in shops or close to the High Cross. Strangers to the town selling 'smythware' were to stand in the open space beside the High Cross, so that their wares could be seen.[9]

Fourteenth-century ordinances, requiring vendors of cloths to carry them in their arms and not to sell them on stalls or benches in the highway, and fulminating against the sale of cloths, half-cloths and remnants in 'inns, chambers and in other places in secret', would not have been issued if the latter had not often been the practice.[10] On a weekly basis, cloth could be purchased every Saturday from the drapers' market in Tucker Street.[11] Annual fairs afforded the opportunity to make more occasional purchases outside the gates of St James's Priory and in the Marsh.[12]

## Selds

This world of street traders, markets and fairs would certainly have been familiar to Worcestre. He would, however, probably have been unfamiliar with the *seld*, a common enough element in the street scene of a century or more before. Research in London and Chester has shown that *selds* were usually off-street private bazaars, subdivided for use by individual traders.[13] The dimensions of some of the properties used as *selds* in Bristol indicate that these were probably similar in form to those in London. The word 'seld', as mentioned in contemporary documents, has sometimes been translated as stall, but the plots occupied by the *selds* that can be firmly identified were too large to have been used as single stalls. *Selds* were located in the more central streets (Fig 7.2). By the early 13th century there were at least six, two newly built, between Welsh Back and Back Street, with others located on both sides of High Street. By the early 14th century they were to be found also below St Leonard's church outside St Leonard's Gate, on the Quay, and in Redcliff and Temple.[14]

At nos.18–20 High Street the *selds* with buildings behind were granted by William Curtelove to St Augustine's Abbey in the early 13th century. This plot was *c* 48ft wide; the division between the front and rear cellar of no.18 (Fig 7.20) may indicate that the *selds* were *c* 20ft in depth. On Welsh Back, at the north-west end of Bristol Bridge, a development of the

*Fig 7.2 Location of selds in High Street by the early 13th century (RHL, PEC).*

1290s provided for certainly two *selds* and possibly for five in all, each approximately 17ft wide and 27ft deep. In 1305 two *selds* at nos.5–6 and 7–8 High Street each occupied a plot *c* 17ft wide; later divisions between the cellars fronting the street and those set further back indicate that each *seld* was probably *c* 22ft deep. At nos.11–13 High Street, the tenement known as Ropeseld by 1309 occupied a plot 30ft wide. The smallest *seld* recorded, *c* 10ft wide, was that at no.47B High Street, granted to St Augustine's Abbey in the early 13th century (Fig 7.2). There is no evidence that *selds* were also used as dwellings, although at nos.5–8 and 18–20 High Street there were buildings behind, in the former the dwelling of the owner of the *seld*.

With the exception of nos.11–13 High Street, still known as the Ropeseld in 1464 but by then an inn, only one reference to *selds* in Bristol has been recorded after the first half of the 14th century. It is for what may be interpreted as stalls in front of no.Xch/8 Wine Street, a shop with *selds* leased in 1404. The *selds* on Welsh Back had certainly been replaced by shops by *c* 1350; the southernmost of the row was by 1345 a corner shop with a solar, by 1377 a shop with a solar built above. Deeds of 1335 and later for nos.5–8 High Street make no reference to *selds*.[15] Their disappearance from the street scene may be linked to the increasing number of storeys being given to the houses fronting the principal streets. *Selds* would have ceased to be commercially viable once a greater rent could be obtained from letting a house of two, three or more storeys. In contrast to London, there are no references to any of the Bristol *selds* having upper floors.[16]

## Shops

In 1312, in Bristol as elsewhere, the collection of the tax known as the 'tallage' would have involved the compilation of a list in the form of a parchment roll recording the payment made by each household. The roll for Bristol survives and, decoded, could provide a street directory of much of the early 14th-century town (Fig 7.3).[17] Even without the exhaustive research that this would necessitate, the roll provides some clues to the distribution of shops within the town by the early 14th century.

Properties named as shops in the Tallage Roll were concentrated especially in the suburban streets. Notable was Back Street, behind Welsh Back, where 29 shops were located; in *c* 1350 these included the 11 new shops of the chantry of Eborard Fraunce (le Frenche) (chapter 6). Similar concentrations were found in the streets leading out of the town on the west. The suburb in Frog Lane (later Frogmore Street) may have consisted almost entirely of shops.

There were possibly as many shops in the more central streets, but, with the exception of a concentration in St Nicholas Street, these seem to have been largely omitted from explicit mention in the Tallage Roll. They are, however, frequently recorded in contemporary deeds. Typical would be the corner shop in the drapers' corner, opposite the south door of Christchurch, with shops either side, part of no.1 High Street, mentioned in a deed of 1285 and predating the construction of the vaulted cellar on the site. Large numbers of shops in the Temple and Redcliff suburbs south of the Avon may have been similarly omitted from the Tallage Roll of 1312.

*Fig 7.3 Extract from the Tallage Roll, 1312 (Fuller 1894–5; s = shop). The extract from the list of names is probably in a walking order, providing in effect a street directory for that date. It commences outside the Marsh Gate with four shops, past another three shops of St Augustine's Abbey and then turns into Back or Baste Street. Here the two shops of Agnes Dawe are followed by many more, showing this (now Queen Charlotte Street) to have been one of the busiest shopping streets in Bristol in 1312.*

| | | |
|---|---|---|
| Johanna Crok — d. quat. s. extra portam maresci … … … | 5 | 4 |
| Abbas Sancti Augustini d. trib. s. ib. … … … … … … | 6 | 0 |
| Robertus de Holhurst h.d. eisdem … … … … … … | 6 | 0 |
| Agnes Dawe — d. duab. s. in Baste Strete … … … … … | 2 | 8 |
| Hospitium Sancti Laurentii h.i.r.d. quinq. s. ib. … … … | 10 | 0 |
| Edwardus le Fleschewere — ib. d. una s. juxta venellam … … | 3 | 0 |
| Cecilia le Clerk h.i.r. d. una s. cum curtilagio … … … … | 5 | 0 |
| Bernard ate Wolde — d. quinq. s. ib. … … … .. … … | 8 | 0 |
| Ricardus de Panys — d. trib. s. ib. … … … … … … | 4 | 0 |
| Magister Hospitii Sancti Johannis — d. duab. s. ib. … .. … | 6 | 0 |
| Galfridus Locking — ib. d. duab. s. … … … … … | 7 | 0 |
| Alicia de Dene — d. trib. s. .. … … … … … | 9 | 0 |
| Walfridus de Wynton h.i.r.d. duab. schophis ib. … … … | 8 | 0 |

THE COMPLEXITIES OF COMMERCE

Certainly by the 15th century it can be seen that in Bristol, as elsewhere, shop owners set out to draw custom through eye-catching ornament to the shop itself, and through the proliferation of signs identifying particular shops to largely illiterate potential customers. At the junction of Peter Street and Chequer Lane, for example, a richly decorated post supported the dragon beam to the corner shop built before 1419 as part of the dwelling house and four shops of Simon Oliver, seneschal or steward to Queen Catherine, for her properties in Bristol (Figs 7.4a and 7.4b).[18] At the corner of Redcliff Street and Fisher Lane a naked female figure supporting a dragon beam similarly served to catch the eye of passers-by (Fig 7.5).

By the 15th century many properties were also individually named for the purposes of identification. Some of these were inns or taverns, such as the Starr at nos.32–4 High Street (p159) or the Horsshedd at no.63 Wine Street (pp162–4), identified as such through either being named specifically as inns, being occupied by innkeepers or through other chance references. However, not all named houses were necessarily inns or taverns.[19] In the 1690s Celia Fiennes noted that as in London 'there are signes to many houses that are not Publick houses'.[20] In Bristol those named houses that cannot be shown to have been public houses were to be found in the principal streets, and were probably shops. In 1650 no.47 the Quay, for example, was known as the 'Anchor Smyth'. This was the dwelling and workplace of three or more generations of the Jones family, makers of anchors. There is no evidence that his house was a tavern or inn.[21]

The form of shops in medieval Bristol is known only from documentary sources, principally early plans and views of the city's main streets. As in other English towns, shops had large unglazed windows with removable shutters, and there seems to have been a very close relationship between space inside and outside the shop. Boards for display were commonly set up outside the shop (*see* Figs 5.36, 6.26 and 6.27), and the large windows opened up the interior to view. The particular goods on sale or in preparation would, therefore, have been immediately apparent to passers-by. By 1470 at least four of the cooks providing take-away food in the High Street had each set up their 'dressing bord' and hearth on the street in front of their houses on what was properly common ground (Fig 7.6). Together hearths and dressing boards, the latter synonymous with the

*Fig 7.4*
*No.6 Peter Street, corner post supporting dragon beam:*
*a) photograph of the 1890s (BRSMG Plates);*
*b) Buckler drawing of the 1820s (The British Library Board, Add MS 36436 fol 289).*

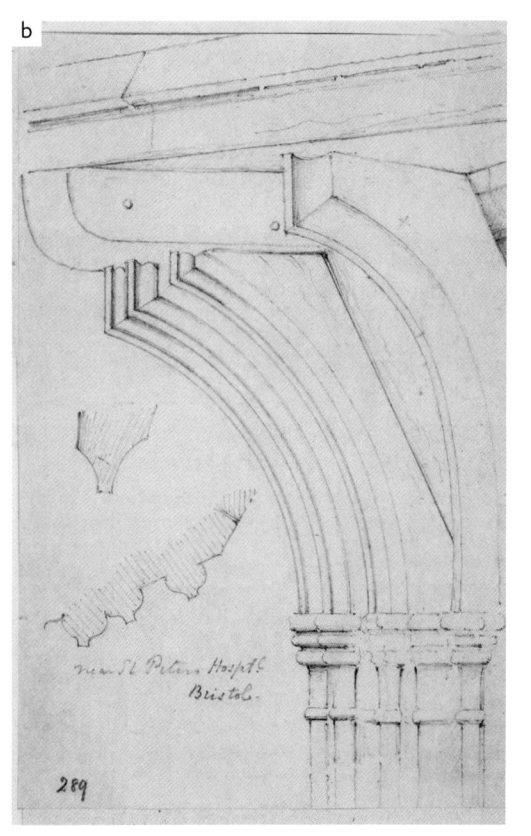

*Fig 7.5 (above)*
*No.113 Redcliff Street, house with female figure supporting dragon beam at corner of Fishers Lane, drawing of 1820s (BRSMG Bristol Streets, R–S, M4135).*

147

*Fig 7.6*
*Reconstructed plans of cellars in High Street, east and west sides (RHL, PEC).*

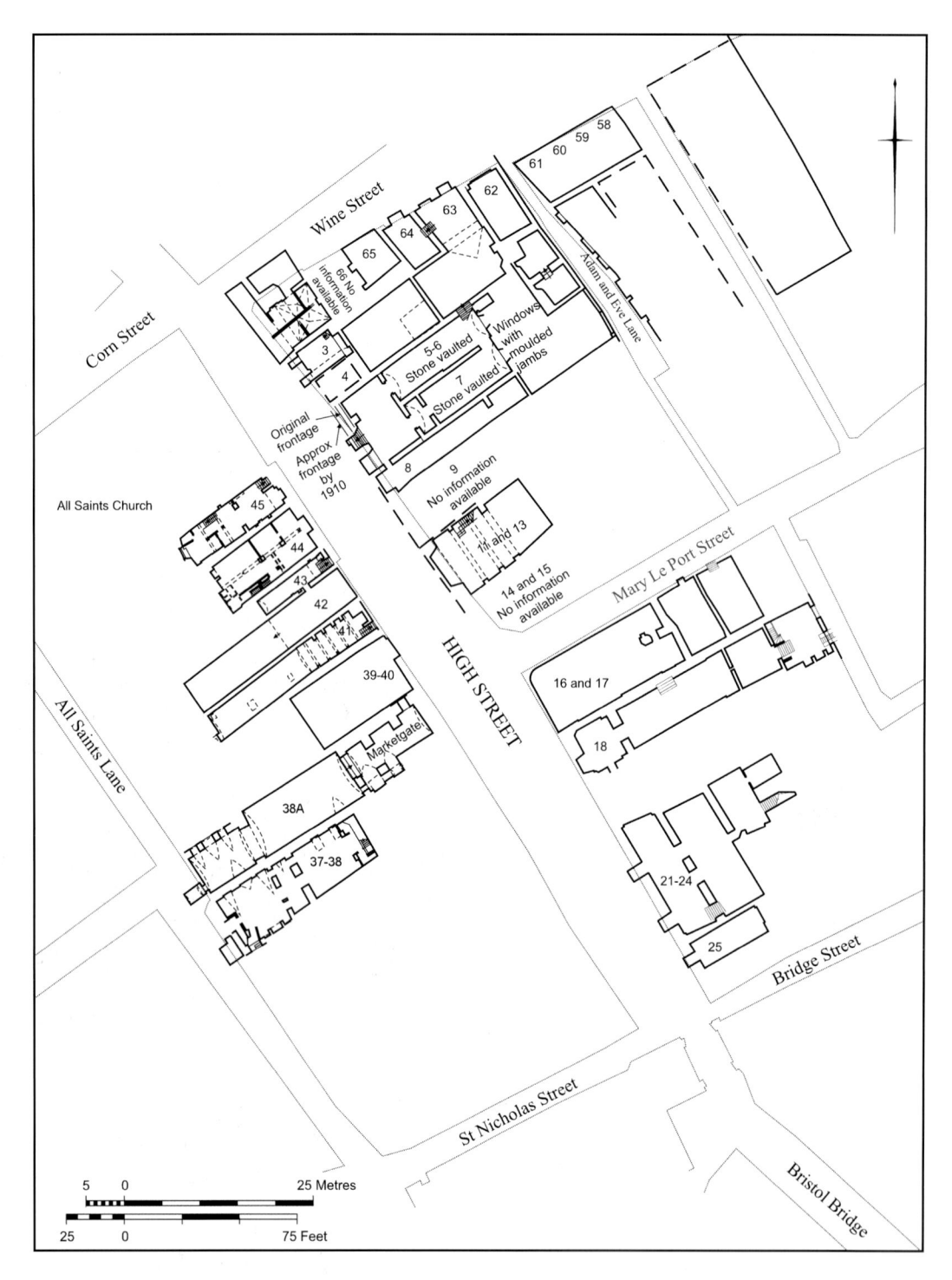

boards making up the stall, took up between 5–8ft of the ground extending into the street. To the council this probably provided an extra source of income, once the encroachments had been legally adjudged. The enticing smell of freshly cooked food drew potential customers to the shop.[22]

Tapsters and brewers had to ensure that their ale was for sale in a 'common place', not in 'solars, chambers or other secret places'. In c 1370 skinners were ordered not to place any 'drynchfates' in any shop, nor in any open space near the High Street.[23] The close association in 14th-century thinking between the open space of the street and the semi-public space occupied by the shop is seen most clearly in the ordinances of 1514–15, which restricted the rights of the town officers to enter the properties of burgesses

THE COMPLEXITIES OF COMMERCE

*Fig 7.7*
*Arcade at no.59 Old Market, photograph of 1941 (NMR BB41/00424).*

for the purposes of arrest. Henceforth this right could only be exercised in respect of 'open houses and none other'. Open houses were defined as open hostelries, taverns, common alehouses and barbers' shops.[24]

Some shops were possibly evident through being set within a covered arcade. The only recorded examples are from Old Market, all of the 17th or early 18th centuries, where nos.59, 73–73A and 74 were provided with arcades on the ground floor. This was a device that made the first-floor living accommodation rather larger since it then over-sailed (lay partly over) the pavement (Figs 7.7 and 7.8). These few examples of such houses from Bristol are comparable to those found in

*Fig 7.8*
*Arcades at nos.73–73A and 74 Old Market, watercolour by H O'Neill, 1822 (BRSMG M2786).*

149

other towns of south-west England, such as Totnes or Dartmouth.

Shops were not necessarily on the street frontage. For some trades an open hall would make an ideal showroom. In this situation the earlier domestic use might at the same time remain evident to the onlooker. For Edward Pickrell, a blacksmith of St Michael's, his shop was clearly a workshop, with anvil, bellows, fire irons and a supply of coal among its contents. His open hall served as a showroom, where customers could inspect goods – among them, in 1617, seven dozen slices and tongs and nine pairs of small andirons. To judge from the quantities, these must have been selling well. His unheated hall also contained an impressive array of weapons, for the most part one of each type: '2 holberds, 1 muskett, flaske and tuch boxe, 1 rest, 3 swords & a rapier, 1 dagger, 1 hedepese, 1 byll with a byll heade'. These took pride of place among his possessions, with the best being left to the Smiths and Cutlers to hang in their hall – taking precedence in his will even over the great anvil and other tools of his trade left to his nephew. As a place of rest for his finest weapons, Pickrell's hall was perhaps both central to his trade and to his perception of his place in society.[25]

John Dowles, a glazier of St Peter's, conducted his trade in a very similar way. Beam and scales would have revealed that his open hall was a place for the conduct of business. At the same time, its furnishings included four assorted weapons, two little ships, as found in some merchants' halls, and at least two tables, together with stools. As described in 1623, the contents of John Dowles's hall were possibly inherited, but would have served also as a means of creating suitable surroundings for his customers.[26]

## Storage in Medieval Bristol: Cellars and Warehouses

In c 1480 William Worcestre was particularly struck by the numbers of cellars or vaults in the principal streets of the town, many since recorded by archaeological fieldwork and documentary research (Fig 7.6). These he counted diligently, drawing first on information from William, Clerk of St Mary le Port, and then in person. He noted that both stone and wood were used in their construction, that on the east side of High Street were 17, on the west side 12, on the north side of Corn Street between St Leonard's Gate and St Werburgh's church 18 and so on: in all amounting to some 142 vaults or cellars.[27] Unfortunately, except in two instances, Worcestre did not record the ways in which cellars or vaults were used.

Many cellars were used for storage. A good number would have accommodated wine, for which the darkness and constant temperature of a stone-vaulted cellar were particularly appropriate. Harris has provided calculations of the storage capacity of the cellars in particular towns in relation to the involvement of their citizens in the wine trade.[28] Towards the end of the 13th century, when the trade was at its height, Bristol was importing more wine than any other English city apart from London.[29] Many of the 142 cellars noted by William Worcestre would have been used for the storage of wine, including those below Haddon's Tavern, later 'the Horsshedd'.[30] In the 1420s Elizabeth, Countess of Berkeley purchased much of her requirements from Bristol merchants; she also paid the cost of transporting it to the quay from the cellars of merchants John Russell, Nicholas Maynes, Richard Page and others, in the High Street and in Redcliff. From there it would be transported principally to Berkeley Haven, but also to Worcester, where it could be used while the countess was in the Midlands. In the autumn of 1420 the countess's butler, Henry Butyler or De La Celer, spent 18 days in Bristol making arrangements for the buying and transporting of the household's wine – perhaps much of this time was spent in cellars.[31]

In some such cellars, the vintner would have certainly needed space in which to receive potential customers, the shop or house above being in a separate occupation. In the High Street, the cellar of no.41, the newly rebuilt Green Lattice, was in 1444 let separately to Richard Haddon, the vintner and proprietor of Haddon's Tavern on the other side of the street. Haddon and his servants were given a licence to enable them to enter the cellar by the gate in the pavement there, and to open and shut a window in the cellar.[32] With entry to the cellar specified in this way, it would appear certain also that the cellar was not itself being used itself as a tavern.

At nos.49/50 Broad Street one divided cellar, formerly used as a tavern or to meet entertainment needs, was possibly adapted to serve entirely as a storage area. The front part of this cellar formerly provided access through a four-centred arched doorway of the 15th century to a larger rear cellar, with a plain two-centred arched vault, this corresponding to the outline of a building certainly in existence by 1411. By 1522 this was the property known as 'the Sarsyns hed'.³³ Subsequently the smaller front cellar was itself divided, with each part now stone-vaulted and the centre wall effectively blocking off the former entrance to the rear (Figs 7.9a and 7.9b). In the absence of evidence for a more decoratively finished front cellar, the division between front and rear cellars might be no more than an architectural solution, directed primarily at the planning of the ground and upper floors.

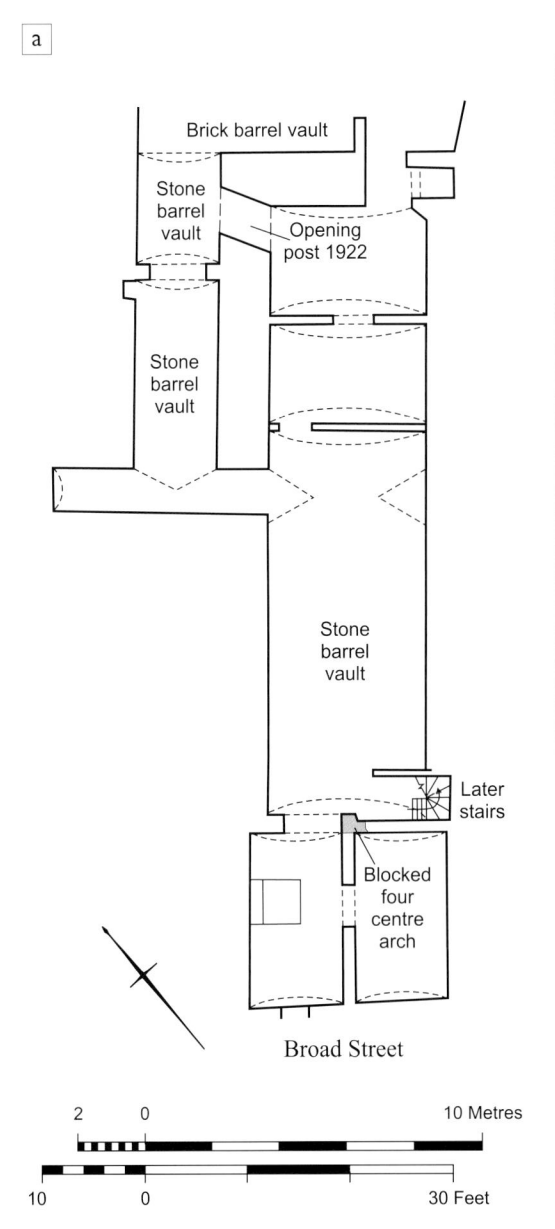

Not all cellars used for storage would have been used for wine. William Worcestre was especially impressed by 'the extremely high and spacious halls of the King, with vaults' in Worshipful Street, 'otherwise the Shambles'. Here, he noted, 'there are 3 extremely deep cellars of the King, beneath three halls of great size and built high, which were established for the safekeeping of wool and merchandise, for loading Bristol ships [bound] for foreign parts beyond the seas'.³⁴ The cellars at nos.44 and 45 High Street, in the Cokyn Rewe, may well have served the needs of the cooks or their clients; each was timber-ceiled, and there were no divisions between a front and rear cellar (Fig 7.6). In 1470 the houses of William Alleyn and John Branvile, both cooks, were each recorded as having stone stairs that constituted a further

*Fig 7.9*
*The cellars at nos.49/50 Broad Street:*
*a) plan of the cellars;*
*b) photograph of blocked doorway to rear cellar, photograph of 1979 (RHL). See Figs 6.5 and 6.6.*

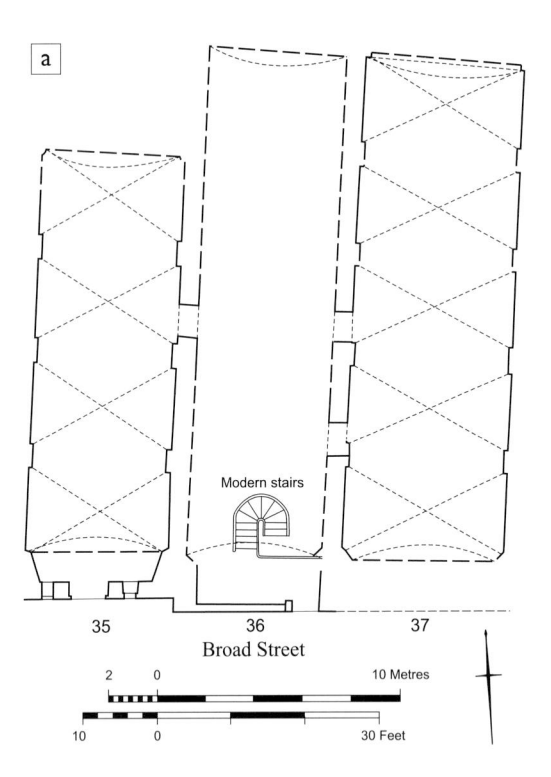

*Fig 7.10*
*The cellars at nos.35–7 Broad Street:*
*a) plan of the cellars (RHL, PEC);*
*b) cellars of no.35, photograph of 1979 (RHL).*

encroachment on the common ground. These stairs provided the access to their cellars, below the two houses now joined as one, in no.44 High Street.

Harris has noted that we may never know the full range of purposes to which the medieval cellar was put.[35] In Bristol a number of cellars are likely to have been used primarily for storage, but their exact purpose cannot yet be established. In Small Street, Broad Street and on the west side of High Street, undivided vaulted cellars of medieval date have been identified below a number of properties (Figs 7.6, 7.9, 7.10a and 7.10b; for Small Street *see* Inventory). In Broad Street, the cellars below nos.43–4 were timber-ceiled but not divided; with no records of separate letting yet traced, they are most likely to have served the needs of the occupier above. In Old Market, the stone-vaulted cellar below the east part of no.59 must certainly have been intended for use by the occupier above, being accessed from the ground floor by a stone vice or stairs (Fig 7.11).

William Worcestre, like many other inhabitants of late medieval and early modern Bristol, used the word cellar, or often 'sellar', to describe two different types of structure, both used for storage. The first was the underground cellar or vault. The second type of cellar was synonymous with the ground floor of a 'storehouse', an above-ground structure on one or more floors, used as a warehouse. Tracing the line of the town walls alongside the Frome quay, Worcestre noted 'the place where new ships are set up and fitted out, and where poles and masts of fir timber as well as anchors lie, and [where are] many warehouses [cellarii] and a great space within the said wall, as far as the first corner of the Key of Bristol'.[36]

The cellars known to Worcestre might have included those that had been owned by William Canynges and which, by 1473, were now possessions of the chantries to his name. These formed part of a property to the west of the Great Tower at the corner of the Quay. In 1473 this was described as 'a Corteplace', one half with a 'Selar lofte'. By 1499 it was comprised of a 'cellar with solar above' and a 'storehouse or masthouse, a ter house and some void ground on the Key'.[37]

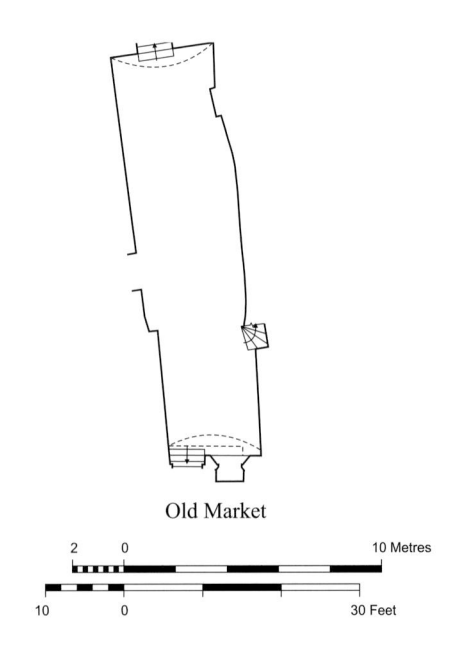

*Fig 7.11*
*No.59 Old Market, plan of the cellar (PEC after RCHME).*

# THE COMPLEXITIES OF COMMERCE

Storage buildings of one or more storeys had been in use before the 15th century. In Redcliff Street the occupants of nos.127–28 each had the use of at least two storehouses, constructed as extensions to the houses on the street frontage between the 14th and 15th centuries (Fig 7.12).[38] From 1452 until at least 1496 no.127 was occupied by dyers – successively Alexander, Joan his widow, Edmund and then his son Richard Newe.[39] They and their neighbours at no.128, also dyers (below), probably used these storehouses for the storage of their cloth, dyeing materials and tools.

These cellars or storehouses were much smaller than two which formed part of the Back Hall belonging to the Corporation, the property once inhabited by the merchants Richard Spicer and Robert Sturmy (chapters 5 and 11). In the 18th century the ground floors of these two stone-walled storehouses were still known as 'cellars' (Fig 7.13a). One of these was described by the photographer Philip E W Street in the 1930s. The ground floor was probably lit by square mullioned windows, and the floors above would have been known to citizens of the 15th century and later as 'lofts'. These, each sub-divided by the roof structure into eight separate bays, formed areas for storage perhaps as equally impressive to visitors as many stone vaults (Fig 7.13b). Street's record of a four-centred arched entrance doorway, and his one photograph of the interior of the southern storehouse, indicates that these two structures could have been built as early as the 15th century. They could therefore have formed part of Spicer's and Sturmy's residence.

A second photograph by Street provides perhaps an impression of what a 'corteplace' might have encapsulated to the 15th- and 16th-century mind (Fig 7.13c). The clerk of Canynges' chantry was not alone in using this term: the same name was used in the 1550s for the court surrounded by various buildings behind no.38 Corn Street, and in 1569 the open space at nos.56–7 Wine Street (later to be the site of the Meal Market) was described as the 'Court Place'.[40] We might interpret 'corteplace' as an open yard of some size, useful to a variety of commercial or manufacturing needs on account of the space provided. Some details of Street's view are unmistakably of the 20th century, but overall his photograph gives an impression of how the open yards adjacent to the storehouses of the Back Hall, or of Canynges' tenement, might have appeared in the 15th and 16th centuries.

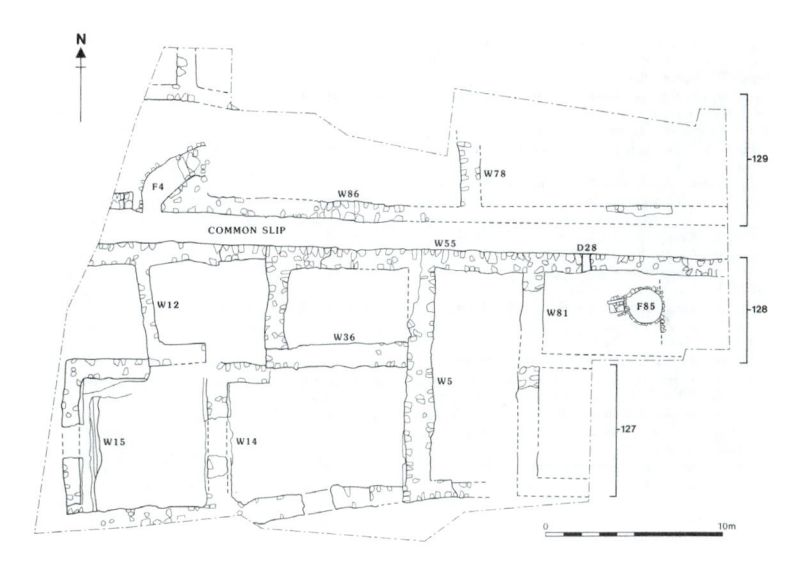

Fig 7.12
No.128 Redcliff Street
(Good 1990/1, Fig 11).

Fig 7.13
The Back Hall, no.6 Welsh Back, storehouses fronting Back Street:
a) extract from plan of 1810 (BRO 04479 (5) fol 26);
b) interior, photograph of 1931
(NMR AA 78/06691 PEWS, 1931);
c) the Back Hall courtyard, photograph of 1931
(NMR AA 78/06690 PEWS, 1931).

# THE TOWN HOUSE IN MEDIEVAL AND EARLY MODERN BRISTOL

*Fig 7.14*
*No.80 Broad Quay, storehouse of early 17th century or earlier, photograph of 1890s (Reece Winstone Archive OB/1588; for location see Inventory).*

Less well recorded than those at the Back Hall is a storehouse which stood at no.80 Broad Quay, at the corner with Alderskey Lane. Photographs show that this also was of two storeys, gabled end on to the quayside and with a hoist over the first-floor loading door.[41] This stood at one corner of the site leased by the Corporation in 1626 to the merchant Alderman Robert Aldworth, who had earlier rebuilt Norton's house (chapter 5). A civic minute of July in that year noted that in consideration of making a new dry dock there was to be a lease to Aldworth of his dwelling house, storehouse and a small dock already made. Archaeological excavations have identified the location of the dock;[42] it can now be seen that the storehouse photographed in the 1890s was on the north side of this dock, against the northern boundary of Aldworth's property and set back behind his dwelling house (Fig 7.14). The building photographed in the 1890s was probably the storehouse used by Aldworth for the storage of shipbuilding materials, built by 1626.

## The Split-Level Commercial Town House

Cellars of medieval date have been recorded in many English towns, their function the subject of considerable discussion. One of the few towns where the overall distribution of such cellars has been studied is Winchester. Here, Keene has argued, largely from the documentary sources, that the concentration of cellars in the heart of the commercial area of the city implied that they had a commercial function, being used for the sale as well as for the storage of goods.[43] Such a relationship could be similarly argued for Bristol. The streets in which William Worcestre recorded medieval cellars were similarly the most important commercial streets. Fieldwork for this research was able to add only one street, Old Market, for a solitary medieval cellar at no.59, to those listed by Worcestre in the 1480s (Fig 7.11).

Roland Harris has argued strongly for the presence in towns during the 12th to 14th centuries of town houses or properties operating commercially on two floors, with a shop at street level and a cellar below serving also as a shop or other commercial outlet.[44] In Bristol, the cellar of no.43 High Street is an example of one such shop. A vaulted cellar at semi-basement level was approached by stone steps from the street and entered through a well-finished stone-arched doorway of the later 14th or 15th century. The cellar was illuminated by a similarly finished window to the street, and if necessary also by lights placed in recesses within the side walls (Figs 7.6 and 7.15).

In 1470 the ground floor above was the shop of John Adames, one of the cooks in Cokyn Rewe. The absence of any access from this to the vaulted cellar below indicates that each functioned as a separate shop. In 1470 both the ground-floor shop and the cellar must have been leased from John Yong, a merchant of London and the owner of the property as a whole.[45] By this date Adames' boards extended forward from his house by 8ft, which must have severely diminished the light entering the cellar. Possibly the cellar had ceased to be used as a shop by that date. Harris has suggested that with the fall in urban property values from the later 14th century, the attractions of using cellars as shops may have diminished.

It was in the principal streets of large medieval towns that the imperative to increase the density of shops through the construction of split-level houses operating commercially on two floors would have been greatest.[46] Property values in medieval Bristol would have been highest in the most commercial streets closest to the carfax. It was here that a new cellar with a complex and highly decorated ribbed vault was constructed, probably in the later 14th century (Figs 7.6, 7.16a and 7.16b). At the very corner of Wine Street and High Street, underneath nos.1 and 2 High Street, this was by the 16th century below three separate ownerships of property. From the available evidence it appears that the only access to the cellar was from the street. Given the level of investment in providing it with such a finely finished vaulted roof, this must have been a shop – most probably for drapery. The site was known as the draper's corner in 1285, while the property above was certainly a tailor's and then a glover's premises between the 16th and 18th centuries.[47]

Close to St Giles's Gate, the front part of the cellar below no.10 Small Street may also have served as a shop. The front to the cellar was completely open, framed by a two-centred chamfered arch of the 13th or 14th century, approached from the street by a set of stone steps (Fig 7.17). In what must have been a high-value site, immediately adjacent to the Quay Head and just within the town gate, this would have been an excellent location for a split-level town house used for commercial purposes on two levels. In this instance, there was a clear separation of occupancy between the two levels. This cellar

*Fig 7.15 (below left) No.43 High Street, photograph of cellar showing entrance, blocked window and recess for light (RHL, PEC).*

*Fig 7.16 Views of corbels in the cellar at no.1 High Street: a) photograph from Pritchard 1908, 297; b and c) photographs probably taken by Bryan St John O'Neil in 1944 (NMR BB80/2567). See Fig 1.4.*

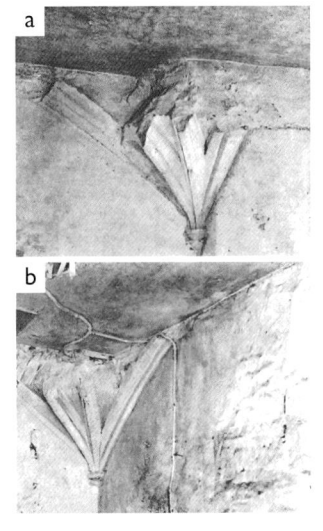

*Fig 7.17
No.10 Small Street,
elevation of cellar
(John Winstone, Reece
Winstone Archive).*

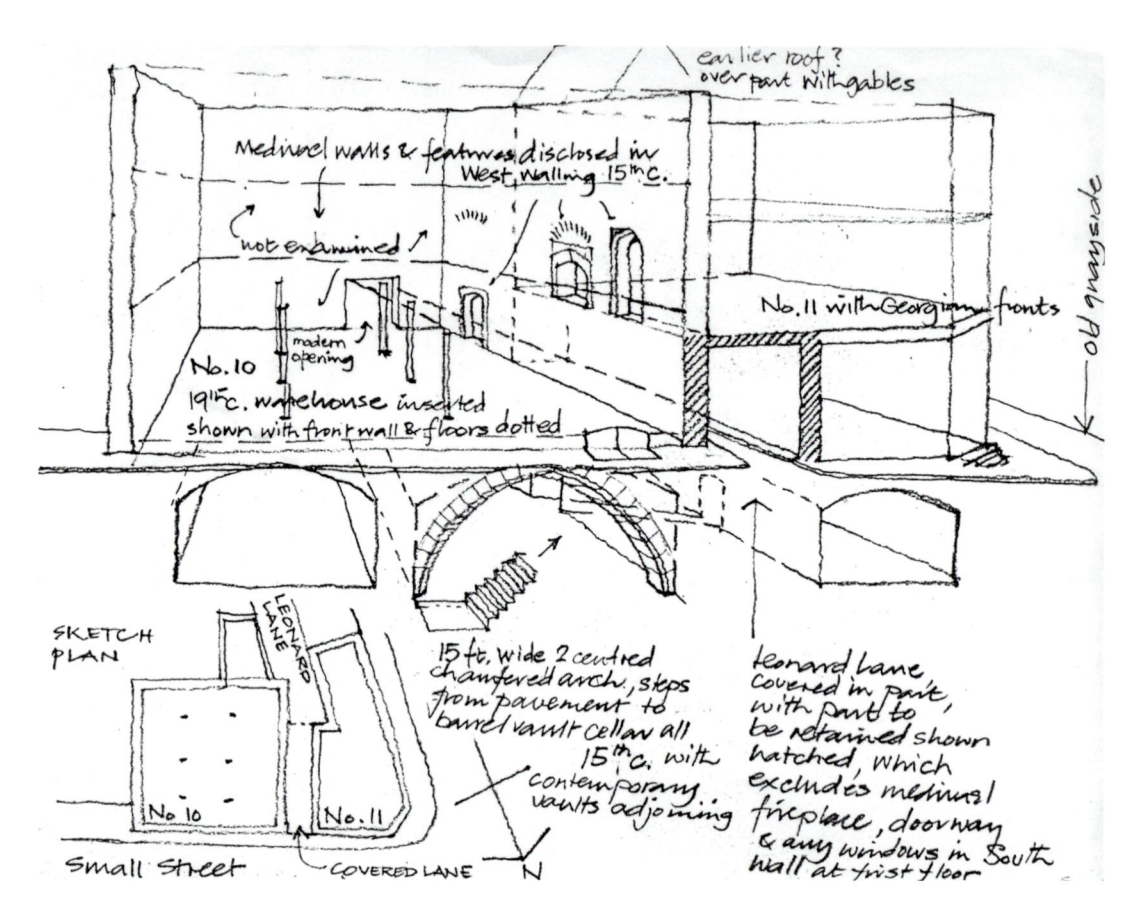

formed part of the adjacent property, no.11, until the 20th century.[48]

Harris has noted how principal streets also on a slope were favoured locations for the siting of split-level houses. Two such sites were no.43 High Street and nos.10 and 11 Small Street, and nos.35 and 37 Broad Street was another. Fronting the steeply sloping street just within St John's Gate, the two cellars in Broad Street were partly at a semi-basement level. Respectively of four and five bays in depth, the groining of the vaults sprang from shallow attached columns of rectangular section (Fig 7.10). With these decorative vaults, each may in the 14th and 15th centuries have been used for the reception of customers.

## The Tavern in Medieval Bristol

Fourteenth-century ordinances for Bristol, similar to those for London, make it clear that ale was sold in a wide range of locations. Every brewer and brewstress who had ale to sell was to have their ale on sale in a public place, 'and not in solars, chambers or other secret places, and that the sign of that ale shall be at the door of the house where that ale will be sold all the time that the said ale is on sale'. Cellars, however, appear to have been a common location for taverns. In London a number of the larger undercrofts in 13th- and 14th-century Cheapside probably served as taverns, offering wine and various entertainments; it has been argued that in London, Winchester and in other towns, there was a strong link between the uses of stone-vaulted cellars and the trade in wine.[49]

It has also been suggested that the architectural distinction made between the front and rear parts of these cellars was one intended to define the drinking and storage areas. The front part for drinking was usually more highly decorated, and the rear part for storage usually plainer, but much larger.[50] Harris has explored further this relationship, highlighting London regulations of the 14th century, which forbade taverners to hang a cloth before the door of the cellar where wine was stored, and emphasising that the narrow stairs by which most cellars were approached would militate against any arrangement whereby taverners would be constantly running up and down from the street or ground floor with foaming jugs.[51] The drinking area was most likely, therefore, to be at the same level as the storage space.

There is now considerable evidence that divided cellars, similar to those in London, Winchester and other towns, were in use in the central streets of Bristol in the 14th and 15th centuries, most probably as taverns. At the corner with St Nicholas Street, no.32 Corn Street was known as the 'peynted taverne' by 1532.[52] Its semi-basement cellar was recorded in the 1850s, when it was thought to have been part of St Leonard's church, demolished c 1766–70; this is now known to have been situated wholly on the opposite side of the street.[53] The cellar was probably of the 12th century, the front part having a vault with plain chamfered ribs and a carved boss at the centre (Fig 7.18). On the frontage to Corn Street were an arched entrance doorway and probably two windows to the side, by then blocked. In the rear wall of this front part of the cellar were three openings with heavy, chamfered pillars and chamfered, two-centred arches. These provided access to the larger, and evidently plainer, rear part of the cellar, divided at the centre by a single plain rib to the vault. On the opposite side of Corn Street at no.35, the cellar has a vault of similar date and form to no.32A, also incorrectly thought to have been part of St Leonard's church. A more decorated cellar fronted on to the street, while a less ornate but larger cellar extended back behind the street frontage.

Similarly divided cellars were constructed in High Street and Broad Street in the later 14th or 15th centuries. These, too, can be interpreted as taverns. Ascending the High Street from the Bridge, one of the first properties on the right was nos.21–4, probably consisting at the ground-floor level of shops on the street frontage and a house with an open hall behind. Below the shops, but accessible only from the street or cellars to the rear, the front cellar had a quadripartite vault of four bays, with chamfered ribs, clustered side columns and three-quarter round columns in the corners. Two bays of this cellar survive (Figs 7.19a and 7.19b).[54] The two wide, four-centred arched

*Fig 7.18 (below left) No.32 Corn Street (at corner with St Nicholas Street), drawing of cellar incorrectly identified as being of St Leonard's church (Bindon 1851).*

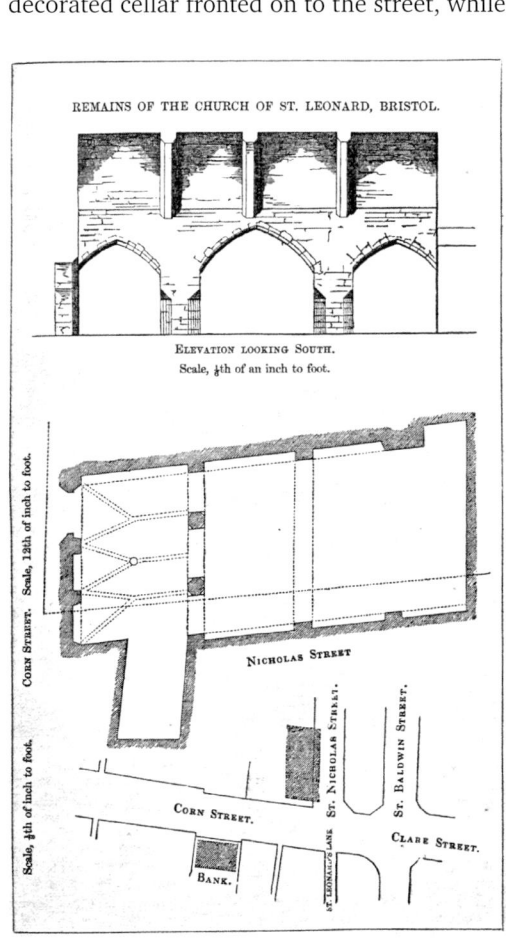

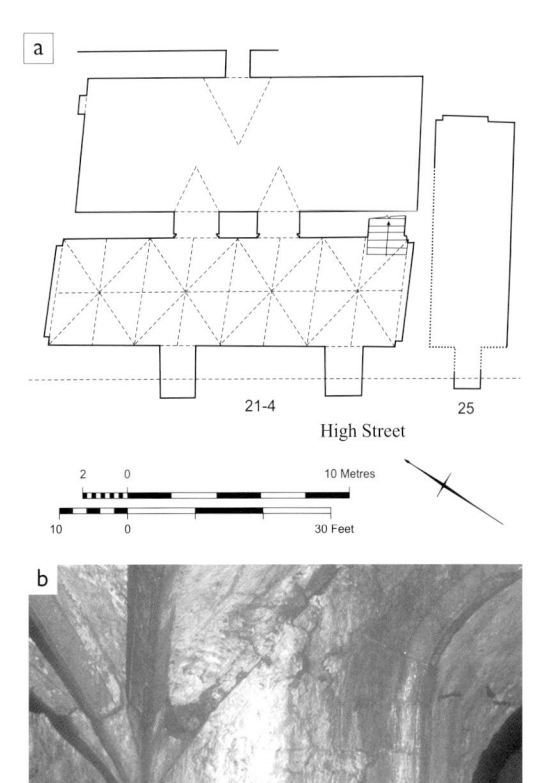

*Fig 7.19 Nos.21–4 High Street: a) plan (RHL); b) photograph of 1979 (M Aston).*

openings leading to the rear cellar would have provided an ample view of this much plainer and larger area where the wine might have been drawn. The documentary evidence also hints at this having been a tavern, it being known as 'the George' by 1532 and held by Hugh Draper, a vintner, by 1556.[55]

Passing the Raven and Boar's Head inns at nos.19–20, of which no plans have been traced, William Worcestre would have observed a similar division between an elaborately vaulted front cellar and a much larger but plain one to the rear at no.18 High Street. This is known only from an architect's plan of 1882. It shows four three-quarter round columns in the corners and possibly a central pillar or later support to the centre of a square vault, with the much larger and plain vaulted cellar to the rear being shown in both plan and section (Fig 7.20). No documentary evidence for the ownership or use of this cellar has been traced.

In two divided cellars the front part was provided with a timber ceiling rather than a stone vault. At nos.5–7 High Street, almost at the carfax, a timber-ceiled cellar 34ft wide spanned the full width of the three houses on the street frontage (Figs 7.21a, 7.21b and 7.21c).

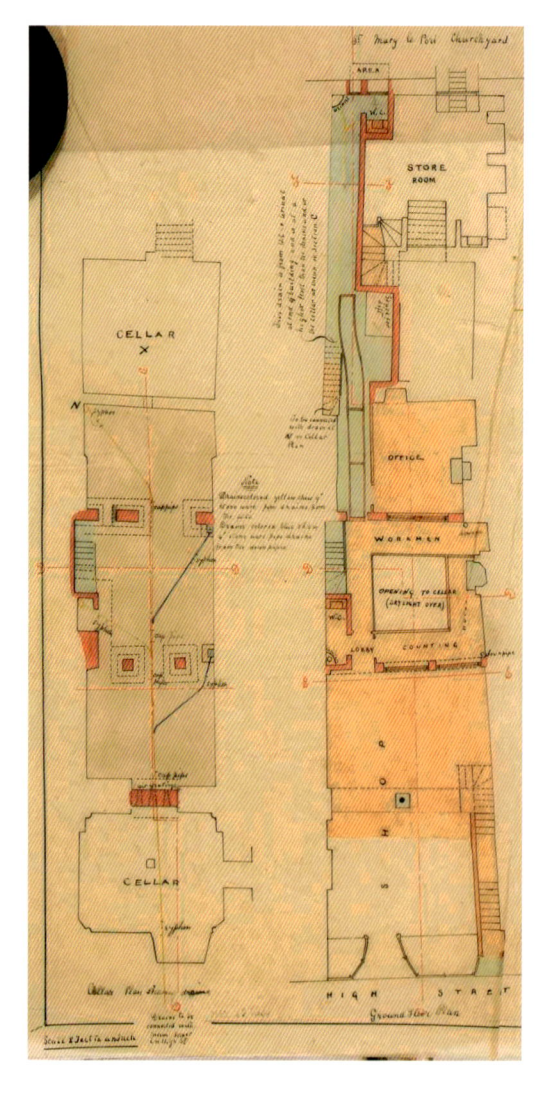

*Fig 7.20 (right) No.18 High Street: architect's plans of cellar and ground floor in 1882 (BRO Building plans vol 19, fol 10a; English Heritage DP 141165).*

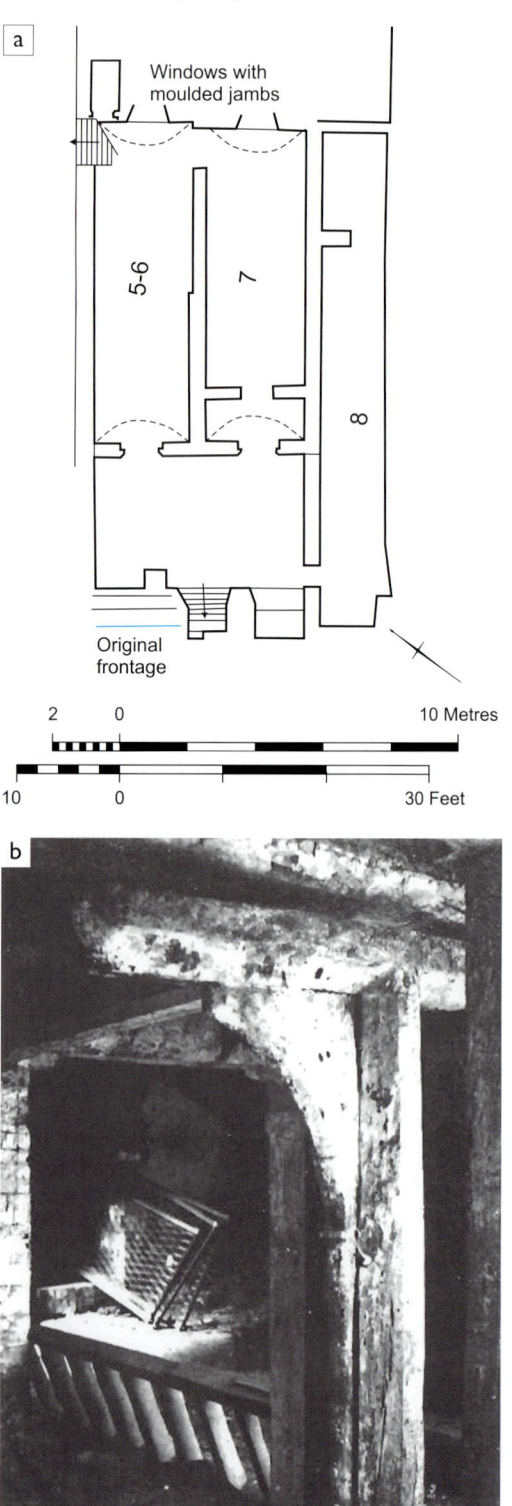

*Fig 7.21 (far right and opposite) Nos.5–7 High Street: a) plan of cellars (RHL, PEC from BRO Building Plans vol 63, fol 47; BRO 6255 (12); b) and (c) photographs of roof support and rear cellar (Pritchard 1920).*

A centrally placed entrance and stone stairs of eight steps leading down to the cellar, as well as the form of the timber roof, were observed by Pritchard in 1914, and recorded on an application for approval of building works.[56] The ceiling was carried on chamfered oak beams c 18in square, supported both by oak uprights, one of which retained an attached shelf and arched bracket, and by large, roughly shaped stone corbels let into the end walls. Behind this single wide cellar lay two barrel-vaulted cellars, each entered through a four-centred arched doorway and having at the rear a splayed window opening, 6ft wide, overlooking a courtyard beyond. These rear cellars were certainly built after 1360–9, the date of the latest coin found embedded in the mortar of the vaulting of no.5 in the course of demolition.

Part of the lands of Witham Priory formed nos.5–7, but unfortunately there is no documentary evidence for their use during the 14th to 15th centuries. However, a second, similarly divided cellar on the opposite side of High Street is better documented. By 1461 nos.35–6 were described as two shops with a share of the inn called 'le Cocke'; in 1566 a deed referred to part of this property as the 'inner part' of 'the Cocke'.[57] This inner part can be interpreted as having been the part recorded in 1890 as having an open roof of late medieval date.[58] Below was a cellar with a two-centred arched vault (*see* Fig 5.13), entered from a courtyard at the rear and in turn providing access to a cellar on the street frontage. This cellar was provided with two entrances to the street and spanned the entire width of the four-storey, 15th-century house above. It appears in section to have been timber-ceiled.

A third timber-ceiled cellar can certainly be associated with a tavern, but cannot, in the absence of any plan or other evidence, be shown to have had a larger and architecturally less ornate cellar to the rear. The roof of the cellar below nos.32–4 High Street perhaps provided clearer headroom than a stone vault, but, with an elaborate finish, it was not necessarily any less expensive to construct. The 19th-century historian George Pryce recorded that below nos.32–4 were flat-roofed cellars. The large transverse beams carrying the floor above were supported by lozenge-shaped pillars of solid oak standing on stone plinths, probably of the 15th century (Figs 7.22a and 7.22b).[59] Pryce's drawing shows that this was probably a single cellar, of at least four bays in depth back from the street and probably of six bays in width.[60] Nos.32–4 were by 1467 'the Starre Tavern'.[61]

*Fig 7.22*
*Nos.32–4 High Street: a) illustration from Pope 1888, Pl. xviii (probably mistakenly labelled as 43); b) drawing of the later 19th century in BCRL Pryce MS.*

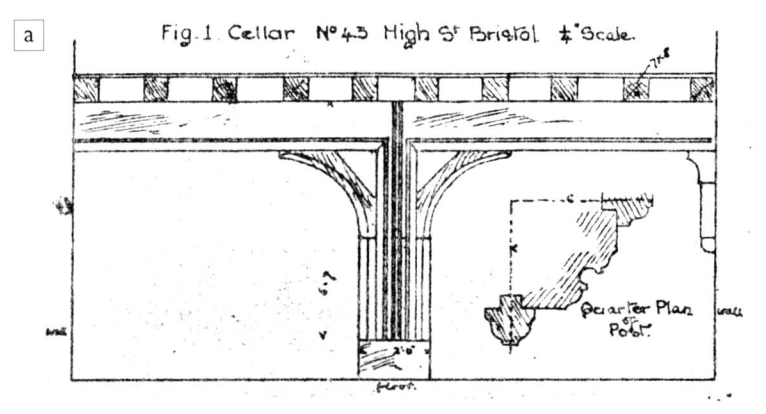

It is possible, though, that by the late 15th century most divided cellars were no longer used as taverns. In the 1480s William Worcestre noted that in All Saints Lane were one or two cellars used 'for the selling of wine'.[62] This might be read as a note of a practice that was now exceptional.

Not all taverns were restricted to the cellar; the larger establishments could occupy rooms on the ground floor as well. The Green Lattice at no.41 High Street, built built between 1439 and 1442, was certainly a tavern in 1467 when the parish of All Saints paid 17d for Roger Kemes to have breakfast there.[63] The part closest to the street would have been a shop on the ground floor, with a parlour and chambers on the floors above. Behind was an open hall of two bays, with a fireplace and chimney on the south wall. This room provided access to those behind, and possibly via a stairs and gallery to the upper rooms on either side (*see* Fig 5.8).

Similarly positioned was the hall of the inn known in the later 15th century as the Cock in the Hoop, at nos.35–6 High Street (chapters 5 and 6). In 1541, when the property was sold to the wealthy merchant John Smythe, this hall was still seen as separate from the shops on the frontage. The property purchased by Smythe was that part of 'the Cocke in the Hope', extending from 'the fore shop' and 'the hawle dore' to 'the farther or ynnar ende'.[64] The open hall survived to 1941, its roof probably of the 15th century (*see* Fig 5.13). At no.30, the Bull or Angel was also from its name possibly a tavern by 1472. This, too, had an open hall set back behind the street frontage and alongside St Nicholas Street. The roof of the hall and a fireplace at the first floor were of the 15th century (Fig 7.23; *see* Fig 5.55).

Behind the street frontage of the White Lion inn in St Thomas Street was possibly a hall similar to those of the taverns in High Street. An illustration of *c* 1870 shows the courtyard of this inn prior to its demolition. A pentice and galleries of the 17th century had been added to an earlier structure, the proportions of this and its roof indicating that it was probably a large open hall (Fig 7.24). This also would have served as the central room of a late medieval tavern.

*Fig 7.23*
No.30 High Street, the Angel, chimneypiece of the 15th century, watercolour by H O'Neill, 1820 (BRSMG M2247).

*Fig 7.24 (opposite page)*
The White Lion, St Thomas Street, possible hall with added galleries, drawing of *c* 1870 by Joseph Wood, deposited by Miss Wood/ Eustace Button [architect] (BRSMG Mb3499 (part)).

THE COMPLEXITIES OF COMMERCE

Court yard of the "White Lion Inn" Thomas Street.
(taken down in the year 1872)

A. Pillar on ground floor .......  ⎫
B. Balusters & handrail .........  ⎬ One inch to a foot
C. Columnette between trusses ...  ⎭
D. Plan of balustrade
E. Section through balcony ....... two feet to an inch

## Taverns and Inns 1550–1750

The way in which a tavern functioned in the late 16th century is best illustrated by the inventory describing the contents of Haddon's Tavern. Known in 1584 as the 'Horsshedd in Wynestreete', it was then owned by the Dean and Chapter of the Cathedral and leased to John Boydell, a vintner. A detailed description of the fittings of the tavern, made after his death (Appendix 2), can be correlated in part with a watercolour, the plan of the cellars and other plans (Fig 7.25).[65] The latter show some internal details and the overall extent of the property, extending from nos.3–4 High Street to no.63 Wine Street. From this information the arrangements of the tavern can be reconstructed (Fig 7.26).

In 1584 the first rooms encountered by the appraisers of Boydell's goods were described as 'The rome benethe called the seller and the shop

*Fig 7.25*
*Nos.3–4 High Street and no.63 Wine Street, cellars of Haddon's Tavern or the Horsshedd, watercolour by J Johnson, 1821 (BRSMG M2352).*

THE COMPLEXITIES OF COMMERCE

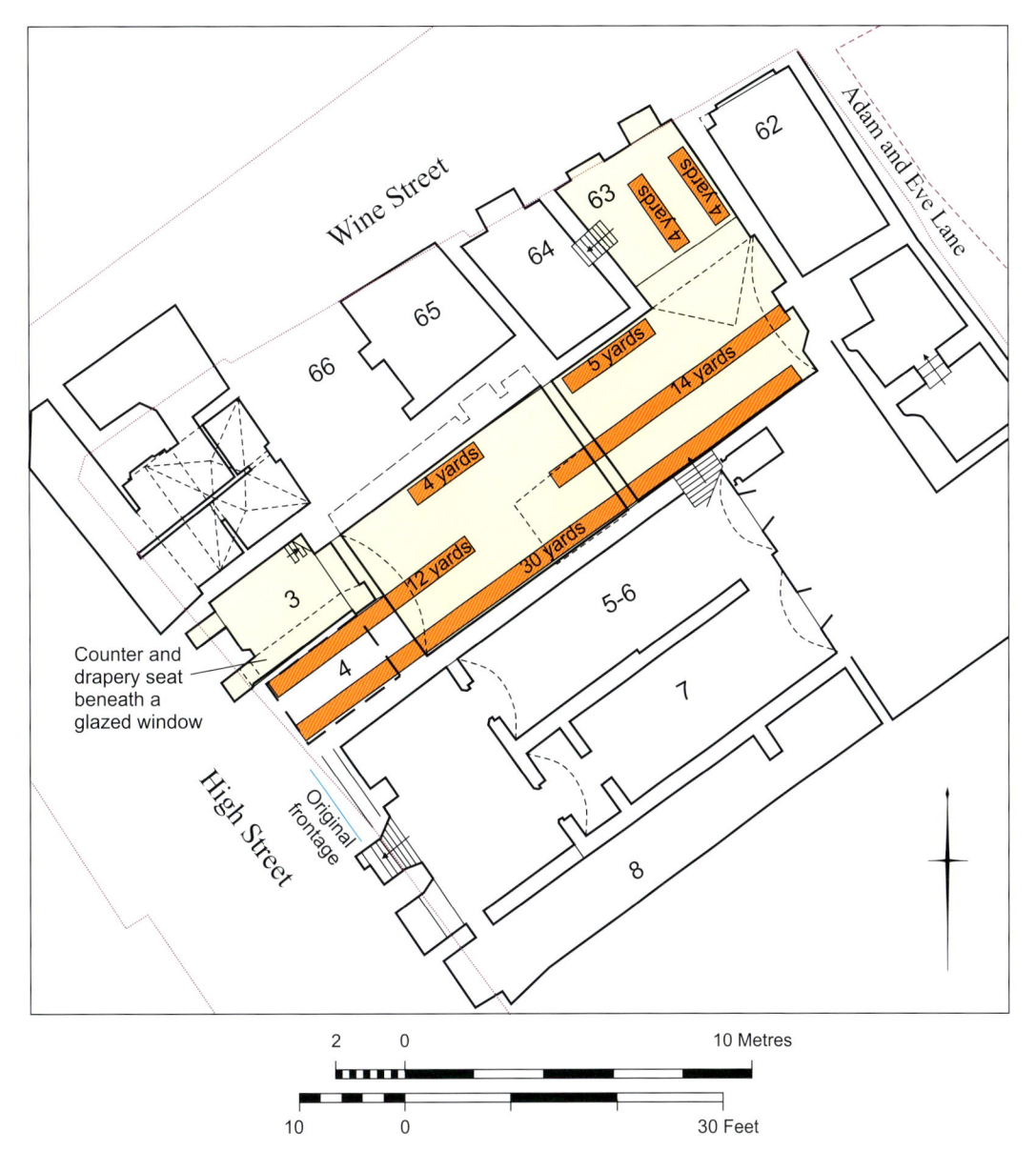

*Fig 7.26*
*Reconstructed plan of the Horssheddin 1584; stillings or supports for wine barrels shown in orange (RHL, PEC).*

thereunto adioyninge'. The cellar was possibly the room beneath no.3 High Street, lit by glass lanterns after dusk. Behind a glazed and barred window was the counter and a drapery seat for 'him or her that receavethe the money for the wyne'. A press to put tavern pots upon was possibly in the cellar, but most of the eight seats, benches and tables for customers were in the adjoining room, where a fire would blaze in the winter months, possibly here or on the ground-floor room above.

The 'great vaulte' and 'the little vault towards Wynestreete' described in 1584 perfectly match the reconstructed plan of the cellars. They were the long, divided vault extending back behind the cellar beneath nos.3 and 4 High Street (where the wine was served) and the cellar at right angles to this, below no.63 Wine Street. These two vaults were used exclusively for wine storage. Two of the 'stillings' or supports for the wine barrels in the great vault were each 90ft long, reaching along the length of the smaller and great cellar extending back from the High Street. The stillings in the Wine Street vault similarly took up most of its length, and it can be estimated that together the two cellars would have housed *c* 32 tuns of wine in 256 barrels.

The main reception room in the tavern was probably the first-floor hall. It rose through two storeys, presumably to the roof, and its walls were lined with drapery hangings. A fireplace, perhaps that on the north wall, is shown on

163

*Fig 7.28 (oppsite page) Fountain Tavern, Tailors' Court:*
*a) plan of the property (PEC after RCHME);*
*b) entrance doorway inscribed with the initials IFM (for John and Mary Freeman), 1692; photograph of 1941 (NMR BB41/00513).*

*Fig 7.27 The Full Moon, Stokes Croft, formerly North Street, plan (PEC after RCHME).*

a much later plan, with stairs giving access to a gallery and the upper chambers. There were tables and forms in this room, but the principal dining and drinking area must have been the great parlour with a table (6ft by 3ft), a window extending the full width of no.63 Wine Street and a glazed and barred counter – possibly a second place at which to pay for drink and food. The hall also provided access to a little parlour and to a lower chamber, both with chambers above. We cannot be certain in which of these rooms Boydell's household lived, but their domestic lives must have been inextricably bound up with the workings and life of the tavern.

By the early 17th century there appears to have been only a shadowy distinction between a tavern and an inn. In All Saints Lane, for instance, the New Inn was later known as the Rummer Tavern.[66] On the whole, the word 'tavern' seems to have been reserved for premises which served wine, but which offered little or no accommodation. The term 'inn' appears to have been used for those which provided accommodation on some scale, though it could be sometimes applied to properties which appeared little different from taverns. To the early 17th-century visitor there might have been little apparent difference between the Cock in the Hoop inn and the Horsshedd tavern. This was a situation similar to that in Winchester, where in the later 17th century the word 'inn' was used to include properties that would earlier have been run by taverners and would later have been known as ale-houses.[67]

In the course of the 17th century, most inn and tavern keepers probably ceased to see the open hall as the central room of their establishment, at least in a public sense. In 1650 George Pearce, the landlord of the White Hart in Broad Street, certainly kept nothing of value in the main part of his hall. Yet the contents of 'the little buttery' in his hall (including a feather bed, two chests, a trunk, a safe and a cupboard) indicate that this is most probably where he lived and slept. His concern for the safety of the takings must have been very similar to that of John Boydell at the Horsshedd. In a private sense, the hall was still the centre of the inn.

Nearly four decades later, in 1687, Elinor Biggs, the keeper of the Swan in Mary le Port Street, still retained a heated hall with a table, benches and settles. In 1691, by contrast, John Holt, innkeeper at the White Lion in St Thomas Street, had no use whatsoever for a room called the hall; it was simply not mentioned in the inventory of his possessions. A room which has been identified above as the former hall had been converted to at least three floors of accommodation, the upper two accessed from galleries overlooking the courtyard (Fig 7.24).

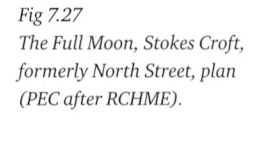

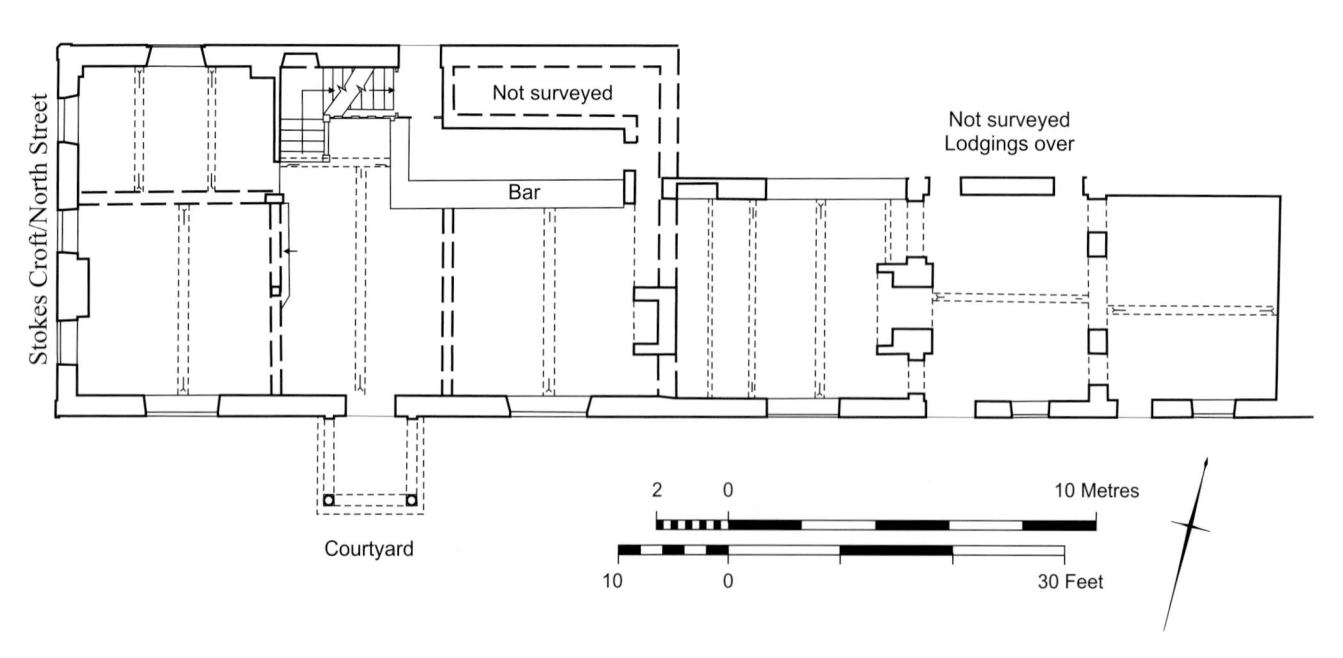

For those building new inns and taverns towards the end of the century, the hall had become the entry to the new premises. This could be seen in two new taverns or inns built in the 1690s. The Full Moon Inn in North Street, Stokes Croft was built c 1696–8.[68] Access to the new inn was through a central portico facing the courtyard, which fronted on to North Street. A wide central entrance and stairs hall then gave access to the two principal rooms on the ground floor, and on each of the floors above (Fig 7.27). Fronting on to the courtyard were probably the kitchen and further lodging rooms.

In Tailors' Court in Broad Street James Freeman, an apothecary, was responsible for the building of the Fountain Tavern in 1692. Access to the new tavern was through Tailors' Court, a lease from the Merchant Tailors being necessary to allow this. An impressive, shell-hood doorway, with the building date and the initials of James and his wife Mary, must have been intended as much to attract potential customers into a new, purpose-built interior as to commemorate the building work. As in the Full Moon, a wide central stairs hall then gave access to the two principal rooms on the ground floor and on each of the floors above (Figs 7.28a and 7.28b). A similar intention was evident in the plan of the New or Rummer Inn in All Saints Lane, rebuilt in *c* 1740 (Figs 7.29a and 7.29b).

Most of the properties known in Bristol as inns by the early 17th century offered a range of accommodation, occupying sites more extensive than that of the Cock in the Hoop. The largest included the Bear in Redcliff Street, with 19 chambers in 1617,[69] the Swan, probably in Mary le Port Street, with ten chambers in 1647,[70] the White Hart in Broad Street, with nine chambers in 1650,[71] the Red Lion at no.7 Redcliff Street, with at least 10 chambers in 1661,[72] the Lamb in Wine Street, with at least 16 chambers in 1687[73] and the White Lion in St Thomas Street, with 15 chambers in 1691.[74] There was also the extensive Guilders Inn between High Street and St Nicholas Street, for which no detailed information is available.[75]

At the White Lion the galleries and rooms overlooking the courtyard possibly resulted from the interior reorganisation of the medieval hall (Fig 7.24). On the second floor the subdivision of the gallery into five sections must have related to the five new and apparently unheated chambers: the Rose, the Bear, the Ship, the Crown and the Half Moon, each accessed from the gallery or 'upper passage'. These names were typical of those accorded to the chambers in all these inns, synonymous with the signs used to identify the different rooms to the illiterate. In both the White Lion in 1691 and the Lamb in 1687, approximately one-third of the chambers were heated.

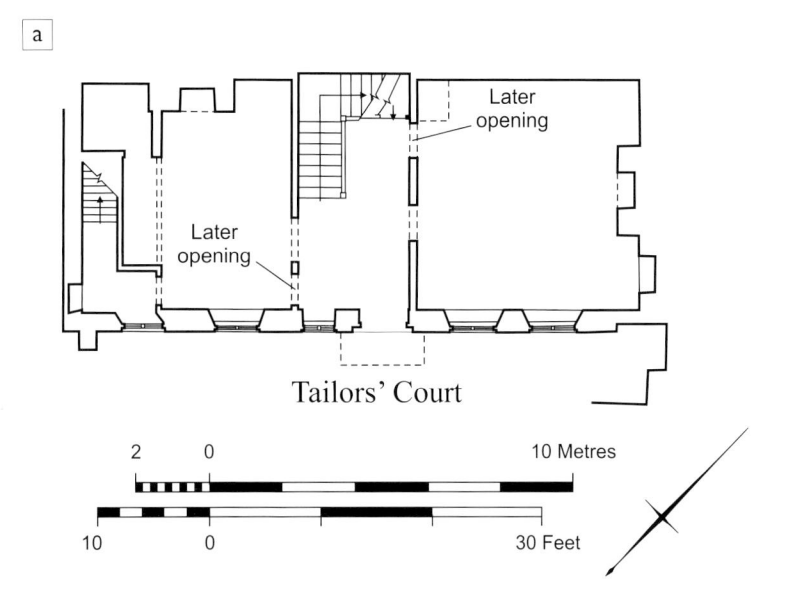

*Fig 7.29
The Rummer, All Saints Lane, built c 1740:
a) plan of the property by John Wood, c 1740 (Royal Academy of Arts, London);
b) entrance hall, photograph of 2002 (RHL).*

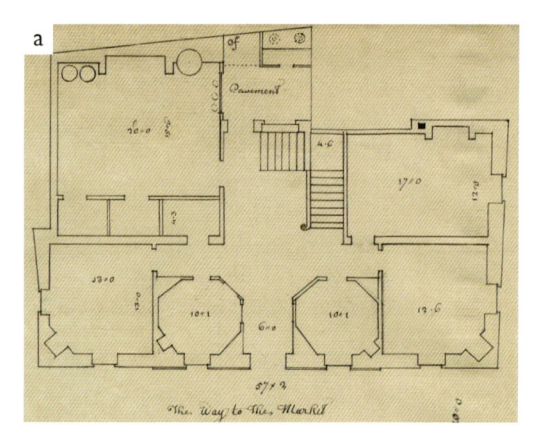

The larger inns were ranged around or alongside a courtyard, often with stabling and other ancillary buildings (Fig 7.30). A plan of Gillows Inn of *c* 1740 shows that the ground floor around such a courtyard could be taken up largely with stabling and storage buildings, apart from the kitchen of the inn and the separately held Guilders Tavern. Accommodation was principally on the upper floors, as at the White Lion in St Thomas Street. Here all but one of the chambers in 1691 was on the upper floors (Fig 7.24). At the Red Lion in Redcliff Street, the occupants of the 10 principal chambers could from the late 17th century overlook the courtyard from galleries at the first and second floor (Fig 7.31).[76]

## Storage in Early-Modern Bristol: Cellars, Storehouses and Warehouses

Bristol may have been at the peak of its life as a trading city in the early modern period. Having recovered from the collapse of the Bordeaux trade, it began to develop its Atlantic connections, still free of serious challenge from other English ports. Commerce generated prosperity for traders within the city, increasing the demand for storage.

By the 17th century cellars seem to have been used exclusively for storage purposes. From the many probate inventories examined, there is no evidence that they were used either as shops or as taverns. In the many new houses built in the second half of the century, some cellars were vaulted in stone, others timber-ceiled. In King Street, citizens representing a variety of occupations and trades lived with either, accepting perhaps the form of construction favoured by the builder and perhaps by the initial occupant or owner of their house. Among merchants living in this street, John Cooke at no.6 possessed a stone-vaulted cellar, while successive occupants of no.33 possessed one built less lavishly in timber.

Successive occupants of nos.1–5 also had the potential benefit of cellars vaulted in stone. At no.5, one of these cellars formed in 1702 a storage area below the dwelling house of Aaron Williams. Its contents (Appendix 2) included 50 herring barrels, 'two tunne' of other barrels and hogsheads, over 1,000 barrel staves of varying types and an assortment of tools

Fig 7.30
*Inns as shown by Ashmead and Plumley, 1828 (RHL, PEC).*

Broad Street, Corn Street and Wine Street

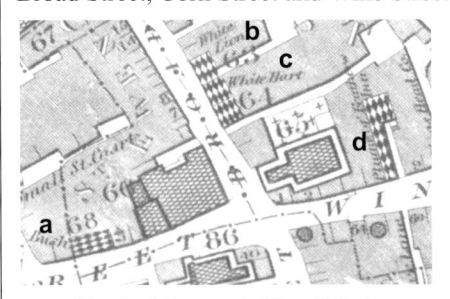

a. The Bush Tavern, b. The White Lion
c. The White Hart, d. The Plume of Feathers

College Place

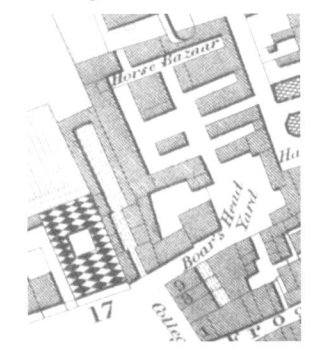

a. Reeves Hotel (17) and
b. The Boar's Head

North Street

Full Moon Inn

West Street

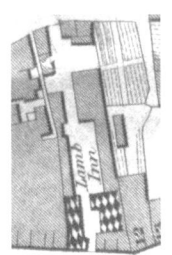

The Lamb

Redcliff Street

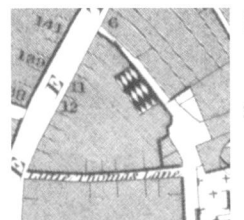

The Red Lion

The Queen's Head

The Angel

St. Michael's Hill

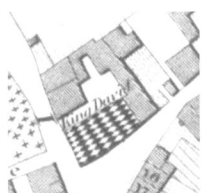

King David

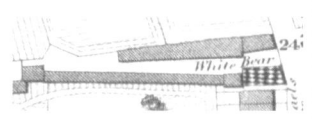

The White Bear

St Thomas Street

a. The Talbot (115) and b. The Bell

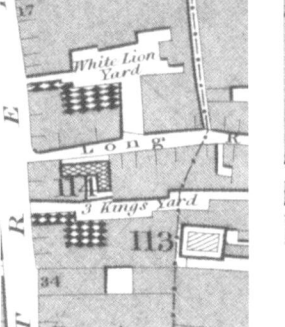

a. The White Lion and b. The Three Kings

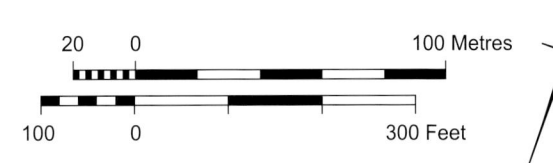

The Three Queens

Temple Gate

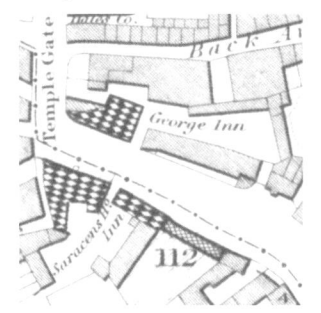

a. The George and
b. The Saracen's Head

*Fig 7.31*
*The Red Lion, Redcliff Street, drawing by S G Tovey [18]48 (BRSMG M2994).*

(Figs 7.32a and 7.32b). Knowing that Williams' house was used to provide lodgings, and aware of its latter-day use as part of the inn, the Llandoger Trow, it would have been tempting to see this stone-vaulted cellar as an area for the storage of alcoholic beverages. As seen in 1702, however, its contents related entirely to Williams' trade as a cooper.

One cellar certainly used for the storage of wine was that mentioned by John Aubrey in explaining how his godfather, the merchant John Whitson, first came into his fortune: 'He was bound apprentice to Alderman Vawr, a Spanish merchant of this City. He was a handsome young fellow; and his old Master (the Alderman) being dead,[77] his Mistress one day called him into the Wine-cellar and had him broach the best Butt in the Cellar for her; and truly he broach't his mistress, who after married him. This story will perhaps last as long as Bristol is a City'.[78]

Vaulted cellars were not, though, absolutely

THE COMPLEXITIES OF COMMERCE

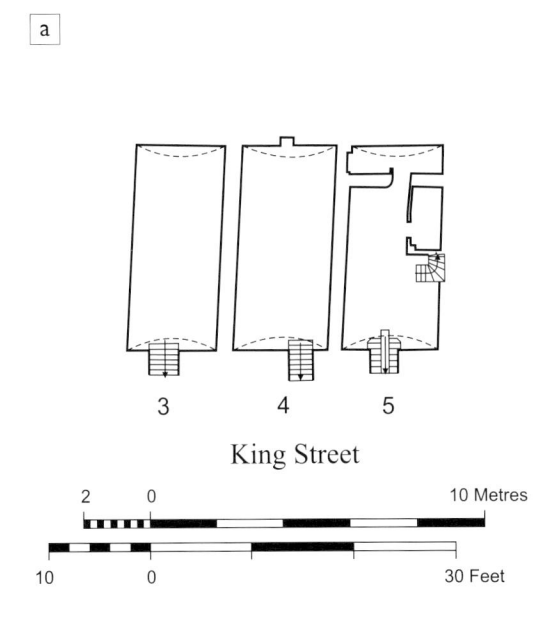

necessary for the storage of wine or ale. Thomas Tippett, a vintner, was responsible for building the Hatchet Inn in Frogmore Street between 1661 and 1675.[79] His cellar was entirely ceiled in timber, though the design of the steps was clearly intended to allow for the easy delivery and collection of barrels (Figs 7.33a and 7.33b). A similar rolling way was constructed for the entrance to the cellar of the Swan with Two Necks in Little Anne Street, built *c* 1715.

For Aaron Williams and Thomas Tippett the cellar was an integral part of the property above, but other citizens of the 17th and 18th centuries continued to use cellars separately. Successive owners of no.18 Small Street held a series of interconnected stone- or brick-vaulted cellars extending under that property, as well as beneath nos.16–17 Small Street and below the Guildhall and no.21 in Broad Street (Fig 7.34). William Colston and Thomas Speed, both merchants, each held no.18 during the course of the 17th century. By 1775 the property was held by Joseph Orlidge and his son, wine merchants – the cellars presumably needed for the storage of their liquid assets.[80] In the north-west corner of Queen Square the cellars below nos.68–73 are still linked with one another, reflecting their use for the storage of wine in the 1890s and 1900s, and possibly suggesting an earlier shared use.[81]

*Fig 7.32*
*Nos.3–5 King Street:*
*a) plan of the property's cellars*
*(RHL, PEC);*
*b) cellar of no.3 showing stone vault, now rendered, photograph of 1992*
*(NMR BB92/23639).*

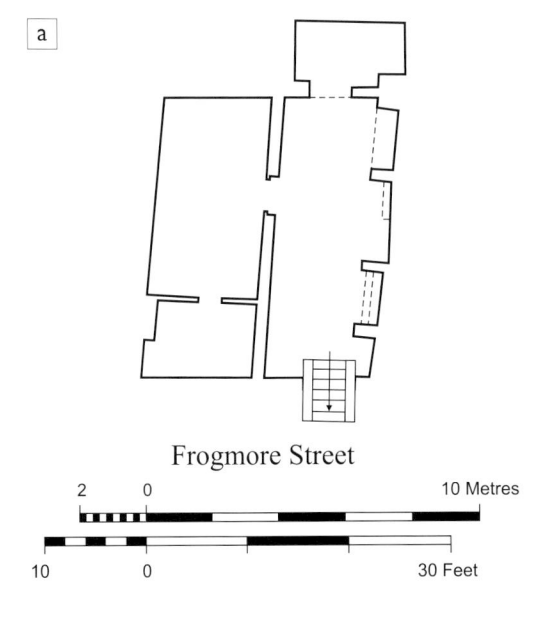

*Fig 7.33*
*The Hatchet, Frogmore Street:*
*a) plan of the plan of the cellars showing rolling way for barrels (RHL, PEC);*
*b) photograph of 1941*
*(NMR BB41/00505).*

169

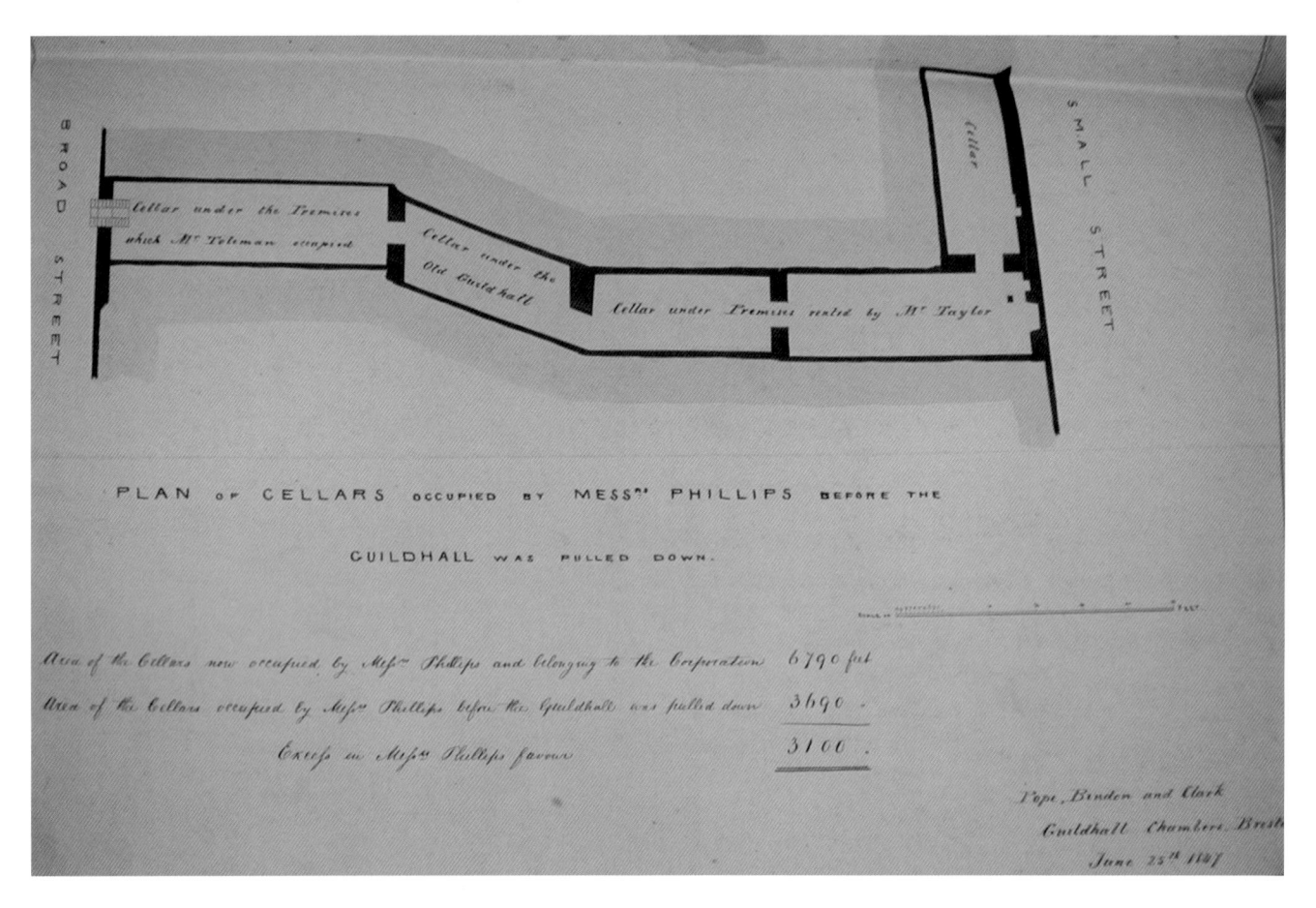

*Fig 7.34*
*Cellars extending from no.18 Small Street to no.21 Broad Street, prior to the rebuilding of the Guildhall in c 1843*
*(BRO 04479(1) fol 104a).*

By the early 17th century storehouses of three storeys were also certainly in use. In 1610 Robert Aldworth and Christopher Cary, both merchants, and Thomas Wade, a shipwright, jointly held a storehouse to the south of the Canynges property, fronting Marsh Street. This consisted of 'three stories (that is to saie) a cellar above ground', held by Aldworth, and 'two lofts one above the other', held by Cary and Wade respectively. Behind, extending back to the Quay, were a further two storehouses, their internal arrangements not described.[82]

The storehouse at no.34 King Street was possibly similar to that held by Aldworth, Cary and Wade in nearby Marsh Street. Built between 1650 and 1658, it adjoined no.33, a house built at the same time on the west side. Both house and storehouse were by 1688 leased by the Corporation of Bristol to Robert Dowding, a rope maker; the storehouse at no.34 was sublet by him to Henry Daniel, a merchant, and is the earliest such structure now surviving in Bristol.[83]

As built, it would have fitted well with the description of the three-storey storehouse in Marsh Street. The only access was direct on to King Street, through a centrally placed entrance on the ground floor or 'cellar'. Goods could also be taken in and out through the doors on the first and second floors or 'lofts', below a hoist placed at eaves level and fixed to the central tie beam of the open roof (Figs 7.35a and 7.35b).

In the 16th and 17th centuries other buildings were also converted to serve as warehouses. Adjacent to the head of the quayside, the church of St Giles had become the property of the Corporation by the mid-14th century and was certainly used as a grain warehouse by the early 17th century.[84] Immediately next to it was the church of St Lawrence, deconsecrated in 1585 and leased then to the merchant William Ellis as a storehouse. This remained in use as a warehouse until the 19th century, by then housing a barilla mill (Fig 7.36).[85]

Former open halls also made ideal storage spaces. In 1611 Humphrey Ellis, a haberdasher, stored a variety of goods in 'the mydle rome called the halle'.[86] In 1620 John Ably, a joiner occupying an extensive property at nos.51–2 the Quay, used his hall for the storage of 41 coffers and chests.[87] Nearly 50 years later, Thomas Andrewes in St Philip's parish used his hall in part for cooking and dining, but also for the

THE COMPLEXITIES OF COMMERCE

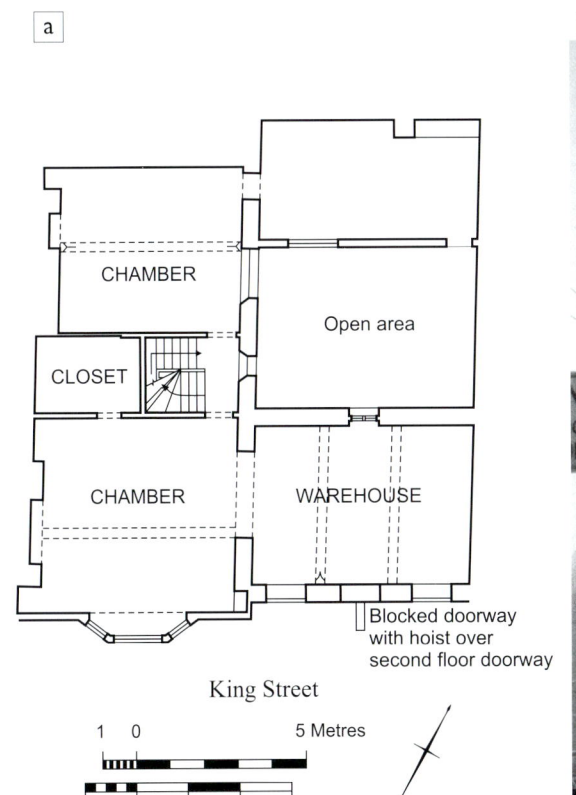

storage of charcoal. In 1669 the appraisers of his possessions counted some 15 sacks of the fuel.[88]

Those involved in the movement of goods in and out of such warehouses would have noticed little difference between working in ones constructed in the 17th century and those built in the first half of the 18th century. The three warehouses built at the rear of nos.50–4 Prince Street, the three-bay warehouse built behind nos.68–70 and the pair of warehouses built behind nos.64–6, were all constructed in the late 1720s (Figs 7.37 and 7.38).[89] Further north along the quayside, a long row of houses south of the Fish Market was replaced by a row of warehouses in the 1770s (Fig 7.39). All were of three storeys with hoists and loading doors, of similar design to that at no.34 King Street.

The relationship between the merchant's house and his warehouse was extremely varied. Location, the fluctuating fortunes of individual businesses and opportunities in the property market all influenced the way in which the merchant's domestic and commercial lives were arranged spatially. By the late 15th century and subsequently, merchants often had the use of storehouses or warehouses sited outside the

Fig 7.35
No.33–4 King Street:
a) plan of the property (RHL, PEC);
b) exterior photograph of 1931 (NMR AA78/06700 PEWS).

Fig 7.36
St Lawrence's church, re-used as a storehouse from 1585, watercolour showing the crypt, T L Rowbotham, 1827; see also Fig 2.14 (BRSMG M2455).

171

*Fig 7.37*
*Warehouses at backs of nos.50–4 to nos.64–6 Prince Street, photograph of the merchant ship Arragon, photograph taken between 1871 when the ship first traded with Bristol and 1882 when it was wrecked on the St Lawrence River (BRSMG, Industrial Museum collection).*

*Fig 7.38*
*Nos.68–70 Prince Street, two warehouses under a single shaped gable, photograph of 1970 (NMR BB70/07249).*

confines of their dwelling house and its adjacent plot of land. On the Quay, the cellars or storehouses belonging to Canynges' chantry were held separately from the two dwelling houses on the same plot on the Marsh Street frontage.[90] On the Quay, the storehouse to the south of the Canynges' property, fronting Marsh Street in 1610, was not linked to the dwellings of either Cary or Wade.[91] In Back Street the two cellars at the Back Hall could not have been used in conjunction with a merchant's own dwelling after Robert Sturmy's death in the 1450s.

Further back from the Quay, at nos.40–1 Baldwin Street, a property belonging to Christchurch parish was rebuilt in c 1545 as a 'storehouse'. In 1696 when leased to Thomas Day, a wine cooper, it was described as 'the great cellar lately converted into two with two lofts and other buildings over'. The two cellars are shown on a plan of 1769 (Fig 7.40). There is no evidence that part of this was a dwelling at any time after 1545.[92] In King Street the storehouse at no.34 was, in the 17th century, used independently of the adjacent house to which it was later linked, and the house of the rope maker Robert Dowding at no.32 lay apart from his storehouse. Only from 1717 was the storehouse apparently leased with the adjacent house at no.33, the two being described as 'a tenement and warehouse'. They were leased then to Thomas Seed, a hooper, and in 1766 to Thomas Clark, a corn merchant.[93]

Similar complexities were to be found in the use of the warehouses behind nos.36–8 Queen Square, three houses backing on to the Avon waterfront. By 1732 Lionel Lyde and Co occupied the bottle warehouse to the rear of no.38. The dwelling house was occupied by Captain Matthew Thomas, a merchant; he evidently had no need of a warehouse here, though it is quite

Fig 7.39
Photograph of the mid-19th century: warehouses on Broad Quay to the S of the Fish Market. From left to right: nos. 21 and 22 the Tontine warehouses of the 1770s to the N of St Stephen's Lane (Manders and Co and Wintle and Co); nos.23–4 Broad Quay to the S of St Stephen's Lane (Taylor and West of England Coal) (Taylor 1872, author's copy.)

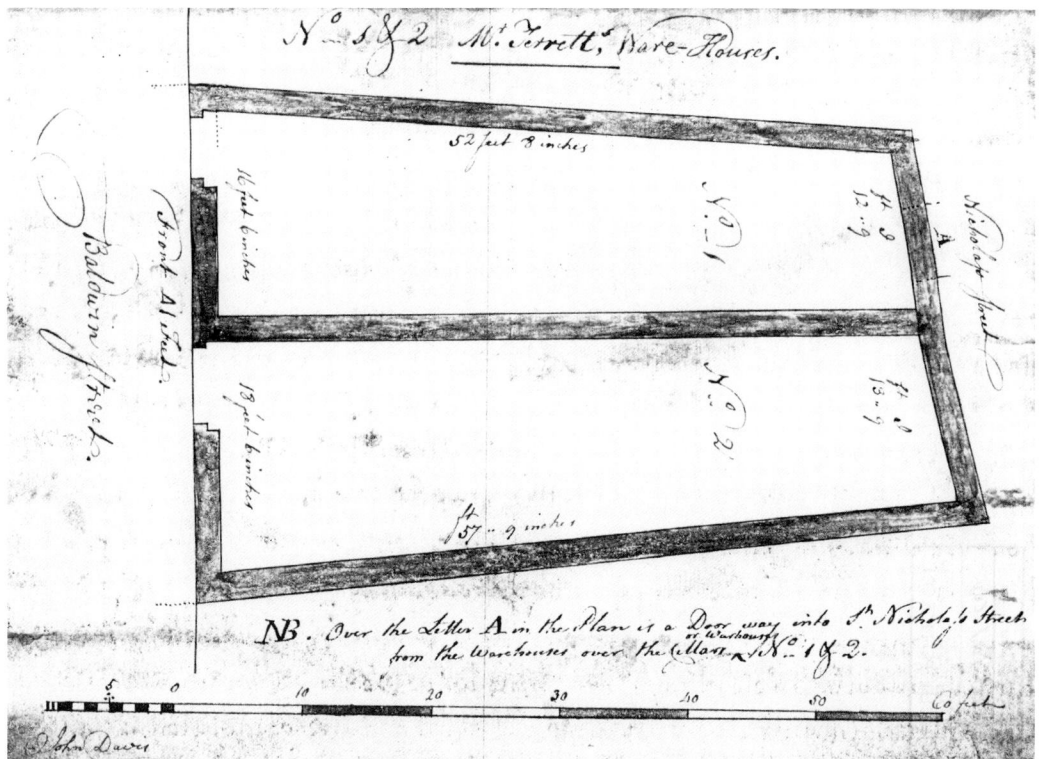

Fig 7.40 (left)
Nos.40–1 Baldwin Street, plan dated to 1769 showing the great cellar, in 1696 described as lately converted 'into two with two lofts and other buildings over' (BRO P/XCh/D1).

possible he held one elsewhere. His neighbour Mrs Wraxall, the occupier of no.37 and the widow of another sea captain and merchant, held a warehouse behind her own house and also one behind no.36. This was the home of the merchant Captain John Davis; he, too, must have had no need of a warehouse, or held one elsewhere (Fig 7.41).[94]

These arrangements represent pragmatic responses to opportunities presented by the ebb and flow of merchant businesses. However, the ideal represented by the close association of dwelling and storehouse was evidently alive in the early 18th century. It is seen most clearly in Prince Street and Queen Street, where architects and developers arranged the new plots to give a dwelling house facing on to the street or square, and a warehouse behind the dwelling facing on to the quayside or back street, a plan that provided both convenience and security.

In the development of nos.50–4 Prince Street, built for Robert Yate in the late 1720s (Fig 7.37; see Fig 8.44), it was the architect's intention that each merchant's house should have a warehouse attached. Nehemiah Champion, Vickris Dickason and Richard Farr, the first merchant owners of nos.50–4, were able to walk across a private courtyard and past the back kitchen through to their warehouse without leaving their own property. It is, though, doubtful whether their workmen or business contacts would have been expected to use this same route from quayside to house. Yate's architect was clear in his own mind that the compter or counter should be close to the front of each house, so that 'People of Business may not have farr to go, and that the Master may see and hear of everything that comes in at his doors'.[95] Similar considerations must have prevailed in the design of nos.68–70. The merchant John Hobbs, the first occupier of no.70 in the 1720s,[96] would have been able to pass directly from his dwelling house across his own courtyard to his warehouse behind on the quay frontage (Fig 7.38).

In several instances merchants held a warehouse which extended behind their own property and an adjacent one. At nos.18–22

*Fig 7.41*
*Nos.36–8 Queen Square, warehouses facing The Grove, photograph of 1970 (NMR BB70/07295).*

Narrow Quay, a single three-storey warehouse of three bays was built in *c* 1725 as one structure behind a curvilinear gable. It took up the whole space behind nos.68–70 Prince Street, the centre-line of the three roofs and the hoist below aligned on the party wall between the two houses. By *c* 1740 nos.68–70 were leased to Joseph Jones, a sailmaker. Jones occupied no.70, holding also the three-bay warehouse formerly leased by John Hobbs. His sub-tenant at no.68 possibly had no need of a warehouse.[97] Further to the east, nos.36–8 Queen Square were rebuilt in the 1740s. The warehouse to the rear belonged solely to no.36 (Fig 7.41).

How long the close association of house and warehouse continued both to be practical and in conformity with changing ideas on the wealthy merchant's way of life is not clear. It may not have lasted beyond the middle of the 18th century. When the quayside south of the former fish market was redeveloped in the 1770s, there was no attempt to integrate storage and the merchant's dwelling house. Instead a row of warehouses was constructed as an investment for those who subscribed to this particular scheme. For the merchants and others who then used these buildings, this was a workplace quite separate from home.

## The Workplace and the Home

The close association between work and home extended beyond the merchant community to embrace a wide range of industries. This can be traced from the 13th century onwards. The occupants of no.128 Redcliff Street were involved in dyeing from the later 13th to the 15th centuries. A house on the street frontage consisted of a smaller room towards the front, interpreted as a shop, and a larger room behind, certainly used for dyeing. On the south side of the house a passage gave access to the yards behind and the Avon; it must also have provided light to the various rooms of the house and its ancillary buildings. In the larger rear room, a circular hearth served as the base for a dyeing vat; this room can be interpreted as the dyeing shop. Since the front room was unheated, and was probably the shop mentioned in contemporary deeds, the living accommodation for the household must have been on the first floor, in the one or more chambers over the front room.[98]

A possibility not stated by the excavator of no.128 was that the larger rear room was a former open hall, now used as a workshop. The room must have been open to the roof, for there was no stack to surround the open hearth which formed the vat base. It need occasion no surprise that a room built as an open hall to a dwelling house was being used as a workshop by the 15th century. As early as the 14th century, townspeople were using their halls as working rather than domestic space. The ordinances of 1346 were explicit in requiring that weavers' looms were to be located not in solars or cellars, but only in halls and shops, next to the street and in sight of the people.[99] In the late 15th century John Gauge's hall was certainly used in this way, with the contents of his hall in 1489 including both cloths and a winding press for the cloth (Appendix 2). Gauge's principal living room was either his unheated parlour or his kitchen.[100] By the 17th century other open halls had been adapted as workplaces by townspeople involved in various trades (pp 112–3).

From at least the 12th century, townspeople also constructed or adapted a variety of buildings specifically as workplaces, usually close to the dwelling on the same tenement plot. At nos.86–7 Redcliff Street, the 13th- and 14th-century occupiers of two adjacent properties were shown, through archaeological excavations, to have possessed stone-walled buildings utilised for dyeing. At no.87 a building housing both a hearth and a vat base were sited immediately behind the dwelling house and shop (chapter 5) on the street frontage. At no.86 a building with two vat bases was similarly located to the rear of the dwelling.[101] In 1473 Richard Thomas, a bell maker, held one of the properties of Canynges' chantry, located in Old Market close to Lawford's Gate. Described as 'a tenement with a bellehouse', the latter was probably a separate structure.[102] The clothier Edmond Jones located the houses for his workforce and probably his workhouse in the Rackhay close to his own dwelling on Welsh Back (chapter 6).

The long tenement plots extending back behind houses in streets such as Redcliff Street and Old Market provided ample space for the construction of buildings to be used in a variety of manufacturing processes. As will be seen below, more evidence is available for the construction of such workshops from the 16th century onwards.

Soap manufacture was an important industry in Bristol by the late 15th century. Owing to the noxious nature of soap manufacture, it would have often been necessary to construct or utilise

*Fig 7.42 (opposite) Whitsun Court Sugar House, Lower Maudlin Street. The house, bearing the initials of the sugar baker Thomas Ellis and his wife Ann, also the date 1666, was probably built as his residence; watercolour by Alfred Parkman of the late 19th century (BRSMG M4596).*

buildings separate from the dwelling house. When Thomas Elyot, the inhabitant of a house at the north end of Redcliff Street, left to his son all his 'ffate, furneys, cestren etc' in 1505, these were probably located in a soap house behind the dwelling house, on the long tenement plot extending back to the Avon with the water essential both for the inward transport of whale fat and for the soap making process.[103] Elyot was one of a number of soap makers whose premises in the 16th and 17th centuries lay close to Bristol Bridge.[104] A second favoured location for this industry was on the south side of Lewin's Mead, most properties here having long tenement plots extending back to the Frome.

By 1533 one such property was held by David Tailor or Ketilwell, a soap maker. Mortgaging his property in 1556, he was obliged to agree that he would not boil soap in the furnace of his soap house more than once a month. The soap house could have been used by a number of the subsequent soap makers who occupied this property, the last possibly being Richard Keene, who purchased it in 1739.[105] The need for such processes to be sited away from the main dwelling house was also highlighted in a city ordinance of 1594, where it was decreed that chandlers, apothecaries and other inhabitants 'should provide themselves with out houses in their gardens, or in other convenient places in the outskirts or suburbs of the cittie for the prevention of the danger of fire'.[106]

In the east part of Castle Street, buildings for industrial or commercial use were being built from the late 1650s in the gardens of newly built houses. At no.56 first Thomas Harris, a cooper, and then Charles Chard, a grocer, made use of a large warehouse which occupied about half the space remaining behind the dwelling and its detached kitchen. The rest was left as garden until at least the mid-18th century.[107] Though shown as a warehouse, this may have served also as a workshop (*see* Fig 6.27). At no.59, the home of Flower Hunt, a tobacco pipe maker, two 'working rooms' were located behind the dwelling house, shown in outline on a late 18th-century plan.[108] In 1672 these contained the forge, tobacco pipe moulds and other tools of his trade.

George Hill, a button mould maker, was a contemporary of Hunt. He lived at no.68 Castle Street, and the arrangement of his house and tenement plot in 1678 followed a similar pattern (Appendix 2).[109] Behind his dwelling was a workshop, its contents again the tools of his trade. The evidence from Castle Street shows that for individual craftsmen the construction of workshops immediately adjacent to one's dwelling was still a preferred way of life in the later 17th century.

Both Hunt and Hill held long tenement plots which extended to the Avon. Those in manufacturing trades who found themselves occupying smaller plots might have adopted the strategy of the soap maker Andrew Gale. His dwelling house, no.14A Castle Street, occupied a relatively small plot with extensive street frontage, used by Gale to maximum advantage as tenements for letting. Gale's workhouse, with the implements and tools necessary for soap making, was in the former Castle Orchard, in Passage Street, about five minutes' walk from his house.[110]

The narrow tenement plots of Lewin's Mead and Castle Street would not have been suitable for sugar refining, which required considerable space for the various processes involved. The first sugar refinery in Bristol was established by Robert Aldworth from *c* 1607 in premises adjacent to his rebuilt house next to St Peter's church (chapters 5 and 8).[111] In this and the second refinery, founded by John Knight from *c* 1654 in the Great House on St Augustine's Back, it is not possible to identify which parts of an existing building structure were utilised for the sugar refining process. The inventories that exist for both properties show that both Aldworth and Knight continued to use these houses as their own residences. A third sugar house was established by five partners, led by the merchant Thomas Ellis, the founder of the Broadmead Baptist congregation. Ellis was responsible for the purchase of part of the former St James's Priory lands in 1665 and is credited with the erection of the sugar house, the two-storey warehouse and millhouse with a loft.[112] The house bearing Ellis's initials and the date 1666 was probably built as his residence (Fig 7.42).

The sugar house established at nos.107–9 Temple Street in 1662 by Richard Lane and John Hine was a similar joint venture. Like Aldworth, Knight and Ellis, Lane and Hine too lived on the premises, in new purpose-built accommodation. The two new houses built by Lane and Hine were immediately adjacent to the sugar house, and are probably the houses shown on a watercolour of 1828 (Fig 7.43).

With a shared investment at risk until the refining process was complete, the manufacture of refined sugar required an investment far beyond that needed for the manufacture of tobacco pipes or buttons. The juxtaposition of home and workplace was a common element in the lifestyles of men such as Flower Hunt and William Ellis. For these citizens, living and manufacturing were inextricably intertwined with the routines of daily domestic life.

In granting leases for building in the Castle, the Corporation made no conditions that would have excluded the noise or fumes associated with these industries from new residential areas. Such conditions appear to have been included in leases for building only from the very end of the 17th century. The first lease for the development of Queen Charlotte Street (Appendix 1), the commencement of Queen Square, stipulated that there were to be no buildings behind the dwelling except as were necessary for the use of the house, such as 'Back Kitchen, warehouses, Outhouses Stables and Coach-house'. Explicitly excluded were smiths' shops and brewhouses, and tenants such as tallow-chandlers or 'any other Tradesmen who by noyse danger of ffire or ill smells shall disturbe or annoye any of the inhabitants'.[113] Such conditions were to be the norm in the granting of leases for larger dwellings in the 18th century.

Such covenants did not necessarily distance the domestic lives of manufacturers from their workplaces. In Castle Street Edward Garlick, an apothecary and a successful varnish manufacturer, had in 1714 recently erected 'a Work' at his premises, the Sign of 'The Distell'. This must either have replaced or been an adaptation of the back kitchen, as still survived on his neighbour's tenement at no.26 (chapter 6). Garlick's works were, however, in due course moved. By 1740 'his turpentine house, lamp-black houses, stills, worms, cisterns, backs, coppers and other utensils' had been moved to the outparish of St Phillip and St Jacob.[114] In 1719 William Bonny, the printer of the city's

*Fig 7.43*
*The two new houses built by Richard Lane and John Hine for their sugar house at no.107 Temple Street (in foreground), watercolour by T L Rowbotham, 1828 (BRSMG M2137).*

first newspaper, *The Bristol Post-Boy*, combined his residence at no.15 Small Street with his printing presses and the tools of his trade, all kept in his 'workhouse'.[115] In Halliers Lane George Daubeny I, the first of three generations of sugar refiners, lived from 1731–41 next to or close to his sugar house, one of the most prosperous businesses in 18th-century Bristol. Two succeeding generations successively rose from merchant-manufacturer to banker status, but chose to live at a greater distance from the works.[116]

## The Increasing Separation of Home and Work

In the first half of the 18th century Edward Garlick I and George Daubeny I were poised to see their families rise to the upper echelons of Bristol society. However, they were also representative of the large number of citizens whose place of work continued to be adjacent to their dwelling. The directories of 1775 and 1801 reveal large numbers of persons in the more central and commercial streets who continued to live in this way: living over the shop, keeping taverns or inns, or involved in manufacturing on a domestic scale. At the same time there were significant new developments, notably the emergence of a small number of companies involved in larger-scale manufacturing, such as Daubeny's sugar refinery, the Bristol Copper Company and Reynolds, Getley and Co – the two last established before 1775 in former high-status residences at nos.5 and 7 Small Street.[117]

There was also the growth of a professional and banking quarter, concentrated in Corn Street, Broad Street and Small Street. The 1801 directory shows an increasing number of attorneys and brokers with business addresses in these streets, but with private addresses in the smarter, entirely residential streets and squares of Clifton and around Brunswick and Portland Squares. By 1775 there were also many entirely residential streets, the dwellings of employers or the employed which will be considered as residential houses in chapter 8. The separation of residence from place of work is a subject to which subsequent chapters will return, but it will be evident that the juxtaposition of work and domestic life continued to be central to many citizens into the second half of the 18th century.

# 8

# The Residential House

In late 15th-century Bristol the distinction made between hallhouse and shophouse was, it may be argued, a signifier of differences in wealth and status. From the documentary, archaeological and architectural data it is evident that shophouses were then built in the busier commercial streets of the city, and were for the most part occupied by households whose resources did not permit the possession of a grander property, replete with an open hall. Hallhouses were more widely distributed across the city, and in the most important commercial streets, such as Broad Street, High Street and Small Street, one could find both shophouses and hallhouses. In these streets hallhouses were occupied by some of the wealthiest inhabitants of the city; but elsewhere, in such thoroughfares as Redcliff Street and St Thomas Street (chapter 5), smaller houses with open halls were possibly the dwellings of the less wealthy. Here the hallhouse and shophouse were not so clearly indicators of differing wealth and status.

From the 16th century onwards an increasingly large part of the population inhabited houses without open or symbolic halls. These houses are termed collectively here as 'the residential house'. Like the medieval house with the open hall, the residential house offered a mode of living for people of widely differing positions in society, ranging from rich to poor. The overall form of the residential house was essentially that of the shophouse, a storeyed dwelling with one or more rooms on each floor stacked one above the other, but with the important difference that the ground floor of the house was given over to residential use: it was not used as retail or working space.

New residential houses were built in large numbers in new developments in the central area and suburbs from the 1650s onwards. By c 1800 such houses occupied a significant proportion of the built-up area of the much expanded city. In the ensuing two centuries, developments of such houses were placed further and further from the city's historic centre. From Bristol's inner Victorian suburbs to the late 20th- and 21st-century estates on the periphery, a sizeable part of its population now lives in residential houses – houses divorced from the place of work. A large part of the city is now residential in function. The city that existed from the 16th to the 18th centuries, characterised by exclusively residential districts around a commercial core, can be seen as an element of emerging modernity.[1] The purpose of this chapter is to examine how the residential house changed through two or more centuries in response to social change.

There has been a tendency to see the Georgian town house as a static, unchanging entity. Elizabeth McKellar has explored how Summerson's focus on the Georgian house and 'Palladian taste' as the 'norm to which classical architecture in this country has returned over and over again' has led to a misleading and simplistic interpretation of later 17th- and early 18th-century London houses.[2] She has shown that the Baroque exterior elevations, timber-framed interior structures and plans characteristic of houses of before the Great Fire distinguished later 17th-century houses from those of Georgian London.[3] Guillery's more recent study of the smaller houses of 18th-century London has underlined how these, too, have been neglected in earlier studies.[4]

For Bristol there has been a similar focus on the Georgian town house. The focus of architectural historians has been very much on style, on aesthetic perceptions and on the identity and work of individual architects. Relatively little attention has been paid to how the Georgian town house functioned: it has been seen internally as a static entity. As for the 17th-century town house, it has been scarcely studied at all. The evidence now available from Bristol affords the opportunity to see how residential houses changed through a period spanning the mid-17th century to the end of the 18th century.

In looking at how the design and use of houses might have changed in this period, cultural context is provided by what has been termed the beginnings of an English urban renaissance, placed in the last quarter of the 17th century. From this time onwards it has been argued that social space became more important in people's minds, and that this was particularly evident in architecture. Prior to this period, Borsay has argued, 'urban architecture paid little attention to questions of aesthetics and planning'.[5] Looking at popular culture in 17th-century Bristol, Jonathan Barry has argued that 'only at the very end of the century did the wealthy abandon the "Tudor", vernacular style of architecture for the neo-classical style'.[6] The adoption by the wealthy of the neoclassical style at the beginning of the 18th century could in turn be linked to aspirations of refinement, gentility and politeness, all much evidenced in the world of consumption.

This chapter will look at the design and use of the residential house in the 17th and 18th centuries. In particular it will explore how the use of domestic space during these centuries characterised housing at different social levels.

## The Several Modes of Houses

The writer and polymath Roger North wrote his influential essay *Of Building* in the 1680s. The work provides an important source for a contemporary viewpoint on the planning and design of houses.[7] North's concerns were centred on south-east and eastern England, and his familiarity with the design of town houses probably came in part from witnessing the rebuilding of London in the two decades after the Great Fire of 1666. However, North also had interests in Bristol. His family held considerable property here, and elsewhere he relates aspects of the life in Bristol of his father-in-law, Sir Robert Cann. Using North's *Of Building*, and his chapter on 'the several modes of houses' in particular, provides a contemporary and meaningful framework for understanding the design of the residential house in late 17th- and early 18th-century Bristol.

Several other key contemporary collections amplify and modify North's categorisation of housing types. The first of these is the book of architectural drawings donated by Richard Rawlinson (1690–1755) to the Bodleian Library at Oxford. The plans in this volume have already been linked by Alison Maguire and Howard Colvin to North's writings.[8] A second important source is the collection of early 18th-century drawings in *The Kingsweston Book of Drawings*; this has especial relevance to the study of houses in Bristol.[9]

In looking at the range of housing types in early modern Bristol we can follow and extend the typological approach adopted by Roger North, moving from the smallest houses to the largest, across the wide spectrum of the urban population. Also like North, we can examine the degree to which houses were planned according to contemporary notions of necessity and convenience. Well into the 18th century and as in London, the form of smaller houses was probably determined by traditional practice rather than by books.[10] Many builders were following vernacular tradition without any direct awareness of contemporary architectural plans – so a further major source for understanding the residential house in 17th- and 18th-century Bristol must be the houses themselves, as recorded or surviving.

The plans of houses considered in this chapter and the next occurred in both the central parts of the city, where, as observed by North, 'divers houses stand contiguously in range', and the suburbs, where similar plans were employed for the design of individual detached or semi-detached houses.[11]

## The Smallest Houses

Neither Roger North nor the compiler of *The Kingsweston Book of Drawings* was concerned with the smallest of urban houses, those consisting of one room on each floor. For contemporary concerns with these smallest of houses, we must turn to the Rawlinson collection, where a number of the 169 published drawings are of town houses. Three such designs (Fig 8.1) were presumably for a town house, its principal room on the ground floor and its first floors lit only from the street.[12] The first design was for a house with a projecting stair turret to the rear, and the third with the stairs within the main body of the house. The second design was a variant of the third, with projecting bays to the street frontage. The first and third of these designs can be found in houses built in Bristol during the 16th to the 18th centuries.

The simplest plan for the house of one room

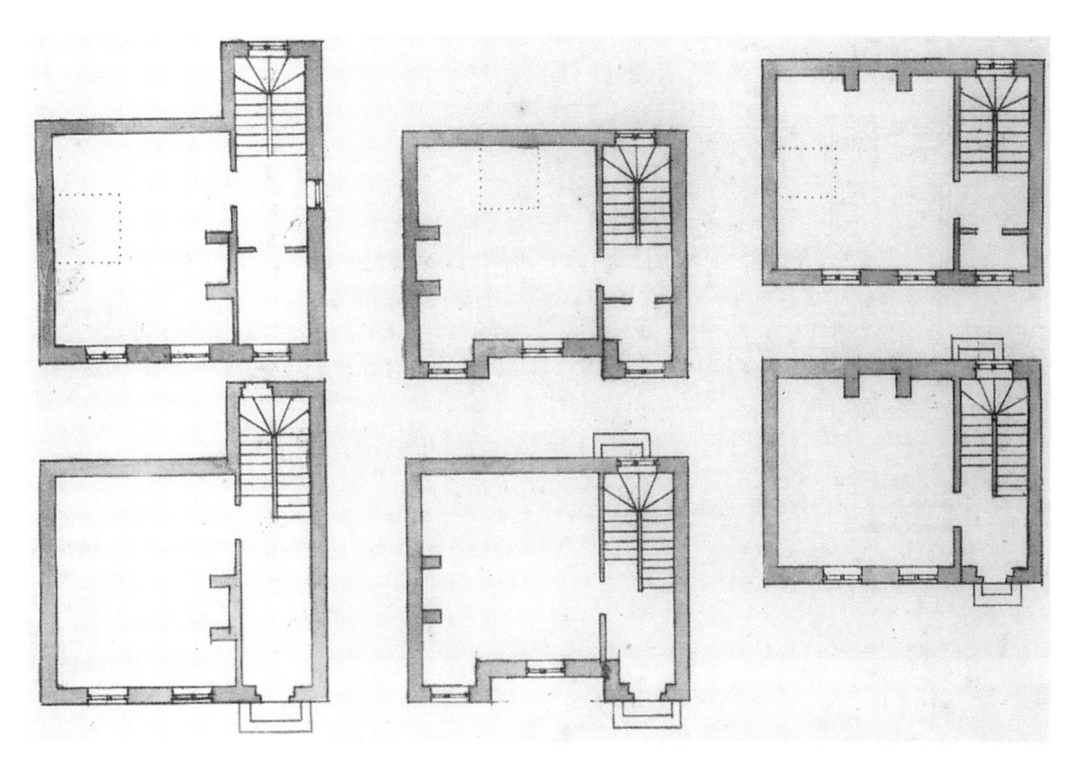

*Fig 8.1*
*Designs of the late 17th century for the smallest town houses (Bodleian Library, Rawlinson collection D.710 fol 17v).*

on each floor was to place the stairs in one corner, providing access to rooms stacked one above the other. Two houses of this plan lay within nos.23–9 St Michael's Hill, a row of four timber-framed houses built by 1637. These were quite substantial buildings, of three storeys and with large prominent gabled frontages (Fig 8.2a). Built to this same plan in the late 17th century was no.8 Pipe Lane, again with the stairs placed between the stack and the rear wall (Fig 8.2b). On the opposite side of what was formerly the same street, nos.68–70 Colston Street are two of a row of ten or more one-room deep houses first occupied in the 1690s (Fig 8.2c). On the hillside above, uphill of Griffin Lane (later Lower Park Row), at least two small houses of similar plan were within a development undertaken on land belonging to the Corporation (Fig 8.2d). Although these houses were situated in a part of the city where many garden houses of similar plan were constructed from the 17th century onwards, these were definitely not occasional residences. They were built as residential houses and were first occupied by artisans or their widows.

Houses of this plan continued to be built into the 18th century. Typical of many smaller houses in Nathaniel Wade's extensive development of *c* 1700–10 was no. 17 Wade Street. The original plan provided one room on each floor, three rooms in all, with the stairs between the stack and the rear wall (Fig 8.2e and 8.3). On the south side of New Street two houses were built *c* 1710 as part of an adjacent development, possibly to the same plan as no.17 Wade Street, with kitchens each of a different plan added at a later date. The houses were evidently refronted in the 19th century, by which date the ground-floor front rooms had become shops (Fig 8.4). Not closely dated, and known of only from historic plans, are two houses of similar plan close to St James's church (see Inventory), to the west of the church (Fig 8.2g) and to the east in Cannon Street (Fig 8.2h).

Many of these smallest houses are known from documentary sources, from early plans, photographs and other illustrations. Using such evidence raises at the same time problems of interpretation; in many cases only archaeological excavation would now demonstrate whether rooms to the rear were part of the original design. In Rosemary Street on the east side of the city, a row of four houses had been built by 1656. The ground floor was the principal room for cooking and living, the upper rooms accessed by a winder stairs set in the corner between stack and rear wall. The inconsistent arrangement of the rooms to the rear indicates that these were possibly added to the houses as first built (Figs 8.5 and 8.6).

In Old King Street nos.3–8 were three pairs of such houses. Each was probably first built, of one

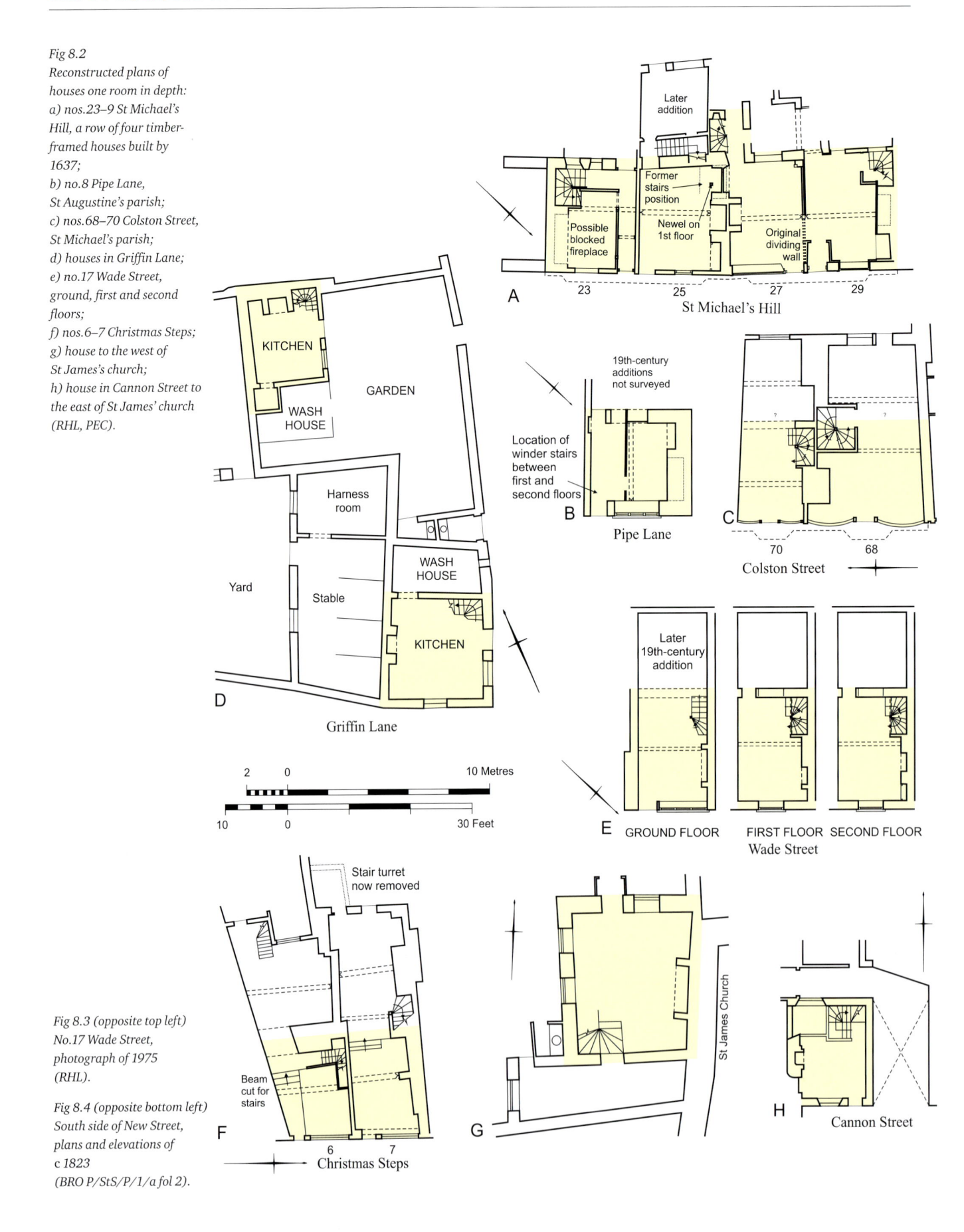

## THE TOWN HOUSE IN MEDIEVAL AND EARLY MODERN BRISTOL

Fig 8.2
Reconstructed plans of houses one room in depth:
a) nos.23–9 St Michael's Hill, a row of four timber-framed houses built by 1637;
b) no.8 Pipe Lane, St Augustine's parish;
c) nos.68–70 Colston Street, St Michael's parish;
d) houses in Griffin Lane;
e) no.17 Wade Street, ground, first and second floors;
f) nos.6–7 Christmas Steps;
g) house to the west of St James's church;
h) house in Cannon Street to the east of St James' church (RHL, PEC).

Fig 8.3 (opposite top left)
No.17 Wade Street, photograph of 1975 (RHL).

Fig 8.4 (opposite bottom left)
South side of New Street, plans and elevations of c 1823 (BRO P/StS/P/1/a fol 2).

# THE RESIDENTIAL HOUSE

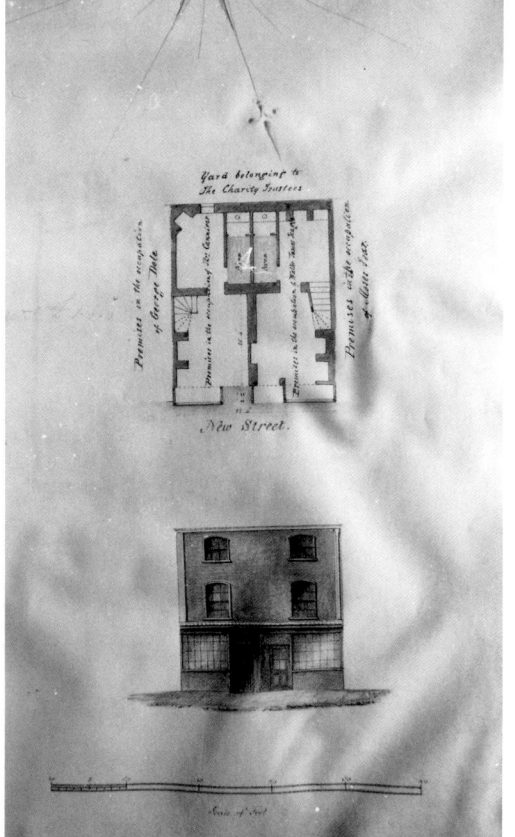

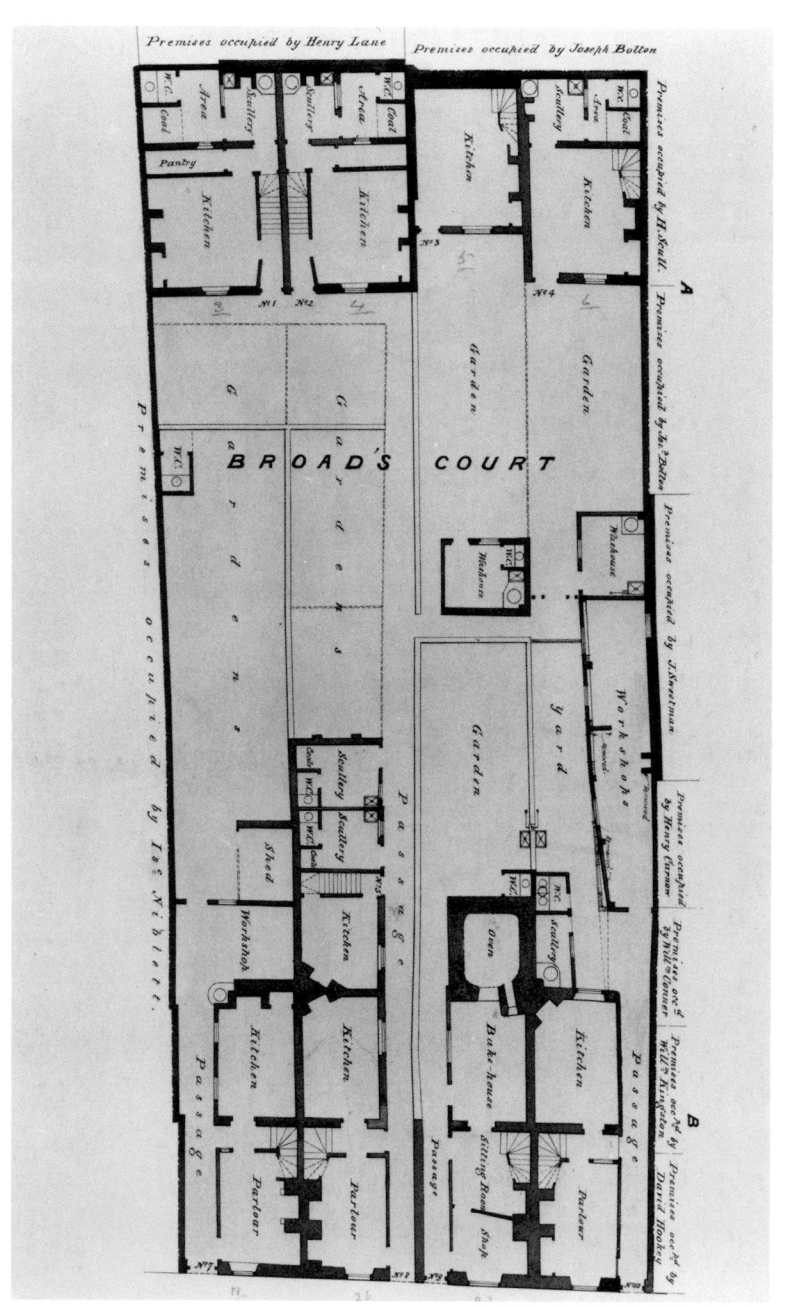

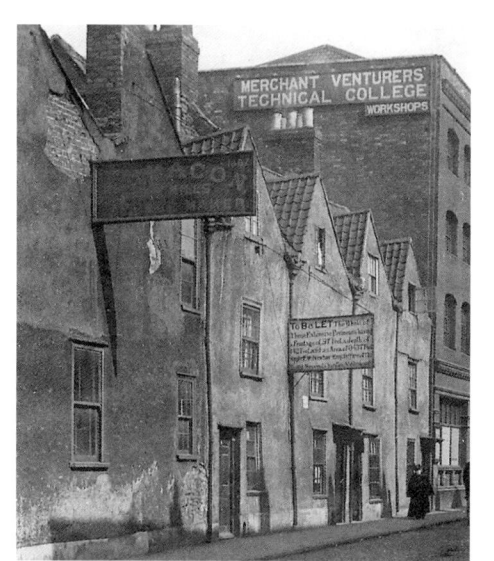

*Fig 8.5 (above)*
*Nos.14–18 (formerly 10, 9, 8 and 7) Rosemary Street, plan of late 19th century (BRO 33041/BMC/12/Pl 2 fol 59).*

*Fig 8.6 (left)*
*Nos.14–18 Rosemary Street (no.18 is closest to the camera), photograph of 1906 (BRO 33041/BMC/12/1).*

183

*Fig 8.7*
*Nos.7 (labelled on the plan as no.6) and 8 Old King Street, plan of 1863, no.7 with a ground-floor stack, that formerly in no.8 by then removed (BRO 33041/BMC/12/Pl 2 fol 32).*

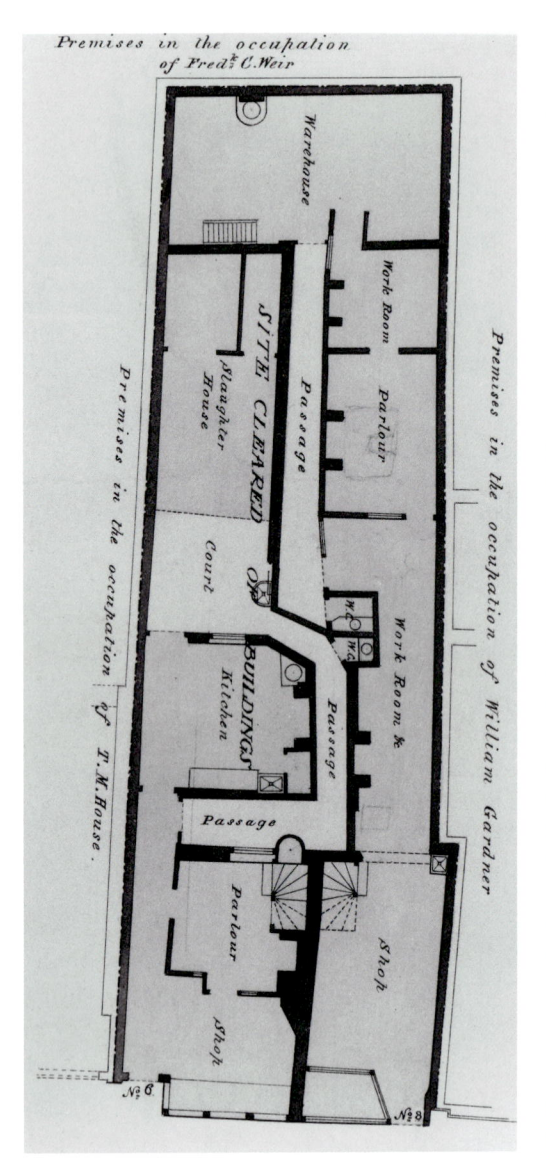

*Fig 8.8 (below right) Nos.3–8 Old King Street, photograph of 1906 (BRO 33041/BMC/12/1).*

*Fig 8.9 (below) West end of row of one-room plan houses built on the south side of the churchyard of St Philip and St Jacob; watercolour of 1823 by T L Rowbotham (BRSMG M2742).*

room in depth and three storeys in height, by 1686 (Figs 8.7 and 8.8). On the south side of St Phillip's churchyard a row of houses of similar plan was built in the late 17th century (Fig 8.9). Three similar one-room deep houses were built after 1685 in Pile Street near St Mary Redcliff church; these too probably extended backwards at a later date (Fig 8.10). Silver Street, to the north of St James's church, appears to have consisted almost entirely of houses of one-room plan, built in the 17th century (Figs 8.11 and 8.12). Between Temple Street and Rose Street, Rose Alley was a development of similar houses built c 1700 (Figs 8.13 and 8.14). To the east, houses of similar plan were built in Rose Street (Figs 8.15 and 8.16).

A more complex design was to place the stairs in an external turret, the first option of the three designs of the compiler of the Rawlinson collection (above). In the house of one room on each floor this provided significantly more living space, and also gave the house a more imposing appearance. On St Michael's Hill no.29 was of this plan, and retains the moulded stone fireplace surround on the first floor (Figs 8.2a and 8.17). On Christmas Steps, known as Queen Street, in 1673, nos.6 and 7 were each originally of similar plan; a large fireplace opening on the ground floor denoted the principal living room of the house (Figs 8.2f and 8.18). On the north side of Johnny Ball Lane, formerly Bartholomew Lane, a garden house of this plan was constructed under a building lease of 1691, with a stairs that appeared not as a prominent turret, but simply as an extension to the side of the house (see Fig 9.45).[13]

THE RESIDENTIAL HOUSE

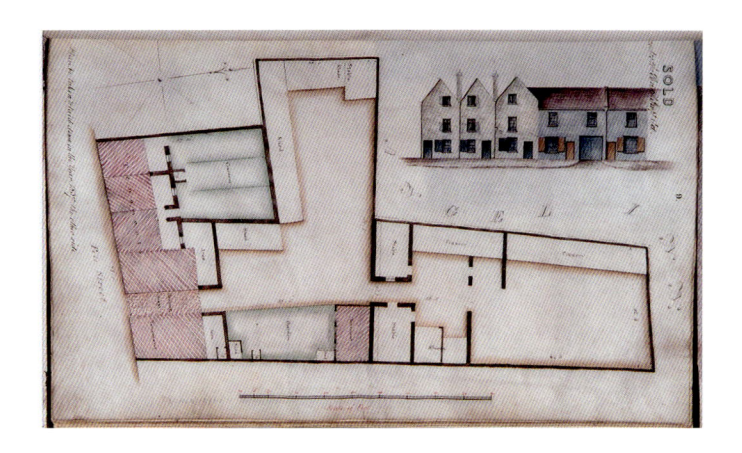

*Fig 8.10 (left)*
*Nos. 12, 13 and 14 Pile Street, row of three one-room-plan houses built after 1685 near St Mary Redcliff church, plan and drawing of 1823 (BRO P/StS/P/1a/fol 9).*

*Fig 8.11 (above)*
*Silver Street and St James's Back looking north, with the one-room house of St John's parish on the right; watercolour of 1824 by E Cashin (BRSMG Mb1).*

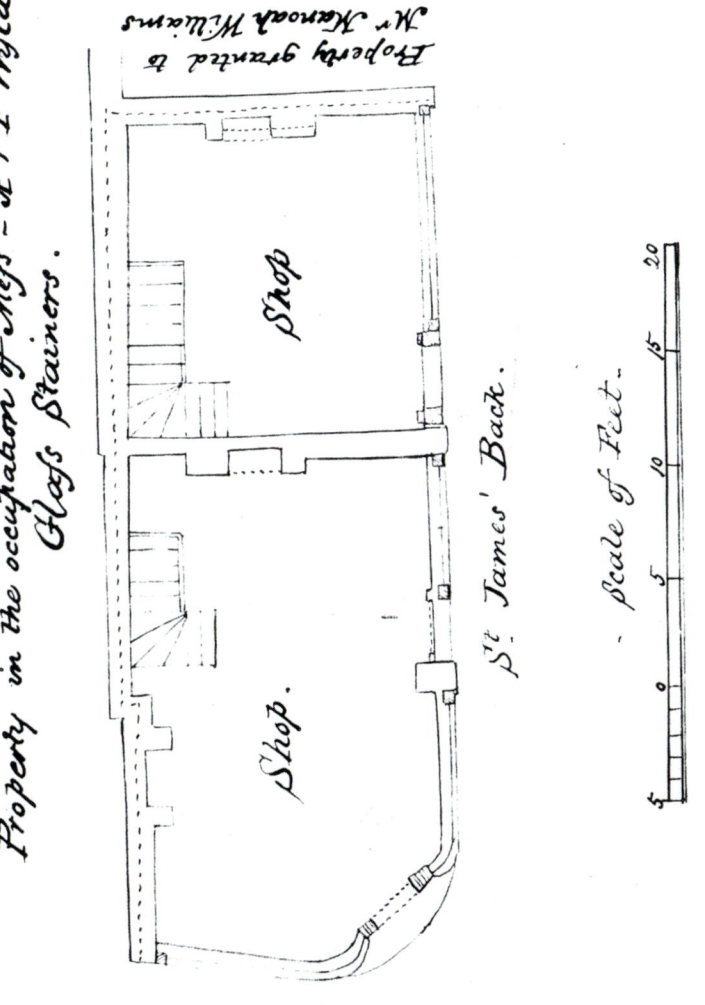

*Fig 8.12 (left)*
*Plans of houses in Silver Street shown in Fig 8.11, probably built as one-room houses of St John's parish (BRO 32226/Box 6/book of plans, 1853, for St John's church, fol 12).*

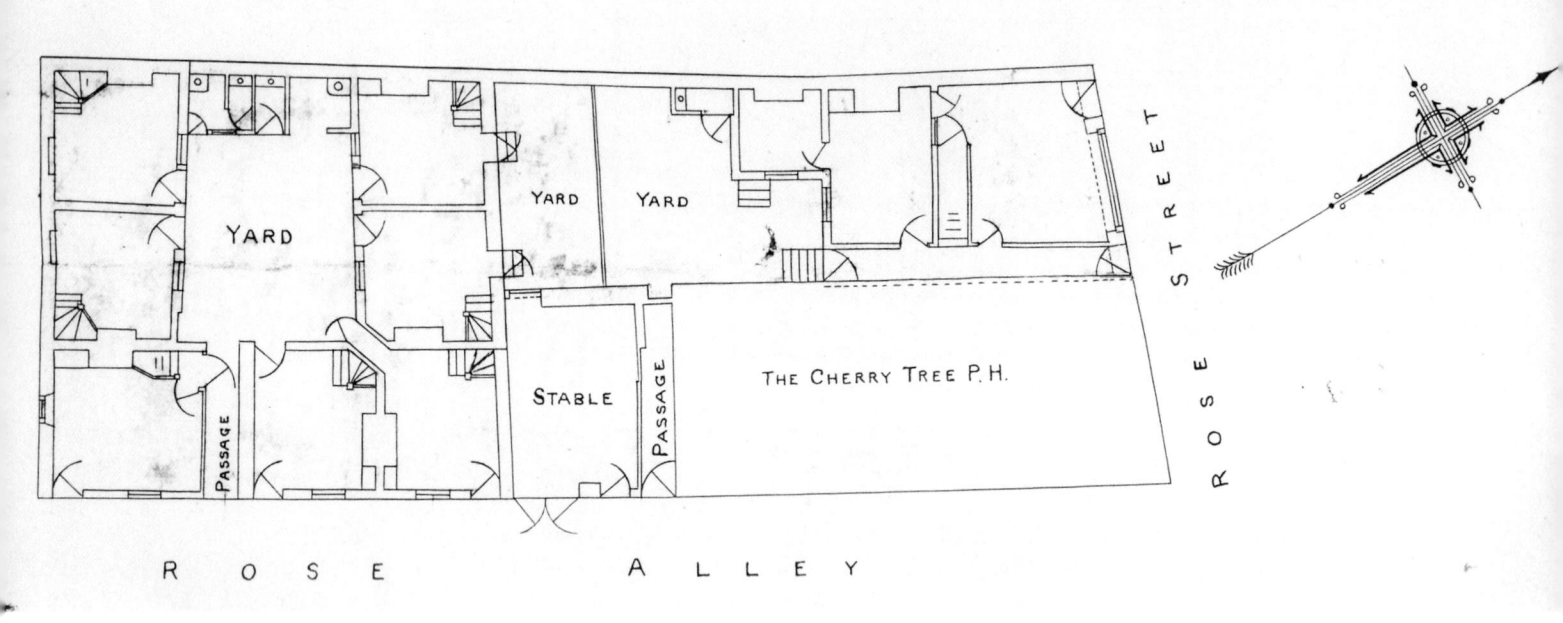

*Fig 8.13
Court of houses of one-room plan in Rose Alley, built c 1700; detailed plan of 1909 from deeds (BRO 3355(r)).*

*Fig 8.14
Row in Rose Alley, built c 1700, drawing of 1910 by Samuel Loxton of exterior (BCRL, Loxton drawing 1686X).*

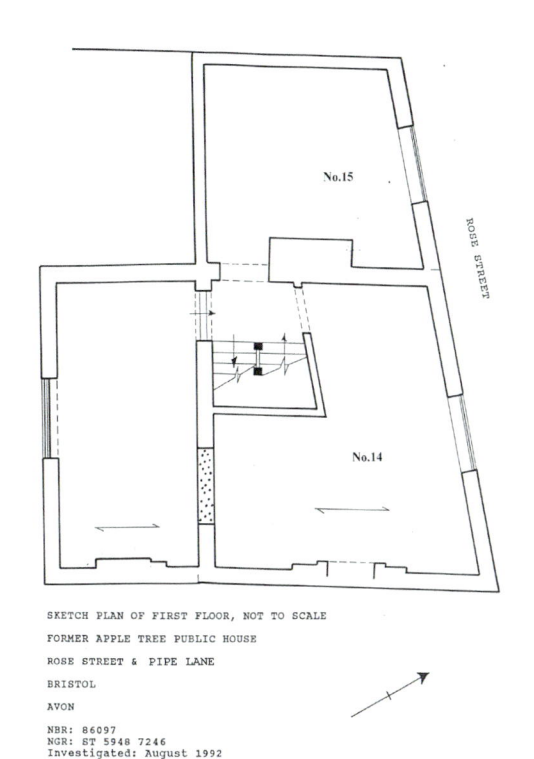

THE RESIDENTIAL HOUSE

*Fig 8.15 (far left)*
*Former 'Apple Tree' public house, corner of Rose Street and Pipe Lane, nos.14–15 Rose Street, plan of ground floor*
*(RCHME).*

*Fig 8.16 (left)*
*Former 'Apple Tree' public house, corner of Rose Street and Pipe Lane, nos.14–15 Rose Street, photograph of 1992*
*(NMR BB92/24057).*

*Fig 8.17 (far left)*
*No.29 St Michael's Hill, moulded stone fireplace surround in first-floor front room, photograph of 2012 (English Heritage DP 152552).*

*Fig 8.18 (left)*
*Nos.6–7 Christmas Steps, two houses of the 15th or 16th century refronted in brick in the late 18th or early 19th century, photograph of 2010 (English Heritage DP 111033).*

## Courtyard Developments

Some one-room houses were built in courts, often on gardens or tenement plots behind main street frontages. This sort of urban infill, common in many towns in the early modern period, provided inner-city housing for the poorer levels of society and demonstrates the abandonment of large city centre residences by the wealthy elite. The process started as early as the 17th century. New Buildings, a courtyard behind the south side of Broadmead, was built by 1673 (Figs 8.19 and 8.20), and Tailors' Court, of which two houses survive, was probably built c 1677 (Figs 8.21 and 8.22).[14]

The process may have intensified after 1750 as the elite flight to the suburbs gathered pace and more space became available in the central parts of the city. By 1828 at least four such houses had been built as nos.1–4 Broad's Court, to the rear of the four 17th-century houses in Rosemary Lane. A mid-19th-century plan shows that each consisted of one room on each of the

## THE TOWN HOUSE IN MEDIEVAL AND EARLY MODERN BRISTOL

*Fig 8.19 (above)
New Buildings, south side of Broadmead, Millerd 1673 (BRSMG).*

*Fig 8.20 (right)
Little St James's Back, in the distance at the end of the street, is the entrance to New Buildings, south side of Broadmead, watercolour of 1825 by T L Rowbotham (BRSMG M2836).*

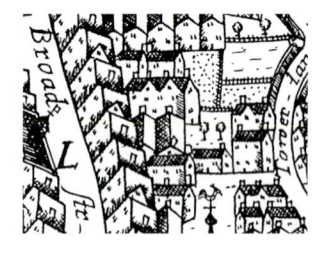

*Fig 8.21 (above)
Tailors' Court, Broad Street, Millerd 1673 (BRSMG).*

*Fig 8.22 (right)
Tailors' Court, Broad Street, photograph of 1930 looking north (NMR AA77/01993, PEWS).*

two floors, a kitchen on the ground floor and a chamber above (Figs 8.5 and 8.6). North of St James's church on the west side of Great James Street (later renamed Whitson Street), West Street was a court built as a new street running the length of a former tenement plot. It contained on the north side a row of seven houses built *c* 1700, each of one room in depth and of three storeys; the ground floors were clearly intended for living accommodation rather than shops (Figs 8.23 and 8.24).

To the north of Lewin's Mead, another 'New Buildings' was a courtyard development of land belonging to the parish of St Nicholas. It was built behind the street frontage *c* 1786 in an existing garden and extended back to Deep Street (Figs 8.25 and 8.26).[15] The design of the uniform frontage to the new side street was of an entirely domestic character; behind the facade were at least six one-room deep houses of varying size. In Gay's Court behind nos.109–10 Temple Street at least five similar, one-room deep houses of varying size had been built by 1789.[16] Though of varying plan and possibly built over a period of time, all were entirely residential in character (Fig 8.27). Similar

188

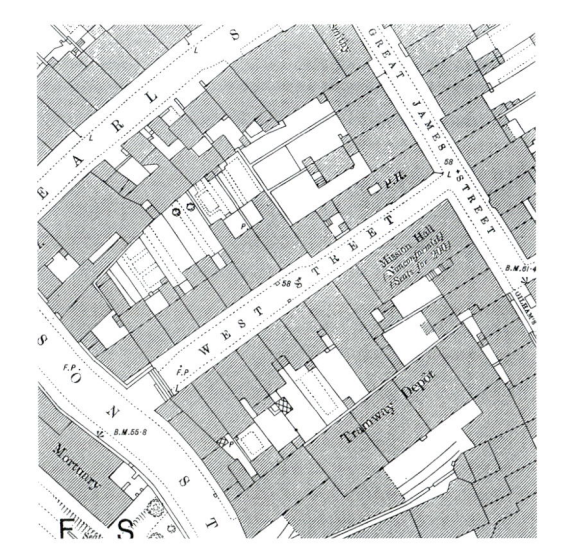

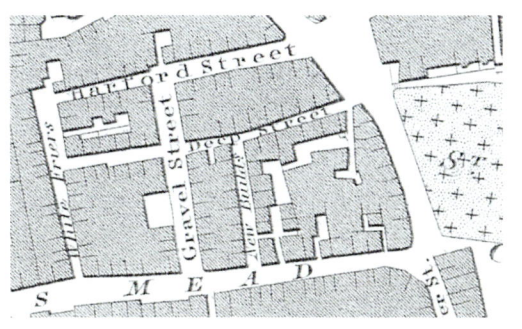

THE RESIDENTIAL HOUSE

*Fig 8.23 (far left, above) West Street, Great St James Street, from OS map of 1885, 1st edition, 1:500 town plan, Gloucestershire, Bristol, sheet LXXI.16.15.*

*Fig 8.24 (far left, below) West Street, Great St James Street, photograph of 1930 (PEWS, NMR AA77/02016).*

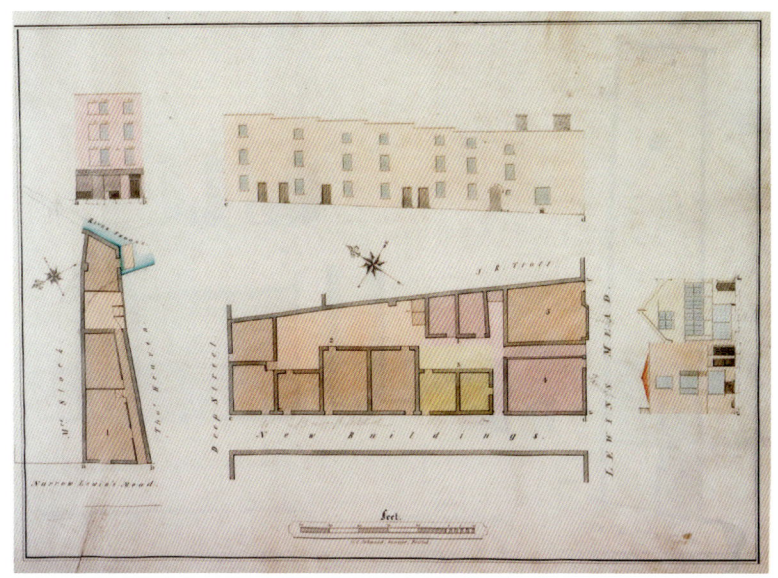

*Fig 8.25 (above, top) New Buildings, north side of Lewin's Mead, from Ashmead and Plumley's map of 1828 (BRO).*

*Fig 8.26 (above, centre) New Buildings, north side of Lewin's Mead, 1820s (BRO 39180 fol 16).*

*Fig 8.27 (left) Gay's Court, 109–110 Temple Street, plan and elevations of c 1828 (BRO P/StT/Ch/31 fol 3).*

developments in courtyards can be seen on plans of properties in Queen Street in 1742 (Fig 8.28) and at no.38 Redcliff Street in *c* 1816–17, where Warry's Court was a development of eight one-room plan houses, probably of *c* 1755 (Fig 8.29).[17]

Similar in size to the workers' houses known to have been provided in the two sugar houses (below), some of these smaller houses could also have been built primarily to rent to skilled wage earners employed in nearby industrial concerns. By the mid-18th century industries such as glass making, pottery manufacture and sugar refining were concentrated in the areas where developments of small houses such as the above can be identified.

189

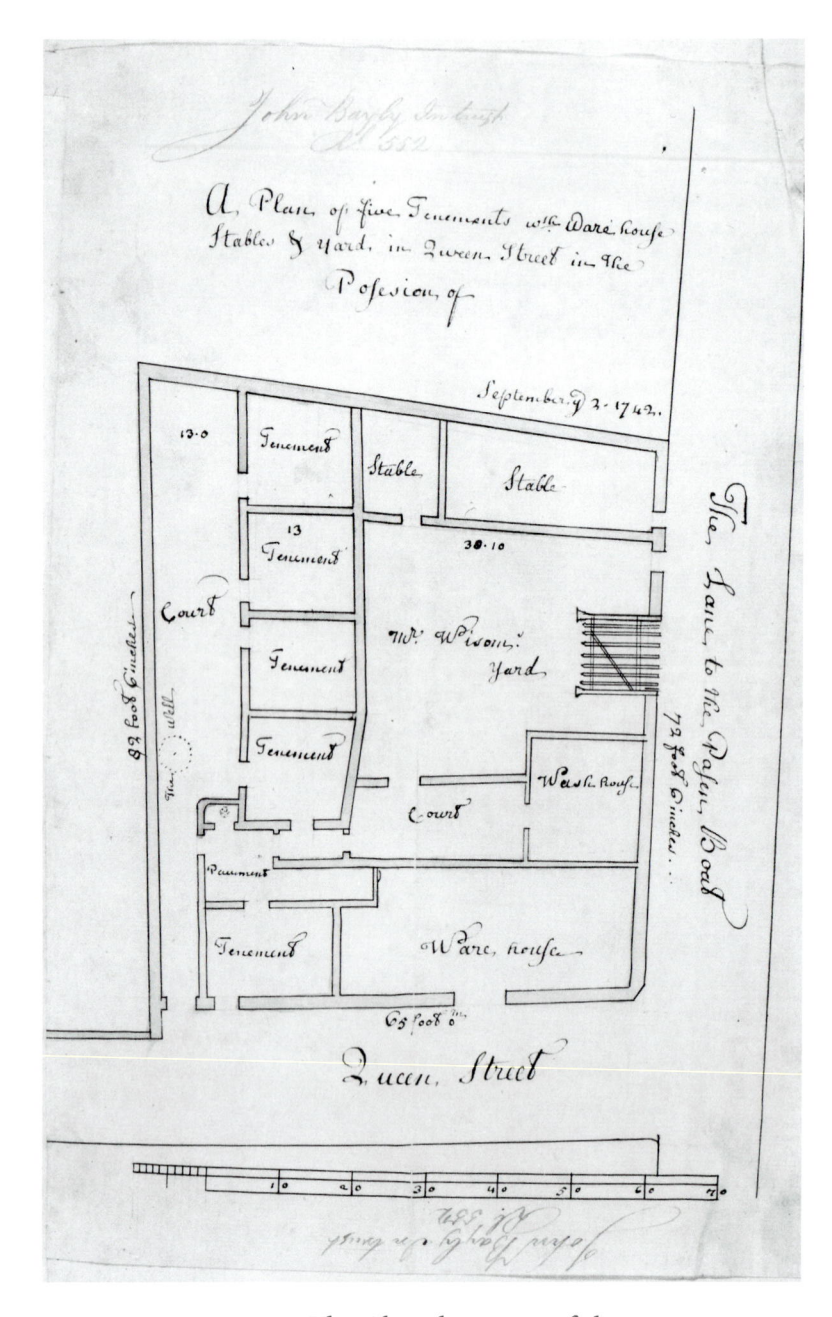

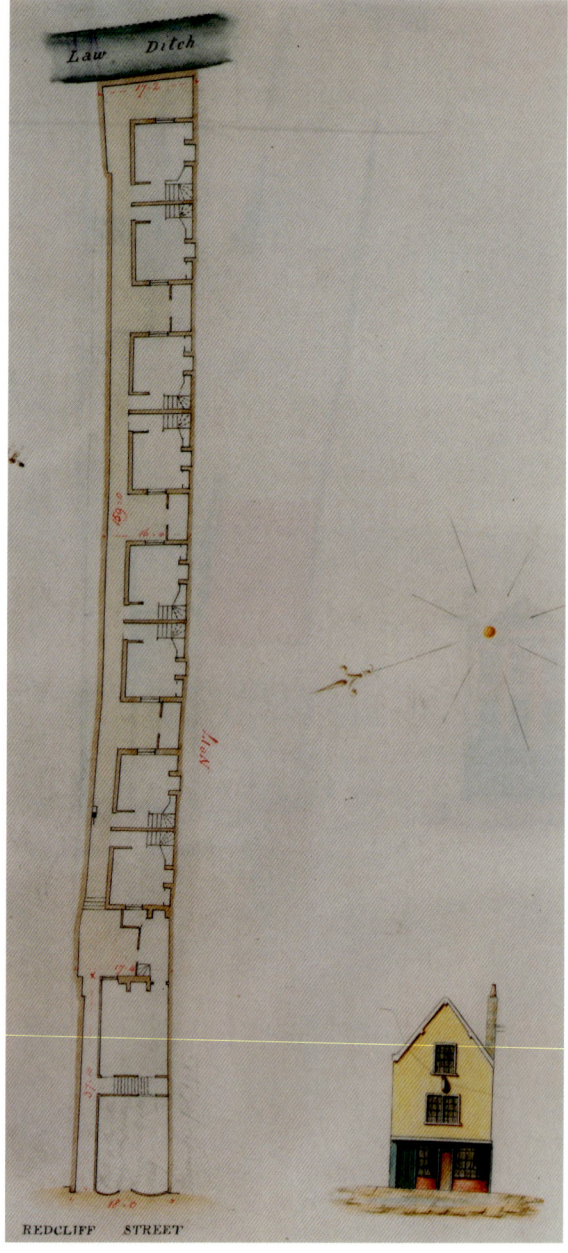

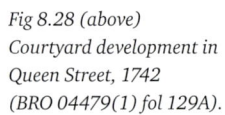

# THE TOWN HOUSE IN MEDIEVAL AND EARLY MODERN BRISTOL

*Fig 8.28 (above)*
*Courtyard development in Queen Street, 1742 (BRO 04479(1) fol 129A).*

*Fig 8.29 (above right)*
*Warry's Court behind no.38 Redcliff Street, plan of c 1816–17 (BRO P/StT/Ch/31 fol 16).*

## The Abandonment of the One-Room Plan

From the 1740s onwards, new developments of houses for artisans were largely of small, two-room deep houses (see below). As in London, the one-room plan was less acceptable by the end of the 18th century; artisans' aspirations were now set higher.[18] Developments such as New Buildings in Lewin's Mead, Gay's Court in Temple Street and Warry's Court in Redcliff Street may have been built for poorer levels of society, crowding into the congested city centre. It is noticeable that houses built in courtyards in the 19th century were smaller in size than the artisan houses of an earlier era: by 1800 the one-room plan had declined in status. Even if this plan did not lead seamlessly to the development of mass back-to-back housing, as was the case in Leeds,[19] it had become the bottom rung of the city's housing ladder.[20]

## Industrial Housing

Some of these smallest houses, particularly those built as rows, may not have been built primarily as speculative developments for rent, but rather by entrepreneurs or industrialists

THE RESIDENTIAL HOUSE

wishing to secure and retain the services of a skilled workforce. To the west of Back Street, immediately beyond the most congested part of the city, James Millerd carefully depicted one courtyard on his map as 'ye Racky' (Fig 8.30). Before the 16th century the Rackhay was probably a large garden, used for the setting up of racks for the drying of dyed cloths.[21] By 1567 10 houses were built here, and by 1646 the garden around which these were built had become an additional burial ground for the parish of St Nicholas. Plans and watercolours of the 1820s show at least 12 houses of the 16th or 17th centuries facing the burial ground – all dwellings of just one room on each floor (Fig 8.31). Four of these on the west side of the garden had small yards less than half the size of each house; the remaining eight houses were without any curtilage beyond the dwelling itself (Figs 8.32a and Fig 8.32b).

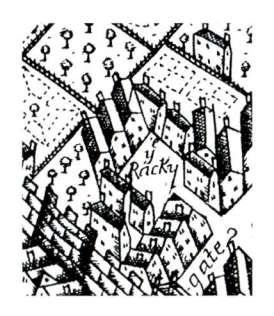

*Fig 8.30*
*The Rackhay in 1673 (BRSMG, Millerd's map of 1673).*

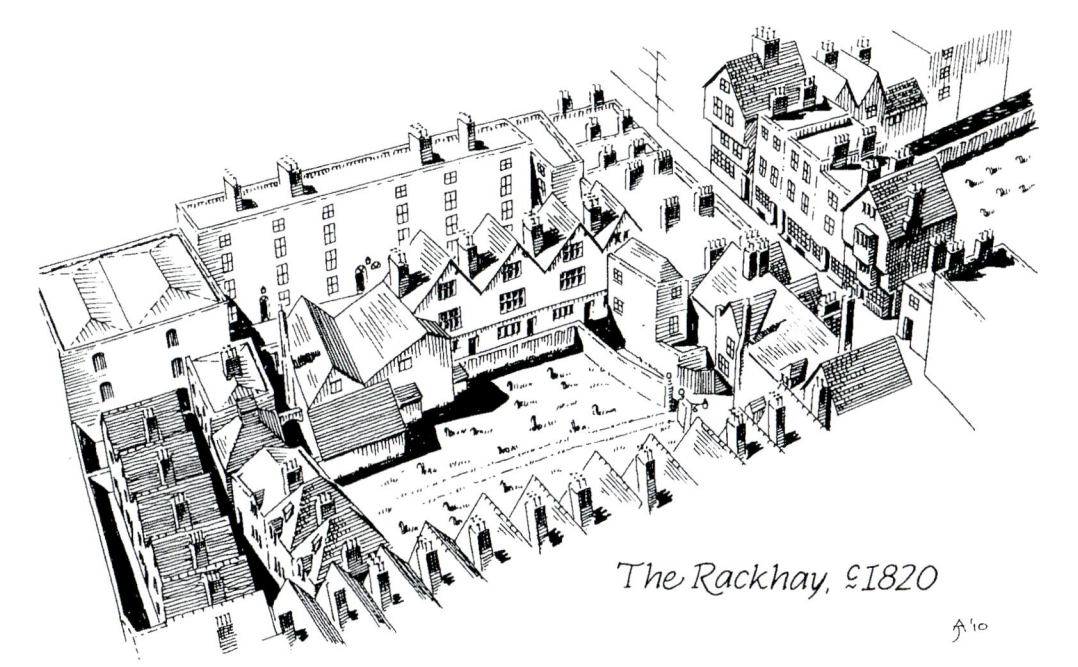

*Fig 8.31*
*The Rackhay: reconstruction of the townscape from documentary sources (JA).*

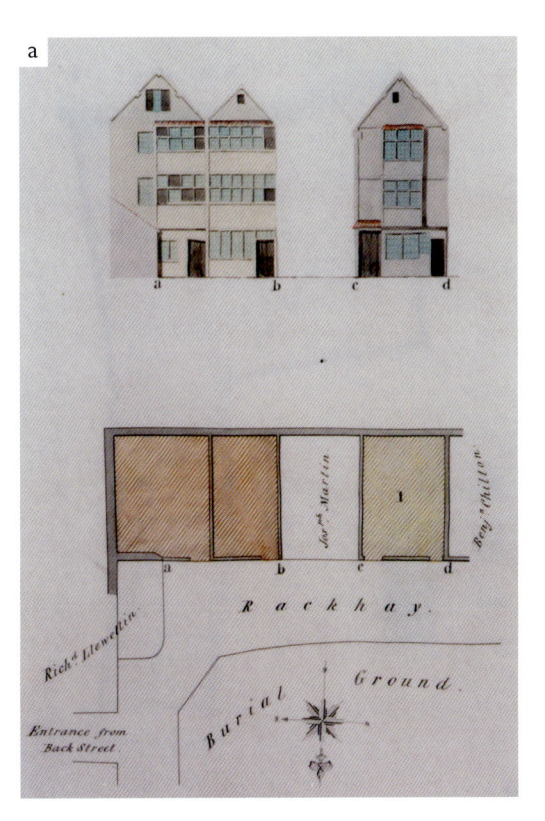

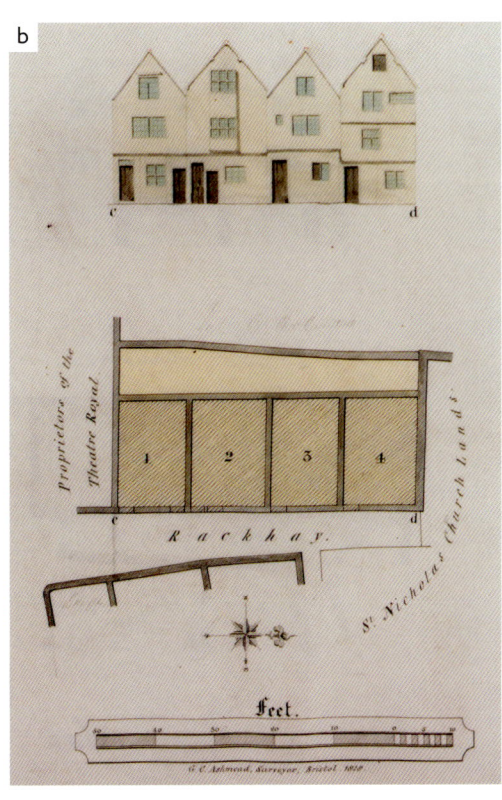

*Fig 8.32*
*The Rackhay in the 1820s: (a–b) – houses recorded in the book of plans of the church lands of St Nicholas (BRO 39180 fols 13–14).*

191

When first recorded in 1567 the 10 houses were all held under a head lease granted to Edmond Jones, a clothier.[22] Possibly these houses were built initially for his workers, employed in his 'wourck house' close to the Rackhay and his own house on Welsh Back (chapter 6).[23] The exceptional provision of light to the upper floors of some of the houses suggests that a form of industrial activity, perhaps weaving, was carried out in the workers' homes.

Provision of housing for textile workers may have been made at an earlier date in St Thomas Street. Here the development of 12 or more small houses already mentioned (see Fig 5.1b), known as 'Haveryngis Rent' by 1506, was probably built in the former garden, known as Averings Hayes.[24] The 'long rowe of houses' was recorded in 1607 and lay in close proximity to racks for the drying of cloths (Fig 8.33). Recent excavations have revealed the constructional details of these houses, confirming that each was of *c* 20ft in depth and therefore probably of one room on each floor (Fig 8.34).[25]

In two further locations, small dwellings of this type were certainly built to house industrial workers. At the Great House on St Augustine's Back, a sugar house or factory from *c* 1653, some 13 workmen's houses were built at a cost of

*Fig 8.33*
*Averings Hayes in 1673 (BRSMG, Millerd's map of 1673).*

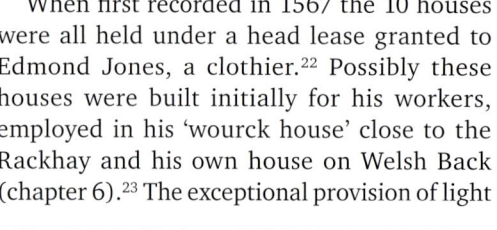

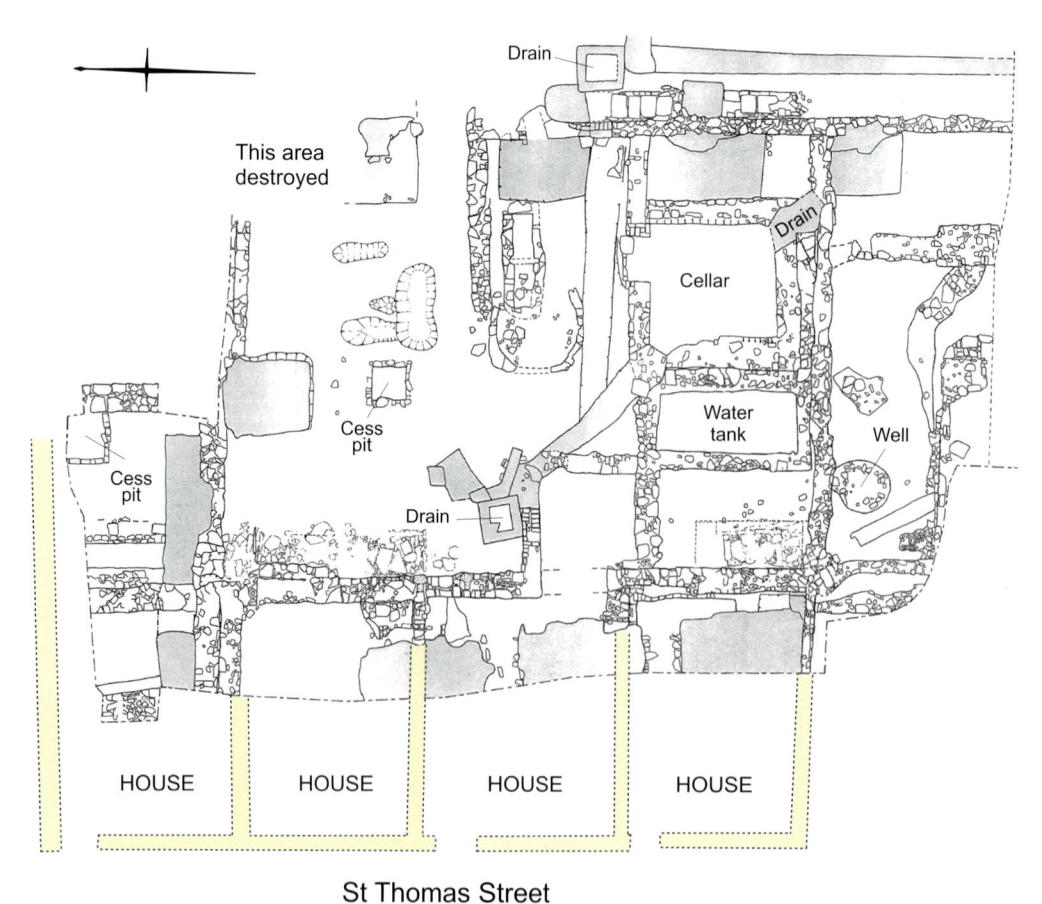

*Fig 8.34*
*Averings Hayes, south end of St Thomas Street, ground-floor plans of houses excavated in 2006 (BaRAS); see also Fig 5.1.*

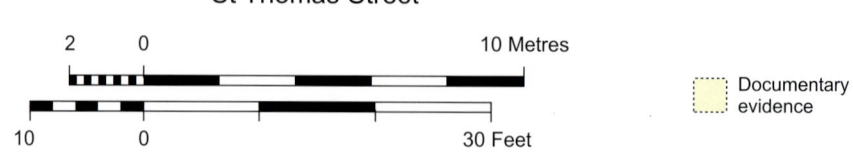

# THE RESIDENTIAL HOUSE

£1,200 for its proprietor John Knight in 1661.[26] Disposed around two sides of a courtyard to the west of the Great House, later named 'Chapel Court', these houses were similar in size to most of those in the Rackhay. Each consisted of three storeys, with one room on each floor and a small yard to the rear (Figs 8.35a, 8.35b and 8.35c).

## Almshouses

A further setting for the house of one-room plan was the almshouse. The earliest almshouse in Bristol was possibly Burton's in Long Row, which claimed to have been founded c 1292. This house was twice later rebuilt, however, so we must turn to others to see the authentic plan and form of a medieval almshouse. At least two were of a similar plan, utilising the form of a long medieval tenement plot set out in the early medieval period (chapter 2). Spencer's Almshouse in Lewin's Mead, founded c 1493, was recorded on both a Braikenridge watercolour and on Ashmead's map of 1828 (Figs 8.36a and 8.36b).[27] This followed the conventional plan of many medieval almshouses with a long row of dwellings; from their appearance, each probably consisted of one room down one side of a long tenement plot. In the 16th century a similar plan was adopted for the almshouses founded by Dr Thomas White in Temple Street, the dwellings for the poor being set out along the north side of the plot purchased for the almshouse (Figs 8.37a and 8.37b).

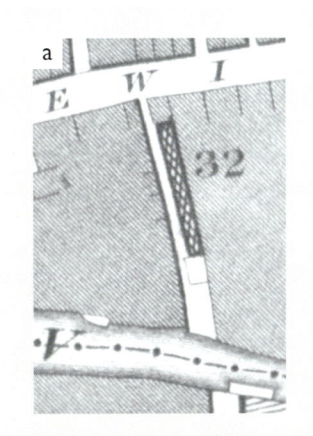

*Fig 8.35 (above)
St Augustine's Place, houses for workers in the sugar refinery, built c 1661:
a) plan from Millerd's map of 1673 (BRSMG);
b) later 19th-century photograph of houses (BRSMG Photographs Box 1, fol L [Lady Huntingdon Court]);
c) OS map, 1884.*

*Fig 8.36 (left)
Spencer's Almshouses, Lewin's Mead:
a) extract from Ashmead's map of 1828;
b) watercolour by H O'Neill, 1821 (BRSMG M2867).*

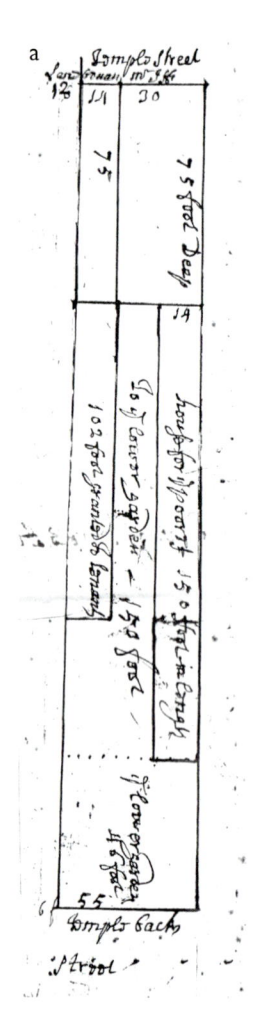

*Fig 8.37 (above and above right)*
*Dr White's Almshouses, Temple Street:*
*a) plan, not dated but probably of the 18th century (BRO 12966/155);*
*b) watercolour by H O'Neill, 1821 (BRSMG M2131).*

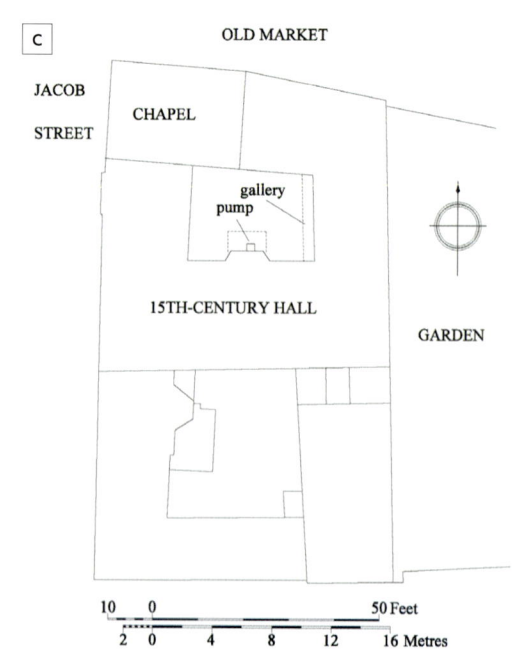

*Fig 8.38 (far right above, centre and below)*
*Trinity Almshouse, south side of Old Market:*
*(a-b) views of the courtyard, drawings by S G Tovey, 1841 (BRSMG M3963–4);*
*c) interpretive plan (RHL) based on plan of c 1850 (BRO 33041/BMC/12/PL8 fol 39).*

A different plan was that adopted for Trinity Almshouse on the south side of Old Market. It was founded before the end of the 14th century and recorded in drawings of the 1820s and of 1841, prior to its later rebuilding. Here the almshouse lodgings were ranged around a small courtyard. Rooms on the ground and first floors were on the east side and rooms with lateral chimneystacks on the south and west. The room on the west was probably an open hall, having one lofty mullioned window overlooking the courtyard (Figs 8.38a, 8.38b and 8.38c).

From the mid-17th century other designs were adopted for newly founded or rebuilt almshouses. These fall into two categories. Firstly, there were at least three almshouses built or rebuilt to appear from the exterior to be one large building. The earliest of these was St Nicholas's almshouse in King Street, built *c* 1656 on land granted to the parish of St Nicholas by the Corporation of Bristol in 1652 – this gift to be commemorated by 'the arms of the city of Bristol, fairly engraven, over the door or entrance of the said almshouse' (Fig 8.39).[28] Another, Burton's almshouse in Long Row, was rebuilt in 1721. This, too, had a single main facade with a commemorative plaque over the entrance, celebrating the original foundation and the rebuilding; but unlike the St Nicholas's almshouse it had separate doorways to the houses either side of the main entrance (Figs 8.40a and 8.40b). The third almshouse, designed so as to appear to be a single building, was Ridley's almshouse at the corner of Milk Street, built *c* 1739. Under the will of Sarah Ridley, who died in 1716, an almshouse for five men and five women was to be built in memory of her and her brother. The trustees, mainly merchants of Bristol, were to buy or build the almshouses 'as they thought best'.[29] Their thoughts were clearly directed to building a single large structure of Classical form, while

THE RESIDENTIAL HOUSE

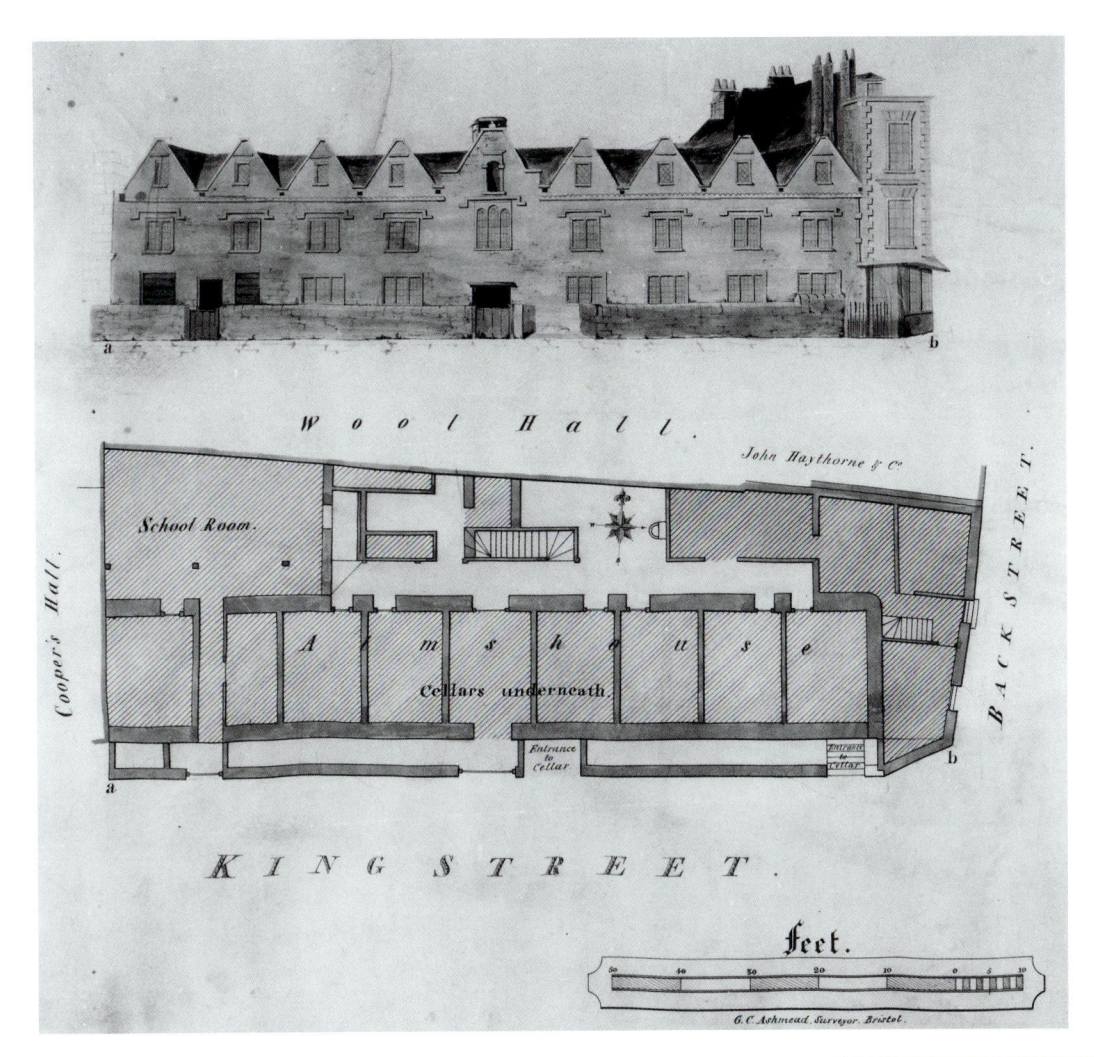

*Fig 8.39*
*St Nicholas's Almhouse, King Street, plan and elevation (BRO 39180).*

*Fig 8.40*
*Burton's Almshouse, Long Row:*
*a) plan of ground floor (drawn for Sir George Oatley by A R P Newman, October 1942, architect's collection, now in University of Bristol Special Collections);*
*b) watercolour by H O'Neill, 1822 (BRSMG M2087).*

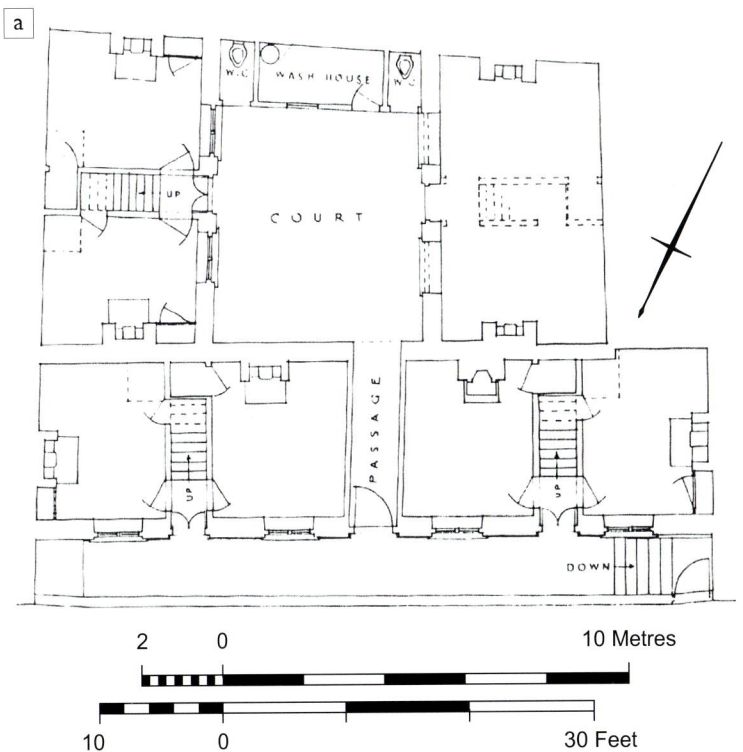

195

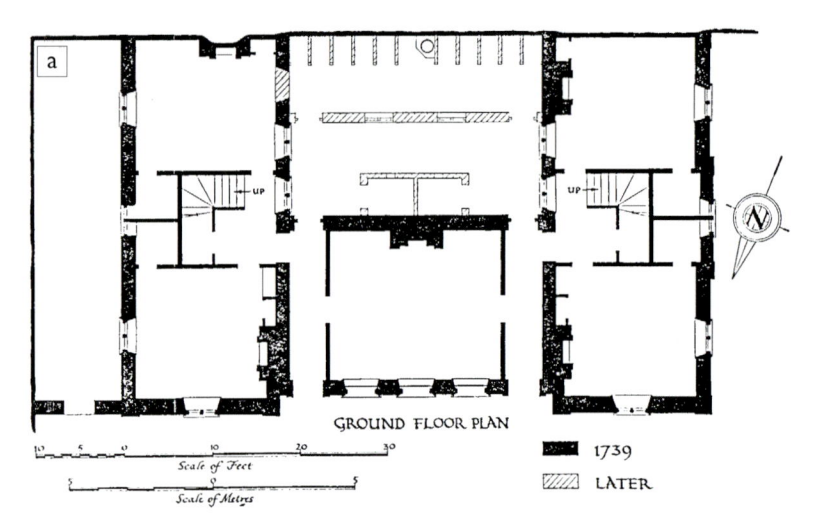

*Fig 8.41*
*Ridley's Almshouse, Milk Street:*
*(a–b) –plan and view (O'Neil 1951, 57–8).*

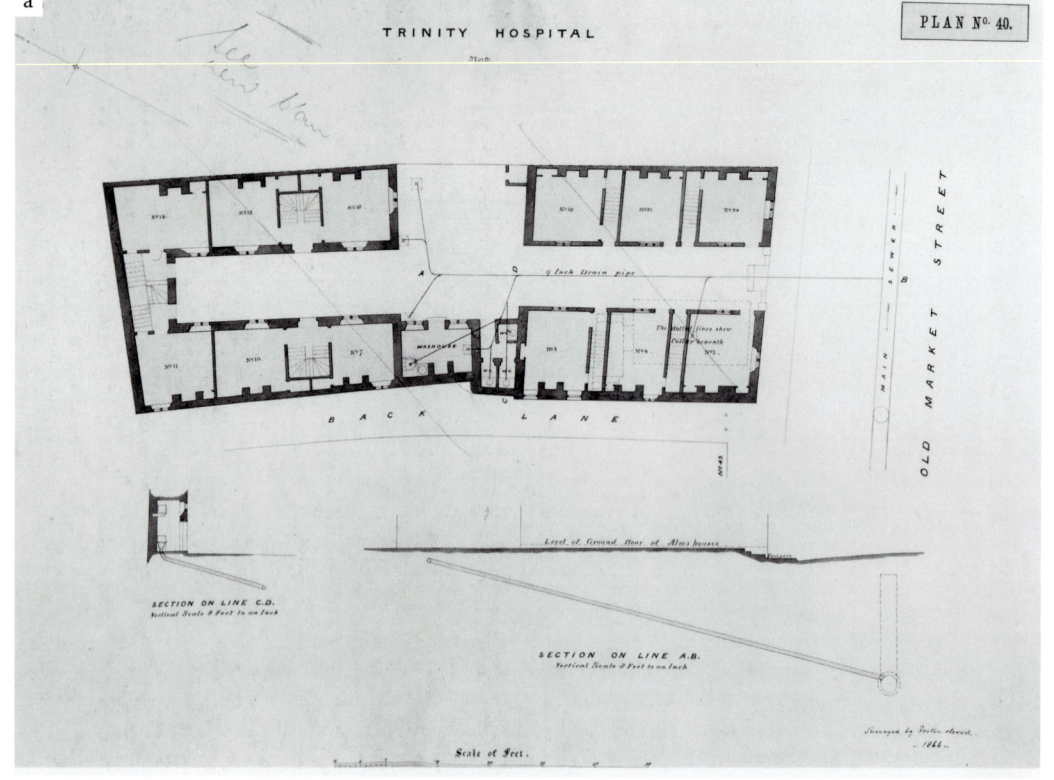

*Fig 8.42*
*Trinity Almshouse, north side of Old Market:*
*a) plan by Foster Wood 1866 (BRO 33041/BMC/12/PL 1 fol 40);*
*b) watercolour by H O'Neill, 1822 (BRSMG M2763).*

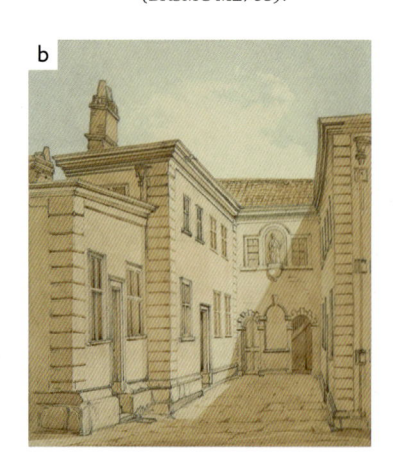

retaining mullioned and transomed windows of a style more appropriate to the 17th century (Figs 8.41a and 8.41b). Perhaps older people needed to be housed in dwellings of an older appearance.

The second solution to rebuilding or planning a new almshouse was to place the lodgings around a courtyard. The north part of the Trinity Hospital on the north side of Old Market was apparently rebuilt in this way in the late 17th or early 18th century; the design can be analysed from the evidence of watercolours of the 1820s and from a plan of 1866 (Figs 8.42a and 8.42b). From these it can be deduced that the ranges of buildings were of two storeys, with the almshouses on each floor. This would not have been evident from looking simply at the exterior of the buildings, which on every side of the courtyard appear to be each of four bays in width, with an entrance doorway set to one side.

Looking at other almshouses in the city, it is evident that this was a widely employed device. The Merchants' Almshouse in King Street (Figs 8.43a and 8.43b) and Colston's Almshouses on St Michael's Hill, two foundations administered by the Society of Merchant Venturers, were of a similar design. Standing within the courtyard of the Merchants' Almshouse, before one half of the complex was destroyed in the Blitz in 1941,

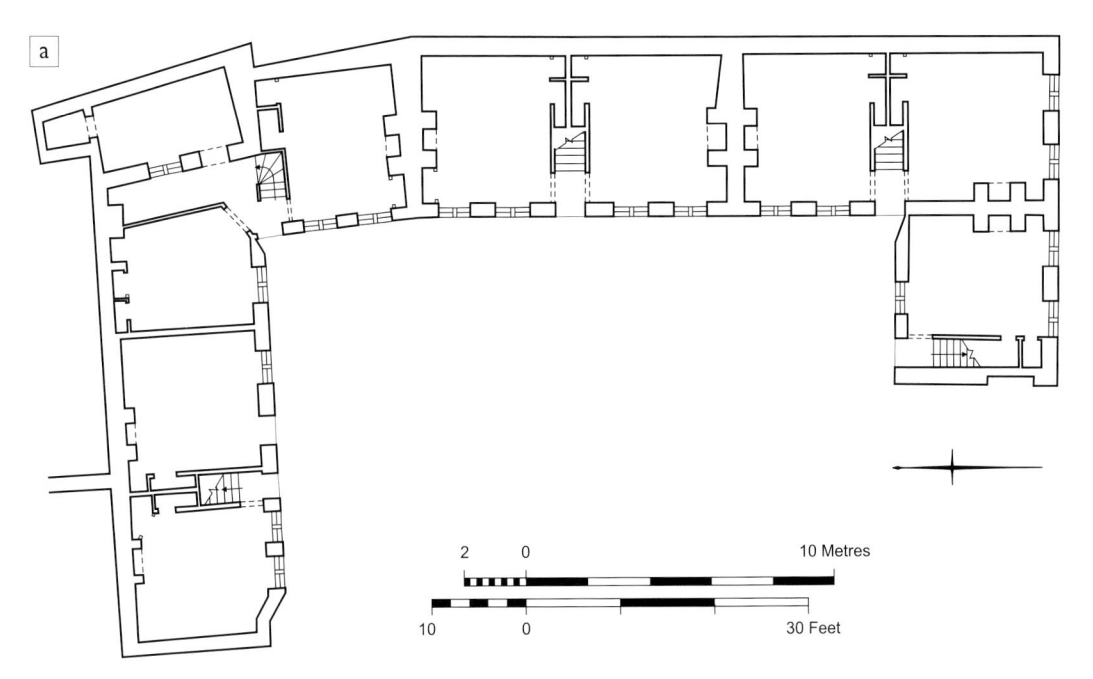

*Fig 8.43
Merchants' Almshouse,
King Street:
a) plan
(RHL, PEC; after BRO
Buildings Plans vol 80,
fol 39b);
b) photograph of 1978
(NMR BB78/9431).*

one would have seen seven apparently separate dwellings; each consisted of two storeys and of five bays in width, with an entrance doorway in the centre. On closer examination, this would have emerged as an illusion. Every centre doorway led to four separate lodgings, each comprising one room with its own internal entrance: a total of 28 almshouses in all.

The elite of Bristol were not alone in their use of this architectural device. In *c* 1780 houses of this plan were built at Milton Abbas in Dorset, to accommodate the dispossessed and forcibly moved inhabitants of the town demolished to create a park for the Earl of Ilchester.[30] In the 1840s Isambard Kingdom Brunel employed the same plan for the workers' housing in the Railway Village at Swindon.[31] The 'kind and generous care', proclaimed in verse on one range facing the courtyard of the Merchants' Almshouse in King Street, was designed to appear more kind and generous than it really was. David Hancock has shown how, 'in extending alms to the needy', merchants 'demonstrated their power and influence over others in society', and how for these merchants 'house building lay at the heart of the construction of social identity'.[32] In Bristol the philanthropic construction and rebuilding of almshouses mirrored the spiritual aspirations and social identity of the merchant elite.

## The One-Room Wide, Two-Room Deep Town House

The smallest of the house types discussed by Roger North in the 1680s was the house of '2 rooms on a floor, with a closet, that is used in the city, and is the comon forme of all late built houses'. North added that this plan was 'not fit for the country, and is confined to cittys where divers houses stand contiguously in range'.[33] In an urban context houses of this type, of two rooms on each floor, were generally placed on a narrow plot, set at right angles to the street. The compiler of the Rawlinson collection, again in the late 17th century, included plans of a number of houses of this type, with variations in the positioning of the stairs and the chimneystacks. The stairs could be placed in the centre of the house, at the end of the hall and also alongside the hall. The chimneystacks could be on the side walls or on internal walls; fireplaces could be central to the room or placed in the corner.[34]

Moving forward to the 1720s, the anonymous compiler of *The Kingsweston Book of Drawings* provided some valuable thoughts on the variations by then deemed most appropriate for this building type in Bristol. Two narrow houses in Prince Street, either side of a larger house destined for a merchant (Fig 8.44), were of identical plan. Each had a front 'best parlour' and a rear 'back parlour', with the stairs at the end of the hall alongside the rear parlour; a counting house and detached kitchen were located in the courtyard to the rear (Appendix 1).[35]

In its simplest form, the two-room deep town house consisted on the ground floor of a parlour and kitchen, or two parlours. Builders utilised the form of the two-room deep shophouse, with the front parlour, often heated, replacing the unheated shop (chapter 6). In most of the earliest two-room deep residential houses, the space provided on the ground floor for the entertainment of visitors was limited to the front room, while the rear part of the house served as the kitchen. A number of the early houses in King Street were of this type, being residential houses rather than shophouses. Built by 1658 (chapter 7), nos.33–4 King Street is now the oldest house in the street; it is the sole survivor of those built there on the north side, up against the city wall. The ground-floor front room is heated by an ornamented fireplace of the mid-17th century, indicating that it was designed as a parlour rather than as a shop (Fig 8.45; *see* Fig 7.35).

On the opposite side of the street nos.3–5 are the surviving houses of a row of five constructed under building leases granted in 1663. Each is of identical plan (Figs 8.46 and 8.47a). The arrangement of the ground floors is similar to that of no.33, both ground-floor rooms being provided with fireplaces. Here, though, there is even stronger evidence for the front room having been intended as a parlour. The earlier plan of each house is indicated by the evidence of ceiling cornices for partitions, since removed, which screened the room from the street door. In each of the houses as built, access to the room was not directly from the street, as for a shop, but only indirectly from the side passage leading to the wider rear room – the latter probably a kitchen. The front room, accessed only from the corridor, could, therefore, be interpreted as a parlour. This was certainly the arrangement of no.5 in 1705, when it contained the possessions of the cooper Aaron Williams. The probate inventory made then of his possessions (Appendix 2) lists the contents of the house room by room, and names the two rooms on the ground floor as the parlour and kitchen.[36]

Similarly planned residential houses were found in Lewin's Mead. In 1689 the contents of the house of the recently deceased wealthy brewer Andrew Hook were enumerated room

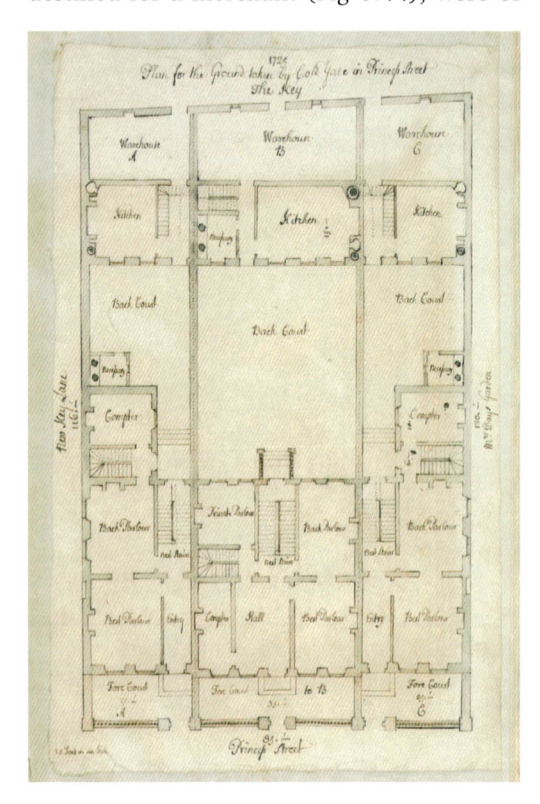

*Fig 8.44*
*Nos.50–4 Prince Street, from* The Kingsweston Book of Drawings *(BRO 33746).*

THE RESIDENTIAL HOUSE

*Fig 8.45
Moulded stone chimneypiece to fireplace in ground-floor front room of no.33 King Street, photograph of 1997 (NMR AA005690).*

*Fig 8.46
Nos.1–5 King Street, photograph of 1937; no.5 (Aaron Williams' house) is closest to the camera (NMR OP07431).*

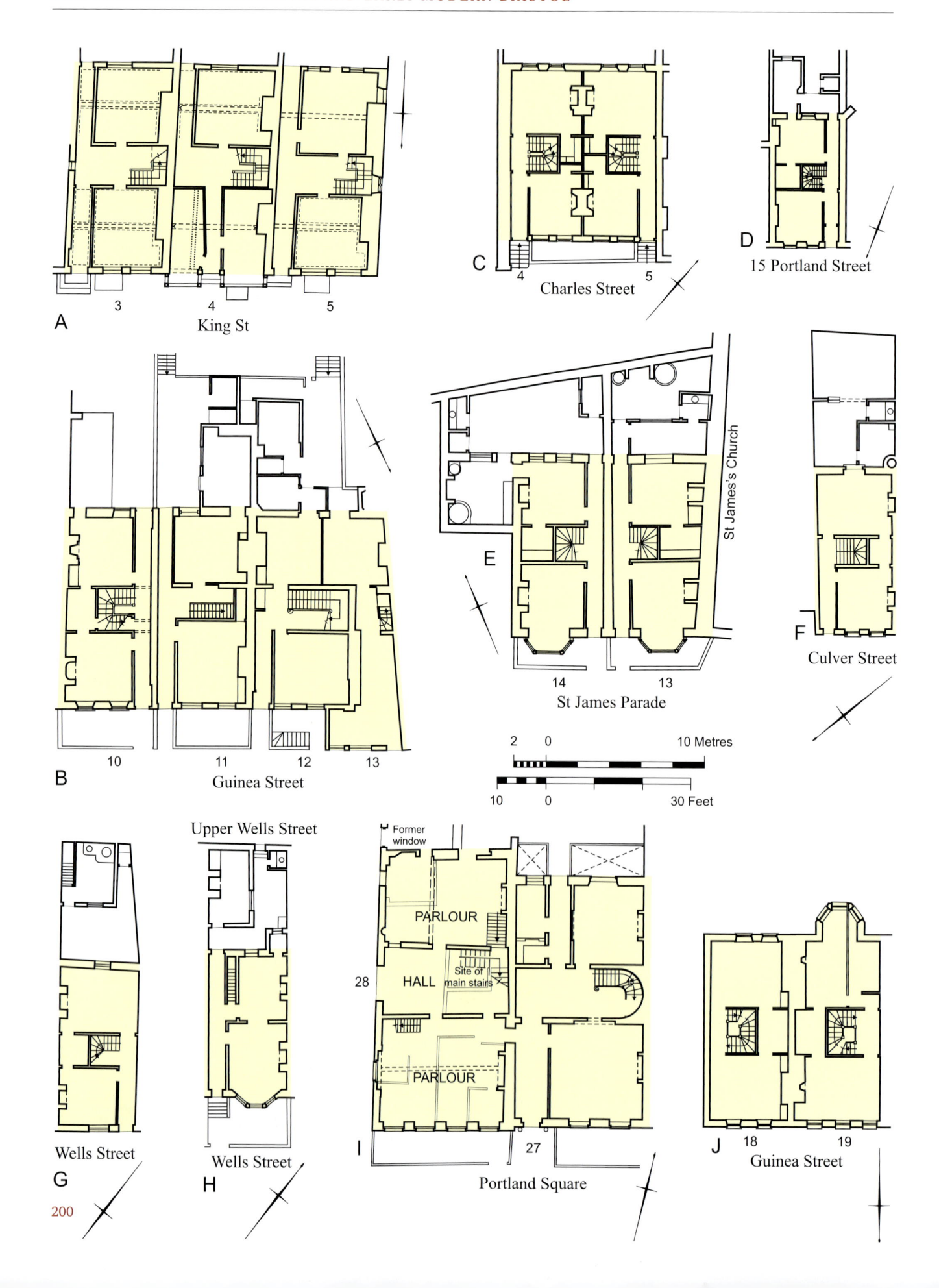

THE TOWN HOUSE IN MEDIEVAL AND EARLY MODERN BRISTOL

A  3  4  5  King St

B  10  11  12  13  Guinea Street

C  4  5  Charles Street

D  15 Portland Street

E  14  13  St James Parade / St James's Church

F  Culver Street

2  0  10 Metres
10  0  30 Feet

G  Wells Street

H  Upper Wells Street / Wells Street

I  28  27  Portland Square
PARLOUR
HALL
Site of main stairs
PARLOUR
Former window

J  18  19  Guinea Street

200

by room for the probate inventory of his possessions. On the ground floor were the kitchen and parlour. Their location is confirmed by the sequence followed on the first floor, which lists first the contents of the 'chamber over the kitchen' and then those of the 'forestreet room over the parlour' (Appendix 2). In 1674 Hook's near neighbour, Henry Dighton, lived in a similarly arranged house.[37]

The form of the larger shophouse with a detached kitchen to the rear could be similarly adapted to provide an entirely residential house. Two parlours could be located on the ground floor of the main part of the dwelling, with the kitchen being sited in a separate building to the rear. Built c 1666 at the corner of Castle Green and Castle Street, no.34 Castle Street would have been readily identifiable as an entirely residential house. Here the two principal rooms on the ground floor were both used as parlours; each was furnished with a full-height stone chimneypiece of the mid-17th century, and the kitchen was set in a separate unit to the rear (Figs 8.48 and 8.49).[38]

## The Central-Stairs Plan

In 1678 Joseph Moxon wrote in his *Mechanick Exercises* that the master-workman would need to consider that 'a Gentleman's House must not be divided as a Shop-keeper's'. It was probably the choice of where to position the staircase that he had in mind. In Bristol the use of the central-stairs plan, where the stair was placed between front and rear rooms, had been almost ubiquitous in houses of the 17th century; it is found, for example, in both the shophouses and residential houses of Castle Street and King Street. In the residential house such a placement of the stairs hid it from the view of those entering the house via the long, narrow side passage alongside the front room. The visual effect of a finely finished stairs, such as those at nos.25–31 (odd) Victoria Street, formerly nos.128–31 St Thomas Street, or at no.16 King Street was not obtained until one was at the very foot of the stairs (Figs 8.50 and 8.51).

The central-stairs plan continued in use well into the 18th century, although by then alternative plans were known and employed in Bristol. It was used in two rows of houses built for, or by, ships' captains in Guinea Street in the 1720s and 1730s. Given their extensive wanderings and experiences of other cultures, it is perhaps a little surprising to find ships'

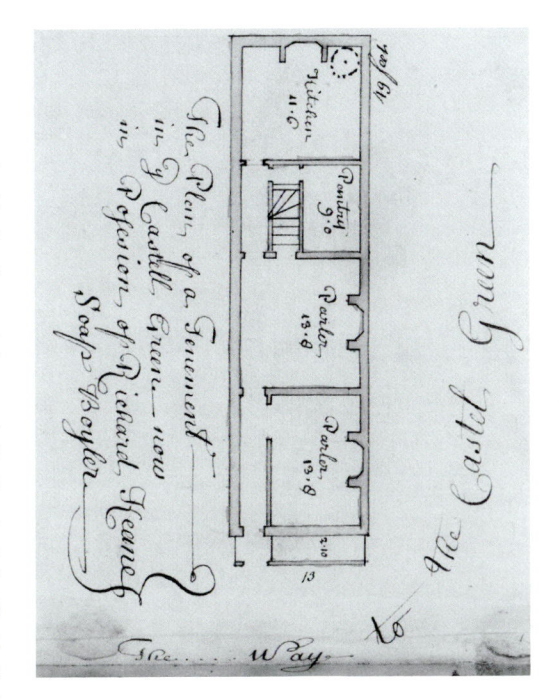

*Fig 8.47 (opposite)*
Plans of houses two rooms in depth with the stairs in the centre (RHL, PEC):
a) nos.3–5 King Street;
b) nos.10–12 Guinea Street;
c) nos.4–5 Charles Street;
d) no.15 Portland Street;
e) nos.13–14 St James's Parade;
f) no.1 Culver Street;
g) no.8 Wells Street;
h) no.2 Wells Street;
i) nos.27-28 Portland Square;
j) nos.18-19 Guinea Street.

*Fig 8.48 (above left)*
No.34 Castle Street, built c 1666, plan of 18th century (BRO 04479(1) fol 85).

*Fig 8.49 (left)*
No.34 Castle Street, chimneypiece in ground-floor rear room dated 1666, photograph of the late 19th or early 20th century (BRSMG Mb993).

*Fig 8.50 (below left)*
No.31 Victoria Street, formerly no.128 St Thomas Street, showing centrally placed stairs, looking down from the second floor, photograph of 1998 (NMR AA98/02835).

*Fig 8.51 (below right)*
No.16 King Street, centrally placed stairs, looking upwards, photograph of 2001 (RHL).

captains showing strongly conservative tastes; or perhaps it rather reveals a hankering for solid and tested forms. Edmund Saunders, himself a ship's captain, seems to have first conceived nos.10–12 Guinea Street as a row of three houses, each with a central stairs (Figs 8.47b and 8.52). Saunders then took and re-planned nos.11–12 for his own use; no.10 remained separately occupied by a succession of ships' captains.

In Guinea Street nos.5–7 were a second row of three, all with a centrally placed stairs, completed between 1744 and 1754 (Figs 8.53 and 8.54).[39] Ships' mariners first occupied two of the houses.[40] The use of the plan in houses of superior quality can be seen at nos.4–5 Charles Street: two houses that were well finished, from the quality of the exterior brickwork to the details of the interior trim and joinery, including the staircases (Figs 8.47c and 8.55). Charles Wesley (the hymn writer and younger brother of John Wesley), who lived at no.4 from 1766–71, judged the house as adequate for the needs of his family. A little to the west of Charles Street, Wesley might have been familiar with the row of houses of similar plan built in the late 17th and early 18th centuries in St James's Parade (Fig 8.47e).

A pair of similarly planned houses, nos.5 and 6 Clifton Wood Road were built c 1774 in an area characterised by aspirations to gentility.[41] The same central-stairs plan was used for the majority of houses in Culver Street and Wells Street, built c 1775 (Figs 8.47f, 8.47g, 8.47h, 8.56a, 8.56b and 8.57); many of the houses built in Somerset Street in the 1770s and 80s were of similar plan (see Inventory). The occasional use of the plan certainly continued into the 1790s, with no.15 Portland Street, Kingsdown built to this plan c 1791 (Fig 8.47d).[42]

The central-stairs plan also continued to be utilised for some of the smallest two-room deep houses, as well as in streets with fewer aspirations to gentility. Formerly known as Smith Street, Ellbroad Street had been the home of tanners and related trades since at least the 15th century. One plot away from a bark mill, and possibly even closer to some of the tanning pits, nos.23–33 comprised 'five good and useful' three-storey houses, rebuilt c 1731.[43] Built on the street frontage of a much larger plot with industrial buildings behind, these houses were entirely residential in use (Figs 8.58 and 8.59). A matching pair of two-room deep houses, nos.110–11 Temple Street were built c 1735 (see Inventory); similar in plan to nos.23–33 Ellbroad

*Fig 8.52*
*Nos.10–12 Guinea Street, photograph of 1998 (NMR BB98/01126).*

THE RESIDENTIAL HOUSE

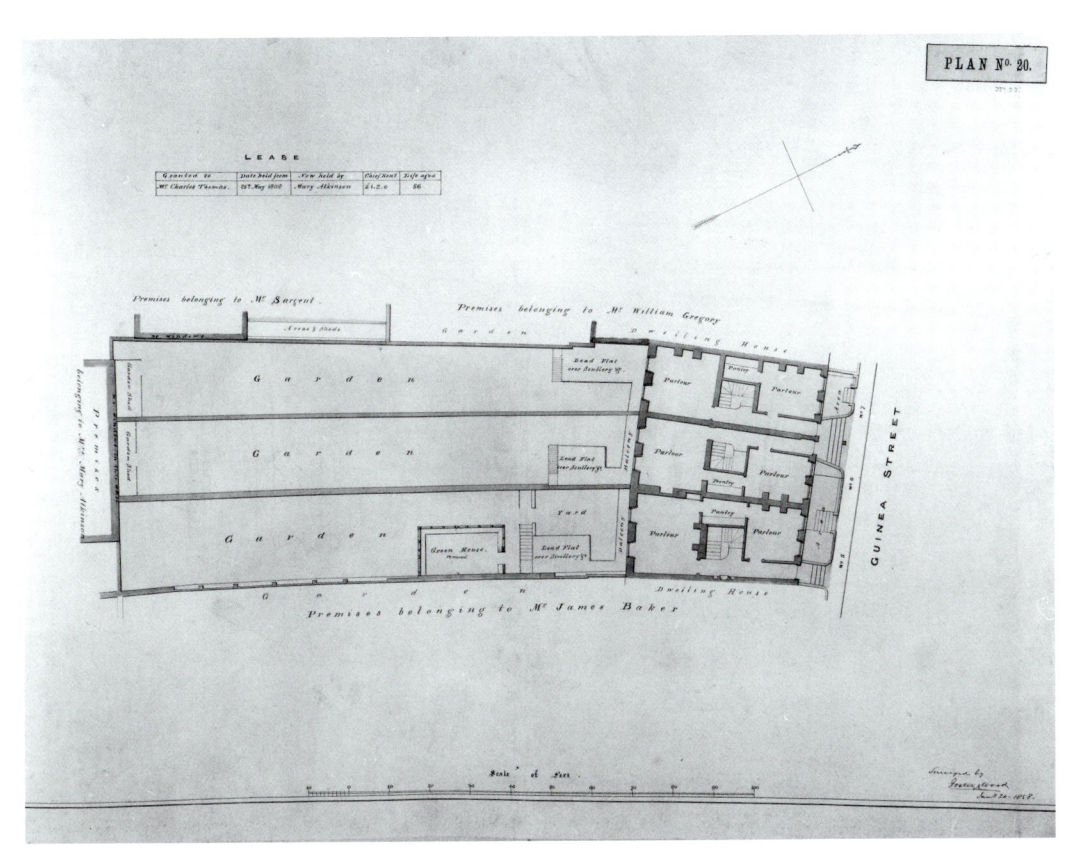

*Fig 8.53*
*Nos.5–7 Guinea Street, plan of ground floor, 1858 (BRO 33041/BMC/12/PL1 fol 20).*

*Fig 8.54 (left)*
*Nos.5–7 Guinea Street, photograph of 1906 (BRO 33041/BMC/12/1).*

*Fig 8.55*
*Nos.4–5 Charles Street, photograph of 2010 (English Heritage DP114106).*

Street, they were among the smallest two-room deep houses built in the 18th century. These houses were built on narrow plots, where the rear-stairs plan was less practical.

Recent research has focused on the use of the central stairs in the context of London and the wider Atlantic world.[44] In Bristol, as in London, a superficial reading of the surviving architectural evidence could lead one to suppose a replacement of the central-stairs plan by one that placed the stairs alongside the rear room – a development that was driven by changing

203

## THE TOWN HOUSE IN MEDIEVAL AND EARLY MODERN BRISTOL

Fig 8.56
Wells Street and Culver Street, ground-floor plans of houses:
a) nos.2 and 4, mid-19th-century plan
(BRO DC/E/40/65/50140);
b) no.12, mid-19th-century plan
(BRO DC/E/40/65/50167).

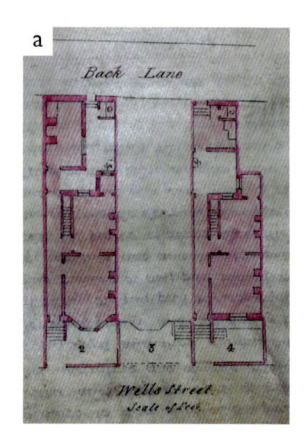

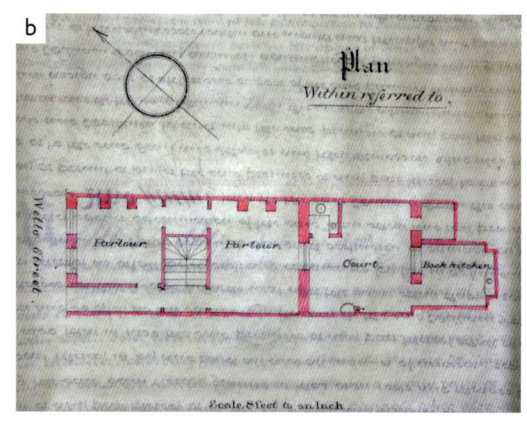

Fig 8.57
Wells Street, west side, photograph of 1960
(Reece Winstone Archive 34749).

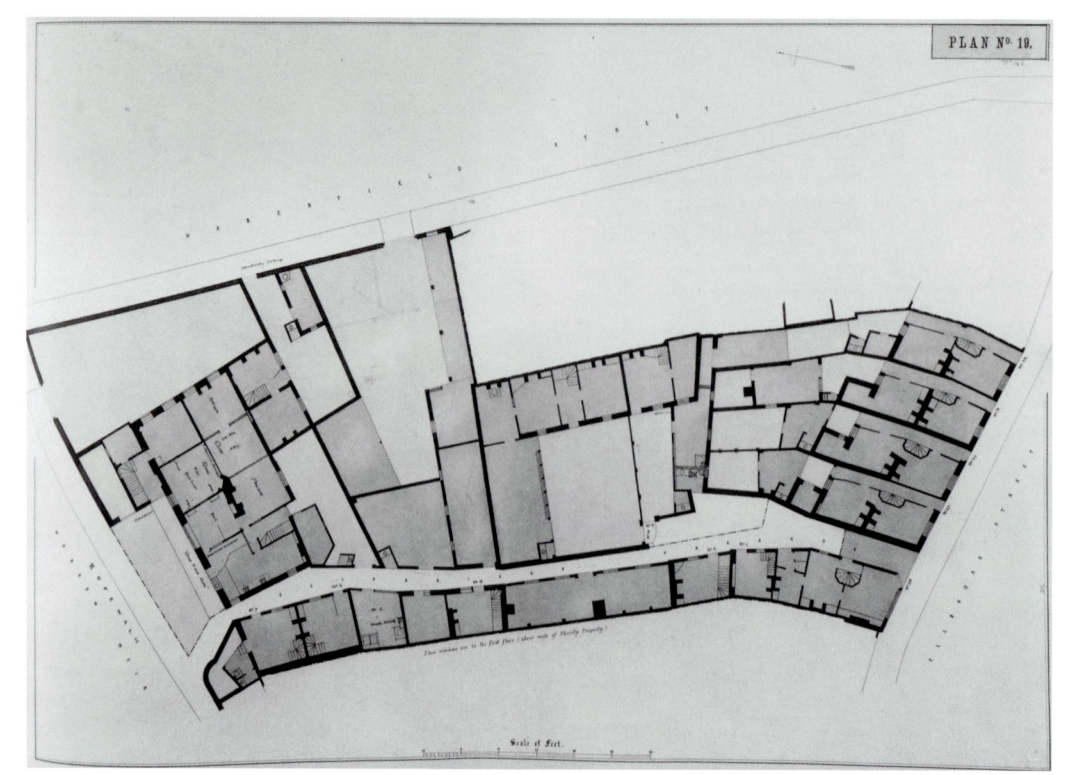

Fig 8.58
Nos.25–33 Ellbroad Street, plan of ground floor, probably of the 1850s
(BRO 33041/BMC/12/PL1 fol 19).

fashion. This idea of simple succession of one form by another is, however, derived from a sample of surviving houses that is weighted in favour of the more prestigious and larger houses with rear staircases. A closer reading of the evidence indicates that the central-stairs plan continued to be used throughout the 18th century, and not only in very modest houses. The Bristol evidence is a useful corrective in showing the persistence of the central-stairs plan at a range of social levels. Different needs, rather than fashion, may have been the determining influence in dictating the choice of plan.

In Bristol, as in the wider Atlantic world, the central-stairs plan was particularly appropriate for houses in multiple occupation. Herman has shown how houses in Portsmouth, New Hampshire were divided vertically, the widow's portion often being one or other of the two vertical halves of the house. Houses in 17th-century Bristol were sometimes divided in similar ways for multiple occupation.[45]

## The Rear-Stairs Plan

Placing the stairs alongside the rear room of the house brought several advantages. The visual impact of a well-finished staircase could now be appreciated from the front door; and within this view the passage through the central wall dividing front and back parts of the house could be finished as an arch, underlining the importance of the route. The stairs could be lit via windows in the rear elevation, emphasising the visual impact still further and overcoming one of the chief drawbacks of the central stairs. The plan also provided advantages for the circulation of space. In the central-stairs house, access from one room to the other on each floor was only possible via the narrow landing at the head of the stairs. In a house with a rear-stairs plan, access could be either via a wider landing or directly between one room and the other.

The earliest house in Bristol to be designed in this way was probably Langton's shophouse at no.12 Welsh Back (chapter 6), built in *c* 1623; the next we know was no.74 Old Market, rebuilt *c* 1699 (Figs 8.60a and 8.61). From the 1700s onwards the majority of two-room deep houses were built to this plan. Close to Guinea Street it was employed in the building of no.9 Redcliff Parade *c* 1768, and for other houses in the same row (Figs 8.60c and 8.62),[46] while close to the church of St Mary Redcliff some of the new row of houses in Colston Parade had rear staircases (Figs 8.60b and 8.63).

Across the river many of the houses in the new streets of St Augustine's and St Michael's parishes were of similar plan, for instance in Orchard Street (Fig 8.64), both on the north (Figs 8.65 and 8.66) and south sides (Figs 8.67 and 8.68), Unity Street, Pipe Lane (Figs 8.69 and 8.70) and Trinity Street (Figs 8.71 and 8.72). On the east side of the city, many of the new houses built in and close to the new Brunswick and Portland Squares were also of this plan (Figs 8.60d and 8.73). In the building of most of the streets of houses on the slopes of Kingsdown, the rear-stairs plan was widely utilised over several decades. It featured in larger houses from King Square (Figs 8.60e and 8.74) and the adjacent streets (Figs 8.75 and 8.76) in the 1750s and 1760s to the building of the north part of Kingsdown Parade in the 1790s (Figs 8.60f and 8.77). The plan was also adopted in smaller houses, built in streets such as Cherry Lane, Portland Street and Alfred Place (Figs 8.60g, 8.60h and 10.36). Rebuilt and new houses on St Michael's Hill were mostly of this plan (Figs 8.60i, 8.60j and 8.60k). In the second half of the 18th century most of the new houses built in Clifton were of this same plan.

*Fig 8.59*
*Nos.25–33 Ellbroad Street, photograph of 1906 (BRO 33041/BMC/12/1).*

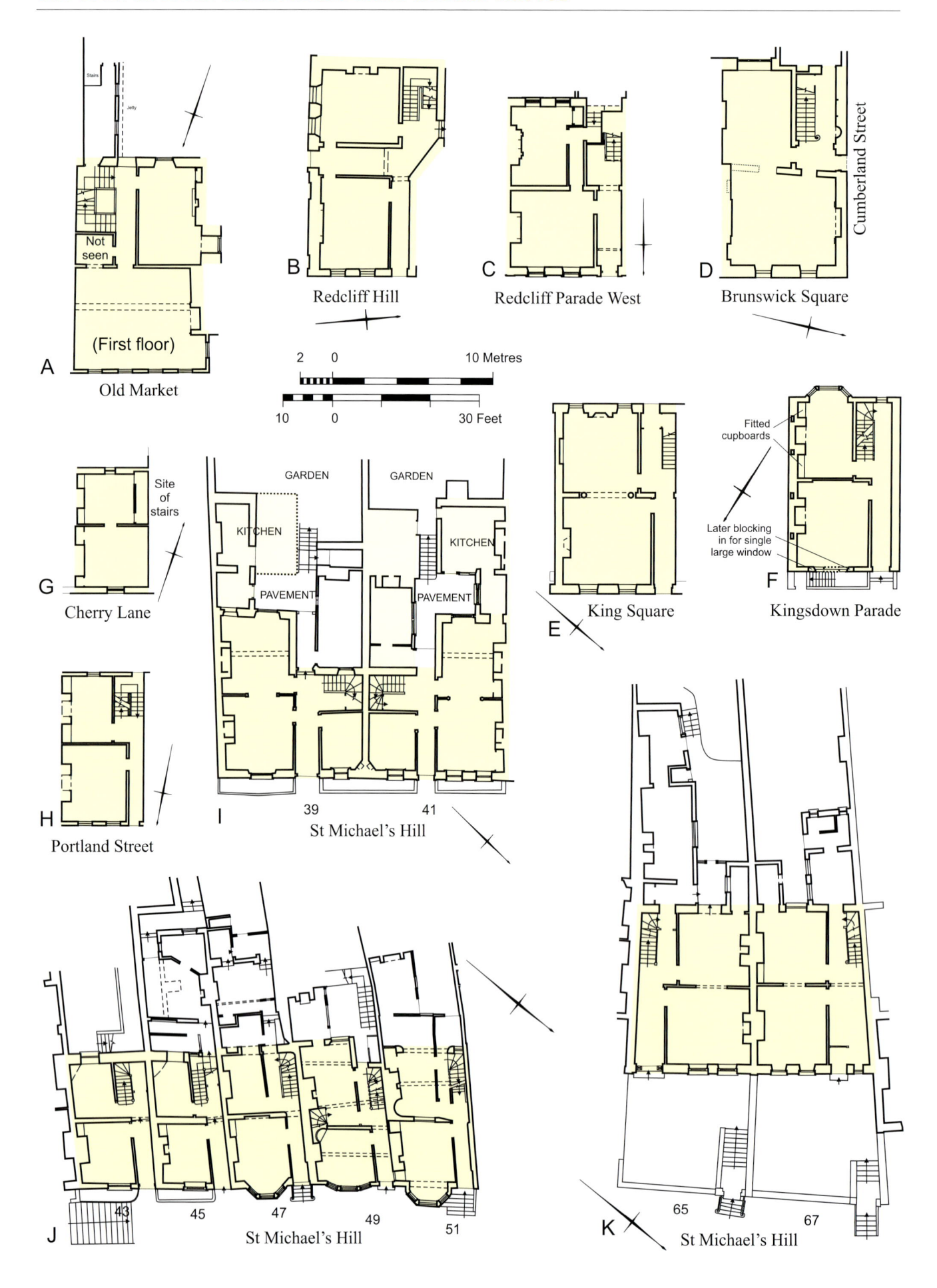

THE TOWN HOUSE IN MEDIEVAL AND EARLY MODERN BRISTOL

A Old Market (First floor)

B Redcliff Hill

C Redcliff Parade West

D Brunswick Square

2 0 10 Metres
10 0 30 Feet

G Cherry Lane — Site of stairs

H Portland Street

I St Michael's Hill — 39, 41 — GARDEN, KITCHEN, PAVEMENT

E King Square

F Kingsdown Parade — Fitted cupboards; Later blocking in for single large window

J St Michael's Hill — 43, 45, 47, 49, 51

K St Michael's Hill — 65, 67

THE RESIDENTIAL HOUSE

*Fig 8.60 (opposite)
Plans of houses two rooms in depth with the stairs alongside the rear room (RHL, PEC):
a) no.74 Old Market;
b) no.51 Redcliff Hill;
c) no.9 Redcliff Parade;
d) no.14 Brunswick Square;
e) no.5 King Square;
f) no.52 Kingsdown Parade;
g) no.16 Cherry Lane;
h) no.16 Portland Street;
i) nos.39-41 St Michael's Hill
j) nos. 43-51 St Michael's Hill
k) nos.65–7 St Michael's Hill.*

*Fig 8.61 (far left)
No.74 Old Market, stairs to first floor, drawing of 1910 by Samuel Loxton
(BCRL Loxton drawings).*

*Fig 8.62 (left)
Redcliff Parade viewed from the north, photograph of 2003
(NMR AA048246, JD).*

*Fig 8.63
Colston Parade, viewed from the east, photograph of 2010 (English Heritage DP 111034).*

207

*Fig 8.64*
*Orchard Street, looking west, photograph of 1941 (NMR BB41/00234).*

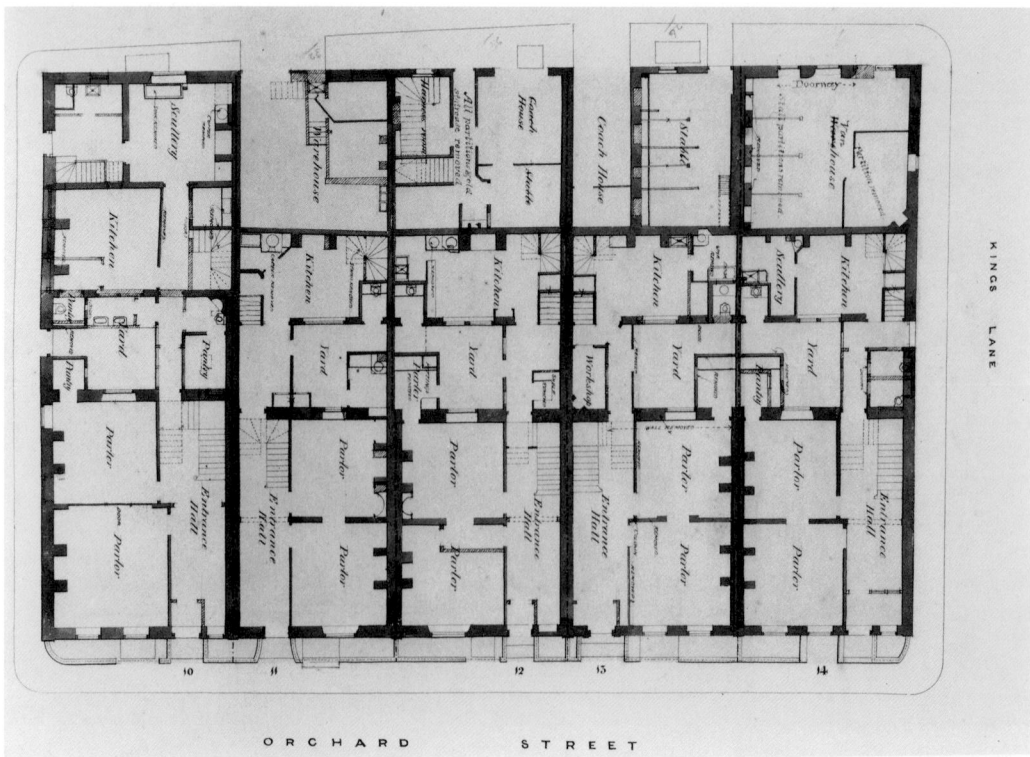

*Fig 8.65*
*Nos.10–14 Orchard Street, plan of the mid-19th century (BRO 33041/BMC/12/PL1 fol 42).*

THE RESIDENTIAL HOUSE

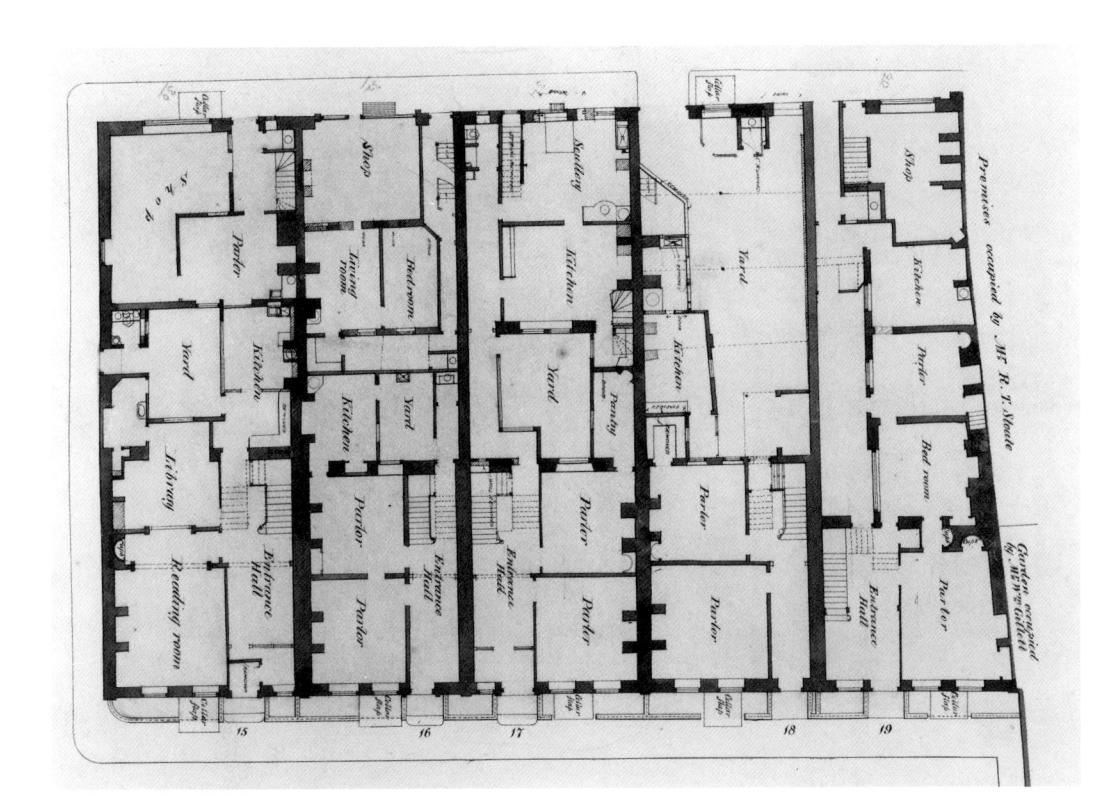

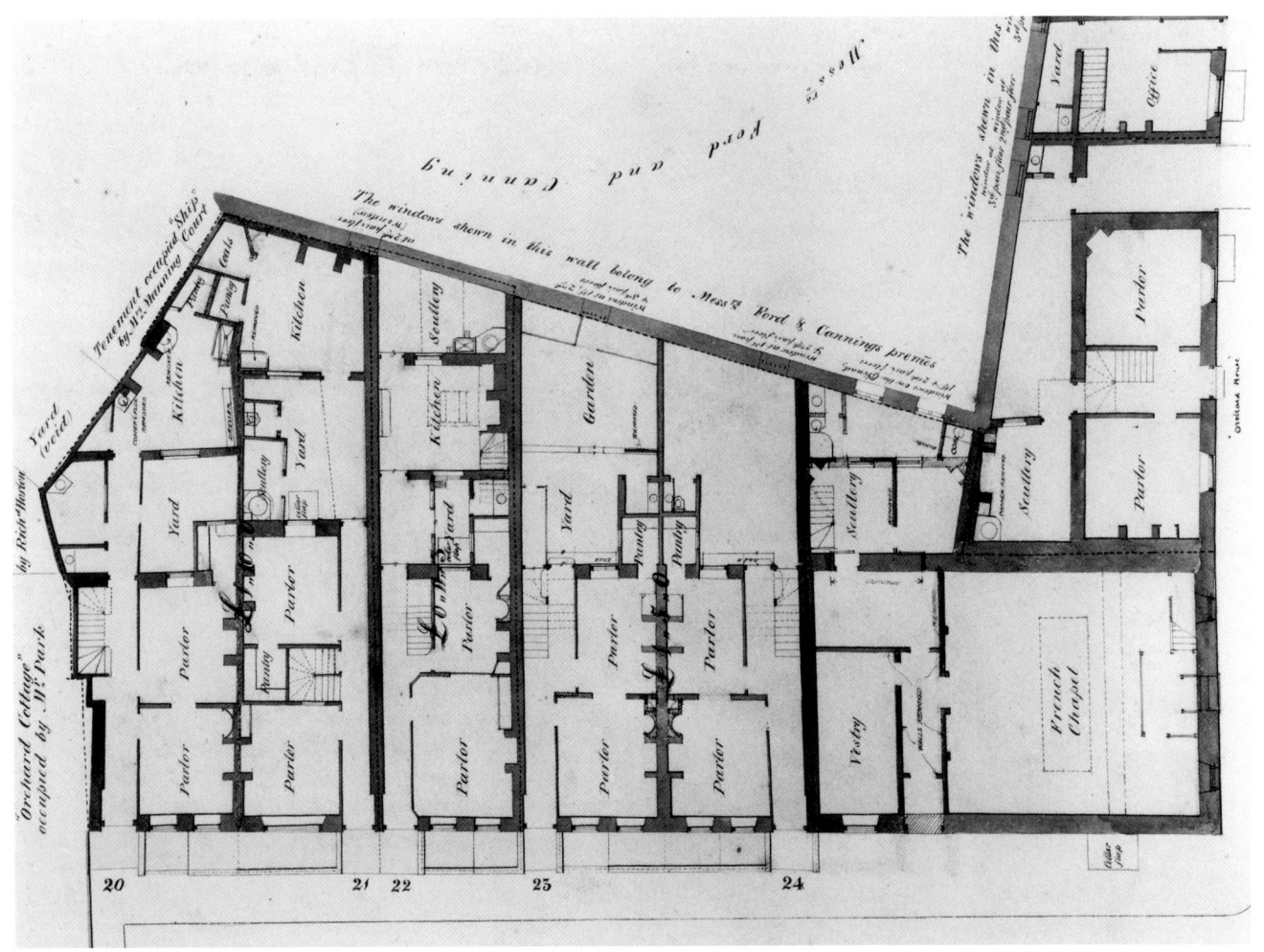

*Fig 8.66*
*Nos.15–19 Orchard Street, plan of the mid-19th century (BRO 33041/BMC/12/PL1 fol 43).*

*Fig 8.67*
*Nos.20–4 Orchard Street, plan of the mid-19th century (BRO 33041/BMC/12/PL1 fol 44).*

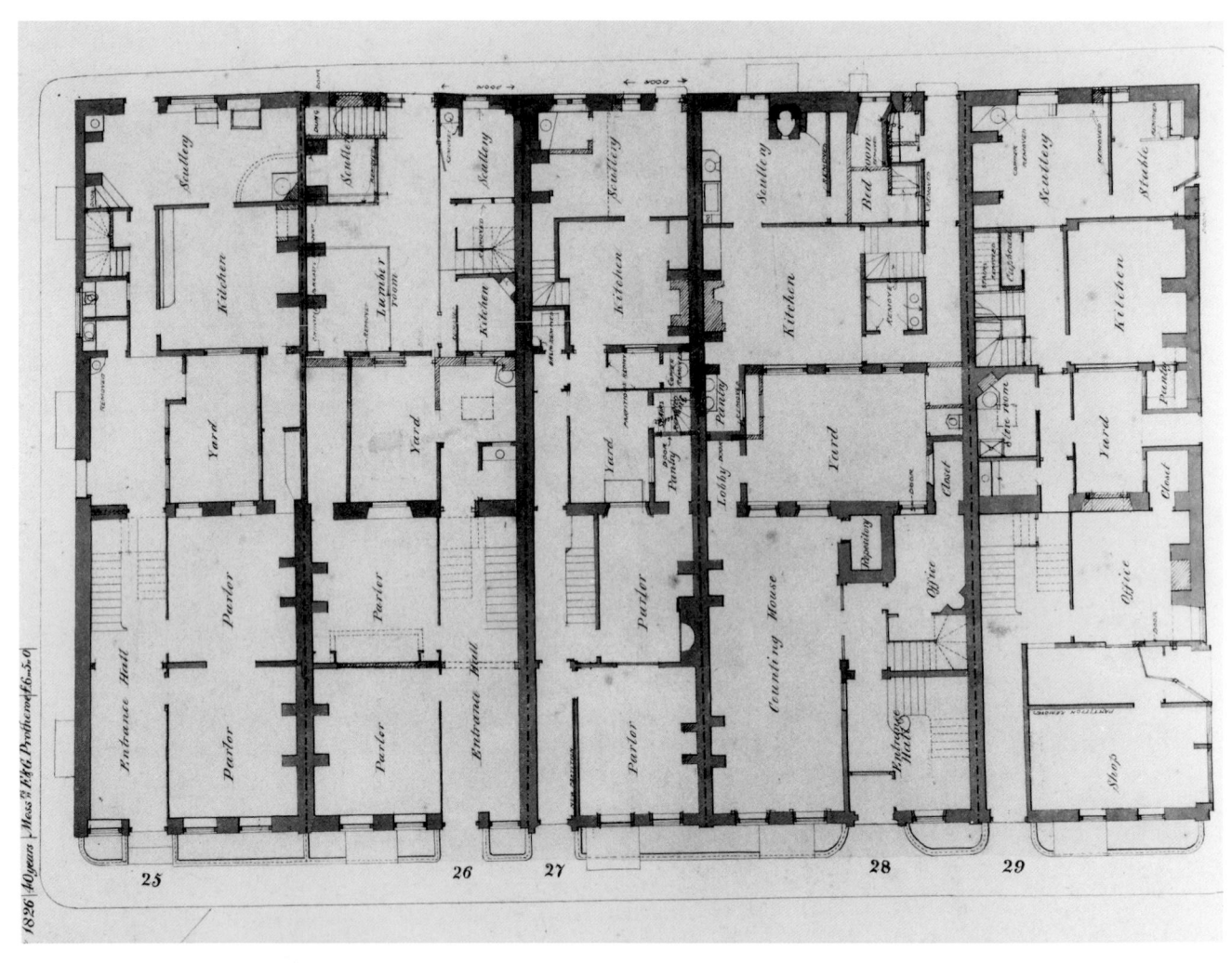

# THE TOWN HOUSE IN MEDIEVAL AND EARLY MODERN BRISTOL

*Fig 8.68*
*Nos.25–9 Orchard Street, plan of the mid-19th century (BRO 33041/BMC/12/PL1 fol 45).*

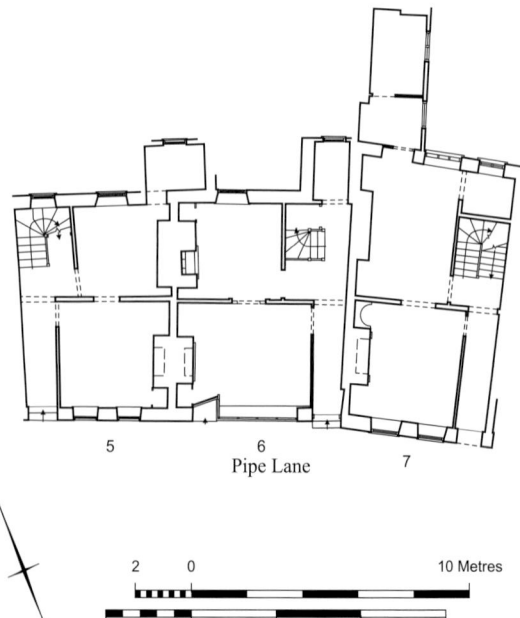

*Fig 8.69*
*Pipe Lane, viewed from the north, photograph of 1930 (PEWS, NMR AA77/01982).*

*Fig 8.70*
*Nos.5–8 Pipe Lane, plan of ground floor (RHL, PEC).*

THE RESIDENTIAL HOUSE

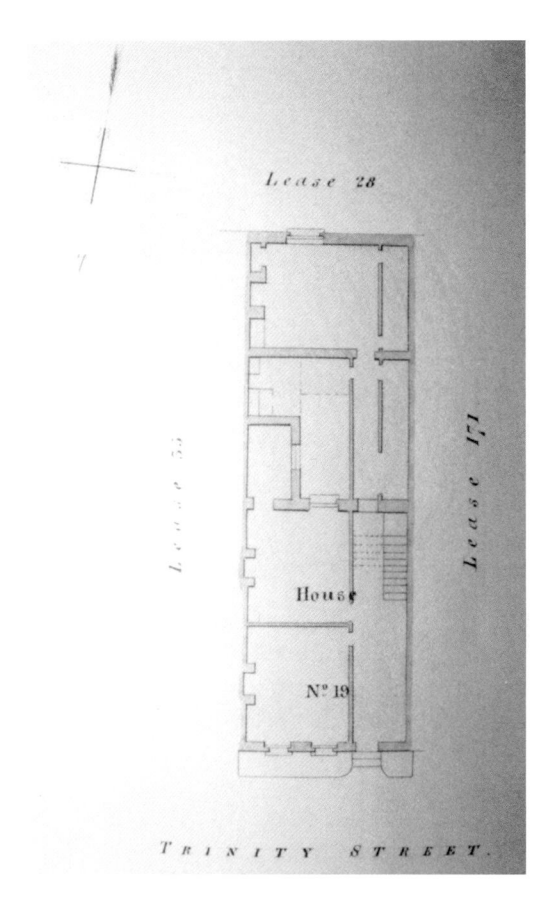

*Fig 8.71 (above left)
Trinity Street, ground-floor plan of house, the only plan of a house in this street that it was possible to locate (Church Commissioners' Book of Plans, lease no.79, plan probably of the mid-19th century).*

*Fig 8.72 (above right)
No.1 Trinity Street, photograph of stairs hall (Dening 1923 Pl xxxvi).*

*Fig 8.73 (left)
No.14 Brunswick Square, photograph of 1965 (NMR AA65/01302).*

211

# THE TOWN HOUSE IN MEDIEVAL AND EARLY MODERN BRISTOL

*Fig 8.74*
*West side of King Square, houses of rear-stairs plan, photograph of 2002 (© Mr Mike Bedingfield LRPS; source English Heritage).*

*Fig 8.75*
*South-east side of Duke Street, houses of rear-stairs plan, photograph of 1942 (NMR A42/02290).*

THE RESIDENTIAL HOUSE

*Fig 8.76*
*South-east side of Carolina Row, houses of rear-stairs plan, photograph of 1942 (NBR AA59/00924, reproduced by permission of English Heritage).*

*Fig 8.77*
*East side of Kingsdown Parade, houses of rear-stairs plan, photograph of 2003 (NMR AA047302).*

## The Two-Room Wide Town House

Roger North had regarded the narrow house built end-on to the street as being typical of cities, but many houses certainly occupied a plot two rooms in width. In their analysis of the plans in the Rawlinson Manuscript volume, Maguire and Colvin categorised these as 'single pile', 'double pile', 'square pile' or 'triple pile'.[47]

### The Single-Pile House

Single-pile houses of two rooms in width were built in Bristol from the late 16th century onwards. This was a popular plan for lodges or garden houses (chapter 9). The White Lodge, consisting of two principal rooms on each floor, was built to this plan *c* 1589, and many more lodges or garden houses were built to this same plan in the 17th and 18th centuries.

This was a plan also used for houses on the periphery of the city. The new houses built around College Green at the end of the 17th century occupied a similar, quasi-rural location to the lodges or garden houses on the hillsides overlooking the city, but were the primary residences of persons connected with, or simply leasing their house from, the Dean and Chapter of the Cathedral. Several of these houses were sketched by the topographical artists Samuel and Nathaniel Buck for their north-west prospect of the city in 1734 (Figs 8.78 and 8.79); no.14 College Green, newly built in 1690, can be seen from the print to have been two rooms wide with a centrally placed stairs.

Houses of this plan were also constructed in some of the new streets laid out within the more built-up parts of the city in the 17th century. In King Street the one house built on a double-width plot was no.6. Although the original arrangements are somewhat masked by an early 18th-century remodelling, the two ground-floor rooms can be interpreted as originally the kitchen and parlour – the former identifiable by a wide chimneystack which can only have been for the kitchen fireplace. On the west side of the house, the parlour is then identifiable by its very much smaller stack. Judging by the positioning of the partition between it and the kitchen, the parlour must have been entered directly from the street, also providing access to the stairs at the rear: a rather different arrangement to that found in the narrower houses (Figs 8.80a and 8.81).

This interpretation is supported by the evidence for the ground-floor usage of nos.20–4 St Michael's Hill, three houses built in the early 1690s (Figs 8.80b and 8.82). In no.22 the architectural evidence suggests the same plan of kitchen and parlour, the latter again entered from the street and providing access to the stairs

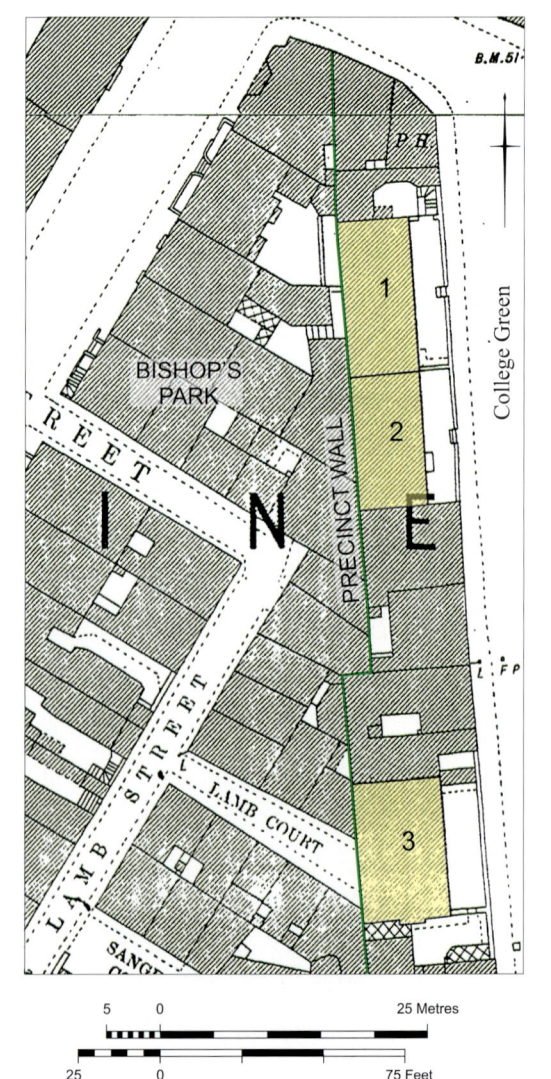

*Fig 8.78*
*Two-room wide, single-pile houses facing on to College Green, as drawn by Samuel and Nathaniel Buck, 1734 (S and N Buck, The North-West Prospect of Bristol, 1734).*

*Fig 8.79*
*The two-room wide, single-pile houses facing on to College Green, as mapped in 1884 (Ordnance Survey sheet LXXV.IV.III).*

THE RESIDENTIAL HOUSE

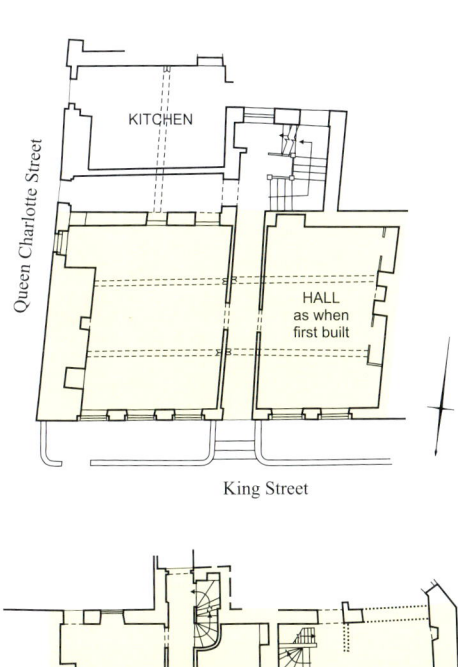

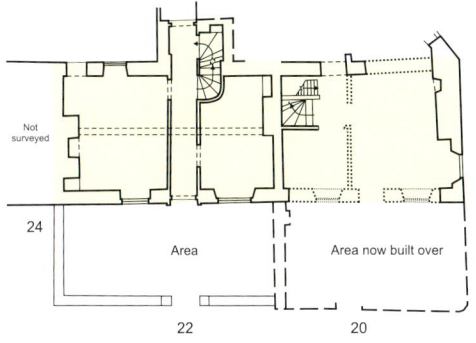

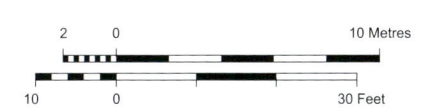

*Fig 8.80 (above left and centre left)
Plans of houses two rooms in width and one room in depth (RHL, PEC):
a) no.6 King Street;
b) nos.20–2 St Michael's Hill.*

*Fig 8.81 (above)
No.6 King Street, photograph of 2012 (English Heritage DP 111038).*

*Fig 8.82 (left)
Nos.20–4 St Michael's Hill, three houses built in the early 1690s, photograph of 1998
(NMR BB98/01255).*

215

THE TOWN HOUSE IN MEDIEVAL AND EARLY MODERN BRISTOL

*Fig 8.83*
*The house for a Bristol merchant (Fig 8.44), The Kingsweston Book of Drawings, plan (c 1724) of proposed ground floor (BRO 33746; English Heritage DP 136014).*

at the rear. Both nos.20 and 24 have been much altered, but surviving evidence and earlier plans can be combined to show that the two houses were originally of a similar plan to no.22. The contents of no.24, the home of a malt dealer Walter Landen, were described in a probate inventory of 1710 (Appendix 2).[48] Here the appraisers commenced their tour of the house in the kitchen. They then passed to the 'wash kitchen', probably in the yard to the rear, and then to the room described as 'the hall and parlour', before ascending the stairs to the first chamber. Read in conjunction with the plan of no.22, the hall and parlour of the inventory can be interpreted as the single room serving literally both functions, entrance area and living room – precisely as at no.6 King Street.

## The Double or Double-Pile House

Houses at least two rooms wide and of two ranges in depth were to be found in London's suburbs by the early 17th century.[49] These were houses of the type that Richard Ligon referred to in 1657 as 'the double house',[50] and that Roger North knew of in the 1680s as the double- or square-pile.

The Rawlinson collection contains a number of plans of houses of this type. In some plans the principal rooms take up only the front range, with the service rooms and stairs placed in a narrower rear range. In the greater number of plans there are four rooms to each floor, with the stairs and entrance hall in the centre. This was the plan adopted for the house of a Bristol merchant, probably Robert Yate, by the unidentified architect responsible for many of the drawings in *The Kingsweston Book of Drawings* (Figs 8.83 and 8.44). Double houses were built in Bristol only from the first decade of the 18th century onwards, some of them as suburban villas (see below and chapter 9). The plans of these houses provide considerable evidence for experimentation in the planning of domestic space in houses which were, at the grandest level, the successors to the sprawling hallhouses of medieval Bristol. Particular areas of concern were the placement and function of the stairs and the location of the kitchen.

The earliest of these houses were built in Queen Square, laid out *c* 1700. A symmetrical row of three houses, nos.36–8 were built 1703–12; no.38 was certainly occupied by 1705 (Figs 8.84a and 8.85). Seen from Queen Square, each house was of five bays, built in brick; each

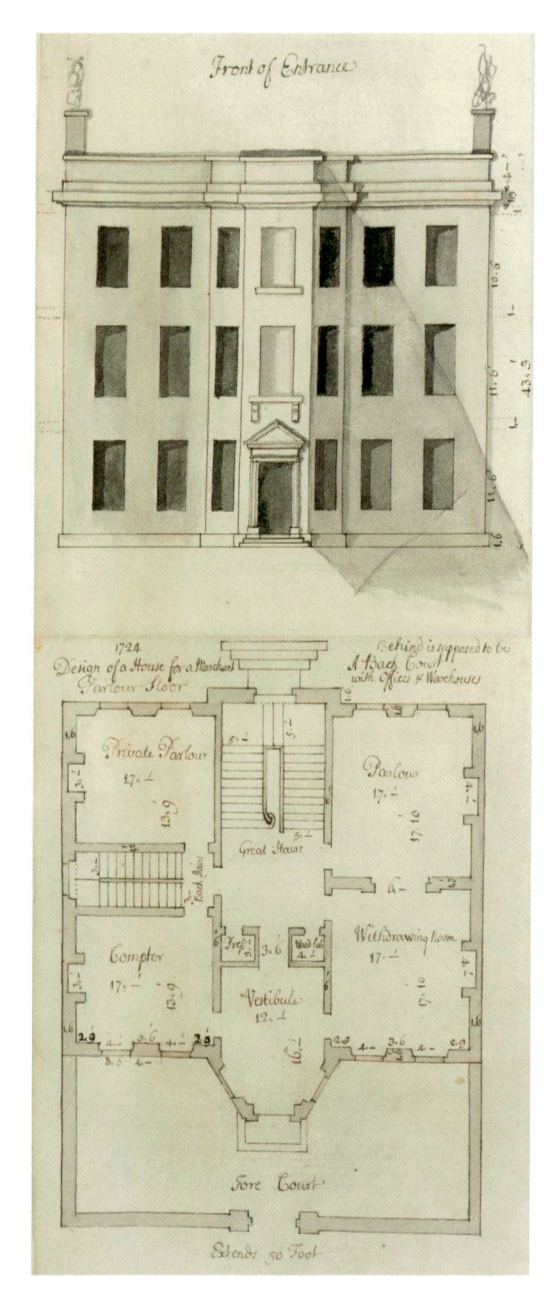

originally possessed moulded stone string courses, bolection-moulded sash frames, projecting keystones and a crowning modillioned eaves cornice of timber. The intended plan for these three houses conformed to the unequal double-pile plan found in the drawings of the Rawlinson collection.[51] In each house one of the two principal rooms took up the entire depth of the house, while the other occupied only the front range. The remaining part of the shallower rear range provided space for the stairs and for two small, unheated closets or back rooms. At no.38 one of these was set between the smaller front parlour and the

THE RESIDENTIAL HOUSE

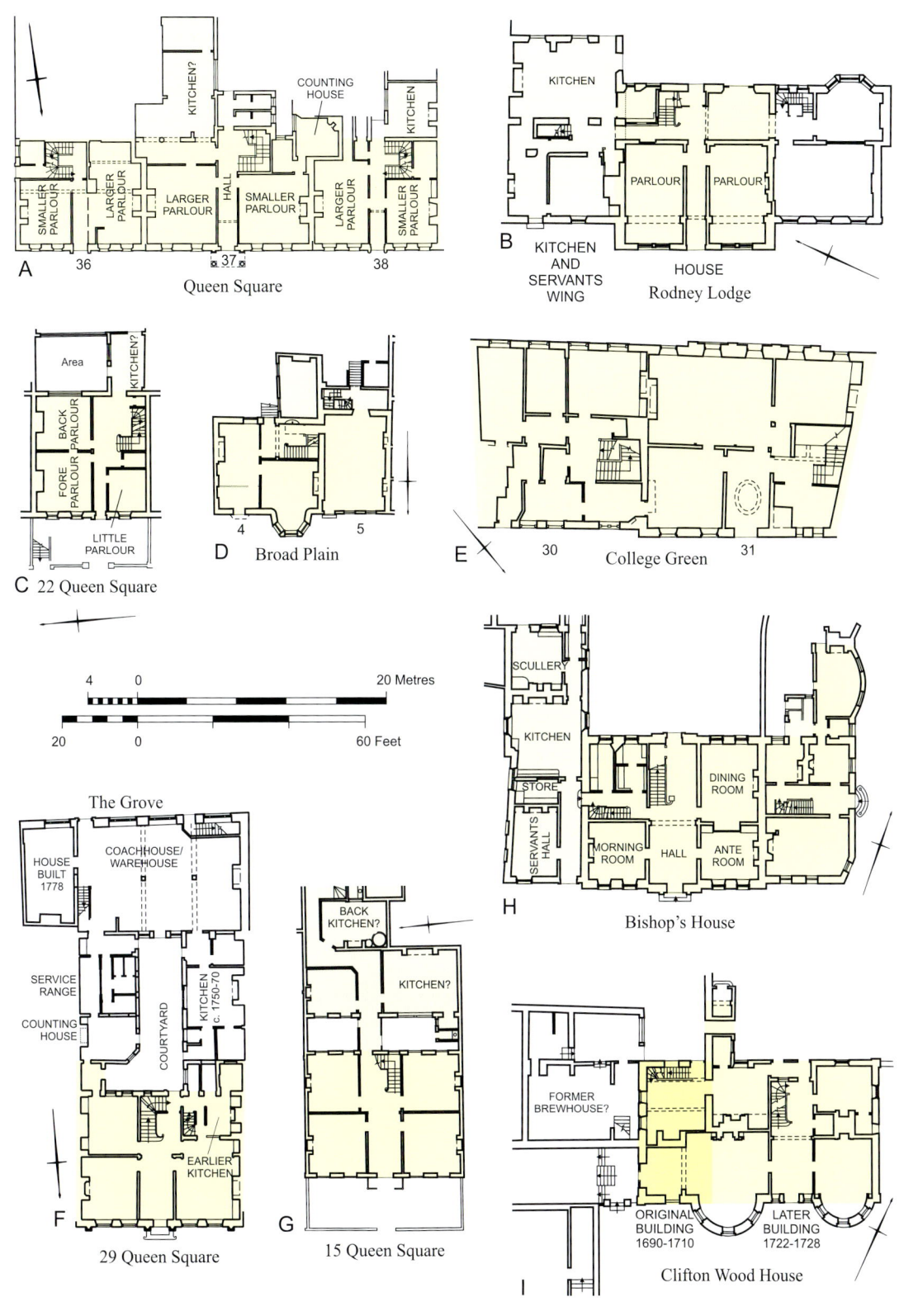

*Fig 8.84 (left and overleaf) Plans of houses of four or more rooms on each principal floor (RHL, PEC):*
*a) nos.36–8 Queen Square;*
*b) Rodney Lodge, Clifton Down Road;*
*c) no.22 Queen Square;*
*d) nos.4–5 Broad Plain;*
*e) nos.30–1 College Green, first floor;*
*f) no.29 Queen Square;*
*g) no.15 Queen Square;*
*h) The Bishop's House, Clifton Hill;*
*i) Clifton Wood House, Clifton Wood Road;*

A Queen Square

B Rodney Lodge

C 22 Queen Square

D Broad Plain

E College Green

The Grove

F 29 Queen Square

G 15 Queen Square

H Bishop's House

I Clifton Wood House

217

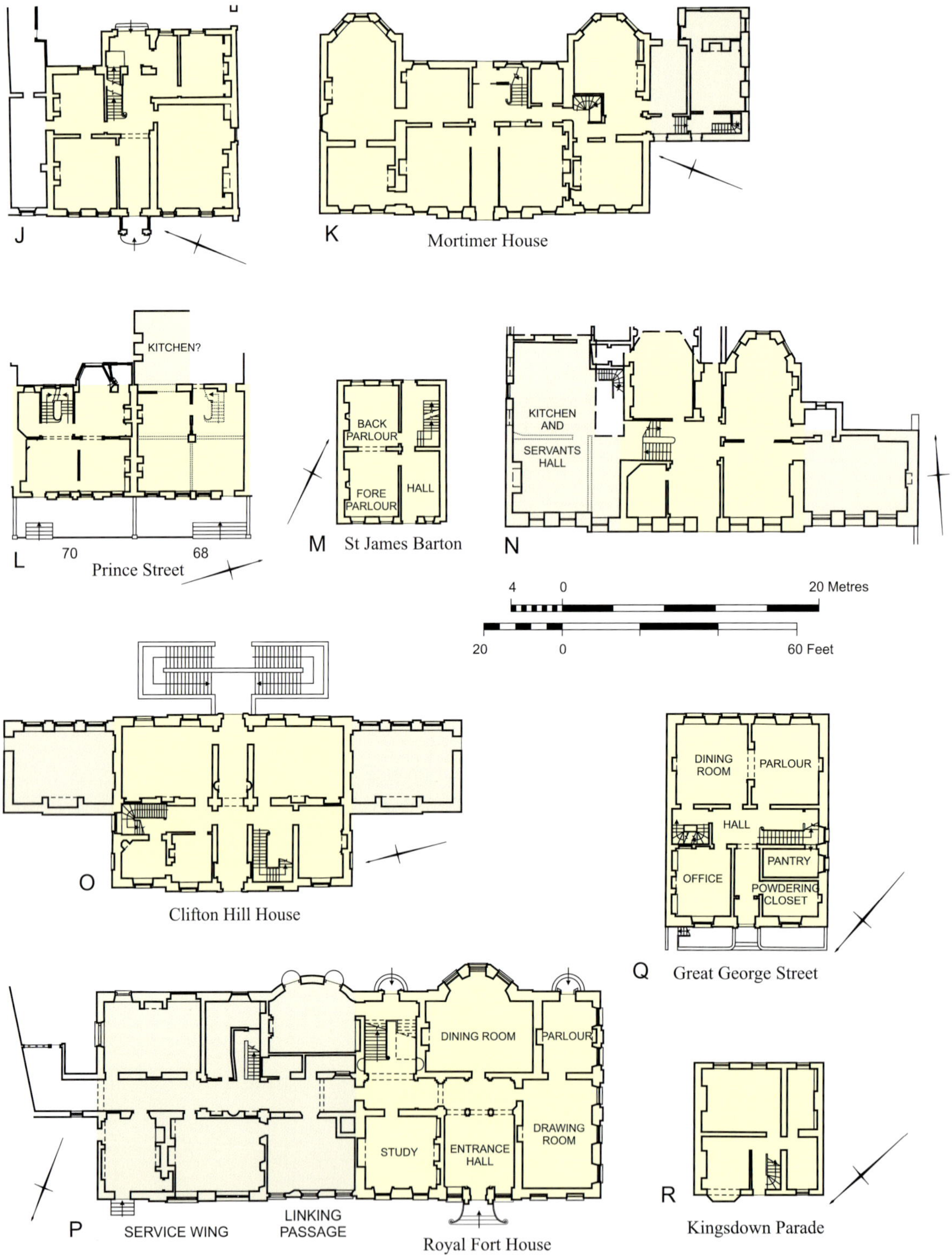

# THE TOWN HOUSE IN MEDIEVAL AND EARLY MODERN BRISTOL

Fig 8.84
Plans of houses of four or more rooms on each principal floor (RHL, PEC):
j) Duncan House, Clifton Down Road;
k) Mortimer House, Clifton Down Road;
l) nos.68–70 Prince Street;
m) no.12 St James's Barton;
n) Clifton Court, now the Chesterfield Nursing Home;
o) Clifton Hill House, as built;
p) Royal Fort House, ground and first floors;
q) no.7 Great George Street;
r) no.22 Kingsdown Parade.

probable site of the kitchen, in a separate but attached range to the rear of the main house.

Overall the three houses were intended to form a symmetrical plan, but the size of the ground-floor principal rooms and closets varied house to house. The asymmetrical plan of each house was in contrast to the appearance of symmetry provided by the elevation to Queen Square and the overall plan. The small size of the back rooms on each floor, and of the narrow hall providing access to the stairs, will be seen to contrast with the planning of some later double houses of a full two rooms in depth.

The unequal double-pile plan continued to be used later in the 18th century, and it was employed in the building of several suburban villas in Clifton. Callendar House, first recorded in 1746, was possibly of this plan.[52] In the development of the Holly Lands in Clifton, this was the plan used for the construction of Mortimer House and Rodney Lodge, formerly Freeman House, in the early 1750s. Duncan House, in the same development, was possibly first intended to be of similar plan, but was then modified in building (Figs 8.84b, 8.84j, 8.84k and 8.86).

The remaining double-pile houses in Queen Square for which evidence survives were built to a full two rooms in depth, or 'square pile' in North's terminology. In 1712 no.22 was first occupied. The overall plan, much altered from 1949 onwards, subdivided the ground floor into four equally sized units, providing two parlours of equal depth on the north side, the stairs on the south-east and a smaller parlour and closet next to the stairs on the south-west (Fig 8.84c).

A modified form of this plan was utilised for the rebuilding of nos.30 and 31 College Green in *c* 1730. In both houses the ground-floor plan can be inferred from what survives on the first floor and above (Figs 8.84e and 8.87). The north-west part of each house was subdivided

*Fig 8.85*
*Nos.36–8 Queen Square, photograph of 1997 (NMR BB97/04503).*

*Fig 8.86*
*Rodney Lodge, formerly Freeman House, Clifton Down Road, built c 1750, exterior, photograph of 1998 (RHL).*

*Fig 8.87*
*Nos.30–1 College Green, viewed from the south, photograph of 1998 (NMR AA98/02824).*

*Fig 8.88*
*Exterior and interior views of houses of Broad Plain: a) nos.3–4, viewed from the west, photograph of 1964 (NMR AA64/02762); b) hall and stairs of no.4, photograph of 1953 (NMR BB78/09299).*

into three units: a front parlour, the stairs and a back parlour. The remaining part of each house was divided to provide two parlours of equal size, except on the ground floor where an entrance hall, asymmetric to the frontage in the case of no.31, led to the stairs and necessitated a smaller front parlour. Elsewhere, on the periphery of the city, double-pile houses were being constructed on the east side of Broad Plain in the late 17th century or early 1700s. The house later to become nos.3–4 Broad Plain was of a similar plan to no.22 Queen Square and the houses at nos.30–1 College Green (Figs 8.84d, 8.88a and 8.88b).

Demolished c 1912, no.15 Queen Square was first occupied in 1711, a year before no.22. It was built to the plan that was to become the generally adopted design for larger double houses in Bristol, providing four rooms to each floor with the stairs at the end of the central entrance hall (Figs 8.84g and 8.89).[53] The surviving no.29 was built to a similar plan from 1709 onwards, although only first occupied from 1720, having two powder closets projecting into the courtyard behind. A central hallway led to the stairs, which then ascended from the ground to the attic floor (Fig 8.84f). Four decades later, in 1762, no.5 Albemarle Row in Hotwells was built to exactly the same plan, including the powder closets.⁵⁴ In the interim Ware's design of 1747 for Clifton Hill House had provided a plan for a very large town house. The central area had been expanded to give a reception hall to the front (in place of the smaller entrance hall of lesser houses) and a rear hall. The stair, to one side of this, was set in a separate, off-centre compartment (Fig 8.90).

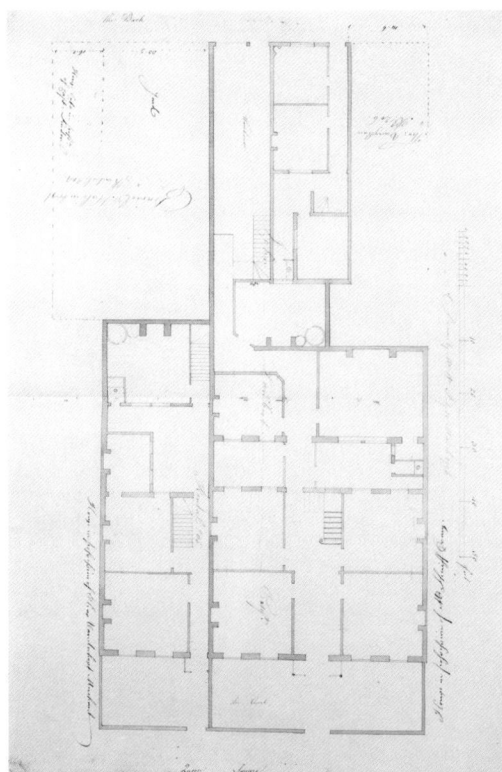

The houses considered up to this point had, as far as is known, a single stair connecting all levels within the building. Others developed alternative arrangements which sought to segregate traffic on social lines. In some houses the main stairs terminated at the first floor, and a separate stairs gave access to the floors above. This was the solution adopted in the design of no.16 Lower Maudlin Street, one of a pair of five-bay, semi-detached houses, built *c* 1726. At the back of the house a wide central hallway provided access to the stairs (Fig 8.95a), which terminated at the first floor; a separate stairs closer to the front of the house provided access to the floors above. This solution was also used in the extension and alteration of Lunsford House, Park Row, to form a house of double-pile plan. The new stairs terminated at the first floor, with a separate stairs giving access to the floors above (*see* Fig 9.71).

The separate stairs, certainly by the time it reached the attic floor, would have served as a servants' stair. A further variation on the central-hall plan was to provide two separate stairs from the ground floor upwards, the lesser stairs being for servants. This was the plan of the former Church House, latterly the Bishop's House, next to Clifton churchyard, dated to 1711 (Figs 8.84h and 8.91; *see* Fig 10.10). Here a servants' stairs is sited to one side of the main stairs, the latter terminating at the first floor and a servants' stair providing the only access to the floors above. This same plan was used in the extension and rebuilding of Clifton Wood House, *c* 1724 (Figs 8.84i, 8.92, 8.93a and 8.93b). Two decades later a similar solution was employed in the design of two detached double houses in Clifton, both built *c* 1750 as part of the same

*Fig 8.89*
*Nos.14 and 15 Queen Square, plan of 1795 (BRO 04479(2) fol 98C).*

*Fig 8.90*
*Isaac Ware's plan of Clifton Hill House (Ware 1768, Pl. 42).*

*Fig 8.91 (bottom)*
*Bishop's House, Clifton Hill, view from the south, photograph of 1942 (NMR A42/02293).*

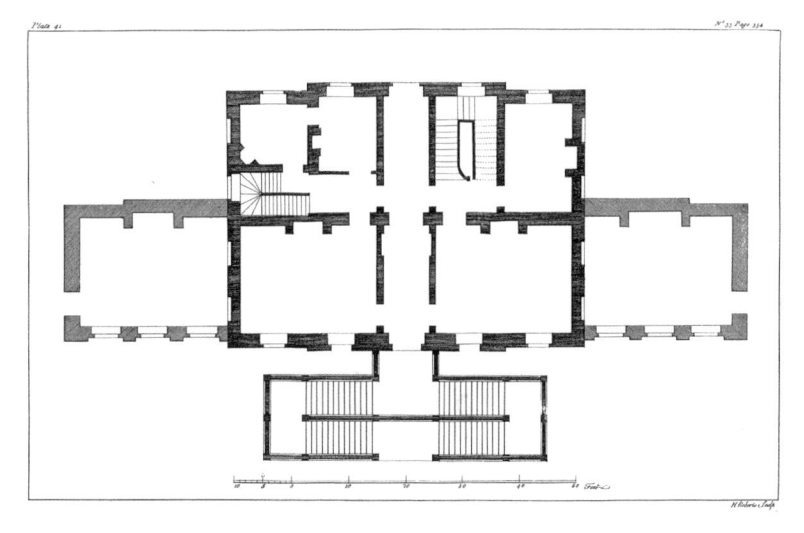

*Fig 8.92*
*Clifton Wood House, view from the west, photograph of 2003 (RHL).*

*Fig 8.93*
*Clifton Wood House:*
*a) the stairs hall (English Heritage DP 135980);*
*b) marquetry to underside of half-landing; photographs of 2011 (English Heritage DP 135982).*

development. In Rodney Lodge and Mortimer House the secondary stairs to the first floor were within an attached kitchen block (Figs 8.84b and 8.84k).

The plan of Clifton Wood House as built in 1724 was broadly similar to that of the central house in Robert Yates's speculative development in Prince Street. Built in the same year, it evidently derived from the plans of 'a house proposed for a merchant' by the unknown compiler of *The Kingsweston Book of Drawings* (Figs 8.44 and 8.83). The plans envisaged that the main, or 'great', stairs would continue upwards to at least the second floor. It would be of interest to know whether the stairs terminated at the first floor in the house in Prince Street as completed.[55]

The unknown compiler's explanatory notes for the proposed merchant's house in Prince Street provide some context for the various arrangements devised for the placement of the stairs in the double house: 'And by it [the Compter] is the back stairs, to the chambers that the young men may at night go to their beds and in the morning come to their business without disturbing or dirtying the best part of the house'. Of the 'great stairs', the compiler wrote, 'the enlargement of the Well upwards gives a better view of the Stairs and Cieling [*sic*], and adds a beauty which cannot be imagind [*sic*] by those who have not seen the experience of it'. The compiler's proposed house accorded a level of privacy to the main stairs: 'a vestibule for the conveniencey [*sic*] of common people attending till they can be spoken to … separated from the stairs that they may not be at liberty to walk about and that the family may pass privately about their affairs'.[56]

The framed, open-well main stairs of the double house was then intended to please and to add beauty to the design of the house; but the motives behind its placement were more complex. A client more moved to overt display might ensure that the main stairs were fully visible from the front entrance. The double-pile design which placed the stairs fully in view can be seen as the two-room deep town house of rear-stairs plan, simply extended to be two rooms in width. The earliest examples of this design were constructed in Prince Street, where nos.66, 68 and 70, built *c* 1725, were each of this plan (Fig 8.84l).[57] Also of this plan was no.12 St James's Barton, a very grand house possibly designed by the architect for no.66 Prince Street and built by 1725 (Figs 8.84m and 8.94).[58]

A family or client intent on maximising privacy might place the stairs to one side of the entrance hall, where the busy family traffic up and down the house was not visible from the street entrance. In this context we might re-examine the ground-floor plans of four houses, all built for merchants of great wealth *c* 1740–90. Clifton Court, now the Chesterfield Hospital, was built *c* 1742 for Nehemiah

# THE RESIDENTIAL HOUSE

Champion and his wife Martha, formerly Goldney, to a full double-pile plan and with the stairs placed to one side of the entrance hall, not visible from the front door of the house (Fig 8.84n).

The design of this house has been attributed to the architect William Halfpenny and might therefore have been known to the architect of Clifton Hill House, built for Paul Fisher to a design by Isaac Ware 1746–50. Ison considered that 'Ware's urbane design exerted a considerable influence on contemporary house building in Bristol' (Figs 8.84o and 8.90). The influence of Ware's design, though, might have extended beyond that of the exterior architecture to the less apparent implications of the plan. The placement of the stairs out of sight from the main entrance implied an emphasis on both privacy and the separation of servants and, as published in 1755, might have been known to James Bridges, the designer of Thomas Tyndall's Royal Fort house in 1760. The new parkland setting of Royal Fort house was private enough, and the stairs were two further lines of sight away from the front entrance to the house. The focus on privacy in Bridge's design is further emphasised by the closure of the top of the main stairs; the first-floor rooms and the secondary stairs to the attic are invisible beyond a closed door (Fig 8.84p).

Similarly the house built in 1790 for John Pinney at no.7 Great George Street was one intended for a Nevis planter and Bristol merchant most concerned with business and his privacy. In Pinney's house the principal rooms were at the back of the house, overlooking the ships and commerce of the quaysides and the city beyond. Neither the stairs nor even the entrance to Pinney's office on the street front were visible from the front door. The finely finished stone stairs with iron balustrade added beauty to the experience of those who ventured beyond the hall; they were located in a private zone, accessible to Pinney, his family and guests. A separate servants' stair provided a link between the basement kitchen, the ground floor and the attic, a route doubtless used by Pinney's Nevisian servant Pero (Fig 8.84q).

Placing the stairs to one side of the entrance hall brought the main circulation point within the house forward to create more private space beyond. This was the strategy adopted for several of the larger houses constructed in Kingsdown Parade in the mid-18th century. Built facing each other across Montague Hill c 1760, nos.20 and 22 were both designed with the stairs to one side of the entrance doorway. The plan had the added virtue of providing an element of public display lacking in other houses, for the stair was clearly visible as a show of elegance through an arched stairs window (Fig 8.84r).

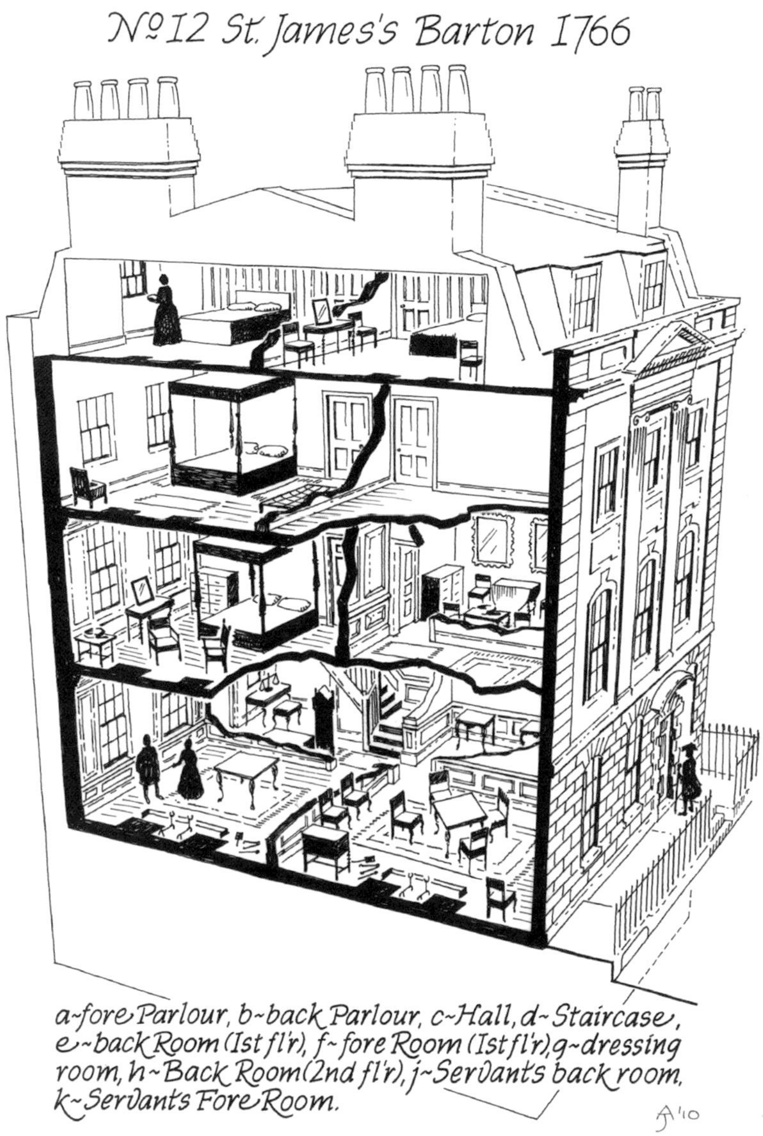

## The Semi-Detached House

The two-room wide town house was sometimes built in the context of the urban row, but a number were built as pairs of semi-detached or as single detached houses. The pairs of semi-detached houses which have been recorded were all houses of high status. In Lower Maudlin Street, for example, nos.16 and 17 were built

*Nº 12 St James's Barton 1766*

a–fore Parlour, b–back Parlour, c–Hall, d–Staircase, e–back Room (1st fl'r), f–fore Room (1st fl'r), g–dressing room, h–Back Room (2nd fl'r), j–Servants back room, k–Servants Fore Room.

*Fig 8.94*
*No.12 St James's Barton, reconstructed from documentary sources including the probate inventory of Thomas Crosby 1766 (Appendix 2) (JA).*

*c* 1726. Each was probably initially of double-pile plan with a centrally placed stairs; they were of five bays and faced in brick of Flemish bond (Fig 8.95a). In Stokes Croft, two such houses were probably built *c* 1729 by John Brock of Bristol, house carpenter, on land leased from St James's church and subject to the erection by Brock of one or more houses on the ground. By the later 19th century the northernmost of these was no.106, a double-pile house with projecting bays on the street frontage; the southernmost house was evidently of a different plan, without

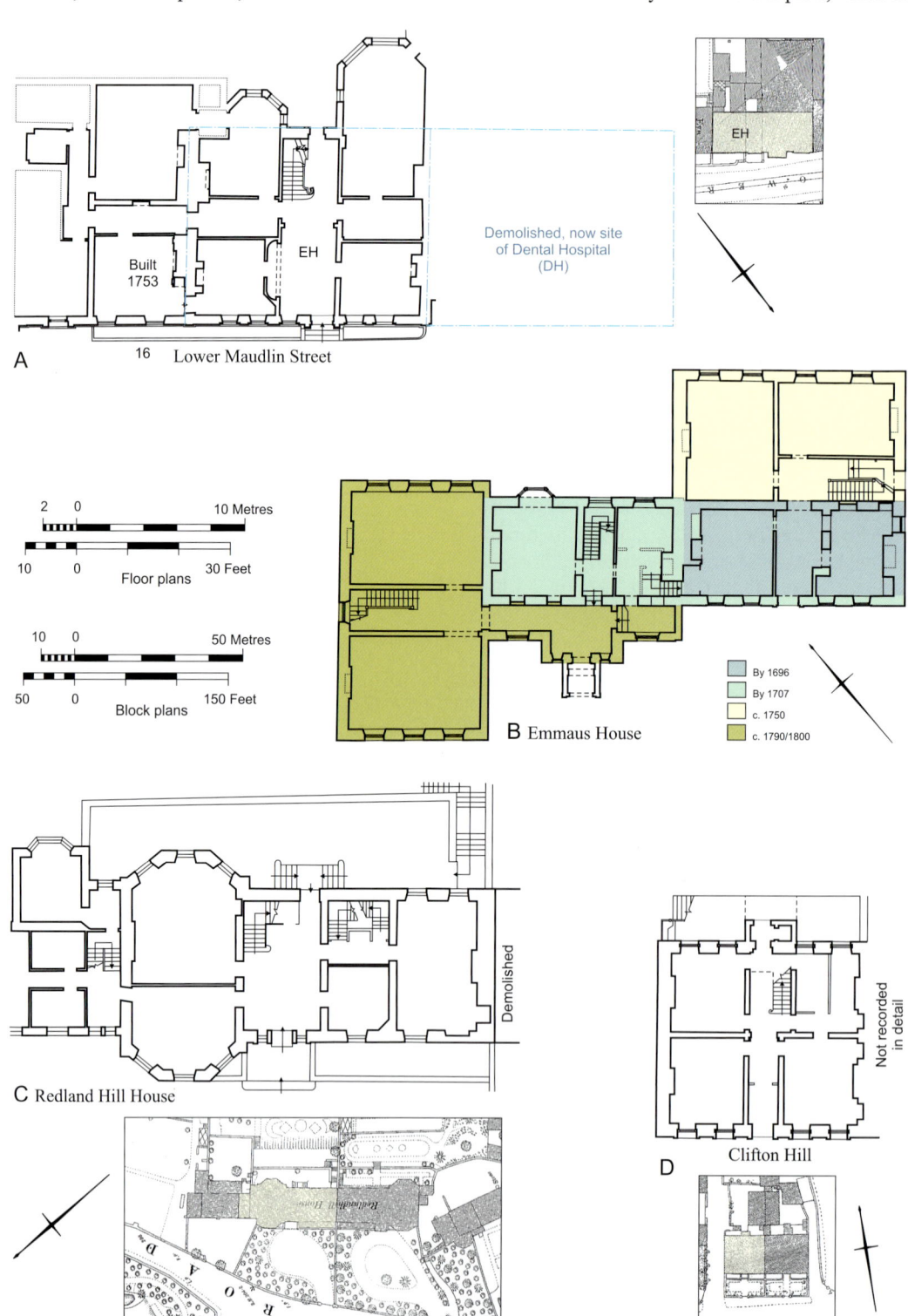

Fig 8.95
Plans of semi-detached houses
(RHL, PEC):
a) nos.16 and 17 Lower Maudlin Street;
b) Emmaus House, nos.1 and 2 The Grove, Clifton Hill;
c) Redland Hill House (and adjacent demolished house), Redland Hill;
d) Beresford and Prospect Houses, nos.1–2 Clifton Hill.

*Fig 8.96*
*Beresford and Prospect Houses, nos.1–2 Clifton Hill (Country Life, 6 September 1962, p 523).*

projecting bays. At roughly the same date the two houses making up Emmaus House, nos.1 and 2 The Grove, were probably rebuilt to the same plan (Fig 8.95b).

Two other pairs of semi-detached villas were constructed in the middle of the 18th century. On Redland Hill, Redland Hill House is the surviving half of a pair of houses of *c* 1770.[59] The plan emphasised the role of the entrance hall, stairs and principal reception room, the latter possessing a stone bay window at each end; a separate servants' stair could be seen as underlining the importance of arrangements for entertainment (Fig 8.95c). The demolished house was of identical overall dimensions to that surviving, so was probably of similar plan. On Clifton Hill another semi-detached pair was built between 1757 and 1763; each owner commissioned their own architect so that each house had its own distinctive elevation (Fig 8.96).[60] One half, formerly Prospect House and now no.2, was certainly of double-pile plan with a central hall and stairs (Fig 8.95d). As Summerson noted of similar houses in London, these semi-detached pairs were 'in effect ordinary terrace houses – the end houses, as it were, in a terrace of two instead of a terrace of twelve or twenty'.[61]

Semi-detached pairs of smaller houses were built in many streets, but notably in the new suburbs of the 18th century. Two such pairs were nos.4 and 5 Charles Street (Fig 8.55) and nos.3 and 4 Clifton Wood Road (Fig 8.97). On the north side of Park Row, nos.8 and 9 were probably the only semi-detached pair built in this street (Fig 8.98). On the north-west side of Kingsdown Parade, nos.57–9 were another

*Fig 8.97*
*Nos.3 and 4 Clifton Wood Road, photograph of 2011 (English Heritage DP 141399).*

*Fig 8.98*
*Nos. 8 and 9 Park Row, probably the only semi-detached pair built in this street, detail from photograph of c 1864 (Winstone 1866–1860, Pl 9, Reece Winstone Archive).*

## The Largest Houses

In the 16th century a number of monastic properties were converted to become some of the largest houses in the city, as happened in other larger towns and cities. On the north-east side of the city Henry Brayne had in the 1540s contrived a large, rambling residence out of the claustral ranges and outbuildings of St James's Priory (*see* Fig 2.16). The layout of the converted monastery was described in detail in a deed of partition of 1579, when it became two separate properties.[64] On St Michael's Hill, the buildings of the nunnery of St Mary Magdalene were converted, by the 1550s, to become the town house of William Gorges the elder, of Wraxall – close by in north Somerset. Situated high above the western edge of the city and with extensive views to the east, the site of the priory was well suited for re-use as a gentry residence.[65]

pair set within a row, along with a variety of other designs.

As in London, the building of a quasi semi-detached row was a fashionable innovation in the late 18th century.[62] The west side of Kingsdown Parade, 85–91 Ashley Road, sometimes referred to as Ashley Place, and Princes Buildings, Clifton were all designed as rows or series of semi-detached houses, again as in London, 'though semi-detached in form … only detached above the first-floor level'.[63] Most of the linking subsidiary blocks have now been raised to the full height of the adjacent houses (Fig 8.99).

Between 1568 and 1574 the claustral buildings of the former Carmelite Priory were demolished or adapted for the construction of the 'Great House on St Augustine's Back'. It was built by John Young, a gentleman and merchant from Wiltshire with trading interests in Bristol; his income perhaps derived principally from the post that he held as customs collector (*see* Fig 2.20). The buildings and site of St Mark's Priory were utilised for first one and then several superior houses, the church being retained by

*Fig 8.99*
*Reconstructed original design for the two sides of the north part of Kingsdown Parade, formerly James's Place, c 1792, drawing by David and Penny Mellor (Mellor 1985, 8–9).*

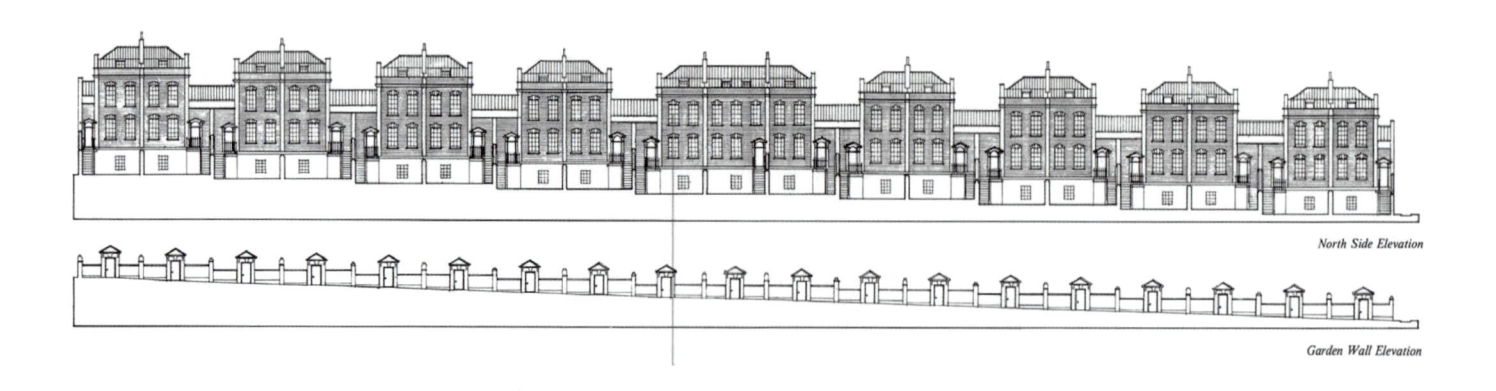

North Side Elevation

Garden Wall Elevation

The Terraces as originally planned

South Side Elevation

the Corporation for its own use (*see* Figs 11.19 and 11.20). The buildings of the Greyfriars, Temple and Augustinian Friars were similarly re-used (*see* Fig 2.15).

Within the Castle, the remains of the great hall were similarly utilised for the construction of the gentry residence inhabited in the 1630s by Francis Brewster; it was later converted to at least three separate large houses (chapter 10). Two decades later, at least four large new houses were built in the 1650s and 1660s within the only recently built Civil War citadel, the Royal Fort (chapter 9).

Two of the largest houses built in the first part of the 17th century fronted on to the Avon close to Bristol Bridge. The 'great house' at the corner of Redcliff Street and Bristol Bridge was constructed in the late 16th century by Robert Rogers, an alderman and wealthy soap maker (Figs 8.100a and 8.100b). On the opposite side of the river, the house of merchant Robert Aldworth, on the south side of St Peter's church and completed *c* 1612, was the rebuilding of a large medieval house (*see* Fig 10.74).[66]

By the end of the 17th century most of these houses had ceased to be used as residences by the wealthy. Aldworth's house at St Peter's, the mansion at St James's Priory and the Great House on St Augustine's Back had all been converted to sugar houses. Brewster's house in the Castle, and those of Hooke and Aldworth alongside the Frome (chapter 9), had been subdivided into smaller houses, with former garden areas now built upon. Rogers' house at the Bridge had become an inn. To the owners who sold these houses for use as sugar factories, or who subdivided them into smaller houses and plots, commerce and profit were more important than having a very large or 'great' residence in, or close to, the centre of the city.

The two suburban houses built by Hooke and Aldworth alongside the Frome were the precursors of the many suburban villas that surrounded the city by the end of the 18th century; some of them have already been mentioned above. These merit closer analysis and discussion alongside the lodge or garden house, the subject of the next chapter.

## Some Conclusions

The residential house can now be set in the wider context of social change. From the 16th and 17th centuries medieval hallhouses were replaced by storeyed residential houses, appropriating the form of the medieval shophouse. The form of the shophouse, a series of separate spaces one above the other, facilitated the process of closure: 'the architectural referents of the open hall became lost and replaced by different rooms, different classes within the household occupying different spaces.'[67] Segregation within the

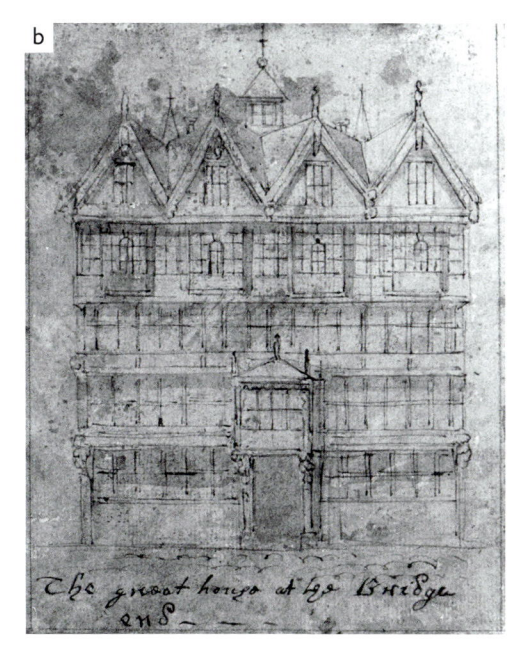

*Fig 8.100*
*The Great House at Bristol Bridge:*
*a) elevation to the Avon, Millerd 1673 (BRSMG);*
*b) elevation to Redcliff Street of 'The great house at the Bridge end', drawing probably of the 18th century (BRSMG Art Gallery Box Bristol Buildings F–G).*

household was further emphasised by the separation of circulation routes for family and servants, especially in relation to the access between floors and, in some cases, the screening of the principal stair from the eyes of callers to the house. In these plan arrangements can be seen the replacement of a single household, using shared space, by a different social relationship which set family apart from its domestic staff.

The fact that certain elements of the storeyed residential house spanned the 17th and 18th centuries undermines the vision of the Georgian house as an unvaried and unvarying entity. Basic plans, single- and double-pile, the central-stairs and rear-stairs plans can be seen to have extended across two centuries. 'Georgian' design, therefore, had strong roots in the 17th century; it did not spring from architects' drawing boards and pattern books as something innovatory in the early 18th century. The same process of evolution can be seen in the use of the detached kitchen, the hierarchical structure of the storeyed house with the servants' rooms in the attic and the distribution of house types and occupants marking the beginnings of a new residential differentiation. All these topics will be examined further in subsequent chapters.

It is useful to return to the question implied at the beginning of this chapter: was the changing form of the house dictated by social change, or did architectural form influence the way that society evolved? It might be claimed that both processes were at work in early modern Bristol. We have seen how the changing nature of the relationships within the household encouraged the development of new plan features, specifically in relation to circulation routes within the larger houses. In this area, social change would appear to be the more powerful driver: it seems unlikely that society changed because new plan forms were imposed upon wealthy clients. Similarly, the wide variety of house types might most logically be seen as a response to the needs of different social levels within Bristol society.

But how might architectural form be a catalyst for social change? The proposition suggests that forms might be imposed upon occupiers of houses, who therefore adjusted their lifestyle and their relationship to society generally in accordance with the way that their environment was laid out. One might accept this readily in the case of byelaw terraced housing of the late 19th-century, or of inter-war suburban housing, or – perhaps the most extreme case – in high-rise blocks of the post-war era: these certainly created new communities and dictated new social relationships and ways of living. But to what extent did it apply in early modern Bristol?

It is not possible to judge the extent to which innovations originating at high social levels were adopted lower down the scale in slavish imitation of fashion and, as a consequence, altered social relations. It is, however, possible to suggest that the range of architectural forms, specifically the wide variety of house size, sent out clear messages about residents' place in society, and may have formalised the hierarchical nature of the urban community. This was unlikely to be a new thing: it is simply that we can study it more fully in the early modern period because we have better evidence.

Housing solutions were certainly imposed in Bristol in this period: once holdings had been amalgamated, or where single tenements were developed for multiple occupation, housing was provided not on an individual basis but speculatively, using models which were deemed appropriate for different levels of society. Thus economic imperatives lay behind the development of individual tenements as courts or yards of houses of one room on each floor, and the exploitation of larger plots of open land produced new forms such as the terrace. The terrace at least, and perhaps also the court, led to new modes of living: the creation of new environments led to new proximities and the development of new communities. Perhaps we can say that the forms of houses provided for different social levels were driven primarily and originally by the practical needs of different types of household, but that these forms, once established and formalised, tended to reinforce and consolidate social change.

Kingsdown Parade has been mentioned several times in this and earlier chapters. Residential houses in this street were of a variety of forms: one- and two-room wide single- and double-pile dwellings; separate and linked semi-detached pairs; and rows of identical, two-room deep houses of the rear-stairs plan. In its completion during the building boom of the 1780s and early 1790s, Kingsdown Parade was a street displaying a transition from heterogeneity or variation to homogeneity or uniformity. As a street of garden houses, it serves also as an introduction to the subject of the next chapter: the lodge or garden house.

# 9

# The Garden House

## Comely Buildings and Pleasant Gardens

In 1673 James Millerd noted the 'comely buildings and pleasant gardens' that had recently begun to appear on St Michael's Hill, part of an 'increase of new buildings' that was evident especially on the west and north sides of the city.[1] These stand out in the distance in the painting of Broad Quay attributed to a painter of the British School, once believed to be the work of Peter Monamy (Fig 9.1). Millerd's map shows a number of houses which would fit this description, set within walled gardens. They were sited particularly on the hillside extending from Stony Hill to the Royal Fort, but also to the south on Redcliff Hill and to the east beyond Old Market (Fig 9.2). At least four of these dwellings were individually named: the Red Lodge and the White Lodge; the Royal Fort; and Baber's Tower, known also as Enderbie's Lodge.

Simplistically these houses might be seen to denote the beginning of a new era of expansion, the development of new suburbs ever further beyond the bounds of the tightly defined medieval city – a process that has continued to the present day. Yet looking closely at some of the suburban houses shown on Millerd's map will reveal a more complex story, centred first on what a 'lodge' signified to the inhabitants of 16th- and 17th-century Bristol. In late medieval England the term 'lodge' had come to be applied to either a place of lodging associated with the forest and the chase or to a secondary residence intended as a place for retreat and seclusion: a place to which the gentry or their betters might resort for 'recreation and pastime'.[2]

These two categories were not mutually exclusive, but it is with the latter that this chapter is principally concerned, in relation to the largely unexplored context of the second residence in the life of the urban elite in the early modern city.[3] The chapter will go on to examine the influence which the lodge or garden house had on places of permanent (rather than intermittent or occasional) residence in the growing city and beyond, specifically in so far as it established a model for the close relationship between house and garden and reflected a desire to create a new type of urban domestic environment.

*Fig 9.1*
*The quayside of Bristol in the early 18th century. The slopes of St Michael's Hill are shown in the distance. British School (BRSMG K514).*

*Fig 9.2*
*Extracts from Millerd's map of 1673 featuring four lodges. Left to right: the Red Lodge; the White Lodge; the Royal Fort; Baber's Tower (BRSMG).*

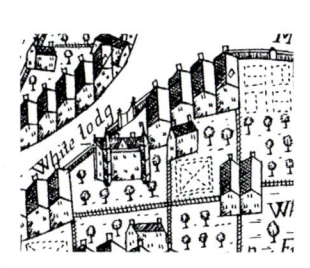

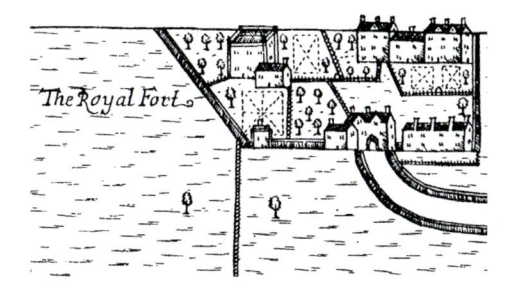

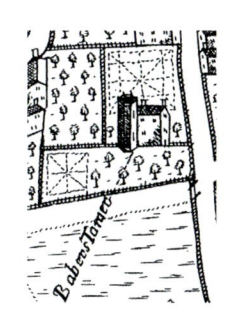

## Lodges

From the early 16th-century properties described as lodges were to be found in increasing numbers in the suburbs and on the periphery of Bristol (Fig 9.3). The earliest lodges recorded were of the 15th century; in 1430 John Crosse took the lease of a 'logge' on the north side of Pile Street.[4] In 1448 a second lodge, that of Isabella Waryn, was recorded at the west end of Tomlinson's Close to the south of Pile Street.[5] More references to lodges date from the 16th century: in 1534 a lodge belonging to the chantries of William Canynges was on Redcliff Hill, close to the church of St Mary Redcliff.[6] By 1547 the property known as Tower Harratz included 'one house called a lodge'.[7] In 1548 nos.8–11 Park Row, a property granted to Mede's chantry in St Mary Redcliff, included a garden and 'le Lodge' held by one Maurice Cradogge (Fig 9.4),[8] and a garden and lodge with a dove house near Lawford's Gate in 1557 was possibly that known later as Baber's Tower.[9]

In St Thomas Street two separate lodges with gardens formed part of the lands of Lord Lisle by 1557,[10] and in the same street a tenement later to become no.61 was described in 1566 as a garden with a lodge, bounded with gardens on either side.[11] By 1588 three lodges had been built to the south and east of Temple churchyard, each set within its own garden.[12] In the precinct of the Greyfriars at least two lodges existed by the 1580s.[13] On the slopes to the west of the city several lodges existed by this same date: in 1578 the merchant John Draper held three gardens on St Michael's Hill, one with a lodge.[14] The Red Lodge was built between 1578 and 1589, and the White Lodge *c* 1588.[15]

Where their owners can be identified, these lodges were for the most part the houses not of the gentry, but of merchants and other wealthy townspeople. In 1548 an orchard and lodge 'buylded upon the same' in Rosemary Lane was held by Margaret Wadhouse, a prosperous tanner's widow.[16] In 1556 the property at Tower Harratz was held by Thomas Launsdowne,

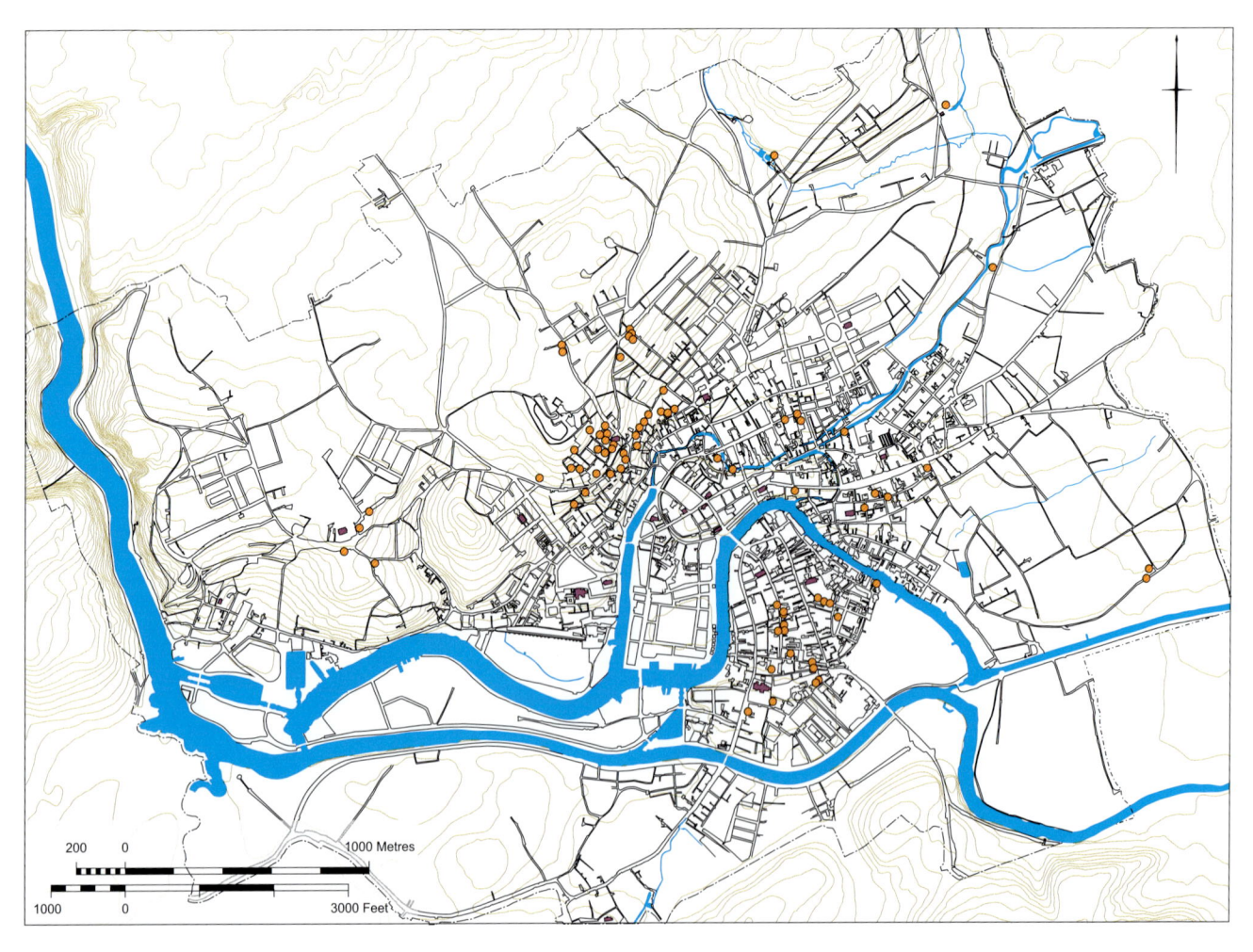

*Fig 9.3*
*Map showing the distribution of lodges and garden houses known to have existed in the suburbs around the city of Bristol between the 15th and 18th centuries, based on the map of 1828 by Ashmead and Plumley, with the addition of contours from the modern Ordnance Survey map (reproduced by permission of Ordnance Survey on behalf of HMSO, © Crown copyright 2014. All rights reserved. Licence number 100046522). (RHL, PEC).*

## THE GARDEN HOUSE

*Fig 9.4
Nos.8–11 Park Row, a property granted to Mede's chantry in St Mary Redcliff in 1548, included a garden and 'le Lodge' held by one Maurice Cradogge. The lodge is no.10, the closer of the two gabled houses shown here on an aerial photograph of 2000 (Reece Winstone Archive, negative no.32638).*

a grocer.[17] In 1568 an orchard, garden and lodge in the suburbs adjoining Earles Mead was occupied by Joan Pacy, widow of Thomas Pacy, an alderman of the city whose residence had been in High Street.[18] This must have been close to another lodge identified on Millerd's map of 1673 as 'the Whitstry' and known before 1690 as 'Earls Mead Lodge' or 'Newfoundland'; the property was once of Edward Pyland, a butcher, and after of Thomas Harris, a brewer.[19] In 1589 a garden with a lodge in Old Market was held by Thomas Younge, a merchant.[20] This was a pattern of ownership which will be seen to have continued into the next century. Among those who owned lodges in 16th- and 17th-century Bristol Sir John Younge, a gentleman and collector of customs for Bristol, was very much the exception.

### The Red Lodge

Younge was responsible for the building of the Red Lodge between 1578 and 1589, within one of the gardens on the hillside above his great house on St Augustine's Back, possibly to a design by the Italian architect Serlio (Figs 9.5.

9.6a and 9.6b). When sited close to the principal residence of a gentleman or person of greater importance, the lodge could take on a function similar to that of the banqueting house, a place for retreat to have desserts following a formal dinner.

The Red Lodge must have fulfilled such a function, although the guests crossing the

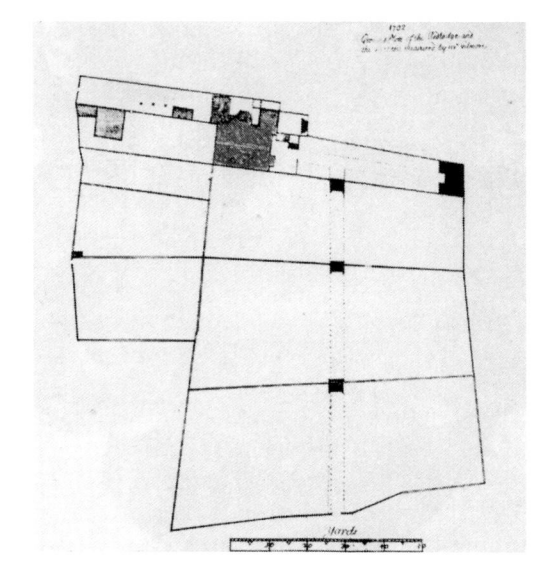

*Fig 9.5
Plan of the Red Lodge and gardens in 1702, from The Kingsweston Book of Drawings (BRO 33746).*

231

# THE TOWN HOUSE IN MEDIEVAL AND EARLY MODERN BRISTOL

*Fig 9.6*
*The Red Lodge:*
*a) view from garden, photograph of 2011 (English Heritage DP 140423);*
*b) Serlio's design, published between 1537 and 1575 and possibly used for its construction (Serlio, eds Hart and Hicks 1996, xxxir (153r)).*

thoroughfare of Trenchard Lane to reach the upper garden would have been conscious that this was no rural idyll. Once below the lodge, steps leading to an open and balustraded loggia (Figs 9.6a and 9.6b) at the ground floor enabled Younge and his guests to move between the delights of the garden and those of the house. On the first and originally the middle floor, a richly finished great parlour or chamber took up two-thirds of the available space of this two-room wide, single-pile house (Figs 9.7 and 9.8). The stair tower may have risen to the roof to provide a viewing platform.

## Other Lodges and their Owners

Contemporaries might have seen the building of the White Lodge in *c* 1588 as an attempt to emulate that of the Red Lodge. Similarly situated on the lower slopes of St Michael's Hill a little to the north, it was of similar size and plan, but had two towers rather than one (Figs 9.9a and 9.9b).[21] Its builder, William Birde, was not a gentleman, but a woollen draper. An immediate reason for its construction was perhaps his need to celebrate in style his year as mayor, commencing in 1589.[22] Birde could not have used his lodge as a place for occasional entertainment in the same way that Sir Robert Younge intended for the Red Lodge. Unlike the latter, the White Lodge was not contiguous with a greater house, and could not have been used as a place of retreat for the desserts following the main meal. Birde's principal residence was at some distance in the centre of the walled city close to Bristol Bridge, at no.59 Baldwin Street (identified as Seyer's chapel of St John in chapter 1). An intensively developed tenement plot in a prime commercial position, it was a suitable location for a prominent draper.[23]

Keeping a second residence as a retreat from the less pleasant aspects of city life was not a new idea. Almost a century before, in 1505, Thomas Elyot, a soap maker, held a property at the north end of Redcliff Street close to Bristol Bridge; here he kept the fat, furnaces and cisterns of his noxious trade. Elyot also kept a second residence in Barton Hundred on the

THE GARDEN HOUSE

*Fig 9.7*
*The Red Lodge, the great parlour on the first floor, photograph of 2003 (NMR AA047227, JD).*

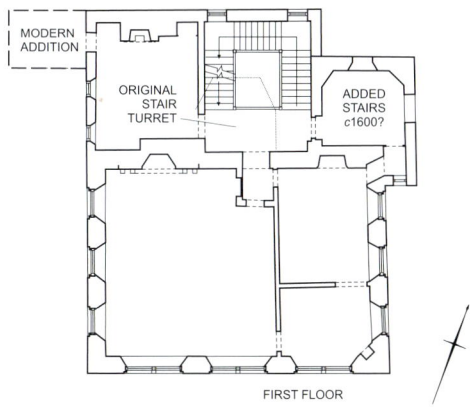

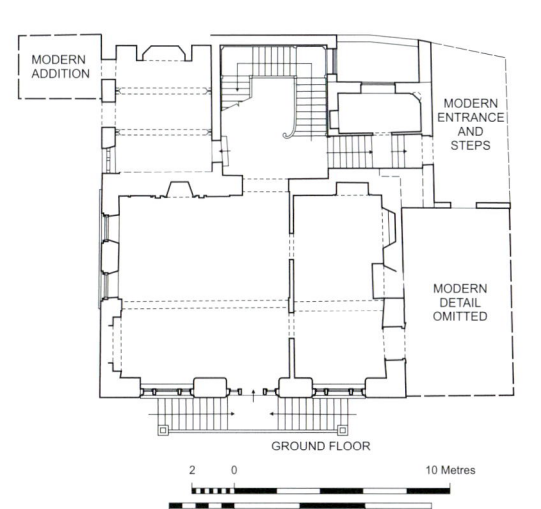

east side of the city, with a cellar used for the storage of wine. This was probably close to St James's churchyard, where he kept a standing, or stall.[24] In 1558 John White, titled 'gentleman', but a linen draper by trade, used the rooms over his shop on Bristol Bridge both for storage and for living accommodation.[25] White, too, had a second residence in Bedminster, on the very southern extremity of the city. In 1578 Francis

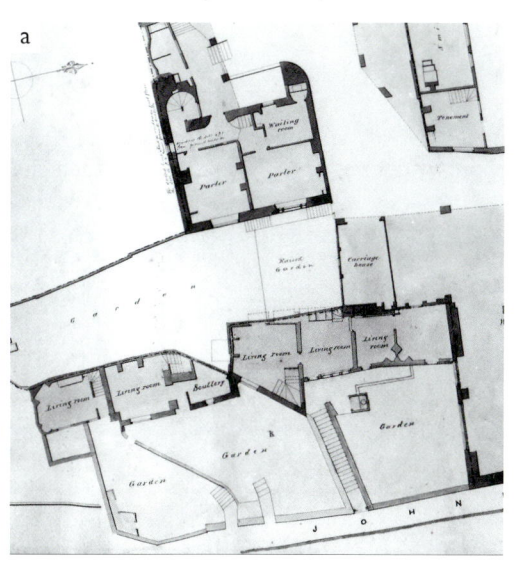

*Fig 9.8 (far left)*
*The Red Lodge, plans of the ground and first floors (RHL, PEC after NF).*

*Fig 9.9 (left and below)*
*The White Lodge, Bristol: a) plan of mid-19th century (extract from BRO 33041/ BMC/12/PL4 fol 9); b) watercolour by H O'Neill, 1821 (BRSMG M2574).*

233

Knight, a mercer, maintained a similar lifestyle, occupying two adjacent tenements in High Street for the purposes of his trade, but also holding for his own use a lodge and garden in Old Market.[26]

One of the earliest lodges known in some detail is possibly a house and its adjacent garden excavated in 1999. Close to what is now Union Street, in medieval times it would have fronted the suburban street known as St James's Back, just outside the Pithay Gate and town wall. This lodge would have comprised several buildings spread across two separate freeholds, both leased by the Cheddar family – merchants whose lands descended ultimately to Lord Lisle, the Crown and then the Corporation of Bristol. The northerly part of the property was described in 1544 as a 'lodge', the southerly part five years later as a 'mansion house and brewhouse'. The array of buildings, courtyards and gardens were first constructed between the early to mid-12th century and the late 13th century (Fig.9.10). Their documented tenurial connections and associated finds, including wine jugs from France and Iberia, indicate that this property just outside the town walls was an elite residence.[27]

In the 17th century many more citizens can be identified as having owned a house in the centre of the city and another on the periphery. In 1634 the merchant George White described his house in Lower Park Row as his dwelling house, but at the same time saw himself as a parishioner of St Werburgh's in the centre of the city.[28] By the 1650s a number of gardens, each containing a lodge, fronted on to Upper Maudlin Street or Johnny Ball Lane, all within the former precinct of St Bartholomew's Hospital (Fig 9.3). With the exception of the White Lodge, all were (or had been) leased to successive generations of individuals whose main residence was in the centre of the city – merchants such as Matthew Haviland, followed by his son Robert; Francis Creswick, followed by his son Henry; and Anthony Gay, succeeded by his widow Martha. Their lodges were among the 19 'garden houses' listed in the Hearth Tax return for St Michael's parish in 1662.[29]

By this date there were certainly more such houses on the slopes of Stony Hill in the adjacent parish of St Augustine's, and in other parishes on the edges of the city. The owners of these lodges, mostly merchants and traders, lived almost exclusively in the central parishes close to the Bridge and carfax. This development of lodges or garden houses had been promoted by those members of the urban elite who managed the estates of the former St Bartholomew's Hospital on behalf of the Corporation.

Above the Bartholomew lands on St Michael's Hill, the 'Little Park' was similarly developed as an estate of garden houses in the 1660s (Fig 9.3).[30] Here certainly were some of the 'comely buildings and pleasant gardens' that Millerd had in mind in 1673. The precincts of the Blackfriars, the former Dominican Friary, and of the Greyfriars, the former Franciscan Friary, were redeveloped in a similar way. Within the former precinct of the Dominican Friary a number of lodges existed by the early 1600s. Immediately north of the former friary church were the lodges of Humphrey Brent, a button maker, of Alice Warren, a widow, and of Richard Warde, a gardener. To the east was the lodge of George Richards, who also at this date held the lease of the Friars' Orchard to the east. Further south, against the Frome, was the lodge of Thomas Stringer, a whittawer (leather finisher).[31] Some

Fig 9.10
Union Street, formerly in St James's Back, plan of 1999–2000 showing excavations of buildings of the late 13th/14th centuries (RHL, PEC, based on plan by BaRAS).

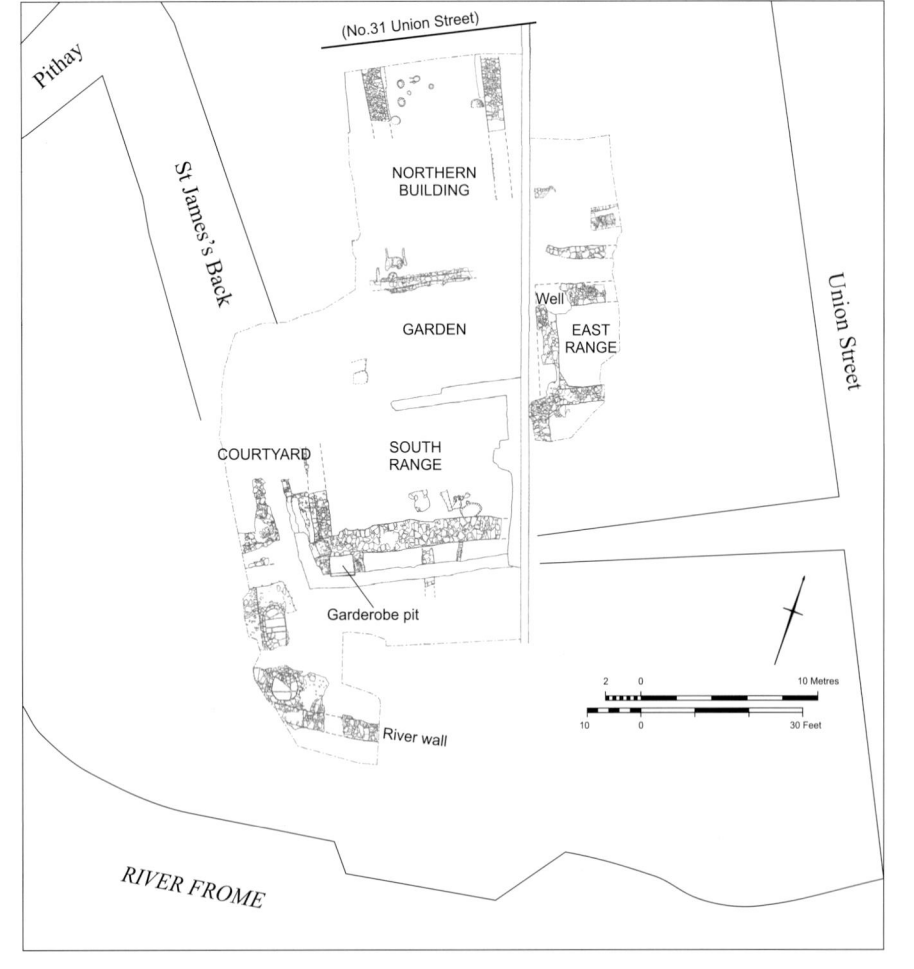

THE GARDEN HOUSE

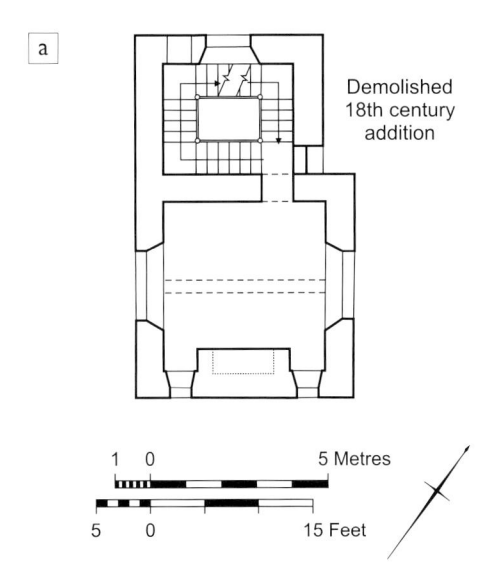

of these lodges were probably adaptations of medieval friary buildings. The use of already ancient buildings might in particular be valued by townspeople wishing to give an air of antiquity to their own lineage and status within the city.

When sold by the Corporation to the mercer Thomas Cole in 1585, the precinct of the Greyfriars was said to have included two lodges, 'one of old building', the other 'late newly built' by Cole. It also subsequently contained two other buildings which were probably lodges. The first of these was one of the monastic buildings, converted to a house by the 18th century (see Fig 2.15). The second was a lodge newly built in the 17th century and still surviving, although heavily rebuilt. Now confusingly renamed 'the abbot's house', it was sited in a street equally confusingly named Blackfriars (Figs 9.11a, 9.11b and 9.11c).[32] A plan of 1808 and a drawing by Loxton of no.4 Stile Lane, William Dunning's house in 1679 (Figs 9.12a and 9.12b), shows a garden house of similar plan, within the development of the Little Park commenced c 1660 (p43).[33]

Even more than their rural counterparts, most of these houses were characterised by the very restricted range of accommodation available for servants and guests. Where an architectural record exists, it can be seen that many of the 17th-century lodges were of one room on each floor, sometimes with an attached stair turret. These houses were of a size for which use of the term 'banqueting house' would have been appropriate, but such lodges could not have been used for banquets in the formal courtly sense as they were not contiguous with

Fig 9.11
Blackfriars, lodge of one room on each floor, built in the former precinct of the Greyfriars, in the street named Blackfriars:
a) plan of the first floor showing fireplace and overhead ceiling beam (RHL, PEC);
b) photograph of exterior, 1955 (NMR BB77/06692, PEWS);
c) photograph of stairs, 1955 (NMR BB77/06695, PEWS).

*Fig 9.12
Lodge in Stile Lane:
a) plan of ground floor, 1808 (not all windows are shown);
b) drawing by Loxton of c 1900
(BCRL Loxton drawings 1761X).*

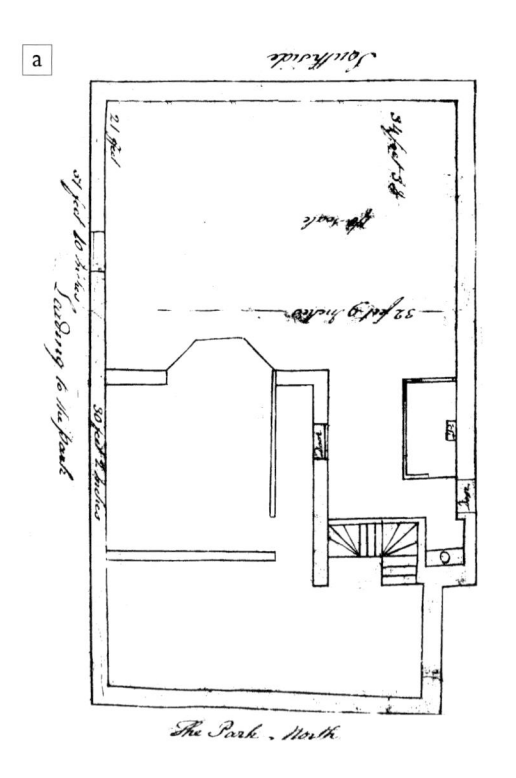

the main residence. In 1649 the Parliamentary Commissioners used the term 'banqueting house' to describe two structures on Stony Hill leased to Thomas Wells, a confectioner whose principal residence was in Broad Street; but this was possibly a piece of London terminology being applied to what citizens of Bristol would have termed a lodge.[34] In 1661 Wells's property (Figs 9.13a, 9.13b, 9.13c, 9.13d and 9.13e) was described in a lease issued in Bristol as 'a garden ground with a lodge therein'.[35]

The early 17th-century lodge within the Greyfriars estate consisted of simply one room on each of the four floors. The rooms were accessed from a well-finished, open-well stair in a turret projecting northwards from the house, with the turret occupying space almost two-thirds of the area of the main part of the lodge (Figs 9.11a, 9.11b and 9.11c). Service accommodation must have been restricted to the ground-floor kitchen and possibly a garret in the roof. The main part of this structure, 20ft square in its external dimensions, was of similar size to the lodge newly built by Cole in 1585 (23½ft by 19½ft).[36] Similar in size and appearance were others on the slopes to the west. Tower-like, these houses were all probably of one room on each floor.[37] The earliest part of a large 17th-century house, later to become the Female Penitentiary in Upper Maudlin Street, built within the same precinct, may have had this plan and was of almost identical size (Figs 9.14a and 9.14b). On St Michael's Hill, a similar structure was situated in the centre of what had become by 1662 the garden house of the merchant Eusebius Brookes; with seven hearths, it had clearly by then been extended (Fig 9.15).

The description of the contents of Richard Jordan's garden house, in the inventory of his possessions made after his death in 1676 (Appendix 2), provides the best insight available into the interior organisation of one of these tower-like houses (Fig 9.16). The lowest floor was a cellar for storage. Above this was a kitchen, and above that a dining room. Above that were the best chamber and a garret above in the roof, the inventory account matching exactly the three hearths noted in the 1662 assessment.

Jordan, a painter, was possessed of considerable wealth. He lived also at his house in Broad Street, a building of the mid-16th century, but kept half of his possessions in what was a sumptuously furnished garden house on the hill, described in 1676 as 'his house in the Parke'; 15 glasses and 17 platters, great and small, indicated the likely scale of entertainment.[38] Gilbert Moore's garden house (*see* Fig 3.23) was smaller than Jordan's; possessing only two hearths in 1662, it consisted probably of just two floors. Heightened by one storey and extended outwards, Moore's garden house survived until destroyed by bombing in 1940–1 (Fig 9.17).

THE GARDEN HOUSE

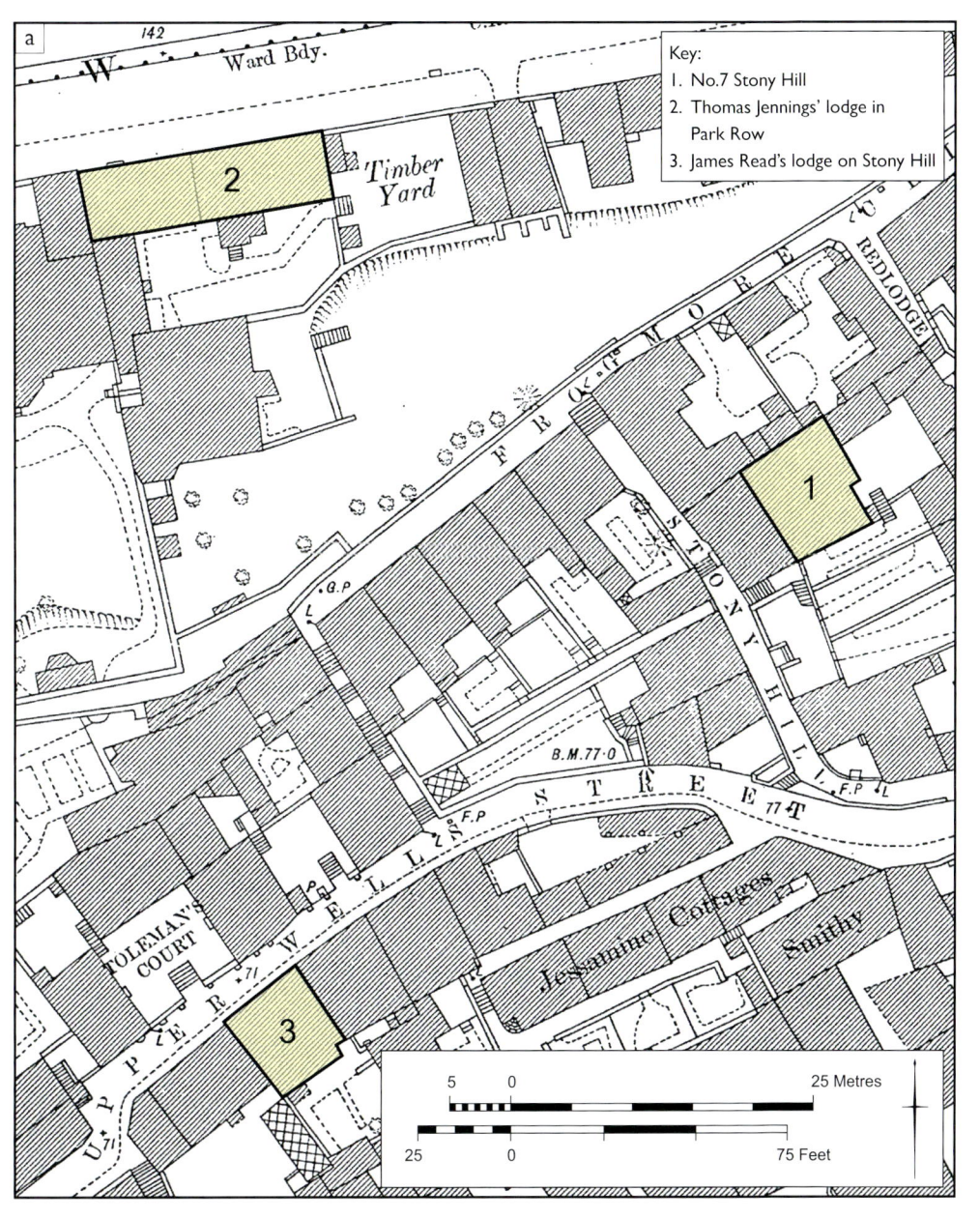

Fig 9.13
Thomas Wells's lodge on Stony Hill:
(a) location plan:
1. No.7 Stony Hill (Thomas Wells)
2. Thomas Jennings' lodge in Park Row
3. James Read's lodge on Stony Hill
(OS map, 1884. 1st edition 1:500 town plan, Gloucestershire, Bristol, sheet LXXI.16.24)
(b) photograph of exterior (BRSMG M3596)
(c) first-floor room (BCRL Loxton drawings)
(d) ceiling detail (BRSMG M3597)
(e) chimneypiece (BRSMG slide);
photographs and drawing all of the late 19th or early 20th centuries.

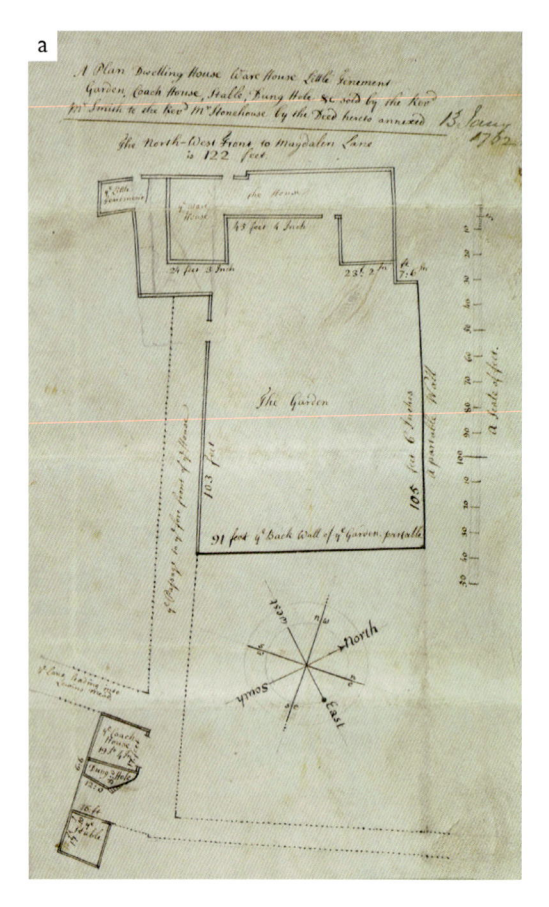

*Fig 9.14*
*Female Penitentiary in Upper Maudlin Street:*
*a) plan of 1762 (BRO 35722/1/9c);*
*b) 19th-century print of exterior, possible early lodge on right (BCRL L.36.7 BRI).*

Two further garden houses noted in 1662 were within gardens fronting St Michael's Hill. Immediately above the row of four early 17th-century, one-room plan houses (nos.23–9) were in 1662 the garden houses of Mrs Elizabeth Cugley and Leonard Hancocke, a soap maker whose main residence overlooked the Avon at the north end of Redcliff Street. Each had just one hearth. That of Mrs Cugley was possibly one of the structures shown on a plan of nos.31–7 St Michael's Hill, c 1813 (Fig 9.18).

On the same hillside to the west of the city, a house in Upper Wells Street was of similar size to the lodge in Greyfriars and that of Richard Jordan. It measured 24ft square externally and consisted of only one room on each of the four floors; that on the first floor had a decorated plaster ceiling (Figs 9.19a and 9.19b). Built c 1654 by James Read, the minister of Little St Augustine's, on a plot close to another leased by Read to Thomas Wall for the construction of a lodge, this may too have been intended to be used as such. A lodge of similar size was the 17th-century part of Rupert House in Upper Church Lane. Built in 1674, 24ft wide and 18ft deep, it was of three storeys and probably had one room on each floor. This was possibly built

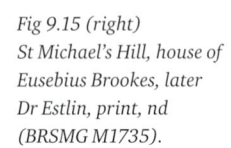

*Fig 9.15 (right)*
*St Michael's Hill, house of Eusebius Brookes, later Dr Estlin, print, nd (BRSMG M1735).*

*Fig 9.16 (below)*
*St Michael's Hill, Richard Jordan's 'house in the Parke', from Millerd's map of 1673 (BRSMG).*

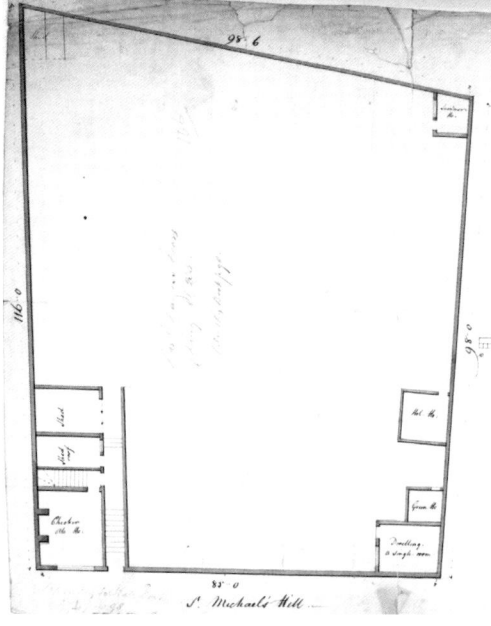

*Fig 9.17 (far left)*
*Gilbert Moore's garden house on St Michael's Hill. The further part of the house is shown here (BRSMG Heber Mardon Bequest, watercolour by E Parkman, nd, Ma.4023).*

*Fig 9.18 (left)*
*Plan of nos.31–7 St Michael's Hill, c 1813, showing the garden with garden house of Mrs Cugley in 1662 (BRO 04479(2) fol 98c; Leech 2000b, 76).*

*Fig 9.19*
*Stony Hill, James Read's lodge: a) exterior view, photograph of 1956 (Reece Winstone Archive K55); b) decorated plaster ceiling to first-floor chamber, photograph of 1960 (Reece Winstone Archive, negative no.35137).*

for another merchant, the initials on the dated chimneypiece probably being those of Richard Stubbs and Mary his wife (Figs 9.20a and 9.20b).

Similar structures could be observed in the 17th century to the south and east of the city. In Jacob Street, the back lane to Old Market, one such house demolished in 1908 is known of only from an account by Pritchard.[39] Of one room on each floor and gabled on all four sides, it must have been very similar in appearance to the

*Fig 9.20*
*Upper Church Lane, Rupert House:*
*a) exterior view from drawing, probably of the early 20th century and by Loxton (BCRL Extra-Illustrated Latimer 16th-century Annals)*
*b) chimneypiece of 1674 (on brackets), photograph late 19th or early 20th century (BRSM Mb1007).*

*Fig 9.21*
*Jacob Street, chimneypiece in Headford House, Jacob Street (BRSMG photographic plate. no.1352, not labelled, but identified as being of the house described by Pritchard and probably of c 1908 (Pritchard 1908, 289–92).*

surviving lodge in the Blackfriars. A chimneypiece on the first floor carried the date 1664, along with initials – perhaps those of Nehemiah Collins and his wife. Collins was Sheriff in 1658, and he was recorded as living at approximately this location in 1662 (Fig 9.21).[40] This was possibly one of a number of lodges fronting on to both sides of Jacob Street. They are shown on Millerd's map of 1673, and possibly survived until at least the early 20th century at nos.71 and the Golden Bowl at the corner with David Street, as well as at nos.37–9 (Fig 9.22). Other lodge-like houses on the east side of the city included the Three Horseshoes on Narrow Weir and a house at Rennison's Bath – the setting of each being enhanced through the proximity to running water (Figs 9.23, 9.24a and 9.24b).

The higher ground around St Mary Redcliff was a favoured area for the siting of such residences, evidently pre-dating St Michael's Hill in its popularity for this purpose. We might link this to the importance of the Redcliff Fee for the cloth trade in the late medieval period, and the prosperity the trade brought, especially to this southern part of the city. In a number of instances the location of lodges appears also to have been linked to the presence of cloth-drying racks; the large garden of a peripheral urban residence for occasional use would lend itself to such purposes. In 1617 the property at nos.54–5 St Thomas Street was described as a tenement, garden, lodge and a rack called 'Parke Corner'.[41]

Further along the same street nos.62–5 consisted in 1572 of two lodges under one roof, together with a garden and two racks.[42] In the same year nos.87–90 were now described as a lodge and garden, together with a rack.[43] On the far side of the suburb south of the river were the lodges built close to Temple churchyard (chapter 3) and in Pyke's Meadow, later the site of the Great Gardens development (chapter 3). In 1568 this was described as 'one acre of meadowe grounde with a lodge or stable standinge at the west ende of the said acre'. Pyke's Meadow was probably the 'one close with three rackes called Teynters … one acre' held by Thomas Nashe, listed in the grant of Temple Fee to the city in 1544.[44]

A house at no.58 Pile Street near St Mary Redcliff church was another lodge, shown on two watercolours of the 1820s from the Braikenridge collection. It evidently consisted of one room on each floor, with that on the first floor featuring a decorated plaster ceiling – of sufficient interest to merit recording at the

THE GARDEN HOUSE

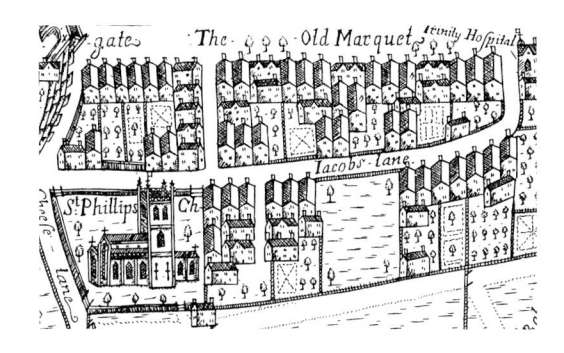

time of its demolition c 1870 (Figs 9.25a, 9.25b and 9.25c). This lodge was described in 1691 as 'a little tenement or lodge and garden', late of Nicholas Pattfield, a wool comber.[45] The juxtaposition of elaborate provision for entertainment and minimal provision for service and sleeping marked this house out as a lodge. At least five other houses named as lodges were sited further to the east or west in the same street.[46]

On the hillside above these, to the east of the churchyard and on the opposite side of Pump Lane, was a large garden, which by 1509 formed part of the endowment of the chantry of William Canynges. A lodge had been built here by 1534. In 1549, at the dissolution of the chantries, it was described as a house or lodge, standing to the east of the churchyard. The lodge and a second smaller building are shown on Millerd's

*Fig 9.22 (above left)*
*Jacob Street, probable lodges shown on Millerd's map of 1673 (BRSMG).*

*Fig 9.23 (above)*
*The Three Horseshoes on Narrow Weir, probably built as a lodge, photograph of 1931 (NMR AA78/06741, PEWS).*

*Fig 9.24*
*Lodge at Rennisons Bath:*
*a) exterior, drawing by Loxton of 1913;*
*b) interior, drawing by Loxton of 1913*
*(BCRL Loxton drawings 85B and 905L).*

241

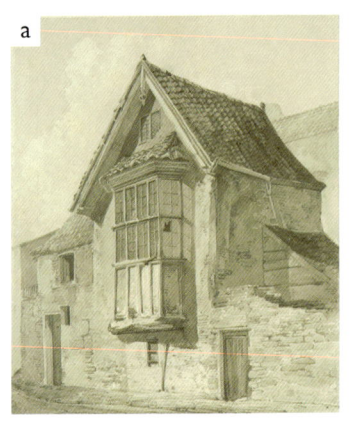

# THE TOWN HOUSE IN MEDIEVAL AND EARLY MODERN BRISTOL

Fig 9.25
Lodge at no.58 Pile Street:
a) watercolour by H O'Neill, 1821
(BRSMG M2039);
b) drawing of c 1870 by Joseph Wood, deposited by Miss Wood/Eustace Button [architect]
(BRO Mb 3499 (part 1));
c) sketch of c 1870
(Reproduced with the kind permission of Devon Heritage Services, N W Deckemant drawings, Z19/31/3/1–17).

Fig 9.26
Lodge first mentioned in 1534 and a second smaller but possibly similar building close to St Mary Redcliff church, as shown on Millerd's map of 1673
(BRSMG).

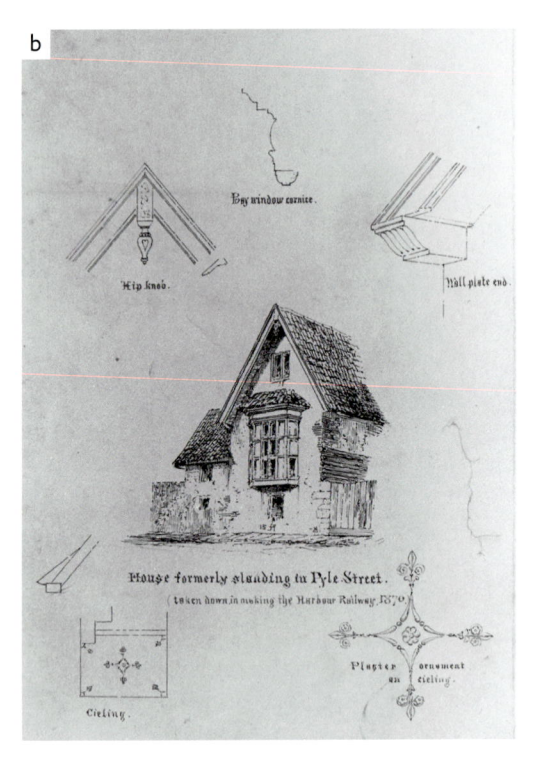

map of 1673 (Fig 9.26).[47] Another lodge on Redcliff Hill, shown on an early illustration and in plan evidently of two rooms on each floor with a central stairs, had by the 19th century become part of the Hope and Anchor Inn (Figs 9.27a and 9.27b). In 1684 this was the garden, lodge and tenement leased to one Daniel Gwillim, by 1692 used as a dwelling house.[48]

On the east side of the city, a house known as Tilly's Court House, in Barton Hill and demolished in 1894, was of the one-room plan. It was of three storeys with a projecting two-storey porch, and originally had one principal room on each floor (Figs 9.28a and 9.28b). The wide mullioned and transomed windows on the ground and first floors were possibly of the 16th century, but both the entrance porch and a carved stone chimneypiece on the first floor bore the date 1658 and the initials of Thomas Harris, a brewer, and his wife Elizabeth. The ground-floor room was finished to a similar standard, also with a carved stone chimneypiece and decorated ceiling, while a massive stairs in the south-east corner provided access to the upper floors. For Thomas and Elizabeth Harris this was probably a second residence, with their principal home being no.58 Castle Street; then newly built, the latter provided at least double the amount of accommodation. Hard times or disenchantment, or possibly the purchase of the Whitstry (Fig 9.29), a larger lodge closer to the city (above), might have occasioned their sale of Tilly's Court House in 1663.[49]

Barton Hill, like St Michael's Hill, was possibly a favoured location for a garden house. Across the road from Tilly's Court House was another larger lodge, now the Rhubarb Tavern (Figs 9.30a, 9.30b and 9.30c), but probably built c 1672 as the garden house of Sir Thomas Day. Mayor in 1687–8, he was a soap maker and the owner of the great house at Bristol Bridge (see Fig 8.100).[50] Like Day, a few among the most prosperous citizens had the use of second residences which offered substantially more accommodation. In the last decades of the 16th

242

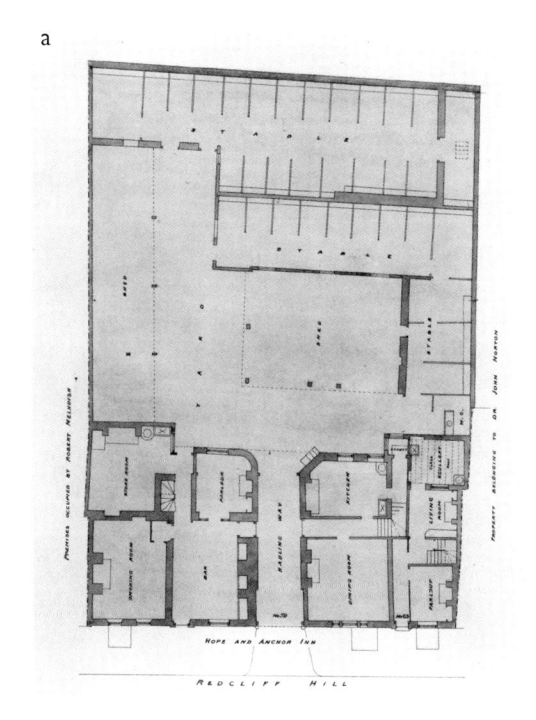

century both the Red Lodge and the White Lodge (above) provided approximately four times the floor space offered by lodges of one-room plan, such as those built in the Greyfriars precinct. While the Red Lodge was certainly planned to function as a banqueting house with only a limited amount of accommodation for servants and for guests staying overnight, the original plan of the White Lodge is uncertain; demolished in 1874, it was recorded only on a 19th-century plan (Fig 9.9).

More is known of two larger lodges built on the slopes of Stony Hill in the 17th century. Built before 1634, in the garden to the north of the Red Lodge, was no.10 Park Row. This garden had belonged to the White family since 1599,[51] and since no.10 was the dwelling house of George White at the time of his death in 1634, it is likely

Fig 9.27
Lodge on Redcliff Hill, by the 19th century part of the Hope and Anchor Inn:
a) in plan of the mid-19th century (BR033041/BMC/12/PL2 fol 53);
b) as shown in drawing by Loxton of 1908 (BCRL Loxton drawings 946M).

Fig 9.28
Tilly's Court House, Barton Hill, as shown in drawings by Loxton:
a) exterior;
b) garden gateway (both in Pritchard 1897).

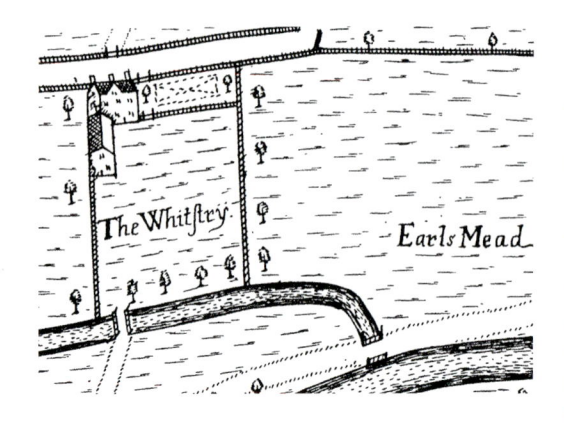

*Fig 9.29*
*The Whitstry, Newfoundland Lane, Millerd's map of 1673 (BRSMG).*

*Fig 9.30*
*The Rhubarb Tavern, formerly Barton Hill House, Queen Anne Road:*
*a) plan of the ground floor (RHL, PEC);*
*b) exterior showing the projecting stair turret on the south side, photograph of 2012 (English Heritage DP 152555);*
*c) chimneypiece with the date 1672 and 'TDA', the initials of Sir Thomas and Lady Anne Day, photograph of 2012 (English Heritage DP 146961).*

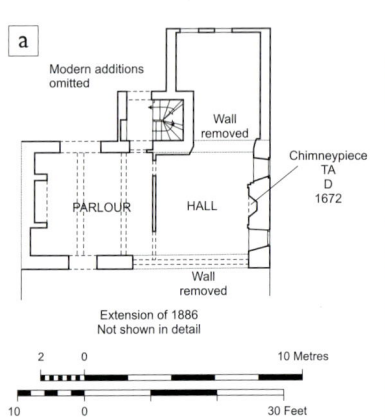

that the house was built for him or at least a member of his family (Figs 9.31a and 9.31b). It was not the only dwelling that White held, for in his will he was said to be of the city centre parish of St Werburgh – probably one of the two George Whites listed as living there in 1610.[52] It would in any event have been improbable that in the early 17th century a merchant of sufficient wealth to make large endowments to the Corporation and others (Figs 9.32a and 9.32b) would have lived only on the hillside above the city. Like William Birde, George White probably lived in the centre of the city and kept a second residence standing in its own large garden, no more than 20 minutes walk away on the hillside to the west. With two rooms on each of the four floors, each separated by the central stairs, no.10 Lower Park Row offered approximately twice the floor area and twice the number of rooms as a lodge of one-room plan;[53] the property could have been intended by White to be his principal residence rather than a lodge, notwithstanding his loyalty to the parish of St Werburgh.

In 1664 no.7 Stony Hill was built for Thomas Wells, confectioner, on the site of the two banqueting houses noted by the Parliamentary Commissioners. Wells died in 1666, leaving to his widow Elizabeth his house on Stony Hill 'new builded', together with the garden, but leaving to her also the house in which he lived in Broad Street.[54] The house on Stony Hill was described in 1692 as 'a lodge … now converted into a fair messuage'.[55] No detailed floor plan has been traced, but photographs and an outline plan show there must have been at least two principal rooms on each floor, in addition to a substantial stairs (Figs 9.13a and 9.13b). The principal chamber on the first floor had a dated chimneypiece with the initials of Wells and his wife Elizabeth (Figs 9.13c and 9.13e), while the ceiling had plasterwork with the allegorical female figure of Abundance and her Horn of Plenty (Figs 9.13c, 9.13d and 9.13e). It is likely that Wells intended to use the house as a second residence. The views of this room, and of that in the lodge of his neighbour James Read

THE GARDEN HOUSE

*Fig 9.31*
*No.10 Lower Park Row:*
*a) plan of the ground floor prior to restoration of the house c 1983 (RHL, PEC after John Bryant;*
*b) restored original frontage to garden on the west, photograph of 2010 (English Heritage DP 114300).*

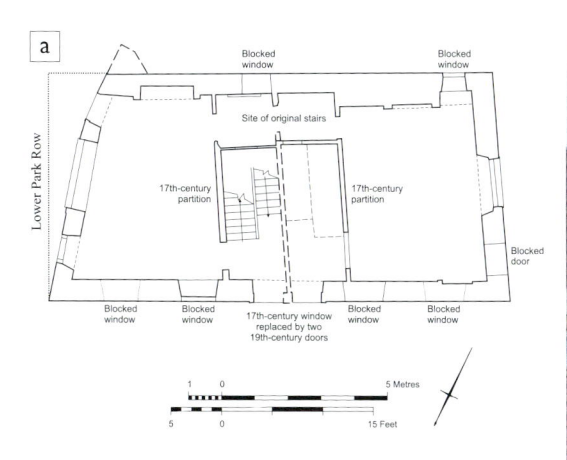

(Fig 9.19), provide two of the best available insights into the interior decor of the mid-17th-century lodge in Bristol.

The garden house of the vintner Ralph Oliffe in Upper Mauldin Street, close to the lodge that later became the Female Penitentiary, must, from its exterior appearance, have been of similar plan (Fig 9.14). However, nothing is known of its interior appearance except from the probate inventory of Oliffe's possessions, where it is described as the 'garden house in Magdalen Lane' (Appendix 2). By the 1750s this had become the house of James Stewart, writing master and historian; a drawing of 1753 prepared for his unpublished history provides the earliest detailed view of one of the 'comely buildings and pleasant gardens' described and shown in outline by Millerd. Like no.10 Lower Park Row, the house first of Oliffe and then Stewart was of three and a half storeys with a central entrance hall, its facade to a walled garden on the east side (Fig 9.33). Oldbury House on St Michael's Hill, the garden house built c 1679–89 by Marmaduke Bowdler, a woollen draper whose city centre residence was at the west end of Bristol Bridge, was of similar plan (Fig 9.34).

Another of Stewart's drawings shows a house of similar form a little to the west of his own house in Upper Maudlin Street, built in the precinct of the former nunnery of St Mary Magdalen at the corner of St Michael's Hill and Horfield Road. In 1708 this was one of 'two heretofore new built houses' built within 'the Upper Maudlens', both possibly garden houses (Fig 9.35).[56]

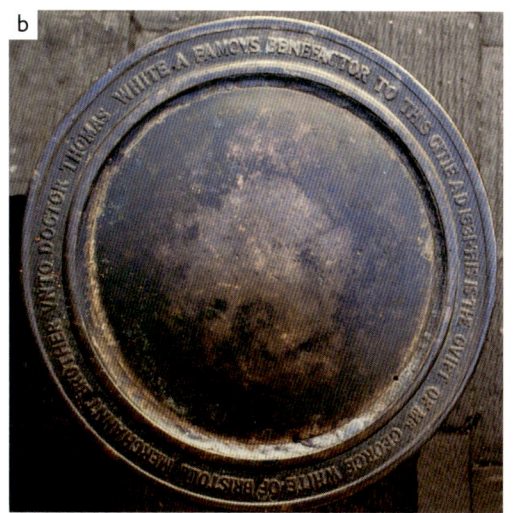

*Fig 9.32*
*Corn Street:*
*a) and b) – 'Nail' given by George White in 1631. One of four brass-turned, flat-topped stands, formerly placed beneath a covered way on the north side of All Saints' Church and used for settling deals, now on the north side of the Exchange; photographs of 2011 (English Heritage DP 114332, 152580).*

245

*Fig 9.33*
*'View of my own dwelling house, taken from the windows of Mr Jackson's upper room', formerly the garden house or lodge of Ralph Oliffe in Upper Maudlin Street, drawing by James Stewart, 1753 (Bodleian Library, Western MS, Gough Somerset 8, fol 20).*

*Fig 9.34*
*Oldbury House, no.121 St Michael's Hill:*
*a) photograph of 2011 (English Heritage DP 141398)];*
*b) plan of ground floor (RHL,PEC after Oatley and Brentnall).*

Other evidence confirms that, notwithstanding the restricted accommodation available in most lodges, such houses were well finished and could be furnished to varying standards of comfort. In 1638 Thurston Harris, a prosperous baker, lived on a tightly constrained tenement plot in Marsh Street adjacent to St Stephen's churchyard. With six well-furnished rooms and a bakehouse, this was certainly his principal residence. Harris's second house at 'Barton hundred', probably the farmhouse called Whitfield Place, was more sparsely furnished, its contents accounting for one-tenth of his moveable wealth. The arrangement of the rooms there precludes it having been of similar plan to the lodge in Blackfriars, or to that of Tilly's Court House on Barton Hill, but it does provide an indication of how such a second residence might be furnished. The five rooms included a heated parlour with seating for six to nine persons, a buttery, an unheated kitchen and two chambers with beds for three persons. Harris and his family probably spent Sundays there, for the contents of the parlour included 'one great bible', an item absent from the house in Marsh Street.[57]

In 1668 Michael Puxton's lodge on Redcliff Hill similarly had only one heated room which certainly served as a kitchen; but it had beds for four persons and tableware for six. Puxton, a wealthy soap maker, lived on a congested plot in Redcliff Street, close to the Bridge. His lodge was near enough to be visited during summer evenings, but the sleeping accommodation indicates that it was also a place in which to stay.[58] In contrast the sparsely furnished lodge or 'garden house' leased by Sir Henry Creswick, in Upper Maudlin Street on St Michael's Hill, contained only two small table boards, a little feather bed, stools and pictures. Creswick possibly made little use of it. The lodge was only 20 minutes walk away from his house in Small Street, but he possessed a larger, much more sumptuously furnished second residence at Hanham Court, some four miles distant.[59] The Hearth Tax return for 1662 provides a further

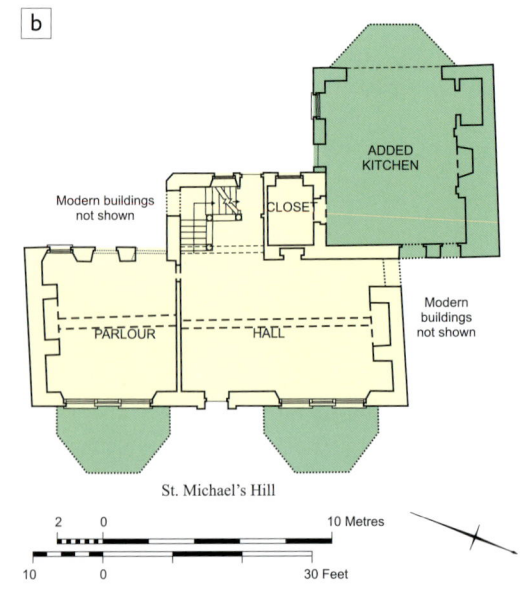

# THE GARDEN HOUSE

*Fig 9.35
'The west view of the remains of the Magdalens taken from Peter Baynton's tomb in St Michs Ch yd', summerhouse and garden houses built in the precinct of St Mary Magdalen, drawing by James Stewart, 1751 (Bodleian Library, Western MS, Gough Somerset 8, fol 17).*

reminder that lodges varied considerably in comfort. Among the 19 garden houses listed for St Michael's parish, the number of hearths ranged from one to five.⁶⁰

By the later 17th century the terms 'garden house' and 'lodge' were for the most part synonymous, except probably for the largest houses, such as the Red or White Lodges. In the religious persecution of the Dissenters in March 1670 the wealthy Baptist benefactor Edward Terrill was recorded as having 'moved his habitation from Corne Street to his Garden house near Lawford's Gate'.⁶¹ At least three of the lodges in Upper Maudlin Street and Johnny Ball Lane, described as 'lodges' in the various city draft leases, were listed among the 19 'garden houses' on St Michael's Hill enumerated in the Hearth Tax return for 1662.

The term 'lodge' was also used more in legal documents. As used by the city surveyors in 1612, it described a property that had the potential to be used as a lodge. The surveyors had set out the terms of a lease to John Rymer, a blacksmith, of a 'lodge' built within a tower on the town wall (Fig 9.36).⁶² The inventory of Rymer's possessions made in 1617 shows that, although the property was described as a lodge in his lease from the Corporation, his use of it was more prosaic: its contents consisted solely of a pair of old bellows and various tools.⁶³ The term 'lodge' was perhaps preferred by the surveyors for the justification that it might provide for an increased rent. Evidence from London has shown the increasing awareness of the importance of amenity and situation in relation to rents in the early 17th century.⁶⁴

A 'lodge' could also be described as a 'summerhouse'. Michael Puxton's second residence on Redcliff Hill was described as a lodge in his will, but as a 'summerhouse' in the probate inventory compiled by the assessors of his possessions. It will be seen that the term 'summerhouse' was increasingly preferred to 'lodge' and 'garden house' in the later 17th and 18th centuries. The contents of Puxton's summerhouse show that these could serve as second residences, and were not necessarily the less substantial structures for daytime use implied in the present-day usage of the term.

Wealthy citizens continued to build summerhouses in this tradition well into the 18th century. In 1730 the merchant David Coombs purchased one of the plots newly laid out for development on the slopes of Kingsdown, on which he had already built a summerhouse. At his death in 1737 this passed to Buckler Weekes, the owner of a house in Upper Maudlin Street which was itself the successor to an earlier garden house, once held by Anthony and then Martha Gay. Just as Weekes' predecessors had found it congenial to have a lodge sited in Upper Maudlin Street above the bustle of the city,

*Fig 9.36
Back of Narrow Wine Street overlooking the Frome, watercolour by H O'Neill, 1821 (BRSMG M2895). In 1612 the bastion or tower in the middle distance formed part of the 'house and garden with a lodge built within the tower on the town wall' leased to John Rymer (Leech 1997a, 185).*

247

so Weekes now found it pleasing to have a summerhouse on Kingsdown, high above his own residence. His summerhouse on Kingsdown cannot have been particularly substantial, being demolished in 1771 for the building of Prospect House (below).[65]

Several plots to the east of Prospect House, at nos.13, 15 and 17 Marlborough Hill, three summerhouses were built on ground which was sold for building in the 1730s. One of these survives within no.13, a later house, c 15ft square in its outside dimensions, with a window to the east; it originally had both a window and an ashlar-faced entrance on the south. A second summerhouse, c 16ft square in its outside dimensions, survives within the ruins of the later no.15. A third, c 16ft square in its outside dimensions, survives as part of the largely later no.17 (Figs 9.37 and 9.38).

Further to the west along the same hillside overlooking the city, gardens with summerhouses of similar dimensions to those on Marlborough Hill were laid out to the east of St Michael's Hill. Some were sited on lands belonging to the Society of Merchant Venturers, and are shown on a map of their possessions here in 1766 (Fig 9.39a). Detailed survey has revealed some of these still surviving above no.27 Horfield Road and alongside Robin Hood Lane (Fig 9.39b).

On the hillside above Horfield Road, Southwell Street was developed in the 1750s by John Smith and Nathaniel Daniel, a carpenter and mason respectively. Their building leases allowed for the construction of either a messuage or a summerhouse.[66] There is no evidence, though, that the latter option was actually exercised. However, at the corner of Kingsdown Parade and Marlborough Hill one such house was built. It was c 22ft square and consisted of two rooms, one on each floor, with a corner window to catch the view along both streets and a vaulted cellar below (Fig 9.40). Set in its own garden, on a plot first leased in the 1730s, and constructed probably in the late 18th century, no.6 Kingsdown Parade must have been one of the last small garden or summerhouses of this type to be newly built in the city.[67]

Summerhouses in the more modern sense of the word were also built from at least the later 17th century. Andrew Hook had one such summerhouse in the grounds of his second

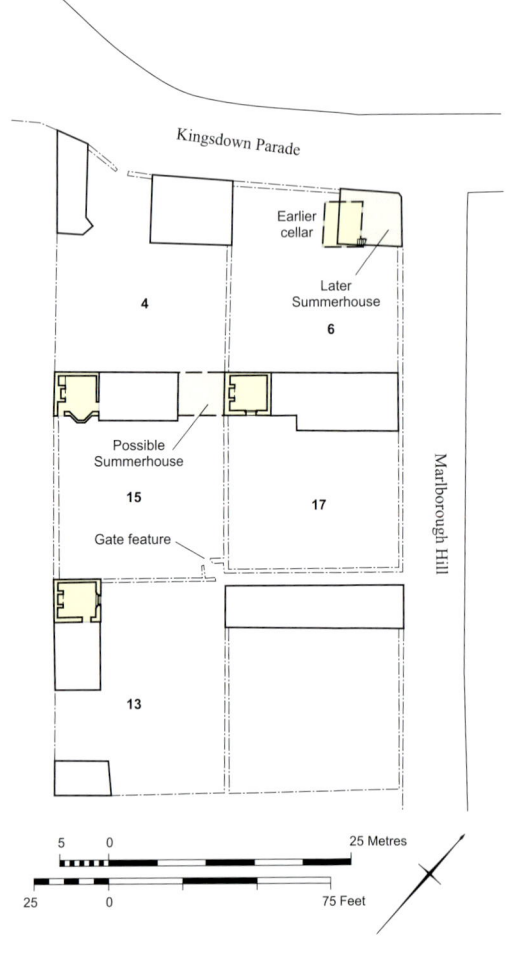

*Fig 9.37 (right) Plan of Marlborough Hill, nos.13, 15 and 17, showing the three summerhouses (RHL, PEC).*

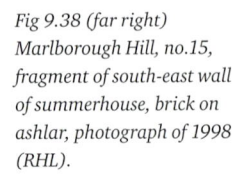

*Fig 9.38 (far right) Marlborough Hill, no.15, fragment of south-east wall of summerhouse, brick on ashlar, photograph of 1998 (RHL).*

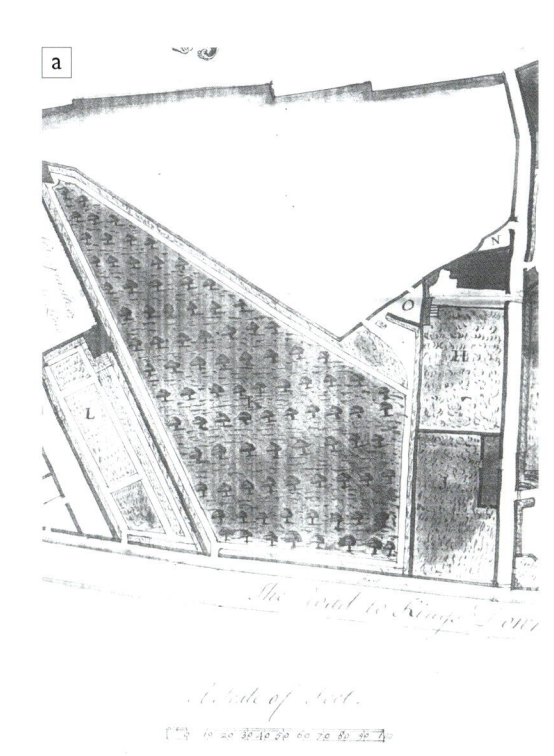

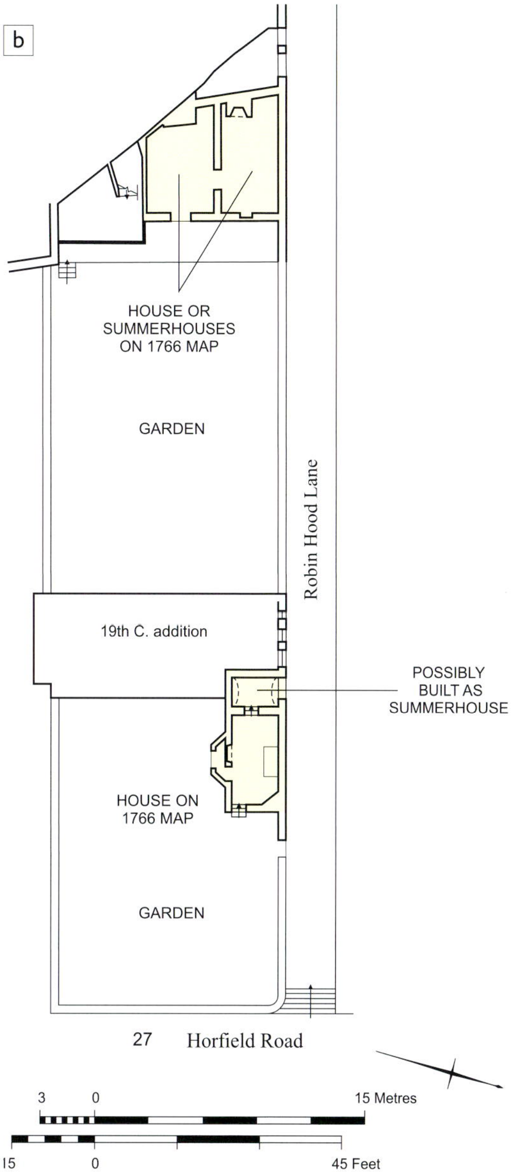

THE GARDEN HOUSE

Fig 9.39
Horfield Road and Robin Hood Lane, summerhouses as shown in:
a) map of 1766 (Merchant Venturers' archives);
b) plan (RHL, PEC, after RCHME).

residence at Ashley Manor (below); its contents in 1689 were a table and ladder (Appendix 2).[68] In the grounds of Oldbury House on St Michael's Hill, the cellar of Edward Bisdee's summerhouse in 1730 contained a parcel of bottled perry; on the floor above were four chairs, a table, a looking glass and a stove grate.[69] These summerhouses were possibly similar in appearance to that at the foot of St Michael's Hill and drawn by James Stewart in 1751 (Fig 9.35).

One of the principal ways in which people impose order on their daily experiences is through the use of naming systems. In the 17th century the terms 'garden house' and 'summerhouse' were increasingly used in preference to 'lodge' to describe a house secondary to a main residence and standing in its own garden. As names that were used regularly to describe a social space, such terms offer clues as to how these houses and gardens were perceived by those who lived in them. A better understanding of these concepts might come from looking at the relationships between house, garden and summer.

The owners of most lodges lived in parishes in the centre of the city. Some of them, such as William Birde of Baldwin Street and Thurston Harris of Marsh Street, had little or no garden. Almost all lodges, in contrast, stood within a garden. Many were built in already existing gardens, some within the former religious

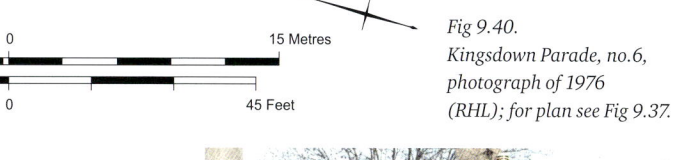

Fig 9.40.
Kingsdown Parade, no.6, photograph of 1976 (RHL); for plan see Fig 9.37.

249

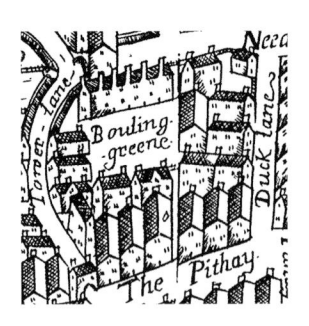

*Fig 9.41*
*Pithay Bowling Green, earlier the site of the Great Lodge, detail from Millerd's map of 1673 (BRSMG).*

precincts such as those of St Bartholomew's Hospital, the Greyfriars and the Blackfriars,[70] others behind the frontages of streets with long tenement plots, notably Old Market, Temple Street and St Thomas Street. Away from the principal streets, such gardens could be of considerable size. Close to the street known as Pithay a house described by 1609 as 'a great lodge' was surrounded by a garden of sufficient extent to have been converted to a bowling green by 1673; this lodge had possibly been abandoned by then, because its environment had become hemmed in and noisy (Fig 9.41).[71] To the south of the surviving lodge in Greyfriars was a herb garden, the individual plots set out as squares, rectangles and circles, defined by cattle bones.[72] Distanced from the busy streets these gardens offered tranquillity, seclusion and privacy, and a welcome escape from the noise, smells and bustle of the city.

It was in this more peaceful setting that the merchant George Lane died in 1614. His main residence lay close to the centre of the city in St Nicholas Street, but he died at his house on St Michael's Hill, known to the appraisers of his goods as 'the house att the hill' (Figs 9.42a and 9.42b).[73] A well-furnished second house with a good number of rooms, its contents included the tools and other items associated with the use of the land surrounding the house: notably rakes and other implements for the garden, three beehives, tools for haymaking, 18 milk pans and cheese-making equipment.[74]

At their second house at the Barton, Thurston Harris's family would have enjoyed a similar close relationship with the tilling and cultivation of the land around, illustrated by a barn complete with pickaxes, a spade and other tools.[75] Retreat to more rural surroundings was also feasible for some citizens. In c 1626 Richard Aldworth acquired the lease of Kingcot, a farm on the west side of the parish of Long Ashton to the west of the city and on the Somerset bank of the Avon (Figs 9.43a, 9.43b and 9.43c).[76] Here Aldworth evidently carried out some refurbishment, with the chimneypiece to the first-floor chamber bearing his initials and those of his wife, Mary. The plan of this house was different from that of the lodges closer to the city. It was determined here by the plan of the existing house, a medieval rural hallhouse, but it still featured a lodge-like projecting stairs turret, probably added by Aldworth.

Travelling from their city centre residence, possibly in All Saints Lane, Aldworth and his wife would have journeyed west from the city to cross the Avon at Rownham Ferry, thence into the parish of Long Ashton.[77] Travelling north out of the city, Robert Winstone and his family possibly made similar visits from no.1 High Street to their second residence later known as Oldbury Court (Fig 9.44). Journeys of similar length would have been necessary for the families visiting their lodges on Barton Hill, the Harris household going to Tilly's Court House or the Days visiting their lodge, now the Rhubarb Tavern.

The use of the term 'garden house' implies a close relationship between two different social spaces – one a cultivated and enclosed ground to be enjoyed, the other a roof under which to live. In Bristol this close relationship was very evident in the siting of lodges in relation to the garden. It would have been possible to place a lodge within its garden so that it was entirely surrounded by its own curtilage; but in practice lodges were for the most part placed to one side. Furthermore, although it was perfectly possible to provide an imposing facade to the street where it could be seen, in practice the principal facade of the lodge invariably fronted on to the garden. The consequences of these decisions can be seen by looking at the relationships between some of the lodges and gardens thus far identified.

Placed in the upper north-east corner of its garden was no.10 Lower Park Row (Fig 9.31). Its principal facade faced on to the garden which lay to the south and west of the house, enabling house and garden together to be in the sun for much of the day. From the house, the garden could be seen in its entirety from each of the four floors. The house itself was positioned so that enjoyment of its architecture was first and foremost for those in the garden. One end wall faced on to the lane. No.7 Stony Hill was similarly positioned. Here the house was placed in the north-west corner of the garden, with its two principal gables and cluster of angled chimneys all in view for those within the garden (Fig 9.13).

This same intimate relationship between house and garden could be seen in two of the lodges or garden houses in the former precinct of the Bartholomews. In Johnny Ball Lane, Richard Paine's small lodge was placed on the north side of its garden, on the side away from the lane (Figs 9.45a and 9.45b). The garden could be viewed in its entirety from the house, while the house, in turn, was best viewed

THE GARDEN HOUSE

a

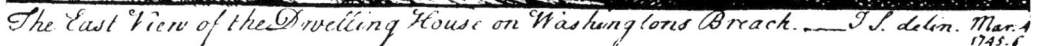

*The East View of the Dwelling House on Washingtons Breach.* — J.S. delin. Mar. 4 1745.6

b

*The West View of the Dwelling House and Mulberry Garden on Washingtons Breach.* J.S. delin. March 3 1745.6

*Fig 9.42
Park Row, Washington's Breach, the 'house att the hill' of the merchant George Lane, later the residence of James Stewart, drawings by James Stewart, 1746:
a) the house;
b) the garden
(Bodleian Library, Western MS, Gough Somerset 8, fols 32, 28).*

251

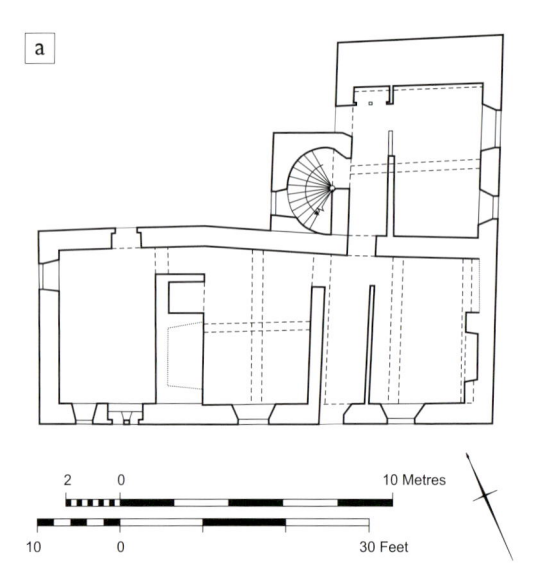

*Fig 9.43*
*Kingcot Farm, Long Ashton:*
*a) plan;*
*b) exterior;*
*c) chimneypiece with the initials of Richard and Mary Aldworth*
*(plan and photographs of 1982, RHL).*

*Fig 9.44*
*Oldbury Court, Robert Winstone's second residence, photograph of c 1908 (Reece Winstone Archive OB4401).*

from within the garden. On the hillside above was the White Lodge (Fig 9.9). This house was positioned against the west side of its much larger plot, with its rear elevation to Upper Maudlin Street and its principal facade looking south over the main part of the gardens.

In each of these properties the integration of house and garden is evident in the arrangements for access to the lodge. Convenience was not the primary consideration, for these were houses that had no direct access to the street: they could only be entered by passing first through the garden. The route to the house formed part of a processional way that served to underline the importance of the juxtaposition of house and garden. The long-demolished elaborate baroque gateway to the garden of the lodge at Tilly's Court House (Fig 9.28) can be read as an architectural statement: the entrance to such a garden house, in which garden and house were joined and used together as one. Subservient to

THE GARDEN HOUSE

a

*Fig 9.45
Richard Paine's small lodge in Bartholomew Lane:
a) watercolour by Burroughs of the early 19th century (BRSMG);
b) detail of plan of c 1857 (extract from BRO 33041/ BMC/12PL4 fol 9); see Figs. 9.3 and 9.9b) for location.*

this entrance was that to the garden of the Manor House in Park Lane (Fig 9.70c); here the entrance to the house itself, visible only from the garden, was also designed to impress (Fig 9.70b).

The garden was thus central to the use of houses that would be visited from time to time rather than lived in permanently. Therein lies the explanation for the use of the second term for the lodge, the 'summerhouse'. Gardens would be most welcoming in summer, and would need most attention then. Visits would

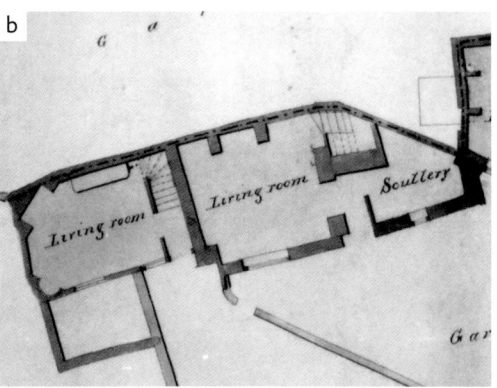

b

also be most easily made at that time of year. Many garden or summerhouses lay within 20 or 30 minutes walk of the central part of the city; on long summer evenings it would be possible to work or relax in one's garden and return before nightfall or early the next morning. On Sundays such pleasure could be prolonged.

## The Secondary Residence in the Country

Almost all the second houses discussed up to this point – whether lodges, garden houses or summerhouses – were located very close to the historic centre of Bristol. Where they now survive, they have been swallowed up by the city's expansion, leaving little impression of the contrast that they originally offered to town centre living. The close connection between main house and garden house was emphasised by the visual link between them: the garden house was almost invariably sited to give views over the bustling city and, as we have seen, the hillsides dotted with second houses were plainly visible from the city streets. Visually and functionally, therefore, lodges and garden houses were part of the city.

There was, however, a second group of residences sited more remotely and different in character, if not in purpose. A small number of wealthy individuals acquired country residences within a few miles of the city which were larger than those here called garden or summerhouses. From an external glance, such houses might appear to be indistinguishable from those of the gentry. Were these the houses of citizens who, having made their fortunes, had forsaken the city to establish themselves as gentry? Things are not always what they seem to be. As with the smaller lodge or garden house, a closer examination of the architecture and historical context of these houses may reveal a more complex story.

By 1668 Sir Henry Creswick had the use of three houses: his house in Small Street; his garden house on St Michael's Hill; and Hanham Court. The last was his country residence, four miles distant from the city and largely of the late 16th century; like his other two houses, its contents were listed in the inventory of 1668. Hanham Court was by the 1660s a substantial residence with some 18 rooms and of sufficient size to be seen as a gentry house (Fig 9.46). Creswick's predecessor at no.20 Small Street, the merchant John Smyth, had similarly

*Fig 9.46*
*Hanham Court, the house belonging to Sir Henry Creswick in 1668, photograph of 1942 (NMR A42/04301).*

acquired Ashton Court (Fig 9.47) as his country residence; as a gentry house this served until the 20th century as the country seat of Smyth's descendants.

At least two of Creswick's contemporaries acquired or built new country residences. Seen independently of their owner's city house, each could have been mistaken for a gentry house. Andrew Hook, a brewer, was the owner and possibly the builder of Ashley Manor, an impressive structure featuring five gabled bays, two storeys with attics and a sundial with the date 1656 over the centre porch (Figs 9.48a, 9.48b and 9.48c).[78] Still more imposing was Sir Robert Cann's residence at Stoke Bishop. This house, of three storeys with attics and of seven bays in width, was built for him in 1669, and its rooms and contents were described in his probate inventory of 1686 (Figs 9.49a, 9.49b, 9.49c and Appendix 2).[79]

All the owners of these houses lived, like Creswick, in the centre of the city. Cann's residence was, by the time of his death in 1686 in Small Street, a few houses away from Creswick's house. Hook's principal residence was in Lewin's Mead, by the later 17th century a street of smart, tightly packed row houses in St James's parish, close to the centre of the city. Did their country houses signify a wish to be seen as gentry or were they primarily places of retreat from the city, as were the smaller lodges and garden houses of their contemporaries? Or did these larger country houses serve other purposes? Since none of these individuals recorded their thoughts on these matters, answers must be sought in comparing their

Fig 9.47
Ashton Court, drawing by J C Buckler of 1827 (SANHS, photograph by RHL).

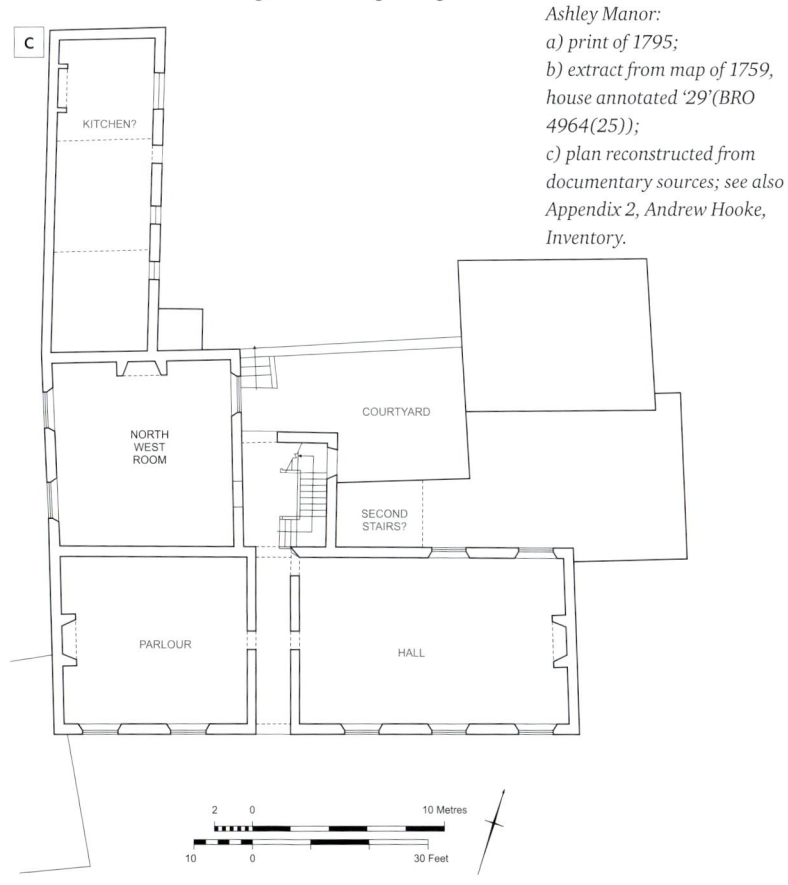

Fig 9.48
Ashley Manor:
a) print of 1795;
b) extract from map of 1759, house annotated '29' (BRO 4964(25));
c) plan reconstructed from documentary sources; see also Appendix 2, Andrew Hooke, Inventory.

# THE TOWN HOUSE IN MEDIEVAL AND EARLY MODERN BRISTOL

*Fig 9.49*
*Stoke Bishop House, now Trinity Theological College:*
*a) plan of ground floor in 1998;*
*b) photograph of south elevation in 1998, showing the porch of 1669, the gables as modified in the late 18th or early 19th century and the windows as rebuilt in the later 19th century (NMR BB98/11789);*
*c) the house in 1686, reconstructed from documentary sources; Cann's earlier lodge is to the left (JA; see also Figs 9.85, 9.86 and 12.11).*

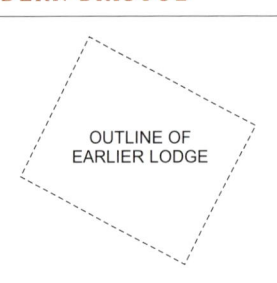

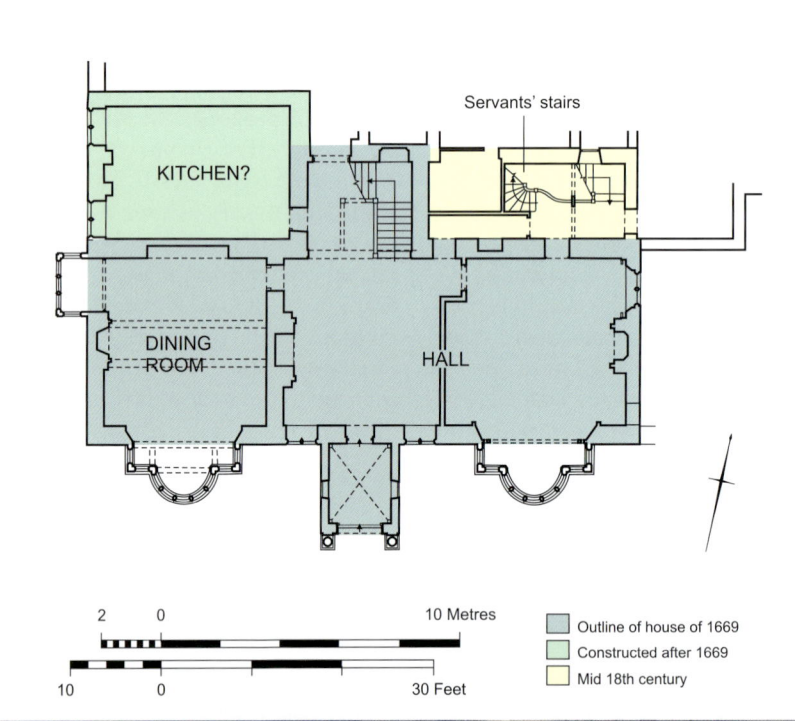

country and town houses, and the furnishings within them.

Seen from a distance the country houses of Cann and Hook certainly looked larger than their town houses, but the size of these new residences was more apparent than real. Each was built to one room in depth, and with just two principal rooms on each floor, the stairs being in the centre. Cann's house was larger in floor area and had an additional reception room on the ground floor, the kitchen first in a detached block to the rear and out of sight; but its internal arrangement was far simpler than indicated by the seven gabled bays of the imposing facade.

When compared with the town residences of their owners, all three of these country residences offered a roughly equivalent amount of accommodation. Hanham Court had been built or re-modelled long before Creswick's father had purchased it in 1638, so it was not designed specifically for the Creswicks' needs. Nevertheless, the 11 chambers at Hanham must have offered roughly the same amount of accommodation for household and guests as did the nine in Small Street. Cann's house at Stoke Bishop was purpose-built to his requirements; the number of chambers, five, was exactly the same as for his Small Street house. Hook's two houses each had four chambers.

The finish and furnishings of each of these country residences also indicates that their owners expected a decor similar to that found in the town house, notably in the bedchambers and in the dining rooms. Sir Henry Creswick's dining rooms at Hanham and in Small Street both provided seating for 13 persons, and each was furnished with pictures on the wall. At Ashley Manor the chimneypieces and decorated ceilings were of a quality that would have fitted perfectly into the wealthiest of houses in the city.

There were also significant differences. Visitors to a gentry house in the mid-17th century would not have been surprised to be shown the great hall and the portraits of their hosts' ancestors, or to be regaled with music before or during the formal meal. For Creswick, Cann and Hook the setting for this formal entertainment was not the house in the country, but that in the town. Creswick's great hall was fitted out to underline perceived ancestry and status; it was in the Small Street house that the visitor could hear his virginals and organ and gaze on the 51 pictures in the two long galleries. Cann's great hall was similarly furnished, with

Stoke Bishop House 1686

a.~Dining Room, b.~Hall, c.~Chamber over the dining room, d.~Chamber over the Hall, e.~Maid's Chamber, f.~Men's Chamber, g.~Nursery, h.~Chamber next to the Nursery, j.~kitchen.

three old muskets, 10 swords and 10 bandeleers signifying his right as a pre-eminent citizen to lead the militia in time of war. Hook's town house was more modern in its design and furnishing. It included no room designated as the hall, but in the entry (or entrance hall) were a pike, six old swords, a carbine, a musket, two pistols and a pair of bandeleers. Open halls and weaponry were significantly absent from their country residences.

The country house was a less formal place, one more designed for leisure and pleasure. At Hanham Court the hall was fitted out for comfort: heated, carpeted and well furnished with chairs, cushions, a leather couch and a clock. There was also a gun room. At Stoke Bishop, Cann's hall was a room in which to relax, or perhaps conduct household business; it was simply furnished with a table, six leather chairs and the tools for the hearth. Hook's parlour at Ashley Manor was furnished even more simply. These three country houses provided their owners with gardens far more extensive than the small plots adjacent to their town houses. In these three houses the only weapons were three guns at Hanham, perhaps for shooting ducks.

It can then occasion no surprise that Creswick, Cann and Hook were each regarded at their deaths as citizens of Bristol, rather than of the rural parishes of their country houses. But moving forward a generation or more, a different picture would emerge. Creswick's son moved permanently to Hanham and styled himself 'gentleman'. Both Stoke Bishop House and Ashley Manor were subsequently extended, and their later owners too were established as gentry. At Ashley Manor these alterations included the provision of more accommodation and a second stairs, the latter a signifier of changed social relations and an increased separation between family and servants (chapter 10).

It is against these complexities that other larger houses, built or extended in the 17th century and in the immediate environs of the city, might also now be seen as the second residences of wealthy citizens. Redland Manor (Figs 9.50a and 9.50b), originally similar in size to Cann's house at Stoke Bishop, was built c 1658 by Francis Gleed, a soap maker who lived at no.55 Wine Street. The design of the chimneypiece in one of the principal rooms of the house at Redland signifies that Gleed intended this also to be for his own use.[80] Sneyd Park at Stoke Bishop (Fig 9.51) was the residence of Joseph Jackson, a merchant and former mayor whose dwelling house in 1658 was in St Nicholas Street.[81]

To the north of the city Oldbury Court near Fishponds (Fig 9.44) was the second residence of Robert Winstone, the glover, builder and owner of the Dutch House at no.1 High Street (see Figs 1.1, 1.2, 1.3, 1.4 and 6.32). Cook's Folly, overlooking the Avon Gorge at Stoke Bishop (Fig 9.80), was built in 1693 by John Cook, merchant and chamberlain of the city and resident of no.6 King Street.[82] On the east side of the city Langton Court in Brislington

*Fig 9.50*
*Redland Manor, photographs taken prior to its demolition c 1890:*
*a) exterior*
*(Reece Winstone Archive OB2425);*
*b) chimneypiece*
*(BRSMG fireplaces).*

THE GARDEN HOUSE

*Sneed Park the Seat of Joseph Jackson Esq*

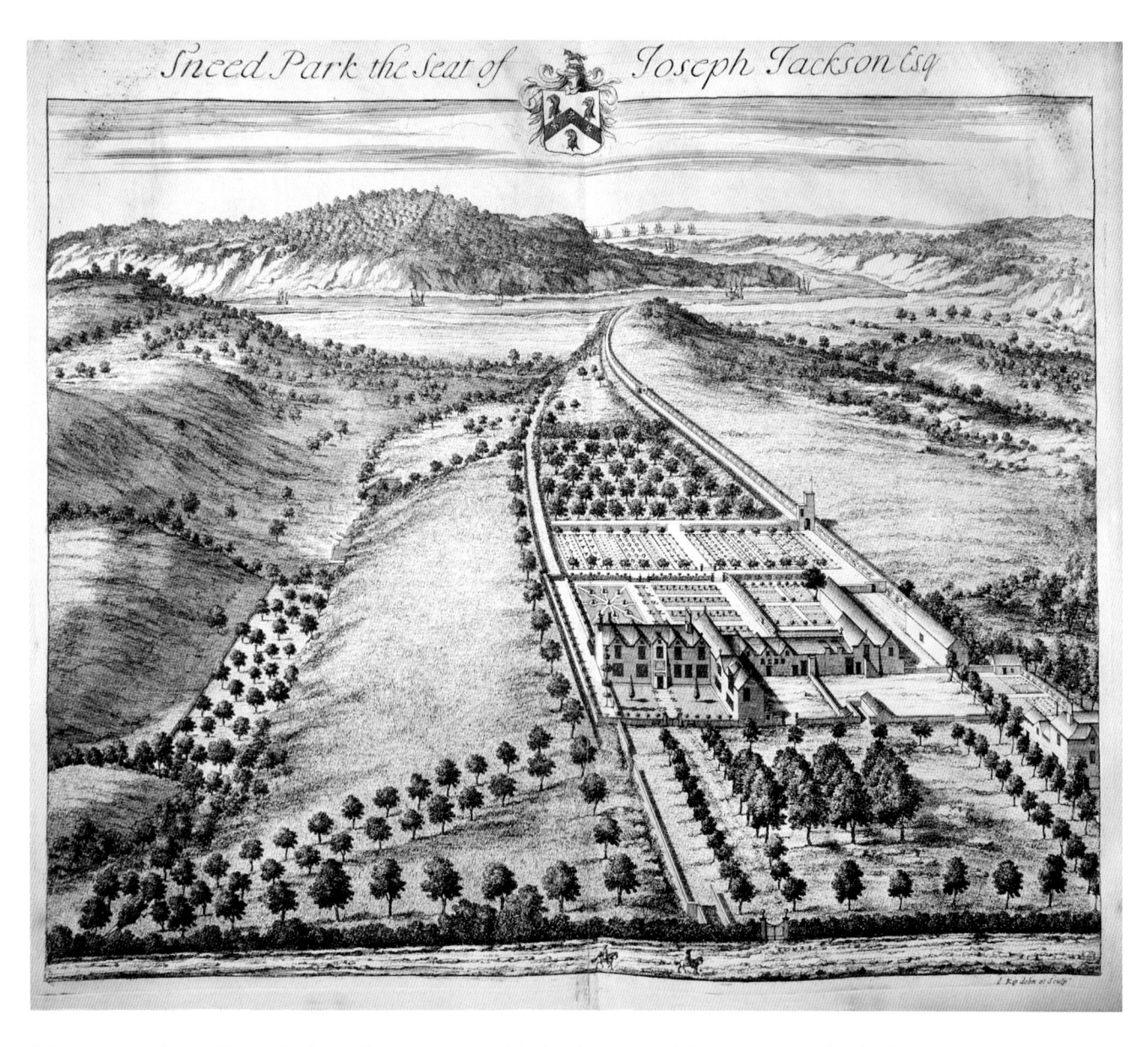

(Figs 9.52a and 9.52b) was in the 17th century the country house of the Langton family; their city residence was the shophouse at no.12 Welsh Back.[83] Langton Court and Cann's house at Stoke Bishop show, in the use of 'Dutch' gables, the influence of the artisan mannerist style – associated by Summerson with a number of London houses that can now be identified as the out-of-town second residences for some citizens of London.[84] There is a hint, therefore, of a common commercial culture in the choice of architectural style.

Some members of Bristol's urban elite continued during the 18th century to use a city residence alongside one set in the city's rural hinterland. Joseph Beck was the wealthy occupant of no.14 St James's Square from 1741 to his death in 1747 (Fig 9.53).[85] He also built Frenchay Manor (Figs 9.54a and 9.54b), five miles from his town house, interpreted by Timothy Mowl as 'a merchant's cheap passport to gentry status … a thin house grossly over-detailed for its small size'.[86] This, though, is a modern judgement; the historical context may provide a different interpretation, and the building of Frenchay Manor must be judged by the canons of early 18th-century taste. Beck described himself as a linen draper of the City of Bristol in his will.[87] His contemporaries may have seen his house as a perfectly acceptable second residence.

The plan of the house indicates that it was designed as a lodge (Fig 9.54a). The ground floor provided only two reception rooms, and

*Fig 9.51*
Sneyd Park, Stoke Bishop (print by Johannes Kip in Atkyns 1712, between pp 804–5).

259

*Fig 9.52*
*Langton Court, Brislington: a) viewed from the south-west, photograph of the later 19th century (NMR BB90/03885); b) detail from Tithe Award map of 1846, north at foot of plan, the photographic view from the direction of parcel number '286' on the plan (BRO EP/A/32/9).*

a disproportionate amount of the available space was given over to a large and grandiose stairs to a first-floor reception room, an arrangement echoing that of the 'Manor House' in Easton (Figs 9.55a, 9.55b and 9.55c). A much meaner stairs provided access to the second floor and its two chambers.

Occupying almost as much floor area as the house was the stable block. For frequent visits from the city, from Beck's family and his guests, this would have been an important part of the necessary arrangements, accommodating both his chariot and horse, of sufficient importance to command an explicit mention in his will. An alternative reading of Frenchay Manor might be as a Bristol merchant's second residence, built much in the tradition of a 17th-century lodge – a property certainly designed to impress with its scale and Classical architecture, but not intended as an entrée to landed society. Beck's life remained firmly rooted in Bristol's commercial activity.

On the west side of the city Clifton was an attractive and convenient location for a second residence. A little over a mile from the centre, it was then a distinct and separate settlement. Close to the summit of the hill, the wealthy draper Whitchurch Phippen acquired in 1701 the lease for what had been the larger of the two manor houses of Clifton. Here he then built a new house of single-pile, central-stairs plan with a distinctive exterior design, now known as Richmond House (Figs 9.56a and 9.56b). The five-bay elevation is characterised by single and paired mullioned and transomed cross-windows below continuous stone hood moulds; these, together with the moulded timber lintels over the windows, echoed 17th-century practice and perhaps gave the house more of an air of antiquity. From afar this heavily glazed exterior must have been very prominent; the views from the house itself were extensive.

The absence of gables, and the five-bay symmetrical design with paired windows to each side of a central bay, would both be repeated in the building of houses in St James's Square (Fig 9.53) in the same decade. Internally, the positioning of windows rather than cupboards in the spaces between chimneystacks

*Fig 9.53*
*Joseph Beck's city residence was at no.14 St James's Square, the house behind the scaffolding, photograph of 1930 (NMR AA77/02022).*

*Fig 9.54 (below)*
*Joseph Beck's house at Frenchay Manor, Frenchay: a) plan of ground floor with suggested names of rooms (RHL, PEC, after plan by Roger E Poole (NMR EE/4600059)); b) photograph of 1942 (NMR AA42/02977).*

and front and back walls echoed a 17th-century preference, as did the centrally placed entrance and stairs hall. The paucity of kitchen and other service accommodation, in a single projecting range to the north, together with the space given over to the stairs, marked the house out as one used intermittently and perhaps mainly for entertainment. In the centre of the city Whitchurch Phippen's principal residence was at no.9 High Street, until his death in 1710.[88]

Further to the east along the crest of the same ridge Whitchurch Phippen's son, also named Whitchurch Phippen, had by 1738 built a second garden house, by then occupied by his widow Jane. Its exterior elevation is of a more modern design, but the plan remains essentially that of many 17th-century lodges – set against the boundary wall to face downhill over the garden and with a well-finished stairs providing access to the one room on each floor (Figs 9.57a and 9.57b).

A neighbour to the Phippens in High Street was Thomas Goldney II, further down the same street and on the same side at no.22. In 1694 Goldney acquired the lease of a house in Clifton across the street from that of the Phippens, followed by the purchase of the freehold of the property in 1705. This house, it can be argued, was used by Goldney's family as a garden house, with the house in High Street being retained as the principal residence.[89] The lease of 1694 was of the house along with 'all statues, figures & flower pots', indicating that the garden was already an important element.[90]

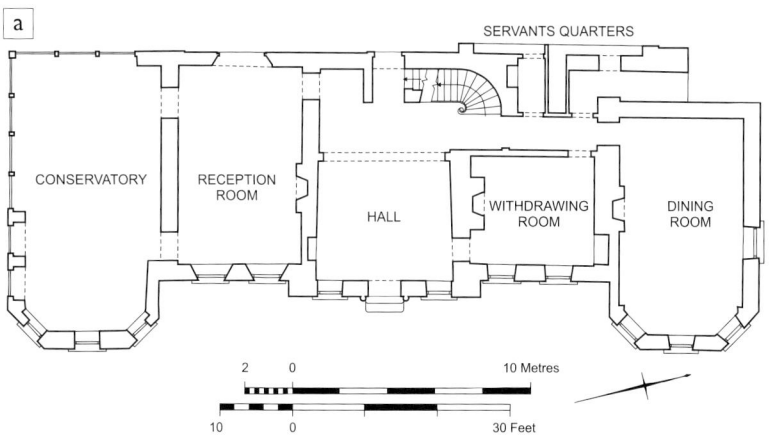

# THE TOWN HOUSE IN MEDIEVAL AND EARLY MODERN BRISTOL

Fig 9.55
Easton Manor House in St Mark's Road:
a) plan from OS map, 1882 (1st edition, 1:500 town plan, Gloucestershire, Bristol, sheet LXXII.13.4);
b) exterior view, drawing by Loxton of late 19th century;
c) stairs hall, drawing by Loxton of late 19th century (BCRL Loxton drawings 918 and 919).

Fig 9.56
Richmond House, Clifton:
a) ground-floor plan and reconstructed elevations of a residence secondary to that in High Street – note the similarity of the design to that of near-contemporary houses in St James's Square (Fig 9.53) (RHL, PEC);
b) photograph of 2011 (NMR DP135989).

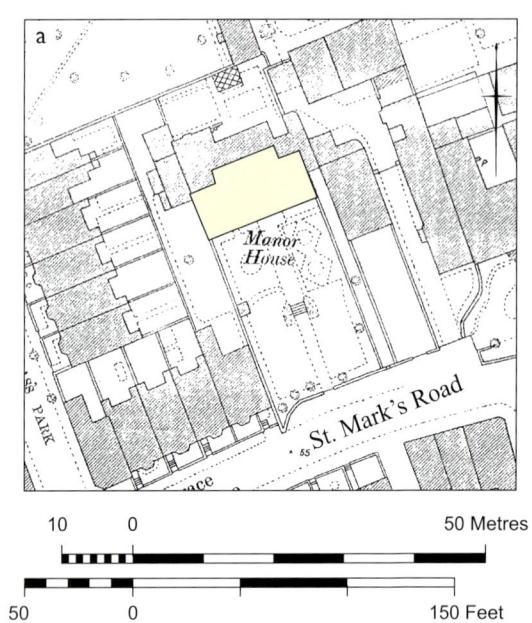

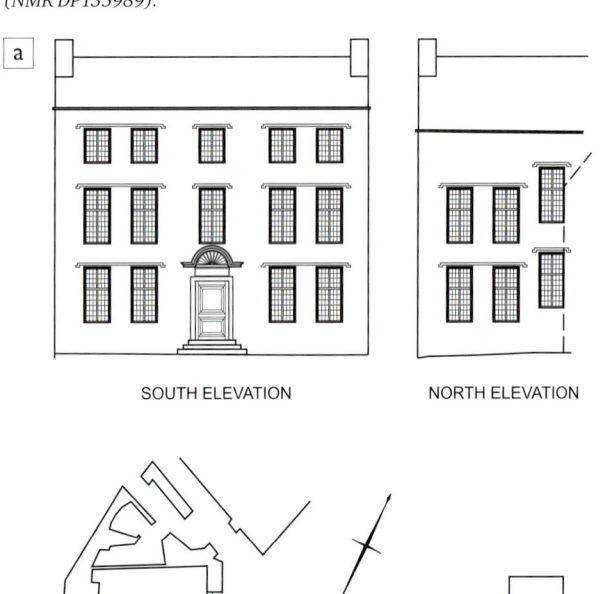

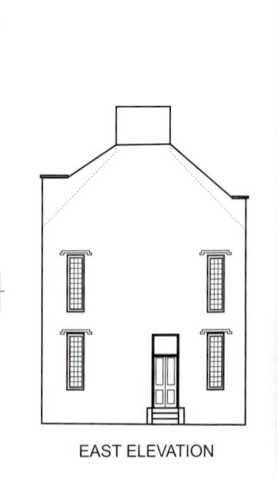

THE GARDEN HOUSE

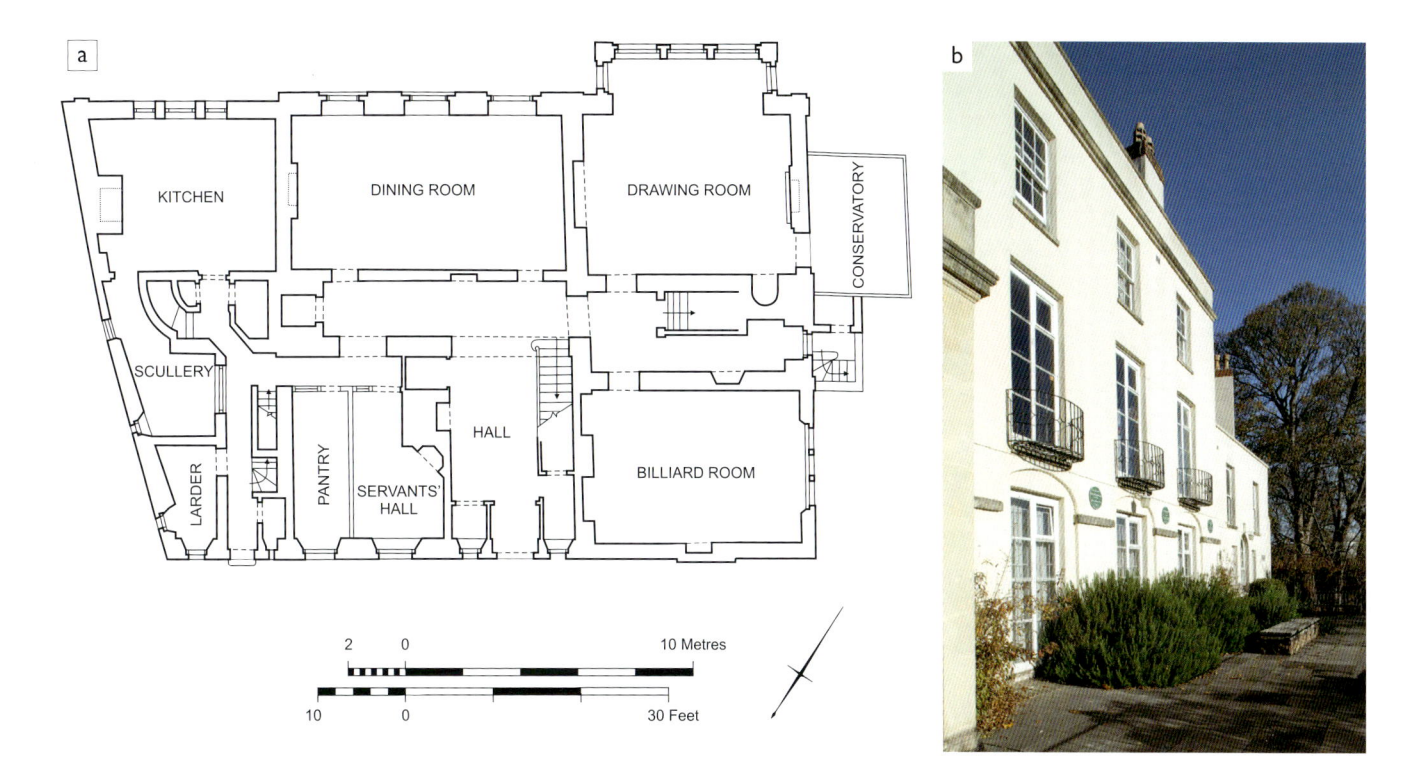

The garden house functioned partly as a place to which his wife Martha could retreat when expecting a child. From 1696 onwards all seven Goldney children recorded by Thomas Goldney II were born at Clifton, rather than in the city centre parish of All Saints. The Clifton house was then extended and altered *c* 1723 by Thomas Goldney, after he had confirmed the title to his purchase made some years before in 1705.[91]

This house, later named Goldney House, was substantially rebuilt by the architect Alfred Waterhouse in 1864–5, and it has been generally assumed by architectural historians that this was essentially a re-facing of the property first rebuilt by Goldney, which must therefore have been a house of five bays in width. The earlier house was in fact only half this width; it is shown in plan as such on Ashmead's map of 1828, on the Ordnance Survey plan of 1885 and on Waterhouse's plan for the rebuilding of Goldney House. The house as extended and altered by Goldney in *c* 1723 was therefore far more typical of lodges and garden houses built in the 17th century, with one room on each floor, the stairs in one corner and a very fine finish to the principal room, here on the ground floor (Figs 9.58a and 9.58b).

In the middle decades of the 18th century there are indications that some Bristol citizens were investing in something rather larger or functionally more complete than a garden house for occasional use. To the west of Richmond House, Clifton Court was built *c* 1742 for Nehemiah Champion and his wife (Martha Goldney). To the casual observer its Palladian facade is not dissimilar to that of Beck's house at Frenchay, but its black glass-slag side walls are a reminder of its owner's industrial interests (Fig 9.59; *see* Fig 8.84n). The accommodation provided in this second residence, following a double-pile plan with a central stairs, exceeded that provided by the typical 17th-century garden house; the building is perhaps best seen instead as a suburban villa. Champion already had a house in the city, at no.33 Prince Street, which he continued to occupy until his death in 1747.

On the slopes below Champion's house was Clifton Wood House (Fig 9.60; *see* Figs 8.84i, 8.92 and 8.93), which from 1746 to at least 1778 was the residence of Richard Farr, mayor in 1763. This also was a house of double-pile plan, being an extension of an earlier garden house of two rooms on each floor. Farr, too, had a city residence, at no.32 Prince Street, next door to Champion's house and highly convenient for his years of office first as Master of the Merchant Venturers in 1762 and then as mayor in 1763. By 1775 he had moved to Park Street. His son Thomas was now the owner of the Blaise Castle estate at Henbury, but also occupied his father's former house in Prince Street, certainly in 1775 when he also became mayor.

Fig 9.57
Manor House, York Place, Clifton:
a) plan of the ground floor (RHL, PEC after plan of 1891–2 (BRO building plans vol 27, fol 31, additional information from survey));
b) much altered elevation to garden, photograph of 2011 (English Heritage DP 135985).

263

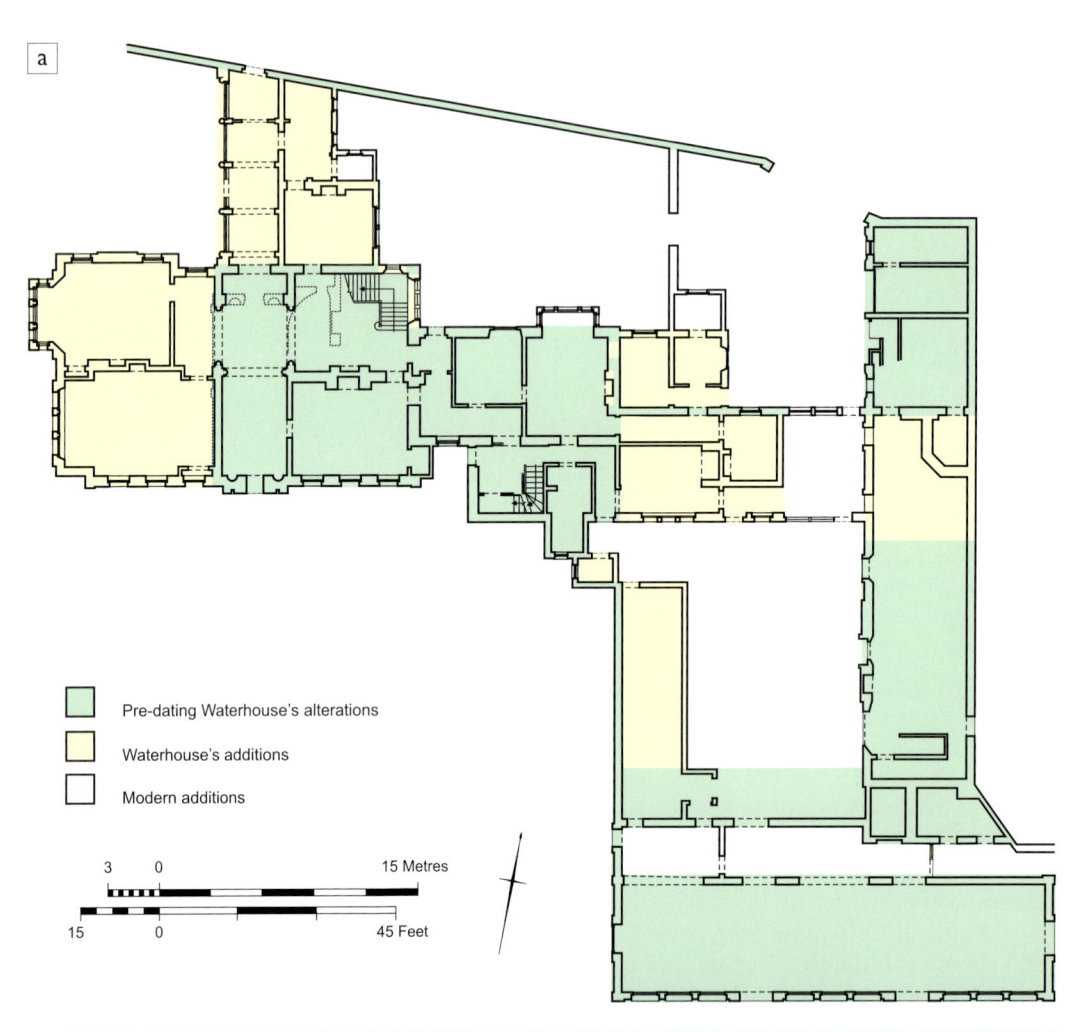

- Pre-dating Waterhouse's alterations
- Waterhouse's additions
- Modern additions

*Fig 9.58*
*Goldney House, Clifton:*
*a) plan of ground floor showing house as first built and later additions (RHL, PEC);*
*b) the house viewed from the south, photograph of 2012 (English Heritage DP 152554).*

# THE GARDEN HOUSE

*Fig 9.59
Clifton Court, photograph of 2003
(NMR AA048163).*

*Fig 9.60
Clifton Wood House, windows with hood moulds in the west wall of the former lodge or garden house, photograph of 2003 (RHL). For location see Fig 8.92.*

Some merchant families certainly did move entirely from the city to the surrounding countryside or villages during the 18th century.[92] Nevertheless, studies of Bristol in the 18th century have perhaps too readily assumed that the existence of merchant residences in Frenchay, Stoke Bishop or Clifton provides evidence for a move away from the city, in some instances a wish by merchants to establish themselves as gentry. In making his will in 1684 Robert Vickris described himself as a merchant, of the City of Bristol and now of Chew Magna in Somerset. He still thought of himself as a citizen. Vickris's body was to be buried in St Nicholas's and brought in procession from Chew, should he die there. His widow was to be given the option of staying in the country house, where she might have 'sufficient firewood and liberty of his orchards and gardens for the recreation of herself and her friends', but also given the option of living in Bristol.[93] It would be of interest to know how Nehemiah Champion and the Farrs, a century or so later, viewed their relationship between city and country, and the extent to which the country residence was still in essence a lodge.

## The Conversion of Lodges and Garden Houses to become Permanent Dwellings

Even by the early 17th century, in Bristol as elsewhere in England, lodges and secondary residences were being converted to become dwellings for permanent occupation. This applied to both those buildings that could be extended and those that already offered two or more rooms of accommodation on each floor. The attractions of a large garden, a view or seclusion may often have outweighed the drawbacks of moving into a house not designed for permanent occupation, notably the restricted amount of accommodation. By the early 1660s a number of houses built as lodges can be shown to have been adapted or simply taken over for permanent occupation.

The size and architectural merits of the Red and White Lodges must have made them eminent candidates for permanent occupation. By the 1660s the occupier of the White Lodge was Captain Richard Ham; this was evidently his only residence. The Red Lodge was sold separately from the Great House on St Augustine's Back in 1599 and had possibly been used as a main residence from 1595 when it was purchased by William Winter; alterations which converted the lodge to a permanent residence included the walling-in of the loggia and the addition of a new stairs wing, all possibly undertaken by Winter.[94] By 1694 no.10 Lower Park Row was certainly being used as a principal residence, with the merchant Hugh Bickham and his family living there.

Smaller lodges were also adapted to permanent occupation, sometimes within a short time of being built. A reading of the architectural evidence may indicate that the minister James Read's house on Stony Hill was built as a lodge, but by the time of his death it was his only residence.[95] With one room on each of the four floors, the accommodation described in the probate inventory of his possessions was restricted to a kitchen, study, chamber and a cockloft. Substantial rents from his property developments meant that Read could have easily afforded a more commodious residence, but he was evidently content with this house, its walled garden and the views over the city to the east (Fig 9.19). In Hownden or Mitchell Lane, a little to the north of nos.52–3 St Thomas Street, a property described from 1566–1673 as a lodge with a stable was by 1717 recorded as being 'now a dwelling house' (Fig 9.61).[96]

Other citizens seized the opportunity afforded by a favourable location to extend a lodge of one-room plan to become a much larger house, possibly to become their main residence. Eusebius Brookes or a predecessor must have rapidly extended the core of a lodge on the summit of St Michael's Hill with a succession of additions, all apparently of the 17th century (Fig 9.15). In Upper Maudlin Street the 17th-century owner of the Female Penitentiary must have made similar extensions (Fig 9.14). At no.13 Marlborough Hill a simpler strategy was adopted in the later 18th century for the enlargement of a one-room plan lodge, built in the 1730s. The existing square house more than doubled in size to consist of two rooms on three floors, each placed either side of a central stairs (Fig 9.62). The former summerhouse became at ground level the kitchen, with the new room becoming the parlour. The high quality of finish to the latter indicated that appearances were important, while its one-brick-thick exterior wall was a reminder that expense was to be kept to the necessary minimum.

On Clifton Hill we have already seen how two families first acquired a garden house and then made their suburban idyll a permanent residence. Thomas Goldney II first leased a garden house and then extended and rebuilt it, possibly as a permanent residence. His near neighbour in High Street, Whitchurch Phippen,

*Fig 9.61 (below)*
*Hownden or Mitchell Lane, lodge, watercolour and plan c 1828*
*(BRO P/StT/Ch/31 fol 5).*

*Fig 9.62 (below right)*
*No. 13 Marlborough Hill, plan of house as extended in the later 18th century (RHL, PEC).*

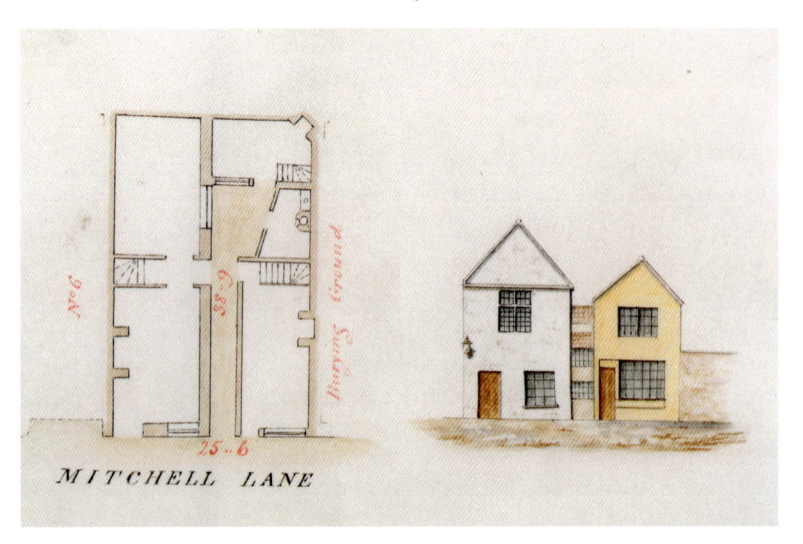

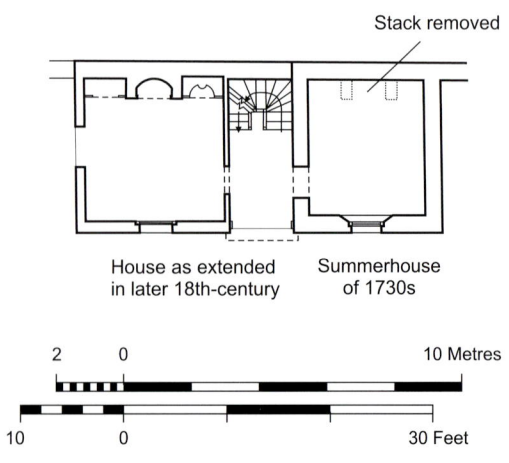

THE GARDEN HOUSE

built a garden house, now Richmond House, in which his son then lived as his permanent home. Further to the north along Clifton Hill the two garden houses built by James Hollidge, now Emmaus House, were both rebuilt and extended to become larger houses suitable as main residences (*see* Fig 8.95b).

## Suburban Villas

While some lodges were adapted to become dwellings, other houses, constructed with the characteristics of the lodge, were intended from the outset to be houses for permanent occupation. The 'comely buildings' noted by James Millerd in 1673 included both lodges and the permanently occupied suburban houses, the plans of some of which have been discussed in chapter 8. 'Pleasant gardens' were an essential feature of life in these houses. In the late 17th century Roger North wrote that 'a villa is quasy a lodge, for the sake of a garden, to retire to injoy and sleep, without pretence of enterteinment of many persons'.[97] Suburban villas that would have been familiar to North, and smaller houses that might not have merited the appellation 'villa', offered the opportunity to escape from the bustle, noise and smell of the city, but still to enjoy its pleasures and partake of urban culture and civility.[98]

In the 17th century the majority of new larger houses being constructed within the city were set at right angles to the street, and were of two rooms in depth with a central staircase. In the design of no.10 Lower Park Row, this town house plan was adapted to the needs of life in the lodge, to become what in the previous chapter has been described as a house two rooms wide and of single-pile plan (Fig 9.31). Freed from the constraints of the narrow, inner city tenement plot, it was possible to position a house of this plan so as to face its garden, the entrance now symmetrical to the front elevation. Making the back wall of the house also the rear wall of the property served to maximise the size of the garden; it also necessitated that the stairs be placed within the main body of the house, between the two principal rooms on each floor. Through minimising the relationship with the street, and in the emphasis thus given to the view over the garden, life in the house was made to feel more secluded and further removed from the bustle of the city than would otherwise have been possible. Further away from the city a different strategy was used for the positioning of houses such as Stoke Bishop House, placed in the centre of its own large grounds and garden (Fig 9.49).

It would be of interest to know if the earliest suburban houses built in the first decades of the 17th century in the Marsh alongside the Frome were of this form, but no detailed evidence has been traced. Both the house built by Sir Humphrey Hooke from 1608 onwards and that lately built by Alderman Robert Aldworth in 1626 are shown on Millerd's map of 1673, each by then with an accretion of later smaller houses (Fig 9.63). Hooke's house was possibly square in plan, its structure surviving partly in nos.40–8 Prince Street as drawn in a plan of 1794 (Figs 9.64a and 9.64b). Aldworth's house was certainly re-fronted in the 1740s. Recorded in 1680 as being set back behind a small court 12ft in depth, its outline could be reconstructed from 19th-century plans and photographs; it showed

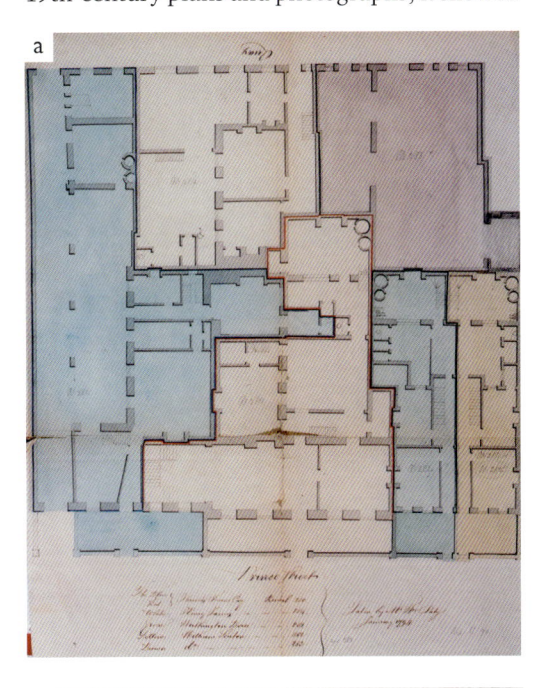

*Fig 9.63*
*The Marsh, Sir Humphrey Hooke's house (left) and Robert Aldworth's house (right), details from Millerd's map of 1673 (BRSMG).*

*Fig 9.64*
*The Marsh, nos.40–42 Prince Street, Sir Humphrey Hooke's house:*
*a) plan of 1794 showing nos. 36–42, nos. 40–42 marked as 'Rl 280' and 'Rl 284' (BRO04479(1) fol 269);*
*b) chimneypiece of 17th century (Reece Winstone Archive OB2131).*

267

*Fig 9.65*
*Castle Green, houses and gardens extending back to the Castle wall, details from Millerd's map of 1673 (BRSMG).*

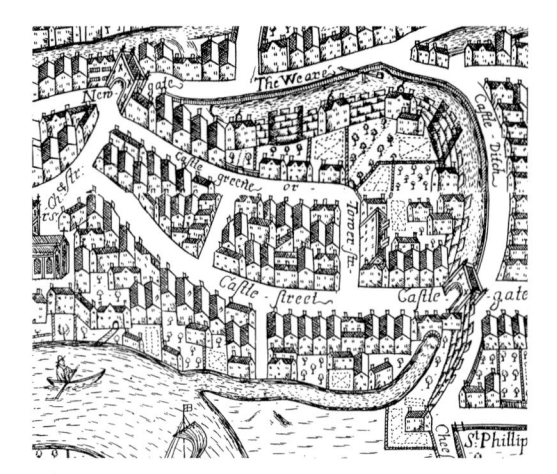

*Fig 9.66*
*Royal Fort:*
*a) plan*
*1  Royal Fort House*
*2  Manor House (Major Harper)*
*3  Cromwell House (John Hicks)*
*4  John Garway's House*
*5  Edward Milner's House (RHL, PEC);*
*b) distant view in drawing by James Stewart, 'The North East View of Prince Rupert's Fort, commonly called the Royal Fort', 1752 (Bodleian Library, Western MS, Gough Somerset 8, fol 19).*

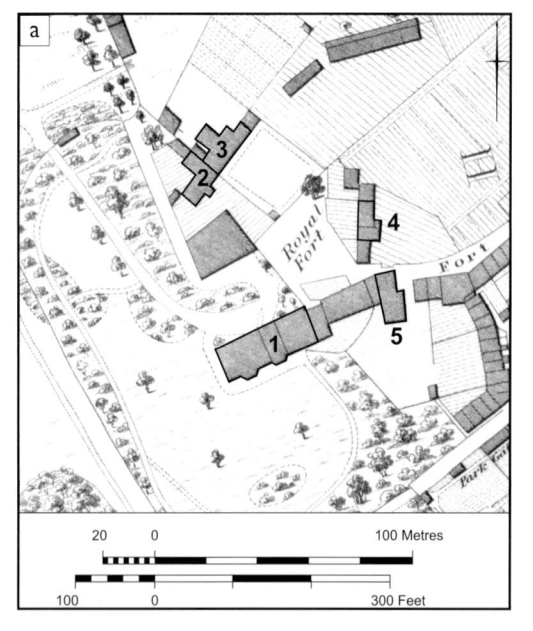

a property of one room in depth, with a centrally placed stair turret behind the main house.

This form of house was sufficiently popular by the 1650s to be adopted in modified form in two new developments of suburban houses. In the redevelopment of the Castle, Castle Green was rebuilt as an enclave of superior dwellings. Millerd's map shows the general context of these houses, set largely on the north side of the street with walled gardens looking north over the former Castle wall to Broadmead and the slopes of Kingsdown. Some houses adapted from existing Castle structures were placed on the street frontage, but other probably new houses were set well back, secluded from the street and the city by house and Castle wall (Fig 9.65).

A second development was that within and around the Royal Fort on the summit of St Michael's Hill. Here several suburban houses, similar in plan to no.10 Lower Park Row, were built in the 1650s and 1660s, each standing in its own walled garden, most well set back from St Michael's Hill (Figs 9.66a and 9.66b). On the east side of the Fort, the house lately built in 1665 by John Hicks, a mercer, was of three storeys and three gabled bays. It faced south over the city, and featured a court in front and a plot of ground for a garden to the rear.

In 1665 the adjacent house was that of Major Harper. Later styled 'manor house', it had apparently been re-roofed in the early 18th century. The two stacks, each with three diagonally set chimneys, revealed its 17th-century or earlier origins, and also indicated a plan of two rooms with a central stairs (Figs 9.67a, 9.67b and 9.67c). A house of similar plan was that built on the ground leased in 1656 to Edward Milner, the swordbearer of the Corporation. This house, to the south of the gate into the Royal Fort, consisted of two bays and possibly featured a centrally placed entrance (Fig 9.68).[99]

In writing of the recent increase of 'comely buildings and pleasant gardens' now much visible on St Michael's Hill, James Millerd would have been aware of these and other houses, similar in plan to no.10 Lower Park Row. Further along Park Row to the west of the Red Lodge, a house drawn by Samuel and Nathaniel Buck in 1734 and shown on an early photograph,[100] was apparently of similar form: facing over the city but also on to its walled garden, of three bays with a central entrance and presumably a stair hall behind (Fig 9.69). By 1662 this was the house of the sugar refiner Thomas Jennings, his only residence in the Hearth Tax returns for that year.[101]

Dwelling in a secluded suburban house continued to be a sufficiently attractive lifestyle for houses to be built or rebuilt in this way into the second part of the 18th century. Above St Michael's church one of the largest houses in the parish, described in 1596 as a 'capital messuage' and one of the 19 garden houses in St Michael's parish in the Hearth Tax return for 1662, was first extended or rebuilt by 1668. It was then totally rebuilt following a fire c 1691.[102] The core of the new house, now known as the Manor House, was of a similar plan to no.10 Lower Park Row with, in the main range, two principal ground-floor rooms used as reception rooms – that with a large, bolection-moulded chimneypiece and overmantel closest to the kitchen most probably a dining room (Figs 9.70a, 9.70b and 9.70c). With two contemporary service wings, the house was clearly rebuilt not as a lodge, but for permanent occupation. As at no.10 Lower Park Row and at the house of Ralph Oliffe, later of James Stewart, the principal facade was to the walled garden, totally enclosed with high walls and with entrance to the house via the garden. The facade to the street was altogether much plainer.

A variation on this plan was for the garden to front on to the street, with the house placed at the end furthest from the frontage, but facing and visible from the street. This was the plan utilised for Oldbury House, the garden house on St Michael's Hill built for Marmaduke Bowdler

Fig 9.67
Royal Fort, nos.2 and 3, houses of Major Harper and John Hicks;
a) drawing by James Stewart, 1752, enlarged detail of Fig 9.66b);
b) drawing by Loxton of Major Harper's house, later styled 'manor house', 1920 (BCRL Loxton drawings D271);
c) photograph of Cromwell House, late 19th or early 20th century (collection of Mrs Janet Schonbeck).

Fig 9.68
Royal Fort, Milner's house, drawing by James Stewart, 1752, enlarged detail of Fig 9.66b).

*Fig 9.69*
*Park Row, in 1662 the house of Thomas Jennings, late 19th-century photograph (Reece Winstone Archive, negative from Winstone 1866–1860 Pl.9).*

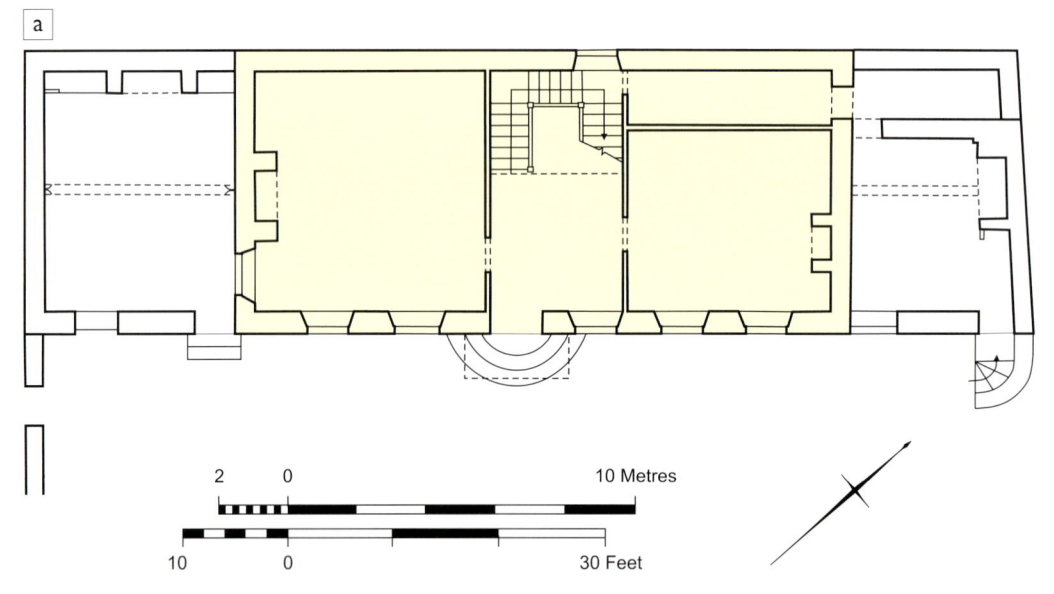

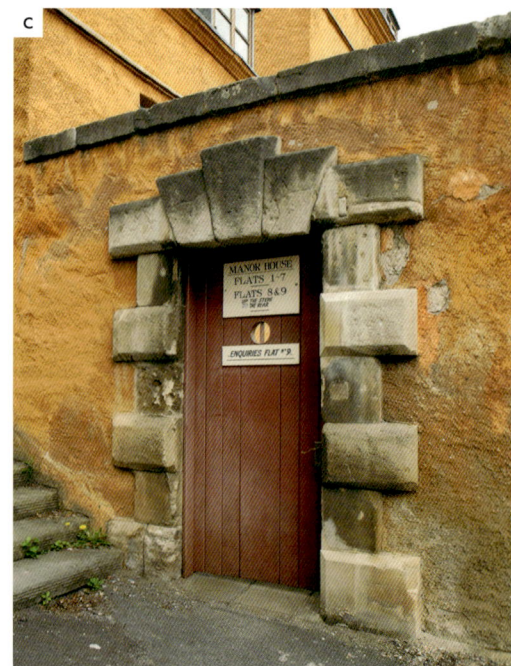

*Fig 9.70*
*Manor House, Park Lane, St Michael's Hill:*
*a) plan*
*(RHL, PEC);*
*b) house, photograph of 2003*
*(NMR AA047089);*
*c) entrance to garden, photograph of 2011*
*(NMR MG 4022).*

c 1679–89 (Fig 9.34). Lunsford House, built c 1738–9, was similarly placed in relation to the garden, but because of the slope was not visible from Park Row below (Figs 9.71a and 9.71b). A further strategy for the siting of a large suburban house was to place it in the middle of the tenement plot, with a garden to the front and another to the rear. This was implemented for the several large houses, Rodney Lodge, Duncan House and Mortimer House, built in the Hollylands development at Clifton in the 1730s (chapter 3). St Michael's Hill House, the out-of-town residence of the pewterer William Going, was similarly sited (Fig 9.83).

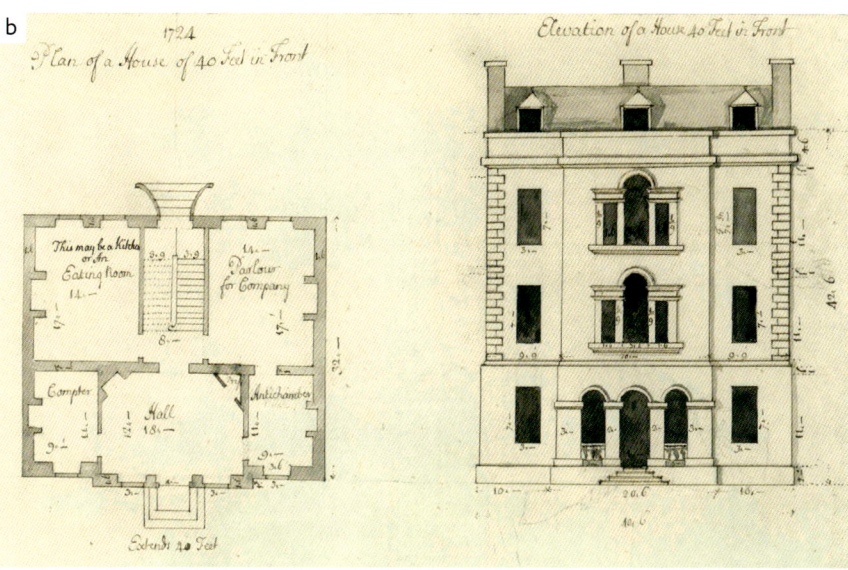

## Garden Houses in Rows

Houses placed at one end of a large garden continued to be built until at least the 1770s. In Southwell Street most of the new houses built in the 1750s were probably of this plan, no.4 being the only one to have been recorded internally (Figs 9.72a, 9.72b and 9.72c). On the north side of Kingsdown Parade houses of similar plan were constructed from 1733 until the 1770s. Most of the houses at the west end of Kingsdown Parade (west of no.65) and no.4 Southwell Street stood at the end of a long walled garden, *c* 40ft wide at the point furthest from the street. The two rooms on each of the upper floors, accessed as at no.25 Kingsdown Parade from a centrally placed, dogleg stairs of minimal proportions, formed part of a plan that would have been perfectly familiar to the 17th-century builder of no.10 Lower Park Row (Fig 9.73).

In both Southwell Street and Kingsdown Parade, and similarly in Sion Hill in Clifton, these houses differed from the lodge-like suburban dwellings so far considered by being built in rows. Yet in their external and internal arrangements, these houses as newly built must have seemed to their inhabitants and visitors to be a world apart from the narrow, two-room deep houses of similar overall size then being constructed in rows, and in much larger numbers, on the east side of Kingsdown Parade and in other new suburban streets. Gardens in Southwell Street and Kingsdown Parade were larger and, placed between high walls on the street and the house behind, had the effect of offering more seclusion. The exterior architecture of the house was principally for those privileged to enter its garden.[103] Inside the house the stairs hall was central, but given less emphasis in architectural display. From within the vista of the long and large garden again offered a different experience.

The east end of Kingsdown Parade was completed in a building campaign that commenced in 1791. The occupants of the new semi-detached houses (chapter 8) on the north side of the street were to enjoy a lifestyle similar to those of the earlier lodge-like houses to the west. Whereas the south side of the new James's Place (later named Kingsdown Parade) consisted almost entirely of row houses fronting the street and built on 20ft-wide plots, the north side was set out as a continuous long row of pairs of houses. Each had a garden *c* 22–25ft wide, sandwiched like those of the earlier houses between a high wall on the street frontage and the house behind (*see* Fig 8.99).

In form the pairs of villas were intended to be very different from the earlier two-room, central-staircase houses in a continuous row. In practice, however, the differences were minimised by the multitude of devices soon employed to infill the lower parts between each pair. As in the earlier houses to the west, the principal facade was to the garden; the rear elevation faced directly on to a back lane, unprepossessing and essentially providing a service entry. A similar arrangement was adopted for houses being built on the north side of Ashley Road from the 1790s onwards. The almost semi-detached villas of Ashley Place (chapter 8) and the more individually designed

*Fig 9.71*
*Lunsford House, Park Row: a) photograph of 1999 (RHL; for detailed plan see Fig 10.4b); b) a house 40ft in width from The Kingsweston Book of Drawings, a design similar to that adopted for Lunsford House (BRO 33746, fol 9; English Heritage DP 136007).*

*Fig 9.72*
*No.4 Southwell Street:*
*a) plan also showing plot boundaries (RHL, PEC, from OS plan of 1885);*
*b) photograph of the exterior;*
*c) photograph of interior showing the stairs (RHL); photographs of 1976.*

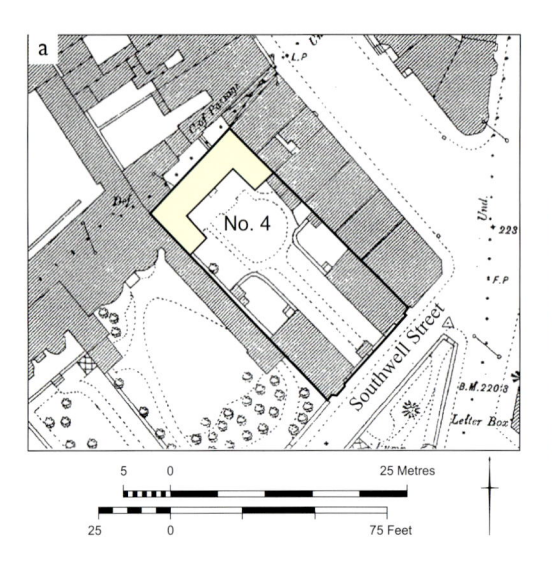

*Fig 9.73 (right)*
*No.25 Kingsdown Parade, plan showing plot boundaries (RHL. PEC, from OS map of 1885, 1st edition, 1:500, Gloucestershire, Bristol, sheet LXXI 16.9).*

*Fig 9.74 (below)*
*The north side of Ashley Road, gardens between houses and the road (Plumley and Ashmead, 1828).*

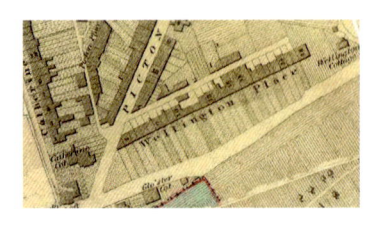

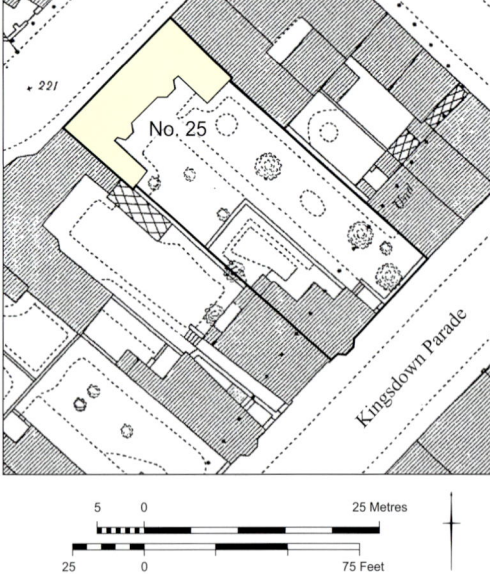

houses of Wellington Place were similarly placed, with a back lane to the rear and long gardens extending forwards on the south side to the country lane later to be named Ashley Road (Fig 9.74).

In the layout of such streets we can see the origins of semi-detachment in the suburbs as a residue of the garden-house tradition: residences open on three sides, with light and air and a degree of seclusion and privacy, set within a soft landscape distinct from the hard world beyond.[104] Houses such as those on the north side of Southwell Street and Kingsdown Parade were 'garden houses': not in the sense of being second residences, but in the core 17th-century meaning of the house and garden constituting one single space. Both the adaptation of lodges to become permanent dwellings and the adoption of the lodge plan into that of the suburban house retained long-lived elements of 17th-century design. The occupants of the new houses in later 18th-century Southwell Street and Kingsdown Parade would have found resonances to their own immediate environment by standing in the gardens of houses such as the Red Lodge, no.10 Lower Park Row and the Manor House in Park Lane. There, as in their own houses, access to the house was principally through the garden, marked with a gateway now of Classical or Gothic design and bounded by high stone walls (Fig 9.75). Their houses too stood at one end of the plot, maximising the size of the garden, while the architecture of the house was first and foremost for its occupants, the garden viewed in its entirety from the house.

## The Suburban House and its Garden: Seeing and Being Seen

No 18th-century views of the gardens in Southwell Street or Kingsdown Parade have been traced, but the intimate relationship between the suburban house and its garden is very evident in James Stewart's views of his own garden in Upper Maudlin Street and of others close by in the 1740s and 1750s (Fig 9.33). By the 1820s garden design had changed, but the same nexus between house and garden was equally apparent in the garden of the Female Penitentiary, the lodge built in the former precinct of the Greyfriars (above), a few houses distant from Stewart's (Fig 9.14).

In the 16th century the occupants of the Red Lodge would have been even less aware of the division between house and garden, marked only by an open loggia (Fig 9.6). A similar effect was achieved in the 18th century, first in the garden of Rupert House in Lower Church Lane (Fig 9.20) and later in that of Prospect House in Prospect Lane (Figs 9.76a and 9.76b). In each a three-storey extension to the existing house was supported at garden level by an open loggia of Classical form. At Prospect House it gave access to a wash kitchen, the pump and a panelled corner cupboard, perhaps for the use of the household.

A lodge such as no.10 Lower Park Row, or a suburban house such as Prospect House, offered both a prospect to the occupants and a display of exclusivity to those more distant. Both houses were placed so as to be at the upper end of the garden, the prospect secured then being over both the garden itself and into the distance. Similar views could be enjoyed from houses such as the Red Lodge, the Manor House on St Michael's Hill and from Marlborough House on Marlborough Hill (Fig 9.77). On the summit of St Michael's Hill the group of houses on the site of the Royal Fort enjoyed a distant view commensurate with their own visibility from afar (Fig 9.1). To see was to be seen.

The importance of the prospect is evident in the architectural treatment given to the fenestration of three of the best recorded 17th-century lodges. At no.10 Lower Park Row tall four-light windows on each floor took in the view from three sides (Fig 9.31). Flooded by

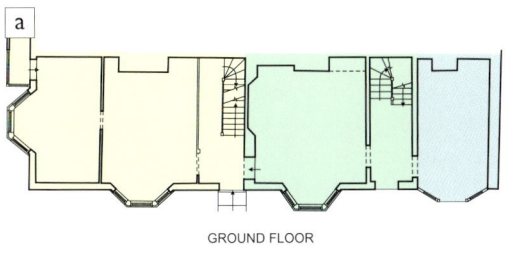

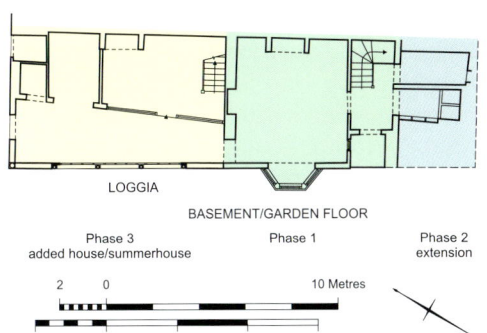

*Fig 9.75*
*Kingsdown Parade, nos.69 (closest to camera) and 71 (in distance), garden entrances, photograph of 2011 (NMR DP 114305–6).*

*Fig 9.76 (far left) Prospect House, Prospect Lane: a) plan (RHL, PEC); b) the loggia, photograph of 1975 (RHL).*

*Fig 9.77 (left) Marlborough Hill, Marlborough House, photograph of 2011 (NMR DP 114328).*

light from the south, it was still considered necessary to ensure the view to the north with small arched windows placed to one side of the two chimneystacks on each of the upper floors. Although built several decades later, Richmond House on the Clifton scarp was of a similar design to no.10 Lower Park Row; the interior on the ground, first and second floors was flooded with light from the tall mullioned and transomed windows on at least three sides (Fig 9.56).

In the smaller lodge in Blackfriars the fenestration was similarly arranged – here for a house of one room on each floor, but with a projecting stair turret on the west side. Windows of two or more lights were placed on each of the walls away from the stack and stairs, flooding the house with light from the south and north; the sides looked away from the city and across the greenery of adjacent gardens. Smaller windows on either side of the chimneystack afforded an optional view on a third side, to the city and the east.

The prospects afforded from such houses were carefully directed. In Blackfriars the chimneystack might logically have been placed on the north side, but control of the view from the lodge was more important than the direction of the sun. Similarly it can be argued that both no.10 Lower Park Row and no.7 Stony Hill were deliberately sited so as to provide a prospect not simply over their own gardens into the distance, but also over the extensive gardens of the Red Lodge.

Prospects could be further enhanced and the eyes of the onlooker further controlled by adding viewpoints such as towers and belvederes. The two largest lodges above the city, the Red and White Lodges, each had towers (Fig 9.2). The Red Lodge had a single stair turret, shown in outline on the plan of 1702 (Fig 9.5) and rising to the roof to afford elevated views. The White Lodge had two, one for the stairs and the other perhaps for a garderobe (Fig 9.9). On the slope below Old Market in Jacob Street the 'mansion house … heretofore used as a lodge'– formerly called 'Enderbie's Castle', but by 1627 known as 'Baber's Tower' – was shown as a dwelling with a tower on Millerd's map (Fig 9.2).[105] To the south of the city the house at Inns Court, embellished with a stairs turret of the 15th century and interpreted as a 'manor house', was also possibly a lodge.[106]

Other lodges incorporated towers on the city wall. One lodge to the south of the city wall included Tower Harratz; as excavated, this lodge has possibly been mistaken for a Civil War defence (Fig 9.78).[107] Behind no.4 Narrow Wine Street another tower in the city wall was used as a lodge in the late 16th and early 17th centuries (Fig 9.36). Towers provided a panoramic view above the level of that otherwise possible. As visitors were taken to the top of the tower, they and their hosts would have been conscious that this was a view for a privileged elite, for those permitted to enter this private space and those able to afford a tower. On the belvedere of a 17th-century lodge, such as Stoke Bishop House, the view from one of the two cupolas on the roof would have offered a similar exclusive vista – underlined for Sir Robert Cann by the adoption of an architectural device used for the Great House at Henbury completed a few years earlier (Fig 9.79).

Two towers built for the view were actually labelled by contemporaries as 'follies'. Overlooking the Avon Gorge was Cook's Folly (Fig 9.80), built by the City Chamberlain John Cook as his garden house or rural retreat from his town house at no.6 King Street. On the Kingsdown scarp Wint's Folly, advertised in 1750 as having a turret or gazebo on the roof, was presumably built by one Wint, and was conspicuous enough to be shown on the Bucks' prospect of Bristol from the south-east (Fig 9.81).

*Fig 9.78*
*Tower Harratz, photograph of excavations, 1994 (Williams 1994/1995 Pl 2).*

THE GARDEN HOUSE

The distant prospect can be shown in other contexts in 17th-century Bristol, as elsewhere, to have certainly been a feature of elite lifestyles. Flat roofs with balustrades appear to have been a feature added in the 17th century to a number of city houses, providing prospects of the street as well as more distant views. The balustraded viewing platform in the centre of Langton's house on Welsh Back would have provided a fine prospect of the river and the progress of shipping, but was also a central feature in a painting which must have been executed for the wealthy owner of this house (chapter 6, see Fig 6.12). On the opposite side of the river, the belvedere to the great house by the Bridge was given prominence on Millerd's map of 1673 (chapter 8, see Fig 8.100). Similar artistic attention to the belvedere was given by the topographical artist Johannes Kip to the cupolas on the roofs of Cann's house at Stoke Bishop and on the Great House at Henbury (Fig 9.79).

In the 18th century the occupants of larger suburban villas frequently enjoyed a prospect. Beyond the city and its immediate confines, Easton Manor was sited so as to face east across the valley of the Frome. On the hillsides to the west of the city many larger suburban villas offered similar, if not finer, prospects. Marlborough House in Marlborough Hill (Fig 9.77) and Observatory House (Fig 9.82) in Somerset Street on the slopes of Kingsdown, as well as St Michael's Hill House (Fig 9.83) and Royal Fort on St Michael's Hill, all faced east over the city towards Bath. On the upper slopes of Clifton Hill, Richmond House, Goldney House, Clifton Hill House and Clifton Court were four of a number of larger houses affording their occupants fine prospects across the Avon to the south (Fig 9.84).

Bristol's setting, with hills rising steeply from the rivers, offered many opportunities for viewpoints. The construction of numerous more modest suburban houses on the slopes to the west of the city in the 18th century opened up prospects to a greater number of individuals and households, but did not necessarily greatly widen the constituency of those who could afford such a view. In 1775 the 11 recorded inhabitants of Kingsdown Parade included three gentlemen, two merchants, the land-surveyor of the customs for Bristol and three prosperous widows. One may well have been the purchaser of the house advertised for letting in 1765, 'a delightful prospect over the city, and the adjacent villages, into Gloucestershire, Somersetshire and Wiltshire'.[108]

As well as affording a prospect, the siting of many garden houses and second residences allowed them to assume a prominent role in the landscape. Houses such as no.10 Lower Park Row, the Red Lodge and the White Lodge, the lodges on Stony Hill and on St Michael's Hill, on

*Fig 9.79*
*The viewing platform above the roof of John Sampson's house at Henbury (shown in print by Johannes Kip in Atkyns 1712, between pp 474–7, Henbury, seat of John Sampson).*

*Fig 9.80*
*Cook's Folly, photograph of the 1890s (Reece Winstone Archive).*

*Fig 9.81*
*Kingsdown, from the south-east prospect of Bristol by S and N Buck, 1734, showing Wint's Folly on left and Marlborough House with its own large garden on the right.*

*Fig 9.82*
*Observatory House, Somerset Street, drawing of the later 19th century (BCRL Seyer MSS 481–4, vol.II, Pt.II, fol 200).*

*Fig 9.83*
*St Michael's Hill House, St Michael's Hill (from Harvey 1904, Pl XXXIV).*

*Fig 9.84*
*The Clifton hillside from Rownhams Mead in 1785, showing from left to right: Emmaus House; Clifton Court, now the Chesterfield Nursing Home; the semi-detached pair of Prospect and Beresford Houses on Clifton Hill; Goldney House; and to the right the engine tower (BRSMG M4178).*

Redcliff Hill and Baber's Tower to the south-east of Old Market were highly visible from afar. Such houses provided what Nicholas Cooper has termed a public display of exclusivity.[109] Many of the suburban houses built on these same hillsides were of equal prominence. Kip's view of Robert Cann's second house at Stoke Bishop did not do justice to its position, prominently sited on the skyline above the valley of the Trym (Fig 9.85). Some of the largest suburban villas of the 18th century were similarly sited.

Exclusivity was accentuated through architectural design, underlining the status, wealth and taste of the owner. During the 16th and 17th centuries the lodge was a feature of elite architecture, associated in a rural context with courtly traditions of banqueting and with the chase.

The lodges of the city were certainly for the most part owned by the urban elite. Like the symbolic open hall, possession of a lodge may have served to underline the status of individuals in a fluid society where fortunes might be won and lost over just a few generations or less. Architectural features consolidated this effect through their reference to history.

As in other houses of the urban elite, heraldry remained an important device to underline the pedigree of the owner of the lodge or villa. Inside the Red Lodge heraldry received prominent display on the portal and chimneypiece of the great parlour. At least one

THE GARDEN HOUSE

*Stoke Bishop the Seat of Sr. Thomas Cann*

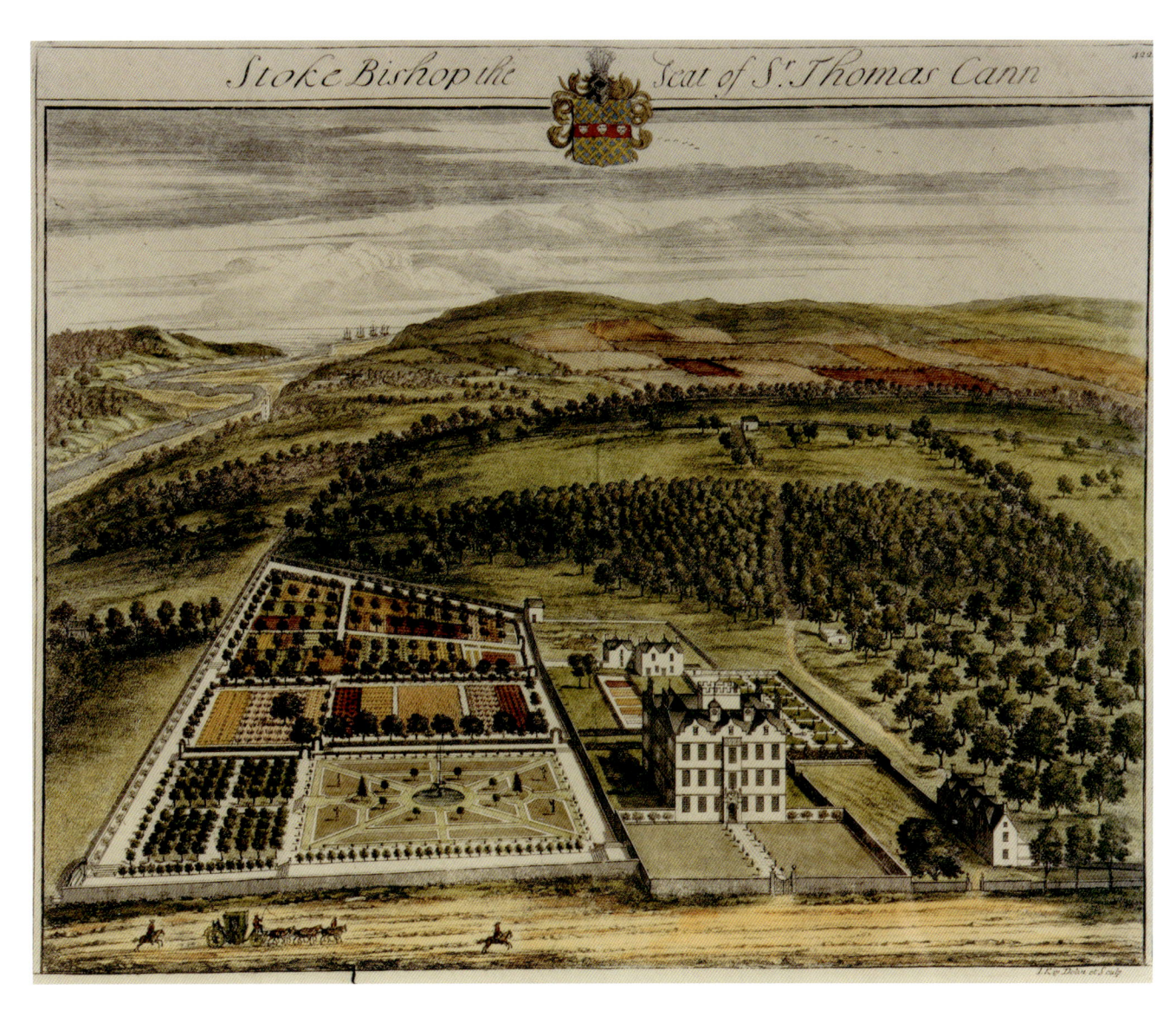

chimneypiece in the White Lodge bore the device of William Bird, 'a pair of compasses surmounted by a dove with an olive branch in its beak', similar but not identical to the arms on his tomb in St Mark's, the Lord Mayor's Chapel.[110]

These displays were relatively restrained alongside that of Cann's arms of 1669. Roger North (whose brother Dudley married Cann's daughter Ann) described Cann's fondness for making a show.[111] Approaching the flamboyant baroque porch of his second house at Stoke Bishop and passing beneath two allegorical angels waiting to push or drop Cann's arms into those of the next visitor, this was a sentiment with which Cann's guests would have agreed (Fig 9.86). Eighty years later a more restrained approach was taken by the architect Isaac Ware in the application of similar detail to Clifton Hill House, the suburban villa of the wealthy linen draper Paul Fisher. Over the entrance to the house were simply the date and initials of Fisher and his wife; the coat of arms appeared only in a corresponding position on the garden side (Fig 9.87).

The selective employment of medieval architectural forms gave the 17th-century lodge an air of antiquity, underlining the chivalrous pedigree of its owner. Sir Henry Creswick, his pedigree underlined by the arms of Elizabeth I hanging in his hall, would have approved of the use of the tower as such a device. His own country residence at Hanham Court (Fig 9.46) was one of several country houses with prospect or stair towers of the 16th century sited in the immediate vicinity of the city. Lodges with towers might have been associated in the mind of the builder or beholder with large or courtly houses in the countryside surrounding Bristol,

*Fig 9.85*
*Stoke Bishop House, well placed for the distant view to the south-west (from a print by Johannes Kip in Atkyns 1712, between pp 804–5).*

277

*Fig 9.86*
*Stoke Bishop House, entrance porch with Sir Robert Cann's arms, photograph of 1998 (NMR BB98/11790).*

*Fig 9.87*
*Clifton Hill House, exterior, photograph of 2003 (NMR AA048151, JD).*

such as Inns Court and Ashton Court in Somerset and Knole Park at Almondsbury, Hanham Court and old Kingsweston House in Gloucestershire.[112]

An alternative to having a tower was to crenellate. By the end of the 15th century a licence to crenellate was more a status symbol than a permit to fortify.[113] By the end of the 17th century a licence was no longer necessary, but several suburban houses sited within the Royal Fort had been supplied with crenellated parapets, perhaps highlighting the association of their owners with the Royal Fort (Figs 9.66, 9.67 and 9.68).

## Conclusion

Medieval towns, and especially cities, have been seen as little islands of capitalism. The investment of wealth in second residences could be seen as one facet of early capitalism – an investment that would convey status and bring both pleasure and fear for the safety of the investment. The possession of a second residence complete with garden might be seen as another element of emerging modernity, one that in Bristol, as in London, was certainly evident by the 15th century.[114]

Attitudes to the possession of a second residence also demonstrate changing views and underline the juxtaposition of material culture and historical context. Not all those who could afford a second house invested in one, perhaps sharing Samuel Pepys's opinion that, following a weekend visit to the Surrey countryside in 1667:

> My resolution is never to keep a country-house, but to keep a coach, and with my wife on the Saturday to go sometimes for a day to this place, and then quit to another place; and there is more variety and as little charge, and no trouble, as there is in a country-house.[115]

Many wealthy Bristol citizens, however, were of different mind. Here, as in London and probably elsewhere, the possession of a garden house as a second residence was very much an element of merchant culture and identity in the early modern city.

The possession of a garden house served many purposes beyond being simply an investment in property: they served principally as places for retreat from the noise and bustle of the city. In Bristol garden houses were places for entertaining and for visiting on a Sunday, offering space for a garden and cultivation which could not be found in the centre of the city. A garden house well beyond the city could serve also as a rural smallholding, as for Richard and Mary Aldworth at Kingcot in the parish of Long Ashton, for instance (Fig 9.43). The merchant George Lane leased a lodge or garden house (Fig 9.42), adjacent to what later became Tyndall's Park; it served both as a rural smallholding and a house that could be used for high-status entertainment. Lane's possessions in the parlour of this house in 1613, including a lute and Venetian glasses, indicate that it served as a dining room, while James Stewart's drawing of 1746 shows the garden still lovingly tended some 100 years later (Fig 9.42b). Such gardens were valued: when James Hollidge leased one of his garden houses at Emmaus House to John Matthews, a gardener in 1710, he stipulated that the fruit trees and standers were to be properly pruned and not removed at the end of the lease.[116]

Garden houses could be visited on summer evenings, especially those closest to the city, such as those built above Johnny Ball Lane, in the Little Park and in the former Greyfriars precinct. They could also provide a Sunday retreat, as probably was the case for the family of Thurston Harris. In 1622 the contents of their house at Barton Regis included a 'great bible', an item absent from their house in the city (above). Proximity to the centre of the city was a selling point as an entry in *The Bristol Weekly Intelligencer* for 8 September 1750 indicated: 'for sale a Mansion House at Stapleton, but one hour's walk from the Exchange in the depth of winter'. From the records of the Goldney family we might deduce that they were also places more amenable to await events such as the birth of a child. On summer evenings and on Sundays the Goldneys and Phippens might well have trod the same path from their town houses in High Street to their garden houses on Clifton Hill. The cluster of residences on Clifton Hill must have offered many opportunities to the elite of Bristol for sociable conviviality. Similar opportunities must have existed on St Michael's Hill, at Barton Hill and in other clusters of second residences (Fig 9.3).

The identification of the garden house or lodge as part of the lifestyle of the wealthier citizens of early modern Bristol has been one of the discoveries made in the course of this study, underlining that this phenomenon was not confined to just gentry and their betters, but the urban elite as well, an element of merchant culture that could be found in London and other large towns.[117] Doubtless more such houses remain to be identified, from documentary and/or architectural evidence: the Keeper's Lodge in the park of Ashton Court to the west of the city, the gabled centre-part of Clancy's Farm in Knowle, to the south, and Inns Court at Knowle West (Figs 9.88, 9.89 and 9.90) are examples of houses that might be added to the corpus of houses built as elite second residences.

*Fig 9.88*
The Keeper's Lodge in the park of Ashton Court to the west of the city, drawing of 1829
(The British Library Board, Buckler Drawings, Add MS 36379 fol 39).

*Fig 9.89*
The gabled centre-part of Clancy's or Lower Knowle Farm, in Knowle, to the south of the city: possibly a lodge, photograph of 1999 (Jon Brett).

*Fig 9.90*
*Inns Court, Knowle West, the 15th-century chamber block with tower and garderobe, possibly part of an elite second residence, drawing of c 1827 by John or John Chessell Buckler (Jackson 2007, 1).*

# 10

# Spaces and Changes

The names, functions and interrelationships of the rooms in the Bristol town house have been discussed at numerous points in previous chapters. The purpose of this chapter is to bring together some of these threads to provide a more detailed analysis of how use of domestic space evolved in the early modern or post-medieval period. The changing roles of specific spaces, and the reasons why houses were modified, reflected developments in society and, in particular, the altering relationships within the household. Evolving architectural forms, therefore, are powerful evidence for wider historical processes in the development of urban life.

## Aspiring to Magnificence: the Hall and Stairs

In 'The Explanation of the Draughts of a House Proposed for a Merchant', dated 1724, the unidentified architect, working on behalf of the merchant and developer Robert Yate, used words such as 'graceful', 'beauty' and 'magnificence' for the areas of the house in which the owner would receive visitors of note (chapter 8). Efforts to achieve these effects were concentrated on the exterior of the house and on interior spaces such as the entrance hall, the stairs and the principal reception rooms. The aspiration to magnificence was most easily accomplished in building by the wealthy. In 17th-century and earlier Bristol, it could be seen in the houses of wealthy merchants such as William Canynges, John Smyth, Robert Aldworth and Sir Henry Creswick (chapter 5). They, too, had sought houses pleasing to the eye. The evidence for houses of the 17th and the 18th centuries provides the opportunity to examine more rigorously how far across the urban population as a whole such intentions extended. How far did the house itself become a means of expressing and achieving aspirations towards gentility or refinement?

We have seen in earlier chapters how, for those at the apex of Bristol's commercial community, the open hall of the medieval hallhouse retained a symbolic value that ensured its continuing use until the end of the 17th century. The first-floor room over the shop in the shophouse was also known before 1600 as the hall, probably on account of its being the most important room in the house; in probate inventories of the 17th century this room was usually named 'the forestreet chamber', showing that use of the term 'hall' for this room was now being abandoned. In the 18th century there was an increasing use of the term 'hall' in its modern sense of being an entry hall; the evidence for this comes from probate inventories of identified houses.

In 1719 no.22 Queen Square (chapter 8) had recently become the home of the mercer and former mayor George Stephens (Appendix 2). The walls of the entrance hall and stairs were lined not with weaponry and armour, but principally with pictures and prints: 10 small pictures and two large pictures in the hall, one large map, four heraldic prints, one landscape, 18 India prints and six large pictures on the stairs.

The contents of no.15 St James's Barton (chapter 8) were described in the inventory of Thomas Crosby taken in 1766 (Appendix 2). There was again a touch of modernity to the contents of his hall. The absence of chairs to sit on, for example, indicated that the room was mainly a space to move through, furnished only with two large square mahogany tables, two green cloths for the tables, one glass lamp and three pieces of old haircloth, the last possibly for polishing shoes. Towards the end of the century, in 1781, the contents of no.16 Queen Square, the house of the wealthy merchant Michael Miller, were appraised (Appendix 2). Miller's hall, contemporary in build with that of no.15 (Fig 10.1), was simply an entrance to his house. It was furnished with a marble table, two mahogany tables, an eight-day clock, a clothes press, four Windsor chairs, a map of Bristol and four prints on the wall; there was also a remnant of haircloth and a shoebag on the floor.

How and why had these changes in the role and status of the hall come about? Miller's hall was closer in character to the entrance vestibule of Victorian mansions than to the hall of a wealthy merchant of the 17th century. At that time men of the wealth and status of Crosby and Miller would probably have held a position of importance in the militia, proclaimed through a display of arms and amour around the entrance hall.

By the early 18th century there was a clear emphasis on the need, at the apex of Bristol society, to make a dramatic architectural statement in the form of an impressive entrance to the house. Yate's architect (chapter 8) raised the ground floor of the proposed merchant's house some 18in above ground level, 'as well as to give a graceful Entrance as for giving light to the Cellars'. Medieval merchants had similarly striven for impact, which they achieved by means of a decorated porch or canopy over the street entrance (chapter 5). The continued value of this sort of display may be inferred from the retention of medieval features in houses of the 17th century. Within the Castle, the remains of the great hall described by William Worcestre in the 1480s had by the 1630s been incorporated into the mansion house of Francis Brewster, the principal tenant. Brewster, or a near contemporary, retained the structure of the medieval vaulted entrance porch, both the exterior buttress wall and the vaulted entrance porch on the inside – probably as a way of adding to the magnificence of his re-modelled house (Figs 10.2 and 10.3). The porch did not, in fact, provide the main entry to the house, but it certainly caught the eye of approaching visitors.

Once inside the entrance door, the clearest differences between the treatment of the entrance in the great medieval town house and its later successors became evident. In the medieval house the entrance had led, either directly or by means of a screens passage, into the open hall – both the ceremonial centre of the house and the point from which other rooms were reached. In the post-medieval town house, the hall eventually cast off other functions to become simply the central point in the pattern of circulation. The critical design consideration became the relationship of the hall to the principal stair, and Bristol's post-medieval houses show considerable variety in this relationship. A number of determining factors included the size of the house, the circulation patterns within it and preferences in architectural effect.

The elevation of the stair to the status of principal display feature can be traced to the 17th century. Entries and stairs on this scale must have been incorporated in the largest houses of the later 16th and the 17th centuries, notably the great houses on St Augustine's Back and at the south end of Bristol Bridge, but few have survived or been recorded. Two recorded examples of the 17th century that we do possess were, like the houses of Yate's architect, situated away from the principal streets.

Both again can be shown to have been owned or occupied by citizens of considerable wealth.

*Fig 10.1*
*No.15 Queen Square, entrance hall*
*(from Dening 1923, Pl v).*

Francis Brewster's conversion of the great hall of the Castle to a residence involved adding a new entry and stairs (Fig 10.4), while Oldbury House, St Michael's Hill, built probably in the 1680s for woollen merchant Marmaduke Bowdler, and by 1704 the house of Lady Phillippa Gore (Appendix 2), was provided with a wide, open-well stair placed symmetrically in the centre of the house, in full view from the entry hall (Fig 10.5; *see* Fig 9.34). Stairs of similar design were to be found from the 1650s in the second residences of wealthy citizens, for instance at Ashley Manor and Stoke Bishop House (*see* Figs 9.48 and 9.49). In two taverns of the 1690s, the Fountain in Tailors' Court and the Full Moon in Stokes Croft, the stairs were similarly placed and finished (Fig 10.6).

The majority of the recorded examples of stairs built on this scale in principal residences of the 17th century belong to the 1690s. Following the destruction of its predecessor by fire, the so-called Manor House in Park Lane, on St Michael's Hill, was rebuilt between 1690 and 1696. The open-well stairs (Fig 10.7) were similar in plan to those of Oldbury House. Being built several years later, however, they were of the fashionable baroque design, in which barley-sugar twist balusters replaced the massive, column-on-vase pattern used for those at Oldbury House. In both these houses the stairs were displayed to those coming through the front entry.

By the early 18th century the relationship between the entrance hall and the stair had become one of the critical considerations for architect and client. In preparing designs for the property that was to become no.52 Prince Street, Robert Yate's architect, the unknown compiler of 'The Explanation of the Draughts of a House Proposed for a Merchant' in *The Kingsweston Book of Drawings* (chapter 8), strived to combine grace with magnificence. He conceived a large and undivided hall featuring two openings, probably arched, in its further end wall, providing glimpses of the stairs and rooms beyond. The 'best stairs' on the plan were the 'great stairs' in the architect's account. This enlarged stair well gave 'a better view of the stairs and ceiling', adding 'a beauty which cannot be imagined by those who have not seen the experience of it'.[1]

No visual record of the interior of no.52 has been traced, but two other houses provide ample evidence of what the architect intended. Yate's own town residence was the Red Lodge, for the rebuilding of which this same architect prepared at least three speculative drawings. One of them, dated 1728, included the additional and optimistic note 'in case of any accident to the Red Lodge', an implied exasperation at his client's unwillingness to accede to a total rebuilding. What Yate did agree to was the raising of the Red Lodge by a further storey and the addition of a new 'great stairs' – rising through three storeys with a wide open well and treads 5ft in width, exactly as recommended for the merchant's house (Fig 10.8).

By 1728 the same unidentified mason–architect had already commenced and probably completed his commission for James Furney, Yate's neighbour, on the north side of Park Row (pp270-1). As rebuilt and extended (Fig 10.9a; *see* Figs 9.71a and 9.71b), nearly one-quarter of the basement, ground and first floors of Lunsford House was taken up by the new great stairs. Each tread was just over 4ft in width and the view upwards was of the bold baroque carving of the stairs and the decorated ceiling (Fig 10.9b). This was a view fully open to the entrance hall, accessed from a small lobby between the stairs and the main or rear door of the house. On the ground and first floors panelled entrance doorways indicated the principal rooms beyond, the placement of those on the ground floor echoing this architect's plan for no.52 Prince Street.

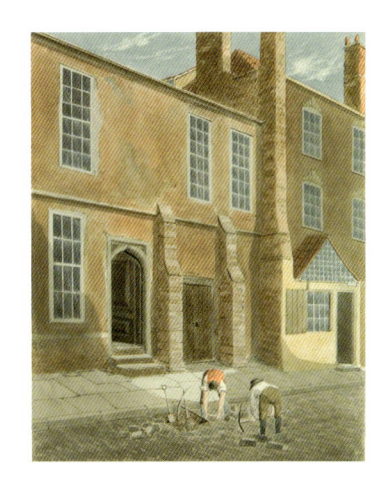

*Fig 10.2*
The exterior buttresses of no.20 Castle Green, removed in 1822 and probably part of the porch to the great hall of the medieval Castle, the entrance to which lay behind the gabled porch on the right hand side of the projecting buttress and chimneystack removed in 1822, watercolour of 1822 by Samuel Jackson (BRSMG M2734).

*Fig 10.3*
The vaulted entrance to the great hall of the Castle. This was retained within Brewster's house, the part that later became no.21 Castle Green; the entrance lay behind the gabled porch shown on the right hand side of Fig 10.2; in the distance can be seen the stairs shown in Fig 10.69 (BRO 20894, photograph probably by Fred Little and taken c 1907).

# THE TOWN HOUSE IN MEDIEVAL AND EARLY MODERN BRISTOL

Fig 10.4
No.20 Castle Green, stairs hall of the 17th century, drawing by Loxton of late 19th or early 20th century (BRSMG M3004).

Fig 10.5 (right)
Oldbury House, no.121 St Michael's Hill, entrance hall and stairs, photograph of 2010 (English Heritage DP 114685).

Fig 10.6 (far right, above)
The Full Moon Inn, Stokes Croft, entrance hall and stairs (Dening 1949, 57).

Fig 10.7 (far right, below)
The Manor House, Park Lane, St Michael's Hill, entrance hall and stairs, photograph of 1952 (NMR BB776710, PEWS).

SPACES AND CHANGES

*Fig 10.8*
*Red Lodge, Park Row. Robert Yate's unknown architect advised in 1724 that the stairs should have 'a beauty which cannot be imagin'd by those who have not seen the experience of it', photograph of 2003 (English Heritage DP 140426).*

From the early 18th century the construction of houses two rooms wide and deep facilitated the placement of a central entry and great stairs – as envisaged in the proposed design of the 'unknown compiler' for a merchant (*see* Fig 8.83). Both Yate and his architect might have been familiar with the house on Clifton Hill, built in 1711 for the Hodges family and latterly known as the Bishop's House. In this building a wide arch across the division between the front and rear parts of the house served to frame the view of the stairs (Fig 10.10).[2] In the city nos.15 and 29 Queen Square were among the first houses designed in this way (*see* Figs 8.84g and 8.84f respectively).

No.15 was first occupied from *c* 1711, its first occupant being the Reverend Strickland Gough. Here the stair hall was slightly wider than the

285

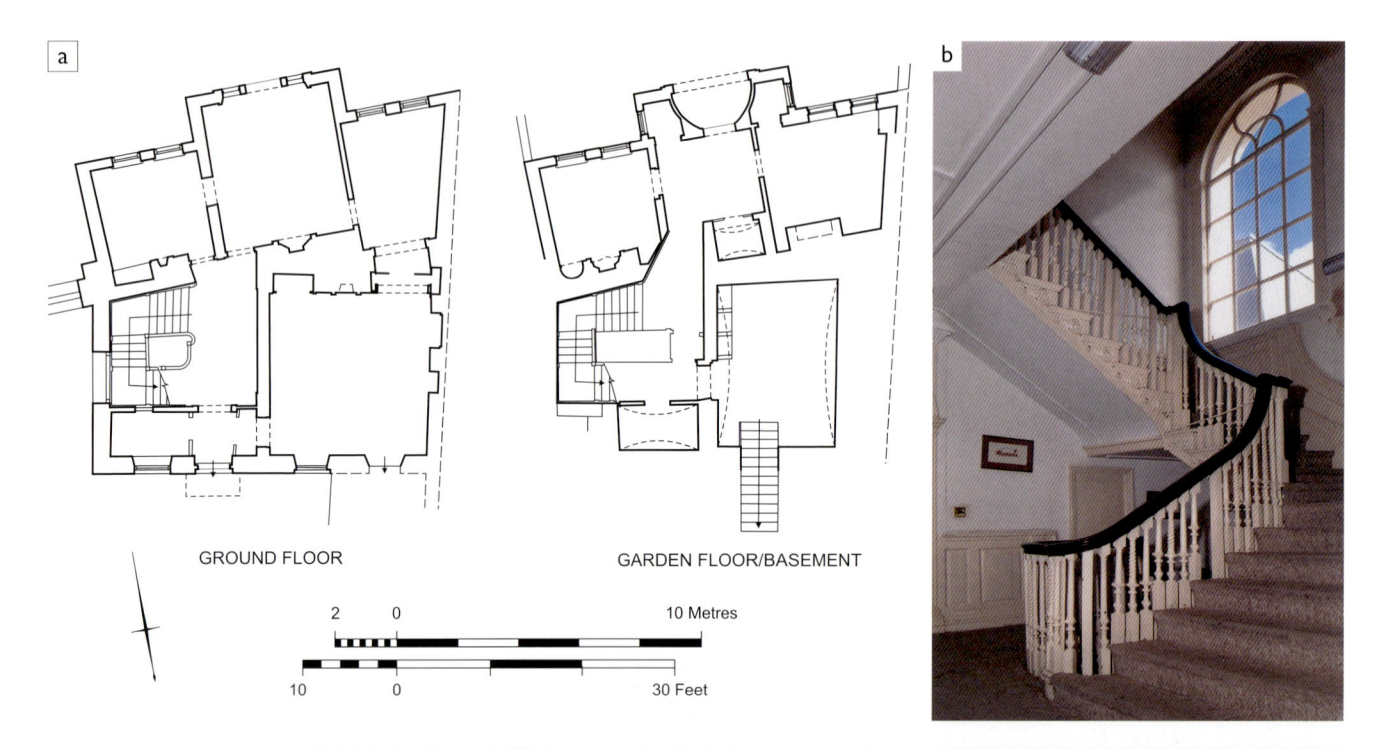

*Fig 10.9*
*Lunsford House, Park Row:*
*a) plan of the ground floor (RHL, PEC after RCHME);*
*b) the main stairs, photograph of 2010 (English Heritage DP 114313).*

*Fig 10.10*
*The Bishop's House, Clifton Hill, entrance hall and stairs, photograph of 1942 (English Heritage AA42/2295).*

entrance hall. The building lease for no.29 was granted to the merchant Nathaniel Day in 1709, but he occupied the house only from 1720. Built to the same plan and at approximately the same date was no.4 Broad Plain. Here the stairs were similarly framed by the wide arch to the entry hall, with the stair hall ornamented by an arched and tiled niche (Fig 10.11; *see* Fig 8.84d). A similar effect was achieved in a number of other houses built before the middle of the 18th century. In Lower Maudlin Street, no.16 (later the Eye Hospital) was one of a pair of

*Fig 10.11
No.4 Broad Plain, entrance hall and stairs, photograph of 1978
(NMR BB78/9299).*

*Fig 10.12
No.16 Lower Maudlin Street, entrance hall and stairs, photograph of 1998
(NMR AA98/02850).*

semi-detached houses, built *c* 1726 for the merchant John Rowe (Appendix 2). Here an imposing central hall and stairs were further embellished with an arched recess for a piece of furniture suitable for display at this point (Fig 10.12; *see* Fig 8.95a).

What was good for a large town house, with two rooms and an entrance hall across its frontage, could also be adapted for use in more modest dwellings. Isaac Ware wrote in the 1760s that 'there is often an air of space and room in throwing back a stair-case; and this may be done to such advantage in a moderate house, as to make it seem much larger than it is, by a great part of it being seen first'.[3] In a narrow house of two rooms in depth, positioning the stairs alongside the rear room enabled it to be seen from the entry in much the same way as with a house of two rooms in width; the size of the arch framing the stairs was limited by the width of the passage or entrance hall from the street. This was the strategy adopted at Langton's house at no.12 Welsh Back (*see* Fig 6.13), built *c* 1623 on a plot only 20ft wide, and at no.74 Old Market, built in the 1690s (*see* Figs 8.60a and 8.61).

From the early 18th century many more one-room wide houses were designed so that the stairs might visibly form part of the entry. In the north-east angle of Queen Square, no.61 Queen Charlotte Street was part of a row commenced in 1699 but itself first occupied in 1711, consisting of two rooms in depth and between 24 and 30ft wide. The stairs, placed alongside the rear room, were framed by the arch between the front and rear parts of the entrance hall (Figs 10.13 and 10.14). On the south side of the square, nos.26–8 were a row of three houses. They were also first occupied c 1711, but each consisted of one and a half rooms in depth, with a width no more than 20ft. The stairs were again placed alongside the rear room, an arch marking the division between the front and rear parts of the hall (Fig 10.52b).

On St Michael's Hill, high above the city, older houses were being replaced in the 1710s by a continuous row of houses of similar plan to no.61 Queen Charlotte Street and nos.26–8 Queen Square.[4] In nos.43–51 St Michael's Hill the stairs were placed alongside the rear room, each stairs visible from the entry to the house (see Fig 8.60j). The first occupant of no.51 as rebuilt c 1712 was Lady Sarah Whetstone; now a widow, she had once lived with her family at Cromwell House in the Royal Fort (see Inventory). A little later in date, of the late 1720s and 1730s, was the row of four houses built in Pipe Lane leading from St Augustine's Back to Trenchard Street. These were also of similar plan, with a winder stairs placed alongside the rear room, framed by the arch from the entrance hall (see Fig 8.70).

In houses of such size, this view from the entry was for most people in the 1710s a new experience. Seeing the stairs from a distance, visitors might well have supposed such houses to be larger than they were in reality, much as the architect Isaac Ware advised half a century later. Ascending the stairs, however, the winders at each landing and the compact design of these houses would have been familiar to the widows, sea captains and genteel persons who predominated among their occupants in the 1710s and 1720s.[5] These features would mark the houses out as being of lesser status than those with generous, open-well stairs.

The advice echoed by Ware was followed most effectively in houses larger than these, but of insufficient width for a room on either side of the stairs. Newly built in 1713, nos.32 and 33 Old Market replaced earlier houses; both were on plots 28ft wide. Plans of 1780 and 1862 show no.32, first probably as built and subsequently as altered to become a shophouse, then its current use. The front entrance hall, originally between one large and one smaller room, opened out to a wide stairs hall occupying over one-third of the width of the house at the rear (Fig 10.15). In wider houses such as these it was also possible to provide a more spacious entrance

*Fig 10.13 (right) No.61 Queen Charlotte Street, plan of ground floor (RHL, PEC after RCHME).*

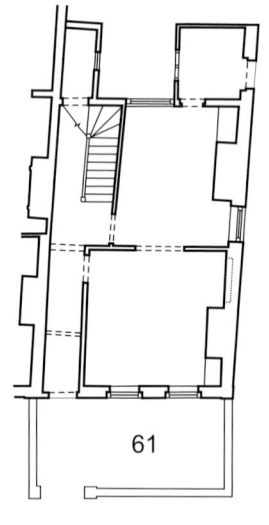

*Fig 10.14 (far right) No.61 Queen Charlotte Street, entrance hall and stairs, photograph of 1995 (NMR BB95/8284).*

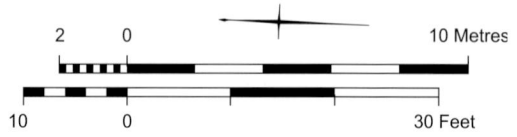

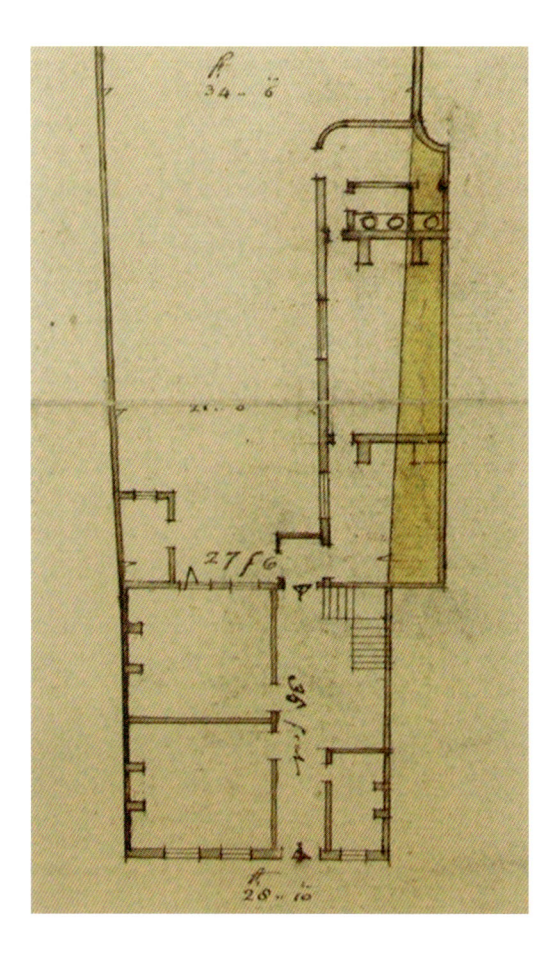

hall, lit by a window to one side of the front door and providing a view of the stairs comparable to that obtained in a wider house (such as nos.15 and 29 Queen Square).

Among the first houses planned in this way were nos.10–19, nos.20–4 and nos.25–9 Orchard Street, all built *c* 1717–22 (*see* Figs 8.65, 8.66, 8.67 and 8.68). The widest of these, first occupied in 1722 by John Becher, Master of the Society of Merchant Venturers, was no.28; its open-well stairs were also the grandest (Fig 10.16). This same arrangement was followed for the majority of the houses built in Prince Street in the 1720s and 1730s. In no.70, one of a pair with no.68, the entrance hall was 15ft wide, the stairs beyond fully framed by the wide arch between the front and rear parts of the house (*see* Fig 8.84l).

In the second half of the 18th century few such houses were built, but the construction of houses with a narrower entrance hall and the stairs alongside the rear room continued apace. In Redcliff Parade, Brunswick Square and King Square the new terraces from the 1750s to the 1770s seem to have been entirely of houses of this plan. Many rebuilt houses were also of this plan, as for instance at nos.68 and 69 Old Market (Fig 10.17). In these houses, as in the building of the north-east part of Kingsdown Parade in the 1790s (Fig 10.18; *see* Fig 8.60f), the view of the stairs from the entry, a largely new experience in the early 18th century, had now become the norm.

In all the houses considered up to this point the visual connection between entry and stair was a governing element of design. There were, however, alternative approaches to this relationship. For many citizens the thoughts of Isaac Ware and Yate's architect on the importance of a graceful entrance and a visually arresting stairs for those entering one's house were of little significance. In most houses of two rooms in depth in 17th-century Bristol, the stairs were

*Fig 10.15 (above left)*
*No.32 Old Market, plan of ground floor c 1780 (BRO 04479 (1) fol 255).*

*Fig 10.16 (above)*
*No.28 Orchard Street, the stairs, photograph of 2003 (NMR AA042257).*

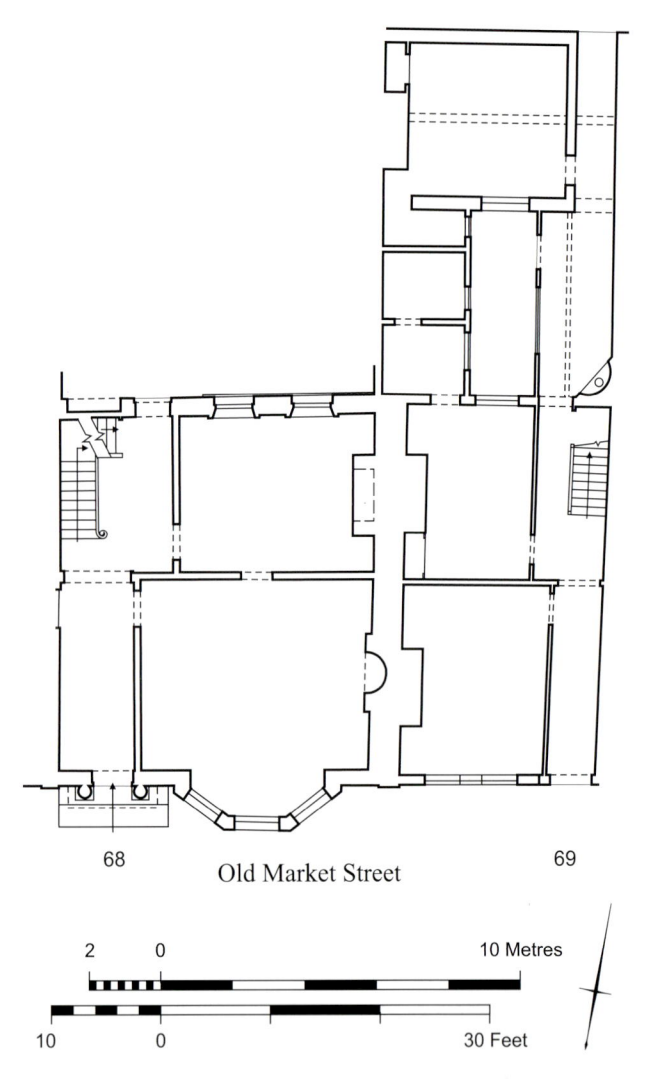

placed in the centre of the house. They were entirely or almost out of sight of the entrance, and sometimes lit only if doors to the front and rear rooms were open to provide light. This was so for most of the houses built in Castle Street and King Street in the 1650s and 1660s, and indeed for most older houses rebuilt throughout the century.

The open-well stairs in many of the King Street houses (Fig 10.19), and for instance those in the row of four next to St Thomas's church (*see* Fig 8.50), would doubtless have delighted many of their inhabitants; to visitors too they would have been impressive demonstrations of the joiner's art. Stairs built around a single newel but with a handrail and balusters were less complex works of joinery, but might still have afforded pleasure in their finish. Neither would, however, have conveyed the same visual impact as the immediately visible stairs in such houses as Oldbury House (Fig 10.5) and Langton's house at no.12 Welsh Back (*see* Figs 6.13 and 6.14).

In many smaller houses of two rooms in depth built during the 17th century, the centrally placed stairs were clearly not designed to impress; they were enclosed, with a door giving access to and from each floor. Between 1684 and 1694 nos.38–9 and 40–1 Old Market Street were both built as a pair. Each had an enclosed stair placed centrally between the front and rear rooms, possibly indicating a functional distinction between the ground and first floors

Fig 10.17 (above)
Nos.68–9 Old Market, plan of ground floor
(RHL, PEC).

Fig 10.18 (right)
No.52 Kingsdown Parade, view of the stairs from the entrance hall, photograph of 2010
(NMR DP114092).

Fig 10.19 (far right)
No.5 King Street, the stairs, photograph of 1992
(NMR BB92/23663; see Figs 8.46–7a).

as there were no reception rooms on the first or upper floors (*see* Figs 6.24 and 6.25). On the opposite side of the street, no.53 was rebuilt in the later 17th century to a similar plan, again with an enclosed stairs.

Even to some citizens living in larger houses the intervisibility of entry and stairs was frequently not of importance in the 17th century. A house of two rooms in width, no.6 King Street was built in the late 1660s. For its late 17th-century occupants, the merchant John Speed and gentleman John Cooke,[6] the entry was to a front hall probably taking up the west half of the ground floor – an impressively large but unheated space that possibly also served some commercial function. To the rear a spacious, open-well stairs was placed in a projecting wing at the back of the house, not though visible from the entrance hall (Fig 10.20; *see* Fig 8.80a). This was a conscious decision of the architect and/or client, since it would have been equally possible to position the stairs in full view of the entry, as at Oldbury House (Fig 10.5).

Similar decisions were made with regard to the building of nos.20–4 St Michael's Hill, a row of three houses, two rooms in width, built in the early 1690s. These three houses were grand enough from the exterior, originally with ball finials to the gables. Inside the stairs were well finished, and could, like those of Oldbury House higher up the hill, have been placed in full sight of the entrance. In no.22, however, where the configuration of the tenement plot obliged the designer to place them inside the main body of the house, the stairs were to one side of the view from the entry, scarcely visible to visitors unless ascending to the first floor (Fig 10.21; *see* Fig 8.80b).

The opportunities and choices to be made by the designers of wider houses such as these were evident in the planning of the larger houses in Queen Square, built in the 1700s and 1710s. In some large houses entry and stairs formed an ensemble designed to impress and please. In other houses of similar width, however, a conscious decision was made to place the stairs at the rear of the house but out of sight of the entrance hall, a plan little different in this respect from no.6 King Street and the houses on St Michael's Hill. In Queen Square nos. 36–8, a row of three houses first occupied between 1705 and 1712, were each planned with a narrow entrance hall that gave access to the principal front rooms and to the rear stairs hall and beyond. Each staircase was framed around

*Fig 10.20*
*No.6 King Street, the stairs, photograph of 2012 (English Heritage DP 146929).*

*Fig 10.21*
*No.22 St Michael's Hill, the stairs, photograph of 1998 (NMR AA98/00271).*

*Fig 10.22*
*Nos.36–8 Queen Square, the stairs in no.38, photograph of 1997 (NMR BB97/4503).*

*Fig 10.23 (below left) No.22 Queen Square, the stairs, photograph of 2001 (Jon Brett).*

*Fig 10.24 (below right) No.31 College Green, the stairs, photograph of 1998 (NMR AA98/02816).*

an open well, affording an impressive sight upwards but not visible from the front hall (Fig 10.22; *see* Figs 8.84a and 8.85).

In some large houses the experience of the entry and stairs was given a more subtle treatment in the 18th century. In no.22 Queen Square, a house built to a full two rooms in width and depth, the stairs were placed to one side rather than centrally at the rear (Fig 10.23; *see* Fig 8.84c); and in the 1720s houses of a similar plan were constructed in College Green (Fig 10.24; *see* Fig 8.87). The plan was adapted and advocated later in the century by Isaac Ware, who observed that 'as to the situation of the stair-case, with respect to the principal door, it is a point much disputed'. Some, he noted, 'prefer the placing the stair case on one side, and there are examples of buildings very beautiful in this way'.[7] This was Ware's own preference in setting out the plan for Clifton Hill House, and was a stratagem employed in the building both of Royal Fort House *c* 1760 and of no.7 Great George Street *c* 1790 (*see* Figs 8.84o–q and 8.90).[8] Further magnificence was achieved in these houses through the installation of a stone stairs or iron balusters, fitted only in the houses of some of the wealthiest members of the city elite (Figs 10.25, 10.26, 10.27 and 10.15). The domestic environments of the wealthiest citizens continued to be distinct.

For many builders choice in the placing and style of the stair was clearly possible.

SPACES AND CHANGES

The decision appears not to have been determined absolutely by wealth or status, however, for different forms were adopted in houses of widely differing sizes and both large and small houses showed a variety of solutions. Choice may have been very much a matter of personal views on how the house should function. Considerations of privacy may have been at work, as we have seen in chapter 8, and fashionable ideas were doubtless more influential with some builders than others.

In the early 18th century, some wealthy owners opted for the fashionable and elegant open-string stairs in full view of the entrance, as in 29 Queen Square. Others, however, perhaps of more conservative taste (or perhaps foreseeing Ware's ideas later in the century), introduced a visual barrier between the two. Cultural influences may have been the most powerful determinants of choice in this element of the town house.

*Fig 10.25 (above left) Clifton Hill House, designed by Isaac Ware for Paul Fisher, the stone stairs, photograph of 2010 (NMR A42/2299).*

*Fig 10.26 (top right) Royal Fort House, the stone stairs, photograph of 2003 (NMR AA042256).*

*Fig 10.27 (left) No.7 Great George Street, the stone stairs, photograph of 2011 (English Heritage DP 141417).*

293

## Living over the Shop: the First-Floor Hall and the Forestreet Chamber

In London the principal first-floor room was, in the 16th and early 17th centuries, known as the hall. This was true of houses both large and small, the latter including many which would in 15th-century Bristol have been called 'shop-houses'.[9] To the inhabitants of Bristol, this room was known very rarely as the hall by the early 17th century. In most houses with a ground-floor shop, it was known as the 'forestreet chamber', 'lodging chamber' or simply 'chamber'. Among some 30 houses with shops described in a sample of probate inventories between 1609 and 1650,[10] there are only three examples in which the appraisers refer to the first-floor principal or front room as the hall. In the house of Guy Hill, a joiner who died in 1635, the first-floor front room was known as the hall.[11] His house was of two rooms in depth, the ground floor comprising a shop and possibly the kitchen, the latter not mentioned in the inventory. In Henry Foxe's house at nos.15–17 Wine Street, the first-floor front room was known as the hall in 1643; it was heated, and used both for sitting and dining.[12]

More can be said of the arrangements of no.49 Wine Street, the third inventory to mention a first-floor hall. At her death in 1641, Mary Reade's house here was evidently of two rooms in depth. On the first floor, the rear room was called the hall. The contents of this room included four chests, a table, nine stools and a low chair, indicating that it was used probably for dining and certainly for daytime living. It also included two beds, suggesting that, despite being called the hall and retaining some of the functions of a principal living room, it had been adapted to serve also as a bedroom. It therefore performed a role similar to that of the multi-purpose parlour in other houses and to the forestreet chamber in many shophouses.

The house passed at Reade's death to her brother William Lymell, who died three years later in 1644. In the inventory of his possessions, this first-floor room was again called the hall, its furnishings similar to those in 1641. The house was then inherited by his widow Elizabeth, who died four years later in 1648.[13] The appraisers drawing up the list of her possessions followed an almost identical route to that taken on the two previous occasions. Coming to the room formerly called the hall, it was identified this time as 'the chamber over the parlor'. It was a room more sparsely furnished than either the parlour or the chamber at the front of the house.

Within a year of Elizabeth Lymell's death, commissioners were preparing a survey of the confiscated lands of the Dean and Chapter of the Cathedral, one of a number of Parliamentary Surveys undertaken throughout England in *c* 1649. In Bristol the greater part of the survey was undertaken by four surveyors, appointed by Parliament in London. In their reports the term 'hall' was generally preferred for the principal living room of the house; the surveys included many houses with first-floor halls over a ground-floor shop.[14]

In the absence of a ground-floor parlour, the room in which visitors were likely to be received was the forestreet chamber. For most townspeople living over the shop, this formed the social centre of the house. Like the parlour as it had been in the 15th century, this was a room used for sleeping as well as for daily living. When in 1591 Elizabeth Pepwell left to her son Timothy all the linen in the chest at 'the beddes hedde in the fore chamber next the streate' in her house in High Street, she was referring to a room that might have easily been called the hall by her contemporaries Mary Reade and Elizabeth Lymell.[15] At no.2 Narrow Wine Street in 1617, John Ryman's 'best upper chamber' was well furnished for dining and sleeping. The table had seating for eight and the bed had a truckle bed below; the windows were hung with curtains, and a musket, holberd, sword and dagger provided a good display for visitors.[16]

Throughout the 17th and 18th centuries many townspeople continued to use the forestreet chamber in this way, living and sleeping in the same room.[17] In 1729 Samuel Daw was living in St Thomas's parish in a three-storey house, two rooms in depth. The ground floor was taken up by the shop and kitchen. Daw's principal living room was the first-floor front room, called 'the fore Room one Story'; the space was used for dining, sitting and sleeping.[18]

The first-floor chamber at the back of the house was sometimes used in the same way. In 1708, William Nicklus, the barber-surgeon at no.26 Castle Street (*see* Fig 6.26), used the first-floor front room as a study and consulting room, keeping there his 40 books on surgery and medicine. The room to the back of the house was used both for sleeping and entertainment, its contents including a table and seven cane chairs.[19]

For other townspeople, the forestreet chamber was assigned only to daytime living. In 1637 William Bysshop, a cloth worker, lived in St Thomas's parish in a house of at least two storeys. Above the ground-floor shop and kitchen were his bedchamber, at the back of the house, and the 'fore chamber'.[20] The latter was not used for sleeping, but only for sitting and dining. A similar use was made of the first-floor front room in some of the houses in Castle Street during the 1660s and 1670s. At no.68, George Hill's first-floor room was clearly intended for dining; its contents consisted solely of a table and form, a coffer and chair (Appendix 2). Such sparseness might indicate that the room had been partly emptied, but this would not have been the case in Flower Hunt's house at no.59. Here the forestreet chamber was furnished with a table and side cupboard, six chairs for dining and six others, two stools and the hearth furniture.[21] To judge from the first-floor fenestration of no.57 (Fig 10.28), built at roughly the same date, this would have been a well-lit and finely finished room.

The use of the first-floor front room for dining continued into the 18th century. At no.16 Queen Square the contents of the first-floor front room of the merchant Michael Miller, named as the 'dining room' in the probate inventory of his possessions in 1781 (Appendix 2), included curtains and blinds for the five windows spanning the greater part of the width of his house (Fig 10.29) and seating for 18 guests. Towards the end of the 18th century Miller's contemporary, merchant Richard Bright, evidently modified the first floor of no.29 Queen Square to provide a large, first-floor room across a little over half the width of his house. This was possibly also to serve as a dining room, or may have been intended for other entertainment (Fig 10.30).

In the 17th century and later the importance of the first-floor front room was also underlined by the chimneypieces installed there. At no.129 St Thomas Street, now no.29 Victoria Street, the overmantel of the chimneypiece was approximately of the same date as the construction of the house, c 1673; displaying the arms of the city and those of the Society of Merchant Venturers (Fig 10.31), it must have been central to marking the status of one of the first occupants. At no.6 Welsh Back, the importance of the first-floor front room was

*Fig 10.28*
*No.57 Castle Street, showing full width window to the forestreet chamber, BRSMG, photograph of the early 20th century by Fred Little (BRO 43455/IM/Ph/1/13).*

*Fig 10.29*
*No.16 Queen Square: the first-floor front room, six windows wide, was the dining room of Michael Miller in 1781, drawing of the late 19th or early 20th century (BCRL Loxton drawings X1672; English Heritage DP 115106).*

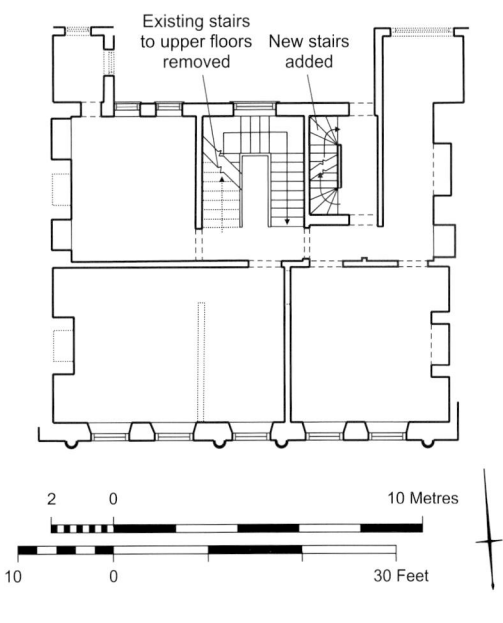

*Fig 10.30*
*No.29 Queen Square, plan of first floor showing alterations to create a larger front room and a new stairs landing, with a separate stairs to the floors above (RHL, PEC after Nicholas Joyce).*

*Fig 10.31*
*No.129 St Thomas Street, now no.29 Victoria Street: overmantel of the chimneypiece. The overmantel, of approximately the same date as the construction of the house, c 1673, displays the arms of the city and those of the Society of Merchant Venturers, photograph of the late 19th or early 20th century (BRSMG Mb 990).*

*Fig 10.32*
*No.45 Broad Quay, Sir Robert Cann's house, chimneypiece portraying his arms and the sacrifice of Isaac, dated 1676, photograph of 1909 (BRSMG Mb1003).*

again marked out by the elaborate chimneypiece displaying the arms of the Langton family (*see* Fig 6.15). At no.45 Broad Quay Sir Robert Cann's first-floor front room was similarly embellished (Fig 10.32).

In this context the first-floor front room in the shophouse had assumed the role formerly accorded to the great parlour (chapter 5). In its decor and furnishing Langton's first-floor front room must to contemporaries have seemed very similar to the great parlours in the houses of John Whitson and Humphrey Brown. Flower Hunt's first-floor front room (above) might have been called a dining room, not as grand as Sir Henry Creswick's but assigned solely to this function. This was certainly a term in use in Bristol by the 1650s. At a modest social level it had been applied to such a room in the house of Richard Berriman, a tobacco pipe maker of St James's parish in 1650.[22] The sole daytime purpose of Berriman's room was indeed dining, but it also included a curtained bed. To the contemporary onlooker, Hunt's dining room would have seemed more like that of another resident of Castle Street, Andrew Gale, who lived at no.14a. Gale's wealth exceeded that of any other recorded inhabitants of houses with shops. His dining room, like Hunt's, looked out on to the street. Its contents in 1684 included the dining table and Russia leather chairs providing seating for 12, a chest and sideboard with a looking glass and drinking glasses, and the hearth furniture. Quite the most expensive item in the room was Gale's large clock with chimes and case, valued at £10 (Appendix 2).[23]

## The Parlour in the 17th-Century Shophouse

By the 17th century, for those who lived in houses with open halls, the parlour had supplanted the hall as the principal heated room of the house for daily living. In such houses, especially those in which the hall had been relegated to a largely symbolic role (chapter 5), the parlour was, by the 17th century, a room for use only in the daytime: citizens who still used this room also for sleeping were now very much the exception. Looking into the parlours of those 17th-century townspeople who lived over the shop, similar distinctions might be observed.

During the 17th and 18th centuries parlours were to be found in many houses with shops, the more so in those which were adaptations of earlier structures. For people who lived over the shop, the parlour could be used both in the daytime and as a room for sleeping at night. In 1611 the furnishings of the barber William Stainred's heated parlour in St Thomas's parish included chairs, stools, a form and a table, indicators of the room's use for sitting and dining. The parlour also contained one of the three beds in the house.[24] Ephraim Goodyear, a wealthy goldsmith, lived in much the same way but with rather more opulence at no.6 Broad Street (Fig 10.33).[25] At the time of his death in 1635 Goodyear was possessed of a heated and very well-furnished parlour. A table and six stools for dining, embroidered stools and gilded leather chairs for sitting, pictures and weaponry on the walls for him, his household and visitors to gaze upon, books of divinity and a curtained bed combine in the inventory to show that this room fulfilled several functions.

For other households, the parlour had now become a room for use only in the daytime. In 1643 one of a row of three houses, nos.15–17 Wine Street, was the shophouse of Henry Foxe, a barber-surgeon. Foxe's 'inner parlour' was, to judge from its contents, his kitchen, next to the shop and a room used possibly also for dining.[26] In Elizabeth Lymell's house in 1648, no.48a or 49 Wine Street, the use made of the ground-floor parlour was very different.[27] The contents included a pair of brass-topped andirons, shovel and tongs in the hearth, cupboards and three chairs; this was a room in which to sit, to keep warm and to read. With a table and six stools, this was also a room that could be used for dining. Immediately behind the shop, it could be readily used for the reception of visitors. In 1628 the parlour of another widow, Margaret Day, would have presented a similar appearance: a heated room, next to the shop, with table, stools and chairs, but no bed.[28]

In assigning a more restricted range of uses to the parlour, the lifestyles of Elizabeth Lymell and Margaret Day might have been seen as more modern. In the hosier Michael Threlkeld's house in All Saints Lane, this more modern use was evident in 1623 in one of his two upper-floor parlours, unheated and used for dining, alongside a more richly furnished and heated parlour used both for sleeping and sitting.[29] Returning to no.6 Broad Street in 1664, one would have observed that Ephraim Goodyear's son Tobias had also adopted this newer, more restricted usage for his parlour.[30] It remained a room for dining, sitting and studying, but there was no longer a curtained bed. His father's musket, sword and birding piece had also been relegated to the little room at the head of the stairs. Tobias Goodyear had abandoned at least two significant elements of his father's lifestyle.

Households who retained a parlour in the 17th century located it at various positions within the house. In the Threlkelds' house both parlours were on the second floor. The Goodyears' parlour was 'a fore streete'. In the houses of Elizabeth Lymell, John Harris (*see* Fig 6.27), Henry Foxe and Margaret Day, the ground-floor room behind the shop was used as a parlour.

## The Parlour in the 18th-Century House

Insights into the placement and function of the parlour in the 18th century, invariably on the ground floor, can be drawn from a number of probate inventories for identified houses in and around Queen Square. One of the first houses to be built in Queen Square, no.55 Queen Charlotte Street was by 1724 the home of the merchant Abraham Hungerford (Appendix 2). The plan was of a two-room deep house with the stairs alongside the rear room. The front room was in

*Fig 10.33*
*The west side of Broad Street, showing Ephraim Goodyear's house at no.6 (the third of the gabled houses from the left), watercolour by T L Rowbotham, 1828 (BRSMG M 2313).*

1724 called the 'fore parlour'; with six stuffed silk chairs, a tea table, a stand for the tea kettle and 'the tea equipage', it was clearly designed for receiving visitors. The 'back parlor' possibly served a similar purpose containing China ware and six cane chairs; close at hand between this room and the kitchen to the rear were the plate, a silver basin, a tea kettle and a coffee pot.

The details of Hungerford's house enable us to identify the front and rear rooms of the nearby nos.59 and 61 in the same street as front and rear parlours, and to glimpse the finish to these rooms: the front parlours with full height panelling; the back parlours with dado or full height panelling; plaster ceiling cornices (Fig 10.34); and, in no.61, a panelled cupboard to one side of the stack. Catering for six visitors might have been the mean in houses of this size in the first decades of Queen Square. On the east side of the square, no.11 was in 1713 the home of the mariner Shadrack Beale (Appendix 2). Beale's parlour was similarly provided with six cane chairs. It differed from Hungerford's in having no tea or coffee equipage, but it did contain a clock, two decanters and glasses. Parlours furnished to cater for half a dozen visitors were to be found elsewhere in the city. Thomas Crosby's house at no.15 St James's Barton, for example, was of a similar plan to the houses in Queen Charlotte Street, and his probate inventory (Appendix 2) enables the front and rear rooms on the ground floor to be identified as the front and back parlours.

Larger houses had more parlours. In 1781 Michael Miller's house at no.16 Queen Square had three: back, fore and little. None were specifically equipped for offering tea or coffee, but all were heated, with seating and a variety of small occasional tables (Appendix 2). In 1720 George Stephens' house at no.22 Queen Square also had three parlours, identically named and similarly furnished (Appendix 2). From a modern plan of the house, made before substantial alterations took place (*see* Fig 8.84c), it can be deduced that the little parlour was the smaller front room, on the same side of the stairs hall as the staircase, while the larger front room was the fore parlour. The back parlour was in a similar position to those at nos.59–61 Queen Charlotte Street.

No records survive of the appearance of the rooms in these two houses, but the surviving rooms of no.29 offer a clue. Number 16 must have been of a similar plan to nos.15 and 29 (*see* Figs 8.84f and g); double-pile with a central stairs, with two rooms on each side of the entrance hall and stairs hall (*see* Fig 8.84g). In no.29 each of these rooms has full-height panelling with a plaster ceiling cornice; in most rooms stone chimneypieces are set below a longitudinal panel serving as the overmantel.

Robert Yate's unidentified architect gave a few clues as to why there should be more than one parlour. Writing in his 'Explanation' of 1724, he specified that one room should be a parlour 'every way full as large as the Withdrawing Room': not a room in which to eat, but one in which 'to sit and converse' after eating. Additionally there was to be a 'private parlour where the Master may treat with any Dealer, or drink a glass with a friend without disturbing the Family; Where the Family when alone may eat, and the young Men when Company is to dine with their Master, that they may have as little occasion as may be to mix and converse with Common Servants from whom they seldom learn any good.'[31] 'Closure', the division of the household into family and servants, the identification of gendered spaces and the desire for privacy within the house are clearly evident in the multiplication of parlours.

## Joining Rooms

Front and back parlours could be directly linked through an arched opening, sometimes of sufficient width to make the two rooms appear as one. In his design of a house for a merchant, Robert Yate's 'unknown compiler' proposed in 1724 that on the right-hand side of the entrance

*Fig 10.34*
*No.59 Queen Charlotte Street, rear parlour, ground floor, photograph of 1995 (NMR BB95/8283).*

hall there should be a 'handsome withdrawing room for the Mistress of the House to entertain Company in, …with a Parlour behind of the same dimensions (and open to it for the greater Magnificence by a double door of Six foot wide when they want to entertain more Freinds [*sic*] than one Room will conveniently hold, or they are inclind to make a Shew)'.³² Such a strategy certainly appears to have been adopted for this house and the two on each side, each house having a 'best parlour' fronting the street and a 'back parlour' behind; unfortunately, no details of the doors survive (*see* Fig 8.44). Over a decade later John Wood the Elder used folding doors to permit a large room over the market hall on the east side of the Exchange to be converted when required to a number of smaller separate rooms (Fig 10.35).

Most examples of recorded houses designed so that front and rear parlours could be joined together are of the late 18th century. Various solutions were employed. For instance, the modest-sized, two-room deep houses in Alfred Place of the early 1790s were provided with doors that folded back beside the walls framing the opening between front and back parlours – as for example at no.20 (Fig 10.36). At no.13 Hope Square, completed in the same decade,

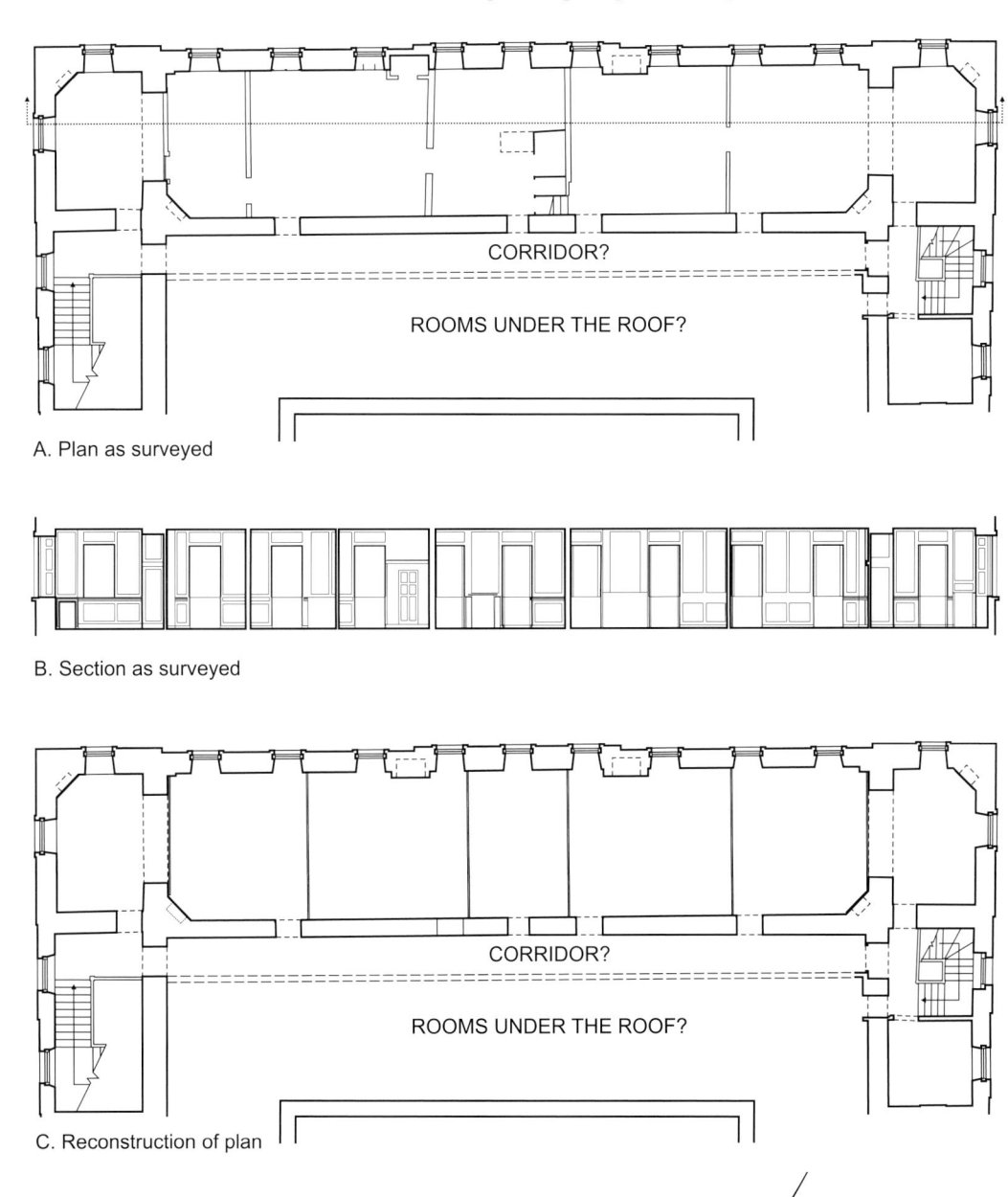

A. Plan as surveyed

B. Section as surveyed

C. Reconstruction of plan

*Fig 10.35*
*The large room over the market hall on the east side of the Exchange, to be converted when required to a number of smaller separate rooms, plan of first floor*
*(RHL, PEC).*

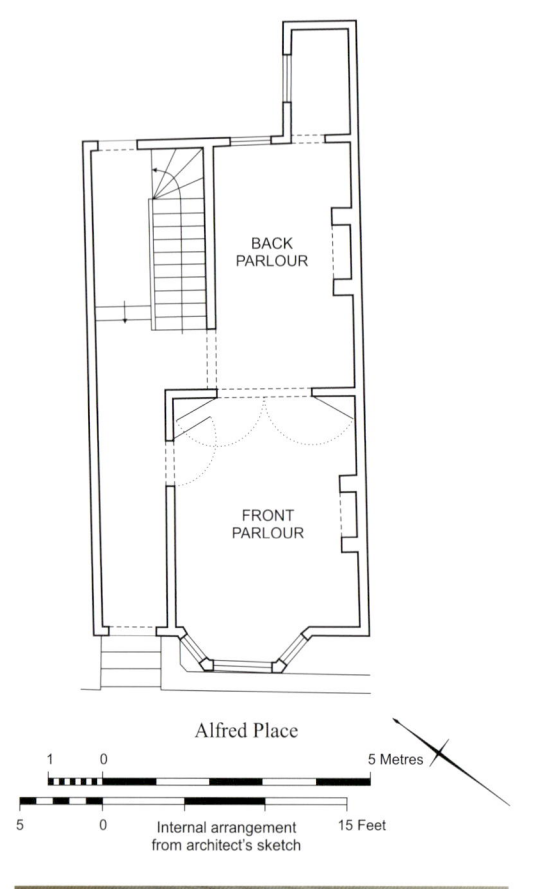

*Fig 10.36*
*No.20 Alfred Place, plan of ground floor showing location of doors that folded back framing the opening between front and back parlours (RHL, PEC after Alan Elkan).*

*Fig 10.37 (right)*
*No.13 Hope Square, the arched opening between the front and back parlours, photograph of 2012 (English Heritage DP 146921).*

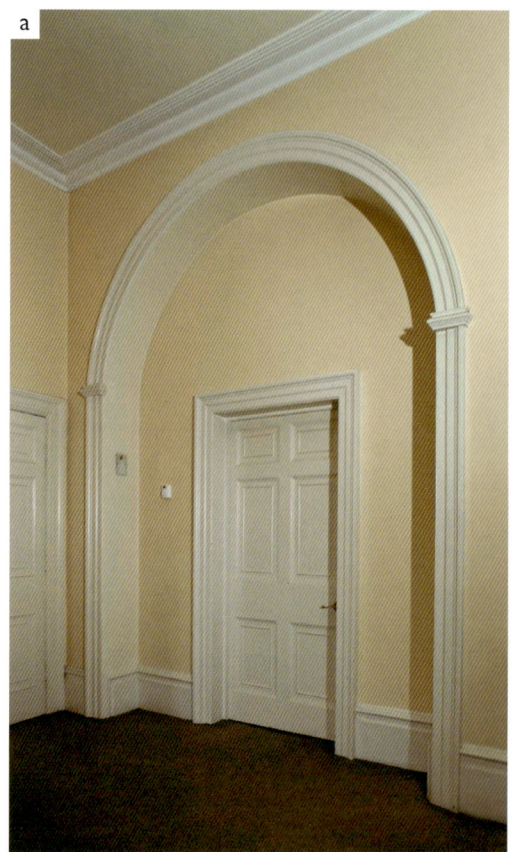

*Fig 10.38 (far right)*
*No.2 Cornwallis Crescent, showing archways, now blocked or altered, between the front and rear rooms: a) on the ground floor, photograph of 2012 (English Heritage DP 146922); b) on the first floor, photograph of 2007 (RHL).*

a smaller arched opening between front and back parlours was framed with fluted Tuscan columns and provided with hinged panelled doors (Fig 10.37). A variation on the strategy of joining two separate rooms was to design two spaces which appeared separate, but in reality were one. At no.2 Cornwallis Crescent, for instance, the archway between the front and rear rooms on the ground and the first floor indicates that the rooms were intended for entertainment and 'making a show', but includes no doors to convert the two spaces into quite separate rooms (Figs 10.38a and 10.38b).

SPACES AND CHANGES

## The Hearth Wall and Other Areas for Display

The most prominent feature of the parlour would often have been the chimneypiece, as in the front and back parlours of no.34 Castle Street, constructed in the 1660s (*see* Figs 8.48 and 8.49), and in the front parlour of no.10 Guinea Street, built *c* 1710 (Fig 10.39; *see* Fig 8.47b). Equally prominent in this room was the arched opening of the display cupboard, the other most prominent feature of the parlour, which could be left open to reveal the contents, shaped shelves and other decoration.

The degree of ornament could vary considerably, from the plain shelves behind the panelled doors of the cupboards on either side of the fireplace at no.52 Kingsdown Parade to the shaped shelves behind similar doors at no.13 Marlborough Hill, or to the richly decorated surround and interior of the display cupboards at a house on Stony Hill and World's End House, Clifton (Figs 10.40a and 10.40b). The most ornate parlour recorded is the Mahogany Parlour at Goldney House (Fig 10.41). Panelled in mahogany, with an ornate chimneypiece and

*Fig 10.39*
*No.10 Guinea Street, chimneypiece in front parlour, photograph of 1998 (NMR BB/9801114).*

*Fig 10.40*
*Display cupboards:*
*a) from a house on Stony Hill*
*(Dening 1923, Pl li);*
*b) from World's End House, Clifton, photograph of 2003 (RHL).*

301

*Fig 10.41*
*Goldney House, Clifton, the Mahogany Parlour built in the 1700s (Dening 1923, Pl lxiv).*

*Fig 10.42*
*Mortimer House, Clifton, chimneypieces of c 1750: (a–b) on ground floor, Rooms G3 and G11; (c–d) on first floor, Rooms 1.3 and 1.4, photographs of 2008 (RHL).*

overmantel, it was mentioned as such in an inventory of 1766 and formed part of Thomas Goldney II's rebuilding of the house in the 1700s (*see* Fig 9.58).[33] The largest assemblage of ornate chimneypieces of the 18th century was in Mortimer House, the residence in Clifton of the especially wealthy Elton family (Fig 10.42). Occasionally furniture such as bookcases might be built into the fabric of the house, as for instance at no.7 Great George Street. Again this was the residence of an especially wealthy owner, of John Pinney, merchant and the owner of sugar plantations on Nevis in the West Indies (Fig 10.43).

Another opportunity for display within the parlour was the provision of an alcove for items of furniture. The earliest such alcove recorded is possibly that in one of the front rooms of no.29 Queen Square, built between 1709 and 1720, when the house was first occupied (Fig 10.44; *see for location* Fig 8.84f). The most elaborate of such alcoves recorded are in the front and rear parlours of no.27 Portland Square, the building of which commenced in the 1790s. In each room the alcoves were framed by elaborately moulded and carved columns of the Corinthian and Ionic orders (Figs 10.45 and 10.46).

SPACES AND CHANGES

*Fig 10.43*
*No.7 Great George Street, showing fitted bookcases (left and right of the fireplace) for the residence of an especially wealthy owner – in this instance John Pinney, merchant and owner of sugar plantations on Nevis in the West Indies, photograph of 2011 (English Heritage DP 141418).*

*Fig 10.44*
*No.29 Queen Square, buffet at rear of ground-floor front parlour, photograph of 1995 (NMR BB95/114).*

# THE TOWN HOUSE IN MEDIEVAL AND EARLY MODERN BRISTOL

*Fig 10.45 (above left)*
*No.27 Portland Square, arched recess in the front parlour, photograph of 2012 (English Heritage DP 146923).*

*Fig 10.46 (above right)*
*No.27 Portland Square, arched recess in the rear parlour, photograph of 2012 (English Heritage DP 146925).*

*Fig 10.47 (right)*
*The house for a Bristol merchant (see Fig 8.44), plan of proposed first floor, from 'The Explanation of the Draughts of a House Proposed for a Merchant' in The Kingsweston Book of Drawings, 1724 (BRO 33746; English Heritage DP 136014).*

## Chambers

Robert Yate's unknown architect had various recommendations for the design of bed-chambers: adjacent to the chambers there were to be closets, which could be used, *inter alia*, for the holding of 'close stools and many other Family necessarys'; in one chamber the bed was placed within a niche, the spaces on either side being a portal to the room and a closet; walls were to be wainscotted only to the height of the windowsills and preferably lined with hangings (less of a fire risk and likely to provide a smell when burnt, to serve as an alarm); floors should be of deal, 'which will enliven the room' and were more appropriate to a room less likely to be 'abusd and dirtied'. The plan by Yate's architect is of especial interest in indicating the positions of the beds within the proposed rooms, parallel to the wall with the fireplace (Fig 10.47).[34]

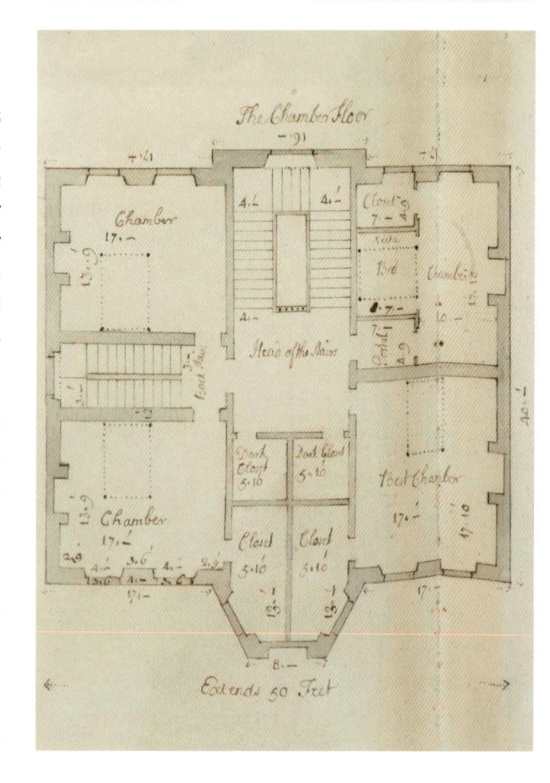

What are not shown on the plan by Yate's architect are the cupboards typically placed in the space between the chimney breast and the side wall of the room. These are features found in many upper chambers of houses built or modified in the 18th century in Bristol. One of the earliest recorded examples is on the first floor of no.22 St Michael's Hill, built in the early 1690s (Fig 10.48). In many instances such cupboards had a single door giving access to a single shelf approximately at door height, with a row of wooden pegs fitted into a moulded rail below the shelf. Examples of this are found at no.69 Old Market, rebuilt in the mid-18th century, and no.10 Guinea Street, built *c* 1720 (Fig 10.49). The cupboards were almost certainly intended for the storage and hanging of clothes.

## The Study

Possessing a study was a mark of gentility or learning. Those who are recorded in probate inventories of the 17th and 18th centuries as having a study included a barber-surgeon, one gentleman, two clerics and an organist.[35] The contents of these studies were principally shelves and books, though Thomas Adeane, the late organist of the cathedral in 1668, also kept there his collection of musical instruments: one pair of Virginals, three Viols, and 'one little hanging Watch with Alarms'. No surviving room has been interpreted as a study, but one back room in the Pole family's house in St James's Square possibly fulfilled this function (Fig 10.50). Although few studies were named in inventories, mention of books in other rooms indicates that merchant society was not necessarily unlearned. An interest in a wide range of subjects including history, theology, English and French literature, the ancient writers and travel is evident, for instance, in Michael Miller's extensive library in 1781 (Appendix 2).

## The Compter or Business Office

The term 'residential house' has been used in this study to mean a house devoted to living, as opposed to the mixture of living and commercial activity represented by the shophouse. The term, however, is one of convenience, and it should not be allowed to suppress the fact that many residential houses were used not simply as dwellings, but also as places where business was transacted. We have seen how some rooms were used for small-scale manufacturing, but a mixture of uses was evident also right at the

*Fig 10.48*
*No.22 St Michael's Hill, built in the early 1690s, showing cupboard between chimneystack and side wall in the north room on the first floor, photograph of 1998 (NMR AA98/00272).*

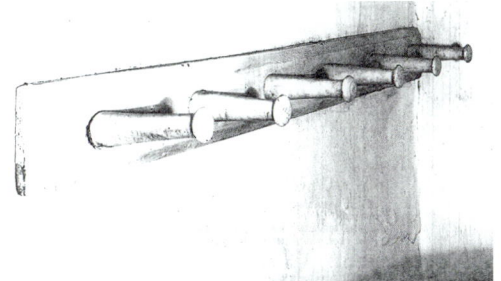

*Fig 10.49*
*No.10 Guinea Street, cupboard interior, row of wooden pegs, photograph of 1998 (NMR BB98/01107).*

*Fig 10.50*
*No.14 St James's Square, back room in house of the Pole family – possibly a study, painting of 1806 (BRSMG K4353).*

apex of Bristol's commercial society, among the leading merchants of the city. These men operated complex businesses spanning, in some cases, three continents and trading in goods, including human beings, of great value. They lay at the heart of the development of the Atlantic economy and of early modern capitalism.

Where were these businesses based? Some activities were undertaken in public spaces and buildings such as the Exchange, but there is little evidence that the routine work of documenting transactions was conducted in purpose-built office accommodation in the city centre; 'chambers' were a rather later development in the provision of business facilities. Instead it is likely that a merchant's business transactions were recorded in a 'compter', a counting house or office, within the residential house.

The plan for three houses in Prince Street drawn up in *c* 1724 (*see* Fig 8.44) shows the formalisation of what must have been a very common arrangement. In the two smaller houses the office was set immediately behind the residential house, accessed from the small lobby beside the servants' stair. In the larger house it lay off the entrance hall, a location which, although segregated from the family accommodation, nevertheless indicated that business and family traffic shared this important circulation space. It is notable that in the three houses in Prince Street, the offices were much more closely connected with the residential spaces than with the warehouses built against the quay at the rear of the plots. Very different types of business activity were conducted in the two areas: one compatible with domestic life; the other focused upon the heavy work of moving goods into and out of the property.

## Servicing the Household: Kitchens and Servants' Rooms

To the writer and polymath Roger North in the 1680s, one of the inconveniences of a house where the rooms lay one above another, in a 'pyle', was that 'all smells that offend are a nuisance to all the rooms, and there is no retiring from them'.[36] Both smells and fumes were realities that had to be considered. The anonymous Bristol compiler's advice to his client in the 1720s was that 'eating rooms should be wainscoted … hangings of stuff are apt to be impregnated by the fumes of victuals'; similar thoughts underpinned his advice not to place the larder or buttery on the ground floor of the main house 'where it is often offensive'.[37] In his design of a house for a merchant the kitchen was therefore set not within the main house, but on the other side of a back court. Along with the placement of the stairs, where to locate the kitchen was one of the principal questions confronting the builder or client for a new or re-designed house.

### Cooking on the Upper Floor

For those citizens living in houses of one room in depth, it was sometimes only possible to locate the kitchen on an upper floor. In 1633 Edward Harsell's house, no.6 Wine Street, built against the south wall of Christchurch, might have been typical.[38] On the ground floor, the shop of this wealthy goldsmith was only 6ft in depth from the street frontage back to the wall of the church. His kitchen can only have been located on the floor above.

In this respect Harsell's lifestyle was similar to that of his near neighbour Isaac Woolfe, a cutler; he lived on the street frontage of the churchyard of Christchurch at no.63 Broad Street. The appraisers of Woolfe's possessions in 1635 referred to his shop as 'his shopp under his dwelling house'.[39] The room on the first floor was named the hall. A table, stools, other chairs and cushions would have indicated that this room was lived in during the daytime, and that it served also for dining with visitors. The presence at the hearth of broaches, gridirons, frying and dripping pans, chafing dishes and other cooking utensils would have made it abundantly clear that this room was also the kitchen. The inhabitants of nos.38–42 Mary le Port Street, built *c* 1648 hard against the north wall of the church and only 14ft in depth on the ground floor, must have cooked in a similar fashion, in kitchens on the first floor (*see* Figs 6.10 and 6.11).[40] Robert Winstone, the wealthy glover, builder and first occupier of the new no.1 High Street, must have lived in a similar way. In the house as rebuilt in 1676, the ground floor must have been given over wholly to his shop, fronting the corner of High Street and Wine Street. The rooms above constituted a house of four floors, with eight rooms, six of them heated (*see* Figs 1.1, 1.2, 1.3 and 6.32). This was clearly built as a dwelling house above the shop. One of these upper rooms must have served also as the kitchen.

## SPACES AND CHANGES

### The Ground-Floor Kitchen

In both shophouses and early residential houses, it was common for the kitchen to be placed at the rear of the house on the ground floor. For most inhabitants of two-room deep shophouses, there was the option of using the room behind the shop as the kitchen. On tightly confined tenement plots, this siting of the kitchen was the most commonly adopted solution. In 1623 Michael Threlkeld, the hosier, was living at a house in All Saints Lane, hemmed in by adjacent properties. His kitchen could only be placed in the main body of the dwelling, behind the shop.[41] In 1647 John Hill, a button mould maker, inhabited a rather smaller house in what was to become Castle Street. This was arranged in a similar way to Threlkeld's house, with the kitchen and shop on the ground floor, but here simply with two chambers and a cockloft above.[42]

Numbers 128–31 St Thomas Street, now nos.25–31 Victoria Street, the row of four houses backing directly on to the churchyard, built c 1673, were probably also arranged in this way. In no.128 the ground-floor rear room was reduced in size in the early 18th century, retaining a probably 5ft-wide fireplace opening and an internal window taking light into the enlarged shop (*see* Figs 6.22 and 6.23). As modified, this was a well-finished room. Its new extent was defined by a moulded plaster ceiling cornice and the fireplace opening framed by a panelled chimneypiece and overmantel. The room on the floor above, however, was of a superior finish. That on the ground floor can only have been the kitchen.

Flower Hunt, a large-scale manufacturer of tobacco pipes at no.59 Castle Street who died in 1672, kept his kitchen in the main body of the house, behind the shop (Fig 10.51).[43] In the 1680s another house further along the same street could have been observed to be of similar plan. At no.69 Castle Street, the house in 1678 of George Hill, a button mould maker, the kitchen was contained within the main body of the house and the space behind utilised for his workhouse, its contents being the tools of his trade (Appendix 2).

In some of the earliest two-room-deep residential houses, the space provided on the ground floor for the entertainment of visitors was limited to the front room, with the rear part of the house serving as kitchen. At no.33 King Street, built by 1658, the ground-floor rear room contains a fireplace 5ft in width, dimensions indicating that it was probably for the kitchen (*see* Fig 7.35). Of a similar plan were nos.3–5 King Street, constructed c 1663 (*see* Fig 8.47a). Each house had a side passage leading from the front entrance to a wider and less private rear room, which can be identified from the wide fireplace opening and the 1705 inventory of Aaron Williams (Appendix 2) as the kitchen. In Lewin's Mead the house of Andrew Hook in 1689 (Appendix 2) was of a similar plan.

From the early 18th century onwards the two-room deep town house with the stairs alongside the rear room was a symbol of aspirations to bourgeois sociability. These aspirations did not always extend as far as removing cooking smells from the ground floor of the house. In the less prosperous streets of the city, builders continued to construct houses of this plan with the rear ground-floor room used as a kitchen. In Little Ann Street the 'Swan with Two Necks', one of the larger houses in Nathaniel Wade's development, was built c 1715 with a rear-stairs plan. The ground and first floors

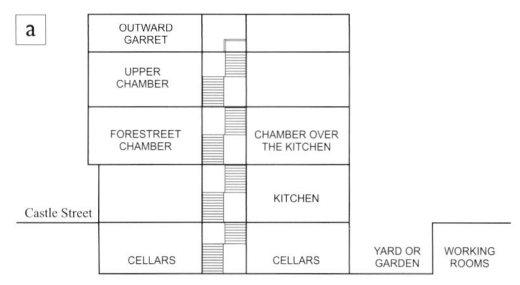

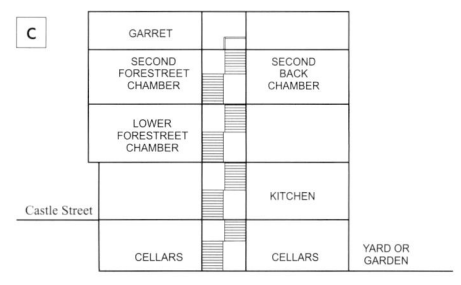

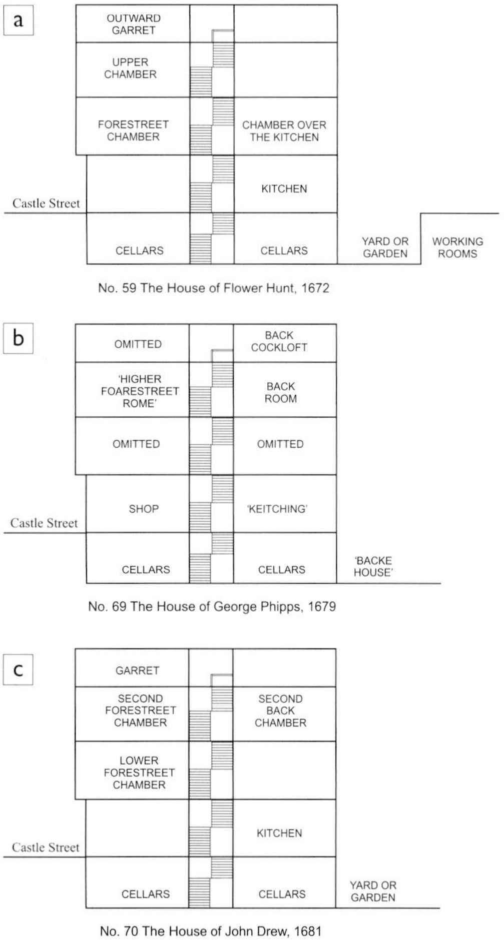

*Fig 10.51*
*Schematic reconstructed sections of houses in Castle Street:*
*a) no.59;*
*b) no.69; and*
*c) no.70*
*(RHL. PEC from probate inventories in Appendix 2).*

have been much altered, but on the second the original arrangements survive. They show that the rear stack was larger than that at the front, originally serving the kitchen on the ground floor below (Fig 10.52a). Houses of this plan may also have been built in more prosperous neighbourhoods. In Queen Square the surviving no.27 (Fig 10.52b) and no.28 were possibly built to this plan. Described only in a probate inventory, no.11 seems also to have had the rear room alongside the stairs as the kitchen (Fig 10.52c).

In the first half of the 18th century a similar approach can be seen in the design of new houses with a central-stairs plan. Nos.22–3 Ellbroad Street displayed aspirations to respectability in the uniformity of the facade to the street, but internally were provided with kitchens in the rear ground-floor rooms (*see* Figs 8.58 and 8.59). Of a similar design were nos.109–110 Temple Street, a matching pair of two-room deep houses built *c* 1735 (*see* Fig 8.27). In these two houses the rear rooms were clearly used as kitchens, furnished with wider fireplaces and coppers for boiling. Sash windows, original or possibly a later alteration, were a move towards gentility, but offset by the need for external shutters to protect the ground-floor windows (one survived in 1818) and the retention of casement windows of an older design at the second floor.

In the building of the largest residential houses only two examples can be cited for placement of the kitchen on the ground floor of the main house. At no.29 Queen Square, occupied from *c* 1720, the central entrance and

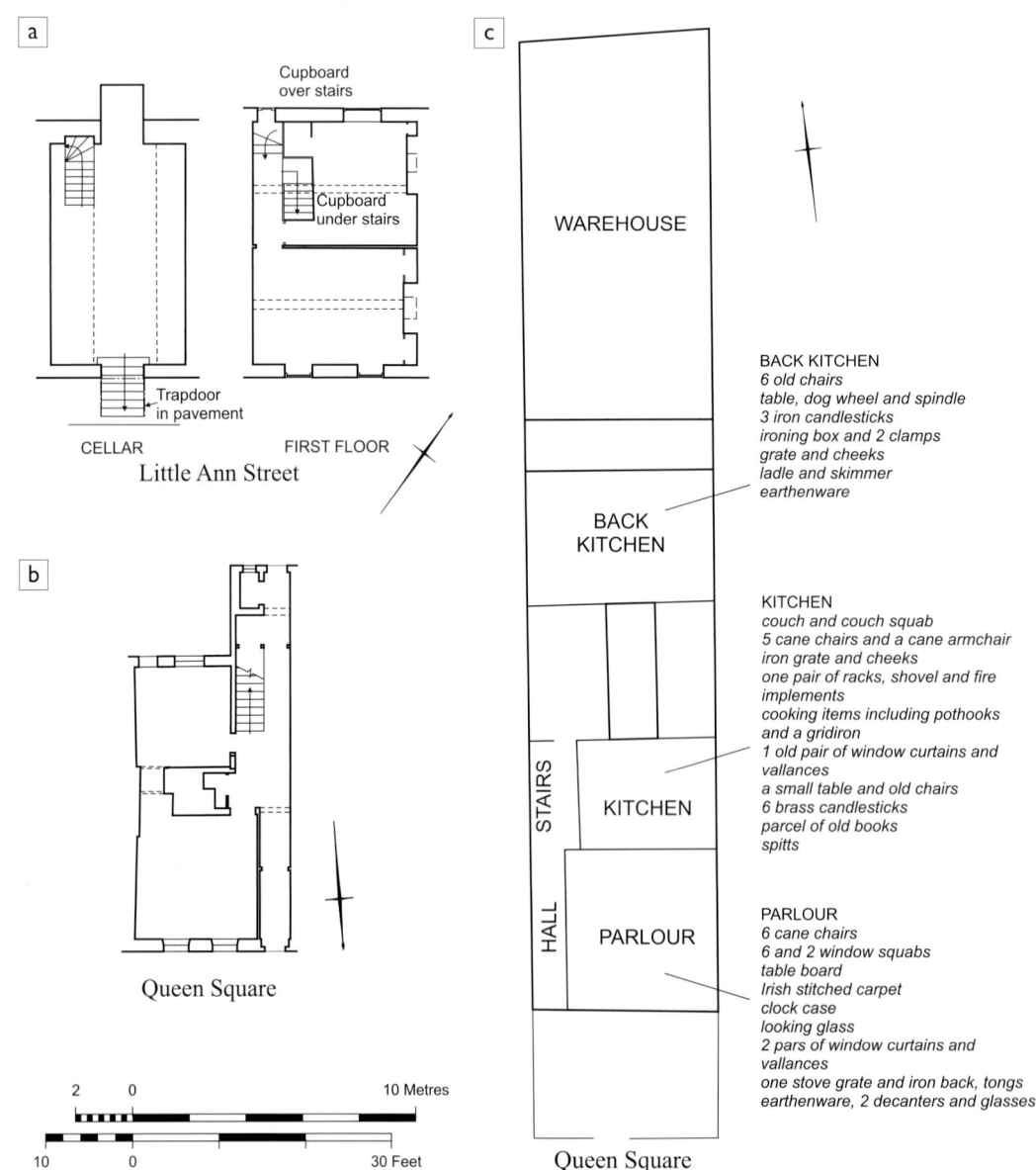

Fig 10.52
Plans of houses with the kitchen on the ground floor (RHL, PEC):
a) 'The Swan with Two Necks', Little Ann Street;
b) no.27 Queen Square;
c) no.11 Queen Square, plan of ground floor (RHL, PEC) from plan of c 1800 (BRO 04479(3) and from inventory of Shadrack Beale, Appendix 2).

stairs hall separated a front and back parlour on one side from a front parlour and a stone-paved kitchen on the other (*see* Fig 8.84f). The conversion before *c* 1750 of this kitchen to become a further panelled room, and the building of a new detached kitchen in the courtyard, shows that this was not considered to be a satisfactory arrangement.

At Clifton Wood House, as rebuilt in 1724, the kitchen was again located in the main part of the house, also in a rear room alongside the central stairs (*see* Fig 8.84i). This might seem surprising in a house provided with a great stairs which, with marquetry inlay and a fitted stair gate, surpassed in sophistication almost all others within what was then England's second city (*see* Fig 8.93). Nevertheless the wide fireplace, originally with a spit rack above, provides conclusive evidence for the identification of the kitchen. Careful reading of the plan shows that the room was only accessible from the exterior of the house or from the older part of the building to the west. Although next to the stairs, it was inaccessible from within the rest of the new house. The adjacent room in the older garden house was possibly still used as a back or secondary kitchen. This may have influenced the thinking of designer and client in placing the main kitchen here rather than across a courtyard.

## The Detached Kitchen

Assigning part of the ground floor to cooking introduced smells and fumes into living space and further restricted the allocation of space for more genteel living. These problems could be overcome in designs where the ground-floor rooms in the main part of the house were designated exclusively as parlours, and where the kitchen was then sited in a separate, detached block to the rear.

We have seen that detached kitchens were a feature of medieval Bristol. On narrow plots these were typically placed behind the hallhouse, as in Christmas Street and Marsh Street (chapter 5). Detached kitchens appear to have been a feature of the urban landscape in south-west England more generally, being recorded elsewhere in Exeter, Totnes and Plymouth. In all these towns the reason for detaching the kitchen from the main body of the house may have been the avoidance of fire.

In the 17th century many houses in Bristol were constructed with detached kitchens. Many of these were shophouses (chapter 6): Langton's house at no.12 Welsh Back built in 1623 has been mentioned several times and may have been one of these. A separate 17th-century building to the rear was possibly its detached kitchen, with servants' accommodation on the floors above (*see* Fig 6.14). A little later, in 1641, Mary Reade, at no.49 Wine Street, lived in a shophouse with a detached kitchen.[44] Although no plan of the house survives, three successive inventories of the 1640s show that the ground floor of the dwelling on the street front was used as shop and parlour while the kitchen lay to the rear, beyond an open pavement.[45]

This same arrangement was possibly that adopted by John Harris, a cooper and the first occupier of no.56 Castle Street, built *c* 1660. It was a plan certainly in existence by the mid-18th century, the rear room of the main house by then the parlour, with the kitchen separate to the rear (*see* Fig 6.27). This was also the plan adopted by the builder William Barrett for the rebuilding of no.35 Old Market in *c* 1705. The front ground-floor room was an unheated shop and the rear room a parlour, interpreted as such from its full-height raised and fielded pine panelling. The kitchen was sited as a detached block to the rear of the main house (*see* Fig 6.24).

Outline plans of tenements in Castle Street in the 18th century could be interpreted as indicating that this was a commonly adopted arrangement (Fig 10.53), but here many of the detached kitchens were possibly secondary to a principal kitchen within the street-frontage dwelling. In William Nicklus's house at no.26 Castle Street, for example, there was both a kitchen in the main dwelling, and a 'back kitchen' (*see* Fig 6.26). The main kitchen was clearly used for cooking, its contents in 1708 including the crane, gridiron, trivet, spit and hooks for the hearth and a full range of utensils. With a table, form and six chairs, together with a looking glass and curtains for the windows, this was a room where the master or his servant spent some time on other matters.[46] In contrast Nicklus's back kitchen included no furniture. With a furnace and boiler, it was certainly used for washing clothes; it also formed a convenient store for 'other lumber things'.

The earliest residential house identified as having a detached kitchen to the rear was no.34 Castle Street, built *c* 1666 at the corner of Castle Green and Castle Street (chapter 3) and shown on a plan of the early 18th century (*see* Fig 8.48). The main house consisted on the ground floor of two parlours, and the kitchen was located in

## THE TOWN HOUSE IN MEDIEVAL AND EARLY MODERN BRISTOL

*Fig 10.53*
*Nos.1–14A Castle Street, plan of early 19th century showing detached kitchens (BRO 04479(3) fol 23b, English Heritage DP 136018).*

*Fig 10.54*
*No.98 Redcliff Street, plan of ground floor, drawing of c 1816–17 (BRO P/StT/Ch/3/31 fol 18).*

a separate building to the rear. Probably of similar date was no.98 Redcliff Street, with matching front and rear rooms and a detached kitchen built out of the former open hall to the rear; the street front was apparently rebuilt in the early 18th century (Fig 10.54).

A surviving house of this plan, no.69 Old Market, is superficially of the early 18th century, though the presence of ovolo-moulded ceiling beams on the first and second floors indicates that the two chimneystacks are of the 17th century (*see* Fig 6.42). On the ground floor these stacks probably served front and rear parlours, originally separated by a centrally placed stairs. The kitchen for no.69 was the ground-floor room in the detached block to the rear. This also had an ovolo-moulded ceiling beam, running into the chimneystack over a wide fireplace opening.

By the early 18th century the plan with two parlours in the main block and a detached kitchen to the rear was adopted widely. It was used on St Michael's Hill, in the development of Queen Square and Orchard Street, and in smaller building schemes elsewhere. On St Michael's Hill, nos.30–2 were built *c* 1709, each with fully panelled front and back parlours on the ground floor and detached kitchens to the rear.[47] On the west side of St Michael's Hill this same plan was used for the 10 houses forming nos.11–29 Old Park Hill, built 1714–22 (Fig 10.55).[48]

Detached kitchens were also provided for some of the smaller early houses built in and around Queen Square. In nos.59 and 61 Queen Charlotte Street, both first occupied in 1711, the front and rear ground-floor rooms have been identified as parlours (p298). The rear room of no.59 has full-height panelling of *c* 1711 and fireplace openings in the front and rear rooms of equal size. The fireplace openings in no.61 are of similar size, inappropriately small for the rear room to have served as a kitchen. Buildings to the rear, now demolished, must have accommodated the kitchens for these houses. On the south side of Queen Square a similar plan was possibly used for nos.26–8, a row of three houses again first occupied in 1711 (Fig 10.52b). However, historic plans provide no evidence for detached kitchens, and on balance it is probable that in each house the kitchen was in the rear room, as in the 'Swan with Two Necks' (Fig 10.52a).

Probate inventories confirm and provide further levels of complexity to these interpretations. From 1718 until his death in *c* 1723 the merchant Abraham Hungerford lived at no.55 Queen Charlotte Street – in 1703 one of the first houses of the Queen Square development to have been occupied.[49] The appraisers of Hungerford's possessions (Appendix 2) proceeded from the upstairs rooms first down to the front parlour, thence to the back parlour and only then to the kitchen, probably placed to the rear of the main house, as in the two nearby houses (nos.59–61 Queen Charlotte Street).

On the east side of Queen Square no.11 was one of three narrow, two-room deep houses occupied from 1710 onwards. From the probate inventory made in 1713 of the possessions of its first inhabitant, the mariner Captain Shadrack Beale (Appendix 2), we would conclude that the ground floor was arranged as parlour and kitchen, with a back kitchen beyond.[50] From the outline plans of the 19th century it could have been concluded that this was a house with two parlours on the ground floor and a detached kitchen behind (Fig 10.52c). Houses were not necessarily used in the way that their builders intended.

In a development commenced as the building of Queen Square was drawing to a close, nos 10–29 Orchard Street were built as four separate rows of houses between 1718 and 1722. In 15 or more of the houses the ground floor was arranged as front and back parlours, with the kitchen placed in a separate building to the rear.

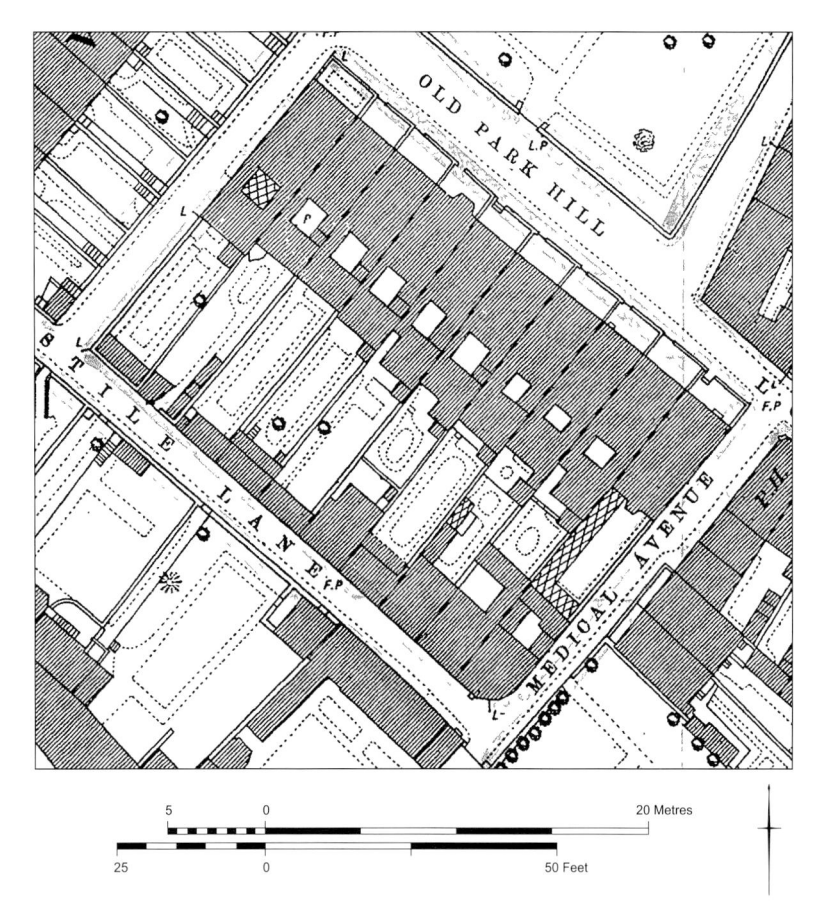

The original arrangements can be best seen in detailed mid-19th-century plans of nos.10–14 and nos.25–9 (*see* Figs 8.65, 8.66, 8.67 and 8.68). Though many houses have been much altered since first built, in several there exist the original chimneypieces, panelling and plaster cornices to the front and back parlours.

Contemporary with the building of Orchard Street was the construction in *c* 1717–19 of four new houses on a smaller plot at Redcliff Back. Two houses remained in 1815, the ground-floor rooms named as parlours, with yards and detached kitchens behind (Figs 10.56a and 10.56b). In the same parish of St Mary Redcliff houses of this plan were still being constructed a decade later. Built *c* 1710, nos.5–7 and 10–12 Guinea Street can be argued to have been designed as two rows, each of three houses. Each house had front and rear ground-floor parlours, vaulted cellars for storage and detached kitchens to the rear (Fig 10.57; *see* Figs 8.47b and 8.52).

In most larger houses, from the building of Queen Square onwards, smells and fumes were avoided through placing the kitchen in a separate range, sometimes detached from the

*Fig 10.55*
*Nos.11–29 Old Park Hill, built between 1714 and 1722, overall plan showing detached kitchens (RHL, PEC, from OS plan of 1884, 1st edition, 1:500 town plan, Gloucestershire, Bristol, sheet LXXI.16.19).*

early 19th-century plan as linking house and warehouse. A probate inventory of 1722 shows that the three rooms on the ground floor of the main house were the fore parlour, little parlour and back parlour. The 'little kitchen' and 'great kitchen & room over' mentioned in the inventory can only have been in the (long since demolished) range to the rear (*see* Fig 8.84c).[51]

Placing the kitchen in a range detached from the main house must also have reduced the risk to the latter from fire, and this was the solution adopted for the placement of the kitchen in other larger houses in Queen Square. At no.15, the great kitchen stood within a range spanning the width of the plot behind the main house (*see* Fig 8.89). The kitchen can be identified from the wide fireplace in the larger room; on the opposite side of a through-passage to what was possibly a housekeeper's room, with the passage providing access to a second kitchen and warehouse beyond. The second kitchen was probably for washing clothes or brewing, containing two large coppers.

No.52 Prince Street, commenced or built in 1725, was of a similar plan, flanked by two houses, nos.50 and 54, forming part of the same development but each of one room in width. All three houses were provided with a detached kitchen, the names of the rooms being among the detail shown on a contemporary plan (*see* Fig 8.44). The plan of the centre house can be identified as that outlined in 'The Explanation of the Draughts of a House Proposed for a Merchant', dated 1724 and seen as a speculative explanation and plan in advance of Robert Yate, the developer, finalising his purchase of the building plot (p198).[52] In the 'Explanation' the compiler explained that it is in 'the Back Court in which the Kitchen and other Offices are proposed', as implemented in the final plan.

Houses with detached kitchens were still being built in 1740 in Prince Street – at this date certainly one of the most fashionable streets in Bristol. Nos.36–8 comprised a matching pair of carefully designed, two-room deep houses, with yards and detached kitchens to the rear (*see* Fig 9.64a). William Paty's detailed plan of 1794 does not name the rooms, but some inferences may be made.[53] In each house the front and rear rooms were parlours, with fireplaces of equal size; the rear parlours provided access to walk-in closets. Accessed from the courtyard were a storage room and privy. Beyond the courtyard was a kitchen with a larger fireplace, two coppers and water pumps.

main house. In the earliest of these houses, the row of nos.36–8 Queen Square, the evidence from no.38 points to the kitchen being in a range projecting backwards from the main house (*see* Fig 8.84a). The kitchen of no.22 Queen Square was similarly located, in the range shown on an

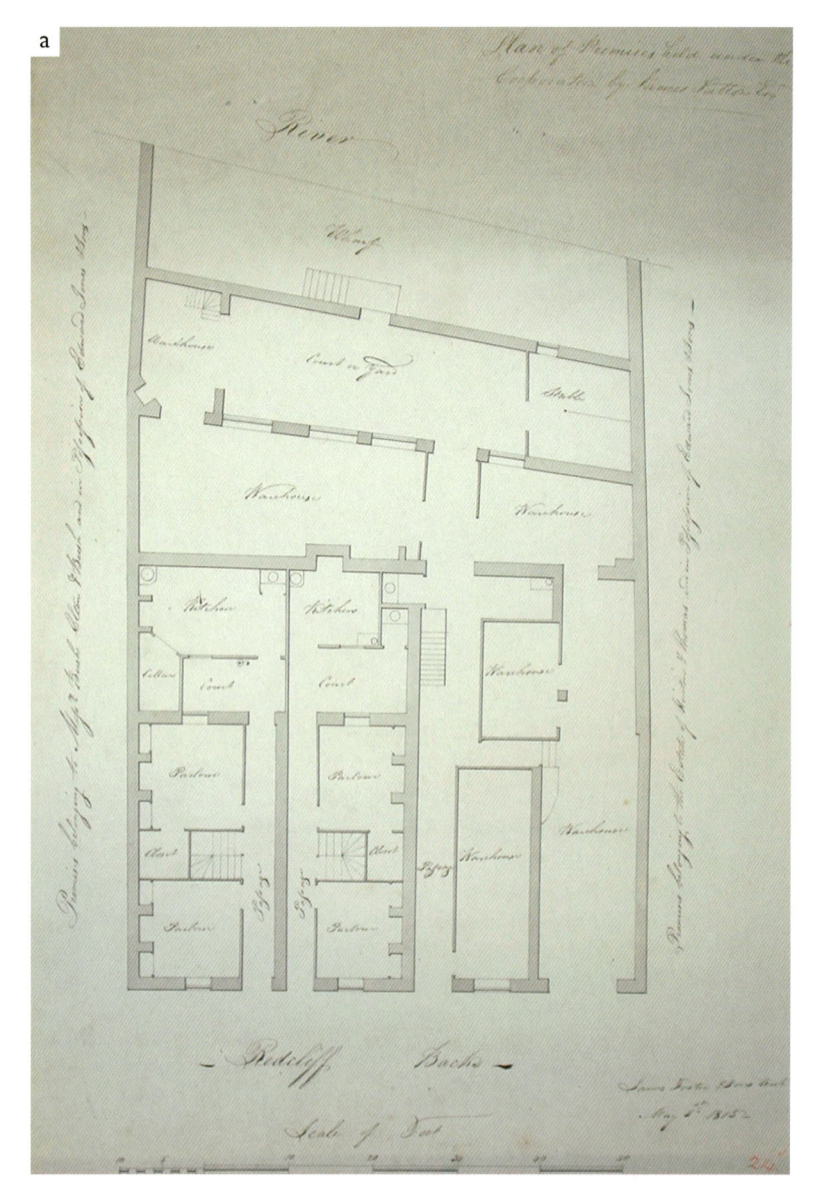

Fig 10.56
Redcliff Back, row of four houses built c 1717–9, with yards and detached kitchens behind:
a) plan of ground floor of 1815
(BRO 04479(4) fol 25);
b) photograph of later 19th century, probably c 1872
(BRSMG Hever Mardon bequest, extra illustrated Bristol Past and Present vol II, Pt iv Ma 4151–4);
Winstone 1874–1866, Pls 41–4).

SPACES AND CHANGES

*Fig 10.57*
*No.10 Guinea Street, rear parlour, photograph of 1998 (NMR BB98/01125).*

From the 1740s detached kitchens were no longer built in an urban context. The only house built with a detached kitchen within the city as a whole appears to have been Royal Fort House, designed by James Bridges for the merchant and gentleman Thomas Tyndall c 1760–1. The design of this house enabled a level of gentility surpassing any of the houses so far mentioned. Royal Fort House itself has been much discussed, but the presence of its kitchen and service quarters has been strangely neglected. Architectural historians have previously seen the kitchen block as an adaptation of an earlier house.[54] Sited to the north of the main house and connected to it by a linking passage, it is certainly contemporary with the house built by James Bridges (*see* Fig 9.66a).

The ovolo-moulded door frames can be compared with those in the service areas of other elite houses of the same date, for instance at Stoke Bishop House and Mortimer House. On Bridges' model of the main house, now preserved and displayed at Royal Fort House, there are also slots for the attachment of the linking passage; the model as it now is must be regarded as incomplete (Fig 10.58). In plan the detached block and linking passage can be seen as part of the overall design. It was possible in this open parkland setting to place the kitchen beyond the main house, removing all service activities and smells of cooking from the main house, but without affecting the view from all but one side. This, indeed, was achieved elsewhere in many country houses.

Within the more built-up streets of the city, the abandonment of the detached kitchen – an enduring arrangement for more genteel living, favoured from at least the later medieval period onwards – can be best understood by looking at new house plans of the 1740s onwards.

*Fig 10.58*
*Bridges' model of Royal Fort House, showing slots between the ground- and first-floor levels for the attachment of a former separate model of the kitchen block with linking passage (English Heritage DP 114330).*

313

## The Basement Kitchen

From the second quarter of the 18th century, initially in the more prosperous neighbourhoods, the kitchen was increasingly sited in the basement, often at the rear of the house.[55] Such houses would usually be lit from the front through the use of a basement well or area, the hillsides of the city often making it possible for the kitchen away from the street to be at ground level on the garden side. Placing the kitchen in the basement brought several advantages.

The space behind the house could now be devoted to the garden, visible from the house, from the rear parlour on the ground floor and from the chambers above. Food prepared in the basement kitchen could be brought directly to a parlour or dining room on the floors above, without having to pass through wind, rain and cold. The kitchen space was no longer visible to visitors, being neither in a rear room nor in a detached block to the rear of the main house. The setting of the entrance hall could now be entirely genteel.

The earliest houses to have been provided with basement kitchens were possibly nos.68–70 Prince Street, built as a pair *c* 1725. There is no evidence for there having been detached kitchens, and in the basement of no.70 the width of the stack indicates that it was for a wide kitchen fireplace.

The change in building practice occurred over a very short period of time. In 1740 houses with detached kitchens were still being built at nos.36–8 in fashionable Prince Street (*see* Fig 9.64a). Three years later no fewer than nine separate houses, all with basement kitchens, had formed part of the new Exchange in Corn Street (*see* Fig 6.35). All were to the designs of John Wood the Elder of Bath. Wood settled in Bath in 1727 and commenced the building there of Queen Square in 1728. Plans of the houses constructed there by Wood provide for the kitchen being placed in the basement.[56]

Among the earliest houses built to this plan in Bristol were nos.4 and 5 Charles Street, built *c* 1743 and first occupied in 1744 (Fig 10.59a).[57] As in many earlier two-room deep houses, the front and rear ground-floor rooms were parlours with fireplace openings of similar size; the rear room in no.5 has its original chimneypiece. The kitchens for each house can be identified as the rear basement room, with traces of the original fireplaces and dressers. Each of these rooms had a conventional flat-plastered ceiling, and was lit from the garden. The front basement rooms were vaulted cellars, providing cool storage adjacent to the kitchen, but restricting the space available for the kitchen proper.

In the suburbs on the same side of the city as Charles Street, this same plan was utilised for the west side of Brunswick Square *c* 1766. At the corner with Cumberland Street no.14 Brunswick Square was completed by *c* 1771 (Fig 10.59b). New rows of houses in the suburb of St Mary Redcliff were being built to the same plan in the 1760s and 1770s. Redcliff Parade, for instance, was built *c* 1768 as a row of 13 houses of substantial proportions overlooking the Avon. The original plan for these houses is preserved best at no.9. Here contemporary plaster cornices and six-panelled doors to the front and rear rooms indicate that the ground floor was arranged as two parlours. The kitchen of no.9 Redcliff Parade was in the rear basement room;

*Fig 10.59*
*Plans of houses with the kitchen on the basement floor:*
*a) nos.4–5 Charles Street;*
*b) no.14 Brunswick Square;*
*c) no.9 Redcliff Parade;*
*d) no.51 Redcliff Hill (RHL, PEC).*

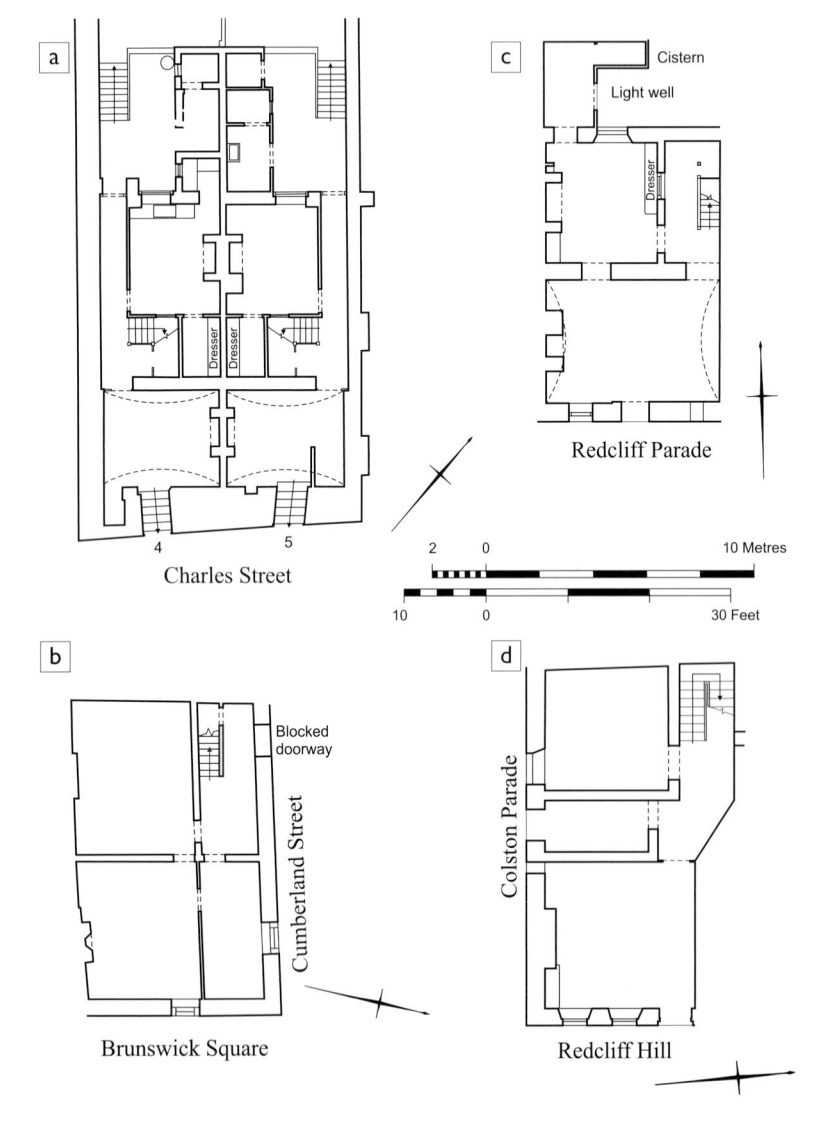

some of the original cast-iron fireplace fittings and the dresser still survive. A door from the basement kitchen provided access to a front cellar, vaulted as at nos.4–5 Charles Street and here providing access to an open area in front of the house (Fig 10.59c).

The same layout was utilised for the development of 12 houses built on Redcliff Hill and in Colston Parade, within a corner site facing the south side of the churchyard of St Mary Redcliff. The original plan for this row is preserved best at no.51 Redcliff Hill, a corner site house arranged as two parlours on the ground floor, a basement kitchen facing Redcliff Hill and a vaulted cellar to the rear (Fig 10.59d). Archaeological excavations have shown that the same plan, of basement kitchen at the rear and vaulted storage cellar to the front, was used during the 1780s in the construction of houses in College Street.[58]

In the new rows of terraced houses constructed or commenced in the building boom of the early 1790s the placement of the kitchen in the basement was universal. Examples included the east row at the north end of Kingsdown Parade and Royal York and Cornwallis Crescents in Clifton.

## Servants' Rooms

It has been noted that 'the investigation of service in 18th-century English town houses typically locates kitchen functions, but seldom the lodgings for the servants who supported the household'.[59] For Bristol, the presence of servants *en masse* was perhaps first noted in the tax assessment of 1696, now published as a listing of the inhabitants of Bristol in 1696. Where these servants were accommodated is evident partly from the houses themselves and partly from probate inventories.

Servants were accommodated principally in the roof space. The suite of garret rooms at the top of a house of *c* 1776 at no.14 Clare Street at the junction with Marsh Street[60] has been described as 'particularly generous' (Fig 10.60 and Appendix 1).[61] The attic rooms of many houses were provided with a finish more simple and less genteel than that of the chambers on the floors below: fireplaces were smaller; plaster ceiling cornices were lacking; roof trusses were often left visible; wall faces were often accommodated within the sloping surfaces of the roof; doors were of two large panels or boarded rather than panelled.

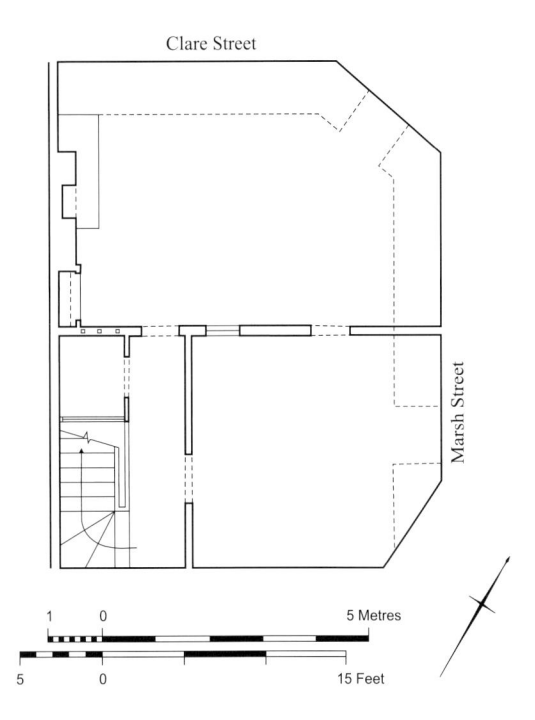

*Fig 10.60*
*No.14 Clare Street, plan of attic floor showing generous space allocated to servants' rooms*
*(RHL, BH, PEC).*

That these upper rooms were of a lower status than those below was also sometimes indicated by a hierarchy of moulding profiles, as noted in studies of the 18th-century architecture of Virginia.[62] More elaborate mouldings would be given to reception rooms and chambers on the floors above; simpler mouldings would be given to door frames and other features on the attic floor. Moulding profiles were similarly used to define service space. At both Stoke Bishop House and Royal Fort House, kitchen and service space of the mid-18th century is defined by the use of a heavy ovolo-moulding, very old-fashioned by the time that these houses were built. Another location for the servants could be the room over the kitchen, if the latter was detached.

Probate inventories sometimes specified the locations of servants' accommodation, but more often catalogued the contents of rooms which might appear to be those of servants. At no.12 St James's Barton the servants to the Crosby household must have been accommodated in 'the Servants Back Room' and 'the Servants Fore Room', both above the second floor (Appendix 2). The contents of these two rooms could have indicated that the latter, overlooking the street (Fig 10.61; *see* Figs 8.84m and 8.94), was for a servant of superior status; it contained a bed with 'China furniture', six chairs and deal (as opposed to mahogany) furniture, both a dressing table and a chest. In contrast the back room held only a bed.

# THE TOWN HOUSE IN MEDIEVAL AND EARLY MODERN BRISTOL

*Fig 10.61*
*No.12 St James's Barton, on the right, viewed from the street: the servants' rooms were above the second floor, photograph of 1957 (NMR AA57/3071).*

The servants' rooms might also be identified by the age of the furniture. In cataloguing the possessions of Sir Robert Cann, the appraisers noted the age of the furniture in the servants' rooms at Stoke Bishop House: in the Maids' Chamber an 'old bedstead'; in the Mens' Chamber 'old rugs and blankets, two old bedsteads' and 'one old chest' (Appendix 2).

With the advent of the basement kitchen, service areas and servants' rooms were thus placed at the opposite margins of the house, with the principal household occupying the space in between. In the very small number of houses with separate service stairs, servants could move between work and their own rooms without interference; but in most houses this was not possible. Most households provided an environment of continual surveillance through the comings and goings in the hall and on the stairs. Where the principal stairs terminated at the first floor, as at Mortimer House in Clifton Down Road, no.16 Lower Maudlin Street, the altered no.29 Queen Square and Clifton Wood House before alteration, the separation of service and servants' quarters from the rest of the household must have been further emphasised: the principal stair, as the only link between ground and first floors, was shared by the whole household – family and servants. However, the second stair, up from first floor to the attics, was used principally by servants and lesser members of the family.

## The Nursery

Attic rooms could also serve as nursery space for children, but those mentioned as such in probate inventories were often probably spaces which had once served this function and were now remembered by that name. In Sir Robert Cann's house at Stoke Bishop in 1686 (Appendix 2) the nursery was listed following the servants' chambers, probably in the attic, but it contained only a bed and six chairs. In Michael Miller's house at no.16 Queen Square (Appendix 2) the attic room described in 1781 as the 'Nursery' was large enough to contain four beds, two of which were 'four-post beds'. Here, too, 'Nursery' was perhaps a former use, one now remembered only in the name of the room. Children were now only evident in the 'Garrett', the contents of which included one 'child's Mahogany chair' and one 'child's cribb'; possibly these were for the child of one of the servants, to whom the two beds in this same room might have belonged. At Abraham Hungerford's house at no.55 Queen Charlotte Street (Appendix 2), the 'nursery' was probably the front attic room – a space remembered as having been the nursery, since all it contained in 1724 was a bed, dressing table, mirror, chest and three chairs. Similarly in Thomas Puxton's house at no.133 St Thomas Street in 1684 'the children's room' now contained only a bed, bolster, rug, blanket and one old bedstead.

## Improvements

In the major changes to the form and planning of the Bristol town house can be read the principal ideas on how to improve living accommodation – essentially by matching the house to the needs and aspirations of the household. Some changes were of less overall significance, but represent ideas on how accommodation might be modified to make dwellings more convenient. In *The compleat Builders Guide* published in 1726, for instance, the writer Richard Neve set out some contemporary notions of 'Improvements'. For Neve two great improvements were 'the

SPACES AND CHANGES

contrivance of closets, in most rooms … for Conveniency' and *painted wainscot*, now so much used … for Cleanliness'.[63] Closets large enough to serve as dressing areas were being provided in new housing from the 1660s onwards, as can be seen from the plans of the houses being built in King Street (Fig 10.62), in the larger houses being built in Queen Square from *c* 1700, for instance at no.38 (Fig 10.63a) and in many houses built thereafter – for example at Mortimer House in Clifton Down Road of *c* 1750 (Fig 10.63b) and in nos.27–8 Portland Square of the 1790s (Fig 10.63c). In many smaller houses built in the 18th century the cupboards provided in the upper chambers may also have served as closets for storage.

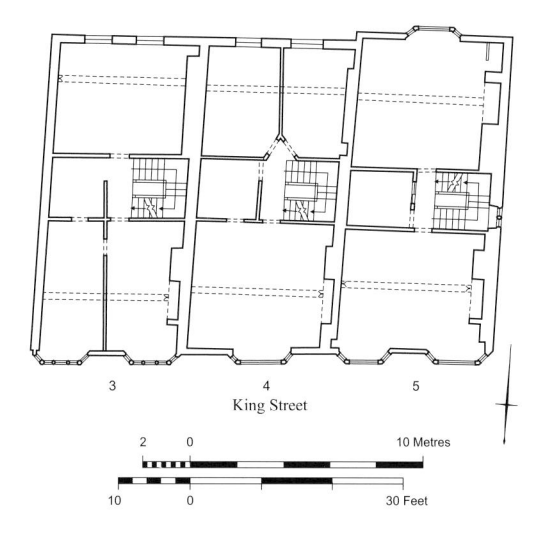

*Fig 10.62*
*Nos.3–5 King Street, plan of first floor (RHL, PEC).*

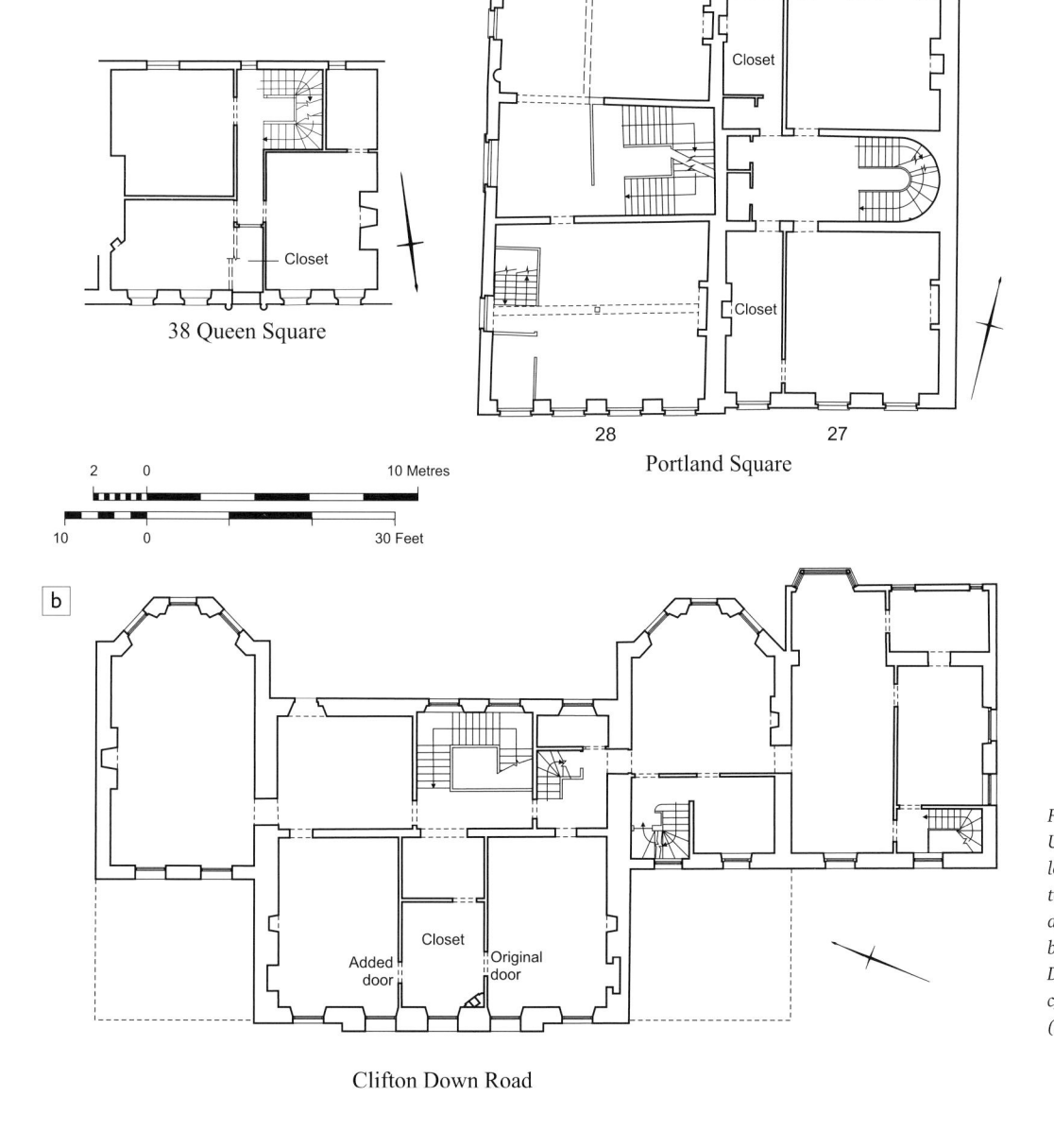

*Fig 10.63*
*Upper-floor plans showing location of closets adjacent to chambers:*
*a) no.38 Queen Square;*
*b) Mortimer House, Clifton Down Road;*
*c) nos.27–8 Portland Square (RHL, PEC).*

Sash windows were another aspect of 'conveniency' ubiquitous in Bristol houses from c 1700. Less often noted have been sash shutters, installed in some houses being constructed in the 1790s building boom. In Kingsdown, for instance, shutters of this type were used at no.16 Portland Street in the ground- and first-floor front rooms of a modest, two-room deep house (Fig 10.64); they were also installed in the compter built overlooking the courtyard of no.29 Queen Square (Fig 10.65). For more superior houses, such as those in Kingsdown Parade, an innovation appearing in the same period was the system of bells by which visitors could announce themselves and through which servants could be summoned, a device for further control and surveillance.[64]

Turning to 'cleanliness', some houses of the early 18th century, such as no.29 Queen Square, had a majority of their rooms provided with full-height panelling. By c 1750 it was much more normal for wainscot to be of dado height, as for instance in the row of four houses built in Pembroke Place, Upper Maudlin Street; here the wainscot was not panelled, but formed of boards butted and glued longitudinally. By the 1790s this form of wainscot was frequently replicated in plaster, as a surbase or dado capped with a timber moulding, as for instance at no.20 Alfred Place and no.52 Kingsdown Parade.

Another aspect of cleanliness was the installation of a wash-basin recess. Recesses with blue and white tin-glazed tiles, some of these being niche tiles, were a feature in a number of smart houses of the 18th century, for instance in Broad Plain (Fig 10.66a) and Portland Square (Fig 10.66b); most of the examples today forming part of the collection of the Victoria and Albert Museum are thought to have come from Bristol.[65] The wash-basin recess could also have a stone basin as at Clifton Wood House (Fig 10.66c), where it was placed close to the exit from the kitchen and may originally have been tiled, and at no.69 Old Market (Fig 10.66d), where a richly decorated basin was installed within the piazza connecting the main house to the detached kitchen (see Fig 6.37d).

The development of arrangements for sanitation can be observed in the progress from cess pit to water closet. Archaeological excavations of medieval domestic sites have demonstrated the existence of cess pits for the disposal of human and household waste, the usual means employed in the larger cities of medieval England.[66] Probate inventories show that close stools were in common use in 16th- and 17th-century Bristol, but how waste was disposed of is not clear. The first evidence for privies or 'necessaries' emerges from the plans of Bristol properties of the 18th century: houses in Prince Street had two-seater privies in the yard or next to the detached kitchen (see Fig 8.44), and other early plans show privies in similar positions (see Fig 8.84g). In poorer areas of the city, privies were sited over water courses where possible (Fig 10.67). It is not known when the water closet was introduced, either on the residential plot as a whole or, more significantly, within the house itself.[67]

SPACES AND CHANGES

*Fig 10.64 (opposite top) No.16 Portland Street (house in centre), Kingsdown. Sash shutters were installed in the ground- and first-floor rooms of this modest, two-room deep house, photograph of 1974 (RHL).*

*Fig 10.65 (opposite below) No. 29 Queen Square, compter or counting house overlooking courtyard, window formerly with sash shutters, photograph of 2003 (RHL).*

*Fig 10.66 (left) Recesses for wash basins: a) no.4 Broad Plain, photograph of 1978 (NMR BB78/9298); b) no.27 Portland Square, photograph of 2005 (RHL); c) Cliftonwood House, photograph of 1937 (NMR OP06503, Ruding Bryan); d) no.69 Old Market, photograph of 1998 (NMR BB98/01587).*

*Fig 10.67 (below) Houses on St James's Back, privies overhanging the Frome, watercolour by S Jackson, 1826 (BRSMG M2834).*

319

## The Changed House

One area of fascination for students of vernacular architecture is looking at the evidence within a building for how it has been changed in the past. Very often such enquiries are driven by a wish to understand the original form of the building. The remaining part of this chapter will draw on information on change to suggest how, and if possible why, Bristol houses were rebuilt and modified through the centuries. What were building owners hoping to achieve by making changes? To answer this question we should look first at complete conversions of older buildings and then at the different categories of modification that have been observed.

### Conversions and Modifications

Some of the largest-scale alterations were those made to older buildings converted to become houses. As has been earlier noted (chapter 2), several of the dissolved religious houses were converted to residences. The Great House on St Augustine's Back (*see* Fig 2.20) was possibly in part an adaptation of the church and claustral buildings of the Carmelite Priory, but without being able to examine its remains archaeologically we shall never know if this was so. Certainly part of the claustral buildings of St James's Priory were altered by Thomas Ellis to become a house within his sugar refinery, retaining at least one window of medieval date (*see* Fig 7.42).

One such conversion that might one day be investigated archaeologically was the great hall within Bristol Castle.[68] It was converted to become the house of Francis Brewster, who acquired the lease of the Castle from the Corporation in 1625. He or a successor retained parts of the medieval building, notably one tower (Fig 10.68a) and the medieval porch (Figs 10.2 and 10.3), but subdivided the interior and inserted new floors so that it became a house of two storeys (Fig 10.68b) and of two rooms in depth with a substantial stairs in the centre (Fig 10.4).

A second stairs of the 17th century (Fig 10.69) was possibly a service stairs for this house. Alternatively, it may have been installed for a new house of central-stairs plan when Brewster's house was further subdivided into three separate dwellings. Either way it was clearly intended that the great hall of the Castle should become domestic space with a contemporary finish. In retaining one tower and part of the medieval entry to the great hall, Brewster, like Thomas Ellis, evidently wished his new house to retain an air of antiquity. The conversion of the great hall of the Castle was essentially similar to the conversion of many medieval hallhouses, noted in an earlier chapter (chapter 5). These too were possibly sometimes

*Fig 10.68*
*Nos.19 and 20 Castle Green, parts of the medieval castle retained in the new house of the 1620s:*
*a) a tower behind no.20, photograph of the early 20th century (BRO 20894);*
*b) no.19 closest to the camera, the street frontage of it and no.20 possibly the west wall of the medieval great hall, photograph of 1930 (NMR AA78/6737).*

# SPACES AND CHANGES

earlier form (*see* Fig 5.35). In Temple Street no.124 appears from the plan of *c* 1816–17 to have been another such hallhouse with a shophouse on the street frontage (*see* Figs 5.11, 5.12, 5.25 and 5.26). Part of the former open hall possibly became an open area within the converted dwelling, while the room to the rear with a substantial fireplace, possibly a kitchen or parlour, remained in use in the new conversion.

## Re-use

Re-using fragments of an older building in its conversion or rebuilding was possibly sometimes for convenience rather than for the allure of antiquity. In the building of no.30 College Green, *c* 1730, a cupboard door of the 17th century (Fig 10.70a) was possibly used because it was to hand on the building site. Similar considerations may have influenced the retention of a section of 17th-century panelling in the back of a first-floor cupboard at no.29 Queen Square in the 1710s (Fig 10.70b). However, we might reasonably ask why a 17th-century chimneypiece was preserved in the rebuilding of no.40 Prince Street (*see* Fig 9.64)? If it was thought worthwhile to provide this 17th-century house with a new Palladian facade (Fig 10.71), then why retain an old chimneypiece inside? Possibly this was to give John Day's house an air of ancestral use, rather like Sir Henry Creswick's decision to display the arms of Elizabeth in his house in Small Street (chapter 5).

*Fig 10.69*
*No.21 Castle Green, new stairs of the 17th century, drawing of an 'ancient staircase in house in Castle Green' by Samuel Loxton, 1907*
*(BRSMG Mb 3005).*

valued for their antiquity, the roofs of no.20 Small Street, Spicer's Hall on Welsh Back and Canynges' House in Redcliff Street being especially notable

Elsewhere in the city, hallhouses were converted to become storeyed dwellings. One such hallhouse was no.44 Broad Street, the insertion of later floors almost concealing its

*Fig 10.70*
*Re-used earlier materials:*
*a) no.30 College Green, c 1730, re-used cupboard door of the 17th century, photograph of 1998 (NMR AA98/02823);*
*b) no.29 Queen Square, section of 17th-century panelling in the back of a first-floor cupboard, photograph of 1995 (NMR BB95/133).*

# THE TOWN HOUSE IN MEDIEVAL AND EARLY MODERN BRISTOL

*Fig 10.71*
*New facade to no.40 Prince Street (Dening 1923, Pl xxxi; see Figs 9.64a and b).*

*Fig 10.72 (below right)*
*No.45 High Street, showing the new baroque facade added c 1700, photograph of late 19th or early 20th century (BRO 01143).*

*Fig 10.73 (below left)*
*Nos.21–4 High Street, re-fronted to match houses in the streets leading to the new Bristol Bridge, watercolour by T L Rowbotham, 1828 (BRSMG M2260).*

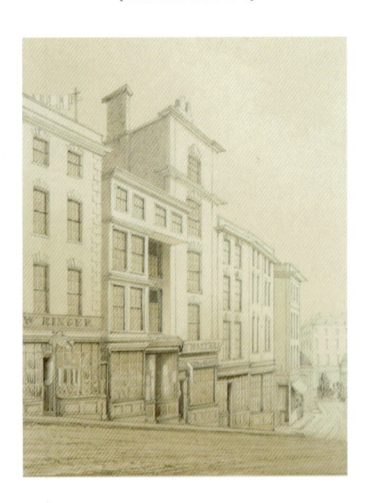

## Re-fronting the House

A house could be made to appear more modern by providing a new front. Instances of this happening before *c* 1800 are most numerous in houses in High Street, one of Bristol's most important commercial streets in the medieval and early modern periods. The new baroque facade to no.45 (Fig 10.72) was provided *c* 1700, when the house was leased to the mercer Samuel Weekes, was 'new built' and known as 'the Hen and Chickens'.[69] Close by, on the opposite side of the street, no.42/3 and nos.21–4, 'The George', were probably re-fronted in the 1760s to match the new houses with similar facades built in Bridge Street and other approaches to the new Bristol Bridge (Fig 10.73). In all these instances the medieval fabric behind the new facades was retained, so the purpose of re-fronting can only have been to change the external appearance. In commercial properties, such as those in High Street, the motive for the

*Fig 10.74*
*Robert Aldworth's new frontage to his house opposite St Peter's church, photograph of 1906 (NMR Country Life Collection CTL01/17031/7033/1).*

change may have been an attempt to attract more business. In other situations, proclaiming status and a change of ownership may have been the main motivation. When Robert Aldworth re-fronted St Peter's Hospital, a large residence facing St Peter's churchyard purchased as Aldworth's town house, the new, decorated bargeboards would have heralded the change in ownership that had taken place (Fig 10.74).

The search for better business may have lain behind the re-fronting of some houses. No.98 Redcliff Street was possibly re-fronted to draw attention to Nicholas Bloome's sugar refinery behind the street frontage. The carefully drawn elevation of the house made *c* 1816–17 shows a single sash window on the attic floor, as if it were lighting the room under a gabled roof behind (Fig 10.75).[70]

Re-fronting could also make rented houses more attractive to prospective tenants. In Temple Street nos.109 and 110 were evidently re-fronted in the late 18th century, in conjunction with the construction of a new court of seven or eight dwellings behind the street frontage (Fig 10.76). The carefully drawn elevation of the street frontage made *c* 1816–17 shows new sash windows on the lower floors, but older mullioned and transomed windows on the

# THE TOWN HOUSE IN MEDIEVAL AND EARLY MODERN BRISTOL

*Fig 10.75*
*No. 98 Redcliff Street, a gabled house of the 17th century or earlier, probably re-fronted, drawing of c 1816–17, detail of Fig 10.54 (BRO P/StT/Ch/31 fol 18).*

*Fig 10.76*
*Nos.109–110 Temple Street, two gabled houses of the 17th century or earlier, probably re-fronted, drawing of c 1816–17 (BRO P/StT/Ch/31 fol 3).*

second floor within what might formerly have been gables.[71]

An early instance of re-fronting was possibly that of no.43 Broad Street, where a stone facade was replaced with one in timber frame *c* 1411 (*see* Fig 6.5). However, this new facade was also part of the structure of the property as rebuilt – with more floors, and possibly therefore attracting a higher rent. This timber facade was replaced in brick when the street was widened in the early 19th century, doubtless for reasons of fashion.

The completion of nos.52 and 54 Kingsdown Parade was in a sense a re-fronting (Fig 10.77; *see* Fig 8.99). Both houses had probably been commenced before the collapse of the building boom in 1793. Removal of wall plaster on the interior face of no.52 exposed blocked former window openings, showing that it was originally intended to have three windows across the front of the house (two windows and the entrance door on the ground floor). Instead both nos.52 and 54 were completed with just one window on each floor, those to the ground- and first-floor chambers of no.52 having on the interior an elaborate surround with fluted Corinthian columns on either side, those to the ground floor serving as shutters (Figs 10.77–8). Here the decision to change the design from that of the adjacent houses was probably made once confidence in the housing market had recovered and when building recommenced; it could have been driven either by changing fashion or economics. Reducing the number of windows on the street elevation would have cut the costs of both labour and materials, even if the existing openings had to be infilled.

## Adding New Rooms

A house could also be made to appear more refined with the addition of a parlour. At no.45 High Street the re-modelling in the early 18th century of the rear room with bolection-moulded panelling was probably another part of Samuel Weekes's modernisation of his property. Originally part of St Michael's Hill, nos.68–70 Colston Street had been built *c* 1692 (*see* Fig 8.2c). In the early 18th century no.70 was nearly doubled in size, being extended backwards by one room on each floor. The new room at the rear of the ground floor – traversed by a cased ceiling beam with beaded mouldings, indicating that this was a polite space – was probably added as a parlour.

Rebuilding the house provided the opportunity to add a new parlour. A house of the 17th century, no.69 Old Market, was rebuilt in the early to mid-18th century, and the commercial character of the first floor has already been mentioned (chapter 6; *see* Figs 6.37d and 6.42). As rebuilt, a smart new back parlour was provided on the ground floor, with a fully panelled hearth wall, chimneypiece, overmantel and a display cupboard with shaped shelves (Fig 10.79). The adjacent house, no.68, was rebuilt *c* 1766 with a front and back parlour, each with full-height panelling and panelled window openings and shutters.

SPACES AND CHANGES

*Fig 10.77 (far left)
No.52 Kingsdown Parade, ground-floor front room, new window surround of c 1800 replacing the two window openings originally intended; the fluted pilasters serve also as shutters (English Heritage DP 114095).*

*Fig 10.78 (left)
No.52 Kingsdown Parade, first-floor front room, new window surround of c 1800 replacing the three window openings originally intended, photograph of 2010 (English Heritage DP 114090).*

*Fig 10.79
No.69 Old Market, the new parlour of the 18th century, photograph of 1998 (NMR BB98/01586).*

The completion of a campaign of building work could be commemorated through the installation of a new chimneypiece with the date recorded. On St Michael's Hill a chimneypiece with the initials of Eusebius and Elizabeth Brookes commemorated in c 1683 the extension of the house later built over by the terrace nos.123–31, a garden house used by Eusebius since at least 1662 (Fig 10.80; *see* Fig 9.15).[72]

## Re-modelling the Stairs

In several instances major alterations to the stairs made a house appear to be more up to date, but also provided a stairs with a shallower ascent. At no.33 King Street the stairs from the ground to the first floor were replaced in the early 18th century (Fig 10.81; *see* Fig 7.35), and the stairs to the floors above were modified at a

325

*Fig 10.80 (right)
Nos.123–31 St Michael's Hill (site of), chimneypiece of 1683 in the house of Eusebius and Elizabeth Brookes, drawing of 1823 (BRSMG Solanders, fireplaces, Estlin's House, fireplace, destroyed October 1823).*

*Fig 10.81 (far right) No.33 King Street, new stairs to the first floor of the early 18th century, photograph of 1997 (RHL).*

*Fig 10.82 No.2 The Grove (Emmaus House), earlier stairs surviving between the first and second floors, photograph of 2011 (English Heritage DP 141405).*

date unknown. In two other instances, at no.28 Queen Square and no.2 The Grove (Emmaus House), stairs of respectively the early 18th and later 17th century were modernised in the late 18th century, but left unaltered on their final ascent to the attic floor – an indication that modification for either aesthetics or convenience was a lesser priority for the rooms used for accommodating servants (Fig 10.82).

In the largest houses the magnificence of the stairs to the upper floors was probably a consideration in undertaking major alterations. At no.29 Queen Square the main stairs above the first floor were removed *c* 1800 to provide a grand entry to a new first-floor reception room taking up a little over half the front of the house (Fig 10.30). This was possibly driven by the fashion in the closing years of the 18th century for large private parties or assemblies known as 'routs', typically for between 40 and 200 persons.[73] Enigmatically the same process in reverse was implemented at Clifton Wood House; here a grand stairs originally terminated at the first floor, but was modified *c* 1800 so as to continue up to the second floor. A separate service stair from the ground to first and second floors was possibly removed at the same time (Fig 10.83, showing the first- and second-floor plans). At the Red Lodge a new grand stair installed in the early 18th century provided access from the ground to both floors above (Fig 10.8; *see* Fig 9.8).

SPACES AND CHANGES

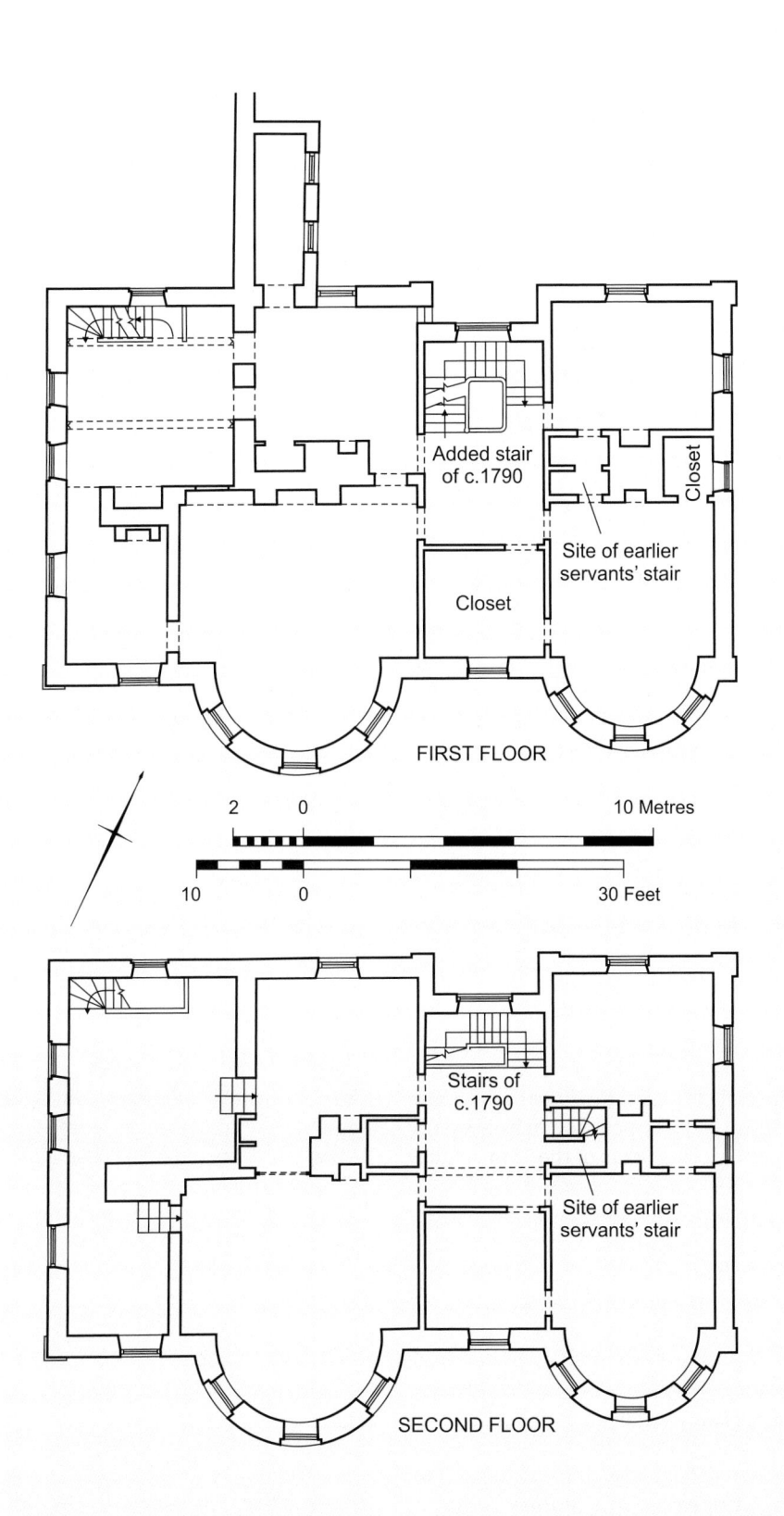

*Fig 10.83*
*Cliftonwood House, plans of first and second floors showing location of removed servants' stair and inserted stairs to second floor (RHL, PEC).*

Added stair of c.1790

Site of earlier servants' stair

Closet

Closet

FIRST FLOOR

2  0          10 Metres
10  0         30 Feet

Stairs of c.1790

Site of earlier servants' stair

SECOND FLOOR

327

## Changing Spaces

This chapter has charted changes in the use of domestic space in Bristol during the early modern period. Two main trends can be observed. The first is the disappearance of quasi-feudal social relations, symbolised in the use of the hall adorned with weaponry, arms and signifiers of ancestry and antiquity. By the end of the 18th century the hall had become simply the entry hall as we know it today, often decorated with pictures on the walls and with the occasional table and chair. As noted in chapter 8, the entrance hall had itself been made a more refined space, providing a view of what Yate's architect called the 'beauty' of the stairs. By the end of the 18th century most larger Bristol houses offered this visual experience.

The disappearance of the hall was also in part the process that Johnson has termed 'closure' – but so too was its replacement by the residential house which utilised the form of the storeyed shophouse to provide a series of segmented, more private spaces. In Bristol changes in housing reveal how the social structure of early modern England 'was moving away from a medieval, feudal pattern towards an early modern, capitalist one'.[74]

The stairs and the form of the residential house or shophouse were critical in maintaining the separation of the master and mistress of the household from the servants, removing the unity of the household formerly present in the open hall. The earlier emphasis on family and the household was replaced by one that underlined wealth and hierarchy.[75] In the segmented storeyed house, with basement kitchen and servants' rooms in the attic, the lives of the master and mistress of the house now separated the domestic and working lives of their servants. The form of the house also enabled surveillance of the servants, but, as Herman has observed, the proximity of the basement kitchen to the street and passing traffic also facilitated resistance and subversion for the servants.[76]

A second change that has been observed is the increasing sophistication apparent in the use of domestic space. In examining *The Refinement of America*, Richard Bushman placed some considerable emphasis on the role of the parlour in the spread of gentility: 'The crucial characteristic of a refined house was a parlor, free of work paraphernalia and beds, and dedicated to formal entertainment and the presentation of the family's most decorative possessions'.[77] In domestic space in Bristol, it was in the parlour that this process of refinement was most evident. Here the room included the most valuable objects, was usually the best decorated room and became the setting for fashionable social activities such as the drinking of tea and coffee, exotic beverages from the Orient and West Indies.

By *c* 1800 Bristol was predominantly a city of two-parlour houses; the majority of the *c* 3,000 new houses added through the developments of the 18th century (chapter 3) were of this plan. In most, some of the built features of the parlour now also appeared in other rooms, notably the panelled cupboards to be found in many first-floor rooms and upper chambers. A considerable section of the population was now conversant with the 'tea equipage' and the lifestyle of the front and back parlour. As Bushman has observed, the increasingly polite use of the parlour generated many new demands for the expanding industrial economy.[78] This is a theme to which we will return when looking at the wider context of Bristol houses in chapter 13.

## Motives for Change

It can be seen then that the motives for converting and modifying included fashion, profit and the enforcement of social behaviour and relations within the house. New facades to commercial buildings not only brought them up to date, but could also attract more custom and bring about economies in building. Conversions of medieval hallhouses into storeyed dwellings reflected social change, but could also bring in an increased rent. New facades, too, could be necessitated by internal modifications intended to increase rents. Yet many internal alterations were in the cause of fashion: creating a new parlour and engineering an impressive stair for routs were for entertainment on wildly differing scales, but were both driven by the wish to impress visitors with the host's refinement and *savoir faire*. Robert Yate's unidentified architect, writing in his 'Explanation' of 1724, and the material evidence of the houses themselves remind us also that lying behind such alterations were the less overt intentions to control both members of the household and their visitors.

# 11

# 'The Company of the town'

*'Just by the water side is a long rope yard which is encompass'd with trees on either side which are lofty and shady, therefore its made choice of for the Company of the town to take the diversion of walking in the evening; this compasses round a large space of ground which is called the Marsh, a green ground.'*

Celia Fiennes, 1702[1]

The traveller and writer Celia Fiennes was describing the population of Bristol perambulating in the evening the perimeter of the Marsh, the open area upon which Queen Square was shortly to be built (Fig 11.1). This might evoke for the reader memories of summer evenings in continental towns and cities, with what might seem to be a sizeable portion of the population strolling the central streets for pleasure and conviviality. In referring to 'the Company of the town', it might be thought that Fiennes saw the townspeople as a single entity. That is a concept that might be challenged, however, as the last several chapters have shown the variety of housing provided in medieval and early modern Bristol. The purpose of this chapter is therefore to examine the changing social and architectural topography of the city during this period. In particular it seeks to ascertain whether an analysis of the architectural evidence can contribute to our understanding of the appearance and development of residential zoning indicative of differences in status and wealth.[2]

This is a topic much studied by historians. In his study *The Widening Gate*, David Sacks has argued that 'Bristol's history between 1450 and 1700 created a center of early modern capitalism out of a medieval commercial town'.[3] Drawing upon his analysis of the housing developments thought to have taken place between 1568 and 1673, the dates of the maps of the city by William Smith and James Millerd,[4] Sacks has linked the provision of new housing to the increase in the city's population in the later 16th and 17th centuries (chapter 3). His study set 'the seventeenth century apart as the beginning of a new period in Bristol's long-term development'.[5] To Sacks the replacement of the Castle by 'a thriving city district' and the change in King Street 'from a mere pathway below the city wall into a thoroughfare with handsome houses on both sides' were manifestations of the changes taking place in the face of the city.[6] From the perspectives gleaned from chapters 2 and 3, we can now agree with Sacks in seeing these new housing developments as a distinctively new occurrence, the first of a succession of land promotions destined to double the extent of the city in the 18th century.

*Fig 11.1*
*The Marsh in 1673, which Celia Fiennes (1702) observed as the 'choice of for the Company of the town to take the diversion of walking in the evening'*
*(BRSMG, Millerd's map of 1673).*

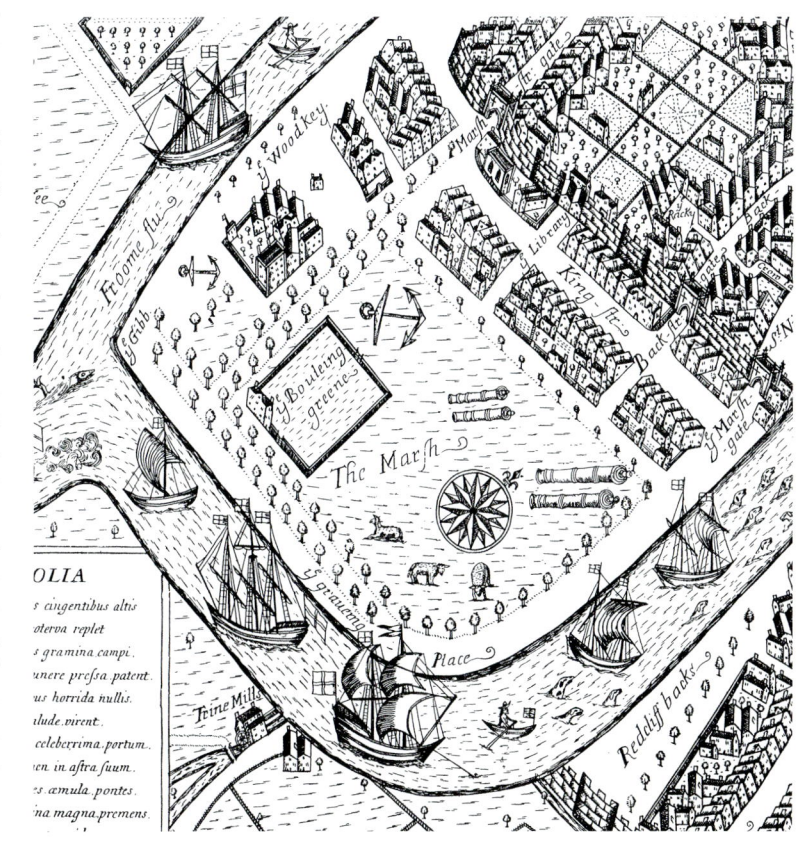

Sacks also indicated some of the complex ways in which the social geography of the city had changed between the 14th century and the 1670s. In the late 14th century the wealthiest members of the community were 'rather evenly distributed' across the city.[7] By the 1520s this had changed radically, with the city's wealthiest inhabitants now concentrated in the centre and portside parishes; in these same areas were large numbers of middling types and also poorer wage earners, the latter concentrated in or close to the markets and wharf sides. The suburbs to the east and to the south of the Avon contained fewer wealthier inhabitants and greater concentrations of wage earners. By the 1670s, Sacks argued, there were now significant concentrations of rich and poor identifiable in the portside and suburban parishes, with the merchants of the portside parishes now living in houses larger than those of many of the middling sort.

Elizabeth Baigent, examining economy and society in Bristol during the 1770s, has sought to place the changes taking place in the social structure of the city 'in the context of wider research on the nature of the *Gemeinschaft–Gesellschaft* transition' – the changes taking place as urban society moved from a focus on community to one centred on the individual.[8] This, too, is a theme that has been manifested in the development of housing in the city from the Middle Ages to the 18th century.

This present study will combine the information from documentary surveys of the city's inhabitants with architectural evidence to analyse the changing social and architectural topography of the medieval and early modern period. It will usefully focus on four points in time when such data is available. The first of these is *c* 1295, the date of the first recorded list of landgable rents, a form of tax levied on each house or plot; the second is the later 15th century, combining the information in the rental of the Canynges' chantries with the insights to be gained from the traveller and writer William Worcestre's description of *c* 1480 (a period from which much more architectural evidence survives). The third date is the later 17th century, for which an even greater body of architectural evidence can be studied alongside the Hearth Tax returns, Millerd's map of 1673 and a detailed tax assessment of 1696, listing all the then inhabitants of the city. The fourth point in time is the later 18th century, drawing on the information provided by the first systematic street directory of the city, compiled by the printer and publisher James Sketchley in 1775.

## The Social and Architectural Topography of the City from *c* 1295

Landgable rents were made to the Crown and in Bristol, as elsewhere, may have originated in Anglo-Saxon times.[9] Those for Bristol of 1295 were evidently recorded in a walking order matching the sequence in which the rents were listed – house by house, up and down the various streets.[10] Among the streets most readily identifiable is Broad Street. The higher landgable rents of 15d were payable on the widest plots, typically *c* 45ft, as for nos.41–3 and nos.51–2. On the latter the Cyder House, a hallhouse recorded in early illustrations and through archaeological excavation (chapter 5), was possibly typical of the elite residences that may have occupied these wide plots (Fig 11.2 A and B).

A second concentration of wealthier residences, visible primarily here from the architectural and archaeological evidence, was at the end of Baldwin Street closest to Bristol

*Fig 11.2*
*Elite housing of the 13th century in Broad Street. The wide tenement plots are those recorded in the landgable rents of 1295 (RHL and PEC, Ashmead 1828 as the base).*

*Fig 11.3*
*Elite housing of the 13th century in Baldwin Street close to Bristol Bridge (RHL and PEC, Ashmead and Plumley 1828 as the base).*

Bridge, where stone houses with halls were to be found on both sides of the street (Fig 11.3). From the identification of these groups of elite residences it can be concluded that zoning by wealth was already probably evident in the architectural topography of the city by the late 13th century – not, as Sacks has argued, a change that took place between the late 14th century and the 1520s. We have no evidence from this period, however, to indicate where the poorest families lived, nor anything to illustrate the types of houses that they occupied.

## The Social and Architectural Topography of the City from the later 15th Century

William Worcestre's account mentions only the houses of his own family and those of the most prominent citizens. Of the latter, the houses of Vyell, Shipward, Norton, Canynges and Sturmy were all either on or very close to the river, but widely scattered across the city (Fig 11.4). A similar mix of properties for the rich and those less affluent could be seen in the distribution of hallhouses and shophouses across the city, notably in High Street (Fig 11.5). Such a mix was not uniform, however. Broad Street, Christmas Street and Small Street, all close to Broad Quay (the quays for ocean-going vessels), were areas principally of elite housing characterised by hallhouses. By this date there was also a new indicator of wealth in the distribution of housing across the city: lodges or second residences. These were widely scattered, from St Michael's Hill on the north to the Redcliff Fee on the south (*see* Fig 9.3).

From the rental of the properties of Canynges' chantries made in 1473, it has been argued in earlier chapters that by the later 15th century a distinction was made between hallhouses and shophouses. Those who lived in the former paid higher rents and were probably therefore wealthier individuals. The display of wealth was most evident in those hallhouses of members of the urban elite which formed part of a complex of buildings arranged around a courtyard, known in Bristol as a 'corteplace' (chapter 5) – another term used in the 1473 rental to describe a particular type of property. Examples of such houses already discussed have included no.20

*Fig 11.4*
*Elite houses of the later 15th century, those mentioned by William Worcestre (ed Neale 2000), recorded 'court places' (ed Leech 1997a) and known courtyard houses (Inventory).*

*William Worcestre (page numbers in ed Neale 2000 in parentheses):*
1  Shipward's house (3, 21, 129)
2  Splendid structure of Norton's residence and houses, St Peter's Hospital (101)
3  Where Oliver, the jurist, Recorder of Bristol, dwelt, no.6 Peter Street (173)
4  The house where Richard Newton, the King's justice, dwelt when he was Recorder of the town of Bristol (197), nos.42–4 Corn Street
5  'The dwelling house with the corner of huge stones, called Vyell's Place ... the said corner house of Henry Vyell' (205), 'a most splendid tower built by John Vyelle Esquire upon the first corner of The Key' (215)
6  The Prior of Bath's house, later of John Smyth et al, no.20 Small Street (209)
7  Canynge's house, no.97 Redcliff Street (215).

*Recorded 'court places' (page numbers in Leech 1997a in parentheses):*
8  No.38C Corn Street, John Cutt's 'corteplace' (62)
9  The Quay, 'corteplace' south of the Great Tower (136–7)
10  Nos.56–7 Wine Street (198).

*Courtyard houses known mainly from archaeological recording (see Inventory):*
11. No.6 Welsh Back
12. Union Street, the lodge/ courtyard complex excavated 2000

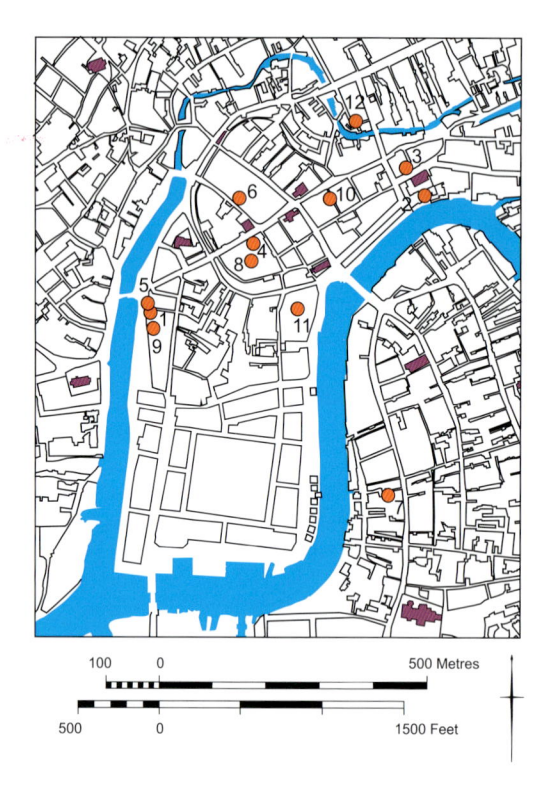

Small Street (*see* Figs 5.14 and 5.42 to 5.47), Canynges' house at no.97 Redcliff Street (*see* Figs 5.37 and 5.38) and Spicer's Hall, later Sturmy's house, at no.6 Welsh Back (*see* Fig 5.33), all characterised also by richly decorated roofs to the open halls.

Previous studies of urban housing in England have identified the courtyard house as a distinct form of urban dwelling, both in London and elsewhere.[11] In Bristol too, courtyard houses were very evident in the later medieval townscape, although, like the other forms of large house, they were found in different parts of the city rather than concentrated in one quarter. To the examples already mentioned could be added others: on the Quay was another property of William Canynges, described in 1473 by the clerk of his chantry as 'a corteplace'. Facing the Avon in front of St Peter's church was the house of the Nortons, this too apparently enclosing a courtyard.

Some of the new houses created out of the former monastic houses were also probably of courtyard plan. In 1579 the buildings of Henry Brayne's mansion formed out of St James's Priory abutted both 'the great green court' and 'the little square green courte', the latter perhaps a former cloister.[12] The Great House on St Augustine's Back (*see* Fig 2.20) may similarly have utilised the monastic cloisters or precinct as a courtyard. These were all the houses of Bristol's wealthiest citizens, located in prime situations both in the central streets of the city and on key sites close to the waterfront.

Hallhouses smaller than those in the elite courtyard developments were differentiated from those of the wealthiest citizens (such as Canynges') by size, a lesser investment in decoration and by the status of their inhabitants. Various examples can be cited. The corbels at no.2 Christmas Street, possibly of the merchant John Stoke and his wife, have already been mentioned (*see* Fig 5.41). The occupants of the hallhouses at no.23 Christmas Street and nos.72 and 144 Redcliff Street in the 14th century and earlier remain unidentified, but no.44 Broad Street (chapters 5 and 10; *see* Fig 5.35) can be shown to have been in the first half of the 15th century the house of Geoffrey John, a draper, also known as John Draper. John held the property as a subtenant to his neighbour John Clyve, mayor in 1412 and 1425, who in turn held the principal lease from the Cheddre family. John was held in sufficiently high regard by Clyve to be granted the remainder of the lease on Clyve's death *c* 1430; he became sheriff in 1414.[13]

Successive occupants of the Green Lattice in High Street, a hallhouse built to serve as a tavern, were variously mercers and merchants. William Warde, the occupant at the time of its 15th-century rebuilding, was a mercer and a proctor of All Saints church; he was of sufficient stature to represent the church on business in London, but did not become mayor or sheriff. A similar picture could be painted of his successors, merchants John Compton and Thomas Cogan. Cogan, though never mayor or sheriff, was wealthy enough at his death in 1486 to leave gilded silver vessels to each of his children, and for their welfare, as children of a member of the city elite, to be the concern of the City Corporation.[14]

This is a sample of the smaller hallhouses that existed, but they certainly indicate a pattern. These were the houses of townsmen of some wealth and stature, but not for the most part of the merchant elite: of these identified inhabitants, only John Draper held high civic office. Only by seeing the internal arrangements of their houses, an opportunity now denied to us by the loss of most of these properties, would we know whether they too had adopted a lifestyle in which the open hall, though central to considerations of rent, was no longer the social centre of the house, but had instead

'THE COMPANY OF THE TOWN'

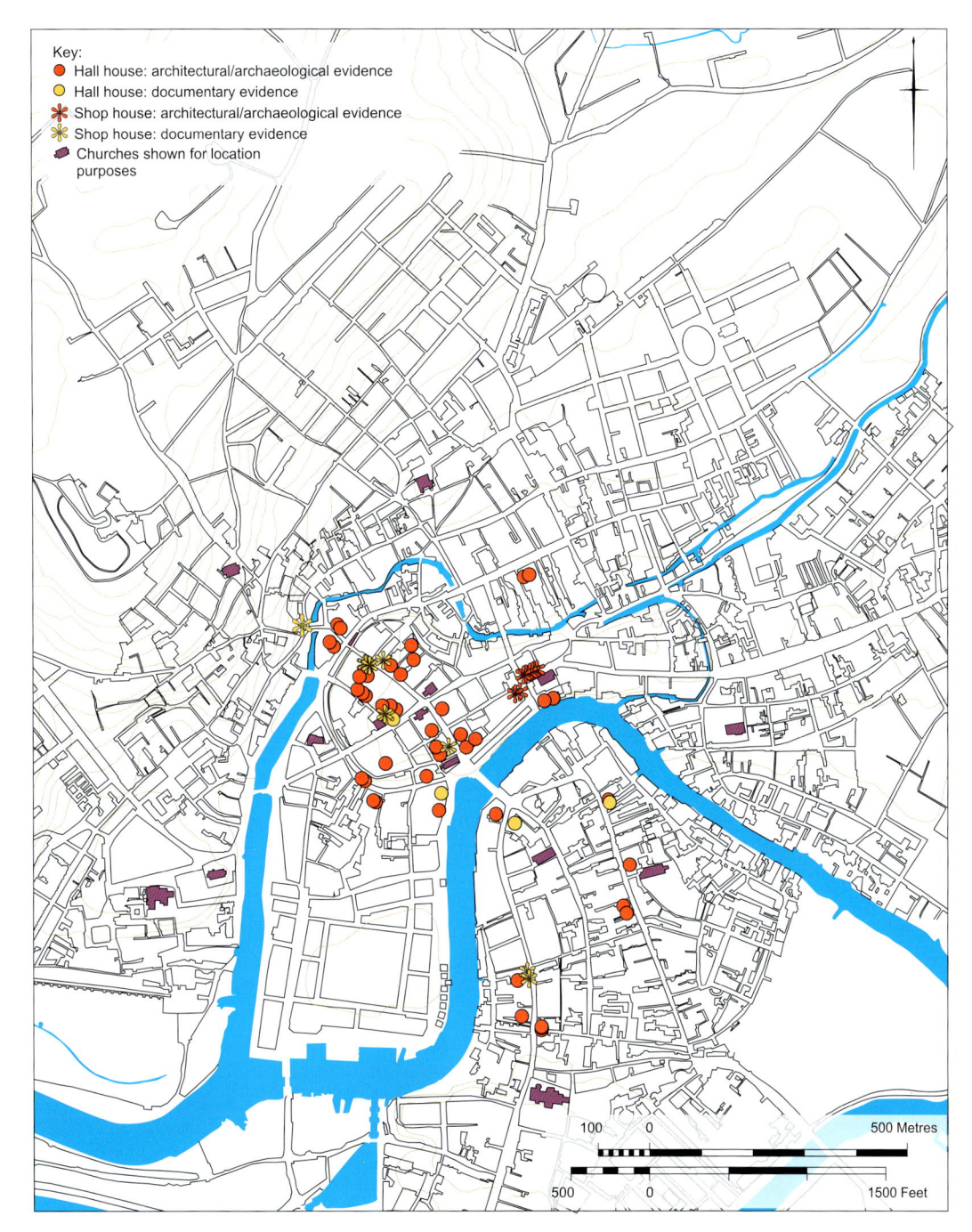

*Fig 11.5*
*The distribution of hallhouses and shophouses by the later 15th century, drawing upon documentary and architectural evidence (RHL and PEC, Ashmead and Plumley 1828 as the base).*

Key:
- Hall house: architectural/archaeological evidence
- Hall house: documentary evidence
- Shop house: architectural/archaeological evidence
- Shop house: documentary evidence
- Churches shown for location purposes

assumed a ceremonial and symbolic function – a statement of position and status. For all these individuals the hallhouse, commonly with an impressive open hall, whether used ceremonially or still as the focus of household life, enabled the status of the family and household to be displayed to visitors. Though concentrated in the central streets of the city, smaller hallhouses were also found in suburban areas such as Redcliff Street on the approach to the city from the south.

Conversely those who lived in shophouses paid lower rents (chapter 5) and may have named the principal room of their houses 'the hall' in emulation of the room in higher-status households. Properties noted as 'shops', sometimes perhaps a shorthand for shophouse (chapter 5), were widely distributed across medieval Bristol. By the early 14th century shops were to be found in most of the streets within the early walled town and the Marsh suburb.[15] Notable within the latter was Back Street, behind

333

Welsh Back, where 29 shops were concentrated; in the Tallage Roll, a taxation assessment of *c* 1350, these included the 11 new shops of Eborard le Frauncey (chapters 6 and 7).

Similar concentrations were found in the streets leading out of the town on the west. The suburb in Frog Lane (later Frogmore Street) may have consisted almost entirely of shops. There were possibly as many shops in the more central streets; with the exception of a concentration in St Nicholas Street, these must have been largely omitted from explicit mention in the Tallage Roll of *c* 1350, but are much mentioned in contemporary deeds.[16] Typical would be the corner shop in the drapers' corner, opposite the south door of Christchurch, with shops either side – part of no.1 High Street, mentioned in a deed of 1285 and predating the construction of the vaulted cellar on the site. Large numbers of shops in the Temple and Redcliff suburbs south of the Avon may have been similarly omitted from the Tallage Roll. Later, in the 15th century, John Haveryng would build the row of shops at the south end of St Thomas Street, revealed in archaeological excavations as houses probably of two rooms in depth. The naming of this development as 'St Mary Reckehey' indicates that it may have served a similar purpose to 'the Rackhay' behind Welsh Back, in 1573 the property of the clothier Edmond Jones. This was a development of houses for cloth workers, employed by a clothier from whom they rented their houses and within a close that contained also the racks for the drying of cloths.

In an urban context, certainly in Bristol by the 15th century, the distinction made by contemporaries between hallhouses and shophouses must remind us that not all houses had an open hall. Moreover, among the houses that could not have been called hallhouses were throughhouses, open halls which had been subdivided. These were open halls, abandoned not simply for mealtimes, but given over to property redevelopment. Here the way of life evoked by Langland (chapter 5) had passed completely. Across the city as a whole many households lived with open halls, but many also without.

Population growth was very marked in the 16th and 17th centuries and the city expanded in all directions, as has been seen in chapter 3. The increased population was not accommodated, however, simply by building more houses. Millerd's map of 1673, largely iconographic in its detail, shows almost all houses as being of three storeys. Survey and documentary sources reveal many pre-18th century houses of four and even five storeys in height. The expansion of the city to accommodate the increasing population was upwards as well as outwards.

A major change not noted by Sacks was that by the early 17th century some members of the city and commercial elite had eschewed the house with the symbolic hall in favour of the shophouse: as in earlier centuries, commerce could be linked to high social status. The hosier Michael Threlkeld (chapter 6), the merchant John Langton (chapter 6) and goldsmith Ephraim Goodyear (chapter 10) were, from the material and documented evidence of the furnishing of their houses, all among the wealthiest citizens in this period. All three decided to live in houses without an open or symbolic hall, choosing instead to live in luxuriously appointed shophouses of two rooms on each floor (chapter 6). As we have seen in previous chapters, each used all or part of the house on the ground floor for the shop; the room above the shop served as the principal living room, the hall or 'forestreet chamber', looking out over the street.

Although it might be assumed that the wealthiest citizens contended for the largest and most prominent residential locations, there is good evidence for departures from this simple picture. Alongside the inertia which followed from inheritance and a limited property market, personal preferences – linked to the location of tenements, to their size, to commerce, to amenity and to other factors – played a role in determining where citizens chose to live. Seyer's 'chapel' at no.59 Baldwin Street was a substantial house built in the mid-13th century, on a plot only 28ft in width, close to High Street and the Bridge. Notwithstanding the small size of the plot, the developer felt confident from its location that building this house here was a worthwhile investment. In the late 16th century this same house was refurbished by William Birde, a wealthy woollen draper. His preference was to live in a house in this location, despite the apparent mismatch between his status and the size of his property, because it offered potential for developing his business.

Looking at the preferences of his neighbours, towards and away from the Bridge, one could begin to construct a wider picture (Fig 11.6). On the opposite side of Baldwin Street, further away from the Bridge, were tenements possessing very limited commercial frontages,

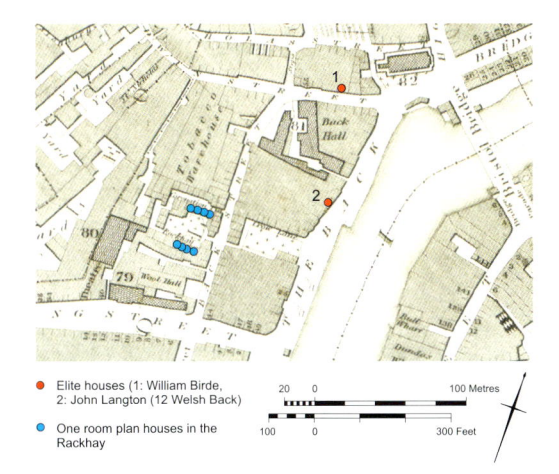

*Fig 11.6 (left)*
*Elite houses and houses of one-room plan of the late 16th and early 17th centuries in Baldwin Street, Welsh Back and the Rackhay (superimposed on the map of 1828).*

- Elite houses (1: William Birde, 2: John Langton (12 Welsh Back))
- One room plan houses in the Rackhay

but with a few of the largest gardens and orchards within the walled area of the city. Here lived some of the wealthiest and most prominent of Birde's contemporaries; to them the amenity of the large garden outweighed the importance of the commercial frontage to the house.

Close by, in the Rackhay, were some of Birde's poorest neighbours; their houses, of one-room plan, occupied almost the total extent of the tenements on which they stood. For them a large garden plot was not a possible option. Here one can see beyond tax returns and counts of hearths to the preferences of individuals, as expressed in their choice of where to live – and to the sharp social division between those for whom such choice existed and those who lived where dwellings were provided.

John Langton's house at no.12 Welsh Back illustrated a further trend, not noted by Sacks but of importance in identifying the emergence of a centre of early modern capitalism. New building was now a means by which an individual might assert newly acquired status. The doorway from Langton's forestreet chamber or hall to the chamber or stairs behind, richly decorated with tropical hardwoods, silver, ivory and mother-of-pearl, bore the initials 'J L' and the date 1628, the year in which Langton became mayor (*see* Fig 6.16). Similarly the woollen draper William Birde possibly celebrated his year as mayor in style, commencing in 1589 with the building of the White Lodge (chapter 9; *see* Fig 9.9), while in Castle Mill Street Robert Adams's new house, bearing the initials 'R A' and the date '1547', possibly commemorated his year as mayor in 1546–7 (Fig 11.7). Initials and a date on the exterior or interior of a building could, however, be no more than a means of displaying status gained through wealth acquired by investment in property. Robert Adams may be a case in point, as may the pewterer Thomas Hobson: he built a new house at no.17 Broad Street (Fig 11.8) in 1622 and displayed its date, his merchant's mark or symbol and the initials of him and his wife on the interior.

Adams's house is the earliest structure in Bristol recorded as bearing initials and a date. There is no evidence that some of the largest dwellings constructed during the 15th and 16th centuries were similarly signed and dated, including Canynges' house and tower in Redcliff Street and John Smyth's rebuilding of no.20 Small Street, although there is evidence from no.2 Christmas Street (chapter 5; *see* Fig 5.41) of a merchant and his wife commemorating their association with the house through their depiction on two of the corbels in the hall. That example apart, we might see here, in the assigning of initials and dates to architectural features, the emergence of what Cary Carson has called a 'rough-and-ready possessive individualism … everywhere starting quite abruptly in the 1580s and 1590s'.[17]

Against all this evidence for the polarisation of wealth and poverty in the late medieval city, one must also note the interdependence of trades and the contacts between persons of greatly varying wealth that this must have created. As the Bristol merchant John Browne wrote in his treatise for the sons and servants of merchants, *The Merchants Avizo*, first published in 1589 and then reprinted in 1590:

> The merchant made the clothier rich
> by venting of his cloth:
> The clothier then sets many at worke,
> And helpeth every crafte. [18]

Finally, we might note that the very poorest quarters of the medieval town possibly remain elusive, unidentified by archaeological, architectural or documentary evidence.

## Elite Architectural Awareness from the 15th to 17th Centuries

Evidence from across the city reveals that the very wealthy also had access to an architectural awareness that extended from Bristol to the metropolis and beyond. From William Worcestre's description it can be concluded that Canynges' tower with bay windows, overlooking the Avon behind Redcliff Street, must have been similar in appearance to Baynard's Castle on the Thames in London (chapter 9). Building in this

*Fig 11.7*
*Castle Mill Street, no.11, Robert Adams's new house, bearing the initials 'R A' and the date '1547', possibly commemorating his year as Mayor in 1546–7, watercolour of 1825 by T L Rowbotham (BRSMG M2705; see also Fig 2.13a).*

*Fig 11.8*
*The pewterer Thomas Hobson's new house at no.17 Broad Street, dated on the interior to 1622, watercolour by H O'Neill, 1806 (BRSMG M2435).*

style possibly indicated Canynges' familiarity with the latest developments in architecture in London. The John Smyth of St Ewen's parish who oversaw the building of the new church house there was possibly the 'Johannes Smyth de Bristoll, Marchaunt' admitted to the Bristol Staple Court in 1513. He may also have been the same John Smyth who later owned and extended no.20 Small Street, the house formerly of Bath Abbey.[19] In the rebuilding and extending of no.20, his own house in Small Street, this John Smyth is likely to have had access himself, or via a master builder, to knowledge of the design of the hammer-beam roof constructed at Hampton Court, first for Cardinal Wolsey and then completed by Henry VIII c 1536, and subsequently by members of the gentry at Beddington in Surrey and Cowdray in West Sussex.[20]

Bristol citizens were evidently aware of architectural writings by the late 16th century. The design of the garden front of John Young's Red Lodge was probably derived from a design by the Italian mannerist architect Sebastiano Serlio (1475–1554), whose writings on architecture were well known in late 16th- and early 17th-century England (see Fig 9.6).[21] In Bristol the Redcliff and Temple Gates were both rebuilt in this period to designs incorporating many elements featured in Serlio's writings (Figs 11.9a and 11.9b).

Knowledge expressed through architecture and art was also a means of asserting authority. In the case of Robert Aldworth, who rebuilt the Nortons' former property, later St Peter's Hospital, this was contrived through a moral message directed at his servants. Aldworth's house was provided with two principal entrances. One faced north to St Peter's churchyard, an integral part of the showy display made by the four richly decorated gables of Aldworth's costly rebuilding, completed in 1612. The plan (see Fig 5.15) shows that this entrance was central to the entrance hall then providing access to the upper hall and great parlour. This would certainly have been the entrance by

*Fig 11.9*
*The city gates rebuilt in the late 16th and early 17th centuries reflected a knowledge of Serlio's designs:*
*a) the Redcliff Gate, drawing by James Stewart, 1751 (Bodleian Library, Western MS, Gough Somerset 8, fol 12);*
*b) the Temple Gate before 1809 (when it was demolished), drawing by H H Holmes said to be of 1819 (BRSMG M2150).*

which Aldworth would have expected honoured guests to arrive at his rebuilt house.

A second entrance to Aldworth's house was on the south side, facing the river – to judge from its 18th-century appearance, an altogether plainer facade. Aldworth did not lay out funds to nearly the same extent on embellishing this side of his house. The only notable decoration was that to the porch, providing access to what later became the kitchen. The porch was certainly as built by Aldworth, bearing the date '1612', his and his wife's initials and his own merchant's mark or symbol. On the inside of the porch, below the plaster ceiling cornice and originally above panelling, were three panels of the theological virtues, Faith, Hope and Charity; a fourth panel depicted the vine, a common symbol of the Christian faith. This can be read as Aldworth's prescriptive Protestant text for servants and others entering by the back door (Fig 11.10). Fides stands between Daniel's companions in the fiery furnace and Jonah and the great fish.

The art of the chimneypiece was the most usual vehicle by which merchants conveyed moral messages to their households and visitors. At no.5 or 6 Redcliff Street an unidentified merchant owner commissioned a chimneypiece, now removed to Wiltshire, portraying St George and the Dragon – the triumph of good over evil (Figs 11.11a and 11.11b).[22] At no.59 Baldwin Street (Seyer's 'chapel'), another unidentified merchant owner selected the Judgement of Solomon for his chimneypiece (Fig 11.12), perhaps wishing to highlight the virtues of wisdom, truth and honesty. The need for discipline in one's personal or public life was perhaps the message to be conveyed by the chimneypiece in Alderman Cann's house at no.45 Broad Quay, depicting the sacrifice of Isaac (see Fig 10.32).[23] The importance of resisting temptation might have been the message to be conveyed in the depiction of the Fall on a chimneypiece in an unidentified house on St Augustine's Back (Fig 11.13).

The chimneypiece was also the vehicle for the wealthiest merchants to demonstrate their knowledge of art and culture. At no.15 Small Street the merchant Humphrey Brown, sheriff in 1619, commissioned for his parlour or dining room a chimneypiece depicting the five senses (see Figs 5.50 and 5.51). His own inclination to proselytising was well illustrated in his will,

*Fig 11.10*
St Peter's Hospital, interior of Robert Aldworth's porch on the river frontage depicting Faith, Hope and Charity. Fides stands between Daniel's companions in the fiery furnace and Jonah and the great fish (Simpson 1926, Pl IV).

*Fig 11.11*
No.5 or 6 Redcliff Street:
a) chimneypiece overmantel and a shelf below it dated '1637', shown on a Braikenridge watercolour (BRSMG M2043);
b) the overmantel removed by Detmar Blow to Lake House, Wilford, Wiltshire – the chimneypiece itself is not certainly from the same house, photograph of 1908 (NMR, Country Life Collection CTL01/11472/15A).

*Fig 11.12 Chimneypiece at no.59 Baldwin Street: the Judgement of Solomon, watercolour by H O'Neill, 1822 (BRSMG M2252).*

*Fig 11.13 Chimneypiece in an unidentified house on St Augustine's Back: the Fall, with the initials 'T B' and the date '1637', watercolour by John Watkins Brett, 1823 (BRSMG M2544).*

which left funds to the City to 'procure, provide and maintaine for ever a Learned sermon or lecture to be preached on every Lords day in the afternoone for ever', in either of St Nicholas's or St Werburgh's churches, 'for the better instructing of the people in the deep misteries of God and of his savinge health'.[24] Brown's near neighbour, the pewterer Thomas Hobson, evidently installed a similar chimneypiece in his new house, built c 1622.[25]

In contrast to John Young's Red Lodge, however, the lodges and suburban houses of Bristol's wealthy citizens in the 17th century were mainly of a conservative design. They employed the vernacular repertoire characteristic of the surrounding region fully, but eschewed the more adventurous forms sometimes used elsewhere for the lodge in a rural context. The gables, finials, bulls-eye windows and diagonally set chimneys applied to lodges such as those in Greyfriars, at Redland Manor and on Stony Hill could be seen on many a south Gloucestershire farmhouse.[26] Shorn of its mannerist porch, even Sir Robert Cann's house at Stoke Bishop was essentially a conservative vernacular design.

That access to architectural knowledge was only for the urban elite is further underlined by the fact that the houses of late medieval and early modern Bristol were for the most part probably designed by craftsmen builders following traditional practice. The City Corporation's building leases of the 1660s and 1670s indicate that by then it was normal for those committing themselves to the construction of new houses to undertake to build them in uniformity with those already existing (chapter 3); this can be seen as a requirement to follow traditional practice. The few surviving records of the construction of late medieval and early modern houses in the city provide plenty of information on sources of materials and costs, but offer no insights into who was responsible for the design. In 1472, at no.31 High Street, the builder simply undertook to construct a house with a specified range of rooms, creating a house of four storeys – excluding an attic and cellar, both of which were possibly provided as part of the traditionally built house of this form. The detailed accounts of the rebuilding of the house in Broad Street (rebuilt by the parishioners of St Ewen's in 1493) contain no payments to any person evidently overseeing the project, other than to John Smyth, one of the two churchwardens in the year following.[27]

## The Social and Architectural Topography of the City in the later 17th and early 18th Centuries

One characteristic of the modern city is the way in which particular districts come in and out of fashion. Looking at the physical expansion of Bristol from the 17th century onwards, we might ask for whom were these new houses first built, and to what extent did their occupancy and use change through time as new and more sought-after neighbourhoods emerged? A guide to the character of different parts of the city is provided by James Millerd's new map of the City of Bristol, published in 1673. Behind the preparation of the manuscript for the engraver there must have been many weeks, if not months and years, of preparation – tramping the streets, climbing the hills surrounding the city, surveying and drawing. Perhaps more than most of his contemporaries, Millerd would have been aware of the varied architectural experiences which walking the streets of the city afforded. Though to a considerable degree iconographic, his map has much to tell us of what was both immediately evident and less obvious in the architectural topography of late 17th-century Bristol – most especially when read in conjunction with what we can see of this architecture from other sources.

The map certainly shows that Millerd was aware of which houses were the largest in the city. He would also have been familiar with the smallest and have been conscious of the extent to which the gradations in house size mirrored the complex layers of society in the early modern city. The largest houses were shown as such on his map, among them the great houses on St Augustine's and Redcliff Backs, each with its own vignette (*see* Figs 2.20 and 8.100a), no.20 Small Street, Spicer's Hall and Langton's House on Welsh Back, the Manor House in Park Lane and Norton's House, later Aldworth's, at St Peter's Hospital. The smallest houses, and especially those in courts, were similarly identified by Millerd, notably the Rackhay and the New Buildings on the south-east side of Broadmead (*see* Fig 8.30).

Millerd must also have been aware of the concentration of houses of the urban elite in Small Street and in the parish of St Werburgh; he showed no.20 Small Street on his map as a much wider than normal residence of special importance. Earlier and until the end of the 17th century houses with open halls ornamented with arms and armour (chapter 5) were still to be found in this district. Such houses symbolically proclaimed the status of their owners and marked out a distinct residential zone within the city (Fig 11.14).

Many of the owners of these houses also possessed second residences on the slopes overlooking the city and in the fields to the east, within the Little Park and the former precincts of St Bartholomew's Hospital, the Greyfriars and Blackfriars (*see* Fig 9.3). By the 1660s these areas too had become distinct residential zones, populated on Sundays and at other times by the wealthiest residents of the city. But it is significant that, despite the attractions of these more spacious surroundings, wealthy families still maintained their ancient residences in the crowded city centre, where the demonstration of power and status was most effective.

An important element in Sacks's delineation of the emergence of the early capitalist city was his identification of the beginnings of residential differentiation. We have seen that such zoning was in fact already evident by the later 13th century, and was also part of the process of change discernible in the 17th century – especially in the development of the Castle and the growth of garden house suburbs. It was also much more evident, as will be seen from the beginning of the 18th century, in the building of new elite neighbourhoods. For Sacks these developments were identified through the changing patterns of wealth distribution and the concentration of particular religious affiliations in certain streets and districts. In the modern city, property or real estate values are often said to be linked to location, not in the first place to the size of the house. Some areas of older properties with larger houses retain a high status; others do not. The changing status of residential districts, over varying lengths of time, is a feature of life in the modern town, reflecting the preferences or fate of those who can or cannot choose where to live.

By the later 17th century most leading citizens, and increasingly also others, lived in houses that were entirely residential and were neither hallhouses nor shophouses. These new residential districts had distinct environmental characters according to the predominant types of houses built within them: environmental character, of course, was a mirror of the social structure of the early modern city.

Sacks has argued that analysis of the Hearth Tax returns showed that further changes had taken place by the 1670s. In the central and transpontine districts of the city, the juxtaposition of rich and poor was much as it had been a century earlier. In the portside and suburban parishes there had been much greater change, however, with significant concentrations of rich and poor now identifiable. The merchants' houses of the portside parishes were on the whole larger than those of the middling sort (shopkeepers and artisans) who now dominated the Castle Precinct and Old Market to the east.[28] Yet Sacks's conclusion that social zoning had become more marked in these quarters needs some qualification. It has been shown by the author elsewhere that the use of the Hearth Tax returns to map relative wealth is fraught with problems. In Bristol, as elsewhere, it can be demonstrated that the houses with the most hearths were very often inns.[29] Most of Sacks's larger houses of the portside parishes were certainly inns.[30]

*Fig 11.14*
*Hallhouses in Broad Street and Small Street ornamented with arms and armour (RHL, PEC; Ashmead and Plumley 1828 as the base).*

The process of increasing residential differentiation was also in part the result of the way in which new developments were planned, reflecting the deliberate intentions of the city elite. In the development of the Castle the two principal new streets emerged as two very different neighbourhoods (*see* Fig 9.65). Castle Green was a street populated largely by the urban elite: the newly laid-out plots were of generous size, and the new houses built there probably included a number of garden houses (chapter 9) or elite second residences. For example, no.10 Castle Green was the house of the wealthy Jackson family, whose principal town residence was at nos.25–7 Small Street and who also owned a suburban house at Sneyd Park (chapter 9).[31] Castle Street was much more a street for the middling sort, many living in shophouses (chapter 6) and including both tradesmen and some professional people.

In the development of the Marsh two residential zones emerged. The first inhabitants of King Street were very much of the middling sort, a similar mix of tradesmen and professional men to that in Castle Street. In contrast Queen Square and Prince Street consisted much more of the residential houses of the urban elite, including many merchants and shipowners (*see* Fig 3.5).

From at least the 1650s storeyed residential houses were being built in or close to streets of medieval origin, such as Frog Lane (later Frogmore Street), Lewin's Mead, Old King Street, the Rackhay, Rosemary Lane (later Rosemary Street), St Augustine's Back (later St Augustine's Parade), St Michael's Hill and Small Street. Some of these had been partly residential neighbourhoods since the 16th century or earlier.[32] Certain of these storeyed residential houses will have replaced unrecorded medieval hallhouses.

Elsewhere new streets began to be built on the periphery of the city as exclusively residential neighbourhoods – that is, as areas where commerce and retail trades were absent. King Street and Castle Green were developed in the 1650s and 1660s as streets mainly of larger residential houses. By 1673 the neighbourhood around the Cathedral was largely of a residential character, and had been so from probably at least the preceding century. To the south and west of the Cathedral was the precinct, within which were located the bishop's palace and the houses of various canons and clerics; some of these houses were new built, while others were modifications of older buildings made in the century following the establishment of the Cathedral out of the lands of St Augustine's Abbey.

The Registrar's house, for instance, was built in 1664 over a gateway of the 12th century (Fig 11.15). Immediately outside and abutting the still surviving Norman gateway to the monastic precinct was the Deanery, the largest of the canon's houses, its structural history less easily understood (Figs 11.16 and 11.17). Beyond the Deanery, the north-west side of College Green was enclosed by three further large houses (*see* Figs 8.78 and 8.79). Also part of the Cathedral lands, the north side of College Green was developed for new housing after 1673; these new houses too were shown on the Bucks' prospect of Bristol from the north-west in 1734 (Fig 11.18). This side of College Green was occupied in part by the superior houses built within the former precinct of St Mark's Priory (Fig 11.19). The occupants of some of these houses, all demolished for the building of Unity Street in *c* 1720, are recorded on a plan of the early 18th century (Fig 11.20).

*Fig 11.15*
*The Cathedral Precinct, the Registrar's house, built in 1664 over a gateway of the 12th century, drawing by J C Buckler, 1811 (BRSMG M1905).*

'THE COMPANY OF THE TOWN'

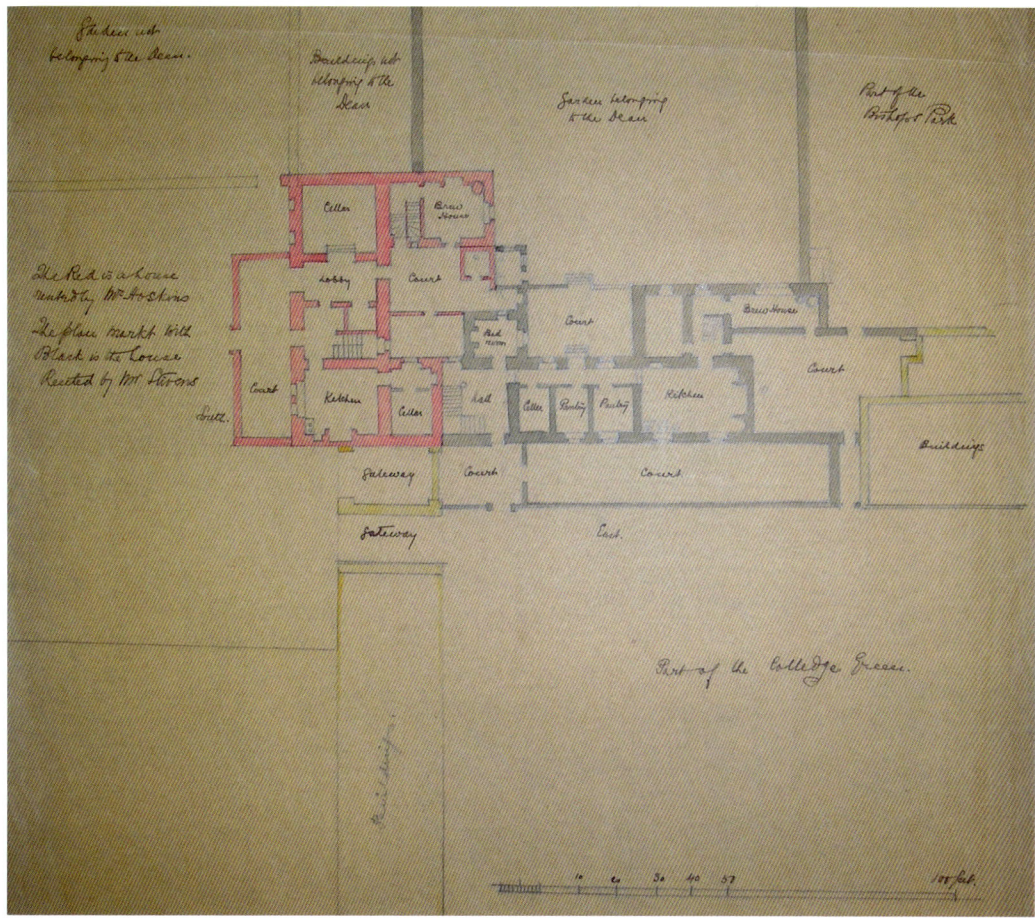

*Fig 11.16 (above)*
*The Cathedral Precinct, the Deanery, drawing by S H Grimm, 1789: nothing is known of its structural and pre-Reformation history (The British Library Board, Add MS 15540 fol 155).*

*Fig 11.17 (left)*
*The Cathedral Precinct, the Deanery: the plan (of the late 18th or early 19th century) indicates that this was a building with a complex history (BRO DC/F/9/1).*

# THE TOWN HOUSE IN MEDIEVAL AND EARLY MODERN BRISTOL

Fig 11.18 (above)
Elite housing on the north side of College Green, detail from the Bucks' view of 1734 (S and N Buck, The North West Prospect of Bristol, 1734).

Fig 11.19 (right)
Elite houses built within the former precinct of St Mark's Priory, later used for the Red Maids' School, watercolour by S Jackson, 1824 (BRSMG M2547).

Fig 11.20
Plan of the early 18th century showing elite houses built within the former precinct of St Mark's Priory (BRO 04479(2) fol 42).

'THE COMPANY OF THE TOWN'

The building of a uniform row of 10 residential houses on the north side of Host Street (Fig 11.21), first occupied in the late 1690s, the building of further rows on either side of St Michael's Hill and the commencement of building on the south side of Broad Plain by *c* 1700 (Fig 11.22) were among the principal developments of larger residential houses in the last three decades of the century.[33]

## 'Artisan' Residential Neighbourhoods

That residential neighbourhoods were not the preserve of the wealthy is evident from developments in the 17th century. Many new small houses for lower-income households were built on the frontages of existing but less commercially important streets. They were located in courtyards or in gardens behind

*Fig 11.21*
*Host Street, new houses of the later 17th century, photograph of c 1870 (BCRL L93.11).*

*Fig 11.22 (below)*
*House of the later 17th century on the south side of Broad Plain, watercolour by T L Rowbotham, 1826 (BRSMG M2782).*

existing houses, for instance in the Rackhay, Tailors' Court (Broad Street) or New Buildings as drawn by Millerd (Figs 8.19 and 8.20), forming socially cohesive enclaves within the city. At the end of the 17th century the construction of new streets lined mainly with tiny, one-room deep houses provided further neighbourhoods of artisan character.

The north end of St James's Back, Silver Street and Narrow Plain, on the south side of the churchyard of St Philip and St Jacob, were made up of clusters or rows of small houses. The smaller residential houses were not necessarily far divorced from the place of work; in some cases they were located to provide accommodation for the workers at an adjacent industrial enterprise. Close by might be found the much larger house of the owner or manager. Elsewhere a workshop or warehouse could be set back behind a house on the street frontage used entirely for residential and domestic purposes. By the end of the 18th century, however, it had become the norm for the more upmarket new developments of such houses to stipulate that a variety of the more noxious trades, such as brewing, smithying or tallow chandling, or any 'noisy noisome or offensive trade or calling' (Appendix 1), be excluded from the curtilage of the tenement as a whole.

In the early 18th century further 'artisan' residential zones were created through the construction of concentrations of small houses, for instance on the east and west sides of the city (*see* Figs 3.18–21 and 3.24). Some of these houses were built on the principal commercial street frontages, as one-room deep shophouses built against the churches of Christchurch and St Mary le Port. Others were constructed on the streets leading out of the city, as on St Michael's Hill. Most, however, were built in less important streets away from the commercial core, as around the churches of St Mary Redcliff and St Philip, in new developments of artisan housing or in courtyard developments. On the east side of the city the estate developed by Nathaniel Wade in the first two decades of the 18th century was built as a mix of one- and two-room deep houses, inhabited almost entirely by artisans and craftsmen. Possibly typical of the smaller houses being built here were no.17 Wade Street and two houses in New Street (*see* Figs 8.3 and 8.4).[34]

In looking at the great mass of the population of early 18th-century London, Earle has emphasised the distinction to be made between housekeepers and lodgers. Housekeepers rented, leased or owned a whole house. Within this there might be lodgers, who would rent rooms or floors of a house. The distinction was also one of status. Housekeepers occupied a position in society seen as superior, often playing a part in the management of local affairs.[35] For Bristol the combined use of architectural and documentary evidence can provide a further clue to identifying the residential zoning of the city.

The houses of one-room plan on St Michael's Hill, in the Rackhay and elsewhere were the smallest houses available to persons of housekeeper status – probably too small even for the accommodation of lodgers. The latter can be said with some certainty because, just over 20 years after the publication of Millerd's map, the assessments made in 1696 for the so-called marriage tax have provided a list of the inhabitants of every single house within the city. In the Rackhay 12 houses of the 17th century or earlier were recorded on the illustrations of the 1820s (*see* Figs 8.30, 8.31 and 8.32).[36] The tax assessment of 1696 lists 12 households, precisely the same number, none with lodgers.[37]

That the inhabitants of even these small houses were moderately prosperous might be inferred from the architectural aspirations evident in the finish of the houses on Christmas Steps and St Michael's Hill. At no.6 Christmas Steps the balustrade to the stair well (Fig 11.23; *see* Figs 8.2f and 8.18) at the first floor provided a touch of gentility. At no.29 St Michael's Hill, in a row of four houses (nos.23–9) of one-room plan (*see* Fig 8.2a), the moulded stone chimneypiece (*see* Fig 8.17) in the first-floor chamber overlooking the street was of a design that could be found in many wealthier households.

If similar evidence of internal finish was available for the houses in Rosemary Lane and the Rackhay, it might have been possible to detect gradations of social status among the households that inhabited these small properties. Where the households of the street-frontage dwellings in Rosemary Lane (*see* Figs 8.5 and 8.6) enjoyed the use of long plots extending back some 140ft,[38] room sufficient for gardens, small vegetable plots and 'necessaries' or privies detached from the dwelling, a majority of the households of the Rackhay had no back yard at all.

Here the documentary sources are in accord with the reading of the architectural evidence. In the row of four houses on St Michael's Hill, three of the households listed included servants.³⁹ In the Rackhay there were no servants among the 12 households listed in 1696. The occupations of the heads of households on St Michael's Hill are not identified, but looking at the context of their four small houses, and conscious of the servants in their midst, we might judge that they enjoyed a status in society superior to that of the Rackhay's inhabitants. Those able to purchase leases in the Rackhay during the first three decades of the 17th century had included a pump maker and a clockmaker; in 1696 the heads of households included a mariner and a victualler. These were the houses of skilled artisans. The skilled workers of the sugar refineries might have enjoyed a similar status.

These small houses would, without exception, have seemed to contemporaries to be of an urban character. Although close to the limits of the city, and still facing north over gardens and fields in 1673, the row of four houses on St Michael's Hill was, and is, distinctly urban in character – a row with each house gabled at right angles to the frontage for economy of space (*see* Fig 8.2a). Although arranged around the large open space of the burial ground and former garden, the small houses of the Rackhay and the workers' houses at the sugar house (*see* Figs 8.30 and 8.35) were similarly disposed. In Rosemary Lane the row of four end-gabled, one-room deep houses was even closer to the city's rural environs, just a few yards from the track that townspeople used to cross the fields towards Earl's Mead (Fig 11.24). Close to where town met countryside, the existence of these end-gabled rows must have helped to define for contemporaries the limits of the close-built city in which space was so much at a premium.

*Fig 11.23*
*No.6 Christmas Steps, the balustrade to the stair well at the first floor, photograph of 1912 (English Heritage DP 146952).*

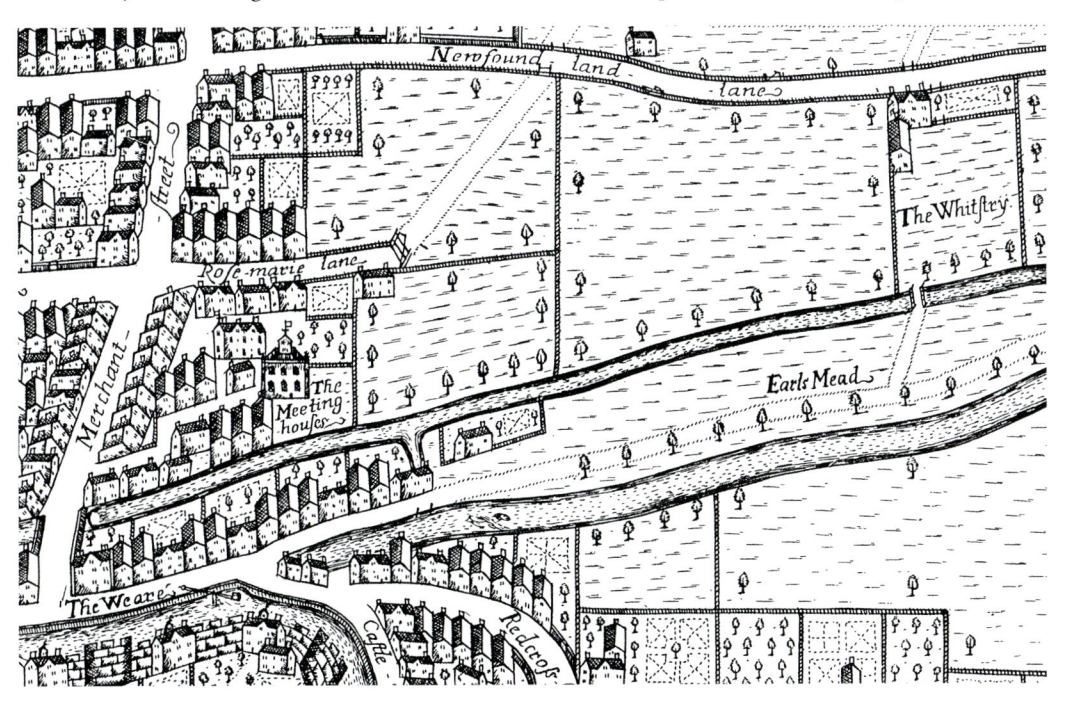

*Fig 11.24*
*Rosemary Lane (later Rosemary Street) and Earl's Mead, urban houses on the rural periphery of the city (BRSMG, Millerd's map of 1673).*

The documentary evidence for the construction of these smaller houses indicates that most were built as speculations to generate rental income. The size of house built might indicate the anticipated market for renting in those particular locations. However, most of the poor probably lived in older, subdivided housing, in the most crowded parishes in the centre of the city. This was certainly so a century later.[40] An outstanding example of subdivision and overcrowding was probably Cock Lane, demolished before c 1740 for the building of the Exchange (chapter 3).

## Second Residences

Some of the smallest houses evident in the city of 1673 were indicative of a far higher social status than those already considered. These were the properties identified in chapter 9 as lodges or garden houses, the second residences of the urban elite. Looking at these, Millerd must have been aware of the privileged backgrounds of their owners. On the slopes above the city on the west he would for example have passed the garden houses of the merchant Richard Stubbs in Upper Church Lane (see Fig 9.20) and the house at no.4 Stile Lane (see Fig 3.23), a few years later the second residence of Samuel Wallis, who became mayor in 1695.[41]

A majority of the owners of garden houses or second residences were members of the urban elite, well able to make such an investment. On the slopes of St Michael's Hill, a majority of the garden houses belonged to residents of the wealthiest city centre parishes ((Fig 11.25; see Fig 3.23)). In some areas the distribution of second residences mirrored the neighbourly relations of the city centre parishes – most notably on the slopes of the Clifton hillside, which in the 18th century supplanted St Michael's Hill as the fashionable area in which to have a garden house or villa (Fig 11.26). Here by the mid-18th century the Goldneys could meet their wealthy neighbours, the Fishers and the Phippens, close by in High Street and close at hand in Clifton. Nearby also were the suburban residences of the Champions, Eltons and Farrs. Similar concentrations of elite owners of garden houses were to be found below Upper Maudlin Street in the Greyfriars and Bartholomews developments and at Barton Hill, and on the western edge of the Downs towards Stoke Bishop where John Elbridge's Cote House lay just across the fields from Stoke Bishop House.[42] The spacious, tranquil character of the 'garden-house suburbs' – exclusive in occupation, but open in landscape form – provided a strong contrast to the assault on the senses experienced in the crowded streets of the city centre.

*Fig.11.25 (below) Garden houses in St Michael's parish in 1662 (BRO F/Tax/A/1): their owners and their city centre residences.*

| Name and number of hearths | St Michael's Hill | Reference | City centre | Reference |
| --- | --- | --- | --- | --- |
| Thomas Shewell 2 | ? | Not located | St Leonard's parish | BRO F/Tax/A/1 |
| John Gonning esq. 2 | 17 Park Row | Leech 2000, 121–2 | 8 Small Street | Leech 1997a, 155 |
| John Hillier 3 | Lunsford House, 15 Park Row | Leech 2000, 117–20 | No.H Corn Street | Leech 1997a, 65 |
| Robert Challoner 1 | ? | Not located | 6 Welsh Back | Leech 1997a, 166 |
| Edward Tyly 5 | 3–4 and 16–18 Old Park | Leech 2000, 93–4 | 44 Mary le Port Street | Leech 1997a, 109 |
| Charles Powell 3 | 2 Back Church Lane | Leech 2000, 96–7 | No other residence | BRO F/Tax/A/1 |
| Henry Jones 5 | Manor House, Park Lane | Leech 2000, 98 | ? No.AA St Nicholas Street | Leech 1997a, 145 |
| Richard Jordan 3 | Park Lane | Leech 2000, 99 | 24 Broad Street | Leech 1997a, 34 |
| Gilbert Moore 2 | 3 Back Church Lane | Leech 2000, 97–8 | c 14 Broad Street | BRO F/Tax/A/1 |
| Elizabeth Cugley 1 | 31–7 St Michael's Hill | Leech 2000, 76 | No other residence | BRO F/Tax/A/1 |
| Leonard Hancocke 1 | 43–7 St Michael's Hill | Leech 2000, 77 | 142 Redcliff Street | BRO P/St.T/D/19 |
| George Lane 3 | ? | Not located | Broad Street, Christchurch parish | BRO F/Tax/A/1 |
| Henry Creswick esq. 1 | Upper Maudlin Street, S side | BRO 04044(1) fol.335 | 20 Colston Street | Leech 1997a, 158-9 |
| John Haggett esq. 4 | Church Steps | Manchee 1831, 2, 119–21 | 5 Wine Street | Leech 1997a, 174 |
| Anthony Gay 3 | Upper Maudlin Street, S side | BRO 04044(1) fol.331 | ? Small Street | Leech 1997a, 153–5; BRO F/Tax/A/1 |
| Elizabeth Browne widow 2 | ? | Not located | St Leonard's parish | BRO F/Tax/A/1 |
| Thomas Walter 2 | ? | Not located | All Saints or St Philip's parish | BRO F/Tax/A/1 |
| Thomas Bevan 1 | ? | Not located | No other residence | BRO F/Tax/A/1 |
| Thomas Langton 2 | Church Steps (Joan Langton) | Manchee 1831, 2, 119–21 | 15 Small Street | Leech 1997a, 157 |

'THE COMPANY OF THE TOWN'

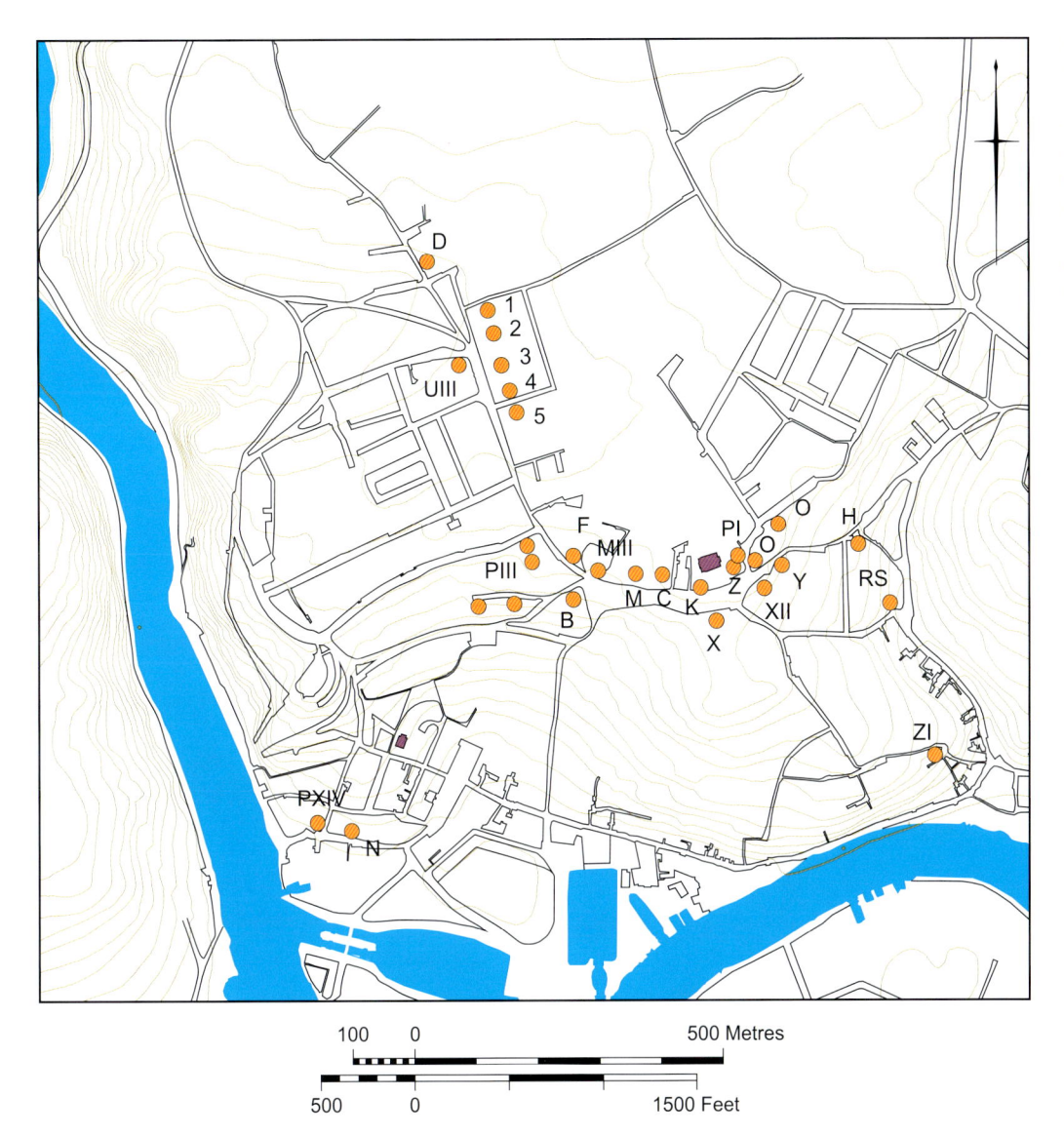

*Fig 11.26*
*Second residences and villas on the Clifton hillside by the mid-18th century; 1-5 are Clifton Down Road; other letters are those used by De Wilstar in his survey of 1746 (BRO SMV/6/5/4/3) (RHL, PEC, Ashmead and Plumley 1828 as base).*

## The Social and Architectural Topography of the late 18th-Century City

James Sketchley published the first street directory of Bristol in 1775. Though arranged in name order, it was clearly based on his own perambulations of the streets; each address was assigned a number in each street, the information being re-sorted for the directory. The city that Sketchley walked was to a considerable extent a new city. Extensive residential districts were reaching out to places that in Millerd's day, a century or more before, had been only fields and gardens. At the same time the older city was now much more densely populated, innumerable houses having been built in alleys and courtyards or created through the subdivision of older properties on the street frontages. Far more so than in 1673, this was a city composed of residential houses, dwellings separated from business or work. It was also a city in which the extremes of rich and poor, evident in the relative size of dwellings, were now much more generally visible. Above the status of those who lived in lodgings, there were many households who still inhabited houses of one room on each floor (Fig 11.27).

Social zoning was not universal in this period, however, for the old proximity of social classes characteristic of earlier times still prevailed in some parts of the city. One of the areas where rich and poor were most closely juxtaposed was on the east side of the city. Here Nathaniel Wade's new estate in Crotwells, a new district populated largely by artisans, lay first in close

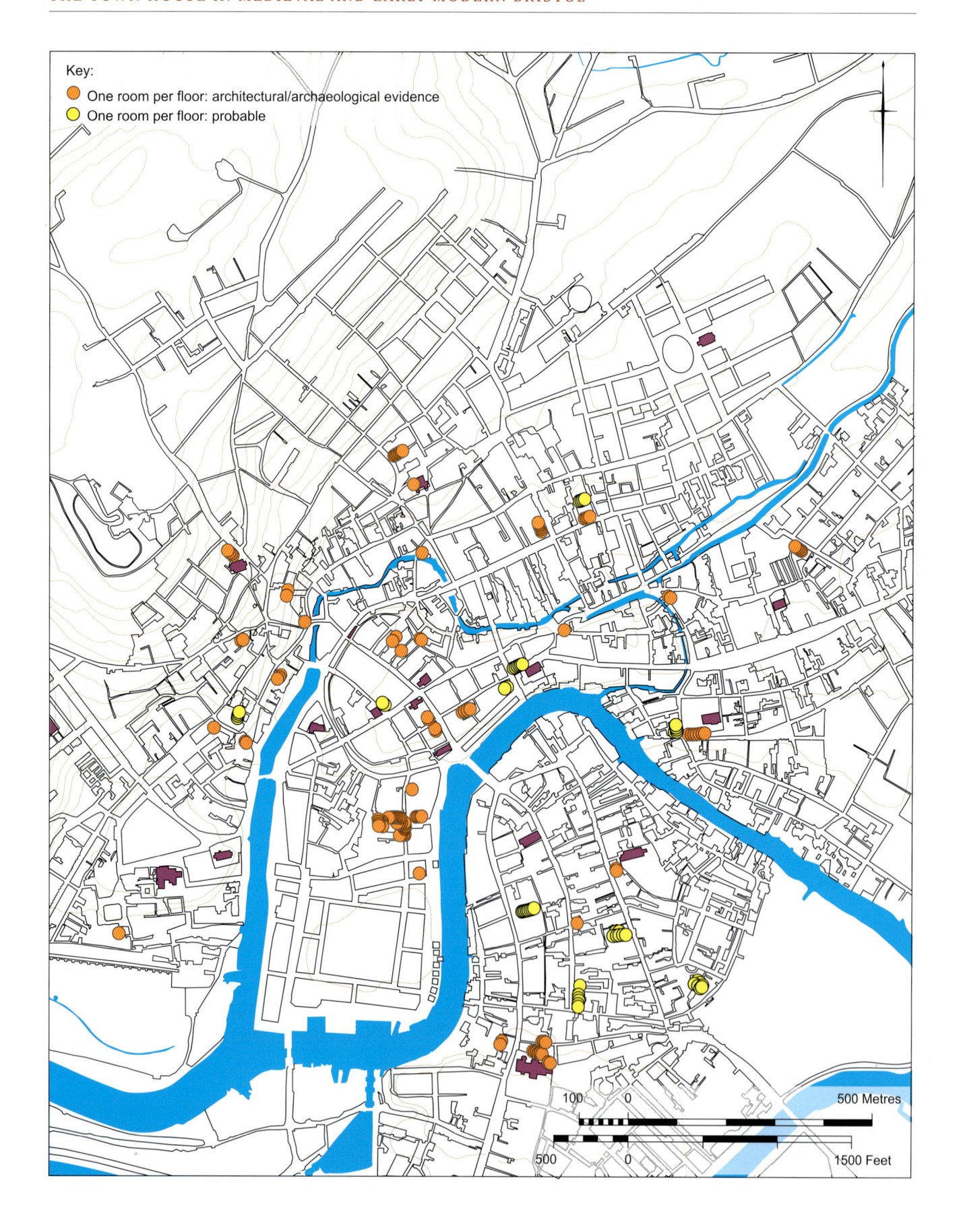

THE TOWN HOUSE IN MEDIEVAL AND EARLY MODERN BRISTOL

Key:
- 🟠 One room per floor: architectural/archaeological evidence
- 🟡 One room per floor: probable

proximity to the newly built, high-status St James's Square and the new houses in St James's Barton. Several decades later, the similarly prestigious Brunswick and Portland Squares were built close by. In the same area of the city, Old Market was another street in which rich and poor lived close to one another.

In 1775 nos.67–9 were the homes of the wealthy merchants Nehemiah and George Champion. The smartly finished business premises at no.69 Old Market (chapter 6; *see* Figs 6.37d and 6.42) had earlier in 1746 been the house of the merchant Samuel Rich. These three houses can be seen as those of merchants who had made a conscious decision to remain physically close to the area in which their business interests were located. Around them teemed the life of the busy working street. In 1775 houses to the east were occupied by a tin-plate worker, cooper, baker, two maltsters, silk-dyer, book-keeper and wheelwright, and those to the west by a victualler, attorney-at-law, leather-dresser and breeches maker, carpenter and carrier.

Doubtless because of the need to satisfy demand from the swelling ranks of Bristol's middling sort, the majority of the new developments in the period 1673–1775 created districts populated by a mix of prosperous tradesmen and professional people. Typical were the developments of the Bishop and Dean and Chapter (College Street, Trinity Street, Culver Street and Wells Street), and the new streets of Kingsdown. Sketchley's entries for College Street in 1775 recorded a variety of occupations: grocer, organ builder, stay maker, timber-merchant, merchant, carpenter, cabinet maker and baker. These were entrepreneurial households plying a variety of trades or professions, but seeking to live in modern houses in fashionable quarters of the city.

Some new developments were much more mixed, and not cheek by jowl with the residences of the urban elite. The houses in Great Gardens were by the middle of the 18th century occupied by a mix of skilled artisans and minor professional people. In 1750 the properties at the south-west corner of Tower Street and Avon Street were occupied by an accountant, a chandler, a cooper, two glassmen, a tidewaiter (customs officer) and a tobacconist.[43] A similar mix was evident in Sketchley's directory of 1775, and in the list of inhabitants' names and occupations preserved in the Quarter Sessions Records relating to the new drainage scheme.

The latter is of especial interest in providing the first glimpse of an enclave occupied by the labouring classes. Jones's Court, on the south side of Avon Street, was one of the many small courts by then already built behind the principal street frontages. Here the inhabitants were principally factory workers or engaged upon piecework, in the manufacture of clothes, furniture, pins, pottery and slippers.[44]

Alongside the new developments of the 18th century, the survival of earlier houses in other streets was an indicator of districts that had become less fashionable in which to live. Examples include notably Lewin's Mead and Old Market.[45] The former had been important as a bypass around the Castle, but with its demolition this was no longer so. Castle Street now offered a more convenient route across the city from east to west and, possibly for this reason, there was now less incentive to invest in new building in Lewin's Mead. The old buildings therefore remained, although large houses were subdivided and the social tone declined: this was no longer a desirable address.

## Middling Houses

It has been noted above that the one-room deep house had became a less attractive housing option by the end of the 18th century; increasingly, many households preferred to live in two-room deep houses, providing double that level of accommodation. In the 18th century many hundreds of houses of this type were built within the numerous new developments beyond the limits of the medieval city, so that by 1775 a wide social spectrum of the city lived in houses of two-room plan. The lowest end of this spectrum was readily evident at nos.110–11 Temple Street and nos.23–33 Ellbroad Street. Both were among the smallest two-room deep houses built in the 18th century and, being situated close to glass works, potteries and tanneries, were within what would have been considered by then to be noxious neighbourhoods. These were the homes of the relatively poor, some of them possibly wage earners in nearby industrial premises.

## The Largest Houses

One great change by 1775 was that whereas in 1673 very few households inhabited houses of three or more rooms on four or more floors, a significant number now did so (Fig 11.28).

*Fig 11.27 (opposite) Distribution of one-room plan houses across the city by the early 18th century; churches shown in purple to aid location (RHL, PEC).*

They constituted an urban elite whose lives were in this context much more distant from those of the urban poor, and whose houses were increasingly distinctive in their debt to architectural knowledge and in their outward display.

The city's first residential squares had been built in the 1700s. Queen Square was developed on land to the south of King Street in 'the Marsh', by the late 17th century an area marked out with tree-lined avenues and bordering upon the houses of Prince Street and the quays. St James's Square was set out on the opposite side of the city, in 'Hobson's Garden' to the south of the road to Thornbury. The 64 or more houses of Queen Square were mostly inhabited by 1711, the occupants of the largest houses including merchants, ship-owners and two former mayors, Abraham Elton and George Stephens.[46] In St James's Square the 16 new houses completed between 1705 and 1715 were first occupied by prosperous households drawn mainly from St James's parish.[47]

The construction of these two squares significantly changed the architectural and social topography of the city. Some 80 new residential houses had been built, enabling an equivalent number of wealthy or prosperous households to relocate themselves in two new neighbourhoods close to, but distinct from, the rest of the city. The geographical separation of the squares from the adjacent streets was emphasised by the form of the square itself. Houses looked inwards to the square and one another rather than to the streets and houses of other parts of the city; the rear boundary walls of the individual houses together formed a continuous boundary or envelope, emphasising the separateness of the square from its neighbours. Standing within the square, citizens were from the 1710s totally surrounded by a social environment uniformly new and consisting of the wealthiest households.

In 1775 James Sketchley noted no.16 (then no.15) Queen Square as the residence of Michael Miller esq. Six years later Miller became one of the few mayors of the city to die while in office, the probate inventory made after his death

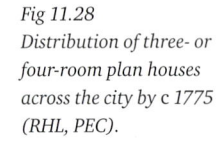

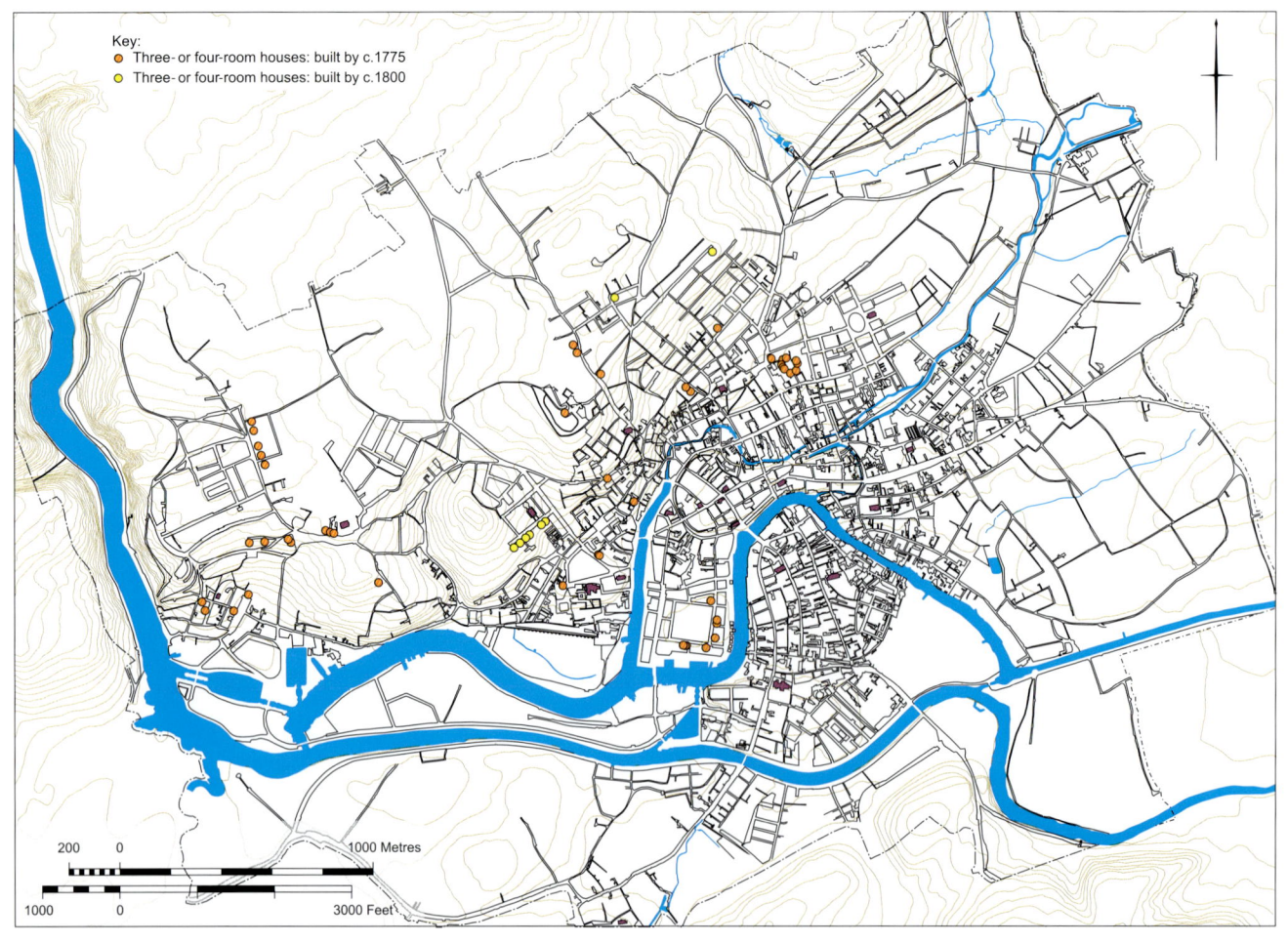

*Fig 11.28 Distribution of three- or four-room plan houses across the city by c 1775 (RHL, PEC).*

giving an unusually detailed insight into the scale of accommodation now available to one of the wealthiest members of the city's ruling elite.[48]

Miller's house had been built more than half a century before and had first been occupied in 1711 by Abraham Elton (son of Sir Abraham, mayor in 1719); Elton himself became mayor in 1742 – and it remained his home until 1747. The plan of 1781 must have been little changed from that when built for Abraham Elton, echoing that of the adjacent house (no.14), recorded in 1795, and that of no.22. The ground floor of Miller's house provided three parlours, 'back', 'fore' and 'little' respectively, together with the entrance and stairs hall, an arrangement that fits exactly the plan of the adjacent no.14 (*see* Fig 8.89). This was a house providing five floors of accommodation, with the equivalent of at least four rooms on each (Appendix 2).

During the 1720s and 1730s several large houses built on slightly narrower plots were likewise first occupied by some of the wealthiest citizens. In Orchard Street John Becher, mayor in 1721 and master of the Society of Merchant Venturers in 1722, was the first occupant of no.28, a house more grand and ornate than others in the same street and the only one to be provided with a back stairs (*see* Figs 8.68 and 10.16). In Prince Street nos.50 and 54 in the same street, built by Robert Yate in the 1730s, on either side of the larger no.52 already mentioned (chapter 8), were of similar size; their first occupants were prominent members of the merchant elite.[49]

There are many more examples. In St James's Barton, no.12 was built on a similar scale *c* 1728.[50] In Clifton a series of similar sized houses, all detached and including Rodney Lodge and Mortimer House, was built *c* 1750 in the development of Hollylands, in what is now Clifton Down Road. In the ensuing decades several of the plots being developed in Kingsdown Parade and Great George Street were filled with houses of a similar size (Fig 11.28). Close to Stokes Croft, no.20 St James's Barton, the home of Sir Isaac Abraham Elton, was by then one of the largest houses in the city (Fig 11.29).[51]

Almost all of these large houses remained the dwellings of some of the wealthiest inhabitants of the city until the end of the century. In 1775 the inhabitants of Queen Square included upwards of 20 persons styled as merchant, among them Miller and Henry Bright, a later owner of no.29 who became mayor in 1771.[52] In Lower Maudlin Street in 1775 Jeremiah Ames, sugar maker and alderman, now lived in John Salmon's house at no.17, while no.16 was now the home of the merchant Thomas Pierce. As respectively the residences of Charles and Joseph Harford, no.1 Dighton Street and the nearby no.12 St James's Barton in 1775 encapsulated the close links and networks of merchant families. Most of the large houses in Prince Street similarly remained the homes of leading merchant families. Prominent in the occupancy of these larger houses were members of the Elton family – not only in Queen Square, but also at no.30 College Green, at no.20

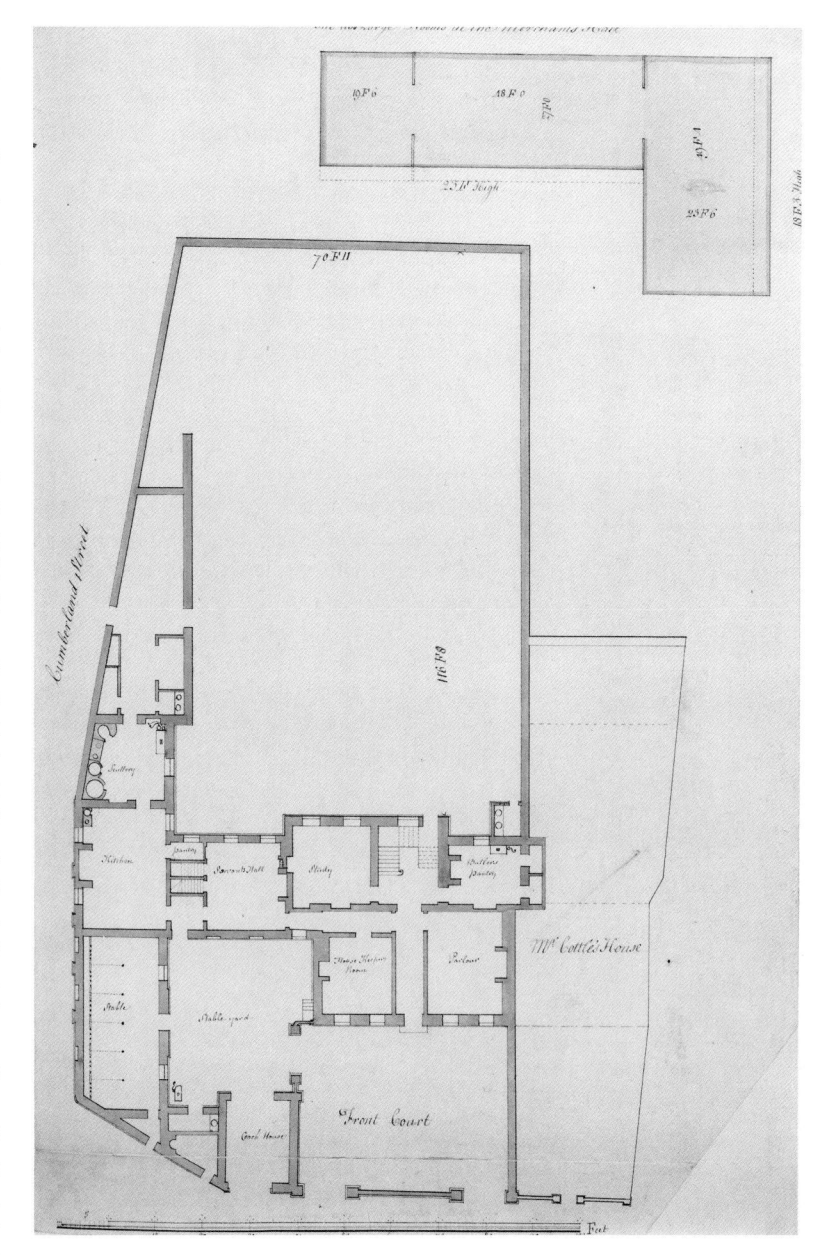

*Fig 11.29*
*No.20 St James's Barton, the home of Sir Isaac Abraham Elton, mayor in 1778, plan of c 1742 (BRO 04479(2) fol 6).*

St James's Barton and at Mortimer House in Clifton Down Road.

It would be incorrect, however, to assume that there was an exact relationship between the status of a household and the size of the house in which it dwelt. In Queen Square nos.36–8 were a row of three wider houses, each occupied by sea captains in the 1710s and 20s.[53] Equally a number of smaller, two-room deep houses can be identified as the homes of persons of considerable wealth and status.

## The Debt to Architectural Knowledge

By 1775 the very wealthy, scattered across the city, had long had access to an architectural awareness that extended beyond Bristol to the metropolis. In the first decades of the 18th century the unknown compiler or architect of many of the designs in *The Kingsweston Book of Drawings* was evidently in the service of Alderman Robert Yate, responsible for the design and building of a row of three new houses in Prince Street and offering advice on how the Red Lodge might be rebuilt.[54] This same architect was certainly concerned with the building of a new house for a member of the Fane family at Henbury. He may also have been responsible for the design of the rebuilt Lunsford House immediately opposite the Red Lodge, the design of which closely matches elements in one of the drawings (*see* Fig 9.71b). A feature of the design of Lunsford House was the separation of the main stairs from the back stairs to the servants' rooms in the attic (Fig 10.9). This was a device used also at Mortimer House and Clifton Wood House in Clifton and at no.16 Lower Maudlin Street, all houses possibly by the same architect.

The unknown compiler certainly held an admiration for the work of Sir John Vanbrugh, so much so that *The Kingsweston Book of Drawings* was once erroneously believed to be the work of Vanbrugh himself. Sir Edward Southwell's employment of Vanbrugh as the architect of Kingsweston House on the west side of the city was another example of the architectural awareness of the Bristol mercantile community. So was the building of Bishopsworth House, a suburban villa or garden house on the south side of the city and closely modelled on the design of Kingsweston House (Fig 11.30).

Most notably in this context, the linen draper Paul Fisher had the knowledge and the funds to employ the prestigious architect Isaac Ware in building Clifton Hill House in the 1740s. In 1756 Ware published *A Complete Body of Architecture*, the first detailed architectural encyclopedia aimed at an English readership and one in which he was sufficiently proud to include Fisher's new villa (*see* Figs 8.90, 9.87 and 10.25).[55] The building of the new villa at Royal Fort in the 1760s showed a similar architectural awareness that extended beyond the merely provincial; Thomas Tyndall's taste and fortunes enabled him to employ James Bridges as his architect and to build the house described by Timothy Mowl as 'arguably as 'arguably the most complete and enchanting Rococo house in Britain'.[56] Houses such as those built for Fisher and Tyndall were, however, exceptional.

### 'Nothing succeeds like excess'

In *c* 1660 at least 30 prosperous citizens, possibly considerably more, had kept a garden house or second residence on the periphery of the city. By *c* 1800 this was no longer so. Notwithstanding some merchants having kept such a second residence until well towards the end of the century, by *c* 1800 what had been an important element of elite lifestyle during the 16th and

*Fig 11.30 Bishopsworth House, photograph of 2012 (English Heritage DP 146938).*

17th centuries was no longer much in evidence. A wealthy citizen wishing to enjoy something of the country air could now live in a larger suburban villa (*see* Fig 9.3). Meanwhile, in streets such as Ashley Road and Kingsdown Parade, whole rows of garden houses were increasingly also for the middle classes.

The increasing exclusivity of the lodge and the larger suburban villa in the 18th century was apparent in both the excesses and the wider awareness of national developments that only a few individuals were able to afford.[57] Joseph Beck's lodge at Frenchay Manor was excessive both in its use of Classical ornament and, along with Easton Manor, in the space given internally to the entrance hall. The mid-century Gothick and black slag excesses of Quaker industrialists, such as William Reeve at Arnos Vale with its villa, castle and bath house (Fig 11.31), Thomas Goldney at Goldney House with its grotto, orangery, canal and water pump tower (Figs 11.32a and 11.32b; *see* Figs 9.58 and 10.41) and the merchant Thomas Farr in building his lodge at Blaise Castle (Fig 11.33), represented conspicuous consumption on a level that few citizens could afford. Both Reeve and Farr became bankrupt. Lodges such as Blaise Castle were not only now exceptional and sufficiently costly to help bankrupt their owners; they also invited ridicule from none other than Jane Austen (in *Northanger Abbey*, 1804):

> "'Blaise Castle!' cried Catherine.
> "What is that?"
> "The finest place in England; worth going fifty miles at any time to see."
> "What! Is it really a castle – an old castle?"
> "The oldest in the kingdom.'" [58]

*Fig 11.31*
Arnos Vale:
a) the house, photograph of 1949 (NMR AA49/04980);
b) the Black Castle, photograph of 1947 (NMR AA47/04224).

# THE TOWN HOUSE IN MEDIEVAL AND EARLY MODERN BRISTOL

*Fig 11.32
Goldney House, Clifton:
a) the grotto, photograph of 2003
(NMR AA042219);
b) the water pump tower, photograph of 2011
(English Heritage DP 141406).*

*Fig 11.33
Blaise Castle, watercolour by J M Field, 1842
(BRSMG).*

354

By the 1720s the wealthiest citizens could enjoy a house which combined the latest fashions with comfort, convenience and gentility. In Prince Street one of the building sites newly leased in 1725 was taken by Robert Yate, the owner and inhabitant of the Red Lodge. Yate's adviser on building matters, 'the unknown compiler', was responsible for an 'Explanation of the Draughts of a House Proposed for a Merchant' (chapter 10). It provides a valuable and almost unique insight from the documentary sources into an architect's ideas on how best to provide his client with a house that embodied contemporary best practice, to a design and finish that only the wealthy could afford.[59] Surviving and recorded houses in the same street provide from the material evidence further insights into the planning and finish of these houses (chapters 8 and 10).

Isaac Ware wrote that 'every thing in a great house should have an air of grandeur'.[60] The entrance hall and stairs, framed recesses, chimneypieces and all manner of panelling and cornicing provided such grandeur, and marked out the houses of the wealthy and powerful both in the central areas and in the suburbs. The interiors of the churches were similarly furnished (Fig 11.34) and to many worshippers would, as in 18th-century Virginia, have marked these out as the spaces of the gentry and wealthy, raising the question 'whose house was it?'[61]

On the opposite side of the city to Prince Street was the populous district described by Defoe and developed by Nathaniel Wade (chapters 3 and 8). Here many of the houses built in the early 18th century made fewer concessions to concerns such as those expressed by Yate's architect. Most of the houses built in new thoroughfares such as New Street and Wade Street consisted of one room on each floor. Planning to provide privacy or a separation between business and the domestic world was of little concern to the builders of these houses.

## The Changing City

The data embedded in Sketchley's directory has been combined with that from contemporary local tax returns to map the social geography of the city in the 1770s (Fig 11.35). From this map Baigent has concluded that the 18th century was 'a critical period in the move to a *Gesellschaft* or class society', a move away from a *Gemeinschaft* or community-based society.[62] The architectural evidence, however, provides some qualifications to these conclusions:

*Fig 11.34*
*'Whose house was it?' The screen in the south aisle of Temple Church (Dening 1923, Pl XLVII) might have reminded some of Thomas Goldney's mahogany parlour (see Fig.10.41).*

Firstly, a move of focus away from community to individual can be seen as beginning in the 15th and 16th centuries, with a wider architectural awareness initially evident in Canynges' new tower and in personalised marks of ownership first appearing in the 1540s.

Secondly, the close juxtaposition of rich and poor that characterised the medieval town was still evident in the late 18th century, most notably on the east side of the city, in the parishes of St James and St Philip and St Jacob.

Thirdly, the emergence of distinct residential zones had begun not in the 18th century, but at a much earlier date. From at least the 15th century onwards the residences of the urban elite were concentrated in the parish of St Werburgh, and especially in Small Street. In the 17th century the laying out of new streets in the demolished Castle and on the edge of the Marsh, and the development of the Little Park as an estate of garden houses, immediately created new distinct residential areas.

The 18th century was certainly a critical period, however, as the construction of new streets and suburbs created a city with much more distinct residential zones. The strength of the architectural evidence for other periods is reinforced by it being in accord, though with some qualifications, with the conclusions reached by Baigent from matching Sketchley's directory of 1775 against contemporary tax returns, from which four distinct areas of the city could be recognised.[63] The first was the group of central commercial parishes with 'high numbers of professional men, distributors and those in high and middle status trades in general'. Here a small number of new houses of the 18th century provided residences for such people (Fig 11.35). 'Secondly, there were the artisan parishes which were largely on the periphery of the city, especially on the unfashionable southern and eastern sides' – although here the architectural evidence can qualify the notion that these were 'unfashionable' areas, notably close to the church of St Mary Redcliff where Colston Parade, Redcliff Parade, Colston Street and Langton Street were all built as genteel fashionable streets (Fig 11.35). A third distinct area encompassed 'the suburban residential parishes on the fashionable northern and western sides of the city', Clifton and areas within the parishes of St Augustine and St Michael and the outparish of St James. The analysis of directory and tax returns also offered some insights into the juxtaposition of rich and poor: 'the rich lived on the main thoroughfares and the poor in the back houses, courts, alleys and ditches immediately adjacent to them'.[64]

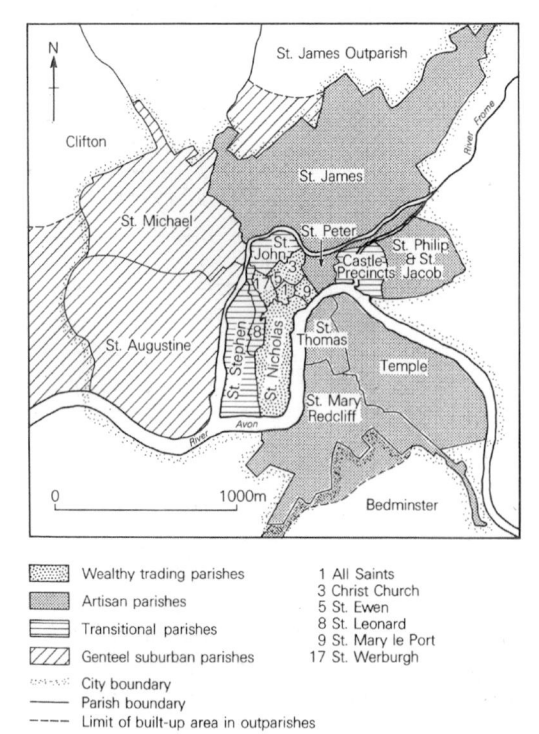

The most critical period, however, was the 17th century, within the centuries during which Sacks saw Bristol emerge as a centre of early modern capitalism. It was in this period, and particularly during the 1650s and 1660s, that the first new streets to be laid out since the 13th century were developed and that the number of second and suburban residences was greatly increased, creating new residential zones distinguished by the status and wealth of their occupants. The origins of some of this newly acquired wealth will be further examined in the next chapter.

*Fig 11.35*
*The social geography of the city in the 1770s (Baigent 1988, Fig 119).*

# 12

# Bristol and the Atlantic World

The passage of time and the ever-changing global economy have obscured and removed the links between Bristol and the Caribbean. During the later 17th and 18th centuries, however, it was these links, centred on the trade in slaves and slave-produced goods, that fuelled the city's growth and brought prosperity to virtually every level of society in Bristol. Madge Dresser's recent study *Slavery Obscured* has underlined many of the connections often overlooked by both contemporaries and historians, focusing especially on the lives of the urban elite, while this author's archaeological research in the Caribbean has highlighted some of the connections between Bristol property developers of the middling sort (chapter 11) such as Llewellin Evans (below) and the Caribbean trade that might otherwise be unknown.[1] These various connections turn our attention to two areas: the extent to which the prosperity and housing stock of Bristol were built upon the profits of the Atlantic trade in slaves and slave-related goods, and the degree to which new buildings on the other side of the Atlantic were influenced by Bristol practice.

## Bristol's Trading Links with America and the Caribbean

Before the 1640s the overseas trade of Bristol was predominantly with Ireland, France and the Iberian peninsula. The trade with the Americas had its origins in the 15th century, with Bristol mariners and merchants ever more present in the western seas (chapter 1). However, McGrath noted that 'although the merchants must be given credit for their encouragement of colonisation in America and Newfoundland, and for their financing Captain James's expedition, the amount of capital they actually invested was small'.

The trade with the Americas grew considerably from the 1650s onwards, as revealed in the shipping figures. Between 1658 and 1660 it was one-seventh of Bristol's total trade, but by 1685–7 it had become one-quarter. This trade was also more important than these figures alone might suggest, because the ships used were bigger and the commodities – tobacco and, increasingly, sugar – were far more valuable than many other traded goods. Also of significance was the fact that the trade consisted of exports as well as of the new imported exotic goods. Exports included iron implements and machinery, copper vessels and glass – all products of industries in which Bristol merchants were investors.[2] Increasingly these would include goods shipped down the Severn to Bristol, the region around Ironbridge being the most famous of the new industrial centres of the Midlands.

The city's merchants and shipowners became deeply involved in the shipment of slaves from Africa following the ending of the London-based Royal African Company's monopoly in 1698.[3] Bristol's industry developed to exploit both these new markets and the new sources of supply. On the south side of the city, in the parishes of Temple and Redcliff, the glass industry had become especially important by the 1740s. Defoe in the 1710s observed in his *A Tour through the Whole Island of Great Britain* that glass bottles were used for the export of beer, cider and wine to the West Indies and for the export of brandy to Africa, all in greater quantities from Bristol than from London.

## Built upon the Profits of the Atlantic Slave Trade

An excavation site in Main Street in Charlestown on the island of Nevis in the Eastern Caribbean was a waterfront plot, on the opposite side of the

Atlantic to its counterparts fronting the quays of Bristol. The archaeology had many resonances of Bristol – in the glass, the ceramics and the clay pipes. Among the last was a pipe stem with the initials 'L E'; similar stems have been found in the abandoned town of Jamestown, further north on Nevis. 'L E' are the initials of Llewellin Evans, well documented as active in clay pipe manufacture until his death in Bristol in 1688.[4] The archaeological evidence tells us that Evans's commercial ventures encompassed trade with the Caribbean and especially with Nevis, since the mid-17th century an island heavily dependent on the production of sugar using African slave labour.[5]

Evans was an investor and developer of property in Bristol during the 1680s. His speculative ventures included the redevelopment of nos.38–41 Old Market (see Figs 3.17, 6.24–5), now part of a row of late 17th-century houses, restored c 1980. Evans was responsible for the rebuilding of nos.38 and 39 and nos.40 and 41. Two adjacent pairs of houses, they were built with economy and very much in the medieval style, gable-end on to the street with timber-framed facades and overhanging jetties at the first floors. The notion that Bristol's links with slavery might only be explored through the grandest merchant houses might have led to these more modest houses being overlooked, but for the clay pipe stems from Nevis: this insight makes it clear that the links were pervasive.

The association between new housing developments in Bristol and the Atlantic trade in slaves and goods related to slavery, notably sugar, tobacco, coffee and chocolate, can be suggested from as early as the mid-17th century. The timing of new housing developments may be linked in a general way with the growing Caribbean trade. In the 1650s and 1660s the first new streets in Bristol since the 13th century were laid out and developed: Castle Street, Castle Green and King Street were all commenced at this time. This was precisely the same period in which the economy of the English Caribbean islands switched to a dramatically profitable dependence on the cultivation of sugar, highly dependent upon slave labour.[6]

Quite when the construction of new housing can be traced back to the profits of trading in slaves and associated goods is not clear. The example of Llewellin Evans is somewhat tenuous in this connection. Much more evident is the case of Edmund Saunders, one of the principal developers of Guinea Street in the parish of St Mary Redcliff. Guinea Street was laid out in the 1700s, its very name a reflection of the concerns of Bristol merchants for the African Guinea coast. Saunders was a slave-ship captain and agent for the sale of slaves. When listed for bankruptcy proceedings in 1740, his goods emphasised his close involvement in the specifically African trade.[7] Of equal significance for assessing Saunders' close association with this part of the Atlantic trade was the design of his own new house in the same street, built c 1718. Saunders' wealth had enabled him to combine what had probably been intended as three separate plots into a single, luxuriously appointed dwelling (see Fig 8.52).[8]

At first sight the building of residential streets and squares such as Prince Street and Queen Square in the first decades of the 18th century might appear to provide evidence of the connection between the slave trade and new house construction, especially as the houses here often included warehouses as part of the plot. However, such a connection is by no means certain. The builders or developers of the plots around the square are best identified through the building leases granted by the City Corporation. The initial occupants of the houses in Queen Square can be identified by the rates paid by them to the two parishes of St Nicholas and St Stephen. Analysis of these shows that only a small percentage of the houses in Queen Square were probably first built or occupied on the profits of the slave and associated trades.[9] Only later in the century could the occupants of many of the houses be shown to have connections with the trade in slaves and related goods.[10]

A much more direct relationship between the individuals involved in the slave trade and investment in property emerges in the construction of new housing on and close to St Michael's Hill. Old Park Hill was developed as a row of 10 houses from 1714 onwards; all were completed and occupied by 1722 (Fig 12.1). The first occupants included John Brickdale, a shipowner, responsible for shipping 220 slaves in 1728, and Mrs Kennah, widow of a Captain William Kennah; he had shipped over 1,300 by 1719. There was also Captain Skinner, who had shipped 1,400 slaves by 1727, and Captain Barry, responsible for over 1,200 by 1729. The ships' captains occupying the remaining houses in the row were similarly involved in the slave trade; only two houses in the row were not so occupied.

Nearby, no.65 St Michael's Hill was built

*Fig 12.1*
*Nos.11–21 Old Park Hill, shown in a photograph of 1952. By c 1730 the individuals living in nos.11–29 Old Park Hill had been directly concerned with the shipment to the Americas of upwards of 15,000 African slaves (NMR BB77/06703). See Fig 10.55 for a plan of the entire row.*

c 1725 by Captain Joseph Barnes, as one of two houses which completed a row of six dwellings in total. There is no evidence that Barnes himself was involved in the Atlantic trade, but his two neighbours in the houses higher up the hill were both directly concerned: Captain John Constant had made three slave trade voyages and Captain Francis Pitts seven. The house below Barnes's was occupied by a widow, Mrs Hollister. Previously, by 1716, her husband Lawrence Hollister had been involved in nine slave voyages.[11]

In and around St Michael's Hill, therefore, we see a direct correlation between the wealth generated by the slave trade and the occupancy of new houses in Bristol. By c 1730 the individuals living in Old Park Hill had been directly concerned with the shipment of upwards of 15,000 slaves – this could well have been called Slavers' Row.[12]

The connection between the slave trade and housing continued throughout the 18th century.

Orchard Street, much closer to the quaysides, had a heavy bias towards shipping and trade among its first residents. In 1731 over half the new residents were sea captains or merchants.[13]

Dresser has shown how by 1775, and as early as the 1740s, the residents of Queen Square were overwhelmingly connected with the Atlantic trade and the trade in slaves in particular. By c 1770 Clifton was similarly 'awash with slave-based wealth'.[14] To the houses cited by Dresser can be added Mortimer House (chapters 8 and 10), yet another residence of the Elton family (Fig 12.2). Along the hillside above the city, much of the development of Kingsdown was also probably linked to slavery-related wealth – one major street in this development was named appropriately Jamaica Street. Dresser has shown also how much of the building development of the 1790s in Clifton and elsewhere was closely related to the Africa/Atlantic- and slave-related trade. James Lockier,

## THE TOWN HOUSE IN MEDIEVAL AND EARLY MODERN BRISTOL

*Fig 12.2*
*Map of Clifton showing properties associated with slavery-based wealth (RHL, PEC, based on Ashmead and Plumley 1828; Dresser 2001, 105–9).*

*Residences of merchants and others with Atlantic trade interests:*
1. Richard Farr – Clifton Wood House
2. Paul Fisher – Clifton Hill House
3. Isaac Elton – Mortimer House
4. Thomas Daniel – Duncan House
5. John Freeman – Rodney Lodge and manor of Clifton
6. Henry Hobhouse – Cornwallis House
7. Josias Jackson – St Vincent's Rocks
8. Thomas Pedler – Beaufort House
9. Samuel Worrall – Church House, later Bishop's House

*Developed by merchants with Atlantic trade interests:*
10. Royal York Crescent

*West Indian families with memorials in Clifton churchyard:*
11. Alleyne (Barbados)
12. Bayly (Jamaica)
13. Mills (St Kitts and Nevis)

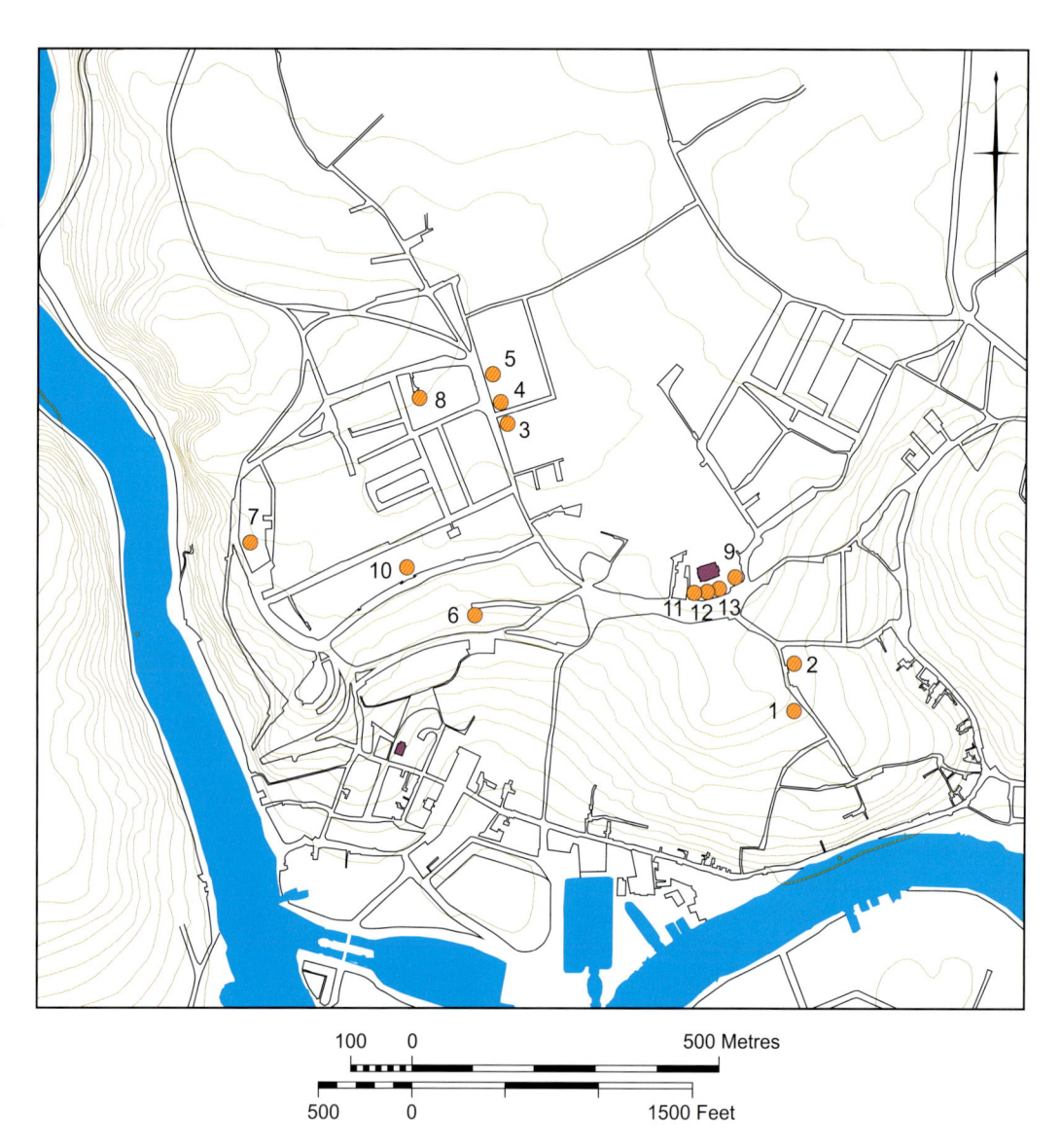

an upholsterer and financier much involved in the development of Kingsdown Parade, Berkeley and Portland Squares on the north and east sides of the city, had interests in the mahogany, Africa and wider Atlantic trades.[15] The building of Royal York Crescent was financed by six merchants, most of whom were linked to the Atlantic trade. In the countryside around Bristol, many new or rebuilt houses had similar links – although, as has been shown, some were initially the second residences of wealthy citizens, not the houses of 'merchants grown rich' who 'moved out to country houses as the eighteenth century wore on'.[16] Oldbury Court and Stoke Bishop House, for instance, were the second residences respectively of Robert Winstone (the builder of the Dutch House at no.1 High Street) and Sir Robert Cann.

### Bristol Practice and New Building in the Americas

The pipe maker Llewellin Evans was not the only property developer in 17th-century Bristol who can be linked with the Caribbean trade. In June 1654, 30 years earlier, the carpenter Thomas Wickham had sent three of his men to Nevis to work as carpenters for John Knight, a planter and a member of a Bristol family deeply involved in sugar production on both sides of the Atlantic.[17] Knight's Nevis plantation was probably that known as Jennings Range, named after the Jennings family with whom the Knights were closely associated.[18] If its 17th-century timber buildings had survived, there might have been preserved for comparative study some evidence of 17th-century Bristol carpentry, for

Wickham's own housebuilding activities in Bristol can be viewed alongside those of Llewellin Evans. One of Wickham's houses survives (*see* Fig 7.35), in a street the wealth of which has indeed been associated with the Caribbean trade.[19] This house is the oldest one in King Street, nos.33–4 on the north side, its association with trade reinforced by its combining domestic quarters and warehousing on a single plot (chapter 7).

The place of Bristol in the 17th- and 18th-century Atlantic worlds is, however, more evident in the general characteristics of urban housing than in the specific details of carpentry and other elements of building. Like Deptford, downstream from London on the Thames, Bristol was a place where builders provided new dwellings meeting 'fresh demands for comfort, privacy, display and fashionability' that were common to seaports and cities around the Atlantic rim.[20]

## Architectural Identity on the 18th-century Atlantic Rim

Recent studies have recognised the similarities between urban houses in many of the different cities and seaports on both sides of the Atlantic in the 18th century.[21] Sea captains voyaging to the east coast of English North America would have seen much to remind them of the urban domestic scene in Bristol, London and other English seaports. The clapboard finish of houses in Southwark and other suburbs of London would have been called to mind travelling the streets of many New England seaports – to the present-day reader these might include such towns as Salem and Boston in Massachusetts and Portsmouth in New Hampshire. The brick exteriors of London and Bristol terraced houses would have been remembered as a mark of wealth while walking the similar streets of Boston, Charleston, Newburyport or Philadelphia. House plans too would often have been familiar, whether those of one-room plan artisan houses or two-room deep houses for the middling sort. Within the latter there would have been the distinction familiar in Bristol between houses with the stairs placed centrally and those with the stairs alongside the rear room. 'Attic rooms … plainly plastered and likely served as servants' quarters' were 'an allocation of household space common to elite late 18th-century town houses around the North Atlantic rim'.[22]

In the detail of these house plans it would, however, have been evident to contemporaries that, depending on where you were, North American practice was of London and south-east England or of Bristol and south-west England. The two-room deep house of 17th-century London and towns in south-east England such as Deptford, Canterbury and Portsmouth typically had a central chimneystack, separating the front and rear rooms and abutted by the stairs. Early 17th-century houses in Jamestown, Virginia and later houses in Norfolk, Virginia and Portsmouth, New Hampshire were of his plan.[23]

In the equivalent house in Bristol, two chimneystacks were placed against the side wall, with the section of the house containing the stairs separating the front and rear rooms, sometimes with a detached kitchen to the rear of the main house. Houses of similar plan were to be found in other towns in southwest England, including Plymouth, Totnes, Dartmouth, Exeter and Taunton; they were also evident in London and Dublin.[24] Houses of the 17th century and later in Charleston, South Carolina (above), Baltimore, Portsmouth (New Hampshire) and Philadelphia were all of this plan, possibly echoing artisan and mercantile links with south-west England.[25] In Charleston some houses were possibly shophouses, with an unheated front room, as in those in Bristol.[26] In looking at Charleston, Herman also noted the ubiquity on the Atlantic rim of the placement of kitchens and servants' quarters to the rear of the main house, a feature encountered both there, in Bristol and in other provincial English seaports, such as the tobacco port of Whitehaven in the north-west.[27]

In the Caribbean such observations could not be made so readily, for houses were built without chimneystacks – not necessary in the year-round warm, tropical climate. One of the best recorded urban rows is in Lime Street, Port Royal in Jamaica.[28] These would have been familiar to Bristol or London mariners and merchants simply as two-room deep houses.

The interior finish of these urban houses around the Atlantic rim would have been immediately recognisable to Bristol sea captains and merchants visiting London or the east coast of America. In the early 18th century, rooms were fully panelled; later in the century full-height panelling was confined to hearth walls and other panelling rose generally only to dado height. The Classical trim or architrave to cornices, doorcases and window surrounds was ubiquitous, and carved Classical pilasters were used in America as in Bristol, when it was intended to make a show. The placement and display of the stairs was another unifying architectural feature: houses in the American colonies show the same range of plans, some having central stairs, some stairs to the rear alongside a back room and visible from the entry.[29] In the internal arrangements for the household the organisation of the servants' quarters would have been similarly familiar. Working areas such as the kitchen were located in the basement, and sometimes a back stairs led direct to the servants' rooms in the attic. Similarities such as these facilitated the intersection of 'social display and performance' with 'the trading world of wharf, countinghouse and merchant society', fitting 'into a larger Atlantic culture steeped in acquisition, display and exchange'.[30]

In the suburbs or on the periphery of these North American seaports, the scatter of smart suburban houses would also have been recognised by the Bristol merchant. Occasionally, as at Newburyport, Massachusetts, such houses would have been the second residences of citizens living in the centre of the town. In the 1690s the lifestyle of the wealthy merchant Daniel Pierce, with his town house close to the quays and his second residence (a smart, brick-built house with projecting porch and stairs turret) on the edge of the countryside, would have been perfectly familiar to any traveller from Bristol cognisant of the town and rural houses of men such as Sir Robert Cann and the brewer Andrew Hooke.[31]

The Penn family, who with other Bristol citizens founded Pennsylvania and the city of Philadelphia, lived a life that displayed many points of similarity to that of a Bristol merchant family. Thomas Penn's country house at Springettsbury on the west side of Philadelphia was intended to be 'a weekend and summer villa, embellished with pleasure gardens, wilderness groves and other amenities'.[32] It was one of a number of such houses on the fringes of the city.[33] Its setting and purpose as a place of retreat and recreation would have been familiar to Penn's father William, the founder of Pennsylvania. He had lived below the slope of St Michael's Hill in Bristol in the 1690s, probably in the garden house in Upper Maudlin Street that later became the Female Penitentiary (chapter 9).[34]

In the 17th and 18th centuries, keeping one house in the city or town and a second residence in the countryside, part of the culture of the Bristol elite, was possibly more widespread in North America than has been appreciated. In Surry County, Virginia, Bacon's Castle, built in the 17th century in the artisan mannerist style to a hall-parlour plan with projecting porch and stair turrets, and not dissimilar to Daniel Pierce's house at Newburyport, would have fitted perfectly as the country residence for a member of the urban elite of 17th-century Jamestown.[35]

In several of the islands of the Eastern Caribbean, recent research has revealed that a number of houses were built as lodges or villas by planters in the 18th century. One of the best documented houses, and one with a connection to Paul Fisher's house, is Olivees on St Kitts, on the hillside to the south of Basseterre. This was the house visited *c* 1775 by Janet Schaw, named by the editor or publishers of her journal as 'a lady of quality'. She described the house as being on a well-raised stone terrace, paved with marble, with spacious open galleries and verandas. The 'great hall' was a large, finely proportioned room which ran the entire length of the front; it had a handsome deep cornice and ample doors, both of dark mahogany and panelling of the same wood. This space constituted the great reception and dining room, the scene of lavish entertainment and hospitality. In addition the house had a drawing room and bedchambers finished and furnished in English style.[36]

This house survives today only as a roofless ruin. A drawing of 1970 (Fig 12.3) shows the house as roofed but evidently abandoned. Prominent, but not notably visible on this, are the stairs forming the exterior entrance. Survey of the ruin is more informative (Fig 12.4). The stairs rise in two flights on each side, originally with a metal balustrade, the sockets for which still remain. The colonnade along the front of the house was paved in white marble, as described by Miss Schaw, probably from the Mediterranean. A separate entrance hall to the rear was paved with limestone slabs similar to Portland stone, but shown from petrological analysis to be from the Poole Harbour region of Dorset.[37] The mahogany panelled hall described by Janet Schaw must have been placed over what is now a cellar open to the sky. One might have interpreted this house as being of two rooms in width, but for her assertion that the principal room extended the full width of the house.

*Fig 12.3*
*Olivees, St Kitts, drawing of 1970 showing the timber house before its demolition and removal*
*(St Christopher Heritage Society).*

*Fig 12.4*
*Olivees, St Kitts, survey of the ruins, 2009 (RHL).*

The documentation for this house extends beyond Miss Schaw's visit to reveal first that it was probably owned by a member of the Mills family, wealthy London merchants and plantation owners.[38] At the time of her visit, however, it was leased to her hosts Lady Isabella Erskine and William Leslie Hamilton. A second strand to the documentation is the existence of the plan of a very similar house built in England. This is Isaac Ware's depiction in 1768 of Clifton Hill House (chapter 11; *see* Fig 8.90), the house that he had recently designed for Paul Fisher, the Bristol merchant – drawing perhaps for the plan of the external stairs on Burlington's design for Chiswick House.[39] The similarities between Olivees and Clifton Hill House are several: most notably the design of the stairs, the arrangement of the four flights of steps and the arched entrance to the basement (*see* Figs 8.90 and 9.87), but also the dimensions of the ground floor and the provision of a hipped roof. The frontage of Olivees was clearly finished in shingles, perhaps a substitute for rusticated stonework. West Indian planters could also call upon pattern books and here, in one of the closest sets of similarities between a Bristol house and one in the West Indies, the design of Olivees must have been so engendered.

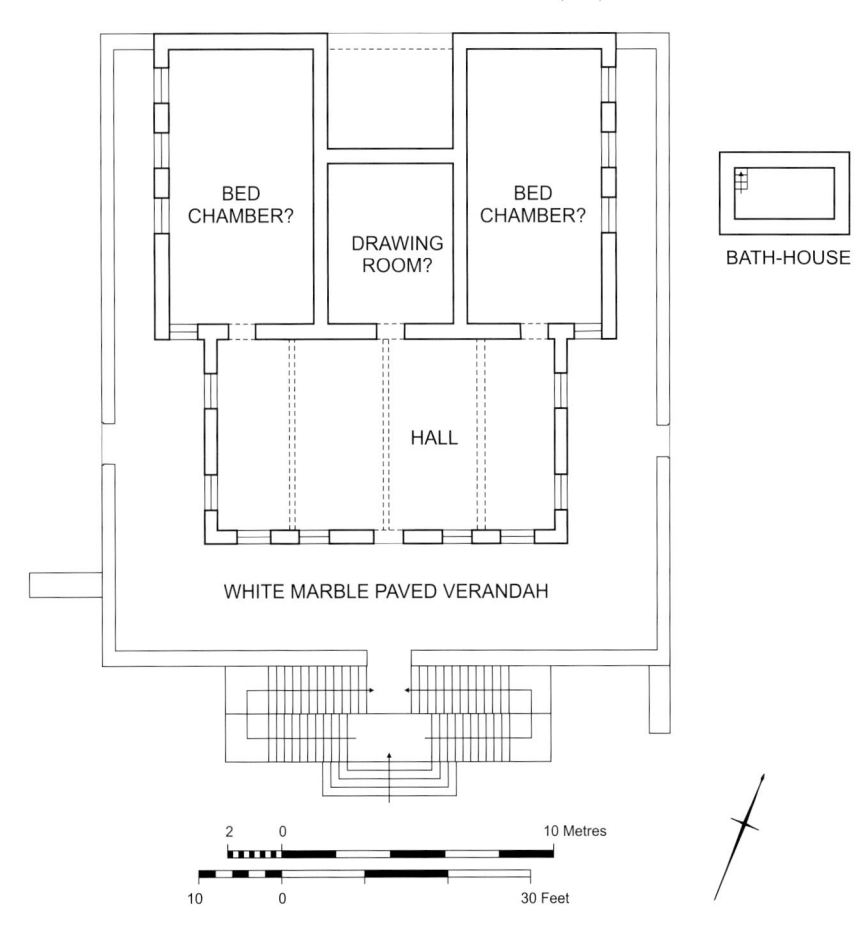

Also on the island of St Kitts, another house of the 18th century gave its name to the Lodge Plantation, a small, square, one-room plan house of emphatically Palladian design (Figs 12.5a and 12.5b). On the neighbouring island of Nevis a number of such houses were built, mostly on the hillsides overlooking the island capital of Charlestown (Fig 12.6).[40] Just as 'garden house' was an appropriate term for such houses on the hillside above Bristol in the 17th century, 'Paris's Garden' was a similarly apposite name for the mountain villa of the owner of a plantation on the edge of Charlestown in 1879.[41]

On Barbados two villa-like houses were sited inland from Speightstown or 'Little Bristol', indicating that the ownership of a second residence on the edge of town was as much a part of Barbados merchant culture as that of Nevis, Bristol or Philadelphia. The plantation house at Alleynedale, two miles from Speightstown in the north part of Barbados, was rebuilt in the later 17th century. The masonry walls of the new house were of coral limestone, with brick quoins to the windows and doorways, and curved gables in the artisan mannerist tradition. Traces of red paint on the coral limestone indicate that it was intended to make the house as a whole appear to be of brick. Almost all of the ground floor was given over to one large room, of which the main, and most of the subsidiary, moulded ceiling beams still survive. From a later drawing, and from survey data, it can be argued that the house was approximately of a cross-plan, with a projecting porch on the north and a wider projecting stairs on the south (Fig 12.7). The plan of Alleynedale, seemingly given over to entertainment, and its proximity when built in the 17th century to the nearby urban centre of Speightstown, indicates that this was possibly a residence secondary to the main concerns of its owner – who may have lived for the most part elsewhere, perhaps in Speightstown.

*Fig 12.5*
*The house at the Lodge Plantation, St Kitts –*
*a Palladian second residence in the Eastern Caribbean:*
*a) plan*
*(RHL, PEC);*
*b) photograph of 2004, the original lodge on the right hand side*
*(R Philpott).*

St Nicholas Abbey, in the north part of Barbados but closer to the Atlantic coast than Alleynedale, has often been claimed as the best preserved stone house from the 17th-century English Caribbean (Fig 12.8a). It was probably built by John Yeamans, a merchant with Bristol connections; he was briefly the owner of the house in the 1660s and early 1670s before moving on to play a major role in the foundation of South Carolina. Both Alleynedale Hall and St Nicholas Abbey were of a two-room, hall-parlour plan with a centrally placed stairs to the rear and a projecting porch at the front.

Possibly the ownership of the Yeamans family explains for the latter the choice of a plan familiar in 17th-century Bristol. Later similarities in the alterations to both Stoke Bishop House and St Nicholas Abbey may also be explained by identifying a further Bristol–Barbados connection. By the later 18th century St Nicholas Abbey was owned by the Cumberbatch family who, like the Yeamans,

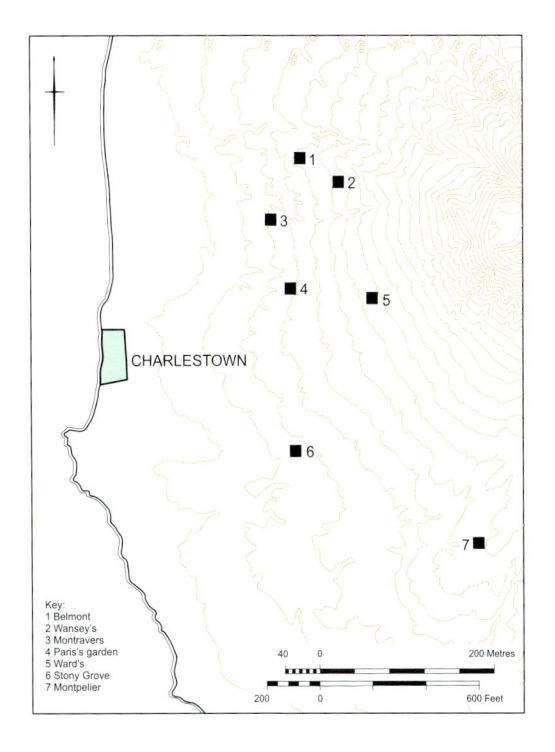

*Fig 12.6*
*Locations of garden houses or villas of the late 18th and early 19th centuries on the hillsides above Charlestown, the capital of Nevis (RHL, PEC).*

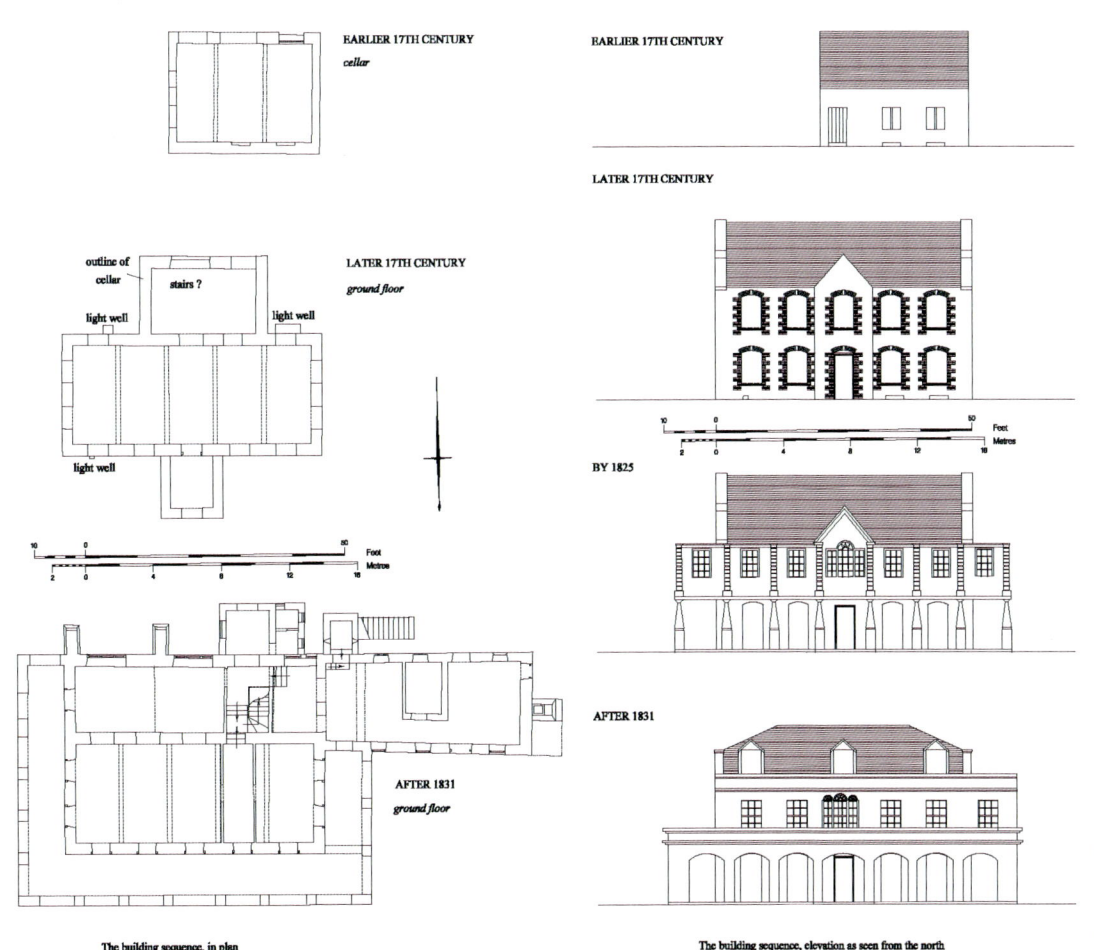

*Fig 12.7*
*The development of Alleynedale House, Barbados (Leech 2002).*

*Fig 12.8*
*Two similar houses with Bristol associations on opposite sides of the Atlantic:*
*a) St Nicholas Abbey, Barbados, photograph of 2008 (RHL);*
*b) Stoke Bishop House, a watercolour of 1791 by J M W Turner (Trinity Theological College).*

had Bristol connections.[42] The shaped gables of St Nicholas Abbey might, along with the insertion of a stairs with a chinois fretwork balustrade, be a modification of the later 18th century, in the rococo style much favoured in contemporary Bristol.[43] This style appears to have also been the inspiration for the modifications to Stoke Bishop House shown on Turner's watercolour of 1791 (Fig 12.8b).

The archaeology and form of the 17th-century house are largely hidden by render and plaster, but some similarities to Bristol architectural features are evident. The window openings are most likely to be similar to those recorded at Alleynedale Hall and in Speightstown, rectangular in stone walling edged with brick quoining (Figs 12.9a and 12.9b). In England this was a technique used most commonly in areas of rubble walling – notably in East Anglia, but also in Bristol, where openings of this construction survive on the former external wall of a manorial building in Clifton, now the Muset Restaurant in Clifton Road (Fig 12.9c).

## An Arena for Mercantile Discourse

By the late 18th century urban houses on both sides of the Atlantic shared many common features. For merchants and mariners crossing the Atlantic, the urban domestic interiors of the Atlantic rim offered a familiar arena that facilitated business and sociable discourse. Following the American Revolution, Elias Vanderhorst was appointed as Consul of the United States for the Port of Bristol in 1792. He settled in Bristol at no.37 Queen Square where, surrounded by the finish, furnishings and contents of his house and others of the square, he might well have been comforted and eased in his duties by recollections of similar environments, for business and pleasure, in the domestic and urban surroundings of his native South Carolina.[44] Vanderhorst, with his background in the plantations of South Carolina, would have been more aware than most of the square's inhabitants of this peculiar juxtaposition of gentility with slave-produced wealth, and the brutality that accompanied it.[45]

## High Water at Bristol Key

'High Water at Bristol Key', the inscription that appears on many Bristol long case clocks of the later 18th century (Fig 12.10), underlined the preoccupation of Bristol citizens, particularly merchants and shipowners, with shipping. Until the construction of the locked 'floating harbour' in c 1804–9,[46] ocean-going ships could only come up the Avon and the lowest reach of the Frome to tie up alongside the quaysides of Broad Quay, Narrow Quay and St Augustine's Back at high tide. High water was the critical time for seeing which ships and what cargoes had arrived on the quaysides. At low tide, just as in William Worcestre's day, great ships still lay 'in the wooze'.

The wealth invested in the construction of houses, in beauty and magnificence, in the acquisition of second residences (some of which became country seats), could be seen as a diversion away from the imperatives of

*Fig 12.9
Rectangular window openings in stone walling edged with brick quoining:
a) Alleynedale House, Barbados, photograph of 2008
(RHL);
b) house in Speightstown, Barbados, photograph of 2011
(Barry Jones);
c) The Muset Restaurant, no.14 Clifton Road, in the former external wall of a manorial building, photograph of 2012
(English Heritage DP 114708).*

*Fig 12.10
'High Water at Bristol Key', part of the face of a long case clock by Wasborough and Mailard, now in a house in Clifton, photograph of 2011
(English Heritage DP 141404).*

commerce – and as one reason, alongside the difficulties of access up the Bristol Channel and Avon Gorge, why Bristol was overtaken in importance by Liverpool from the late 18th century onwards. A more significant factor in Liverpool's ascendancy, however, was its proximity to the much richer, expanding industrial hinterland of the north-west.

Symbolically this change in Bristol's fortunes could be seen as having commenced with the construction of Queen Square, where merchants now looked inwards to a polite, genteel, exclusive space as well as outwards over their warehouses on to the river and commercial streets – the view that the earlier houses of merchants such as William Canynges, the Nortons, Robert Sturmy, the Aldworths and John Langton had enjoyed. The former mayor and draper George Stephens who, before his death *c* 1718/19 (Appendix 2), had moved from Bristol Bridge to live at no.22 Queen Square, might be seen as typifying this change.

The siting of many second residences and country houses can be taken, however, to reflect a continuing concern with commerce and shipping. In depicting Cann's house at Stoke Bishop, by then owned by Sir Thomas Cann, Johannes or Jan Kip took care to ensure that the view included the estuary of the Avon and ships progressing towards Bristol. Kip's views of this

*Fig 12.11*
*Stoke Bishop House: the principal viewpoint for the distant river and shipping was the battlemented platform above the main stairs, photograph of 1998 (NMR BB98/11795).*

*Fig 12.12*
*Thomas Tyndall's Royal Fort House was a notable landmark, rising above the vista of harbour and shipping. The latter provide the principal focus of this painting (of which this is a detail) of 1785 by Nicholas Pocock, possibly commissioned to celebrate the completion of the 32-gun frigate shown on the right, below Tyndall's house on the skyline above (BRSMG K742).*

house, Kingsweston House and John Sampson's house at Henbury all showed a similar concern in depicting the platforms or cupolas from which the owner, family and guests could observe the distant view of river and shipping (*see* Figs 9.79, 9.85 and 13.2). At Stoke Bishop House the principal viewpoint for the distant river and shipping was the battlemented platform above the main stairs (Fig 12.11). Closer to the city, the hillsides above the Avon offered similar viewpoints. From the garden terraces of Goldney House successive Thomas Goldneys were able to observe shipping progressing up the river, while Thomas Tyndall's new Royal Fort House of 1760 (chapter 8) was a notable landmark rising above the vista of harbour and shipping (Fig 12.12).[47]

The ring of smart suburban houses around the city also symbolised an enduring theme in the social geography of the medieval and early modern city. From corteplaces, hallhouses and shophouses to residential houses, second residences and suburban villas, the design and location of a citizen's house asserted, reflected and documented aspiration and status. The imperatives and complexities of merchant capitalism determined and were facilitated by the structure of urban housing. At the end of the 18th century what could be afforded was also closely related to the trade in slaves and slave-produced commodities, notably sugar, but also tobacco and chocolate. The visible gentility of the late 18th-century city was, like that of other cities and seaports around the Atlantic rim, built upon a trade and lives immersed in the brutality of plantation slavery.[48] The next and final chapter will look more closely at these interconnections in Bristol and beyond across the eight centuries studied in this book.

# 13

# Merchant Capitalism and the Streets of Bristol

*Freed from all storms the tempest and the rage*
*Of billows, here we spend our age.*
*Our weather beaten vessels here repair*
*And from the Merchants' kind and generous care*
*Find harbour here; no more we put to sea*
*Until we launch into Eternity.*
*And lest our Widows whom we leave behind*
*Should want relief, they too a shelter find.*
*Thus all our anxious cares and sorrows cease*
*Whilst our kind Guardians turn our toils to ease.*
*May they be with an endless Sabbath blest*
*Who have afforded unto us this rest.*

This verse, affixed to the exterior of the Merchants' Almshouse in King Street, turns our attention to the merchants and the poorer members of Bristol society whose houses have been studied over the last 12 chapters. Almost valedictory in intent, it serves appropriately as an introduction to summing up the conclusions of this study.

Throughout the period studied Bristol was a commercial city, centred upon its harbour. Wealth was for the most part generated by trade; the social elite was composed mainly of merchants, and the architecture of the city reflects this. So Bristol stands as an example of what commerce made of a city, with the aspirations of its merchant elite, what we might term the early modern order of merchant capitalism, discernible in the city's form and fabric.[1]

## Civic Building

These aspirations were very evident in the programmes of civic building undertaken over many centuries. The long-lived urban elite had its origins in the foundation of the Saxon *burh* (chapter 2). Within three centuries of the establishment of the town, feudal lords were busy in extending its area, with the result that by the beginning of the 14th century Bristol was one of the largest towns in England. The officials of the new borough were then responsible for a series of interlinked and broadly contemporary projects: the diversion of the Frome, the rebuilding of the Bridge in stone and the building of new walls – all possibly undertaken for commerce and prestige rather than defence.

These works must have been immensely disruptive. To comprehend the scale of the changes in the 13th century we need to visualise the new suburb of the Redcliff Fee (*see* Figs 2.2 and 2.4) extending southwards to its parish church, and the demolitions that must have occurred here when a new town wall and ditch separated that part of the suburb around the church from the part of the town enclosed by a wall to the north. Similar excavations and demolitions would have occurred on the north of the town, in the extension of the walled area northwards to the Frome.

Planning and rebuilding on this scale were not undertaken again until the 17th century, when Bristol, formerly focused in its trading on Europe, notably France, Spain and the Mediterranean, began to develop transatlantic connections. New streets were set out in the 1650s for the first time since the 12th or 13th centuries, introducing distinct, socially differentiated neighbourhoods into the life of the city. This process was given a renewed impetus from *c* 1700 onwards with the development of urban squares and new streets on an unprecedented scale. Major civic schemes of the 18th century again had a commercial imperative. The building of an Exchange, the rebuilding of the Bridge in 1764–8, the opening of a new market and the construction of new streets were all followed early in the 19th century with the opening of the Floating Harbour – so named because the locking of the Avon enabled ships to remain afloat within the harbour whatever the state of the tide. Most of these new developments necessitated the demolition of whole streets and the relocation of their inhabitants to other parts of the city.

## Town Houses

Richard Britnell has said that 'one of the characteristic features of modern capitalism has been the challenge to old elites by capitalists and entrepreneurs who have made money. Capitalism implies the possibility of social ascent through trade for the fortunate few'.[2] Transformations such as these were evident in the building of the largest urban houses from the early medieval period onwards, as well as in the fortunes of individuals whose houses have been studied. Earlier chapters have shown how the form of the medieval house, centred upon the open hall, was appropriated to assert the status of the urban elite, with emphases on lineage and rank being especially important. In an urban context this was not always successful. Screens or entry passages could become rights of way for townspeople; halls could be subdivided to form multiple dwellings, or be given over to purposes other than communal eating such as showrooms or warehouses. Whereas in a rural context the disappearance of the open hall was linked to changing social relations, the process that Johnson has termed 'closure',[3] in an urban context its late survival was linked to the aspirations of the urban elite and served to differentiate this group from lesser members of the community. The largest storeyed residential houses of 18th-century Bristol's squares and smarter residential streets were the successors of the courtyard houses and larger open halls of the late medieval city.

Several large medieval houses can be directly linked to social ascent and changing fortunes. In the 14th and 15th centuries members of the Canynges family emerged from comparative obscurity to become one of the city's wealthiest merchant dynasties.[4] The elaborate open hall of Canynges' house in Redcliff Street reflected the wealth of this family in the 14th or early 15th centuries, but by the later 15th century it had become no more than the entrance to the courtyards and larger house beyond – a hall in the modern sense of being an entry passage. A second such house, much discussed in earlier chapters, was no.20 Small Street, purchased at the Dissolution by John Smyth – a merchant whose family origins are, like those of the Canynges, clouded in obscurity.[5] A new chamber block and the re-roofing of the open hall in the style of the new hammer-beam roof at Hampton Court were additions of the mid-16th century, through which Smyth possibly celebrated and asserted his wealth and new purchases from the Crown. A century later, Small Street remained a location in which new wealth could assert its status in society and the militia. The Creswicks were the new residents of what had been Smyth's house at no.20, fit now to receive an embattled king and his sons (chapter 5).

In the preceding chapters much has been made of the distinction made in the rental of 1473 between hallhouses and shophouses – terms that formed part of the everyday vocabulary of the 15th century for citizens wishing to distinguish between different classes or types of houses. It has been suggested in earlier chapters that the terms 'hallhouse' and 'shophouse' possibly encapsulated a distinction between houses with an open hall and houses where the hall was a ceiled room over a ground-floor shop. This might have equated for the most part to a distinction between larger and smaller houses, between those of rich and less wealthy townspeople, as mapped by Pearson for the towns of Kings Lynn and Salisbury.[6] What is significant about the distribution of these types of houses in Bristol is that, while some central streets were clearly the most prestigious residential areas, there is little sign in the Middle Ages of a strict social segregation: rich and poor still appear to have lived in close proximity.

The evidence from Bristol has pointed to this proximity disappearing from the later 17th and early 18th century, with the development of suburbs that were increasingly differentiated socially. The 16th- to early 17th-century date suggested by Sacks for the development of exclusively wealthy portside parishes has been shown to have been based too much on the counting of hearths, the houses with the most hearths being in fact inns rather than residences. At the same time the earlier chapters of this present study have shown that different house types cannot be correlated absolutely with social status, at least from the 17th century. Some shophouses close to the quaysides could be quite grand dwellings, suitable as residences for the urban elite, notably Langton's house at no.12 Welsh Back, Cann's house on Broad Quay and the shophouses at nos.128–31 St Thomas Street, built *c* 1673 (chapter 6).

Summerson's focus on Nicholas Barbon as the instigator of speculative building in early

17th-century London[7] has perhaps obscured the extent to which the design of the storeyed residential house, so characteristic of 17th- and 18th-century cities such as London and Bristol, and most frequently of two rooms in depth with the stairs linking the separate floors, was based on that of the storeyed, late medieval shophouse. The building of these houses in such large numbers from the 1650s onwards transformed the appearance and fabric of Bristol, to the extent that by the end of the 18th century a large part of the population must have lived in what we might term two-parlour, storeyed residential houses.

The town house played a critical role in affirming the position of the merchant elite in the medieval and early modern town and city. In the medieval period, and extending nearly to the end of the 17th century, larger hallhouses and particularly those fronting courtyards provided a means of displaying both wealth and status. Larger storeyed residential houses fulfilled the same role from the late 16th century onwards, the earliest of these being the great houses on St Augustine's Back and at the south end of Bristol Bridge on Redcliff Back (*see* Figs 2.10, 8.100a and 8.100b).

The construction of many hundreds of large and smaller storeyed residential houses in the 17th and 18th centuries formed a fundamental part of the process of creating a city with distinct residential neighbourhoods. These were much as mapped by Baigent (chapter 10), but needing perhaps some reassessment of what constituted an 'artisan parish'.

By the 18th century, and to some extent from an earlier date, houses were almost without exception constructed to principles which possibly made hierarchy in society seem natural. Ground and first floors were areas for the display of wealth through panelling, plaster cornices, six-panelled doors, open strings and hardwood handrails to the stairs. As one ascended through the house, panelling and plasterwork became increasingly absent. Doors were reduced first to four panels and then two, and the stairs to the uppermost storeys were given closed strings, a less expensive option than the alternative open string with the sides of the individual steps exposed to view (chapter 10). These changes were also ones of economy, ways of making money go further. However, with reception rooms on the ground and first floors and servants' rooms on the upper floors, they also underlined cognitive links between expenditure, status and the design of the house. Such unwritten design principles were part of that same early modern order of merchant capitalism.

## Second Houses – Lodges and Garden Houses

A second major change in the townscape was the encirclement of the city with the second residences of the urban elite. This was a major focus for the investment of capital and for leisure, most evident as an element of merchant culture in the city centre parishes containing Broad Street, Corn Street and Small Street. The occasional use of such residences, and the corresponding primacy of the urban house, has sometimes been overlooked by historians assuming that merchants were setting themselves up as gentry. This did happen, but in succeeding generations. From the evidence of houses, probate inventories and other documentary sources we can see that John Smyth of Small Street and Ashton Court, and Robert Cann of Corn Street and Stoke Bishop House, regarded themselves first as citizens of Bristol; but their descendants used the same country houses to project themselves as gentry.

The urban elite, not just merchants but others as well, thus created a distinct suburban landscape that has made a long-lasting contribution to today's townscape. It might be seen as part of that early modern order of merchant capitalism; also as possibly the inspiration for placing gardens to the front of rows of terraced houses, very much part of the design of the modern city.

## The Urban Elite – Display and Illusion

In these changes to the form and fabric of the city, display and illusion played an important part. Most obviously there is the use of the open hall, much discussed above, but several further examples can be given. In 1724 Robert Yate's unknown compiler wrote of various devices to enhance the 'magnificence' and 'beauty' of the house for a merchant, including double doors between the front and rear parlours for when they are 'inclined to make a shew' and the importance of the 'great stairs' (chapter 10). The great stairs were certainly an important element

*Fig 13.1*
*An early design for the re-fronting of Kingsweston House, showing the house as depicted by Johannes Kip. The U-shaped plan with the stair turrets is echoed or possibly still retained in Vanbrugh's later re-fronting or rebuilding (BRO 33746 fols 115–7).*

in the design of elite houses by the early to mid-17th century, evident in Langton's house at no.12 Welsh Back (*see* Figs 6.12–16) and in the building of a new house out of the remains of the great hall of the Castle (*see* Figs 10.2, 10.3 and 10.4).

Display also provided opportunities for the assertion of individual identity and possession. In challenging the notion of 'Georgianisation', Carson has noted that throughout Anglo–American society 'personalized marks of ownership appear everywhere, starting quite abruptly in the 1580s and 1590s'.[8] In Bristol the earliest houses bearing dates were in Steep Street, of 1540 (Inventory Fig 1370) and in Castle Mill Street, Robert Adams's house at no.11 with his initials and the date 1547 carved into the bargeboards (Inventory Fig 183). The row of houses nos.23–4 and 26 Broad Street, built *c* 1544 out of the munificence of Dr Thomas White, bore only his initials (Inventory Fig 110). As noted by Carson, 'house-proud men and women carved ... and painted their initials, names, significant dates, and other identifying devices on personal possessions in the seventeenth century as never before or since'.[9] This was certainly true of houses in 17th-century Bristol, and might be linked to individualism taking precedence over community, as noted by Cooper in analysing the development of the gentry house.[10]

Access to architectural knowledge played an important part in furthering illusions about the city and its elite. New city gates made use of designs by Serlio, and to underline the authority of the city made reference to a Roman past that it had never possessed. A design by Serlio formed also the core of the design for Sir John Young's new Red Lodge in the 1580s (*see* Fig 9.6b). Sir Edward Southwell's house at Kingsweston was effectively re-fronted by Sir John Vanbrugh, an architect whose work was also in theatre design. Illustrations in *The Kingsweston Book of Drawings* include other plans for the conversion of the earlier house, showing elements depicted by Kip in the early 18th century and still echoed in the plan as it survives today (Figs 13.1 and 13.2).[11]

Close to the commercial centre of the city, a few wealthy individuals were able to acquire sufficient land to create landed estates, smaller than that of Southwell but still offering both a quasi-rural idyll and longer-term possibilities for investment and property development. Urban estates such as Tyndall's Park[12] and Goldney's garden[13] were highly visible and made a lasting impact on the landscape of the city. Looking down on the city from the slopes above, these larger urban gardens could be compared to those in Annapolis, an element of what we might term the early modern order of merchant capitalism.

There is, however, little evidence for 'falling gardens' revealing a knowledge of mathematics and the rules of perspective, as evident in Annapolis. A design by the surveyor Jacob de Wilstar for one such garden above Hotwell Road, not certainly ever built, was for a series of parterres set out across a walled garden falling down the hillside below Clifton Wood (Inventory Fig 532).

The lodges or garden houses surrounding the city provided further opportunities for illusion and display. The 17th-century garden house was entered often from the garden, with the house more clearly visible only once the garden was entered, and otherwise best seen from a distance. This same device was applied from the mid-18th century onwards to whole rows of garden houses, most notably on the north side of Kingsdown Parade, but also in Ashley Road and in other locations around the city.

## The Rococo and the Gothick

Mowl has highlighted the significance of the 18th-century addiction to new building in the rococo and Gothick styles, identifying the rococo as 'the art form of bourgeois capitalism' much loved by a number of wealthy owners of new houses. Among them were the merchants Paul Fisher and Thomas Tyndall at Clifton Hill House and Royal Fort House respectively, and the brass founder William Reeve at Arnos Court.[14] The Gothick revival might be considered also in the context of providing an air of antiquity to new wealth, much as the display of Elizabeth I's

*Fig 13.2*
*Kingsweston House in the early 18th century. Beyond are the River Severn and the shipping that underpinned Bristol's commerce (print by Johannes Kip in Atkyns 1712, between pp 476–7).*

arms had served to underline the lineage of Sir Henry Creswick. At Arnos Court William Reeve placed the rebuilt medieval Lawford's Gate between his new house and the Black Castle (see Fig 11.31b). By 1791 (see Fig 12.8b) the gables and windows of Stoke Bishop House, built c 1669, had been given a Gothick makeover by the merchant descendants of Sir Robert Cann – developments replicated on the far side of the Atlantic by a similar re-modelling of St Nicholas Abbey on Barbados (see Fig 12.8a). But by the 1790s the Gothick was also a popular style in its own right, as evidenced by its use for the design of the basement cupboards at no.52 Kingsdown Parade (Inventory Fig 658).

### Display, Illusion and Charity

The aspirations of the merchant elite of Bristol were evident also in their giving to charitable causes, among the highest recorded in England in the period 1480 to 1660. Charitable giving in Bristol during these years exceeded proportionately that of London, and was substantially more than whole counties such as Hampshire, with a population eight times that of Bristol.[15] Detailed analysis of the charitable donations of the Bristol elite revealed some of their interests: education and its close links to apprenticeships, the removal of poverty, municipal improvements and the establishment of a library were all of greater importance than donations to religious purposes and the needs of those outside Bristol. 'Bristol, urban community though it was, remained almost perversely parochial, bestowing no more than 0.79% of all its great charitable wealth on the needs of other regions.'[16] A brief examination of the housing provided by merchants for the poor revealed another dimension to their charity. 'The Merchants' kind and generous care', acknowledged in the verse placed upon their almshouse in King Street, was, together with the design of this and other almshouses, intended to appear more kind and generous than it really was. Typically these almshouses appeared to consist of several separate, generously wide houses. This was an architectural illusion; in reality each of these consisted of four separate one-room dwellings (chapter 8).

We have seen that a similar illusion was accomplished in the building of Wood's Exchange – so successfully that today its component parts are largely forgotten. What appeared from the exterior as one large public building was in fact made up of a number of separate components: a tavern, a coffee house, various market halls and a number of houses for commercial people. The opening of the Exchange in 1740 encapsulated the relationship between the urban elite and the townspeople, preceded by a hierarchically ordered procession and concluding with the distribution of ale and the throwing of copper coins to the populace.[17]

## Urban Housing, the Atlantic Trade and the Williams Thesis

In concluding, we might look finally at urban housing in Bristol in the context of the wider Atlantic world. We have seen that after the urban expansion of the 12th and 13th centuries, Bristol was next expanded in area from the mid-17th century onwards (chapter 3). Several events or trends were possibly of significance here. Sugar cultivation emerged as the means of making a rapid fortune in Barbados and the Leeward Islands during the 1640s and 1650s. In this same period the West Indian and American trades were becoming much more important to Bristol merchants, so much so that by c 1660 they represented one-seventh of the city's trade.[18] It was in this very period that the new streets in the Castle precinct and the Marsh were first set out for new building. By 1686–7 the Atlantic commerce represented between one-quarter and one-third of Bristol's overseas trade and, as McGrath identified, 'its real importance was more than these figures suggest, for the ships engaged were bigger and the commodities more valuable than in other trades'.[19]

Eric Williams's thesis, that the slave trade and the sale of slave-produced sugar provided the capital and the demand for manufactured goods that were a key element in sparking and fuelling the Industrial Revolution in the later 18th century, could be usefully re-examined in the context of the expansion of Bristol (and London) in the later 17th and early 18th centuries.[20] The expansion of these cities coincided precisely with the sugar boom in the English West Indies and the growth in the Atlantic trade that then followed. That Bristol remained a commercial city well into the 18th century is demonstrated most powerfully by the development of the Marsh. Here Prince Street and Queen Square were lined by large merchant houses, with sophisticated principal elevations and plans which reflected mercantile aspirations to gentility. Yet in the back streets behind these houses the traffic to and from the merchants' warehouses, located at the rear of their dwellings, revealed the origin of the wealth which gave the city's elite their place in society.

This study has examined the material evidence for changing living patterns in one of England's great historic cities. It has used the evidence of urban development and of housing to demonstrate cultural change, for the city's topography and the different forms of housing represent the result of a number of deliberate and significant choices in the way in which the wealthier citizens elected to live and present themselves to the world – choices which can often be traced from the medieval period through to the 17th and 18th centuries. These developments have been seen in the wider context of economic change, specifically the emergence of a capitalist, mercantile society, with the order of merchant capitalism evident in the setting and form of urban housing. The link between such momentous shifts in economy and culture on the one hand, and the nature of urban living on the other, is one of the many areas of research and enquiry which it is hoped that this study might stimulate.

This study might also encourage further research into the social and architectural topography of English towns (chapter 11) – drawing first on the results of property history analysis outlined in chapter 1 to correlate (in many of the above chapters) the information contained in probate inventories with identified houses. Such research could also consider the important evidence from topographical drawings, historic photographs and plans of long-demolished houses alongside the data drawn from those that still remain, an approach in England pioneered to some extent by Schofield's work on London and referred to in chapter 1. For Bristol itself, much scope for such explorations remains. For several centuries it was England's second city. Its remarkable legacy of surviving pre-19th-century houses, combined with equally noteworthy city archives and records preserved elsewhere and a rich buried archaeological resource, will ensure that much still remains to be discovered and written upon in the future.

# APPENDIX 1

### Documents Relating to the Building of Bristol Houses (ordered by date)

### 1472  No.31 High Street (BRO P.AS/D/HS/C/9)

This endenture made betwene Alison Chestre of Brystowe wydowe sumtyme the wyf of Harry Chestre of Brystowe draper on the oon partie and Stephen Morgan of Brystowe carpenter on the other partie witnesseth that the seide Stephen hath covenaunted with the same Alice and hym byndeth by these presentes to make wele werkmanly and surely of good tymbre and bordys a newe hows in the high strete of Brystowe with flores wyndowes dorrys and partesons and all other thyngis of tymbre werk belongyng to the same hows excepte latthes and latyces; whiche seide newe hows shalbe sette betwene the ten[emen]t called The Bull on the oon partie and the ten[emen]t in whiche oon John A Cork corviser nowe dwelleth yn on the other partie, conteynying in length xix fote and v ynches of assise and in wydnes x fote and iiij ynches. And the seide Stephen shall make in the seid hows a shop and a hall above the same with an oryell, a chambre above the hall with an oryell and another chambre above that, by the feste of Annunciation of oure Lady nexte commyng. For whiche hows soo to be made by the same Stephen the seide Alson graunteth and hir byndeth by this present to paye unto the seide Stephen vj li xiij s. iiij d. sterlinges; that ys to sey atte feste of the Natyvitee of our Lorde next commyng iij li.; atte florying of the seide hows xxxiij s. iiij d., and atte ende of the same werk xl s. Also hit ys accorded that hit shalbe lefull to the same Stephen to have and take as his owne all the oold tymbre of the seide oold hows without any geyneseying of the same Alson or any other for hir or in hir name. In witnes whereof the parties forseid to thise endentures entrechaungeably have sette theire seales. Yoven the xvij daye of the moneth of Novembre in the xij yere of the regne of Kynge Edward the fourthe.

### 1699  No.51 Queen Charlotte Street (BRO 04335(8) fol 124)

The Mayor and Burgesses to John Reade, Doctor of Divinity and vicar of St Nicholas, a lease for the term of five lives of 'so much of the said void ground of the said Marsh … as shall contein forty foot in breadth inwards and to run of the same breadth down towards the River Avon in length about One hundred & five foot as it is now layd out allotted and marked by the Citys Oficers and workemen … under the yearly rent of forty shillings, being one shilling for each foot in front to be payable quarterly cleer of all Taxes and deductions whatsoever to commence from Michaelmas One thousand Seaven hundred. The which ground the said Dr Read hereby agrees to build upon in manner following (vizt.). To have a Court enclosed with a Brickwall the whole breadth of the front of his house of Tenn foot in Breadth from the outside of the Court wall to the Outside of the housewall To build the whole front of the house with Brick the Quoines of which with freestone which is to extend to the full breadth of the said ground. The whole house to be built of the heighth of forty foot and all except the front to be built with stone the first and second stories to be eleaven foot in heighth including beams and joists The third story to be tenn foot in heighth and the fourth eight foot with canterliners also montdellians under the tile over the walls so that the whole front on the inside of the house be in heighth forty compleat foot That he enclose the whole ground except the said front with Stone wall and have no building towards the River but what shal be for the necessary use of … the house such as Back Kitchen warehouses Outhouses Stables and Coach-house but no Tenement to be lett out to any sort of Tenants particularly no Smiths Shopp Brewhouse nor to any Tallow-Chandler or to any other Tradesmen who by noyse danger of fire or ill smells shall disturbe or annoy any of the Inhabitants who shall build neer it for Compleating which building he is allowed two years from Christmas next and he is at his own charge to Pitch Twelve foot in depth before the front and Tenn foot in depth behind the said house and to continue it Repaired and Amended.

*Transcript after Ison 1952, 141–2*

### 1725  Nos.50–4 Prince Street (33, 32, 31) (BRO 04335(10) fol 21)

1725 It is agreed between the Surveyors of the Lands belonging to the Mayor Burgessses and Commonalty of the City of Bristol of the one part and Robt. Yate of the same City Esq. of the other part as follows (that is to say) that the said Robt. Yate in consideration of the rents, covenants and Agreements herinafter mencioned shall have granted unto him eighty four foot in the fron of voyd ground situate in the parish of Saint Stephen within the said City at the lower end of the Key being lands lately made use of as yards for

Shipcarpenters and containing in length from Princes Streete thereon on or towards the East unto the Key on or towards the west in the middle part thereof one hundred and twenty eight foot or thereabouts from the outside of a court wall intended to be made next Princes Streete aforesaid between a Garden Wall belonging to a Dwelling house now in the possession of Mrs Elizabeth Day on or towards the North part and with other part of the same void ground intended to be left open as a Lane or Street of the breadth of thirty foot on or toward the South parte and intended to be called South Lane[.] **To hold** the said ground to the said Robert Yate his Execrs. Admrs. and Assignes for the term of three years to commence from Lady day next to the intent that within that time he or they may build a Mansion house or houses thereon paying the rent of a pepper corne at the end of the said terme (if lawfully demanded) and from and after the Expiration of the said Three Years **To hold** the said Ground and all buildings that shall be thereon erected unto the said Robert Yate his Execrs. Admrs. and Assignes for a further term of fifty one years to commence from Lady Day one thousand seven hundred and twenty nine at the yearly rent of Eight pounds Eight shillings of lawfull British money clear of all manner of Taxes whether Parliamentary or otherwise payable at the feasts of Saint Michael the Archangel and the Annunciation of the Blessed Virgin Mary by equal portions with covenants for distress and reentry on non payment of rent and reenjoyment till satisfaction shall be made for rent in arrear and charges [.] The said Robt. Yate is to covenant and also to be obliged in the severall sums of fifty pounds of lawfull British money that before the feast of Saint Michael the Archangel which shall be in the year of our Lord one Thousand seven hundred and twenty nine he his Execrs. Admrs. and Assignes shall and will build one or more Substantiall house or houses of eighty four foot in front upon the same ground hereby agreed for in manner following (that is to say) Ten foot of the said ground hereby agreed for of the whole length thereof in the front is to be inclosed with a brick wall and to be left and used as a Court and no building, structure of other manner of Ediface whatsoever to be erected thereon (porches excepted) and that no porches shall be extended above five foot from the wall of Such structure and at the Extent of the Court Westward is to be the foundation and front of the house or houses and from the Grass Tabling upwards all the front is to be of brick or hewn stone, no house to be less than twenty five foot in front and three stories high besides the garrett all windows in the front to be sashes, the joists to be coffer – every Room on the first floor is to be the height of Tenn foot and an half and every room in the second floor also ten foot and an half and every room in the Third floor nine foot in the Clear excluding beams and joysts all other outward walls in building on the said ground to be of good Stone and all Timber Iron work and other materials to be Substantiall the Outward Doors and windows to be Arched with Stone or brick no Timber to be used in Chimneys or Mantelpieces or discharges but to be done with stone or brick Arches [.] The said Robert Yate his Execrs. Admrs. and Assignes is not nor are to build any stables or to use any part of the said Ground for Timber Deal Blockmakers or Carpenters Yards or Erect any mean Sordid buildings on the Back part of the said Ground to be receptacles for poor people & nor to let any house thereon for Shops for Smith's work houses for Tallors Chandlers or any other Shopps for Tradesmen or Artificers to Annoy the Neighbouring Inhabitants by Ill smells danger of fires or otherwise but to build the back part of the said Ground Either in to Warehouses or dwelling houses and if dwelling houses the same are to be of the same dimensions as those next Princes Streete aforesaid the voyd ground or streete in the front without the court wall to the middle part thereof and one Moyety or half parte of south lane aforesaid from end to end and ten foot from the wall next the Key the breadth of the whole ground is to be pitched or paved before the said feast day of Saint Michael the Archangel one thousand seven hundred twenty and nine and from that time always afterwards at the proper Costs and Charges of the said Robert Yate his Execrs. Admrs. & Assignes to be kept pitched or paved repaired and amended during the said tenure of fifty one years that the Trees now growing in the said Princes Streete shall within six months time be cut down or rooted out that no other trees shall be planted in the said streete during the Terme and estate hereby contracted for And the said Robert Yate his Execrs. Admrs. and Assignes to keep the pitching or paveing free and open and not to lay or suffer to be laid any Timber or other Incumbrances to remain on any part thereof And the said Robert Yate is to covenant to keep all buildings that shall be erected on the said ground and all Gowts links and other Easements in good repair during the said terme of fifty one years and at the end thereof to leave them for the Mayor Burgesses Commonalty are to covenant for quiet enjoyment during the terme aforesaid under the said rents and Covenents.

Robert Yate

### 1772 A House in Clare Street (in the deeds for Nos.16–24 (BRO 40766/9))

1772 Counterpart of the conveyance from John Lewis and Thomas Paty to John Powell, who was to lay out at least £500 in erecting and finishing a good and substantial messuage or dwelling house on plot of ground released, to front Clare Street in a 'regular manner so as to contain and fill up the whole breadth, to range in such said front with the strait line and trench towards Clare Street aforesaid cut and marked out on the same plott of ground as directions for placing the front of such said messuage …' It included the following stipulations:

- the house to be erected in a workmanlike manner, and the front on the north side to be well built with 'the best red stock bricks except the architraves to the windows, facia and sill courses, bases, cornice and coping of the parapett wall which shall be of good freestone well cleaned and finished'.

- the house to be separated from the adjacent dwellings 'with good freestone pillasters and that there shall be no wooden story post or storyhead to any of the shop windows or doorways but instead thereof there shall be good freestone arches'.

- the house to be 'of three stories in height from the level of the parlour, shop or principal floor (exclusive of garretts in the roofing) … viz. a principal or ground story, a second story and an attick story, and that such parlour shop or principal story shall be eleven feet high in the clear, that such second story shall be ten feet high in the clear, that such attick story shall be eight feet and six inches high in the clear and that the garretts shall be six feet high in the clear'.

- the roofing to be 'raised and built uniformly and according to the design and elevation thereof prepared by the said Thomas Paty … the front of such roofing towards Clare Street shall be covered with the best blue slate or Cornish tiles…'.

- the east wall to be 'a partable wall, if built with stone not less than twenty inches thick, if built with brick not less than [words omitted]'.

## 1792   No.52 Kingsdown Parade (BRO xeroxes of documents not in BRO/44)

The building lease for no.52 Kingsdown Parade, part of James Lockier's James's Place development (chapters 3 and 12), was accompanied by a separate contract of 17 September 1792. This was between Charles Melsom, a sworn measurer or surveyor acting on behalf of the developers, and James Pope, a mason and the builder of the house, and it set out the constructional details for the house to be built in some considerable detail:

'…the Dwelling house shall be in and front to James's Place aforesaid and that the Basement Story shall be Eight feet high in the clear at the least from the level of the Kitchen floor and shall be built in such front with stone at least two feet thick and Stuccoed Smooth plaistered or rough cast That there shall be in front of the said Basement Story an Area of three feet wide at the least from the level of the Kitchen up to the level of the said Street called James's Place with Steps to descend as an Entrance to such Kitchen floor That on the top of such Basement Story there shall be laid a freestone course or base of ten inches deep and that thereon the whole remainder of the said northward front shall be built and Carried up with the best red front brick and that such brick front shall be not less than fourteen inches thick That the Joists of the Parlour floor shall be nine inches deep and two inches thick at the least and shall be laid at Proper Distances not exceeding Twelve inches in the clear That the Parlour Story shall be Ten feet in height in the clear That the first Chamber floor joists shall also be Nine inches deep and two Inches thick at the least and likewise laid at proper distances and that such first Chamber story shall be Nine feet and Six inches high in the clear and the second Chamber or Attick floor joists shall be Eight inches Deep and two inches thick at the least and also laid at proper distances and that such Attick Story shall be Nine feet high in the Clear and that the roof of the said house shall be covered with tile That there shall be two Saish Windows in the parlour and three Saish Windows in each of the Chamber and Attick stories and that all such windows shall have uniform freestone Cills and Arches That there shall be a Two bed Cornice over and at a Proper distance from the Arches of the Windows of the Attick Story upon which there shall be carried up a brick Parapet wall and that the said Parapet Wall shall be coped with freestone That there shall be freestone Pilasters of Eighteen inches wide carried up on the Eastward and Westward sides of the said house on the North front thereof and that the same Pilasters and also the Walls at the said eastward and westward sides shall be partable between the Messuage to be built and those to be erected on the next lots adjoining hereto on the Eastwardmost and Westwardmost sides and such party walls shall be of the full standard thickness That the Door or entrance of the said house shall have freestone jambs and pediment uniform with the other houses built or intended to be built in this Rank of Buildings And that the South front thereof facing Somerset Street shall be built with stone and rough cast and shall range in a Strait and direct line and be uniform with the other intended buildings to form a range of Twenty one houses aforesaid not having any projection Except there may be a Bow Window in the Parlour thereof That the garden of the said Messuage or Tenement shall be laid out on the South front thereof extending from such front the Depth of the said Ground as herein before ascertained and that the said walls parting said garden from those on the Eastwardmost and Westwardmost sides thereof shall be Partable Walls and shall be of no greater height in the whole than Eight feet nor less than Six feet That the said Messuage or Tenement and Buildings hereby contracted to be set up shall be built with the best materials and the same Messuage or Tenement or the Area Doors windows front walls or any part thereof shall never afterwards be altered so as to thereby in any respect to destroy the Uniformity of the said range of Twenty one houses and buildings of which the hereby contracted to be erected and built will form a part That there shall be set up and made at the Costs and Charges as of the said James Pope his heirs and assignees in the said street called James's Place in the north front of the said

Messuage or Tenement hereby contracted to be built and the whole breadth of the said hereby contracted for ground a neat Iron railing or Palisade upon a Stone base of Ten Inches high uniform with the other houses on each side thereof for the purpose of railing in the said Area And there shall also be made at the costs of the said James Pope his heirs or assignees without the said railing and close thereto the whole front of the said Ground a Paved footway of four feet wide And the remainder of the said street called James's Place from such paved footway to the middle of such street shall at the like Costs and Charges of the said James Pope be pitched and that the same railing, pitching and paving shall be for ever hereafter kept in good order and repair And that there shall not be at any time hereafter any erection or buildings set upon the said Garden on the Southward front of the said house of any greater height than ten feet or that will annoy or obstruct the houses on the westward side hereof And also that there shall not be at any time hereafter carried on or exercised in the said premises hereby contracted to be erected any noisy noisome or offensive trade or calling.'

# APPENDIX 2
# Inventories

## Introduction

Many of the probate inventories to which reference has been made can be found transcribed in volumes published by the Bristol Record Society. This Appendix is principally of inventories proved in the Prerogative Court of Canterbury and now held in the National Archives at Kew, but it includes some proved in Bristol and of relevance to this study. This selection of inventories is included in Appendix 2 to provide information on the arrangement of identified houses and the names and uses of rooms; in some instances the contents of particular rooms are summarised, and the values of specific items have not therefore been included.

Not all of the inventories were made for probate. Some, such as those of no.58 Kingsdown Parade and that of John Boydell, list the fixtures of buildings being leased – a precaution taken by the owner to ensure that these were all returned on the termination of the lease.

Two sets of inventories are included here. The first comprises inventories of the 15th century, of which only that of John Foster can be linked to an identified house. With the exception of Foster's inventory, all of these are in the National Archives. These inventories are presented in order of date. The second set of inventories included here comprises a selection of those that can be linked to identified houses, most of which are referred to in the text or *The Selective Inventory of Recorded Houses*. These inventories are presented in street and house order.

## Inventories of the 15th century

### 1489, John Gauge (PROB 2/30)

*Inventory of the goods of John Gauge …*

#### In the Haull

| | |
|---|---|
| In primis … [illeg] of old [illeg] conteynyng … the yeard iijd | viijs vjd |
| Item … Bancard of grene Wedmoll price | xijs |
| Item … of floxe val | ijs |
| Item trestylles price | xijd |
| Item ij old ffor … val | iiijd |
| Item i wyndyng presse for cloth price | viijs |
| Item iij [illeg] and vi pavys price | iiijs |
| Summa xxiiijs xd | |

#### In the Parloure

| | |
|---|---|
| In primis iij coferynges of red Wedmol old conteynyng in length and brede xx yeardes price the yeard ijd | ijs iiijd |
| Item ij old bancards ij of red Wedmoll & a nother of grene Wedmoll price oon with a nother | xxd |
| Item v quysshons of tapestry price | iijs |
| Item i bolster of floxe price | xijd |
| Item i [lyt]ell foldyng tabull price | vjd |
| Summa xiiijs | |

#### In the Buttry

| | |
|---|---|
| In primis iiij latyn Basyns with iij Ewers price | |
| Item ij quarte potts & viij pynts price | vjd |
| Item x candels[tick]s price oon with a nother | iijs |
| [Item…] Basyn of Tynne price | |
| [Item] [illeg] [pl]aters vij potyngers & vij Sallsers [illeg] price | |

Summa xvjs xd

#### In the Kechyn

| | |
|---|---|
| In primis vj crokks grete and small & a possenet and a lytell pankin weyng xxx li price the lli ijd ob price | iijs ixd |
| Item v old pannes, a papps … & … … [weyn]g [illeg] lli price the lli ijd | vjs viijd |
| [Item … ] fryeng panns price | viijd |
| [Item …. ] ij broches [illeg] …. | |
| [g]redeyrone ij pothoks & a pavyng shovell weyng xl lli price the lli ob ijd | |

Summa xvs iijd

#### In the Shop

weyng xl lli price the lli ob ijd
Summa iijs

#### In the Chambre

[end of first and only surviving fragmentary page]

### 1492, Inventory of John Foster

The historian and Bristol City Librarian George Pryce summarised the inventory of John Foster (Pryce 1861, 557), but provided no source. No inventory is to be found in the National Archives, and it is possible that Pryce's source was papers formerly belonging to Foster's Hospital and retained in Bristol.

The rooms listed were the hall, parlour, buttery, kitchen, one chief or best chamber, two other chambers and cellars.

In the hall and other 'ordinary appartments' were weapons, viz spears, poleaxes, gloves etc; also 14 green cushions, a table supported by tressels and a branch of laten tin, with five candlesticks.

In the bedroom were a spruce coffer, three smaller ones, a carpet and a feather bed and bolster, with a green coverlet.
The inventory also lists his plate.

Foster's house can be identified as 16–17 Small Street (for references to this and other identifications see the separate *Selective Inventory of Recorded Houses*, also Leech 1997a and 2000b).

## 1494, Inventory of possessions of John Parkyns [Perkyns] (PROB2/767)

Appraiser: Richard Russell

### In the Hall

| | |
|---|---|
| In primis a folding tabyll with a cupbord lok and key | vijs |
| Item iij turned stoles olde | ixd |
| Item the halle hanged with bawdekykn ij peces | vjs viijd |
| Item ij bankers A cupborde cloth of grene saye | xd |
| Item vj olde quysshons stuffed with flokkes | ijs |
| Item i cupborde pleyn an almery for mete lok and key | ijs vjd |
| Item v basons of laton iiij Ewers an hangyng candelstyk iiij Candelstykkes weyng vj$^{xx}$lb at ijd ob le lb | xijs vjd |
| Item ij Aundeirons in the chymney & a pothoke | vs |
| Summa xxxvijs iijd | |

### In the Parloure

| | |
|---|---|
| Item a folding table of sprewse lok and key | vjs viijd |
| Item ij turned stoles a cupbord pleyn lok and key | vs |
| Item iij coferings of steyned cloth olde | iijs iiijd |
| Item i banker of grene cloth olde and iiij olde quyshons | xxd |
| Item ij AundeIrons for the chymney | xijd |
| Item iij tynne potts to set in flowres | xijd |
| Item ij candilstikks | xijd |
| Item i bedstede | xijd |
| Item ij federbedds and ij bolsters | xvjs |
| Item i coverlyte of Norwiche makyng | vs |
| Item ij blanketts | ijs iiijd |
| Item i celer A tester of peinted cloth and iij curteyns of bokeram | vjs viijd |
| Item i federbed and a bolster | vjs |
| Item i coveryng of Norwiche makyng olde | xxd |
| Summa lviijs iiijd | |

### In the Botery

| | |
|---|---|
| Item xviij platers vj disshes and iiij sawsers | viijs |
| Item viij peauter potts iij potells and v pynts | iiijs |
| Item iiij peauter basons | ijs iiijd |
| Item v laton basons pond | |
| Item iij pleyn candilstikks | ijs vjd |
| Item i chafyng dissh of laton | xijd |
| Summa xvijs xd | |

### In the Chambre by the halle

| | |
|---|---|
| Item a bedstede | xijd |
| Item a federbed and a bolster | xiijs iiijd |
| Item a blanket and a quylt | iijs iiijd |
| Item a counterpoynt of olde tapisery | vs |
| Item i celer a tester and ij curteyns of reade saye olde | iijs iiijd |
| Item iiij chests pleyn | xxs |
| Item ij pyllowes febyll | xvjd |
| Item v peyrs of shets and a shete olde | xvs |
| Item iij peire of course shets | vjs viijd |
| Item iiij table clothes olde | vjs viijd |
| Item vj napkyns and iiij pillowberes | ijs vjd |
| Summa iijli xviijs ijd | |

### In the Kechyn

| | |
|---|---|
| Item v platers vj disshes iiij potyngers | vjs viijd |
| Item iij great pannys of brasse | xiijs iiijd |
| Item iiij ketylls | vjs viijd |
| Item ij brasse potts and a postnet | xijs |
| Item iiij broches of Iron | vjs viijd |
| Item A peire of Rakkes And A Trevet | ijs |
| Item all other lomber there | xijd |
| Summa xlviijs iiijd | |

### In the Meynes Chambre

| | |
|---|---|
| Item a matras A bolster and a bedstede | ijs |
| Item a coverlite of Norwiche makyng | xvjd |
| Item a celer a tester ij curteyns and ij steyned clothes | vjs viijd |
| Summa xs | |

In his will of 1494 (TNA PROB 11/10/112) Parkyns stated his wish to to be buried in the chapel of St John the Baptist, in the church of St Ewen's – the meeting place of the Guild of Merchant Tailors, to which he presumably belonged.

## 1496, Giles George (PROB 2/121)

### Inventory of the goods of Giles George

### In the Hall

| | |
|---|---|
| In primis a hangyng of .... worke pryce | illeg |
| Item a table borde pryce | illeg |
| Item a cubborde pryce | illeg |
| Item a Carpett to the same | illeg |
| Item a Rede Banker pryce | illeg |
| Item xix quysshons pryce | xxs |
| Item a Rounde Table pryce | ijs |
| Item ij chayres pryce | vjs |
| Item iiij stolys pryce | ijs |
| Item a payre of andyrons | iijs iiijd |
| Item a Schortt forme pryce | viijd |
| Item a myster pryce | vs |
| Item a Brawnche with v Candylstyks | vjs viijd |
| Summa iiij li ijs viijd | |

### In the best Chambre

| | |
|---|---|
| In primis a hangyng off stayned clothe pryce | xs |
| Item a selour and a testour off borde Elysaunder pryce | xxs |
| Item ij counterpoyntts pryce | xxs |
| Item ij fetherbedes with ij bolsters | illeg |
| Item a payre of blanketts pryce | illeg |
| Item a cobbord pryce | illeg |
| Summa… [illeg] | |

### In a nothyr Chambre

| | |
|---|---|
| In primis ij fethyr beddys | illeg |
| Item ij counterpoyntts pryce | xxvjs |
| Item a coverlyght of worsted pryce | ijs |
| Item a selour and a testour of stayned worke pryce | xxvjs |
| Item ij chestys pryce | xiijs iiijd |
| Item vj quysshons pryce | ijs |
| Item a cheste pryce | vjs viijd |
| Item iij coffyres pryce | vs |
| Item iij lytyll sosers pryce | iijs |
| Summa… vjli [illeg] | |

### In the Buttery

| | |
|---|---|
| In primis xvj bassyns of laten pryce | [illeg] |
| Item iiij Ewers pryste | [illeg] |
| Item xxij candylstyks pryce | [illeg] |
| Item vj pottell potts pryce | [illeg] |
| Item iiij quartt potts pryce | [illeg] |
| Item iiij chafyng dyschys | [illeg] |
| Summa iijli [illeg] | |

## APPENDIX 2

### In a nothyr chamber

| | |
|---|---|
| In primis a selour and a testour with hangyng of stayned worke | xs |
| Item a fethyrbed pryce | [illeg] |
| Item iij payrs of blanketts pryce | [illeg] |
| Item a whyte coverlyght with flowers | [illeg] |
| Item a counterpoynt pryce | [illeg] |
| Item a banker of countersett tapistrie | [illeg] |
| Item a coverlyght of whyte | [illeg] |
| Item a quyltt pryce | [illeg] |
| Item a coverlyght off rede | [illeg] |
| Item a counterpoynt with flowers | [illeg] |
| Item a banker pryce | ijs |
| Item ix costrells of grene saye | xxvjs |
| Item an olde coverlyght of saye | xxd |
| Item viij pyllowys pryce | viijs |
| Item ix quysshons of rede | ijs |
| Item a nothyr quylt pryce | xxd |
| Item a tabylbord with a payre of trestylls pryce | xxs |
| Item a banker pryce | iiijs |
| Item iij coffyrs pryce | [illeg] |
| Summa vli | [illeg] |

### In the Kechyn

| | |
|---|---|
| In primis ii grett pots | |
| Item a grete panne pryce | |
| Item iiij lytell potts pryce | viij |
| Item v pannys pryce | xs |
| Item ij lytyll posnetts pryce | ijs |
| Item xi pannys pryce | xxs |
| item ij Garnyshe off vessell | xxs |
| item ij chafurs pryce | vs |
| item a morter of brasse pryce | xiijs iiijd |
| item ij trevetts pryce | vjd |
| item iij Spytts pryce | [illeg] |
| item a fyre panne pryce | [illeg] |
| item a payre of tongys | [illeg] |
| item iij potthoks pryce | [illeg] |
| item a Sclysse pryce | [illeg] |
| item a fleshehoke pryce | [illeg] |
| item a skewor Skemor prye | [illeg] |
| item a payre of covyrons | xxd |
| item a Gyrdyrn pryce | iiijd |
| Summa… v li vijd | |

### Napery

| | |
|---|---|
| In primis x payrs off courrse shetts pryce… | xxx |
| Item viij payrs of othyr shetts | [illeg] |
| Item xxviij napkyns pryce | [illeg] |
| Item iiij tabylclothys of Dyaper | [illeg] |
| Item ij playn tabyleclothys | x [illeg] |
| Item ij towells of Dyaper | iij[illeg] |
| Item viij towells of Irysh cloth | |
| Summa vijli iiijs | |

### Plate

Not noted, but value totalled xliij li vijs viijd.

In her will of 1496 Giles George alias Swayne, widow, asked that her body be buried in the churchyard of St John the Baptist (TNA PROB 11/10 sig.25).

## 1500, Inventory of Possessions of Thomas Keynes (PROB 2/172)

### In the halle

| | |
|---|---|
| In primis a hangyng of grene saye | [illeg] |
| Item ij bankers and ij window cloths of the same price | vjd |
| Item xij bills and iiij pollaxes price | xjs |
| Item viij polleaxes [?] price | ijs |
| Item viij sterys [?] price | [illeg] |
| Item a folding tabull price | xijd |
| Item a [illeg] price | ijd |
| Item a myster price | xxd |
| Item ij stolys price | vjd |
| Summa xixs ijd | |

### In the parlor

| | |
|---|---|
| Item a hangyng of grene saie price | viijs |
| Item ij bankers and a cupborde cloth of the same price | vjd |
| Item a spruse table price | vijs viijd |
| Item vi [illeg] | xxd |
| Item a cupborde price | iiijd |
| Item vj old quysshons of tapstry | xxd |
| Item a scale price | iijd |
| Item a fethrbedd with a bolster price | vjs viijd |
| Item a pair of shets price | ijs |
| Item a coverlet price | iijs ijd |
| Item a pair of Aundyrons | xvjd |
| Summa xxvjs | |

### In the butry

| | |
|---|---|
| Item a garneshe of pewter vessalle price | viijs |
| Item xv [illeg] basyns with xij Silver [?] [illeg] | xxs |
| Item xij candilsticks price | iijs |
| Item vj flour potts price | xijd |
| Item iij pottell potts price | xijd |
| Item ix litill potts price | xviijd |
| Item a brasen mortar with a pestell price | ijs |
| Item a [illeg] of Iersh cloths price | ijd |
| Summa xxxvijs iiijd | |

### In the kechen

| | |
|---|---|
| Item v greate potts of bras price | xxs |
| Item viij lasse [?] potts of bras price | xijs iiijd |
| Item viij smale brasen pannes price | vjs |
| Item a longe Brandyron price | vjd |
| Item ij tryvetts price | ijd |
| Item ij broches price | viijd |
| Item ij pothoks price | ijd |
| Item ij litel cobberts price | vjd |
| Summa lis ijd | |

### In the Bruehows and Yeldyng hous

| | |
|---|---|
| Item v vats price | xs |
| Item xxx trendilles [?] price | xvs |
| Item ij old [illeg] –nds price | xlixs |
| Item ij messhyng vats price | xs |
| Item xxx stands price | xs |
| Summa iiij li ixs | |

### In the malt loft

| | |
|---|---|
| Item a bushell mesure price | vjd |
| Item xxij wey of barley malt price | xxli |
| Summa xxli vjd | |

383

### In the fore chambre

| | |
|---|---|
| Item ij pecs of grene saie price | ijs |
| Item a fethrbedde with a bolstre price | xs |
| Item a seler and tester of grene saie with iij price | xvjs iiijd |
| Item a pair of blankets price | xijd |
| Item a coverlet price | xvjd |
| Item iiij litill cofurs price | iiijs |
| Item ij bedsteds price | vjd |
| Item a spruse table price | vs |
| Item ij tables of Seynt Johns hedd | viijd |
| Summa xxxs xd | |

### In Naprye

| | |
|---|---|
| Item a beryng shete price | iijs iiijd |
| Item a pair of fyne shets price | vjs viijd |
| Item iiij pair of corse shets price | viijs |
| Item x other pairs of corse shets price | xiijs iiijd |
| Item xi diaper napkyns price | iijs |
| Item iiij pillowe berys price | iiijd |
| Item ij playne towelles a diaper towell a tablecloth of diaper a tableclothe of twylly and a tableclothe of canvas | ixs |
| Summa xlvjs iiijd | |

### In the newe Chambre

| | |
|---|---|
| Item a scarlet gown furred with calabre price | xls |
| Item a crymyssyn gown lyned price | xxxs |
| Item a violet gown lyned price | vjs viijd |
| Item ij coverletts of tapstry work price | xxd |
| Item a banker of [illeg] price | iiijs |
| Item a riding gown of scarlet price | vjs viijd |
| Item a cofre price | xijd |
| Item a tablebourd with ij tressills price | xxd |
| Summa vli xs | |

### Plate

In gilt plate
Not noted
In plate parcell gilt
Not noted

### In the Servauntes Chambre

| | |
|---|---|
| Item a matras with a bolster a pair of shetes a paire blankets and a coverlet price | iiijs viijd |
| Summa iiijs viiid | |

### In Speratt Detts

| | |
|---|---|
| Item in sperat detts | xijs xjd |
| Total iiij^xx [?] xix li xiiijs xjd | |

Thomas Keynes was bailiff in 1469 (Veale 1953, 106).

In his will of 1499 Thomas Keynes, burgess, asked for his body to be buried in the cemetery of the parish church of St James, presumably the parish in which he lived; he left to his wife Joan a tenement in Marshfield and another at Brokehouse (TNA PROB 11/12/122).

## 1503, Thomas Mason (PROB 2/471)

### Inventory of Thomas Mason merchawnd appraised by John Kemys and Mr James Botiller

### In the Hall

| | | |
|---|---|---|
| Furst | an old hanging of green seye & ij fourmys | ijs |
| Item | xv course clothis price | xx li |
| Summa | | xxli ijs |

### In the Parlour

| | | |
|---|---|---|
| Furst | a hanging [illeg] | [illeg] |
| Item | vi quysshons ij bank[ers] [illeg] | [illeg] |
| Item | a –bourde and a counter bord | [illeg] |
| Item | ij andirons | xxd |
| Item | iij [illeg] price | xijd |
| Summa | | xjs iiijd |

### In the Buttry

| | | |
|---|---|---|
| Furst ij basons ij lavones of laten | | ijs |
| Item | ij chafing disshes & iiij bolle candellstickks | iijs |
| Item | iiij potell potts of pewter and iiij quartes | iijs |
| Item | ij paynt potts price | viijd |
| Item | a garnyssh of vessell | xviijs |
| Item | a mister & ij flower potts | xijd |

### In his Mayne Chambre

| | | |
|---|---|---|
| Furst | a hangyng of grene saye | iijs |
| Item | a solar and a tester of steyned worke | iijs |
| Item | a bedsted price | vjd |
| Item | a fethurbed and a bolster | xiijs iiijd |
| Item | a counterpane of old tapistrie | xs |
| Item | a pair of shetes and a pair of blanketts | iiijs |
| Item | iiij cofurs price | viijs |
| Item | ij bolsters & iiij pelows | iijs |
| Item | iij course clothis | vi li |
| Item | a short grene gowne | vs |
| Item | a old grene gowne | iiijs |
| Item | a old violet gowne | viijs |
| Item | a blew gowne | xs |
| Item | a murrey gown lined with blak | xs |
| Item | a longe old grene gowne | viijs |
| Item | a old short Russet gowne | iiijs |
| Item | a violet jaquet | ijs |
| Item | in a [?]coffer shetes fine & course xiiij peir price | xxiiijs |
| Item | a dosen of plain Napkins | ijs |
| Item | ij tabulcloths of diaper | xs |
| Item | iij plaine tabulcloths | iiijd |
| Item | ij small cofers | ijs |
| Summa xij li xviijs xd | | |

### In the Maydens Chamber

| | | |
|---|---|---|
| Furst | a fethurbed & a coveryng | ijs |
| Item | a silar and a tester | ijs |
| Item | ij pere of blankettes and ij mantells | vjs |
| Item | x stone of wole and flokkes | xxxs |
| Item | lxxx li of Irysh wole | xs |
| Summa ljs | | |

### In the Kichyn

| | | |
|---|---|---|
| Furst | ij brase pottes | viijs |
| Item | iiij little pannys and ij cawdyrons | vjs |
| Item | xviij li of pewter | vjs |

| Item | a chaffron & ij rekkes & a brandiron | ijs |
| Item | ij small rackes a gridiorn & a dripping panne | ijs |
| Item | ij litle brochis | vid |
| Item | a pewter pot & a fork | vid |
| Summa xxvs | | |

*In the Selour*

| Furst | vij ton of salt price | iiijli |
| Item | a litle salt with a cover of v [illeg] | xxs |
| Item | a dosen of silver sponys | xxvjs viijd |
| Item | a little maser | illeg |
| Item | in Redi Money | iiij li |
| Summa xli xvjs viiid | | |

*Sperat detts*

| Furst | Hugh Colston | xxxiijs iiijd |
| Item | George Meke | xiiijs |
| Summa  cl li xxxs xd [?] | | |

In his will of 1502 Thomas Mason, merchant, left 'all my goods moveable unto Margaret my wife wherever they may be found beyond the see or on this side the see', his body to lie in the church of St Stephen, and whole cloths left to his son Thomas, daughters Margerie and Jenner, and a child yet to be born (TNA PROB 11/13).

# A Selection of Probate Inventories with Links to Identified Houses (ordered by street and house name or number)

## Ashley Manor and Lewin's Mead, 1689, Andrew Hook (TNA PROB/7599)

This inventory (here summarised) is of his possessions in two houses, his town centre house in Lewin's Mead and his secondary residence, garden house or lodge, Ashley Manor. The contents of the former are appraised first.

*Kitchen*
Pair of iron grates, 4 spits, chopping knives, pot hooks, one iron [?] heater, tongs, fork, slice, 2 side irons and fender, warming pann, small oval table, one Spanish table and side table, 3 turned chairs, 2 leather chairs & 3 cushions, one cane with a silver head, 2 joint stools, 1 small looking glass, pewter, 10 brass candlesticks, 2 brass [illeg], 1 brass chaffing dish, 1 pair of brass snuffers, one brass pepper box, brass candle box, quantity of brass

*Back Kitchen*
One long iron grate, tongs, slice & fork, bright crane, 2 iron racks, a [illeg] frying pans, iron dripping pan, spit & cleaver, Latin ware, 3 turned chairs & one joint stool & 4 small stools, 1 small settle, a cub and trencher rack, 1 iron chaffing dish, 2 big wooden trenchers, 2 iron boxes and champs and stands, 1 brass bottle, earthen ware

*Summerhouse*
1 Dutch table & frame

*Parlour*
Oval table, 9 rushy leather chairs, fire grate with brass heads, pair of andirons, wax candlestick & a brass single branch candlestick

*Chamber over the kitchen*
Feather bed & bolster bedstead, curtains, vallins, rugs, blankets & [illeg], 9 cane chairs, one green couch, 1 little table & a looking glass, one pair of little brass dogs, tongs & slice of brass with 2 brass hooks, glasses on the clavy with figures

*In the passage*
One clock

*Forestreet Room over the Parlour*
Chest of drawers & a table & 2 stands, 2 folding tables, 1 large looking glass, one pair of brass andirons, brass tongs & slice & hooks, 3 large earthen flower pots, 2 basons, 2 plates of Flemish ware, 1 large sullybub glass & 4 other glasses

*In the second Chambre over the Kitchen*
Feather bed and bolster, 2 pillows & bedstead, one suite of blew curtains & vallins, a counterpaine of the same & two blankets, 2 India quilts, 2 blue window curtains & [illeg], chairs covered with blue serge, case of drawers & side board, dressing box & looking glass, one sullybub glass & 2 other glasses, one small pair of brass andirons

*In the Closet in the same Chambre*
Flint bottle, two crewetts, eight [?] marmalid glasses, one glass funnel, two custard cupps, one earth sullybub cup, a little flint bottle with a silver head, a little lignumvitae tumbler tipt with silver & one straw pannier

*In the Closet att the Staires Head*
One close stool and pann, three brushes, a voider dust pan and ceive and two old trunks

*In the forestreet Chamber on the same floor*
One feather bed and bolster, two feather pillows, one green rug, two blankets and a paire of druggett curtens & vallins, one chest of drawers, one skreene, one Standish, one yello embrodied chayre, two stooles, two cushions ditto, four needlework stooles and a chayre, one stand, two great trunks and a little one, one paire of dogs with brass heads, one pair of andirons with brasses, one paire of tongs and slice and bellows, one fender, some glasses on the clavy, two pin cushions and a comprase & purse, two old boxes and trunk

*In Andrews Chamber*
One bedstead, one feather bed and bolster, curtains, vallins, rugs, blankets & appts, one truckle bedstead, bed, bolster and coverlid and blankets, one Spanish table, two chests, one close stool & pan

*In the Cockloft*
Two wainscot chests, one still compleat (list of linen then follows, including 20 napkins)

*In the Entry*
1 pike & 6 leather buckets, 6 old swords, a carbine, a musquett, 2 pistols and a paire of bandyleers

*In the outward Buttery*
One [illeg] tubb, one large tray, two washing tubs, six chopping boards, a wooden [illeg] a earthen pan & four wooden sawcers, three payles, one wooden horse, a wooden hursy, one wooden fender, one washing tubb, one barge and case of old knives
A parcel of books
Lumber and goods

*Goods in the house at Ashley*

*Parlour*
Table board [only item]

*Kitchen*
1 table board, 5 chairs, 1 ceive

*Chamber over the Kitchen*

Pair of andirons with brasses & 3 leather chairs

*Chamber over the Parlour*

*Buttery on the same floor*

3 small pots with covers, leather [illeg] of Dutch earthen ware, one [illeg] yarn, one line & some old iron

*In the second Kitchen Chamber*

One bedstead, matt & cord, 1 pair of carpatteen curtains & vallens, one red rug & a low wrought stool, one small box

*In another Chamber on the same floor*

One feather bolster, one rug, five sheets, five blankets, one bedstead matt & cord & iron rods

*In the Cockloft*

One truckle bedstead & rod, one 'old fashion bedstead' and rod

*In the Backside*

One wheelbarrow, one cart, one putt, one winnow, one ladder, one old spade, old lumber

*In the Stable*

One ladder, one curry comb, a razt rope, one spade, one howe, one lead halste hundred, a collar & heames and one pecke

*In the Court*

One pair of wheels and one puncheon

*In the inwards Kitchen*

4 pewter dishes & 3 pewter saucers, all [illeg]
One great brass vessel, another middling & one small, one brass crock [illeg]
One brass candlestick & a pair of brass heads
One frying pan, one pair of iron dogs, one iron slice
One table board, one turned chair, one folding chair, one cupbd, three joint stools, three earthen platters

*Upper Chamber*

One old bedstead & chairs

*Wash house*

2 barges, one tub, one washing pan, a rudder, a ceive, one coal rake, pair of tongs & iron fork, one iron door & frame for a furnace, one wooden horse, one hand peece & one dog wheel
One furnace
One hook

*Buttery*

One iron drag & a ball

*Fore Chamber*

One bedstead, matt & cord, 1 pair of brass andirons, one case of drawers & a joint stoole

*Upper Chamber*

Bed stead, flock bed & bolster, red rug, 2 other bolsters, 1 matt & cord, 1 table, 1 joint stool, 2 marking irons, 2 iron hoops & an old reaping hook with some other old iron
One hatchet

*Summerhouse in the Garden*

One table

One Dutch ladder

[The inventory then proceeds to list items found in various parcels of ground close to the house]

Then leases of various properties in Bristol (3 tenements in Lewin's Mead and 3 tenements in Corn Street).

For no.23 Broad Street see under Park Lane below.

### No.68 Castle Street, 1678, George Hill (BRO Inventory 1684/19)

An Inventory taken October 28th 1678 of the Goods Chattells and Debts oweing to belonging and Apperteineing unto George Hill Button mould maker Of the Castle Precints in the City of Bristoll Deceased And appraised by Thomas Kill John Bristow and Christopher Loosly

*In the Kitching*

| | | £ | s | d |
|---|---|---|---|---|
| Imprimus | Of Pewter 25li by estemacon at 7d per li | 00 | 14 | 07 |
| Item | For 3 brass kittles and brass Candle Sticks a Small paire of Scales and Small ladle and Skillet | 01 | 10 | 00 |
| Item | A paire of grates One forke one sliss 2 pair of tongues 3 Spitts 2 driping pans one great 2 paire of pott hooks one small paire of Andirons | 00 | 10 | 00 |
| Item | One settle one Biffett 2 formes one small Table board 2 chaires one joint stoole and Other things of small value | 00 | 09 | 06 |

*In the Shop*

| Item | One Small Table board | 00 | 01 | 06 |
|---|---|---|---|---|

*In the Seller*

| Item | One kinderkin of Ale and remaines of another | 00 | 07 | 00 |
|---|---|---|---|---|

*In the –1t [1st] Chamber*

| Item | Two Flock-beds 2 paire of Sheets 3 blankitts Two Ruggs one feild bedstid matt & boards One paire of Red Flaning Curtains – 2 flock boulsters 2 feather pillows 1 trundle bedsted matt and cord | 03 | 10 | 00 |
|---|---|---|---|---|
| Item | One Side board Cupboard and Great Chest one Small Table board 3 Leather Chaires one small turned Chaire one box | 01 | 00 | 06 |

*In the forestreet Roome*

| Item | One Table board one long form one Coffer one Greene Chair | 00 | 09 | 06 |
|---|---|---|---|---|

*In the upper Chamber*

| Item | Two flock small beds two small bolsters One sheete one blanket two old Coverleds and one halfe headed bedsted one trundle bed-sted | 00 | 08 | 09 |
|---|---|---|---|---|

*In the Work-house*

| Item | Of working tools that is to say Two hatchetts two small Axes Four iron wedges three Lathes for working Irons two hold-fasts two Saws six small files | 00 | 09 | 05 |
|---|---|---|---|---|

| Item | for wearing Apparell | 01 | 11 | 06 |
| Item | In desperate debts for Ale and for Button moulds | 02 | 07 | 08 |

The will of George Hill is of interest in complementing the above Inventory with further details of the occupancy and contents of individual rooms (BRO will George Hill, 1678).

## No.70 Castle Street, 1681, John Drew (BRO inventory 1681/20)

A true and perfect Inventory of all and singular the goods chattles rights & creditts which were of John Drew late of the Citty of Bristoll housecarpenter ~ decd taken and appraised the [blank] Anno R – Carol Secdi nunc [?] Angl etc Tricesimo Domi 168– by John Hollester cordwinder and Thomas Kill sergemaker as fol's (vizt)

|  | £ | s | d |
|---|---|---|---|
| Imprimus The decds mony in Purse and wearing apparell | 06 | 00 | 00 |

### In the lower forestreet Chamber

| one bed and bedsteed with a suite of curtains vallians & appertenances & one truckle bedsteed | 02 | 10 | 00 |
| All the linnen of severall sorts | 02 | 08 | 00 |
| one table four joined stooles twoe cases of drawers six leather chaires one chest one trunk & some other small goods | 03 | 00 | 00 |

### In the Second forestreet Chamber

| one feather bed with a sute of curtains & vallians, bedsteed and the appertenances | 04 | 10 | 00 |
| one table board one sideboard & one box | 00 | 12 | 00 |

### In the Second back Chamber

| one bed bedsteed & the appertenances one truckle bedsteed with a bed & the appertenances | 01 | 15 | 00 |
| one chest one coffer and one box | 00 | 07 | 00 |

### In the Garrett

| one bedsteed and frame of a Crane | 00 | 06 | 00 |

### In the lower Romth backwards

| Two chaires Twoe low stooles and one pair of fire doggs | 00 | 08 | 00 |

### In the Kichen

| five joint stooles one Sideboard–cupboard three small chaires one cradle with the appertenances & one small case of boxes | 01 | 05 | 00 |
| one table one chaire some earthen ware & some other small things | 00 | 07 | 06 |
| Six pewter plates fourteen pewter dishes and some other small pewter | 01 | 07 | 00 |
| four small brass candlesticks one warming pan three brass crocks three kettles twoe skilletts one spice morter & one ladle all brass | 02 | 00 | 00 |
| one pair of racks one fire shovell and tongs one frying pan three small spitts one dripping pan one box & irons one pair of fire doggs all iron with other small iron ware | 01 | 00 | 00 |
|  | 27 | 15 | 06 |

[fol 2]

### In the Cellar

| one small furnace some beare caske & brewing vessels and other lumber goods | 01 | 12 | 00 |
| four chattel leases | 150 | 00 | 00 |
| In mony and plate | 03 | 00 | 00 |
|  | 154 | 12 | 00 |
|  | 27 | 15 | 06 |
|  | 182 | 07 | 06 |

His will shows that the house was partly let to his two tenants, Richard Bryant and Jane Brickett, widow.

The will of John Drew made in 1680 (BRO wills) bequeathed various properties, including his dwelling house in the Castle, to be enjoyed by his wife Dorcas (so long as she remained unmarried) and his children, the dwelling house in his occupation and also that of his tenants Richard Bryant and Jane Brickett, widow.

## Nos.3–4 High Street, Haddon's Tavern, The Horse's or Nag's Head 1575, John Boydell (BRO 04421(a) fols 324–5)

The Horse's or Nag's Head was located at the corner of High Street and Wine Street. For Boydell's will see Wadley 1886, 214–5.

### The messuage or tenement called the Horsshedd

### The Rome benethe called the Seller and the Shop thereunto adioyninge

Imprimis ij severall seates with table bordes and benches to the same and a glasse windowe all glased in that parte of the said seller wich adioynethe to the tenement in the tenure of the same William Yeman the elder

Item viij other seates with their table bordes and benches in the other parte of that seller and in the shopp thereunto adoiyninge and a lettice windowe in the same shoppe

Item a drapery coffer for to putt bread in with ij severall romes in the same and ij springe locks and keys thereunto

Item a presse with iiij romes to set tavern potts uppon

Item a seate of drapery with iij cupbordes and lockes and keis to the same for him or her that receavethe the money for the wyne a glasse windowe all glased and barrs of iorn to the same behynde the same seate

Item also a cownter behinde the said seate adoiyninge to the said seate with a table boorde in yt and a glasse windowe all glased with barrs of iorn to the same

Item iij glass lannterns

Item an iron hearthe for fyer in the shoppe

### The greate Parlor aforestrete

Item all the drapery worke aboute the about said parlour upto the sealinge with the benches and mollers to the same & a portall conteyninge in all lij yards di

Item a glasse wyndowe all glassed reachinge along all the parlor afore with ba[rres]

of iorn to the same and di casements of iron

Item a table bourde of v yardes longe and a yarde brode uppon a frame with xij joyned stooles

Item at thende of the said parlor a little cownter with ij shelves rounde about the same a glasse wyndowe all glased in the same counter with iron barrs in the same wyndowe

## The Haull

Item all the drapery worke of the Botterye there beinge a yarde and iij quarters highe with the mollers upon the same and upon the same drapery of the butterye, be sett lettice wyndowes of half an elle depe and in lengthe aboute iij yardes and a di with molers upon the same with a drapery dore to the said butterye and locke and key thereunto and in the same butery be iiij formes

Item in the said haull all the sealinge worke or drapery worke reachinge from the flower of the sealinge of the gallery begininge at the greate parlor dore to the chamber dore and over the chamber dore and so to the little parlor dore, all the sealinge worke or drapery worke as highe as the lower parte of the gallery beginninge at the little parlor dore and so to the chimney of the haull with mollers upon the same and a benche of drapery worke from the said little parlor dore to the said chymney another benche of drapery worke from the chamber dore to the little parlor dore with a a byffett and lock and key to the same, all the sealinge worke reachinge from the staiers cominge up to the said haull to the staier that goethe upp to the gallery with a a benche of drapery to the same, which sealinge worke or drapery reachethe from the said benche to the sealinge of the said gallerye and a byffet with a lock and kaye to the said benche more in the said haull a table bourde of vir and iij yardes iij quarters longe and nighe a yarde broade with a joyned fframe to the same and ij formes of a yarde and a half long a pece, ij glasse wyndowes all glassed with barres of iron which doe gyve light into the said haull

## The little Parlor

Item all the wayneskotte and drapery worke in the said parlor that is to saie the drapery worke from the dore unto the chymney and from the chymney to the wyndowe reachinge from the flower to the sealinge of the parlor with molers upon the same a pece of drapery for the chimney in the sommer tyme with a dore of waynskotte to the said parlor a benche of drapery of that parte that the wyndowe standethe a great glasse wyndowe throughe glased with barrs of iron and ij casements of iron, a buttery with turned pyllers and under the said posts drapery worke, and a yarde and a half in higheth a table bourde of ij yards di longe and iij quarters of a yarde broade uppon a frame in the said parlor, a joyned fforme of ij yards and better in the said parlor ij shelves rounde aboute the buttery with a dore and a lock and a key to the said buttery, more two halfe doores with a bolt of iron goinge out of the said buttery to the hawll abovsaid

## The lower Chamber adioyninge to the Haull

Item a great glasse windowe windowe all glased with barrs of iron and ij casements to the same
    Item a doore to the same with lock and key and ij bolts of iron

## The Chamber over the said lower Chamber

Item ij standinge bedsteds with fretted posts with testers and molere to the same
    Item a glass wyndowe all glased with barrs of iron and a casement of iron
    Item a portall doore of drapery with a latche and a catche to the same
    Item a doore to the same chamber with lock and kay to the same
    Item a table bourde of ij yardes longe and a yarde broade with a frame to the same

## The Chamber afore towardes Wynestrete

Item a very faire lettice windowe cutt owte of the whole tymber with ij tymber casements to the same
    Item to the same chamber a doble doore with lock and key ij bolts of yron and staples to the same and a barr of yron to goe overthwart the said doore with a staple to make fast the same
    Item a counter in the same chamber with a boorde and iiij shelves in the said counter
    a glasse wyndowe with barrs of yron and a casement and a doore to the said counter with lock and key

## The Chamber over the little Parlor

Item a glasse windowe with barrs of yron

## The Entry goinge into the Kytchyn

Item a wyndowe not glassed havinge five barrs of iron in the same
    Item over the back doore a light with xij barrs of yron

## The little Vault towards Wynestreete

Item ij wyndowes with barrs of iron
Item iiij styllinges to lay wynes upon of iiij yardes and di longe a pece vj ynches highe and v ynches broade every of them

## The greate Vaulte

Item one pr of stillings of xxxtie yardes a pece vj ynches highe and v ynches brad evry of them
    It a paire of styllings of xij yardes a pece six ynches highe & v ynches thick evry of them
    It a paire of styllings of xiiij yardes di a pece by vj ynches highe & v ynches thick evry of them
    It a paire of styllings of v yardes a pece vj ynches highe & v ynches thick evry of them
    It a paire of styllings of iiij yardes a pece vj ynches highe & v ynches thick evry of them
    (Plate and goblets not noted)

## The tenement in the Highe Streete wherein William Yeman the elder now dwelleth

## The Haule

Imprimis all the wainscott there with the benches cont in all xliij yardes di
    Item all the glasse in the windowes there and the barrs of iorn to the same
    Item a buttery with the shelves

## The Parlor

Item all the wayneskott there with the benches cont in all xltie yards one foote
    Item all the glasse in the windowes there with the lettice to the same
    Item a buttery and a counter with there shelves

## The Kytchin

Item an iron barr in the chymney with the shelves there

## The Aller

Item an oulde cheste

## No.5 King Street, 1702, Aaron Williams (TNA PROB 5/4420)

A true and perfect Inventory of all and Singular the goods chattells and creditts of Aaron Williams late of the City of Bristol *Cooper* – deceased which since his death are come to the hands possession or knowledge of Sarah Williams widow the Relict and Administratrix of the said deced made as followeth (vizt)

### In the forestreet Chamber of his Dwelling House

|  | £ | s | d |
|---|---|---|---|
| One Suite of Camlett Curtains with a white inside | 02 | 05 | 00 |
| One white Quilt | 00 | 15 | 00 |
| One blankett | 00 | 02 | 00 |
| One feather bed bolster & paire of pillowes | 02 | 00 | 00 |
| Six Chaires One Stoole | 01 | 00 | 00 |
| One bedstead laceing buckram tester and Rods | 00 | 16 | 00 |
| One paire of brass Andirons | 00 | 07 | 00 |
| One looking Glass | 00 | 04 | 00 |
| One dressing table | 00 | 01 | 00 |
| Linnen of Several Sorts for the house | 01 | 10 | 00 |

### In the next Roome

| | | | |
|---|---|---|---|
| One Suite of Druggatt Curtains and loose Cases to five Chaires | 00 | 18 | 00 |
| One Old feather bed bolster and two pillowes | 01 | 10 | 00 |
| One Old pantado Quilt | 00 | 05 | 00 |
| One Old Rugg and paire of blanketts | 00 | 04 | 00 |
| One bedstead matt Cord and Rods | 00 | 10 | 00 |
| Two Old white window Curtains and vallens with a Curtain Rod | 00 | 01 | 06 |
| One looking Glass | 00 | 08 | 00 |
| One table Stand & dressing box | 00 | 09 | 00 |
| Two Chest of drawers | 01 | 02 | 00 |
| One Chest | 00 | 12 | 00 |
| One paire of brass Andirons | 00 | 07 | 00 |

### In the forestreet Roome next above

| | | | |
|---|---|---|---|
| One feather bed and bolster | 01 | 02 | 00 |
| One bedstead matt Cord & Rods with a buckram Tester | 00 | 08 | 00 |
| One Chest of drawers | 00 | 06 | 00 |
| One Chest | 00 | 07 | 00 |
| four Old green chaires | 00 | 02 | 06 |
| One Old turned Chaire and one matted Chaire | 00 | 01 | 00 |

### In the next Roome backward

| | | | |
|---|---|---|---|
| One Old Suite side & foot Carpett Curtains | 00 | 03 | 06 |
| One Old bed bolster and pillow of flocks and feathers | 00 | 18 | 00 |
| Two Ruggs two blanketts | 00 | 09 | 00 |
| One Old bedstead matt Cords and Rods | 00 | 04 | 00 |

### In the next Roome

| | | | |
|---|---|---|---|
| One Old Suite of Curtains | 00 | 03 | 00 |
| One flock bed and bolster | 00 | 10 | 00 |
| Two Old Ruggs and One blankett | 00 | 03 | 06 |
| One bedstead matt Cord tester & rodds | 00 | 08 | 00 |
| wearing apparell of the deceased | 01 | 00 | 00 |

### In the upper Roome

| | | | |
|---|---|---|---|
| One Old bed two bolsters & One pillow | 00 | 10 | 00 |
| One halfe headed bedstead matt & cord | 00 | 05 | 00 |

### In the Parlour

| | | | |
|---|---|---|---|
| Two Carpetts | 00 | 08 | 00 |
| One Oval Table | 00 | 10 | 00 |
| Tenn leather Chaires at 2$^s$ 6$^d$ per chaire | 01 | 05 | 00 |
| One arme'd leather Chaire | 00 | 01 | 06 |
| One paire of brasses and an Iron fender | 00 | 05 | 00 |

### In the Kitchen

| | | | |
|---|---|---|---|
| Two window Curtains & Rod | 00 | 05 | 00 |
| One Skreen | 00 | 07 | 00 |
| One table | 00 | 02 | 06 |
| Three Joint Stooles | 00 | 02 | 00 |
| One old Settle | 00 | 02 | 00 |
| One round table | 00 | 02 | 06 |
| for Earthen ware | 00 | 02 | 06 |
| Three Old Chaires | 00 | 01 | 00 |
| One warming pan | 00 | 02 | 06 |
| pewter of all sorts 1$^c$ 3$^{qrs}$ 01$^l$ at 7$^d$ per pound | 05 | 14 | 11 |
| two paire of twisted brass Candlesticks | 00 | 08 | 00 |
| One pestle and Mortar | 00 | 01 | 00 |
| One paire of Candlesticks | 00 | 01 | 00 |
| A single Candlestick | 00 | 01 | 00 |

### Cask [marginal, appears to indicate contents of cellar]

| | | | |
|---|---|---|---|
| 48 herring barrels at 2$^s$ 3$^d$ per barrel | 05 | 08 | 00 |
| Two barrells of Old herrings at 10$^s$ per barr'l | 01 | 00 | 00 |
| Two tunn of barrels & hogsheads at 30$^s$ per – | 03 | 00 | 00 |
| Sixteene dry kilderkins at 1$^s$ 2$^d$ per – | 00 | 18 | 08 |
| Fifteen Small dry Casks at 9$^d$ per – | 00 | 11 | 03 |
| Three West India barrells at 3$^s$ per – | 00 | 09 | 00 |
| Eleven Rundletts of Several Sizes | 00 | 18 | 00 |
| One Old bony | 00 | 04 | 00 |
| Fifteen Old Casks | 00 | 10 | 00 |
| 760 hering barrel staves | 02 | 06 | 00 |
| 50 heads | 00 | 06 | 00 |
| 76 Liquor hogshead Staves | 00 | 13 | 09 |
| Old Lumber in the back Shopp | 00 | 05 | 00 |
| Nine score of West India barrell Staves at 1$^s$ 8$^d$ per Score | 00 | 15 | 00 |
| Iron hoops 18$^l$ at 2$^d$ per li | 00 | 03 | 00 |
| In the backside Old lumber | 00 | 04 | 00 |
| One Old lave & turn | 00 | 05 | 00 |
| One Joynter & turn | 00 | 02 | 00 |
| Two Axes Two Adds One Sheering hatchet & Round Share | 00 | 01 | 06 |
| One adds Bungborer & paring knife | 00 | 01 | 06 |
| Three paire of Compasses | 00 | 00 | 10 |
| One parring ladder & plane | 00 | 01 | 00 |
| Twenty Six Toaches of twiggs | 00 | 08 | 08 |

### More in the Kitchen

| | | | |
|---|---|---|---|
| One brass pott One Bell mettle One plate  } | | | |
| Two kettles 32lb at 9$^d$ per lb  } | 01 | 04 | 00 |
| Iron 7 lb at 1$^d$ per lb | 00 | 00 | 07 |
| One grate Two pair of tongs Two Shovells One Trippett five spits fender & paire of holders Two boxes & Irons & One new fork | 00 | 19 | 06 |
| Money in his purse at the time of his death | 00 | 00 | 06 |

An account of moneyes & debts – reced by the said Sarah Williams since the death of the said Aaron Williams [not transcribed here]

## No.58 Kingsdown Parade, 1811 (BRO 40563/8)

This is not a probate inventory, but an inventory of fixtures in a house about to be leased. This inventory is of particular value in giving the contemporary names of rooms in a house typical of the many hundreds of houses constructed in the building boom of the early 1790s.

*Back Garrett*

One small iron grate
Wire grating for window with lock
One bell pull with cranks

*Front Garrett left hand side*

One wire window grating with lock
One small iron grate

*Garret passage*

One bell complete

*Second floor, Back Bed Room*

One bath stove grate
One bell with two pulls
One rowler blind
One cupboard with shelves and Pins

*Second Floor, Front bed room – right hand side*

One rowler blind

*Front Bedroom – left hand side*

Two rowler blinds
One bell with two pulls
One Bath stove grate
Two cupboards on each side of fire place with shelves

*First Floor, Back Bed Room*

One rowler blind
One Bell with two Pulls
Cupboard on each side fireplace with shelves
One door bolt with a pull
One bath stove grate

*Drawing Room*

Three rowler blinds
One Logister (?) Legister [?] bright stove, quite new
Two bell pulls

*First Window in Stairs*

One rowler blind
Three iron rods across window frame

*Second Window in Stairs*

Three iron rods across window

*Stairs*

Brass eyes fixed for rods up to the second floor complete

*[Ground Floor (Street Level)]*

*Back Parlour*

Three rowler blinds to bow window
One Bath stove grate
One bell pull

*China Pantry*

Dresser and shelves complete
And bell and pull next the door

*Front Parlour*

Two rowler blinds
One Bath stove grate
One bell with two pulls
Two sets of French blinds to window

*Passage to front Door*

One lamp and lamp irons complete over the front door
Two mahogany Hat rails with brass pins complete
One extra door covered with green bays [sic] and brass nailed in the passage
One brass lamp hook

*Garden Level*

*Kitchen*

One grate with two swing crows
Two spit hooks
One ash pit grate
Smoak [sic] jack and chains
One crane one oven
and hot dresser
One dresser with shelves, cupboards and drawers
One rowler for reel towel

*Cooks Pantry*

One dresser with shelves and hooks
One wire lattice to the window
And one shutter

*Front Cellar*

Two oak beer Horses (one small one large)
Three sliding boards to coal house

*Servants Pantry*

Three shelves
One bottle drainer
Meat hooks
And wire lattice over the door

*Back Kitchen*

One common grate
Two cupboards with doors and shelves
And small boiler
And clamp kiln
Two shelves
Fixed table for cleaning knives &c with drawer
One soft water pump with trow complete

*Back Area*

One inclosed [sic] canvas meat cupboard [ironmongery]
One patent lock and key to wine cellar door
Locks and keys to every door except the garrets
Door plates to drawing room, parlour and best bedroom

Witness         R Harrison
James Leman     James Moore

Note: for the inventory of Andrew Hooke's house in Lewin's Mead, see Ashley Manor above.

# No.16 Lower Maudlin Street, 1729, John Rowe (TNA PROB3 28/91)

A True & Perfect Inventory of All & Singular the Goods Chattles & Credits of John Rowe late of the City of Bristoll Esq. deced taken valued & appraised on the 17th 18th & 25th days of Aprill anno domi 1729 By Virtue of a Commission Issued under the Seal of the Prerogative Court of Canterbury directed to us whose names are underwritten doth follow vizt./

### In the back upper Room

|  | £ | s | d |
|---|---|---|---|
| One press bedstead mill Puff bed feather Bolster and Pillow With a Rugg and Blankett | 2 | 0 | 0 |
| Two Cloathes Hussys |  | 6 | 0 |
| Two Battle Pieces seaventeen Prints & a mappe | 0 | 17 | 0 |
| Seaventeen prints more | 0 | 4 | 0 |
| Three India Pictures | 0 | 15 | 0 |
| One hair line & one Old Wooden chair | 0 | 3 | 0 |
| One Bedstead with Wrought furniture and lined with Striped Dimitty and one Counterpane | 10 | 0 | 0 |
| One Pair of ten Quarter Whitney Blankets | 0 | 14 | 0 |
| One Quilt | 0 | 18 | 0 |
| One Old Oaken Chest | 0 | 4 | 0 |

### In the little back Roome, the same floor

| Eight Old Cushions | 0 | 4 | 0 |
|---|---|---|---|
| One Portugal floor matt | 0 | 4 | 0 |
| Six Old Boxes, Two Old Trunks, Five Old Turkey Worked Seates And Backs of Chairs | 0 | 10 | 0 |
| Two China Sconces | 0 | 2 | 6 |
| One Bucking Cloth | 0 | 3 | 6 |

### In the Servts. Roome the same floor fore street

| One Bedstead with Plodd furniture, feather Bed and Bolster four Blankets one quilt and Two Pair of window Curtains and Rods | 3 | 15 | 0 |
|---|---|---|---|
| One Dressing Table and Skreen Glass | 0 | 15 | 0 |
| Four Old Cane Chaires | 0 | 15 | 0 |
| One Iron Fender | 0 | 2 | 0 |
| Two Pictures in the Closet | 0 | 1 | 0 |
| One Old Pair of Bellows | 0 | 0 | 6 |

### In the other Roome the same floor

| Three Old Blankets & One Old Quilt | 0 | 11 | 0 |
|---|---|---|---|
| Yellow Cheyney Hangings | 1 | 2 | 6 |
| Three Pillows & One Pillow Case | 0 | 5 | 0 |
| Three Old Cane Chaires One Armed Ditto | 0 | 6 | 0 |
| Two Iron dogs with Brass Heads | 0 | 2 | 0 |
| [fol 2] |  |  |  |
| One Oak Case of drawerers [sic] | 0 | 19 | 0 |
| One Ironing Board with Tressells and Covered with Green Kersey & One Small Table | 0 | 10 | 0 |

### Linnen

| Four Pair of Holland Sheets | 4 | 0 | 0 |
|---|---|---|---|
| Four Pair of Old fine Sheets | 1 | 13 | 0 |
| Five Pair of Sheets | 3 | 18 | 0 |
| Five Pair of Servts Sheets | 2 | 3 | 0 |
| Nine Pair of Old Servts Sheets | 1 | 8 | 0 |
| Twelve Pair of Pillow Cases | 1 | 1 | 0 |
| One Suite of fine damask Table Linnen Consisting of One Large Table Cloth & Twelve Napkins | 5 | 0 | 0 |
| One damask Table Cloth & eleven Napkins | 1 | 3 | 0 |
| One diaper Table Cloth & eleven Napkins | 1 | 4 | 0 |
| One Small diaper Table Cloth & twenty Napkins | 1 | 7 | 6 |
| One Small Table Cloth & Six Napkins | 0 | 11 | 0 |
| Two Small Table Cloths & eleven Napkins | 0 | 6 | 8 |
| Two Small Table Cloths & seaventeen Napkins | 0 | 11 | 6 |
| Two Small Table Cloths & nine Napkins | 0 | 8 | 0 |
| Five Hugabag Table Cloths & Twenty Napkins very old | 0 | 11 | 6 |
| Five Table Cloths & Five Napkins | 0 | 11 | 6 |
| Five diaper Towells seaventeen Coarse Towells | 0 | 7 | 0 |
| Nineteen Ordinary Coarse Napkins | 0 | 4 | 6 |
| Nine Servts Table Cloths | 0 | 7 | 3 |
| Nine Coarse Cloths | 0 | 5 | 6 |
| Twelve Coarse Ordinary Towells | 0 | 1 | 6 |

### In the Redd Roome

One Red Bed with Curtains & Valians (not valued in this Appraism.t being bespoke by the deced in his Life time but delivered since his death & paid for by Mrs Rowe out of the Deceds Moneys

| Three Cane Chairs & One Arm'd Do with Squabbs | 1 | 4 | 0 |
|---|---|---|---|
| One Dressing Table with Case & One Skreen Glass | 0 | 15 | 0 |
| One Close Stool & Pan | 0 | 5 | 0 |
| Two Pair of Linnen Curtains Two Pair of Muslin Do & One Pair of Old Stuffe Window Curtains | 0 | 13 | 0 |

### In the Roome over the Little Parlour

| One Black Japand Cabinet with Gilt frame | 3 | 0 | 0 |
|---|---|---|---|
| One Skreen Table & Two Old Stands | 0 | 6 | 6 |
| Three Black Cane Chairs One Arm'd Do & Three Squabbs | 1 | 8 | 0 |
| One family Picture with Gilt frame | 0 | 15 | 0 |
| One Muskett & Bayonett One Blunderbuss & One Pair of Screwed Pistolls | 1 | 15 | 0 |
| Four Old Curtain Rodds | 0 | 2 | 8 |
| [fol 3] |  |  |  |

### In the Green Roome

| One Green Camblett Bed with Curtains & Vallians | 6 | 0 | 0 |
|---|---|---|---|
| One feather Bed & Bolster with a Check Case One Pair of large fine Blanketts One Pair of Coarse Do One Quilt One Pair of fine Sheets Six Pillows & Pillow Cases | 7 | 2 | 0 |
| One Easy Chair One Case of Drawers on a frame Two Cane Chairs & One arm'd Do with Two Squabbs | 3 | 10 | 0 |
| One Dressing Table One Skreen Glass One Brass Hearth with Creepers Slice Tongs & Brass Fender | 1 | 14 | 0 |

### In the Roome over the Kitchin

| One old Chest of Drawers on a frame Three Cane Chairs One Small Stove Grate | 1 | 5 | 0 |
|---|---|---|---|

### In the Closett within the same Roome

| One Truckle bedstead with flock Bed & Bolster & feather Bolster One Pair of Sheets One Blankett Three Ruggs | 1 | 8 | 6 |
|---|---|---|---|

### In the Stair Case

| One Pendulum Clock & Case | 4 | 12 | 6 |
|---|---|---|---|

### In the Hall

| Two Windsor Chairs | 0 | 10 | 0 |
|---|---|---|---|
| One Oval Walnutt Table | 0 | 8 | 0 |

### In the little Parlour

| | £ | s | d |
|---|---|---|---|
| One large Sconce Glass One Mohogony Folding Card Table Three Cane Chairs One Arm'd Dº with a Squabb One Hand Bell | 3 | 6 | 0 |
| One hand Tea Table One Old Pair of Bellows An Old Slice Tongs & Poker & a small Piece of Sale Cloth | 0 | 3 | 0 |

### In the best Parlour

| | £ | s | d |
|---|---|---|---|
| Six Black Cane Chairs One Arm'd Dº & One Black Card Table lined with velvet | 3 | 9 | 0 |
| One Pier Glass One Tea Table One Skreen Table Two Glass Sconces & a Pair of Glass Armes | 3 | 9 | 0 |
| One Stove Grate a Pitt Grate Slice Tongs & Poker | 1 | 3 | 0 |
| One Old Tea Table | 0 | 4 | 6 |
| A Parcell of China Ware some being broken | 3 | 17 | 0 |
| A dozⁿ of Ivory halfted Knives & forks in a Case | 1 | 5 | 0 |

### In the Pantry

| | £ | s | d |
|---|---|---|---|
| A Parcell of Delfe ware a Small Parcell of China Ware A Hand Tea Table Hand Maid & Corner Cupboard | 1 | 7 | 0 |

### In the best Kitchin

| | £ | s | d |
|---|---|---|---|
| Five Wooden Chairs & Two Tables | 1 | 0 | 0 |
| One Warming Pan, One Copper frying Pan, Ten brass Candlesticks, One Brass Ring One Chaffing Dish One Mortar One Tea Kettle & Lamp One Chocolate Pott Two Coffee Pott, One Copper Coale Pan One Other Tea Kettle | 3 | 6 | 6 |
| One Kitchin Grate fender Slice Tongs Corner Irons ThreeSpits One Gridiron One Tripett, Ash Pitt Grate, One Chopping Knife Pothooks & an Iron Plate Heater [fol 4] | 2 | 10 | 7 |
| Two Ironing Boxes & Heaters | 0 | 5 | 6 |
| Twenty Pewter Dishes Big & Small Twenty One Old Pewter Plates & Three Dozn of best Pewter Plates | 5 | 10 | 3 |
| Three Brass Potts One Brass Dish Kettle One Bellmettle Skillet & One Bellmettle Posnett | 2 | 8 | 0 |

### In the back Kitchin

| | £ | s | d |
|---|---|---|---|
| One Fire Skreen One old Tin Watering Pott One Chopping Block & chopping Bench One Bason Two Sauce Panns One Pair of Iron Racks One Pye Board & One Knife Board | 0 | 8 | 8 |

### In the Kitchin Pantry

| | £ | s | d |
|---|---|---|---|
| Five Knives & forks One Knife Baskett One Copper Pott | 0 | 4 | 0 |
| Two Brass Pollidds | 0 | 6 | 0 |
| One Brass Pair of Scales & Weight One Brass Scimmer Two Ladles One Egg Spoon One Pewter Cullender Six Peices of Tin Ware & some wooden ware | 0 | 11 | 0 |

### In the Parlour unfinish't

| | £ | s | d |
|---|---|---|---|
| Six Brewing Tubbs One Stepp Ladder One Sale Cloth & Ten Yards of narrow Sale Cloth | 2 | 9 | 0 |

### In the Cellar

| | £ | s | d |
|---|---|---|---|
| Three Kilderkins Two Barrells One Firkin Three Horses One Hen Cubb One Bottle Rack & abt. Four dozn. Bottles One Bellmettle Pott One Powdering Tubb One Scald Pott & One Pan | 1 | 11 | 6 |

### Plate

Listed but not noted here

| | £ | s | d |
|---|---|---|---|
| The Deced's Wearing Apparell, One Old Silver Watch One Pockett Book Two Old Swords Two Pair of Gold Buttons & Several odd small Gold Rings | 10 | 10 | 0 |
| A Parcell of Books in Law History Divinity Classicks & Miscellanies [no value given] | | | |
| One Garden Rowler with Iron work't handle | 0 | 14 | 0 |
| Cash in house (over & besides the Broad Gold after menconed) | 5 | 5 | 0 |
| Twelve Peices of Broad Gold 23ˢ each & eleven peices of Dº value 25ˢ each (wch. are alledged to have been given by the decd to his wife in lieu of a Pair of Diamond Earings [no value given] | | | |
| One Gold Watch Two Diamond Rings One Small Dº One small Gold Chain Two Plain Gold Rings & a small Enamell'd Watch wch. are not valued in this Appraismemt. Being claimed by the deced's widow as her Paraphenalia | | | |
| One Saddle Bridle wth. Housing & Holster Cases | 0 | 15 | 0 |

[Appraisers:]
Daniel Shewring
Matthew Bowen
William Elliott
Luke Shewring

Debts due to the deceased at the time of his death and book debts Both listed in detail, not noted here.

## No.8 Park Lane in the Little Park and no.23 Broad Street, 1676/7, Richard Jordan (BRO Inventory 1677/27)

Little Park was Jordan's garden house; for no.23 Broad Street, see Fig 6.2.

An Inventory indented of the goods moneys chattels and debts which were of Richard Jordan, Painter deceased taken and appraised by Jonathan Sandford Sopemaker and John Price Carpenter the Seventh day of february in the yeer of our Lord God One Thousand Six hundred Seaventy Six

### Imprimus in his house in the Park

### In the Garrett

| | £ | s | d |
|---|---|---|---|
| a half headed bedsteed a millpuffe bedd and bolster and a mat and bedd cord | 00 | 10 | 00 |
| one wooden close stoole a flasket and a hamper with beanes | 00 | 03 | 00 |

### Item in the upper Chamber

| | £ | s | d |
|---|---|---|---|
| one bed steed matt and cord | 00 | 06 | 00 |
| The greene curtaines & valians about the bed steed | 00 | 04 | 00 |
| The feather bedd there and case | 00 | 10 | 00 |
| A bolster and pillow of the same | 00 | 05 | 00 |
| A millpuffe bedd and bolster | 00 | 06 | 06 |
| A redd rugg and a white blanket | 00 | 07 | 06 |
| A truckle bedsteed matt and cord bedd bolster and coverledd | 00 | 10 | 00 |
| One stoole one chaire one little table & one box | 00 | 06 | 06 |
| One paire of creepers with brasse topps a Glass Case and a brush | 00 | 03 | 06 |
| One Case of drawers | 01 | 00 | 00 |
| One Oaken Chest | 00 | 07 | 00 |
| Trifles upon the Clavy peece | 00 | 00 | 06 |

| | | | |
|---|---|---|---|
| Fower white flannen Curtaines & valaines | 00 | 05 | 00 |
| One greene Rugg One redd Rug and a White hamacke | 00 | 15 | 00 |
| One Pincushion | 00 | 01 | 00 |
| fower other greene Curtaines and valaines Two Carpets Two Cushions | 00 | 15 | 00 |
| One bucking Cloth and One bagg | 00 | 01 | 00 |
| Eleaven paire of sheetes | 02 | 15 | 00 |
| One paire of holland sheetes | 00 | 10 | 00 |
| fower table clothes & Six Side board Clothes | 01 | 00 | 00 |
| Three dozen of Table napkins | 01 | 00 | 00 |
| Seaven pillow cases | 00 | 10 | 00 |
| Two mantles and One Cotten coate | 00 | 10 | 00 |
| Two pillow cases and a child's mantle One Small pillow Three Towels | 00 | 03 | 06 |

*Item in the Dyning Roome*

| | | | |
|---|---|---|---|
| One feild bed steed | 00 | 06 | 00 |
| One feather bedd & bolster & an old blanket | 01 | 00 | 00 |
| five pictures and an Escutcheon | 00 | 10 | 00 |
| One Oval Table and Three joint stooles | 01 | 00 | 00 |
| Eleaven leather chaires | 01 | 02 | 00 |
| Fifteene Glasses on the Clavy | 00 | 03 | 00 |
| One paire of bellowes | 00 | 01 | 06 |
| One paire of long Andirons One paire of short Andirons & Two paire of slice & tongs all with Brasses | 00 | 08 | 00 |
| One old side Cupboard | 00 | 02 | 06 |
| Three shirtes | 00 | 06 | 00 |
| In Pewter (vizt) One cupp Seaventeene platters great & Small Two pie plates Nine trencher plates Six porringers Eight sawcers Three candlesticks Two Tankards Two mustard potts One Sawce cup One bottle One halfe pinte pott One flagon | 02 | 00 | 00 |
| In brasse fower candlesticks One pestell and mortar One paire of Snuffers One chafing dish | 00 | 07 | 00 |

*Item in the Kitchen*

| | | | |
|---|---|---|---|
| One Table board with a drawer fower joint stooles One leather chaire Two matted chaires One greene Stoole | 00 | 11 | 00 |
| Earthen ware of Severall Sorts | 00 | 06 | 08 |
| Woodden ware of Severall Sorts | 00 | 07 | 00 |
| One looking glasse | 00 | 02 | 06 |
| Iron ware (vizt) a Crane a paire of Racks Two paire of Andirons one of them with brasse heads Two fire forks One flesh fork fower Spits One paire of tongs & Slice Two Gridirons One Jacke Two stands One chopping knife & One mincing knife One barr One paire of doggs One paire of pothooks Two Hangells Brasse ware One warming pann One great kettle One little kettle Two crocks Two skillets Three ladles | 03 | 00 | 00 |
| | 01 | 10 | 00 |
| One small deske Two bibles One Testament and Two other small books | 00 | 05 | 00 |

*In the Cellar*

| | | | |
|---|---|---|---|
| Wood cole caske Earthern panns And other lumber | 01 | 00 | 00 |

*In the Kitchen more*

| | | | |
|---|---|---|---|
| two course table clothes and a napkin | 00 | 02 | 06 |

*In the Pavement*

| | | | |
|---|---|---|---|
| One leaden Cisterne | 03 | 00 | 00 |

*Item in his Dwelling House in Broad Streete*

| | | | |
|---|---|---|---|
| One old bed steed matt and cord | 00 | 05 | 00 |
| Item one bedd bolster and Rug | 00 | 07 | 00 |
| One old Chest fower pillowes & one bolster case | 00 | 10 | 00 |
| One Trunke and One deske | 00 | 01 | 00 |
| One cradle One Twigg chaire | 00 | 02 | 00 |
| One Table board Three joint stooles | 00 | 07 | 00 |
| One other bed steed Matt and Cord | 00 | 05 | 00 |
| One sett of curtaines and valaines and Curtaine rodds | 00 | 03 | 00 |
| One feather bedd One flocke bedd One feather bolster One flocke bolster Three feather pillowes Two rugs and Two blankets | 02 | 00 | 00 |
| One chest and a frame | 00 | 08 | 00 |
| Iron ware (vizt) a paire of tongs and slice a paire of dogs an old barr One Crane a paire of Andirons One Crocke One frying pan One Chafing dish and One Candlestick | 00 | 10 | 00 |
| Item one clothe suite and an haire Cloake | 04 | 00 | 00 |
| One greene sett rug | 00 | 16 | 00 |
| Six Cushions | 00 | 05 | 00 |
| One brasse Crocke | 00 | 03 | 00 |
| One brasse kettle | 00 | 01 | 06 |
| One Table board One joint stoole One Side Cupboard Two turned chaires Two matted chaires | 00 | 07 | 00 |
| Item his plate forty fower Ounces Three Quarters | 11 | 03 | 09 |
| Item Three Chattle lease houses | 140 | 00 | 00 |
| Item in ready money | 012 | 12 | 11½ |
| Item in debts | 026 | 00 | 00 |
| Summa totalis | ccxxxili | iis | x½d |

Ph Jordan

## No.55 Queen Charlotte Street, Abraham Hungerford, 1724 (TNA PROB3 23/135)

One of the first houses to be constructed in the development of the Square, no.55 Queen Square was just a few houses away from no.51 (Appendix 1).

The following inventory is summarised, focusing on the names and contents of the rooms with the values given in the original omitted:

*Nursery*

A bedstead etc, half headed bedstead etc, two sets of window curtains, one old dressing table, one small looking glass, one small chest and three old chairs

*Room 2 pair of Stairs backwards*

Used for domestic storage, contents not noted in detail.

*Chamber one pair of Stairs*

(No mention of grate or hearth furniture.)
Bedstead with mohair furniture, 'one easy chair' six window curtains, 6 stuffed chairs, two stools, one cane chair, two glass candlesticks, a pair of 'fine Holland sheets', other linen.

*Room one pair of Stairs backwards*

A bedstead with green furniture and window curtains, printed hangings, linen, a fire grate, six Dutch matting chairs, a close stool.

*In the Closet in the same Room*

(Possibly a cupboard) one case of drawers and one trunk.

*In the fore Parlour*

2 large sconces
4 small sconces
1 large pier glass
1 tea table with 'the tea equipage'
2 sets of Calico window curtains and 1 pair of window squabbs
1 set of Dwigar window curtains and 1 pair of window squabbs
6 stuffed silk chairs
brass hearth, creepers etc.
1 stand for a tea kettle
1 small oval table

*Back Parlour [from its contents probably the dining room]*

6 cane chairs and squabbs
1 set of window curtains
1 stove grate and fender
1 pair of glass sconces
1 set of mock tapestry hanging
Chinaware
2 tables
Then follows a list of the plate, silver basin, tea kettle and coffee pot

*In the closet in the back Parlour*

paper hangings
parcel of books
leather chair

*Kitchen*

large grate and fender
cooking ware, dishes etc.
1 square table and 5 chairs

*Cellar*

Casks, tubs and bottle rack

*In the house of the deceased at Wickwar*

[not noted here]

## No.11 Queen Square, Shadrack Beale, mariner, 1713 (PROB 4/4403)

Appraised 31 March 1713 by William Humfrey, Michael White, George Irish and Athelstan Tyndall and John Hipsly and others.

The following inventory is summarised, focusing on the names and contents of the rooms with the values given in the original here omitted:

*Garrett*

drawers, cupboard, bed stead etc, window curtains, vallens

*Forestreet Chamber two pair of Stairs*

bed stead and 2 chairs

*Back chamber two pair of stairs*

tester bed with appts. curtains, vallens etc, feather bed, 3 Irish stich'd chairs, iron dogs, looking glass and 2 old round Dutch boxes [from Beal's travels?]

*Forestreet Chamber one pair of Stairs*

bed stead with raised tester, curtains etc, feather bed, bolster etc, looking glass, 6 black cane chairs, black case of drawers, black table and drawer

*Back Chamber one pair of Stairs*

curtained bed with feather bed, bolster etc, 6 cane chairs, small table and drawer, pair of calico window curtains and vallens etc, brass andirons, small looking glass

*Closet in same Chamber*

1 Irish stich'd chair, 3 old chairs

*Ground floor*

*Parlour*

6 cane chairs, 6 window squab and 2 ditto, table board, Irish stich'd carpet, clock case, looking glass, 2 pairs of window curtains, vallens etc, one stove grate and iron back, tongs etc, earthenware, 2 decanters and glasses

*Kitchen*

Couch, couch squab, 5 cane chairs and cane arm chair, iron grate and cheeks, 1 pr of racks, shovel etc, cooking items including pothooks, gridirons etc
[definitely the main cooking kitchen]
1 old pair of window curtains, vallens etc small table and chairs, 6 small brass candlesticks, parcel of old books, spits

*Chamber over back Kitchen*

2 half headed bed steads with flock beds etc, 5 brewing tubs etc, parcel of bottles

*Back Kitchen*

6 old chairs, table, dog wheel and spindle, 3 iron candlesticks, ironing box and 2 clamps, grate and cheeks, ladle and skimmer, earthenware

*Cellar*

barrels, kilderkins

*Plate*

in all 69 oz at                                             £17. 05. 00
Then linen, pewter not noted in detail here.
His interest in ship *Flying Horse* and its cargo uncertain
Lease of his dwelling house for about 49 years to come
Total                                                       £233. 07. 11

## No. 16 Queen Square, Michael Miller, 1781 (PROB31/694 no.446)

The very detailed inventory of Michael Miller, who died 31 July 1781, is summarised, focusing on the names and contents of the rooms with the values of individual items given in the original here omitted.

The inventory first of all summarises the cash, notes, lottery tickets and promissory notes left by the deceased.

The rooms and contents are as follows:

### Back Parlour

Large picture of Edward Elton esq delivered to him. Looking glass with gilt frame, 2 large prints, 2 middle do. 2 smaller do., one Guiandole [girandole], 2 oval pictures, 1 mahogany inlaid side board, mahogany card table, one small mahogany folding table, 2 mahogany elbow chairs, horse hair buttons with brass nails, 6 mahogany chairs ditto, 2 window blinds, 2 yellow window curtains, 1 firescreen, 1 steel grate, fender, tongs, poker, slice, Turkey carpet and two drawings glazed
Valued and appraised at the sum of £32 10s

### Fore Parlour

Large pier glasss, chimney glass with sconces, 2 window curtains, 2 window blinds, 6 India prints gilt framed, 2 mahogany elbow chairs yellow damask with brass nails, 8 mahogany chairs ditto ditto, mahogany card table, small mahogany table, steel grate with fender, tongs, poker, slice, 1 large Wilton carpet with green covering
Valued and appraised at the sum of £44 0s 6d

### Little Parlour

1 mahogany bureau with book case, 6 walnut chairs horse hair bottomed, 1 mahogany wash hand stand, 8 pictures various sorts framed, 1 very old carpet, 1 brass fender, 1 fire shovel, tongs and poker, 1 mahogany folding screen, 1 yellow window curtain, 1 small mahogany wine cooler and mirrour
Valued and appraised at the sum of £9 18s 6d

### Hall

1 large marble table, 2 large mahogany tables, 1 8 day clock, 1 clothes press, 4 Windsor chairs, a map of Bristol, 4 prints, 1 blind, a remnant of hair cloth & shoebag
Valued and appraised at the sum of £17 0s 0d

### Bed Chamber first Story

30 Japan dressing boxes, 2 Japan bottles, 1 Japan dressing glass, 9 bead ear rings, 1 pair shoe and knee buckles, a flower picture in a frame, 1 magic lanthorne, 1 print of Alexander, 1 small looking glass, 1 print of our Saviour, mahogany press bed, 1 cotton bed with 2 window curtains of the same, mahogany fluted bedstead, milpuff bed, bolster and 2 pillows, 1 great chair, 6 mahogany elbow chairs, 1 mahogany night stool, 1 mahogany wash hand stand, 1 Wilton carpet & green covering thereto, 1 mahogany Pembroke table, 1 toilet table, 1 brass fender, slice, tongs and poker, 1 mattrass, and 1 mahogany comb tray
Valued and appraised at the sum of £45 14s 6d

### Dining Room

2 large looking glasses, 2 large looking glasses with sconces, two guiandoles [girandoles], 2 mahogany elbow chairs & 16 mahogany chairs covered with red Harrateen, cushions & red checks, 5 red Harateen curtains, 5 Venetian blinds, 6 large glazed prints, 1 small do., 2 mahogany card tables, 1 steel grate, fender tongs & poker 1 India 6-leaved screen & 2 chimney boards covered in India paper
Valued and appraised at the sum of £61 1s 6d
1 mahogany firescreen worked with silk
Valued 10s

### Back Room first Story

A picture of Shakespeare, 1 marble side board mahogany framed, 1 small empty trunk, 1 brass fender & grate, 1 sopha covered with crimson morine and check case, 1 iron compass, fender & one set of fire irons
Valued and appraised at the sum of £10 19s 6d

### Yellow Room

yellow morine bed with 2 window curtains of the same, 1 mahogany fluted bedstead, milpuff bed & feather bolster, 4 walnut chairs with yellow check covers, 1 small Wilton carpet, 2 bedside carpets, 1 deal table with yellow stuff covering, 1 gilt frame dressing glass, 3 prints & 1 double mahogany chest of drawers
Valued and appraised at the sum of £17 1s 0d

### Green room

green damask bed with 2 window curtains of same, 1 feather bed, mattress, bolster & 2 pillows, 1 elbow chair & 6 chairs walnut with green cheque covers, 1 Wilton carpet, 1 gilt frame dressing glass, 1 mahogany framed looking glass, 1 deal table with blue stuff covering, 1 mahogany night stool, 3 large prints, 1 small print, 1 small do, 1 mahogany double chest of drawers, 1 mahogany wash hand stand with china basin & bottle, 1 iron fender, 2 china chamber pots, a slice, tongs & poker
Valued and appraised at the sum of £30 18s 0d

### In the Nursery

2 oak bedsteads, 2 cotton beds with 2 window curtains of same, 2 four post bedsteads, 2 milpuff beds & bolsters, 6 walnut chairs with cheque bottoms, 1 deal table covered with red stuff, 1 mahogany double chest of drawers, 1 mahogany framed dressing glass and toilet table, slice, tongs & poker, 1 steel fender, 1 very old Turkey carpet, 1 bedside carpet & 1 round deal table
Valued and appraised at the sum of £19 17s 6d

### Closet in the Nursery

milpuff bed & bolster, oak bedstead, mahogany chest of drawers
Valued and appraised at the sum of £2 2s 8d

### Back Room second Story

1 oak bedstead and milpuff bed with cheque furniture, 1 deal table, 1 small mahogany framed looking glass, 2 walnut chairs with cheque covers, 1 mahogany fluted bedstead, 1 feather bed bolster & 2 pillows harrateen furniture
Valued and appraised at the sum of £15 12s 6d

### Garrett
1 Oak bedstead, feather bed & bolster, one oak bedstead milpuff bed & bolster, 1 mahogany childs chair, 1 childs crib, a lark cage, 1 deal wardrobe, 1 old matt & 1 long dusting brush
Valued and appraised at the sum of £8 9s 0d

### In the Laundry
1 large cloths horse, small ditto, iron fender slice, tongs & tin fender, 2 deal ironing boards, 2 tressells, 2 ironing boxes with stands & 2 pair of heaters, 1 old deal folding table, 3 flat irons, 1 large barbam iron, 1 deal plate rack, 2 deal boxes, 7 mahogany dish stands, 1 old cupboard, 1 ironing cloth, 1 bendezer, 13 pattipans, 1 buffet, 1 dresser, 5 shelves
Valued and appraised at the sum of £3 16s 0d

### Kitchen
1 brass warming pan, 1 spice mortar and pestle, 2 flat candlesticks, 2 ditto, 1 skimmer, 1 dish kettle and cover, 1 copper warming pan, one ditto, plate warmer, 1 ditto, coal scoop, 1 ditto scuttle, 1 ditto large boiler & cover, 1 ditto oval stew pan & cover, 1 ditto large saucepan, 1 ditto dish cover, 1 ditto stewpan, 2 ditto ditto & cover, 6 ditto small saucepans, 1 dito small pott & cover, 3 ditto tea kettles, 1 bell mettle kettle, 1 chocolate pot, 1 pair of scales & weights & 1 copper beer pot
Then   pewter   ) all in the
       Iron   ) kitchen
       Tinware ) all inclusive
Valued and appraised at the sum of £27 6s 0d

### Passage
1 lamp, chopping block, 2 pails & 1 bucket, iron chaffing dish, ash cart, brush & mop cupboard
Valued and appraised at the sum of £1 14s 0d
Then sundry other household furniture not listed by room.

### Fixtures
2 door lamps, deal dresser & shelves in closet in back room, first storey
2 chimney boards in the dining room
lanthorne on the stairs
bins & cheese rack in the wine cellar
7 iron curtain rods, old mirror & prints, mahogany book shelf, smoke jack & chains, kitchen grate & brass front hobb grate in bedchamber
two sash windows in the couinting house
grate & hobbs crane in the warehouse
one alphabet cupboards drawers & a nest of sample drawers
Valued and appraised at the sum of £30 2s 0d
Then Plate, jewels & trinkets at great level of detail
       China & glass   "   "   "   "   "
       Books           "   "   "   "   "
Total for estate £3245 19s 0d

## No.22 Queen Square, 1718/19, George Stephens (TNA PROB 3 19/50)

Appd 2 Jan 1718/19 by William Bush, John Wraxall, William Reeve, Richard Bayly, Peter Muggleworth, Joseph Fowles, John Payne, Matthew Bowen, Jacob Hollister, Isaac Cotther et al
Trade goods (several membranes), wool, worsteds, linen
Household Goods (include)

|  | £ | s | d |
|---|---|---|---|

### Garrett
Domestic storage including cheese rack & boards, saddle etc, lanthorne, bottles & garden glasses — 1  11  6

### Servants Room
Suite of curtains and valances with tester bed stead and flock bed but with 2 feather pillows, blankets, sheets, 2 cane chairs, dressing table & looking glass, 2 pairs of window curtains — 4  4  0

### Room next the servants, Forestreet
2 pairs of window curtains, 5 cane chairs, 3 ditto black, 1 Press bed stead and all pillows, blankets etc — 3  9  6

### Black Room
linen, drawers, coffer, 2 pictures of William & Mary, step ladder, pair of leaves for an ovalTable, 2 pairs window curtains, 2 leaves for the windows — 4  0  0

### Passage on the same Floor
old chest & linen — 2  11  6

### Blew Room
standing bed stead and counterpane with Feather bed etc, 2 stools, 4 chairs, rug and chest of drawers on a frame, dressing table, linen, one union sett, 2 pairs window curtains, one suite paper hangings — 16  2  6

### Red Room
Crimson mohair bed & counterpane lined with white satin, feather bed, bolster, pillows etc – calico counterpane, one case curtains and rods, 2 pairs of muslin curtains, 6 small chairs & 1 elbow ditto, 7 mohair cushions, dressing table & cover, looking glass, bellows & a hand brush — 40  9  0

### Irish stich Room
1 camblett bed lined with stuff, calico Quilt etc, 2 pairs window curtains & valences, 6 cane chairs, 2 square stools, dressing table, box & boxes, tea table, 2 sconces, brush [?for hearth], one suite Irish stich hangings — 19  11  0

### Fore Parlour
6 elbow chairs, 6 cushions, 2 pairs of window Curtains & valences, one glass, 1 Dutch table, 1 card table, 4 glass sconces 2 window squabs, 3 sash shades for the windows — 17  3  0

### Little Parlour
one cane couch, one couch squab, 5 cane chairs, 5 cushions, — 3  11  0
1 Dutch table, 1 pair of window curtains & 1 window squab

### Back Parlour
large glass, 2 pairs of window curtains & Vallancess, one 'easy' chair, 5 small chairs, 2 elbow chairs, 1 small table, 1 square table, 2 glass Sconces, 7 squabs — 9  10  0

### In the Staircase
large map, 4 prints of heraldry, 1 Landskip, 2 large India prints, 4 lesser India prints 12 small India prints, 6 large pictures — 5  7  0

### Hall
12 [illeg], 3 ladder chairs, 1 oval table, 10 small Pictures, 2 Large pictures — 2  6  6

## Little Kitchen

3 ladder chairs, 1 table, napkin press, 1 window
curtain etc      1   6   0

## In Great kitchen & Room over

4 ladder chairs, 1 wooden chair, 1 glass, 1 oval table, 1 chair,
1 square table, 2 pairs curtains & vallions, Bedstead, 1 matt,
flock bed, bolster, pillow, 3 blankets, sheets and rug    2   3   9

## Cellar

Domestic storage including tubs & 9 kinderkins

House in Queen Square valued at £1000

## House on the Bridge

[The rooms of this house are not identified except for the 'dark room'. From the contents listed (beds, tables, chairs etc), this house was used both for sleeping and living; it had perhaps been Stephens' residence at an earlier date or possibly used for his employees. The contents of the house were valued at £8 9s 9d. Following this section the inventory returns to the back kitchen, probably of the house first described and identified here as being no.22 Queen Square.]

## Back Kitchen

barrel furnace, iron work, iron boiler, iron work, scales and balance, small still and appts
Brass and pewter are all listed separately, as is silver plate and all his 'China ware' including 1 teapot coloured, valued £9 5s 6d, 12 teacups & saucers etc.
The inventory then returns to the house on the bridge.
2 shop candlesticks, 2 brass kettles, 2 small candlesticks
The total value of his possessions is given as £12113, 14s 9¼d.

## No.12 St. James's Barton, 1766, Thomas Crosby (PROB 31/516/0.696)

A true and perfect Inventory of all and singular the goods Chattles and Credits of Thomas Crosby late of the City of Bristol deced. which since his death have come to the hands possession or knowledge of Rachel Crosby Widow the Relict and sole executrix named in the last Will and Testament of the said deceased taken valued and appraised the twenty fourth day of July in the Year of our Lord 1766 by Thomas Purnell and Richard Symes and given in and exhibited by virtue of the solemn Declaration or Affirmation of the said Rachel Crosby and are as follows to wit:

### In the fore Parlour

| | £ | s | d |
|---|---|---|---|
| Six Mahogany chairs with mixt Damask Cases and one Elbow Ditto | 5 | 0 | 0 |
| Two sets green mixt Damask Window Curtains | 2 | 10 | 0 |
| One Mahogany Card Table with Leather Case | 0 | 12 | 0 |
| One Mahogany Tea Chest one shagreen Case with Bottles | 0 | 18 | 0 |
| Four pieces Scotch Carpet | 1 | 5 | 0 |
| One Stove Grate Fire Shovel Tongs Poker and Brass Fender | 2 | 5 | 0 |
| One Wilton Carpet | 3 | 10 | 0 |

### In the back Parlour

| | | | |
|---|---|---|---|
| One Mahogany carved Tea Table | 1 | 1 | 0 |
| One large Stove Grate broken back Fire Shovel Tongs Poker and Brass carved Fender | 3 | 5 | 0 |
| One piece Scotch Carpet | 0 | 5 | 6 |

### In the Hall

| | | | |
|---|---|---|---|
| Two large square Mahogany Dining Tables | 4 | 4 | 0 |
| Two Green cloaths for Ditto | 0 | 15 | 0 |
| One Glass Lamp | 0 | 11 | 0 |
| Three pieces old Hair Cloth | 0 | 5 | 0 |

### In the Staircase

| | | | |
|---|---|---|---|
| One eight day Clock | 4 | 10 | 0 |
| One Mahogany Buroe | 3 | 10 | 0 |
| One Pewter Ink stand three penknives one Padlock one Nippers and Nuttcrackers one set of small Money Scales & Weights one Ivory Knife for folding Paper | 0 | 5 | 6 |
| Four pieces Scotch Carpet | 1 | 7 | 0 |
| One Leather Stool one small Hair Trunk | 0 | 3 | 6 |

### In the Closet in the Stair Case

| | | | |
|---|---|---|---|
| One large Stove Grate Fire Shovel Tongs Poker and Brass Fender | 3 | 0 | 0 |

### In the back Room first Story

| | | | |
|---|---|---|---|
| One four post Bedstead sacking cord etc with Mahogany Foot Pillars two sets Yellow Morine Window Curtains Rails etc | 4 | 16 | 0 |
| One Feather Bed Bolster and two Pillows in a check Case | 5 | 5 | 0 |
| One Mattrass and Check Counterpane and two Remnants of Check | | 1 | 8 |
| One Easy Chair with a green Morine Case & one Cotton Case to Ditto | 3 | 15 | 0 |
| One Mahogany double Case of Drawers | 6 | 0 | 0 |
| One ditto Bureau dressing Table and one swing dressing Glass with Drawers | 3 | 10 | 0 |
| One Mahogany Wash hand stand | 0 | 10 | 6 |
| Four white & Carpet Quilts | 5 | 15 | 0 |
| Three pair large fine Blankets | 2 | 8 | 0 |
| Three pair small coarse Ditto | 1 | 1 | 0 |

### In the fore Room first Story

| | | | |
|---|---|---|---|
| One Bedstead with Cotton furniture and two sets Window Curtains Rails etc to Do | 15 | 15 | 0 |
| One Wilton Floor Carpet and two Bedside Carpets | 3 | 0 | 0 |

### In the dressing Room

| | | | |
|---|---|---|---|
| One double chest of Drawers | 6 | 0 | 0 |
| Six Mahogany Chairs with Cotton Case one Elbow Do | 4 | 18 | 0 |
| Two Pier Glasses in Mahogany Frames and Gilt | 6 | 10 | 0 |
| One Mahogany Wash hand Stand | 0 | 10 | 6 |
| One small Mahogany Flap Table | 0 | 15 | 0 |

### In the Back Room 2d Story

| | | | |
|---|---|---|---|
| One four Post Bedstead with Green Morine Furniture two sets Window Curtains Rails etc | 6 | 10 | 0 |
| Six Virginia Walnut Chairs with green Morine Bottoms and one Close Stool Chair Ditto with Pewter Pan | 3 | 15 | 0 |
| One small Glass in Mahogany Frame | 2 | 5 | 0 |
| One Mahogany dressing Table with Drawers and swing Glass with drawers | 2 | 1 | 0 |
| One Milpuff Bed and Bolster | 1 | 15 | 0 |
| One old Floor Scotch Carpet two Bedside Do | 0 | 15 | 0 |

### In the Servants back Room

| | | | |
|---|---|---|---|
| One Feather Bed with check case Bolster and two pillows | 5 | 5 | 0 |

### In the servants fore Room

| | | | |
|---|---|---|---|
| One Bedstead with green China Furniture | 1 | 1 | 0 |
| Two Linen Quilts one flock Bolster | 1 | 2 | 0 |
| Six Rush bottom Chairs | 1 | 4 | 0 |
| One Deal dressing Table and small swing Glass | 0 | 7 | 6 |
| One Deal Cloth Chest | 0 | 6 | 0 |
| Two Crimson Check Window Curtains Rails etc | 1 | 5 | 0 |

### In the Laundery

| | | | |
|---|---|---|---|
| Four Windsor Chairs | 1 | 4 | 0 |
| One old Step Ladder and one stand for brushing cloaths | 0 | 4 | 0 |

### In the Kitchen

| | | | |
|---|---|---|---|
| One water Dish and six water plates | 1 | 14 | 0 |
| One Dozen and six best plates | 0 | 18 | 0 |
| One dozen smaller Do 10$^s$ and six best soop plates 7$^s$ | 0 | 17 | 0 |
| One tureen 7$^s$ one Oval Dish with a Plate 7$^s$ | 0 | 14 | 0 |
| Twelve Dishes of different sizes | 1 | 3 | 6 |
| Two soop Dishes 4$^s$ 6$^d$ one pint Cup and one old Cullender 3$^s$ | 0 | 7 | 6 |
| One large Copper pott and cover | 0 | 7 | 6 |
| One Copper Fish Kettle and Cover | 0 | 16 | 0 |
| One ditto small pot and Cover | 0 | 4 | 0 |
| One large sauce Pan and Cover four small Ditto and one small Lamp and odd Brass | 0 | 13 | 0 |
| Two Copper Stew pans | 0 | 7 | 0 |
| One brass dish kettle | 0 | 5 | 0 |
| One small Bell Mettle Kettle | 0 | 3 | 0 |
| One Pestle and Mortar two Ladles & one skimmer | 0 | 6 | 6 |
| Six brass Candlesticks | 0 | 10 | 6 |
| One brass Warming Pan Chocolate pot and brass trippett | 0 | 9 | 0 |
| One Tea Kettle and Brass Bason | 0 | 4 | 6 |
| Fifteen pieces of Tin Ware | 0 | 5 | 0 |
| One Copper Coal Carrier | 0 | 7 | 6 |
| One Spit one pair Racks six seives | 0 | 2 | 6 |
| Two Lead Trays and two small Leaves | 0 | 8 | 0 |
| One Fire shovel Tongs Poker and trippett two fenders and Gridirons | 0 | 9 | 0 |
| One Frying Pan Cleaver Chopping Knife Bellows and Rolling Pin | 0 | 6 | 0 |
| One Mahogany Tray and Tea Board | 0 | 9 | 6 |
| Sixteen Knives and Forks and Knife Box | 0 | 4 | 0 |
| Four board bottom Chairs | 0 | 8 | 0 |
| One large fire screen Tin'd | 0 | 7 | 6 |
| One Sugar Knife two brass Cocks | 0 | 2 | 0 |
| One washing tub one Beer stooper one Beer horse one small Tubb one close Hussey | 0 | 7 | 0 |
| One bottle rack one Bucking Basket three Coal Boxes two brushes one Rubber one Flat Block one Soap Box and two Bowles | 0 | 12 | 6 |
| Earthenware Glass Bottles etc | 0 | 4 | 6 |
| One Lead Tobacco Canister & 2 Bottle Boards | 0 | 1 | 6 |

### China Ware

| | | | |
|---|---|---|---|
| One small blue and white punch Bowl one salad Bason crack'd | 0 | 4 | 0 |
| Five burnt Fruit Plates | 0 | 7 | 6 |
| Seventeen blue and white plates broke and whole | 0 | 14 | 0 |
| Six Coffee Cups Milk pot one small Jarr one Tea Pot and Stand one Boat two Chocolate Cups | 0 | 10 | 6 |
| One Jugg | 0 | 3 | 6 |
| Ten Tea Cups twelve Saucers one Slop Bason and Stand one Butter plate | 0 | 8 | 6 |

### Glass Ware

| | | | |
|---|---|---|---|
| Three Glass Decanters three Tumblers two Salts Fourteen Wine Glasses | 0 | 18 | 0 |
| One Steel Snuffers and Stand | 0 | 4 | 6 |

### Plate

[AQ25]

| | | | |
|---|---|---|---|
| Twelve Knives and twelve Forks in a Shagreen Case | 2 | 10 | 0 |
| Two Butter Dishes 20$^{oz}$ at 6$^s$ 6$^d$ | 6 | 10 | 0 |
| Two half pint Canns 15$^{oz}$ 10 $^{pwts}$ @ 6$^s$ | 4 | 13 | 0 |
| One pint Cann | 3 | 3 | 0 |
| Three Casters 13$^{oz}$ 5$^{pwts}$@6.6 | 4 | 6 | 1½ |
| One small salver 7:18 @ 6:6 | 2 | 11 | 4 |
| One Sauce Spoon 6:5 at 6 | 1 | 17 | 6 |
| Ten Table Spoons five Tea Do 20$^{oz}$ @6 | 6 | 0 | 0 |
| One plain Gold Watch | 7 | 7 | 0 |
| One Do old Silver Do | 2 | 10 | 0 |
| One pair old plain gold sleve Buttons one pair Stone set in gold | 1 | 10 | 0 |
| To cash paid William Rogers of Bath in exchange with four old Candlesticks for two prs of New Silver Ditto as per Receipt | 23 | 19 | 0 |
| Three Books | 0 | 7 | 6 |

### Linen

| | | | |
|---|---|---|---|
| Two large Damask Table cloths | 1 | 10 | 0 |
| One large and one small Ditto | 1 | 0 | 0 |
| Three Diaper Tablecloths for Breakfast | 0 | 6 | 0 |
| Eight Huckaback Ditto | 1 | 4 | 0 |
| Nine smaller Ditto | 0 | 18 | 0 |
| Four Ditto shaving Cloths | 0 | 4 | 0 |
| Twenty five Diaper Napkins | 0 | 15 | 6 |
| Six Huckaback hand Towels | 0 | 3 | 0 |
| Nineteen Russia hand Ditto | 0 | 4 | 0 |
| Six pair fine Sheets | 5 | 8 | 0 |
| Six pair coarse Ditto | 2 | 8 | 0 |
| Three pair Ditto Do | 1 | 11 | 6 |
| Twenty two pillow cases | 1 | 0 | 0 |
| Six Bolster cases | 0 | 9 | 0 |
| Six servants small Table Cloths | 0 | 3 | 0 |
| Seven Reel Towells | 0 | 4 | 6 |
| Twelve Knife Cloths | 0 | 1 | 0 |
| Wearing Apparel Wollen Linen etc | 30 | 0 | 0 |

### In the Stable & Coach house

| | | | |
|---|---|---|---|
| One post Charriot Harness for 2 Horses | 21 | 0 | 0 |
| Two Coachhorses | 28 | 0 | 0 |
| One Hackney Saddle one postillion Ditto two Bridles one Whip | 0 | 13 | 6 |
| Two Corn Bins | 0 | 15 | 0 |
| Five Horse Cloths good and bad currycombs Brushes etc | 0 | 10 | 6 |
| One Stable Lanthorn and two Buckets | 0 | 4 | 0 |
| Some small things that may possibly be omitted | 0 | 5 | 0 |
| | 321 | 15 | 11½ |

The document continues with debts owed to deceased from individuals in Jamaica, Pennsylvania, Philadelphia and Maryland; also from the Brazil Company of Holywell in Flint. The largest debts included £4,000 owed by Thomas Goldney and the Coalbrooke Dale Company.

## No.24 St. Michael's Hill, 1710, Walter Landen (BRO 1710/20/a)

A true and perfect Inventory of all and Singular the Goods and Chattles rights Debts & Credits of Walter Landen late of the City of Bristoll Maltman done taken and appraised the 4th day of July 1710 by James Millerd and Benjamin Chaddock as followeth Vizt./

|  |  | £ | s | d |
|---|---|---|---|---|
| Imprs. | The Decds wearing Apparell | 02 | 00 | 00 |

*In the Kitchen*

|  |  | | | |
|---|---|---|---|---|
| | a paire of fire-Grates Racks & Crane, two paire of slice & tongs a fender & fork and two Spitts | 01 | 05 | 0 |
| | One Trunk, one Chest of Drawers & an old Cupboard | 00 | 10 | 0 |
| | Two Small Tables | 00 | 05 | 0 |
| | One Settle & Seaven Ordinary Chayres | 00 | 05 | 0 |
| | Brass Wares in the Kitchen | 01 | 00 | 0 |
| | 1cwt 2qt 12li of pewter att 7d | 05 | 05 | 0 |
| | an old Musquet and Birding peece | 00 | 10 | 0 |
| Item | *In the Wash Kitchen* | | | |
| | three Kettle-potts, two Sawce pans, a Skillett, Scimmer and fryeng pan | 01 | 00 | 0 |
| Item | *In the Hall and Parlor* | | | |
| | two table boards | 00 | 07 | 0 |
| | Five ordnry Cane Chayres | 00 | 02 | 0 |
| | Twelve leather Chayres | 00 | 12 | 0 |
| | One Brass Clock | 03 | 0 | 0 |
| | A large folding table | 00 | 10 | 0 |
| | Two Couches and a paire of bellows | 01 | 05 | 0 |
| | One press Bed | 01 | 10 | 0 |
| | One fire Grate & fender, two Slice & tongs, a paire of Andirons Creepers and Trippett | 01 | 10 | 0 |
| | One looking-Glass | 00 | 12 | 0 |
| | One Silver Tankard Cawdle Cupp and Can qt. 30. oz | 07 | 10 | 0 |
| Item | *In the first Chamber* | | | |
| | One Bed Bedsteed, Bolster Green Curtenes, Curtain Rods Rugg & a paire blankets | 03 | 00 | 0 |
| Item | *In the two Garretts* | | | |
| | one bedsteed red rug & blanket, two drogett Curtains & one ordinary Chest | 01 | 02 | 6 |
| | One Chest of Drawers & a little Table, one Dressing Box & two Chayres & an old Trunke | 01 | 00 | 0 |
| | One Bed Bedsteed bolster pillowes Curtens, red Rugg and blanket | 03 | 00 | 0 |
| Item | *In the second Chamber* | | | |
| | One old Chest of Drawers | 00 | 05 | 0 |
| | three old blankets & one old Quilt | 00 | 07 | 0 |
| | One Bedsteed, Curtains & Rods, and one Small Looking Glass | 02 | 00 | 0 |
| | One Bedsteed more | 00 | 05 | 0 |
| Item | *In the third Chamber* | | | |
| | three black Chayres | 00 | 10 | 0 |
| | One Chest of Drawers & one old rotten table | 00 | 07 | 0 |
| | One paire of brass Doggs | 00 | 02 | 6 |
| | One Bed Bedsteed Bolster, Kidderminster Curtains and an old Quilt | 02 | 10 | 0 |
| | A parcel of Earthen Ware & figures | 00 | 4 | 0 |
| Item | *In the brewing House* | | | |
| | brewing Tubb Cooler & Casks | 01 | 00 | 0 |
| | five dozen of Napkins | 00 | 12 | 6 |
| | Six Table Clothes | 00 | 06 | 0 |
| | Sixteen paire of Sheets att 4s 6d per paire | 03 | 04 | 0 |
| | Six pillow Cases | 00 | 06 | 0 |
| Item | Eight old towels | 00 | 02 | 0 |
| | One Malt Mill with all belonging to it | 03 | 00 | 0 |
| | A Mill Horse | 00 | 10 | 0 |
| | A Bay Mare | 04 | 00 | 0 |
| | Lomber & small things omitted | 00 | 10 | 0 |
| | Two Hundred and Eighty Seaven Bushells of Malt att 4s 11d per Bushell | 66 | 11 | 1 |
| | James Millerd Benj. Chaddock Apprs./ | 123 | 12 | 7 |

(Details of debts omitted in this transcription)

## Oldbury House, No.121 St. Michael's Hill, 1704, Lady Phillippa Gore (BRO 14183(2) fols 50–65)

An Inventory [c 1704] of the contents of a house on St Michael's Hill prepared in the course of a lawsuit in Chancery, the Gore family of Barrow versus Joseph Knight brother of Sir John Knight of Bristol, two schedules attached to Joseph Knight's Complaint (see also BCRL Jeffries, vol 20, miscellaneous):

### Schedule 1

*In the Parlour*

[fol 50]

|  | £ | s | d |
|---|---|---|---|
| One fine Clock | 04 | 00 | 00 |
| One Table two Stanns | 02 | 02 | 06 |
| One Great looking Glasse | 00 | 15 | 00 |
| One Landskipp Skreene and Three Pictures | 00 | 10 | 00 |
| One Sett of Steele Andirons fire pann and Tongs | 00 | 10 | 00 |
| Six Land Skipps | 00 | 06 | 00 |
| Six Cane Chaires two Great Cane Chaires | 00 | 16 | 00 |
| [fol 51] | | | |
| One long Couch | 00 | 05 | 00 |
| One Greate Cusheon | 00 | 00 | 06 |
| One Hanging Shelf and Things over the Chimney of Dutch Earth | 00 | 05 | 00 |
| One fine reppeating Clock | 03 | 00 | 00 |

*In the Kitchen*

|  | £ | s | d |
|---|---|---|---|
| One Iron Grate two racks All things belonging to itt | 01 | 15 | 00 |
| Five dozen Pewter Plates | 00 | 15 | 00 |
| One new hoop for Rime | 00 | 01 | 00 |

# APPENDIX 2

Twelve Pewter Dishes with
Six Mazarines  02  00  00
[fol 52]

### In the Hall

Six Cane Chaires  00  12  00
One Great Clapp Table  00  06  00
Foure Land Skipps  00  08  00

### In the Staire Case

Severell Land Skipps  00  05  00

### In the Chamber fore Strangers

One Crimson Mohaire Bedd
Lyned with Alemode
Imbroidered Quilt a feather Bed
Bolster and two pillowes
Three Blanketts One Holland
Quilt one Stained Calicoe
Quilt for Greate Cane
Chaires and Mohaire Cusheons  12  00  00
[fol 53]
One Greate Looking Glasse Table and Stanns  03  00  00
One greate Tortoise Shell Cabbinett  10  00  00
One little Amber Cabinett
By Chance broke to Pieces and not worth anything  00  00  00
Two Landskipps five little Pictures  00  10  00
Foure little Silk Indian Curtaines made in to two
Very Old  00  02  06
A Sett of brass Andirons with brass fender
Fire pann and tongs  00  10  00
[fol 54]
One hanging Shelfe with China and other Toyes
on the Chimney and on the Great Cabinet  00  05  00

### In the Lady Gores Closset

One Looking Glasse serverall little Pictures a Hanging
Shelfe Silver Ink box and Silver Case  00  10  00
Two Window Curtaines made
in to One Cane Stooles and Cushions  00  05  00

### In the Chamber where Dame Phillippa Gore lay

A Grey Cloth bedd
[fol 55]
Lined with blue Tabby
a blew Quilt of the
same One Holland Quilt
a Stained Calicoe Quilt
a fether bedd a Bolster
two Pillowes three blankets  00  05  00
one Great Chaire lined
with blew Tabby One
Great looking Glass Table and Stanns  01  10  00
Stooles and Cloth Chaires  00  08  00
A Sett of Steel Andirons
fire pann and tongs  00  05  00
Things on the Chimney  00  01  00
One Chest of Drawers Inlaid  00  15  00
[fol 56]
One plaine Chest of Drawers  00  10  00
One Guilt Leather Skreene  00  10  00

### In the Nursery

One bedd bolster and
two Pillowes One Pallett
bedd bolster and two
Pillowes a Suite of White and Blew
Floured Curtaines lyned with
White Callicoe – Chaires of
The Same – three Blanketts
One Callicoe Quilt to
the Pallett bed and two blanketts  03  00  00
One paire of Andirons fire Pann and tongs  00  05  00
[fol 57]
One blew Stuff Printed Skreene  00  05  00
Two Beds for Servants
with Stuffe Curtains Valance
two bolster and foure
Blankets two Course Ruggs  01  00  00
Three paire of brass Candle Sticks  00  03  00
Item the Silver basket  30  00  00
One Lockett  00  15  00
a Gold Seale with
Armes with a Cornelian  01  10  00

### In Lynnen – In a little Chest

Four paire of Common
Eight Diaper Table Clothes
[fol 58]
Fourteen Common Towells Six
paire of Pillow Cases
Two Dozen and tenn
Huckaback Napkins two dozen of Old Napkins  02  00  00

### In a Cubboard

Six paire of Canvas one paire of Old Sheets  00  05  00

### In another Chest

One dozen of Damaske Napkins One dozen of
fine Diaper Napkins three Diaper Table Cloths two
Damaske Table Clothes One dozen of Common
diaper Napkins  01  10  00
[fol 59]

### In a haire Trunk

One large Child bedd
Sheet One paire of
Fine sheets three paire
Of fine Pillow beeres
Four diaper Table Cloths
One Damaske Table Cloath
One Damaske Towell two
Dozen fine Diaper Napkins
One Dozen and Nine
Damaske Napkins  02  00  00

### In a Greate Truncke

Three paire of Sheets
foure paire Sheets
three paire of new
[fol 60]
Callicoe Sheets three Old
Callicoe Sheets Six Callicoe

Cubboard Cloathes Eight paire
Of Pillow beeres foure
Diaper Towells Twenty three
new Towells two little
Damaske Table Cloathes One
paire of fine large Sheets 02 10 00
J: Hiccocks

## Schedule 2

The Second Schedule containing a Particular of sundry household Stuffe and other things remaining in the dwelling house of the Defendt Joseph Knight att the
[fol 61]
    Time of the death of his late wife and now in his Custody which are and not included in the Schedule to the Deed mentioned in the Complts bill as the said Defendt Apprehends

### In the best Parlour

| | | | |
|---|---|---|---|
| One Small Japan Table and Stanns | 00 | 05 | 00 |
| One large black Japan Table and Looking Glasse | 04 | 00 | 00 |
| One Japan Cabinett & frame | 05 | 00 | 00 |
| Two hanging Shelves | 00 | 10 | 00 |
| [fol 62] | | | |
| One Looking Glasse over the Chimney | 01 | 00 | 00 |
| One Picture over the Chimney | 00 | 02 | 06 |
| One black Iron hearth Doggs fire Shovel and tongs With Silver Gilt heads | 00 | 10 | 00 |
| Three Images | 00 | 03 | 00 |
| Six Elbow Chaires with Silke bottoms | 01 | 10 | 00 |
| Three Silke Window Curtaines | 00 | 15 | 00 |
| One Gilt leather Skreen | 01 | 10 | 00 |
| Gilt leather hangings to the Roome | 03 | 00 | 00 |
| A parcel of Delph Jarrs and China Ware | 02 | 00 | 00 |
| [fol 63] | | | |
| A parcel of China Ware in the Cupboard | 00 | 10 | 00 |

### In the little Parlour

| | | | |
|---|---|---|---|
| One weather Glasse | 00 | 05 | 00 |
| One Harpsicord | 02 | 00 | 00 |
| Two Window Curtains | 00 | 02 | 00 |
| Three Pictures | 00 | 03 | 00 |
| Six Old Cusheons | 00 | 01 | 06 |
| Two bags and a Small Parcel of China Ware on the Chimney piece and some odd things | 00 | 05 | 00 |
| One Table board | 00 | 02 | 00 |
| One looking Glasse | 00 | 10 | 00 |
| [fol 64] | | | |

### In the Hall and Stair Case

| | | | |
|---|---|---|---|
| A parcel of Pictures Greate & Small | 03 | 00 | 00 |
| Two Sconces and Foure Little Images | 00 | 01 | 06 |

### In the Kitchen

| | | | |
|---|---|---|---|
| A Table and Some odd Things | 00 | 05 | 00 |
| A parcel of Pewter and Potts | 01 | 00 | 00 |

### In the Chamber for Company

| | | | |
|---|---|---|---|
| A parcel of Pictures and Some odd things | 00 | 05 | 00 |

### In Lady Gores Closett

| | | | |
|---|---|---|---|
| Soome Pictures and little books & other things | 00 | 05 | 00 |
| [fol 65] | | | |

### In the Chamber where Lady Gore lay

| | | | |
|---|---|---|---|
| The hangings of a Roome a Picture an Easy Chaire and Some Odd things and Carpet | 04 | 00 | 00 |

### In the Closett within

| | | | |
|---|---|---|---|
| Foure stooles a Parcel of Pictures and Hangings | 01 | 10 | 00 |
| One Gold Watch and Trinketts | 06 | 00 | 00 |

### In the Brewhouse Chamber

| | | | |
|---|---|---|---|
| One Old blew bedd with all its furniture | 01 | 00 | 00 |

### In the Brewhouse

| | | | |
|---|---|---|---|
| A parcel of Tubbs & barrel | 01 | 00 | 00 |
| Two Silver Rings for Dishes | 01 | 00 | 00 |

J:Hiccocks

Note: a second inventory for this house is the probate inventory for Edward Bisdee, baker, made in 1731 (PROB3/30/20).

This lists the rooms in the house as follows:

On the second floor there were a study of books, the farthermost room, a middle chamber and a hither room.

On the first floor there were a counting room, a room adjoining, another room with a closet within, a middle room and a green room with a closet adjoining.

On the ground floor were a best parlour, a little parlour, the hall, and a pantry, a little room next to the kitchen, a pump house, a kitchen, the brew house, a stable, coach house, cart house, laundry and a summerhouse.

No.8 Small Street – for the inventory of Sir Robert Cann's house, see Stoke Bishop House below.

## No.20 Small Street, 1557, John Smythe, merchant (BRO AC/F8/1)

Appraised by Giles White, Thomas Marshall and Robert Presh

### The Hall

| | | | |
|---|---|---|---|
| In primis the hangings of grene saye | | | xxs |
| Item | iij pecs of grene say for bankers | | vs |
| " | vii panes in the same hall | | xiiijs |
| | In the same hall xviij cushions of Tapstrie | | xxiiijs |
| Item | iij bordes in the hall | | vs |
| | Summus | iijli | viijs |

### The Parlor

| | | | |
|---|---|---|---|
| Item | in the parlor a table with a frame and a cupborde | | viijs |
| – | xviij stoles | | xijs |
| – | ij Luxborne chaires | | vs |
| – | twoo carpets | | xxs |
| – | the hanginges of redd and grenesay belonging unto The same parlor | | xls |
| – | ij panes | | iiijs |
| – | ij little doggs of yron and a plate of yron for the chimney | | iiijs |
| – | a slice and a paire of tongs | | ijs |
| | Summus | iiijls | xvs |

### The Buttry

| | | | |
|---|---|---|---|
| Item | in the butttry two olde cofers | | ijs |
| – | one cupborde | | ijs |
| – | iiij garnishe of pewter vessel | | viik li |
| – | ij dosen of podage dishes | | xxs |
| – | ix laten basons | | lxs |

|   |   |   |
|---|---|---|
| – | x laten candelsticks and ten pewter candilsticks | xxs |
| – | ij pottle pots iiijs iij^or a quarte potts iiij^s | viijs |
| – | a greate looking glasse | ijs |
|   | Summus | xjli iijs |

### The Kechin

|   |   |   |
|---|---|---|
| Item | ij bordes | ijs |
| – | vij broches | vijs |
| – | ij racks of yron to holde the brochesvs |  |
| – | xij crokkes | iij li |
| – | v pannes | xxvs |
| – | one posnet ijs iij pankins at xvjd the pece | vjs |
| – | iiij^or kettills | viijs |
| – | one bruyng kettle | vis viijd |
| – | iiij hanginges and iiij pott hokes | iiijs |
| – | iiij dripping pannes | iiijs |
|   | Summus | vi li vijs viijd |

### The Shop

|   |   |   |
|---|---|---|
| Item | a cupboard with a trymer over him | vs |
| – | a beme of yron and a paire of scales | vis viijd |
| – | iij c waytes in lead | xvs |
| – | xiij tones of yron at xli the tonne | cxxx li |
| – | a packing presse | vs |
|   | Summus | cxxxj li xjs viijd |

### The Chamber over the Parlour

|   |   |   |
|---|---|---|
| Item | a bedstead | xxs |
| – | ij fetherbedds one flokbedd one bolster} |  |
| – | and ij pillows } | vli |
| – | a paire of fustian blankets to the same bed | vis viijd |
| – | a coverlet of arras worke | iiij li |
| – | curtens and vallens of sarsenet to the same bed | xxvjs viijd |
| – | a cupboard & a little square table | iiijs |
| – | ij carpetts of dornix to the same | vs |
| – | ij Luxborne chaires | vs |
| – | a paire of Andirons a plate a fire shovel a paire of tongs and a little paire of dogs | xxvjs viijd |
| – | the hangings of grene and red say | xxxs |
|   | Summus | xv li iijs |

### The little Chamber within the Parlour Chamber

|   |   |   |
|---|---|---|
| Item | a bedsted | iijs iiijd |
| – | a flokbedd a fether bed a bolster of fethers | xxxs |
| – | a paire of blankets | iiis iiijd |
| – | a coverlet | xs |
| – | hangings of grene say | vis viijd |
|   | Summus | Liijs iiijd |

### The Gallery by the Chappell

|   |   |   |
|---|---|---|
| Item | iij cofers | xxs |
|   | Summus | xxs |

### The grete Chamber

|   |   |   |
|---|---|---|
| Item | hangings of olde grene say | xiijs iiijd |
| – | ii bedsteds | xxvjs viijd |
| – | ii featherbeds ij flokbedds ij bolsters of fethers and iiij pillows | iiij li |
| – | ij pairs of blanketts | vis viijd |
| – | ij coverlets | Ls |
| – | curtens of grene say | xvjs |
| – | a cupborde | ijs iiijd |
| – | a folding borde | iijs iiijd |

|   |   |   |
|---|---|---|
| – | iij Cofers | xviijs |
| – | a paire of little Aundirons | ijs |
|   | Summus | xli xviijs iiijd |

### The little Chamber within the same

|   |   |   |
|---|---|---|
| Item | a carved bedsted after the old fashion | vis viijd |
| – | a fetherbed a flokbedd a bolster and ij pillows | xxs |
| – | a paire of blankets and a coverlet | xvjs |
| – | a cofer and a rounde table | ijs |
|   | Summus | xliijs viijd |

### The Chamber over the Shop

|   |   |   |
|---|---|---|
| Item | a bedstede | xxs |
| – | a tester and curtens of grene sarcenet | xls |
| – | a fether bed a flok bedd a bolster and ij pillows | iijli |
| – | a pair of fustian blankets | vis viijd |
| – | a coverlett | xls |
| – | the hangings of grene and red say | xls |
| – | iiij cofers | xxvis viijd |
| – | a pair of Aundirons a paire of tongs and a fire shovel | vis viijd |
| – | ij Luxbone chaires | vs |
|   | Summus | vs |

### The Closet

|   |   |   |
|---|---|---|
| Item | a presse | xiijs iiijd |
| – | a folding table | ijs |
|   | Summus | xvis iiijd |

### The ij Chambers for servants

|   |   |   |
|---|---|---|
| Item | ij bedstedes | vs |
| – | ij flok bedds one fether bed and ij bolsters of fethers | xxvis viiid |
| – | ij paire of blanketts | iiijs |
| – | ij coverletts | xs |
| – | ij old cofers | ijs |
|   | Summus | xlvijs viijd |

The detailed list of Smyth's apparel, befitting a merchant who could purchase former monastic properties from the Crown, then follows (not noted here). Further inventories for the same property were made the following the death of his wife Joan in 1560 (BRO AC/F8/2) and the death of Sir Henry Creswick in 1668 (see chapter 5 for references and further discussion).

## Stoke Bishop House, Stoke Bishop, 1686, Sir Robert Cann (TNA PROB4/11206)

Sir Robert Cann held leases of tenements in Bitton, a tenement in Corn Street, two tenements in King Street, a house near Frome Gate and two houses in Broad Street (held from the Company of Merchant Tailors).

The Inventory is of the contents of two houses – Cann's principal residence in the city, the south part of no. 8 Small Street, and his house at Stoke Bishop, Stoke Bishop House – which are here summarised:

### In the house where Lady Cann dwells situate in Smalestreet in Bristoll

Linen, not noted

### Chamber over the great Parlour

Item a little tableboard, several old chairs, stools and pictures, pair of brass andirons, slice and tongs, a little scripture, and one iron chest

| | | | |
|---|---|---|---|
| Valued at | £x | 0s | 0d |

### Dining Room
large tableboard, two small sidetables, one couch, a dozen and a half old fashioned chairs, six stools, a few old pictures and glasses, a large pair of brass andirons, a small pair of brass andirons and a brass slice and tongs
Valued at £ix xs 0d

### Chamber next the Dining room
pair of brass andirons, brass slice and tongs, small pair of andirons with brass heads, one sideboard, an old looking glass, three old pictures and an old carpet
Valued at £iii 0s 0d

### In the Room where Sir Robert usually lodged
nest of drawers, sydeboard, an old chest and three trunks, four old chairs, one old looking glass, a little pair of brass andirons and other old lumber
Valued at £iiii 0s 0d

### Maids' Chamber
an old case of drawers and sideboard, two old chests, a small pair of brass andirons
Valued at £I vs 0d

### In the Little Parlour
little tableboard with an old carpet, five old leather chairs, with [illeg] two pairs of brass andirons, slice and tongs
Valued at £ii xs 0d

### The Hall
old tableboard, two sideboards, 18 old cushions, three old muskets, 10 swords, 10 bandoliers, six joined stools and six buckets, 15 old pictures, four old sconces, an old cushion, two old carpets
Valued at £iii xs 0d

### Lower Parlour
tableboard, sideboard, couch, seven chairs, two cushions, five joined stools, two old carpets, one small looking glass, two sconces, two pairs of andirons with brass heads and a pair of brass slice and tongs
Valued at £iiii 0s 0d

### In the Gallery
Eight truncks, two scriptores and two chests
Valued at £iiii 0s 0d

### In the Chamber next the maids
two little side tables, an old chest of drawers, two chairs, two stools, pair of brass andirons and two old pictures, one stand and an old looking glass
Valued at £i xs 0d

### Kitchen
| | | | |
|---|---|---|---|
| four cwt pewter | £xiiij | 0s | 0d |
| one and a half cwt of all sorts of brass | £vi | 0s | 0d |
| two cwt of all sorts of iron | £0 | xviiis | 0d |
| 20 dozen bottles | £i | xs | 0d |

### Garden House
| | | | |
|---|---|---|---|
| Tableboard, old carpet, six old leather chairs | £i | 0s | 0d |
| half ton of Spanish iron | £vi | 0s | 0d |
| nine tons of logwood since sold One Hundred and Eighty Pounds | £clxxx | 0s | 0d |
| Also wood, lumber in the sellar and about the house and for things forgotten | £v | 0s | 0d |
| Also in Sir William Poole's house in Small Street old tables, beds etc | £iii | 0s | 0d |
| Item: old goods remaining in the house at Compton | £ii | 0s | 0d |

### In the house at Stoke Bishop in the County of Gloucester

### Dining Room
looking glass, oval tableboard, small side table, a dozen of turkey-work chairs, two small pairs of brass andirons, slice and tongs, an old wrought and two leather chairs
Valued at £ix xs 0d

### Hall
Tableboard, six leather chairs, two pairs of brass andirons, slice and tongs
Valued at £ii xs 0d

### Chamber over the Dining Room
small feather bed, bedsted, matt
Valued at £ii 0s 0d

### Chamber over the Hall
feather bed, two blankets, pillow, one bedsted and mat eight chairs, two stools, two cupboards and a stand
Valued at £ii xs 0d

### Maids' Chamber
old bedsted, with flock bed, coverlet and blankets
Valued at £i vs 0d

### Men's Chamber
two flock beds with old rugs and blankets, two old bedsteds and one old chest
Valued at £ii xs 0d

### Nursery
one bedsted, mat and cord, one bolster and six small cane chairs
Valued at £i xs 0d

### Chamber next to the Nursery
old case of drawers, old looking glass, old chair and bedsted
Valued at £0 xviis 0d

### Kitchen
| | | | |
|---|---|---|---|
| Pewter by weight | £iiij | xvis | 0d |
| 3 spits, 2 iron racks, iron dogs, bar and fender, pair of tongs, 2 fire shovels, fire fork, ¾cwt at 1d per pound | £0 | viis | 0d |
| old tableboard, 2 leather chairs and a stool | £0 | iis | 0d |
| 13 cows | £0 | xxxs | 0d |
| 7 horses | £xlij | 0s | 0d |
| 4 yearlings calves | £111j | xs | 0d |
| 2 coaches with the harness etc | £xl | 0s | 0d |
| All the plough harness | £x | 0s | 0d |
| 3 saddles | £iii | 0s | 0d |
| 22 tons of hay | £xxxiiij | 0s | 0d |
| And other farm items | | | |
| Total | £11,366 | 14s | 5d |

## Upper Maudlin Street, immediately east of Johnny Ball Lane, Ralph Oliffe, 1684 (TNA PROB4 /12120)

The inventory is of an unidentified inn as his main residence and a garden house. It is included here for the interest of the garden house, which is shown on a drawing of James Stewart (*see* Fig 9.33). The rooms in the inn and their contents (which included wines valued at £1507) are not noted here.

| *At the garden house in Magdalin lane* | £ | s | d |
|---|---|---|---|
| One old bedstead matt & cord one side cupboard a paire of wooden dogs | 0000 | 18 | 00 |
| a parcel of clavy glasses | 0000 | 05 | 00 |
| six high chayres & tappestry worke | 0000 | 05 | 00 |
| five pictures | 0003 | 00 | 00 |
| a paire of wooden dogs | 0000 | 8 | 00 |
| a parcel of clavy glasses | 0000 | 10 | 00 |
| six green chayres a green carpet two tables a screen five paire of wooden dogs a paire of plaine iron dogs a paire of billoses a parcel of glasses in the clavy a looking glass six pictures a twigg chayre and cushion two burning glasses | 0003 | 01 | 00 |
| a bedstead cord and matt with curtains rods a small sydetable and a truncke | 0000 | 14 | 00 |
| a feather bed two bolsters three blankets a coverlet curtaines needle work vallyns | 0006 | 00 | 00 |
| a suite of fine Holland curtaines and vallians and counterpaine for chayres a paire of cotten blankets three lallies curtaines & looking glass | 0003 | 17 | 00 |
| a bedstead in the cock loft | 0000 | 08 | 00 |
| a small furnace an iron grate a pair of iron dogs one iron crane a jack a Rose water still and brass foot a brass engine three brass pots two brass skillets and posnet one kettle a watering cann bastering ladle skimmer a close stoole and pann five dozen of eathern wares one dozen of platters three chayres one chafing dish | 0008 | 11 | 06 |

*In the summerhouse*

| | | | |
|---|---|---|---|
| one oval table four pictures one carpet two leather stooles and a furnes [furnace] | 0001 | 07 | 00 |
| In bad debts | 2273 | 18 | 00 |
| Debts due on several bonds | 0227 | 00 | 00 |
| | 4958 | 02 | 05 |

# NOTES

## Preface and Acknowledgements

1. Leech 1975; Aston and Leech 1977; Leech 1981a.
2. Leech 1981b.
3. Barley 1974.

## Chapter 1

1. These include the Survey of London and studies by the former Royal Commission on the Historical Monuments of England of larger towns, such as Salisbury, Stamford, Whitehaven and York, and many smaller towns, such as Dorchester and Poole in Dorset or Pickering in North Yorkshire. To these should be added some of the accounts in the Victoria County History volumes, notably Jones on Tewkesbury, Coventry and Warwick. Notable studies by individual researchers make interesting reading. These include: Brown (1999) on the Rows of Chester; Clarke *et al*'s study of Sandwich (2010); Laithwaite's work (1973 and 1984) in Burford and Totnes; Martin (2004) on the houses of Winchelsea; O'Neill's study (1953) of the Rows in Great Yarmouth; Jones's studies (1984 and 1987) of Lincoln houses; Smith and Carter (1983), the publications of the Norwich Survey; Pantin on Oxford (1947); Parker's study (1971) of the making of Kings Lynn; Portman's study (1966) of Exeter houses; Schofield (1995) on medieval London houses; Summerson (1969) and more recently McKellar (1999) and Guillery (2004) on post-Fire London houses; and Taylor's work (1974) on the houses of Taunton.
2. Pantin 1962–3 and 1963 have been particularly influential on subsequent studies, for instance Platt 1976, Grenville 1997 and Schofield 1995.
3. Grenville 1997, 165–93; Schofield 1995.
4. Grenville 1997, 171.
5. Harris R 1994, 405.
6. Smith 1983, apparently overlooked by Grenville (1997), Harris (1994) and Quiney 2004.
7. Quiney 2004.
8. *Medieval Archaeology*, **49** (2005), 484–6.
9. Herman 2005.
10. McKellar 1999, 34.
11. Ibid, 17–18; Summerson 1969.
12. Guillery 2004, 5.
13. Williams 1944.
14. Britnell 1993, 230.
15. Palliser 1994, 140.
16. Ibid.
17. Ibid, 138.
18. Ibid, 149.
19. Foyle 2004, 296.
20. Potter 1976, 37–8.
21. Lobel and Carus-Wilson 1975, 11.
22. Williamson 1962; Jones 2006.
23. Sacks 1991, 19–53.
24. Latham and Matthews (eds) 1974, 234; Defoe 1724-6, 361.
25. Carus-Wilson 1967; Sacks 1985, 1991; Morgan 1993.
26. McGrath 1952, 1953, 1968; Barry 1985a, 1985b.
27. Barry 1985b, 79–80.
28. Ibid, 77.
29. Sacks 1991, 331–62.
30. Notably Dresser 2001.
31. Nicholls and Taylor 1881.
32. See Bibliography for abbreviations and references for the series of publications by Reece and John Winstone.
33. Dening 1923; Ison 1952; Mowl 1991.
34. Gomme *et al* 1979, 11-91.
35. This study has used the copy in Bristol City Museum and Art Gallery, reproduced in facsimile.
36. BRSMG M3073.
37. S and N Buck 1734, *The North-West Prospect of the City of Bristol*; S and N Buck 1734, *The South-East Prospect of the City of Bristol*.
38. Bodleian Library, Western MS, Gough Somerset 2.
39. Bristol City Museum and Art Gallery and the Society of Merchant Venturers; British Library.
40. Gill 1973; Stoddard 1981, 17; Greenacre and Stoddard 1986; Greenacre 2005; Greenacre 1982; Stoddard 2001.
41. Skelton 1831; Nicholls and Taylor 1881.
42. Bindon 1851.
43. Pryce 1861; Bristol City Reference Library manuscripts.
44. Pope 1888.
45. *Bristol Observer*, published weekly; Loxton drawings, Bristol City Reference Library.
46. See Bibliography: Thomas, N 1986.
47. BRO 20894(32); copies of Street's photographs are held also in Bristol City Museum and Art Gallery and in the National Monuments Record, Swindon.
48. *Winstone 1928–1933*, 22–4; *Winstone 1963–1975*, 5.
49. Ponsford 1969.
50. I am most grateful to Bob Jones of Bristol City Council for these statistics.
51. Seyer 1821–3.
52. Cronne 1946, 3.
53. Evans 1816, 441.
54. See Inventory, corner of Corn Street, Temple Street, nos.39/40 High Street, no.59 Baldwin Street.
55. Skelton 1831, pl. xxxv.
56. Bindon 1851.
57. Pantin 1962–3, 1963; Portman 1966; Parker 1971; Laithwaite 1995; Schofield 1995; for further references, see also Wood 1965.
58. Keene 1985.
59. Ibid, 1, 442.
60. Keene 1989, 206.
61. Leech 1997a, 14, entry for no.59 Baldwin Street.
62. Masters and Ralph 1967, xxviii.
63. BRO 04335(10) fol 2; BRSMG, Braikenridge Notebook a.32; Leech 1997a, 14.
64. Currie 1988, 6.
65. Hartley 1953, 1.
66. West 1999, 2–3.
67. Johnson 1997, 15.
68. Williams 1950, 225–7.
69. Pearson 2009, 5, 9–10; but see also Pearson 2007 for an informed discussion of Smith's paper.
70. Pantin 1963; Pearson (2007, 43) argues that 'late medieval urban houses had their own lines of descent, and that the influences are often likely to have gone from town to country'.
71. Pantin 1963, 445–58; Schofield 1995, 34–44.
72. Bourdieu 1989, 172.

## Chapter 2

1. Lobel and Carus-Wilson 1975, 2–3; Grinsell 1986, Grinsell 1973, 12–14.
2. Haslam 1984, 264; Leech 2009a.

NOTES

3   Whitelock (ed) 1961, *Anglo-Saxon Chronicle* entries for 1016.
4   Lawson 2004, 13.
5   Nenk, Margeson and Hurley 1991, 132; see also Price and Ponsford 1979a; Leech 1997b.
6   Lobel and Carus-Wilson 1975, 2–3.
7   Biddle and Hill 1971; Haslam (ed) 1984, see especially Barnstaple.
8   Imperial measurements are given here as this was the form of measurement used in the period being discussed. It is interesting to note that the Anglo-Saxon streets were so often laid out using units of 10 feet.
9   See plans in Biddle and Hill 1971 and Haslam (ed) 1984, also Platt and Coleman-Smith 1975, 22.
10  Leech 1997b.
11  Keene 1989, 201.
12  Conzen, 1968; Baker *et al* 1992.
13  Leech 1997a, xiii.
14  Whitelock (ed) 1961, *Anglo-Saxon Chronicle* entries for 1051, 1063 and 1068.
15  Morris 1989, 210; Morris leaves open Dawson's assertion that the street plan is of *c* 1100.
16  Leech 1997b, 23.
17  Smith 1970; Carus-Wilson and Lobel 1975; see Dawson 1986 for further references.
18  Leech 1997b, 22–3.
19  Leech 1997a, 184–94.
20  Winterbottom and Thomson (eds) 2007, 447.
21  Darlington (ed) 1928, 32–4.
22  Vince and Barton 1988.
23  See p 3, note 20.
24  A third site with an earthfast structure was found at Rupert Street. It was excavated by M W Ponsford in 1970, but no detailed report or plan has ever been published (reported on in Wilson and Moorhouse 1971, 152).
25  Watts and Rahtz 1985, 78; metric building measurements as quoted in report.
26  Ponsford 1979, 91–3, 178 where Building D is identified as 'late Saxon settlement'; see also Watts and Rahtz 1985, 80 for a comparison between the Mary Le Port Street building and Building D within the Castle.
27  Patterson 1973, 82, 39.
28  Ponsford 1979, 69–70 argues that there was no gate here. However, he was apparently unaware of the reference to the 'netheryate' at approximately this point in the perambulation set out in the charter of 1373 elevating Bristol to a county, see Harding (ed) 1930, 149–65.
29  For St James's Fair see Patterson 1973, 53–5; for the Dominican friars see Leighton 1933.
30  Leech 1997b.
31  Harding (ed) 1930, 4–5.
32  Taylor 1875, 275–8.
33  Veale (ed) 1933, 99; Patterson 1973, 171.
34  Nicholson and Hillam 1987, 141.
35  Veale (ed) 1933, 100; Bickley (ed) 1900, **1**, 7–9.
36  Leech 2009a.
37  Leech 1997b.
38  Patterson 1973, 82.
39  BRO 5139(450).
40  Patterson 1973, 164.
41  Leech 1997b, 25–6.
42  Lobel and Carus-Wilson 1975, 7; Leech 1997b.
43  The bridge is shown first on William Smith's map of 1568 (BL Sloane MS 2596 fol 77). It then appears on Millerd's map of 1673 and on several later illustrations; houses are mentioned by the mid-14th century (Bickley (ed) 1900, **1**, 3–4 correlated with Veale (ed) 1953, 22–3).
44  Leech 1997b, 28–9.
45  See Keene 1989, 204.
46  Leech 1997a, 14, the above mentioned being owned by different landlords from the early 14th century.
47  Latimer 1903; Ross (ed) 1959, 285.
48  See Keene 1989, 218.
49  Leech 1997b.
50  Leech 1997a, 49.
51  Ibid, 6.
52  Ibid, 4.
53  Ibid, 6.
54  Ibid.
55  Wadley 1886, 98.
56  Leech 1997a, 79–80, xxv Map 7.
57  Leech 1997a, 82–3.
58  Leech 1997a, 161; Veale (ed) 1931, 302, entries 25–8.
59  Boore 1984.
60  Good 1990/91.
61  Leech 1997a, 8.
62  Ibid, 77.
63  Ibid, 7–8.
64  Ibid, 8–9.
65  Ibid, 40–1.
66  Ibid, 158.
67  Ibid, 50–2.
68  Ibid, 79–80.
69  Ibid, 74–5.
70  Ibid, 72–3.
71  Ibid.
72  BRO 04696(2), 83.
73  Wadley 1886, 209–10.
74  Leech 1997a, 60–1.
75  The absence of new developments is evident in the research summarised in Leech 1997a.
76  Wadley 1886, 122.
77  Leech 1997a, 110–11.
78  GRO P329/MI 4.
79  Leech 1997a, 90.
80  Ibid, 62.
81  Ibid, 188.
82  Ibid, 124.
83  *Latimer 17th century Annals* (see Bibliography for abbreviations and references for the series of historical publications by John Latimer), 216.
84  Leech 1997a, 121–2.
85  Ibid, 42.
86  Ibid, 78.
87  Ibid, 46.
88  Bickley (ed) 1900, **1**, 2–7.
89  Leech 1997a, 118.
90  Latham (ed) 1947, 27.
91  A photograph by Reece Winstone shows that part of the north claustral range survived until the 1960s (*Winstone 1960–1962*, 121); see pp 236–8.
92  Bettey 1990, 12.
93  Leighton 1933; Ridgeway and Watts (eds) 2013 was published too late to be considered here. See also Inventory.
94  BRO 5535(1–9).

# Chapter 3

1   As defined by Chalklin 1974, 73–140.
2   Barry 1991, 200, citing various sources.
3   This total is based on the figures which follow in this chapter.
4   *Latimer 17th-century Annals*, 113; BRO 04026(23).
5   Chalklin 1989, 107.
6   BRO 04335(1).
7   BRO 00347(13) states that Wickham's grant abutted the almshouses.
8   BRO 04335(5).
9   BRO 04043(3) fol 615.
10  See Inventory, entry for no.1 Redcliff Street.
11  *Latimer 18th-century Annals*, 408, 425, 496.
12  First shown on the revision of Millerd's map of 1673, published in 1710 (BL K. Top.37.32).
13  BRO DC/A/8/1 Chapter Minutes 1663–1751; DC/A/8/2, ibid.1751–1801.
14  BRO DC/E/1/6 fol 308, the grant of land for a street from Frog Lane (later Frogmore Street) showing that the land leased was intended as a new development.
15  BRO DC/E/40/28/2.
16  BRO 05492(1–26).
17  BRO 05502.
18  For other provincial towns see Chalklin 1974.
19  BRO 6226(5), Lamp and scavenging rates (collected to pay for the lighting and cleaning of the streets) for the parish of St James.
20  BRO 04335(8) fol 195 for the draft leases for nos.35–7.
21  BRO 04335(8) fol 163 and (10) fol 60.
22  Defoe 1724–6, 362.
23  BRO Modern Records, deeds from compulsory purchases.

406

24 References for this section are in Leech 2000d.
25 References for this section are in Ison 1952, 204–9, 220–3.
26 Matthews 1801.
27 Ison 1952, 220.
28 Leech 2000b, 81–108.
29 Ibid, 94–6.
30 Hall 1949, 141,156.
31 BRO 05677 and Poor Rate returns for 1699 onwards, parish of St Augustine's.
32 *Latimer 18th-century Annals*, 227.
33 *Bristol Weekly Intelligencer*, 2 December 1749.
34 *Latimer 18th-century Annals*, 333.
35 Ison 1952, 212; the new road being constructed by the Corporation c 1758 and referred to by Ison (ibid, 211) was most probably the street linking College Green and the new Unity and Orchard Streets to the new streets in the Bishop's Park.
36 Ison 1952, 214; BRO EP/A/25/StGBH/4.
37 Jones 1992, 31.
38 Ison 1952, 157–161.
39 The three houses were Freeman House (later named Rodney Lodge), Duncan House and Mortimer House.
40 Jones 1992, 117; Mowl 1991, 140.
41 Evidence is from the published maps and from BRO P/StMR/ deeds.
42 Ward 1978, 5.
43 Ison 1952, 27–8.
44 Ward 1978, 9.
45 Borsay 1991.
46 Ison 1952, 21–3; Ward 1978, 4; Mowl 1991, 10–19.
47 Ison 1952, 141.
48 BRO DC/E/40/48/2.
49 BRO 04335(4) fols 111, 136, 135.
50 BRO 04335(4) fol 41; a platform was a ground plan or design.
51 BRO 04335(4) fol 57.
52 BRO 04335(5) fol 5.
53 Ibid.
54 BRO 04335(8) fol 195.
55 For an even more detailed specification from the late 18th century, see Appendix 1, lease for a property in 1792 in Kingsdown Parade; copied from the deeds for no.52 Kingsdown Parade by the author during his residence 1975–9.
56 BRO, copies of documents not in BRO/44.
57 In the removal of decayed plaster, the intended but blocked openings were observed by the author as above.
58 BRO 26138(2) conveyance of 13 June 1792.
59 BRO P/Temple/Ag4/fol 213.
60 BRO Quarter Sessions papers, Avon and Tower Street being within the Great Gardens development.
61 Ison 1952, 221.
62 *Latimer 17th-century Annals*, 475–6.
63 Barry 1991, 212–3.
64 Defoe, 1724–6, 73; http://www.montpelier.org/history/name_origin.cfm; I am indebted to Eleanor Leech for this reference.
65 BRO 04026(23).
66 Ison 1952, 141-2, 152-3; Ponsford 1979, 62.
67 BRO 04335(4) fol 45; 04335(6) fol 18; 04335(9) fol 142; 04335(11) fol 157; 04043(4) fol 398 and 04779(3) fol 18, the last two referring to 'NR' [new rental] fol 528.
68 BRO 04335(5) fol 5.
69 Ponsford 1979, 217–30, tabulates the various developers, with many errors of identification.
70 Hall 1949, 141, 156.
71 Buchanan and Cossons 1969, 119.
72 Ward 1978, 4.
73 Ibid, 5–7.
74 Ibid.

## Chapter 4

1 Morris 1947.
2 Defoe 1724–6, 362.
3 Palliser 1994, 145–6, with reference also to Maitland.
4 Ibid, 132–3.
5 Keene 1985, **1**, 399.
6 Oxford English Dictionary.
7 Leech 1997a, 41–2.
8 With the deeds of the church, BRO P/St JB/D/2/101; Leech 1997a, 160–1.
9 BRO P/AS/D/HS B 6 (243).
10 BRO P/AS/HS C 10.
11 BRO P/AS/D/HS E 9 (188).
12 BRO P/AS/D/HS E 10 (197).
13 Deeds of no.52 Kingsdown Parade.
14 Good 1990/1, 32.
15 Boore 1982, 9.
16 Deeds for no.52 Kingsdown Parade.
17 Bickley (ed) 1900, 2, 225–6.
18 Masters and Ralph (eds) 1967, 14.
19 Williams 1950, 245, 231.
20 Strong 1967, deed CS B 1.
21 Strong 1967, deed NA 39.
22 Leech 1997a, 180–1.
23 Ibid, 80; BRO 04696 (2) p 262; for cellars, see Inventory.
24 BRO 00471(3).
25 Boore 1982.
26 Pantin 1962/3, 205–6; Pantin 1963.
27 Keene 1989, 223.
28 BRO P/StJB/D/2/15 and 24.
29 Leech 1997a, 7–8; BRSMG M2126.
30 Leech 1997a, 167.
31 Ibid, 12–13.
32 Ibid, 199–200 for further references for this interpretation.
33 See chapter 5 for further discussion of street doorways.

## Chapter 5

1 Parts of this chapter first appeared in a paper in *Vernacular Architecture* (Leech 2000a).
2 BRO 171(1); for references to the rental of 1473 see chapter 1.
3 Wadley 1886, 98; in the 16th-century accounts for St Mary Redcliff the houses are those referred to 'Haveryng's' (BRO P/StMR/Churchwarden's accounts).
4 Burrell 1931, **1**, 292.
5 Mercer 1975, 20–2.
6 Johnson 1993, 1994, 1996.
7 Williams 1981, Building 1; dendrochronological dating from the Dundas Wharf excavations necessitates that the published 13th- and 14th-century dates for sites in Bristol excavated prior to the work at Dundas Wharf are pushed back by up to 100 years, see Nicholson and Hillam 1987, also Ponsford 1991.
8 Pantin 1962–3, Pl XXIII.
9 Nicholls and Taylor 1881, 200.
10 Gaimster, Margeson and Hurley 1990, 168; Jones 1986.
11 For London see Schofield, 1995, 33; for Kings Lynn see Taylor and Richmond 1989, 260–6; for Stamford see RCHME 1977, lii.
12 For a discussion of this custom see Wood 1965, 369–80.
13 Priestley and Corfield 1982, 93–123.
14 Pearson 2000, lxix–cii.
15 BRO P/StJB/D/274 for no.21 Broad Street in 1606 and 33288(40) for no.18 Small Street in 1587 are examples. This category of inventory needs both to be better known and to be distinguished by the unwary from those made for probate; for the discussion of the Sevenoaks House see Pearson 2000, lxxi–lxxii.
16 The author's transcript of the return for 1664 is deposited in the Bristol Record Office. The 1666 and later returns for Bristol are possibly arranged differently, listing the individual lodgers and sub-tenants of houses in multiple occupation; for the important distinction between housekeepers and lodgers etc see Earle 1994, 167.
17 For a useful summary of references see Bedell 2000, 223–5.
18 Keene 1985 **1**, 175–6.
19 Williams 1981.
20 Jones 1983, 37–9.
21 Dolman and Jobbins' plan showed only the part of Spicer's House to the north of the through-passage, leading Pantin to conclude, incorrectly, that this was its full extent. The part to the south was not let separately from the rest of Spicer's Hall until the 18th century. The two tenements to the north were let separately, at least from 1463 (Leech 1997a, 166–7).

## NOTES

22  PRO PROB 2/121.
23  BRO will and probate inventory 1618/14; 04479(2) fol 55.
24  BRO inventories 1643/5 and 1646/3. The inventories of both Barnard and Mary Benson list as the upper rooms a lodging, middle and backwards or lower chamber, corresponding to the tripartite arrangement of the ground floor, the 'middle chamber' most probably over the hall.
25  Neale (ed) 2000, 214.
26  Schofield 1995, 41, 217.
27  Williams 1950, 58–62 for his London connections and Edward IV's visit of 1461.
28  Wadley 1886, 145–7.
29  The inventories of Keynes, Mason and Parkyns are PRO PROB2/172,471,767. Foster's inventory cannot now be traced, but is summarised by Pryce 1861, 557. Together with three other inventories in PROB 2, these are the only inventories traced for before 1558 and provide a valuable insight into the domestic life of wealthier townspeople during the late 15th and early 16th centuries.
30  Wadley 1886, 125, the will of Edmund Bierden, 1384. His estate included a property adjacent to that of the Kalendars, well documented and identified as no.25 Christmas Street; see also Latimer 1903, 131.
31  Identified as no.2 Christmas Street, a house belonging to the Kalendars, from the abuttals given in documents relating to no.3 (Veale (ed) 1950, 130; Livock (ed) 1966, 7, 85; BRO 04041 fol 95, 00859 (5); corbels illustrated in Pritchard 1911, 72–3.
32  BRO P/StT/D/261; Sir John Walshe, who sold the property in 1535, was probably the son of John Walshe, the executor and defaulter of John Foster's will, see also Manchee 1831, **1**, 82.
33  PRO PROB 2/5.
34  PRO PROB 2/8.
35  Roberts and Parker 1992a, 2–9.
36  Roberts and Parker 1992b, 346–7, 378.
37  BRO AC/F8/1; the inventory of his widow Joan, made in 1560, is almost identical in content, BRO AC/F8/2.
38  Vanes (ed) 1975, 27.
39  Leech 1997a, 158-9.
40  Vanes (ed) 1975, 79.
41  Leech 1997a, 157; BRO Inventories 1623/8; *Latimer 17th century Annals*, 497.
42  Hirst 1927.
43  Stairs within the gallery are recorded in a number of 17th-century houses.
44  McGrath (ed) 1968, 80–9; Dick (ed) 1972, 477–8.
45  The rooms were listed in a schedule attached to a mortgage deed of 1648, transcribed by Simpson 1926, 215.
46  BRO inventory 1628/14.
47  Leech 1997a, 159; *Latimer 17th century Annals*, 183.
48  McGrath (ed) 1968, 92–7.
49  The gateway and the arched corbel for the jetty above are visible on a drawing of the 1820s, BRSMG Mb.7.
50  Leech 1997a, 58; BRO inventory 1618/76.
51  Livock (ed) 1966, 172-6, probably no.7 Broad Street (Leech 1997a, 32).
52  Schofield (1995, 66) concluded that 'open halls had been abandoned in up-to-date houses in the region … this development must have been shared by London houses, though evidence is sparse'. In the context of the evidence presented here, a distinction can now be made between the halls of the wealthiest members of the urban community and others. For the former, Schofield's conclusion must be reconsidered.
53  For a discussion of the evidence from London and other towns see Leech 2000a.
54  McGrath 1968, xxxi.
55  Cooper 1999, 275–89.
56  Ross 1951, 85.
57  Leech 1997a, 180.
58  Williams 1950, 55–62.
59  Wadley 1886, 145–7.
60  Vanes (ed) 1975, 25–7.
61  McGrath (ed) 1968, 93.
62  Pearson 1994, 134–5.
63  Priestley and Corfield 1982, 93–123.
64  Powicke 1962, 223.
65  Walker 1954.
66  Boynton 1967, 14.
67  Adams 1910, 112–3.
68  Walker 1954, 45.
69  Ibid, 17.
70  PRO PROB 4/11206.
71  PRO PROB 4/7599.
72  Boynton 1967, 212–3.
73  Walker 1954, 7.
74  Adams 1910, 113–4.
75  *Latimer 16th century Annals*, 61; Hall 1949, 123.
76  *Latimer 16th century Annals*, 53.
77  *Latimer 17th century Annals*, 183, 331–2.
78  Pearson 1994, 134.
79  Priestley and Corfield 1982, 93–123.
80  None have been identified in the large number of inventories now examined by the author.
81  Western 1965, 7.
82  BRO inventory 1612/8.
83  BRO inventory 1612/3.
84  BRO inventory 1613/5.
85  For inventories of this period see George & George 2002 (eds).
86  BRO inventory 1643/57.
87  BRO inventory 1678/5; Leech 1997b, 39.
88  BRO inventory 1611/17.
89  BRO inventory 1668/51.
90  BRO inventory 1617/43 will of Edward Pickrell.
91  BRO DC/E/3/1; Leech 1997a, 202; BRO inventory 1623/19.
92  BRO inventories 1618/62 and 1628/8.
93  BRO inventory 1611/30.
94  Leech 1997a, 73, 199; see also pp 162-4 above and Appendix 2, 387-8.
95  Vanes (ed) 1975, 25–9.
96  BRO 00566(14).
97  Leech 1997a, 76–7.
98  Neale (ed) 2000, 123.
99  Neale (ed) 2000, 85.
100  Leech 1997a, 7–8.
101  BRSMG M2301.
102  BRSMG Braikenridge Notebook K.23.
103  Leech 1997a, 8; also of interest here is the use of the term 'hallehouse'.

## Chapter 6

1  For the use of the term 'shophouse' in 1473, see chapter 1.
2  Salzman 1967, 598.
3  Williams 1950, 225–31.
4  Smith 1983, 95–6; it can be argued that the term 'shophouse' was most probably applied to shops with dwelling space above.
5  Corfield and Keene 1990, 36.
6  Short 1980; RCHME 1981, lix; Moran 1994, 32, 34.
7  Smith 1983, 95.
8  See Schofield (ed), 1987.
9  Parker 1971, 66, notes that in one such row the upper rooms were called solars, but nevertheless concludes that they may not have been intended as dwellings; Smith 1983, 96.
10  Keene 1985 **1**, 239, concluded that in Winchester 'shops were similar in size to cottages and may often have served as domestic accommodation'.
11  For Tackley's Inn, Oxford and the parallels in Chester and elsewhere see Brown (ed) 1999, 559.
12  Leech 1997a, 6,110.
13  BRO P/StJB/D178–80; BRSMG M2441, Braikenridge Notebook 2.
14  Leech 1997a, 166–7.
15  The numbering follows that in Leech 1997a.
16  23–5 Abchurch Lane in Schofield (ed) 1987, 100–3.
17  RCHME 1981, 225–6.
18  For the dispute between the Fraternity of St John the Baptist and the parishioners of St John the Baptist, see BRO P/StJB/D/98, 138, 142.
19  BRO P/StJB/D/2/15.
20  Leech 1997a, 164.
21  Ibid, 42.
22  Ibid, 77–8.
23  Wadley 1886, 75.
24  Leech 1997a, 53.
25  Ibid, 48–9.

26 Ibid, 48.
27 Ibid, 173.
28 Ibid, 46.
29 The Tallage Roll of 1312 lists a number of shops which were also explicitly dwellings, see Fuller 1894–5, 171–278.
30 Salzman 1967, 483–5.
31 Leech 1997a, 172.
32 Wadley 1886, 217.
33 Smith 1983, 96.
34 Leech 1997a, 80–2; no.44 was then two separate shops.
35 Bickley (ed) 1900, 227; Veale (ed) 1933, 132–47; the proclamations made in the 14th century were evidently repeated in the 1450s. For evidence of cookshops in 16th-century London, see Schofield 1987, 20, 70–1, 85–7.
36 Veale (ed) 1933, 140–5.
37 Leech 1997a, 48, 79.
38 For York see RCHME 1981; for Tewkesbury see Jones 1968, 129; for Battle see Martin and Martin 1977.
39 Leech 1997a, 110–11; Lang and McGregor (eds) 1993, 17.
40 The numbering given in Leech 1997a.
41 BRO inventory 1618/14 and will of Thomas Clement; Leech 1997a, 68–9 for the two houses held by him and John Stibbens.
42 Leech 1997a, 170–4; see Wadley 1886 for the wills of John Holland and George Rowley.
43 BRO inventory 1633/31.
44 Leech 1997a, 172–3.
45 BRO 5139 (193).
46 BRO inventory 1618/14.
47 Pritchard 1906b, 270.
48 Notably Broad Street, Broad Weir, High Street, Mary le Port Street, Redcliff Street, the Shambles, St Nicholas Street, St Thomas Street, Temple Street and Wine Street; for the Parliamentary Survey of 1649 see BRO DC/E/3/2.
49 Including Broadmead, Corn St, Frog Lane and Cow Lane, Host Street, Lewin's Mead, Pipe Lane, St Augustine's Back and Tower Lane.
50 BRO inventory 1623/63.
51 The new house was New Place at Shedfield, designed by Edwin Lutyens (Weaver 1914, 175–82).
52 Latimer 1903.
53 For the inventories of Andrew Gale (1682) see TNA PROB5/4412; John Bisse (1628) see BRO 1628/8; Nicholas Stacy (1624) see BRO 1624/64.
54 A plaque on the exterior gives the date 'c.1456', but the leases of the parish of St Thomas are unequivocal in giving a building date of c 1673, for which see BRO P/StT/D/151–3, 171–91.
55 BRO 04335(7) fol 33, 130; BRO 04335(8) fol 163,195.

56 BRO inventory 1708/37.
57 BRO 04479(1) fol 86.
58 BRO 04335(4) fol 66.
59 BRO 04335(4) fol 68, (5) fol 83.
60 BRO P/StJB/D/154.
61 BRO P/Tem/H/1 no.29.
62 Guillery 2004, 225; Earle 1989, 206–18; Leech 1996.
63 BRO Building Plans vol 19 fol 45.
64 BRO 6170(1) a.
65 BCRL, elevation drawings of Bristol streets.
66 Wood 1745, 21.
67 BRO 792/1, lease of 25 September 1805, with references to earlier leases.
68 Jordan et al 1999, 200.

## Chapter 7

1 John Baptiste Malchair lived from 1731 to 1812; see Barley 1974 for his topographical drawings.
2 See, for instance, Winchester (Keene 1985 (**1**), 248–365).
3 Neale (ed) 2000, 23.
4 Leech 1997a and BRS volumes forthcoming.
5 Briggs 2009.
6 Neale (ed) 2000, 7 *et seq*.
7 Bickley (ed) 1900, **2**, 27.
8 Ibid, **2**, 231.
9 Veale (ed) 1933, 147–8.
10 Bickley (ed) 1900, **1**, 35 and **2**, 71.
11 Bickley (ed) 1900, **2**, 54.
12 Cronne (ed) 1946, 27, 31, 62, 137.
13 Keene 1990, 38–40; see also Brown (ed) 1999, 18–20.
14 Leech 1997a, 73, 82,162; Fuller 1894/5, 222–78.
15 Leech 1997a, 73–5, 162-3, 173.
16 See endnote 13.
17 Leech 1997a, xiv.
18 Ibid, 111.
19 Keene 1985, 167.
20 Morris (ed) 1947, 238.
21 Leech 1997a, 138.
22 Bickley (ed) 1900, **1**, 132–4.
23 Veale (ed) 1933, 142; Bickley (ed) 1900, **2**, 30.
24 Stanford (ed) 1990, 9.
25 BRO inventory 1617/43, will of Edward Pickrell.
26 BRO inventory 1623/19.
27 Neale (ed) 2000, 40–69.
28 Harris 1994.
29 James 1971, 10, 95, 97.
30 Neale (ed) 2000, 65–9 for Worcester's count of cellars in High, Corn, Broad and Wine Streets, also St Nicholas Street and Pithay.
31 Ross 1951, 97–8.
32 Leech 1997a, 80.
33 Ibid, 43.
34 Neale (ed) 2000, 11.

35 Harris 1994, 245.
36 Neale (ed) 2000, 23.
37 Williams 1950, 225–6; Leech 1997a, 136–7.
38 Good 1990/91, 39.
39 BRO P/StJB/D/2 and Wadley 1886,145,166.
40 Leech 1997a, 62,198.
41 *Winstone 1890s*, Pl 65.
42 Good 1987, 25–34: the excavations were not correlated with the historic landscape.
43 Keene 1985, **1**, 166.
44 Harris 1994, especially chapter 2.
45 Bickley (ed) 1900, **2**, 133.
46 Harris 1994, 117.
47 For the history of these properties see Leech 1997a, 72–3.
48 Ibid, 156–7.
49 Keene 1990, 187–90; Keene 1985, **1**, 166–7.
50 Keene 1985, **1**, 167.
51 Harris 1994, 232–3.
52 Bindon 1851, 128–9.
53 Leech 1997a, 59.
54 A plan was published by Pope, 1888. The part of the cellar under nos.23–4, destroyed in *c* 1928, was described by Pritchard 1929, 235–6.
55 BRO 04026(1); Leech 1997a, 76, 77, 79.
56 Pritchard 1920, 127–34; BRO 35438/63/47.
57 Leech 1997a, 79.
58 BRO 35438/26, fol 26.
59 Pryce 1861, 16–17. A section through the same cellar, incorrectly numbered as no.43 (which had a stone vault and not a timber roof; Fig 7.6), is provided by Pope 1888, pl xviii; a more general view of the same is in the Pryce manuscripts in Bristol City Reference Library. Bindon 1851, 120 describes the part of the cellar then surviving below no.32.
60 Pryce's drawing possibly appears fanciful, but other drawings in the same collection, notably of the cellars below nos.21–4, can be shown to be acceptably accurate.
61 Leech 1997a, 78.
62 Neale (ed) 2000, 17.
63 Burgess 2000, 63.
64 BRO 00566(14).
65 BRO 04421(a), fols 324–5 for the inventory, the earliest traced for any Bristol inn or tavern.
66 Leech 1997a, 2.
67 Keene 1985, **1**, 168-9.
68 BRO F/Tax/A/20/StJ(b) records this property at the same position in the listing as that for 1704, when it was the 'Full Moone' held by Mr Jacob (BRO L&S Rate, StJ, 1704 fol 17).
69 BRO inventory of John Thrupp vintner, 1617/60.
70 George and George (ed) 2002, 159–61.
71 Ibid, 166–7.

72  George and George (ed) 2005, 8–11.
73  Ibid, 156–60.
74  PRO PROB4/11301.
75  BRO inventory 1661/29.
76  George and George (ed) 2005, 8–11.
77  *Latimer 17th century Annals*, 103 correctly identifies that Aubrey was mistaken here and that Whitson's master had been Nicholas Cutt, a wine merchant.
78  Dick (ed) 1972, 477.
79  The date '1606' is painted on the exterior, probably from the date of a licence for the Hatchet being granted. However, the inn was apparently constructed between 1661 – when it was the 'roofelesse tenement', the property of the Dean and Chapter leased to William Pascall pewterer – and 1675, when it was leased, with a garden, to John Lloyd brewer of Bristol. The inn was then described as 'lately erected and new built by Thomas Tippett late of the Same Citty Vintner deceased'. BRO DC/E/1/2 fol 135; DC/E/1/3 fols 76, 400.
80  Leech 1997a, 33, 158.
81  Various of the houses were leased to the wine merchant Alfred Smith, no.69 from 1892, nos.70 and 71 from 1903 (BRO 09082(1) fols 254–6); the cellars of no.68 were possibly linked through an agreement not noted in the leases. See Inventory.
82  Leech 1997a, 99.
83  BRO ancient lease 1712 (1).
84  Leech 1997a, 118.
85  Barilla was the ash of burnt seaweed imported from Spain and the Levant, then ground up to make soda. Stoddard 2001, 24.
86  BRO inventory 1611/30.
87  Leech 1997a, 139; BRO inventory 1620/1.
88  BRO inventory 1669/3.
89  BRO 33746; Bold 1990.
90  Leech 1997a, 98, 99, 136–72.
91  Ibid, 99.
92  Ibid, 9.
93  See Inventory.
94  See Inventory.
95  Bold 1990, 79.
96  BRO 04043(4) fol 531.
97  See Inventory.
98  Good 1990/91, 41.
99  Bickley (ed) 1900, **2**, 3–4.
100  PRO PROB 2/30.
101  Williams 1981a, 16–22.
102  Williams 1950, 225.
103  Wadley 1886, 174.
104  For instance, Richard Rogers the elder (Wadley 1886, 258) and Henry Slye (BRO 04041 fol 107).
105  BRO 11178 (1–3).
106  Quoted in Hall 1957, 127.
107  BRO 04043(4) fol 400 and earlier rentals.
108  BRO 04043(4) fol 398 and earlier rentals; for his inventory see George and George (ed) 2005, 52–3.
109  BRO 04043(4) fol 394 and earlier rentals.
110  BRO 04041 fol 202; PRO PROB5/4412.
111  Jones 1996, 2.
112  Hall 1944, 3, 19.
113  Ison 1952, 141–2.
114  Hall 1961, 135.
115  PRO PROB3/18/93; no evidence of the former printing works was noted in the survey of this property.
116  Hall 1965, 1966.
117  Leech 1997a, 153–5.

## Chapter 8

1  Jordan *et al* 1999 saw the increasing abandonment of the city centre from the mid-19th century onwards as another element in emerging modernity.
2  McKellar 1999, 158–63.
3  For pre-Great Fire London town house plans see Schofield 1995; Leech 1996.
4  Guillery 2004.
5  Borsay 1977, 588.
6  Barry 1985, 77.
7  Colvin and Newman (eds) 1981.
8  Maguire 1992.
9  Downes 1967; Bold 1990.
10  Guillery 2004, 51.
11  Colvin and Newman (eds) 1981, 70.
12  McKellar 1999, 165, taken from Bodleian MS Rawl. D.710 fol 17v.
13  BRSMG Bristol Streets, D–K, watercolour of Johnny Ball Lane, back of 32 Maudlin Street, April 1865 by H H Burroughs; BRO 38041/12/PL4/9; BRO 04479(3) fol 57; 04335(8) fol 62.
14  BRO 4954(6) fol 11.
15  Manchee 1831, **2**, 162.
16  BRO P/StT/D/28: by 1789 the property was converted into two tenements, with garden ground adjoining, whereon were late erected five small messuages, in the tenure of George Carmarthen, carpenter.
17  Manchee 1831, **2**, 470–1.
18  Guillery 2004, 222.
19  Beresford 1971.
20  For instance Weare's Buildings in Bedminster, see Everleigh 2003, 231.
21  Leech 1997a, 6.
22  Ibid.
23  Wadley 1886, 217.
24  BRO P/StMR/D.
25  Information from B Williams of BaRAS.
26  Hall 1949, 121, 141, 156.
27  Sampson 1909, 84; Sampson's paper is the principal source for the historical information on the almshouses discussed here.
28  Manchee 1831, **2**, 199.
29  O'Neil 1951.
30  RCHME 1970, 197–9.
31  Cattell and Falconer 1995, 52–3.
32  Hancock 1995, 319–20.
33  Colvin and Newman (eds) 1981, 69–70.
34  McGuire 1992, 146–7.
35  Bold 1990, 77.
36  PRO inventory PROB5/4420.
37  PRO inventory PROB4/2.
38  The feature on the street frontage is thus enigmatic, having all the appearance of a bulk, but with no evidence of a shop behind.
39  Leases of nos.5–7 were granted to Joseph Thomas, a tiler and plasterer, in 1744 and 1754 (BRO 04335(12) fol 21 and 1395(4).
40  In 1754 nos.5–7 were occupied by Joseph Thomas (above), Isaac Wheeler and Richard Jenkins, both mariners (BRO 1395(4)).
41  BCPD file 82560, plan of ground floor and notes drawn from owners' title deeds for the house.
42  As seen in 1973 by the author, who lived then at no.16.
43  BRO 04335(10) fol 173, bargain of 6 November 1731.
44  Guillery 2004; Guillery and Herman 1999.
45  The inventory of John Drew for no.70 Castle Street indicates that some rooms were not in his possession at his death in 1681 (BRO inventory 1681/20); at no.68 Castle Street Katherine Bason left the use of the lower backward chamber to her daughter Sarah at her death in 1675 (BRO inventory 1675/6 and will).
46  The deeds for no.9 Redcliff Parade (with the owner) commence with a building lease of that date.
47  Maguire (ed) 1992, 144–6.
48  BRO Inventory 1710/20a.
49  Cooper 1999, 149–54.
50  Ligon 1657, 142.
51  Maguire (ed) 1992, 144.
52  On de Wilstar's map of 1746 (BRO SMV/Plans), this was the house of Parson Taylor.
53  The plan (BRO 04479(2) fol 98C) is dated to 1795 by that being the year in which David Evans was sheriff.
54  Ison 1952, 201.
55  No detailed plans of this house, no.52 (formerly no.32) Prince Street, have been traced in the Urban Sanitary Authority Building Plans in the BRO, or in Corporation leases relating to the property.
56  Bold 1990, 78–9.
57  Ison 1952, 162.
58  BRO Scavenging rates for 1725, parish of St James.
59  Evans 2000, 212; I am grateful to William Evans for other information relating to this house.

60 Ison 1952, 204 gives a date of *c* 1765 for the construction, but cites no source; the dates of 1757 and 1763 are given by Little 1962, 523, who must have had access to title deeds or other records relating to the construction of the two houses. From the evidence presented, Prospect House was designed by William Paty, Beresford House by Thomas Manley.
61 Summerson 1995, 6–7.
62 Guillery 2004, 186.
63 Summerson 1995, 6.
64 Latimer 1898.
65 BRO 28960(1).
66 Simpson 1926.
67 Johnson 1993, 107.

## Chapter 9

1 Parts of this chapter first appeared as Leech 2003a.
2 Cooper 1999, 109–28.
3 To the author's knowledge, Girouard 1990, 279–80 is the only writer to have noted the multiplicity of second residences in close proximity to late medieval and early modern Bristol.
4 Bickley 1899, 80, 83.
5 Ibid, 84–5.
6 Williams 1950, 241, 253.
7 BRO 00022–00024.
8 Leech 2000b, 112.
9 BRO 04421(a) fol 413.
10 Livock (ed) 1966, 56.
11 BRO P/StT/D/15.
12 BRO 04421(a) fol 480.
13 BRO 35722.
14 Wadley 1886, 224.
15 The Red Lodge was built *c* 1579 (timbers bearing the initials 'IY' have been dated to 1579 (ADS dendrochronology database)) and completed by 1585, see the inquisition noted in Maclean 1890–1, 239–40; for the White Lodge, see note 21 below.
16 BRO 04421(a) fol 418.
17 Livock (ed) 1966, 8; Leech 1997a, 107.
18 BRO 04421(a) fols 455–6; Strong 1967, NA 71 (m).
19 Leech 2000d.
20 BRO 26166(139).
21 The building of the White Lodge is dated by a chimneypiece bearing the date 1588, see BRSMG Braikenridge Notebook a.32.
22 Latimer 1903, 137.
23 Leech 1997a, 14.
24 Wadley 1886, 174.
25 PRO PROB11/12 Welles; Way 1921.
26 BRO 04421(a), fol 478.
27 BRSMG 1999/23 and 2000/25 are the accession numbers for the excavation archive. A preliminary report by R Jackson was given in Gaimster and Bradley (eds) 2001, 259; for the full report see Jackson 2010.

28 Manchee 1831, **2**, 132.
29 BRO Tax/F/A/1, where these are described as garden houses.
30 Leech 2000b, 81–108.
31 Leech 2000d.
32 The building is dated to the 17th century from the ovolo-moulded ceiling beam on the first floor. The moulding is similar to that found in houses in King Street, built in the 1660s.
33 Leech 2000b, 103–4.
34 BRO DC/E/3/2 fol 107.
35 BRO DC/E/40/57.
36 BRO 35722(1).
37 Tower-like lodges were being built also in early 17th-century London, for instance the New River Head Water House of 1613 (*Survey of London* vol 47 forthcoming).
38 The only illustration so far traced of Jordan's house is its depiction on Millerd's map of 1673.
39 Pritchard 1908, 289–92.
40 BRO transcription of the Hearth Tax (F/Tax/1A) by the author.
41 BRO 04041 fol 298; 04335(5) fol 98.
42 BRO P/StMR/D/1/a–b; D/4/1.
43 BRO P/StMR/D/4/1; the rent of 9s enables the property to be traced.
44 Latham (ed) 1947, 100. The subsequent history of Pyke's Meadow can be traced through the records relating to the collection of the annual rent of 20s. In 1627 this was paid by 'Mr Pikes for an acre of ground behind the Friers in fee farme' (Livock (ed) 1966, 150). In *c* 1650 the meadow was similarly described in the earliest surviving detailed rental of the city lands (BRO 04041 fol 9). By 1715 this rent was paid by Joseph Haskins (in 1700 it had been paid by John Haskins); the acre of ground with a lodge was then held by Joseph Haskins and Joseph Foot (BRO 04043(1) fol 1 and 04043(2) fol 2). By 1743 Joan Haskins, a widow, was paying the 20s rent, with the former acre of ground and a lodge 'now built on and called Avon Street' in the possession of James Tucker carpenter 'and many others' (BRO 04043(4) fol 7).
45 BRO P/StMR/D/6; P/StMR/D/E/1.
46 Other lodges in Pile Street were at nos.12–16, 17–18, 33, 58 and Averyng Hayes.
47 BRO P/StMR/D; Williams 1950, 241, 253; deeds of the 17th and 18th centuries enable the site of the lodge to be closely identified.
48 BRO 04335(7) fol 139, (9) fol 42, (10) fol 127; 04044(1) fol 271; 04479(3) fol 128 provides the location and shows the property later known as the Hope and Anchor.
49 Pritchard 1897; BRO F/Tax/A/1 for Castle Ward.
50 Dening 1949, 103.

51 BRO 5535(16 and 19).
52 PRO E179/116/482, assessment of 1610.
53 Bryant and Winstone 1983.
54 PRO PROB11/325 sig 121.
55 BRO DC/E/3/2 fol 99; DC/E/40/57.
56 BRO 6609 (31).
57 BRO 09463(5) a; 6685/6.
58 BRO inventory 1668/43 and will.
59 McGrath (ed) 1968, 92–100.
60 BRO F/Tax/A/1 fol 36b and correlation with entries for other parishes, in McGrath (ed) 1968 and Leech 1997a; for other parishes garden houses certainly existed, but are not separately identified.
61 Hayden 1974, 128.
62 Leech 1997a, 184–5.
63 BRO inventory 1617/48.
64 Leech 1996, 231.
65 Mrs Wilson's deeds for Prospect House, noted in 1975.
66 BRO 19522, deeds for no.26 Southwell Street recite deeds relating to the development of the field known as 'The Three-cornered Handkerchief'.
67 The deeds as seen by the author *c* 1975 commenced with a building lease of the 1730s.
68 PRO PROB4/7599.
69 PRO PROB3/30/20.
70 By 1618 two lodges were similarly sited in the former precinct of the Blackfriars. Both were set back behind the Rosemary Lane frontage, to the north and east of the former Friary buildings (Leech 2000d for references).
71 BRO P/AS/D/F18.
72 Egan 1990, 172.
73 BRO, will of George Lane 1613; Leech 2000b, 42–3.
74 McGrath (ed) 1968, 71–9.
75 BRO 09463(5) a.
76 Nott (ed) 1935, 244.
77 Leech 1997a, 2.
78 PRO PROB4/7599.
79 PRO PROB4/11206; Kingsley (1992, 232) interpreted Robert Cann's purchase of land at Stoke Bishop as one 'on which to build a house and establish his family as landed gentry'.
80 *Winstone 1879–1874*, Pl 120 and *1880s* Pl 133; BRO F/Tax/A/1 correlated with Leech 1997a, 198.
81 McGrath (ed) 1968, 60.
82 *Latimer, 17th century Annals*, 489.
83 The Langton family acquired the manor of Brislington in the 17th century, see McGrath (ed) 1968, 131–3.
84 Summerson 1953, 97–105; Leech 2009b, 175–7.
85 BRO P/StJames/lamp rates.
86 Mowl 1991, 41, 53.
87 PRO PROB/11/754 sig 142.

## NOTES

88 BRO lamp and scavenging rates and land tax assessments for the parish of All Saints: the entries in which record Whitchurch Phippen as living at no.9 High Street until his death in 1710.
89 BRO St Nicholas's parish lamp and scavenging rates.
90 Stembridge 1998, 88.
91 Stembridge 1998, 20.
92 For instance Thomas Goldney II and III both lived permanently at Goldney House; Henry Hobhouse moved from no.46 Queen Square to Cornwallis House Clifton in 1765; Levi Ames moved from no.15 Lower Maudlin Street to Clifton Wood House before 1792.
93 McGrath (ed) 1968, 68–71.
94 BRO 5535(6) and survey, see Inventory.
95 BRO will and inventory of James Read 1675/59.
96 BRO P/StT/D/15–22.
97 Cooper 1999, 128.
98 Ibid, 128–9.
99 Leech 2000b, 60–1; the rooms are described in the inventory of 1738 of the possessions of John Elbridge (BRO AC/WO/10(18).
100 *Winstone 1866–60*, Pl 9.
101 BRO F/Tax/A/1 entries for St Augustine's correlated with 04335(5) fol 4.
102 Leech 2000b, 98–9.
103 This could be said of these houses even today; at the time of writing there are still no photographs of most of the north side of Kingsdown Parade on the English Heritage 'Images of England' website.
104 I am indebted to Peter Guillery for this suggestion.
105 BRO 33041/BMC/6/14 lease no.5.
106 Jackson 2007.
107 BRO 00022–00024; 04479(5) fols 100–1; recent excavations may have mistakenly concluded that the walls of this 16th-century and later house were part of a Civil War gun battery, see Williams (ed) 1994/1995, 74.
108 Mellor 1987, 33.
109 Cooper 1999, 128–9.
110 BRSMG Braikenridge Notebook a.32.
111 North 1826, 121.
112 For the Gloucestershire houses see Kingsley 1992.
113 Johnson 2002, 23–4, 120–1.
114 For London see Leech 2003a.
115 Latham and Matthews (eds) 1974, 339–40.
116 BRO 1281(3).
117 For the lodge or garden house in early modern London see Leech 2003a.

### Chapter 10

1 Bold 1990, 79.
2 Ison 1952, 23; Jones 1992, 37; Mowl 1991, 13–14.
3 Ware 1768, 326.
4 Leech 2000b, 77–9.
5 BRO lamp and scavenging rates for St Michael's parish, 1703–75.
6 BRO 04335(5) fol 92.
7 Ware 1768, 326.
8 Ison 1952, 192, 219.
9 Schofield 1995.
10 The sample being that making up the volume of inventories transcribed by George and George 2002, 7–168.
11 BRO inventory 1635/41.
12 BRO inventory 1643/33; Leech 1997a, 178.
13 BRO inventories 1641/41, 1644/36 and 1648/12.
14 BRO DC/E/3/2.
15 Wadley 1886, 270.
16 BRO inventory 1617/48.
17 For instance Robert and Agatha Robbins, BRO inventory 1643/73; Thomas and Katherine Bason at no.61 Castle Street, BRO inventories 1673/2 and 1675/6; John Drew at no.70 Castle Street, BRO inventory 1681/20.
18 BRO inventory 1729/11.
19 BRO inventory 1708/37.
20 BRO inventory 1633/7 transcribed in George and George (eds) 2002, 71–2.
21 BRO inventory 1672/26 transcribed in George and George (eds) 2005, 52–3.
22 BRO inventory 1650/1.
23 PRO PROB 5/4412.
24 BRO inventory 1611/74.
25 BRO inventory 1635/33; Leech 1997a, 32.
26 BRO inventory 1643/33; Leech 1997a, 178.
27 BRO inventory 1648/12; Leech 1997a, 196.
28 BRO inventory 1628/23.
29 BRO inventory 1623/63; Leech 1997a, 3.
30 BRO inventory 1664/19; Leech 1997a, 32.
31 Bold 1990, 79.
32 Ibid, 79.
33 For the inventory of 1766 see Stembridge (ed),1998, 150–4.
34 Bold 1990, 80–1.
35 William Nicklus, the barber-surgeon at no.26 Castle Street in 1708 (*see* Fig 6.22 for ground-floor plan), used the first-floor front room as a study and consulting room, keeping there his 40 books on surgery and medicine (BRO inventory 1708/37); inventories of George Baldwin 1613, Thomas Palmer 1639 and Thomas Adeane 1668 (George and George (eds), 2002); inventory of Tobias Higgins 1699 (PRO PROB4/1811).
36 Colvin and Newman (eds) 1981, 69.
37 Bold 1990, 79–80.
38 BRO inventory 1633/31; Leech 1997a, 172.
39 BRO inventory 1635/98; Leech 1997a, 49–50.
40 Leech 1985.
41 BRO inventory 1623/63; Leech 1997a, 3.
42 BRO inventory 1647/16.
43 BRO inventory 1672/26; Leech 2006, 86–9 (where Fig 10.3 incorrectly identifies Hunt's house as no.57).
44 See end note 13.
45 BRO inventories 1641/41, 1644/36 and 1648/12; Leech 1997a, 196.
46 BRO inventory 1708/37.
47 Observed by the author *c* 1977.
48 Leech 2006a, 86-9.
49 BRO St Nicholas 1/J14; PRO PROB 3/23/135.
50 BRO St Nicholas 1/J14; PRO PROB 4/4403.
51 BRO St Nicholas 1/J14; PRO PROB 3/19/50 for George Stephens.
52 BRO 33746; Bold 1990.
53 BRO 04479(1) fol 269.
54 Ison 1952, 192; Mowl 1991, 86; the earlier house was of a different configuration, see Leech 2000b, 54–6.
55 By the 1720s this was also the practice in London (Cruickshank and Burton 1990, 52).
56 Ison 1980, 105–8.
57 Brown 1993, 23.
58 Holt and Leech 2011, 128–38.
59 Herman 2005, 137.
60 BRO 00748.
61 Herman 2005, 138.
62 Chappell 1984, 3–4.
63 Neve 1726, 72.
64 A plan for the bells and bellwires of a house is in *The Kingsweston Book of Drawings* (Downes 1967, Fig 89).
65 Archer 1997, 426–7.
66 For instance in Peter Street (Boore 1982) and in Redcliff Street (Jones 1983).
67 A design for a water closet is in *The Kingsweston Book of Drawings* (Downes 1967, Fig 90).
68 Part of the area formerly occupied by the great hall, later by nos.19–21 Tower Street, has remained undeveloped since the Second World War.
69 Leech 1997a, 82.
70 BRO P/St T/Ch/3/31 fol 18; Nicholas Bloome was the lessee from 1738 onwards (BRO P/St T/D/102–4).
71 BRO P/St T/Ch/31/fol 3; the date of re-fronting is uncertain.
72 Leech 2000b, 49–51.
73 For routs see *Latimer 18th century Annals*, 528.
74 Johnson 1993, 176.
75 The links between elite building and changes in society are discussed at length by Cooper 1999, 3–18.
76 Herman 2005, 146–7.
77 Bushman 1993, 251.
78 Ibid, 263.

## Chapter 11

1. Morris (ed) 1947, xxii–xxiii, 238.
2. The concept of exploring the architectural and social topography of the city is taken from Herman's study (1995) of Portsmouth, New Hampshire.
3. Sacks 1991, 331–62.
4. Based on a straightforward comparison between the two maps, Smith's of dubious value in its portrayal of the city's extent, some misunderstanding of the city's expansion between these years was inevitable. Notably Old Market and Broadmead were existing suburbs first laid out in the 12th century, not 'significant new neighborhoods' of the period 1568–1673. Similarly the suburbs extending beyond the walls on the south side of the city, and much of the area close to the Cathedral, were developments of the medieval period, but largely omitted from Smith's map. Elsewhere the conclusions drawn by Sacks in respect of new developments are broadly correct, and point the way to how the emergence of the early modern city might be better understood.
5. Sacks 1991, 353.
6. Ibid, 355.
7. Ibid, 146–9.
8. Baigent 1988, 110.
9. The name 'landgable' comes from the Anglo-Saxon 'land gavel', a form of tribute rather than any reference to house gables.
10. Leech 2006a, 83–4.
11. Pantin 1962–3 and 1963; Schofield 1995.
12. Latimer 1898.
13. BRO 00859(5) and Veale (ed) 1933, 218; Leech 1997a, 42.
14. Leech 1997a, 80; Burgess (ed) 1995, 76; Veale (ed) 1950, 59 and 154–5 for John Compton and Thomas Cogan.
15. Leech 1997a for references.
16. Ibid.
17. Carson 1994, 553.
18. McGrath 1957, 5.
19. Bettey 1978, 3–4; chapter 5 above.
20. Howard 1987, 111–12.
21. Hart and Hicks (eds), 1996, xxxi–xxxiv.
22. Now at Lake House, Wilford, see photographs in NMR and BRSMG M2043.
23. Pritchard 1909, 326–8.
24. Leech 1997a, 157; McGrath 1968, 53–6.
25. See Inventory for details.
26. See Hall 1983 for many examples.
27. Masters and Ralph (eds), 1967, xxvii, 11–143.
28. Sacks 1991, 356–7.
29. Leech 2006a, 92–3.
30. See Leech 2006a; Table 10.5 for the identification of inns in the ward of St Thomas.
31. For no.10 Castle Green see BRO 00349(15); for nos.25–7 Small Street see Leech 1997a, 159. No.10 Castle Green may have been let, however, the Jacksons being absent from the Hearth Tax returns for the Castle Precincts.
32. See Inventory and Leech 1997a.
33. For the south side of St Michael's Hill see Leech 2000b; for the north side see Inventory.
34. No.17 Wade Street was first discussed in Leech 1981, 17.
35. Earle 1994, 167; for the use of the term housekeeper in Bristol see Manchee 1831, 1, [All Saints].
36. BRO 39180 fols 12–14.
37. Ralph and Williams (eds), 1968, 146.
38. BRO 04479(3) fol 140b.
39. Ralph and Williams (eds), 1968, 125, first four entries.
40. Baigent 1988, 120.
41. For Stubbs see Leech 2000b, 83–4; for Wallis see Leech 2000b, 103–4, his city centre residence was in Baldwin Street, see Leech 1997a, 121–2.
42. See Inventory entries for houses on Clifton Hill, for Cliftonwood House, Upper Maudlin Street and Barton Hill.
43. BRO 00437.
44. BRO Chamberlain boxes 1799, Quarter Sessions papers, list of the inhabitants' names whose gouts or drains communicate with the common sewer to the parish of Temple.
45. See Inventory for many examples.
46. Poor rates for the parish of St Nicholas; *Latimer 18th century Annals*, 534–5.
47. Poor rates for the parish of St James.
48. TNA PROB31/694 no.446 for 1781.
49. These were Nehemiah Champion (no.50), Vickris Dickinson (no.52) and Richard Farr (no.54) (Poor Rate for St Stephen's parish, occupancy of properties traced back from the first street directory of 1775).
50. Ison 1952, 163–4; the house was probably built for a member of the Scandrett family (Poor Rate for St James's parish). No references are given for Ison's association of the house with the Elton family, which is possibly based on an incorrect identification of the location of Abraham Elton's house. See also Appendix 2 for the inventory of Thomas Crosby and below for Elton's house (Fig 11.29).
51. BRO 03683(1–6); the title deeds for no.21 St James's Barton the adjacent house, record that no.20 was 'the capital messuage … where Sir Isaac Abraham Elton, who rebuilt the same, dwelt'.
52. For addresses see Sketchley 1775. *Latimer 18th century Annals*, 536.
53. See Inventory.
54. Downes 1967, Bold 1990; see also chapter 8 and this chapter above.
55. Bold and Chaney (ed) 1993, 108, provides a wider context for Ware's work.
56. Mowl 1991, 62.
57. Oscar Wilde, *A Woman of No Importance*, Act III, 1916, Small (ed) 1993.
58. Jane Austen, *Northanger Abbey*, 1804, Kinsley and Davie (eds) 2003, 60.
59. Bold 1990, who underlines that this account is of more than local interest.
60. Ware 1758, 293.
61. For a discussion of these issues and the furnishing of the church in 18th-century Virginia see Upton 1986; for illustrations of the interiors of other Bristol churches in the 18th century see Dening 1923.
62. Baigent 1988, 109, 124.
63. Ibid, 118.
64. Ibid, 120.

## Chapter 12

1. See especially Dresser 2001 and Leech 2004, where parts of this chapter first appeared.
2. McGrath 1968, xxiv.
3. Richardson (ed) 1986, viii.
4. BRO Inventory 1688/19.
5. Dunn 1973, 120–5.
6. Ibid, 188–223.
7. Dresser 2001, 101–2.
8. The rate assessments for the parish of St Mary Redcliff indicate that after the bankruptcy sale these became separate houses once again.
9. See Inventory entries for Prince Street and Queen Square.
10. Dresser 2001, 105–8.
11. Leech 2004, 160–1.
12. Leech 2000b, 91–6.
13. BRO P/St Aug/Poor Rates, working back from 1775.
14. Dresser 2001, 105–9.
15. Ibid, 109; for Lockier's involvement in the Kingsdown development see BRO 35887.
16. Dresser 2001, 111.
17. Nott and Ralph (eds) 1948, 160.
18. Hall 1949, 117–8; Oliver 1909–18 (*Caribbeana*, **4**), 106; John Rylands Library, Stapleton MS. 2/1.
19. Dresser et al 1998, 12.
20. Guillery and Herman 1999, 77.
21. See especially Herman 1997 and 2005; Guillery 2004.
22. Herman 2005, 41.
23. For Jamestown see Cotter 1994, 45–51; for Norfolk, Virginia see Herman 2005, 47; for Portsmouth ibid, 157.

24  For Plymouth see NMR red boxes; for Totnes see Laithwaite 1984 and 1995; for Dartmouth and Exeter see Thorp 1995; and for Taunton see Taylor 1974. Peter Guillery points out that this variant of the central-stairs plan was also to be found in London and Dublin.
25  For Charleston, South Carolina see Herman 2005, 67, 123, 130, 221; for Baltimore ibid, 109; for Portsmouth, New Hampshire ibid, 111; for Philadelphia ibid, 144, 197.
26  Herman 2005, 105.
27  Ibid, 135.
28  http://nautarch.tamu.edu/portroyal/prmap3.html.
29  Herman 2005, 1–32.
30  Ibid, 59.
31  Leech 2009b, 184.
32  Maclean and Reinberger 1999, 34.
33  Ibid, 36 and 44; Reinberger 1996, 1998; Reinberger and Maclean 1997; Maclean and Reinberger 1999.
34  Ralph and Williams (eds) 1968, 84. The entry for William Penn, his wife Hannah and their servant Jane Andrews correlated with property deeds for St James's parish.
35  Leech 2009b, 183–5.
36  Andrews 1921, 107.
37  Petrological analysis by Drs Jim Andrews and Ian West, University of Southampton, for the author.
38  Wareham nd., 1–2.
39  Harris 1994, Pl 67, Pl 97 et seq.
40  These villas and gardens are discussed at greater length in Leech 2013, 47–52.
41  Iles's map of Nevis in 1879 shows two places with Paris's name. One is the now ruined plantation mill and house on the north side of Charlestown; the other is higher up the mountain and now the ruins surveyed by the author in 2004. 'Parris's Garden' is shown on a map of Mountravers dated to 1879, the original privately held in Boston, Mass. A copy has been kindly given to the author by David Small.
42  Discussed in Dresser 2001, 109–10.
43  Mowl and Earnshaw 1999.
44  For the concept of vernacular gentility in this context, and for a wider discussion of houses in London and south-east England seen alongside those in North America, see Guillery 2004, 277.
45  Explored at length in Dresser 2001, 96–128.
46  Buchanan and Cossons 1969, 39.
47  This painting is analysed and discussed in Greenacre 1982, 64. A painting now in a private collection shows Thomas Goldney's tower as a similarly prominent landmark, ibid, 37, Pl 17.
48  This paradox is much explored in Dresser 2001.

## Chapter 13

1  Glassie (1968 and 1975), Deetz (1996), Leone (1988 and 2005) and Johnson (2005) have all written at length on Georgianisation or the Georgian Order of Merchant Capitalism. This concept has been critiqued by Carson (1994), who has argued for a longer trajectory of the changes linked to emerging individualism and merchant capitalism. The evidence from Bristol fits comfortably alongside that outlined by Leone for Annapolis, but supports Carson's longer timescale.
2  Britnell 1993, 228.
3  Johnson 1993, 1996.
4  Williams 1950.
5  Bettey 1978.
6  Pearson 2009.
7  Summerson 1969, 38–51.
8  Carson 1994, 553.
9  Carson 1994, 554.
10  Cooper 1999, 3–5.
11  Downes 1987, 343.
12  Bettey 1997.
13  Stembridge 1991 and 1996.
14  Mowl 1991, 62–92, Mowl and Earnshaw 1999, 251–84.
15  Jordan 1959, 24–8.
16  Ibid, 363.
17  Leech 1999b, 19–20.
18  McGrath 1968, xxi.
19  Ibid.
20  Williams 1944.

# BIBLIOGRAPHY

## References

### Abbreviations

| | |
|---|---|
| BaRAS | Bristol and Region Archaeological Services |
| BCPD | Bristol City Planning Department |
| BCRL | Bristol City Reference Library |
| BL | British Library |
| BRO | Bristol Record Office |
| BRSMG | Bristol City Museum and Art Gallery |
| Devon R O | Devon Record Office |
| EH | English Heritage |
| GRO | Gloucestershire Record Office |
| *Latimer 16th century Annals* | Latimer, J 1908 *The Annals of Bristol in the Sixteenth century* |
| *Latimer 17th century Annals* | Latimer, J 1900 *The Annals of Bristol in the Seventeenth Century* |
| *Latimer 18th century Annals* | Latimer, J 1893 *The Annals of Bristol in the Eighteenth Century* |
| *Latimer 19th century Annals* | Latimer, J 1887 *The Annals of Bristol in the Nineteenth Century* |
| Leech 1997a | 'The Topography of Medieval and Early Modern Bristol, Part 1: Property Holdings in the Early Walled Town and Marsh Suburb North of the Avon'. *Bristol Record Society* **48** |
| Leech 2000b | 'The St Michael's Hill Precinct of the University of Bristol. The Topography of Medieval and Early Modern Bristol, Part 2'. *Bristol Record Society* **52** |
| NMR | National Monuments Record |
| OS | Ordnance Survey |
| PRO | Public Record Office, now The National Archives |
| RCHME | The Royal Commission on the Historical Monuments of England |
| SANHS | Somerset Archaeological and Natural History Society |
| SRO | Somerset Record Office |
| SRS | Somerset Record Society volumes |
| Suff RO | Suffolk Record Office |
| TNA | The National Archives |
| *Winstone 1845–1900* | Winstone, R 1983 *Bristol as it was 1845–1900* |
| *Winstone 1850s* | Winstone, R 1978 *Bristol in the 1850s* |
| *Winstone 1866–1860* | Winstone, R 1972 *Bristol as it was 1866–1860* |
| *Winstone 1874–1866* | Winstone, R 1971 *Bristol as it was 1874–1866* |
| *Winstone 1879–1874* | Winstone, R 1968 *Bristol as it was 1879–1874*, 2nd edition revised |
| *Winstone 1880s* | Winstone, R 1962 *Bristol in the 1880s* |
| *Winstone 1890s* | Winstone, R 1973 *Bristol in the 1890s* |
| *Winstone 1920s* | Winstone, R 1977 *Bristol in the 1920s* |
| *Winstone 1928–1933* | Winstone, R 1979 *Bristol as it was 1928–1933* |
| *Winstone 1934–1937* | Winstone, R 1986 *Bristol as it was 1934–1937* |
| *Winstone 1953–1956* | Winstone, R 1969 *Bristol as it was 1953–1956* |
| *Winstone 1960–1962* | Winstone, R 1981 *Bristol as it was 1960–1962* |
| *Winstone 1963–1975* | Winstone, J 1990 *Bristol as it was 1963–1975* |

### Works cited in the text

Adams, W 1910 *Chronicle of Bristol*. Bristol: J W Arrowsmith

Alcock, N W 1993 *People at Home: Living in a Warwickshire Village, 1500–1800*. Chichester: Phillimore

Alexander, M and Harward, C 2011 'Harbourside, Bristol: Investigations from 2003–2008' in Watts, M (ed) *Medieval and Post-Medieval Development within Bristol's Inner Suburbs.* 79–119. Cirencester: Cotswold Archaeology

Andrews, E W (ed) 1921 *Journal of a Lady of Quality: being the Narrative of a Journey from Scotland to the West Indies, North Carolina and Portugal in the Years 1774–1776*. New Haven: Yale University Press

Anon 1944 'Buildings in Bristol of Architectural or Historic Interest Damaged or Destroyed by Enemy Action, 1940–42'. *Trans Bristol Gloucestershire Archaeol Soc* **65**, 167–74

Archer, M 1997 *Delftware: the Tin-glazed Earthenware of the British Isles*. London: HMSO

Arts Council of Great Britain 1982 *John Sell Cotman 1782–1842*. London: The Herbert Press

Ashmead, G and Plumley, J 1828 *To the Right Worshipful the Mayor … This plan of the City of Bristol and its suburbs, is … dedicated, by … G.C. Ashmead. Commenced in the year 1813, by the late John Plumley; and completed to the year 1828, by Geo. C. Ashmead. Engraved by S. Turrell. Scale, 500 feet [= 65 mm]*. Bristol; London: G.C. Ashmead: Smith & Son.

Aston, M and Leech, R H 1977 *Historic Towns in Somerset*. Bristol: Committee for Rescue Archaeology in Avon, Gloucestershire and Somerset.

Atkin, M and Evans, D H 2002 'Excavations in Norwich 1971–1978 Part III'. *E Anglian Archaeol* **100**

Atkyns, R 1712 *The Ancient and Present State of Gloucestershire*. London: W Bowyer for Robert Gosling

Baigent, E 1988 'Economy and Society in Eighteenth-Century English Towns: Bristol in the 1770s' in Denecke, D and Shaw, G (eds) *Urban Historical Geography: Recent Progress in Britain and Germany*. Cambridge Studies in Historical Geography **10**. Cambridge: Cambridge University Press, 109–24

Baker, N *et al* 1992 'From Roman to Medieval Worcester: Development and Planning in the Anglo-Saxon City'. *Antiquity* **66**, 65–74

Barley, M W 1974 *A Guide to British Topographical Collections*. London: Council for British Archaeology

Barrett, W 1789 *The History and Antiquities of Bristol*. Bristol: William Pine

Barry, J 1985a *The Cultural Life of Bristol, 1640–1775*. Unpublished D. Phil. thesis, University of Oxford

Barry, J 1985b 'Popular Culture in Seventeenth-Century Bristol' *in* Reay, B (ed) *Popular Culture in Seventeenth-Century England*. London: Croom Helm, 59–90

Barry, J 1991 'Provincial Town Culture 1640–1680: Urbane or Civic?' *in* Pittock, J H and Wear, A A (eds) *Interpretation and Cultural History*. London: Macmillan, 198–234

Barton, K J 1964 'The Excavation of a Medieval Bastion at St Nicholas's Almshouses, King Street, Bristol'. *Medieval Archaeol* **8**, 184–212

Beachcroft, G and Sabin, A (eds) 1938 'Two compotus rolls of Saint Augustine's Abbey, Bristol (for 1491–2 and 1511–12)'. *Bristol Record Society* **9**

Beacon Planning 2010 *Chesterfield, no 3 Clifton Hill, Clifton, Bristol Historic Building Assessment. October 2010*: Stow-cum-Quy, Cambridge: Beacon Planning Ltd

Bedell, J 2000 'Archaeology and Probate Inventories in the Study of 18th-Century Life'. *J of Interdiscplinary Hist* **31:2**, 223–5

Beresford, M W 1971 'The Back-to-Back House in Leeds 1787–1937' *in* Chapman, S D (ed) *The History of Working-Class Housing: a Symposium*, 98–102. Newton Abbot: David & Charles

Bettey, J H 1978 *The Rise of a Gentry Family: the Smyths of Ashton Court c.1500–1642*. Bristol: Bristol Branch of the Historical Association, the University, Bristol

Bettey, J 1982 'Calendar of the correspondence of the Smyth family of Ashton Court, 1548–1642'. *Bristol Record Society* **35**

Bettey, J 1990 *The Suppression of the Religious Houses in Bristol*. Bristol: Bristol Branch of the Historical Association, the University, Bristol

Bettey, J 1997 'The Royal Fort and Tyndall's Park: the development of a Bristol landscape'. Bristol: Bristol Branch of the Historical Association, the University, Bristol

Bettey, J 2007 'Records of Bristol Cathedral'. *Bristol Record Society* **59**

Beverley, S Margeson, S, and Hurley, M 1991 'Medieval Britain and Ireland in 1990'. *Medieval Archaeol* **35**, 126–238

Bickley, F B 1899 *A Calendar of Deeds (chiefly relating to Bristol), collected by George Weare Braikenridge, F.S.A.* Edinburgh: Constable

Bickley, F B (ed) 1900 *The Little Red Book of Bristol, volumes 1 and 2*. Bristol and London: Hemmons and Sotheran & Co

Biddle, M and Hill, D 1971 'Late Saxon Planned Towns', *Antiq. J* **51**, 70–85

Bindon, J 1851 'On the Desecrated and Destroyed Churches of Bristol'. *Archaeol J*. **20**, 118–41

Bold, J 1988 *Wilton House and English Palladianism*. London: HMSO for the Royal Commission on the Historical Monuments of England

Bold, J 1990 'The Design of a House for a Merchant, 1724'. *Architect History* **33**, 75–82

Bold, J and Chaney, E 1993 *English Architecture Public and Private: Essays for Kerry Downes*. London and Rio Grande: Hambledon Press

Boore, E J 1982 'Peter Street Excavations'. *Bristol Avon Archaeol* **1**, 7–11

Boore, E J 1984 *Excavations at Tower Lane, Bristol*. Bristol: City of Bristol Museum and Art Gallery

Boore, E 1990/1 'The Minster House, Bristol Cathedral'. *Bristol Avon Archaeol* **9**, 43–8

Borsay, P 1977 'The English Urban Renaissance: The Development of Provincial Urban Culture c.1680–c.1760'. *Social Hist* **5**, 581–603

Borsay, P 1991 *The English Urban Renaissance, Culture and Society in the Provincial Town 1660–1770*. Oxford: Oxford University Press

Bourdieu, P 1989 *Distinction. A social critique of the judgement of taste*, translated from the French by Richard Nice. London: Routledge

Boynton, L 1967 *The Elizabethan Militia 1558–1638*. London: Routledge

Briggs, K 2009 'OE and ME *cunte* in place-names'. *Journal of the English Place Name Society* **41**, 26–39

Bristol City Council, 1988 *Ashton Court Mansion: Historic Development and Future Potential*. Bristol: Bristol City Council

Bristol City Museum and Art Gallery nd [c 1970] *Guide to the Georgian House*. Bristol: Bristol City Museum and Art Gallery

Bristol and Region Archaeological Services 1994a *Archaeological Evaluation of Belmont Street/St Mark's Road, Easton, Bristol for Modus Associates*. Bristol: Bristol City Museum and Art Gallery

Bristol and Region Archaeological Services 1994b *Archaeological Recording at Belmont Street/St Mark's Road, Easton, Bristol for Sovereign Housing Association*. Bristol: Bristol City Museum and Art Gallery

Bristol and Region Archaeological Services 1997 *Archaeological Evaluation at The Redoubt, Temple Quay, Bristol, Report No.374/1997*. Bristol: Bristol and Region Archaeological Services

Bristol and Region Archaeological Services 2003 *Archaeological Watching brief at No.6 Denmark Street & No.1 Mark Lane, Bristol Report No.1030/2003*. Bristol: Bristol and Region Archaeological Services

Bristol and Region Archaeological Services 2007 *Archaeological Desk-based Assessment of No.47 Langton Court Road, Brislington, Bristol*. Bristol: Bristol and Region Archaeological Services

Britnell, R H 1993 *The Commercialisation of English Society, 1000–1500*. Cambridge: Cambridge University Press

Brown, A (ed) 1999 *The Rows of Chester: The Chester Rows Research Project*. London: English Heritage

Brown, R W 1993 *Charles Wesley Hymn Writer, Notes on Research carried out to establish the location of his residence in Bristol during the period 1749–1771*. Bristol: privately printed (available at no.4 Charles Street)

Bryant, J and Kear, D 1982 'An 18th century bakery at Christmas Steps, Bristol'. *Bristol Avon Archaeol* **1**, 45–9

Bryant, J and Winstone, J 1983 'A Seventeenth Century House at 10 Lower Park Row, Bristol'. *Bristol Avon Archaeol* **2**, 45–7

Buchanan, R A and Cossons, N 1969 *The Industrial Archaeology of the Bristol Region*. Newton Abbot: David & Charles

Buchanan, R A and Cossons, N 1970 *Industrial Archaeology in Pictures: Bristol*. Newton Abbot: David & Charles

Buck, Samuel and Nathaniel, 1734 *The North West Prospect of the City of Bristol*, drawn and engraved by S and N Buck

Buck, Samuel and Nathaniel, 1734 *The South East Prospect of the City of Bristol*, drawn and engraved by S and N Buck

Buck, Nathaniel 1774 *To the Nobility, Clergy and Gentry, who were the Generous Promoters & Encouragers of this Work by Subscription, This Collection of XXIV perspective Views of the Ruins of ye most noted Abbeys & Castles in the County of York, etc., is greatfully inscrib'd their most oblig'd humble Servt., Samuel [and Nathaniel] Buck.* [14 Collections of 24 plates each, of views in England and Wales. Collections 1 & 2 by Samuel Buck, Collections 3–14 by Samuel and Nathaniel Buck, with 3 sets of 24 plates each, of views in Wales (set 3 having 12 extra plates), and with 2 volumes of towns, castles, & country seats in England & Wales]. London: Robert Sayer

Burgess, C (ed) 1995 'The Pre-Reformation Records of All Saints, Bristol: Part 1'. *Bristol Record Society* **46**

Burgess, C (ed) 2000 'The Pre-Reformation Records of All Saints, Bristol: Part 2'. *Bristol Record Society* **53**

Burnside, A 2009 *A Palladian Villa in Bristol, Clifton Hill House and the People who lived there.* Bristol: Redcliffe Press

Burrell, A (trans) 1931 *Piers Plowman: the vision of a people's Christ.* New York: Everyman

Bushman, R 1993 *The Refinement of America.* New York: Vintage Books

Carson, C 1994 'The Consumer Revolution in Colonial British America: Why demand?' in Carson, C et al 1994 *Of Consuming Interests – The Style of Life in the Eighteenth Century*. Charlottesville and London: United States Capitol Historical Society by the University Press of Virginia, 483–697

Carus-Wilson, E M 1967 *Medieval Merchant Venturers*, 2 edn. London: Methuen

Carus-Wilson, E M (ed) 1967 'The Overseas Trade of Bristol in the Later Middle Ages', 2 edn. *Bristol Record Society,* **20**

Cattell, J and Falconer, K 1995 *Swindon: The Legacy of a Railway Town.* London: HMSO for the Royal Commission on the Historical Monuments of England

Chalklin, C W 1974 *The Provincial Towns of Georgian England. A Study of the Building Process 1740–1820*. London: Edward Arnold

Chalklin, C W 1989 'Estate Development in Bristol, Birmingham and Liverpool, 1660–1720' in Chalklin, C W and Wordie, J R (eds) *Town and Countryside: The English Landowner in the National Economy 1660–1860.* London: Unwin Hyman, 102–15

Chappell, E 1984 'Looking at Buildings' in *Fresh Advices: A Research Supplement*. Williamsburg: Colonial Williamsburg Foundation

City and County of Bristol Guardians of the Poor, 1901 *Opening of the New Board Room ... at St Peter's Hospital.* Bristol: Guardians of the Poor

Clarke, H et al 2010 *Sandwich: A Study of the Town and Port from its Origins to 1600.* Oxford: Oxbow Books

Collins, A 1812 *Collins's Peerage of England ... Greatly augmented, and continued to the present time, by Sir Egerton Brydges.* London: F C & J Rivington

Colvin, H and Newman, J (eds) 1981 *Of Building – Roger North's Writings on Architecture.* Oxford: The Clarendon Press

Conder, E and Were, F 1907 'The Heraldry of some of the Citizens of Bristol between the years 1662 and 1688'. *Trans Bristol Gloucestershire Archaeol Soc* **30**, 273–82

Conzen M R G 1960 'Alnwick, Northumberland; a study in town plan analysis'. *Institute of British Geographers Publications* **27**

Conzen, M R G 1968 'The Use of Town Plans in the Study of Urban History' in Dyos, H J (ed) *The Study of Urban History.* Leicester: Leicester University Press, 113–30

Cooper, N 1999 *Houses of the Gentry 1480–1680.* New Haven and London: Yale University Press

Corfield, P J 1982 *The Impact of English Towns 1700–1800*. Oxford: Oxford University Press

Corfield, P J and Keene, D 1990 *Work in towns 850–1850*. Leicester: Leicester University Press

Cotter, J 1994 *Archaeological Excavations at Jamestown, Virginia.* Virginia: Cumberland: Archaeological Society of Virginia Special Publications **3**

Cronne, H A (ed) 1946 'Bristol Charters 1378–1499'. *Bristol Record Society* **11**

Crossley-Evans, M E 2010 'Christ Church, City, its fabric and Re-building during the eighteenth century' in Crossley-Evans, M (ed) *'A Grand City' – 'Life, Movement and Work', Bristol in the eighteenth and nineteenth centuries, Essays in Honour of Gerard Leighton, F.S.A.* Bristol: Bristol and Gloucestershire Archaeological Society, 73–97

Cruishank, D and Burton, N 1990 *Life in the Georgian City.* Harmondsworth: Viking

Currie, C R J 1988 'Time and Chance: Modelling the Attrition of Old Houses'. *Vernacular Architect* **19**, 1–9

Darlington, R R (ed) 1928 'Vita Wulfstani'. *Camden Soc* 3rd ser **40**, 32–4

Dawson, D 1986 'Handlist of Medieval Places of Worship within the 1373 Boundaries of the City of Bristol'. *Bulletin CBA Churches Committee* **24**, 2–15

Deetz, J 1996 (revised) *In small things forgotten – an archaeology of early American life*. New York: Doubleday

Defoe, D 1724–6 *A Tour through the Whole Island of Great Britain,* abridged and edited by P Rogers. Harmondsworth: Penguin Books

Dening, C F W 1923 *The Eighteenth-Century Architecture of Bristol.* Bristol: J W Arrowsmith

Dening, C F W 1949 *Old Inns of Bristol*, 4 edn. Bristol and London: John Wright and Sons Ltd and Simpkin Marshall Ltd

Dick, O L (ed) 1972 *Aubrey's Brief Lives.* Harmondsworth: Penguin Books

Dickinson, J C 1976 'The Origins of St Augustine's, Bristol' in McGrath, P and Cannon, J (eds) *Essays in Bristol and Gloucestershire History.* Bristol: Bristol and Gloucestershire Archaeological Society, 109–26

Dollman, F T and Jobbins, J R 1863 *An Analysis of Ancient Domestic Architecture, Exhibiting the Best Existing Examples in Great Britain.* London: Atchley and Co

Downes, K 1967 'The Kings Weston Book of Drawings'. *Architect Hist* **10**, 9–88

Downes, K 1987 *Sir John Vanbrugh, a Biography*. London: Sidgwick & Jackson

Dresser, M et al 1998 *Slave Trade Trail Around Central Bristol*. Bristol: Bristol Museums and Art Gallery

Dresser, M 2001 *Slavery Obscured. The Social History of the Slave Trade in an English Provincial Port.* London and New York: Continuum

Dunn, R S 1973 *Sugar and Slaves, The Rise of the Planter Class in the English West Indies, 1624–1713.* New York and London: W W Norton and Co

Earle, P 1989 *The Making of the English Middle Class: Business, Society and Family Life in London, 1660–1730*. London: Methuen

Earle, P 1994 *A City full of People*. London: Methuen

Egan, G 1990 'Post-Medieval Britain in 1989'. *Post-Medieval Archaeol* **24**, 159–211

Elton, M 1994 *Annals of the Elton Family: Bristol Merchants and Somerset Landowners.* Stroud: Alan Sutton

Evans, J 1816 *A Chronological Outline of the History of Bristol and the Stranger's Guide through its streets and neighbourhoods.* Bristol: John Evans

Evans, W 2000 'Redland Hill House and Redland Hill Chapel, Bristol', *Trans Bristol Gloucestershire Archaeol Soc* **118**, 206–12

Everleigh, D 2003 *Bristol, the Photographic Collection, a Compilation of Bristol 1850–1919 & Bristol 1920–1969.* Stroud: Sutton Publishing

Forman, H C 1956 *Tidewater Maryland Architecture and Gardens.* New York: Bonanza Books

Foyle, A 2004 *Bristol* (Pevsner Architectural Guides). New Haven and London: Yale University Press

Fradgley, N et al 1995 'The Chamber over the Hall: two early post-medieval houses in Hampshire'. *Proc Hampshire Fld Club Archaeol Soc* **51**, 107–36

Fuller, E A 1894–5 'The Tallage of 6 Edward II (Dec 16, 1312) and the Bristol rebellion'. *Trans Bristol Gloucestershire Archaeol Soc* **19**, 171–278

Gaimster, D R M, Margeson, S and Hurley, M 1990 'Medieval Britain and Ireland in 1989'. *Medieval Archaeol* **34**, 162–252

Gaimster, M and Bradley, J 2001 'Medieval Britain and Ireland, 2000'. *Medieval Archaeol* **45**, 233–379

Galster, G 1966 *Sylloge of Coins of the British Isles* **7**. 'Royal Collection of Coins and Medals, National Museum, Copenhagen. Pt 2 Anglo-Saxon Coins, Aethelraed'. London: Oxford University Press for the British Academy

Garner, T and Stratton, A 1911 *The Domestic Architecture of England during the Tudor Period, volumes 1 and 2.* London: Batsford

George, E and George, S (eds) 2002 'Bristol Probate Inventories Part 1: 1542–1650'. *Bristol Record Society* **54**

George, E and George S (eds) 2005 'Bristol Probate Inventories Part II: 1657–1689'. *Bristol Record Society* **57**

George, E and George S (eds) 2008 'Bristol Probate Inventories, Part III: 1690–1804'. *Bristol Record Society* **60**

Gill, J 1973 *The Bristol Scene. Views of Bristol by Bristol Artists from the Collection of the City Art Gallery*. Bristol: Bristol and West Building Society

Girouard, M 1990 *The English Town.* London and New York: Guild Publishing

Glassie, H 1968 *Pattern in the material folk culture of the eastern United States.* Philadelphia: University of Pennsylvania Press

Glassie, H 1975 *Folk Housing in Middle Virginia: a structural analysis of historic artifacts.* Knoxville: University of Tennessee Press

Gomme, A, Jenner, M and Little, B 1979 *Bristol, an Architectural History*. London: Lund Humphries

Good, G L 1987 'The Excavation of Two Docks at Narrow Quay, Bristol, 1978–9'. *Post-Medieval Archaeol* **21**, 25–126

Good, G L 1990/91 'Some aspects of the Development of the Redcliffe Waterfront in the light of Excavation at Dundas Wharf'. *Bristol Avon Archaeol* **9**, 29–42

Good, G L 1992 'Excavation at Water Lane, by Temple Church, Bristol 1971'. *Bristol Avon Archaeol* **10**, 2–41

Greenacre, F 1982 *Marine Artists of Bristol, Nicholas Pocock and Joseph Walter*. Bristol: City of Bristol Museum and Art Gallery

Greenacre, F 2005 *From Bristol to the Sea: Artists, the Avon Gorge and Bristol Harbour*. Bristol: Redcliffe Press in association with Bristol City Museums and Art Gallery

Greenacre, F and Stoddard, S 1986 *The Bristol Landscape: the watercolours of Samuel Jackson 1794–1869*. Bristol: Bristol City Museum and Art Gallery

Grenville, J 1997 *Medieval Housing.* London: Routledge

Grinsell, L et al 1973 *Sylloge of Coins of the British Isles* **19**. 'Bristol City Museum and Art Gallery, Bristol. Ancient British Coins and Coins of the Bristol Mint' in Bristol and Gloucester Museums, 'Ancient British Coins and Coins of the Bristol and Gloucestershire Mints'. London: Oxford University Press for the British Academy

Grinsell, L 1986 *The Bristol Mint*. Bristol: City of Bristol Museum and Art Gallery

Grosart A B (ed) 1886–8 *The Lismore Papers* (Family muniments, preserved in Lismore Castle), 2 ser 10 vols. London: privately printed

Guillery, P 2004 *The Small House in Eighteenth-Century London: a Social and Architectural History*. New Haven and London: Yale University Press

Guillery, P and Herman, B 1999 'Deptford Houses: 1600 to 1800'. *Vernacular Architect* **30**, 58–84

Hall, I V 1944 'Whitson Court Sugar House, Bristol, 1665–1824'. *Trans Bristol Gloucestershire Archaeol Soc* **65**, 1–97

Hall, I V 1949 'John Knight, junior, Sugar Refiner at the Great House on St Augustine's Back (1654–1679)'. *Trans Bristol Gloucestershire Archaeol Soc* **68**, 110–64

Hall, I V 1957 'Temple St. Sugar House under the first partnership of Richard Lane and John Hine (1662–78)'. *Trans Bristol Gloucestershire Archaeol Soc* **76**, 118–40

Hall, I V 1961 'The Garlicks, two Generations of a Bristol family'. *Trans Bristol Gloucestershire Archaeol Soc* **80**, 132–59

Hall, I V 1965 'The Daubenys: Part I under George Daubeny I'. *Trans Bristol Gloucestershire Archaeol Soc* **84**, 113–40

Hall, I V 1966 'The Daubenys: Part II'. *Trans Bristol Gloucestershire Archaeol Soc* **85**, 175–201

Hall, L J 1983 *The Rural Houses of North Avon and South Gloucestershire 1400–1720. Bristol City Museum and Art Gallery Monograph* **6**. Bristol: City of Bristol Museum and Art Gallery

Hancock, D 1995 *Citizens of the World: London Merchants and the Integration of the British Atlantic Community, 1735–1785*. Cambridge: Cambridge University Press

Harding, N D (ed) 1930 'Bristol Charters 1155–1373'. *Bristol Record Society* **1**

Harrington, D (ed) 2001 *Kent Hearth Tax Assessment Lady Day 1664.* London: British Record Society, Hearth Tax Series **2**

Harris, J 1994 *The Palladian Revival, Lord Burlington, His Villa and Garden at Chiswick.* New Haven and London: Yale University Press

Harris, J 2007 *Moving Rooms: the Trade in Architectural Salvage.* New Haven and London: Yale University Press

Harris, R B 1994 *The Origins and Development of English Townhouses Operating Commercially on Two Floors.* Unpublished Oxford DPhil. thesis, University of Oxford

Hart, V and Hicks, P 1996 *Sebastiano Serlio on Architecture, Volume One, Books I–V of 'Tutte L'Opere D'Architettura et Prospetiva' by Sebastiano Serlio.* New Haven and London: Yale University Press

Hartley, L P 1953 *The Go-Between.* London: Hamilton

Harvey, A 1904 'The Architecture of the Later Renaissance in Bristol'. *Proc Clifton Antiq Club* **5**, 210–35

Haslam, J 1984 'The Towns of Devon' in Haslam, J (ed) *Anglo-Saxon Towns in Southern England*. Chichester: Phillimore

Hayden, R 1974 'The Records of a Church of Christ in Bristol, 1640–1687'. *Bristol Record Society* **27**

Herman, B L 1995 'The Architectural and Social Topography of Early-Nineteenth-Century Portsmouth, New Hampshire' *in* Cromley, E C and Hudgins, C L (eds) *Gender, Class, and Shelter, Perspectives in Vernacular Architecture* **5**. Knoxville: University of Tennessee Press, 225–42

Herman, B L 1997 'The Embedded Landscapes of the Charleston Single House' *in* Adams, A and McMurry, S (eds) *Exploring Everyday Landscapes, Perspectives in Vernacular Architecture* **8**. Knoxville: University of Tennessee Press, 41–57

Herman, B L 2005 *Town House: Architecture and Material Life in the Early American City 1780–1830*. Chapel Hill: University of North Carolina Press

Hillaby, J and Sermon, R 2007 'Jacob's Well, Bristol: Further Research'. *Bristol Avon Archaeol* **22**, 97–105

Hirst, H C M 1927 'A 17th century house and chimneypiece in Small Street, Bristol'. *Trans Bristol Gloucestershire Archaeol Soc* **49**, 203–20

Holt, R and Leech, R H 2011 'Cabot House, Deanery Road, Bristol: Investigations in 2008' *in* Watts, M (ed) 2011 *Medieval and Post-Medieval Development within Bristol's Inner Suburbs* 121–44. Cirencester: Cotswold Archaeology

Horrox, R (ed) 1994 *Fifteenth Century Attitudes*. Cambridge: Cambridge University Press

Howard, M 1987 *The Early Tudor Country House: Architecture and Politics 1490–1550*. London: George Philip

Hudelston, C R 1937 'Canynges House, Bristol'. *The Gloucestershire Countryside* **2 no 10**, 193–4

Hulton, P H (ed) 1959 'Drawings of England in the seventeenth century by Willem Schellinks, Jacob Esselens and Lambert Doomer'. *The Walpole Society* **25**

Hutchinson, M 2003 *Number 57, the History of a House*. London: Headline Publishing

Ireson, Sister Kathleen 2006 *Emmaus – The Story of a House*. Bristol: Burleigh Press

Ison, W 1952 *The Georgian Buildings of Bristol*. London: Faber and Faber

Ison, W 1980 *The Georgian Buildings of Bath from 1700 to 1830*, revised edn. Bath: Kingsmead

Jackson, R 2000 '15 to 29 Union Street', 143–4 *in* Williams, B (ed) 'Review of Archaeology 1999–2000'. *Bristol Avon Archaeol* **18**, 139–51

Jackson, R 2006 *Excavations at St James's Priory, Bristol*. Oxford: Oxbow Books

Jackson, R 2007 *A Roman Settlement and Medieval Manor House in South Bristol, Excavations at Inns Court*. Bristol: Bristol and Region Archaeological Services

Jackson, R 2010 *The Archaeology of the medieval Suburb of Broadmead, Bristol, excavations in Union Street, 2000*. Bristol: Bristol and Region Archaeological Services

James, M K (ed) 1971 *Studies in the Medieval Wine Trade*. Oxford: The Clarendon Press

Jeayes, I H 1892 *Catalogue of the Muniments in Berkeley Castle*. Bristol: Jeffries & Sons

Jenks, S (ed) 2006 'Robert Sturmy's Commercial Expedition to the Mediterranean'. *Bristol Record Society* **58**

Jenner, M 2002 *22–24 Queen Square and 42 and 43 Welsh Back, Architectural and historical assessment*. Bristol: privately printed

Johnson, M 1993 *Housing culture – traditional architecture in an English landscape*. Washington: Smithsonian Institute Press

Johnson, M 1994 'Houses and History'. *Archaeol J* **151**, 435–9

Johnson, M 1996 *An Archaeology of Capitalism*. Oxford: Blackwell

Johnson, M 1997 'Vernacular Architecture: the loss of innocence'. *Vernacular Architect* **28**, 13–19

Johnson, M 2002 *Behind the Castle Gate, From Medieval to Renaissance*. London and New York: Routledge

Johnson, M J 2005 *English Houses 1300–1800: Vernacular Architecture, Social Life*. Oxford: Blackwell

Jones, D 1992 *A History of Clifton*. Chichester: Phillimore

Jones, D 1996 *Bristol's Sugar Trade and Refining Industry*. Bristol: Bristol Branch of the Historical Association, the University, Bristol

Jones, E 2006 'The Matthew of Bristol and the Financiers of John Cabot's 1497 voyage to North America'. *Engl Hist Rev* **121**, 778–95

Jones, R H 1983 'Excavations at 68–72 Redcliff Street, 1982'. *Bristol Avon Archaeol* **2**, 37–9

Jones, R H 1986 *Excavations in Redcliffe 1983–5, survey and excavation at 95–97 Redcliff Street, Bristol*. Bristol: City of Bristol Museum and Art Gallery

Jones, S 1968 'The Borough of Tewkesbury: Social life and Buildings' *in* Elrington, C R (ed) *Victoria County History: History of the County of Gloucester* **8**. Oxford: Oxford University Press for the Institute of Historical Research, 122–31

Jones, S et al 1984 *The Survey of Ancient Houses in Lincoln, Priorygate to Pottergate, Houses to the South and West of the Minster*. Lincoln: Lincoln Civic Trust

Jones, S et al 1987 *The Survey of Ancient Houses in Lincoln 2, Houses to the South and West of the Minster*. Lincoln: Lincoln Civic Trust

Jordan, S et al 1999 'Emerging Modernity in an Urban Setting: nineteenth-century Bristol revealed in property surveys'. *Urban History* **26:2**, 190–210

Jordan, W K, 1959 *Philanthropy in England 1480–1660: a study of the Changing Pattern of English Social Aspirations*. London: Allen and Unwin

Keene, D 1985 *Winchester Studies* **2** *Survey of Medieval Winchester, Parts 1 and 2*. Oxford: The Clarendon Press

Keene, D 1989 'The Property Market in English towns, A.D.1100–1600' *in* Vigueur, J M (ed) *D'une ville à l'autre: structures matérielles et organisations dans les villes Européennes*. Rome: Ecole Française de Rome

Keene, D and Harding, V 1985 'A Survey of Documentary Sources for Property Holding in London before the Great Fire'. *London Record Society Publications* **22**

Keene, D 1990 'Shops and Shopping in Medieval London' *in* L Grant (ed), *Medieval art, architecture and archaeology in London, British Archaeological Association Conference Transactions for the year 1984*. London: British Archaeological Association

Kelly, A 2003 *Queen Square Bristol*. Bristol: Redcliffe Press

King, A 2007 'Archaeological excavation, building survey & watching brief at 22–30 West Street, Old Market, Bristol'. *Bristol Avon Archaeol* **22**, 1–46

Kingsley, N 1989 *The Country Houses of Gloucestershire Vol.1 (1500–1660)*. Cheltenham: N Kingsley

Kingsley, N 1992 *The Country Houses of Gloucestershire Vol.2 (1660–1830)*. Chichester: Phillimore

Kinsley, J and Davie, J (eds) 2003 Jane Austen *Northanger Abbey* (Oxford World's Classics). Oxford: Oxford University Press

Kirby, I (ed) 1970 *Diocese of Bristol, Catalogue of the Records of the Bishops and Archdeacons and of the Dean and Chapter*. Bristol: Bristol Corporation

Laithwaite, M 1973 'The Buildings of Burford: a Cotswold Town in the fourteenth to nineteenth centuries' *in* Everitt, A (ed) *Perspectives in English Urban History*. London: Macmillan, 60–90

Laithwaite, M 1984 'Totnes Houses 1500–1800' *in* Clark, P (ed) *The Transformation of English Provincial Towns: 1600–1800*. London: Hutchinson, 13–61

Laithwaite, M 1995 'Town Houses up to 1660' *in* Beacham, P (ed) *Devon Building: an Introduction to Local Traditions*. Tiverton: Devon Books

Lang, S and McGregor, M 1993 'Tudor Wills proved in Bristol 1546–1603'. *Bristol Record Society* **44**

Latham, R C (ed) 1947 'Bristol Charters 1509–1899'. *Bristol Record Society* **12**

# BIBLIOGRAPHY

Latham, R and Matthews, W (eds) 1974 *The Diary of Samuel Pepys* **9**, 1668–1669. London: Bell

Latimer, J 1887 *The Annals of Bristol in the Nineteenth Century*. Bristol: W F Morgan

Latimer, J 1893 *The Annals of Bristol in the Eighteenth Century*. Bristol: Privately printed

Latimer, J 1898 'Ancient Bristol Documents: A Deed relating to the partition of the property of St James's Priory, Bristol'. *Proc Clifton Antiq Club* **4**, 109–38

Latimer, J 1900 *The Annals of Bristol in the Seventeenth Century*. Bristol: W George's & Sons

Latimer, J 1903 'The Maire of Bristowe is Kalendar: its list of civic officers collated with contemporary legal MSS'. *Trans Bristol Gloucestershire Archaeol Soc* **26**, 108–37

Latimer, J 1908 *The Annals of Bristol in the Sixteenth Century*. Bristol: J W Arrowsmith

Lawson, M K 2004 *Cnut. The Danes in England in the early eleventh century*. Stroud: Tempus

Leech, R H 1975 *Small Medieval Towns in Avon. Archaeology and Planning*. Bristol: Committee for Rescue Archaeology in Avon, Gloucestershire and Somerset.

Leech, R H 1981a *Historic Towns in Gloucestershire*. Bristol: Committee for Rescue Archaeology in Avon, Gloucestershire and Somerset.

Leech, R H 1981b *Early Industrial Housing. The Trinity Area of Frome, Somerset. RCHME Supplementary Series* **3**. London: HMSO

Leech, R H 1985 'The seventeenth-century and later houses to the north of the church', S9.12 [microfiche] in Watts, L and Rahtz, P *Mary-le-Port, Bristol: excavations 1962–3*. Bristol: Bristol City Museum and Art Gallery

Leech, R H 1996 'The prospect from Rugman's Row: the row house in late sixteenth- and early seventeenth-century London'. *Archaeol J* **153**, 201–42

Leech, R H 1997a 'The Topography of Medieval and Early Modern Bristol, Part 1: Property holdings in the Early Walled Town and Marsh Suburb North of the Avon'. *Bristol Record Society* **48**

Leech, R H 1997b 'The medieval defences of Bristol revisited' *in* Keene, L (ed) *Almost the Richest City, Bristol in the Middle Ages*. London: British Archaeological Association Conference Transactions **19**, 19–30

Leech, R H 1999a 'Row and terrace – urban housing in the seventeenth- and eighteenth-century English City' *in* Eagan, G *et al The Archaeology of the British 1600–1800: Views from Two Worlds*. London: Society for Post-Medieval Archaeology **and** Williamsburg: Society for Historical Archaeology

Leech, R H 1999b 'The processional city: some issues for historical archaeology', *in* Tarlow, S and West, S (eds) *The Familiar Past? Archaeologies of later historical Britain*, 19–34. London: Routledge

Leech, R H 1999c *An Historical and Architectural Survey and Analysis of the Exchange, Corn Street, Bristol*. Romsey: Cultural Heritage Services Client Report 1998/1999/107

Leech, R H 1999d *Draft proposal for the inclusion of Jacob's Well, Bristol, in the Schedule of Ancient Monuments*. Report prepared for and deposited with Bristol City Council Planning Department

Leech, R H 2000a 'The symbolic hall: historical context and merchant culture in the early modern city'. *Vernacular Architecture* **30**, 1–10

Leech, R H 2000b 'The St Michael's Hill Precinct of the University of Bristol. The Topography of Medieval and Early Modern Bristol, part 2'. *Bristol Record Society* **52**, 1–133

Leech, R H 2000c 'Owners and tenants, gardens and houses: the site in the late sixteenth to eighteenth centuries' *in* Jackson, R 'Archaeological excavations at Upper Maudlin Street, Bristol, in 1973, 1976 & 1999'. *Bristol Avon Archaeol* **18**, 71–5

Leech, R H 2000d 'Appendix 3: Detailed histories of properties in each street' *in Archaeological Desktop Evaluation of the Broadmead Redevelopment Site*, Bristol and Region Archaeological Services. Bristol: Bristol and Region Archaeological Services

Leech, R H 2002 'Alleyndale Hall, Barbados – A Plantation House of the Seventeenth Century'. *Journal of the Barbados Museum and Historical Society* **48**, 123–41

Leech, R H 2003a 'The garden house: merchant culture and identity in the early modern city' *in* Lawrence, S (ed) *Archaeologies of the British, Explorations of Identity in Great Britain and its Colonies 1600–1945,* One World Archaeology Series **46**. London: Routledge, 76–8

Leech, R H 2003b *Clifton Wood House, Randall Road, Clifton, Bristol, An Archaeological Desk-Based Assessment and Building Assessment*. Romsey: Cultural Heritage Services Client Report 2003/2004/156

Leech, R H 2003c 'The setting and the Environs', 11–52 *in* Drury, M (ed) 2003 *St Mary Redcliffe Conservation Plan*. Salisbury: Michael Drury Architects

Leech, R H 2004 'The Atlantic world and industrialisation: Contexts for the structures of everyday life in early modern Bristol' *in* Barker, D and Cranstone, D (eds) *The Archaeology of Industrialisation. Society for Post-Medieval Archaeology Monograph*. Leeds: Maneys, 157–64

Leech, R H 2006a 'Bristol: the Hearth Tax as a decodeable street directory' *in* Barnwell, P S and Airs, M (eds) *Houses and the Hearth Tax, the Later Stuart House and Society. CBA Research Report* **150**. York: Council for British Archaeology, 83–94

Leech, R H 2006b 'The Bishop's Park', 67–70 *in* Cox, S, Barber, A and Collard, M 'The Archaeology and History of the Former Bryan Brothers' Garage Site, Deanery Road, Bristol: the evolution of an urban landscape'. *Trans Bristol Gloucestershire Archaeol Soc* **124**, 55–71

Leech, R H 2009a 'Arthur's Acre, an Anglo-Saxon bridgehead at Bristol'. *Trans Bristol Gloucestershire Archaeol Soc* **127**, 11–20

Leech, R H 2009b 'Charlestown to Charleston – urban and plantation connections in an Atlantic setting' *in* Shields, D (ed) *Material Culture in Anglo-America, Regional Identity and Urbanity in the Tidewater, Lowcountry and Caribbean*. Charleston: College of Charleston

Leech, R H 2010a 'Richmond House and the Manor of Clifton' *in* Crossley-Evans, M (ed) *'A Grand City' – 'Life, Movement and Work', Bristol in the eighteenth and nineteenth centuries, Essays in Honour of Gerard Leighton, F.S.A*. Bristol: Bristol and Gloucestershire Archaeological Society, 27–46

Leech, R H 2010b 'Documentary evidence', 106–13 *in* Colls, K 'The Avon Floodplain at Bristol'. *Trans Bristol Gloucestershire Archaeol Soc* **128**, 73–120

Leech, R H 2011 'On the waterfront – the early medieval landscape setting of St Augustine's, Bristol' *in* Cannon, J (ed) *Studies in the Art and Architecture of Bristol Cathedral*. University of Bristol Medieval Studies series, 20–31

Leech, R H 2013 'Lodges, garden houses and villas – the urban periphery in the early modern Atlantic world' *in* Dresser, M (ed) *Slavery and the English Country House*. London: English Heritage, 46–56

Leech, R H and Bryant, J 2000 *Archaeological Desktop Evaluation of the Broadmead Redevelopment Site, Bristol*. Bristol: Bristol and Region Archaeological Services

Leighton, W 1933 'The Black Friars, now Quaker's Friars, Bristol'. *Trans Bristol Gloucestershire Archaeol Soc* **55**, 151–90

Leone, M P 1988 'The Georgian Order as the Order of Merchant Capitalism in Annapolis, Maryland', *in* Leone, M (ed) *The Recovery of Meaning*. Washington: Smithsonian Institute Press

Leone, M P 2005 *The Archaeology of Liberty in an American Capital, Excavations in Annapolis*. Berkeley, Los Angeles and London: University of California Press

Ligon, R 1657 *A true & exact history of the island of Barbados*. London: Humphrey Moseley, edited and annotated by E J Hutson, 2000. Barbados: Barbados National Trust

Lindley, E S 1961 'A John Smyth bibliography'. *Trans Bristol Gloucestershire Archaeol Soc* **80**, 121–31

Little, A W 1907 *Bristol Castle, Guidebook to the remains of Bristol Castle*. Bristol: privately printed in Narrow Wine Street (copy in BCRL)

Little, B 1962 'The Georgian Houses of Clifton'. *Country Life*, 6 September 1962, 520–3

Little, B (ed) 1971 *Sketchley's Bristol Directory 1775*. Bath: Kingsmead Reprints

Little, B 1988 *Stoke Bishop and Stoke House*. Bristol: privately printed, copy given to RCHME for NMR by Trinity Theological College

Livock, D M (ed) 1966 'City Chamberlains' Accounts in the 16th and 17th centuries'. *Bristol Record Society* **24**

Lobel, M D and Carus-Wilson, E M 1975 *Bristol* [fascicule from *The Atlas of Historic Towns*, **2**]. London: The Scholar Press

Maclean, J 1890–1 'The Family of Yonge, or Young, and on The Red Lodge' *Trans Bristol Gloucestershire Archaeol Soc* **15**, 227–45

Maclean, E and Reinberger, M 1999 'Springettsbury, a lost estate of the Penn family'. *Journal of the New England Garden History Society* **7**, 34–45

Maguire, A 1992 'A Collection of seventeenth-century Architectural Plans'. *Architect Hist* **35**, 140–82

Manchee, T J 1831 *The Bristol Charities*, 2 volumes. Bristol: T J Manchee

Martin, D and Martin, B 1977 'A row of "wealdens" in Battle'. *Historic Buildings in Eastern Sussex* **1.1** (Rape of Hastings Architectural Survey), 3–5

Martin, D and Martin, B 2004 *New Winchelsea, Sussex, A Medieval Port Town*. London: Heritage Marketing and Publications Ltd

Masters, B R and Ralph, E (eds) 1967 *The church book of St Ewen's, Bristol, 1454–1584*. Bristol: Records section of the Bristol and Gloucestershire Archaeological Society

Matthews, W 1801 *Matthews's Commercial Directory 1801*, disc 1 of 1. Bristol: Bristol Historical Databases Project, Faculty of Humanities, University of the West of England

McGrath, P V 1949 'The Wills of Bristol Merchants in the Great Orphan Books'. *Trans Bristol Gloucestershire Archaeol Soc* **68**, 91–109

McGrath, P V (ed) 1952 'Records relating to the Society of Merchant Venturers of the City of Bristol in the seventeenth century'. *Bristol Record Society* **17**

McGrath, P V 1953 'The Society of Merchant Venturers and the Port of Bristol'. *Trans Bristol Gloucestershire Archaeol Soc* **72**, 105–28

McGrath, P V 1957 *The Merchants Avizo by I[ohn]B[rowne], Marchant, 1589*. Harvard: Baker Library, Harvard Graduate School of Business Administration

McGrath, P V (ed) 1968 'Merchants and Merchandise in seventeenth century Bristol', 2 edn. *Bristol Record Society* **19**

McGrath, P V and Williams, M E 1979 *Bristol Inns and Alehouses in the Mid-Eighteenth Century*. Bristol: City of Bristol

McKellar, E 1999 *The Birth of Modern London*. Manchester: Manchester University Press

Mellor, P 1985 *A Kingsdown Community*. Bristol: Coordination Colin Greenslade

Mellor, P 1987 *A Kingsdown Collection*. Bristol: Coordination Colin Greenslade

Mercer, E 1975 *English Vernacular Houses: a study of traditional farmhouses and cottages*. London: HMSO

Millerd, J 1673 *An exact delineation of the famous city of Bristol and its suburbs*. Bristol: James Millerd (facsimile by Messrs Waterlow and Sons Limited 1950)

Millerd, J c 1710 *An exact delineation of the famous city of Bristol and its suburbs* [with revisions]. Bristol: James Millerd (copy in British Library Map Room)

Moran, M 1994 'Shropshire Dendrochronology Project – Phase Two'. *Vernacular Architect* **25**, 31–6

Morgan, K 1993 *Bristol and the Atlantic Trade in the Eighteenth Century*. Cambridge: Cambridge University Press

Morris, C (ed) 1947 *The Journeys of Celia Fiennes*. London: The Cresset Press

Morris, R K 1989 *Churches in the Landscape*. London: Dent

Mortimer, R 1971 'Minute book of the men's meeting of the Society of Friends in Bristol, 1667–1686'. *Bristol Record Society* **26**

Mowl, T 1991 *To Build the Second City, Architects and Craftsmen of Georgian Bristol*. Bristol: Redcliffe Press

Mowl, T and Earnshaw, B 1988 *John Wood: architect of obsession*. Bath: Millstream

Mowl, T and Earnshaw, B 1999 *An Insular Rococo: Architecture, Politics and Society in Ireland and England, 1710–1770*. London: Reaktion Books Ltd

Neale, F (ed) 2000 'William Worcestre: The Topography of Medieval Bristol'. *Bristol Record Society* **51**

Nenk, B *et al* 1991 'Medieval Britain and Ireland in 1991' in *Medieval Archaeol* **35**, 126–238

Neve, R 1726 *Neve's The City and Country Purchaser and Builder's Dictionary*. A Reprint of the Work subtitled *The Compleat Builders Guide,* published 1726. Newton Abbot: David & Charles Reprints 1969

Nicholls, J F and Taylor, J 1881 *Bristol Past and Present*, 3 vols. Bristol: J W Arrowsmith

Nicholson, R B and Hillam, J 1987 'A dendrochronological analysis of oak timbers from the early medieval site at Dundas Wharf, Bristol'. *Trans Bristol Gloucestershire Archaeol Soc* **105**, 133–45

North, R 1826 *The lives of the Right Hon. Francis North, Baron Guilford ... The Hon. Sir Dudley North ... and the Hon. and Rev. Dr. John North*. 3 vols, London: Henry Colburn

Nott, H E 1935 'The Deposition Books of Bristol Vol.1 1643–1647'. *Bristol Record Society* **6**

Nott, H E and Ralph, E 1947 'The Deposition Books of Bristol Vol.II 1650–1654'. *Bristol Record Society* **13**

Oliver, V L (ed) 1909–18 *Caribbeana: being Miscellaneous Papers Relating to the IIistory, Genealogy, Topography, and Antiquities of the British West Indies*, **1–6**

O'Neill, B H St J 1951 'Ridley's Almshouses, Bristol'. *Trans Bristol Gloucestershire Archaeol Soc* **70**, 54–63

O'Neill, B H St J 1953 'Some seventeenth-century houses in Great Yarmouth'. *Archaeologia* **95**, 141–80

Palliser, D M 1994 'Urban society' *in* Horrox, R (ed) 132–49

Pantin, W A 1947 'The development of domestic architecture in Oxford'. *Antiq J* **27**, 120–50

Pantin, W A 1962–3 'Medieval English town-house plans'. *Medieval Archaeol* **6–7**, 202–39

Pantin, W A 1963 'Some medieval English town houses. A Study in adaptation', 445–78 in Foster, I L L and Alcock, L (eds) *Culture and Environment, essays in Honour of Sir Cyril Fox*. London: Routledge & Kegan Paul

Parker, V 1971 *The Making of Kings Lynn. Secular Buildings from the 11th to the 17th century*. London and Chichester: Phillimore

Patterson, R B 1973 *Earldom of Gloucester Charters, The Charters and Scribes of the Earls and Countesses of Gloucester to A.D. 1217*. Oxford: The Clarendon Press

Paul, R 1912 'The Plan of the Church and Monastery of St Augustine, Bristol', *Archaeologia* **63**, 231–50

Peare, C O 1956 *William Penn, a Biography*. London: Dennis Dobson

Pearson, S 1994 *The medieval houses of Kent: an historical analysis*. London: HMSO

Pearson, S 2000 'The Kent Hearth Tax Records: Context and Analysis, xxiii–cii in Harrington, D (ed) *Kent Hearth Tax Assessment Lady Day 1664*. London: British Record Society, Hearth Tax Series **2**

Pearson, S 2007 'Rural and urban houses 1100–1500: "Urban adaptation" reconsidered', 43–63 in Giles, K and Dyer, C (eds) *Town and Country in the Middle Ages, Contrasts, Contacts and Interconnections*, 1100–1500. Leeds: Maney, for the Society for Medieval Archaeology

Pearson, S 2009 'Medieval houses in English Towns: form and location'. *Vernacular Architect* **40**, 1–22

Pevsner, N 1958 *The Buildings of England: North Somerset and Bristol*. Harmondsworth: Penguin Books

Pittock, J H and Wear, A (eds) 1991 *Interpretation and Cultural History*. Basingstoke: Macmillan

Platt, C 1976 *The English Medieval Town*. London: Martin Secker and Warburg

Platt, C and Coleman-Smith, R 1975 *Excavations in Medieval Southampton 1953–1969*. Leicester: Leicester University Press

Ponsford, M W 1969 'Bristol'. *Archaeol Rev* **4**, 54–5

Ponsford, M W 1975 *Excavations at Greyfriars, Bristol*. Bristol: City of Bristol Museum

Ponsford, M W 1979 *Bristol Castle: Archaeology and the History of a Royal Fortress*. Unpublished M. Litt thesis, University of Bristol.

Ponsford, M W 1991 'Dendrochronological dates from Dundas Wharf, Bristol and the dating of Ham Green and other medieval pottery' in Lewis, E (ed) *Custom and Ceramics. Essays presented to Kenneth Barton*. Wickam: APE

Ponsford, M W et al 1989 'Archaeology in Bristol 1989'. *Bristol Avon Archaeol* **8**, 41–5

Pope, T S 1888 'Notes on old Bristol houses'. *Proc Clifton Antiq Club*, **1**, 172–4

Portman, D 1966 *Exeter Houses, 1400–1700*. Exeter: University of Exeter

Potter, K R (ed) 1976 *Gesta Stephani, Oxford Medieval Texts*. Oxford: The Clarendon Press

Powicke, M 1962 *Military Obligation in Medieval England. A study in Liberty and Duty*. Oxford: The Clarendon Press

Price, R and Ponsford, M 1979a 'Excavation at the Town Wall, Bristol, 1974' in *Rescue Archaeology in the Bristol Area: 1, Monograph* **2**. Bristol: City of Bristol Museum and Art Gallery, 15–27

Price, R and Ponsford, M 1979b 'Survey and excavation near St Peter's Churchyard, Bristol, 1972' in *Rescue Archaeology in the Bristol Area: 1*, Monograph **2**. Bristol: City of Bristol Printing and Stationery Department, 35–55

Priest, G 2003 The *Paty Family. Makers of Eighteenth-Century Bristol*. Bristol: Redcliffe Press

Priestley, U and Corfield, P J 1982 'Rooms and room use in Norwich housing, 1580–1730'. *Post-Medieval Archaeol* **16**, 93–123

Pritchard, J E 1893–1896 'The Registrar's House, Bristol'. *Proc Clifton Antiq Club* **3**, 204–9

Pritchard, J E 1897–1899a 'Bristol Castle: Existing Remains'. *Proc Clifton Antiq Club* **4**, 17–19

Pritchard, J E 1897–1899b 'Vanishing Bristol. A Plea for the More Careful Recording of Existing Relics of Old Domestic Architecture in Bristol'. *Proc Clifton Antiq Club* **4**, 48–57

Pritchard, J E 1899 'Bristol Tokens of the XVIth and XVIIth Centuries'. *Numis Chron* **19**, 350–61

Pritchard, J E 1900 'Bristol Archaeological Notes for 1900'. *Trans Bristol Gloucestershire Archaeol Soc* **23**, 262–75

Pritchard, J E 1900–1903a 'Bristol Archaeological Notes for 1900'. *Proc Clifton Antiq Club* **5**, 43–56

Pritchard, J E 1900–1903b 'Bristol Archaeological Notes for 1901'. *Proc Clifton Antiq Club* **5**, 128–40

Pritchard, J E 1901 'Bristol Archaeological Notes for 1901'. *Trans Bristol Gloucestershire Archaeol Soc* **24**, 274–82

Pritchard, J E 1903 'Bristol Archaeological Notes for 1902'. *Trans Bristol Gloucestershire Archaeol Soc* **26**, 138–49

Pritchard, J E 1904 'Bristol Archaeological Notes for 1903'. *Trans Bristol Gloucestershire Archaeol Soc* **27**, 327–39

Pritchard, J E 1906a 'Bristol Archaeological Notes for 1904'. *Trans Bristol Gloucestershire Archaeol Soc* **29**, 127–41

Pritchard, J E 1906b 'Bristol Archaeological Notes for 1905'. *Trans Bristol Gloucestershire Archaeol Soc* **29**, 265–83

Pritchard, J E 1908 'Bristol Archaeological Notes for 1908'. *Trans Bristol Gloucestershire Archaeol Soc* **31**, 288–309

Pritchard, J E 1909 'Bristol Archaeological Notes for 1909', *Trans Bristol Gloucestershire Archaeol Soc* **32**, 313–33

Pritchard, J E 1911 'Bristol Archaeological Notes for 1910'. *Trans Bristol Gloucestershire Archaeol Soc* **34**, 65–89

Pritchard, J E 1913 'Bristol Archaeological Notes for 1912'. *Trans Bristol Gloucestershire Archaeol Soc* **36**, 103–29

Pritchard, J E 1918–1919a 'The Work of the Society – Past and Future'. *Trans Bristol Gloucestershire Archaeol Soc* **41**, 11–25

Pritchard, J E 1919–1919b 'An Archaeological Survey – An Archaeological Revival'. *Trans Bristol Gloucestershire Archaeol Soc* **41**, 129–39

Pritchard, J E 1920 'Bristol Archaeological Notes, 1913–1919'. *Trans Bristol Gloucestershire Archaeol Soc* **42**, 125–48

Pritchard, J E 1922 'Bristol Archaeological Notes 1920–1923, including the latest 'Chatterton Find'. *Trans Bristol Gloucestershire Archaeol Soc* **44**, 79–99

Pritchard, J E 1923 'Tobacco Pipes of Bristol of the XVIth Century and their Makers'. *Trans Bristol Gloucestershire Archaeol Soc* **45**, 165–91

Pritchard, J E 1926a 'The Pithay, Bristol'. *Trans Bristol Gloucestershire Archaeol Soc* **48**, 251–73

Pritchard, J E 1926b 'Bristol in Norman Times'. *Bristol Times and Mirror*, 2 February 1926

Pritchard, J E 1929 'Bristol Archaeological Notes for 1924–1929'. *Trans Bristol Gloucestershire Archaeol Soc* **51**, 225–43

Prout, J S 1893 *Picturesque antiquities of Bristol. From the original drawings by J. S. Prout*. Bristol: E Smith

Pryce, G 1854 *Memorials of the Canynges' Family and their times ... To which is added memoranda relating to Chatterton*. Bristol: J W Arrowsmith

Pryce, G 1861 *A Popular History of Bristol, Antiquarian, Topographical and Descriptive, from the Earliest Period to the Present Time*. Bristol: W Mack

Quiney, A 2004 *Town Houses of Medieval Britain*. New Haven & London: Yale University Press

RCHME 1963 *Monuments Threatened or Destroyed. A Select List: 1956–1962*. London: HMSO

RCHME 1970 *An Inventory of Historical Monuments in the county of Dorset, Vol 3, Central Dorset, Part 2*. Edinburgh: HMSO

RCHME 1977 *The Town of Stamford: an Inventory of Historical Monuments*. London: HMSO

RCHME 1981 *An Inventory of the Historical Monuments in the City of York, Vol* **5**, *The Central Area*. London: HMSO

Ralph, E and Williams, M E 1968 'The inhabitants of Bristol in 1696'. *Bristol Record Society* **25**

Reinberger, M 1996 'Eighteenth-century suburbanization in Philadelphia: patterns on the land and the Quaker beliefs of William Penn'. *Proceedings of the Council of Educators in Landscape Architecture*, 113–21

Reinberger, M 1998 'Belmont: The Bourgeois Villa in Eighteenth Century Philadelphia'. *Journal of the Southeast Chapter of the Society of Architectural Historians* **9**, 13–39

Reinberger, M and Maclean, E 1997 'Isaac Norris's Fairhill, architecture, landscape and Quaker ideals in a Philadelphia colonial country seat'. *Winterthur Portfolio* **32:4**, 243–74

Richardson, M (ed) 1986 'Bristol, Africa and the eighteenth-century slave trade to America. Vol.1: the years of expansion 1698–1729'. *Bristol Record Society* **38**

Ridgeway, V and Watts, M (eds) 2013 *Friars, Quakers, Industry and Urbanisation. The Archaeology of the Broadmead Expansion Project, Cabot Circus, Bristol, 2005–2008*, Cirencester and London: Consortium of Cotswold Archaeology and Pre-Construct Archaeology.

Roberts, E and Parker, K (eds) 1992a *Southampton Probate Inventories 1447–1575 Volume 1 Southampton Records Series* **34**

Roberts, E and Parker, K (eds) 1992b *Southampton Probate Inventories 1447–1575 Volume 2 Southampton Records Series* **35**

Robinson, T O 1981 *The Longcase Clock*. Woodbridge: Antique Collectors' Club

Rocque, J 1742 *A Plan of the City of Bristol, Surveyed and Drawn by John Rocque, Engraved by John Pine*. Bristol: B Hickey

Ross, C D 1951 'The household accounts of Elizabeth Berkeley, Countess of Warwick, 1420–1'. *Trans Bristol and Gloucestershire Archaeol Soc* **70**, 81–105

Ross, C D (ed) 1959 'Cartulary of St. Mark's Hospital Bristol'. *Bristol Record Society* **21**

Ross, K 2004 *Report on Bishop's House, Clifton Hill, Bristol*. Upton Cheyney: the House Historians

Sacks, D H 1985 *Trade, Society and Politics in Bristol, 1500–1640*, 2 vols. New York: Garland Publishing

Sacks, D H 1991 *The Widening Gate: Bristol and the Atlantic Economy, 1450–1700*. Berkeley: University of California Press

Salzman, L F 1967 *Building in England down to 1540: a documentary survey*. Oxford: The Clarendon Press

Sampson, W A 1909 'The Almshouses of Bristol'. *Trans Bristol Gloucestershire Archaeol Soc* **32**, 84–108

Schama, S 1987 *The Embarrassment of Riches. An interpretation of Dutch culture in the Golden Age*. London: Collins

Schofield, J (ed) 1987 The *London Surveys of Ralph Treswell*. London Topographical Society Publication **135**

Schofield, J A 1995 *Medieval London Houses*. New Haven and London: Yale University Press

Seyer, S 1821/1823 *Memoirs, Historical and Topographical, of Bristol*, 2 volumes. Bristol: Norton

Short, P 1980 'The Fourteenth-Century Rows of York'. *Archaeol J* **137**, 86–136

Simpson, J J 1926 'St Peter's Hospital, Bristol'. *Trans Bristol Gloucestershire Archaeol Soc* **48**, 193–226

Skelton, J S 1831 *Etchings of the antiquities of Bristol, from original sketches by the late Hugh O'Neil*. Bristol: London: Davey and Muskett; Longman, Rees, Orme, Brown and Green

Small, I (ed) 1993 *A Woman of No Importance* (first published by Oscar Wilde in 1916). London: A & C Black

Smith, G M 1917 *A History of the Bristol Royal Infirmary*. Bristol: J W Arrowsmith

Smith, J T 1983 '[The] English Town House in the XVth and XVIth centuries' *in* Chastel, A and Guillaume, J (eds) *La Maison de Ville à la Renaissance*. Paris: Picard, 89–98, 183–6

Smith, M G 1970 *The Medieval Churches of Bristol*. Bristol: Bristol Branch of the Historical Association, the University, Bristol

Smith, R and Carter, A 1983 'Function and site: aspects of Norwich buildings before 1700'. *Vernacular Architect* **14**, 5–18

Stanford, M (ed) 1990 'The Ordinances of Bristol'. *Bristol Record Society* **41**

Stembridge, P K 1982 *Thomas Goldney (1696–1768): aspects of the life of a Bristol merchant*. M. Litt thesis University of Bristol

Stembridge, P K 1991 *Thomas Goldney, man of property*. Bristol: University of Bristol

Stembridge, P K 1996 *Thomas Goldney's garden: the creation of an eighteenth century garden*. Bristol: Avon Gardens Trust

Stembridge, P K 1998 'The Goldney Family – A Bristol Merchant Dynasty'. *Bristol Record Society* **49**

Stocker, D 1999 *Notes on the Stocker Family*, typescript privately circulated

Stoddard, S 1981 *Mr Braikenridge's Brislington*. Bristol: City of Bristol Museum and Art Gallery

Stoddard, S 2001 *Bristol before the Camera: The City in 1820–30*. Bristol: Redcliffe Press

Stone, G F 1909 *Bristol: as it was and as it is. A record of fifty years' progress ... Illustrated by S. J. Loxton, reprinted, with additions, from the 'Bristol Evening News', 1908–1909*. Bristol: Walter Reid

Strong, P L 1967 *All Saints, City of Bristol, Calendar of Deeds*. London: submitted for London University Diploma in Archive Administration (copy in BRO)

Summerson, J 1953 *Architecture in Britain, 1530–1830*, London: Penguin

Summerson, J 1969 *Georgian London*. Harmondsworth: Penguin Books

Summerson, J 1995 'The beginnings of an early Victorian suburb'. *London Topographical Record* **27**, 1–48

Tatum, G B 1976 *Philadelphia Georgian*. Middletown CT: Wesleyan University Press

Taylor, J 1872 *A Book about Bristol; Historical, Ecclesiastical and Biographical, from original research*. London and Bristol: Houlston and Sons, Thomas Kerslake & Co and William George

Taylor, J 1885 *Picturesque Old Bristol. A series of fifty-two etchings by Charles Bird, with letterpress by John Taylor.* Bristol: Frost and Reed.

Taylor, J 1875 'The church of Holy Cross, Temple, Bristol'. *J Brit Archaeol Ass*, 275–82

Taylor, R 1974 'Town Houses in Taunton, 1500–1700'. *Post-Medieval Archaeol* **8**, 63–79

Taylor, R and Richmond, H 1989 '28–32 King Street, Kings Lynn'. *Norfolk Archaeol* **40**, 260–85

Thomas, N 1986 'J.E. Pritchard and the Archaeology of Bristol'. *Trans Bristol Gloucestershire Archaeol Soc* **104**, 7–25

Thornton, P 1993 *Authentic Decor: the Domestic Interior 1620–1920.* London: Weidenfield and Nicolson

Thorp, J 1995 'Town Houses of the late seventeenth and early eighteenth centuries' *in* Beacham, P *Devon Building: An introduction to local building traditions*, 2 edn. Tiverton, England: Devon Books, 122–3

Turner, L G 1911 *Original Records of Early Nonconformity under Persecution and Indulgence.* London: Unwin

Upton, D 1986 *Holy things and profane: Anglican churches in colonial Virginia*. Cambridge, Massachusettts: MIT Press

Vanes, J (ed) 1975 'The Ledger of John Smythe'. *Bristol Record Society* **28** [a reprint of the Royal Commission on Historical Manuscripts publication of 1974]

Veale, E W W (ed) 1931 'The Great Red Book of Bristol, Introduction Part 1, Burgage Tenure in Mediæval Bristol'. *Bristol Record Society* **2**

Veale, E W W (ed) 1933 'The Great Red Book of Bristol, Text Part 1'. *Bristol Record Society* **4**

Veale, E W W (ed) 1937 'The Great Red Book of Bristol, Text Part 2'. *Bristol Record Society* **8**

Veale, E W W (ed) 1950 'The Great Red Book of Bristol, Text Part 3'. *Bristol Record Society*, **16**

Veale, E W W (ed) 1953 'The Great Red Book of Bristol, Text Part 4'. *Bristol Record Society*, **18**

Vince, A and Barton, K J 1988 'Early English medieval pottery in Viking Dublin' and 'The medieval pottery of Dublin' *in* Mac Niocaill, G and Wallace, P F (eds) *Keimelia: Studies in Medieval Archaeology in Memory of Tom Delaney*. Galway: Galway University Press, 254–324

Wadley, T P 1886 *Notes or Abstracts of the Wills Contained in the Great Orphan Book of Wills*. Bristol: C T Jefferies and Sons

Walker, D (ed) 1998 *The Cartulary of St Augustine's Abbey, Bristol, Gloucestershire Record Series Volume* **10**. Bristol: J W Arrowsmith for the Bristol and Gloucestershire Archaeological Society

Walker, G G 1954 *The Honourable Artillery Company 1537–1926*, 2 edn. Aldershot: Gale and Polden Ltd

Ward, J R 1978 'Speculative Building at Bristol and Clifton'. *Business History* **20**, 3–18

Ware, I 1768 *A Complete Body of Architecture, adorned with plans and elevations from original designs; in which are interspersed some designs of Inigo Jones*. London: Rivington (facsimile reprint of: Farnborough: Gregg, 1971)

Wareham, T nd *Introduction to the Mills Archive*. London: Manuscript introductory text at the Docklands Museum

Warren, R H 1907 'The Medieval Chapels of Bristol'. *Trans Bristol Gloucestershire Archaeol Soc* **30**, 181–211

Watts, L and Rahtz, P 1985 *Mary-le-Port, Bristol: excavations 1962–3.* Bristol: City of Bristol Museum and Art Gallery

Way, L J U 1921 'Some Miscellaneous Bristol Deeds'. *Trans Bristol Gloucestershire Archaeol Soc* **42**, 97–123

Weare, G E 1893 *A Collectanea relating to the Bristol Friars Minors, Gray Friars, and their convent, together with a concise history of the dissolution of the houses of the Four Orders of Mendicant Friars in Bristol.* Bristol: W Bennett

Weaver, L 1914 *Houses and Gardens by E .L. Lutyens*. London: Country Life

Wells-Cole, A 1997 *Art and Decoration in Elizabethan and Jacobean England. The Influence of Continental Prints, 1558–1625*. New Haven and London: Yale University Press

West, S 1999 'Introduction', 2–3 *in* Tarlow, S and West, S (eds) *The Familiar Past? Archaeologies of later historical Britain*. London: Routledge

Western, J B 1965 *The English militia in the 18th century, the story of a political issue 1660–1802*. London: Routledge

Whitelock, D et al 1961 *The Anglo-Saxon Chronicle*. London: Eyre and Spottiswoode

Williams, B 1981 *Excavations in the medieval suburb of Bristol, 1980*. Bristol: City of Bristol Museum and Art Gallery

Williams, B 1982 'Excavations at Bristol Bridge, 1981'. *Bristol Avon Archaeol* **1**, 12–15

Williams, B 1988 'The Excavation of Medieval and Post-Medieval Tenements at 94–102 Temple Street, Bristol' 1975 *Trans Bristol Gloucestershire Archaeol Soc* **106**, 107–68

Williams, B (ed) 1992 'Archaeology in Bristol 1990–92'. *Bristol Avon Archaeol* **10**, 53–6

Williams, B 1994/5 'Bristol and Region Archaeological Survey Projects 1994'. *Bristol Avon Archaeol* **12**, 70–5

Williams, B (ed) 2006 'Review of Archaeology 2006' *Bristol Avon Archaeol* **21**, 107–24

Williams, E 1944 *Capitalism & slavery*. Chapel Hill: University of North Carolina Press

Williams, E E 1950 *The chantries of William Canynges in St Mary Redcliffe Bristol*. Bristol: William George Sons Ltd

Williamson, J A 1962 *The Cabot Voyages and Bristol Discovery under Henry VII....* Cambridge: Cambridge University Press

Wilson, D M and Moorhouse, S 1971 'Medieval Britain in 1970'. *Medieval Archaeol* **15**, 124–79

Winstone, J 1990 *Bristol as it was 1963–1975*. Bristol: Reece Winstone Archive and Publishing

Winstone, J 1993 *Bristol Trade Cards*. Bristol: Reece Winstone Archive and Publishing

Winstone, R 1962 *Bristol in the 1880s*. Bristol: Reece Winstone.

Winstone, R 1968 *Bristol as it was 1879–1874* (2nd edition revised). Bristol: Reece Winstone

Winstone, R 1969 *Bristol as it was 1953–1956*. Bristol: Reece Winstone

Winstone, R 1971 *Bristol as it was 1874–1866*. Bristol: Reece Winstone

Winstone, R 1972 *Bristol as it was 1866–1860*. Bristol: Reece Winstone

Winstone, R 1973 *Bristol in the 1890s*. Bristol: Reece Winstone

Winstone, R 1977 *Bristol in the 1920s*. Bristol: Reece Winstone

Winstone, R 1978 *Bristol in the 1850s*. Bristol: Reece Winstone

Winstone, R 1979 *Bristol as it was 1928–1933*. Bristol: Reece Winstone

Winstone, R 1981 *Bristol as it was 1960–1962*. Bristol: Reece Winstone

Winstone, R 1983 *Bristol as it was 1845–1900*. Bristol: Reece Winstone

Winstone, R 1986 *Bristol as it was 1934–1937*. Bristol: Reece Winstone

Winterbottom, M and Thomson, R M (eds) 2007 *Gesta Pontificum Anglorum: The History of the English Bishops (William of Malmesbury)*. Oxford: Oxford University Press

Wood, J 1745 *Description of the Exchange of Bristol*. Bath: J Leake

Wood, M 1965 The *English Mediaeval House*. London: Dent

# INDEX

Page numbers in **bold** refer to figures.

## A

*A Complete Body of Architecture* (Ware) 352
Ably, John 170
Abyndon's Inn 23
Adames, John 155
Adams, Robert 335, **335**, 372
Adeane, Thomas 305
Æthelræd II, King (979–1016) 13
Albemarle Row 220–1
Aldworth, Richard and Mary 250, **252**, 279
Aldworth, Robert 106, 154, 170, 176, 227, 267–8, **267**, 281, 323, **323**, 336–7, **337**
ale, sale ordinances 156
Alfred Place 205, 299, **300**, 318
All Saints church 65
All Saints Lane 65, 66, 160, 164, 165, **166**, 250, 297, 307
Alleyn, William 151–2
Alleynedale House, Barbados 364, **365**, 366
almshouses 369, 374
   chimneystacks 194
   earliest 193
   plans 193–4, **194**, **195**, 196–7, **196**, **197**
   windows 196
American Revolution 366
Ames, Jeremiah 351
Andrewes, Thomas 170–1
Apperlugh, Roger 65
arcades 149–50, **149**
archaeological excavations 7
   Averings Hayes 192, **192**
   Baldwin Street, no.59 8, **9**
   Broad Quay 154
   Charlestown, Nevis 358
   College Street 315
   Greyfriars, 1973 **30**
   Redcliff Hill 315
   Redcliff Street, 1982 69
   Tower Harratz, 1994 **274**
   Union Street 234, **234**
archaeological recording 7
architectural awareness, elite 335–8, **336**, **337**, **338**, 352, 372
architectural design, and status 276–7, **278**, **279**
architectural form, and social change 228
architectural identity, Atlantic Rim 361–6, **363**, **364**, **365**, **366**, **367**
architectural innovation, diffusion of 1
Arnos Court 373–4
Arnos Vale 353
   The Black Castle **353**, 374
*Arragon* (ship) **172**
Arthur, Edmund 24–5
Arthur family 20
Arthur's Acre **19**, 20
artisan residential neighbourhoods 343–6, **345**, 356
Ashley Manor 110–11, 249, 255, **255**, 257, 258, 283, 385–6
Ashley Place 271–2
Ashley Road 56, 226, 271, **272**, 353, 373
Ashton Court 255, **255**, 371
   Keeper's Lodge 279, **279**
aspirations, expression of 281
Assize of Arms, 1181 110
Atlantic Rim, the
   architectural identity 361–6, **363**, **364**, **365**, **366**, **367**
   lodges 364–5, **364**, **365**
   and mercantile discourse 366
Atlantic trade 2, 12, 33, 58, 306, 357
   and property investment 357–60, **359**, **360**
   the Williams thesis 374–5
attic rooms 315
Aubrey, John 106, 168
Austen, Jane 353
authority, asserting 336–7
Averings Hayes 192, **192**
Avon, River 13, 21
Avon Street 46, 56, 349

## B

Baber's Tower (Enderbie's Lodge) 229, **229**, 230, 276
Back Street 22, 119, 145, 146, 333–4
back-plot development 33
Bacon's Castle, Surry County, Virginia 362
Bagot, Clement 97
Baigent, Elizabeth 330, 356, 371
Baker, Thomas 61
Bakers' Hall 31, **31**
Baldwin, George 112
Baldwin Street 18, 22, 36, 38
   no.15 23
   nos.15/16 86
   nos.15/16 and 17 73, **73**
   nos.31–4 78, 114–15
   nos.33–5 67, **67**, 84
   nos.36–9 24, **24**, 78
   nos.40–1 173, **173**
   nos.43–4 22
   elite housing 330–1, **331**, 335
   le Thoroughouse 68
   shophouses 118–19
   through-houses 114–15
   trades 144
   warehouses 173, **173**
Baldwin Street, no.59 64, 78, 232, 334
   archaeological excavations 8, **9**
   chapel of St. John 7, 8, **8**, **9**, **10**
   chimneypieces 337, **338**
   laver 88–9
   ownership 8
   plan **10**
   rent 22
banking houses 140–2, **141**, **142**
banqueting houses 235–6, 243
Baptist Mills 58, **58**
Barbados 364–6, **365**, **366**, **367**
Barbon, Nicholas 370–1
Barnes, Joseph 359
Barratt, William 41
Barrett, William 132
Barrs Leaze 42, **42**
Barry, Jonathan 3–4, 33, 180
Bartholomew Lane 184, **253**
Barton Hill 242–3, **243**, 245, 346
Barton hundred 246
Barton Regis 279
Bassett, Anthony 124–5
Baste Street 22
Bath 50
Bath Priory 98
Bath Street 36, 54, 55, 138
Battle 11, 69
Baynard's Castle 95, **95**, 335
Beale, Shadrack 298, 311, 394
Becher, John 289, 351
Beck, Joseph 259–60, **261**, 353
Beck, Stephen 142
bedchambers 295, 304–5. *see also* sleeping arrangements
Bell Lane 14
Belle Vue 45
Benson, Barnard 93
Benson, Mary 93
Beresford House, Clifton Hill **224**, 225, **276**
Berkeley Castle 109
Berkeley Haven 150
Berkeley Square 45, 48, 50, **51**, 360
Berriman, Richard 296
Bevill, John 112
Bickham, Hugh 266
Biggs, Elinor 164
Bindon, John 6, 8
Birde, William 8, 232, 244, 334, 335

Bishop's House, Clifton Hill **217**, 221, **221**, 285, **286**
Bishop's Park 39–40, **40**
Bishopsworth House 352, **352**
Bisse, John 129
Black Castle, the, Arnos Vale **353**, 374
Blackfriars, lodges 234–5, **235**, 240, 274
Blaise Castle 263, 353, **354**
blind arcades **75**, 85–7, **86**, **87**
Blind Steps 38, 114
Blinkers Steps 42
Bloome, Nicholas 323
Bonny, William 177–8
bookcases 302, **303**
books 305
Borsay, Peter 4, 180
boundary disputes 60–2, **61**
boundary surveys 60
boundary walls 60–1, 62–3, **62**, **63**, 350
Bourdieu, Pierre 12
Bowdler, Marmaduke 245, 269–70, 283
Boydell, John 162–4
Boynton, Lindsay 110, 111
Braikenridge, George Weare 6, 10
Brandon Hill 6, **51**
Branville, John 151–2
brass works 58, **58**
Brayne, Henry 31, 226, 332
Brent, Humphrey 234
Brewster, Francis 227, 282, 283, 320
Brick Leaze 42, **42**
Brickdale, John 358
Bridge Street 14, 36, **38**, 138, 322
Bridges, James 223, **313**, 352
Bright, Henry 351
Bright, Richard 295
Bristol
   commercial core 142
   comparison with London 3
   decline 367
   Elizabeth I visit of 1574 111
   expansion 2, 23, 338, 374
   foundation 13
   legacy 375
   literature 2–5
   location 3, 13
   setting 275
   social geography, 1770s 355–6, **356**
   wealth 1

Bristol Bridge 10, 21, **21**, 144, 322, 330–1
   the Great House 227, **227**, 275
   rebuilding 36, **37**, **38**
Bristol Castle 11, 16, 33, **34**, 329
   conversion 320–1, **320**, **321**
   development, late 17th and 18th centuries 50
   hall 282, 283, **283**
   Site D 17
   stairs 320, **321**
Bristol Cathedral 7, 340
   Bishop's Park 39–40, **40**
   Dean and Chapter 33, 39–40, **39**, **40**, 50, 349
Bristol Central Reference Library 8
Bristol Channel 13
*Bristol Observer* 7
*Bristol Past and Present* 4
*Bristol Post-Boy, The* 177–8
Bristol Record Office 8
Britnell, Richard 2, 370
Broad Plain **217**, 220, **220**, 286, **287**, 318, **319**, 343, **343**
Broad Quay 229, **229**, 370
   no.45 296, **296**, 337
   no.80 154, **154**
   storehouses 154, **154**
   warehouses 171, **173**
Broad Street 15, 16, 73, 236, 371
   no.1 64
   no.6 297, **297**
   no.17 335, **335**
   no.21 169, **170**
   nos.22–5 78, 81, **82**
   nos.23–4 119, **119**, 120, 372
   nos.23–30 119
   no.26 372
   nos.33 and 34 60–1, **61**
   no.34 24
   no.35 63, **63**, 112–13, 156
   nos.35–7 **152**
   no.37 156
   nos.41–2 27, **139**, 140–1, **141**
   nos.41–3 121
   no.43 24–5, 27, 60, 120, 120–1, **120**, 122, 123, 324
   nos.43–4 152
   no.44 64, 91, **92**, 93, **120**, 321, 332
   nos.49/50 **120**, 150–1, **151**
   nos.51–2 (the Cyder House) 8, 23, 64–5, **65**, 80, **80**, 27, **120**, 121, **121**, 330
   nos.54–5 27, 121, 129–30, **130**

   no.61 121
   no.63 306
   13th–15th centuries 27
   1700 59, **59**
   cellars 150–1, **151**, 152, **152**, 156
   elite housing 330, **330**, 331
   extensions **28**
   inns 167
   landgable rents 330
   medieval infill 22
   shophouses **119**, 120, 120–1, **120**, **121**
   taverns 164, 165
   the White Hart 164, 165
Broadmead 10, 17, 18, **18**, 33, 144
Broad's Court 33, 187
Brock, John 224
Brookes, Eusebius 236, **238**, 266, 325, **326**
Broun, Robert 114, 115
Brown, Humphrey 104, 296, 337–8
Browne, John, *The Merchants Avizo* 335
Brunel, Isambard Kingdom 197
Brunswick Square 42, **43**, 50, 56, 205, **206**, **211**, 289, 314, **314**, 349
Buck, Samuel and Nathaniel 6, 214, **214**
Buckler, J C **255**
builders 338
building boom, late 17th and 18th centuries 44, 48, **48**, 50
building covenants 52–4
building leases 57, 338
building sample 10
building survival 10–11
Bullock's Park 44–5
burgages 15–16
burgesses 20–1
Burgesses Revolt, 1312 26
*burh* 13, **14**, 369
   medieval period 16–17
   and street layout 14–15
Burton's almshouse 194, **195**
Bury St Edmunds 56
Bushman, Richard, *The Refinement of America* 328
business offices 305–6
Butcher, John 102, 109
Butcher, Nathaniel 106–7
Butter Lane 46
Bysshop, William 295

# C

Cabot, John 3
Callendar House, Clifton Down Road 219
Callowhill Street 42, 56
Cann, Sir Robert 109, 110, 180, 255, 257, 258, 274, 275, 276, 277, **277**, 296, **296**, 316, 337, 338, 371, 402, 403–4
Cann, Sir Thomas 367–8
Cannon Street 181, **182**
Canterbury 361
Canynges, William 68, 93–6, 109, 114, 115, 152, 281, 332
Canynges' chantry 173, 175, 331
Canynges' House 72, 84, **94**, **95**, **96**, 321, 332, 335–6, 370
capitalism
   development of 4, 339
   merchant 368, 369–75
Caribbean, the 357, 358, 360–1, 361
Carmelite Friary 32, **32**, 226, 320
Carolina Row 213
Carson, Cary 335, 372
Cart Lane 46
Carus-Wilson, Eleanor 3
Cary, Christopher 170
Cashin, E **185**
Castle Green 33, 50, 56, 268, **268**, **283**, **284**, 320, **321**, 340, 358
Castle Mead 33
Castle Mill Street 28, **28**, 335, **335**, 372
Castle Orchard 33, 35, **35**
Castle Street 11, 33, 50, 56, 290, 307, 340, 349, 358
   nos.1–14a **310**
   nos.5 and 6 50
   no.7 50, **52**, 57
   no.8 50
   no.14a 176, 296–7
   nos.15–16 50, 52
   nos.22–3 52
   no.26 134, **134**, 294–5, 309
   no.34 201, **201**, 301, 309–10
   no.56 134, **134**, 176, 309
   no.57 **295**
   no.59 57, 176, 295, 307, **307**
   no.68 176, 295, 386–7
   no.69 307, **307**
   no.70 134–5, **135**, 307, 387
   nos.71 and 72 **135**
central-stairs plan houses 201
commercial buildings 176
workshops 177

Cathedral Precinct
  the Deanery 340, **341**
  the Registrar's house 340, **340**
Catherine, Queen 147
Cave Street 42
cellars
  access 150–1, **151**, 152, 157, 159
  Broad Street 150–1, **151**, 152, **152**
  commercial function 154–6
  corbels **155**
  Corn Street 150
  distribution 154
  divided 156–60, **157**, **158**, **159**, 163
  early-modern 166, 168–9, **169**, **170**
  hallhouses 71, 73, **77**, 113
  High Street **148**, 150
  light 155
  long 73
  medieval period 7, 8
  Old Market **152**
  plans 151, **151**, **152**, **157**, **158**, **169**, **170**
  purpose 151–2
  roof structure 155, 158, **158**, 159, **159**, 166, 168–9
  shophouses 120, 121
  size 151–2
  Small Street **152**
  split-level commercial town houses 154–6, **155**, **156**
  stairs 151–2, 159
  storage capacity 150
  summerhouses 248, 249
  warehouses 173, **173**
  windows 155, 157
cess pits 318
Champion, George 349
Champion, Nehemiah 174, 222–3, 263, 265, 349
Champion, William 58
Chapel Court 193, **193**
Chapel Row 45
Chard, Charles 176
charitable donations 374
Charles I, King 108, 111
Charles II, King 108
Charles Street **200**, 202, **203**, 225, 314, **314**, 315
Charleston, South Carolina 361
Charlestown, Nevis 357–8, 364, **365**
Charlotte Street 42, 45, 50

Cheddar family **234**
Cheddre, John 22
Cheese Lane 57
Chequer Lane 66, **66**, 147
Cherry Lane 205, **206**
Chester 145
Chester, William 31, 32
Chestre, Alison 61, 117, 121, 122
children, accommodation 316
chimneypieces 102, 104, **105**, 106, **107**, 125, 128, **128**, 314, 325, **326**
  Ashley Manor 257
  country residences 257, 258, **258**
  first-floor halls 295–6, **296**, 344
  heraldry 276
  lodges 238, 240, **240**, 242, 250, **252**, 276–7
  moral messages 337, 337–8, **338**
  one-room wide, two-room deep houses 198–201, **201**
  parlours 301–2, **301**, **302**, 337–8
  re-use 321
  suburban villas **267**, 269
  taverns 160, **160**
chimneypots 130
chimneys and chimneystacks 71, 361
  almshouses 194
  kitchens 310
  placement 274
  shophouses 118, **120**, 123, 130, 132
  suburban villas 268–9
  two-room wide single-pile houses 214
Chiswick House 363
Christchurch 22, 120, 124
Christmas Steps **182**, 184, **187**, 344, **345**
Christmas Street 21
  no.1 73, **73**
  no.2 73, 97, **97**, 332, 335
  no.24 7, 64, 73, **74**, 86, 97
  no.27 61
  elite housing 331
  kitchens 309
  shophouses 121
Church Street 46
churches 344, **348**
  adaptation of redundant 28–9, **29**, **30**, 31, 170, **171**, 320
  conversion to warehouses 170, **171**

interiors 355, **355**
  medieval period **14**, 16
Cilver Street 56
Cissbury 13
City Museum and Art Gallery 8
  Braikenridge collection 6
city surveyors 247
civic building 369–70
civic expenditure 111
civic identity 112
Clancy's Farm, Knowle 279, **279**
Clare Street 38, **39**, 315, **315**, 378–9
Clarence Road 48
Clark, Thomas 173
Clarke Street 42
class society, transition to 355–6
Classical architecture 49, 49–50
cleanliness 318
Clement, Thomas 124, 125
Clifton 45, **45**, 48, 50, 205, **276**, 359–60, **360**
Clifton Court 218, 263, **265**, 275, **276**
Clifton Down Road **347**
  Callendar House 219
  Duncan House **218**, 219, 270
  Freeman House 219
  Mortimer House **218**, 219, 222, 270, 302, **302**, 313, 316, 317, **317**, 351, 352
  Rodney Lodge **217**, 219, **219**, 222, 270, 351
Clifton Hill
  Beresford House **224**, 225, **276**
  Bishop's House **217**, 221, **221**, 285, **286**
  Prospect House **224**, 225, **273**, **276**
Clifton Hill House **218**, 221, **221**, 223, 275, 277, **278**, 292, **293**, 352, 363, 373
Clifton manor 33
Clifton Wood 373
Clifton Wood House **217**, 221–2, **222**, 263, **265**, 309, 316, 318, **319**, 326, **327**
Clifton Wood Road 202, 225, **225**
close stools 318
closets 304, 317
cloth sales 144–5
Clovill, Humphrey 92, 93, 112
Clyve, John 332
Cnut, King (1016–35) 13
Cock Lane 25, 346

coffee house 138
Cogan, Thomas 332
Cokkes, Alice 109
Cokyn Rewe, the 122
Coldharbour II 95
Cole, Thomas 235, 236
collapse of 1793 38
College Green 50, **51**, 214, **214**, 217, 219–20, **220**, 292, 321, **321**, 340, **342**, 351
College Place, inns **167**
College Street 40, 349
Collins, Nehemiah 240
Colston Parade 48, 205, **207**, 356
Colston Street 48, 169, 181, **182**, 324, 356
Colston's Almshouses 196–7
Colvin, Howard 180
commerce, and status 334
common places 148
Commonalty, the 22
Community, sense of 60, 355–6
Company of the town, the **329**
*compleat Builders Guide, The* (Neve) 316–17
compters 305–6
Compton, John 113, 332
conservatism 338
conspicuous consumption 353, **354**, 355
Constant, John 359
conversions 320–1, **320**, **321**, 328
Cook, John 258, 274
Cooke, Isaac 45
Cooke, John 166, 291
cooking 122–3. *see also* kitchens
cooking utensils 306, 309
Cook's Folly 258, 274, **275**
cookshops 122–3
Coombs, David 247
Cooper, Nicholas 276
corbels 97, **97**
cordwainers 144
Corn Street 15, 23, 73, 98, 371
  no.32 157, **157**
  no.32A 157
  no.35 **139**, 141–2, **142**, 157
  no.37 121
  no.38 153
  no.49 **92**, 92–3, 140, **140**
  no.63 108
  cellars 150, 157
  endowments **245**
  inns **167**
  John Cutt's properties 25–6, **25**
  taverns 157

427

Cornwallis Crescent 45, 50, **63**, 300, **300**, 315
Corporation, the 31–2, 33, 49, 50, 136, 181, 235
 building leases 338
 endowments 244, **245**
 estate, late 17th and 18th centuries 33, **34**, 35–6, **35**, **36**, **37**, **38**, **38**, **39**
 expenditure 111
 houses with shops development 136, 138, 140
corteplaces 12, 153, **153**
Cote House 346
counters, hallhouses 106, **106**
country estates 109
country property 110
country residences 254–5, **255**, **256**, 257–61, **257**, **259**, **260**, **261**, **264**, 265, 278
 chimneypieces 257, 258, **258**
 double or double-pile house 263
 furnishings 257
 halls 257–8
 kitchens 257, 261
 parlours 258
 Pennsylvania 362
 siting 275–6, 367–8
 stairs 257, **262**, 263
 Sunday retreats 279
 Virginia 362
 windows 260–1, **265**
county status 3, 110
courtyard houses 12, 331–2, **332**, 371
courtyards
 hallhouses 80–1, **82**, 83, 94
 residential houses 187–9, **188**, **189**, **190**
 shophouses **120**
 taverns 166, **166**
Coventry 2, 11, 69
Cradocke, William 112
Cradogge, Maurice 230
craftsmen builders 338
crenellations 278
Creswick, Francis 234
Creswick, Sir Henry 108–9, 109, 111, 246, 254–5, **254**, 257, 258, 277, 281, 296, 374
Cromwell House 56, 268–9, **268**, **269**, 288
Cronder, Nathaniel 125
Crosby, Thomas 281, 282, 298, 397–9
Crosse, John 230

Crotwells 41, **41**, 50, 57, 347, 349
Cugley, Elizabeth 238, **239**
cultural meanings 4
Culver Close 39, **40**, 56
Culver Street 50, **200**, 202, **204**, 349
Cumberland Street 42
cupboards 304–5, **305**, 317, 321, **321**, 328
curfew 64
Currie, Christopher 10
Curtelove, William 145
Curtis, John 65, 66
Cutt, John 25–6, **25**, 32
Cyder House, the, nos.51–2 Broad Street 8, 23, 27, 64–5, **65**, 80, **80**, 120, 121, **121**, 330

## D

Darby, Abraham 57
Dartmouth 150, 361
Daubeny, George, I 178
David Street 240
Davis, John 174
Daw, Samuel 294
Day, John 321
Day, Margaret 297
Day, Alderman Nathaniel 33, 44–5, 286
Day, Thomas 173, 242–3
De Cobyndone, John 26–7
De Ely, Adam 20
De Temple, Adam 67
Dean Street 42
Deanery Road 40
Defence Street 14, 120, 124
defences 14, **14**, **18**, 20–1, 23
Defoe, Daniel 3, 41, 56, 59, 357
Dening, Charles 4
Deptford 361
developers 58
development, late 17th and 18th centuries
 Bristol Castle 50
 the building boom 44, 48, **48**, 50
 the Corporation estate 33, **34**, 35–6, **35**, **36**, **37**, **38**, **38**, **39**
 Council committees 56–7
 Dean and Chapter of the Cathedral 39–40, **39**, **40**, 50, 349
 developers 58
 drainage 56

 the East and North-East 40–2, **41**, **42**, **43**
 the English urban renaissance 49–50, **49**, **51**, 52–4, **52**, **53**, **54**, **55**
 entrepreneurial households 347, 349
 housing uniformity 50, 52–4, **52**, **53**, **54**, **55**
 institutional and individual 40–6, **41**, **42**, **43**, **44**, **45**, **46**, **47**, **48**
 the North and West 43–5, **43**, **44**, **45**
 South of the City 46, **46**, **47**, 48, **48**
 speculative builders 57–8, **58**
 street names 56–7
 urban design 49–50, **49**
Deyos, Michael 52
Dickason, Vickris 174
Dighton, Henry 33, 44
Dighton Street 351
dining rooms 108, 296–7
Dinnyng, John 67, 121
display space
 alcoves 302, **304**
 bookcases 302, **303**
 cupboards 301, **301**
 hearth walls 301–2, **301**, **302**
Dissenters, religious persecution of 247
documentary record 7–8, **8**, **9**, **10**, **10**
Dolphin Street 14, 16, 26, 28, **28**, 36, 120, 138, **138**
Dominican Friary 31–2, 42, **42**, 144
Dominican Priory **31**
door frames 313
doors
 medieval period tenements 63–4, **63**, **67**
 shophouses 128, **129**
 taverns 165, **165**
double or double-pile house 216, **216**, **217**, **218**, **219**
 country residences 263
 earliest 216
 plans 216, **216**, **217**, **218**, 219–21, **221**
 principal rooms 216, 219
 privacy 222–3
 reconstruction **223**
 stairs 219, 221–3, **221**, **222**
Dowding, Robert 170, 173
Dowles, John 113, 150
Dowry Square 45

drainage 19, 56, 65–7, **66**, 349
Draper, Hugh 158
Draper, John 230, 332
Dresser, Madge, *Slavery Obscured* 357, 359
Drew, John 134–5, 387
Drew, Robert **52**
Droys, John 69
Droys rent roll 69
drunkenness 63–4
Dublin 361
Duke Street **212**
Duncan House, Clifton Down Road **218**, 219, 270
Dundas Wharf 23
Dunning, William 235
Dunster, John 121
Durham 111
Dutch gables 259
Dutch House, no.1 High Street 4, **5**, **6**, 25, 136, **137**, 146, 306, 334, 360
dyers and dyeing 144, 175

## E

Earle, P 344
Earles Mead 231
earlier materials, re-use 321, **321**
East Street 42
Easton Manor 275, 353
Easton Manor House 260, **262**
economic context 3
Edgyn, Arthur 25
Edward IV, King 95
Edward the Elder (899–925) 13
Elbridge, John 346
Elderton, Harry 58
elite housing
 15th-century 330, 331, **332**
 Baldwin Street 330–1, **331**
 Broad Street 330, **330**, 331
 concentration **330**, 339, 356
 conservatism 338
 display of wealth 371–3, **372**, **373**
 excess 352–3, **353**, **354**, 355
 and inertia 334–5
 late 17th and 18th centuries 338–40, **339**, **340**, **341**, **342**, 343, **343**
 late 18th-century 349–52, **350**, **351**
 medieval period 330–1, **330**, **331**

plot sizes 351
Small Street 339, 356
Elizabeth, Countess of Berkeley 150
Elizabeth I, Queen 111, 373–4
Ellbroad Street 202, **204**, **205**, 308, 349
Ellis, Humphrey 113, 170
Ellis, Thomas 57, 176, 320
Elton, Abraham 57, 350, 351
Elyot, Thomas 176, 232–3
Emmaus House, the Grove **224**, 225, 267, **276**, 279, 326
English urban renaissance 49–50, **49**, **51**, 52–4, **52**, **53**, **54**, **55**
entrance halls 282, 328
  architectural statement 282
  aspiration to magnificence 281
  Atlantic Rim houses 362
  development of 281–2
  displays 281, 287
  doorways 283
  furnishings 281–2
  panelling 283
  recesses 287
  size 288–9, 353
  stair framing 285–7, **286**, **287**
  and stairs **284**, **288**
  stairs as principal display feature 282–3
  view of stairs 288–90, **289**, **290**
  windows 289
entrepreneurial households 347, 349
Erle, Richard 25
Evans, John 7–8, 50
Evans, Llewellin 41, 132, 357, 358, 360–1
Excestre, Nicholas 26, 119
Exchange, the 36, **37**, 299, **299**, 306, 314, 369, 374
  houses with shops 138–9, **138**
exclusivity, public display of 276–8, **276**, **277**, **278**, **279**
Exeter 118, 309, 361
'The Explanation of the Draughts of a House Proposed for a Merchant' 281, 298, 304–5, **304**, 312, 355
exports 357

# F

factory workers 349
falling gardens 372–3
family life, location of 90–3

Farr, Richard 174, 263
Farr, Thomas 263, 353
Female Penitentiary, Upper Maudlin Street 236, **238**, 266, 362
Field, J M **354**
Fiennes, Celia 59, 147, 329
Fillyngham, John 121
fireplaces 123
  kitchens 307, 308, 309, 311
  lodges **235**
  parlours 312
  residential houses 184, **187**, 198, **199**
  tenements, medieval period 26
first-floor halls 294–7, **295**, **296**
Fisher, Edward 41
Fisher, Paul 277, 352, 362, 363, 373
Fitz Gregory, William 20
FitzHamon, Mabel 17
Fitzharding, Robert 17, 19, 20
Fletcher, Anthony, and Stevenson, Deborah, *Order and Disorder in Early Modern England* 2
Floating Harbour, the 366, 369
follies 274
food and food preparation 122–3. *see also* kitchens
forestreet chambers 68, 281, 294–7, **295**
Foster, John 381
Fountain Tavern, Tailors' Court 165, **165**
Foxe, Henry 297
Frampton, Walter 24
Fraternity of St. John the Baptist 60, 120
Freeland Place 45
Freeman, Francis 45
Freeman, James 165
Freeman House, Clifton Down Road 219
Frelynge, John 124
Frenchay Manor 259–60, **261**, 353
Frog Lane 10, 17, 39, 126, 146, 334, 340
Frogmore Street 17, **18**, 39, 126, 146, 169, **169**, 334, 340
Frome, River 13, **14**
  diversion of **18**, **19**, 20, 369
furlong alignments 15
Furney, James 283
furnishings
  Atlantic Rim houses 362
  country residences 257

dining rooms 296–7
entrance halls 281–2
forestreet chambers 294–7
garden houses 236
halls 91, 92, 93, 96–7, 98, 100, 103–4, 108–9, 110, 113
lodges 246
nurseries 316
parlours 97, 102, 106, 108, 297, 298, 328
probate inventories 381–404
second residences 246
servants' accommodation 315–16
shophouses 125, 294, 295, 296–7
shops 150
studies 305
summerhouses 249
taverns 387–8

# G

Gale, Andrew 129, 176, 296–7
galleries, hallhouses 83–4, **84**
garden houses 12, 43, 184, 278–9, **279**, **280**, 353, 371
  accommodation 245
  Barton Hill 242–3, **244**
  conversion to permanent dwellings 265–7, **266**
  definition 247
  distribution **230**
  function 278–9
  furnishings 236
  gardens 229, 245, 250, 271, 279, 373
  hearths 236, 238, 246–7
  the Little Park 234, **235**
  Millerd on 229
  plans **239**, **244**, **246**, 269–70
  prospect 273–5
  in rows 271–2, **272**
  St. Michael's Hill 238, **239**
  St. Michael's parish 346, **346**
  siting 275–6, 279
  stairs **244**, 271, **272**
  suburbs 339
  as Sunday retreats 279
  Upper Mauldin Street 245, **246**. *see also* lodges
gardens 265, 278
  distance from city 254
  falling 372–3
  garden houses 229, **239**, 245,

250, 271, 279, 373
gateways **243**
and lodge access 252–3
lodges 230, 231, 234, 241, 249–50, **251**, 252–4, **252**, **253**, 254, 336
medieval period tenements 62
prospect 273–4
the Red Lodge **231**, **232**, 273, 336, 372
relationship to houses 249–50, **251**, 252–4, **252**, **253**, 254, 272, 273–4
residential houses 187, 267
shophouses 118
size 250, 272
suburban houses 273–8
suburban villas 267, 269–70
urban estates 372–3
Garlick, Edward 177, 178
Garway, John **268**
Gauge, John 175, 381
Gaunts' Hospital 31
Gay, Anthony 234
Gay's Court 188, **189**, 190
Gaywode, John 96, 97, 98, 109, 122
*Gemeinschaft–Gesellschaft* transition 330, 355–6
gentry, the, and merchants 109
gentry houses 109
Geoffrey of Coutances 16
George, Giles 91, 93, 382–3
Georgian architecture, literature 4
Georgian design 228
Gibbs, Henry 57
Gillows Inn 65, 66, **166**
glasshouses 143, **143**
glassworks 57
Gleed, Francis 258
Gleson, Harry 132
Gloucester, Earls of 17, 20
Gloucester, Hawisia, Countess of 17
Gloucester, Robert, Earl of 17, 18–19, 20
Gloucester, William, Earl of 20
Gloucester Street 42
Goby, Walter 65
Goddard, Richard 98
Goldney, Thomas II 261, 263, 266, 302, 353
Goldney House 261, 263, **264**, 266, 275, **276**
grotto 353, **354**
Mahogany Parlour 301–2, **302**

# INDEX

viewpoint 368
water pump tower 353, **354**
Goldney's garden 372
Gonning, William 270
Gooch, Thomas, Bishop of Bristol 39–40
Goodyear, Ephraim 297, **297**, 334
Goodyear, Tobias 297
Gore, Lady Phillippa 283, 399–401
Gorges, William, the Elder 226
Gothick style 373–4
Gotley, Richard 40, 56
Gough, the Reverend Strickland 285–6
Great Anne Street 56
Great Gardens, the 46, **46**, **47**, 53, 56, 240, 349
Great George Street 41, 45, 50, 56, **218**, 223, 292, **293**, 302, **303**, 351
Great House, Bristol Bridge 227, **227**, 275
Great House, Henbury 275, **275**
Great House, Redcliff Street 227, **227**
Great House, St. Augustine's Back **32**, 266, 320, 332
Great James Street 188, **189**
Great Lodge, the, Pithay 250, **250**
Green, Jonathan 46
Grenville, Jane 1
Greyfriars 273, 279
lodges 234–6, 243, 250, 338
Greyfriars church 29, **30**, 31, 32
Griffin Lane 181, **182**
Griffiths, Phillip 61
Grimm, Samuel Hieronymous 6
Grope Lane 21, 22
Gropecuntelane 67, 118, 121, 144
Grove, The, Emmaus House **224**, **225**, 267, **276**, 279, 326
Guildhall, the 169
Guillery, Peter 2, 179
Guinea Street 46, **200**, 201–2, **202**, **203**, 301, **301**, 305, **305**, 311, **313**, 358
Gwillim, Daniel 242

# H

Haddon, Richard 113, 150
Haddon's Tavern 7, 150, 162–4, **162**, **163**, 387–8
Halfpenny, William 223
hallhouses 11, 118, 179, 334, 339
access 84
blind arcades 75, 85–7, **86**, **87**
cellars 71, 73, **77**, 113
construction 71–2, **72**, **73**
conversion 320–1, 328
conversion into shophouses 140–2, **140**
counters 106, **106**
courtyards 80–1, **82**, 83, 94
decline of the hall 93–8
definition 11–12, 69, 370
demise of 71, 112–14, 328
development of 69–71, **70**
dining rooms 108
distribution 331–2, **333**
galleries 83–4, **84**
halls. see halls
hearths 72, **72**, 88
heating 88, 89, 113
kitchens 90, 92
lavers 88–9
light 64–65, **72**, 85
living accommodation 91, 92, 112
living rooms 69, 91, 92, 112
location of family life 90
London 69, 98
modernisation, 17th century 92–3
multiple occupation 89
parlours. see parlours
planning 71–3, 72, 78, 80–1
plans 74–7, **78**, **79**, **80**, **81**, **83**, **88**, **90**, **94**, **95**, **99**, **103**, **106**
plot sizes 71–2, 78, 83
porches 84–5, **84**, **85**
probate inventories 89
ranges 73, 78, **79**, 81, **82**, **83**
redundancy 115
rents 331–2, 370
roof structure 88, **88**, 116
rural 83
screens 87, **87**, **88**
service rooms 69
sleeping arrangements 97
social action within 71
social and architectural topography 332–3, **333**
and social change 71
stairs 91
street frontage 69
subdivision 115
as taverns 113–14
through-passages 83, 84, 91, 93–4
windows 72, 85, 86, 91, 94–5, **95**
Halliers Lane 21, 178
halls 334, 370
Atlantic Rim houses 362
Bristol Castle 320
and city status 111
and civic identity 112
conversion to warehouses 170–1
country residences 257–61
decline of 90, 93–8
displays of weaponry 98, 104, 110, 111, 112, 282, 294, 328, 339, **339**
first-floor 294–7, **295**, **296**, 344
function 98, 112
furnishings 91, 92, 96–7, 98, 100, 103–4, 108–9, 110, 111–12, 112, 113
hallhouses 69, 71, 75, **77**, 89–93, **96**
and legitimacy 108
in lesser houses 112–14, **113**
modernisation, 17th century 92–3
and national politics 111–12
roof structure 98, 100, **100**, 113
shophouses 122
as social centre 89–93
and status 108–9, 109–11, 116
symbolic 97, 98, **99**, 100, **100**, 102–4, **103**, 108–9, 109–11, 111–13, 281, 297, 332–3, 334
taverns 164–5
use 89–93, 109
as workshops 112–13, 175
Ham, Richard 266
Hampton Court 336
Hancock, David 197
Hancocke, Leonard 238
Hanham Court 254–5, **254**, 257, 258, 277
Hanover Street 42
Harding, Daniel 125
Harding, Thomas 50, 52, **52**, 57
Harford, Charles and Joseph 351
Harold Godwinsson 16
Harper, Major 268–9, **269**
Harris, John 125, 134, 156, 297, 309
Harris, Roland 1, 150, 152, 154–5
Harris, Samuel 125
Harris, Thomas 125, 176, 231, 242
Harris, Thurston 246, 250, 279
Harsell, Edward 124, 306
Hasard, John 121
Haskins, Joseph 46, 53, 56
Haveryng, John 22, 69, 334
Haviland, Matthew 234
Haviland, Robert 234
Hawkys, John 61
hearth furniture 89
Hearth Tax returns 89, 234, 246–7, 269, 330, 339
hearth walls, parlours 301–2, **301**, **302**
hearths 69, **70**, 72, **72**, 88, 306
garden houses 236, 238, 246–7
lodges 246–7
parlours 106
probate inventories 89
shophouses 122–3
shops 147
heating
braziers 123
hallhouses 88, 113
houses with shops 138
lodges 246–7
parlours 297, 298
shophouses 118, 122–3, 125, 129–30, 132, 294
and social structure 118
taverns 164, 165
Henry VIII, King 111
heraldry 104, 276–7
Herman, Bernard 1, 205, 328, 361
Hicks, John 268, **269**
High Cross 144
High Street 15
no.1 25, 136, **137**, 146, 306, 334, 360
nos.1–2 119, 155, **155**
nos.3–4 387–8
nos.5–7 158–9, **158**
nos.5–8 146
nos.9 and 10 25
nos.11–13 (the Ropeseld) 146
no.18 158, **158**
nos.18–20 145, 146
nos.19–20 158
nos.21–4 78, 87, **87**, 157–8, **157**, 322, **322**
nos.21–5 24, **24**, 113, 119
nos.28–29 121
nos.29–31 28, **28**
no.30 113, **113**, 160, **160**
no.31 28, 61, 119, 338, 377
nos.32–4 (The Starr) 147, 159, **159**
nos.33–4 113–14

nos.35–6 (the Cock in the Hoop) 27–8, **27**, 73, **77**, 114, 119, 123, 159, 160
no.39 65–6
nos.39–40 25
no.41 73, **74**, 150, 160
nos.42 and 43 61, **61**, 322
nos.42–7 122
no.43 155, **155**, 156
nos.44 and 45 151–2
no.45 322, **322**, 324
no.47B 146
cellars **148**, 150, 155, **155**, 156, 157–9, **157**, **158**, **159**, 163
drainage 65, 65–6
the Green Lattice 160, 332
medieval tenements 23
*selds* 145, 146
shophouses 117–42
shops **146**
street frontages 10
taverns 113–14, 123, 157–8, **157**, 158–9, **158**, **159**, 160, **160**, 162–4, **162**, **164**, **165**
'High Water at Bristol Key' 366, **367**
Hill, George 176, 295, 307, 386–7
Hill, Guy 294
Hill, John 307
Hobbs, John 174, 175
Hobson, Thomas 335, **335**, 338
Hobson's Garden 40
Holidge, James 267, 279
Hollister, Lawrence 359
Hollister Street 42
Holmes, H H **336**
Holt, John 164
Holwey, Jeremy 134
home, the, relationship with the workplace 175–8, **177**
Honourable Artillery Company 110
Hook, Andrew 110–11, 198, 201, 248–9, 255, 257, 258, 307, 385
Hook, Sir Humphrey 267, **267**
Hooke, William 65
Hope and Anchor Inn 242, **243**
Hope Square 299–300, **300**
Host Street 44, 343, **343**
Hotwell Road 372–3
Hotwells, the 45
house building, late 17th and 18th centuries 33
house names 147
house types 11–12

household segregation 221, 227–8, 298, 315, 315–16, **316**, 328, 355
households
  communal 90
  numbers 344–5
housekeepers 344
houses with shops
  design 136
  entrances **139**
  heating 138
  plans 138, **138**, **139**, **140**
  purpose 139
  stairs 138
  street frontages **139**, **140**
housing uniformity 50, 52–4, **52**, **53**, **54**, **55**
Hownden or Mitchell Lane lodge 266, **266**
Howse, Reynold 98
Hungerford, Abraham 297–8, 311, 316, 393–4
Hunt, Flower 57, 176, 177, 295, 296, 307
Hurrell, RIchard 121

# I

Ilchester, Earl of 197
improvements 316–18, **317**, **318**, **319**
individualism 335, 356
  asserting 335, **335**, 372
industrial economy 328
industrial housing 57–8, **58**, 189–93, **190**, **191**, **192**, **193**
Industrial Revolution 2, 374
industrial structures 143, **143**
infill, medieval period 22–3
inns 144, 147, 164, 165, 166, **167**. *see also* taverns
Inns Court, Knowle West 279, **280**
Innys, Andrew 140
intramural lanes 23
Ireland, links to 17
iron foundry 57
Ison, Walter 4, 223

# J

Jackson, Joseph 258
Jackson, Alderman Miles 57
Jackson, S **319**
Jacob Street 239, 240, **240**, **241**

Jamaica Street 359
James's Place 53, 62–3, 271
Jamestown, Virginia 361
Jay, John 119
Jennings, Thomas 269, **270**
Jennings Range, Nevis 360–1
John, Geoffrey 332
Johnny Ball Lane 184, 234, 247, 250, 279
joining rooms 298–300, **299**, **300**
Jones, Edmond 122, 129, 175, 192, 334
Jones, Joseph 175
Jones, Teague 112
Jones's Court 349
Jordan, Richard 236, 238, **238**

# K

Keene, Richard 176
Keeper's Lodge, Ashton Court 279, **279**
Kemes, Roger 160
Kent 89, 112
Kerdif, John de 18
Keynes, Thomas 96–7, 383–4
Kill, Thomas 135
King Square 50, 205, **206**, **212**, 289
King Street 35, **35**, 49–50, 56, 329, 340, 358, 374
  nos.1–5 **49**, 166, 168, **169**, **199**, **200**
  nos.2–5 52
  nos.3–5 198, 307, 317, **317**
  no.5 **290**, 389
  no.6 166, 214, **215**, 290, 291, **291**
  nos.6–8 52, 57
  no.16 201
  no.32 173
  no.33 166, 307, 325–6, **326**
  no.33–4 **171**
  nos.33–4 198, **199**, 361
  no.34 170, 171, 173
  cellars 166
  central-stairs plan houses 201, **201**
  improvements 317, **317**
  single-pile houses 214, **215**
  warehouses 171, **171**, 173
Kingcot Farm, Long Ashton 250, **252**
Kings Lynn 370

Kingsdown 33, 44, **44**, **45**, 48, 50, 205, 248, 275, 359
Kingsdown Parade 228, 315, 351, 353, 360, 373
  no.6 248, **249**
  no.20 223
  no.22 **218**, 223
  no.25 271, **272**
  no.46 **53**
  no.48 **53**
  no.50 **53**
  no.54 **53**, 324
  nos.57–9 225–6
  no.58 390
  no.79 54, **54**
  garden houses 272
  improvements 318
  prospect 275
  rear-stairs plan houses 205, **206**, 212
  semi-detached houses 225–6, **226**
  summerhouses 248, **249**
Kingsdown Parade, no.52 53, 62, **248**, **290**, 324, **325**, 379–80
  display cupboards 301
  front elevation **53**
  Gothick style 374
  improvements 318
  rear elevation **53**
*Kingsweston Book of Drawings, The* 180, 198, **198**, 216, **216**, 222, 283, 352, 372
Kingsweston House 352, 368, 372, **372**, **373**
Kingswood 59
Kitchen, Robert 130
kitchens 90, 306
  access 309, 315
  Atlantic Rim houses 362
  basement 314–15, **314**, 316, 328
  ceilings 310, 314
  chimneystacks 310
  cooking utensils 306, 309
  country residences 257, 261
  detached 309–13, **310**, **311**, **312**, **313**
  fireplaces 307, **308**, 309, 311
  ground-floor 307–9, **307**, **308**
  hallhouses 92
  location 15, 307–9, 311–12
  lodges 236
  medieval period 309
  one-room wide, two-room deep houses 198, 201

431

# INDEX

residential houses 181, 307, 309–13, **310**, **311**, **312**, **313**
second 312
shophouses 123–4, 134, 135, 136, 294, 297, 307, 309
smells and fumes 309, 311–12
two-room wide houses 216
upper floor 306
windows 308, 309
Knight, Francis 233
Knight, John 43, 57, 176, 193, 360–1
Knights Templar 18–19, 20
Knowle, Clancy's Farm 279, **279**
Knole West, Inns Court 279, **280**

## L

Lamb Street 40
Landen, Walter 216, 399
landgable rents 330
Lane, George 250, **251**, 279
Lane, Richard 44
Langley, Philip 24, **24**, 65–6, 66, 309
Langton, John **127**, 287, 334, 335, 372
Langton Court 258–9, **260**
Langton Street 48, 356
Launsdowne, Thomas 230–1
lavers 88–9
Law Ditch 19
Lawford's Gate 230, 374
Lawrence Lane 22
Le Frenche, Eborard 22, 114, 119, 146, 334
leases 57, 177, 338
Leeds 190
Leicester, Earl of 111
leisure 4
Lens, Bernard 6
Leonard Lane 14, 22, 63
Lewin's Mead 11, 18, **18**, 49, 307, 340, 349, 385
nos.65, 66, 67, 68, 69 49
no.69 49
no.70 49
New Buildings 188, **189**, 190
one-room wide, two-room deep houses 198, 201
shophouses 118
soap house 176
Spencer's Almshouse 193, **193**
libraries 305
light

cellars 155
disputes 65
hallhouses **72**, 85
medieval period tenements 64–5, **64**, **65**
stairs 205.
see also windows
literature
Bristol 2–5
Georgian architecture 4
town house 1–2
Little, Bryan 5
Little Ann Street, Swan with Two Necks 307–8, **308**, 311
Little Hanover Street 42
Little Park, the 43, **43**, 234, 235
Little St James's Back **188**
Liverpool 3, 367
living accommodation
hallhouses 91
shophouses 118, 120, 121, 122
Spicer's Hall 90–1, **91**
living rooms
hallhouses 69, 91, 92, 112
shophouses 70
Lloyd, Henry 41
Lockier, James 58, 359–60
locks 64
Lodge Plantation, St Kitts 364, **364**
lodgers 344
lodges 12, 371
access 242, 252–3
accommodation 235–6, **237**, 242, 246
Atlantic Rim 364–5, **364**, **365**
Baber's Tower (Enderbie's Lodge) 229, **229**, 230, 276
Blackfriars 234–5, **235**, 240, 274
ceilings **237**, 238, **239**, 240–1, 244
chimneypieces **237**, 240, **240**, 242, 250, **252**, 276–7
conservatism 338
conversion to permanent dwellings 265–7, **266**
crenellated 278
definition 229, 247
distance from city 254
distribution 230, **230**
earliest 230–1, **231**
exclusivity 353
fireplaces **235**
function 231, 243
furnishings 246

gardens 230, 231, 234, 241, 249–50, **251**, 252–4, **252**, **253**, 254
gateways **243**
Greyfriars 234–6, **243**, 250, 338
heating 246–7
Jacob Street 239, 240, **240**, 241
kitchens 236, 246
orchards 230, 231
ownership 230–1, 234
parlours 232, **233**
Pile Street 230, 240–1, **242**
plans **231**, **233**, **235**, 236, **236**, **238**, **243**, 244, **245**, 253
position in garden 250, 252
Rennisons Bath **241**
rents 247
the Royal Fort 229, **229**
Rupert House 238–9, **240**
St. Mary Redcliff 240–2, **242**, **243**
St. Michael's Hill 236, **238**, 266, 275
St. Thomas Street 240
siting 231, 275–6
size 235–6, 238–9
stairs 235, **235**, 236, **241**, 244, 266, 283, **284**, **285**, 326
and status 276–7
Stile Lane **236**
Stony Hill 236, **237**, 238, **239**, 243–5, **245**, 250, 252, 266, 275, 338
summerhouses 247–9, **247**, **248**, **249**
Tilly's Court House 242, **243**, 252–3
towers 274–5, 277–8
Union Street 234, **234**
the Whitstry 231, 242, **244**
windows 242.
see also garden houses; Red Lodge, the; White Lodge, the
London 278, 344, 375
banqueting houses 236
Baynard's Castle 95, **95**
central-stairs plan houses 203, 205
Coldharbour II 95
comparison with Bristol 3
courtyard houses 332, **332**
first-floor halls 294
Great Fire 3
hallhouses 69, 98
Lincoln's Inn Fields 50
medieval town houses 1
militia 110, 111, 112

residential houses 179, 361
selds 145, 146
semi-detached houses 226
shophouses 118, 120, 122, 136
taverns 156, 157
town houses 371
wealth 1
westward expansion 2
London Bridge 21
Long Row 19
longhouses 20
Lord Mayor's Chapel 31
Love Lane 144
Lower Castle Street 28, **28**
Lower Maudlin Street 221, 223–4, **224**, 286–7, **287**, 316, 351, 352, 391–3
Loxton, Samuel 7, **186**, 321
Lunsford House, Park Row 221, 270, **271**, 283, **286**, 352
Lymell, Elizabeth 297
Lymell, William 294

## M

McGrath, Patrick 3, 357, 374
McKellar, Elizabeth 2, 179
Madison, James 56
Magdalens, the 245, **247**
magnificence, aspiration to 281
Maguire, Alison 180
Malchair, John Baptiste 143, **143**
Manor House (Major Harper) 268–9, **268**, **269**
Manor House, Park Lane 253, 269, **270**, 272, 283, **284**
Manor House, St. Michael's Hill 253, 272
Manor House, York Place 261, **263**
maps 4
Ashmead and Plumley, 1828 **36**, **37**, **39**, **40**, **41**, **42**, **43**, **45**, **47**, **51**, **52**, **189**, **263**, **272**
first 6
Millerd's, 1673 **34**, **35**, 40, 191, **191**, **192**, **193**, 229, **238**, 241–2, **242**, **244**, 245, **250**, 267, 268, **268**, 329, 330, 334, 338–9, 344
Rocque's 1742 42, 44, **44**, 46, **47**
Smith, William 329
Tithe Award, 1846 **260**
Mariners' Guild hall, Virgin Lane 86
Markes, Walter 52

markets **38**
Marlborough Hill **266**, 301
  boundary walls **62**
  summerhouses 248, **248**
Marlborough House **273**, 275
marriage 109
marriage tax 344
Marsh, the 18, **18**, 21, 33, **34**, **35**, 49, 73, 340
  development of 35, 374
  perambulation 329, **329**
  suburban villas 267–70
Marsh Street 22, 144, 170, 309
Marsh wall, the 11
Marston, Henry 112
Mary le Port Street 15, 17, 114, 115, 120
  nos.38–42 125, **126**, 306
  shophouses 125, **126**
  the Swan 164, 165
  taverns 164, 165
  trades 144
Mason, Kathryn 122
Mason, Thomas 96–7, 384–5
Mason, William 57
Maynes, Nicholas 150
Meadow Street 42
meals 90
medieval period 1, 3, **14**, 20–1, 23–6, **151**, **152**, 356
  13th-century developments 21–2
  15th–16th-century development 24, **25**, 26
  Bristol Bridge 21, **21**
  *burh* 16–17
  cellars 7, 8, 150–2, 154–5
  churches **14**, 16
  civic building 369
  drainage 19
  elite housing 330, 330–1, **330**, **331**
  expansion 16, 17–20, **18**, **19**
  housing stock 3
  housing survival 3
  infill 22–3
  later period 22–3
  meaning of house 117
  porches 282
  quay **14**, 21
  rents 21, 23
  residential zoning 331
  shophouses 118–23, **119**, **120**, **121**
  shops 146, **146**, 147–50
  social and architectural topography 330, 330–1, **330**
  social mobility 370
  storage **148**, 150–4, **151**, **152**, **153**, **154**
  storehouses 152–4, **153**, **154**
  taverns 156–60, **157**, **158**, **159**, **160**, **161**
  town houses 17
  town walls 20–1
  towns 2
  trade 17
  wine trade 3
  *see also* tenements, medieval period
Melsom, Charles 53
Mercer, Eric 71
merchant capitalism 368, 369–75
merchants
  country property 110–11
  dwellings 173
  endowments 244, **245**
  and the gentry 109
  houses 339
  move from city to country 265
  spatial lives 171, 173, 173–5
  status 109–10
Merchants' Almshouse, the 196–7, **197**, 369
*Merchants Avizo, The* (Browne) 335
Meredith, Nicholas 108–9
mid-16th-century, lack of development 32
middling houses 349
militia, the 110, 111, 112, 257–8
Miller, Michael 281–2, 295, 298, 305, 316, 350–1, 395–6
Millerd, James 4, 6, **34**, **35**, 40, 191, **192**, **193**, 229, **238**, 241–2, **242**, **244**, **250**, 267, 268, 269, 329, 330, 334, 338–9
Mills Coates, Matthew 58
Milner, Edward 268, **268**, 269
Milner's house 268, **268**, 269
Milton Abbas 197
mint 13
Mitchell Lane 19
modernity, emerging 179, 278
modifications
  conversions 320–1, **320**, **321**
  motivation 328
  new rooms 324–5, **325**, **326**
  re-fronting 322–4, **322**, **323**, **324**, **325**, 328
  re-use of earlier materials 321, **321**
  stairs 325, 326, **326**, **327**
Monamy, Peter 229, **229**
monasteries, dissolution of 29, 44
Monmouth's Rebellion 112
Montagues, the 44
Montpelier 56
Moore, Gilbert 129, 236
moral messages, chimneypieces **337**, 337–8, **338**
Morgan, Kenneth 3
Morgan, Stephan 28, 117
Morgan, Thomas 58
Morris, Edward 92, 93, 112, 140
Mortimer House, Clifton Down Road **218**, 219, 222, 270, 302, **302**, 313, 316, 317, **317**, 351, 352
mouldings 302
Mountjoy, Edmund 57
Mowl, Timothy 4, 259, 352
Moxon, Joseph 201
musical instruments 305
muster rolls 110

# N

Narrow Plain 344
Narrow Quay 174–5
Narrow Weir 42
  the Three Horseshoes 240, **241**
Narrow Wine Street 66, **247**, 294
Nemot, Richard 121
Neve, Richard 316–17
Nevis 357–8, 360–1, 364, **365**
New Buildings 33, 187, **188**
New Cut, the 48, 50, **51**
New Hampshire 361
New Street 181, **183**, 355
Newburyport, Massachusetts 362
Newgate 16
Nicholls, James, and Taylor, John, *Bristol Past and Present* 6
Nicklus, William 129, 134, 294–5, 309
Noades, John 46
non-domestic buildings, survival 143
Norfolk, Virginia 361
Norman Conquest, 1066 16
North, Roger 180, 198, 214, 216, 267, 277, 306
North Street, inn 164–5, **167**
Norton, Walter and Isabella 24, **24**, 115
Norton's House 78, **79**
nurseries 316

# O

Observatory House 275, **276**
occupation, multiple 89, 205
Old King Street 181, 184, **184**, 340
Old Market 10, 17, 18, **18**, 23, 349
  no.32 288, **289**
  no.33 **289**
  no.35 309
  nos.35–7 52, **52**
  nos.35–41 41, **41**, 132, **133**
  no.38 358
  no.39 358
  no.40 358
  no.41 358
  no.59 149, **149**, 152, **152**, 154
  nos.67–9 349
  nos.68–9 289, **290**, 324
  no.69 **139**, 142, **142**, 289, 305, 310, 318, **319**, 324, **325**
  nos.73–73A and 74 149, **149**
  no.74 126–7, 205, **207**, 287
  cellars 152, **152**
  lodges 231
  rear-stairs plan houses 205, **206**, 207, **209**–13
  shophouses 118
  shops 149, **149**
Old Market Street 290–1
Old Park Hill 43, 310, **311**, 358, 359, **359**
Oldbury Court 250, **252**, 258, 360
Oldbury House, St. Michael's Hill 245, **246**, 249, 269–70, 283, **284**, 290, 291, 399–401
Oliffe, Ralph 245, 269
Olivees, St Kitts 362–3, **363**
Oliver, Simon 26, 147
one room per floor houses 347, **348**, 349
O'Neill, H **32**, **73**, **74**, **120**, **139**, **195**, **196**, **233**, **247**
open houses 149
open-hall houses 11, 69, **70**
Orchard Street 36, **36**, 50, 56, 57, 205, **208**–10, 289, **289**, 311, 351, 359
orchards 230, 231
Orlidge, Joseph 169
Ormond, Duke of 111
ownership 8
  lodges 230–1, 234

# P

Pacy, Joan 231
Page, Richard 150
Paine, Richard 250, **253**
Palliser, David 2
Pantin, William 1, 2, 11–12
Paragon, the 45, 50
Paris 21, 50
Park Lane, Manor House 269, **270**, 283, **284**
Park Row
    nos.8 and 9 225, **226**
    nos.8–11 230, **231**
    no.10 243–5, **245**, 250, 266, 267, 271, 272, 273, 274, 275
    'house att the hill' 250, **251**
    Lunsford House 221, 270, **271**, 283, **286**, 352
    suburban villas 269, **270**
Park Street 44–5, 50, **51**
Parkyns, John 96–7, 382
Parliamentary Survey, 1649 125–6, 294
parlours 108, 112, 115, 351
    17th-century 297
    18th-century 297–8, **298**
    accommodation 97
    Ashley Manor 258
    bookcases 302, **303**
    buffets **303**
    chimneypieces 104, **105**, 106, **107**, 301–2, **301**, **302**, 337–8
    country residences 258
    decoration 298
    detached 104, **104**
    display alcoves 302, **304**
    display cupboards 301, **301**
    fireplaces 312
    front 298, **304**, 310, 328
    functions 97, 297
    furnishings 97, 102, 106, 106–7, 108, 297, 328
    great **101**, 104, **104**, **105**, 106–9, **106**, **107**
    hallhouses 92
    hearth walls 301–2, **301**, **302**
    hearths 106
    heating 297, 298
    importance of 97–8
    joining rooms 298–300, **299**, **300**
    lodges 232, **233**
    one-room wide, two-room deep houses 198–213
    rear 298, **298**, **303**, **304**, 310, 328
    shophouses 297
    and the spread of gentility 328
    two-room wide houses 220
    United States of America 328
    wainscoting 104
    windows 106
Pattfield, Nicholas 241
Paty, Thomas 138
Paty, William 312
Paul Street 42
Pearce, George 164
Pearson, Sarah 11, 111
Pembroke Place 318
Pembroke Street 42
Penn, William 56, 362
Penn family 42, **42**, 50, 56, 57, 58, 362
Penn Street 42, 56
Pennsylvania 362
Pepwell, Elizabeth 294
Pepys, Samuel 3, 278
perambulation, evening 329, **329**
Perry, James 41
Peter Street 66, 138
    no.A 123–4, **123**, **124**
    nos.A, 1–3 26
    nos.1-4 123–4, **123**, **124**
    nos.4–6 26
    15th-century development 26, **26**
    extensions **28**
    shophouses 119
    shops 147, **147**
Phelypp, Sir Matthew 98
Philadelphia 3
Philadelphia Street 42, 56
philanthropy 197, 374
Phippen, Whitchurch 260–1, 266–7
Phythian-Adams, Charles 2
Pickrell, Edward 113, 150
Pierce, Daniel 362
Pierce, Thomas 351
Pile Street 19, 22, 184, **185**, 230, 240–1, **242**
Pinney, John Frederick 223, 302, **303**
Pipe Lane 46, 181, **182**, 205, **210**, 288
Pithay 130, **131**, 250
Pithay Bowling Green 250
plan units 15
Plumb, Jack H 4
Plymouth 309, 361
Polygon, the 45, 50
Ponsford, Michael 16, **30**
Pope, James 53
Pope, Thomas Shackleton 6, 7
popular culture 180
population 33, 329, 334, 347
porches 282, **283**, 337, **337**
    hallhouses 84–5, **84**, **85**
Portland Square 42, **43**, 48, 50, 56, **200**, 205, 302, **304**, 317, **317**, 318, **319**, 349, 360
Portland Street **200**, 202, 205, **206**, 318, **318**
Portsmouth 361
Portsmouth, New Hampshire 361
Portwall, the 21
powder closets 220–1
Powell, James 57
Power, the Reverend John 45
Powicke, Maurice 110
Prelat, William and Joan 27, 121
preservation 143
Prince Street 35, **36**, 49, 56, 340, 352, 355, 358, 374
    no.32 263
    nos.36–8 312, 314
    no.40 321
    no.50 312, 351
    nos.50–4 174, 198, **198**, 377–8
    no.52 283, 312, 351
    no.54 312, 351
    nos.66, 68 and 70 222
    nos.68–70 174, 175, **218**, 314
    compters 306
    double or double-pile house 222
    warehouses 171, **172**, 174
Prince's Buildings 45
Pritchard, John 7, 159
Pritchard Street 42
privacy 67, 222–3, 228, 293, 355
privies 318, **319**
probate inventories 8, 10, 89, 91, 96, 98, 103, 104, 125, 134–5, 198, 201, 216, 247, 281, 294, 298, 311, 312, 315, 350–1, 381–404
property investment, and the slave trade 357–60, **359**, 360
property values 115, 155, 339
Prospect House, Clifton Hill **224**, 225
Prospect Lane 273, **273**
Pryce, George 6–7, 159, **159**
public rights of way, through-houses 115
Pump Lane 241–2
Puxton, Michael 246, **247**
Puxton, Thomas 316
Pye, Henry 65
Pyke's Meadow 240
Pyland, Edward 231
Pyll, William 66

# Q

Quarter Sessions Records 349
Quay, The **14**, 21, 26–7, **27**
    no.7 22
    no.47 147
    nos.51–2 170
    shophouses 117, 120
    street trading 144
Quay Lane 22
Quay Street 22
Queen Charlotte Street 49, 52, **146**, 288, **288**
    no.51 377
    no.55 311, 316, 393–4
    no.59 297–8, **298**
    nos.59–61 298, 311
    lease 177
Queen Square 35, **35**, **36**, 40, 49–50, 50, 52, 54, 56, 57, 297–8, 340, 358, 367, 374
    no.11 298, **308**, 311, 394
    no.14 351
    no.15 **217**, 220, 282, **282**, 285–6, 289, 312
    no.16 281–2, 295, **295**, 298, 316, 350–1, 395–6
    no.22 **217**, 219, 281, 292, **292**, 298, 312, 396–7
    nos.26–8 288, 311
    no.27 308, **308**
    no.28 308, 326
    no.29 **217**, 220, 286, 289, 293, 295, **295**, 302, **303**, 308–9, 316, 318, **318**, 321, 326, 351
    nos.36–8 173–4, **174**, 175, 216, **217**, 219, **219**, 291–2, **292**, 312, 352
    no.37 366
    no.38 317, **317**
    nos.68–73 169
    construction 350
    courtyard developments 190
    improvements **317**
    inhabitants 351, 352
    warehouses 173–4, **174**
Queen Street 35
    courtyard developments 189, **189**
Quiney, Anthony 1

## R

Rackhay, the 22–3, 191, **191**, 335, **335**, 344, 345
Rawlinson, Richard 180, 198, 214, 216
Read, James 238, **239**, 244–5, 266
Reade, Mary 294, 309
rebuilding 10, 26–8, **27**, **28**
red light districts 144
Red Lodge, the 229, **229**, 231–2, 243, 272, 352
  building date 230, **232**
  chimneypieces 276
  conversion to permanent dwellings 266
  design **232**, 372
  gardens **231**, **232**, 273, 336
  great parlour 232, **233**
  heraldry 276
  plans **231**, **233**
  siting 275
  stairs 283, **285**, 326
Redcliff Back 311, **312**
Redcliff Fee 19, **19**, 21, 144, 369
Redcliff Gate 336, **336**
Redcliff Hill **206**, 230, 247, **314**, 315
Redcliff Parade 48, 205, **207**, 289, 314–15, **314**, 356
Redcliff Parade West **206**
Redcliff Street 19, 23, 64, 112, 321
  no.1 36
  no.5 337, **337**
  no.6 337, **337**
  no.7 165
  no.9 205
  no.38 135–6, **137**, 189
  no.69 90
  nos.69–72 69
  nos.69–78 **70**
  no.70 90
  nos.70–2 72
  no.72 332
  nos.86–7 175
  no.87 72, **72**, 90
  no.94 86
  nos.95–7 93–6, **94**
  no.97 (Canynges' House) 72, 84, 321, 332, 335–6, 370
  nos.97–8 86, 86–7, **86**, **95**, **96**
  no.98 310, **310**, 323, **323**
  no.113 147, **147**
  nos.117–123 86
  no.122 332
  nos.127–9 62
  nos.127–28 153, **153**
  no.128 175
  no.144 72, **72**, 85, 332
  the Bear 165
  dyers 144
  the Great House 227, **227**
  inns **167**
  the Red Lion **167**, **168**
  shophouses 117, 129
  shops **147**
  soap house 176
  storehouses 153, **153**
  sugar refinery 323
  taverns 165, 166, **167**, **168**
  Warry's Court **189**, 190, **190**
Redland Hill House **224**, 225
Redland Manor 258, **258**, 338
Redyngeslane 114, 115
Reeve, William 353, 373–4
*Refinement of America, The* (Bushman) 328
re-fronting 322–4, **322**, **323**, **324**, **325**, 328
religious buildings
  adaptation of redundant 31–2, **31**, **32**, 332
  adaptation of redundant churches 28–9, **29**, **30**, **31**, 170, **171**, 320
religious persecution 247
Rennison's Bath 240, 241
rent rolls 69, 118
rents 8, 69, 331–2, 333, 370
  lodges 247
  medieval period 21, 23
Repton, Humphry 48, **48**
residential differentiation 339–40
residential districts, status 339
residential houses 328, 347
  aesthetics 180
  almshouses 193–7, **193**, **194**, **195**, **196**, **197**
  archaeological excavation 181
  Atlantic Rim 361–6, **363**, **364**, **365**, **366**, **367**
  the Caribbean 361
  central-stairs plan **200**, 201–3, **201**, **202**, **203**, **204**, 205, **205**
  courtyard developments 187–9, **188**, **189**, **190**
  distribution, three- or four-room plan houses 349–52, **350**
  emergence of 178, 179–80
  evolution 228
  fireplaces 184, **187**
  form 179
  gardens 187, 267
  industrial 189–93, **190**, **191**, **192**, **193**
  interpretation 179
  kitchens 181, **182**, 307, 309–13, **310**, **311**, **312**, **313**
  the largest 226–7, **227**
  Massachusetts 362
  multiple occupation 205
  New Hampshire 361
  one room per floor 347, **348**, 349
  one-room wide, two-room deep 198–213, **198**, **199**, **200**, **201**, **201**, **202**–13, 287–8
  plans 228
  plans, almshouses 193–4, **194**, **195**, 196–7, **196**, **197**
  plans, central-stairs plan houses **200**, **203**, **204**
  plans, courtyard developments 188–9, **189**, **190**
  plans, industrial housing 191, **191**
  plans, one-room wide, two-room deep 198, **198**, 200, **200**, **201**, 203–4, **206**, **211**
  plans, rear-stairs plan houses 205, **206**, **208**–10, **211**
  plans, semi-detached houses 223–6, **224**
  plans, smallest houses 180, 180–97, **181**, **182**, **183**, **184**, **184**, **185**, **186**, **187**
  plans, two-room wide houses 214–23, **215**, **216**, **217**, **218**, **219**, **220**, **221**
  privacy 222–3
  rear-stairs plan 205, **206**–13
  segregation 227–8
  semi-detached 223–6, **224**, **225**, **226**
  the smallest 180–1, **181**, **182**, **183**, 184, **184**, **185**, **186**, **187**
  and social change 228
  social context 227–8
  and social zoning 371
  South Carolina 361
  stairs 181, **181**, 184, 198, 267
  street frontages **186**
  suburban villas 267–70, **267**, **268**, **269**, **270**, **271**
  two-room deep 190, 349, 361
  two-room wide double or double-pile house 214, 216, **216**, **217**, **218**, 219–23, **219**, **220**, **221**, **222**, **223**, 267
  two-room wide single-pile houses 214, **214**, **215**, 216
  types 180
  and the urban renaissance 180
  vernacular tradition 180
  Virginia 361
  *see also* country residences; garden houses; lodges
residential squares 350
residential zoning 329, 356, 370, 371
  artisan residential neighbourhoods 343–6, **345**
  later 17th and early 18th centuries 339, **339**
  medieval period 331
  re-use 321, **321**
Rhubarb Tavern, Barton Hill 242–3, **244**, **245**
Rich, Samuel 142, 349
Richards, George 234
Richmond House 260–1, **262**, 267, 274, 275
Ridley, Sarah 196
Ridley's almshouse 194, 196, **196**
Robert, son of Swein 20
Rococo style 352, 366, 373
Rodney Lodge, Clifton Down Road **217**, 219, **219**, 222, 270, 351
Rogers, Robert 227
roof structure
  Atlantic Rim houses 363
  Bakers' Hall **31**
  cellars 155, 158, **158**, 159, **159**, 166, 168–9
  corbels 97, **97**
  hallhouses 88, **88**, 116
  halls 98, 100, **100**, 113
  hammer-beam 336
  Small Street, no.20 (Colston's House) 98, **99**, 100, **100**, **101**
  trusses 100, **100**
rope-house 144
Roper, Robert 22
Ropeseld, the 146
ropewalk 22
Rose Alley 184, **186**
Rose Street 46, 184, **187**
Rose Tavern, the 25
Rosemary Lane 187, 230, 344, **345**
Rosemary Street 33, **183**

# INDEX

Rowbotham, T L **59**, **63**, **87**, 115, **171**, 177, 184, **322**, **335**, **343**
Rowe, John 286–7, 391–2
Royal African Company 357
Royal Fort House 50, **218**, 223, **268**, 292, **293**, 313, **313**, 315, 368, **368**, 373
Royal Fort, the 227, 229, **229**, 268–9, **268**, **269**, 275, 278, 352
Royal York Crescent 45, 50, 315, 360
Rupert House, Upper Church Lane 238–9, **240**, 273
Russell, John 150
Ryder, Thomas 65, 66
Rye House Plot, the 112
Ryman, John 294
Rymer, John 247

# S

Sacks, David, *The Widening Gate* 3, 4, 329–30, 331, 334, 339, 356
St. Andrew's Church 7
St. Augustine's Abbey 17, 17–18, 20, 23, 33, 145, 146
St. Augustine's Back 192–3, **193**
  chimneypieces 337, **338**
  Great House **32**, 266, 320, 332
  sugar refinery 43, 44, 176, 192–3, **193**
St. Bartholomew's Hospital 32, 234, 250
St. Ewen's church 8, 22
St. Giles church 170
St. James's Back 234, **234**, **319**, 344
St. James's Barton **218**, **223**, 349
  nos.9–19 40, **41**
  no.12 315, 351, 397–9
  no.15 281, 298
  no.20 351, 351–2, **351**
St. James's Parade **200**, 202
St. James's Priory 17, 25, 31, 226, 320
St. James's Square 40, **41**, 50, 56, 259, 260–1, **261**, **262**, 305, **305**, 349, 350
St. Jude's 41
St. Kitts
  Lodge Plantation 364, **364**
  Olivees 362, **363**
St. Lawrence's church **29**, 170, **171**
St. Leonard's church 157, **157**
St. Mark's Hospital church 35–6
St. Mark's Priory 226–7, 340, **342**
St. Mary le Port 344
St. Mary Magdalene nunnery 31, 226
St. Mary Redcliff 22, 143, **143**, 230, 314, 344, 356
  lodges 240–2, **242**, **243**
St. Mary Redcliff chantry 11, 12
St. Mary Redcliff church 46, **47**, 143, **143**
St. Michael's Hill 11, 43, 205, **206**, **229**, 344
  nos.20–2 **215**
  nos.20–4 **215**, 216, **291**
  no.22 85–6, **105**, 305, **305**
  nos.23–9 181, **182**
  no.24 399
  no.29 184, **187**, 344
  nos.30–2 310
  nos.43–51 **288**
  no.65 358–9
  nos.123–31 325, **326**
  garden houses 238, **239**, 245, **246**, 346, **346**
  households 345
  inns **167**
  lodges 236, **238**, 266, 275
  Manor House 253, 272
  Oldbury House 245, **246**, 249, 269–70, 283, **284**, 290, 291, 399–401
  summerhouses 248, **249**
St. Michael's Hill House 270, 275, **276**
St. Nicholas Abbey, Barbados 365–6, **366**, 374
St. Nicholas Street 7, 14, 15, 22, 24, 59, **59**, 60, 66, 104, 106
  nos.22–8 80–1, **81**, **82**, 85–6, **105**
  nos.38–42 23
  John Cutt's properties 26
  shops 146
  taverns 157
  through-houses 114, 115
  trades 144
St. Nicholas's almshouse 194, **195**
St. Nicholas's church 22, 60
St. Nicholas's gate 14, 15
St. Peter's Hospital 323, **323**, 336–7, **337**
St. Stephen's church 38
St. Stephen's Street 38, **39**
St. Thomas Street 19, 20, 22, 36, 112, **143**, 150

nos.54–5 240
no.61 135, **136**
nos.62–5 240
nos.68–78 69, **70**
nos.87–90 240
nos.128–31 130, 131 132, **132**, 201, 307, 370
no.129 **295**, **296**
no.133 316
Haveryng's Row 123, 334
inns **167**
lodges 230, 240
weavers 144
White Lion inn 160, **161**, 164, 165, **167**
St. Vincent's Parade 45
Salle, Thomas 98
Sampson, John **275**, 368
Sandwich 11, 69
Sandy, Walter 57
sanitation 318
Saunders, Edmund 202, 358
Saville Place 45
Saxon period 13–16, **14**, 369
  burgages 15–16
  *burh* 13, **14**, 16
  coins 13, **13**
  street broadening 15
Scadepulle 22
Schaw, Janet 362–3
Schofield, John 1, 12, 375
Seager, John 113
second residences 232–4, 242, 244, 279, **280**, 371
  Atlantic Rim 362
  distribution 346, **347**
  furnishings 246
  principle residences 255
  siting 367–8
  social and architectural topography 339, 346, **346**, **347**
  summerhouses 247–8, **247**, **248**, **249**
  terminology 249
  *see also* country residences
security, medieval period tenements 62–4, **63**
Seed, Thomas 173
segregation 298, 315, 315–16, **316**, 328, 355
*selds* 145–6, **145**
semi-detached houses 223–6, **224**, **225**, **226**, 271, 272
Serlio, Sebastiano 231, 336, 372
servants 298

accommodation 309, 315–16, **315**, **316**, 362
segregation 221, 228, 328
Sevenoaks house 89
Severn estuary 13
Seyer, the Reverend Samuel 7, 8, 115
Seynt Mary Reckehey 22–3
shipbuilding 144
shipping, preoccupation with 366
shophouses 11, 38, 69, 116, 179, 227, 281
  access 121
  cellars 120, 121
  characteristics 117–18
  Charleston, South Carolina 361
  chimneypieces 125
  chimneystacks 118, 120, **120**, 123, 130, 132
  contents 134–5
  conversion from hallhouses 140, **140**
  cooking 122–3
  courtyards **120**
  definition 69, 69–70, 370
  dining rooms 296–7
  distribution **333**
  as dwellings 118, 120–1
  fireplaces 123
  first-floor halls 294–7, **295**, **296**
  forestreet chambers 294–5
  furnishings 125, 294, 295, 296–7
  gardens 118
  ground floor 70
  hallhouse 119
  halls 122
  hearths 122–3
  heating 118, 122–3, 125, 129–30, 132, 134–6, 294
  kitchens 123–4, 134, 136, 294, 297, 307, 309
  later Middle Ages 118–23, **119**, **120**, **121**
  living accommodation 70, 118, 120, 121, 122
  locations **117**, 142
  medieval period 118, 118–23, **119**, **120**, **121**
  occupants 124–6, 129
  Parliamentary Survey, 1649 125–6
  parlours 297
  plans 120, **120**, **121**, 124, **125**, 126–7, **126**, 130, **130**, **131**, **132**, **133**, 134–5, **135**, **136**, **137**

436

post-medieval 123–36, **123**, **124**, **125**, **126**, **127**, **128**, **129**, **130**, **131**, **132**, **133**, **134**, **135**, **136**
probate inventories 125, 134–5
purpose 142
rear-stairs plan 205
rent rolls 118
rents 331–2, 333, 370
sleeping arrangements 295, 297
social and architectural topography 333–4, **333**
social centre 122
solars 121
stairs 126–8, **127**, 134, 135
street frontages 119, **119**, **127**, 128
structure 119
value 124
shops 123, 146–50, **146**, **147**, **148**, **149**
arcades 149–50, **149**
density 155
display spaces 150
distribution 334
dressing boards 147–8
furnishings 150
hearths 147
identification 147
medieval period 146, **146**, 147–9
ornamentation 147, **147**
windows 147
Shot Tower, the 7
Silver Street 184, **185**, 344
single-pile houses 214, **214**, **215**, 216
Sion Hill 271
Skelton, Joseph 6, 8
Sketchley, James 330, 347, 349, 350, 355, 356
slave trade 4, 12, 306, 357, 368, 374–5
and property investment 357–60, **359**, **360**
*Slavery Obscured* (Dresser) 357, **359**
sleeping arrangements 304–5
hallhouses 97
shophouses 295, 297
Small Street 15, 25, 108–9, 371
nos.3–4 139, **139**
nos.3–9 14
nos.5 and 7 178
no.10 63, **63**, 155–6, **156**
no.11 156
no.15 104, **104**, **105**, 337–8

nos.16–17 96, 102, 102–4, **102**, **103**, 169, 381
no.18 169, **170**
nos.25–6 84, **84**, 119, **119**
nos.25–7 340
cellars 152, 155–6, **156**
elite housing 331, 339, 356
extensions **28**
Small Street, no.20 (Colston's House) 23, 78, **78**, 85, 116, 321, 332, 339, 370
chamber block 100
chimneypieces 102
extension 336
ground floor 100, 102
hall roof 98, 100, **100**
parlour wing **101**, 102
plan **99**
probate inventory 98, 401–2
stair tower 100
Smith, Jarrit 39
Smith, John 1, 4, 12
Smith, William 4, 329
Smith Street 202
Smyth, John 336, 370, 371
Smythe, John **78**, 98, 108–9, 109, 111, 114, 160, 254–5, 281, 401–2
Sneyd Park 258, **259**, 340
soap manufacture 57, 175–6
social and architectural topography 329–30, 375
15th-century 330, 331–5, **332**, **333**, **335**
artisan residential neighbourhoods 343–6, **345**, 356
entrepreneurial households 349
and inertia 334–5
late 18th-century 347, **348**, 349–52, **350**, **351**
later 17th and early 18th centuries 338–40, **339**, **340**, **341**, **342**, **343**, 344–6, **345**, **346**
medieval period 330, 330–1, **330**, **331**
middling houses 349
second residences 339, 346, **346**, 347
social geography, 1770s 355–6, **356**
social context 1
social mobility 370
social relations 328, 370
social segregation 221, 227–8, 298, 315–16, **315**, **316**, 328, 355

social structure 328
social zoning 339, 347, 349, 370, 371
Society of Merchant Venturers 33, 45, 196–7, 248, 295, **296**
Somerset Square 48
Somerset Street 48, 202
sources, bias 10–11
South Cadbury 13
South Carolina 361, 366
Southampton 15, 98
Southwark 361
Southwell, Sir Edward 352
Southwell, Sir Richard 372
Southwell Street 271, 272, **272**
speculative builders, late 17th and 18th centuries 57–8, **58**
Speed, Thomas 169
Spencer's Almshouse 193, **193**
Spicer, Richard 67, 67–8, 90, 93, 118–19, 119, 153
Spicer's Hall 22, 23, 67, 68, 321, 332
blind arcades 86, **86**, **87**
courtyard 81, 83
gallery 83–4, **84**
hall 83, 90–1
living accommodation 91
parlour 93
plan **83**, **88**, **90**
porch 84, **84**
private accommodation 91
roof construction 88, **88**, 91
screens 87
stairs 91
storied accommodation 90–1
street frontages 91, **91**
through-passages 83, 91
war damage 86, **87**
windows 85, 86, 91
spiritual aspirations 197
split-level commercial town houses 154–6
Stacy, Nicholas 129
Stainred, William 297
stair halls **284**, 285–6
stairs
Atlantic Rim houses 362
balusters 283, 290, 292, 344, **345**, 371
Bristol Castle 320, **321**
cellars 151–2, 152, 159
central-stairs plan **200**, 201–3, **201**, **202**, **203**, **204**, 205, **205**
country residences 257, **262**, 263

cultural influences 293
as display of wealth 371–2
double or double-pile house 219, 221–3, **221**, **222**
enclosed 290–1
and entrance halls **284**, **288**
external turret 184
framing 285–7, **286**, **287**, 291–2
garden houses **244**, 271, **272**
hallhouses 91
handrails 290
houses with shops 138
light 205
lodges 235, **235**, 236, **241**, 244, 266, 283, **285**, 326
one-room wide, two-room deep houses 198, 287–8
open-well 283, 290, **291**
placement 283, 287–8, **288**, 290, **290**, 292
as principal display feature 282–3
principle 316
and privacy 293
rear-stairs plan 205, **206–13**
re-modelling 325, 326, **326**, **327**
residential houses 184, 267
second 316, 320, **321**
segregation 221, 228, 328
semi-detached houses 225
service 316, 326, **327**, 352
shophouses 126–8, **127**, 134, 135
stone 292, **293**
suburban villas 268
taverns 283, **284**
treads 283
view from the entry 288–90, **289**, **290**
visibility 290–2
visual impact 205
windows 205
Stakepenny 20
Stanton, John 46
status 2, 344
and architectural design 276–7, **278**, **279**
city 111
and commerce 334
display 273–8, **273**, **274**, **275**, **276**, **277**, **278**, **279**, **280**, 335
and halls 108–9, 109–11, 116
and heraldry 276–7
and house location 368
individual 110–11

and lodges 276–7
and the militia 110
residential districts 339
shophouses occupiers 126
Statute of Winchester, 1285 110
Steep Street 372
Stepefast, Stephen 63, **63**
Stephens, George 281, 298, 350, 367, 396–7
Stephens, Matthew 52
Stewart, James 6, 245, **247**, 249, 251, **268**, **269**, 273, 279, **336**
Stibbens, John 124
Stile Lane 235, 346
Stocking, Thomas 40
Stoke, John and Alice 97, **97**, 332
Stoke Bishop 110
Stoke Bishop House 255, 258, 267, 275, 313, 360, 365, **366**, 367, 371
  accommodation 257
  conservatism 338
  Dutch gables 259
  elevation **256**
  Gothick style 374
  great hall 257–8
  nursery 316
  plan **256**
  porch 277, **278**
  probate inventory 402–4
  prospect 274
  reconstruction **257**
  servants' accommodation 315, 316
  siting 276, **277**, 367–8
  and St Nicholas Abbey 366, **366**
  stairs 283
  viewpoint 368
Stokes Croft 224
  the Full Moon 164–5, **164**
Stony Hill 234, 274, 301, **301**
  lodges 236, **237**, 238, **239**, 243–5, **245**, 250, 252, 266, 275, 338
storage
  early-modern 166, 168–71, **169**, **170**, **171**, 172, 173–5, **173**, **174**
  increasing demand for 166
  medieval period **148**, 150–4, **151**, **152**, **153**, **154**
  storehouses 152–4, **153**, **154**, 170, **171**
  warehouses 170–1, **171**, **172**, 173–5, **173**, **174**, 306, 344
  *see also* cellars

storehouses 152–4, **153**, **154**, 170, **171**
Stratton Street 42
Street, George Edmund 7
Street, Philip E W 7, 153, **153**
street directory 330, 347
street frontages
  Castle Street 10
  hallhouses 69
  High Street 10
  houses with shops **139**, 140
  medieval period tenements 67–8, **67**
  Old Market 10
  re-fronting 322–4, **322**, **323**, **324**
  residential houses **186**
  semi-detached houses 224–5, **225**
  shophouses 119, **119**, **127**, 128
  Spicer's Hall 91, **91**
  suburban villas 269
street layouts 50
  and the *burh* 14–15
street names 56–7
street trading 144–5
stringehouse 25
Stringer, Thomas 234–5
Stubbs, Richard 239, 346
studies 305, **305**
study scope 5–6
Sturmy, Robert 67–8, 153, 173
suburban villas 227, 263, 267–70, **267**, **268**, **269**, **270**, **271**, 275, 352, **352**, 353
suburbs 179, 229
  garden house 339
sugar refining 176–7, **177**, 178, 189, 227
  Redcliff Street 323
  St. Augustine's Back 43, 44, 176, 192–3, **193**
sugar trade 357, 374
summerhouses 247–9, **247**, **248**, **249**, 253–4
Summerson, John 2, 179, 225, 259, 370–1
Sunday retreats 279
Surry County, Virginia, Bacon's Castle 362
Surrey Street 42
Sussex 112
Swan with Two Necks, Little Ann Street 307–8, **308**, 311
Swindon, Railway Village 197

symbolic halls 97, 98, **99**, 100, **100**, 102–4, **103**, 108–9, 109–11, 111–13, 281, 297, 332–3, 334

## T

Tailor, David 176
Tailors' Court 60, **60**, 120, **164**, 187, **188**, 344
  Fountain Tavern 165, **165**
Tallage Rolls 146, **146**, 334
Taunton 361
taverns 113–14, 123, 144
  1550–1750 162–6, **162**, **163**, **164**, **165**, **166**
  access 164–5
  accommodation 165, 166
  arrangements 162–4
  cellars 156–60, **157**, 163
  chimneypieces 160, **160**
  counters 164
  courtyards 166, **166**
  doors 165, **165**
  drinking areas 156
  entrance hall **166**
  furnishings 387–8
  ground floor 160, **160**
  halls 164–5
  heating 164, 165
  identification 147, 156
  London 156, 157
  medieval period 156–60, **157**, **158**, **159**, **160**, **161**
  names 165
  plans **157**, **158**, **163**, **164**, **165**, **166**
  reception room 163–4
  stairs 283, **284**
  stillings 163
  storage areas 156
  windows 164
  *see also* inns
tax assessment, 1696 330, 344
Taylor, William 135
Temple Church 19, **355**
Temple Fee 19, **19**, 21, 32, **32**, 144
Temple Gate 167, 336, **336**
Temple Street 19, 20, 250
  nos.4–7 75
  no.5 23, 64, **64**, 73, **75**, 85, 86
  nos.9 and 10 136
  no.17 67, **67**
  nos.107–9 176, **177**
  nos.109–10 308, 323–4, **324**

  nos.110–11 202–3, 349
  no.124 73, **76**, 83, 84, **85**, 97, 321
  almshouses 193, **194**
  weavers 144
tenement histories 8, 10
tenements, medieval period 16, 17, 18, 22
  amalgamations 25–6
  boundary disputes 60–2, **61**
  boundary surveys 60
  boundary walls 60–1, 62–3, **62**, **63**
  configuration 60
  definition 60
  density 59
  doors 63–4, **63**, **67**
  drainage 65–7, **66**
  fires 26
  forestreet chambers 68
  gardens 62
  halls 68
  light 64–5, **64**, **65**
  locks 64
  mentality 59–60
  ownership rights 60–2
  privacy 67
  security 62–4, **63**
  shops 67
  solars 67
  street doorways 67–8
  street frontages 67–8, **67**
  subdivision 23–5, **24**
  windows 64–5, **64**, **65**, **67**
tenements, Saxon period burgages 15–16
Terrill, Edward 247
Tewkesbury 11, 69
  Church Row 123
  Church Street 69, **70**
Thebaud, Thomas 26
Thomas, Matthew 173–4
Thomas, Richard 98, 175
Thomas Street 112
Thones 309
Threlkeld, Michael 93, 126, 297, 307, 334
through-houses 25, 114–15, 116
Tilly's Court House 242, **243**, 252–3
Tinker's Close 43, **44**
Tippett, Thomas 169
tobacco 357
Totnes 150, 309, 361
Tower Harratz 56, 230, 230–1, 274, **274**

Tower Lane 14, 15, 22, 23, 60–3, 65
Tower Street 33, 46, 50, 53, 56, 349
towers 94–5, **95**, 274–5, 277–8, 335
town house literature 1
town houses 370–1
   earliest 17
   medieval period 17
   role 371
town walls 14, **14**, 18, **18**, 20–1, 118
towns 1, 2
trade
   growth of 3
   medieval period 17
   *see also* Atlantic trade
trade links 357
trades, distribution 144
Trinity Almshouse 194, **194**, 196, **196**
Trinity Street 39, **39**, 50, 56, 205, **211**, 349
Tucker Street 20, 144, 144–5
tuckers 144
Tudor vernacular architecture 3, 180
Turner, J M W 366, **366**
turrets 184
two-room wide houses 214
   double or double-pile 216, **216**, **217**, **218**, 219–23, **219**, **220**, **221**, **222**, **223**
   kitchens 216
   plans **215**, 267
   semi-detached 223–6, **224**, **225**, **226**
   single-pile 214, **214**, **215**, 216
Tyndale, George 33, 45
Tyndall, Elton and Co 140–2
Tyndall, Thomas 223, **313**, 352, 368, **368**, 373
Tyndall's Park 48, **48**, 50, 372

## U

Union Street 36, 38, **38**, 56, 136, 234, **234**
United States of America 1, 328, 357
Unity Street 36, **36**, 56, 205, 340
Upper Church Lane 346
Upper Maudlin Street 234, 246–7, 247, 273, 318, 346
Female Penitentiary 236, **238**, 266, 362
   garden houses 245, **246**
Upper Wells Street **200**, 238
urban capitalism, development of 4
urban design, late 17th and 18th centuries 49–50, **49**
urban estates 372–3
urban planning 49, 50
urban renaissance, the 33, 180

## V

Vanbrugh, Sir John 352, 372
Vanderhorst, Elias 366
vernacular tradition 338
Vickris, Robert 265
Victoria Street 50, **132**, **201**, 307
viewing platforms 274, 275, 368, **368**
views and viewpoints 273–5
Viking raids 13
Vine Row 43
Virgin Lane, Mariners' Guild hall 86
Virginia 315, 355, 361, 362
visual record 6–7
Vyell, Thomas 61

## W

Wade, Nathaniel 33, 41, **41**, 56, 57, 181, 344, 347, 355
Wade, Thomas 170
Wade Street 56, 181, **182**, **183**, 344, 355
Wadhouse, Margary 230
wainscoting 104, 304, 317, 318
Wall, Thomas 238
Wallis, Samuel 346
Wanstre, John 60–1
wanton women 144
Ward, John 48
Warde, Richard 234
Warde, William 332
Ware, Isaac 223, 277, 287, 288, 292, **293**, 352, 355, 363
Ware, John 108
warehouses 170–1, **171**, **172**, 173–5, **173**, **174**, 306, 344
Warren, Alice 234
Warwick, Earl of 111
wash-basin recesses 318, **319**
washbasins 89
water closets 318
Water Street 42
wealth
   concentration 330
   display of 331–2, 371, 371–3, **372**, **373**
   inequalities 2
   origins 356
   and the slave trade 357–60, **360**
weaponry, displays of 98, 104, 110, 111, 112, 294, 328, 339, **339**
weavers 144
Weekes, Buckler 247–8
Weekes, Samuel 322, 324
Welles, Thomas 61
Wellington Place 272
Wellington Street 48
Wells, Thomas 56, 236, **237**, 244
Wells Street 39, 50, 56, **200**, 202, **204**, 349
Welsh Back 67, 321
   no.6 295–6
   nos.6–9 (Spicer's Hall). *see* Spicer's Hall
   nos.7A and 7B 119
   the Back Hall 153, **153**
   elite housing **335**
   *selds* 145, 145–6, **146**
   shophouses 119, 121, 205
   storehouses 153, **153**
Welsh Back, no.12 126–30, 205, 287, 290, 309, 335, 370
   ceiling 128
   chimneypieces 128, **128**
   display of wealth 372
   doors 128, **129**
   forestreet chamber 128–9, **129**
   plan **128**
   stairs **127**
   street frontages **127**, 128
Welyschote, John 8, 22
Wesley, Charles 202
West Street **189**
Weston, Edmond 22
Whetstone, Lady Sarah 288
White, George 234, 243–4, **245**
White, John 232
White, Thomas 119, 193, 372
White Lodge, the 214, 229, **229**, 232–4, **233**, 243, 252, 335
   building date 230, 232
   chimneypiece 277
   conversion to permanent dwellings 266
heraldry 277
ownership 8, 232
plans **233**
siting 275
Whiteing, Peter 53
Whitfield Place 246
Whitson, John 26, 104, 106, 107, 168, 296
Whitson Street 188
Whitstry, the 231, 242, **244**
Whitsun Court Sugar House 176, **177**
Wickham, Thomas 360–1
*Widening Gate, The* (Sacks) 3, 4, 329–30, 331, 334, 339, 356
William of Malmesbury 13
Williams, Aaron 166, 168, 198, **199**, 307, 389
Williams, Eric 2, 374–5
Williams, Llewllyn 58
wills 8, 10, 89, 265, 337–8
Wilmot Crescent 50, **52**
Wilstar, Jacob de 372–3
Winchester 8, 90, 154, 156, 157
windows
   almshouses 196
   Atlantic Rim houses 366, **367**
   blocked 324
   cellars 155, 157
   country residences 260–1, **265**
   entrance halls 289
   forestreet chambers **295**
   hallhouses **72**, 85, 86, 91, 94–5, **95**
   improvements 318, **318**
   kitchens 308
   lodges 242
   medieval period tenements 64, **64**, 65, **67**
   parlours 106
   placing 273–4
   prospect 273–4
   replacement 323–4, **323**, **325**
   sash 318, **318**, 323, **323**
   shops 147
   shutters 318, **318**, 324, **325**
   stairs 205
   storehouses 153
   taverns 164
Windsor Terrace 45
Wine Street 15, 16, 23, **125**
   no.6 306
   nos.15–17 297
   no.23 65
   no.24 65
   no.48a 297

no.49 294, 297, 309
no.55 258
nos.56–7 153
no.63 (the Horsshedd) 68, 147
nos.64–6 68, 119
inns **167**
*selds* 146
shophouses 119, 121
taverns 113, 165
through-houses 114, 115
Xch/5 125, **125**
Xch/6 124, **125**

Xch7 **125**
Xch/8 146
wine trade 150
Winstone, Reece 4, 7
Winstone, Robert **4**, 136, 250, **252**, 258, 306, 360
Winter, William 266
Wint's Folly 274, **275**
Witham Priory 159
Wood, John, the Elder 36, 138, 299, 314
Woolfe, Isaac 306

Worcestre, William 94, 114, 144, 150, 151, 152, 158, 160, 282, 330, 331, **332**, 335
workplace, the, relationship with the home 4, 175–8, **177**
workshops 175–8, 344
World's End House 301, **301**
Worrall, Samuel 39–40, 45
Worshipful Street 14, 15, 144, 151
Wulfstan, Bishop of Worcester 17
Wyatt, James 50
Wylkyns, William 64

# Y

Yate, Robert 174, 222, 281, 282, 283, 285, 298, 298–9, 304–5, 328, 351, 352, 355, 371
Yeamans, John 365
Yong, John 155
York 1, 90, 118, 120
York Road 50
York Street 42
Young, Sir John 32, 111, 226, 231
Younge, Sir Robert 232
Younge, Thomas 231